instat

INTERNATIONAL STATISTICS SOURCES

Subject Guide to Sources of International Comparative Statistics

MICHAEL C. FLEMING
Professor of Economics
Department of Economics
Loughborough University

and

JOSEPH G. NELLIS
Professor of International Management Economics
School of Management
Cranfield University

Volume 1

ROUTLEDGE

London and New York

First published in 1995
by Routledge
11 New Fetter Lane, London EC4P 4EE
29 West 35th Street, New York, NY 10001

Printed in Great Britain by TJ Press (Padstow), Cornwall

Printed on acid-free paper

British Library Cataloguing in Publication Data
A catalogue record for this book is available from the British Library.

Library of Congress Cataloging-in-Publication Data
A catalog record for this book has been requested.

ISBN 0-415-08634-5 (set)
0-415-11358-X (Volume 1)
0-415-11359-8 (Volume 2)

Contents

Volume 1

Contents

Volume 2

Acknowledgements

The compilation of ***instat*** represents the fruit of several years of work by a team of people and the co-operation of a large number of organizations. In particular, we would like to acknowledge formally the work done by the team of researchers and secretaries who have been responsible for contacting many hundreds of organizations around the world, compiling a comprehensive list of relevant publications and then undertaking the mammoth task of inputting details of all the information contained in these publications. The main team has included, at various times, the following:

Diane Billing
Ben Delves
Russell Dickerson
Jayne Dunne
Georgina Litt
Helen Litt
Heather Jennings
Joanne Tayler
Joyce Tuson
Chris Williams

In addition, a large number of temporary staff has been involved, particularly during the final stages of the project. We are grateful for the effort they have shown when working under considerable pressure to meet the final publication deadline.

We would especially like to express our appreciation of the work done by our two personal assistants, Joyce Tuson and Chris Williams, who have helped to steer the project through to completion from the very beginning with their usual professionalism and good humour. Joyce Tuson has also undertaken a great deal of the inputting work, which has required meticulous care and attention. Diane Billing also deserves a special word of thanks for undertaking a particularly onerous part of the work in the final stages of the project. We hope that they and the rest of the team feel that their efforts have all been worthwhile.

We would also like to acknowledge the co-operation of all the organizations around the world who have responded to our enquiries and who, in many cases, have supplied complimentary copies of their publications.

Thanks are also due to the staff of our respective university libraries for their help in obtaining many other publications through the inter-library loan system and tracing bibliographical details.

Many staff at Routledge have been involved with the project over the years since it was commissioned. We would especially like to thank the editorial staff who have provided technical advice and support throughout the project – as well as for their patience and understanding as deadlines have come and gone!

Throughout the project we have been fortunate to have the loving support of our families who, as always, have had to bear the burden of coping with the trials and tribulations of authorship almost as much as the authors themselves. As ever, mere words of appreciation cannot make up for the many months of absence and, often, ill-temper resulting from the pressure of the work. Needless to say, perhaps, they are as pleased as we are to see the completion of the ***instat*** project!

Michael C. Fleming
Loughborough University

Joseph G. Nellis
Cranfield University

Introduction to *instat*

The purpose of *instat*

Instat provides a comprehensive subject guide to sources of international statistical data. Its essential purpose is to allow users to trace sources of international data on particular subjects easily and quickly. The attempt has been made to cover all international sources of statistical data published by both public and private bodies. Altogether, around 400 sources are included. Purely national sources, restricted to data for one country, are not covered. The publications indexed are, generally speaking, the latest editions available at the time of preparation of ***instat***: 1991 to mid-1994.

The organization and scope of *instat*

User needs have been the major consideration in the design and development of the book. For this reason it is organized by *subject* rather than source. All or most users can be expected to start an enquiry by seeking information on a particular subject, such as population or production; few, if any, are likely to begin with a knowledge of *sources*. Subjects are analysed at two levels:

- A cross-classification of 46 broad subject areas and source publications – given in the **Overview of Subjects and Sources** section

- Detailed subject sub-classifications, which are covered in 46 separate subject sections in Volumes 1 and 2

The purpose of the **Overview** is to provide users with a quick source of reference to all main subjects and their sources. It allows the user to see at a glance both the range of sources in which a particular subject area is covered and the range of subjects covered in any one source.

The detailed subject sub-classifications bring all of the material from the diverse range of sources together under a strict subject arrangement, organized into 46 chapters. These chapters provide the core of the ***instat*** guide.

All publications and their sources are referred to by code in the body of the ***instat*** guide. Full bibliographical details of these publications, arranged by ***instat*** codes, are given in Appendix A. Two further appendices, Appendix B and Appendix C, provide additional alphabetical indexes: the first arranged by title of publication, the second by the name of the organization responsible for each publication.

No restriction has been imposed as to the range of subject matter included in ***instat.*** It covers, therefore, not only the full range of economic, political, business and social statistics, but also statistics concerning many other areas of interest such as the environment, science and technology, defence and climate. The wide coverage will be evident from the list of the 46 subject areas given in the Contents.

In summary, the key features of the organization and scope of ***instat*** are:

- Classification of the available international statistical data according to subject
- Comprehensive coverage of all international sources
- Comprehensive coverage of subjects

The coverage of *instat*

The sources covered are confined to what may be termed international statistical publications – in the main serial publications. It is important to be clear about the coverage of this term. It covers publications which are issued primarily as a means of supplying statistical data, as such, on a regular or fairly regular basis. Many reports and studies are issued, often by the organizations covered in ***instat***, which contain extensive statistical data but whose main purpose is not the publication of statistical data as such. The statistics they contain are generally only an adjunct to the subject of the report and are derived from other sources. These publications are often convenient sources of statistical information which may include valuable commentaries but they are outside the scope of ***instat***. However, apart from statistical serial publications, we do cover recent non-serial publications that provide convenient collections of data drawn from a variety of sources.

As indicated above, the objective is to provide comprehensive coverage of the publications of all organizations which publish international statistical data. We have attempted to accomplish this task by contacting every organization throughout the world which was known or thought likely to publish such data. The response to our enquiries was very good but inevitably, perhaps, a one hundred per cent response rate was not achieved. Naturally, we have endeavoured to minimize the effect of this by using alternative means of tracing the relevant publications of such organizations. Nonetheless, it is possible that some sources have been omitted. If any such cases come to the notice of users of ***instat***, we should be grateful if these could be brought to our attention.

How to use *instat*

Organization of *instat*

Instat is published in two volumes and organized in three main parts as follows:

- An analysis of broad subject areas and sources – given in the **Overview of subjects and sources** section
- Detailed sub-classifications of subjects and their sources – given in 46 subject sections in Volumes 1 and 2
- A set of four Appendices containing information on publications and organizations as follows:

Appendix A	Index of publications arranged by ***instat*** code: full bibliographical details
Appendix B	Index of publications arranged by title of publication
Appendix C	Index of sources arranged by name of organization
Appendix D	Names and addresses of organizations

To trace sources of statistical data on a particular subject, users should consult either the **Overview** section, or the relevant **Subject Section** or the **Subject Index**, depending on whether the nature of the topic in which they are interested is general, specific or very specific. The use and structure of the book is described in more detail below.

The overview of subjects and sources

This part of ***instat*** is solely concerned with broad subject areas – 46 broad subject areas in all. These are cross-referenced to the publication sources in which the relevant data are published. The **Overview** is, therefore, structured as a matrix with a row for each main subject and a column for each publication source. Hence, this allows the user to see at a glance both the range of sources in which a particular subject is covered and, conversely, the range of subjects covered in any one source. Thus the **Overview** serves a dual purpose depending on whether the subject or the publication source is of primary interest.

Each cell of the **Overview** matrix indicates whether or not a publication source contains data on a particular subject and, if so, whether it is a major or a minor source using the following key:

■ Major source indexed in the subject chapters
● Minor source indexed in the subject chapters
○ Minor source not indexed in the subject chapters, but cross-referenced to other subject chapters

Minor sources are defined as those which contain data that are subsidiary to the main subject. For example, many international volumes contain information about the size of the population in each country but are not the primary source of population statistics.

Publication codes in *instat*

All publication sources are assigned an alphanumeric code: an alphabetic prefix denotes the organization responsible for the publication(s) and a numerical suffix defines a particular publication. For example, publications of the United Nations are coded UN1, UN2, etc. Full bibliographical information is given in Appendix A.

Detailed sub-classifications of subjects

This part of ***instat*** represents the core of the book. It consists of 46 chapters, one for each broad subject area, providing much more detailed subject breakdowns than those given in the **Overview** matrix described above. Each chapter is arranged according to a common format (explained in more detail below).

The information in each subject chapter is organized under successively more detailed sub-headings, cross-referenced once again to publication sources, and arranged in alphabetical order. Information is then given about each statistical category as follows:

- Sub-categories of the data available
- Units of measurement
- Whether or not the publication contains time series data and, if so, the frequency
- Territorial coverage
- Source – gives ***instat*** publication code and table identifier

A full cross-referencing system is adopted for subjects which appear under alternative headings.

The terms used to refer to sub-categories of data in different publications vary from one source to another. From the point of view of classification in ***instat*** this presents a dilemma. On the one hand, it would be helpful to have a standardized set of terms. On the other hand, to use terms which are not used in the source publications themselves would not be helpful to users in tracing the data in the original sources. On balance, it is important to retain the use of the terms used in the original sources in so far as possible, and, in the main, this is the approach adopted in ***instat***.

Details of publications and organizations

Throughout ***instat,*** publication references are given by means of the coding system described above. Full bibliographical information about each publication, including details of the particular volume indexed, are given in **Appendix A**, arranged in alphanumeric order according to the ***instat*** coding system. The publication details given in **Appendix A** follow a common format as follows:

- Title
- Publisher
- Place of publication
- Edition and date of publication of the volume indexed
- Frequency of publication
- ISBN and/or ISSN numbers

An important reason for specifying the edition and date of publication of the volume indexed is to permit the data to be readily located. Thus, where appropriate, table numbers referring to these volumes are given in the 46 individual subject chapters. It also provides, of course, a point of reference indicating how up to date the information about a particular source is and is also useful as a benchmark when publications are discontinued or change their names.

Two further appendices, **Appendix B** and **Appendix C**, provide additional classifications of publications and the organizations responsible for them. **Appendix B** is arranged alphabetically according to the *titles* of publications while **Appendix C** is arranged alphabetically according to the *names* of the organizations. The names and addresses of the organizations covered by ***instat*** are listed in **Appendix D.**

Abbreviations and acronyms

Many abbreviations and acronyms are used in the published sources covered by ***instat***. These, and others used in this book, are listed at the front of Volumes 1 and 2.

Definitions of country groupings

Details of countries covered within particular geographical groupings and their appropriate abbreviations or acronyms are also listed at the front of Volumes 1 and 2; for example, the countries within the OECD (Organization for Economic Co-operation and Development).

Subject index

Finally, a **Subject Index** provides a further alternative means of locating information about a particular topic. It acts as a conventional means of reference and includes synonyms cross-referenced to the broad and detailed subject headings used in the subject chapters. In the main, it provides a guide to the subject information classified in the main body of ***instat***. It is thus a means of pinpointing quickly the subject information given there.

Summary

In summary, ***instat*** provides three options to the user for locating statistical information about particular topics. These vary according to the degree of detail in the information required. The options are as follows:

- For broad subject information, consult the **Overview of subjects and sources** section
- For information within the broad subject areas, consult the subject chapters 1 to 46
- For references to specific topics, consult the **Subject index**

Finally, for details concerning publication sources and the organizations responsible, consult Appendices A to D.

Abbreviations and acronyms

A	annually
AA	agricultural area
ACP	African, Caribbean and Pacific
AEA	Association of European Airlines
AGR	average growth rate
agric	agricultural
AIDS	acquired immuno-deficiency syndrome
alh	average length of haul
API	American Petroleum Institute
APO	Asian Productivity Organization
App	appendix
ARA	Amsterdam, Rotterdam, Antwerp
ASEAN	Association of South-East Asian Nations
ASEANS	Association of South-East Asian Nations Secretariat
ASFR	average spot freight rates
avlble	available
AWU	annual worker unit
Bags	60 kilograms
BB	Basil Blackwell Limited
b/cd	barrels per calendar day
b/d	barrels per day
BERD	expenditure on research and development in the business enterprise sector
BFI	Baltic Freight Index
BGS	British Geological Survey
bl	barrel
BOD	biochemical oxygen demand
BOF	basic oxygen furnace

BP	British Petroleum plc
BPB	British Paper and Board Industry Federation
BSU	British size unit
Btu	British thermal units
C	coniferous
CAA	Civil Aviation Authority
CAPMoN	Canadian Air and Precipitation Monitoring Network
Carib	Caribbean
CARICOM	Caribbean Community
CBE	cocoa butter equivalent
CBI	Confederation of British Industry
CCS	Caribbean Community Secretariat
cd	cadmium
CE	Council of Europe
CEEC	Central and Eastern European countries
CF	capital formation
CFA Franc	Franc of the "Communauté Financière Africaine"
CFC	chlorofluorocarbons
cgal	cents gallon
CH	Croom Helm Limited
CIA	Chemical Industries Association
CICPE	Comité International pour le Contrôle des Performances en Élevage
c.i.f.	cost insurance freight
CIRFS	Comité International de La Rayonne et des Fibres Synthétiques
CIS	Commonwealth of Independent States–see EECISC
CMEA	Council for Mutual Economic Assistance
CO	carbon monoxide
CO_2	carbon dioxide
cons	consumption

COS	Chamber of Shipping
CPITN	Community periodontal index of treatment needs
CS	Commonwealth Secretariat
CSFR	Czech and Slovak Federal Republics
CSR	thousand cubic metres
ctry	country
CTQ	sum of the guaranteed quantities (milk) for deliveries and direct sales
Cu	cubic
Cuf/d	cubic feet per day
Curr exp	current expenditure
cwe	carcass weight equivalent
D	daily
DAC	Development Assistance Committee (OECD)
DAE	dynamic Asian economies
defs	definitions
DDSR	debt and debt service reduction
DFS	duty-free shops
DM	Deutschmarks
DMEC	developed market-economy country
dmt	dry metric tonne
doz	dozen
DPI	domestic product of industry
DR	direct-reduced
DSC	Drewry Shipping Consultants Limited
dt	quintal
dwct	dead-weight cargo tonnes
dwt	dead-weight tons
E	European
EAA	European Aluminium Association

EAF	electric arc furnace
EAGGF	European Agricultural Guidance and Guarantee Fund
EAT	Elsevier Advanced Technology
EC	European Community
ECE	Economic Commission for Europe (UN)
ECMT	European Conference of Ministers of Transport
ECU	European currency unit
ECSC	European Coal and Steel Community
EDF	European Development Fund
EEC	European Economic Community
EECISC	Eastern Europe, CIS area and China
EFTA	European Free Trade Association
EIB	European Investment Bank
EKS	Elteto-Köves-Szule
elec	electricity or electrical
EM	Euromonitor
EMCF	European Monetary Co-operation Fund
EMEP	Co-operative programme on monitoring and evaluation of the long range transmission of air pollutants in Europe
EPI	European Paper Institute *or* expanded programme on immunization
EPO	European Patent Office
equiv	equivalent
ESA	European system of integrated economic accounts (EC)
ESCAP	Economic and Social Commission for Asia and the Pacific
est	estimate or estimated
ESU	European size unit
EUR 9	Total of 9 member states of the EEC (Definitions of Country Groupings)
EUR 10	Total of 10 member states of the EEC (Definitions of Country Groupings)
EUR 11	Total of 11 member states of the EEC (Definitions of Country Groupings)

EUR 12	Total of 12 member states of the EEC (Definitions of Country Groupings)
F	Fearnleys
FAO	Food and Agriculture Organization
FDI	foreign direct investment
FEOGA	Fonds Européen d'Orientation et de Garantie Agricole (European Agricultural Guidance and Guarantee Fund)
FNOCL	Fédération Nationale des Organismes de Contrôle Laitier
FF	French francs
f.o.b.	free on board
FOL	F O Licht
FSU	former Soviet Union
fte	full-time equivalents
G	E A Gibson Shipbrokers Limited
g	gram
GAP	gross agricultural product
GATT	General Agreement on Tariffs and Trade
GBAORD	government budget appropriations for outlays for research and development
GCC	Gulf Co-operation Council
GD	Gill and Duffus Group Limited
GDP	gross domestic product
GERD	gross domestic expenditure on research and development
GFCF	gross fixed capital formation
GNP	gross national product
govt	government
GP	General Publications
GRA	general resources account
grt	gross registered tonnage
gsp	generalized system of preferences
gt	gross tonnage

GVA	gross value added
GWe	gigawatt equivalent
GWh	gigawatt hour
h	hour
ha	hectare
HERD	higher education expenditure on research and development
HI	Horwath International
hl	hectolitre
hun	hundred
HIV	human immuno-deficiency virus
HWU	million kilowatt hours
I	irregular
IADB	Inter-American Development Bank
IAEA	International Atomic Energy Agency
IAHP	International Association of Horticultural Producers
IARC	International Agency for Research on Cancer
IATA	International Air Transport Association
IBA	International Bauxite Association
IBRD	International Bank for Reconstruction and Development (World Bank)
ICAC	International Cotton Advisory Committee
ICAO	International Civil Aviation Organization
ICCAT	International Commission for the Conservation of Atlantic Tunas
ICCO	International Cocoa Council Organization
ICOR	incremental capital-output ratios
ICP	International Comparison Project (UN)
IDA	International Development Association
IDF	International Dairy Federation
IEA	International Energy Agency
IFAD	International Fund for Agricultural Development

IFC	International Finance Corporation
IFIA	International Fertilizer Industry Association
IISI	International Iron and Steel Institute
ILO	International Labour Organization
ILZSG	International Lead and Zinc Study Group
IMF	International Monetary Fund
IMWF	International Metalworkers' Federation
ind	industry *or* index
INPFC	International North Pacific Fisheries Commission
INRO	International Natural Rubber Organization
int	international
IP	Institute of Petroleum
IPC	International Patent Classification
IPHC	International Pacific Halibut Commission
IPU	Inter-Parliamentary Union
IRF	International Road Federation
IRTU	International Road Transport Union
IRSG	International Rubber Study Group
ISA	International Sugar Agreement
ISBN	International Standard Book Number
ISCED	International Standard Classification of Education
ISIC	International Standard Industrial Classification of all Economic Activities
ISL	Institute of Shipping Economics and Logistics
ISO	International Sugar Organization
ISSB	Iron and Steel Statistics Bureau
ISSN	International Standard Serial Number
ISTA	ISTA Mielk GmbH
ITC	International Tea Committee
ITMF	International Textile Manufacturers Federation

ITTC	International Tropical Timber Council
ITTO	International Tropical Timber Organization
ITU	International Telecommunication Union
IUR	International Union of Railways
IWC	International Whaling Commission
IWhC	International Wheat Council
IWS	International Wool Secretariat
JM	Johnson Matthey
JP	Jaakko Pöyry
kcal	kilocalorie
kg	kilogram
kg/an	kilograms per animal
kg/c	kilograms per capita
kgoe	kilogram oil equivalent
km	kilometre
km^2	square kilometre
km/h	kilometres per hour
KOE	kilograms of oil equivalent
kVa	kilovolt-ampere
KW	kilowatt
kWh	kilowatt hours
l	litre
LDCs	less-developed countries
ldt	light deadweight tonnes
LIBOR	London interbank offered rate
LNG	liquefied natural gas
LRS	Lloyds Register of Shipping
ltd	light displacement weight
LPG	liquefied petroleum gas

LU	livestock units
LME	London Metal Exchange
m	metre
M	monthly
MAC	Macmillan Press Limited
MB	Metal Bulletin Books Limited
m^2	square metre
MDCs	more-developed countries
mg/l	milligrams per litre
MHPPE	Ministry of Housing, Physical Planning and the Environment (Netherlands)
MJ	mega joules *or* Mining Journal
MLC	Meat and Livestock Commission
mm	millimetre
MPS	System of Material Product Balances
MVA	manufacturing value added
MW	megawatt
MWe	megawatt equivalent
μg	microgram
N	nitrogen
NABS	Nomenclature for Analysis and Comparison of Scientific Programmes and Budgets
NACE/CLIO	Classification of goods derived from NACE for use in ESA and input-output tables
NACE	Nomenclature Générale des Activités dans les Communautés Européennes (General Industrial Classification of Economic Activities in the European Communities)
nat curr	national currency
NATO	North Atlantic Treaty Organization
NC	non-coniferous
NCM	Nordic Council of Ministers and the Nordic Statistical Secretariat
nge	natural gas equivalent
ngl	natural gas liquids

NH_3	ammonia
nes	not elsewhere specified
NMP	net material product
NNP	net national product
nos	numbers
NO_2	nitrogen dioxide
NO_X	nitrogen oxides
nrt	net registered tonnage
NST	Nomenclature Uniforme des Marchandises pour les Statistiques des Transport
NTM	non-tariff measures
N_2O	nitrous oxide
NWAFO	North West Atlantic Fisheries Organization
NWE	North West Europe
NWE/ARA	North West Europe/Amsterdam Rotterdam Antwerp
OCBN	Organization Commune Benin Niger des Chemins de Fer et des Transports
OCTG	oil-country tubular goods
ODA	Overseas Development Administration *or* Official Development Assistance
ODF	official development financing
OECD	Organization for Economic Co-operation and Development
OGA	other gainful activity
OHF	open hearth furnace
OIVV	Office International de la Vigne et du Vin
ONATRA	Office National des Transports
OPEC	Organization of Petroleum Exporting Countries
ORS	oral rehydration solution
ORT	oral rehydration therapy
oz	ounces troy
p	piece
PAX	passengers

PC	The Population Council
PCE	private consumption expenditure
PKF	Pannel Kerr Forster
PPI	Pulp and Paper International
ppl	pence per litre
ppm	parts per million
PPP	purchasing power parity
PPS	purchasing power standard
PQLI	physical quality of life index
pse	producer subsidy equivalents
q	quintal
Q	quarterly
Recip	recipient
Reg	region
R & D	research and development
Ro/Ro	roll-on/roll-off
R/P	reserves/production
RSE	research and development scientists and engineers
S	sulphur
s.a.	seasonally adjusted
SATRA	SATRA (Shoe and Allied Trades Research Association) Footwear Technology Centre
SBP	special boiling point spirit (industrial spirit)
SDR	special drawing rights
SEAR	South East Asia Region
SFIA	Sea Fish Industry Authority
SGM	standard gross margin
SIDF	Saudi Industrial Development Fund
SILICs	severely-indebted lower income countries
SIMICs	severely-indebted middle income countries

SITC	Standard International Trade Classification
SMMT	Society of Motor Manufacturers and Traders Limited
SNA	System of National Accounts (UN)
SNCZ	Société National des Chemins de Fer Zairois
SOEC	Statistical Office of the European Communities (Eurostat)
SO_2	sulphur dioxide
SPC	South Pacific Commission
S'pore	Singapore
SPWP	secondary-processed wood products
sq km	square kilometre
sq m	square metre
TEU	20 feet equivalent unit
TFS	tin-free steel
thou	thousand
TJ	terajoule
toe	ton of oil equivalent
tpe	tons products equivalent
TPER	total primary energy requirements
TPES	total primary energy supply
TSP	total suspended particulates
TWh	terawatt hour
UAA	utilized agricultural area
UDC	Universal Decimal Classification
UN	United Nations
UNCTAD	United Nations Conference on Trade and Development
UNDP	United Nations Development Programme
UNESCO	United Nations Educational, Scientific and Cultural Organization
UNFPA	United Nations Fund for Population
UNHCR	United Nations High Commission for Refugees

UNICEF	United Nations Children's Fund
UNIDO	United Nations Industrial Development Organization
USA	United States of America
USG	United States Gulf
USSR	Union of Soviet Socialist Republics
veh-km	vehicle-kilometre
VICES	Vienna Institute for Comparative Economic Studies
VOC	volatile organic compounds
WB	World Bank
WBMS	World Bureau of Metal Statistics
WC	Wye College
WFP	World Food Programme
WHO	World Health Organization
WIPO	World Intellectual Property Organization
WMO	World Meteorological Organization
WOCA	world-outside-centrally-planned-economies areas
WS	worldscale
WSR	thousand metric tons
WTI	West Texas intermediate
WTO	World Tourism Organization
yr	year
yrly	yearly

Definitions of country groupings

ACP	African, Caribbean and Pacific countries (signatories to the LOMÉ Convention)
APO	Asian Productivity Organization Bangladesh, Fiji, Hong Kong, India, Indonesia, Iran (Islamic Republic of), Japan, Korea, Malaysia, Mongolia, Nepal, Pakistan, Philippines, Singapore, Sri Lanka, Taiwan (Republic of China), Thailand, Vietnam
ASEAN	Association of South-East Asian Nations Brunei, Malaysia, Singapore, Indonesia, Philippines, Thailand
CARICOM	Caribbean Community countries Antigua-Barbuda, Bahamas, Barbados, Belize, Dominica, Grenada, Guyana, Jamaica, Montserrat, St Kitts-Nevis, St Lucia, St Vincent-Grenadines, Trinidad and Tobago
CEEC	Central and Eastern European countries Albania, Bulgaria, Czechoslovakia, Hungary, Poland, Romania, USSR, Yugoslavia
CICPE	Members of Comité International pour le Contrôle des Performances en Élevage. As at 1991 the member countries were: Austria, Belgium, Canada, Czechoslovakia, Denmark, England and Wales, Federal Republic of Germany, Finland, France, Greece, Ireland, Israel, Italy, Japan, Jersey, Luxembourg, Netherlands, New Zealand, Northern Ireland, Norway, Portugal, Scotland, Slovenia, South Africa, Spain, Sweden, Switzerland, Tunisia, United States of America, Zimbabwe, Australia
CIS	Commonwealth of Independent States – see EECISC
EC	European Community Coverage defined as EC9, EC12, EUR9, EUR10, EUR11 or EUR12 (*qv*)
EC9	Total of 9 member states of the former EEC West Germany, France, Italy, Netherlands, Belgium, Luxembourg, United Kingdom, Ireland, Denmark
EC12	Total of 12 member countries of the EC Germany, France, Italy, Netherlands, Belgium, Luxembourg, United Kingdom, Ireland, Denmark, Greece, Spain, Portugal
ECMT	European Conference of Ministers of Transport Austria, Belgium, Czech and Slovak Federal Republics, Denmark, Finland, France, Germany, Greece, Hungary, Ireland, Italy, Luxembourg, Netherlands, Norway, Poland, Portugal, Spain, Sweden, Switzerland, Turkey, and United Kingdom. (Associate Member countries: Australia, Canada, Japan, New Zealand, the United States. Observer country: Morocco)
EEC	European Economic Community – see EC

EECISC	Eastern Europe, the Commonwealth of Independent States (CIS area), and China. *Eastern Europe*: Albania, Bulgaria, Czechoslovakia, Hungary, Poland, Romania, Yugoslavia and the Baltic Republics of Estonia, Latvia and Lithuania *Commonwealth of Independent States (CIS)*: Russia, Armenia, Azerbaijan, Belorussia, Kazakhstan, Kirgizia, Moldova, Tajikstan, Turkmenistan, Ukraine and Uzbekistan. For the sake of convenience, non-members Georgia and Mongolia are also included
EFTA	European Free Trade Association Austria, Finland, Iceland, Norway, Sweden, Switzerland (and Liechtenstein)
ESCAP	Economic and Social Commission for Asia and the Pacific Afghanistan, Australia, Bangladesh, Cook Islands, Fiji, Hong Kong, India, Indonesia, Iran (Islamic Republic of), Japan, Korea (Republic of), Malaysia, Myanmar, Nepal, New Zealand, Niue, Pakistan, Papua New Guinea, Philippines, Samoa, Singapore, Solomon Islands, Sri Lanka, Thailand, Tonga, Vanuatu
EUR9	Total of 9 member states of the EEC – see EC9
EUR10	EUR9 plus Greece
EUR11	EUR10 plus Spain
EUR12	EUR11 plus Portugal
ICCO	Members of International Cocoa Organization. As at 30 June 1992 the member countries were: *Exporting members*: Brazil, Cameroon, Côte d'Ivoire, Ecuador, Gabon, Ghana, Grenada, Guatemala, Haiti, Jamaica, Mexico, Nigeria, Papua New Guinea, Samoa, Sierra Leone, Togo, Trinidad and Tobago, Venezuela *Importing members*: Belgium/Luxembourg, Bulgaria, Czechoslovakia, Denmark, Finland, France, Germany, Greece, Hungary, Ireland, Italy, Japan, Netherlands, Norway, Portugal, Russian Federation, Spain, Sweden, Switzerland, United Kingdom, Yugoslavia
MPS countries	Afghanistan, Albania, Bulgaria, China, Cuba, Czechoslovakia, Germany – former German Democratic Republic, Hungary, Korea (Democratic People's Republic), Mongolia, Poland, USSR, Vietnam
NATO	North Atlantic Treaty Organization Belgium, Denmark, France, Germany, Greece, Iceland, Italy, Luxembourg, Netherlands, Norway, Portugal, Spain, Turkey, United Kingdom, Canada, United States of America
NORDIC countries	Denmark, Finland, Iceland, Norway, Sweden
OECD	Organization for Economic Co-operation and Development Austria, Belgium, Canada, Denmark, France, Germany, Greece, Iceland, Ireland, Italy, Luxembourg, Netherlands, Norway, Portugal, Spain, Sweden, Switzerland, Turkey, United Kingdom, United States, Japan, Finland, Australia, New Zealand The former Yugoslavia took part in some of the work of the OECD (agreement of 28 October 1961)
OECD – Europe	All European member countries of OECD, i.e. EC countries plus Austria, Finland, Iceland, Norway, Sweden, Switzerland, Turkey

OECD Major Seven	Canada, France, Germany, Italy, Japan, United Kingdom, United States of America
OECD Total	All member countries of OECD, i.e. countries of OECD-Europe plus Canada, United States of America, Japan, Australia and New Zealand
OPEC	Organization of Petroleum Exporting Countries The members at 1991 were: Abu Dhabi, Algeria, Dubai, Ecuador, Gabon, Indonesia, Iran, Iraq, Kuwait, Libya, Neutral (Divided) Zone, Nigeria, Qatar, Ras al Khaimah, Saudi Arabia, Sharjah, Venezuela
SEAR	South-East Asia Region Bangladesh, Bhutan, DPR Korea, India, Indonesia, Maldives, Mongolia, Myanmar, Nepal, Sri Lanka, Thailand
SNA countries	Countries in North America and Western Europe (except Yugoslavia) together with Australia, Israel, Japan, New Zealand and South Africa

Overview of subjects and sources

The **Overview of subjects and sources** is a matrix in which each column denotes one of 399 ***instat*** publication codes and each row denotes one of the 46 subject categories. Full bibliographical details of the publications denoted by the ***instat*** codes are given in Appendix A.

Major and minor sources

A distinction is made in the matrix between *major* and *minor* publication sources which are indexed in the relevant subject chapters. In addition, some publications also contain statistical information which is merely incidental in nature. For example, many international volumes contain details about size in terms of population, national income, land area, etc. but such details may not be the primary focus of the publication concerned. In such cases, therefore, the publication is not indexed as a source of such data in the relevant subject chapters but simply cross-referenced as appropriate. Such cases, however, are indicated in the matrix. Major and minor publication sources are denoted in the matrix by use of the following symbols:

■	Major source indexed in the subject chapters
●	Minor source indexed in the subject chapters
○	Minor source not indexed in the subject chapters, but cross-referenced to other subject chapters

Thus, to illustrate the use of the three classificatory symbols, it will be seen, for example, that *Oil and Energy Trends*, coded BB1 on page 3 of the matrix, is denoted as a major source of energy statistics (Subject 17), a minor source for industries (Subject 25), international trade and finance (Subject 27), prices (Subject 37) and shipping (Subject 41) but as a non-indexed minor source for production (Subject 38).

General sources

Some statistical publications are collections of data covering a wide range of different subjects. The *UN Statistical Yearbook* (***instat*** code UN50) is one such example. While such sources are important, they do not cover any one subject in great detail, and thus we do not treat them as major sources for any particular subject. Such sources can be identified in the **Overview of subjects and sources** matrix by the large number of subjects covered, showing the relevant publication as a minor source only.

Use of the overview matrix

The **Overview** matrix can be used in one of two ways:

(a) to locate major and minor publication sources which cover a particular subject area by reading along the relevant row

(b) to identify the range of subject areas covered in any one publication source by reading down the relevant column

Overview of subjects and sources

SUBJECT	PUBLICATION CODE				
	AEA1	AEA2	AEA3	AEA4	APO1
1. ACCIDENTS					
2. AGRICULTURE					
3. CIVIL AVIATION	■	■	■	■	
4. CLIMATE					
5. COMMODITIES					
6. COMMUNICATIONS					
7. CONSTRUCTION					
8. CONSUMPTION					
9. CRIME AND JUSTICE					
10. CULTURE					
11. DEFENCE					
12. DEVELOPMENT AND AID					
13. DISTRIBUTION					
14. DRUGS					
15. EDUCATION AND TRAINING					
16. EMPLOYMENT AND UNEMPLOYMENT					●
17. ENERGY					
18. ENVIRONMENT					
19. FINANCE					
20. FISHING					
21. FORESTRY					
22. HEALTH					
23. HOUSING					
24. INCOME AND WEALTH					
25. INDUSTRIES	●	●	●	●	
26. INTELLECTUAL PROPERTY					
27. INTERNATIONAL TRADE AND FINANCE					
28. LABOUR					■
29. LAND					
30. LIVING COSTS AND STANDARDS					
31. MIGRATION					
32. MINERALS					
33. MINING AND QUARRYING					
34. NATIONAL ACCOUNTS					●
35. PARLIAMENT AND PUBLIC AFFAIRS					
36. POPULATION AND VITAL STATISTICS					
37. PRICES					
38. PRODUCTION					
39. REFUGEES					
40. SCIENCE AND TECHNOLOGY					
41. SHIPPING					
42. SOCIAL INDICATORS					
43. TAXATION					
44. TOURISM					
45. TRANSPORT	●	●	●	●	
46. WELFARE					

PUBLICATION CODE								
ASEANS1	BB1	BB2	BB3	BB4	BGS1	BGS2	BP1	BP2
●								
●								
●								
●					■	■	●	○
●								
							○	●
●								
●								
●								
●								
●	■	■		■	○		■	■
●		●						
●								
●								
●								
	●	●	○	○	○	○	○	○
●	●	●		●	○	○	●	●
●								
●					■	■	○	
●								
●								
●								
●	●	●	●				●	●
●	○	●			○	○	●	●
●								
●	●	●	■					
●								
●								
●								

Overview of subjects and sources

SUBJECT	PUBLICATION CODE				
	BPB1	CAA1	CBI1	CCS1	CCS2
1. ACCIDENTS		■			
2. AGRICULTURE					
3. CIVIL AVIATION		■			
4. CLIMATE					
5. COMMODITIES	○				
6. COMMUNICATIONS					
7. CONSTRUCTION					
8. CONSUMPTION	●				
9. CRIME AND JUSTICE					
10. CULTURE					
11. DEFENCE					
12. DEVELOPMENT AND AID					
13. DISTRIBUTION					
14. DRUGS					
15. EDUCATION AND TRAINING					
16. EMPLOYMENT AND UNEMPLOYMENT					
17. ENERGY					
18. ENVIRONMENT					
19. FINANCE					
20. FISHING					
21. FORESTRY					
22. HEALTH					
23. HOUSING					
24. INCOME AND WEALTH					
25. INDUSTRIES	■				
26. INTELLECTUAL PROPERTY					
27. INTERNATIONAL TRADE AND FINANCE				■	■
28. LABOUR					
29. LAND					
30. LIVING COSTS AND STANDARDS			■		
31. MIGRATION					
32. MINERALS					
33. MINING AND QUARRYING					
34. NATIONAL ACCOUNTS					
35. PARLIAMENT AND PUBLIC AFFAIRS					
36. POPULATION AND VITAL STATISTICS					
37. PRICES					
38. PRODUCTION	●				
39. REFUGEES					
40. SCIENCE AND TECHNOLOGY					
41. SHIPPING					
42. SOCIAL INDICATORS					
43. TAXATION					
44. TOURISM					
45. TRANSPORT		○			
46. WELFARE					

PUBLICATION CODE								
CE1	CH1	CIA1	CIRFS1	COS1	CS1	DSC1	DSC2	EAA1
	●				●			
			●				○	○
					●			
		●	●		●		●	●
					●			
	●				●			
	●	●	●		●	●		
	●				●		●	
	●	●			●	●		
					●			
	●	■	■	○		○	○	●
	●	●	●	●	●	●	●	●
	●				●			
					●			
●								
								■
	●						●	
■	●				●			
		●		●	●	●	●	
	●	●	●		●	●	●	●
				■		■	■	
					●			
				○	●	○		
					●			

Overview of subjects and sources

SUBJECT	PUBLICATION CODE				
	EAT1	EAT2	EC1	EC2	EC3
1. ACCIDENTS					
2. AGRICULTURE			●	■	■
3. CIVIL AVIATION					
4. CLIMATE					
5. COMMODITIES	○				●
6. COMMUNICATIONS		■			
7. CONSTRUCTION					
8. CONSUMPTION	●		●		
9. CRIME AND JUSTICE					
10. CULTURE					
11. DEFENCE					
12. DEVELOPMENT AND AID			●		
13. DISTRIBUTION					
14. DRUGS					
15. EDUCATION AND TRAINING			●		
16. EMPLOYMENT AND UNEMPLOYMENT				●	
17. ENERGY					
18. ENVIRONMENT					
19. FINANCE			●		
20. FISHING					
21. FORESTRY					
22. HEALTH			●		
23. HOUSING					
24. INCOME AND WEALTH			●	●	
25. INDUSTRIES	○		○		○
26. INTELLECTUAL PROPERTY					
27. INTERNATIONAL TRADE AND FINANCE	●	●	●		
28. LABOUR					
29. LAND					
30. LIVING COSTS AND STANDARDS					
31. MIGRATION					
32. MINERALS	■				
33. MINING AND QUARRYING					
34. NATIONAL ACCOUNTS			●		
35. PARLIAMENT AND PUBLIC AFFAIRS					
36. POPULATION AND VITAL STATISTICS			●		
37. PRICES				●	●
38. PRODUCTION	●	●	●	●	
39. REFUGEES					
40. SCIENCE AND TECHNOLOGY					
41. SHIPPING					
42. SOCIAL INDICATORS					
43. TAXATION					
44. TOURISM					
45. TRANSPORT					
46. WELFARE					

PUBLICATION CODE								
EC4	EC5	EC6	EC7	EC8	EC9	EC10	EC11	EC12
					●			
■	■	■	■	■	●			
					●			
		●						
		●	○		●			
					●			
		●	●		●			
					●			
					●		●	
					●		●	
					●			
					●			
		●			●			
		■			●			
		■			●			
					●		■	
		●			●			
○	○	○	○	○	●			○
		●	●		●	■		
					●			
		●		●	●		●	
					●			
					●			
		●			●			
		●			●		■	
●	●	●			●			
		●	●	○	●			
					●			
					●			
					●			■
					●			

SUBJECT	PUBLICATION CODE				
	EC13	EC14	EC15	EC16	EC17
1. ACCIDENTS					
2. AGRICULTURE			■		
3. CIVIL AVIATION					
4. CLIMATE					
5. COMMODITIES					
6. COMMUNICATIONS					
7. CONSTRUCTION					
8. CONSUMPTION					
9. CRIME AND JUSTICE					
10. CULTURE					
11. DEFENCE					
12. DEVELOPMENT AND AID					
13. DISTRIBUTION					
14. DRUGS					
15. EDUCATION AND TRAINING					
16. EMPLOYMENT AND UNEMPLOYMENT					
17. ENERGY					
18. ENVIRONMENT					
19. FINANCE					
20. FISHING					
21. FORESTRY					
22. HEALTH					
23. HOUSING					
24. INCOME AND WEALTH					
25. INDUSTRIES	○	○	○		
26. INTELLECTUAL PROPERTY					
27. INTERNATIONAL TRADE AND FINANCE					
28. LABOUR					
29. LAND					
30. LIVING COSTS AND STANDARDS				●	●
31. MIGRATION					
32. MINERALS					
33. MINING AND QUARRYING					
34. NATIONAL ACCOUNTS					
35. PARLIAMENT AND PUBLIC AFFAIRS					
36. POPULATION AND VITAL STATISTICS					
37. PRICES				■	■
38. PRODUCTION			●		
39. REFUGEES					
40. SCIENCE AND TECHNOLOGY					
41. SHIPPING					
42. SOCIAL INDICATORS					
43. TAXATION					
44. TOURISM					
45. TRANSPORT	■	■			
46. WELFARE					

PUBLICATION CODE								
EC18	EC19	EC20	EC21	EC22	EC23	EC24	EC25	EC26
●								
●	■				■			■
●								
●	■							
	●							○
●								
●								
●	●							○
●								
●					●			
●								
●								○
●								
●								■
●								
●								
●					●	■		○
●	○							●
●	●						■	
●								
●	●							
●								
		●						
●								
●								●
●		■						
●								○
●	●							○
●								
●								
●								
●								
			■	■				

Overview of subjects and sources

SUBJECT	PUBLICATION CODE				
	EC27	EC28	EC29	EC30	EC31
1. ACCIDENTS					
2. AGRICULTURE			●		
3. CIVIL AVIATION					
4. CLIMATE					
5. COMMODITIES					
6. COMMUNICATIONS					
7. CONSTRUCTION					
8. CONSUMPTION		●		○	○
9. CRIME AND JUSTICE					
10. CULTURE					
11. DEFENCE					
12. DEVELOPMENT AND AID					
13. DISTRIBUTION					
14. DRUGS					
15. EDUCATION AND TRAINING					
16. EMPLOYMENT AND UNEMPLOYMENT			■		
17. ENERGY		■		■	■
18. ENVIRONMENT					
19. FINANCE					
20. FISHING					
21. FORESTRY					
22. HEALTH					
23. HOUSING					
24. INCOME AND WEALTH					
25. INDUSTRIES		○	■	○	○
26. INTELLECTUAL PROPERTY					
27. INTERNATIONAL TRADE AND FINANCE	■			○	○
28. LABOUR			■		
29. LAND					
30. LIVING COSTS AND STANDARDS					
31. MIGRATION					
32. MINERALS					
33. MINING AND QUARRYING					
34. NATIONAL ACCOUNTS					
35. PARLIAMENT AND PUBLIC AFFAIRS					
36. POPULATION AND VITAL STATISTICS			●		
37. PRICES	●	●			
38. PRODUCTION				○	○
39. REFUGEES					
40. SCIENCE AND TECHNOLOGY					
41. SHIPPING					
42. SOCIAL INDICATORS					
43. TAXATION		●			
44. TOURISM					
45. TRANSPORT					
46. WELFARE					

PUBLICATION CODE

EC32	EC33	EC34	EC35	EC36	EC37	EC38	EC39	EC40
			●					
			●	●				
		○		●	○	○	○	○
	○	●	●					
			●					
			●					
				●				
			●					
	●		●	●				
■	■	■	●	●				
		■	●					
			●	●				
			●					
			●					
			●					
			●	●				
	○		●	●				
○	○	○	●	●				
	○		●	●	■	■	■	■
	●		●	●				
		■	●					
		●						
			●	●				
			●					
		●	●	●				
●	●		●	●				
	○	○	○	●				
			●					
●								
			●					
			●					

Overview of subjects and sources

SUBJECT	PUBLICATION CODE				
	EC41	EC42	EC43	EC44	EC45
1. ACCIDENTS					
2. AGRICULTURE			■	■	■
3. CIVIL AVIATION					
4. CLIMATE					
5. COMMODITIES	○				
6. COMMUNICATIONS					
7. CONSTRUCTION					
8. CONSUMPTION		●			
9. CRIME AND JUSTICE					
10. CULTURE					
11. DEFENCE					
12. DEVELOPMENT AND AID					
13. DISTRIBUTION					
14. DRUGS					
15. EDUCATION AND TRAINING					
16. EMPLOYMENT AND UNEMPLOYMENT					●
17. ENERGY					
18. ENVIRONMENT					
19. FINANCE					
20. FISHING					
21. FORESTRY					
22. HEALTH					
23. HOUSING		●			
24. INCOME AND WEALTH					
25. INDUSTRIES			○	○	○
26. INTELLECTUAL PROPERTY					
27. INTERNATIONAL TRADE AND FINANCE	■				
28. LABOUR			○		
29. LAND					●
30. LIVING COSTS AND STANDARDS		■			
31. MIGRATION					
32. MINERALS					
33. MINING AND QUARRYING					
34. NATIONAL ACCOUNTS					
35. PARLIAMENT AND PUBLIC AFFAIRS					
36. POPULATION AND VITAL STATISTICS		●			
37. PRICES					
38. PRODUCTION				○	○
39. REFUGEES					
40. SCIENCE AND TECHNOLOGY					
41. SHIPPING					
42. SOCIAL INDICATORS		●			
43. TAXATION					
44. TOURISM					
45. TRANSPORT					
46. WELFARE					

PUBLICATION CODE								
EC46	EC47	EC48	EC49	EC50	EC51	EC52	EC53	EC54
							○	
	○						●	
						●	●	
	○						●	○
						●	■	
		■					●	■
			○				●	
■								
	■							
							■	
○	○	○			■	■	■	
○	○						●	○
							■	
	●							
							●	
			■				●	
		●				●		
○	○				■	■	■	○
				■				
			●					

SUBJECT	PUBLICATION CODE				
	EC55	EC56	EC57	EC58	EC59
1. ACCIDENTS					
2. AGRICULTURE			■	■	
3. CIVIL AVIATION					
4. CLIMATE					
5. COMMODITIES			○	○	
6. COMMUNICATIONS					
7. CONSTRUCTION					
8. CONSUMPTION	●		○	●	
9. CRIME AND JUSTICE					
10. CULTURE					
11. DEFENCE					
12. DEVELOPMENT AND AID					
13. DISTRIBUTION					
14. DRUGS					
15. EDUCATION AND TRAINING		○			
16. EMPLOYMENT AND UNEMPLOYMENT	●	■			
17. ENERGY					
18. ENVIRONMENT					
19. FINANCE			○	○	■
20. FISHING					
21. FORESTRY					
22. HEALTH					
23. HOUSING					
24. INCOME AND WEALTH	●		●	●	
25. INDUSTRIES	■	○	○	●	
26. INTELLECTUAL PROPERTY					
27. INTERNATIONAL TRADE AND FINANCE	●				●
28. LABOUR		○			
29. LAND			●	●	
30. LIVING COSTS AND STANDARDS					
31. MIGRATION					
32. MINERALS					
33. MINING AND QUARRYING					
34. NATIONAL ACCOUNTS					
35. PARLIAMENT AND PUBLIC AFFAIRS					
36. POPULATION AND VITAL STATISTICS		○	○		
37. PRICES	○		●	●	●
38. PRODUCTION	○		○		
39. REFUGEES					
40. SCIENCE AND TECHNOLOGY					
41. SHIPPING					
42. SOCIAL INDICATORS					
43. TAXATION	●				
44. TOURISM					
45. TRANSPORT					
46. WELFARE					

PUBLICATION CODE								
EC60	EC61	EC62	EC63	EC64	EC65	EC66	EC67	EC68
						○		
○			●					●
					●			
○	○				●			
				■				
		■						●
●	●	●						
				○				●
●			●					●
	●							
					●			
								■
■	■	■	■		●		■	
●					●			
	○		●			■	○	
			○	○				●
		●						

SUBJECT	PUBLICATION CODE				
	EC69	EC70	EC71	EC72	EC73
1. ACCIDENTS				●	
2. AGRICULTURE	●				
3. CIVIL AVIATION	●				
4. CLIMATE					
5. COMMODITIES					
6. COMMUNICATIONS					
7. CONSTRUCTION		●			
8. CONSUMPTION			○	●	
9. CRIME AND JUSTICE				●	
10. CULTURE				●	
11. DEFENCE					
12. DEVELOPMENT AND AID				●	
13. DISTRIBUTION			■		
14. DRUGS					
15. EDUCATION AND TRAINING	●			●	
16. EMPLOYMENT AND UNEMPLOYMENT	●	●	○	●	
17. ENERGY	●				
18. ENVIRONMENT				●	
19. FINANCE	●		○		●
20. FISHING					
21. FORESTRY					
22. HEALTH	●			●	
23. HOUSING	●	○		●	
24. INCOME AND WEALTH	●				
25. INDUSTRIES	●	■	■		
26. INTELLECTUAL PROPERTY					
27. INTERNATIONAL TRADE AND FINANCE		●			
28. LABOUR				●	
29. LAND	●				
30. LIVING COSTS AND STANDARDS				●	
31. MIGRATION	●				
32. MINERALS					
33. MINING AND QUARRYING					
34. NATIONAL ACCOUNTS	●				●
35. PARLIAMENT AND PUBLIC AFFAIRS				●	
36. POPULATION AND VITAL STATISTICS	●			●	●
37. PRICES		○			●
38. PRODUCTION	○	●			
39. REFUGEES			○		
40. SCIENCE AND TECHNOLOGY					
41. SHIPPING	●				
42. SOCIAL INDICATORS	●			■	
43. TAXATION			●		
44. TOURISM				●	
45. TRANSPORT	●			●	
46. WELFARE				●	■

PUBLICATION CODE								
EC74	EC75	EC76	EC77	EC78	EC79	EC80	EC81	ECMT1
						●		■
						■		
○								
						■		
	○	●						
■						○		
	●	■	■	●		●	■	
						●		
	○	●						
	●	■	■					
●	■	■	■	○		○		
				●	○			
	●							
								●
				●	○			
								●
				○				
	●		○					
						■		
				■	■			
				○		■		■

Overview of subjects and sources

SUBJECT	PUBLICATION CODE				
	ECMT2	ECMT3	EDFM1	EFTA1	EM1
1. ACCIDENTS		●			
2. AGRICULTURE			■		●
3. CIVIL AVIATION					●
4. CLIMATE					
5. COMMODITIES			○		○
6. COMMUNICATIONS					●
7. CONSTRUCTION					○
8. CONSUMPTION			○		●
9. CRIME AND JUSTICE					
10. CULTURE					●
11. DEFENCE					●
12. DEVELOPMENT AND AID					
13. DISTRIBUTION					●
14. DRUGS					
15. EDUCATION AND TRAINING					●
16. EMPLOYMENT AND UNEMPLOYMENT	●				●
17. ENERGY	●				●
18. ENVIRONMENT					●
19. FINANCE					●
20. FISHING					●
21. FORESTRY					●
22. HEALTH					●
23. HOUSING					●
24. INCOME AND WEALTH					
25. INDUSTRIES	○	○			●
26. INTELLECTUAL PROPERTY					
27. INTERNATIONAL TRADE AND FINANCE			○	■	●
28. LABOUR					○
29. LAND					●
30. LIVING COSTS AND STANDARDS					●
31. MIGRATION					
32. MINERALS					○
33. MINING AND QUARRYING					○
34. NATIONAL ACCOUNTS					●
35. PARLIAMENT AND PUBLIC AFFAIRS					
36. POPULATION AND VITAL STATISTICS					●
37. PRICES			○		●
38. PRODUCTION			○		●
39. REFUGEES					
40. SCIENCE AND TECHNOLOGY					
41. SHIPPING	●				●
42. SOCIAL INDICATORS					○
43. TAXATION					
44. TOURISM					●
45. TRANSPORT	■	■			●
46. WELFARE					○

PUBLICATION CODE

EPI1	EPO1	F1	F2	F3	FAO1	FAO2	FAO3	FAO4
					■	■		
○				○	○	○	○	○
○								
					●			
							■	■
■		○	○	○	○		○	○
	■							
○		○		○		■		●
					●			
				○				
					○			
		●			●			
○					●		○	○
		■	■	■				
		○	○	○				

SUBJECT	PUBLICATION CODE				
	FAO5	FAO6	FAO7	FAO8	FNOCL1
1. ACCIDENTS					
2. AGRICULTURE	■	■	■		■
3. CIVIL AVIATION					
4. CLIMATE					
5. COMMODITIES	○	○	○	○	○
6. COMMUNICATIONS					
7. CONSTRUCTION					
8. CONSUMPTION	●				
9. CRIME AND JUSTICE					
10. CULTURE					
11. DEFENCE					
12. DEVELOPMENT AND AID					
13. DISTRIBUTION					
14. DRUGS					
15. EDUCATION AND TRAINING					
16. EMPLOYMENT AND UNEMPLOYMENT					
17. ENERGY					
18. ENVIRONMENT					
19. FINANCE	●				
20. FISHING					
21. FORESTRY				■	
22. HEALTH					
23. HOUSING					
24. INCOME AND WEALTH					
25. INDUSTRIES	●		○	○	○
26. INTELLECTUAL PROPERTY					
27. INTERNATIONAL TRADE AND FINANCE	●			●	
28. LABOUR					
29. LAND					
30. LIVING COSTS AND STANDARDS					
31. MIGRATION					
32. MINERALS					
33. MINING AND QUARRYING					
34. NATIONAL ACCOUNTS					
35. PARLIAMENT AND PUBLIC AFFAIRS					
36. POPULATION AND VITAL STATISTICS					
37. PRICES	●	●			
38. PRODUCTION	○	○	○	○	○
39. REFUGEES					
40. SCIENCE AND TECHNOLOGY					
41. SHIPPING					
42. SOCIAL INDICATORS					
43. TAXATION					
44. TOURISM					
45. TRANSPORT					
46. WELFARE					

PUBLICATION CODE								
FOL1	FOL2	FOL3	G1	G2	GATT1	GATT2	GATT3	GATT4
■	■	■			■	■		
○	○	○			○	○	○	○
							■	
	○				○	○		
○	○	○	○	○				
●	●	●			■	■	■	■
	●				●	●	●	●
○	○	○				○	●	
			■	■				

SUBJECT	PUBLICATION CODE				
	GATT5	GP1	HI1	IADB1	IAEA1
1. ACCIDENTS					
2. AGRICULTURE	■				
3. CIVIL AVIATION					
4. CLIMATE					
5. COMMODITIES	○				
6. COMMUNICATIONS					
7. CONSTRUCTION					
8. CONSUMPTION	○				
9. CRIME AND JUSTICE					
10. CULTURE					
11. DEFENCE					
12. DEVELOPMENT AND AID					
13. DISTRIBUTION		●			
14. DRUGS					
15. EDUCATION AND TRAINING					
16. EMPLOYMENT AND UNEMPLOYMENT			○		
17. ENERGY					■
18. ENVIRONMENT					
19. FINANCE			○	●	
20. FISHING					
21. FORESTRY					
22. HEALTH					
23. HOUSING					
24. INCOME AND WEALTH					
25. INDUSTRIES			○		○
26. INTELLECTUAL PROPERTY					
27. INTERNATIONAL TRADE AND FINANCE	○			■	
28. LABOUR					
29. LAND					
30. LIVING COSTS AND STANDARDS					
31. MIGRATION					
32. MINERALS					
33. MINING AND QUARRYING					
34. NATIONAL ACCOUNTS				●	
35. PARLIAMENT AND PUBLIC AFFAIRS					
36. POPULATION AND VITAL STATISTICS				●	
37. PRICES		○		●	
38. PRODUCTION	○				●
39. REFUGEES					
40. SCIENCE AND TECHNOLOGY					
41. SHIPPING					
42. SOCIAL INDICATORS					
43. TAXATION					
44. TOURISM			■		
45. TRANSPORT					
46. WELFARE					

PUBLICATION CODE								
IAHP1	IARC1	IATA1	IBA1	ICAC1	ICAC2	ICAO1	ICAO2	ICAO3
		●				■	●	
■				○	○			
		■				■	■	■
				■	■			
○			●	●	●			
				●	●			
		○						
		○	●				○	○
	■							
○		○	○			○	○	○
●				●	●			
○								
			■					
○		○	●		●			
○		○	●	●	●			
		●				○	○	○

SUBJECT	PUBLICATION CODE				
	ICAO4	ICAO5	ICAO6	ICAO7	ICAO8
1. ACCIDENTS					
2. AGRICULTURE					
3. CIVIL AVIATION	■	■	■	■	■
4. CLIMATE					
5. COMMODITIES					
6. COMMUNICATIONS					
7. CONSTRUCTION					
8. CONSUMPTION					
9. CRIME AND JUSTICE					
10. CULTURE					
11. DEFENCE					
12. DEVELOPMENT AND AID					
13. DISTRIBUTION					
14. DRUGS					
15. EDUCATION AND TRAINING					
16. EMPLOYMENT AND UNEMPLOYMENT					
17. ENERGY					
18. ENVIRONMENT					
19. FINANCE					
20. FISHING					
21. FORESTRY					
22. HEALTH					
23. HOUSING					
24. INCOME AND WEALTH					
25. INDUSTRIES	○	○	○	○	○
26. INTELLECTUAL PROPERTY					
27. INTERNATIONAL TRADE AND FINANCE					
28. LABOUR					
29. LAND					
30. LIVING COSTS AND STANDARDS					
31. MIGRATION					
32. MINERALS					
33. MINING AND QUARRYING					
34. NATIONAL ACCOUNTS					
35. PARLIAMENT AND PUBLIC AFFAIRS					
36. POPULATION AND VITAL STATISTICS					
37. PRICES					
38. PRODUCTION					
39. REFUGEES					
40. SCIENCE AND TECHNOLOGY					
41. SHIPPING					
42. SOCIAL INDICATORS					
43. TAXATION					
44. TOURISM					
45. TRANSPORT	○	○	○	○	○
46. WELFARE					

PUBLICATION CODE								
ICAO9	ICAO10	ICCAT1	ICCO1	ICCO2	ICCO3	IDF1	IEA1	IEA2
			■	■	■	■		
■	■							
			●	●	●	○		
				●	○	○	○	●
								●
							■	■
							●	
		■						
○	○	○					○	○
			○	●			●	●
			○	●	○		○	●
			○	●	○		○	○
○	○							

SUBJECT	PUBLICATION CODE				
	IEA3	IEA4	IEA5	IEA6	IEA7
1. ACCIDENTS					
2. AGRICULTURE					
3. CIVIL AVIATION					
4. CLIMATE					
5. COMMODITIES					
6. COMMUNICATIONS					
7. CONSTRUCTION					
8. CONSUMPTION	●	○	○		●
9. CRIME AND JUSTICE					
10. CULTURE					
11. DEFENCE					
12. DEVELOPMENT AND AID					
13. DISTRIBUTION					
14. DRUGS					
15. EDUCATION AND TRAINING					
16. EMPLOYMENT AND UNEMPLOYMENT					
17. ENERGY	■	■	■	■	■
18. ENVIRONMENT					
19. FINANCE					
20. FISHING					
21. FORESTRY					
22. HEALTH					
23. HOUSING					
24. INCOME AND WEALTH					
25. INDUSTRIES	○	○	○	○	○
26. INTELLECTUAL PROPERTY					
27. INTERNATIONAL TRADE AND FINANCE	●	○	○	●	●
28. LABOUR					
29. LAND					
30. LIVING COSTS AND STANDARDS					
31. MIGRATION					
32. MINERALS					
33. MINING AND QUARRYING					
34. NATIONAL ACCOUNTS					
35. PARLIAMENT AND PUBLIC AFFAIRS					
36. POPULATION AND VITAL STATISTICS					
37. PRICES				●	
38. PRODUCTION	●	○	○		●
39. REFUGEES					
40. SCIENCE AND TECHNOLOGY					
41. SHIPPING					
42. SOCIAL INDICATORS					
43. TAXATION				●	
44. TOURISM					
45. TRANSPORT					
46. WELFARE					

PUBLICATION CODE								
IEA8	IEA9	IEA10	IEA11	IEA12	IFA1	IISI1	IISI2	IISI3
					■			
		○			○	■	■	■
●	●	●		○	●	●		●
●	●							
■	■	■	■	■				
○	○	○	○	○	●	○	○	○
●	●	●	●	○	●			●
		●						
●	●	●	●	○	●		●	●

SUBJECT	PUBLICATION CODE				
	IISI4	IISI5	IISRP1	ILO1	ILO2
1. ACCIDENTS					
2. AGRICULTURE					
3. CIVIL AVIATION					
4. CLIMATE					
5. COMMODITIES	■	■	■		
6. COMMUNICATIONS					
7. CONSTRUCTION					
8. CONSUMPTION	●	●			
9. CRIME AND JUSTICE					
10. CULTURE					
11. DEFENCE					
12. DEVELOPMENT AND AID					
13. DISTRIBUTION					
14. DRUGS					
15. EDUCATION AND TRAINING					
16. EMPLOYMENT AND UNEMPLOYMENT		●		■	■
17. ENERGY					
18. ENVIRONMENT					
19. FINANCE					
20. FISHING					
21. FORESTRY					
22. HEALTH					
23. HOUSING					
24. INCOME AND WEALTH				■	
25. INDUSTRIES	○	○	○	○	○
26. INTELLECTUAL PROPERTY					
27. INTERNATIONAL TRADE AND FINANCE	●	●			
28. LABOUR				■	
29. LAND					
30. LIVING COSTS AND STANDARDS					
31. MIGRATION					
32. MINERALS					
33. MINING AND QUARRYING					
34. NATIONAL ACCOUNTS					
35. PARLIAMENT AND PUBLIC AFFAIRS					
36. POPULATION AND VITAL STATISTICS					■
37. PRICES					
38. PRODUCTION	●	●			
39. REFUGEES					
40. SCIENCE AND TECHNOLOGY					
41. SHIPPING					
42. SOCIAL INDICATORS					
43. TAXATION					
44. TOURISM					
45. TRANSPORT					
46. WELFARE					

PUBLICATION CODE								
ILO3	ILO4	ILO5	ILO6	ILO7	ILZSG1	ILZSG2	IMF1	IMF2
				■				
				○				
					■	○		
				○				
					●			
■	■	■	■	■				
				○				
				○				
				○				
				■				
○	○	○	○	○	○	○		
					●		■	■
				■				
					■	■		
				○	■	■		
■	■	■	■					
					●	●		
					●	●		
				○				

SUBJECT	PUBLICATION CODE				
	IMF3	IMF4	IMF5	IMF6	IMF7
1. ACCIDENTS					
2. AGRICULTURE			○		
3. CIVIL AVIATION					
4. CLIMATE					
5. COMMODITIES					
6. COMMUNICATIONS			○		
7. CONSTRUCTION			○		
8. CONSUMPTION					
9. CRIME AND JUSTICE					
10. CULTURE					
11. DEFENCE			○		
12. DEVELOPMENT AND AID					
13. DISTRIBUTION					
14. DRUGS					
15. EDUCATION AND TRAINING			○		
16. EMPLOYMENT AND UNEMPLOYMENT				●	●
17. ENERGY			○		
18. ENVIRONMENT					
19. FINANCE			■	■	■
20. FISHING					
21. FORESTRY					
22. HEALTH			○		
23. HOUSING			○		
24. INCOME AND WEALTH			○		
25. INDUSTRIES					
26. INTELLECTUAL PROPERTY					
27. INTERNATIONAL TRADE AND FINANCE	■	■		■	■
28. LABOUR					
29. LAND					
30. LIVING COSTS AND STANDARDS					
31. MIGRATION					
32. MINERALS					
33. MINING AND QUARRYING			○		
34. NATIONAL ACCOUNTS			■	●	●
35. PARLIAMENT AND PUBLIC AFFAIRS					
36. POPULATION AND VITAL STATISTICS				●	●
37. PRICES				●	●
38. PRODUCTION				●	●
39. REFUGEES					
40. SCIENCE AND TECHNOLOGY					
41. SHIPPING					
42. SOCIAL INDICATORS					
43. TAXATION			●		
44. TOURISM					
45. TRANSPORT			○		
46. WELFARE			○		

PUBLICATION CODE								
IMWF1	INPFC1	IP1	IPHC1	IPU1	IPU2	IRF1	IRRI1	IRSG1
						●		
							■	
		○					○	■
		●					○	●
							●	
							○	
		■						
	■		■					
■							○	
●	○		○				○	○
		●				●	○	●
○								
							○	
●								
				■	■			
							○	●
		●				●	○	●
		●						
						●		
						■		

SUBJECT	PUBLICATION CODE				
	IRSG2	IRTU1	ISL1	ISL2	ISO1
1. ACCIDENTS			●	●	
2. AGRICULTURE					■
3. CIVIL AVIATION		●			
4. CLIMATE					
5. COMMODITIES	■			●	●
6. COMMUNICATIONS					
7. CONSTRUCTION					
8. CONSUMPTION	●				○
9. CRIME AND JUSTICE					
10. CULTURE					
11. DEFENCE					
12. DEVELOPMENT AND AID					
13. DISTRIBUTION					
14. DRUGS					
15. EDUCATION AND TRAINING					
16. EMPLOYMENT AND UNEMPLOYMENT		●		●	
17. ENERGY					
18. ENVIRONMENT					
19. FINANCE					
20. FISHING				●	
21. FORESTRY					
22. HEALTH					
23. HOUSING					
24. INCOME AND WEALTH					
25. INDUSTRIES	○	○	○	○	
26. INTELLECTUAL PROPERTY					
27. INTERNATIONAL TRADE AND FINANCE	●			●	○
28. LABOUR					
29. LAND					
30. LIVING COSTS AND STANDARDS					
31. MIGRATION					
32. MINERALS					
33. MINING AND QUARRYING					
34. NATIONAL ACCOUNTS					
35. PARLIAMENT AND PUBLIC AFFAIRS					
36. POPULATION AND VITAL STATISTICS					
37. PRICES	●		●	●	●
38. PRODUCTION	●		●		○
39. REFUGEES					
40. SCIENCE AND TECHNOLOGY					
41. SHIPPING		●	■	■	
42. SOCIAL INDICATORS					
43. TAXATION					
44. TOURISM					
45. TRANSPORT	●	■			
46. WELFARE					

PUBLICATION CODE								
ISO2	ISO3	ISSB1	ISSB2	ISSB3	ISTA1	ISTA2	ITC1	ITMF1
■	■				■	■	■	
●	●	■	■	■	○	○	○	○
●	●					○	●	●
							●	
								●
								●
		○	○	○	○	○	○	■
●	●	●	○	●	●	●	●	●
								●
						●	●	
●	●					●	●	
●	●	●			○	○	○	○

SUBJECT	PUBLICATION CODE				
	ITMF2	ITMF3	ITTO1	ITU1	IUR1
1. ACCIDENTS					
2. AGRICULTURE					
3. CIVIL AVIATION					
4. CLIMATE					
5. COMMODITIES	●	○	○		
6. COMMUNICATIONS				■	
7. CONSTRUCTION					
8. CONSUMPTION	●				
9. CRIME AND JUSTICE					
10. CULTURE					
11. DEFENCE					
12. DEVELOPMENT AND AID					
13. DISTRIBUTION					
14. DRUGS					
15. EDUCATION AND TRAINING					
16. EMPLOYMENT AND UNEMPLOYMENT			○	○	●
17. ENERGY					
18. ENVIRONMENT					
19. FINANCE				○	○
20. FISHING					
21. FORESTRY			■		
22. HEALTH					
23. HOUSING					
24. INCOME AND WEALTH					
25. INDUSTRIES	■	■	○	○	○
26. INTELLECTUAL PROPERTY					
27. INTERNATIONAL TRADE AND FINANCE			○		
28. LABOUR					
29. LAND			●		
30. LIVING COSTS AND STANDARDS					
31. MIGRATION					
32. MINERALS					
33. MINING AND QUARRYING					
34. NATIONAL ACCOUNTS					
35. PARLIAMENT AND PUBLIC AFFAIRS					
36. POPULATION AND VITAL STATISTICS					
37. PRICES					
38. PRODUCTION			○		
39. REFUGEES					
40. SCIENCE AND TECHNOLOGY					
41. SHIPPING					
42. SOCIAL INDICATORS					
43. TAXATION					
44. TOURISM					
45. TRANSPORT					■
46. WELFARE					

PUBLICATION CODE								
IWC1	IWhC1	IWhC2	IWhC3	IWS1	JM1	JP1	LRS1	LRS2
								■
	○	■	■	●				
○		○	○	■	○	○		
		○	●	●	○			
	■							
■								
						●		
○				○		■	○	○
		○	●	●				
					■			
		○	●			●		
○		○	○	○	○	○	○	
							■	■

Overview of subjects and sources

SUBJECT	PUBLICATION CODE				
	LRS3	LRS4	MAC1	MAC2	MAC3
1. ACCIDENTS					
2. AGRICULTURE			●	●	●
3. CIVIL AVIATION			●	●	●
4. CLIMATE			●	●	
5. COMMODITIES			●	●	○
6. COMMUNICATIONS			●	●	●
7. CONSTRUCTION					
8. CONSUMPTION					
9. CRIME AND JUSTICE					
10. CULTURE				●	
11. DEFENCE					
12. DEVELOPMENT AND AID					
13. DISTRIBUTION					
14. DRUGS					
15. EDUCATION AND TRAINING			●	●	●
16. EMPLOYMENT AND UNEMPLOYMENT			●	●	●
17. ENERGY			●	●	
18. ENVIRONMENT					
19. FINANCE			●	●	●
20. FISHING		○	●	●	
21. FORESTRY				●	
22. HEALTH					
23. HOUSING					
24. INCOME AND WEALTH			●	●	●
25. INDUSTRIES	■	○	○	○	
26. INTELLECTUAL PROPERTY					
27. INTERNATIONAL TRADE AND FINANCE			●	●	●
28. LABOUR			●	●	●
29. LAND					
30. LIVING COSTS AND STANDARDS					
31. MIGRATION				●	●
32. MINERALS			○	○	○
33. MINING AND QUARRYING					
34. NATIONAL ACCOUNTS			●	●	●
35. PARLIAMENT AND PUBLIC AFFAIRS					
36. POPULATION AND VITAL STATISTICS			●	●	●
37. PRICES			●	●	●
38. PRODUCTION	○	○	●	●	●
39. REFUGEES					
40. SCIENCE AND TECHNOLOGY					
41. SHIPPING	○	■	●	●	●
42. SOCIAL INDICATORS					
43. TAXATION					
44. TOURISM					
45. TRANSPORT		○	●	●	●
46. WELFARE					

PUBLICATION CODE								
MB1	MB2	MHPPE1	MJ1	MLC1	MMB1	NATO1	NCM1	NWAFO1
							●	
				■	■		●	
							●	
							●	
○	■		○	○	○		○	
							●	
							●	
○	○	●	●	●	●		●	
							●	
							●	
						■		
							●	
							●	
							●	
				●	●	○	●	
							●	
							●	
		●	●		●	○	●	
							●	■
							●	
							●	
		■					●	
		●					●	
○	○		○	○	○		●	○
							●	
●		○	●	●	●		●	
							●	
		●		●			●	
		●						
		●					●	
○	○		■					
■			■				●	
		●			●		●	
							●	
		●		●	●		●	
●	●	●	●	●	●		●	
○	○		●	○	○		●	
							●	
							●	
		●						
		●					●	
							●	
							●	
		●					●	

SUBJECT	PUBLICATION CODE				
	LRS3	LRS4	MAC1	MAC2	MAC3
1. ACCIDENTS					
2. AGRICULTURE			●	●	●
3. CIVIL AVIATION			●	●	●
4. CLIMATE			●	●	
5. COMMODITIES			●	●	○
6. COMMUNICATIONS			●	●	●
7. CONSTRUCTION					
8. CONSUMPTION					
9. CRIME AND JUSTICE					
10. CULTURE				●	
11. DEFENCE					
12. DEVELOPMENT AND AID					
13. DISTRIBUTION					
14. DRUGS					
15. EDUCATION AND TRAINING			●	●	●
16. EMPLOYMENT AND UNEMPLOYMENT			●	●	●
17. ENERGY			●	●	
18. ENVIRONMENT					
19. FINANCE			●	●	●
20. FISHING		○	●	●	
21. FORESTRY				●	
22. HEALTH					
23. HOUSING					
24. INCOME AND WEALTH			●	●	●
25. INDUSTRIES	■	○	○	○	
26. INTELLECTUAL PROPERTY					
27. INTERNATIONAL TRADE AND FINANCE			●	●	●
28. LABOUR			●	●	●
29. LAND					
30. LIVING COSTS AND STANDARDS					
31. MIGRATION				●	●
32. MINERALS			○	○	○
33. MINING AND QUARRYING					
34. NATIONAL ACCOUNTS			●	●	●
35. PARLIAMENT AND PUBLIC AFFAIRS					
36. POPULATION AND VITAL STATISTICS			●	●	●
37. PRICES			●	●	●
38. PRODUCTION	○	○	●	●	●
39. REFUGEES					
40. SCIENCE AND TECHNOLOGY					
41. SHIPPING	○	■	●	●	●
42. SOCIAL INDICATORS					
43. TAXATION					
44. TOURISM					
45. TRANSPORT		○	●	●	●
46. WELFARE					

PUBLICATION CODE

OECD6	OECD7	OECD8	OECD9	OECD10	OECD11	OECD12	OECD13	OECD14
						○		
						○		
						■		
			■					■
■	■							
●	○							
○	○		○	○				
○								
						○		
		■	■	■		●	■	○
					■			
●								
						●		
○								

SUBJECT	PUBLICATION CODE				
	OECD15	OECD16	OECD17	OECD18	OECD19
1. ACCIDENTS					
2. AGRICULTURE					
3. CIVIL AVIATION					
4. CLIMATE					
5. COMMODITIES				○	
6. COMMUNICATIONS					
7. CONSTRUCTION					
8. CONSUMPTION				●	
9. CRIME AND JUSTICE					
10. CULTURE					
11. DEFENCE					
12. DEVELOPMENT AND AID					
13. DISTRIBUTION					
14. DRUGS					
15. EDUCATION AND TRAINING					
16. EMPLOYMENT AND UNEMPLOYMENT	■	■		●	■
17. ENERGY					
18. ENVIRONMENT					
19. FINANCE		●		●	
20. FISHING					
21. FORESTRY					
22. HEALTH					
23. HOUSING					
24. INCOME AND WEALTH		■			
25. INDUSTRIES	○	■		■	
26. INTELLECTUAL PROPERTY					
27. INTERNATIONAL TRADE AND FINANCE		■	■	●	
28. LABOUR					
29. LAND					
30. LIVING COSTS AND STANDARDS					
31. MIGRATION					
32. MINERALS					
33. MINING AND QUARRYING					
34. NATIONAL ACCOUNTS					
35. PARLIAMENT AND PUBLIC AFFAIRS					
36. POPULATION AND VITAL STATISTICS					■
37. PRICES	■			●	
38. PRODUCTION	■	■		●	
39. REFUGEES					
40. SCIENCE AND TECHNOLOGY					
41. SHIPPING					
42. SOCIAL INDICATORS					
43. TAXATION					
44. TOURISM					
45. TRANSPORT					
46. WELFARE					

PUBLICATION CODE								
OECD20	OECD21	OECD22	OECD23	OECD24	OECD25	OECD26	OECD27	OECD28
●								
						■		
					○	○		
	●	●						
		●			●	●		
	●	●						
●								
●	●	●	■		●			
	●	●			●			
●								
	●	●						
		●						
		●						
●								
●	●	●						
●	●	●	■					○
					○	○		
	●	●		●	●	●	■	●
●		●	■					
	●	●						■
●								
	●	●	■		●			
	●	●			●	●		
				■				
		●			■			
■								
	●	●			○			

SUBJECT	PUBLICATION CODE				
	OECD29	OECD30	OECD31	OECD32	OECD33
1. ACCIDENTS					■
2. AGRICULTURE				○	●
3. CIVIL AVIATION					
4. CLIMATE					
5. COMMODITIES					○
6. COMMUNICATIONS					
7. CONSTRUCTION				●	
8. CONSUMPTION				○	○
9. CRIME AND JUSTICE					
10. CULTURE					
11. DEFENCE					
12. DEVELOPMENT AND AID					
13. DISTRIBUTION					
14. DRUGS					
15. EDUCATION AND TRAINING					
16. EMPLOYMENT AND UNEMPLOYMENT	●			■	
17. ENERGY			■		●
18. ENVIRONMENT					■
19. FINANCE				●	
20. FISHING					
21. FORESTRY					■
22. HEALTH					
23. HOUSING				●	
24. INCOME AND WEALTH	○			■	
25. INDUSTRIES			○	○	●
26. INTELLECTUAL PROPERTY					
27. INTERNATIONAL TRADE AND FINANCE				●	●
28. LABOUR				●	
29. LAND					■
30. LIVING COSTS AND STANDARDS					
31. MIGRATION					
32. MINERALS					○
33. MINING AND QUARRYING					
34. NATIONAL ACCOUNTS	■			■	●
35. PARLIAMENT AND PUBLIC AFFAIRS					
36. POPULATION AND VITAL STATISTICS				●	●
37. PRICES				■	
38. PRODUCTION			●		○
39. REFUGEES					
40. SCIENCE AND TECHNOLOGY					●
41. SHIPPING					
42. SOCIAL INDICATORS					
43. TAXATION					
44. TOURISM		■			●
45. TRANSPORT		○			●
46. WELFARE	○			○	

PUBLICATION CODE								
OECD34	OECD35	OECD36	OECD37	OECD38	OECD39	OECD40	OECD41	OECD42
				○				
				●			○	○
						■		
●	■	■	■					●
								○
				■				
■	●			●			○	●
					■		■	●
							○	
				●				
								■
								●

SUBJECT	PUBLICATION CODE				
	OECD43	OECD44	OECD45	OECD46	OECD47
1. ACCIDENTS					
2. AGRICULTURE					
3. CIVIL AVIATION					
4. CLIMATE					
5. COMMODITIES			○		○
6. COMMUNICATIONS		○			
7. CONSTRUCTION					
8. CONSUMPTION			○		
9. CRIME AND JUSTICE					
10. CULTURE					
11. DEFENCE					
12. DEVELOPMENT AND AID					
13. DISTRIBUTION					
14. DRUGS					
15. EDUCATION AND TRAINING					
16. EMPLOYMENT AND UNEMPLOYMENT			○	○	○
17. ENERGY					●
18. ENVIRONMENT					
19. FINANCE				○	
20. FISHING	■				
21. FORESTRY					
22. HEALTH					
23. HOUSING					
24. INCOME AND WEALTH					
25. INDUSTRIES	○	○	■	○	○
26. INTELLECTUAL PROPERTY					
27. INTERNATIONAL TRADE AND FINANCE	●	■	○	●	
28. LABOUR					
29. LAND					
30. LIVING COSTS AND STANDARDS					
31. MIGRATION					
32. MINERALS					■
33. MINING AND QUARRYING					
34. NATIONAL ACCOUNTS					
35. PARLIAMENT AND PUBLIC AFFAIRS					
36. POPULATION AND VITAL STATISTICS					
37. PRICES				○	
38. PRODUCTION	●		○		○
39. REFUGEES					
40. SCIENCE AND TECHNOLOGY					
41. SHIPPING					
42. SOCIAL INDICATORS					
43. TAXATION					
44. TOURISM		○		■	
45. TRANSPORT		○			
46. WELFARE					

PUBLICATION CODE								
OIVV1	OPEC1	OPEC2	PC1	PKF1	PKF2	PPI1	SATRA1	SFIA1
■								
○	○	○				●	○	
●	●	●				○	●	
							○	
	■	■						
	○	○	○	○	○			
								■
						●		
			○					
○	○	○		○	○	■	■	○
●	●		○			○	●	●
○								
	●							
	●		■					
	●	●						○
●	●	●				○	●	
	●	●						
			●					
				■	■			
	●							
			○					

SUBJECT	PUBLICATION CODE				
	SMMT1	SMMT2	SPC1	SPC2	UN1
1. ACCIDENTS					
2. AGRICULTURE					○
3. CIVIL AVIATION					●
4. CLIMATE					
5. COMMODITIES			○		○
6. COMMUNICATIONS					
7. CONSTRUCTION					
8. CONSUMPTION					○
9. CRIME AND JUSTICE					
10. CULTURE					
11. DEFENCE					
12. DEVELOPMENT AND AID				●	
13. DISTRIBUTION					
14. DRUGS					
15. EDUCATION AND TRAINING					●
16. EMPLOYMENT AND UNEMPLOYMENT					●
17. ENERGY					●
18. ENVIRONMENT					
19. FINANCE					
20. FISHING					
21. FORESTRY					
22. HEALTH					
23. HOUSING					
24. INCOME AND WEALTH					
25. INDUSTRIES	■	■			
26. INTELLECTUAL PROPERTY					
27. INTERNATIONAL TRADE AND FINANCE		●		●	●
28. LABOUR					
29. LAND					●
30. LIVING COSTS AND STANDARDS			■	●	
31. MIGRATION					
32. MINERALS					
33. MINING AND QUARRYING					
34. NATIONAL ACCOUNTS				●	●
35. PARLIAMENT AND PUBLIC AFFAIRS					
36. POPULATION AND VITAL STATISTICS				●	●
37. PRICES			■	●	●
38. PRODUCTION	●	●			●
39. REFUGEES					
40. SCIENCE AND TECHNOLOGY					
41. SHIPPING					●
42. SOCIAL INDICATORS					■
43. TAXATION					
44. TOURISM				●	
45. TRANSPORT	○	○			●
46. WELFARE					

PUBLICATION CODE								
UN2	UN3	UN4	UN5	UN6	UN7	UN8	UN9	UN10
●	●	●	●					
●	●	●	●					
				○			○	●
●	●	●	●					
●	●	●	●					■
				●	●	●	●	●
							●	
●	●	●	●					
●	●	●	●	●				●
●	●	●	●	■	■	■	■	●
●	●	●	●					
●	●	●	●					
●	●	●	●					
●	●	●	●					
								■
				○	○	○	○	■
●	●	●	●	●	●	●	●	●
				○				
				■				
●	●	●	●					
●	●	●	●					●
●	●	●	●					●
●	●	●	●	●	●	●	●	●
●	●	●	●					
●	●	●	●					
●	●	●	●					

SUBJECT	PUBLICATION CODE				
	UN11	UN12	UN13	UN14	UN15
1. ACCIDENTS					
2. AGRICULTURE					
3. CIVIL AVIATION			●		
4. CLIMATE					
5. COMMODITIES	■	●		●	●
6. COMMUNICATIONS					
7. CONSTRUCTION					
8. CONSUMPTION	●		●		
9. CRIME AND JUSTICE					
10. CULTURE					
11. DEFENCE					
12. DEVELOPMENT AND AID					
13. DISTRIBUTION					
14. DRUGS					
15. EDUCATION AND TRAINING					
16. EMPLOYMENT AND UNEMPLOYMENT			●		
17. ENERGY	●		●		
18. ENVIRONMENT					
19. FINANCE					
20. FISHING					
21. FORESTRY					
22. HEALTH					
23. HOUSING					
24. INCOME AND WEALTH					
25. INDUSTRIES	■		●	○	
26. INTELLECTUAL PROPERTY					
27. INTERNATIONAL TRADE AND FINANCE	●	■		■	■
28. LABOUR					
29. LAND			●		
30. LIVING COSTS AND STANDARDS					
31. MIGRATION					
32. MINERALS					
33. MINING AND QUARRYING					
34. NATIONAL ACCOUNTS			●		
35. PARLIAMENT AND PUBLIC AFFAIRS					
36. POPULATION AND VITAL STATISTICS					
37. PRICES					
38. PRODUCTION	●				
39. REFUGEES					
40. SCIENCE AND TECHNOLOGY					
41. SHIPPING			●		
42. SOCIAL INDICATORS					
43. TAXATION					
44. TOURISM					
45. TRANSPORT			■		
46. WELFARE					

PUBLICATION CODE								
UN16	UN17	UN18	UN19	UN20	UN21	UN22	UN23	UN24
○						●		
●						●		
					○	○		●
●								
		■						
○	○			○	●			
●	●							
●								
●								
●								
●	●					○		
●	●	●	●					
				■	■	●		
●						■		
						○		
						●		
●	●							
●	●	●						
●		●						
○		○		○	○	●		
○				○	●	○	■	■
●			●			●		
			■					
●	●							
●	●							
●	●		■			●		
○	○	●		○	●			
■	■		●					
●						●		
●								

SUBJECT	PUBLICATION CODE				
	UN25	UN26	UN27	UN28	UN29
1. ACCIDENTS					
2. AGRICULTURE	○				
3. CIVIL AVIATION					
4. CLIMATE					
5. COMMODITIES				■	
6. COMMUNICATIONS	●				
7. CONSTRUCTION		●			
8. CONSUMPTION		○			●
9. CRIME AND JUSTICE					
10. CULTURE					
11. DEFENCE	●				
12. DEVELOPMENT AND AID	●				
13. DISTRIBUTION					
14. DRUGS					■
15. EDUCATION AND TRAINING	●				
16. EMPLOYMENT AND UNEMPLOYMENT	●		■		
17. ENERGY			●	●	
18. ENVIRONMENT	●				
19. FINANCE			●		
20. FISHING					
21. FORESTRY					
22. HEALTH	●	●			
23. HOUSING		■			
24. INCOME AND WEALTH	●		●		
25. INDUSTRIES	○		■		
26. INTELLECTUAL PROPERTY					
27. INTERNATIONAL TRADE AND FINANCE					●
28. LABOUR	○		●		
29. LAND	●	■			
30. LIVING COSTS AND STANDARDS	●	○			
31. MIGRATION					
32. MINERALS				○	
33. MINING AND QUARRYING				●	
34. NATIONAL ACCOUNTS	●				
35. PARLIAMENT AND PUBLIC AFFAIRS					
36. POPULATION AND VITAL STATISTICS	●	●			
37. PRICES	○				
38. PRODUCTION			●	■	○
39. REFUGEES					
40. SCIENCE AND TECHNOLOGY					
41. SHIPPING					
42. SOCIAL INDICATORS	●	●			
43. TAXATION	●				
44. TOURISM					
45. TRANSPORT		●			
46. WELFARE	●				

PUBLICATION CODE								
UN30	UN31	UN32	UN33	UN34	UN35	UN36	UN37	UN38
				■				
	○	○	○		●			
●				●				
■								
					●			
		●			●			
					●			
					●			
							■	
				○	○			
●	○	■	■	●	●			●
					●			
	○				●			
					●			
						■	■	■
					●			
		●		●	●	○		
○				○	●			
	■	●			●			
	○	○			●			

SUBJECT	PUBLICATION CODE				
	UN39	UN40	UN41	UN42	UN43
1. ACCIDENTS					
2. AGRICULTURE		■			●
3. CIVIL AVIATION					●
4. CLIMATE					
5. COMMODITIES		○			●
6. COMMUNICATIONS					
7. CONSTRUCTION					●
8. CONSUMPTION					
9. CRIME AND JUSTICE					
10. CULTURE					
11. DEFENCE					
12. DEVELOPMENT AND AID			■		
13. DISTRIBUTION					●
14. DRUGS					
15. EDUCATION AND TRAINING					
16. EMPLOYMENT AND UNEMPLOYMENT					
17. ENERGY					○
18. ENVIRONMENT					
19. FINANCE					●
20. FISHING					
21. FORESTRY					
22. HEALTH					
23. HOUSING					●
24. INCOME AND WEALTH					
25. INDUSTRIES		○			
26. INTELLECTUAL PROPERTY					
27. INTERNATIONAL TRADE AND FINANCE					●
28. LABOUR		●			
29. LAND					
30. LIVING COSTS AND STANDARDS					
31. MIGRATION					●
32. MINERALS					○
33. MINING AND QUARRYING					○
34. NATIONAL ACCOUNTS				■	●
35. PARLIAMENT AND PUBLIC AFFAIRS					
36. POPULATION AND VITAL STATISTICS	■				●
37. PRICES		●			●
38. PRODUCTION					●
39. REFUGEES			■		
40. SCIENCE AND TECHNOLOGY					
41. SHIPPING					
42. SOCIAL INDICATORS					
43. TAXATION					
44. TOURISM					
45. TRANSPORT					●
46. WELFARE					

PUBLICATION CODE								
UN44	UN45	UN46	UN47	UN48	UN49	UN50	UN51	UN52
●			■					
●	●					●		
●	●					●		
○	○			■	■	○		
●						●		
	●							
●	●				○	●		
		●						
						●		
						●	●	
●	●	●				●		
●	●	●				●		
●	●					●		
●								
●	●					●		
●						●		
●						●		
●	●	●				●		
●	●	●						
●						●		
○	○				○	●		
						●		
●	●			○	○	●		■
	○					○		
●	●					●		
●	●					○		
	●					○		
●	○					●		
●	●	●				●		
●	●	●				●		
●	●					●		
●	●				○	●		
							■	
●						●		
●	●					●		
		■				○		
						●		
●						●		
●	●		●			●		
	●							

SUBJECT	PUBLICATION CODE				
	UN53	UN54	UN55	UNCTAD1	UNCTAD2
1. ACCIDENTS					
2. AGRICULTURE			●	●	
3. CIVIL AVIATION					
4. CLIMATE					
5. COMMODITIES					
6. COMMUNICATIONS			●		
7. CONSTRUCTION					
8. CONSUMPTION				●	
9. CRIME AND JUSTICE					
10. CULTURE					
11. DEFENCE					
12. DEVELOPMENT AND AID				●	
13. DISTRIBUTION					
14. DRUGS					
15. EDUCATION AND TRAINING			●	●	
16. EMPLOYMENT AND UNEMPLOYMENT			●	●	
17. ENERGY			●	●	
18. ENVIRONMENT					
19. FINANCE					
20. FISHING					
21. FORESTRY					
22. HEALTH			●	●	
23. HOUSING					
24. INCOME AND WEALTH					
25. INDUSTRIES					○
26. INTELLECTUAL PROPERTY					
27. INTERNATIONAL TRADE AND FINANCE	■		●	●	●
28. LABOUR				●	
29. LAND				●	
30. LIVING COSTS AND STANDARDS					
31. MIGRATION					
32. MINERALS					
33. MINING AND QUARRYING					
34. NATIONAL ACCOUNTS				●	
35. PARLIAMENT AND PUBLIC AFFAIRS					
36. POPULATION AND VITAL STATISTICS		■	●	●	
37. PRICES				●	●
38. PRODUCTION			●	●	
39. REFUGEES					
40. SCIENCE AND TECHNOLOGY					
41. SHIPPING				○	■
42. SOCIAL INDICATORS				●	
43. TAXATION					
44. TOURISM			●		
45. TRANSPORT			●	●	●
46. WELFARE					

PUBLICATION CODE								
UNCTAD3	UNCTAD4	UNCTAD5	UNESCO1	UNICEF1	UNICEF2	UNIDO1	VICES1	WB1
		●					●	●
○	■						○	
			■		●		●	
							●	
●							●	○
			■					○
		●			●	●		■
							●	
		●	■	●	■		●	●
		●	●			●	●	●
							●	○
		●						
		●			●		●	
		●		●	■		●	●
							●	●
					●	●	●	○
○						■	●	
●	■	●				●	●	
						●		○
		●	●					●
							●	
■	○							
○								
		●			●		●	●
		●	●	●	●		●	●
●	●	●			●		●	
●		●				●	●	
		●	■			●		
		●						
		●			●		○	■
		●						
							●	
				■	■		●	●

SUBJECT	PUBLICATION CODE				
	WB2	WB3	WB4	WB5	WB6
1. ACCIDENTS					
2. AGRICULTURE					○
3. CIVIL AVIATION					
4. CLIMATE					
5. COMMODITIES					
6. COMMUNICATIONS					
7. CONSTRUCTION					
8. CONSUMPTION					●
9. CRIME AND JUSTICE					
10. CULTURE					
11. DEFENCE					
12. DEVELOPMENT AND AID	■	■	■		
13. DISTRIBUTION					
14. DRUGS					
15. EDUCATION AND TRAINING					
16. EMPLOYMENT AND UNEMPLOYMENT	●				
17. ENERGY					
18. ENVIRONMENT					
19. FINANCE					●
20. FISHING					
21. FORESTRY					
22. HEALTH					
23. HOUSING					
24. INCOME AND WEALTH					
25. INDUSTRIES					○
26. INTELLECTUAL PROPERTY					
27. INTERNATIONAL TRADE AND FINANCE	●	■	■		●
28. LABOUR					
29. LAND					
30. LIVING COSTS AND STANDARDS					
31. MIGRATION				■	
32. MINERALS					
33. MINING AND QUARRYING					
34. NATIONAL ACCOUNTS	●				●
35. PARLIAMENT AND PUBLIC AFFAIRS					
36. POPULATION AND VITAL STATISTICS				■	
37. PRICES	●				●
38. PRODUCTION					
39. REFUGEES					
40. SCIENCE AND TECHNOLOGY					
41. SHIPPING					
42. SOCIAL INDICATORS					
43. TAXATION					
44. TOURISM					
45. TRANSPORT					
46. WELFARE					

PUBLICATION CODE								
WBMS1	WBMS2	WBMS3	WBMS4	WC1	WFP1	WHO1	WHO2	WIPO1
						●		
				■				
○	○	○	■		○			
●	○	●	○	●	○			
					■			
						●		
				●		●		
				●				
						■	■	
○	○	○	○	○				
								■
●		●	●	●	○			
				●				
				●				
■	■	■	●					
●								
				●				
				●		●	●	
●	●	●		●	●			
●	○	●	●					
						●	●	
					○			
				●		●		

SUBJECT	PUBLICATION CODE				
	WIPO2	WIPO3	WMO1	WTO1	WTO2
1. ACCIDENTS					
2. AGRICULTURE					
3. CIVIL AVIATION					
4. CLIMATE			■		
5. COMMODITIES					
6. COMMUNICATIONS					
7. CONSTRUCTION					
8. CONSUMPTION					
9. CRIME AND JUSTICE					
10. CULTURE					
11. DEFENCE					
12. DEVELOPMENT AND AID					
13. DISTRIBUTION					
14. DRUGS					
15. EDUCATION AND TRAINING					
16. EMPLOYMENT AND UNEMPLOYMENT					
17. ENERGY					
18. ENVIRONMENT					
19. FINANCE					
20. FISHING					
21. FORESTRY					
22. HEALTH					
23. HOUSING					
24. INCOME AND WEALTH					
25. INDUSTRIES					
26. INTELLECTUAL PROPERTY	■	■			
27. INTERNATIONAL TRADE AND FINANCE					
28. LABOUR					
29. LAND					
30. LIVING COSTS AND STANDARDS					
31. MIGRATION					
32. MINERALS					
33. MINING AND QUARRYING					
34. NATIONAL ACCOUNTS					
35. PARLIAMENT AND PUBLIC AFFAIRS					
36. POPULATION AND VITAL STATISTICS					
37. PRICES					
38. PRODUCTION					
39. REFUGEES					
40. SCIENCE AND TECHNOLOGY					
41. SHIPPING					
42. SOCIAL INDICATORS					
43. TAXATION					
44. TOURISM				■	■
45. TRANSPORT				○	
46. WELFARE					

PUBLICATION CODE								
WTO3	WTO4							
○	○							
○								
	○							
■	■							
○	○							

instat

GUIDE TO SUBJECTS AND SOURCES

Sections 1 – 24

1 ACCIDENTS

1 ACCIDENTS

Subject	Categories	Units	Time series Yes/No Frequency		Territorial coverage	Source (Table no.)
1.1 AIR – see also under Transport (1.9) and Section 3						
1.1.1 Accidents and Incidents						
Accidents and incidents	By type of operation and aircraft mass	nos	No		World	ICAO1 (I)
Aeroplanes	By type of operation and aircraft mass	nos	No		World	ICAO1 (I)
Aeroplanes	By type of operation and power plant	nos	No		World	ICAO1 (II)
Aircraft destroyed	By type of operation and aircraft mass	nos	No		World	ICAO1 (I)
Aircraft destroyed	By type of operation and power plant	nos	No		World	ICAO1 (II)
Civil aviation	By flying category	nos	No		World	ICAO2 (1.5)
Helicopters	By type of operation and aircraft mass	nos	No		World	ICAO1 (I)
Occurrences	Fatal, non fatal, by type of operation and aircraft mass	nos	No		World	ICAO1 (I)
Occurrences	Fatal, non fatal, by type of operation and power plant	nos	No		World	ICAO1 (II)
Fatal Accidents – see also under Fatalities (1.1.2)						
Accidents		nos	Yes	A	IATA members	IATA1
Number aboard	Crew, passengers	nos	Yes	A	IATA members	IATA1
Number injured	Crew, passengers	nos	Yes	A	IATA members	IATA1
Number of third parties	Crew, passengers	nos	Yes	A	IATA members	IATA1
1.1.2 Fatalities						
Fatal accident rates		rate	Yes	A	IATA members	IATA1
Fatal passenger aircraft accidents by phase of flight	Jet aircraft, all aircraft, total	nos, %	Yes	A	World	CAA1 (13)
Fatal passenger aircraft accidents	Jet aircraft	nos, hours	Yes	A	World	CAA1 (7)
Fatal passenger aircraft accidents	Non-jet aircraft	nos, hours	Yes	A	World	CAA1 (8)
Fatal passenger aircraft accidents	Total	nos, hours	Yes	A	World	CAA1 (6)
Fatalities, commercial air transport	Scheduled and unscheduled services	nos	Yes	A	World	ICAO2 (1.6)
Fatalities occurring in fatal passenger aircraft accidents	Jet, all aircraft	nos, %	Yes	A	World	CAA1 (11)
Fatalities occurring in passenger aircraft involved in mid-air collisions	Scheduled passenger, scheduled passenger and another category	nos	Yes	A	World	CAA1 (12)
Fatality rates		rate km	Yes	A	IATA members	IATA1
Mid-air collisions involving fatalities	Phase take-off, en route, approach, landing. engine type, scheduled, other	nos	Yes	A	World	CAA1 (14)
Number killed	Crew, passengers	nos	Yes	A	IATA members	IATA1
Number of fatalities	Crew, PAX, other, by type of operation and aircraft mass	nos	No		World	ICAO1 (I)
Number of fatalities	Crew, PAX, other, by type of operation and power plant	nos	No		World	ICAO1 (II)
Passenger traffic and fatal accident rates	By region	km, nos	Yes	A	World	CAA1 (10)
Scheduled and non-scheduled passenger fatality rates		nos, km	Yes	A	World	CAA1 (9)

1 ACCIDENTS

Subject	Categories	Units	Time series Yes/No Frequency		Territorial coverage	Source (Table no.)
1.2 GENERAL						
Deaths from external causes	By cause	rate	Yes	10 yrly	OECD	OECD20 (29.1)
1.3 INDUSTRIAL						
1.3.1 General						
Accidents	By selected characteristics	rate	No		OECD	OECD20 (30.2B)
Fatal occupational injuries	By branch of activity	rate	Yes	10 yrly	OECD	OECD20 (15.1)
Occupational injuries, general level	Number, workers involved, work-days not worked	nos	Yes	A	World	ILO7 (31A)
Persons injured	By country, by major industry divisions, lost work	nos	No		SEAR countries	WHO1 (64)
Persons seriously injured in work accidents	By selected characteristics	rate	Yes	10 yrly	OECD	OECD20 (30.2A)
1.3.2 Persons Injured and Workdays Lost						
Agriculture, hunting forestry and fishing	Number, workers involved, work-days not worked	nos	Yes	A	World	ILO7 (31B)
Agriculture, hunting, forestry and fishing		nos	No	I	World	ILO7 (29)
Community, social and personal services		nos	No	I	World	ILO7 (29)
Community, social and personal services	Number, workers involved, work-days not worked	nos	Yes	A	World	ILO7 (31B)
Construction		nos	No	I	World	ILO7 (29)
Construction	Number, workers involved, work-days not worked	nos	Yes	A	World	ILO7 (31B)
Electricity, gas and water	Number, workers involved, work-days not worked	nos	Yes	A	World	ILO7 (31B)
Electricity, gas, water		nos	No	I	World	ILO7 (29)
Financing, insurance, real estate, business services		nos	No	I	World	ILO7 (29)
Financing, insurance, real estate, business services	Number, workers involved, work-days not worked	nos	Yes	A	World	ILO7 (31B)
Manufacturing		nos	No	I	World	ILO7 (29)
Manufacturing	Number, workers involved, work-days not worked	nos	Yes	A	World	ILO7 (31B)
Mining and quarrying	Number, workers involved, work-days not worked	nos	Yes	A	World	ILO7 (31B)
Mining, quarrying		nos	No	I	World	ILO7 (29)
Total		nos	No	I	World	ILO7 (29)
Total	Number, workers involved, work-days not worked	nos	Yes	A	World	ILO7 (31B)
Trade, restaurants and hotels		nos	No	I	World	ILO7 (29)
Trade, restaurants and hotels	Number, workers involved, work-days not worked	nos	Yes	A	World	ILO7 (31B)

Subject	Categories	Units	Time series Yes/No Frequency		Territorial coverage	Source (Table no.)
Transport, storage and communication	Number, workers involved, work-days not worked	nos	Yes	A	World	ILO7 (31B)
Transport, storage, communication		nos	No	I	World	ILO7 (29)
1.3.3 Rates of Fatal Injuries						
Agriculture, hunting, forestry and fishing		rate	No	I	World	ILO7 (30)
Community, social and personal services		rate	No	I	World	ILO7 (30)
Construction		rate	No	I	World	ILO7 (30)
Electricity, gas, water		rate	No	I	World	ILO7 (30)
Financing, insurance, real estate, business services		rate	No	I	World	ILO7 (30)
Manufacturing		rate	No	I	World	ILO7 (30)
Mining, quarrying		rate	No	I	World	ILO7 (30)
Total		rate	No	I	World	ILO7 (30)
Trade, restaurants and hotels		rate	No	I	World	ILO7 (30)
Transport, storage, communication		rate	No	I	World	ILO7 (30)
1.4 NATURAL DISASTERS						
Disasters, major	Extent of damage	nos	Yes	I	OECD	OECD33 (8.1C)
1.4.1 Climatic and Meteorological						
Type of disaster	Type	nos	Yes	I	OECD	OECD33 (8.1C)
1.4.2 Floods						
Major and related losses, extent of damage	Deaths, type	nos, US$	Yes	I	OECD	OECD33 (8.1A)
1.4.3 Geological						
Extent of damage	Human deaths, injured, homeless	nos	Yes	I	OECD	OECD33 (8.1B)
Houses damaged, destroyed	Type	nos	Yes	I	OECD	OECD33 (8.1B)
Natural disasters, major	Type	nos	Yes	I	OECD	OECD33 (8.1B)
		US$	Yes	I	OECD	OECD33 (8.1B)
1.4.4 Hazardous Substances						
Accidents	Origin of accident, products involved, deaths, injured, evacuated	nos	Yes	I	World	OECD33
1.4.5 Oil Spills from Tankers						
Deaths and injuries	Deaths, injured, name of ship, flag, country affected, quantity spilled	US$, tonnes	Yes		World	OECD33 (8.2)
1.5 RAIL – see also under Transport (1.9) and Section 45						
Accidents, killed or injured		nos	No		EC	EC80 (2.22)

1 ACCIDENTS

Subject	Categories	Units	Time series Yes/No Frequency	Territorial coverage	Source (Table no.)
1.6 ROAD – see also under Transport (1.9) and Section 45					
Accident severity indices	By road user category killed per 1000 casualties	rate	No	ECMT countries	ECMT1 (6)
Accidents, elements involved	By pedestrian and vehicle type	nos	No	EC	EC80 (3.18)
Accidents, damage	Number of cases, casualties of which killed, injured	nos	Yes A	ASEANS	ASEANS (9.5)
Accidents, alcohol abuse		nos	No	EC, Canada, USA	UN47 (5)
Accidents	By country, injury to persons, number injured, number killed, rate per vehicle, kms, accidents	nos, vehicle, km, %, % injury	Yes A	World	IRF1 (VII)
Accidents	By nature and surroundings	nos	Yes A	EC, Canada, USA	UN47 (3)
Accidents causing casualties, killed	By type of road	nos	No	ECMT countries	ECMT1 (10)
Accidents causing casualties, deaths within 30 days	By type of road	nos	No	ECMT countries	ECMT1 (10)
Accidents causing casualties, casualties (killed and injured)	By type of road	nos	No	ECMT countries	ECMT1 (10)
Accidents causing casualties		%	No	ECMT countries	ECMT1 (10)
Accidents causing casualties	By type of road	nos	No	ECMT countries	ECMT1 (10)
Accidents causing casualties	Motorways, overall road network	%	No	ECMT countries	ECMT1 (11)
	By sex and age groups	rates	No	OECD	OECD20 (30.1B)
Accidents causing casualties		ratio	No	ECMT countries	ECMT1 (3)
Casualties	Motorways, overall road network	%	No	ECMT countries	ECMT1 (11)
Death from motor vehicle accidents	By sex and age, and distribution by mode of transport	rates, %	No	OECD	OECD20 (29.2)
Deaths, number of road motor vehicles		ratio	No	ECMT countries	ECMT1 (3)
Deaths within 30 days	Motorways, overall road network	%	No	ECMT countries	ECMT1 (11)
Deaths within 30 days per 1000 accidents causing casualties on motorways		nos	No	ECMT countries	ECMT1 (11)
Deaths within 30 days per 1000 accidents causing casualties on other roads		nos	No	ECMT countries	ECMT1 (11)
Deaths within 30 days per 100km of motorways		nos	No	ECMT countries	ECMT1 (11)
Injured		nos	Yes I	EC, Canada, USA	UN47 (1)
Injuries and fatalities	By country, by accidents	nos	No	EC	EC18 (10.6)
Killed		nos, % change	Yes A	ECMT countries	ECMT1 (1A)
Killed	By road-user category	%	No	ECMT countries	ECMT1 (4)
Killed and injured		nos, % change	Yes A	ECMT countries	ECMT1 (1B)
Killed and injured		nos	Yes 5 yrly	EC	ECMT3
Killed and injured		nos	Yes A	EC	EC80 (3.13)
Killed and Injured		nos	Yes I	EC, Canada, USA	UN47 (2)
Killed and injured		nos	Yes I	EC	EC80 (1.3)
Killed and injured	By category and age group	nos	Yes A	EC, Canada, USA	UN47 (4)
Killed and injured	By country	nos	No	EC	EC35
Killed and injured	By road-user category	%	No	ECMT countries	ECMT1 (5)
Number killed per million road users	By road-user category	rate	No	ECMT countries	ECMT1 (7)
Personal injury, death,		nos	Yes A		EC9 (7.11)
Personal injury	Total built-up areas	nos	Yes A	EC	EC80 (3.13)

Subject	Categories	Units	Time series Yes/No Frequency		Territorial coverage	Source (Table no.)
Persons seriously injured	By sex and age groups	rates	Yes	10 yrly	OECD	OECD20 (30.1A)
Traffic casualties	By sex and age group	nos	No		EC	EC80 (3.15)
Traffic casualties	By sex and age group	rate	No		EC	EC80 (3.16)
Traffic casualties	By transport type	nos	No		EC	EC80 (3.14)
Traffic casualties	By transport type and age	nos	No		EC	EC80 (3.17)
1.7 SAFETY						
Persons afraid to walk alone in their neighbourhood at night	By selected characteristics	%	No		OECD	OECD20 (31.1)
1.8 SEA – see also under Transport (1.9) and Sections 41 and 45						
Lives lost	By category, per capita	nos	Yes	A	World	LRS2
Losses, geographical distribution	By how lost, region	nos	No		World	LRS2
Losses, category of ship	By ship type, how lost	nos, tonnage	No		World	LRS2 (3)
Losses	By age at time of loss	years, nos, grt-gt	Yes	A	World	ISL2 (1.4.2)
Losses	By flag	nos, tonnage	Yes	A	World	LRS2 (5)
Losses	By flag	nos, grt-gt	Yes	A	World	ISL2 (1.4.1)
Losses	By how, lost, flag, size, age	nos	No		World	LRS2 (1, 2a, 2b)
Losses	By how lost	gross tonnage, % of tonnage, nos	No		World	LRS2
Losses	By nature of casualty	nos, grt-gt, grt-gt-%	Yes	A	World	ISL2 (1.4.3)
Losses	Total loss, total loss by casualty	grt, gt, dwt, nos	Yes	A, Q, M	World	ISL1 (1.4.1-2)
Merchant fleets	By how lost	nos, tonnage	Yes	A	World	LRS2 (8)
1.9 TRANSPORT – see also under Air (1.1), Rail (1.5), Road (1.6), Sea (1.8) and Section 45						
Fatalities and injuries,		nos	Yes	A	ESCAP countries	UN44

2 AGRICULTURE

2.1 ACCOUNTS

2.2 ANIMAL FEEDSTUFFS

2.3 CAPITAL FORMATION

2.4 COCOA INDUSTRY

2.5 CONSUMPTION
- 2.5.1 Fruit and Vegetables
- 2.5.2 Meat
- 2.5.3 Milk and Dairy Products
- 2.5.4 Sugar
- 2.5.5. Total
- 2.5.6 Wine

2.6 DEVELOPMENT

2.7 EARNINGS

2.8 EMPLOYMENT

2.9 ENERGY CONSUMPTION

2.10 ENVIRONMENTAL PRESSURES
- 2.10.1 Air
- 2.10.2 Foodstuffs and Human Health
- 2.10.3 Soil
- 2.10.4 Water

2.11 EQUIPMENT

2.12 FERTILIZERS AND PESTICIDES
- 2.12.1 Consumption
- 2.12.2 Prices
- 2.12.3 Production
- 2.12.4 Subsidies
- 2.13.5 Trade

2.13 FINANCE
- 2.13.1 General
- 2.13.2 Subsidies
- 2.13.3 Taxes

2.14 FOOD SUPPLY

2.15 INCOMES

2.16 INTERNATIONAL TRADE
- 2.16.1 Animal Feed
- 2.16.2 Crops
- 2.16.3 Livestock and Meat
- 2.16.4 Milk and Dairy products
- 2.16.5 Sugar
- 2.16.6 Total
- 2.16.7 Wine and Beer

2.17 LAND USE AND IRRIGATION

2.18 LIVESTOCK

2.19 MILK, CHEESE AND OTHER LIVESTOCK PRODUCTS

2.20 MILK INDUSTRY
- 2.20.1 Enterprises
- 2.20.2 Finance and Prices
- 2.20.3 Products

2.21 NATIONAL ACCOUNTS

2.22 OILSEEDS, OILS, FATS AND OILMEALS

2.23 PRICES

2.24 PRODUCTION
- 2.24.1 Cereal Crops
- 2.24.2 Fruit and Vegetables
- 2.24.3 General

2.25 SELF-SUFFICIENCY

2.26 STRUCTURE OF HOLDINGS

2.27 SUGAR INDUSTRY

2.28 TEA INDUSTRY

2.29 TRANSPORT

2.30 WINE INDUSTRY

2.1 ACCOUNTS

Subject	Categories	Units	Time series Yes/No	Frequency	Territorial coverage	Source (Table no.)
Accounts, agricultural		ECU	Yes	A	EC	EC9 (5.22)
Accounts, agricultural		volume indices	Yes	A	EC	EC9 (5.23)
Accounts, agricultural	Overall figures at current prices and exchange rates	ECU	Yes	A	EEC	EC6 (IG 1)
Accounts, agricultural	Overall figures at 1980 prices and exchange rates	ECU	Yes	A	EEC	EC6 (IG 2)

2.2 ANIMAL FEEDSTUFFS

Subject	Categories	Units	Time series Yes/No	Frequency	Territorial coverage	Source (Table no.)
Animal feedstuffs		tonnes	Yes	A	EC	EC6 (ID17)
Compound feedingstuffs	By type of animal	tons	Yes	A	EUR12	EC57 (6.28)
Compound feedingstuffs	For dairy cows	tons	Yes	A	EUR12	EC57 (6.29)
Compound pig	Fattening pigs	ECU, nat curr	Yes	A, M	EC	MLC1 (-)
Compound pig	Rearing pigs	ECU, nat curr	Yes	A, M	EC	MLC1 (-)

2.3 CAPITAL FORMATION - see also National Accounts (2.21) and Section 34

Subject	Categories	Units	Time series Yes/No	Frequency	Territorial coverage	Source (Table no.)
Fixed capital formation, gross	At current prices and exchange rates and at investment rate	ECU, %	Yes	A	EC	EC26 (A.0.11)
Fixed capital formation, gross	At current prices and exchange rates	ECU	Yes	A	EC	EC26 (A.1-A.1.12)
Fixed capital formation, net	At current prices and exchange rates	ECU	Yes	A	EC	EC26 (A.1- A.1.12)
Fixed capital formation, gross	At current prices	nat curr	Yes	A	EC	EC26 (A.2.1-A.2.12)
Fixed capital formation, net	At current prices	nat curr	Yes	A	EC	EC26 (A.2.1-A.2.12)
Fixed capital formation, gross	By region	ECU	Yes	A	EC	EC26 (C.0.3)
Fixed capital formation, gross	Current prices and exchange rates	ECU	Yes	A	EC	EC6 (IG 7)
Fixed capital formation, gross	1980 prices and exchange rates	ECU	Yes	A	EC	EC6 (IG 8)

2.4 COCOA INDUSTRY

Subject	Categories	Units	Time series Yes/No	Frequency	Territorial coverage	Source (Table no.)
Butter, imports		tonnes	Yes	3 per year	Selected countries	EDFM1 (5)
CBE usage current and potential CBE usage	By country, by production, potential displacement	tonnes, %	No		EC	ICCO3(20)
Chocolate and chocolate products		US$, tonne	Yes	A	World	FAO2 (76)
Chocolate and chocolate products	By country	tonnes	Yes	A, Q	World	ICC02 (9)
Chocolate and chocolate products	By country	tonnes	Yes	A, Q	World	ICC02 (14)
Cocoa, powder and cake	By country	tonnes	Yes	A, Q	World	ICC02 (7)
Cocoa, coffee and tea	Output, by countries	nos	No		The Americas and Australasia	MAC2 (D6)
Cocoa, coffee and tea	By crop type, country	tonnes	Yes	A	Africa and Asia	MAC1 (D4)
Cocoa, quality of buffer stock	By total, % defective	tonnes, %	No		World	ICC01 (2)
Cocoa and cocoa products	destination of exports, by cocoa product, by country	tonnes	Yes	A, Q	World	ICC02 (20-29)
Cocoa and cocoa products	Origin of imports, by cocoa product, by country	tonnes	Yes	A, Q	World	ICC02 (20-30)
Cocoa and total tree-stock, annual plantings	By producing country, by type of tree-stock	ha	No		World	ICCO3(15)

2 AGRICULTURE

Subject	Categories	Units	Time series Yes/No Frequency		Territorial coverage	Source (Table no.)
Cocoa areas and production	By area, yields, production, by country	ha, kg, ha, tonnes	Yes		World	ICCO3 (5)
Cocoa areas and yields	By producing country, by type of tree-stock	ha, kg, ha	No		World	ICCO3(16)
Cocoa bean, net imports into consuming countries		tonnes	Yes	3 per year	Selected countries	EDFM1 (4)
Cocoa beans,	By country, re-exports	tonnes	Yes	A, Q	World	ICC02 (5)
Cocoa beans, grindings	By country	tonnes	Yes	A, Q	World	ICC02 (3)
Cocoa beans		tonnes	Yes	A	World	UN50 (1)
Cocoa beans		US$, tonne	Yes	A	World	FAO2 (72)
Cocoa beans	Area harvested, yield, production, by country, region	ha, kg, ha, tonnes	Yes	A	World	FAO7 (85)
Cocoa beans	By country	tonnes	Yes	A, Q	World	ICC02 (4)
Cocoa beans	By country	tonnes	Yes	A, Q	World	ICC02 (10)
Cocoa beans	By country	tonnes	Yes	A	World	ICC02 (2)
Cocoa beans	Gross crop, grindings surplus, deficit, end of season stocks, buffer stocks, price	tonnes, %, US$, SDR	Yes	A	World	ICC02 (1)
Cocoa beans	Total	kg, ha	Yes	A	World	FAO1 (79)
Cocoa beans and cocoa products in beans equivalent, net exports	By country, 5 year average	tonnes, %	Yes	A	World	ICC01 (6)
Cocoa beans and cocoa products in beans equivalent, net imports	By country, 5 year average	tonnes %	Yes	A	World	ICC01 (7)
Cocoa butter		US$, tonne	Yes	A	World	FAO2 (75)
Cocoa butter	By country	tonnes	Yes	A, Q	World	ICC02 (6)
Cocoa butter	By country	tonnes	Yes	A, Q	World	ICC02 (11)
Cocoa consumption	By region, by major consuming country	tonnes	Yes		World	ICCO3 (4)
Cocoa elasticity coefficients of apparent final consumption	By country, by model, error, price, income	%, nos	No		World	ICCO3(17)
Cocoa market, global balance	By production, grindings,	tonnes, %, SDR, tonne	Yes		World	ICCO3 (1)
Cocoa market development	By production, grindings, total stocks, prices, income growth	tonnes, %, SDR, tonnes	No		World	ICCO3(21)
Cocoa market development	By production, grindings, total stocks, prices, income growth	tonnes, %, SDR, tonne	No		World	ICCO3(22)
Cocoa paste, liquor	By country	tonnes	Yes	A, Q	World	ICC02 (8)
Cocoa paste, liquor	By country	tonnes	Yes	A, Q	World	ICC02 (13)
Cocoa paste		US$, tonne	Yes	A	World	FAO2 (74)
Cocoa powder and cake		US$, tonne	Yes	A	World	FAO2 (73)
Cocoa powder and cake	By country	tonnes	Yes	A, Q	World	ICC02 (12)
Cocoa projected production	By country of origin	tonnes	No		World	ICCO3(13)
Cocoa projections of final consumption	By country	tonnes	No		World	ICCO3(18)
Cocoa projections of shares of world consumption	By country	%	No		World	ICCO3(19)
Cocoa stocks	By grindings, closing stock, stocks-grinding ratio	tonnes, %	Yes		World	ICCO3 (2)
Cocoa trees, immature	By year of bearing, mature yield	years, %	No		World	ICCO3 (3)
Copra	Production, by country, region	tonnes	Yes	A	World	FAO7 (33)
Futures market: London terminal market	First three futures	£ per tonne	No		London closing prices	EDFM1 (8)
Futures market: London terminal market	High, lows	£ per tonne	Yes	A	London	EDFM1 (10)
Futures market: New York terminal market	First three futures	$ per tonne	No		New York settlement prices	EDFM1 (9)

Subject	Categories	Units	Time series Yes/No Frequency		Territorial coverage	Source (Table no.)
Futures market: New York terminal market	High, lows	$ per tonne	Yes	A	New York	EDFM1 (11)
Grindings		tonnes	Yes	3 per year	World	EDFM1 (1b)
Grindings	By continent,country	tonnes, %	Yes	A	World	ICCO1 (5)
Grindings		tonnes	Yes	3 per year	World	EDFM1 (3)
Liquor, imports		tonnes	Yes	3 per year	Selected countries	EDFM1 (6)
Powder, imports		tonnes	Yes	3 per year	Selected countries	EDFM1 (7)
Prices, physical	Spot Ghana Amsterdam ex-store	£ per tonnes	No		Ghana Amsterdam	EDFM1 (12)
Prices, cocoa product	Cocoa butter, cocoa powder	£ per tonne	Yes	A,M	Netherlands, USA	EDFM1 (13)
Prices, miscellaneous		SDRs per tonne £ per tonne cif $ per tonne fob	Yes	A	Selected countries	EDFM1 (14)
Prices	By average, highest, lowest	SDRs, tonne US cents, lb	No		World	ICCO1 (8)
Production, ICCO members share	By agreements, average grindings, exports, imports	tonnes, %	No		ICCO members	ICCO1 (9)
Production		tonnes	Yes	3 per	World	EDFM1 (1b)
Production	By continent,country	tonnes, %	Yes	A	World	ICCO1 (4)
Production		tonnes	Yes	3 per year	World	EDFM1 (2)
Shipment positions, nearest - Ghana cif UK		£ per tonnes cif	No		Ghana UK	EDFM1 (12)
Stock-consumption ratio		tonnes	Yes	3 per year	World	EDFM1 (1b)
Stocks, sale of	By origin, port, % defect	tonnes, US$	No		World	ICCO1 (1)
Stocks		tonnes	Yes	3 per year	World	EDFM1 (1b)
Supply and demand	By crop	tonnes	Yes	3 per	World	EDFM1 (1a)
Tonnage, net warrant	By crop-year, by country	tonnes	Yes	A	World	ICCO1 (3)
2.5 CONSUMPTION - see also Section 8						
2.5.1. Fruit and Vegetables						
Cocoa, per caput	By country	kg, head	Yes	A	World	ICCO2 (19)
Cocoa	By final consumer, by country	tonnes	Yes	A	World	ICCO2 (18)
Crops	By use,consumer, by product	tonnes	Yes	A	EC	EC19 (V)
Food, nonfood	By type	tonnes	Yes	2 yrly	Selected Asian countries	IRRI1 (63)
Food	By type	kg, year	Yes	2 yrly	Selected Asian countries	IRRI1 (63)
Grape products	Wine, grape juice, fresh grapes, raisins	hl, q	No		World	OIVV1 (G)
Grapes	Pressings,fruit consumption of raisins, table grapes, wine grapes,	q	No		World	OIVV1 (E)
Rice, milled, carry-over stocks	By country and geographical region	tonnes	Yes	A	Selected Asian countries	IRRI1 (64)
Rice calorie supply	By country and calorie supply	%	Yes	A	World	IRRI1 (62)

Subject	Categories	Units	Time series Yes/No	Frequency	Territorial coverage	Source (Table no.)
Rice supply, utilization balances	Production,	tonnes	Yes	2 yrly	Selected Asian countries	IRRI1 (63)
	stock changes,	tonnes	Yes	2 yrly	Selected Asian countries	IRRI1 (63)
	net trade (exports and imports)	tonnes	Yes	2 yrly	Selected Asian countries	IRRI1 (63)
Wheat		tonnes	Yes	A	World	IWHC3 (A.3)
2.5.2 Meat						
Animal products, human consumption	By product	kg, head, yr	Yes	A	EC	EC7 (IV)
Animals and animal products	By animal,product, by consumer	tonnes	Yes	A	EC	EC7 (IV)
Beef and veal	Total, per capita	tonnes, %, kg, capita	Yes	A	World	GATT2 (5)
Beef and veal	Total and per head	tonnes, kg per head	Yes	A	OECD	OECD26
Beef and veal	Carcass weight	tonnes, %	Yes	A	Selected countries	GATT1 (5)
Beef apparent consumption, veal	Per head	head, kg	Yes	A	EC	UN34 (V)
Edible offal	Total and per head	tonnes, kg per head	Yes	A	OECD	OECD26
Horse meat	Total and per head	tonnes, kg per head	Yes	A	OECD	OECD26
Meat, other	Total and per haed	tonnes, kg per head	Yes	A	OECD	OECD26
Meat		tonnes, %	Yes	A	Selected countries	GATT1 (-)
Meat	Carcass weight	tonnes, kg, capita, %	Yes	A	World	GATT1 (16)
Meat	Carcass weight	tonnes, %	Yes	A	Selected countries	GATT1 (-)
Meat	Carcass weight	tonnes, %	Yes	A	Selected countries	GATT1 (-)
Meat	Ready to cook	tonnes, kg, capita, %	Yes	A	World	GATT1 (20)
Meat total	By meat type and by country, consumption	tonnes, kg per year per head	Yes	A	OECD	OECD26
Meat total	Total and per head	tonnes, kg per year	Yes	A	OECD	OECD26
Mutton, lamb and goat meat	Total and per head	tonnes, kg per head	Yes	A	OECD	OECD26
Pig meat, apparent consumption	Per head	kg, %	Yes	A	EC	UN34(XX)
Pig meat	Total, per capita	tonnes, % kg, capita	Yes	A	World	GATT2 (16)
Pig meat	Total and per head	tonnes, kg per head	Yes	A	OECD	OECD26
Poultry meat,apparent consumption	Per head	kg, %	Yes	A	EC	UN34 (XLIX)
Poultry meat	Ready to cook basis total, per capita	tonnes, % kg, capita	Yes	A	World	GATT2 (20)
Poultry meat	Total and per head	tonnes, kg per head	Yes	A	OECD	OECD26
Sheep meat, apparent consumption	Per head	kg, %	Yes	A	Selected European countries	UN34 (XXXV)
Sheep meat	Total, per capita	tonnes, cwe, kg, capita, %	Yes	A	World	GATT2 (24)
2.5.3 Milk and Dairy Products - see also under Milk, Cheese and other Livestock Products (2.19), Milk Industry (2.20) and Section 5						
Butter		tonnes, indices	No		World	GATT5 (2B)
Butter and ghee, cheese, dry milk	By production	Tonnes	Yes	A	World	FAO6(30)
Butter and margarine		kg, head	Yes	A	EC	MMB1 (119)
Cheese	By cheese, fresh cheese	kg, head	Yes	A	EC	MMB1 (120)
Cheeses		tonnes, indices	No		World	GATT5 (4B)
Cream and dairy ice cream		kg, head	Yes	A	EC	MMB1 (118)
Milk, liquid	By type	kg, head	Yes	A	EC	MMB1 (116)
Milk, deliveries		tonnes, indices	No		World	GATT5 (1)

Subject	Categories	Units	Time series Yes/No Frequency	Territorial coverage	Source (Table no.)
Milk fat, protein		kg, head	Yes A	EC	MMB1 (121)
Milk powder, skimmed		tonnes, indices	No	World	GATT5 (5B)
Yogurt and condensed milk	Total	kg, head	Yes A	EC	MMB1 (117)
2.5.4 Sugar - see also under Sugar Industry (2.27)					
Sugar consumption	Raw value	tonnes	Yes A	EC	FOL2 (191)
Sugar deliveries	By consumption, export, buyers, consumers	tonnes	Yes A	EC	FOL2 (191)
2.5.5 Total					
Consumer expenditure on food, drink and tobacco	By household	%	No	EC	WC1 (-)
Expenditure, household consumption as a proportion of total consumer expenditure of households	Food, beverages and tobacco	%	No	EC	WC1 (-)
Final consumption	Total at current prices, volume index numbers, per inhabitant, expenditure for food	ECU, indices ECU %	Yes A	EC	EC6 (IA 9)
Food	By food type	kg, head, nos, head	Yes A	VICES and Yugoslavia	VICES1 (II/3)
Food availability	Total products, animal, vegetable	calories per person per day % change	No	Selected countries	UN22 (II-3.3.2a)
Human consumption	By type	kg, per capita	Yes A	World	EC6 (IA 6)
Intermediate agricultural, total	Total prices and exchange rates, as % of final agricultural output, volume and price indices at current and 1985 prices %, indices	ECU	Yes A	EC	EC26 (A.0.2)
Intermediate agricultural, total	At current prices and exchange rates	ECU	Yes A	EC	EC26 (A.1- A.1.12)
Intermediate agricultural, final	At current prices	nat curr	Yes A	EC	EC26 (A.2.1-A.2.12)
Intermediate agricultural	By region	ECU	Yes A	EC	EC26 (C.0.2)
Intermediate agricultural	By type at current prices and exchange rates	ECU	Yes A	EC	EC26 (A.1-A.1.12)
Intermediate agricultural	By type at current prices	nat curr	Yes A	EC	EC26 (A.2.1-A.2.12)
Intermediate consumption, as percentage of final agricultural output		%	Yes A	OECD	OECD5 (II.5)
Production, consumption and self-supply levels of selected produce	By country, by wheat, barley, fruits, dates, red meat, fish, poultry, to eggs	tonnes, %	No	GCC	CH1 (7.12) CH1 (7.19)
2.5.6 Wine - see also under Wine Industry (2.30)					
Wine		hl	Yes 4 yr	World	OIVV1 (H)
Wine		l, capita	No	World	OIVV1 (I)
Wine	Domestic use by consumer	hl	No	World	OIVV1 (K)
2.6 DEVELOPMENT - see also Section 12					
Agricultural and total development expenditures	By country	US$	No	GCC	CH1 (7.10)
2.7 EARNINGS - see also under Incomes (2.15) and Section 24					
Farm wage rates		nat curr, day	Yes A	Selected Asian countries	IRRI1 (82)
Labour costs	By type of job, permanent adult agricultural workers	nat curr, US$	Yes A	EC and North America	UN40 (XXII)

Subject	Categories	Units	Time series Yes/No Frequency		Territorial coverage	Source (Table no.)
		US$, day	Yes	A	Selected Asian countries	IRRI1 (83)
Wages	By countries	indices	Yes	A	EC	MAC3 (B5,A-D)
2.8 EMPLOYMENT - see also Sections 16 and 36						
Agricultural holdings, AWU	Total, family members, non-family members	nos	Yes	A	EC	EC29 (II, 14)
Agricultural labour force	Total	per capita	Yes	A	Selected Asian countries	IRRI1 (81)
Agricultural population	Total, agricultural, farm population as % of total population	nos, %	No		Selected countries	UN22 (II- 3.1.8)
Agricultural population	Total	per capita	Yes	A	Selected Asian countries	IRRI1 (80)
Agriculture, economically active population	Total, in agriculture	nos, %	Yes	A	ASEAN	ASEANS1 (3.1)
Dual activity, farming	Of holder who is also manager, of members of holders family	nos	No		EC	EC45(AX)
Economically active population in the primary sector		nos	Yes	A	OECD, World	OECD33 (12.3)
Education: Diplomas	By type	nos	No		Selected countries	UN22 (II- 3.1.9)
Education: Professional qualification	By country and type	nos	No		EC	EC23 (-)
Employment	As a share of total employment	%	Yes	A	EC	EC2 (A2)
Employment	By sector	'000, %	No		EC	WC1 (-)
Employment in agriculture	As % of civilian employment	%	Yes	A	OECD	OECD5 (II.2)
Employment in agriculture	Civilian labour	%	Yes	A	EC	MMB1(11)
Farm population, ratio to cultivated land	By ratio and % change dweller, %	ha per farm	No		Selected countries	UN22 (II- 3.1.7)
Labour force, farm holdings	By workers, work time, annual work units, age classes of holder	nos	No		EC	EC45 (AIX)
Labour force, farm holdings	By worker, by age class of holder, by work-time of holder, by size class of holding, by country	nos	No		EC	EC45 (B)
Labour force, farm holdings	AWU, number of persons, distribution of the holders-by work time, per age, OGA, by type of farming by country	nos, %	No		EC	EC45 (C)
Labour force, farm holdings	By worker, by age class of holder, by work time of holder, by country,region	nos	No		EC	EC45 (D)
Labour force, agricultural	By holders, family workers, non-family workers	nos	No		EC	EC9 (5.17)
Labour input	Family in annual work units (AWU)	indices	Yes	A	EC	EC2 (A37)
Labour input	Total in annual work units (AWU)	indices	Yes	A	EC	EC2 (A36)
Manual workers, full-time		nos	No		EC	EC23 (I.1)

Subject	Categories	Units	Time series Yes/No Frequency		Territorial coverage	Source (Table no.)
Manual workers	By country, provision of benefits in kind and work type	nos	No		EC	EC23 (-)
Manual workers	By country, provision of benefits in kind, by sex and age group	nos, %	No		EC	EC23 (-)
Manual workers	By country and region	nos	No		EC	EC23 (III.1- III.7)
Manual workers	By farm size and sex	nos	No		EC	EC23 (I.2)
Manual workers	By provision of benefits in kind and by sex	nos	No		EC	EC23 (I.4)
Manual workers	By sex and age group	nos	No		EC	EC23 (I.5)
Manual workers	By work type and sex	nos	No		EC	EC23 (I.3)
Population, employment and contribution to GDP	Population, employment milk as % of production	nos, %	No		EC	MMB1(10)
Work in agriculture	Total, family, non-family members	nos	Yes	A	EC	EC6 (IA2.3)
Work units per holding	Total, with OGA, without OGA, by size of holding and type of farming	nos	No		EC	EC43 (-)
Work units per holding	Total, with AET, without AET, by size of holding and type of farming	awu per hundred holdings	No		EC	EC43 (-)

2.9 ENERGY CONSUMPTION - see also Section 17

Subject	Categories	Units	Time series Yes/No Frequency		Territorial coverage	Source (Table no.)
Energy consumption		toe	Yes	A	OECD	OECD33 V
Energy consumption		tpe, % change	No		Selected countries	UN22 (II- 3.2.4a)
Energy consumption and production and the efficiency of seven agricultural systems	By energy input, hectare, by energy output, hectare, yield, productivity, surplus energy income	mj, %, mj, ha-yr, mj, person-day, energy ratio	No		Selected countries	UN22 (II 3.2.4b)
Energy consumption	per capita	toe	No		Developing countries	UNCTAD5 (1.4)

2.10 ENVIRONMENTAL PRESSURES-see also Section 18

2.10.1 Air

Subject	Categories	Units	Time series Yes/No Frequency		Territorial coverage	Source (Table no.)
Ammonia emissions, theoretical,	Calculated on the basis of head of cattle and NH_3	tonnes	No		Selected countries	UN22 (4.4.2c)
Emission coeffiecients						
Livestock emissions: methane into the air		tonnes	No		Selected countries	UN22 (II- 4.4.2d)
Livestock emissions: N_2O to the air		tonnes	No		Selected countries	UN22 (II-4.4.2e)

2.10.2 Foodstuffs and Human Health

Subject	Categories	Units	Time series Yes/No Frequency		Territorial coverage	Source (Table no.)
Heavy metals, residues, in foodstuffs fruit, citrus, eggs, meat, milk	By plant origin, vegetables	nos, %	No		Selected countries	UN22 (II-and 4.5.2)
Pesticide residues in foodstuffs, fruit, citrus	By plant origin, vegetables	nos, %	No		Selected countries	UN22 (II-and 4.5.1)
Radioactivity in foodstuffs, fruit, citrus, eggs, meat, milk	By plant origin, vegetables	nos, %	No		Selected countries	UN22 (II-and 4.5.3)

2 AGRICULTURE

Subject	Categories	Units	Time series Yes/No Frequency	Territorial coverage	Source (Table no.)
2.10.3 Soil					
Animal excreta production	By animal	tonnes	No	Selected countries	UN22 (4.4.1)
Chemical deterioration	By loss of nutrients,and or organic matter, soil pollution, acidification, salinization, alkalinization	ha	No	Selected countries	UN22 (II-4.2.2e)
Fertilizing elements, amounts of, corresponding to animal excreta		tonnes	No	Selected countries	UN22 (4.4.2b)
Fertilizing matter in excreta, coefficients of content		% of dry matter	No	Selected countries	UN22 (4.4.2a)
Natural phosphates	By phosphorus and cadmium content	%, cd, kg, cd, kg p	No	Selected countries	UN22 (II-4.2.2g)
Nitrogen balance in agricultural land	By input, by output	kg N, ha	No	Selected countries	UN22 (II-4.6.2)
Nitrogen cycle, guideline values of, in agricultural land	By input, by output	kg N, ha	No	Selected countries	UN22 (II-the 4.6.1)
Organic farming methods, area of holdings and number of producers	By area, as % of total	ha, %	No	EC	UN22 (II-5.5.1)
Physical deterioration	By water erosion, by wind erosion,	ha	No	Selected countries	UN22 (II- 4.2.2c)
	by soil compaction, by water logging	ha	No	Selected countries	UN22 (II-4.2.2d)
Sewage sludge and proportion used for agriculture	By production, by disposal	tonnes, %	No	Selected countries	UN22 (II- 4.2.2i)
Soil degradation, human induced					
Soil degradation	By type, by degree	sq km	No	EC, and North America	UN22 (II-4.2.2a,b)
2.10.4 Water					
Concentrations and fumigants and their admixtures measured in shallow and deep groundwater	By compound, area, sample, depth, concentration	m, nos, µg	No	Selected countries	UN22 (II-4.3.1n)
Freshwater run-off		cu km	No	EC, North and Central America, USSR	UN22 (II-4.3.1a)
Herbicide, concentrations of, (other than triazines) measured in shallow and deep groundwater	By compound, area, sample, depth, concentration	m, nos, µg	No	Selected countries	UN22 (II-4.3.1m)
Insecticides and nematicides, concentrations of, in groundwater	By compound, area, sample, depth, concentration	m, nos, µg	No	Selected countries	UN22 (II-4.3.1i)
Pesticide monitoring, for public drinking-water supplies	By raw water, furnished water	nos, µg, %	No	Selected countries	UN22 (II-of 4.3.1u)
Triazine herbicides, residues of, measured in the upper groundwater of treated fields	By compound, area, sample, depth, concentration	m, nos, µg	No	Selected countries	UN22 (II-4.3.1k)
Triazine herbicides, concentrations of, and their transformation products in water	By compound, area, sample, concentration	nos, µg	No	Selected countries	UN22 (II-4.3.1l)
Water pollution through nitrates	By samples, samples with nitrate concentration, national limit	nos, %	No	Selected countries	UN22 (II-4.3.1c)
Water pollution through pesticides	Pesticides in ground water	nos, %	No	Selected countries	UN22 (II-4.3.1f)
2.11 EQUIPMENT					
Combine harvesters	By crop,harvester % change	nos, ha,	No	Selected countries	UN22 (II-3.2.5b)
Farm machinery	Machinery in service, by country	nos	Yes A	ESCAP	UN44
Machinery	By country	nos	No	EC	EC18 (7.3)

Subject	Categories	Units	Time series Yes/No Frequency		Territorial coverage	Source (Table no.)
Mechanization	Area of arable land per tractor	ha	Yes	A	Latin American and Caribbean countries	UN45 (50)
Tractors		US$, nos	Yes	A	World	FAO2 (129)
Tractors	By land,crops per tractor % change	nos, ha	No		Selected countries	UN22 (II-3.2.5a)
Tractors	Units in service	nos	Yes	A	Latin American and Caribbean countries	UN45 (326)
Tractors and combine harvester-threshers		nos	Yes	A	Nordic countries	NCM1(64)
Tractors and combined harvester-threshers		nos	Yes	A	OECD World	OECD33 (12.4)
Tractors in use	Threshers	nos	Yes	A	World	UN50 (73)
Tractors; harvester-threshers, milking machines	Total	nos	Yes	A	World	FAO1 (118)

2.12 FERTILIZERS AND PESTICIDES

2.12.1 Consumption

Subject	Categories	Units	Time series Yes/No Frequency		Territorial coverage	Source (Table no.)
Commercial fertilizers, deliveries	By country, by type	tonnes	No		EC	EC18 (7.4)
Commercial fertilizers	Consumption,	tonnes	Yes	A	OECD, World	OECD33 (12.6C)
Fertilizer per hectare	By agricultural area, arable land and permanent crops, and per caput	kg	Yes	A	World	FAO5 (10)
Fertilisers	By type	tonnes	Yes	A	World	FAO5 (1)
Fertilizer, consumption	From chemical sources	tonnes	Yes	A	Selected Asian countries	IRRI1 (75)
Fertilizer, use	From chemical sources	tonnes	Yes	A	Selected Asian countries	IRRI1 (76)
Fertilizer, consumption	By type	tonnes,	No		Selected countries	UN22
Fertilizer consumption		per hectare	No		Developing countries	UNCTAD5 (1.4)
Fertilizers, consumption	Total	tonnes	Yes	A	Latin American and Caribbean countries	UN45 (325)
Fertilizers	Consumption, imports, exports	tonnes	Yes	A	World, ESCAP	UN44 (p3)
Fertilizers consumption	Nitrogen	kg	Yes	A	Nordic countries	NCM1(65)
Fertilizing and plant protection practices on wheat cultivation	By use of chemicals	ha, nos	No		Selected countries	UN22 (II-3.2.8c)
Fertilizing and plant protection practices fruit trees	By use of chemicals	ha, nos	No		Selected countries	UN22 (II-3.2.8d)
Fertilizing practices, wheat cultivation	By application of fertilizers, by type of fertilizer	kg, ha, tonnes, ha	No		Selected countries	UN22 (II-3.2.7d)
Fertilizing practices, fruit trees	By application of fertilizers, by type of fertilizer	kg, ha, tonnes, ha	No		Selected countries	UN22 (II-3.2.7e)
Pesticides consumption	By type	kg, % change	No		Selected countries	UN22 (II-3.2.8a,b)
Mineral fertilizers		% change				(II-3.2.7b)
Mineral fertilizers	By type, per hectare	kg, ha	No		Selected countries	UN22 (II-3.2.7c)
Nitrogenous, phosphate and potash fertilizer	Total	tonnes	Yes	A	World	FAO5 (32)
Nitrogenous		tons	Yes	A	World	UN50 (74)
Nitrogenous	Consumption,	tonnes	Yes	A	OECD, World	OECD33 (12.6A)
Nitrogenous fertilizer		tonnes	Yes	A	World	FAO5 (20)
Nitrogenous fertilizer	By economic class	tonnes	Yes	A	World	FAO5 (2)
Pest control	By pest control measure, treated area, quantity sold, total expenditure	ha, nos	No		Selected countries	UN22 (II-3.2.8e)

Subject	Categories	Units	Time series Yes/No	Frequency	Territorial coverage	Source (Table no.)
Pesticide levels in human milk		mg/kg	Yes	Selected	Selected countries	UNCTAD5
Pesticides, consumption	Total, by type	tonnes	No		OECD	OECD33 (12.7A)
Pesticides, consumption	Trends	indices	Yes	A	Selected countries	OECD33 (12.7B)
Phosphate		tons	Yes	A	World	UN50 (75)
Phosphate	Consumption,		Yes	A	OECD, World	OECD33 (12.6B)
Phosphate fertilizer		tonnes	Yes	A	World	FAO5 (24)
Phosphate fertilizer	By economic class	tonnes	Yes	A	World	FAO5 (3)
Potash	Calories	tonnes, nos	Yes	A	World	UN50 (76)
Potash fertilizer		tonnes	Yes	A	World	FAO5 (28)
Potash fertilizer	By economic class	tonnes	Yes	A	World	FAO5 (4)
Urea, home deliveries		tonnes, % years	Yes	A	World	IFA1 (-) (4.44)
2.12.2 Prices						
Mixed and complex fertilisers		nat curr, US$	Yes	A	World	FAO5 (37)
Nitrogenous, phosphatic, potassic	Weighted average prices paid by farmers per 100 kg of plant nutrient	nat curr	Yes	A	EC and North America	UN40 (XVIA, XVIIA, XVIIIA)
Nitrogenous, phosphatic	Prices paid by farmers per metric ton of specified fertilizers	%, nat curr, US$, tonnes	Yes	A	EC and North America	UN40 (XVIB, XVIIB, XVIIIB)
Nitrogenous fertilizer		nat curr, US$	Yes	A	World	FAO5 (34)
Phosphate fertilizer		nat curr, US$	Yes	A	World	FAO5 (35)
Plant nutrients	Prices paid by farmers per metric ton of specified fertilizers	%, nat curr, US$	Yes	A	EC and North America	UN40 (XIX)
Plant nutrients	Weighted average prices paid by farmers per 100 kg	nat curr	Yes	A	EC and North America	UN40 (XX)
Potash fertilizer		nat curr, US$	Yes	A	World	FAO5 (36)
Retail prices of nitrogen from urea		nat curr, tonnes US$, tonnes	Yes	A	Selected Asian countries	IRRI1 (77, 78)
World prices of major fertilizers	By fertilizer grade	US$, tonnes fob raw materials	Yes	A	Selected countries	IRRI1 (79)
2.12.3 Production						
Ammonia production capacity		tonnes	No		World	FAO5 (13)
Fertilizer	By type	tonnes	Yes	A	World	FAO5 (1)
Fertilizer production capacity	By country, by type	tonnes	No		GCC	CH1 (7.11)
Fertilizers	Nitrogenous, phosphate fertilizers, by country	tonnes	Yes	A	ESCAP	UN44
Fertilizers and pesticides	By type, By country	tonnes	Yes	A	ESCAP	UN44
Nitrogenous, phosphate and potash fertilizer	Total	tonnes	Yes	A	World	FAO5 (29)
Nitrogenous fertilizer		tonnes	Yes	A	World	FAO5 (17)
Nitrogenous fertilizer	By economic class	tonnes	Yes	A	World	FAO5 (2)
Phosphate fertilizer		tonnes	Yes	A	World	FAO5 (21)
Phosphate fertilizer	By economic class	tonnes	Yes	A	World	FAO5 (3)
Phosphoric acid production capacity		tonnes	No		World	FAO5 (14)
Phosphorus		kg	Yes	A	Nordic countries	NCM1(65)
Potash (technical grade)		tonnes	Yes	A	World	FAO5 (7)
Potash fertilizer		tonnes	Yes	A	World	FAO5 (25)
Potash fertilizer	By economic class	tonnes	Yes	A	World	FAO5 (4)
Potassium		kg	Yes	A	Nordic countries	NCM1(65)
Rock phosphate		tonnes	Yes	A	World	FAO5 (11)
2.12.4 Subsidies						
Fertilizer subsidy	Total	nat curr	Yes	A	World	FAO5 (38)
Mixed and complex fertilizer		nat curr, US$	Yes	A	World	FAO5 (42)
Nitrogenous fertilizer		nat curr, US$	Yes	A	World	FAO5 (39)
Phosphate fertilizer		nat curr, US$	Yes	A	World	FAO5 (40)

Subject	Categories	Units	Time series Yes/No Frequency		Territorial coverage	Source (Table no.)
Potash fertilizer		nat curr, US$	Yes	A	World	FAO5 (41)
2.12.5 Trade						
Ammonia		tonnes	Yes	A	World	FAO5 (15)
Fertilizer	By type	tonnes	Yes	A	World	FAO5 (1)
Fertilizer	Crude, manufactured	US$	Yes	A	World	FAO2 (130,131)
Nitrogenous, phosphate and potash fertilizer	Total	tonnes	Yes	A	World	FAO5 (30-31)
Nitrogenous fertilizer		tonnes	Yes	A	World	FAO5 (18-19)
Nitrogenous fertilizer	By economic class	tonnes	Yes	A	World	FAO5 (2)
Pesticides		US$	Yes	A	World	FAO2 (132)
Pesticides	Sales, type	tonnes	Yes	A	Nordic countries	NCM1(66)
Phosphate fertilizer		tonnes	Yes	A	World	FAO5 (22-23)
Phosphate fertilizer	By economic class	tonnes	Yes	A	World	FAO5 (3)
Phosphoric acid		tonnes	Yes	A	World	FAO5 (16)
Potash fertilizer		tonnes	Yes	A	World	FAO5 (26-27)
Potash fertilizer	By economic class	tonnes	Yes	A	World	FAO5 (4)
Potash re-exports (complex fertilizer)		tonnes	Yes	A	World	FAO5 (8)
Rock phosphate		tonnes	Yes	A	World	FAO5 (12)
Urea, exports		tonnes, %	Yes	A	World	IFA1 (-)
Urea, exports	Origin, destination	tonnes	No		World	IFA1 (-)
Urea, granular	Share of production	%	No		World	IFA1 (-)
Urea production		tonnes, %	Yes	A	World	IFA1 (-)
2.13 FINANCE						
2.13.1 General - see also under Incomes (2.15)						
EAGGF expenditure		ECU	Yes	A	EC	WC1 (-)
EAGGF guarantee expenditure	By product	ECU, %	Yes	A	EC	WC1 (-)
EAGGF guidance and guarantee expenditure by member state	Total	ECU	No		EC	WC1 (-)
EC financial perspective	Total	ECU	No		EC	WC1 (-)
Income, net of total agricultural labour	At current prices and exchange rates and as % of net value added at factor cost	ECU, %	Yes	A	EC EC	EC26 (A.0.9)
Income, net of agricultural family labour	At current prices and exchange rates and as % of net value added at factor cost	ECU, %	Yes	A	EC	EC26 (A.0.10)
Income, net of total agricultural labour	At current prices and exchange rates	ECU	Yes	A	EC	EC26 (A.1-A.1.12)
Income, net of agricultural family labour	At current prices and exchange rates	ECU	Yes	A	EC	EC26 (A.1-A.1.12)
Income, net of total agricultural labour	At current prices	nat curr	Yes	A	EC	EC26 (A.2.1-A.2.12)
Income, net of family agricultural labour	At current prices	nat curr	Yes	A	EC	EC26 (A.2.1-A.2.12)
Indebtedness, investments and subsidies	Product average by country	pse, nat curr, US$, %, ECU	Yes	A	Selected countries and EC	UN22 (II-3.1.14)
Indebtedness, investments and subsidies		ha, nos,	Yes	10 yrly	Selected countries	UN22 (II- 3.1.15)
Interest, agricultural	By region	ECU	Yes	A	EC	EC26 (C.0.3)
Operating surplus, net	By current prices, 1985 prices	PPS (US$)	Yes	A	OECD	OECD5 (III.2.A,III.2.B)
Operating surplus, net	Current prices	nat curr	Yes	A	OECD	OECD5 (III.2.C)
Operating surplus, net	At current prices and exchange rates and as % of net value added at factor cost	ECU, %	Yes	A	EC EC	EC26 (A.0.8)

2 AGRICULTURE

Subject	Categories	Units	Time series Yes/No Frequency		Territorial coverage	Source (Table no.)
Operating surplus, net agricultureal	At current prices and exchange rates	ECU	Yes	A	EC	EC26 (A.1-A.1.12)
Operating surplus, net agricultural	At current prices	nat curr	Yes	A	EC	EC26 (A.2.1-A.2.12)
Operating surplus, net	By region	ECU	Yes	A	EC	EC26 (C.0.1)
Payments agricultural	By region	ECU	Yes	A	EC	EC26 (C.0.3)
Structural funds	Budget	ECU, %	Yes	A	EC	WC1 (-)
Structure of EC budget revenue	Total	ECU, %	Yes	A	EC	WC1 (-)
2.13.2 Subsidies						
Subsidies	At current prices and exchange rates and as % of final agricultural output	ECU, %	Yes	A	EC	EC26 (A.0.4)
2.13.3 Taxes						
Taxes linked to production (excl VAT)	At current prices and exchange rates and as % of final agricultural output	ECU, %	Yes	A	EC	EC26 (A.0.5)
2.14 FOOD SUPPLY						
Ascorbic acid	Total,vegetable, animal products	milligrams	Yes	3 yrly	World	FAO1 (117)
Beef and veal		tonnes, %	Yes	A	World	GATT2 (4)
Beta-carotene equivalent	Total,vegetable, animal products	micrograms	Yes	3 yrly	World	FAO1 (112)
Butter, stocks		tonnes, indices	Yes	A	World	GATT5 (2E)
Calcium	Total,vegetable, animal products	milligrams	Yes	3 yrly	World	FAO1 (109)
Calories	Total,vegetable, animal products	nos	Yes	3 yrly	World	FAO1 (106)
Cheese, stocks		tonnes, indices	Yes	A	World	GATT5 (4E)
Crops, final stock	Of which: market, by product	tonnes	Yes	A	EC	EC19 (V)
Crops, change in stocks	Of which: market, by product	tonnes	Yes	A	EC	EC19 (V)
Fat	Total,vegetable, animal products	grams	Yes	3 yrly	World	FAO1 (108)
Food, health and nutrition	Food production, calories and proteins population per physician, nurse and hospital bed access to safe water	indices grammes nos %	No		Developing countries	WB1 (-)
Food supply	Protein	grams	Yes	A	World	UN50 (77)
Iron	Total,vegetable, animal products	milligrams	Yes	3 yrly	World	FAO1 (110)
Milk, production and disposals	By type, % of total	tonnes, %	No		EC	MMB1(33)
Milk, total utilisation whole	By product, usage	tonnes, %	No		EC	MMB1(36)
Milk powder, skimmed		tonnes, indices	Yes	A	World	GATT5 (5E)
Milk production and disposals	By type, % of total	tonnes, %	No		EC	MMB1(30)
Milk skimmed, total utilisation	By product, usage	tonnes, %	No		EC	MMB1(37)
Milk skimmed total utilisation	By product, total	tonnes, %	No		EC	MMB1(32)
Milk total utilisation, whole	By product, total	tonnes, %	No		EC	MMB1(31)
Milk utilisation by dairies, whole	By product, usage	tonnes, %	No		EC	MMB1(35)
Milk utilisation on farms, whole	By type	tonnes, %	No		EC	MMB1(34)
Niacin	Total,vegetable, animal products	milligrams	Yes	3 yrly	World	FAO1 (116)
Protein	Total,vegetable, animal products	grams	Yes	3 yrly	World	FAO1 (107)
Retinol	Total,animal products	micrograms	Yes	3 yrly	World	FAO1 (111)

Subject	Categories	Units	Time series Yes/No Frequency		Territorial coverage	Source (Table no.)
Retinol equivalent	Total,vegetable, animal products	micrograms	Yes	3 yrly	World	FAO1 (113)
Riboflavin	Total,vegetable, animal products	milligrams	Yes	3 yrly	World	FAO1 (115)
Thiamine	Total,vegetable, animal products	milligrams	Yes	3 yrly	World	FAO1 (114)
Wheat, carry-over stocks		tonnes	Yes	A	World	IWhC3 (A.4)
Wine		hl	No		World	OIVV1 (J)
2.15 INCOMES						
Compensation of employees, change in		%	Yes	A	EC	EC2 (A7)
Compensation of employees	By region	ECU	Yes	A	EC	EC26 (C.0.3)
Compensation of employees	At current prices and exchange rates and as % of net value added at factor cost	ECU, %	Yes	A	EC EC	EC26 (A.0.7)
Income, net, from agricultural activity of the total labour input	Per annual work unit (EC Indicator 2)	indices	Yes	A	EC	EC2 (A22)
Income, net, from agricultural activity of family labour input	Per annual work unit (EC Indicator 3)	indices	Yes	A	EC	EC2 (A23)
Income, net, change in family labour input	Total labour input,	%	Yes	A	EC	EC2 (A7)
Income and milk price	Farms represented, total output,by size of dairy herd	nos, %, ECU	No		EC	EC58 (5.6)
Income and milk price	Farms represented, total output,by size of dairy herd	nos, % ECU	YES	A	EUR10	EC57 (5.3)
Income and milk price	Farms represented total output,	ECU, %	Yes	A	EC	EC58 (5.5)
Income and milk price	Farms represented	ECU, %	Yes	A	EUR10	EC57 (5.2)
Income and milk production	Normal and less favoured areas	ECU, %, tonnes	Yes	A	EUR10	EC57 (5.8)
Income on type 41 and all holdings	Yearly growth rate	ECU, %	Yes	A	EC	EC57 (5.9)
Income per AWU	Farms with dairy cows, type of farming	ECU, indices	Yes	A	EUR10	EC57 (5.7)
Income per farm	By size of dairy herd	ECU, %	Yes	A	EC	EC58 (5.7)
Income per farm	By size of dairy herd	ECU, %	Yes	A	EUR10	EC57 (5.4)
Income per farm	Farms with dairy cows, type of farming	ECU, indices	Yes	A	EUR10	EC57 (5.6)
Income per farm	Yearly growth rate	ECU, %	Yes	A	EUR10	EC57 (5.5)
Manual workers, full-time	Hourly earnings and number of hours paid	nat curr, hrs	No		EC	EC23 (I.1)
Manual workers, gross hourly earnings		indices	No		EC	EC23 (I.2)
Manual workers, gross hourly earnings	By work type and sex	indices	No		EC	EC23 (I.3)
Manual workers, gross hourly earnings	By provision of benefits in kind and by sex	indices	No		EC	EC23 (I.4)
Manual workers, gross hourly earnings	By sex and age group	indices	No		EC	EC23 (I.5)
Manual workers, hours paid per month	By country, provision of benefits in kind and work type	hrs	No		EC	EC23 (-)
Manual workers, gross hourly earnings	By country, provision of benefits in kind and work type	nat curr	No		EC	EC23 (-)

2 AGRICULTURE

Subject	Categories	Units	Time series Yes/No Frequency		Territorial coverage	Source (Table no.)
Manual workers, gross hourly earnings	By country, provision of benefits in kind, by sex and age group	nat curr, indices	No		EC	EC23 (-)
Manual workers, number hours paid	By country and region	hrs	No		EC	EC23 (III.1-III.7)
Manual workers, gross hourly earnings	By country and region	nat curr	No		EC	EC23 (III.1-III.7)
Net income	As % of net value added	%	Yes	A	OECD	OECD5 (II.7)
Net income from agriculture		US$	Yes	A	OECD	OECD5 (II.10)
Net income from agriculture	By current prices, 1985 prices	PPS (US$)	Yes	A	OECD	OECD5 (III.2.A, III.2.B)
Net income from agriculture	Current prices	nat curr	Yes	A	OECD	OECD5 (III.2.C)
Net value added in agriculture at factor cost	Per annual work unit (AWU) (EC Indicator 1) major components	indices	Yes	A	EC	EC2 (A21, A8-A20)
Professional qualification, gross hourly earnings	By country and type	nat curr	No		EC	EC23 (-)
Real net income of family workers per work unit		indices	Yes	A	EC	EC6 (IG11)
Real net income of total labour force per work unit		indices	Yes	A	EC	EC6 (IG10)
Seasonal workers, gross daily earnings		nat curr, ECU	No		EC	EC23 (IV.1-IV.2)
Seasonal workers, number hours worked		hrs	No		EC	EC23 (IV.1-IV.2)

2.16 INTERNATIONAL TRADE - see also Section 27

2.16.1 Animal Feed

Subject	Categories	Units	Time series		Territorial coverage	Source
Animal feed, imports of	By product	tonnes	Yes	A	EC	WC1 (-)
Copra cake and meal		US$, tonne	Yes	A	World	FAO2 (89)
Cottonseed cake and meal		US$, tonne	Yes	A	World	FAO2 (85)
Fodder, imports and exports	By types of feed	g, tonnes,	No		Selected countries	UN22 (II-3.1.10c)
Groundnut cake and meal		US$, tonne	Yes	A	World	FAO2 (84)
Linseed cake and meal		US$, tonne	Yes	A	World	FAO2 (86)
Meat meal		US$, tonne	Yes	A	World	FAO2 (92)
Oilseed cake and meal (other)		US$, tonne	Yes	A	World	FAO2 (91)
Oilseed cake and meal and other vegetable oil residues		US$, tonne	Yes	A	World	FAO2 (82)
Palm kernel cake and meal		US$, tonne	Yes	A	World	FAO2 (90)
Rapeseed cake and meal		US$, tonne	Yes	A	World	FAO2 (88)
Soybean cake and meal		US$, tonne	Yes	A	World	FAO2 (83)
Sunflower cake and meal		US$, tonne	Yes	A	World	FAO2 (87)

2.16.2 Crops

Subject	Categories	Units	Time series		Territorial coverage	Source
Animal oils, fats and greases (except lard)		US$, tonne	Yes	A	World	FAO2 (116)
Apples		US$, tonne	Yes	A	World	FAO2 (57)
Bananas		US$, tonne	Yes	A	World	FAO2 (56)
Barley		US$, tonne	Yes	A	World	FAO2 (41)
Barley	Imports, exports	tons	No		World	IWhC2 (12)
Bran and milling by-products		US$, tonne	Yes	A	World	FAO2 (81)
Castor beans		US$, tonne	Yes	A	World	FAO2 (107)
Castor oil		US$, tonne	Yes	A	World	FAO2 (127)
Cereals, imports and production	By high, middle, low income	tonnes, kg	No		World	CS1 (15)
Cereals	Total	US$, tonne	Yes	A	World	FAO2 (37)
Cereals (other)		US$, tonne	Yes	A	World	FAO2 (45)
Citrus fruit (other)		US$, tonne	Yes	A	World	FAO2 (55)
Coarse grains	Imports,exports	tonnes	Yes	A	World	IWhC3 (A.7)

2 AGRICULTURE

Subject	Categories	Units	Time series Yes/No Frequency		Territorial coverage	Source (Table no.)
Coarse grains	Imports, exports	tons	No		World	IWhC2 (10)
Coconut oil		US$, tonne	Yes	A	World	FAO2 (125)
Coconuts	In shell and desiccated	US$, tonne	Yes	A	World	FAO2 (60, 61)
Coffee	All types	US$, tonne	Yes	A	World	FAO2 (71)
Copra		US$, tonne	Yes	A	World	FAO2 (104)
Corn, external trade	By countries	tonnes, hectolitres	Yes	A	EC	MAC3 (C10
Cotton lint		US$, tonne	Yes	A	World	FAO2 (110)
Cottonseed		US$, tonne	Yes	A	World	FAO2 (100)
Cottonseed oil		US$, tonne	Yes	A	World	FAO2 (118)
Crops	Total, intra-EUR12, by product	tonnes	Yes	A	EC	EC19 (V)
Crops	Total, intra-EUR12, resources, by product	tonnes	Yes	A	EC	EC19 (V)
Dates		US$, tonne	Yes	A	World	FAO2 (65)
Durum wheat	By destination	tons	Yes	A	Selected countries	IWhC2 (30B)
Flax, fibre, tow and waste		US$, tonne	Yes	A	World	FAO2 (112)
Grain, shipments of	By grain type	shipments	Yes	A, M, Q	Selected countries	IWhC2 (16)
Grain: ocean freight rates	On selected routes	rate	No		Selected countries	IWhC2 (31)
Grapes, table		q	Yes	4 yr	World	OIVV1(Q)
Grapes, table		q	Yes	4 yr	World	OIVV1 (P)
Grapes		US$, tonne	Yes	A	World	FAO2 (58)
Groundnut oil		US$, tonne	Yes	A	World	FAO2 (119)
Groundnuts	Total	US$, tonne	Yes	A	World	FAO2 (98)
Honey (natural)		US$, tonne	Yes	A	World	FAO2 (70)
Hops		US$, tonne	Yes	A	World	FAO2 (52)
Jute and bast fibres		US$, tonne	Yes	A	World	FAO2 (111)
Lemons and limes		US$, tonne	Yes	A	World	FAO2 (54)
Linseed		US$, tonne	Yes	A	World	FAO2 (106)
Linseed oil		US$, tonne	Yes	A	World	FAO2 (123)
Maize, (corn)	Imports, exports	tons	No		World	IWhC2 (11)
Maize		US$, tonne	Yes	A	World	FAO2 (42)
Maize oil		US$, tonne	Yes	A	World	FAO2 (128)
Malt		US$, tonne	Yes	A	World	FAO2 (47)
Milled rice, imports	By country and geographical region	tonnes, US$ cif	Yes	A	World	IRRI1 (7,8)
Milled rice, exports	By country and	tonnes, US$ fob	Yes	A	World	IRRI1 (9,10)
Oats		US$, tonne	Yes	A	World	FAO2 (44)
Olive oil		US$, tonne	Yes	A	World	FAO2 (120)
Onions		US$, tonne	Yes	A	World	FAO2 (51)
Oranges, tangerines and clementines		US$, tonne	Yes	A	World	FAO2 (53)
Palm nut kernels		US$, tonne	Yes	A	World	FAO2 (105)
Palm oil		US$, tonne	Yes	A	World	FAO2 (124)
Palm-kernel oil		US$, tonne	Yes	A	World	FAO2 (126)
Peaches		US$, tonne	Yes	A	World	FAO2 (63)
Pears		US$, tonne	Yes	A	World	FAO2 (62)
Pepper		US$, tonne	Yes	A	World	FAO2 (78)
Pimento		US$, tonne	Yes	A	World	FAO2 (79)
Pineapple	Fresh and canned	US$, tonne	Yes	A	World	FAO2 (64, 66)
Potatoes		US$, tonne	Yes	A	World	FAO2 (48)
Pulses		US$, tonne	Yes	A	World	FAO2 (49)
Raisins		q	Yes	4 yr	World	OIVV1 (S)
Raisins		q	Yes	4 yr	World	OIVV1 (T)
Raisins		US$, tonne	Yes	A	World	FAO2 (59)
Rape, colza and mustard oils		US$, tonne	Yes	A	World	FAO2 (122)
Rape and mustard seeds		US$, tonne	Yes	A	World	FAO2 (103)
Rice, tariff and non-tariff measures	By rice type, duty and/or tax levy in importing and exporting countries	$, tonnes, %	Yes	2 yrly	Selected countries	IRRI1 (96, 97)
Rice		US$, tonne	Yes	A	World	FAO2 (40)

2 AGRICULTURE

Subject	Categories	Units	Time series Yes/No Frequency		Territorial coverage	Source (Table no.)
Rubber, natural		US$, tonne	Yes	A	World	FAO2 (108)
Rye		US$, tonne	Yes	A	World	FAO2 (43)
Sales of grain and products	Importer, exporter	tons	No		Selected countries	IWhC2 (8)
Sesame seed		US$, tonne	Yes	A	World	FAO2 (102)
Silk		US$, tonne	Yes	A	World	FAO2 (109)
Sisal and other agave fibres		US$, tonne	Yes	A	World	FAO2 (113)
Sorghum	Imports, exports	tons	No		World	IWhC2 (13)
Soybean oil		US$, tonne	Yes	A	World	FAO2 (117)
Soybeans		US$, tonne	Yes	A	World	FAO2 (99)
Sunflower seed		US$, tonne	Yes	A	World	FAO2 (101)
Sunflowerseed oil		US$, tonne	Yes	A	World	FAO2 (121)
Tea		US$, tonne	Yes	A	World	FAO2 (77)
Tobacco (unmanufactured)		US$, tonne	Yes	A	World	FAO2 (97)
Tomatoes (fresh)		US$, tonne	Yes	A	World	FAO2 (50)
Vanilla		US$, tonne	Yes	A	World	FAO2 (80)
Wheat	Weekly export and import by selected wheats quotations	US$ per tonne	No		Selected countries	IWhC2 (24)
	by selected coarse grains	US$ per tonne	No		Selected countries	IWhC2 (25)
Wheat and flour	Imports,exports imports forecast, sales, by supplying country	tonnes	Yes	A	World	IWhC3 (A.2) (12C)
Wheat and flour cumulative shipments	By destination	tons	Yes	A	Selected countries	IWhC2 (30A
Wheat and flour including durum	Imports, exports	tons	No		World	IWhC2 (9)
Wheat and meslin		US$, tonne	Yes	A	World	FAO2 (39)
Wheat and wheat flour	In wheat equivalent	US$, tonne	Yes	A	World	FAO2 (38)
Wheat flour		US$, tonne	Yes	A	World	FAO2 (46)
Wheat flour: reported freight	Cumulative fixtures	tonnes	No		Selected countries	IWhC2 (32)
Wheat trade: export licences issued	Cumulative, food aid and donations	tons	No		EC	IWhC2 (28A)
Wheat trade:awards granted under "free market"	By crop	tons, ECU, US$ export tenders	No		EC	IWhC2 (28B)
Wheat trade:awards granted under intervention	By crop	tons, ECU, export tenders	No		EC	IWhC2 (28C)
Wheat trade:export refunds and import levies	By crop	ECU, US$	No		EC	IWhC2 (29)
Wool	Greased and degreased	US$, tonne	Yes	A	World	FAO2 (114,115)
2.16.3 Livestock and Meat						
Animals, live	By type	tonnes	Yes	M	EC	EC7 (I)
Animals, live	By type	tonnes	Yes	M	EC	EC7 (I)
Animals and animal products	Total, intra-EC, by animal, product	tonnes	Yes	A	EC	EC7 (IV)
Animals and animal products	Total, intra-EC, resources, by animal, product	tonnes	Yes	A	EC	EC7 (IV)
Bacon, ham, salted and dried pig meat	By exports, imports	tonnes	Yes	A	World	MLC1 (-)
Bacon, ham and other dried, salted or smoked pig meat	Exports, imports	tonnes, %	Yes	A	Selected European countries	UN34 (XXVI)
Beef and veal, exports	By type, country of destination	tonnes, cwe	Yes	A	Selected countries	MLC1 (-)
Beef and veal, imports	By type, country of origin	tonnes, cwe	Yes	A	Selected countries	MLC1 (-)
Beef and veal, fresh, chilled or frozen		tonnes cwe, %	Yes	A	World	GATT2 (10)
Beef and veal, other than fresh, chilled or frozen		tonnes cwe, %	Yes	A	World	GATT2 (11)
Beef and veal, fresh, chilled or frozen		tonnes, cwe, %	Yes	A	World	GATT2 (7)

Subject	Categories	Units	Time series Yes/No	Frequency	Territorial coverage	Source (Table no.)
Beef and veal, other than fresh, chilled or frozen		tonnes, cwe, %	Yes	A	World	GATT2 (8)
Beef and veal, fresh, chilled and, or frozen	Carcass weight	tonnes,% equivalent	Yes	A	World	GATT1 (7)
Beef and veal, other than fresh, chilled and, or frozen	Canned, cooked etc	tonnes, %	Yes	A	World	GATT1 (8)
Beef and veal, fresh, chilled	Carcass weight and, or frozen	tonnes, % equivalent	Yes	A	World	GATT1 (10)
Beef and veal, other	Canned, cooked etc fresh, chilled and, or frozen	tonnes, %	Yes	A	World	GATT1 (11)
Beef and veal		tonnes	Yes	A	OECD	OECD26
Beef and veal	By exports, imports	tonnes	Yes	A	World	MLC1 (-)
Beef and veal	Exports, imports	tonnes	Yes	A	Selected European countries	UN34 (X)
Beef and veal	Imports, exports	tonnes	Yes	A	Selected European countries	UN34 (XI)
Beef and veal	Volume of exports by principal regions of destination	tonnes	Yes	A	Western Europe and Hungary	UN34 (XVI)
Beef and veal trade with third countries	By exports, imports, type, total	tonnes, cwe tonnes product weight	Yes	A	EC	MLC1 (-)
Bovine cattle		US$, nos	Yes	A	World	FAO2 (8)
Cattle, beef and veal	Value of imports and exports	US$	Yes	A	Western Europe	UN34(XII)
Cattle, beef and veal	Estimated volume of imports	tonnes, %	Yes	A	Western Europe	UN34 (XIII)
Cattle, beef and veal	Estimated volume of net trade	tonnes	Yes	A	Western Europe	UN34 (XIV)
Cattle, beef and veal	Volume of gross imports by principal regions of origin	tonnes	Yes	A	Western Europe	UN34(XV)
Cattle and calves, live	Exports, imports	head, %	Yes	A	Selected European countries	UN34 (VIII)
Cattle and calves, live	Imports, exports	head	Yes	A	Selected European countries	UN34 (IX)
Cattle and calves, live		nos, %	Yes	A	World	GATT2 (9)
Cattle and calves, live		nos, %	Yes	A	World	GATT2 (6)
Cattle and calves, live	Carcass weight	tonnes,% equivalent	Yes	A	Selected countries	GATT1 (6)
Cattle and calves, live	Carcass weight	tonnes, % equivalent	Yes	A	Selected countries	GATT1 (9)
Horse Meat		tonnes	Yes	A	OECD	OECD26
Livestock	By exports, imports	head	Yes	A	World	MLC1 (-)
Meat, total		tonnes	Yes	A	OECD	OECD26
Meat, other		tonnes	Yes	A	OECD	OECD26
Meat, exports	Carcass weight	tonnes, %	Yes	A	World	GATT1 (18)
Meat	Exports, imports, carcass weight	tonnes, %	Yes	A	Selected countries	GATT1 (-)
Meat	Exports, imports, carcass weight	tonnes, %	Yes	A	Selected countries	GATT1 (-)
Meat	Exports, imports, carcass weight	tonnes, %	Yes	A	Selected countries	GATT1 (-)
Meat	Imports, exports, carcass weight	tonnes, %	Yes	A	World	GATT1 (21, 22)
Meat	Imports, exports, carcass weight	tonnes, %	Yes	A	World	GATT1 (17, 25, 26)
Meat (canned)		US$, tonne	Yes	A	World	FAO2 (22)
Meat (dried and salted)		US$, tonne	Yes	A	World	FAO2 (19)
Meat (fresh, chilled or frozen)		US$, tonne	Yes	A	World	FAO2 (11)
Meat (fresh)	Bovine, sheep, swine, poultry, and horse	US$, tonne	Yes	A	World	FAO2 (12-16)

2 AGRICULTURE

Subject	Categories	Units	Time series Yes/No Frequency		Territorial coverage	Source (Table no.)
Meat (other prepared)		US$, tonne	Yes	A	World	FAO2 (25)
Meat and edible offal (dried and salted)		US$, tonne	Yes	A	World	FAO2 (21)
Meat and meat products of the USSR	Imports, exports	tonnes	Yes	A	USSR	UN34 (LV)
Meat exports by main trading countries	By countries	nos	No		The Americas and Australasia	MAC2 (D14)
Meat extracts		US$, tonne	Yes	A	World	FAO2 (23)
Mutton, lamb and goat meat		tonnes	Yes	A	OECD	OECD26
Offal, edible		tonnes	Yes	A	OECD	OECD26
Offal (fresh and edible)		US$, tonne	Yes	A	World	FAO2 (17)
Offal (fresh)		US$, tonne	Yes	A	World	FAO2 (18)
Pig meat, canned	By exports, imports	tonnes	Yes	A	World	MLC1 (-)
Pig meat, exports, imports	By type, country of destination	tonnes, cwe	No		Selected countries	MLC1 (-)
Pig meat		tonnes	Yes	A	OECD	OECD26
Pig meat	Imports, exports	tonnes, %	Yes	A	Selected European countries	UN34 (XXVII)
Pig meat (dried and salted)		US$, tonne	Yes	A	World	FAO2 (20)
Pig meat trade with third countries	By exports, imports, type, total	tonnes, cwe	Yes	A	EC	MLC1 (-)
Pigmeat		tonnes, cwe, %	Yes	A	World	GATT2 (18)
Pigmeat		tonnes, cwe, %	Yes	A	World	GATT2 (17)
Pigs, live	Exports, imports	head, %	Yes	A	Selected European countries	UN34 (XXIII)
Pigs, live	Imports, exports	head, %	Yes	A	Selected European countries	UN34 (XXIV)
Pigs, pork, bacon and ham	Value of imports and exports	US$, %	Yes	A	Western Europe	UN34 (XXVIII)
Pigs, pork, bacon and ham	Estimated volume of imports and exports	tonnes	Yes	A	Western Europe	UN34 (XXIX)
Pigs, pork, bacon and ham	Estimated volume of net trade	tonnes	Yes	A	Western Europe	UN34 (XXX)
Pigs, pork, bacon and ham	Volume of gross imports by principal regions of origin	tonnes	Yes	A	Western Europe	UN34 (XXXI)
Pigs		US$, nos	Yes	A	World	FAO2 (10)
Pork	By exports, imports	tonnes	Yes	A	World	MLC1 (-)
Pork	Exports, imports	tonnes, %	Yes	A	Selected European countries	UN34 (XXV)
Poultry, chicks	By type of poultry, by type of stock	nos	Yes	M	EC	EC7 (II)
Poultry, chicks	By type of poultry, by type of stock	nos	Yes	M	EC	EC7 (II)
Poultry meat		tonnes, cwe, %	Yes	A	World	GATT2 (22)
Poultry meat		tonnes, cwe, %	Yes	A	World	GATT2 (21)
Poultry meat		tonnes	Yes	A	OECD	OECD26
Poultry meat	By principal regions of destination	tonnes	Yes	A	Western Europe, Bulgaria and Hungary	UN34 (LIV)
Poultry meat	Exports, imports	tonnes, %	Yes	A	Selected European countries	UN34 (LII)
Poultry meat	Imports, exports	tonnes	Yes	A	Selected European countries	UN34 (LIII)
Prepared, preserved and sausages	By exports, imports	tonnes	Yes	A	World	MLC1 (-)
Principal livestock export products by main trading countries	By countries	nos	No		The Americas and Australasia	MAC2 (D16)
Sausages		US$, tonne	Yes	A	World	FAO2 (24)
Sheep and goats		US$, nos	Yes	A	World	FAO2 (9)
Sheep and lambs live (including goats)	Exports, imports	head, %	Yes	A	Selected European countries	UN34 (XXXVIII)

Subject	Categories	Units	Time series Yes/No Frequency	Territorial coverage	Source (Table no.)
Sheep and sheep meat, live	Estimated value of imports	tonnes, %	Yes A	Western Europe	UN34 (XLIII)
Sheep and sheep meat, live	Estimated volume of net trade	tonnes	Yes A	Western Europe	UN34 (XLIV)
Sheep and sheep meat, live	Volume of gross imports by principal regions of origin	tonnes	Yes A	Western Europe	UN34 (XLV)
Sheep live	Imports, exports	head, %	Yes A	Selected European countries	UN34 (XXXIX)
Sheep meat, imports	By type, country of origin	tonnes	Yes A	Selected countries	MLC1 (-)
Sheep meat		tonnes, cwe, %	Yes A	World	GATT2 (26)
Sheep meat	By imports	tonnes	Yes A	World	MLC1 (-)
Sheep meat	Exports, imports	tonnes, %	Yes A	Selected European countries	UN34 (XL)
Sheep meat	Imports, exports	tonnes, %	Yes A	Selected European countries	UN34 (XLI)
Sheep and sheep meat, live	Value of imports and exports	US$, %	Yes A	Western Europe	UN34 (XLII)
Sheep meat trade with third countries	By exports, imports, type, total	tonnes, cwe	Yes A	EC	MLC1 (-)
Sheepmeat		tonnes, cwe, % tonnes, cwe	Yes A	World	GATT2 (25)

2.16.4 Milk and Dairy Products

Subject	Categories	Units	Time series Yes/No Frequency	Territorial coverage	Source (Table no.)
Butter, source of imports	To, from country	tonnes	Yes A	EC	MMB1(98)
Butter, destination of exports	From, to country	tonnes	Yes A	EC	MMB1(99)
Butter		tonnes, indices	No	World	GATT5 (2C1)
Butter		tonnes, indices	No	World	GATT5 (2D)
Butter		US$, tonne	Yes A	World	FAO2 (31)
Butter	By destination	tonnes	No	World	GATT5 (2C2)
Casein, source of imports	To, from country	tonnes	Yes A	EC	MMB1 (112)
Casein, destination of exports	From, to country	tonnes	Yes A	EC	MMB1 (113)
Cheese, source of imports	To, from country	tonnes	Yes A	EC	MMB1 (100)
Cheese, destination of exports	From, to country	tonnes	Yes A	EC	MMB1 (101)
Cheese and curd		US$, tonne	Yes A	World	FAO2 (32)
Cheeses		tonnes, indices	No	World	GATT5 (4C1)
Cheeses		tonnes, indices	No	World	GATT5 (4D)
Cheeses	By destination	tonnes	No	World	GATT5 (4C2)
Condensed milk, sweetened, source of imports	To, from country	tonnes	Yes A	EC	MMB1 (102)
Condensed milk, sweetened, destination of exports	From, to country	tonnes	Yes A	EC	MMB1 (103)
Condensed milk, unsweetened, source of imports	To, from country	tonnes	Yes A	EC	MMB1 (104)
Condensed milk, unsweetened, destination of exports	From, to country	tonnes	Yes A	EC	MMB1 (105)
Cream destination of exports	From, to country	tonnes	Yes A	EC	MMB1(93)
Cream source of imports	To, from country	tonnes	Yes A	EC	MMB1(92)
Dairy ice cream, source of imports	To,from country	tonnes	Yes A	EC	MMB1(96)
Dairy ice cream, destination of exports	From, to country	tonnes	Yes A	EC	MMB1(97)
Dairy products, exports	By destination, product	tonnes	Yes A	EC	MMB1 (114,115)
Eggs	In or out of shell, liquid, frozen or dried	US$, tonne	Yes A	World	FAO2 (33-36)
Lard and other rendered fat		US$, tonne	Yes A	World	FAO2 (93)
Margarine and other fats		US$, tonne	Yes A	World	FAO2 (94)
Milk, liquid, source of imports	To, from country	tonnes	Yes A	EC	MMB1(90)
Milk, liquid, destination of exports	From, to country	tonnes	Yes A	EC	MMB1(91)
Milk and cream	All types and by type	US$, tonne	Yes A	World	FAO2 (26-30)
Milk fat, anhydrous		tonnes, indices	No	World	GATT5 (3B1)
Milk fat, anhydrous	By destination	tonnes	No	World	GATT5 (3B2)
Milk powder, skimmed		tonnes, indices	No	World	GATT5 (5C1)

2 AGRICULTURE

Subject	Categories	Units	Time series Yes/No Frequency		Territorial coverage	Source (Table no.)
Milk powder, skimmed	By destination	tonnes	No		World	GATT5 (5C2)
Milk powder, whole		tonnes, indices	No		World	GATT5 (6B1)
Milk powder, whole	By destination	tonnes	No		World	GATT5 (6B2)
Milk powder, skimmed		tonnes, indices	No		World	GATT5 (5D)
Milk powder, whole, source of imports	To, from country	tonnes	Yes	A	EC	MMB1 (106)
Milk powder, whole, destination of exports	From, to country	tonnes	Yes	A	EC	MMB1 (107)
Milk products, fresh, other, source of imports	To, from country	tonnes	Yes	A	EC	MMB1(94)
Milk products, fresh, other destination of exports	From, to country	tonnes	Yes	A	EC	MMB1(95)
Preserved whey, source of imports	To, from country	tonnes	Yes	A	EC	MMB1 (110)
Preserved whey, destination of exports	From, to country	tonnes	Yes	A	EC	MMB1 (111)
Skimmed milk powder, source of imports	To, from country	tonnes	Yes	A	EC	MMB1 (108)
Skimmed milk powder, destination of exports	From, to country	tonnes	Yes	A	EC	MMB1 (109)
2.16.5 Sugar						
Glucose, isoglucose and dextrose trade	By imports, exports, by country	tonnes	Yes	A	EC	FOL2 (196)
Molasses	By imports and exports	tonnes	Yes	A	World	FOL3 (72-77)
Molasses	By production and harvest	tonnes	Yes	A	World	FOL3 (78-80)
Raw and white sugar	By imports and exports	tonnes	Yes	A, M	Selected Countries	FOL3 (34-39)
Raw and white sugar trade	By imports, exports, by country	tonnes	Yes	A, M	Selected countries	FOL2 (192-195)
Sugar, exports, imports	Estimates, change, forecast	tonnes, %	Yes	A	Selected countries	GATTI (1)
Sugar, exports, imports, net	By country	tonnes	Yes	A	World	FOL3 (32, 33)
Sugar	Total, raw and refined	US$, tonne	Yes	A	World	FAO2 (67-69)
Sugar exports	By main trading countries	nos	No		The Americas and Australasia	MAC2 (D15)
Surplus, deficit stocks	Above and below normal working stocks	tonnes	Yes	A	World	FOL3 (40, 41)
2.16.6 Total						
Agricultural, exports	By countries	tonnes, score,	Yes	A	EC	MAC3 (C11)
Agricultural products	% of the f.o.b value of total exports of goods	%	Yes	A	Latin American and Caribbean countries	UN45 (51)
Agricultural products	Import volume, import unit value and import value	indices	Yes	A	World, economic regions and classes	FAO2 (1)
Agricultural products by main trading countries	Exports, by countries	nos	No		The Americas and Australasia	MAC2 (D17)
Agricultural trade, value	By country, by product	US$	Yes	A	World	FAO2 (133-196)
Agriculture, fish and forestry		US$	Yes	A	World	FAO2 (5)
Agricutural products	Export volume, export unit value and export value	indices	Yes	A	World, economic regions and classes	FAO2 (3)
Agricutural products	Total	US$	Yes	A	World	FAO2 (6)
EC external trade, agricultural products by import	By country	ECU	Yes	A	EUR 12	EC6 (IA12)
EC external trade, agricultural products by export	By country	ECU	Yes	A	EUR 12	EC6 (IA13)
EC external trade of member states, agricultural products	Extra EC imports	ECU	No	1989	EC	EC6 (IA14)
EC external trade of member states, agricultural products	Extra EC exports	ECU	No	1989	EC	EC6 (IA15)
EC trade general summary	By commodity, import, export	ECU	Yes	A	EC	EC6 (IA11)
Fishing and forestry products,		hl, cu m, nos				

Subject	Categories	Units	Time series Yes/No Frequency		Territorial coverage	Source (Table no.)
Food (excl fish)		US$	Yes	A	World	FAO2 (7)
Food (excl fish)	Export volume, export unit value and export value	indices	Yes	A	World, economic regions and classes	FAO2 (4)
Food (excl fish)	Import volume, import unit value and import value	indices	Yes	A	World, economic regions and classes	FAO2 (2)
Food and agricultural products, trade balance, external		ECU	No		EC	WC1 (-)
Food and agricultural products	Share of exports in exports of all products	%	No		EC	WC1 (-)
Food and agricultural products	Share of imports in exports of all products	%	No		EC	WC1 (-)
World exports and EC external trade		US$	Yes	A	EC	WC1 (-)
2.16.7 Wine and Beer						
Beer		US$, tonne	Yes	A	World	FAO2 (96)
Wine, vermouth and similar beverages		US$, tonne	Yes	A	World	FAO2 (95)
Wine		hl	Yes	4 yr	World	OIVV1 (L)
Wine		hl	Yes	4 yr	World	OIVV1(M)
Wine	Total, appellation	hl	No		World	OIVV1(N)
Wine	Total,	hl	No		World	OIVV1(N)
2.17 LAND USE AND IRRIGATION - see also Section 29						
Age distribution	Type 41 holdings	age, %	Yes	2 yrly	EC	EC57 (6.13,14)
Agricultural area, woods and forests utilised		ha; % of UAA	No		EC	WC1 (-)
Agricultural area	Arable land, permanent crops, permanent pasture, forest area, irrigated land	ha	Yes	A	Latin American and Caribbean countries	UN45(301)
Agricultural area	Utilised	ha	No		EC	WC1 (-)
Agricultural area utilized	By size group of holding	ha	No		EC	EC9 (5.16)
Agricultural area utilized	Type 41 holdings	nos	Yes	2 yrly	EC	EC57 (6.12)
Agricultural land, use for greenhouses		ha, % change	No		Selected countries	UN22 (II-3.2.12)
Apple tree density	By age and production zone	ha	No		EC	EC15 (I.3)
Apple Tree density	By country and production zone	ha	No		EC	EC15 (I.2)
Apple tree density	By variety, density and age	ha	No		EC	EC15 (I.4)
Apple tree density	By variety and age class	ha, %	No		EC	EC15 (I.5)
Apple tree density	By variety and country	ha	No		EC	EC15 (I.1)
Apricot tree density	By age and production zone	ha	No		EC	EC15 (IV.3)
Apricot tree density	By age class and variety	ha, %	No		EC	EC15 (IV.5)
Apricot tree density	By density and production zone	ha	No		EC	EC15 (IV.2)
Apricot tree density	By variety, age class and density	ha	No		EC	EC15 (IV.4)
Apricot tree density	By variety and production zone	ha	No		EC	EC15 (IV.1)
Arable and combined land, net change in area	By combined land, non-permanent meadows	ha	No		EC	UN22 (II 3.1.2)
Arable and permanent cropland		sq km	Yes	A	OECD, World	OECD33 (12.1A)
Arable land, use of	By crops, fallow	ha	No		Nordic countries	NCM1(55)

2 AGRICULTURE

Subject	Categories	Units	Time series Yes/No Frequency	Territorial coverage	Source (Table no.)
Arable land		%	No	Developing countries	UNCTAD5 (1.4)
Arable land and gardens		ha	No	Nordic countries	NCM1(54)
Area, population, agriculture		ha, per capita, nos	Yes A	EC	EC6 (IA2.2)
Area harvested, 11 main products	% of total area harvested	%	Yes A	Latin American and Caribbean countries	UN45 (48)
Broad areas	Main crops	ha	Yes A	EC	EC6 (IB 1)
Broad areas	Total, by type	ha	Yes A	EC	EC6 (IA2.1)
By arable, permanent crops permanent pasture		ha	No	Selected countries	UN22 (II-3.1.1)
Cereal, potato and sugar beet crops, area	By countries	ha	Yes A	EC	MAC3 (C1)
Cereals, dried pulses, industrial crops, oilseeds, fresh vegetables, and fodder, area used for production	From arable land	ha, indices	Yes A	EC	EC58 (6.20)
Cereals, dried pulses, industrial crops, oilseeds, fresh vegetables, and fodderArea used for production	Type 41 holdings from arable land	ha, indices	Yes A	EUR 10	EC57 (6.27)
Citrus trees, small-fruited	By variety and production zone	ha	No	EC	EC15 (VII.1)
Citrus trees, small-fruited	By density class and production zone	ha	No	EC	EC15 (VII.2)
Citrus trees, small-fruited	By age class and production zone	ha	No	EC	EC15 (VII.3)
Citrus trees, small-fruited	By age class, density and variety	ha	No	EC	EC15 (VII.4)
Citrus trees, small-fruited	By age class and variety	ha, %	No	EC	EC15 (VII.5)
Cotton and tobacco, area and output	By countries, area,output	nos	No	The Americas and Australasia	MAC2 (D5)
Crop, land use	By product	ha	Yes A	EC	EC19 (I)
Crops, area and output, Mediterranean	By countries	ha, tonnes	Yes A	EC	MAC3 (C4)
Crops	Areas, yields and production, by product	tonnes, ha, kg, ha	Yes A	EC	EC19 (II)
Crops and grass, arable, cereals and sugar beet area	Per dairy cow and head of cattle type 41 holdings	area, %	Yes 2 yrly	EC	EC58 (6.21)
Crops and grass, arable, cereals and sugar beet area	Per dairy cow and head of cattle	area, %	Yes 2 yrly	EUR 9	EC57
Drainage		ha, % change	No	Selected countries	UN22 (II-3.2.6a)
Flax, groundnuts and soya beans area	By countries	nos	No	The Americas and Australasia	MAC2 (D3)
Fruit	Pure stand areas, harvested production, by fruit	tonnes, ha,	Yes A	EC	EC19 (III)
Grassland, permanent		sq km	Yes A	OECD, World	OECD33 (12.1B)
Irrigated area		ha, % change	No	Selected countries	UN22 (II-3.2.6b)
Irrigated area		sq km	Yes A	OECD, World	OECD33 (12.2)
Irrigation techniques	By surface and localised techniques	%	No	Selected countries	UN22 (II-3.2.6d)
Land area	By country, by arable crops, permanent crops, irrigated, non-irrigated	ha	No	GCC region	CH1 (7.1)
Land use, agriculture	By type of land use	ha, %	Yes A	ASEAN	ASEANS1 (3.2)
Land use	Arable, crops, grassland wooded	ha	No	World	EC9 (5.1)

Subject	Categories	Units	Time series Yes/No Frequency		Territorial coverage	Source (Table no.)
Land use	Arable, pastoral, irrigated, unirrigated, forest and woodland, by country	ha	Yes	A	ESCAP	UN44
Land use	Arable - by crop, permanent grassland, permanent crops - by crop kitchen gardens	ha	No		EC	EC9 (5.2)
Land use	By country	ha	No		EC	EC18 (7.1)
Land use	By land area and type	ha	Yes	5 yrly	Selected Asian countries	IRRI1 (68)
Land use	By type of crop, type of animal	holdings	No		EC	EC9 (5.17)
Land use	Number of holdings, area under crops, by type of crop, by size class of holding, by country	nos	No		EC	EC45 (B)
Land use	Number of holdings, area under crop, by type of crop, by country,region	nos	No		EC	EC45 (D)
Land use	Number of holdings, area, by type of farming, by country	nos	No		EC	EC45 (C)
Land use and irrigation	By country, by use	ha	No		EC	EM1 (1903)
Lemon tree density	By age class, density and variety	ha	No		EC	EC15 (VI.4)
Lemon tree density	By age class and production zone	ha	No		EC	EC15 (VI.3)
Lemon tree density	By age class and variety	ha, %	No		EC	EC15 (VI.5)
Lemon tree density	By density class and production zone	ha	No		EC	EC15 (VI.2)
Lemon tree density	By variety and production zone	ha	No		EC	EC15 (VI.1)
Main arable crops area	By country, crop type	ha	Yes	A	Africa and Asia	MAC1 (D1)
Main arable crops area	Cities	nos	No		The Americas and Australasia	MAC2 (D1)
Orange tree density	By age class, country and production zone	ha	No		EC	EC15(V.3)
Orange tree density	By age class, variety and density	ha	No		EC	EC15(V.4)
Orange tree density	By age class and variety	ha, %	No		EC	EC15(V.5)
Orange tree density	By density class and production zone	ha	No		EC	EC15(V.2)
Orange tree density	By variety and production zone	ha	No		EC	EC15(V.1)
Peach tree density	By age class, variety and density	ha	No		EC	EC15 (III.4)
Peach tree density	By age class and production zone	ha	No		EC	EC15 (III.3)
Peach tree density	By age class and variety	ha, %	No		EC	EC15 (III.5)
Peach tree density	By density, country and production zone	ha	No		EC	EC15 (III.2)
Peach tree density	By production zone	ha	No		EC	EC15 (III.1)
Pear tree density	By age and production zone	ha	No		EC	EC15 (II.3)
Pear tree density	By age class and variety	ha, %	No		EC	EC15 (II.5)
Pear tree density	By country and production zone	ha	No		EC	EC15 (II.2)
Pear tree density	By variety, density and age	ha	No		EC	EC15 (II.4)
Pear tree density	By variety	ha	No		EC	EC15 (II.1)

2 AGRICULTURE

Subject	Categories	Units	Time series Yes/No	Frequency	Territorial coverage	Source (Table no.)
Rice, rough, harvested area	By country and geographical region	ha	Yes	A	World	IRRI1 (2)
Rice, area planted (or harvested), modern varieties		ha	Yes	A	Selected Asian countries	IRRI1 (65)
Rice area, irrigated		ha	Yes	A	Selected Asian countries	IRRI1 (69)
Rice area, irrigated	as % of total rice area	%	Yes	A	Selected Asian countries	IRRI1 (70)
Rice area	Irrigated, rain-fed, upland, % classified based on dominant water regime	%	Yes	A	World	IRRI1 (72)
Rice area planted (or harvested)	as % of total rice area, modern varieties	%	Yes	A	Selected Asian countries	IRRI1 (66)
Soil suitability and topography	By suitability for type of crop, by land slope	ha	No		Selected countries	UN22 (II-3.1.3)
Utilization of water for irrigation	By area, quantity used, source, quality	ha, cu m per yr	No		Selected countries	UN22 (II-3.2.6c)
Vegetables	Harvested crops area, harvested production, yield, by vegetable	tonnes, ha, kg, ha	Yes	A	EC	EC19 (III)
Vineyards and output of wine, area	By countries, area,output	nos	No		The Americas and Australasia	MAC2 (D8)
Vineyards and output of wine area	By countries	ha, hl	Yes	A	EC	MAC3 (C3)
Wooded and utilized agricultural	By grassland, crop, arable	ha	No		EC	EC69 (IV.1)

2.18 LIVESTOCK

Subject	Categories	Units	Time series Yes/No	Frequency	Territorial coverage	Source (Table no.)
Agricultural production	By member state, meat type	%	No		EC	MLC1 (-)
Animal output, final	By current prices, 1985 prices, crop	PPS (US$)	Yes	A	OECD	OECD5 (II.A, II.1.B)
	current prices	nat curr	Yes	A	OECD	OECD5 (III.1.C)
Animal output	As % of final agricultural output	%	Yes	A	OECD	OECD5 (II.4)
Animals, non-bovine	Significance of non-bovine animals, distribution of holdings by number of selected animals, distribution of holdings with selected animals by agricultural area	nos, %	No		EC	EC45 (VII)
Animals, bovine	Significance of bovine animals, distribution of holdings by number of selected bovine animals, agricultural area in use	nos, %	No		EC	EC45 (AVI)
Animals, slaughter weight	By type	kg/carcass	Yes	A	EC	EC7 (IV)
Animals	Number of holdings, number of animals, by type of animal, by country,region	nos	No		EC	EC45 (D)
Animals	Number of holdings, number of animals, by type of animal, by size class of holding, by country	nos	No		EC	EC45 (B)
Animals and animal products	Changes in stocks, by animal,product	tonnes	Yes	M	EC	EC7 (IV)

Subject	Categories	Units	Time series Yes/No	Frequency	Territorial coverage	Source (Table no.)
Animals and animal products	Gross indigenous production, usable production, by animal, product	tonnes	Yes	A	EC	EC7 (IV)
Animals killed	By type	nos	Yes	A	Nordic countries	NCM1(71)
Animals slaughtered	By meat type and by country	nos	Yes	A	OECD	OECD26
Artificial insemination and embryo transfer	By cattle	nos	Yes	10 yrly	Selected countries	UN22 (II-3.2.11)
Livestock		nos 1000	Yes	A	Central Africa	UN5 (15)
Beef and buffalo meat, mutton and goat meat, pig meat	Carcass weight	head/kg tonnes	Yes	A	World	FAO1 (98)
Beef and buffalo meat	By production	head, kg, an, tonnes	Yes	A	World	FAO6 (24)
Beef and buffalo meat	Production, by country,region	tonnes	Yes	A	World	FAO7 (95)
Beef and veal, total		tonnes	Yes	A	OECD	OECD26
Beef and veal, slaughtered, total		tonnes	Yes	A	OECD	OECD26
Beef and veal		tonnes	Yes	A	EC	EC6 IE10)
Beef and veal	Carcass weight	head/kg	Yes	A	World	FAO1 (92)
Beef and veal	Carcass weight	tonnes	Yes	A	World	GATT1 (4)
Beef and veal	Net	indices, tonnes	Yes	A, M	EC	EC36
Beef and veal	Beef, veal	tonnes, %	Yes	A	World	GATT2 (3)
Beef and veal exports	Destination exporting	tonnes, %	Yes	A	Seven major countries	GATT1 (II)
Beef and veal production	From indigenous animals	tonnes, %	Yes	A	EC	UN34 (I)
Beef and veal stocks	Carcass weight	tonnes, %	Yes	A	World	GATT1 (4)
Breeding sow holdings	By herd size	head, %	No		EC	MLC1 (-)
Breeding sows in different herd size	By breeding sows	head, %	No		EC	MLC1 (-)
Breeds, number of	By breeds used	nos	No		Selected countries	UN22 (II-3.2.2b)
Breeds, endangered and extinct	By domestic animals only	nos	No		Selected countries	UN22 (II-3.2.2c)
Buffalo meat	Carcass weight	head/kg	Yes	A	World	FAO1 (93)
Calves, heifers and cows		head	Yes	A, M	EC	EC58 (2.4,2.5,2.6)
Calves, seasonal movement	Actual,values, moving average, index, mean index, standard deviation	head	Yes	A, M	EUR 9	EC58 (2.7)
Calves slaughtered, number		head	Yes	A, Q	Selected European countries	UN34 (III)
Cattle, numbers	Adult cattle, calves	nos, %	Yes	A	World	GATT2 (1)
Cattle, slaughter	Adult cattle, calves	nos, %	Yes	A	World	GATT2 (2)
Cattle, buffaloes, camels	Kind	head	Yes	A	World	FAO1 (89)
Cattle, buffaloes, pigs	By production	head	Yes	A	World	FAO6 (22)
Cattle	Kind	head, %	Yes	A	EUR9, EUR10	EC57 (2.3,2.4)
Cattle	May and December, surveys, by kind	head, %	No		EC	EC58 (2.1, 2.2)
Cattle	Total, by kind	head	Yes	A	EC	MLC1 (-)
Cattle and calf		head, %	Yes	A	World	GATT1 (2)
Cattle and calf numbers	Total	head, %	Yes	A	World	GATT1 (1)
Cattle and horses		head, % change	No		Selected countries	UN22 (II-3.2.2e)
Cattle and horses	Number of, per agricultural area	head, % change	No		Selected countries	UN22 (II-3.2.2i)
Cattle breeding structure	Total, %	nos	Yes	A	EC	EC6 (IE 5)
Cattle in different herd size	By cattle	head, %	No		EC	MLC1 (-)
Cattle livestock composition	Kind	%	No		EC	EC57 (2.5)
Cattle numbers	Month of census or sample	head, %	Yes	A, M	EC	UN34 (IV)
Cattle numbers	Total, by type	head, %	Yes	A	EC	EC6 (IE 1)
Cattle slaughtered, number		head	Yes	A, Q	Selected European countries	UN34 (II)

2 AGRICULTURE

Subject	Categories	Units	Time series Yes/No	Frequency	Territorial coverage	Source (Table no.)
Chicken and ducks		heads	Yes	A	World, ASEAN	ASEANS1 (3.5.4)
Chicken numbers	Census	pieces, %	Yes	A	EC	UN34 (XLVIII)
Chickens, ducks, turkeys		nos	Yes	A	World	FAO1 (91)
Cow-in-milk, milk production and yield	kg per animal	head, tonnes,	No		Selected countries	UN22 (II-3.2.2g)
Cows, rate of growth	Dairy cows	%	Yes	A	EC	EC57 (2.2)
Cows, other	Principal types of farming	%	Yes	2 yrly	EC	EC57 (6.22)
Cows	Dairy and other	indices	Yes	A	EC	EC57 (2.1)
Cows and buffaloes		heads	Yes	A	World, ASEAN	ASEANS1 (3.5.1)
Cows per holding with other cows	According to community typology	%	Yes	2 yrly	EC	EC57 (6.23)
Cows slaughtered ratio to number of cows		%, nos	Yes	A	EUR 12	EC58 (2.3)
Dairy cow holdings	By herd size	head, %	No		EC	MLC1 (-)
Dairy cows in different herd size	By cows	head, %	No		EC	MLC1 (-)
Edible offal, total		tonnes	Yes	A	OECD	OECD26
Edible offal, slaughtered, total		tonnes	Yes	A	OECD	OECD26
Eggs and poultry, chicks placed	By type of poultry, by type of stock	nos	Yes	M	EC	EC7 (II)
Eggs and poultry, hatcheries	Chicks hatched, eggs in incubation, by type of poultry, by type of stock	nos	Yes	M	EC	EC7 (II)
Ewe premium payments	Total	ECU, nat curr	Yes	A	EC	MLC1 (-)
Goat meat	Carcass weight	head/kg	Yes	A	World	FAO1 (95)
Hatcheries structure	Total	nos	Yes	A	EC	EC6 (IE 7)
Hen eggs, evaporated and condensed	By production milk, honey	tonnes	Yes	A	World	FAO6 (31)
Holders other cows	Non-dairy	head	Yes	2 A	EUR12	EC57 (6.19)
Holders with other cows, rate of growth	According to farming size	nos, %	Yes	2 yrly	EC	EC58 (6.10)
Holders with other cows	According to farming size	nos	Yes	2 yrly	EC	EC58 (6.9)
Holdings	By herd size	head, %	No		EC	MLC1 (-)
Holdings	By herd size	head, %	No		EC	MLC1 (-)
Horse and poultry meat, total	Carcass weight	head/kg	Yes	A	World	FAO1 (97)
Horse meat, total		tonnes	Yes	A	OECD	OECD26
Horse meat, slaughtered, total		tonnes	Yes	A	OECD	OECD26
Horses, mules, asses	Kind	head kg dw kg dw	Yes	A	World	FAO1 (88)
Live imports, exports	Total	tonnes	Yes	A	EC	MLC1 (-)
Livestock, numbers	By type and country	nos	Yes	A	Africa and Asia	MAC1 (D10)
Livestock, numbers	By countries	nos	No		The Americas and Australasia	MAC2 (D9)
Livestock, quantum indices		indices	Yes	A	Latin American and Caribbean countries	UN45 (298)
Livestock, mid year estimate	By type	nos	Yes	A	Nordic countries	NCM1(61)
Livestock, regional distribution	By dairy and other cows	head, %	No		EC	MLC1 (-)
Livestock, regional distribution of	By region	head, %	No		EC	MLC1 (-)
Livestock, other	Total, by type	head, %	Yes	A	EC	EC6 (IE 3)
Livestock, numbers	By countries	nos	Yes	A	EC	MAC3 (C59)
Livestock						
Livestock		nos 1000	Yes	A	East and Southern Africa	UN4(15)
Livestock		nos 1000	Yes	A	North Africa	UN2(15)
Livestock		nos 1000	Yes	A	West Africa Africa	UN3(15)

Subject	Categories	Units	Time series Yes/No Frequency		Territorial coverage	Source (Table no.)
Livestock	By country, by cows, sheep, goats, camels	nos	No		GCC	CH1 (7.9)
Livestock	By country, by horses, cattle, pigs, sheep, goats	nos	No		EC	EM1 (1904)
Livestock	By country	nos	No		EC	EC18 (7.8)
Livestock	By type	head	No		EC	EC69 (IV.3)
Livestock	By type	head	Yes	A	World	EC6(1A 3)
Livestock	By type	nos	Yes	A	VICES and Yugoslavia	VICES1 (I, 5)
Livestock	Cattle, pigs, sheep and goats	nos	No		World	EC9 (5.6)
Livestock	Kind, cows, and other	head	Yes	A	World	UN50 (69)
Livestock	Livestock, products, by country	nos, tonnes	Yes	A	ESCAP	UN44
Livestock	Number of holdings, number of animals, average (heads), by type of farming, by country	nos	No		EC	EC45 (C)
Livestock	By country, by cattle, pigs, sheep and goats	nos	No		EC	EC35 (-)
Livestock in units	Total, by type	livestock unit	Yes	A	EC	EC6 (IE 4)
Livestock numbers	By type	nos	Yes	A	OECD	OECD26
Livestock numbers	By livestock, by member states	head, %	No		EC	WC1 (-)
Livestock products		indices	Yes	A	World	UN50 (1)
Livestock products	Total, production	indices	Yes	A	World	FAO1 (7)
Livestock products	Total, production per capita	indices, per capita	Yes	A	World	FAO1 (12)
Livestock regional distribution	By total pigs, breeding sows	head, %	No		EC	MLC1 (-)
Meat, total	Production, by country, region,	tonnes	Yes	A	World	FAO7 (94)
Meat, output	By countries	nos	No		The Americas and Australasia	MAC2 (D12)
Meat, summary of world production	By meat type	tonnes	Yes	A	World	ISTA2(-)
Meat, gross indigenous		tonnes	Yes	A	OECD	OECD26
Meat, other total		tonnes	Yes	A	OECD	OECD26
Meat, slaughtered, total		tonnes	Yes	A	OECD	OECD26
Meat, dressed carcass weight	By meat type and by country	kg	Yes	A	OECD	OECD26
Meat, gross indigenous	By meat type and by country	tonnes	Yes	A	OECD	OECD26
Meat, total		tonnes	Yes	A	EC	EC6 (IE 9)
Meat, net production	Slaughterings by type of animal	tonnes	Yes	M	EC	EC7 (I)
Meat, gross indigenous production	By type of animal	tonnes	Yes	M	EC	EC7 (I)
Meat, output	By countries	tonnes	Yes	A	EC	MAC3 (C8)
Meat		tonnes	Yes	A	World	UN50 (1)
Meat	By country	tonnes	Yes	A	Africa and Asia	MAC1 (D11)
Meat	By production	tonnes, % change		No	Selected countries	UN22 (II-3.2.2h)
Meat	By type	tonnes	No		World,	EC9 (5.7)
Meat	By type	tonnes	Yes	A	VICES and Yugoslavia	VICES1 (I, 5)
Meat other, slaughtered, total		tonnes	Yes	A	OECD	OECD26
Meat production	By country, by product	tonnes	No		EC	EM1 (1906)
Meat production (slaughterings)	By type	tonnes	Yes	A	World	EC6 (IA 4)
Milk, cows	By yield and production	head, kg, an, tonnes	Yes	A	World	FAO6 (28)
Milk, buffalo, sheep, goat	By production	tonnes	Yes	A	World	FAO6 (29)

2 AGRICULTURE

Subject	Categories	Units	Time series Yes/No Frequency	Territorial coverage	Source (Table no.)
Mutton, lamb and goat meat, total		tonnes	Yes A	OECD	OECD26
Mutton, lamb and goat meat, slaughtered, total		tonnes	Yes A	OECD	OECD26
Mutton and lamb	Carcass weight	head/kg nat curr, kg	Yes A	World	FAO1 (94)
Pig breeding structure	Total, %	nos	Yes A	EC	EC6 (IE 6)
Pig meat, total		tonnes	Yes A	OECD	OECD26
Pig meat, slaughtered, total		tonnes	Yes A	OECD	OECD26
Pig meat	By production	head, kg, an, tonnes	Yes A	World	FAO6 (25)
Pig meat	Carcass weight	head/kg	Yes A	World	FAO1 (96)
Pig meat	Production, by country, region	tonnes	Yes A	World	FAO7 (97)
Pig meat	Reference prices	nat curr,	Yes A, M	EC	MLC1 (-)
Pig meat production	From indigenous animals	tonnes, %	Yes A	EC	UN34 (XVII)
Pig numbers	By census	head	Yes A	EC	UN34 (XIX)
Pig numbers	Total, by type	head, %	Yes A	EC	EC6 (IE 2)
Pigmeat		tonnes, cwe	Yes A	World	GATT2 (15)
Pigmeat		tonnes	Yes A	EC	EC6 (IE 11)
Pigs, sheep, goats	Kind	head	Yes A	World	FAO1 (90)
Pigs		head	Yes A	EC	EC57 (6.24)
Pigs		heads	Yes A	World, ASEAN	ASEANS1 (3.5.3)
Pigs	Number of, per agricultural area	head per ha, % change	No	Selected countries	UN22 (II-3.2.2j)
Pigs	Total, by kind	head	Yes A	EC	MLC1 (-)
Pigs in different herd size	By pigs	head, %	No	EC	MLC1 (-)
Pigs slaughtered, number		head	Yes A	Selected European countries	UN34 (XVIII)
Pork	Net	indices, tonnes	Yes A, M	EC	EC36
Poultry		tonnes	Yes A	EC	EC6(IE 13)
Poultry and pigs		head, % change	No	Selected countries	UN22 (II-3.2.2f)
Poultry meat, total		tonnes	Yes A	OECD	OECD26
Poultry meat, slaughtered, total		tonnes	Yes A	OECD	OECD26
Poultry meat, meat, offals	By production	tonnes	Yes A	World	FAO6 (27)
Poultry meat	Production, by country, region	tonnes	Yes A	World	FAO7 (98)
Poultry meat	Ready to cook basis	tonnes, %	Yes A	World	GATT2 (19)
Poultry meat production		tonnes, %	Yes A	EC	UN34 (XLVI)
Poultry slaughtered		tonnes, pieces	Yes A, Q	Selected European countries	UN34 (XLVII)
Production		tonnes, %	Yes A	Selected countries	GATT1 (-)
Production	Carcass weight	tonnes, %	Yes A	Selected countries	GATT1 (-)
Production	Carcass weight	tonnes, %	Yes A	Selected countries	GATT1 (-)
Production	Carcass weight	tonnes, %	Yes A	World	GATT1 (23)
Production	Carcass weight	tonnes	Yes A	World	GATT1 (15)
Production	Ready to cook	tonnes, %	Yes A	World	GATT1 (19)
Production gross indigenous	By type	head	Yes A	EC	EC6 (IE 8)
Self-sufficiency	Total	%	Yes A	EC	MLC1 (-)
Sheep, cattle	Reference basic price	ECU, kg	Yes A, M	EC	MLC1 (-)
Sheep, representative market prices	By price	nat curr,	Yes A, M	EC	MLC1 (-)
Sheep, goats, chickens	By production	head, nos	Yes A	World	FAO6 (23)
Sheep		head	Yes A	EC	EC57 (6.25)
Sheep	Total, by kind	head	Yes A	EC	MLC1 (-)
Sheep and goat meat	By production	head, kg, an, tonnes	Yes A	World	FAO6 (26)
Sheep and goat numbers	Census	head	Yes A	EC	UN34 (XXXIV)
Sheep and goats		head, % change	No	Selected countries	UN22 (II-3.2.2d)
Sheep and goats meat	Production, by country, region	tonnes	Yes A	World	FAO7 (96)

Subject	Categories	Units	Time series Yes/No	Frequency	Territorial coverage	Source (Table no.)
Sheep meat		tonnes, cwe	Yes	A	World	GATT2 (23)
Sheep meat production	From indigenous animals	tonnes, %	Yes	A	EC	UN34 (XXXII)
Sheep slaughtered, number		head	Yes	A, Q	Selected European countries	UN34 (XXXIII)
Sheep population		By head	Yes	A	World	IWS1 (1)
Sheepmeat and goatmeat		tonnes	Yes	A	EC	EC6 (IE 12)
Sheeps and goats		heads	Yes	A	World, ASEAN	ASEANS1 (3.5.2)
Slaughtered meat, total	By meat type and by country	tonnes	Yes	A	OECD	OECD26
Slaughtered production	Total	tonnes	Yes	A	EC	MLC1 (-)
Slaughterings	By country, by cattle, pigs, sheep, goats	nos	No		EC	EC18 (7.9)
Slaughterings	Total	head	Yes	A	EC	MLC1 (-)
Stocking rate	Type 41 holdings, yield, feed, milk production	LU, ha	No		EUR 9	EC57 (6.18)

2.19 MILK, CHEESE AND OTHER LIVESTOCK PRODUCTS - see also under Livestock (2.18) and Milk Industry (2.20)

Subject	Categories	Units	Time series Yes/No	Frequency	Territorial coverage	Source (Table no.)
Animal products	By country, by product	tonnes	No		EC	EC18 (7.10)
Animal products	By current prices, 1985 prices	PPS (US$)	Yes	A	OECD	OECD5 (II.I.A, II.1.B)
Animal products	Current prices	nat curr	Yes	A	OECD	OECD5 (III.1.C)
Animal products	By type	tonnes	Yes	A	VICES and Yugoslavia	VICES1 (I/5)
Butter, output	By countries	nos	No		The Americas and Australasia	MAC2 (D11)
Butter, balance	By supply and demand	tonnes	Yes	A	EC	MMB1(62)
Butter, disappearance	Total	tonnes	Yes	A	EC	MMB1(63)
Butter, cheap sales	By type of measure	tonnes	Yes	A	EC	MMB1(64)
Butter, stocks	Average	indices tonnes	Yes	A, M	EC	EC36
Butter, dairy		indices tonnes	Yes	A, M	EC	EC36
Butter, output	By countries	tonnes	Yes	A	EC	MAC3 (C7)
Butter		tonnes, indices	No		World	GATT5 (2A)
Butter		tonnes	No		EC, USA, USSR, Canada, Japan	EC9 (5.8)
Butter		tonnes	Yes	A	EC	EC6(IE 21)
Butter movement in intervention	By entries, outgoings	tonnes	Yes	A	EC	MMB1(66)
Butter production	Total	tonnes	Yes	A	EC	MMB1(60)
Butter stocks	Public, commercial	tonnes	Yes	A	EC	MMB1(65)
Butter supplies and disappearance	By stocks, production imports, exports,	tonnes	No		EC	MMB1(59)
Casein production	Total	tonnes	Yes	A	EC	MMB1(89)
Casein supplies and disappearance	By production, exports imports	tonnes, ratio	No		EC	MMB1(88)
Cattle and buffalo hides, fresh; sheepskins, fresh; goatskins, fresh		tonnes	Yes	A	World	FAO1 (105)
Cheese, butter and ghee, evaporated and condensed milk		tonnes	Yes	A	World	FAO1 (101)
Cheese		tonnes	No		EC, USA, USSR, Canada, Japan	EC9 (5.8)
Cheese		tonnes	Yes	A	EC	EC6(IE 22)
Cheese disappearance	Total	tonnes	Yes	A	EC	MMB1(71)
Cheese production	By type and variety	tonnes	No		EC	MMB1(70)
Cheese production	Total	tonnes	Yes	A	EC	MMB1(68)
Cheese production index	By index, weekly avg	avg daily	Yes	M	EC	MMB1(69)
Cheese supplies and disappearance	By stocks, production imports, exports	tonnes	No		EC	MMB1(67)

2 AGRICULTURE

Subject	Categories	Units	Time series Yes/No Frequency		Territorial coverage	Source (Table no.)
Cheeses		tonnes, indices	No		World	GATT5 (4A)
Cows milk, output	By countries	nos	No		The Americas and Australasia	MAC2 (D10)
Cows milk, output	By countries	tons	Yes	A	EC	MAC3 (C6)
Cream		tonnes	Yes	A	EC	EC6(IE 17)
Cream sales by dairies	By fat content	tonnes	Yes	A	EC	MMB1(57)
Dairy products	By country, by product	tonnes	No		EC	EM1 (1905)
Eggs, hen	Production, by country, region	tonnes	Yes	A	World	FAO7 (104)
Eggs		tonnes	No		EC, USA, USSR, Canada, Japan	EC9 (5.8)
Eggs		tonnes	Yes	A	Nordic countries	NCM1(63)
Eggs	Total	tonnes	Yes	A	EC	EC6(IE 23)
Eggs (hen), and excluding hen eggs,		tonnes	Yes	A	World	FAO1 (103)
Eggs (hen)		tons	Yes	A	World	UN50 (71)
Fresh produce		tonnes	Yes	A	EC	EC6(IE 16)
Hen eggs		tonnes	Yes	A	World	UN50 (1)
Honey	Production, by country, region	tonnes	Yes	A	World	FAO7 (105)
Meat, milk production		1000 tons	Yes	A	Central Africa	UN5 (16)
Milk, buffalo	Production, by country, region	tonnes	Yes	A	World	FAO7 (101)
Milk, cow, whole, fresh	Production, by country, region	tonnes	Yes	A	World	FAO7 (100)
Milk, goat	Production, by country, region	tonnes	Yes	A	World	FAO7 (103)
Milk, sheep	Production, by country, region	tonnes	Yes	A	World	FAO7 (102)
Milk, total	Production, by country, region	tonnes	Yes	A	World	FAO7 (99)
Milk, whole powder disappearance	Total	tonnes	Yes	A	EC	MMB1(77)
Milk, cows (whole fresh)	Milking cows, yield, and production	head, kg tonnes	Yes	A	World	FAO1 (99)
Milk, buffalo, sheep, goat		tonnes	Yes	A	World	FAO1 (100)
Milk, concentrated		tonnes	Yes	A	EC	EC6(IE 18)
Milk		tonnes	No		World	EC9 (5.8)
Milk		tonnes	Yes	A	World	UN50 (1)
Milk		tons	Yes	A	World	UN50 (70)
Milk	By country	tonnes	Yes	A	Africa and Asia	MAC1 (D12)
Milk (raw material), whole		tonnes	Yes	A	EC	EC6(IE 15)
Milk and milk products	By type	tonnes	Yes	M	EC	EC7 (III)
Milk disappearance, condensed	Total	tonnes	Yes	A	EC	MMB1(74)
Milk fat, anhydrous		tonnes, indices	No		World	GATT5 (3A)
Milk powder, skimmed	By production, balance, imports, exports	tonnes	Yes	A	Selected countries	ISTA2 (-)
Milk powder, whole and semi-skimmed supplies and disappearance	By production, imports exports	tonnes, ratio	No		EC	MMB1(75)
Milk powder, whole and semi-skimmed production	By type	tonnes	Yes	A	EC	MMB1(76)
Milk powder, skimmed production index	By weekly average	indices	Yes	M	EC	MMB1(80)
Milk powder, skimmed, balance	By supply and demand	tonnes	Yes	A	EC	MMB1(81)
Milk powder, skimmed, stocks	Public, commercial	tonnes	Yes	A	EC	MMB1(82)
Milk powder, skimmed, annual movements in intervention	By buying in, outgoings	tonnes	Yes	A	EC	MMB1(83)
Milk powder, skimmed, disposal from intervention stocks	By type of use	tonnes	Yes	A	EC	MMB1(84)
Milk powder, skimmed		tonnes, indices	No		World	GATT5 (5A)
Milk powder, whole		tonnes, indices	No		World	GATT5 (6A)
Milk powder, skimmed		indices tonnes	Yes	A, M	EC	EC36
Milk powder, skimmed stocks	Average	indices tonnes	Yes	A, M	EC	EC36
Milk powder, cream and whole		tonnes	Yes	A	EC	EC6(IE 19)

Subject	Categories	Units	Time series Yes/No	Frequency	Territorial coverage	Source (Table no.)
Milk production, condensed	Total, type	tonnes	Yes	A	EC	MMB1(73)
Milk products	By type of product	tonnes	Yes	A	EC	MMB1(58)
Milk sales	By treatment, type of liquid milk	tonnes	No		EC	MMB1(56)
Milk supplies and disappearance, condensed	By stocks, production, imports, exports	tonnes	No		EC	MMB1(72)
Milk utilization, whole	By type	tonnes	Yes	A	EC	EC6(IE 14)
Milk-dried; whole, skimmed and buttermilk, whey (dry)		tonnes	Yes	A	World	FAO1 (102)
Milk: production index	By indices, weekly average	indices	Yes	M	EC	MMB1(61)
Milk: sales by dairies to domestic market	By type of milk	tonnes	Yes	A	EC	MMB1(55)
Milk: skim milk and skim powder fed to animals	By type, calves, other animals, total	tonnes skim milk equivalent	Yes	A	EC	MMB1(85)
Milk: skimmed and buttermilk powder supplies and disappearance	By stocks, production imports, exports	tonnes, ratio	No		EC	MMB1(78)
Milk: skimmed and buttermilk powder production	By type	tonnes	Yes	A	EC	MMB1(79)
Milk: skimmed milk and buttermilk powder		tonnes prodn=100	Yes	A	EC	EC6(IE 20)
Production	Meat, milk	1000 tons	Yes	A	North Africa	UN2 (16)
Whey powder production	Total	tonnes	Yes	A	EC	MMB1(87)
Whey powder supplies and disappearance	By production, exports imports	tonnes, ratio	No		EC	MMB1(86)
Wool, greasy	Production, by country, region	tonnes	Yes	A	World	FAO7 (106)
Wool, greasy		tonnes	Yes	A	World	UN50 (1)
Wool, silk	By type and production	tonnes	Yes	A	World	FAO6 (32)
Wool		tons	Yes	A	World	UN50 (72)

2.20 MILK INDUSTRY - see also under Milk, Cheese and Other Livestock Products (2.19) and Section 25

2.20.1 Enterprises

Subject	Categories	Units	Time series Yes/No	Frequency	Territorial coverage	Source (Table no.)
Breed distribution	Dairy herds	%	No		EC	MMB1(16)
Butter producing enterprises	By annual output	tonnes, %	No		EC	MMB1(48)
Cheese enterprises	By type of manufacture	tonnes, nos	No		EC	MMB1(50)
Cheese producing enterprises	By annual output	tonnes, %	No		EC	MMB1(49)
Condensed milk enterprises	By annual output	tonnes, %	No		EC	MMB1(51)
Dairy co-operatives	By organizations, market share	nos, %	No		EC	MMB1(53)
Dairy companies, major	By turnover, intake	nat curr, %	No		EC	MMB1(54)
Dairy herds, size structure	By herds	%, nos	No		EC	MMB1(17)
Dairy herds, size structure	By cows	%, nos	No		EC	MMB1(18)
Dairy herds, average size	By cows per herd	head, %	Yes	A	EC	MMB1(19)
Enterprises, number	Total	nos	Yes	A	EC	MMB1(44)
Enterprises, size structure	By annual milk intake	tonnes, %	No		EC	MMB1(46)
Enterprises, size structure	By output of liquid milk and products	tonnes, %	No		EC	MMB1(47)
Milk, average intake	Per enterprise	tonnes	Yes	A	EC	MMB1(45)
Milk powder enterprises	By annual output	tonnes, %	No		EC	MMB1(52)
Number of organizations	By annual milk intake	nos	Yes	3 yrly	EUR 9	EC57 (6.30)
		tons, %	No		EUR 9	EC57 (6.31)
Producers	Total, full-time farming	nos, %	Yes	A	EC	MMB1(20)
Wholesale quotas		Ton,%			Netherlands, Belgium, England and Wales	EC57 (1.3)

2.20.2 Finance and Prices

Subject	Categories	Units	Time series Yes/No	Frequency	Territorial coverage	Source (Table no.)
Advertising expenditure	Generic by product	nat curr, ECU,	No		EC	MMB1 (122)
Agricultural budget	Appropriations and expenditure	ECU	Yes	A	EC	MMB1 (2)

2 AGRICULTURE

Subject	Categories	Units	Time series Yes/No Frequency		Territorial coverage	Source (Table no.)
Butter, cheese, whole and skim milk powder, world prices	By product	US$/tonne fob	Yes	A	World	MMB1 (131)
Cessation schemes, national	Total payment, compensation, maximum payment, number of producers	ECU, kg, nos	No		EC10	EC58 (1.2)
Cessation schemes, EC	Provisional and forecast results	ECU	Yes	A	EC	EC58 (1.3)
Co-responsibility levy	Revenue and payments	ECU	Yes	A	EC	MMB1 (7)
FEOGA guarantee section	Appropriations and expenditure	ECU	Yes	A	EC	MMB1 (3I, 3II)
Food aid expenditure and appropriations	By quantities and payments	tonnes, ECU	Yes	A	EC	MMB1 (4)
Milk, target and intervention prices	By product	ECU, kg, ppl £/tonne	Yes	A	EC	MMB1(5I)
Milk, target and intervention prices	By product	nat curr per kg/litre	No		EC	MMB1 (5II)
Milk, intervention price equivalent	Butter, skim powder	ECU/kg	No		EC	MMB1 (6)
Promotional expenditure	By per head, by country	US$	No		Selected countries	IDF1 (3)
Promotional expenditure	By type	US$	No		World	IDF1 (V.3-5)
Subsidies and fixed prices	By product	ECU/tonne £/tonne	No		EC	MMB1 (8)
Threshold prices	By pilot products	ECU/tonne £/tonne	Yes	A	EC	MMB1 (9)
2.20.3 Products						
Agricultural production, final	By product	%, ECU	No		EC	MMB1(13)
Butter production	By country	tonnes	Yes	A	Eastern Europe	MMB1 (128)
Butterfat, solids-not-fat, balance	By supply and demand	tonnes	Yes	A	EC	MMB1(29)
Cattle population	By heifers, cows, dairy cows	head, %	No		EC	MMB1(14)
Cheese, butter, milk powder and condensed milk, world trade	By total, % of total	tonnes, %	Yes	A	World	MMB1 (130)
Consumption, total	By milk product, by country	tonnes	No		World	IDF1 (I)
Consumption, per capita	By milk product, by country	kg	No		World	IDF1 (II)
Consumption of cream, butter and cheese	By per head, by country	kg	No		World	IDF1 (2)
Consumption of liquid milk	By per head, by country	kg	Yes	A	World	IDF1 (1)
Consumption of milk fat and proteins	By per head, by country	kg	No		World	IDF1 (4)
Cows milk, world production	By area	tonnes	Yes	A	World	MMB1 (126)
Cows milk, production	By country	tonnes	Yes	A	Eastern Europe	MMB1 (127)
Dairy cows	Total	head	Yes	A	EC	MMB1(15)
Dairy products, trade	By product, exports, imports	tonnes	No		World	MMB1 (124)
Dairying in CIS	By population, production, supplies, sales, type	Per capita, tonnes, %	No		CIS	MMB1 (129)
Milk, average content	By fat	%	Yes	A	EC	MMB1(24)
Milk, average content	By protein	%	Yes	A	EC	MMB1(25)
Milk, production	Cows milk	tonnes	Yes	A	EC	MMB1(26)
Milk, balance	By supply and demand	tonnes	Yes	A	EC	MMB1(29)
Milk, resources	By member state	ECU	Yes	A	EC	MMB1 (1)
Milk, national and Community cessation schemes	Quantities, % of CTQ	tons/%	Yes	A	EC	EC57 (1.4)
Milk	By production	tonnes	Yes	A	Nordic countries	NCM1(63)
Milk	By yield, cow, production, consumption, prospective members of EC	kg, tonnes	No		Selected countries	MMB1 (125)
Milk and dairy products	By cows, product	head, tonnes	No		World	MMB1 (123)
Milk consumption, intermediate	By size of herd	%	Yes	A	EC	EC58 (5.1)
Milk consumption, intermediate	By size of herd	%	Yes	A	EUR10	EC57 (5.1)

Subject	Categories	Units	Time series Yes/No Frequency		Territorial coverage	Source (Table no.)
Milk delivered to dairies, quota	By quota	tonnes	Yes	A	EC	MMB1 (23II)
Milk delivered to dairies	By deliveries quota, direct sales quota	tonnes	No		EC	MMB1 (23I)
Milk delivered to dairies	Cows milk	tonnes	Yes	A	EC	MMB1(27)
Milk delivered to dairies	Relative to quota	%	Yes	A	EC	MMB1 (23III)
Milk deliveries, seasonal movement	Actual, moving average, index, mean index, standard deviation	tons	Yes	A, M	EC	EC58 (3.1)
Milk deliveries, seasonal movement	Actual,moving average, index,mean index, standard deviation	tons	Yes	A	EUR10	EC57(3.2)
Milk deliveries	Per holding	tons/%	Yes	2 yrly	EUR10	EC57 (3.5)
Milk deliveries	Quotas,% production	tons	Yes	A	EC	EC57 (1.2)
Milk deliveries	Regional share	%	?		Germany, France United Kingdom	EC57 (3.1)
Milk deliveries index	By indices	indices, tonnes	Yes	M	EC	MMB1(28)
Milk production, national	By country, by cows, farms, herd, % butter-fat, % protein	nos, kg, %	Yes	A	CICPE member countries	FNOCL1 (-)
Milk production, quantities, guaranteed		tons	Yes	A	EUR10 and EUR12	EC58 (1.1)
Milk production	Average per recorded cow by country, by product-ion, % butterfat, % protein	kg, %	Yes	A	CICPE member countries	FNOCL1 (-)
Milk production	By size of herd, physical performance on type 41 holdings	per farm	No		EC	EC58 (6.7)
Milk production	By size of herd	per farm	No		EUR 10	EC57 (6.16)
Milk production	By size of herd	tonnes	Yes	A	EC	EC58 (3.3)
Milk production	By size of herd	tonnes	Yes	A	EUR 10	EC57 (3.4)
Milk production	Fresh, manufactured, delivery ratio	%	?		EUR 9	EC57 (4.1)
Milk production	Physical performance on type 41 holdings	per farm	Yes	A	EC	EC58 (6.8)
Milk production	Physical performance on type 41 holdings	per farm	Yes	A	EUR 10	EC57 (6.17)
Milk production	Yield on holding by size of herd	kg, %	Yes	A	EC	EC58 (3.2)
Milk production	Yield on holding by size of herd	kg, %	Yes	A	EUR 10	EC57 (3.3)
Milk recording, position	By country, by cows, herds, % recorded cows, cows, % recorded herds,	nos, %	Yes	A	CICPE member countries	FNOCL1 (-)
Milk recording	By cows, herds, average production	head, kg, %	No		EC	MMB1(21)
Milk yields	By cows	kg, cow	Yes	A	EC	MMB1(22)
Substitute products	By substitute, by country	tonnes	No		World	IDF1 (III)

2.21 NATIONAL ACCOUNTS - see also Section 34

Subject	Categories	Units	Time series Yes/No Frequency		Territorial coverage	Source (Table no.)
Agriculture contribution to GDP	By current prices, fixed prices	nat curr	No		Selected countries	UN22 (II-3.1.12,13)
Capital formation	By current prices, 1985 prices	PPS (US$)	Yes	A	OECD	OECD5 (III.3.A, III.3.B)
Capital formation, gross and net fixed	Current prices	nat curr	Yes	A	OECD	OECD5 (III.3.C)
GDP share	% of total GDP at constant 1980 prices	%	Yes	A	Latin American and Caribbean countries	UN45 (47)

2 AGRICULTURE

Subject	Categories	Units	Time series Yes/No Frequency		Territorial coverage	Source (Table no.)
Growth	Average annual rates	indices	Yes	A	Latin American and Caribbean countries	UN45 (46)
Investment rate in agriculture		%	Yes	A	OECD	OECD5 (II.6)
Purchasing power parities (PPP) conversion rates		US$	Yes	A	OECD	OECD5 (II.11)
Value added, gross		US$	Yes	A	OECD	OECD5 (II.9)
Value added, gross, market and factor cost	By current prices, 1985 prices	PPS (US$)	Yes	A	OECD	OECD5 (III.2.A, III.2.B)
Value added gross, market and factor cost	Current prices	nat curr	Yes	A	OECD	OECD5 (III.2.C)
Value added, net	By current prices, 1985 prices	PPS (US$)	Yes	A	OECD	OECD5 (III.2.A, III.2.B)
Value added, net	Current prices	nat curr	Yes	A	OECD	OECD5 (III.2.C)
Value added and income	By current prices, 1985 prices	PPS (US$)	Yes	A	OECD	OECD5 (III.2.A, III.2.B)
Value added and income	Current prices	nat curr	Yes	A	OECD	OECD5 (III.2.C)

2.22 OILSEEDS, OILS, FATS AND OILMEALS

Subject	Categories	Units	Time series Yes/No Frequency		Territorial coverage	Source (Table no.)
Castor beans	Total	kg/ha	Yes	A	World	FAO1 (39)
Copra, palm kernels, palm oil	By production	tonnes	Yes	A	World	FAO6 (33)
Cotton seed, olives, olive oil	By production	tonnes	Yes	A	World	FAO6 (34)
Crushings, net imports of oilseeds	By seed type	tonnes	Yes	A	World	ISTA2 (-)
Crushings	By seed type, by country	tonnes	Yes	A	World	ISTA2 (-)
Groundnut oil and meal, balance	By stocks, production imports, exports, disappearance	tonnes	Yes	A	World	ISTA1 (-)
Groundnuts, in shell	Area harvested, yield, production, by country, region	ha, kg/ha, tonnes	Yes	A	World	FAO7 (25)
Groundnuts, olive oil and linseed	By crop type, country	metric quintals	Yes	A	Africa and Asia	MAC1(D3)
Groundnuts, shelled	Production, yield, harvested area	tonnes, t/ha, ha	Yes	A	World	ISTA1 (-)
Groundnuts, crushings and trade	Crushings, exports, imports	tonnes	Yes	A	World	ISTA1 (-)
Groundnuts (in shell)		tonnes	Yes	A	World	UN50 (1)
Groundnuts in shell	By area harvested, yield and production	ha, kg/ha, tonnes	Yes	A	World	FAO6 (35)
Groundnuts in shell	Total	kg/ha	Yes	A	World	FAO1 (38)
Linseed	Area harvested, yield, production, by country, region	ha, kg/ha, tonnes	Yes	A	World	FAO7 (30)
Linseed	Total	kg/ha	Yes	A	World	FAO1 (43)
Oil cake	Total	tonnes	Yes	A	EC	EC6 (ID11)
Oil crops, cakes equivalent	Production, by country, region	tonnes	Yes	A	World	FAO7 (41)
Oil crops, oil equivalent	Production, by country, region	tonnes	Yes	A	World	FAO7 (40)
Oil crops, output	By countries	nos	No		The Americas and Australasia	MAC2 (D4)
Oil fats, price premiums or discounts	Selected oils, fats, meals	US$/tonne	Yes	A	World	ISTA2 (-)
Oil meals, new supplies	By production, imports exports, new supplies	tonnes	Yes	A	World	ISTA1 (-)
Oilmeals, major	By supply and demand	tonnes	Yes	A	World	ISTA2 (-)
Oilmeals, supply and demand balance	By meal type,	tonnes	Yes	A	World	ISTA2 (-)

Subject	Categories	Units	Time series Yes/No Frequency	Territorial coverage	Source (Table no.)
	by country	tonnes	Yes A	World	ISTA2 (-)
Oilmeals, world summary balance	Opening stocks, production, imports, exports, disappearance, ending stocks	tonnes	Yes A	World	ISTA2 (-)
Oilmeals balance	By meal type	tonnes	Yes A	World	ISTA2 (-)
Oils, balance	By oil type, stocks, production, imports, exports, disappearance	tonnes	Yes A	World	ISTA1 (-)
Oils and fats, balance	By seed type	tonnes	Yes A	World	ISTA2 (-)
Oils and fats, supply and demand balance	By oil, fat, country	tonnes	Yes A	World	ISTA2 (-)
Oils and fats	By country	tonnes	Yes A	World	ISTA2 (-)
Oils and fats	Disappearance	kg	Yes A	World	ISTA2 (-)
Oils and fats	Summary balances	tonnes	Yes A	World	ISTA2 (-)
Oilseed and oleaginous fruit	Total	tonnes	Yes A	EC	EC6 (ID10)
Oilseed crop balance	By stocks, imports, crushings, other use	tonnes	Yes A	World	ISTA2 (-)
Oilseeds, boost in output affecting imports of oilseed	By crops, imports, crushings, share	tonnes, %	Yes A	EC	ISTA2 (-)
Oilseeds, imports, exports	By country, by product	tonnes	Yes A	World	ISTA2 (-)
Oilseeds, imports and exports	By product, country	tonnes	Yes A	World	ISTA1 (-)
Oilseeds, production, yields and harvested area	By oilseed type	tonnes, t/ha, ha	Yes A	World	ISTA2 (-)
Oilseeds, major	By type, crushings, exports, imports	tonnes	Yes A	World	ISTA2 (-)
Oilseeds, crude oils, fats, meals, grains	Lowest representative price for nearest forward bulk shipment	US$/tonne	Yes A	World	ISTA2 (-)
Oilseeds, exports, imports	By seed type	tonnes	Yes A	World	ISTA2 (-)
Oilseeds, summary of world supply and demand balance	By meal type	tonnes	Yes A	World	ISTA2 (-)
Oilseeds	Major stocks, production disappearance, by country	tonnes	Yes A	World	ISTA2 (-)
Olive oil, total	Production by country, region	tonnes	Yes A	World	FAO7 (37)
Palm kernels, palm oil, hempseed	Total	kg/ha	Yes A	World	FAO1 (48)
Palm kernels	Production, by country, region	tonnes	Yes A	World	FAO7 (34)
Palm oil	Production, by country, region	tonnes	Yes A	World	FAO7 (35)
Rapeseed	Area harvested, yield, production, by country, region	ha, kg/ha, tonnes	Yes A	World	FAO7 (28)
Rapeseed	By area harvested, yield and production	ha, kg/ha, tonnes	Yes A	World	FAO6 (36)
Rapeseed	Total	kg/ha	Yes A	World	FAO1 (41)
Safflower oil	By imports, exports	tonnes	Yes A	Selected countries	ISTA2 (-)
Safflower seed	Area harvested, yield, production, by country, region	ha, kg/ha, tonnes	Yes A	World	FAO7 (31)
Safflower seed	By imports, exports	tonnes	Yes A	Selected countries	ISTA2 (-)
Safflower seed	Total	kg/ha	Yes A	World	FAO1 (44)
Sesame seed	Area harvested, yield, production, by country, region	ha, kg/ha, tonnes	Yes A	World	FAO7 (29)
Sesame seed	Total	kg/ha	Yes A	World	FAO1 (42)
Soybeans	By area harvested, yield and production	ha, kg/ha, tonnes	Yes A	World	FAO6 (37)
Sunflower		tonnes	Yes A	Latin American and Caribbean countries	UN45 (319)
Sunflower seed	Area harvested	ha	Yes A	Latin American and Caribbean countries	UN45 (307)

Subject	Categories	Units	Time series Yes/No Frequency		Territorial coverage	Source (Table no.)
Sunflower seed	By area harvested, yield and production	ha, kg/ha, tonnes	Yes	A	World	FAO6 (38)
Sunflower seed	Total	kg/ha	Yes	A	World	FAO1 (40)
Sunflower seeds	Area harvested, yield, production, by country, region	ha, kg/ha, tonnes	Yes	A	World	FAO7 (27)
2.23 PRICES						
Agricultural, price series of international significance	By crop	nat curr, US$/tonnes	Yes	A	World	FAO1 (119)
Agricultural, index numbers of prices received by farmers and prices paid by farmers	All agricultural products, all requisites	indices	Yes	A	World	FAO1 (120)
Agricultural	Producer prices, goods and services consumed, goods and services contributing to agricultural investment agricultural investment, by country	Nominal indices deflated indices	Yes	A	EC	EC9 (5.20)
Agricultural production, EC price indices	By input	indices	Yes	A	EC	EC6 (IF 5)
Agricultural production inputs, purchase prices	By feedingstuffs, fertilizers, motor fuels and fuels for heating	ECU/kg	Yes	A	EC	EC6 (IF 3)
Agricultural products, EC indices of producer prices	By products	indices	Yes	A	EC	EC6 (IF 4)
Agricultural products	EC index of producer prices					
Agricultural products	Indices of average prices received by farmers	indices	Yes	A	EC and North America	UN40 (1)
Animal products, selling prices	By type	ECU/kg	Yes	A	EC	EC6 (IF 2)
Barley	Average prices received by farmers per 100 kg of barley for livestock feeding	nat curr	Yes	A	EC and North America	UN40 (IIIA)
Barley	Average prices received by farmers per 100 kg of barley for brewing weighted average prices (unit values) received by farmers per 100 kg for all forms of utilization	nat curr	Yes	A	EC and North America	UN40 (IIIB)
Beef, average price received by producers		nat curr/kg, %	Yes	A	World	GATT2 (12)
Beef, average retail price		nat curr/kg	Yes	A	World	GATT2 (13)
Beef, average or representative export prices		US$/tonne	Yes	A	World	GATT2 (14)
Beef, average or representative import prices		US$/tonne	Yes	A	World	GATT2 (14)
Beef	By cut	nat curr/kg	Yes	A, M	EC	MLC1 (-)
Beef	By forequarter, hind-quarter, side	nat curr/kg	Yes	A, M	EC	MLC1 (-)
Beef	Live adult bovine	ECU/kg	Yes	M, Q	EC	EC3 (-)
Beef and veal levies	Frozen	ECU/kg	Yes	M	EC	EC3 (-)
Beef or certain beef cuts, retail prices		nat curr, kg, indices	Yes	A, Q	Selected European countries	UN34 (VI)
Beef price, average	Received by producers	nat curr/kg, %	Yes	A	World	GATT1 (12)
Beef price, average retail		nat curr/kg, %	Yes	A	World	GATT1 (13)
Bovine animal levies	Live	ECU/kg	Yes	M	EC	EC3 (-)
Broilers or poultry, producer prices		nat curr, kg, lb	Yes	A, Q	Selected European countries	UN34 (LI)

Subject	Categories	Units	Time series Yes/No Frequency		Territorial coverage	Source (Table no.)
Butter and margarine	By retail prices	nat curr/kg	Yes	A	EC	MMB1(42)
Calf, finished	By type	nat curr/	Yes	A, M	EC	MLC1 (-)
Calf, rearing	By type, liveweight	nat curr/	Yes	A, M	EC	MLC1 (-)
Calves	Live	ECU/kg	Yes	M, Q	EC	EC3 (-)
Cattle	Average prices received per 100 kg live weight for the most representative type of grade	nat curr	Yes	A	EC and North America	UN40 (VIIIA)
Cattle	Weighted average prices (unit values) received by farmers per 100 kg live weight for all types and grades of beef cattle (excluding calves)	nat curr	Yes	A	EC and North America	UN40 (VIIIB)
Cattle, finished	By type of cattle	nat curr/	Yes	A, M	EC	MLC1 (-)
Cattle or beef, producer prices		nat curr, kg	Yes	A, Q	Selected European countries	UN34(VII)
Cereal levies			Yes	M, Q	EC	EC3 (-)
Cereals	All varieties	ECU/t	Yes	M, Q	EC	EC3 (-)
Cheeses, selected	By retail price	nat curr/kg	Yes	A	EC	MMB1(43)
Coarse grain export prices	Based on official f.o.b quotations	US$/tonne	Yes	A, M	World	IWhC3 (A.8)
Cocoa beans, prices of international significance	London Terminal Market New York Coffee, Sugar and Cocoa Exchange	£/tonne, USc/lb	Yes	A, M	World	ICC02 (17)
Cocoa beans	Daily and indicator prices	SDR's/tonne, USc/lb	Yes	A, M	World	ICC02 (15)
Cocoa beans	Daily prices	USc/lb	Yes	A, M	World	ICC02 (16)
Commodity prices, indices of world market	Commodity groups	indices	Yes	2 yrly	World	UN40 (3)
Compound feed for dairy cows	At grass	ECU/kg	Yes	A, M	Ireland	EC58 (5.3)
Compound feed for dairy cows	Stall fed	ECU/kg	Yes	A, M	EC	EC58 (5.4)
Compound or mixed feed, prices paid by farmers per 100 kg	Raw protein content, type of feed by kind of animal or fowl	%, nat curr, US$	Yes	A	EC and North America	UN40(XV)
Consumer price changes	At December and June for 12-months periods	nos	Yes	6 M	EC and North America	UN40 (2)
Cows milk, producer prices		ECU/kg	Yes	A, M	EC	EC58 (5.2)
Crop products, selling prices	By type	ECU/kg	Yes	A	EC	EC6 (IF 1)
Egg levies		ECU/kg	Yes	Q	EC	EC3 (-)
Eggs	Gate prices	ECU/kg	Yes	M, Q	EC	EC3 (-)
Eggs	Ratios of egg prices to prices paid by farmers for feed for laying hens	ratios	Yes	A	EC and North America	UN40 (7)
Export prices	Average or representative	US$/tonnes	Yes	A	World	GATT1 (14)
Export prices	Rice, wheat and corn	US$, tonnes fob	Yes	A	World	IRRI1 (93)
Fats and oils, oilcakes and meals: revised FAO indices of international market prices	By type, annual averages, monthly averages	indices	Yes	A, M	World	FAO6 (1)
Feed grain	Weighted average prices paid by farmers per 100 kg, by type	nat curr	Yes	A	EC and North America	UN40 (XIIIA, B, C)
Foodstuffs, consumer price indices	By type	indices	Yes	A	EC	EC6 (IF 6)
Fowls	Ratios of prices of fowls for meat production to prices paid by farmers for feed for broilers	ratios	Yes	A	EC and North America	UN40 (6)

2 AGRICULTURE

Subject	Categories	Units	Time series Yes/No	Frequency	Territorial coverage	Source (Table no.)
Fowls for meat production	Average prices received for the most representative type of young chickens raised for meat production per 100 kg live weight	nat curr	Yes	A	EC and North America	UN40 (X)
Hen eggs	Average prices received by farmers per 100 kg of eggs sold to wholesalers	nat curr	Yes	A	EC and North America	UN40 (XIA)
Hen eggs	Weighted average prices (unit values) received by farmers per 100 kg for all types of sales	nat curr	Yes	A	EC and North America	UN40 (XIB)
Import levies, minimum		ECU/kg	Yes	M, Q	EC	EC3 (-)
Import prices	Average or representative	US$/tonnes	Yes	A	World	GATT1 (14)
Indices, nominal price	Total, crop products, animal and animal products	indices, %	Yes	Q	EUR 10	EC5 (1)
Indices, deflated price	Total, crop products, animal and animal products	indices, %	Yes	Q	EUR 10	EC5 (1)
Indices, nominal price	Goods and services	indices, %	Yes	Q	EUR 10	EC5 (3)
Indices, deflated price	Goods and services	indices, %	Yes	Q	EUR 10	EC5 (3)
Indices	By fertilizer, per unit of plant nutrient paid by farmers for fertilizers	indices	Yes	A	EC and North America	UN40 (11)
Lamb, finished	By type, deadweight	kg dw nat curr/kg	Yes	A, M	EC	MLC1 (-)
Lamb	By cut	nat curr/kg	Yes	A, M	EC	MLC1 (-)
Maize, cassava, fishmeal and soybean meal	By product and quotation, international market	US$, tonnes	Yes	A, Q	World	UN34 (LVI)
Meat	By cut	nat curr/kg	Yes	A	EC	MLC1 (-)
Milk, producer	3.7%fat, ex-farm, exc VAT and co- responsibility levy	nat curr, ECU/kg	Yes	A	EC	MMB1(39)
Milk, producer price and target price	By ex-farm, levy, transport, deliveries	nat curr/kg	Yes	A	EC	MMB1(40)
Milk, retail prices	By shop price	nat curr/kg	Yes	A	EC	MMB1(41)
Milk	Ratios of whole milk prices to prices paid by farmers for feed for dairy cows by type of feed	ratios	Yes	A	EC and North America	UN40 (9)
Milk product levies		ECU/kg	Yes	M, Q	EC	EC3 (-)
Oats and maize	Average prices received by farmers per 100 kg of feed oats	nat curr	Yes	A	EC and North America	UN40 (IVA, VA)
Oats and maize	Weighted average prices (unit values) received by farmers per 100 kg for all forms of utilization	nat curr	Yes	A	EC and North America	UN40 (IVB, VB)
Oilcake	Selected international oilcake and other feed prices by type of feed	US$/tonne	Yes	A	Selected countries	UN40 (8)
Oilcakes	Prices paid by farmers per 100 kg	nat curr, US$	Yes	A	EC and North America	UN40 (XIV)
Olive oil	All types	ECU/kg	Yes	M, Q	EC	EC3 (-)
Pig, finished	By deadweight	nat curr/kg	Yes	A, M	EC	MLC1 (-)
Pig meat	By price	nat curr/kg	Yes	A, M	EC	MLC1 (-)
Pigmeat levies		ECU/kg	Yes	Q	EC	EC3 (-)
Pigs	Average prices received per 100 kg live weight for the most representative grade	nat curr	Yes	A	EC and North America	UN40 (IXA)

Subject	Categories	Units	Time series Yes/No Frequency	Territorial coverage	Source (Table no.)
Pigs	By type of feed Ratios of pig prices to prices paid by farmers for feed for pigs	ratios	Yes A	EC and North America	UN40 (5)
Pigs	Weighted average prices (unit values) received by farmers per 100 kg live weight for all grades	nat curr	Yes A	EC and North America	UN40 (IXB)
Pigs or pig meat, producer prices		nat curr, kg indices	Yes A, Q	Selected European countries	UN34 (XXII)
Plant protection products	Prices paid by farmers per 100 kg active matter physical state, packing	%/nat curr/US$	Yes A	EC and North America	UN40 (XXI)
Pork	By cut	nat curr/kg	Yes A, M	EC	MLC1 (-)
Pork	Pigs, cuts, piglets	ECU/kg PAB	Yes M, Q	EC	EC3 (-)
Pork or certain pork cuts, retail prices		nat curr, kg indices	Yes A, Q	Selected European countries	UN34 (XXI)
Potatoes	Average prices received by farmers per 100 kg of potatoes for direct human consumption (main crop only)	nat curr	Yes A	EC and North America	UN40 (VIA)
Potatoes	Weighted average prices (unit values) received by farmers per 100 kg for all forms of utilization (main crop only)	nat curr	Yes A	EC and North America	UN40 (VIB)
Poultry	Gate prices	ECU/kg	Yes Q, M	EC	EC3 (-)
Poultry levies		ECU/kg	Yes Q	EC	EC3 (-)
Poultry meat, retail prices		nat curr, indices	Yes A, Q	Selected European countries	UN34 (L)
Price indices, ISTA world market	By oilseeds, food oils fats, oilmeals, all products	indices	Yes A	World	ISTA2 (-)
Price indices, nominal	By agricultural product, by country	indices	Yes A	EC	EC4 (-)
Price indices, deflated	By agricultural product, by country	indices	Yes A	EC	EC4 (-)
Price indices, nominal	Goods and services currently consumed by agriculture, goods and services contributing to	indices	Yes A	EC	EC4 (-)
Price indices, deflated	Goods and services currently consumed by agriculture, goods and services contributing to agricultural investment, by country	indices	Yes A	EC	EC4 (-)
Price indices, rates of change	Total, crop products, animal products	indices, %	Yes Q	EC	EC5 (2)
Price indices, rates of change					
Price indices, nominal	Goods and services	indices, %	Yes Q	EC	EC5 (4)
Price indices, deflated	Goods and services	indices, %	Yes Q	EC	EC5 (4)
Price indices	By feed, fertilizers, plant protection products, agricultural wage rates	indices	Yes A	EC and North America	UN40 (10)
Price indices of plant protection products		indices	Yes A	EC and North America	UN40 (12)
Price series of international significance	By product and quotations	local units	Yes A, M	World	FAO6 (68)
Prices, change in (real)	By type of output and input	%	Yes A	EC	EC2 (A5)
	indices of final output	indices	Yes A	EC	EC2 (A26)
	indices of intermediate consumption in agriculture	indices	Yes A	EC	EC2 (A31)

2 AGRICULTURE

Subject	Categories	Units	Time series Yes/No Frequency		Territorial coverage	Source (Table no.)
Purchase prices	By means of agricultural production	nat curr, ECU	Yes	A	EC	EC4 (-)
Raw and white sugar	Price premiums or discounts	nos	Yes	D	Selected capital cities	FOL2 (190)
Rice, prices international market	Government to government contract, and private trade	US$, tonnes fob, %	Yes	A	Selected Asian countries	IRRI1 (95)
Rice, milled	Wholesale price	nat curr/tonnes, US$/tonnes	Yes	A	Selected Asian countries	IRRI1 (88, 89)
Rice, milled	Retail price	nat curr/tonnes US$/tonnes			Selected Asian countries	IRRI1 (90, 91)
Rice	All varieties	ECU/t	Yes	M, Q	EC	EC3 (-)
Rice	Farm harvest price ofnat rough rice	curr/tonnes, US$/tonnes	Yes	A	Selected Asian countries	IRRI1 (86, 87)
Rice	Government support, procurement price of rough rice, milled rice	nat curr/tonnes US$/tonnes	Yes	A	Selected Asian countries	IRRI1 (84, 85)
Rice export prices, FAO index	By private trade, bilateral contracts, grain type	indices	Yes	A	World	IRRI1 (94)
Rice import levies		ECU/t	Yes	M, Q	EC	EC3 (-)
Selling prices, crop products	By crop product, by country	nat curr, ECU	Yes	A	EC	EC4 (-)
Selling prices, animal products	By animal product, by country	nat curr, ECU	Yes	A	EC	EC4 (-)
Sheep	Lambs	ECU/kg, PAB	Yes	M, Q	EC	EC3 (-)
Sheep levies	Live	ECU/kg	Yes	M, Q	EC	EC3 (-)
Sheep meat or for certain cuts, retail prices		nat curr, indices	Yes	A, Q	Selected European countries	UN34 (XXXVI)
Sheep or sheep meat, producer prices		nat curr	Yes	A, Q	Selected European countries	UN34 (XXXVII)
Sheepmeat levies	Frozen	ECU/kg	Yes	M, Q	EC	EC3 (-)
Sugar, raw and white	Market price	nat curr/lb, nat curr, tonne	Yes	D	Selected capital cities	FOL2 (189)
Sugar beet	Average prices realized per 100 kg for the whole of the harvest	nat curr	Yes	A	EC and North America	UN40 (VIIB)
Sugar beet	Average sugar content of the harvest	%	Yes	A	Selected countries	UN40 (VIIB)
Sugar beet	Contract prices paid to producers per 100 kg	nat curr	Yes	A	EC and North America	UN40 (VIIA)
Sugar levies	Dry, syrup	ECU/kg	Yes	M	EC	EC3 (-)
Veal	By cut	nat curr/kg	Yes	A, M	EC	MLC1 (-)
Weaner	By liveweight	nat curr/	Yes	A, M	EC	MLC1 (-)
Weighting scheme	By agricultural product by country	indices	No		EC	EC4 (-)
Wheat and maize	Selected international export prices	US$/kg	Yes	2 yrly	USA	UN40 (4)
Wheat and rye	Basic fixed prices paid to producers per 100 kg	nat curr	Yes	A	EC and North America	UN40 (IA, IIA)
Wheat and rye	Weighted average prices (unit values) received by farmers per 100 kg for all types and all sales	nat curr	Yes	A	EC and North America	UN40 (IB, IIB)
Wheat export prices	Based on official f.o.b. quotations	US$/tonne	Yes	A, M	World	IWhC3 (A.5)
Whole milk	Average fat content	%	Yes	A	Selected countries	UN40 (XIIA)
Whole milk	Average prices received by farmers per 100 kg of milk delivered to dairies for all forms of utilization	nat curr	Yes	A	EC and North America	UN40 (XIIA)

Subject	Categories	Units	Time series Yes/No	Frequency	Territorial coverage	Source (Table no.)
Whole milk	Weighted average prices (unit values) received by farmers per 100 kg for all types of sales	nat curr	Yes	A	EC and North America	UN40 (XIIB)
Wine	All types	ECU,%, Vol, HL	Yes	M, Q	EC	EC3 (-)

2.24 PRODUCTION - see also under Livestock (2.18), Milk, Cheese and other Livestock, Products (2.19), Milk Industry (2.20), Oilseeds, Oils, Fats and Oilmeals (2.22), Sugar Industry (2.27), Tea Industry (2.28), Wine Industry (2.30) and Section 38

2.24.1 Cereal Crops - see also under General (2.24.3)

Subject	Categories	Units	Time series Yes/No	Frequency	Territorial coverage	Source (Table no.)
Agricultural production	By country, by grain	tonnes	Yes	A	Asia and Pacific	UN43 (-)
Agriculture, yield	By crop	q/h	Yes	A	VICES and Yugoslavia	VICES1 (I/5)
Arable, cereal and potato	Type 41, 81 and all other holdings	nos/ha/%	Yes	2 yrly	EC	EC58 (6.17, 6.18,6.19)
Barley, production	Total	kg/ha/ tonnes	Yes	A	World	FAO1 (19)
Barley, production		tons	Yes	A	World	UN50 (60)
Barley		tonnes	Yes	A	EC	EC6 (ID 7)
Barley		tonnes	Yes	A	World	UN50R (1)
Barley		tons	Yes	A	World	IWhC2 (4)
Barley	Area harvested, yield, production, by country, region	ha, kg/ha, tonnes	Yes	A	World	FAO7 (4)
Barley	By area harvested, yield and production	ha, kg/ha, tonnes	Yes	A	World	FAO6 (7)
Beans (dry)	By area harvested, yield and production	ha, kg/ha, tonnes	Yes	A	World	FAO6 (40)
Cereal, potato and sugar beet crops, output	By countries	hl, tonnes	Yes	A	EC	MAC3 (C2)
Cereal, production	Total	indices	Yes	A	World	FAO1 (8)
Cereal, production per capita	Total	indices/per	Yes	A	World	FAO1 (13)
Cereal, production	By country, by product	tonnes	No		EC	EM1 (1907)
Cereal crops, principal	By country, by area, tonnes, yield, production	ha, tonnes/ha,	No		Selected countries	CH1 (7.7)
Cereals, total	Area harvested, yield, production, by country, region	ha, kg/ha, tonnes	Yes	A	World	FAO7 (1)
Cereals, production (total)	Total	kg/ha/ tonnes	Yes	A	World	FAO1 (15)
Cereals, production		tons	Yes	A	World	UN50 (57)
Cereals, total	By area harvested, yield and production	ha, kg/ha, tonnes	Yes	A	World	FAO6 (15)
Cereals		indices	Yes	A	World	UN50 (1)
Cereals	By area harvested, production and yield	ha, tonnes, kg/ha	No		Selected countries	UN22 (II- 3.2.1a)
Cereals	By cereal type	tonnes	Yes	A	World,	UN44 (p1)
Cereals	By type	tonnes	No		World	EC9 (5.4)
Cereals	Total	tonnes	Yes	A	EC	EC6 (ID 4)
Chick-peas	By area harvested, yield and production	ha, kg/ha, tonnes	Yes	A	World	FAO6 (39)
Coarse grains		tonnes	Yes	A	World	IWhC3 (A.6)
Crop rotations	By type of crop	nos	No		Selected countries	UN22
Crop yields	By type of crop	kg/ha	Yes	10 A	EC	EC9 (5.3)
Crops, production	Principal crops	1000 tons	Yes	A	North Africa	UN2(17)
Crops, production	Principal crops	1000 tonnes	Yes	A	West Africa	UN3 (4-2)
Crops, production	Principal crops	1000 tons	Yes	A	West Africa	UN3 (17)
Crops, production	Principal crops	1000 tonnes	Yes	A	East and Southern Africa	UN4 (4-2)
Crops, production	Principal crops	1000 tons	Yes	A	East and Southern Africa	UN4 (17)
Crops, production	Agricultural	nos	Yes	A	Central Africa	UN5 (14)

2 AGRICULTURE

Subject	Categories	Units	Time series Yes/No Frequency	Territorial coverage	Source (Table no.)
Crops, production	Principal crops	1000 tonnes	Yes A	Central Africa	UN5 (4-2)
Crops, production	Principal crops	1000 tons	Yes A	Central Africa	UN5 (17) (II-past 3.2.10)
Crops, principal	Production by crop, by country	tonnes	Yes A	ESCAP	UN44
Crops, principal	Area by crop, by country	ha	Yes A	ESCAP	UN44
Crops, principal	Sown area, by crop, by country	ha	Yes A	ESCAP	UN44
Crops, harvested	By production	tonnes	Yes A	Nordic countries	NCM1(57)
Crops, harvested, average yield	By production	ha	Yes A	Nordic countries	NCM1(59)
Crops, production	By country, by crop	tonnes	No	EC	EM1 (1908)
Crops, harvested	By production	ha/kg	No	EC	EC69 (IV.2)
Crops, harvested, excluding fruit and vegetables	By production	ha	Yes A	EC	EC6 (ID 1)
Crops	By type	tonnes	Yes A	VICES and Yugoslavia	VICES1 (I/5)
Durum wheat		tonnes	Yes A	EC	EC6 (ID 6)
Durum wheat	By production,	tons	Yes A	World	IWhC2 (20A)
	by trade,	tons	Yes A	World	IWhC2 (20B)
	by closing stocks	tons	Yes A	World	IWhC2 (20C)
Genetic diversity in agriculture	By variety	nos	No	Selected countries	UN22 (II- 3.2.1c)
Genetic diversity in agriculture	Wheat, by number of banks, species, cultivars	nos	No	Selected countries	UN22 (II- 2.6.1)
Genetic diversity in agriculture	Wheat, by principal variety, % of total area	nos, %	No	Selected countries	UN22 (II- 3.2.1d)
Grain, harvested	By production	tonnes	Yes A	Nordic countries	NCM1(58)
Grain supply, disappearance		tons	No	World	IWhC2 (19)
Grains, coarse		tons	Yes A	World	IWhC2 (2)
Maize, production	Total	kg/ha/	Yes A	World	FAO1 (20)
Maize		tonnes	Yes A	EC	EC6 (ID 8)
Maize		tonnes	Yes A	Latin American and Caribbean countries	UN45 (320)
Maize	Area harvested, yield, production, by country, region	ha, kg/ha, tonnes	Yes A	World	FAO7 (5)
Maize	Area harvested	ha	Yes A	Latin American and Caribbean countries	UN45 (308)
Maize	By area harvested, yield and production	ha, kg/ha, tonnes	Yes A	World	FAO6 (8)
Maize (corn), production		tons	Yes A	World	UN50 (62)
Maize (corn)		tonnes	Yes A	World	UN50 (1)
Maize (corn)		tons	Yes A	World	IWhC2 (3)
Meat, milk, production		1000 tons	Yes A	Central Africa	UN5 (16)
Millet	By area harvested, yield and production	ha, kg/ha, tonnes	Yes A	World	FAO6 (9)
Millet	Total	kg/ha/	Yes A	World	FAO1 (23)
Millet and Sorghum	Area harvested, yield, production, by country, region	ha, kg/ha, tonnes	Yes A	World	FAO7 (8)
Mixed Grain	Area harvested, yield, production, by country, region	ha, kg/ha, tonnes	Yes A	World	FAO7 (9)
Oats, production		tons	Yes A	World	FAO1 (22)
Oats, production		tons	Yes A	World	UN50 (61)
Oats		tons	Yes A	World	IWhC2 (6)
Oats	Area harvested, yield, production, by country, region	ha, kg/ha, tonnes	Yes A	World	FAO7 (7)
Oats	By area harvested, yield and production	ha, kg/ha, tonnes	Yes A	World	FAO6 (10)

Subject	Categories	Units	Time series Yes/No Frequency	Territorial coverage	Source (Table no.)
Peas (dry)	By area harvested, yield and production	ha, kg/ha, tonnes	Yes A	World	FAO6 (41)
Pulses (total)	By area harvested, yield and production	ha, kg/ha, tonnes	Yes A	World	FAO6 (42)
Rice, paddy	By area harvested, yield and production	ha, kg/ha, tonnes	Yes A	World	FAO6 (11)
Rice, rough, production	By country and geographical region	tonnes	Yes A	World	IRRI1 (1)
Rice, rough, yield	By country and geographical region	tonnes/ha	Yes A	World	IRRI1 (3)
Rice		tonnes	Yes A	Latin American and Caribbean countries	UN45(314)
Rice	Area harvested	ha	Yes A	Latin American and Caribbean countries	UN45(303)
Rice (paddy)		tonnes	Yes A	World	UN50 (1)
Rice (rough or paddy)		tons	Yes A	World	UN50 (59)
Rice (rough or paddy)	Total	kg/ha tonnes	Yes A	World	FAO1 (17,18)
Rye		tons	Yes A	World	IWhC2 (7)
Rye	Area harvested, yield, production, by country, region	ha, kg/ha, tonnes	Yes A	World	FAO7 (6)
Rye	By area harvested, yield and production	ha, kg/ha, tonnes	Yes A	World	FAO6 (12)
Rye	Total	kg/ha/	Yes A	World	FAO1 (21)
Sorghum		tonnes	Yes A	Latin American and Caribbean countries	UN45 (323)
Sorghum		tons	Yes A	World	IWhC2 (5)
Sorghum	Area harvested	ha	Yes A	Latin American and Caribbean countries	UN45 (311)
Sorghum	By area harvested, yield and production	ha, kg/ha, tonnes	Yes A	World	FAO6 (13)
Sorghum	Total	kg/ha/	Yes A	World	FAO1 (24)
Wheat, production	Total	kg/ha tonnes	Yes A	World	FAO1 (16)
Wheat, production		tons	Yes A	World	UN50 (58)
Wheat, including durum	Area, yield, production	ha, tonnes, quintals/ha	Yes A	World	IWhC3 (A.1)
Wheat, common		tonnes	Yes A	EC	EC6 (ID 5)
Wheat		tonnes	Yes A	Latin American and Caribbean countries	UN45 (324)
Wheat		tonnes	Yes A	World	UN50 (1)
Wheat		tons	Yes A	World	IWhC2 (1)
Wheat	Area harvested, yield, production, by country, region	ha, kg/ha, tonnes	Yes A	World	FAO7 (2)
Wheat	Area harvested	ha	Yes A	Latin American and Caribbean countries	UN45 (312)
Wheat	By area harvested, yield and production	ha, kg/ha, tonnes	Yes A	World	FAO6 (14)
Wheat supply, disappearance	Estimated and forecast	tons	No	World	IWhC2 (17)
2.24.2 Fruit and Vegetables - see also under General (2.24.3)					
Almonds, pistachios, hazelnuts (filberts)	Total	kg/ha	Yes A	World	FAO1 (76)
Almonds	Production, by country, region	tonnes	Yes A	World	FAO7 (77)
Apples, grapes, wine	By production	tonnes	Yes A	World	FAO6 (18)

2 AGRICULTURE

Subject	Categories	Units	Time series Yes/No Frequency		Territorial coverage	Source (Table no.)
Apples	Production, by country, region	tonnes	Yes	A	World	FAO7 (61)
Apricots	By production	tonnes	Yes	A	World	FAO6 (61)
Apricots	Production, by country, region	tonnes	Yes	A	World	FAO7 (63)
Artichokes	Area harvested, yield, production, by country, region	ha, kg/ha, tonnes	Yes	A	World	FAO7 (44)
Artichokes	By production	tonnes	Yes	A	World	FAO6 (49)
Artichokes	Total	kg/ha	Yes	A	World	FAO1 (51)
Avocados, mangoes, pineapples	Total	kg/ha	Yes	A	World	FAO1 (73)
Bananas, plantains, papayas	Total	kg/ha	Yes	A	World	FAO1 (74)
Bananas, grapefruit and pomelos, raisins	By production	tonnes	Yes	A	World	FAO6 (20)
Bananas	Production, by country, region	tonnes	Yes	A	World	FAO7 (56)
Bananas and plantains		tonnes	Yes	A	Latin American and Caribbean countries	UN45 (315)
Beans, dry	Area harvested, yield, production, by country, region	ha, kg/ha, tonnes	Yes	A	World	FAO7 (15)
Beans, green	Area harvested, yield, production, by country, region	ha, kg/ha, tonnes	Yes	A	World	FAO7 (48)
Beans, dried		tonnes	Yes	A	Latin American and Caribbean countries	UN45(318)
Beans, dried	Area harvested	ha	Yes	A	Latin American and Caribbean countries	UN45(306)
Beans, dry	Total	kg/ha	Yes	A	World	FAO1 (32)
Beans, green	Total	kg/ha	Yes	A	World	FAO1 (60)
Broad beans, dry	Area harvested, yield, production, by country, region	ha, kg/ha, tonnes	Yes	A	World	FAO7 (16)
Broad beans, dry	Total	kg/ha	Yes	A	World	FAO1 (33)
Cabbages	Area harvested, yield, production, by country, region	ha, kg/ha, tonnes	Yes	A	World	FAO7 (43)
Cabbages	By production	tonnes	Yes	A	World	FAO6 (48)
Cabbages	Total	kg/ha	Yes	A	World	FAO1 (50)
Cantaloupes and other melons	Area harvested, yield, production, by country, region	ha, kg/ha, tonnes	Yes	A	World	FAO7 (50)
Cantaloupes and other melons	Total	kg/ha	Yes	A	World	FAO1 (64)
Carrots	By production	tonnes	Yes	A	World	FAO6 (58)
Carrots	Total	kg/ha	Yes	A	World	FAO1 (62)
Cashew nuts, chestnuts, walnuts	Total	kg/ha	Yes	A	World	FAO1 (77)
Cashew nuts	Production, by country, region	tonnes	Yes	A	World	FAO7 (75)
Cassava		tonnes	Yes	A	Latin American and Caribbean countries	UN45(321)
Cassava	Area harvested, yield, production, by country, region	ha, kg/ha, tonnes	Yes	A	World	FAO7 (13)
Cassava	Area harvested	ha	Yes	A	Latin American and Caribbean countries	UN45(309)
Cassava	Total	kg/ha	Yes	A	World	FAO1 (28)
Castor beans	Area harvested, yield, production, by country, region	ha, kg/ha, tonnes	Yes	A	World	FAO7 (26)

Subject	Categories	Units	Time series Yes/No Frequency		Territorial coverage	Source (Table no.)
Cauliflower	Area harvested, yield, production, by country, region	ha, kg/ha, tonnes	Yes	A	World	FAO7 (46)
Cauliflowers	By production	tonnes	Yes	A	World	FAO6 (50)
Cauliflowers	Total	kg/ha	Yes	A	World	FAO1 (53)
Cherries, sour	Production, by country, region	tonnes	Yes	A	World	FAO7 (64)
Cherries	Production, by country, region	tonnes	Yes	A	World	FAO7 (65)
Chestnuts	Production, by country, region	tonnes	Yes	A	World	FAO7 (76)
Chick peas	Area harvested, yield, production, by country, region	ha, kg/ha, tonnes	Yes	A	World	FAO7 (18)
Chick peas	Total	kg/ha	Yes	A	World	FAO1 (35)
Chillies and peppers, green	By production	tonnes	Yes	A	World	FAO6 (54)
Citrus fruit		tonnes	Yes	A	EC	EC6 (ID15)
Citrus fruits and bananas	By crop type, country	tonnes	Yes	A	Africa and Asia	MAC1 (D5)
Cocoa beans		tonnes	Yes	A	World	FAO6 (6)
Coconuts, copra, tung oil	Total	kg/ha	Yes	A	World	FAO1 (47)
Coconuts	Production, by country, region	tonnes	Yes	A	World	FAO7 (32)
Coffee, green	Area harvested, yield, production, by country, region	ha, kg/ha, tonnes	Yes	A	World	FAO7 (84)
Coffee, green	Total	kg/ha	Yes	A	World	FAO1 (78)
Coffee, green		tonnes	Yes	A	World	UN50 (1)
Coffee		tonnes	Yes	A	World	FAO6 (6)
Coffee		tons	Yes	A	World	UN50 (65)
Coffee	Area harvested	ha	Yes	A	Latin American and Caribbean countries	UN45(304)
Cow peas, dry	Area harvested, yield, production, by country, region	ha, kg/ha, tonnes	Yes	A	World	FAO7 (20)
Crops, harvested, vegetables	By production	ha	Yes	A	EC	EC6 (ID 2)
Crops, harvested, fruit	By production	ha	Yes	A	EC	EC6 (ID 3)
Cucumbers and gherkins	By production	tonnes	Yes	A	World	FAO6 (52)
Cucumbers and gherkins	Total	kg/ha	Yes	A	World	FAO1 (55)
Currants	By production	tonnes	Yes	A	World	FAO6 (66)
Currants	Production, by country, region	tonnes	Yes	A	World	FAO7 (73)
Dates, mangoes, pineapples	By production	tonnes	Yes	A	World	FAO6 (19)
Dates	Production, by country, region	tonnes	Yes	A	World	FAO7 (69)
Eggplants	By production	tonnes	Yes	A	World	FAO6 (53)
Eggplants	Total	kg/ha	Yes	A	World	FAO1 (56)
Figs	Production, by country, region	tonnes	Yes	A	World	FAO7 (68)
Fruit, excl. melons total	Production by country, region	tonnes	Yes	A	World	FAO7 (52)
Fruit, output	By countries	nos	No		The Americas and Australasia	MAC2 (D7)
Fruit, fresh (excluding citrus)		tonnes	Yes	A	EC	EC6 (ID14)
Fruit	Total fresh fruit, apple citrus, dried	tonnes	No		World	EC9 (5.5)
Fruit and vegetable production	By country, by product, yield	tonnes/ha, tonnes	No		GCC	CH1 (7.8)
Garlic	By production	tonnes	Yes	A	World	FAO6 (55)
Garlic	Total	kg/ha	Yes	A	World	FAO1 (59)
Grapefruit and pomelo	Production, by country, region	tonnes	Yes	A	World	FAO7 (60)
Grapefruit and pomelos, citrus fruit nes apricots	Total	kg/ha	Yes	A	World	FAO1 (72)

2 AGRICULTURE

Subject	Categories	Units	Time series Yes/No Frequency		Territorial coverage	Source (Table no.)
Grapes	Area harvested, yield, production, by country, region	ha, kg/ha, tonnes	Yes	A	World	FAO7 (53)
Grapes	Total	kg/ha	Yes	A	World	FAO1 (65)
Green beans	By production	tonnes	Yes	A	World	FAO6 (56)
Green chillies and peppers	Total	kg/ha	Yes	A	World	FAO1 (57)
Green coffee		tonnes	Yes	A	Latin American and Caribbean countries	UN45(316)
Green peas	By production	tonnes	Yes	A	World	FAO6 (57)
Hazelnuts (filberts)	Production, by country, region	tonnes	Yes	A	World	FAO7 ()79
Lemons and limes, oranges, tangerines, mandarines, clementines and satsumas	By production	tonnes	Yes	A	World	FAO6 (21)
Lemons and limes	Production, by country, region	tonnes	Yes	A	World	FAO7 (59)
Lentils	Area harvested, yield, production, by country, region	ha, kg/ha, tonnes	Yes	A	World	FAO7 (19)
Lentils	Total	kg/ha	Yes	A	World	FAO1 (36)
Lupins	Area harvested, yield, production, by country, region	ha, kg/ha, tonnes	Yes	A	World	FAO7 (23)
Nuts		tonnes	No		World	EC9 (5.5)
Olives	Production, by country, region	tonnes	Yes	A	World	FAO7 (36)
Onions, dry	Area harvested, yield, production, by country, region	ha, kg/ha, tonnes	Yes	A	World	FAO7 (47)
Onions, dry	Total	kg/ha	Yes	A	World	FAO1 (58)
Onions	By area harvested, yield and production	ha, kg/ha, tonnes	Yes	A	World	FAO6 (46)
Oranges, tangerines, mandarins, clementines and satsumas, lemons and limes	Total	kg/ha	Yes	A	World	FAO1 (71)
Oranges	Production, by country, region	tonnes	Yes	A	World	FAO7 (57)
Papayas	By production	tonnes	Yes	A	World	FAO6 (67)
Peaches and nectarines	By production	tonnes	Yes	A	World	FAO6 (62)
Peaches and nectarines	Production, by country, region	tonnes	Yes	A	World	FAO7 (66)
Pears	By production	tonnes	Yes	A	World	FAO6 (60)
Pears	Production, by country, region	tonnes	Yes	A	World	FAO7 (62)
Peas, dry	Area harvested, yield, production, by country, region	ha, kg/ha, tonnes	Yes	A	World	FAO7 (17)
Peas, green	Area harvested, yield, production, by country, region	ha, kg/ha, tonnes	Yes	A	World	FAO7 (49)
Peas, dry	Total	kg/ha	Yes	A	World	FAO1 (34)
Peas, green	Total	kg/ha	Yes	A	World	FAO1 (61)
Pigeon peas	Area harvested, yield, production, by country, region	ha, kg/ha, tonnes	Yes	A	World	FAO7 (21)
Pineapples	Production, by country, region	tonnes	Yes	A	World	FAO7 (70)
Plantains	By production	tonnes	Yes	A	World	FAO6 (59)
Plums	By production	tonnes	Yes	A	World	FAO6 (63)
Plums	Production, by country, region	tonnes	Yes	A	World	FAO7 (67)
Potatoes, sweet	Area harvested, yield, production, by country, region	ha, kg/ha, tonnes	Yes	A	World	FAO7 (12)

Subject	Categories	Units	Time series Yes/No Frequency	Territorial coverage	Source (Table no.)
Potatoes, production		tons	Yes A	World	UN50 (64)
Potatoes		tonnes	Yes A	EC	EC6 (ID 9)
Potatoes		tonnes	Yes A	World	UN50 (1)
Potatoes	Area harvested, yield, production, by country, region	ha, kg/ha, tonnes	Yes A	World	FAO7 (11)
Potatoes	By area harvested, yield and production	ha, kg/ha, tonnes	Yes A	World	FAO6 (43)
Potatoes	Total	kg/ha	Yes A	World	FAO1 (26)
Pulses, total	Area harvested, yield, production, by country, region	ha, kg/ha, tonnes	Yes A	World	FAO7 (14)
Pulses, total	Total	kg/ha	Yes A	World	FAO1 (31)
Pumpkins, squash and gourds	Total	kg/ha	Yes A	World	FAO1 (54)
Pumpkins, squash and gourds	By production	tonnes	Yes A	World	FAO6 (51)
Raisins	Production, by country, region	tonnes	Yes A	World	FAO7 (55)
Raspberries	By production	tonnes	Yes A	World	FAO6 (65)
Raspberries	Production, by country, region	tonnes	Yes A	World	FAO7 (72)
Rice, paddy	Area harvested, yield, production, by country, region	ha, kg/ha, tonnes	Yes A	World	FAO7 (3)
Roots and tubers, total	Total	kg/ha	Yes A	World	FAO1 (25)
Roots and tubers	Area harvested, yield, production, by country, region	ha, kg/ha, tonnes	Yes A	World	FAO7 (10)
Roots and tubers	By area harvested, production and yield	ha, tonnes, kg/ha	No	Selected countries	UN22 (II- 3.2.1b)
Soya beans		tonnes	Yes A	Latin American and Caribbean countries	UN45(322)
Soya beans	Area harvested	ha	Yes A	Latin American and Caribbean countries	UN45(310)
Soybeans, production		tons	Yes A	World	UN50 (63)
Soybeans	Area harvested, yield, production, by country, region	ha, kg/ha, tonnes	Yes A	World	FAO7 (24)
Soybeans	Total	kg/ha	Yes A	World	FAO1 (37)
Strawberries, raspberries, currants	Total	kg/ha	Yes A	World	FAO1 (75)
Strawberries	By production	tonnes	Yes A	World	FAO6 (64)
Strawberries	Production, by country, region	tonnes	Yes A	World	FAO7 (71)
Sugar, apples, pears, peaches and nectarines, plums	Total	kg/ha	Yes A	World	FAO1 (70)
Sweet potatoes	Total	kg/ha tonnes	Yes A	World	FAO1 (27)
Tangerines, mandarins, satsumas, clementines	Production, by country, region	tonnes	Yes A	World	FAO7 (58)
Taro	Total	kg/ha	Yes A	World	FAO1 (30)
Tea		tonnes	Yes A	World	FAO6 (6)
Tomatoes	Area harvested, yield, production, by country, region	ha, kg/ha, tonnes	Yes A	World	FAO7 (45)
Tomatoes	By area harvested, yield and production	ha, kg/ha, tonnes	Yes A	World	FAO6 (47)
Tomatoes	Total	kg/ha tonnes	Yes A	World	FAO1 (52)
Treenuts, total	Production, by country,region	tonnes	Yes A	World	FAO7 (74)
Vegetable	Total	tonnes	Yes A	EC	EC6 (ID13)

2 AGRICULTURE

Subject	Categories	Units	Time series Yes/No	Frequency	Territorial coverage	Source (Table no.)
Vegetables, fruits, berries and nuts, total production	Total	kg/ha	Yes	A	World	FAO1 (49)
Vegetables	Tomatoes	tonnes	No		World	EC9 (5.5)
Vegetables and melons	Production, by country, region	tonnes	Yes	A	World	FAO7 (42)
Vetches	Area harvested, yield, production, by country, region	ha, kg/ha, tonnes	Yes	A	World	FAO7 (22)
Walnuts	Production, by country, region	tonnes	Yes	A	World	FAO7 (78)
Watermelons	Area harvested, yield, production, by country, region	ha, kg/ha, tonnes	Yes	A	World	FAO7 (51)
Watermelons	Total	kg/ha	Yes	A	World	FAO1 (63)
Yams	Total	kg/ha	Yes	A	World	FAO1 (29)
2.24.3 General						
Agricultural, production quantum indices		indices	Yes	A	Latin Amerian and Caribbean countries	UN45 (296)
Agricultural, final	At current prices and exchange rates	ECU	Yes	A	EC	EC26 (A.1-A.1.12)
Agricultural, final	At current prices	nat curr	Yes	A	EC	EC26 (A.2.1-A.2.12)
Agricultural, final	By region	ECU	Yes	A	EC	EC26 (C.0.2)
Agricultural crops, quantum indices		indices	Yes	A	Latin American and Caribbean countries	UN45 (297)
Agricultural output, final	By current prices, 1985 prices	PPS (US$)	Yes	A	OECD	OECD5 (II.1.A, OECD5 (II.1.B)
Agricultural output, final	By 1985 prices and 1985 PPPs	US$	Yes	A	OECD	OECD5 (II.8)
Agricultural output, final	By current prices, 1985 prices	PPS (US$)	Yes	A	OECD	OECD5 (III.2.A,III.2.B)
Agricultural output, final	Current prices	nat curr	Yes	A	OECD	OECD5 (III.2.C)
Agricultural output, gross	Total, crop, animal, index at constant prices, average annual growth rate at constant prices	indices, %	Yes	A	VICES and Yugoslavia	VICES1 (I/5)
Agricultural output	At current and 1985 prices and exchange rates, as % of EC final agricultural output, volume and price indices	ECU, %, indices	Yes	A	EC	EC26 (A.0.1)
Agricultural production, total	Total	indices/per capita	Yes	A	World	FAO1 (10)
Agricultural production, growth rates	Total, per capita, annual average growth rates of food production	%	Yes	A	World	UNCTAD1 (6.5)
Agricultural production, domestic	By country	US$	No		GCC	CH1 (7.5)
Agricultural production, food	Production,labour force, per capita	%GDP, %,	Yes		World	UN55
Agricultural production		nos	Yes	A	East and Southern Africa	UN4(14)
Agricultural production		nos	Yes	A	North Africa	UN2(14)
Agricultural production		nos	Yes	A	West Africa Africa	UN3(14)

2 AGRICULTURE

Subject	Categories	Units	Time series Yes/No	Frequency	Territorial coverage	Source (Table no.)
Agricultural production	"Price scissors"[1] of intermediate consumption, trends in	indices	Yes	A	EC	EC2 (A35)
Agricultural production	Annual average growth rate					
Agricultural production	By country, all commodities, cereals	indices	Yes	A	Asia and Pacific	UN43 (-)
Agricultural production	By country	index	No		EC	EC18 (7.5)
Agricultural production	By country	indices	No		EC	EM1 (1901)
Agricultural production	By crop	%/tonnes	No		World, developing ACP	EC1 (I3-I12)
Agricultural production	By final production	ECU	No		EC	WC1 (-)
Agricultural production	By high, middle, low income	indices, tonnes	No		World	CS1 (14)
Agricultural production	By produce	tonnes	Yes	A	World,	FAO6 (5)
Agricultural production	By production	tonnes	Yes	A	World	FAO1 (14)
Agricultural production	By type of output and input, indices of final output, indices of intermediate consumption in agriculture	%, indices	Yes	A	EC	EC2 (A, 24,29)
Agricultural production	By type of output and input indices of final output indices of intermediate consumption in agriculture	%, indices	Yes	A	EC	EC2 (A, 29, 32)
Agricultural production	By type of output and input, indices of final output, indices of intermediate consumption in agriculture	%	Yes	A	EC	EC2 (A, A28, A33)
Agricultural production	Food,	indices	Yes	A	World	UN50 (56)
Agricultural production	Indices of intermediate consumption in agriculture	indices	Yes	A	EC	EC2 (A30)
Agricultural production	Net value added at factor cost, share in net domestic product at factor cost	%	Yes	A	EC	EC2 (A1)
Agricultural production	Productivity of intermediate consumption, trends in	indices	Yes	A	EC	EC2 (A34)
Agricultural production	Total	indices	Yes	A	World	FAO1 (5)
Agricultural production	Total and per capita	%	No		World	FAO6 (2)
Agricultural production	Agricultural production, food production, cereal	indices	Yes	A	ASEAN	ASEANS1 (3.3)
Agricultural products in the EC	By country, by product	%	No		EC	EC35 (-)
Agriculture, share of in the GDP	GVA GDP	%	No		EC	WC1 (-)
Agriculture		indices, tonnes	Yes	A	ESCAP	UN44 (pp5, 10)
Agriculture	Food, cereals, total and per capita production, by country	indices	Yes	A	ESCAP	UN44
Agriculture	Total and per capita food and agricultural production	indices	Yes	A	World, ESCAP	UN44 (p1)
	All commodities					
Animal, final	At current and 1985 prices and exchange rates, as % of final agricultural output, volume and price indices	ECU, %, indices	Yes	A	EC	EC26 (A.0.1.1)
Animal, final	At current prices and exchange rates	ECU	Yes	A	EC	EC26 (A.1-A.1.12)
Animal, final	By region	ECU	Yes	A	EC	EC26 (C.0.2)

1 Nominal index of prices of final output divided by the nominal index of prices of intermediate consumption.

2 AGRICULTURE

Subject	Categories	Units	Time series Yes/No Frequency		Territorial coverage	Source (Table no.)
Animal, final	At current prices	nat curr	Yes	A	EC	EC26 (A.2.1-A.2.12)
Animal	By type at current prices and exchange rates	ECU	Yes	A	EC	EC26 (A.1-A.1.12)
Animal	By type at current prices	nat curr	Yes	A	EC	EC26 (A.2.1-A.2.12)
Arable crops, output	Cities	nos	No		The Americas and Australasia	MAC2 (D2)
Arable crops	By country, crop type	tonnes, hectolitres	Yes	A	Africa and Asia	MAC1 (D2)
Cotton	By country	tonnes	Yes	A	Africa and Asia	MAC1 (D7)
Cotton (lint), fibre crops nes natural rubber	Total	kg/ha	Yes	A	World	FAO1 (87)
Cotton (lint)		tonnes	Yes	A	World	UN50 (1)
Cotton (lint)		tons	Yes	A	World	UN50 (68)
Cotton lint, sisal, natural rubber	By production	tonnes	Yes	A	World	FAO6 (16)
Cotton lint	Area harvested, yield, production, by country, region	ha, kg/ha, tonnes	Yes	A	World	FAO7 (93)
Cotton seed, olives, olive oil	Total	kg/ha	Yes	A	World	FAO1 (46)
Cottonseed	Production, by country, region	tonnes	Yes	A	World	FAO7 (39)
Crop, final	At current and 1985 prices and exchange rates, as % of final agricultural output, volume and price indices	ECU, %, indices	Yes	A	EC	EC26 (A.0.1.1)
Crop, final	At current prices and exchange rates	ECU	Yes	A	EC	EC26 (A.1-A.1.12)
Crop, final	By region	ECU	Yes	A	EC	EC26 (C.0.2)
Crop, final	At current prices	nat curr	Yes	A	EC	EC26 (A2.1-A.2.12)
Crop	By type at current prices and exchange rates	ECU	Yes	A	EC	EC26 (A.1-A.1.12)
Crop	By type at current prices	nat curr	Yes	A	EC	EC26 (A.2.1-A.2.12)
Crop	Usable production, by product	tonnes	Yes	A	EC	EC19 (V)
Crop output, final	By current prices, 1985 prices	PPS (US$)	Yes	A	OECD	OECD5 (11.1.A, II.1.B)
Crop output	As % of final agricultural output	%	Yes	A	OECD	OECD5 (II.3)
Crop production		indices	Yes	A	World	UN50 (1)
Crop production	By country, by selected crop	ql/ha	No		EC	EC18 (7.7)
Crop production	By type	tonnes/ hectolitres	Yes	A	World	EC6 (IA 5)
Crop production	Total	indices	Yes	A	World	FAO1 (6)
Crop production per capita	Total	indices/per capita	Yes	A	World	FAO1 (11)
Crop rotations	By type of crop	nos	No		Selected countries	UN22
Crops, production	Principal crops	1000 tonnes	Yes	A	West Africa	UN3 (4-2)
Crops, production	Principal crops	1000 tons	Yes	A	West Africa	UN3 (17)
Crops, production	Principal crops	1000 tonnes	Yes	A	East and Southern Africa	UN4 (4-2)
Crops, production	Principal crops	1000 tons	Yes	A	East and Southern Africa	UN4 (17)
Crops, production	Principal crops	1000 tons	Yes	A	North Africa	UN2(17)
Crops, production	Agricultural	nos	Yes	A	Central Africa	UN5 (14)
Crops, production	Principal crops	1000 tonnes	Yes	A	Central Africa	UN5 (4-2)
Crops, production	Principal crops	1000 tons	Yes	A	Central Africa	UN5 (17)
Crops, production	Agricultural	nos	Yes	A	Central Africa	UN5 (14)
Crops, production	Principal crops	1000 tonnes	Yes	A	Central Africa	UN5 (4-2)
Crops, production	Principal crops	1000 tons	Yes	A	Central Africa	UN5 (17)

Subject	Categories	Units	Time series Yes/No Frequency		Territorial coverage	Source (Table no.)
Crops, permanent, distribution of holdings	By area under selected permanent crops	%	No		EC	EC45 (AIVB)
Crops, permanent, holdings	Holdings with permanent crops and area under permanent crops, by type	nos	No		EC	EC45 (AIVA)
Crops, principal, production		1000 tonnes	Yes	A	North Africa	UN2(4-2)
Crops under glass	significance of crops under glass and distribution of holdings according to area of crops under glass	nos, %	No		EC	EC45(AV)
Final output, intermediate consumption, gross value-added, subsidies		ECU, %	No		EC	EC69 (IV.4)
Flax fibre and tow	Area harvested, yield, production, by country, region	ha, kg/ha, tonnes	Yes	A	World	FAO7 (90)
Flax fibre and tow	Total	kg/ha	Yes	A	World	FAO1 (83)
Food, production		per capita	Yes	A	Central Africa	UN5 (4-1-2)
Food, growth in production	Average annual rates	indices	Yes	A	Latin American and Caribbean countries	UN45 (49)
Food, per capita, quantum indices		indices	Yes	A	Latin American and Caribbean countries	UN45 (300)
Food, quantum indices		indices	Yes	A	Latin American and Caribbean countries	UN45 (299)
Food and agricultural production	By total	indices	Yes	A	World	FAO6 (4)
Food production		indices	Yes	A	World	UN50 (1)
Food production		per capita	Yes	A	East and Southern Africa	UN4 (4-1-2)
Food production		per capita	Yes	A	North Africa	UN2 (4-1-2)
Food production		per capita	Yes	A	West Africa	UN3 (4-1-2)
Food production	By country	indices	No		EC	EM1 (1902)
Food production	Total	indices	Yes	A	World	FAO1 (4)
Food production	Total and per capita	%	No		World	FAO6 (3)
Food production per capita	Total	indices/per capita	Yes	A	World	FAO1 (9)
Forestry, paper products, production	By country, by product	tonnes, m	No		EC	EM1 (1909)
Growth rates, agricultural	Total, per capita,	%	Yes	A	World	UNCTAD1 (6.5)
Harvest volumes	By country, by selected crop	tonnes	No		EC	EC18 (7.6)
Hemp fibre and tow	Total	kg/ha	Yes	A	World	FAO1 (84)
Hops	Area harvested, yield, production, by country, region	ha, kg/ha, tonnes	Yes	A	World	FAO7 (87)
Hops	Total	kg/ha	Yes	A	World	FAO1 (81)
Jute, jute-like fibres	Area harvested, yield, production, by country, region	ha, kg/ha, tonnes	Yes	A	World	FAO7 (92)
Jute and jute-like fibres	By production	ha, kg/ha,	Yes	A	World	FAO6 (17)
Jute and jute-like fibres	Total	kg/ha	Yes	A	World	FAO1 (85)
Meat, milk production		1000 tons	Yes	A	Central Africa	UN5 (16)
Meat, milk production		1000 tons	Yes	A	East and Southern Africa	UN4 (16)
Meat, milk production		1000 tons	Yes	A	West Africa	UN3 (16)
Natural rubber		tonnes	Yes	A	World	UN50 (1)
Net value-added at factor cost and per work unit		indices	Yes	A	EC	EC6 (IG 9)
Production, current prices and exchange rates		ECU	Yes	A	EC	EC6 (IG 1)

2 AGRICULTURE

Subject	Categories	Units	Time series Yes/No Frequency		Territorial coverage	Source (Table no.)
Production, 1980 prices and exchange rates		ECU	Yes	A	EC	EC6 (IG 2)
Production, current prices and exchange rates		ECU	Yes	A	EC	EC6 (IG 4)
Production, current prices and exchange rates	Percentage of final production of the EC	%	No	1989	EC	EC6 (IG 5)
Production, current prices and exchange rates	Percentage of final production of each country	%	No	1989	EC	EC6 (IG 6)
Rubber, natural	Production, by country, region	tonnes	Yes	A	World	FAO7 (89)
Rubber, natural		tonnes	Yes	A	World, ESCAP	UN44 (p1)
Rubber	By country	tonnes	Yes	A	Africa and Asia	MAC1 (D9)
Seed cotton		tonnes	Yes	A	Latin American and Caribbean countries	UN45(313)
Seed cotton	Area harvested, by country, region	ha	Yes	A	World	FAO7 (38)
Seed cotton	Area harvested	ha	Yes	A	Latin American and Caribbean countries	UN45(302)
Seed cotton	Total	kg/ha	Yes	A	World	FAO1 (45)
Sisal	Area harvested, yield, production, by country, region	ha, kg/ha, tonnes	Yes	A	World	FAO7 (91)
Sisal	Total	kg/ha	Yes	A	World	FAO1 (86)
Tobacco		tonnes	Yes	A	World	UN50 (1)
Tobacco		tons	Yes	A	World	UN50 (67)
Tobacco	By area harvested, yield and production	ha, kg/ha, tonnes	Yes	A	World	FAO6 (45)
Tobacco	By country	tonnes	Yes	A	Africa and Asia	MAC1 (D8)
Tobacco leaves	Area harvested, yield, production, by country, region	ha, kg/ha, tonnes	Yes	A	World	FAO7 (88)
Tobacco leaves	Total	kg/ha	Yes	A	World	FAO1 (82)
Tree crop production, principal	By country, by type	tonnes	No		GCC	CH1 (7.6)
Value addd gross,	Agriculture as % of GDP	%	Yes	A	OECD	OECD5 (II.1)
Value added, gross (at market prices)	At current prices	nat curr	Yes	A	EC	EC26 (A.2.1-A.2.12)
Value added, gross (at factor cost)	At current prices	nat curr	Yes	A	EC	EC26 (A.2.1-A.2.12)
Value added, net (at factor cost)	At current prices	nat curr	Yes	A	EC	EC26 (A.2.1-A.2.12)
Value added, gross (at market prices)	By region	ECU	Yes	A	EC	EC26 (C.0.1)
Value added, gross (at factor cost)	By region	ECU	Yes	A	EC	EC26 (C.0.1)
Value added, net (at factor cost)	By region	ECU	Yes	A	EC	EC26 (C.0.1)
Value added, gross (at market prices)	At current prices and exchange rates	ECU	Yes	A	EC	EC26 (A.1-A.1.12)
Value added, gross (at factor cost)	at current prices and exchange rates	ECU	Yes	A	EC	EC26 (A.1-A.1.12)
Value added, net (at factor cost)	At current prices and exchange rates	ECU	Yes	A	EC	EC26 (A.1-A.1.12)
Value added, net (factor cost)	At current prices and exchange rates and as % of EC net value added at factor cost	ECU, %	Yes	A	EC	EC26 (A.0.6)
Value added, gross	At current and 1985 prices and exchange rates, as % of final agricultural output, volume and price indices	ECU, %, indices	Yes	A	EC	EC26 (A.0.3)

Subject	Categories	Units	Time series Yes/No Frequency		Territorial coverage	Source (Table no.)
Value added, gross, at factor cost, by groups of economic branches	Agriculture, forestry fisheries, industry, services, total	ECU, %	Yes	A	EC	EC6 (IA 7)
Volume index numbers		indices	Yes	A	EC	EC6 (IG 3)
2.25 SELF-SUFFICIENCY						
Butter, self-sufficiency	By type	%	No		EC	EC9 (5.14)
Cereal supply balance sheets	imports, exports, domestic uses, production change in stocks	tonnes	No		EC	EC9 (5.11)
Cheese, self-sufficiency	By type	%	No		EC	EC9 (5.14)
Crop products, self-sufficiency	By type of crop	%	No		EC	EC9 (5.14)
Meat, self-sufficiency	By type	%	No		EC	EC9 (5.14)
Meat supply balance sheets	By type, imports and exports, domestic use, production change in stocks	tonnes	No		EC	EC9 (5.13)
Oils and fats, self-sufficiency	By type	%	No		EC	EC9 (5.14)
Self-sufficiency	By product	%	No		EC	WC1 (-)
Self-sufficiency ratios	By butterfat and solids-not-fat	ratios	Yes	A	EC	MMB1(38)
Sugar supply balance sheets	imports, exports, domestic uses, production change in stocks	tonnes	No		EC	EC9 (5.12)
Wheat supply balance sheets	Imports, exports, domestic uses, production change in stocks	tonnes	No		EC	EC9 (5.11)
Wine supply balance sheets	Imports, exports, domestic uses, production change in stocks	tonnes	No		EC	EC9 (5.12)
2.26 STRUCTURE OF HOLDINGS						
Agricultural area, utilized	Per holding	ha	No		EC	WC1 (-)
Agricultural holdings	By size and no, % type of cattle	nos, %	No		EC	MMB1(12)
Agricultural land tenure and number of enterprises	By type of land tenure number of enterprises	ha, nos	No		Selected countries	UN22 (II- 3.1.6)
Agricultural population	By country, by time worked on the holding	nos	No		EC	EC35 (-)
Arable land, distribution of holdings	By area under selected arable land crops	%	No		EC	EC45 (A IIIB)
Arable land, holdings	Holdings with arable land and area under arable land, by type	nos	No		EC	EC45 (A IIIA)
Cows, other, number,	According to size of holding	head/%	Yes	2 yrly	EC	EC58 (6.12)
Cows, dairy, number	According to size of holding	head/%	Yes	2 yrly	EC	EC58 (6.3)
Cows, other, number	Rate of growth according to size of holding	head/%	Yes	2 yrly	EC	EC58 (6.13)
Cows, dairy, number	Rate of growth according to size of holding	%	Yes	2 yrly	EC	EC58 (6.4)
Cows, other, number	Holdings with other cows and other cows per holding according to community typology	nos/head/%	Yes	A	EC	EC58 (6.11)

2 AGRICULTURE

Subject	Categories	Units	Time series Yes/No Frequency		Territorial coverage	Source (Table no.)
Cows, dairy, number	Holdings with dairy cows and cows per holding according to community typology	nos/head/%	Yes	2 yrly	EC	EC58 (6.5)
Dairy cows, number	According to size of holding	head/%	Yes	2 yrly	EUR9	EC57 (6.5)
Dairy cows, number	Rate of growth according to size of holding	%	Yes	2 yrly	EUR9	EC57 (6.6)
Dairy cows, number	According to community typology	head/%	Yes	2 yrly	EC	EC57 (6.7)
Dairy cows, number	By principal types of farming	%	Yes	2 yrly	EC	EC57 (6.8)
Dairy cows, number	Holdings with dairy cows and cows per holding according to community typology dairy cows according to farming size	nos/head %	Yes	2 yrly	France	EC57 (6.9)
Farm holdings	By number and area	no	No		Selected Asian countries	IRRI1 (73)
Farm holdings (SGM)	Production as % of their type of farming	%	No		EC	EC44 (3a)
Farm holdings (SGM)	Production as % of their type of farming	%	No		EC	EC44 (3)
Farm specialization	By speciality crop, animal production, field crops	nos	No		Selected countries	UN22 (II- 3.1.5b)
Farming, type	Number of holdings by principal type of farming, by country, region	nos	No		EC	EC45 (D)
Farming, holdings	Holdings, AWU, economic size, AWU, holding, ecomomic size, holding, economic size, AWU, by type of farming	nos, ECU	No		EC	EC43 (-)
Farming, tenure	By type	%	No		EC	EC45 (AXII)
Farming, typology	Proportion of regional SGM supplied by one or two types of farming or by holdings practising them	nos	No		EC	EC44 (4)
Farming, type of	Specialized, mixed	holdings	No		EC	EC9 (5.18)
Farms, number of	By area category	ha	No		Selected countries	UN22 (II- 3.1.4)
Farms	By size and distribution	nos, ha	No		Selected Asian countries	IRRI1 (74)
Farms	Field crops, horticulture, permanent crops, grazing livestock, granivores, total	% of SGM	No		EC	EC44 (2)
Holders, number	With dairy cows	head/%	Yes	2 yrly	EC	EC57 (6.1)
Holders, number	With dairy cows according to farming size	nos/%	Yes	2 yrly	EUR9	EC57 (6.2)
Holders, number	With dairy cows according to farming size	nos/%	Yes	2 yrly	EC	EC58 (6.1)
Holders, numbers	Rate of growth, with	%	Yes	2 yrly	EC	EC58 (6.2)

Subject	Categories	Units	Time series Yes/No Frequency		Territorial coverage	Source (Table no.)
Holders with another gainful activity	According to size of standard gross margin on type 41 holdings	%	No		EUR9	EC57 (6.15)
Holdings, number and area	Farm size class	ha UAA, nos;%, ha	No		EC	WC1 (-)
Holdings, labour force and area	By size of holding and age of holder	nos/hectares	No		EC	EC69 (IV.5)
Holdings, percentage of	With other cows according to community typology	%	Yes	2 yrly	EC	EC57 (6.21)
Holdings, economic size per holding	Total, with OGA, without OGA, by size of holding and type of farming	ECU	No		EC	EC43 (-)
Holdings, farm type	By type of farming	nos	No		EC	EC45 (AVIII)
Holdings, in less favoured areas	Number and significance of holdings, by type of crop in less favoured areas	nos, %	No		EC	EC45 (AXI)
Holdings, number	Total, with OGA, without OGA, by size of holding and type of farming	nos	No		EC	EC43 (-)
Holdings, average economic size	By principal types of farming	ESU	No		EC	EC45 (AIID)
Holdings, agricultural area	Average agricultural area in use, by holder's time worked, by holder's age, by principal type of farming	ha	No		EC	EC45 (AIIC)
Holdings, economic size	Distribution of holdings, by size classes, by member state	nos, %	No		EC	EC45 (AIIB)
Holdings, physical size	Distribution of holdings, by size classes, by member state	nos, %	No		EC	EC45 (AIIA)
Holdings, number and area	By country	nos, ha, %	No		EC	EC35 (-)
Holdings, agricultural	By size group	nos	No		EC	EC9 (5.15)
Holdings, agricultural	By size group	nos	No		EC	EC9 (5.18)
Holdings, number and area , by AA size category		nos total	Yes	2 yrly	EC	EC6 (IC 4)
Holdings, number and standard gross margin	Total, by ESU category	nos	Yes	2 yrly	EC	EC6 (IC 5)
Holdings, number and standard gross margin	Total, by ESU category	nos	Yes	2 yrly	EC	EC6 (IC 6)
Holdings	According to ESU, type 41,with cows	%	Yes	2 yrly	EC	EC57 (6.10)
Holdings	According to ESU, type 41,with cows	%	Yes	2 yrly	EC	EC58 (6.6)
Holdings	By number	'000	No		EC	WC1 (-)
Holdings	By size class, total, in less favoured areas, in mountain areas, by country	nos	No		EC	EC45 (B)
Holdings	Holdings with male cattle pigs and sheep, and male cattle, pigs and sheep per holding according to community typology	nos/head/%	Yes	2 yrly	EC	EC58 (6.14,6.15, 6.16)

2 AGRICULTURE

Subject	Categories	Units	Time series Yes/No Frequency		Territorial coverage	Source (Table no.)
Holdings	Number of holdings, utilized AA, SGM and AWUs	ha, ESUs	Yes	2 yrly	EC	EC6 (IC 1)
Holdings	Total, in less favoured areas, in mountain areas, agricultural area, by country, region	nos	No		EC	EC45 (D)
Holdings	With and without cattle	ha/nos	No		Nordic countries	NCM1(60)
Holdings	With dairy cows according to community typology	%	Yes	2 yrly	EC	EC57 (6.4)
Holdings	With dairy cows by type of farming	%	Yes	2 yrly	EC	EC57 (6.3)
Holdings	With other cows, by principal types of farming	%	Yes	2 yrly	EC	EC57 (6.20)
Holdings by size of arable land		nos/%	No		Nordic countries	NCM1(56)
Labour force	Number of persons AWUs	nos/AWUs	Yes	2 yrly	EC	EC6 (IC 7)
Land use	By crops	nos	Yes	2 yrly	EC	EC6 (IC 8)
Legal personality and holding management		nos	Yes	2 yrly	EC	EC6 (IC 2)
Livestock farming	By breeding stock	nos	Yes	2 yrly	EC	EC6 (IC 9)
Main crops	By country, by crop	nos	No		EC	EC35 (-)
Production, regions in community	Field crops, horticulture, permanent crops, grazing livestock, granivores, total	% of SGM	No		EC	EC44 (2a)
Production structure	Field crops, horticulture, permanent crops, grazing livestock, granivores, total	% of SGM	No		EC	EC44 (1)
Production structure	Field crops, horticulture, permanent crops, grazing livestock, granivores by region	% of SGM	No		EC	EC44 (1a)
Socialist agricultural holdings	By country, by state holdings, cooperatives	nos	No		EC	EC18 (7.2)
Tenure, types		nos	Yes	2 yrly	EC	EC6 (IC 3)
2.27 SUGAR INDUSTRY						
Alcohol	By imports, exports, country	hl	Yes	A	World	FOL1 (144-145)
Beet	By crop year	tonnes	Yes	A	World	FOL3 (11)
Beet and cane	By type	tonnes, %	Yes	A	World	FOL3 (7)
Cane	By crop year	tonnes	Yes	A	World	FOL3 (12,13)
Centrifugal sugar	By crop year	tonnes	Yes	A	World	FOL3 (8,9,10)
Import levy		ECU/kg	No		EC	FOL1 (-)
Molasses	By imports, exports, country	tonnes	Yes	A	World	FOL1 (137-143)
Production	By exporter	tonnes	Yes	A	World	FOL1 (-)
Sugar, centrifugal, raw	Production, by country, region	tonnes	Yes	A	World	FAO7 (82)
Sugar, non-centrifugal	Production, by country, region	tonnes	Yes	A	World	FAO7 (83)
Sugar, imports, exports	By country of origin, by country of destination	tonnes	Yes	A	World	ISO3 (-)

Subject	Categories	Units	Time series Yes/No Frequency		Territorial coverage	Source (Table no.)
Sugar	Beginning stock, production, consumption, change stock, ending stock. import, export		No		World	ISO1 (-)
Sugar	By country, imports, exports, production, consumption, stocks, total	tonnes	Yes	A, M	World	ISO2 (-)
Sugar	By imports, exports, production, consumption, stocks,	tonnes	Yes	A	World	ISO3 (-)
Sugar	By production, consumption end year stocks, exports imports,net exports and imports, free market net imports and exports, per caput consumption, ISA daily price	tonnes, kgs, cents per lb	Yes	A	World	ISO3 (-)
Sugar balance, world	By stocks, imports production, exports	tonnes, %	Yes	A	World	FOL3 (14)
Sugar balances by countries	By stocks, imports exports, production, consumption	tonnes	Yes	A	World	FOL3 (15-23)
Sugar beet cultivation	By number of growers, acreage planted	nos, ha	Yes	A	World	ISO1 (1)
Sugar beets	Area harvested, yield, production, by country, region	ha, kg/ha, tonnes	Yes	A	World	FAO7 (81)
Sugar beets	Total	kg/ha	Yes	A	World	FAO1 (68)
Sugar cane, sugar beets, sugar (raw)	By production	tonnes	Yes	A	World	FAO6 (44)
Sugar cane		tonnes	Yes	A	Latin American and Caribbean countries	UN45 (317)
Sugar cane	Area harvested, yield, production, by country, region	ha, kg/ha, tonnes	Yes	A	World	FAO7 (80)
Sugar cane	Area harvested	ha	Yes	A	Latin American and Caribbean countries	UN45 (305)
Sugar cane	Total	kg/ha	Yes	A	World	FAO1 (67)
Sugar centrifugal (raw value)	Total	kg/ha	Yes	A	World	FAO1 (69)
Sugar economy, evolution	By country, production consumption, exports, imports, net trade	tonnes	Yes	A	New York, London Paris	ISO1 (-)
Sugar production		tonnes	Yes	A	EC	EC6 (ID12)
Sugar production	By output, raw value	tonnes	Yes	A	EC	FOL2 (191)
Sugar production and consumption	By producer, surplus,	tonnes	No		World	ISO1 (-)

2.28 TEA INDUSTRY

Subject	Categories	Units	Time series Yes/No Frequency		Territorial coverage	Source (Table no.)
Extensions, replacements and replantings		ha	Yes	A	Selected countries	ITC1 (A1)
Imports	By origin, destination	kg per kg	Yes	A	Selected countries	ITC1 (H4)
Planted		ha	Yes	A	Selected countries	ITC1 (A)
Price quotations, (London), monthly	By type	pence per kg	Yes	A, M	UK	ITC1 (F1)
Prices (London), average	By month	pence per kg	Yes	A, M	UK	ITC1 (F2)
Prices (London), annual average	By country	pence per kg	Yes	A	World	ITC1 (F3)
Prices (producing countries), annual average	By type and country	nat curr per kg	Yes	A	Selected countries	ITC1 (F4-F5)

Subject	Categories	Units	Time series Yes/No Frequency	Territorial coverage	Source (Table no.)
Production		tonnes	Yes A	World	UN50 (1)
Production		tons	Yes A	World	UN50 (66)
Production	Area harvested, yield, production, by country,region	ha, kg/ha, tonnes	Yes A	World	FAO7 (86)
Production	Total	kg/ha	Yes A	World	FAO1 (80)
Supply and absorption of tea	By exporters, importers, production, exports	tonnes	Yes A	World	ITC1 (G1)
Tea, world production		% share	Yes A	Major producing countries	ITC1 (B1)
Tea, according to manufacture	By type	tonnes	Yes A	Selected countries	ITC1 (B2)
Tea, world production		% share	Yes A	Producing countries	ITC1 (C1)
Tea, retained	By country	tonnes	Yes A	Producing countries	ITC1 (-)
Tea, value	By country, exporter	US$	Yes A	Selected countries	ITC1 (-)
Tea, imports	By destination	tonnes, US$	Yes A	World	ITC1 (C2-C20)
Tea, imports, re-exports	By country of origin	tonnes, US$	Yes A	World	ITC1 (D2, D6-5,D17-D25,D27-D43)
Tea, re-exports of tea	By country of destination	tonnes, US$	Yes A	World	ITC1 (D4,D16)
Tea, imports, re-exports, net imports, apparent consumption per head		tonnes, kg	Yes A		ITC1 (D5)
Tea, consumption of tea in producing countries		tonnes	Yes A	Selected countries	ITC1(D44)
Tea, quantities sold (London)	By country	tonnes	Yes A	Selected countries	ITC1 (F6)
Tea, quantities sold and average prices	By country, CIF, FOB	tonnes, pence	Yes A	Selected countries	ITC1 (F7-F8)
Tea, quantities sold (producing countries)	By type	tonnes	Yes A	Selected countries	ITC1 (F9-F10)
Tea, apparent consumption per head	By country	tonnes, kg,	Yes 6 M	Selected countries	ITC1 (G2)
Tea, production		kg	Yes A	Selected countries	ITC1 (H)
Tea, exports	By origin, Destination	kg	Yes A	Selected countries	ITC1 (H1-H3, H5)
Tea imports for consumption	By country	tonnes	Yes A	World	ITC1 (D1)
Tea imports in packages	By country of origin	tonnes, US$	Yes A	Selected countries	ITC1 (D3)
Tea including green tea	By produce	tonnes	Yes A	World	ITC1 (B)
Tea including green tea	By produce	tonnes	Yes A	World	ITC1 (C)
Tea retained for consumption	By imports	%	Yes A	World	ITC1 (D1A)

2.29 TRANSPORT - see also Sections 41 and 45

Subject	Categories	Units	Time series Yes/No Frequency	Territorial coverage	Source (Table no.)
Freight Rates, heavy grains	Port of origin to port of destination	US$/tonne	Yes A, M	World ports	IWhC3 (A.9)

2.30 WINE INDUSTRY

Subject	Categories	Units	Time series Yes/No Frequency	Territorial coverage	Source (Table no.)
Areas grubbed or no longer cultivated	By production, class potential yield, by region	ha	No	EC	EC8 (6.0P)
Areas grubbed or no longer cultivated	By production, class actual yield, by region	ha	No	EC	EC8(6.1A)
Grapes		q	Yes 4 yr	World	OIVV1 (C)
Grapes	Wine grapes, table grapes, grapes for drying	q	No	World	OIVV1(D)
Grape vines, area planted		ha	Yes 4 yr	World	OIVV1(A)
Grape vines, area planted	By type	ha	No	World	OIVV1 (B)
Grape-must or wine, production	By production, potential yield, alcoholic strength %, by region	hl	No	EC	EC8 (7.0)
Grape-must or wine, production	By production, actual yield, alcoholic strength %, by region	hl	No	EC	EC8 (7.1)
Grapes, table		q	Yes 4 yr	World	OIVV1(O)
Raisins		q	Yes 4 yr	World	OIVV1 (R)

Subject	Categories	Units	Time series Yes/No Frequency		Territorial coverage	Source (Table no.)
Viticulture	Vine area, production, by region	ha, hl	No		Principal wine producing countries	OIVV1(U)
Wine, raisins, dates	Total	kg/ha	Yes	A	World	FAO1 (66)
Wine		hl	Yes	4 yr	World	OIVV1 (F)
Wine	By country	ha	Yes	A	Africa and Asia	MAC1 (D6)
Wine	Production, by country, region	tonnes	Yes	A	World	FAO7 (54)
Wine	Total	tonnes	Yes	A	EC	EC6(ID16)
Wine-grape vine areas, planted	By production, class, actual yield, by region	ha	No		EC	EC8 (5.1)
Wine-grape vine areas, replanted	By production, class potential yield, by region	ha	No		EC	EC8 (6.0R)
Wine-grape vine areas, replanted	By production, yield class, by region	ha	No		EC	EC8 (6.-R)
Wine-grape vine areas, planted	By production, yield class, by region	ha	No		EC	EC8 (6.-P)
Wine-grape vine areas production	By production, class, potential yield, by region	ha	No		EC	EC8 (5.0)

3 CIVIL AVIATION

3.1 AIR CARRIERS

3.2 EMPLOYMENT AND LABOUR COSTS
- 3.2.1 General
- 3.2.2 Pilots

3.3 ENERGY

3.4 FINANCE
- 3.4.1 Airport and Route Facilities
- 3.4.2 Comparative Financial Data – Non-Scheduled Operators
- 3.4.3 Comparative Financial Data – Scheduled Airlines
- 3.4.4 Financial Accounts by Airline
- 3.4.5 General
- 3.4.6 IATA Members' Corporate Financial Results
- 3.4.7 IATA Members' International Scheduled Financial Results
- 3.4.8 Scheduled Airlines

3.5 FLEET STATISTICS
- 3.5.1 Fleet Statistics by Air Carrier
- 3.5.2 Fleet Statistics by Aircraft Type
- 3.5.3 General
- 3.5.4 IATA Members' Aircraft Fleet
- 3.5.5 Non-Scheduled Operator's Fleet - Personnel and Utilization
- 3.5.6 Non-Scheduled Operators' Traffic Coefficients - Utilization per Aircraft
- 3.5.7 Scheduled Airline Fleet – Personnel and Utilization
- 3.5.8 Scheduled Airline Traffic Coefficients – Utilization per Aircraft

3.6 SAFETY/ACCIDENTS

3.7 TRAFFIC
- 3.7.1 Airport and En-route Traffic
- 3.7.2 All Services of Commercial Airlines
- 3.7.3 All Services of Charter Airlines
- 3.7.4 All Services of Non-Scheduled Operators
- 3.7.5 All Services of Scheduled Airlines
- 3.7.6 All-Freight Services
- 3.7.7 Charter Services
- 3.7.8 Charter Services of Scheduled Airlines

3.7.9 IATA Members' Air Transport Operations
3.7.10 On-Flight Origin and Destination
3.7.11 Traffic by Flight Stage

Subject	Categories	Units	Time series Yes/No Frequency		Territorial coverage	Source (Table no.)
ACCIDENTS - see under Safety/Accidents (3.6) and Section 1						
3.1 AIR CARRIERS – see also under Traffic (Section 3.7)						
Airlines		nos	No		EC	EC9 (7.6)
National airlines, kilometres flown	By country, by passengers, goods carried	nos,% tonnes,	No		EC	EM1 (2212)
Tonne-kilometres performed	By region	tonne-kms	Yes	A	World	ICAO2 (1.22)
3.2 EMPLOYMENT AND LABOUR COSTS – see also under Fleet Statistics (3.5.5 and 3.5.7)						
3.2.1 General						
IATA Members						
Employees	By type	% change, nos	Yes	A	IATA members	IATA1 (-)
Employees	By type	nos, % change				
Production per employee		% change, ratio	Yes	A	IATA members	IATA1 (-)
Non-scheduled Operators						
Personnel	Country, operator, flight, other, total	nos	No		World	ICAO6 (D3)
Personnel	International and domestic scheduled services, non-scheduled operators	nos	No		World	ICAO2 (3.1-3.3)
Scheduled International and Domestic Airlines						
Number of personnel	Country, airline, type of staff	nos	No		World	ICAO6 (D1-D2)
Remuneration, average annual	Country, airline, type of staff	nat curr $US	No		World	ICAO6 (D1- D2)
Total expenditure	Country airline, type of staff	$US	No		World	ICAO6 (D1-D2)
3.2.2 Pilots						
Civil pilot licences	By pilot category	nos	No		World	ICAO2 (1.4)
Civil pilot licences	By pilot category	nos	Yes	A	World	ICAO2 (2.2)
3.3 ENERGY - see also Section 17						
Energy consumption	Forms of energy	TJ	Yes	A	EC, USA, Canada	UN13 (5)
3.4 FINANCE						
3.4.1 Airport and Route Facilities						
Airport financial data, capital investment, gross	By state, city, airport	nat curr	Yes	A	World	ICAO3 (IA)
	By state, city, airport, type	nat curr, US$	Yes	A	World	ICAO3 (IIA)
Airport financial data, expenses	By state, city, airport	nat curr	Yes	A	World	ICAO3 (IA)
	By state, city, airport by type	nat curr, US$	Yes	A	World	ICAO3 (IIA)
Airport financial data, income	By state, city, airport	nat curr	Yes	A	World	ICAO3 (IA)
	By state, city airport, by source	nat curr	Yes	A	World	ICAO3 (IIA)
En-route facility financial data, capital investment, gross	By state	nat curr	Yes	A	World	ICAO3 (IB)
	By state, type	nat curr, US$	Yes	A	World	ICAO3 (IIB)
En-route facility financial data, expenses	By state	nat curr	Yes	A	World	ICAO3 (IB)
	By state, type	nat curr, US$	Yes	A	World	ICAO3 (IIB)

3 CIVIL AVIATION

Subject	Categories	Units	Time series Yes/No Frequency		Territorial coverage	Source (Table no.)
En-route facility financial data, income	By state,	nat curr	Yes	A	World	ICAO3 (IB)
	By state, source	nat curr, US$	Yes	A	World	ICAO3 (IIB)
3.4.2 Comparative Financial Data Non-Scheduled Operators						
Revenues and expenses per tonne-km performed and available	By source or type, by country, by operator	nos	Yes	A	World	ICAO5 (D)
Revenues, expenses, profit (or loss)	By source or type, by country, by operator	nos	Yes	A	World	ICAO5 (D)
3.4.3 Comparative Financial Data Scheduled Airlines						
Assets	By type, by country, by airline	US$	Yes	A	World	ICAO5 (B)
Liabilities	By type, by country, by airline	US$	Yes	A	World	ICAO5 (B)
Operating expenses per tonne-km performed	By type, by country, by airline	US$	Yes	A	World	ICAO5 (B)
Operating expenses per tonne-km available	By type, by country, by airline	US$	Yes	A	World	ICAO5 (B)
Operating expenses,	By type, by country, by airline	US$, %	Yes	A	World	ICAO5 (B)
Operating result	By type, by country, by airline	US$	Yes	A	World	ICAO5 (B)
Operating revenues per tonne-km performed	Scheduled, non-scheduled services by source, by country by airline	US$	Yes	A	World	ICAO5 (B)
Operating, revenues,	Scheduled, non-scheduled services by source, by country, by airline	US$, %	Yes	A	World	ICAO5 (B)
Operating revenues per tonne-km available	Scheduled, non-scheduled services by source, by country by airline	US$	Yes	A	World	ICAO5 (B)
Profit, loss, net	By country, by airline	US$	Yes	A	World	ICAO5 (B)
Retained earnings	By country, by airline	US$	Yes	A	World	ICAO5 (B)
3.4.4 Financial Accounts by Airline						
Balance sheet	Scheduled airlines, non-scheduled operators, by airline or operator	US$	Yes	A	World	ICAO5 (C, D)
Profit and loss statement	Scheduled airlines, non-scheduled operators, by airline or operator	US$	Yes	A	World	ICAO5 (C, D)
Retained earnings statement	Scheduled airlines, non-scheduled, operators, by airline or operator	US$	Yes	A	World	ICAO5 (C, D)
Revenue traffic	Scheduled airlines, non-scheduled operators, by airline or operator	US$	Yes	A	World	ICAO5 (C, D)
Tonne-km available	Scheduled, non-scheduled, by type	nos	Yes	A	World	ICAO5 (C, D)
Tonne-km performed	Scheduled, non-scheduled, by type	nos	Yes	A	World	ICAO5 (C, D)

Subject	Categories	Units	Time series Yes/No Frequency		Territorial coverage	Source (Table no.)
3.4.5 General						
Operating expenses	All types	US$	Yes	A	World	ICAO2 (1.25-1.26)
Operating expenses	International scheduled services, non-scheduled operators	US$	No		World	ICAO2 (3.1-3.3)
Operating result		US$	Yes	A	World	ICAO2 (1.25)
Operating result	International scheduled services, non-scheduled operators	US$	No		World	ICAO2 (3.1-3.3)
Operating revenues		US$	Yes	A	World	ICAO2 (1.25-1.26)
Operating revenues	International scheduled Services, non-Scheduled operators	US$	No		World	ICAO2 (3.1-3.3)
Profit or loss		US$	Yes	A	World	ICAO2 (1.25)
Revenues	By type of carrier for non-scheduled services	US$	Yes	A	World	ICAO2 (1.27)
Yield predictions predictions and forecast, average annual change		%	Yes	A	EC	AEA4 (-)
3.4.6 IATA Members' Corporate Financial Results						
Net result		US$, % change	Yes	A	IATA members	IATA1 (-)
Operating expenses		US$, % change	Yes	A	IATA members	IATA1 (-)
Operating result		US$, % change	Yes	A	IATA members	IATA1 (-)
Operating revenues		US$, % change	Yes	A	IATA members	IATA1 (-)
Scheduled Airlines						
Load factor	Scheduled, non-scheduled services	%	Yes	A	World	ICAO5 (A3)
Operating expenses	By type	US$	Yes	A	World	ICAO5 (A1)
Operating expenses per tonne km performed	By source	US$	Yes	A	World	ICAO5 (A2)
Operating result	By type	US$	Yes	A	World	ICAO5 (A1)
Operating result per tonne-kms performed	By source	US$	Yes	A	World	ICAO5 (A2)
Operating revenues	By source	US$	Yes	A	World	ICAO5 (A1)
Operating revenues per tonne km performed	By source	US$	Yes	A	World	ICAO5 (A2)
Passenger-kms	Scheduled services	nos	Yes	A	World	ICAO5 (A3)
Tonne -kms performed	Scheduled services, by source	nos	Yes	A	World	ICAO5 (A3)
Tonne-kms available	Non-scheduled services, by source	nos	Yes	A	World	ICAO5 (A3)
3.4.7 IATA Members' International Scheduled Financial Results						
Net interest charges		US$, % change	Yes	A	IATA members	IATA1 (-)
Operating expenses		US$, % change	Yes	A	IATA members	IATA1 (-)
Operating revenues		US$, % change	Yes	A	IATA members	IATA1 (-)
Unit cost		US$, % change	Yes	A	IATA members	IATA1 (-)
Yields		US$, % change	Yes	A	IATA members	IATA1 (-)
3.4.8 Scheduled Airlines' System						
Operating and net results		US$	Yes	A	World, IATA,	IATA1 (-)
Operating expenses	By type	% change, US$	Yes	A	World, IATA,	IATA1 (-)

3 CIVIL AVIATION

Subject	Categories	Units	Time series Yes/No Frequency		Territorial coverage	Source (Table no.)
Operating revenues	Scheduled passenger, freight, mail, total scheduled, charter, incidental	% change, US$	Yes	A	World, IATA,	IATA1 (-)
Turnover (IATA clearing house statistics)		US$	Yes	A, M	IATA and non-IATA members	IATA1 (-)
Unit cost	Expense per available tonne-kilometre	% change	Yes	A	World, IATA	IATA1 (-)
Yield	Revenue per tonne-kilometre performed, by service	US$	Yes	A	World, IATA	IATA1 (-)
3.5 FLEET STATISTICS						
3.5.1 Fleet Statistics by Air Carrier						
Aircraft hours flown, total	International and domestic scheduled services, non-scheduled operators	hrs	No		World	ICAO2 (3.1-3.3)
Aircraft, civil, on register	Aircraft of 9000kg and over by classification category and model, by commercial air transport operators and by other operators by country	nos	No		World	ICAO8 (C)
Aircraft, civil, on register	Aircraft of 9000kg and over by manufacturer and model by commercial air transport operators and by other operators by country	nos	No		World	ICAO8 (-)
Aircraft, civil, on register	Aircraft under and over 9000kg by aircraft classification by commercial air transport operators, and by other operators by country	nos	No		World	ICAO8 (-)
Aircraft, civil, on register in ICAO contracting states	Aircraft under and over 9000kg by manufacturer and model type, commercial air transport operators, other operators	nos	No		World	ICAO8 (B)
Aircraft, number of	International and domestic scheduled services, non-scheduled operators	nos	No		World	ICAO2 (3.1-3.3)
Aircraft-km performed	International and domestic scheduled services, non-scheduled operators	kms	No		World	ICAO2 (3.1-3.3)
Civil aircraft	By operator	nos	No		World	ICAO2 (1.2)
Departures	Aircraft type, carrier scheduled revenue, non-scheduled revenue, scheduled, non-scheduled, international and domestic airlines and operators	nos	No		World	ICAO6 (C1-C4)
Fleet, commercial air transport operators	By class of aircraft of 9000kg and over	nos, %	Yes	A	World	ICAO8 (A)

Subject	Categories	Units	Time series Yes/No Frequency		Territorial coverage	Source (Table no.)
Hours flown	Aircraft type, carrier scheduled revenue, non-scheduled revenue, scheduled, non-scheduled, international and domestic airlines and operators	nos	No		World	ICAO6 (C1-C4)
Number of aircraft	Aircraft type, carrier, Total, acquired, disposed of scheduled, non-scheduled, international and domestic airlines and operators	nos	No		World	ICAO6 (C1-C4)
Revenue-hours, average daily	Aircraft type, carrier scheduled revenue, non-scheduled revenue, scheduled, non-scheduled, international and domestic airlines and operators	nos	No		World	ICAO6 (C1-C4)
Size of aircraft	Aircraft type, carrier, seats Take-off weight scheduled, non-scheduled, international and domestic airlines and operators	nos tonnes	No		World	ICAO6 (C1-C4)
3.5.2 Fleet Statistics by Aircraft Type						
Number of aircraft	Aircraft type, carrier, total acquired, disposed of	nos	No		World	ICAO6 (B1-B4)
Size of aircraft	Aircraft type, carrier, seats, Take-off weight	nos tonnes	No		World	ICAO6 (B1-B4)
Utilization of aircraft						
Departures	Aircraft type, carrier, scheduled revenue, non-scheduled revenue	nos	No		World	ICAO6 (B1-B4)
Hours flown	Aircraft type, carrier, scheduled revenue, non-scheduled revenue	nos	No		World	ICAO6 (B1-B4)
Revenue-hours, average daily	Aircraft type, carrier	nos	No		World	ICAO6 (B1-B4)
3.5.3 General						
Aircraft		nos	No		EC	EC9 (7.6)
Aircraft	Of non-scheduled operators, by category	nos	Yes	A	World	ICAO2 (1.11)
Aircraft	Of scheduled airlines by category	nos	Yes	A	World	ICAO2 (1.9)
Civil aircraft	By type	nos	Yes	A	World	ICAO2 (1.1)
Civil aircraft on register	By type	nos	No		EC	EC80 (6.1)
Civil aircraft on register	By type	nos	Yes	A	World	ICAO2 (2.1)
Civil flying	By aircraft numbers and hours flown	nos	No		World	ICAO2 (1.3)
Fixed wing aircraft	Of commercial carriers by category	nos	Yes	A	World	ICAO2 (1.7)
Fleet Orders and deliveries	Of commercial carriers by manufacturer and model	nos	No		World	ICAO2 (1.8)
Passenger aircraft scheduled and charter operations	By haul type, number of aircraft, revenue hours per aircraft, airline	nos, hours, kms	Yes	A	World	AEA2 (-)

Subject	Categories	Units	Time series Yes/No Frequency	Territorial coverage	Source (Table no.)
Tonne-kms performed	By type	tonne-kms	Yes A	World	ICAO2 (1.21)
Turbo-jet aircraft	Of non-scheduled operators, by type	nos	No	World	ICAO2 (1.12)
Turbo-jet aircraft	Of scheduled airlines by type	nos	No	World	ICAO2 (1.10)
3.5.4 IATA Members' Aircraft Fleet					
Age, average	By type	years		IATA members	IATA1
In service	By type	nos		IATA members	IATA1
On order	By type	nos		IATA members	IATA1
Year of delivery	By type	nos		IATA members	IATA1
3.5.5 Non-scheduled Operators' Fleet – Personnel and Utilization					
Fleet	Country, operator	nos	No	World	ICAO6 (A2)
Personnel	Country, operator	nos	No	World	ICAO6 (A2)
Revenue-hours flown	Country, operator	nos	No	World	ICAO6 (A2)
Revenue-kms flown	Country, operator	nos	No	World	ICAO6 (A2)
Type of operator	Country, operator	type	No	World	ICAO6 (A2)
3.5.6 Non-Scheduled Operators' Traffic Coefficients – Utilization per Aircraft					
Revenue					
Distance per hour flown	Country, operator	km/h	No	World	ICAO6 (A4)
Load capacity available	Country, operator	kg	No	World	ICAO6 (A4)
Passenger load factor	Country, operator	%	No	World	ICAO6 (A4)
Passengers carried	Country, operator	nos	No	World	ICAO6 (A4)
Seats available	Country, operator	nos	No	World	ICAO6 (A4)
Total load carried	Country, operator	kg	No	World	ICAO6 (A4)
Type of operator	Country, operator	types	No	World	ICAO6 (A4)
Weight load factor	Country, operator	%	No	World	ICAO6 (A4)
3.5.7 Scheduled Airline Fleet – Personnel and Utilization					
Aircraft	Country-airline	nos	No	World	ICAO6 (A1)
Aircraft departures	Revenue - scheduled, non-scheduled, country-airline	nos	No	World	ICAO6 (A1)
Aircraft hours flown	Revenue - scheduled, non-scheduled, non-revenue, total country-airline	nos	No	World	ICAO6 (A1)
Kilometres flown	Revenue - scheduled, non-scheduled, country-airline	nos	No	World	ICAO6 (A1)
Persons	Country-airline	nos	No	World	ICAO6 (A1)
Type of airline	Types, country-airline	nos	No	World	ICAO6 (A1)
3.5.8 Scheduled Airline Traffic Coefficients – Utilization per Aircraft					
Cargo load	Country-airline	kg	No	World	ICAO6 (A3)
Distance per hour flown	Country-airline	km/h	No	World	ICAO6 (A3)
Load capacity available	Country-airline	kg	No	World	ICAO6 (A3)
Mail load	Country-airline	kg	No	World	ICAO6 (A3)
Passenger load	Country-airline	kg	No	World	ICAO6 (A3)
Passenger load factor	Country-airline	%	No	World	ICAO6 (A3)
Passengers carried	Country-airline	nos	No	World	ICAO6 (A3)
Seats available	Country-airline	nos	No	World	ICAO6 (A3)
Type of airline	Country-airline	type	No	World	ICAO6 (A3)
Weight load factor	Country-airline	%	No	World	ICAO6 (A3)
3.6 SAFETY/ACCIDENTS – see also Section 1					
Accidents and incidents	By type of operation	nos	No	World	ICAO1 (I)
Accidents and incidents, aircraft destroyed	By type of operation and aircraft mass	nos	No	World	ICAO1 (I)

Subject	Categories	Units	Time series Yes/No Frequency		Territorial coverage	Source (Table no.)
Accidents and incidents, fatalities	Crew, pax, other by type of operation and aircraft mass	nos	No		World	ICAO1 (I)
Accidents and incidents, occurrences	Fatal, non fatal by type of operation and aircraft mass	nos	No		World	ICAO1 (I)
Accidents and incidents, reports	By type of operation and aircraft mass	nos	No		World	ICA1 (II)
Accidents to aeroplanes, reports	By type of operation and aircraft mass	nos	No		World	ICAO1 (I)
Accidents to aeroplanes, reports	By type of operation and power plant	nos	No		World	ICAO1 (II)
Accidents to aeroplanes, aircraft destroyed	By type of operation and aircraft mass	nos	No		World	ICAO1 (I)
Accidents to aeroplanes, aircraft destroyed	By type of operation and power plant	nos	No		World	ICAO1 (II)
Accidents to aeroplanes, fatalities	Crew, pax, other by type of operation and aircraft mass	nos	No		World	ICAO1 (I)
Accidents to aeroplanes, fatalities	Crew, pax, other by type of operation and power plant	nos	No		World	ICAO1 (II)
Accidents to aeroplanes, occurrences	Fatal, non fatal by type of operation and aircraft mass	nos	No		World	ICAO1 (I)
Accidents to aeroplanes, occurrences	Fatal, non fatal by type of operation and power plant	nos	No		World	ICAO1 (II)
Accidents to helicopters, reports	By type of operation and aircraft mass	nos	No		World	ICAO1 (I)
Accidents to helicopters, aircraft destroyed	By type of operation and aircraft mass	nos	No		World	ICAO1 (I)
Accidents to helicopters, fatalities	Crew, pax, other by type of operation and aircraft mass	nos	No		World	ICAO1 (I)
Accidents to helicopters, occurrences	Fatal, non fatal by type of operation and aircraft mass	nos	No		World	ICAO1 (I)
Civil aviation	By flying category	nos	No		World	ICAO2 (1.5)
Commercial air transport	Involving passenger fatalities for both scheduled and unscheduled services	nos	Yes	A	World	ICAO2 (1.6)
Fatal accident rates		rate	Yes	A	IATA members	IATA1
Fatal accidents, number aboard	Crew, passengers	nos	Yes	A	IATA members	IATA1
Fatal accidents, number	Crew, passengers	nos	Yes	A	IATA members	IATA1
Fatal accidents, number injured	Crew, passengers	nos	Yes	A	IATA members	IATA1
Fatal accidents, number killed	Crew, passengers	nos	Yes	A	IATA members	IATA1
Fatal accidents, number of third parties	Crew, passengers	nos	Yes	A	IATA members	IATA1
Fatal passenger aircraft accidents	Jet aircraft	nos, hours	Yes	A	World	CAA1 (7)
Fatal passenger aircraft accidents by phase of flight	Jet aircraft, all aircraft total	nos, %	Yes	A	World	CAA1 (13)
Fatal passenger aircraft accidents	Non-jet aircraft	nos, hours	Yes	A	World	CAA1 (8)
Fatal passenger aircraft accidents	Total	nos, hours; kms	Yes	A	World	CAA1 (6)
Fatalities occurring in fatal passenger aircraft accidents	Jet, all aircraft	nos, %	Yes	A	World	CAA1 (11)
Fatalities occurring in passenger aircraft involved in mid-air collisions	Scheduled passenger; scheduled passenger and another category	nos	Yes	A	World	CAA1 (12)
Fatality rates		rate	Yes	A	IATA members	IATA1

3 CIVIL AVIATION

Subject	Categories	Units	Time series Yes/No Frequency		Territorial coverage	Source (Table no.)
Fatality rates, passenger	Between scheduled and non-scheduled passenger services	nos, kms	Yes	A	World	CAA1 (9)
Mid-air collisions involving fatalities	Phase: take-off, en route, approach, landing Engine type: scheduled, other	nos	Yes	-	World	CAA1 (14)
Passenger traffic and fatal accident rates	By region, annual averages, departures	kms, nos	Yes	A	World	CAA1 (10)
3.7 TRAFFIC						
Aircraft seat-kilometres	Scheduled services by national flag carrier	seat-kms	No		EC	EC80 (6.4)
Aircraft tonne-kilometres	All services by national flag carrier	tonne-kms	No		EC	EC80 (6.4)
Aircraft tonne-kilometres	Non-scheduled services by national flag carrier	tonne-kms	No		EC	EC80 (6.4)
Aircraft tonne-kilometres on offer	Scheduled services by national flag carrier	tonne-kms	No		EC	EC80 (6.4)
Aircraft tonne-kilometres run	Scheduled services by national flag carrier	tonne-kms	No		EC	EC80 (6.4)
Aircraft weight load factor	Scheduled services by national flag carrier	%	No		EC	EC80 (6.4)
Aircraft-kilometres	All services by national flag carrier	aircraft-kms	No		EC	EC80 (6.4)
Aircraft-kilometres	Non-scheduled services by national flag carrier	aircraft-kms	No		EC	EC80 (6.4)
Aircraft-kilometres	Scheduled services by national flag carrier	aircraft-kms	No		EC	EC80 (6.4)
Freight carried	Scheduled services by national flag carrier	tonnes	No		EC	EC80 (6.4)
Passenger load factor	Scheduled services by national flag carrier	%	No		EC	EC80 (6.4)
Passenger-kilometres	All services by national flag carrier	passenger-kms	No		EC	EC80 (6.4)
Passenger-kilometres	Non-scheduled services by national flag carrier	passenger-kms	No		EC	EC80 (6.4)
Passenger-kilometres	Scheduled services by national flag carrier	passenger-kms	No		EC	EC80 (6.4)
Passengers carried	Scheduled services by national flag carrier	nos	No		EC	EC80 (6.4)
3.7.1 Airport and En-Route Traffic						
Aircraft departures	Total, international and domestic for all services and freight services	nos	No		World	ICAO2 (1.18)
Aircraft movements, commercial total	State, city, airport	nos	Yes	A	World	ICAO4 (B)
Aircraft movements, domestic, total	State, city, airport	nos	Yes	M	World	ICAO4 (C)
Aircraft movements, international scheduled	State, city, airport	nos	Yes	M	World	ICAO4 (C)
Aircraft movements, international non-scheduled	State, city, airport	nos	Yes	M	World	ICAO4 (C)
Aircraft movements, total	State, city, airport	nos	Yes	A	World	ICAO4 (B)
Aircraft movements. commercial air transport	State, city, airport	nos	Yes	M	World	ICAO4 (C)
Airport traffic	By state, city, airport, total, international	traffic units	Yes	A	World	ICAO3 (IA)
Airports having highest commercial traffic volume		tonnes; %	No		World	ICAO4 (1)
All freight, mail services	Embarked, disembarked, total, direct transit	nos	Yes	M	World	ICAO4 (C)

Subject	Categories	Units	Time series Yes/No Frequency		Territorial coverage	Source (Table no.)
All other movement	Embarked, disembarked, total, direct transit	nos	Yes	M	World	ICAO4 (C)
Commercial air transport	Embarked, disembarked, total, direct transit	nos	Yes	M	World	ICAO4 (C)
Commercial international passengers	State, city airport	nos	Yes	A	World	ICAO4 (B)
Domestic	State, city, airport	nos	Yes	A	World	ICAO4 (B)
En-route traffic	By state, total, international	nos	Yes	A	World	ICAO3 (IB)
Freight, all freight, mail services	Embarked, disembarked, total, direct transit	tonnes	Yes	M	World	ICAO4 (C)
Freight, all other movement	Embarked, disembarked, total, direct transit	tonnes	Yes	M	World	ICAO4 (C)
Freight, commercial air transport	Embarked, disembarked, total, direct transit	tonnes	Yes	M	World	ICAO4 (C)
Freight, domestic	State, city, airport	tonnes	Yes	A	World	ICAO4 (B)
Freight, domestic, total	Embarked, disembarked, total, direct transit	tonnes	Yes	M	World	ICAO4 (C)
Freight, international	State, city, airport	tonnes	Yes	A	World	ICAO4 (B)
Freight, international non-scheduled	Embarked, disembarked, total, direct transit	tonnes	Yes	M	World	ICAO4 (C)
Freight, international scheduled	Embarked, disembarked, total, direct transit	tonnes	Yes	M	World	ICAO4 (C)
Freight, total	State, city, airport	tonnes	Yes	A	World	ICAO4 (B)
Highest traffic volume	By airport	nos	No		World	ICAO2 (4.2)
International	State, city, airport	nos	Yes	A	World	ICAO4 (B)
International aircraft movements	City, airport rank order	nos, % change	No		World	ICAO4 (A3)
International freight tonnes loaded plus unloaded	City, airport rank order	nos, % change	No		World	ICAO4 (A2)
International passengers embarked plus disembarked	City, airport rank order	nos, % change	No		World	ICAO4 (A1)
Mail, all freight, mail services	State, city, airport	nos	Yes	M	World	ICAO4 (C)
Mail, all freight/mail services	Embarked, disembarked, total, direct transit	tonnes	Yes	M	World	ICAO4 (C)
Mail, all other movement	Embarked, disembarked, total, direct transit	tonnes	Yes	M	World	ICAO4 (C)
Mail, all other movement	State, city, airport	nos	Yes	M	World	ICAO4 (C)
Mail, commercial air transport	Embarked, disembarked, total, direct transit	tonnes	Yes	M	World	ICAO4 (C)
Mail, domestic	State, city, airport	tonnes	Yes	A	World	ICAO4 (B)
Mail, domestic, total	Embarked, disembarked, total, direct transit	tonnes	Yes	M	World	ICAO4 (C)
Mail, international	State, city, airport	tonnes	Yes	A	World	ICAO4 (B)
Mail, international non-scheduled	Embarked, disembarked, total, direct transit	tonnes	Yes	M	World	ICAO4 (C)
Mail, international scheduled	Embarked, disembarked, total, direct transit	tonnes	Yes	M	World	ICAO4 (C)
Mail, total	State, city, airport	tonnes	Yes	A	World	ICAO4 (B)
Passengers, domestic, total	Embarked, disembarked, total, direct transit	nos	Yes	M	World	ICAO4 (C)
Passengers, international scheduled	Embarked, disembarked, total, direct transit	nos	Yes	M	World	ICAO4 (C)
Passengers, international non-scheduled	Embarked, disembarked, total, direct transit	nos	Yes	M	World	ICAO4 (C)
Passengers, embarking and disembarking	Total services	nos	Yes	A	Nordic countries	NCM1 (151)
Principal airport traffic	By type	nos	No		World	ICAO2 (4.1)
Total	State, city, airport	nos	Yes	A	World	ICAO4 (B)
Total aircraft movements rank order	City, airport	nos, % change	No		World	ICAO4 (A3)
Total freight tonnes loaded plus unloaded	City, airport	nos, % change	No		World rank order	ICAO4 (A2)

3 CIVIL AVIATION

Subject	Categories	Units	Time series Yes/No Frequency		Territorial coverage	Source (Table no.)
Total passengers embarked plus disembarked	City, airport rank order	nos, % change	No		World	ICAO4 (A1)
3.7.2 All Services of Commercial Airlines						
Air traffic	Aircraft-km passengers carried, passenger-km, tonne-km of freight	nos	Yes	A	Latin American and Caribbean countries	UN45 (358)
Air traffic	Freight, passengers	tons, nos 1000	Yes	A	Central Africa	UN5(29)
Air traffic	Freight, passengers	tons, nos 1000	Yes	A	East and Southern Africa	UN4(29)
Air traffic	Freight, passengers	tons, nos 1000	Yes	A	North Africa	UN2(29)
Air traffic	Freight, passengers	tons, nos 1000	Yes	A	West Africa	UN3(29)
Aircraft departures	By airline, operator by country	nos	No		World	ICAO9 (A)
Aircraft departures	Total	nos	Yes	A	World	ICAO2 (1.17)
Aircraft hours	By airline, operator by country	aircraft-hours	No		World	ICAO9 (A)
Aircraft hours	Total	hours	Yes	A	World	ICAO2 (1.17)
Aircraft hours	Total, international and domestic for all services and freight services	hours	No		World	ICAO2 (1.18)
Aircraft kilometres	Total, international and domestic for all services and freight services	kms	No		World	ICAO2 (1.18)
Aircraft km	Total	kms	Yes	A	World	ICAO2 (1.17)
Aircraft movements			Yes	I	EC	EC80 (1.6)
Aircraft tonne-km	International and national	tonne-kms	No		EC	EC80 (6.3)
Aircraft, average speed of	Total and for domestic and international	kms/hr	Yes	A	World	ICAO2 (1.19)
Aircraft-kilometres	By airline, operator by country	aircraft-kms	No		World	ICAO9 (A)
Aircraft-km	International and national	aircraft-kms	No		EC	EC80 (6.3)
Available seat-kilometres	International, domestic	nos, % change	Yes	A	World, IATA	IATA1 (-)
Available seat-kilometres	International, domestic	nos, % change	Yes	A	World, IATA	IATA1 (-)
Available tonne-kilometres	International domestic,	nos, % change	Yes	A	World, IATA	IATA1 (-)
Available tonne-kilometres	International, domestic	nos, % change	Yes	A	World, IATA	IATA1 (-)
Aviation activities	By type	nos	No		World	ICAO2 (2.4)
Block speeds, average, of passenger services	International, domestic	kms/hour	Yes	A	World	CAA1 (2)
Civil aviation	Distance flown	km, tonne-km, passenger-km	Yes	A	ESCAP region, developing ESCAP region	UN44 (p6, 11)
Civil aviation	Summary, by country passenger-km,	nos, km, tonne-km,	Yes	A	ESCAP countries	UN44
Civil aviation traffic			Yes	M	Asia and Pacific	UN43
Civil aviation traffic	By countries	nos	No		The Americas and Australasia	MAC2 (G7)
Civil aviation traffic	By country, traffic type	ton-kilometre, nos	Yes	A	Africa and Asia	MAC1 (G6)
Commercial aviation	By countries, passenger kms passengers kms, and freight ton/kms	nos, ton/kms	Yes	A	EC	MAC3 (F7,A,B)

Subject	Categories	Units	Time series Yes/No Frequency		Territorial coverage	Source (Table no.)
Distribution	By carrier type, passenger-kilometres and freight tonne-kilometres performed	kms	No		World	ICAO2 (1.14)
Flights, passenger aircraft	By jet and non-jet, departures	hours, nos	Yes	A	World	CAA1 (4)
Freight	By country	tonnes	No		EC	EM1 (2211)
Freight (tonne/km)	Total international	nos	Yes	A	World	UN50 (136)
Freight services	By cargo traffic and revenue, aircraft operating data	tonnes, kms, %	Yes	A	World	AEA2 (-)
Freight tonne kilometres	By airline, region, % change, ranking	%, tonne km	Yes	A	World	AEA1 (-)
Freight tonnes carried	By airline, by country, scheduled, non-scheduled (revenue) flights	freight-tonnes	Yes	A	World	ICAO9 (E1)
Freight tonnes carried	By airline, operator, by country	freight-tonnes	No		World	ICAO9 (A)
Freight tonnes carried	International, domestic	nos, % change	Yes	A	World, IATA	IATA1 (-)
Freight tonnes carried	Total	tonnes	Yes	A	World	ICAO2 (1.17)
Freight tonnes carried	Total, international and domestic for all services and freight services	tonnes	No		World	ICAO2 (1.18)
Freight-tonnes carried	By airline, operator, by country	freight-tonnes	Yes	A	World	ICAO9 (D1)
Freight-tonnes carried	By country, airline and type of operation (international, domestic) by type of scheduled airline (international, domestic)	freight-tonnes	Yes	A, M	World	ICAO9 (B-C)
Goods, international	Entering the country, leaving the country	tonnes	Yes	A	EC, USA	UN13 (4)
Growth rates, scheduled and non-scheduled air traffic in terms of passenger km performed	Total	nos, kms	Yes	A	World	CAA1 (5)
International service	Percentage of total tonne-kilometres performed	%	Yes	A	World	ICAO2 (1.23)
Intra European region developments in 1991 traffic	By country, market change, passengers	nos, %	No		EC	AEA4 (-)
Journey distance per passenger	Total and for domestic and International	kms	Yes	A	World	ICAO2 (1.19)
Km flown	Total, international	nos	Yes	A	World	UN50 (136)
Load-factor		%	No		EC	EC9 (7.6)
Mail (tonne/km)	Total international	nos	Yes	A	World	UN50 (136)
Overall load factor	By airline, region, points change, ranking	%	Yes	A	World	AEA1 (-)
Passenger kilometres	Total, international	nos	Yes	A	World	UN50 (136)
Passenger kilometres	By airline, region, % change, ranking	%, kms	Yes	A	World	AEA1 (-)
Passenger load factor	By airline, operator by country	%	No		World	ICAO9 (A)
Passenger load factor	By airline, region, point change, ranking	%	Yes	A	World	AEA1 (-)

3 CIVIL AVIATION

Subject	Categories	Units	Time series Yes/No	Frequency	Territorial coverage	Source (Table no.)
Passenger load factor	By country, airline and type of operation (international, domestic) by type of scheduled airline (international, domestic)	%	Yes	A, M	World	ICAO9 (B-C)
Passenger load factor	International, domestic	nos, % change	Yes	A	World, IATA	IATA1 (-)
Passenger load factor	Total	%	Yes	A	World	ICAO2 (1.17)
Passenger load factor	Total and for domestic and international	%	Yes	A	World	ICAO2 (1.19)
Passenger load factor	Total, international and domestic for all services	%	No		World	ICAO2 (1.18)
Passenger numbers		nos	Yes	I	EC	EC80 (1.6)
Passenger services	By passenger cargo, total traffic and revenue aircraft operating data	km, %, nos, US$, US cents, hours tonnes	Yes	A	World	AEA2 (-)
Passenger services	Proportion of jet hours, departures	hours	Yes	A	World	CAA1 (3)
Passenger services, all	By aircraft hours flown, passengers carried, number of departures, average stage distance, average number of passengers per aircraft	km, nos	Yes	A	World	CAA1(1)
Passenger traffic highest,	By city pairs	nos	No		World	ICAO2 (1.20)
passenger km performed		passenger-kms	Yes	A	World	ICAO2 (1.23)
Passenger-kilometres	By airline, operator by country	passenger-kms	No		World	ICAO9 (A)
Passenger-kilometres	By airline, operator, by country	passenger-kms	Yes	A	World	ICAO9 (D1)
Passenger-kilometres	International and national	passenger-kms	No		EC	EC80 (6.3)
Passenger-kilometres flown	International, domestic	nos, % change	Yes	A	World, IATA	IATA1 (-)
Passenger-kilometres performed	By country, airline and type of operation (international, domestic) by type of scheduled airline (international, domestic)	passenger-kms	Yes	A, M	World	ICAO9 (B-C)
Passenger-kilometres performed, international	By airline, operator, by country	passenger-kms	Yes	M	World	ICAO9 (D2)
Passenger-km		no-km	No		EC	EC9 (7.6)
Passenger-km	By country	nos	No		EC	EM1 (2210)
Passenger-km performed	By region	passenger-kms	Yes	A	World	ICAO2 (1.15)
Passenger-km performed	International and domestic scheduled services, non-scheduled operators	passenger-kms	No		World	ICAO2 (3.1-3.3)
Passenger-km performed	Total	passenger-kms	Yes	A	World	ICAO2 (1.17)
Passenger-km performed	Total, international and domestic for all services	passenger-kms	No		World	ICAO2 (1.18)
Passengers	By airline, region, % change, ranking	%, nos	Yes	A	World	AEA1 (-)
Passengers carried	By airline, operator by country	nos	No		World	CAO9 (A)

Subject	Categories	Units	Time series Yes/No Frequency		Territorial coverage	Source (Table no.)
Passengers carried	By airline, operator, by country	nos	Yes	A	World	ICAO9 (D1)
Passengers carried	International and national	nos	No		EC	EC80 (6.3)
Passengers carried	International, domestic	nos, % change	Yes	A	World, IATA	IATA1 (-)
Passengers carried	Total	nos	Yes	A	World	ICAO2 (1.17)
Passengers carried	Total, international and domestic for all services	nos	No		World	ICAO2 (1.18)
Passengers carried	Total, international	nos	Yes	A	World	UN50 (136)
Passengers per flight		nos	Yes	A	World	ICAO2 (1.24)
Passengers per flight, average number of	Total and for domestic and International	nos	Yes	A	World	ICAO2 (1.19)
Passengrs carried	By country, airline	nos	Yes	A, M	World	ICA09 (B-C)
Seat availability		nos	No		EC	EC9 (7.6)
Seat kilometres	By airline, region, change, %, km ranking	%	Yes	A	World	AEA1 (-)
Seat-kilometres available	By airline, operator by country	seat-kms	No		World	ICAO9 (A)
Seat-kilometres available	By airline, operator, by country	seat-kms	Yes	A	World	ICAO9 (D1)
Seat-kilometres available	By country, airline and type of operation (international, domestic) by type of scheduled airline (international, domestic)	seat-kms	Yes	A, M	World	ICAO9 (B-C)
Seat-kilometres available	International, domestic	nos, % change	Yes	A	World, IATA	IATA1 (-)
Seat-km available	Total	seat-kms	Yes	A	World	ICAO2 (1.17)
Seat-km available	Total ,international and domestic for all services	seat-kms	No		World	ICAO2 (1.18)
Speed of aircraft, average		kms/hour	Yes	A	World	ICAO2 (1.24)
Stage distance flown, average, per aircraft departure		kms	Yes	A	World	ICAO2 (1.24)
Stage distances flown per aircraft departure, average	Total and for domestic and International	kms	Yes	A	World	ICAO2 (1.19)
Tonne kilometres, available	By airline, region, % change, ranking	%	Yes	A	World	AEA1 (-)
Tonne kilometres, total	By airline, region, % change, ranking	%	Yes	A	World	AEA1 (-)
Tonne-kilometres performed	International, domestic. passengers, freight and mail	nos, % change	Yes	A	World, IATA	IATA1 (-)
Tonne-kilometres available	By airline by country, scheduled, non-scheduled (revenue) flights	tonne-kms	Yes	A	World	ICAO9 (E1)
Tonne-kilometres available	By airline, operator, by country	tonne-kms	No		World	ICAO9 (A)
Tonne-kilometres available	By airline, operator, by country	tonne-kms	Yes	A	World	ICAO9 (D1)
Tonne-kilometres available	By country, airline and type of operation (international, domestic) by type of scheduled airline (international, domestic)	tonne-kms	Yes	A, M	World	ICAO9 (B-C)
Tonne-kilometres available	International and domestic scheduled services, non-scheduled operators	tonne-kms	No		World	ICAO2 (3.1-3.3)

3 CIVIL AVIATION

Subject	Categories	Units	Time series Yes/No	Frequency	Territorial coverage	Source (Table no.)
Tonne-kilometres available	Total	tonne-kms	Yes	A	World	ICAO2 (1.17)
Tonne-kilometres available	International, domestic	nos, % change	Yes	A	World, IATA	IATA1 (-)
Tonne-kilometres performed	By airline by country, scheduled, non-scheduled (revenue) flights, freight, mail	tonne-kms	Yes	A	World	ICAO9 (E1)
Tonne-kilometres performed	By airline, operator, by country	tonne-kms	No		World	ICAO9 (A)
Tonne-kilometres performed	By airline, operator, by country	tonne-kms	Yes	A	World	ICAO9 (D1)
Tonne-kilometres performed	By country, airline and type of operation (international, domestic) by type of scheduled airline (international, domestic) by passengers, freight, mail	tonne-kms	Yes	A, M	World	ICAO9 (B-C)
Tonne-kilometres performed	International and domestic scheduled services, non-scheduled operators	tonne-kms	No		World	ICAO2 (3.1-3.3)
Tonne-km available		tonne-kms	Yes	A	World	ICAO2 (1.23)
Tonne-km performed	By service type	tonne-kms	Yes	A	World	ICAO2 (1.13)
Tonne-km performed	For passengers, mail and freight by region	tonne-kms	Yes	A	World	ICAO2 (1.16)
Tonne-km performed	Total	tonne-kms	Yes	A	World	ICAO2 (1.23)
Tonne-km performed, available services	Scheduled, non-scheduled	nos	Yes	A	World	ICAO5 (App)
Tonne-kms available	Passengers, freight and mail, and total for all services and all freight services only	tonne-kms	No		World	ICAO2 (1.18)
Tonne-kms performed	Passengers, freight and mail, and total for all services and all freight services only	tonne-kms	No		World	ICAO2 (1.18)
Tonne-kms performed	Total and for passengers, mail and freight	tonne-kms	Yes	A	World	ICAO2 (1.17)
Total all services	By cargo traffic and revenue on all service	tonnes, kms, % US$, US cents	Yes	A	World	AEA2 (-)
Total traffic and capacity		%, tonnes, kms	Yes	A	World	AEA2 (-)
Traffic	By country, by type	nos	No		EC	EC18 (10.10)
Traffic	Freight, passengers	tons, nos 1000	Yes	A	Central Africa	UN5(29)
Traffic	Passengers, goods	nos, tonnes, passenger-km, tonne-km	Yes	A	World	IRTU1
Traffic - average annual growth rate	Loaded, unloaded	%Yes	A		Africa	UN1(41)
Traffic, commercial	By EC airport and type	nos, tonnes	No		EC	EC80 (6.2)
Traffic, sea and air	goods, passengers	tonnes, nos	No		EC	EC69 (VI.5)
Weight load factor		%	Yes	A	World	ICAO2 (1.23)
Weight load factor		%	Yes	A	World	ICAO2 (1.24)
Weight load factor	By airline by country, scheduled, non-scheduled (revenue) flights	%	Yes	A	World	ICAO9 (E1)
Weight load factor	By airline, operator, by country	%	No		World	ICAO9 (A)

Subject	Categories	Units	Time series Yes/No	Frequency	Territorial coverage	Source (Table no.)
Weight load factor	By country, airline and type of operation (international, domestic) by type of scheduled airline (international, domestic)	%	Yes	A, M	World	ICAO9 (B-C)
Weight load factor	International, domestic	nos, % change	Yes	A	World, IATA	IATA1 (-)
Weight load factor	Passengers, freight and mail, and total for all services and all freight services only	%	No		World	ICAO2 (1.18)
Weight load factor	Total	%	Yes	A	World	ICAO2 (1.17)
Weight load factor	Total and for domestic and international	%	Yes	A	World	ICAO2 (1.19)
3.7.3 All Services of Charter Airlines						
Passenger-kilometres flown	International, domestic	nos, % change	Yes	A	World, IATA	IATA1 (-)
Tonne-kilometres available	International, domestic	nos, % change	Yes	A	World, IATA	IATA1 (-)
Tonne-kilometres performed	International, domestic. passengers freight and mail	nos, % change	Yes	A	World, IATA	IATA1 (-)
3.7.4 All Services of Non-Scheduled Operators						
Aircraft departures	By airline, operator, by country	nos	Yes	A	World	ICAO9 (D1)
Aircraft hours	By airline, operator by country	aircraft-hrs	Yes	A	World	ICAO9 (D1)
Aircraft hours, non-revenue	By airline, operator by country	aircraft-hrs	Yes	A	World	ICAO9 (D1)
Aircraft-kilometres	By airline, operator, by country	aircraft-kms	Yes	A	World	ICAO9 (D1)
Non-scheduled operators	By type, by country, by carrier	nos	Yes	A	World	ICAO5 (App)
Tonne-kilometres performed	Operator by country by type of operation (international, domestic)	tonne-kms	Yes	A	World	ICAO9 (E2)
Tonne-kilometres available	Non-scheduled services, by source	nos	Yes	A	World	ICAO5 (A3)
3.7.5 All Services of Scheduled Airlines						
Air traffic	Freight, passengers	tons, nos 1000	Yes	A	Central Africa	UN5(29)
Air traffic	Freight, passengers	tons, nos 1000	Yes	A	East and Southern Africa	UN4(29)
Air traffic	Freight, passengers	tons, nos 1000	Yes	A	North Africa	UN2(29)
Air traffic	Freight, passengers	tons, nos 1000	Yes	A	West Africa	UN3(29)
Aircraft departures	By country, airline and type of operation (international, domestic) by type of scheduled airline (international, domestic)	nos	Yes	A, M	World	ICAO9 (B-C)
Aircraft hours	By country, airline and type of operation (international, domestic) by type of scheduled airline (international, domestic)	aircraft-hrs	Yes	A, M	World	ICAO9 (B-C)

3 CIVIL AVIATION

Subject	Categories	Units	Time series Yes/No Frequency		Territorial coverage	Source (Table no.)
Aircraft-kilometres	By country, airline and type of operation (international, domestic) by type of scheduled airline (international, domestic)	aircraft-kms	Yes	A, M	World	ICAO9 (B-C)
Freight tonnes carried	International, domestic	nos, % change	Yes	A	World, IATA	IATA1 (-)
Passenger load factor	International and domestic scheduled services	%	No		World	ICAO2 (3.1-3.2)
Passenger-kilometres flown	International, domestic	nos, % change	Yes	A	World, IATA,	IATA1 (-)
Passengers carried	International and domestic scheduled services	nos	No		World	ICAO2 (3.1-3.2)
Scheduled airlines	Services by type, by country, by airline	nos	Yes	A	World	ICAO5 (App)
Scheduled traffic		nos	No		World	ICAO2 (2.3)
Tonne-kilometres performed	International, domestic, passengers, freight and mail	nos, % change	Yes	A	World, IATA	IATA1 (-)
Tonne-kilometres available	International, domestic	nos, % change	Yes	A	World, IATA	IATA1 (-)
Tonne-kms performed	Scheduled services, by source	nos	Yes	A	World	ICAO5 (A3)
Traffic	Passsenger-km and cargo tonne-km flown on: total scheduled services, international scheduled services	nos	Yes	A	ASEAN	ASEANS1 (5.4.2)
Traffic, civil aviation	Km flown on, total scheduled services, international scheduled services	nos	Yes	A	ASEAN	ASEANS1 (5.4.1)
3.7.6 All-Freight Services						
Aircraft departures	By airline by country, scheduled, non-scheduled (revenue) flights	nos	Yes	A	World	ICAO9 (E1)
Aircraft departures	International, domestic	nos, % change	Yes	A	World, IATA	IATA1 (-)
Aircraft hours	By airline by country, scheduled, non-scheduled (revenue) flights	aircraft-hrs	Yes	A	World	ICAO9 (E1)
Aircraft-kilometres	By airline by country, scheduled, non-scheduled (revenue) flights	aircraft-kms	Yes	A	World	ICAO9 (E1)
Available tonne kilometres	International, domestic	nos, % change	Yes	A	World, IATA	IATA1 (-)
Freight-tonnes carried	International, domestic	nos, % change	Yes	A	World, IATA	IATA1 (-)
Hours flown	International, domestic	nos, % change	Yes	A	World, IATA	IATA1 (-)
Kilometres flown	International, domestic	nos, % change	Yes	A	World, IATA	IATA1 (-)
Number of flights	By station-pair by airline	nos	Yes	A	World	ICAO10 (-)
Tonne-kilometres performed	Freight, mail international, domestic	nos, % change	Yes	A	World, IATA	IATA1 (-)
Type of aircraft	By station-pair by airline		Yes	A	World	ICAO10 (-)

Subject	Categories	Units	Time series Yes/No Frequency		Territorial coverage	Source (Table no.)
Weight load factor	International, domestic	nos, % change	Yes	A	World, IATA	IATA1 (-)
3.7.7 Charter Services						
Aircraft departures	International, domestic	nos, % change	Yes	A	World, IATA,	IATA1 (-)
Available tonne kilometres	International, domestic	nos, % change	Yes	A	World, IATA	IATA1 (-)
Hours flown	International, domestic	nos, % change	Yes	A	World, IATA	IATA1 (-)
Kilometres flown	International, domestic	nos, % change	Yes	A	World, IATA	IATA1 (-)
Passenger kilometres flown	International, domestic	nos, % change	Yes	A	World, IATA	IATA1 (-)
Tonne kilometres performed	International, domestic	nos, % change	Yes	A	World, IATA	IATA1 (-)
3.7.8 Charter Services of Scheduled Airlines						
Passenger-kilometres flown	International, domestic	nos, % change	Yes	A	World, IATA	IATA1 (-)
Tonne-kilometres performed	International, domestic, passengers, freight and mail	nos, % change	Yes	A	World, IATA	IATA1 (-)
Tonne-kilometres available	International, domestic	nos, % change	Yes	A	World, IATA	IATA1 (-)
3.7.9 IATA Members' Air Transport Operations						
Scheduled services, aircraft departures	International, domestic	nos, % change	Yes	A	IATA	IATA1 (-)
Scheduled services, hours flown	International, domestic	nos, % change	Yes	A	IATA	IATA1 (-)
Scheduled services, kilometres flown	International, domestic	nos, % change	Yes	A	IATA	IATA1 (-)
3.7.10 On-Flight Origin and Destination						
Between countries of AEA airlines	By on-flight origin and destination, passengers flights, freight, mail	nos, tonnes	No		Selected countries	AEA3 (-)
Between countries of AEA airlines and other countries in the AEA	By on-flight origin and destination, passengers flights, freight, mail	nos, tonnes	No		Selected countries	AEA3 (-)
Freight traffic		tonnes	No		World	ICAO7
Mail traffic		tonnes	No		World	ICAO7
Passenger Numbers		nos	No		World	ICAO7
3.7.11 Traffic by Flight Stage						
Scheduled Services - International Operations (Revenue Traffic)						
Freight	By station-pair by airline	tonnes	Yes	A	World	ICAO10 (-)
Mail	By station-pair by airline	tonnes	Yes	A	World	ICAO10 (-)
Number of flights	By station-pair by	nos	Yes	A	World	ICAO10 (-)
Passenger load factor	By station-pair by airline	%	Yes	A	World	ICAO10 (-)
Passenger seats available	By station-pair by airline	nos	Yes	A	World	ICAO10 (-)
Payload capacity, total	By station-pair by airline, revenue traffic	tonnes	Yes	A	World	ICAO10 (-)
Revenue passengers carried	By station-pair by airline	nos		A	World	ICAO10 (-)

3 CIVIL AVIATION

Subject	Categories	Units	Time series Yes/No Frequency		Territorial coverage	Source (Table no.)
Station-pairs	Distance	kms	Yes	A	World	ICAO10 (-)
Type of aircraft	By station-pair by airline		Yes	A	World	ICAO10 (-)

4 CLIMATE

Subject	Categories	Units	Time series Yes/No Frequency		Territorial coverage	Source (Table No.)
Atmospheric pressure	By CLIMAT station, by country	mb	Yes	M	World	WMO1
Humidity	By CLIMAT station, by country	%	Yes	M	World	WMO1
Latitude, normal temperature, precipitation, sunshine	Capital cities or other available sites	m, mm, °C, hours	No		World	UN16 (9)
Precipitation		mm	No		Nordic countries	NCM1 (4)
Precipitation		mm	Yes	A	EC	EC6 (IA1)
Precipitation	By city	mm	No		The Americas and Australasia	MAC2 (A1)
Precipitation	By city	mm	Yes	A	Africa and Asia	MAC1 (A1)
Precipitation	By CLIMAT station, by country	mm	Yes	M	World	WMO1
Precipitation	Monthly total, deviation from the mean, 1mm plus, by station	mm, days	Yes	M	EC	EC19 (IV)
Rainfall - see Precipitation						
Seasonal temperature deviations		°C	Yes	A	EC	UN22 (I-1.1.1)
Seasonal temperature deviations		°C	Yes	A	EC	UN22 (I-1.1.1)
Sunshine	By CLIMAT station, by country	hours	Yes	M	World	WMO1
Temperature		°C	No		Nordic countries	NCM1 (5)
Temperature		°C	Yes	A	EC	EC6 (IA1)
Temperature	By city	°C	Yes	A	Africa and Asia	MAC1 (A2)
Temperature	By city	mm	No		The Americas and Australasia	MAC2 (A2)
Temperature	By CLIMAT station, by country	°C	Yes	M	World	WMO1
Temperature	By state, by height,	mm	No		Central and Eastern Europe	EC18 (2.2)
Temperature	Monthly average, deviation from the mean, mean maximum, mean minimum, by station	°C	Yes	M	EC	EC19 (IV)
Temperature, precipitation, sunshine	Capital cities or other available sites	m, mm, °C, hours	No		World	UN16(9)
Vapour pressure	By CLIMAT station, by country	mb	Yes	M	World	WMO1
Water exchange	Monthly total potential evapotranspir., total hydrologic balance, by station	mm	Yes	M	EC	EC19 (IV)

5 COMMODITIES

5.1 CONSUMPTION

- 5.1.1 Agricultural Commodities
- 5.1.2 Cement
- 5.1.3 Metals, Ores, Minerals and Chemicals
- 5.1.4 Textiles, Clothing and Footwear

5.2 INTERNATIONAL TRADE

- 5.2.1 Agricultural Commodities
- 5.2.2 Fish and Fish Products
- 5.2.3 General
- 5.2.4 Manufactured Commodities
- 5.2.5 Meat and Livestock Products
- 5.2.6 Metals, Ores, Minerals and Chemicals
- 5.2.7 Mining and Oil
- 5.2.8 Textiles, Clothing, Leather and Footwear
- 5.2.9 Wood and Forestry Products

5.3 PRICES

- 5.3.1 Agricultural Commodities
- 5.3.2 Meat and Livestock Products
- 5.3.3 Metals, Ores, Minerals and Chemicals
- 5.3.4 Textiles, Clothing and Footwear

5.4 PRODUCTION

- 5.4.1 Agricultural Commodities
- 5.4.2 Energy
- 5.4.3 Fish and Fish Products
- 5.4.4 Meat and Livestock Products
- 5.4.5 Metals, Ores, Minerals and Chemicals
- 5.4.6 Textiles, Clothing and Footwear
- 5.4.7 Wood and Forestry Products

5.5 SUPPLY AND DISTRIBUTION

- 5.5.1 Agricultural Commodities
- 5.5.2 Metals, Ores, Minerals and Chemicals
- 5.5.3 Textiles

5 COMMODITIES

Subject	Categories	Units	Time series Yes/No	Frequency	Territorial coverage	Source (Table no.)
5.1 CONSUMPTION - see also under Production (5.4), International Trade (5.2) and Section 8						
5.1.1 Agricultural Commodities - see also Section 2						
Cocoa						
CBE usage, preliminary estimates of current and potential in the EC	By country, by production potential displacement-	tonnes, %	No		EC	ICCO3 (20)
Chocolate and chocolate products	By country	tonnes	Yes	A, Q	World	ICC02 (9)
Chocolate and chocolate products	By country	tonnes	Yes	A, Q	World	ICC02 (14)
Cocoa, powder and cake	By country	tonnes	Yes	A, Q	World	ICC02 (7)
Cocoa, sale of stocks	By origin, port, % defect	tonnes, US$	No		World	ICCO1 (1)
Cocoa	By consumption	tonnes	Yes	A	World	UNCTAD4 (2.12.6)
Cocoa	By country, per capita	kg/head	Yes	A	World	ICC02 (19)
Cocoa	By final consumer, by country	tonnes	Yes	A	World	ICC02 (18)
Cocoa (beans) production and trade	By country	tonnes, %	Yes	A	World	ISL2 (2.3.23)
Cocoa and cocoa products	Destination of exports, by cocoa product, by country	tonnes	Yes	A, Q	World	ICC02 (20-29)
Cocoa and cocoa products	Origin of imports, by cocoa product, by country	tonnes	Yes	A, Q	World	ICC02 (20-30)
Cocoa beans	By country	tonnes	Yes	A, Q	World	ICC02 (4)
Cocoa beans	By country	tonnes	Yes	A, Q	World	ICC02 (10)
Cocoa beans	By production	tonnes	Yes	A	World	UNCTAD4 (2.12.1)
Cocoa beans	Quantity and value of exports and imports	tonnes, US$	Yes	A	World	UNCTAD4 (2.12.2, 2.12.3)
Cocoa beans and cocoa products, net exports of	By country, 5 year average	tonnes, %	Yes	A	World	ICC01 (6)
Cocoa beans and cocoa products, net imports of	By country, 5 year average	tonnes %	Yes	A	World	ICC01 (7)
Cocoa butter	By country	tonnes	Yes	A, Q	World	ICC02 (6)
Cocoa butter	By country	tonnes	Yes	A, Q	World	ICC02 (11)
Cocoa paste, liquor	By country	tonnes	Yes	A, Q	World	ICC02 (8)
Cocoa paste/liquor	By country	tonnes	Yes	A, Q	World	ICC02 (13)
Cocoa powder and cake	By country	tonnes	Yes	A, Q	World	ICC02 (12)
Cocoa products	Quantity and value of exports and imports	tonnes, US$	Yes	A	World	UNCTAD4 (2.12.4, 2.12.5)
Consumption of cocoa, globally-adjusted	By region, by major consuming country	tonnes	Yes		World	ICCO3 (4)
Consumption of cocoa,elasticity coefficients	By country, by model, error, price, income	%, nos	No		World	ICCO3 (17)
Consumption of cocoa, projections	By country	tonnes	No		World	ICCO3 (18)
World cocoa market development	By production, grindings, total stocks, prices, income growth	tonnes, %, SDRs/tonnes	No		World	ICCO3 (21)
World cocoa market development	By production, grindings, total stocks, prices, income growth	tonnes, %, SDRs/tonne	No		World	ICCO3 (22)
World cocoa stocks, evolution in relation to world grindings	By grindings, closing stock, stocks-grinding ratio	tonnes, %	Yes		World	ICCO3 (2)
World consumption of cocoa, projections of shares	By country	%	No		World	ICCO3 (19)
World grindings	By continent, country	tonnes, %	Yes	A	World	ICC01 (5)
General						
Bananas	Consumption, apparent	tonnes	Yes	A	World	UNCTAD4 (2.8.4)
Coffee	By consumption	bags	Yes	A	World	UNCTAD4 (2.11.4)

5 COMMODITIES

Subject	Categories	Units	Time series Yes/No Frequency		Territorial coverage	Source (Table no.)
Tea	By consumption	tonnes	Yes	A	World	UNCTAD4 (2.13.4)
Tobacco	By consumption	tonnes	Yes	A	World	UNCTAD4 (2.26.4)
Rubber						
Rubber	By country	tonnes	Yes	A	Malaysia, peninsular	IRSG1 (16)
					Singapore	IRSG1 (17)
					Indonesia	IRSG1 (18)
					Thailand	IRSG1 (19)
					Sri Lanka	IRSG1 (20)
Rubber	By major sectors	tonnes	Yes	A, Q	World	IRSG1 (37)
Rubber	By type of rubber	tonnes	No		USA	IRSG1 (29)
					Brazil	IRSG1 (30)
					France	IRSG1 (31)
					Germany	IRSG1 (32)
					UK	IRSG1 (33)
					Australia	IRSG1 (34)
					India	IRSG1 (35)
					Japan	IRSG1 (36)
Rubber	Latex, total	tonnes	Yes	A	Malaysia, peninsular	IRSG1 (16)
					Singapore	IRSG1 (17)
					Indonesia	IRSG1 (18)
					Thailand	IRSG1 (19)
					Sri Lanka	IRSG1 (20)
Rubber latex, natural		tonnes	Yes	A	World	IRSG2 (17)
Rubber latex, natural		tonnes	Yes	A, M	World	IRSG1 (23)
Rubber latex, natural		tonnes	Yes	M	World	IRSG1 (23)
Rubber latex, natural, net imports		tonnes	Yes	A, M	World	IRSG1 (22)
Rubber, apparent consumption	By non-reporting country	tonnes	Yes	A	World	IRSG2 (6)
Rubber, consumption	Total, synthetic, per capita	kg	Yes	A	World	IISRP1 (15,16)
Rubber, consumption, actual	Type of rubber, elastomer type	tonnes	Yes	A	World	IISRP1 (-)
Rubber, consumption, forecast	Type of rubber, elastomer type	tonnes	No		World	IISRP1 (1-4)
Rubber, natural		tonnes	Yes	A	World	IRSG2 (8)
Rubber, natural		tonnes	Yes	A	World	IRSG2 (9)
Rubber, natural		tonnes	Yes	M	World	IRSG1 (1, 13)
			Yes	A	World	IRSG2 (1, 13)
Rubber, natural	By consumption	tonnes	Yes	A	World	UNCTAD4 (2.28.4)
Rubber, natural	In producing country	tonnes	Yes	M	World	IRSG1 (14)
Rubber, natural	Quantity and value of exports and imports	tonnes, US$	Yes	A	World	UNCTAD4 (2.28.2, 2.28.3)
Rubber, natural , consumption, production	Natural synthetics, 1946-60	tonnes	Yes	A	World	IRSG2 (47)
Rubber, natural , gross imports to major non-producing countries		tonnes	No		World	IRSG1 (21)
Rubber, natural and synthetic	By country	tonnes	Yes	A	World	IRSG2 (3)
Rubber, natural and synthetic	By country	tonnes	Yes	M	World	IRSG1 (3)
Rubber, natural and synthetic	By major sector	tonnes	Yes	A	World	IRSG2 (25)
Rubber, natural and synthetic	By major sector	tonnes	Yes	M	World	IRSG1 (37)
Rubber, natural consumption	1900-45	tonnes	Yes	A	World	IRSG2 (45)
Rubber, natural, net imports		tonnes	Yes	A, M	World	IRSG1 (12)
Rubber, SBR values		nat curr, tonne	Yes	A	World	IRSG2 (21)
Rubber, sheet, gross exports	By grade	tonnes	Yes	A, M	Malaysia, Indonesia Thailand	IRSG1 (10)
Rubber, synthetic		%	Yes	A	World	IRSG2 (4)
Rubber, synthetic		%	Yes	M	World	IRSG1 (4)
Rubber, synthetic		tonnes	Yes	A	World	IRSG2 (16)
Rubber, synthetic		tonnes	Yes	A	World	IRSG2 (17)

Subject	Categories	Units	Time series Yes/No Frequency		Territorial coverage	Source (Table no.)
Rubber, synthetic		tonnes	Yes	M	World	IRSG1 (2, 28)
		tonnes	Yes	A	World	IRSG2 (2, 23)
Rubber, synthetic	By destination	tonnes	Yes	A	World	IRSG1 (26)
Rubber, synthetic, net imports		tonnes	Yes	A, M	World	IRSG1 (27)
Rubber. technically-specified	By grade	tonnes	Yes	M	World	IRSG1 (11)
	By grade	tonnes	Yes	A	World	IRSG2 (10)
Tyre and tyre products	By polymer type	%	No		World	IISRP1 (10,11)
Tyres	Car, truck	tonnes	Yes	A, Q	Major exporting countries	IRSG1 (40)
Tyres and tubes, total		tonnes	Yes	A	EC	EC53 (5.52)
Sugar						
Consumption, world	By country, per capita	kgs	Yes	A	World	ISO3 (-)
Consumption	By country	tonnes	Yes	A, M	World	ISO2 (-)
Consumption	By country	tonnes	Yes	A	World	ISO3 (-)
Consumption	Total, net		No		World	ISO1 (-)
Stocks	By country	tonnes	Yes	A, M	World	ISO2 (-)
Stocks	By country	tonnes	Yes	A	World	ISO3 (-)
Sugar, raw	By production	tonnes	Yes	A	World	UNCTAD4 (2.9.1)
Sugar, raw and refined	Total, value of exports and imports	US$	Yes	A	World	UNCTAD4 (2.9.2, 2.9.3)
Sugar, raw and refined	Quantity of exports and imports	tonnes	Yes	A	World	UNCTAD4 (2.9.4, 2.9.5)
Sugar		tonnes	Yes	A	EC	EC53 (5.40)
Sugar	By consumption	tonnes	Yes	A	World	UNCTAD4 (2.9.6)
Sugar (centrifugal and raw), production and trade	By country	tonnes, %	Yes	A	World	ISL2 (2.3.20)
Sugar agreement			No		World	ISO1 (-)
5.1.2 Cement						
Cement		tonnes	Yes	A	World	UN10 (16)
5.1.3 Metals, Ores, Minerals and Chemicals - see also Sections 32 and 33						
Aluminium, primary	By consumption	tonnes	Yes	A	World	UNCTAD4 (3.1.12)
Aluminium, primary and secondary	By consumption	tonnes	Yes	A	World	UNCTAD4 (3.1.13)
Copper, refined	By consumption	tonnes	Yes	A	World	UNCTAD4 (3.2.11)
Lead		tonnes	Yes	A, M	Peru	ILZSG1 (22)
Lead	By principal uses	tonnes	Yes	A, M	US	ILZSG1 (24)
Lead	By principal uses	tonnes	Yes	A, M	Japan	ILZSG1 (20)
Lead	By principal uses	tonnes	Yes	A, M	UK	ILZSG1 (23)
Lead	By principal uses	tonnes	Yes	A, M	Italy	ILZSG1 (19)
Lead	By principal uses	tonnes	Yes	A, M	Germany	ILZSG1 (18)
Lead	Metal consumption	tonnes	Yes	A	Eastern Europe Socialist countries	ILZSG1 (9)
Lead	By principal uses	tonnes	Yes	A, M	Australia	ILZSG1 (15)
Lead	By principal uses	tonnes	Yes	A, M	France	ILZSG1 (17)
Lead	By principal uses	tonnes	Yes	A, M	Canada	ILZSG1 (16)
Lead, refined	By principal uses	tonnes	Yes	A, M	Mexico	ILZSG1 (21)
Lead, recovery of secondary lead	Refined lead and lead alloys, remelted lead and lead alloys	tonnes	Yes	A, Q	World	ILZSG1 (11)
Lead, refined		tonnes	Yes	A	EC, US, Japan	ILZSG1 (2)
Lead, refined		tonnes	Yes	A, Q	Western World	ILZSG1 (1)
Lead, refined		tonnes	Yes	A, M	World	ILZSG1 (7)
Lead, total refined		tonnes, %	Yes	A	Western World	ILZSG1 (25)
Lead, total refined		tonnes, %	Yes	A	World	ILZSG1 (25)
Nickel, unwrought	By consumption	tonnes	Yes	A	World	UNCTAD4 (3.6.9)
Scrap consumption	By country, region	tonnes	Yes	A	World	IISI4 (23)

5 COMMODITIES

Subject	Categories	Units	Time series Yes/No	Frequency	Territorial coverage	Source (Table no.)
Stainless steel, consumption	By product group	tonnes	No		Western world	WBMS4 (-)
Stainless steel, consumption	Total	tonnes	Yes	A	Western world	WBMS4 (-)
Steel, apparent consumption	Estimated change	tonnes, %	No		Industrialised countries	IISI1 (5, 8)
Steel, apparent consumption	Estimated change	tonnes, %	No		Developing countries	IISI1 (6, 9)
Steel, apparent consumption	Estimated change	tonnes, %	No		World	IISI1 (7, 10)
Steel, apparent consumption	Estimated change	tonnes, %	No		Industrialised countries	IISI3 (2)
Steel, apparent consumption	Estimated change	tonnes, %	No		Developing countries	IISI3 (3)
Steel, apparent consumption	Estimated change	tonnes, %	No		World	IISI3 (4)
Steel, crude, apparent consumption	By country, region	tonnes	Yes	A	World	IISI4 (10)
Steel, crude, apparent consumption	By country, region, per capita	kg	Yes	A	World	IISI4 (11)
Steel, finished, apparent consumption	By country, region	tonnes	Yes	A	World	IISI4 (12)
Steel, consumption	By country, by product	tonnes	No		World	MB1 (-)
Steel industry	by fuel type and by industrial process	tonnes,cu m, mwh, gj	No		EC, USA, Canada and Japan	UN11 (7)
Steel industry raw materials	By type	tonnes	No		EC, USA, Canada and Japan	UN11 (5)
Tin metal, primary	By consumption	tonnes	Yes	A	World	UNCTAD4 (3.9.8)
Tin metal, secondary	By consumption	tonnes	Yes	A	World	UNCTAD4 (3.9.9)
Tungsten ore	By consumption	tonnes	Yes	A	World	UNCTAD4 (3.10.4)
Zinc		tonnes	Yes	A, M	Peru	ILZSG1 (47)
Zinc		tonnes	Yes	A	Western World	ILZSG1 (26)
Zinc	By principal uses	tonnes	Yes	A, M	Australia	ILZSG1 (40)
Zinc	By principal uses	tonnes	Yes	A, M	Canada	ILZSG1 (41)
Zinc	By principal uses	tonnes	Yes	A, M	France	ILZSG1 (42)
Zinc	By principal uses	tonnes	Yes	A, M	Germany	ILZSG1 (43)
Zinc	By principal uses	tonnes	Yes	A, M	Italy	ILZSG1 (44)
Zinc	By principal uses	tonnes	Yes	A, M	Japan	ILZSG1 (45)
Zinc	By principal uses	tonnes	Yes	A, M	Mexico	ILZSG1 (46)
Zinc	By principal uses	tonnes	Yes	A, M	UK	ILZSG1 (48)
Zinc	By principal uses	tonnes	Yes	A, M	US	ILZSG1 (49)
Zinc, refined		tonnes	Yes	A, M	World	ILZSG1 (32)
Zinc, refined		tonnes	Yes	A, M	EC, US, Japan	ILZSG1 (27)
Zinc, metal		tonnes	Yes	A	Eastern Europe Socialist countries	ILZSG1 (34)
Zinc, recovery of secondary zinc	Refined zinc metal, remelted zinc and direct use of secondary materials	tonnes	Yes	A, Q	World	ILZSG1 (36)
Zinc, total refined		tonnes	Yes	A	Western world	ILZSG1 (50)
Zinc, total refined		tonnes	Yes	A	World	ILZSG1 (50)
5.1.4 Textiles, Clothing and Footwear						
Chemical fibres	By country	tonnes, %	Yes	A	World	ICAC2 (pp81-100)
Consumption	By fibre type,	tonnes	No		Selected countries	ITMF2 (3.2-3.5)
Consumption summary	By fibre type	tonnes	No		Selected countries	ITMF2 (3.1)
Cotton		bales	Yes	A	World	ICAC2 (pp18-19)
Cotton	By calender year	bales	Yes	A	World	ICAC2 (pp20-21)
Cotton	By consumption	tonnes	Yes	A	World	UNCTAD4 (2.31.9)
Cotton (mill use)	By country	tonnes, %	Yes	A	World	ICAC2 (pp81-100)
Cotton (total)		tonnes	Yes	A	China, E. Europe, CIS, India, US, EC, Pakistan, E. Asia	ICAC2

Subject	Categories	Units	Time series Yes/No Frequency	Territorial coverage	Source (Table no.)
Jute	By production	tonnes	Yes A	World	UNCTAD4 (2.32.6)
		tonnes	Yes A	EC	EC53 (5.22)
Virgin wool consumption at the spinning stage		%, kg	Yes A	World	IWS1 (16)
Wool	By consumption	tonnes	Yes A	World	UNCTAD4 (2.34.6)
Wool	By country	tonnes, %	Yes A	World	ICAC2 (pp81-100)
5.2 INTERNATIONAL TRADE - see also under Production (5.4) and Section 27					
5.2.1 Agricultural Commodities					
General					
Agricultural raw materials	Value of exports, imports	US$	Yes A	World	UNCTAD4 (1.8, 1.9)
Bananas	Quantity and value of exports and imports	tonnes, US$	Yes A	World	UNCTAD4 (2.8.2, 2.8.3)
Coarse grains production and trade	By country, destination	tonnes	Yes A	World	ISL2 (2.3.17.3-4)
Coarse grains, import and exports	By destination	tonnes	Yes A	World	ISL2 (2.3.17.4.12)
Cocoa beans, re-exports	By country	tonnes	Yes A, Q	World	ICC02 (5)
Coconut oil	Quantity and value of exports and imports	tonnes, US$	Yes A	World	UNCTAD4 (2.22.1, 2.22.2)
Coffee	Quantity and value of exports and imports	tonnes, US$	Yes A	World	UNCTAD4 (2.11.2, 2.11.3)
Coffee (green) production and trade	By country	tonnes, %	Yes A	World	ISL2 (2.3.21)
Commodities, share of three leading, in total exports by developing countries	By commodity	%	No	Developing countries	UNCTAD4 (A.7)
Commodity exports, direction	By origin and destination, total agricultural raw materials	%	Yes 2 A	World	UNCTAD4 (1.27)
Copra	Quantity and value of exports and imports	tonnes, US$	Yes A	World	UNCTAD4 (2.21.2, 2.21.3)
Direction of commodity exports	By origin and destination, all food items	%	Yes 2 A	World	UNCTAD4 (1.26)
Exports and imports, gross	By country of origin, sugatr type	tonnes	Yes A	World	ISO3 (-)
Food, all items	Value of exports, imports	US$	Yes A	World	UNCTAD4 (1.6, 1.7)
Grains, coarse	Quantity and value of exports and imports	tonnes, US$	Yes A	World	UNCTAD4 (2.7.1, 2.7.2)
Groundnut oil	Quantity and value of exports and imports	tonnes, US$	Yes A	World	UNCTAD4 (2.18.1, 2.18.2)
Groundnuts	Quantity and value of exports and imports	tonnes, US$	Yes A	World	UNCTAD4 (2.17.2, 2.17.3)
Imports by developed market economy countries of selected commodities	By commodity, raw and processed forms	$, %	No	Developed and developing countries	UNCTAD4 (A.6)
Natural rubber latex, net imports		tonnes	Yes M	World	IRSG1 (22)
		tonnes	Yes A	World	IRSG2 (16)
Natural rubber, gross imports	Into major non-producing countries	tonnes	Yes Q	World	IRSG1 (21)
		tonnes	Yes A	World	IRSG1 (12)
Natural rubber, net exports		tonnes	Yes M	World	IRSG1 (9)
		tonnes	Yes A	World	IRSG2 (8)
Natural rubber, net imports into consuming countries		tonnes	Yes A	World	IISRP1 (12)
Natural rubber, net imports		tonnes	Yes M	World	IRSG1 (12)
		tonnes	Yes A	World	IRSG2 (11)

5 COMMODITIES

Subject	Categories	Units	Time series Yes/No Frequency		Territorial coverage	Source (Table no.)
Oilseeds, fats, oils, oil cakes and meals	Value of exports and imports	US$	Yes	A	World	UNCTAD4 (2.15.1, 2.15.2)
Palm kernel oil	Quantity and value of exports and imports	tonnes, US$	Yes	A	World	UNCTAD4 (2.24.1, 2.24.2)
Palm nuts and kernels	Quantity and value of exports and imports	tonnes, US$	Yes	A	World	UNCTAD4 (2.23.2, 2.23.3)
Palm oil	Quantity and value of exports and imports	tonnes, US$	Yes	A	World	UNCTAD4 (2.25.2, 2.25.3)
Peppers	Quantity and value of exports and imports	tonnes; US$	Yes	A	World	UNCTAD4 (2.14.3, 2.14.4)
Rice	Quantity and value of exports and imports	tonnes, US$	Yes	A	World	UNCTAD4 (2.6.2, 2.6.3)
Rice production and trade	By country	tonnes	Yes	A	World	ISL2 (2.3.18)
Rice, paddy	By production	tonnes	Yes	A	World	UNCTAD4 (2.6.1)
Rubber products	By product, total	units, tonnes	Yes	A	World	UN28 (-)
Rubber, natural	By production	tonnes	Yes	A	World	UNCTAD4 (2.28.1)
Rubber, natural,	Net exports, imports	tonnes	Yes	A, M	World	IRSG1 (9)
Rubber, synthetic, exports		tonnes	Yes	M	World	IRSG1 (25)
		tonnes	Yes	A	World	IRSG2 (20)
Rubber, synthetic, exports	By destination	tonnes	Yes	M	World	IRSG2 (26)
Rubber, synthetic, gross exports		tonnes	Yes	A, M	World	IRSG1 (25)
Rubber, technically specified, gross exports	By grade	tonnes	Yes	A, M	Malaysia Indonesia Thailand	IRSG1 (11)
Sheet rubber, gross exports	By grade	tonnes	Yes	M	World	IRSG1 (10)
	By grade	tonnes	Yes	A	World	IRSG2 (9)
Soybean oil	Quantity and value of exports and imports	tonnes, US$	Yes	A	World	UNCTAD4 (2.20.1, 2.20.2)
Soybean oil, imports and exports	By country	tonnes/%	Yes	A	World	ISL2 (2.3.19.2)
Soybean production and trade	By country	tonnes, %	Yes	A	World	ISL2 (2.3.19.1)
Soybeans	Quantity and value of exports and imports	tonnes, US$	Yes	A	World	UNCTAD4 (2.19.2, 2.19.3)
Spices	Quantity and value of exports and imports	tonnes, US$	Yes	A	World	UNCTAD4 (2.14.1, 2.14.2)
Sugar Exports			No		World	ISO1 (-)
Sugar Exports	By country	tonnes	Yes	A	World	ISO3 (-)
Sugar Exports	By country	tonnes	Yes	A, M	World	ISO2 (-)
Sugar Exports	By country of destination	tonnes	Yes	A	World	ISO3 (-)
Sugar Exports to free market, net	By country	tonnes	Yes	A	World	ISO3 (-)
Sugar Exports to free market, net	By country	tonnes	Yes	A, M	World	ISO2 (-)
Sugar Exports, net	By country	tonnes	Yes	A	World	ISO3 (-)
Sugar Exports, net			No		World	ISO1 (-)
Sugar Imports	By country	tonnes	Yes	A, M	World	ISO2 (-)
Sugar Imports	By country, by country of origin	tonnes	Yes	A	World	ISO3 (-)
Sugar Imports from the free market net	By country	tonnes	Yes	A	World	ISO3 (-)
Sugar Imports to free market, net	By country	tonnes	Yes	A, M	World	ISO2 (-)
Sugar Imports, exports			No		World	ISO1 (-)
Sugar Imports, net	By country	tonnes	Yes	A	World	ISO3 (-)
Synthetic rubber, net imports		tonnes	Yes	M	World	IRSG1 (21)
		tonnes	Yes	A	World	IRSG2 (22)
Tea	By production	tonnes	Yes	A	World	UNCTAD4 (2.13.1)
Tea	Quantity and value of exports and imports	tonnes, US$	Yes	A	World	UNCTAD4 (2.13.2, 2.13.3)
Tea production and trade	By country	tonnes, %	Yes	A	World	ISL2 (2.3.22)
Tobacco	By product, total	tonnes, units	Yes	A	World	UN28 (-)

Subject	Categories	Units	Time series Yes/No Frequency		Territorial coverage	Source (Table no.)
Tobacco	Quantity and value of exports and imports	tonnes, US$	Yes	A	World	UNCTAD4 (2.26.2, 2.26.3)
Tobacco (unmanufactured) production and trade	By country	tonnes, %	Yes	A	World	ISL2 (2.3.24)
Tropical beverages	Value of exports and imports	US$	Yes	A	World	UNCTAD4 (2.10.1, 2.10.2)
Vegetable oilseeds, oleaginous fruits and oils	Value of exports and imports	US$	Yes	A	World	UNCTAD4 (2.16.2, 2.16.3)
Wheat	By production	tonnes	Yes	A	World	UNCTAD (2.5.1)
Wheat and wheat flour	Quantity and value of exports and imports	tonnes, US$	Yes	A	World	UNCTAD4 (2.5.2, 2.5.3)
Wheat flour		tonnes	Yes	A, M	World	UN35 (21)
Wheat production and trade	By region, country	tonnes	Yes	A	World	ISL2 (2.3.17.1-2)
Wheat, imports and exports	By destination	tonnes	Yes	A	World	ISL2 (2.3.17.2.12)
5.2.2 Fish and Fish Products - see also Section 20						
Fishery commodities	Value of exports and imports	US$	Yes	A	World	UNCTAD4 (2.3.1, 2.3.2)
5.2.3 General						
Commodities,	Value of exports; imports total 18 integrated programme	US$	Yes	A	World	UNCTAD4 (1.13, 1.14)
Commodities	By country, SITC, sections and groups, by imports, exports	US$	Yes	A	World	UN24 (2-3)
Commodities	Principal exporters, importers	US$	Yes	A	World	UNCTAD4 (1.17, 1.18)
Commodities	Exports; imports	US$	Yes	A	World	UNCTAD4 (1.15, 1.16)
Countries of provenance and destination	By imports, exports, country	US$	Yes	A	World	UN24 (1)
Exports	By SITC section and trading partners, by country or area	tonnes, US$	No		World	UN15
Imports	By SITC section and trading partners, by country or area	tonnes, US$	No		World	UN15
Merchandise trade	Value of exports; imports	US$	Yes	A	World	UNCTAD4 (1.1, 1.2)
Primary commodities, share in all merchandise trade values	By region; exports; imports	%	Yes	A	World	UNCTAD2 (1.19)
Primary commodities, share of regions in wold total trade values	Exports; imports	%	Yes	A	World	UNCTAD2 (1.21)
Primary commodities, share of exports in GDP	By country	%	Yes	A	World	UNCTAD2 (1.22)
Primary commodities	Value of exports including; excluding fuels	US$	Yes	A	World	UNCTAD4 (1.3, 1.4)
Primary commodities	Value of imports excluding fuels	US$	Yes	A	World	UNCTAD4 (1.5)
Trade, classification by broad economic categories	By imports and exports, by commodities	US$	Yes	A	Asia and Pacific	UN24 (4)
5.2.4 Manufactured Commodities						
Beer		hectolitres	Yes	A	EC	EC53 (5.41)
Beverages	By product, total	h, tonnes	Yes	A	World	UN28 (-)
Cars, trucks	Exports	nos	Yes	Q	Major countries	IRSG1 (40)
Cars, trucks	Exports	nos	Yes	A	Major countries	IRSG2 (31, 32)
Cars,.trucks	Exports	nos	Yes	Q	Major countries	IRSG1 (41)
Cars, trucks	Exports	nos	Yes	A	Major countries	IRSG2 (33, 34)

5 COMMODITIES

Subject	Categories	Units	Time series Yes/No Frequency		Territorial coverage	Source (Table no.)
Cereals and cereal preparations	Value of exports and imports	US$	Yes	A	World	UNCTAD4 (2.4.1, 2.4.2)
Cigarettes		pieces	Yes	A	EC	EC53 (5.42)
Cigars and cigarillos		pieces	Yes	A	EC	EC53 (5.43)
Compound feedingstuffs		tonnes	Yes	A	EC	EC53 (5.44)
Engineering products	Between countries in the EC region (total)	US$	No		EC	UN14 (3)
Engineering products	Between geographical and/or economic regions (total)	US$	No		World	UN14 (2)
Engines, turbines and machinery	By product, total	units, kilowatts horsepower, spindles, kVA	Yes	A	World	UN28 (-)
Exports (total)		US$, %, growth	No		World	UN14 (1)
Manufactured commodities	By destination (total)	US$	No		World	UN14 (6a,b)
Manufactured commodities	By region and country of destination (total)	US$,%	No		World	UN14 (4)
Manufactured commodities	Exports by region and country of destination	US$	No		World	UN14 (7)
Manufactured commodities	Main exporter (total)	US$	No		Selected countries	UN14 (5b)
Manufactured commodities	Main exporter and by commodity group (total)	US$	No		World	UN14 (5a)
Manufactured commodities	Professional scientific and controlling instruments and apparatus; photographic apparatus and equipment, optical goods; watches and clocks by region and country of destination	US$	No		World	UN14 (9)
Manufactured miscellaneous commodities	By product, total	units, metres	Yes	A	World	UN28 (-)
Metal products, fabricated	By product, total	units tonnes	Yes	A	World	UN28 (-)
Porcelain, china and glass	By product, total	tonnes,units, metres	Yes	A	World	UN28 (-)
Radio and television receivers, communication equipment and electrical appliances	By product, total	units, tonnes	Yes	A	World	UN28 (-)
Transport equipment	By product, total	units, grt, horsepower	Yes	A	World	UN28 (-)
5.2.5 Meat and Livestock Products - see also Section 2						
Animals live, meat and meat preparation	Value of exports and imports	US$	Yes	A	World	UNCTAD4 (2.1.1,2.1.2)
Beef and veal	By production	tonnes	Yes	A	World	UNCTAD4 (2.2.1)
Bovine hides and skins	Availability	tonnes	Yes	A	World	UNCTAD4 (2.27.4)
Bovine meat	By consumption	tonnes	Yes	A	World	UNCTAD4 (2.2.4)
Bovine meat	By exports and imports, quantity and value	tonnes, US$	Yes	A	World	UNCTAD4 (2.2.2, 2.2.3)
Butter		tonnes	Yes	A	EC	EC53 (5.39)
Cattle and buffalo hides, fresh	By production	tonnes	Yes	A	World	UNCTAD4 (2.27.3)
Hides, skins and furskins, undressed	Value of exports and imports	US$	Yes	A	World	UNCTAD3 (2.27.1,2.27.2)
Margarine		tonnes	Yes	A	EC	EC53 (5.38)
5.2.6 Metals, Ores, Minerals and Chemicals - see also Sections 25, 32 and 33						
General						
Manufactures of metal	By region and country of destination	US$	No		World	UN14 (8)

Subject	Categories	Units	Time series Yes/No Frequency		Territorial coverage	Source (Table no.)
Mineral fuels	Value of exports	US$	Yes	A	World	UNCTAD4 (1.12)
Minerals, ores and metals	Value of exports; imports	US$	Yes	A	World	UNCTAD4 (1.10, 11)
Iron and steel						
Alloy steel, exports	By country, by product	tonnes	No		Selected countries	ISSB2 (-)
Bars and flats	By country, by product	tonnes	No		World	ISSB1 (-)
Bars, rods and sections	By export, import, type	tonnes	Yes	A	World	WBMS4 (-)
Cold finished bars	By country, by destination	tonnes	No		World	ISSB3 (5)
Cold finished/cold formed and forged sections	By country, by destination	tonnes	No		World	ISSB3 (8)
Cold formed sections, wire, narrow strip	By country, by product	tonnes	No		World	ISSB1 (-)
Cold reduced plate and sheet in coil and lengths	By country, by destination	tonnes	No		World	ISSB3 (13)
Cold rolled sheet	By export, import, thickness, type	tonnes	Yes	A	World	WBMS4 (-)
Cold rolled strip	By country, by destination	tonnes	No		World	ISSB3 (15)
Cold rolled strip	By export, import thickness, type	tonnes	Yes	A	World	WBMS4 (-)
Deformed reinforcing bars and rods	By country, by destination	tonnes	No		World	ISSB3 (2)
DR iron	By production, imports	tonnes	Yes	A	Developing countries	IISI3 (-)
Drawn line, single	By country, by destination	tonnes	No		World	ISSB3 (24)
ECSC products, total	By country, by destination	tonnes	No		World	ISSB3 (30)
Electrical sheet and strip	By country, by destination	tonnes	No		World	ISSB3 (19)
Flat products	By production, imports, exports	tonnes	Yes	A	Developing countries	IISI3 (-)
Forged blooms, billets, slabs and bars	By country, by destination	tonnes	No		World	ISSB3 (25)
Forgings - unworked	By country, by destination	tonnes	No		World	ISSB3 (27)
Heavy sections 80mm and over	By country, by destination	tonnes	No		World	ISSB3 (7)
High speed flat products, coated sheet and strip	By country, by product	tonnes	No		World	ISSB1 (-)
Hot rolled and cold rolled plate and sheet	By country, by product	tonnes	No		World	ISSB1 (-)
Hot rolled bars and flats in lengths	By country, by destination	tonnes	No		Selected countries	ISSB3 (4)
Hot rolled coils	By export, import, thickness	tonnes	Yes	A	World	WBMS4 (-)
Hot rolled light sections	By country, by destination	tonnes	No		World	ISSB3 (6)
Hot rolled plate	By export, import, thickness	tonnes	Yes	A	World	WBMS4 (-)
Hot rolled plate 3mm thick or more	By country, destination	tonnes	No		World	ISSB3 (11)
Hot rolled sheet up to 3mm thick	By country, by destination	tonnes	No		World	ISSB3 (12)
Hot rolled strip	By country, by destination	tonnes	No		World	ISSB3 (14)
Hot rolled strip	By export, import	tonnes	Yes	A	World	WBMS4 (-)
Hot rolled wide strip	By country, by destination	tonnes	No		World	ISSB3 (10)
Hot rolled wide strip and plate	By country, by product	tonnes	No		World	ISSB1 (-)
Ingots and semis	By country, by product	tonnes	No		World	ISSB1 (-)

5 COMMODITIES

Subject	Categories	Units	Time series Yes/No Frequency		Territorial coverage	Source (Table no.)
Ingots and semis	By production, imports, exports	tonnes	Yes	A	Developing countries	IISI3 (-)
Ingots, blooms and billets	By export, import	tonnes	Yes	A	World	WBMS4 (-)
Ingots, blooms, billets and slabs	By country, by destination	tonnes	No		World	ISSB3 (1)
Iron and steel	By production; exports; imports	tonnes	Yes	A	World	BGS2 (-)
Iron and steel basic industries	By product, total	tonnes	Yes	A	World	UN28 (-)
Iron and steel, importers and exporters, major	Net	tonnes	No		World	IISI5 (-)
Iron and steel, products	Exports; production	tonnes, %	Yes	A	World	IISI5 (-)
Iron and steel, trade by area	Exports; imports;	tonnes	No		World	IISI5 (-)
Iron ore	Apparent consumption	tonnes	No		World	IISI5 (-)
Iron ore	By production exports; imports	tonnes	Yes	A	World	BGS2 (-)
Iron ore	By production, imports	tonnes	Yes	A	Developing countries	IISI3 (-)
Iron ore	By production; quantity	tonnes	Yes	A	World	UNCTAD4 (3.3.1)
Iron ore	Quantity of exports and imports	tonnes	Yes	A	World	UNCTAD4 (3.3.5, 3.3.7)
Iron ore	Value of exports and imports	US$	Yes	A	World	UNCTAD4 (3.3.4, 3.3.6)
Iron ore exports, imports	By country, region	tonnes	Yes	A	World	IISI4 (21, 22)
Iron, scrap, ore and ferro alloys	By country, by product	tonnes	No		World	ISSB1 (-)
Long products	By product, imports, exports	tonnes	Yes	A	Developing countries	IISI3 (-)
Metals, non-ferrous	By product, total	tonnes	Yes	A	World	UN28 (-)
Mineral products, other non metallic	By product, total	units, metres tonnes	Yes	A	World	UN28 (-)
Otherwise worked	By export, import, type	tonnes	Yes	A	World	WBMS4 (-)
Pellets	By production, imports	tonnes	Yes	A	Developing countries	IISI3 (-)
Pig iron	Apparent consumption;	tonnes	Yes	A	World	ISII1 (-)
Pig iron	By production, imports	tonnes	Yes	A	Developing countries	IISI3 (-)
Pig iron exports, imports	By country, region	tonnes	Yes	A	World	IISI4 (18, 19)
Rails, sleepers, fishplates, sole-plates, points, switches, crossings etc	By country, by destination	tonnes	No		World	ISSB3 (9)
Railway tyres, wheels and axles	By country, by destination	tonnes	No		World	ISSB3 (26)
Scrap exports, imports	By country, region	tonnes	Yes	A	World	IISI4 (24, 25)
Scrap iron	Apparent domestic supply	tonnes	No		World	IISI5 (-)
Seamless tubes	By production, imports, exports	tonnes	Yes	A	Developing countries	IISI3 (-)
Sections	By country, by product	tonnes	No		World	ISSB1 (-)
Steel castings -unworked	By country, by destination	tonnes	No		World	ISSB3 (28)
Steel industry raw materials	By type	tonnes	Yes	A, Q	EC, USA, Canada and Japan	UN11 (4)
Steel products	By type	tonnes	Yes	A, Q	EC, USA, Canada and Japan	UN11 (4)
Steel products summary	By country, by product	tonnes	No		World	ISSB1 (-)
Steel products, ECSC	By country, by product	tonnes	No		World	ISSB1 (-)
Steel products, ECSC	By country, by year	tonnes	Yes	A	Selected countries	ISSB1 (-)
Steel products, total	By country, by destination	tonnes	No		World	ISSB3 (29)
Steel products, total	By country, by year	tonnes	Yes	A	Selected countries	ISSB1 (-)
Steel trade as percentage of world steel production	By crude steel equivalent, finished steel	tonnes, %	Yes	A	World	IISI4 (9)
Steel tube and pipe fittings	By country, by destination	tonnes	No		World	ISSB3 (23)

Subject	Categories	Units	Time series Yes/No Frequency		Territorial coverage	Source (Table no.)
Steel tubes and pipes - seamless	By country, by destination	tonnes	No		World	ISSB3 (21)
Steel tubes and pipes - welded	By country, by destination	tonnes	No		World	ISSB3 (22)
Steel, crude		tonnes	Yes	A	EC	EC53 (5.9)
Steel, crude	Imports, exports	tonnes	Yes	A	EC, USA and Japan	EC53 (1.13)
Steel, destinations	By country, by product	tonnes	No		World	ISSB3 (-)
Steel, exporting countries	By country, by product	tonnes	No		Selected countries	ISSB3 (-)
Steel, exports and imports of semi-finished and finished products	By country	tonnes	Yes	A	World	IISI4 (7, 8)
Steel, exports of semi-finished and finished products	By commodity and by region and country of destination, by total and by country	tonnes	No		EC	UN48 (4)
Steel, exports, imports	By country of origin, steel type	tonnes	No		World	WBMS4 (-)
Steel, finished rolled	By type	tonnes	No		EC	EC53 (5.11)
Steel, net trade and apparent consumption	By slab production, estimated deliveries imports, exports	tonnes	No		Western world	WBMS4 (-)
Steel, special	Non-alloy steel ingots, alloy steel ingots	tonnes	No		EC	EC53 (5.10)
Steel, total exports of semi-finished and finished products	By exporting country	tonnes, %	Yes	A	Selected countries	UN48 (1)
Steel, total exports of semi-finished and finished products	By region and country of destination	tonnes, %	Yes	A	Selected countries	UN48 (2)
Tinplate and TFS sheet and strip	By country, by destination	tonnes	No		World	ISSB3 (16)
Tubes	By country, by product	tonnes	No		World	ISSB1 (-)
Tubes and pipes	By export, import, type	tonnes	Yes	A	World	WBMS4 (-)
Tubes, forgings and cast products	By country, by product	tonnes	No		World	ISSB1 (-)
Welded tubes	By production, imports, exports	tonnes	Yes	A	Developing countries	IISI3 (-)
Wire	By export, import	tonnes	Yes	A	World	WBMS4 (-)
Wire rod	By export, import,	tonnes	Yes	A	World	WBMS4 (-)
Wire rod and other hot rolled bars	By country, by destination	tonnes	No		World	ISSB3 (3)
Wire rods, reinforcement, rails	By country, by product	tonnes	No		World	ISSB1 (-)
Worked flat products, other	By country, by destination	tonnes	No		World	ISSB3 (20)
Zinc coated sheet and strip, other	By country, by destination	tonnes	No		World	ISSB3 (17, 18)
Lead						
Lead		tonnes	Yes	A, M	EC, America Africa, Oceania	ILZSG1 (13)
Lead	Antimonial lead, ores, concentrates, lead bullion, refined lead	tonnes	Yes	A, M	Japan	ILZSG1 (20)
Lead	By production; exports; imports	tonnes	Yes	A	World	BGS2 (-)
Lead	Concentrates, refined lead	tonnes	Yes	A, Q	USSR	ILZSG1 (10)
Lead	Ores, concentrates refined lead	tonnes	Yes	A, M	Canada	ILZSG1 (16)
Lead	Ores, concentrates refined lead, lead bullion	tonnes	Yes	A, M	UK	ILZSG1 (23)
Lead	Ores, concentrates, lead bullion, refined lead	tonnes	Yes	A, M	Australia	ILZSG1 (15)

5 COMMODITIES

Subject	Categories	Units	Time series Yes/No Frequency		Territorial coverage	Source (Table no.)
Lead	Ores, concentrates, refined lead	tonnes	Yes	A, M	Italy	ILZSG1 (19)
Lead	Ores, concentrates, refined lead	tonnes	Yes	A, M	Peru	ILZSG1 (22)
Lead	Ores, concentrates, refined lead	tonnes	Yes	A, M	US	ILZSG1 (24)
Lead	Ores, concentrates, lead bullion, refined lead	tonnes	Yes	A, Q	Eastern Europe, Socialist countries	ILZSG1 (14)
Lead	Refined lead	tonnes	Yes	A, M	Mexico	ILZSG1 (21)
Lead	Refined lead, lead bullion	tonnes	Yes	A, M	France	ILZSG1 (17)
Lead metal	Quantity and value of exports and imports	tonnes, US$	Yes	A	World	UNCTAD4 (3.4.5, 3.4.6)
Lead metal, primary	By consumption	tonnes	Yes	A	World	UNCTAD4 (3.4.7)
Lead metal, primary	By production	tonnes	Yes	A	World	UNCTAD4 (3.4.4)
Lead ore	Quantity and value of exports and imports	tonnes, US$	Yes	A	World	UNCTAD4 (4.2, 3.4.3)
Lead, ores and concentrates		tonnes	Yes	A, M	EC, Africa America, Oceania	ILZSG1 (12)
Lead, refined	Ores, concentrates, lead bullion, refined lead	tonnes	Yes	A, M	Germany	ILZSG1 (18)
Minerals and Chemicals						
Alumina	By production, exports; imports	tonnes	Yes	A	World	BGS2 (-)
Alumina	Quantity and value of exports and imports	tonnes, US$	Yes	A	World	UNCTAD4 (3.1.7, 3.1.8)
Alumina, bauxite and aluminium	By production, exports, imports, type, country	tonnes	Yes	A	World	BGS1 (-)
Aluminium	By production, exports; imports	tonnes	Yes	A	World	BGS2 (-)
Aluminium	Quantity and value of exports and imports	tonnes, US$	Yes	A	World	UNCTAD4 (3.1.10,3.1.11)
Ammonia, synthetic		tonnes	Yes	A	EC	EC53 (5.19)
Antimony	By production, exports; imports	tonnes	Yes	A	World	BGS2 (-)
Arsenic	By production, exports; imports	tonnes	Yes	A	World	BGS2 (-)
Asbestos	By production, exports, imports of unmanufactured asbestos by country	tonnes	Yes	A	World	BGS1 (-)
Barytes	By production, exports, imports, by country	tonnes	Yes	A	World	BGS1 (-)
Bauxite	By production exports; imports	tonnes	Yes	A	World	BGS2 (-)
Bentonite and Fullers earth	By production, exports, imports, type, country	tonnes	Yes	A	World	BGS1 (-)
Beryl	By production, country	tonnes	Yes	A	World	BGS1 (-)
Bismuth	By production exports; imports	tonnes	Yes	A	World	BGS2 (-)
Borates	By production, country	tonnes	Yes	A	World	BGS1 (-)
Bromine	By production, exports, imports, country	kg	Yes	A	World	BGS1 (-)
Butadiene		tonnes	Yes	A	EC	EC53 (5.13)
Cadmium	By production exports; imports	tonnes	Yes	A	World	BGS2 (-)
Cement		tonnes	Yes	A	EC	EC53 (5.12)

Subject	Categories	Units	Time series Yes/No Frequency		Territorial coverage	Source (Table no.)
Chemical products	By SITC Section, by countries of origin, destination with world countries	US$	No		World	UN12
Chemical products, total	By countries of origin, destination with world countries	US$	No		World	UN12
Chemicals and chemical products	By product, total	tonnes	Yes	A	World	UN28 (-)
Chlorine		tonnes	Yes	A	EC	EC53 (5.20)
Chromium	By production exports; imports	tonnes	Yes	A	World	BGS2 (-)
Chromium ores and concentrates	By production, exports, imports, by country by type	tonnes	Yes	A	World	BGS1 (-)
Coal	By production exports; imports	tonnes	Yes	A	World	BGS2 (-)
Cobalt	By production exports; imports	tonnes	Yes	A	World	BGS2 (-)
Commodity exports, direction of	By origin and destination; total minerals and ores	%	Yes	2 yrly	World	UNCTAD4 (1.28)
Commodity exports, direction of	By origin and destination; total mineral fuels	%	Yes	2 yrly	World	UNCTAD4 (1.29)
Copper	By production exports; imports	tonnes	Yes	A	World	BGS2 (-)
Copper ore	Quantity and value of exports and imports	tonnes; US$	Yes	A	World	UNCTAD4 (3.2.2, 3.2.3)
Copper, unrefined	By production	tonnes	Yes	A	World	UNCTAD4 (3.2.4)
Copper, unrefined	Quantity and value of exports and imports	tonnes, US$	Yes	A	World	UNCTAD4 (3.2.50, 3.2.6)
Diamond	By production, exports, imports, by type, country	carats	Yes	A	World	BGS1 (-)
Diatomite	By production, exports, imports, country	tonnes	Yes	A	World	BGS1 (-)
Ethylene		tonnes	Yes	A	EC	EC53 (5.15)
Feldspar	By production, exports, imports, country	tonnes	Yes	A	World	BGS1 (-)
Ferro-alloys	By production exports; imports	tonnes	Yes	A	World	BGS2 (-)
Ferromanganese	Quantity and value of exports and imports	tonnes, US$	Yes	A	World	UNCTAD4 (3.5.5, 3.5.6)
Fluorspar	By production, exports, imports, country	tonnes	Yes	A	World	BGS1 (-)
Formaldehyde		tonnes	Yes	A	EC	EC53 (5.18)
Germanium	By production exports; imports	tonnes	Yes	A	World	BGS2 (-)
Gold	By production; exports; imports	kg	Yes	A	World	BGS2 (-)
Graphite	By production, exports, imports, country	tonnes	Yes	A	World	BGS1 (-)
Gypsum	By production, exports, imports, type, country	tonnes	Yes	A	World	BGS1 (-)
Iodine	By production, exports, imports, country	kg	Yes	A	World	BGS1 (-)
Kaolin	By production, exports, imports, country	tonnes	Yes	A	World	BGS1 (-)
Lithium	By production; exports; imports	tonnes	Yes	A	World	BGS2 (-)

5 COMMODITIES

Subject	Categories	Units	Time series Yes/No Frequency	Territorial coverage	Source (Table no.)
Lithium minerals	By production, exports, imports, type, country	tonnes	Yes A	World	BGS1 (-)
Magnesite	By production	tonnes	Yes A	World	BGS1 (-)
Magnesite and magnesia	By exports, imports, by type, by country	tonnes	Yes A	World	BGS1 (-)
Magnesium	By production; exports; imports	tonnes	Yes A	World	BGS2 (-)
Manganese ore	Quantity and value of exports and imports	tonnes, US$	Yes A	World	UNCTAD4 (3.5.2, 3.5.3)
Mercury	By production; exports; imports	kg	Yes A	World	BGS2 (-)
Mica	By production, imports, exports, type, country	tonnes	Yes A	World	BGS1 (-)
Molybdenum	By production; exports; imports	tonnes	Yes A	World	BGS2 (-)
Nepheline syenite	By production, country	tonnes	Yes A	World	BGS1 (-)
Nickel	By production; exports; imports	tonnes	Yes A	World	BGS2 (-)
Nickel ore	Quantity and value of exports and imports	tonnes, US$	Yes A	World	UNCTAD4 (3.6.2, 3.6.3)
Nickel, intermediate products	Quantity and value of exports and imports	tonnes,US$	Yes A	World	UNCTAD4 (3.6.5, 3.6.6)
Nickel, unwrought	Quantity and value of exports and imports	tonnes, US$	Yes A	World	UNCTAD4 (3.6.7, 3.6.8)
Niobium	By production; exports; imports	tonnes	Yes A	World	BGS2 (-)
Perlite	By production, country	tonnes	Yes A	World	BGS1 (-)
Phosphate rock	By production, exports, imports, country	tonnes	Yes A	World	BGS1 (-)
Phosphate rock	Quantity and value of exports and imports	tonnes, US$	Yes A	World	UNCTAD4 (3.7.2, 3.7.3)
Platinum	By production; exports; imports	kg	Yes A	World	BGS2 (-)
Polyethylene		tonnes	Yes A	EC	EC53 (5.17)
Potash	By production, exports, imports, type, country	tonnes	Yes A	World	BGS1 (-)
Propylene		tonnes	Yes A	EC	EC53 (5.14)
Rare earth minerals	By production, type, exports, imports, country	tonnes	Yes A	World	BGS1 (-)
Rare earths	By production; exports; imports	tonnes	Yes A	World	BGS2 (-)
Rubber, synthetic		tonnes	Yes A	EC	EC53 (5.16)
Salt	By production, type, exports, imports, country	tonnes	Yes A	World	BGS1 (-)
Selenium	By production; exports; imports	tonnes	Yes A	World	BGS2 (-)
Sillimanite	By production, exports, imports, type, country	tonnes	Yes A	World	BGS1 (-)
Silver	By production; exports; imports	kg	Yes A	World	BGS2 (-)
Strontium minerals	By production, country	tonnes	Yes A	World	BGS1 (-)
Sulphur	Quantity and value of exports and imports	tonnes, US$	Yes A	World	UNCTAD4 (3.8.2, 3.8.3)
Sulphur and pyrites	By production, type, exports, imports, country, (sulphur content)	tonnes	Yes A	World	BGS1 (-)
Sulphuric acid		tonnes	Yes A	EC	EC53 (5.21)
Talc	By production, type, exports, imports, country	tonnes	Yes A	World	BGS1 (-)
Tantalum	By production; exports; imports	tonnes	Yes A	World	BGS2 (-)

Subject	Categories	Units	Time series Yes/No Frequency		Territorial coverage	Source (Table no.)
Tellurium	By production; exports; imports	tonnes	Yes	A	World	BGS2 (-)
Tin	By production; exports; imports	tonnes	Yes	A	World	BGS2 (-)
Tin metal	Quantity and value of exports and imports	tonnes, US$	Yes	A	World	UNCTAD4 (3.9.6, 3.9.7)
Tin metal, secondary	By production	tonnes	Yes	A	World	UNCTAD4 (3.9.5)
Tin ore	Quantity and value of exports and imports	tonnes, US$	Yes	A	World	UNCTAD4 (3.9.2, 3.9.3)
Titanium	By production; exports; imports	tonnes	Yes	A	World	BGS2 (-)
Titanium materials	By production, type, exports, imports, country	tonnes	Yes	A	World	BGS1 (-)
Tungsten	By production; exports; imports	tonnes	Yes	A	World	BGS2 (-)
Tungsten ore	By production	tonnes	Yes	A	World	UNCTAD4 (3.10.1)
Tungsten ore	Quantity and value of exports and imports	tonnes, US$	Yes	A	World	UNCTAD4 (3.10.2, 3.10.3)
Uranium	By production; exports; imports	tonnes	Yes	A	World	BGS2 (-)
Vanadium	By production; exports; imports	tonnes	Yes	A	World	BGS2 (-)
Vermiculite	By production, country	tonnes	Yes	A	World	BGS1 (-)
Wollastonite	By production, country	tonnes	Yes	A	World	BGS1 (-)
Zirconium minerals	By production, type, exports, imports, country	tonnes	Yes	A	World	BGS1 (-)
Zinc						
Zinc		tonnes	Yes	A, M	World	ILZSG1 (38)
Zinc	By production; exports; imports	tonnes	Yes	A	World	BGS2 (-)
Zinc	Concentrates, slab zinc	tonnes	Yes	A, Q	Eastern Europe Socialist countries	
Zinc	Ores, concentrates, refined zinc	tonnes	Yes	A, M	Australia	ILZSG1 (40)
Zinc	Ores, concentrates, refined zinc	tonnes	Yes	A, M	Canada	ILZSG1 (41)
Zinc	Ores, concentrates, refined zinc	tonnes	Yes	A, M	France	ILZSG1 (42)
Zinc	Ores, concentrates, refined zinc	tonnes	Yes	A, M	Germany	ILZSG1 (43)
Zinc	Ores, concentrates, refined zinc	tonnes	Yes	A, M	Mexico	ILZSG1 (46)
Zinc	Ores, concentrates, refined zinc	tonnes	Yes	A, M	Peru	ILZSG1 (47)
Zinc	Ores, concentrates, refined zinc	tonnes	Yes	A, M	US	ILZSG1 (49)
Zinc	Ores, concentrates, refined zinc	tonnes	Yes	A, Q	Eastern Europe, Socialist countries	ILZSG1 (39)
Zinc	Refined zinc	tonnes	Yes	A, M	Italy	ILZSG1 (44)
Zinc	Refined zinc	tonnes	Yes	A, M	Japan	ILZSG1 (45)
Zinc	Zinc alloys, refined zinc	tonnes	Yes	A, M	UK	ILZSG1 (48)
Zinc, ores and concentrates		tonnes	Yes	A, M	World	ILZSG1 (37)
Zinc, refined		tonnes	Yes	A, Q	USSR	ILZSG1 (35)

5 COMMODITIES

Subject	Categories	Units	Time series Yes/No Frequency		Territorial coverage	Source (Table no.)
5.2.7 Mining and Oil - see also Sections 17 and 33						
Bauxite	By production, quantity	tonnes	Yes	A	World	UNCTAD4 (3.1.1)
Bauxite	Quantity of exports and imports	tonnes	Yes	A	World	UNCTAD4 (3.1.3, 3.1.5)
Bauxite	Value of exports and imports	US$	Yes	A	World	UNCTAD4 (3.1.2, 3.1.4)
Coal	By type, total	tonnes	Yes	A	World	UN28 (-)
Ferrous and non-ferrous metal ores	By type, total	tonnes, kilogrammes	Yes	A	World	UN28 (-)
Non-metallic minerals and fertilizers	By type, total	tonnes, cu m, carats	Yes	A	World	UN28 (-)
Petroleum and natural gas	Total	tonnes	Yes	A	World	UN28 (-)
Petroleum and coal	By product, total	tonnes, metres, terajoules, units	Yes	A	World	UN28 (-)
5.2.8 Textiles, Clothing, Leather and Footwear						
Abaca	Quantity and value of exports and imports	tonnes, US$	Yes	A	World	UNCTAD4 (2.33.9, 2.33.10)
Carpets, total		sq m	Yes	A	EC	EC53 (5.48)
Cotton		bales	Yes	A	World	ICAC2 (pp22-23)
Cotton		bales	Yes	A	World	ICAC2 (pp24-25)
Cotton	By country	tonnes	Yes	A	World	ICAC2 (pp101-156)
Cotton	By country	tonnes	Yes	A	World	ICAC2 (pp101-156)
Cotton	Quantity and value of exports and imports	tonnes, US$	Yes	A	World	UNCTAD4 (2.31.4, 2.31.5)
Cotton	Commitments for	tonnes	No		World	ICAC1 (p6)
Cotton (total)		tonnes	Yes	A	E. Asia, EC, China, E.Europe, CIS	ICAC1 (p2)
Cotton (total)		tonnes	Yes	A	US, CIS, India Francophone Africa, Australia, China Pakistan	ICAC1 (p2)
Cotton and cotton yarn	Value of exports and imports	US$	Yes	A	World	UNCTAD4 (2.31.1, 2.31.2)
Cotton fabric		tonnes	Yes	A	World	ICAC2 (pp74-75)
Cotton fabric		tonnes	Yes	A	World	ICAC2 (pp76-77)
Cotton yarn		tonnes	Yes	A	World	ICAC2 (pp68-69)
Cotton yarn		tonnes	Yes	A	World	ICAC2 (pp70-71)
Cotton yarn	Quantity of exports and imports	tonnes	Yes	A	World	UNCTAD4 (2.31.7, 2.31.8)
Fabrics. total		tonnes	Yes	A	EC	EC53 (5.46)
Hard fibres and hard fibres manufactures	Value of exports and imports	US$	Yes	A	World	UNCTAD4 (2.33.1, 2.33.2)
Hard fibres manufactures	Quantity of exports and imports	tonnes	Yes	A	World	UNCTAD4 (2.33.3, 2.33.4)
Jute	By consumption	tonnes	Yes	A	World	UNCTAD4 (2.32.9)
Jute and jute products	Value of exports and imports	US$	Yes	A	World	UNCTAD4 (2.32.1, 2.32.2)
Jute products	Quantity of exports and imports	tonnes	Yes	A	World	UNCTAD4 (2.32.7, 2.32.8)
Knitted or crocheted fabric		tonnes	Yes	A	EC	EC53 (5.47)
Leather and leather products	By product, total	tonnes, metres, pairs	Yes	A	World	UN28 (-)
Sisal	Quantity and value of exports and imports	tonnes, US$	Yes	A	World	UNCTAD4 (2.33.6, 2.33.7)
Textile fibres, natural	Value of exports and imports	US$	Yes	A	World	UNCTAD4 (2.30.1, 2.30.2)
Textiles	By product, total	tonnes, metres	Yes	A	World	UN28 (-)

Subject	Categories	Units	Time series Yes/No	Frequency	Territorial coverage	Source (Table no.)
Wearing apparel	By product, total	pairs, units, metres, tonnes	Yes	A	World	UN28 (-)
Wool, grower country	By wool type; raw wool destination	kg	No		World	IWS1 (6)
Wool, virgin	By actual weight	kg	Yes	A	World	IWS1 (7)
Wool, virgin	Share held by main producers	%	Yes	A	World	IWS1 (8)
Wool, virgin	By actual weight	kg	Yes	A	World	IWS1 (9)
Wool, clean dry-combed; c.i.f.; London	Monthly average prices	UK pence/kg	Yes	A	World	IWS1 (12)
Wool, greasy	By average price	nat curr per kg	Yes	A	Australia; New Zealand; South Africa	IWS1 (11)
Wool, virgin	Share held by main producers	%	Yes	A	World	IWS1 (10)
Wool, total	Value of exports and imports	US$	Yes	A	World	UNCTAD4 (2.34.2, 2.34.3)
Wool, greasy and degreased	Quantity of exports and imports	tonnes	Yes	A	World	UNCTAD4 (2.34.4, 2.34.5)
Wool and hair tops (including slivers)	By imports and exports	kg	Yes	A	World	IWS1 (18)
Wool woven fabrics	Imports and exports	kg	Yes	A	World	IWS1 (24)
Woollen yarns (worsted and woollen)	Imports and exports	kg	Yes	A	World	IWS1 (21)
Yarn		tonnes	Yes	A	EC	EC53 (5.45)
5.2.9 Wood and Forestry Products - see also Section 21						
Paper, board and pulp	By production, imports, exports	tonnes	Yes	A	World	PPI1 (-)
Paper and board		tonne	Yes	A	EC	EC53 (5.51)
Paper and paper products	By product, total	tonnes, metres	Yes	A	World	UN28 (-)
Particle board		cu m	Yes	A	EC	EC53 (5.49)
Pulp for paper and board		tonnes dried	Yes	A	EC	EC53 (5.50)
Roundwood, non-coniferous industrial	By production	cu m	Yes	A	World	UNCTAD4 (2.29.1)
Wood, non-coniferous	Quantity and value of exports and imports	cu m, US$	Yes	A	World	UNCTAD4 (2.29.2, 2.29.3)
Wood and wood products	By product, total	metres, units, tonnes	Yes	A	World	UN28 (-)
5.3 PRICES - see also Section 37						
5.3.1 Agricultural Commodities - see also Section 2						
Cereals	All varieties	ECU, t	Yes	M, Q	EC	EC3 (-)
Cocoa beans, prices of international significance	London Terminal Market New York Coffee, Sugar and Cocoa Exchange	£/tonne, USc/lb	Yes	A, M	World	ICC02 (17)
Cocoa beans	Daily and indicator prices	SDRs/tonne, USc/lb	Yes	A, M	World	ICC02 (15)
Cocoa beans	Daily and indicator prices by average, highest, lowest	sdrs, tonne US cents, lb	No		World	ICC01 (8)
Cocoa beans	Daily prices	USc/lb	Yes	A, M	World	ICC02 (16)
Commodities - market price and raw material price indices	By commodity	indices	Yes	A, M	World	ISL2 (2.3.26)
Commodity prices	By commodity	lbs, US$, tonne, kg	Yes	A, M	World	ISL2 (2.3.27)
Milk product levies		ECU, kg	Yes	M, Q	EC	EC3 (-)
Natural rubber prices		nat curr	Yes	M	Major cities	IRSG1 (44)
		nat curr	Yes	A	Major cities	IRSG2 (35)
Olive oil	All types	ECU, kg	Yes	M, Q	EC	EC3 (-)
Primary commodities, free market prices and price indices		indices, US$ per metric ton	Yes	A	World	UNCTAD4 (A.1)

5 COMMODITIES

Subject	Categories	Units	Time series Yes/No Frequency		Territorial coverage	Source (Table no.)
Primary commodities, instability indices and trends in monthly market prices	By commodity	%	No		World	UNCTAD4 R(A.2)
Rice	All varieties	ECU, t	Yes	M, Q	EC	EC3 (-)
Rubber, natural		nat curr/ tonne	Yes	A	World	IRSG2 (14)
Rubber, natural	By grade	nat curr/ tonne	Yes	A, M	New York, London Tokyo, Kuala Lumpur Singapore	IRSG1 (44)
Rubber, natural		£ or $/tonne	Yes	A	London, New York	IRSG2 (25)
Rubber, synthetic		nat curr/ tonne	Yes	A	World	IRSG2 (20)
Rubber, synthetic	By type	nat curr/ tonne	Yes	A,, Q	UK, Germany, Italy	IRSG1 (45)
Rubber, SBR export values		nat curr/ tonne	Yes	A, M	USA, France, UK Germany, Japan, Republic of Korea Taiwan	IRSG1 (43)
Rubber, natural prices - INRO daily market indicator	Daily high, low, monthly average	Singapore cents	Yes	M	Malaysia	IRSG2 (36)
Rubber, synthetic, prices		Singapore cents	Yes	Q	Major countries	IRSG1 (45)
		Singapore cents	Yes	A	Major countries	IRSG2 (37)
Rubber, synthetic, export values		Singapore cents	Yes	M	Major countries	IRSG1 (43)
		Singapore cents	Yes	A	Major countries	IRSG2 (38)
Rubber, natural prices		nat curr	Yes	A	London, New York	IRSG2 (46)
Sugar, daily spot prices and selected economic indicators	By sugar type, differentials	US cents per lb, %, SDRs/US$, indices	Yes	A, M	World	ISO1 (-)
Sugar, ISA daily price	By monthly averages	US cents per lb	Yes	A, M	World	ISO1 (-)
Sugar, free market daily spot prices	By monthly averages, sugar type	US cents per lb fob	Yes	A, M	World	ISO1 (-)
Sugar, prices, daily spot	By highest, lowest ISA	tonnes	Yes	D	London, New York,	ISO2 (-)
Sugar, prices	By London, New York and ISA daily price monthly averages	£ tonnes, US cents, US$	Yes	A,D, M	World	ISO3 (-)
Sugar, prices of white refined	By country and locality wholesale and retail	US cents	Yes	A	Selected countries	ISO3 (-)
Sugar levies	Dry, syrup	ECU, kg	Yes	M	EC	EC3 (-)
Wine	All types	ECU, %vol, hl	Yes	M, Q	EC	EC3 (-)
5.3.2 Meat and Livestock Products						
Beef	Live adult bovine	ECU/kg	Yes	M, Q	EC	EC3 (-)
Bovine animal levies	Live	ECU/kg	Yes	M	EC	EC3 (-)
Calves	Live	ECU/kg	Yes	M, Q	EC	EC3 (-)
Eggs	Gate prices	ECU/kg	Yes	M, Q	EC	EC3 (-)
Pork	Pigs, cuts, piglets	ECU/kg pab	Yes	M, Q	EC	EC3 (-)
Poultry	Gate prices	ECU/kg	Yes	Q, M	EC	EC3 (-)
Sheep	Lambs	ECU/kg/pab	Yes	M, Q	EC	EC3 (-)
5.3.3 Metals, Ores, Minerals and Chemicals						
Ferrous metals, spot prices, small	By country, by product	nat curr	No		World	MB1 (-)
Ferrous metals, merchants' buying price,	By country, by type	nat curr	No		World	MB1 (-)
Iron ore	By country	nat curr	No		World	MB1 (-)
Lead, refined	London Metal Exchange LME prices, COMEX daily MB international quotation	£/tonne	Yes	A, M	London, USA	ILZSG1 (4)

Subject	Categories	Units	Time series Yes/No	Frequency	Territorial coverage	Source (Table no.)
Non-ferrous metals prices	By country, by metal prices, Chicago buying price	nat curr USc/lb	No		World	MB1 (-)
Zinc	London Metal Exchange	US$/tonne	Yes	A, M	London, USA	ILZSG1 (29)

5.3.4 Textiles, Clothing and Footwear

Subject	Categories	Units	Time series Yes/No	Frequency	Territorial coverage	Source (Table no.)
Cotton	Changes in consumer prices	%	Yes	A	World	ICAC2 (p79)
Cotton	Changes in domestic product	%	Yes	A	World	ICAC2 (p78)
Cotton (New York futures)		USc/lb	Yes	A	New York	ICAC2 (pp61-63)
Cotton (North Europe)		USc/lb nat curr/lb	Yes	A, M	World Japan, Germany	ICAC2 (pp56-59)
Polyester		nat curr/kg	Yes	M	US, Taiwan, Italy	ICAC2 (p60)

5.4 PRODUCTION - see also under Consumption (5.1), International Trade (5.2) and Section 38

5.4.1 Agricultural Commodities - see also Section 2

Subject	Categories	Units	Time series Yes/No	Frequency	Territorial coverage	Source (Table no.)
Age-specific yield of immature cocoa trees	By year of bearing, mature yield	years, %	No		World	ICCO3 (3)
Agricultural commodities	By commodity, principal developing	tonnes; units; pairs, cu	No		Principal Developing	UNCTAD4 (A.4)
Animal feedstuffs		tonnes	Yes	A	EC	EC6 (ID17)
Bananas	By production	tonnes	Yes	A	World	UNCTAD4 (2.8.1)
Bananas	Consumption, apparent	tonnes	Yes	A	World	UNCTAD4 (2.8.4)
Barley		tonnes	Yes	A	EC	EC6 (ID 7)
Beef and veal	Net	indices, tonnes	Yes	A, M	EC	EC36
Beer	By countries	nos	No		The Americas and Australasia	MAC2 (E21)
Beer	By country	ha	Yes	A	Africa and Asia	MAC1 (E27)
Butter, stocks	Average	indices, tonnes	Yes	A, M	EC	EC36
Butter, dairy		indices, tonnes	Yes	A, M	EC	EC36
Cassava	Area harvested, production	ha, tonnes	Yes	A	World, ASEAN	ASEANS1 (3.4.7) (3.4.8)
Cereals	Total	tonnes	Yes	A	EC	EC6 (ID 4)
Citrus fruit		tonnes	Yes	A	EC	EC6 (ID15)
Coarse grains, production and trade	By country, destination	tonnes	Yes	A	World	ISL2 (2.3.17.3-4)
Cocoa, ICCO members share in production grindings, exports, imports	By agreements, average	tonnes, %	No		ICCO	ICC01 (9)
Cocoa, quality of buffer stocks	By total, % defective	tonnes, %	No		World	ICC01 (2)
Cocoa, net warrant tonnage	By crop-year, by country	tonnes	Yes	A	World	ICC01 (3)
Cocoa, world production	By continent, country	tonnes, %	Yes	A	World	ICC01 (4)
Cocoa, projected production	By country of origin	tonnes	No		World	ICCO3 (13)
Cocoa, annual plantings of cocoa and total tree-stock	By producing country, by type of tree-stock	ha	No		World	ICCO3 (15)
Cocoa, equivalent mature areas and yields	By producing country, by type of tree-stock	ha, kg/ha	No		World	ICCO3 (16)
Cocoa	Area harvested, production	ha, tonnes	Yes	A	World, ASEAN	ASEANS1 (3.4.17) (3.4.18)
Cocoa (beans), production and trade	By country	tonnes, %	Yes	A	World	ISL2 (2.3.23)
Cocoa areas and production	By area, yields, production, by country	ha, kg/ha, tonnes	Yes		World	ICCO3 (5)

5 COMMODITIES

Subject	Categories	Units	Time series Yes/No	Frequency	Territorial coverage	Source (Table no.)
Cocoa Beans, summary data	Gross crop, grindings surplus, deficit, end of season stocks, buffer stocks, price	tonnes, %, US$, tonne, SDRs, tonne	Yes	A	World	ICC02 (1)
Cocoa beans, grindings	By country	tonnes	Yes	A, Q	World	ICC02 (3)
Cocoa beans	by country	tonnes	Yes	A	World	ICC02 (2)
Coffee	Area harvested, production	ha, tonnes	Yes	A	World, ASEAN	ASEANS1 (3.4.20) (3.4.21)
Coffee	By consumption	bags	Yes	A	World	UNCTAD4 (2.11.4)
Coffee	By production	tonnes	Yes	A	World	UNCTAD4 (2.11.1)
Coffee (green), production and trade	By country	tonnes, %	Yes	A	World	ISL2 (2.3.21)
Copra		tonnes	Yes	A	World, ASEAN	ASEANS1 (3.4.19)
Copra	By production	tonnes	Yes	A	World	UNCTAD4 (2.21.1)
Cotton	Area harvested, production	ha, tonnes	Yes	A	World, ASEAN	ASEANS1 (3.4.22) (3.4.23)
Fresh fruit (excluding citrus)		tonnes	Yes	A	EC	EC6 (ID14)
Groundnut	Area harvested, production	ha, tonnes	Yes	A	World, ASEAN	ASEANS1 (3.4.13) (3.4.14)
Groundnuts in shell	By production	tonnes	Yes	A	World	UNCTAD4 (2.17.1)
Harvested crops, vegetables	By production	hectares	Yes	A	EC	EC6 (ID 2)
Harvested crops, fruit	By production	hectares	Yes	A	EC	EC6 (ID 3)
Harvested crops (excluding fruit and vegetables)	By production	hectares	Yes	A	EC	EC6 (ID 1)
Maize		tonnes	Yes	A	EC	EC6 (ID 8)
Maize	Area harvested, production	ha, tonnes	Yes	A	World, ASEAN	ASEANS1 (3.4.3) (3.4.4)
Natural Rubber,1900-45	Production, stocks	tonnes	Yes	A	World	IRSG2 (45)
		tonnes	Yes	A	World	IRSG2 (45)
Oil cake	Total	tonnes	Yes	A	EC	EC6 (ID11)
Oil palm	Area harvested, production	ha, tonnes	Yes	A	World, ASEAN	ASEANS1 (3.4.24) (3.4.25)
Oilseed and oleaginous fruit	Total	tonnes	Yes	A	EC	EC6 (ID10)
Palm kernels	By production	tonnes	Yes	A	World	UNCTAD4 (2.23.1)
Palm oil	By production	tonnes	Yes	A	World	UNCTAD4 (2.25.1)
Pepper	Area harvested, production	ha, tonnes	Yes	A	World, ASEAN	ASEANS1 (3.4.26) (3.4.27)
Potatoes		tonnes	Yes	A	EC	EC6 (ID 9)
Potatoes	Area harvested, production	ha, tonnes	Yes	A	World, ASEAN	ASEANS1 (3.4.9) (3.4.10)
	production	tonnes				(3.4.30)
Rice, production and trade	By country	tonnes	Yes	A	World	ISL2 (2.3.18)
Rice	Area harvested, production	ha, tonnes	Yes	A	World, ASEAN	ASEANS1 (3.4.1), (3.4.2)
Rubber, natural	Production, stocks	tonnes	Yes	A, M	World	IRSG1 (1)
Rubber, natural,		tonnes	Yes	A, M	World	IRSG1 (14)
Rubber, natural		tonnes	Yes	A, M	World	IRSG1 (13)
Rubber, natural		tonnes	Yes	A	World	IRSG2 (10)

Subject	Categories	Units	Time series Yes/No Frequency	Territorial coverage	Source (Table no.)
Rubber, natural	Production, stocks	tonnes	Yes A	World	IRSG2 (25)
Rubber, natural	Production, stocks	tonnes	Yes A	World	IRSG2 (1)
Rubber, natural in producing countries		tonnes	Yes A	World	IRSG2 (11)
Rubber, synthetic	Production, stocks	tonnes	Yes A	World	IRSG2 (2)
Rubber, natural and synthetic		tonnes	Yes A	World	IRSG2 (3)
Rubber, natural and synthetic		tonnes	Yes A, M	World	IRSG1 (3)
Rubber, synthetic		%	Yes A, M	World	IRSG1 (4)
Rubber, synthetic		%	Yes A	World	IRSG2 (4)
Rubber, synthetic		tonnes	Yes A	World	IRSG2 (18)
Rubber, synthetic	Production, stocks	tonnes	Yes A, M	World	IRSG1 (2)
Rubber, synthetic		tonnes	Yes A, M	World	IRSG1 (28)
Rubber, natural		tonnes	Yes A, M	World	IRSG1 (7)
Rubber, area under plantation	Estates, smallholdings	ha	No	World	IRSG1 (46)
Rubber, natural	By country	tonnes	Yes A	World	IRSG2 (7)
Rubber, synthetic		tonnes	Yes A	World	IRSG2 (15)
Rubber, synthetic		tonnes	Yes A, M	World	IRSG1 (24)
Rubber, technically specified		tonnes	Yes A, M	World	IRSG1 (8)
Rubber, natural and synthetic	By production	tonnes	Yes A	World	ISL2 (2.3.12.1-2)
Rubber, natural		tonnes	Yes A, M	World	UN35 (9)
Rubber, production, 1946-60	Natural synthetics	tonnes	Yes A	World	IRSG2 (47)
Rubber, areas under plantation		ha	No	Various countries	IRSG1 (46)
		ha	No	Various countries	IRSG2 (18)
Rubber, synthetic rubber	By area and by type	tonnes	Yes A	World	IISRP1 (5,6)
	By producer	tonnes	No	World	IISRP1 (32)
Rubber, synthetic	By area	tonnes	Yes A	World	IISRP1 (30)
Rubber, synthetic	By type	tonnes	Yes A	World	IISRP1 (31,33)
Rubber, synthetic	By type	tonnes	No	World	IISRP1 (34-46)
Rubber, synthetic	Production, by type	tonnes	No	World	IISRP1 (32,34)
Rubber, multi-purpose plants	Capacity	tonnes	No	World	IISRP1 (47)
Rubber, proposed facilities	Capacity	tonnes	No	World	IISRP1 (48)
Rubber	Area harvested, production	ha, tonnes	Yes A	World, ASEAN	ASEANS1 (3.4.28) (3.4.29)
Rubber	By major sector	tonnes	Yes A	World	IRSG2 (5)
Rubber		tonnes	Yes M	Asia and Pacific	UN43(-)
Rubber	By type capacities	metric tons	No	World	IRSG1 (47)
Rubber	By type	metric tons	No	World	IRSG2 (24)
Rubber	By type of rubber	tonnes	No	USA	IRSG1 (29)
				Brazil	IRSG1 (30)
				France	IRSG1 (31)
				Germany	IRSG1 (32)
				UK	IRSG1 (33)
				Australia	IRSG1 (34)
				India	IRSG1 (35)
				Japan	IRSG1 (36)
Rubber	Latex, total	tonnes	Yes A, M	Malaysia, peninsular	IRSG1 (16)
				Indonesia	IRSG1 (18)
				Thailand	IRSG1 (19)
				Sri Lanka	IRSG1 (20)
Rubber goods, indices of production		indices	Yes A, M	USA, France, UK Germany, Japan, Italy	IRSG1 (42)
Rubber industry: growth rates	Type of rubber	tonnes, %	Yes A	World	IISRP1 (-)
Sorghum	Area harvested, production	ha, tonnes	Yes A	World, ASEAN	ASEANS1 (3.4.5) (3.4.6)
Soybean, production and trade	By country	tonnes, %	Yes A	World	ISL2 (2.3.19.1)
Soybeans	Area harvested, production	ha, tonnes	Yes A	World, ASEAN	ASEANS1 (3.4.15) (3.4.16)

5 COMMODITIES

Subject	Categories	Units	Time series Yes/No Frequency		Territorial coverage	Source (Table no.)
Soybeans	By production	tonnes	Yes	A	World	UNCTAD4 (2.19.1)
Sugar		tonnes	Yes	A	EC	EC6 (ID12)
Sugar		tonnes	Yes	M	Asia and Pacific	UN43 (-)
Sugar	By production, consumption end year stocks, exports imports,net exports and imports, free market net imports and exports, per caput consumption, ISA daily price	tonnes, kgs, cents per lb	Yes	A	World	ISO3 (-)
Sugar, estimates of production and consumption	By producer, surplus,	tonnes	No		World	ISO1 (-)
Sugar, evolution of the sugar economy	By country, production consumption, exports, imports, net trade	tonnes	Yes	A	New York, London Paris	ISO1 (-)
Sugar, beginning stock			No		World	ISO1 (-)
Sugar, production			No		World	ISO1 (-)
Sugar, production	By country	tonnes	Yes	A, M	World	ISO2 (-)
Sugar, production	By imports, exports, consumption, stocks,	tonnes	Yes	A	World	ISO3 (-)
Sugar, production	By sugar type, country	tonnes	Yes	A	World	ISO3 (-)
Sugar (centrifugal and raw), production and trade	By country	tonnes, %	Yes	A	World	ISL2 (2.3.20)
Sugar beet cultivation	By number of growers, acreage planted	nos, ha	Yes	A	World	ISO1 (1)
Sugar cane	Area harvested,	ha,	Yes	A	World, ASEAN	ASEANS1
Sweet potatoes	Area harvested, production	ha, tonnes	Yes	A	World, ASEAN	ASEANS1 (3.4.11) (3.4.12)
Synthetic		tonnes	Yes	A, M	World	UN35 (31)
Tea, production and trade	By country	tonnes, %	Yes	A	World	ISL2 (2.3.22)
Tea	Area harvested, production	ha, tonnes	Yes	A	World, ASEAN	ASEANS1 (3.4.32) (3.4.33)
Tobacco	Area harvested, production	ha, tonnes	Yes	A	World, ASEAN	ASEANS1 (3.4.34) (3.4.35)
Tobacco	Cigars, cigarettes,	nos, tonnes	No		EC, USA, USSR, Canada, Japan	EC9 (4.12)
Tobacco (unmanufactured), production and trade	By country	tonnes, %	Yes	A	World	ISL2 (2.3.24)
Tobacco leaves	By production	tonnes	Yes	A	World	UNCTAD4 (2.26.1)
Tyres		nos	Yes	A, M	World	UN35 (32)
Tyres	Car, truck	nos	Yes	A, Q	World	IRSG1 (38)
Tyres	Car commercial vehicle	nos	Yes	A	World	IRSG2 (22)
Tyres, car and truck		nos	Yes	A, Q	World	IRSG1 (39)
Tyres, radialisation	New, replacement, car, truck	%	Yes	A	Selected countries	IRSG2 (29, 30)
Vegetable oilseeds	By production	tonnes	Yes	A	World	UNCTAD4 (2.16.1)
Vegetables	Total	tonnes	Yes	A	EC	EC6 (ID13)
Wheat, common		tonnes	Yes	A	EC	EC6 (ID 5)
Wheat, durum		tonnes	Yes	A	EC	EC6 (ID 6)
Wheat, production and trade	By region, country	tonnes	Yes	A	World	ISL2 (2.3.17.1-2)
Wheat flour		tonnes	Yes	A, M	World	UN35 (21)
Wheat flour		tonnes	Yes	M	Asia and Pacific	UN43 (-)
Wine	Total	tonnes	Yes	A	EC	EC6 (ID16)

Subject	Categories	Units	Time series Yes/No Frequency		Territorial coverage	Source (Table no.)
5.4.2 Energy - see also Sections 17, 33 and 38						
Coal		tonnes	Yes	A	World, ASEAN	ASEANS1 (4.2.3)
Coal		tonnes	Yes	M	Asia and Pacific	UN43 (-)
Coal	By country and type	tonnes	Yes	A	Africa and Asia	MAC1 (E2)
Coal, output	By country	nos	No		The Americas and Australasia	MAC2 (E2)
Coal, production and consumption	By country	toe, tonnes	Yes	A	World	ISL2 (2.3.3.1-2)
Crude petroleum, output	By country	nos	No		The Americas and Australasia	MAC2 (E3)
Crude petroleum		cu m	Yes	M	Asia and Pacific	UN43 (-)
Crude petroleum		tonnes	Yes	A	World, ASEAN	ASEANS1 (4.2.1)
Crude petroleum	By country	tonnes	Yes	A	Africa and Asia	MAC1 (E3)
Crude petroleum	By production; exports; imports	tonnes	Yes	A	World	BGS2 (-)
Electric energy, output	By country	nos	No		The Americas and Australasia	MAC2 (E22)
Electric energy	By country	kWh	Yes	A	Africa and Asia	MAC1 (E2)
Electricity		kWh	Yes	M	Asia and Pacific	UN43 (-)
Gas producing countries and reserves		cu m	Yes	A	World	ISL2 (2.3.2.2.1-2)
Gas production, offshore	By country	cu feet, day,%	Yes	A	World	ISL2 (2.3.2.3)
Manufactured gas		TJ	Yes	A	ASEAN	ASEANS1 (4.1.1)
Natural gas, output	By country	nos	No		The Americas and Australasia	MAC2 (E4)
Natural gas		cu m	Yes	M	Asia and Pacific	UN43 (-)
Natural gas		TJ	Yes	A	World, ASEAN	ASEANS1 (4.2.2)
Natural gas	By country	cu m	Yes	A	Africa and Asia	MAC1 (E4)
Natural gas	By production	cu m	Yes	A	World	BGS2 (-)
Natural gas	Production	cu m	Yes	A	World	ISL2 (2.3.2.1)
Oil, producing, reserves, refining, consuming	By country	tonnes, %	Yes	A	World	ISL2 (2.3.1.3.1-4)
Oil production, offshore daily average	By country	b/d,%	Yes	A	World	ISL2 (2.3.1.2)
Oil production	By country	tonnes, %	Yes	A	World	ISL2 (2.3.1.1)
Petroleum products		cu m	Yes	M	Asia and Pacific	UN43 (-)
Petroleum products		tonnes	Yes	A	World, ASEAN	ASEANS1 (4.1.4)
5.4.3 Fish and Fish Products - see also Section 20						
Fish catches, nominal and trade	By country	tonnes, %, US$	Yes	A	World	ISL2 (2.3.25.1-2)
5.4.4 Meat and Livestock Products - see also Section 2						
Beef and veal		tonnes	Yes	A	ASEAN	ASEANS1 (4.1.5) (4.1.2)
Meat		tonnes	Yes	M	Asia and Pacific	UN43 (-)
Pork	Net	indices, tonnes	Yes	A, M	EC	EC36
Skimmed milk powder, stocks	Average	indices, tonnes	Yes	A, M	EC	EC36
Skimmed milk powder		indices, tonnes	Yes	A, M	EC	EC36
5.4.5 Metals, Ores, Minerals and Chemicals - see also Section 32, 33 and 38						
Iron and Steel						
Alloy, others	By country	tonnes	No		World	ISSB2 (28)
Alloy products, other, total	By country	tonnes	No		World	ISSB2 (20)
Castings	Total, by type	tonnes	Yes	A	World	WBMS4 (-)
Coke production	By country, region	tonnes	Yes	A	World	IISI4 (26)

5 COMMODITIES

Subject	Categories	Units	Time series Yes/No	Frequency	Territorial coverage	Source (Table no.)
Cold finished bars and drawn wire	By country	tonnes	No		World	ISSB2 (22)
Cold finished bars and sections	By country	tonnes	No		World	ISSB2 (14)
Cold finished bars and sections	By country	tonnes	No		World	ISSB2 (4)
Cold rolled plate and sheet	By country	tonnes	No		World	ISSB2 (18)
Cold rolled plate and sheet	By country	tonnes	No		World	ISSB2 (8)
Cold rolled strip	By country	tonnes	No		World	ISSB2 (19)
Cold rolled strip	By country	tonnes	No		World	ISSB2 (9)
Crude steel; production	By region, by country, total	tonnes	Yes	M	World	IISI4 (3, 3a)
Crude steel, world production	By production	tonnes	Yes	A	World	IISI4 (1)
Crude steel, output	By countries	nos	No		The Americas and Australasia	MAC2 (E9)
Crude steel		tonnes	Yes	A	EC,	EC9 (4.36)
Crude steel		tonnes	Yes	A	World, ASEAN	ASEANS1 (4.1.6)
Crude steel		tonnes	Yes	M	Asia and Pacific	UN43 (-)
Crude steel	By process	tonnes, %	No		World	IISI5 (-)
Crude steel	By production	tonnes	Yes	A	Developing countries	IISI3 (-)
Crude steel	Growth rates	tonnes, %	Yes	A	World	IISI5 (-)
Crude steel production, BOFs	By country, region	tonnes, %	Yes	A	World	IISI4 EAFs (27,28)
Crude steel production, OHFs	By country, region	tonnes, %	Yes	A	World	IISI4 (29)
Crude steel production, trade in steel products, trade by area	By country, exports, destination	tonnes, %	Yes	A	World	ISL2 (2.3.5.1-3)
Crude steel production	By country, region, % change	tonnes, % change	Yes	M, Q	EC	IISI2 (-)
Crude steel production	By country, total	tonnes	Yes	A	World	IISI4 (2)
Crude steel production	By country, by year	tonnes	Yes	A	World	ISSB1 (-)
Crude steel production	By process, by country, by % of total production	tonnes, %	Yes	A	World	IISI4 (4)
Drawn wire	By country	tonnes	No		World	ISSB2 (15)
Drawn wire	By country	tonnes	No		World	ISSB2 (5)
Hot rolled and cold finished flat products	By country	tonnes	No		World	ISSB2 (23)
Hot rolled and forged bars and sections	By country	tonnes	No		World	ISSB2 (13)
Hot rolled and forged bars and sections	By country	tonnes	No		World	ISSB2 (3)
Hot rolled and forged ingots and semis	By country	tonnes	No		World	ISSB2 (11)
Hot rolled and forged ingots and semis	By country	tonnes	No		World	ISSB2 (1)
Hot rolled and forged rods and bars	By country	tonnes	No		World	ISSB2 (21)
Hot rolled plate, sheet and narrow strip	By country	tonnes	No		World	ISSB2 (7)
Hot rolled plate	By country	tonnes	No		World	ISSB2 (16)
Hot rolled wide and narrow strip and hot rolled sheet	By country	tonnes	No		World	ISSB2 (17)
Hot rolled wide strip	By country	tonnes	No		World	ISSB2 (6)
Ingots	By production	tonnes	Yes	A	Developing countries	IISI3 (-)
Ingots	Total, by type	tonnes	Yes	A	World	WBMS4 (-)
Ingots and semis	By production, imports, exports	tonnes	Yes	A	Developing countries	IISI3 (-)
Iron and steel	Pig iron, steel, finished rolled products	tonnes	No		World, EC, USA, USSR, Canada, Japan	EC9 (4.34)
Iron ore		tonnes	Yes	M	Asia and Pacific	UN43 (-)
Iron ore	By country	tonnes	Yes	A	Africa and Asia	MAC1 (E5)
Iron ore	Total ore mined, % iron content	tonnes, %	No		World, EC, USA USA, USSR, Canada, Japan	EC9 (4.33)
Iron ore, output	By countries	nos	No		The Americas and Australasia	MAC2 (E5)

Subject	Categories	Units	Time series Yes/No	Frequency	Territorial coverage	Source (Table no.)
Iron ore production	By country, region	tonnes	Yes	A	World	IISI4 (20)
Iron production	By country, region	tonnes	Yes	A	World	IISI4 (14)
Iron production	By country, region, by type	tonnes	Yes	A	World	IISI4 (17a)
Iron products of the steel industry	By type	tonnes	Yes	A, Q	EC, USA Canada and Japan	UN11 (1)
Liquid steel for casting	By production	tonnes	Yes	A	Developing countries	IISI3 (-)
Pellet production	By country, region	tonnes	Yes	A	World	IISI4 (15)
Pig iron, production	By country	tonnes, %	Yes	A	World	ISL2 (2.3.4)
Pig iron	By country, region, % change	% change	Yes	M	EC	IISI2 (-)
Pig iron	By country	tonnes	Yes	A	Africa and Asia	MAC1 (E16)
Pig iron and ferro-alloys		tonnes	Yes	A, M	World	UN35 (34)
Pig iron production	By country, region	tonnes	Yes	A	World	IISI4 (17)
Pig iron production	By country, by year	tonnes	Yes	A	World	ISSB1 (-)
Pig-iron, output	By countries	nos	No		The Americas and Australasia	MAC2 (E8)
Seamless and welded linepipe	By country	tonnes	No		World	ISSB2 (25)
Seamless and welded OCTG	By country	tonnes	No		World	ISSB2 (26)
Seamless tube production	By country, region	tonnes	Yes	A	World	IISI4 (31)
Sinter production	By country, region	tonnes	Yes	A	World	IISI4 (16)
Slabs, blooms and billets	Total, by type	tonnes	Yes	A	World	WBMS4 (-)
Stainless steel	By country	tonnes	No		World	ISSB2 (27)
Stainless steel production	By country, region	tonnes	Yes	A	World	IISI4 (33)
Stainless steel products	By country	tonnes	No		World	ISSB2 (10)
Steel, continuous cast semis	By production	tonnes	Yes	A	Developing countries	IISI3 (-)
Steel, long products	By product, imports, exports	tonnes	Yes	A	Developing countries	IISI3 (-)
Steel, flat products	By production, imports, exports	tonnes	Yes	A	Developing countries	IISI3 (-)
Steel, seamless tubes	By production, imports, exports	tonnes	Yes	A	Developing countries	IISI3 (-)
Steel, welded tubes	By production, imports, exports	tonnes	Yes	A	Developing countries	IISI3 (-)
Steel, finished and semi-finished products for sale	By production	tonnes	Yes	A	Developing countries	IISI3 (-)
Steel, production	By country, by region % of total crude steel production	tonnes, %	Yes	A	World	IISI4 (5)
Steel, continuously-cast	By output	tonnes, %	Yes	A	World	IISI5 (-)
Steel, high speed products	By country	tonnes	No		World	ISSB2 (24)
Steel, total special tube products	By country	tonnes	No		World	ISSB2 (29)
Steel, production	By country, by product	tonnes	No		World	MB1 (-)
Steel, crude		tonnes	Yes	A, M	World	UN35 (35)
Steel industry	Employees	nos	Yes	A	World	IISI5 (-)
Steel industry raw materials	By type	tonnes	Yes	A, Q	EC, USA. Canada and Japan	UN11 (1)
Steel ingots and castings	By country	tonnes	Yes	A	Africa and Asia	MAC1 (E17)
Steel intensity of GDP	By country, region	kg per US$	Yes	A	World	IISI4 (13a,b)
Steel makers, top	By producer, by ranking, output, change	tonnes, %	No		World	MB1 (-)
Steel products, finished and semi-finished	By type	tonnes	Yes	A, Q	EC, USA. Canada and Japan	UN11 (2)
Steel tube production	By country, region	tonnes	Yes	A	World	IISI4 (30)
Steel-producing companies, largest	Crude steel output	tonnes	Yes	A	World	IISI5 (-)
Steel-producing countries, major	Crude steel	tonnes	Yes	A	World	IISI5 (-)
Welded tube production	By country, region	tonnes	Yes	A	World	IISI4 (32)
Wire rod and other hot rolled bars in coil	By country	tonnes	No		World	ISSB2 (12)
Wire rod and other hot rolled bars in coil	By country	tonnes	No		World	ISSB2 (2)

5 COMMODITIES

Subject	Categories	Units	Time series Yes/No Frequency		Territorial coverage	Source (Table no.)
Metals: Lead, Zinc and Other						
Alumina, production	By country	tonnes	Yes	A	World	ISL2 (2.3.7)
Aluminium	By country	nos	No		The Americas and Australasia	MAC2 (E10)
Aluminium	By country	tonnes	Yes	A	Africa and Asia	MAC1 (E18)
Aluminium	Primary, secondary	tonnes	Yes	A, M	World	UN35 (36)
Antimony ore	By country	tonnes	Yes	A	Africa and Asia	MAC1 (E12)
Bauxite	By country	tonnes	Yes	A	Africa and Asia	MAC1 (E11)
Chromium, nickel and vanadium ores	By country	tonnes	Yes	A	Africa and Asia	MAC1 (E7)
Copper, lead, tin and zinc	By country, primary, secondary	nos	No		The Americas and Australasia	MAC2 (E11)
Copper, smelter		tonnes	Yes	A, M	World	UN35 (37)
Copper, refined		tonnes	Yes	A, M	World	UN35 (38)
Copper (smelter copper), production	By country	tonnes	Yes	A	World	ISL2 (2.3.8)
Copper ore	By country	tonnes	Yes	A	Africa and Asia	MAC1 (E8)
Copper ore and concentrates		tonnes	Yes	M	Asia and Pacific	UN43 (-)
Gold and silver	By type, country	tonnes	Yes	A	Africa and Asia	MAC1 (E14)
Lead, concentrates		tonnes	Yes	A, Q	Western World	ILZSG1 (1)
Lead	Mine production metal production	tonnes	Yes	A	Eastern Europe. Socialist countries	ILZSG1 (9)
Lead	By production; exports; imports	tonnes	Yes	A	World	BGS2 (-)
Lead	Ores, concentrates lead bullion refined lead antimonial lead	tonnes	Yes	A, M	Japan	ILZSG1 (20)
Lead	Ores, concentrates refined lead	tonnes	Yes	A, M	Mexico	ILZSG1 (21)
Lead	Ores, concentrates refined lead	tonnes	Yes	A, M	Italy	ILZSG1 (19)
Lead	Ores, concentrates refined lead	tonnes	Yes	A, M	Peru	ILZSG1 (22)
Lead	Ores, concentrates refined lead	tonnes	Yes	A, M	France	ILZSG1 (17)
Lead	Ores, concentrates refined lead	tonnes	Yes	A, M	US	ILZSG1 (24)
Lead	Ores, concentrates lead bullion refined lead	tonnes	Yes	A, M	Australia	ILZSG1 (15)
Lead	Ores, concentrates refined lead	tonnes	Yes	A, M	Canada	ILZSG1 (16)
Lead	Ores, concentrates lead bullion refined lead	tonnes	Yes	A, M	Germany	ILZSG1 (18)
Lead	Ores, concentrates lead bullion refined lead	tonnes	Yes	A, M	UK	ILZSG1 (23)
Lead	Primary, secondary	tonnes	Yes	A, M	World	UN35 (39)
Lead, mine production		tonnes	Yes	A	EC, US, Australia	ILZSG1 (2)
Lead, mine production		tonnes	Yes	A, M	World	ILZSG1 (5)
Lead, recovery of secondary lead	Refined lead and lead alloys, remelted lead and lead alloys	tonnes	Yes	A, Q	World	ILZSG1 (11)
Lead, refined		tonnes	Yes	A	EC, US, Japan	ILZSG1 (2)
Lead, refined		tonnes	Yes	A, Q	Western World	ILZSG1 (1)
Lead, refined		tonnes	Yes	A, M	World	ILZSG1 (6)
Lead, totals	Mine production refined metal production	tonnes, %	Yes	A	World	ILZSG1 (25)
Lead, totals	Mine production refined metal production	tonnes, %	Yes	A	Western World	ILZSG1 (25)
Lead, refined, production, consumption and trade		tonnes	Yes	A	World	ISL2 (2.3.10)
Lead and zinc ores	By country	tonnes	Yes	A	Africa and Asia	MAC1 (E9)

Subject	Categories	Units	Time series Yes/No	Frequency	Territorial coverage	Source (Table no.)
Lead ores and concentrates		tonnes	Yes	M	Asia and Pacific	UN43 (-)
Manganese ore	By country	tonnes	Yes	A	Africa and Asia	MAC1 (E6)
Mercury, molybdenum, tungsten concentrates	By type, country	tonnes	Yes	A	Africa and Asia	MAC1 (E13)
Metals	Aluminium, copper, zinc, tin, lead	tonnes	No		World, EC, USA USSR, Canada, Japan	EC9 (4.3)
Non-ferrous metals, production and consumption	By country, by metal	tonnes	Yes	A	World	MB1 (-)
Non-ferrous metals, output	By country	nos	No		The Americas and Australasia Countries	MAC2 (E6)
Tin		tonnes	Yes	A, M	World	UN35 (40)
Tin concentrates	By country	tonnes	Yes	A	Africa and Asia	MAC1 (E10)
Tin metal		tonnes	Yes	A	World, ASEAN	ASEANS1
Tin metal		tonnes	Yes	M	Asia and Pacific	UN43 (-)
Zinc	By production; exports; imports	tonnes	Yes	A	World	BGS2 (-)
Zinc	Concentrates slab zinc	tonnes	Yes	A, Q	Western World	ILZSG1 (26)
Zinc	Mine production refined zinc	tonnes	Yes	A, M	EC, Canada Australia, Japan	ILZSG1 (27)
Zinc	Mine production metal production	tonnes	Yes	A	Eastern European Socialist countries	
Zinc	Ores, concentrates refined zinc	tonnes	Yes	A, M	Australia	ILZSG1 (40)
Zinc	Ores, concentrates refined zinc	tonnes	Yes	A, M	Canada	ILZSG1 (41)
Zinc	Ores, concentrates refined zinc	tonnes	Yes	A, M	France	ILZSG1 (42)
Zinc	Ores, concentrates refined zinc	tonnes	Yes	A, M	Germany	ILZSG1 (43)
Zinc	Ores, concentrates refined zinc	tonnes	Yes	A, M	Italy	ILZSG1 (44)
Zinc	Ores, concentrates refined zinc	tonnes	Yes	A, M	Mexico	ILZSG1 (46)
Zinc	Ores, concentrates refined zinc	tonnes	Yes	A, M	Peru	ILZSG1 (47)
Zinc	Ores, concentrates refined zinc	tonnes	Yes	A, M	US	ILZSG1 (49)
Zinc	Primary, secondary	tonnes	Yes	A, M	World	UN35 (41)
Zinc	Refined zinc ore, concentrates	tonnes	Yes	A, M	Japan	ILZSG1 (45)
Zinc, metal		tonnes	Yes	A, M	World	ILZSG1 (31)
Zinc, mine production		tonnes	Yes	A, M	World	ILZSG1 (30)
Zinc, recovery of secondary zinc	Refined zinc metal, remelted zinc and direct use of secondary materials	tonnes	Yes	A, Q	World	ILZSG1 (36)
Zinc, totals	Mine production refined metal production	tonnes	Yes	A	World	ILZSG1 (50)
Zinc, totals	Mine production refined metal production	tonnes	Yes	A	Western World	ILZSG1 (50)
Zinc, refined, production, consumption and trade		tonnes	Yes	A	World	ISL2 (2.3.9)
Zinc ore and concentrates		tonnes	Yes	M	Asia and Pacific	UN43 (-)
Minerals and Chemicals - see also Section 32						
Alumina, bauxite and aluminium	By production, exports, imports, type, country	tonnes	Yes	A	World	BGS1 (-)
Alumina	By production, exports; imports	tonnes	Yes	A	World	BGS2 (-)
Alumina	By production	tonnes	Yes	A	World	UNCTAD4 (3.1.6)

5 COMMODITIES

Subject	Categories	Units	Time series Yes/No Frequency		Territorial coverage	Source (Table no.)
Aluminium	Availability: mining production, domestic recovery imports, utilization: consumption, exports	tonnes	No		EC, USA, Japan	EC9 (4.4)
Aluminium	By production, exports; imports	tonnes	Yes	A	World	BGS2 (-)
Aluminium	By production	tonnes	Yes	A	World	UNCTAD4 (3.1.9)
Ammonia		tonnes	No		World, EC, USA USSR, Canada, Japan	EC9 (4.7)
Antimony	Availability: mining production, domestic recovery imports, utilization: consumption, exports	tonnes	No		EC, USA, Japan	EC9 (4.4)
Antimony	By production, exports; imports	tonnes	Yes	A	World	BGS2 (-)
Arsenic	By production, exports; imports	tonnes	Yes	A	World	BGS2 (-)
Asbestos	By production, exports, imports of unmanufactured asbestos by country	tonnes	Yes	A	World	BGS1 (-)
Barytes	By production, exports, imports, by country	tonnes	Yes	A	World	BGS1 (-)
Bauxite	By production exports; imports	tonnes	Yes	A	World	BGS2 (-)
Bentonite and Fullers earth	By production, exports, imports, type, country	tonnes	Yes	A	World	BGS1 (-)
Beryl	By production, country	tonnes	Yes	A	World	BGS1 (-)
Bismuth	By production exports; imports	tonnes	Yes	A	World	BGS2 (-)
Borates	By production, country	tonnes	Yes	A	World	BGS1 (-)
Bromine	By production, exports, imports, country	kg	Yes	A	World	BGS1 (-)
Cadmium	By production exports; imports	tonnes	Yes	A	World	BGS2 (-)
Caustic soda		tonnes	No		EC, USA. USSR, Canada, Japan	EC9 (4.6)
Cement		tonnes	Yes	A, M	World	UN35 (33)
Cement		tonnes	Yes	A	World	UN10 (16)
Cement		tonnes	Yes	A	World, EC, USA USSR, Canada, Japan	EC9 (4.5)
Cement		tonnes	Yes	A	World, ASEAN	ASEANS1 (4.1.3)
Cement		tonnes	Yes	M	Asia and Pacific	UN43 (-)
Chlorine		tonnes	No		EC, USA, USSR Canada, Japan	EC9 (4.6)
Chromium	Availability: mining production, domestic recovery imports, utilization: consumption, exports	tonnes	No		EC, USA, Japan	EC9 (4.4)
Chromium	By production exports; imports	tonnes	Yes	A	World	BGS2 (-)

Subject	Categories	Units	Time series Yes/No Frequency		Territorial coverage	Source (Table no.)
Chromium ores and concentrates	By production, exports, imports, by country by type	tonnes	Yes	A	World	BGS1 (-)
Coal	By production exports; imports	tonnes	Yes	A	World	BGS2 (-)
Cobalt	Availability: mining production, domestic recovery imports, utilization: consumption, exports	tonnes	No		EC, USA, Japan	EC9 (4.4)
Cobalt	By production exports; imports	tonnes	Yes	A	World	BGS2 (-)
Copper	Availability: mining production, domestic recovery imports, utilization: consumption, exports	tonnes	No		EC, USA, Japan	EC9 (4.4)
Copper	By production exports; imports	tonnes	Yes	A	World	BGS2 (-)
Copper ore	By production	tonnes	Yes	A	World	UNCTAD4 (3.2.1)
Copper, refined	By production	tonnes	Yes	A	World	UNCTAD4 (3.2.7)
Copper, refined	By production, secondary	tonnes	Yes	A	World	UNCTAD4 (3.2.8)
Copper, refined	Quantity and value of exports and imports	tonnes, US$	Yes	A	World	UNCTAD4 (3.2.9, 3.2.10)
Crude steel	By production	tonnes	Yes	A	World	UNCTAD4 (3.3.9)
Diamond	By production, exports, imports, by type, country	carats	Yes	A	World	BGS1 (-)
Diatomite	By production, exports, imports, country	tonnes	Yes	A	World	BGS1 (-)
Feldspar	By production, exports, imports, country	tonnes	Yes	A	World	BGS1 (-)
Ferro-alloys	By production exports; imports	tonnes	Yes	A	World	BGS2 (-)
Ferromanganese	By production	tonnes	Yes	A	World	UNCTAD4 (3.5.4)
Fluorine	Availability: mining production, domestic recovery imports, utilization: consumption, exports	tonnes	No		EC, USA, Japan	EC9 (4.4)
Fluorspar	By production, exports, imports, country	tonnes	Yes	A	World	BGS1 (-)
Germanium	By production exports; imports	tonnes	Yes	A	World	BGS2 (-)
Gold	By production; exports; imports	kg	Yes	A	World	BGS2 (-)
Graphite	By production, exports, imports, country	tonnes	Yes	A	World	BGS1 (-)
Gypsum	By production, exports, imports, type, country	tonnes	Yes	A	World	BGS1 (-)
Iodine	By production, exports, imports, country	kg	Yes	A	World	BGS1 (-)

5 COMMODITIES

Subject	Categories	Units	Time series Yes/No Frequency		Territorial coverage	Source (Table no.)
Iron	Availability: mining production, domestic recovery imports, utilization: consumption, exports	tonnes	No		EC, USA, Japan	EC9 (4.4)
Iron and steel	By production; exports; imports	tonnes	Yes	A	World	BGS2 (-)
Iron ore	By production exports; imports	tonnes	Yes	A	World	BGS2 (-)
Kaolin	By production, exports, imports, country	tonnes	Yes	A	World	BGS1 (-)
Lead	Availability: mining production, domestic recovery imports, utilization: consumption, exports	tonnes	No		EC, USA, Japan	EC9 (4.4)
Lead ore	By production	tonnes	Yes	A	World	UNCTAD4 (3.4.1)
Liquid steel for casting	By production	tonnes	Yes	A	Developing countries	IISI3 (-)
Lithium	By production; exports; imports	tonnes	Yes	A	World	BGS2 (-)
Lithium minerals	By production, exports, imports, type, country	tonnes	Yes	A	World	BGS1 (-)
Magnesite	By production	tonnes	Yes	A	World	BGS1 (-)
Magnesite and magnesia	By exports, imports, by type, by country	tonnes	Yes	A	World	BGS1 (-)
Magnesium	By production; exports; imports	tonnes	Yes	A	World	BGS2 (-)
Manganese	Availability: mining production, domestic recovery imports, utilization: consumption, exports	tonnes	No		EC, USA, Japan	EC9 (4.4)
Manganese ore	By production	tonnes	Yes	A	World	UNCTAD4 (3.5.1)
Mercury	Availability: mining production, domestic recovery imports, utilization: consumption, exports	tonnes	No		EC, USA, Japan	EC9 (4.4)
Mercury	By production; exports; imports	kg	Yes	A	World	BGS2 (-)
Mica	By production, imports, exports, type, country	tonnes	Yes	A	World	BGS1 (-)
Mineral commodities	By commodity	tonnes	No		Principal developing countries	UNCTAD4 (A.5)
Minerals, non-metallic	By countries	nos	No		The Americas and Australasia	MAC2 (E7)

Subject	Categories	Units	Time series Yes/No Frequency		Territorial coverage	Source (Table no.)
Molybdenum	Availability: mining production, domestic recovery imports, utilization: consumption, exports	tonnes	No		EC, USA, Japan	EC9 (4.4)
Molybdenum	By production; exports; imports	tonnes	Yes	A	World	BGS2 (-)
Nepheline syenite	By production, country	tonnes	Yes	A	World	BGS1 (-)
Nickel	Availability: mining production, domestic recovery imports, utilization: consumption, exports	tonnes	No		EC, USA, Japan	EC9 (4.4)
Nickel	By production; exports; imports	tonnes	Yes	A	World	BGS2 (-)
Nickel, unwrought	By production	tonnes	Yes	A	World	UNCTAD4 (3.6.4)
Nickel ore	By production	tonnes	Yes	A	World	UNCTAD4 (3.6.1)
Niobium	Availability: mining production, domestic recovery imports, utilization: consumption, exports	tonnes	No		EC, USA, Japan	EC9 (4.4)
Niobium	By production; exports; imports	tonnes	Yes	A	World	BGS2 (-)
Paper	Newsprint, wood pulp	tonnes	No		World, EC, USA, USSR, Canada, Japan	EC9 (4.13)
Pellets	By production	tonnes	Yes	A	World	UNCTAD4 (3.3.2)
Perlite	By production, country	tonnes	Yes	A	World	BGS1 (-)
Phosphate	Availability: mining production, domestic recovery imports, utilization: consumption, exports	tonnes	No		EC, USA, Japan	EC9 (4.4)
Phosphate rock	By production, exports, imports, country	tonnes	Yes	A	World	BGS1 (-)
Phosphate rock	By production	tonnes	Yes	A	World	UNCTAD4 (3.7.1)
Pig iron	By production	tonnes	Yes	A	World	UNCTAD4 (3.3.8)
Platinum	By production; exports; imports	kg	Yes	A	World	BGS2 (-)
Potash	By production, exports, imports, type, country	tonnes	Yes	A	World	BGS1 (-)
Potash, phosphate, nitrogenous	Production and trade	tonnes, %	Yes	A	World	ISL2 (2.3.11.1-3)
Rare earth minerals	By production, type, exports, imports, country	tonnes	Yes	A	World	BGS1 (-)
Rare earths	By production; exports; imports	tonnes	Yes	A	World	BGS2 (-)
Raw asbestos, phosphate rock, potash and sulphur	By type, country	tonnes	Yes	A	Africa and Asia	MAC1 (E15)

Subject	Categories	Units	Time series Yes/No Frequency		Territorial coverage	Source (Table no.)
Salt	By production, type, exports, imports, country	tonnes	Yes	A	World	BGS1 (-)
Selenium	By production; exports; imports	tonnes	Yes	A	World	BGS2 (-)
Sillimanite	By production, exports, imports, type, country	tonnes	Yes	A	World	BGS1 (-)
Silver	By production; exports; imports	kg	Yes	A	World	BGS2 (-)
Sinter	By production	tonnes	Yes	A	World	UNCTAD4 (3.3.3)
Strontium minerals	By production, country	tonnes	Yes	A	World	BGS1 (-)
Sulphur	By production	tonnes	Yes	A	World	UNCTAD4 (3.8.1)
Sulphur and pyrites	By production, type, exports, imports, country	tonnes (sulphur content)	Yes	A	World	BGS1 (-)
Sulphuric acid, hydrochloric acid, nitric acid and caustic soda	By countries	nos	No		The Americas and Australasia	MAC2 (E18)
Sulphuric acid		tonnes	Yes	M	Asia and Pacific	UN43(-)
Sulphuric acid	By country	tonnes	Yes	A	Africa and Asia	MAC1 (E24)
Talc	By production, type, exports, imports, country	tonnes	Yes	A	World	BGS1 (-)
Tantalum	Availability: mining production, domestic recovery imports, utilization: consumption, exports	tonnes	No		EC, USA, Japan	EC9 (4.4)
Tantalum	By production; exports; imports	tonnes	Yes	A	World	BGS2 (-)
Tellurium	By production; exports; imports	tonnes	Yes	A	World	BGS2 (-)
Tin	Availability: mining production, domestic recovery imports, utilization: consumption, exports	tonnes	No		EC, USA, Japan	EC9 (4.4)
Tin	By production; exports; imports	tonnes	Yes	A	World	BGS2 (-)
Tin metal, primary	By production	tonnes	Yes	A	World	UNCTAD4 (3.9.4)
Tin ore	By production	tonnes	Yes	A	World	UNCTAD4 (3.9.1)
Titanium	Availability: mining production, domestic recovery imports, utilization: consumption, exports	tonnes	No		EC, USA, Japan	EC9 (4.4)
Titanium	By production; exports; imports	tonnes	Yes	A	World	BGS2 (-)
Titanium materials	By production, type, exports, imports, country	tonnes	Yes	A	World	BGS1 (-)

Subject	Categories	Units	Time series Yes/No Frequency		Territorial coverage	Source (Table no.)
Tungsten	Availability: mining production, domestic recovery imports, utilization: consumption, exports	tonnes	No		EC, USA, Japan	EC9 (4.4)
Tungsten	By production; exports; imports	tonnes	Yes	A	World	BGS2 (-)
Uranium	By production; exports; imports	tonnes	Yes	A	World	BGS2 (-)
Vanadium	Availability: mining production, domestic recovery imports, utilization: consumption, exports	tonnes	No		EC, USA, Japan	EC9 (4.4)
Vanadium	By production; exports; imports	tonnes	Yes	A	World	BGS2 (-)
Vermiculite	By production, country	tonnes	Yes	A	World	BGS1 (-)
Wollastonite	By production, country	tonnes	Yes	A	World	BGS1 (-)
Zinc	Availability: mining production, domestic recovery imports, utilization: consumption, exports	tonnes	No		EC, USA, Japan	EC9 (4.4)
Zirconium	Availability: mining production, domestic recovery imports, utilization: consumption, exports	tonnes	No		EC, USA, Japan	EC9 (4.4)
Zirconium minerals	By production, type, exports, imports, country	tonnes	Yes	A	World	BGS1 (-)
Mining and Quarrying - see also Sections 33 and 38						
Bauxite		tonnes	Yes	A	World, ASEAN	ASEANS1 (4.2.8)
Bauxite		tonnes	Yes	A	World	UN35 (16)
Coal		tonnes	Yes	A, M	World	UN35 (11)
Copper ore		tonnes	Yes	A, M	World	UN35 (17)
Copper ore		tonnes	Yes	A	World, ASEAN	ASEANS1 (4.2.6)
Crude petroleum	Specific gravity	tonnes	Yes	A, M	World	UN35 (14)
Iron ore		tonnes	Yes	A	World, ASEAN	ASEANS1 (4.2.5)
Iron ore	Metal content	tonnes	Yes	A, M	World	UN35 (15)
Lead ore		tonnes	Yes	A, M	World	UN35 (18)
Lignite and brown coal		tonnes	Yes	A, M	World	UN35 (12)
Manganese ore		tonnes	Yes	A	World, ASEAN	ASEANS1 (4.2.7)
Natural gas	Heat value	terajoules	Yes	A, M	World	UN35 (13)
Ores	Copper, lead, zinc, tin, bauxite, potash	tonnes	No		World, EC, USA USSR, Canada, Japan	EC9 (4.2)
Salt		tonnes	Yes	A	World, ASEAN	ASEANS1 (4.2.9)
Tin concentrates		tonnes	Yes	A, M	World	UN35 (19)
Tin in concentrates		tonnes	Yes	A	World, ASEAN	ASEANS1 (4.2.4)
Zinc ore		tonnes	Yes	A, M	World	UN35 (20)

Subject	Categories	Units	Time series Yes/No Frequency		Territorial coverage	Source (Table no.)
5.4.6 Textiles, Clothing and Footwear						
Abaca	By production	tonnes	Yes	A	World	UNCTAD4 (2.33.8)
Artificial and synthetic fibres	By countries	nos	No		The Americas and Australasia	MAC2 (E17)
Blankets	By production, wool type	kg	Yes	A	World	IWS1 (27)
Carpets, woven	By production, wool type	kg	Yes	A	World	IWS1 (28)
Carpets, tufted	By production, wool type	kg	Yes	A	World	IWS1 (29)
Cotton, production, trade and consumption		bales, %	Yes	A	World	ISL2 (2.3.13.1-2)
Cotton		ha, tonnes	Yes	A	US	ICAC1 (p9)
Cotton	By production	tonnes	Yes	A	World	UNCTAD4 (2.31.3)
Cotton (all types)		bales	Yes	A	World	ICAC2 (pp12-13)
Cotton (harvested area)		acres	Yes	A	World	ICAC2 (pp14-15)
Cotton (total)		tonnes	Yes	A	China, US, CIS, India, Pakistan Brazil	ICAC1 (p2)
Cotton (yield)		lbs/acre	Yes	A	World	ICAC2 (pp16-17)
Cotton consumption, raw	By country	nos	No		The Americas and Australasia	MAC2 (E12)
Cotton fabric		tonnes	Yes	A	World	ICAC2 (pp72-73)
Cotton spindles	By country	nos	Yes	A	Africa and Asia	MAC1 (E19)
Cotton spindles	By country	nos	No		The Americas and Australasia	MAC2 (E13)
Cotton tissues, output	By country	nos	No		The Americas and Australasia	MAC2 (E15)
Cotton yarn, production	By country	tonnes	Yes	A	World	ISL2 (2.3.16)
Cotton yarn,output	By country	nos	No		The Americas and Australasia	MAC2 (E14)
Cotton yarn		tonnes	Yes	A, M	World	UN35 (22)
Cotton yarn		tonnes	Yes	A	World	ICAC2 (pp66-67)
Cotton yarn		tonnes	Yes	M	Asia and Pacific	UN43 (-)
Cotton yarn	By country	tonnes	Yes	A	Africa and Asia	MAC1 (E20)
Cotton yarn	By production	tonnes	Yes	A	World	UNCTAD4 (2.31.6)
Fibre	Man made fibres; natural	kg	Yes	A	World	IWS1 (2)
Fibre - share	Man made fibres; natural	%	Yes	A	World	IWS1 (3)
Hand knitting yarn	By production, wool type	kg	Yes	A	World	IWS1 (26)
Jute	Quantity and value of exports and imports	tonnes, US$	Yes	A	World	UNCTAD4 (2.32.4, 2.32.5)
Jute and jute-like fibres	By production	tonnes	Yes	A	World	UNCTAD4 (2.32.3)
Non-cellulosic fibres	Continuous filaments, discontinuous filaments	tonnes	Yes	A, M	World	UN35 (29)
Rayon and acetate filaments and fibres	Continuous filaments, discontinuous filaments	tonnes	Yes	A, M	World	UN35 (27)
Sisal	By production	tonnes	Yes	A	World	UNCTAD4 (2.33.5)
Sweaters	By production, wool type	kg	Yes	A	World	IWS1 (25)
Synthetic filaments	By country	tonnes	Yes	A	Africa and Asia	MAC1 (E22)
Tops and slivers of wool and hair wool	By production	kg	Yes	A	World	IWS1 (17)
Vegetable textile yarns, other than cotton	Flax, ramie, true hemp jute, other vegetable	tonnes	Yes	A, M	World	UN35 (24)
Wool, manufacturing stage	By region	kg, %	Yes	A	World	IWS1 (14)
Wool, final stage	By region	kg, %	Yes	A	World	IWS1 (15)
Wool, (dirty), production	By country	tonnes/%	Yes	A	World	ISL2 (2.3.14)
Wool, greasy	By production	tonnes	Yes	A	World	UNCTAD4 (2.34.1)
Wool - greasy		kg	Yes	A	World	IWS1 (4)
Wool - greasy	Share held by main producers	%	Yes	A	World	IWS1 (5)
Wool and hair tops (including slivers)	By imports and exports	kg	Yes	A	World	IWS1 (18)
Wool industry indicators	By country	nos	No		The Americas and	MAC2 (E16)

Subject	Categories	Units	Time series Yes/No	Frequency	Territorial coverage	Source (Table no.)
Wool predominant woollen fabrics	By production	kg	Yes	A	World	IWS1 (23)
Wool predominant woollen yarns	By production	kg	Yes	A	World	IWS1 (20)
Wool predominant worsted fabrics	By production	kg	Yes	A	World	IWS1 (22)
Wool predominant worsted yarns	By production	kg	Yes	A	World	IWS1 (19)
Wool woven fabrics	Imports and exports	kg	Yes	A	World	IWS1 (24)
Wool yarn, production	By country	tonnes	Yes	A	World	ISL2 (2.3.15)
Wool yarn		tonnes	Yes	A, M	World	UN35 (25)
Wool yarn	By country	tonnes	Yes	A	Africa and Asia	MAC1 (E21)
Woollen fabrics and yarns		tonnes	No		World, EC, USA USSR, Canada, Japan	EC9 (4.11)
Woollen woven cloth		sq m	Yes	M	Asia and Pacific	UN43 (-)
Woollen yarn		tonnes	Yes	M	Asia and Pacific	UN43 (-)
Woollen yarns (worsted and woollen)	Imports and exports	kg	Yes	A	World	IWS1 (21)
Wools, spinning stage	By region	kg, %	Yes	A	World	IWS1 (13)
Woven cotton fabrics		units	Yes	A, M	World	UN35 (23)
Woven rayon and acetate fabrics	Metres	units	Yes	A, M	World	UN35 (28)
Woven woollen fabrics		units	Yes	A, M	World	UN35 (26)
Yarn, tissues, wool	output, consumption				Australasia	
5.4.7 Wood and Forestry Products - see also Section 21						
Paper		tonnes	Yes	A	ASEAN	ASEANS1 (4.1.7)
Paper and board production	By grade, country	tonnes	Yes	A	World	PPI1 (-)
Plywood		tonnes, cu m, sq m	Yes	A	ASEAN	ASEANS1 (4.1.8)
Pulp, paper and board production and trade	By country, consumption	tonnes, nos mills	Yes	A	World	PPI1 (-)
Pulp production	By grade, country	tonnes	Yes	A	World	PPI1 (-)
Sawn wood	By country	cu m	Yes	A	Africa and Asia	MAC1 (E25)
Timber industry indicators	By countries	nos	No		The Americas and Australasia	MAC2 (E19)
Wood pulp	By country	tonnes, dry weight	Yes	A	Africa and Asia	MAC1 (E26)
Wood pulp	Paper and board, newsprint	tonnes	No		World, EC, USA, USSR, Canada, Japan	EC9 (4.13)
5.5 SUPPLY AND DISTRIBUTION						
5.5.1 Agricultural Commodities - see also Section 2						
Cocoa: global supply/demand balance in the world cocoa market	By production, grindings,	tonnes, %, SDRs/tonne	Yes		World	ICCO3 (1)
Rubber, synthetic, capacities	By type and country	tonnes	Yes	2yr	World	IRSG1 (47)
Rubber, stocks		tonnes	Yes	A	Malaysia, peninsular	IRSG1 (16)
					Singapore	IRSG1 (17)
					Indonesia	IRSG1 (18)
					Thailand	IRSG1 (19)
					Sri Lanka	IRSG1 (20)
Rubber, opening and closing stocks, new supply	By type of rubber	tonnes	No		USA	IRSG1 (29)
					Brazil	IRSG1 (30)
					France	IRSG1 (31)
					UK	IRSG1 (33)
					India	IRSG1 (35)
					Japan	IRSG1 (36)
Rubber, natural, stocks in producing countries		tonnes	Yes	A	World	IRSG2 (12)
Rubber, natural, stocks in producing countries		tonnes	Yes	A, M	World	IRSG1 (15)
Rubber, natural, stocks in consuming areas		tonnes	Yes	A	World	IRSG2 (13)
Rubber, natural, stocks in consuming areas		tonnes	Yes	A, M	World	IRSG1 (5)
Rubber, synthetic, reported stocks		tonnes	Yes	A, M	World	IRSG1 (6)

5 COMMODITIES

Subject	Categories	Units	Time series Yes/No	Frequency	Territorial coverage	Source (Table no.)
Rubber, synthetic, reported stocks		tonnes	Yes	A	World	IRSG2 (19)
Rubber, natural		tonnes	Yes	M	World	IRSG1 (1)
Rubber, natural		tonnes	Yes	A	World	IRSG2 (1)
Rubber, natural	In producing countries	tonnes	Yes	M	World	IRSG1 (15)
Rubber, natural	In producing countries	tonnes	Yes	A	World	IRSG2 (15)
Rubber, natural, reported	In consuming area	tonnes	Yes	M	World	IRSG1 (5)
Rubber, natural , reported	In consuming area	tonnes	Yes	A	World	IRSG2 (5)
Rubber, synthetic		tonnes	Yes	M	World	IRSG1 (2)
Rubber, synthetic, reported	In consuming area	tonnes	Yes	M	World	IRSG1 (6)
Rubber, reported	In consuming area	tonnes	Yes	A	World	IRSG2 (6)
Rubber, production, 1900-45		tonnes	Yes	A	World	IRSG2 (45)
Rubber, production, 1946-60	Natural synthetics	tonnes	Yes	A	World	IRSG2 (47)
Rubber, purchases or deliveries from government stockpiles	Natural	tonnes	Yes	A	World	IRSG2 (47)
Rubber, production, 1946-60	Natural synthetics	tonnes	Yes	A	World	IRSG2 (47)
Rubber, estimated stocks	Natural synthetics	tonnes	Yes	A	World	IRSG2 (47)
Rubber, government stockpiles	Natural	tonnes	Yes	A	World	IRSG2 (47)
Rubber, total	By type, by area	tonnes, %	Yes	A	World	IISRP1 (8,13)
Rubber, total	Natural, synthetic	tonnes	Yes	A	World	IISRP1 (14)
Rubber, shipments, synthetic	Area and type	tonnes	Yes	A	World	IISRP1 (9)
Rubber supply	Synthetic, by type	tonnes	Yes	A	World	IISRP1 (7)
Stocks		tonnes	Yes	A	World	IRSG2 (45)
Sugar, stocks	By country	tonnes	Yes	A, M	World	ISO2 (-)
Sugar, total	By country	tonnes	Yes	A, M	World	ISO2 (-)
Sugar, change stock			No		World	ISO1 (-)
Sugar, ending stock			No		World	ISO1 (-)
		tonnes	Yes	A	World	IRSG2 (2)
5.5.2 Metals, Ores, Minerals and Chemicals - see also Sections 32 and 33						
Iron and steel scrap movements,	By type of movement	tonnes	No		EC, USA, Canada and Japan	UN11 (6)
Lead, reported metal stocks		tonnes	Yes	A,, Q	Western Europe	ILZSG1 (1)
Lead, stocks	Producer consumer London Metal Exchange	tonnes	Yes	A	EC, US, Japan	ILZSG1 (3)
Lead, stocks	Consumers merchants	tonnes	Yes	A, M	Germany	ILZSG1 (18)
Lead, stocks	Primary secondary	tonnes	Yes	A, M	Japan	ILZSG1 (20)
Lead, stocks		tonnes	Yes	A, M	UK	ILZSG1 (23)
Lead, stocks	Producers consumers stockpile	tonnes	Yes	A, M	US	ILZSG1 (24)
Lead, stocks		tonnes	Yes	A, M	Canada	ILZSG1 (16)
Lead, stocks		tonnes	Yes	A, M	Australia	ILZSG1 (15)
Lead, refined metal stocks	Commercial stocks, (producers consumers merchants London Metal Exchange) non-commercial stocks	tonnes	Yes	A, M	World	ILZSG1 (8)
Steel industry deliveries and receipts	By product type	tonnes	No		EC, USA Canada and Japan	UN11 (3)
Steel products, total deliveries of steel products	By grade, by type by country	tonnes	Yes	A	World	IISI4 (6, 6a)
Zinc, metal stocks	Commercial stocks non-commercial stocks	tonnes	Yes	A, M	World	ILZSG1 (33)
Zinc, stocks	Producers consumers merchants London Metal Exchange	tonnes	Yes	A, M	Western World	ILZSG1 (26)

Subject	Categories	Units	Time series Yes/No	Frequency	Territorial coverage	Source (Table no.)
Zinc, stocks	Producers consumers merchant London Metal Exchange	tonnes	Yes	A, M	EC, US, Japan	ILZSG1 (28)
Zinc, stocks		tonnes	Yes	A, M	Australia	ILZSG1 (40)
Zinc, stocks		tonnes	Yes	A, M	Canada	ILZSG1 (41)
Zinc, stocks	Consumers, merchants	tonnes	Yes	A, M	Germany	ILZSG1 (43)
Zinc, stocks	Consumers, producers, merchants	tonnes	Yes	A, M	Japan	ILZSG1 (45)
Zinc, stocks	Consumers	tonnes	Yes	A, M	UK	ILZSG1 (48)
Zinc, stocks	Producers, consumers, merchants	tonnes	Yes	A, M	US	ILZSG1 (49)
5.5.3 Textiles - see also Section 25						
Cotton	Distribution	bales	Yes	A	World	ICAC2 (p1)
Cotton	Supply	bales	Yes	A	World	ICAC2 (p1)
Cotton	Use, by country	ha, tonnes kg, ha	No		World	ICAC1 (pp13-14)
Cotton	Use, by country	ha, tonnes kg/ha	No		World	ICAC1 (pp15-16)
Cotton	Use, by country	acres, bales lbs/acre	No		World	ICAC2 (pp4-5)
Cotton	Use, by country	acres, bales lbs/acre	No		World	ICAC2 (pp6-7)
Cotton	Use, by country	acres, bales lbs/acre	No		World	ICAC2 (pp8-9)
Cotton	Use, by country	acres, bales lbs/acre	No		World	ICAC2 (pp10-11)
Cotton	Use,by major importers, exporters	tonnes	Yes	A	World	ICAC1 (p2)
Cotton	Use	acre, bales lbs/acre	Yes	A	World	ICAC2 (p2)
Cotton (ending stocks)		bales	Yes	A	World	ICAC2 (pp26-27)
Cotton (extra-fine)		bales	Yes	A	World	ICAC2 (p3)
Cotton (extra-fine)		tonnes	Yes	A	World	ICAC1 (p12)
Cotton (ratio of ending stocks to use)			Yes	A	World	ICAC2 (pp64-65)

6 COMMUNICATIONS

6.1 ADVERTISING

6.2 CINEMA

6.3 GENERAL

6.4 NEWSPAPERS

6.5 POSTAL SERVICES

6.6 TELECOMMUNICATIONS

- 6.6.1 Equipment Market
- 6.6.2 Finance
- 6.6.3 Major Carriers
- 6.6.4 Major Equipment Suppliers
- 6.6.5 Radio
- 6.6.6 Staff
- 6.6.7 Telegraph and Telex
- 6.6.8 Telephone, Modem and Fax
- 6.6.9 Television
- 6.6.10 Traffic

Subject	Categories	Units	Time series Yes/No	Frequency	Territorial coverage	Source (Table no.)
6.1 ADVERTISING						
Direct marketing	By country, by volume of direct mail	nos	No		EC	EM1 (1309)
Expenditure	By country	nat curr	No		EC	EM1 (1301)
	by country, by medium	US$	No		EC	EM1 (1302)
Outdoor advertising	By country, by sites	nos	No		EC	EM1 (1308)
6.2 CINEMA						
Screens, attendances, revenue		nos, nat curr	No		EC	EM1 (1307)
Seating capacity		nos	Yes	A	ASEAN	ASEANS1 (9.3.2)
6.3 GENERAL						
Communication profile	By form of communication	per thou, %, per person	No		Industrial countries	UN25 (34)
Communications	Mail, telegraph, telephone, telex, television, radio, by country	nos	Yes	A	ESCAP	UN44
Communications	Mail, telephones, radios, TV	nos million/1000	Yes	A	North Africa	UN2 (31)
Communications	Mail, telephones, radios, TV	nos million/1000	Yes	A	West Africa	UN3 (31)
Communications	Mail, telephones, radios, TV	nos million/1000	Yes	A	East & Southern Africa	UN4 (31)
Communications	Mail, telephones, radios, TV	nos million/1000	Yes	A	Central Africa	UN5 (31)
Main indicators of communications	By high, middle, low income	nos	No		World	CS1 (34)
Transport & communications	Motor vehicles, telephones, TV receivers in use	per 1000 population	Yes		World	UN55
6.4 NEWSPAPERS						
Circulation		nos	Yes	A	ASEAN	ASEANS1 (9.3.1)
Consumer publications, mainstream	By country, by circulation, audited publications	nos	No		EC	EM1 (1305)
National newspapers, number	By country, by nationals, Sundays	nos	No		EC	EM1 (1303)
National newspapers, circulation	By country, by daily, Sunday	nos	No		EC	EM1 (1304)
6.5 POSTAL SERVICES						
Letter mail	Domestic, foreign of which received, sent	nos	Yes	A	ASEAN	ASEANS1 (5.5.1)
Letters and packets dispatched	National and international traffic by type	nos	No		EC	EC80 (8.1)
Mail traffic	By country	nos	Yes	A	Africa and Asia	MAC1 (G7)
Mail traffic	Letters, parcels, money orders	nos	Yes	A	Nordic countries	NCM1 (158)
Postal and telegraph services	By countries	nos	Yes	A	EC	MAC3 (F8)
Postal and telegraph traffic	By countries	nos	No		The Americas and Australasia	MAC2 (G8)

Subject	Categories	Units	Time series Yes/No Frequency		Territorial coverage	Source (Table no.)
6.6 TELECOMMUNICATIONS						
6.6.1 Equipment Market						
Data terminal equipments connected to dedicated public data networks	By number	nos	Yes	A	Selected countries	ITU1 (413)
Data terminal equipments on public telephone and telex networks	By number	nos	Yes	A	Selected countries	ITU1 (411)
Private leased circuits	By number	nos	Yes	A	Selected countries	ITU1 (412)
Production	By country, product	US$	Yes	A	World	EAT2 (2.1)
Production	By country, product	US$	Yes	A	World	EAT2 (2.2)
Trade	By imports, exports, country, product	US$	Yes	A	World	EAT2 (2.3-2.4)
6.6.2 Finance						
Telecommunication Services - Expenditure						
All telecommunication services	Total	nat curr	Yes	A	Selected countries	ITU1 (76)
Depreciation		nat curr	Yes	A	Selected countries	ITU1 (762)
Income minus expenditure for the telecommunication services		nat curr	Yes	A	Selected countries	ITU1 (77)
Interest paid		nat curr	Yes	A	Selected countries	ITU1 (763)
Operational		nat curr	Yes	A	Selected countries	ITU1 (761)
Other expenditure		nat curr	Yes	A	Selected countries	ITU1 (765)
Taxes		nat curr	Yes	A	Selected countries	ITU1 (764)
Telecommunication Services - Income						
All telecommunication services	Total	nat curr	Yes	A	Selected countries	ITU1 (75)
Annual rentals		nat curr	Yes	A	Selected countries	ITU1 (712)
Calls		nat curr	Yes	A	Selected countries	ITU1 (713)
Connection charges		nat curr	Yes	A	Selected countries	ITU1 (711)
Other transmission services etc.	By data, facsimile	nat curr	Yes	A	Selected countries	ITU1 (74)
Telegram service, public	Total	nat curr	Yes	A	Selected countries	ITU1 (72)
Telephone service	Total	nat curr	Yes	A	Selected countries	ITU1 (71)
Telex service	Total	nat curr	Yes	A	Selected countries	ITU1 (73)
Telecommunication Services - Investments						
Gross investments, including land and buildings		nos	Yes	A	Selected countries	ITU1 (81)
Gross investments, excluding land and buildings		nos	Yes	A	Selected countries	ITU1 (82)
Gross investments, telephone services		nos	Yes	A	Selected countries	ITU1 (83)
Gross investments, telephone switching equipment		nos	Yes	A	Selected countries	ITU1 (84)
Investments, as a share of GDP in %		%	Yes	A	Selected countries	ITU1 (93)
Investments, as a share of GFCF in %		%	Yes	A	Selected countries	ITU1 (94)
6.6.3 Major Carriers						
Main lines	By country	%	Yes	A	World	EAT2 (3.2-3.5)
Profiles of major telecommunications countries	By country, company, financial indicators	nat curr	No		World	EAT2 (3.3-3.6)
Top thirty leader table	By company, country, revenues, employees	US$	No		World	EAT2 (3.1)
6.6.4 Major Equipment Suppliers						
Profiles of major suppliers financial information	By country, company,	nat curr	Yes	A	World	EAT2 (6.2-6.2.20)
Top twenty leader table	By country, company	US$	No		World	EAT2 (6.1)
6.6.5 Radio – see also under Television (6.6.9)						
Programmes	By function and by type of institution	hours, %	No		World	UNESCO1 (10.3)
Radio, television sets	By country, region	per thou	No		UNICEF assisted countries	UNICEF2

Subject	Categories	Units	Time series Yes/No Frequency	Territorial coverage	Source (Table no.)
Radio and television	By countries receiving licences	nos	Yes A	EC	MAC3 (F10)
Radio and television sets in use	By countries	nos	No	The Americas and Australasia	MAC2 (G10)
Radio licences	By country	nos	No	EC	EC18 (10.13)
Radio receivers		nos, 1000	Yes A	North Africa	UN2 (6-4-1)
Radio receivers		nos, 1000	Yes A	West Africa	UN3 (6-4-1)
Radio receivers		nos, 1000	Yes A	East & Southern Africa	UN4 (6-4-1)
Radio receivers		nos, 1000	Yes A	Central Africa	UN5 (6-4-1)
Radios		nos, rate	No	World	UN16 (14B)
Receiver licences	Per thousand inhabitants	nos	Yes A	VICES region, VICES countries and Yugoslavia	VICES1 (II, 4)
Receivers	In use, licences issued	nos, per capita	Yes 5 A	World	UNESCO1 (10.1)
Receivers	Total	nos, per capita	Yes 5 A	Continents, major areas and groups of countries	UNESCO1 (6.9)
Receivers	In use	nos	Yes A	ASEAN	ASEANS1 (9.3.3)
Stations	By country, by commercial non-commercial	nos	No	EC	EM1 (1306)
Transmitters		nos	Yes 5 A	Continents, major areas and groups of countries	UNESCO1 (6.8)
6.6.6 Staff					
Operating staff		nos	Yes A	Selected countries	ITU1 (52)
Other staff		nos	Yes A	Selected countries	ITU1 (54)
Technical staff		nos	Yes A	Selected countries	ITU1 (53)
Total staff		nos	Yes A	Selected countries	ITU1 (51)
6.6.7 Telegraph and Telex					
Telegrams	National and international	nos	Yes A	EC	EC80 (8.2)
Telegraph and telex services	Telegrams, telex, telex messages	nos	Yes A	Nordic countries	NCM1 (160)
Telegraph services	Domestic, foreign of which received sent	nos	Yes A	ASEAN	ASEANS1 (5.5.2)
Telex	National and international and suscriber lines	mins	Yes A	EC	EC80 (8.2)
Telex calls		nos	Yes A	ASEAN	ASEANS1 (5.5.4)
Telex lines	By country	nos	No	EC	EM1 (2003)
Telex traffic	By country	mins	No	EC	EM1 (2004)
Telegrams	By country	nos	Yes A	Africa and Asia	MAC1 (G8)
6.6.8 Telephone, Modem and Fax					
Cellular radio telephones, penetration	By country	nos	No	EC	EM1 (2005)
Cellular radio telephones availability	By country, by systems, users	nos	No	EC	EM1 (2006)
Fax systems	By country	nos	No	EC	EM1 (2007)
Modems		nos	Yes A	EC	EC80 (8.2)
Telephone calls, international outgoing	Number of calls average annual change	nos, %	No	World	GATT3 (16)
Telephone calls, national	By calls, minutes, pulses	nos	Yes A	Selected countries	ITU1 (131c,m,p)
Telephone calls, local	By calls, minutes, pulses	nos	Yes A	Selected countries	ITU1 (1311c,m,p)
Telephone calls, national trunk (toll)	By calls, minutes, pulses	nos	Yes A	Selected countries	ITU1 (1312c,m,p)

6 COMMUNICATIONS

Subject	Categories	Units	Time series Yes/No Frequency	Territorial coverage	Source (Table no.)
Telephone calls, outgoing international	Total, calls, minutes pulses	nos	Yes A	Selected countries	ITU1 (132c,m,p)
Telephone calls, total	By calls, minutes, pulses	nos	Yes A	Selected countries	ITU1 (133cmp)
Telephone calls		nos	Yes A	EC	EC80 (8.2)
Telephone calls		nos	Yes I	EC	EC80 (1.6)
Telephone lines, main lines		nos, nos per capita	No	World, EC, USA USSR, Canada, Japan	EC9 (7.1)
Telephone lines, main lines		nos	Yes A	Selected countries	ITU1 (112)
Telephone lines, main lines	Connected to private branch exchanges (PBX) etc	nos	Yes A	Selected countries	ITU1 (113)
Telephone lines, connected to automatic exchanges		%	Yes A	Selected countries	ITU1 (114)
Telephone lines, equipped for direct customer	International dialling destinations	%	Yes A	Selected countries	ITU1 (115)
Telephone lines, residential		%	Yes A	Selected countries	ITU1 (116)
Telephone lines, connection capacity of local public switching exchanges equipment	By subscriber terminal	nos	Yes A	Selected countries	ITU1 (117)
Telephone lines, main lines					
Telephone lines, new applications		nos	Yes A	Selected countries	ITU1 (121)
Telephone lines, demand, total	Including transfers	nos	Yes A	Selected countries	ITU1 (122)
Telephone lines, waiting list		nos	Yes A	Selected countries	ITU1 (123)
Telephone lines	By category	nos, rate, %	No	World	UN16 (14B)
Telephone main lines		per capita	Yes A	Selected countries	ITU1 (91)
Telephone services	By countries	nos	Yes A	EC	MAC3 (F9)
Telephone services	Number of telephones, telephone traffic	nos	Yes A	Nordic countries	NCM1 (159)
Telephone stations		nos	Yes A	EC	EC80 (8.2)
Telephone stations		nos	Yes I	EC	EC80 (1.6)
Telephone stations (sets)	By all kinds	per capita	Yes A	Selected countries	ITU1 (92)
Telephone stations (sets)	By type, by area connected to the public network	nos	Yes A	Selected countries	ITU1 (111)
Telephone traffic	By country	nos	No	EC	EM1 (2002)
Telephones		nos, rate	Yes A	VICES region, VICES countries and Yugoslavia	VICES1 (II, 4)
Telephones	By country	nos	No	EC	EC18 (10.12)
Telephones in use		nos, rate	Yes A	World	UN50 (137)
Telephones in use	By countries	nos	No	The Americas and Australasia	MAC2 (G9)
Telephones in use	By country	nos	No	EC	EM1 (2001)
Telephones in use		nos	Yes A	ASEAN	ASEANS1 (5.5.3.1)
Telephones in use	Number in use	nos	Yes A	ESCAP region, developing ESCAP region	UN44 (11)
Television licences	By country	nos	No	EC	EC18 (10.14)
Trunk and international circuit ends	Connected to manual switching exchanges, automatic switching exchanges	nos	Yes A	Selected countries	ITU1 (118) (119)
6.6.9 Television – see also under Radio (6.6.5)					
Licensed		nos	Yes I	EC	EC80 (1.6)
Media access	By country, by ownership of media equipment	%	No	EC	EM1 (1310)
Media access	By country, by cable, direct to home satellite television	nos, %	No	EC	EM1 (1311)

Subject	Categories	Units	Time series Yes/No Frequency		Territorial coverage	Source (Table no.)
Programmes	By function and by type of institution	hours, %	No	I	World	UNESCO1 (10.4)
Receiver licences		nos, rate	Yes	A	VICES region, VICES countries, and Yugoslavia	VICES1 (II, 4)
Receivers		nos,	No		World, EC, nos per capita, USA, USSR, Canada, Japan	EC9 (7.1)
Receivers	In use, licences issued, per capita	nos	Yes	5 A	World	UNESCO1 (10.2)
Receivers	Total	nos, per capita	Yes	5 A	Continents, major areas and groups of countries	UNESCO1 (6.11)
Receivers in use		nos	Yes	A	ASEAN	ASEANS1 (9.3.3)
Stations	By country, by commercal, non-commercial	nos	No			EM1 (1306)
Television sets	By country	nos	No,		EC	EC72 (11.14)
Televisions		nos, rate	No		World	UN16 (14B)
Transmitters		nos	Yes	5 A	Continents, major areas and groups of countries	UNESCO1 (6.10)
6.6.10 Traffic						
Telecommunications traffic, outgoing	By major partner Origin and destination	%	No		World	GATT3 (17)

7 CONSTRUCTION

7 CONSTRUCTION

Subject	Categories	Units	Time series Yes/No	Frequency	Territorial coverage	Source (Table no.)
7.1 EARNINGS						
Wages		indices	Yes	Selected years	EC	MHPPE1 (-)
Wages and salaries		ECUs	No		EC by region	EC76 (-)
Wages and salaries of employees		nat curr	Yes	A	World	UN18 (-)
7.2 EMPLOYMENT						
Employees		nos	Yes	A	World	UN18 (-)
Employees	By country	nos	No		EC	EC18 (8.11)
Employees	By firm size	nos	Yes	A	World	UN10 (12)
Employment expectations	By industry	nos	Yes	M	EC	EC70
Persons engaged		nos	Yes	A	World	UN18 (-)
7.3 INDUSTRY						
Construction industry		indices	Yes	A	World	UN10 (11)
Employees	By firm size	nos	Yes	A	World	UN10 (12)
Investments - cost of new fixed assets acquired	Machinery, transport and by the construction industry other , equipment buildings etc	nat curr	Yes	A	World	UN18 (-)
Investments - gross additions to fixed assets of the construction industry	Machinery, transport and other equipment, buildings etc	nat curr	Yes	A	World	UN18 (-)
Number of reporting units		nos	No		EC	EC76 (-)
Number of firms	By size	nos	Yes	A	World	UN10 (12)
Number of statistical units		nos	Yes	A	World	UN18 (-)
7.4 MATERIALS						
Building materials	By type	nos, sq m,	Yes	A	World	UN10 (14)
Building materials price indices	By type	indices	Yes	A	World	UN10 (15)
Cement		tonnes	Yes	A	World	UN10 (16)
Input and output prices	Indices	indices tonnes, cu m	Yes	A	World	UN10 (13)
7.5 PRICES						
Building materials price indices	By type	indices	Yes	A	World	UN10 (15)
Input and output prices	Indices	indices	Yes	A	World	UN10 (13)
Non-residential construction	Implicit price index	%	Yes	A	OECD, EC	OECD32 (8.7)
Price expectations	By industry	nos	Yes	M	EC	EC70
Residential construction	Implicit price index	%	Yes	A	OECD, EC	OECD32 (8.6)
7.6 PRODUCTION – see also Section 23						
7.6.1 Authorized, Permits Issued						
Authorized Dwelling Construction						
All dwellings - floor area		sq m	Yes	A	World	UN18 (-)
All dwellings - number		nos	Yes	A	World	UN18 (-)
Dwelling construction authorized	Co-operatives By type of investor (public, private)	nos	Yes	A	World	UN18 (-)
Dwellings construction authorized	Urban, rural by location	nos	Yes	A	World	UN18 (-)
Dwellings created by restoration and conversion (authorized) - floor area		sq m	Yes	A	World	UN18 (-)

7 CONSTRUCTION

Subject	Categories	Units	Time series Yes/No	Frequency	Territorial coverage	Source (Table no.)
Dwellings created by restoration and conversion (authorized) - number		nos	Yes	A	World	UN18 (-)
New construction authorized in non-residential buildings - floor area		sq m	Yes	A	World	UN18 (-)
New construction authorized in non-residential buildings - number		nos	Yes	A	World	UN18 (-)
New construction authorized in residential buildings - floor area		sq m	Yes	A	World	UN18 (-)
New construction authorized in residential buildings - number	One- or two-dwelling buildings, multi-dwelling buildings	nos	Yes	A	World	UN18 (-)
Rooms in all dwellings authorized		nos	Yes	A	World	UN18 (-)
	State and local governments, other public bodies	nos	Yes	A	World	UN18 (-)
			Yes	A	World	UN18 (-)
Construction Authorized: New Building						
All buildings - floor area		sq m	Yes	A	World	UN18 (-)
All buildings - number		nos	Yes	A	World	UN18 (-)
All buildings - tender value		nat curr	Yes	A	World	UN18 (-)
Building construction	By type	nos, cu m	Yes	A	World	UN18 (-)
Non-residential buildings - floor area	Industrial, commercial, educational, health, other	sq m	Yes	A	World	UN18 (-)
Non-residential buildings - number	Industrial, commercial, educational, health, other	nos	Yes	A	World	UN18 (-)
Non-residential buildings - tender value	Industrial, commercial, educational, health, other	nat curr	Yes	A	World	UN18 (-)
Permits issued	Total and residential	nat curr	Yes	A, Q, M	OECD	OECD21 (-)
Residential buildings - floor area		sq m	Yes	A	World	UN18 (-)
Residential buildings - tender value		nat curr	Yes	A	World	UN18 (-)
Residential buildings -number	One- or two-dwelling buildings, multi-dwelling buildings	nos	Yes	A	World	UN18 -)
Building construction, value	By type of building	nat curr	Yes	A	World	UN18 (-)
7.6.2 Expectations						
Activity assured	Construction as a whole, building, housing, other buildings, public works (civil engineering)	months	No		EC	EC70
Limits to production	None, demand, weather, labour, materials, others, construction as a whole, building, housing, other buildings, public works (civil engineering)	indices	Yes	M	EC	EC70
Trends of activity	Construction as a whole building, housing other buildings, public works (civil engineering)	indices	Yes	M	EC	EC70
7.6.3 Orders						
New Orders	Total, residential	nat curr, indices	Yes	A, M	OECD	OECD22
Order Books	Construction as a whole, building, housing, other buildings, public works (civil engineering)	indices	Yes	M	EC	EC70

Subject	Categories	Units	Time series Yes/No Frequency		Territorial coverage	Source (Table no.)
7.6.4 Output - Non-Residential						
Buildings	Residential, non-residential	nat curr	Yes	A	World	UN18 (-)
Civil engineering		nat curr	Yes	A	World	UN18 (-)
Construction, total	Residential, non-residential, activity (value added in civil engineering constant prices)	index	Yes	A	World	UN18 (-)
Non-residential construction	Implicit price index	%	Yes	A	OECD, EC	OECD32 (8.7)
Non-residential construction	Percentage of GDP	%	Yes	A	OECD, EC	OECD32 (6.10)
Repairs and maintenance		nat curr	Yes	A	World	UN18 (-)
7.6.5 Output - Residential – see also Section 23						
All dwellings	By type of investor, (public, private), state and local governments, other public bodies, Co-operatives	nos, sq m	Yes	A	World	UN18 (-)
All dwellings - floor area		sq m	Yes	A	World	UN18 (-)
All dwellings - number		nos	Yes	A	World	UN18 (-)
Buildings	Residential, non-residential	nat curr	Yes	A	World	UN18 (-)
Dwelling construction	Authorized, completed, started	nos	Yes	A	World	UN18 (-)
Dwellings - created by restoration and conversion (completed) - number		nos	Yes	A	World	UN18 (-
Dwellings - created by restoration and conversion (completed) - floor area		sq m	Yes	A	World	UN18 (-)
Dwellings completed	By location and investor	nos	Yes	A	World	UN18 (-)
Dwellings completed	By type	nos, cu m	Yes	A	World	UN18 (-)
Dwellings completed by location	Urban, rural	nos	Yes	A	World	UN18 (-)
Housing starts	Construction index	nos, indices	Yes	A, Q, M	OECD	OECD21 (-)
Index numbers of construction	Residential, non-residential, activity (value added in civil engineering constant prices)	index	Yes	A	World	UN18 (-)
New dwelling construction in non-residential buildings - floor area		sq m	Yes	A	World	UN18 (-)
New dwelling construction in non-residential buildings - number		nos	Yes	A	World	UN18 (-)
New dwelling construction in residential buildings - floor area		sq m	Yes	A	World	UN18 (-)
New dwelling construction in residential buildings - number	One- or two-dwelling buildings, multi-dwelling buildings	nos	Yes	A	World	UN18 (-)
Residential construction	Implicit price index	%	Yes	A	OECD, EC	OECD32 (8.6)
Residential construction	Percentage of GDP	%	Yes	A	OECD, EC	OECD32 (6.9)
Rooms, dwellings completed		nos	Yes	A	World	UN18 (-)
Work, put in place	Total, residential, private sector,	nat curr	Yes	A, M	OECD	OECD22
Work, in progress	Total, dwellings	nat curr,	Yes	A, Q	OECD	OECD22
7.6.6 Output - Total						
All buildings - floor area		sq m	Yes	A	World	UN18 (-)
All buildings - number		nos	Yes	A	World	UN18 (-)
All buildings - tender value		nat curr	Yes	A	World	UN18 (-)
Buildings	Residential, non-residential	nat curr	Yes	A	World	UN18 (-)

7 CONSTRUCTION

Subject	Categories	Units	Time series Yes/No	Frequency	Territorial coverage	Source (Table no.)
Buildings completed	By type	sq m, nos, nat curr	No		World	UN10 (9)
Buildings, completed	By type of building	nos, cu m	Yes	A	World	UN18 (-)
Buildings completed	Total, by type of building	nos	Yes	A, M	OECD	OECD22
Construction		indices	Yes	A, M	OECD	OECD22
Construction		indices	Yes	A, Q, M	OECD	OECD21
Construction	% of gross fixed investment at constant 1980 prices	%	Yes	A	Latin American and Caribbean countries	UN45 (64)
Construction	At constant market prices	US$	Yes	A	Latin American and Caribbean countries	UN45 (120)
Construction	Buildings	nos	Yes	A	Central Africa	UN5 (25)
Construction	Buildings	nos	Yes	A	East and Southern Africa	UN4 (25)
Construction	Buildings	nos	Yes	A	North Africa	UN2 (25)
Construction	Buildings	nos	Yes	A	West Africa	UN3 (25)
Construction activity	By country or area	indices	Yes	A	World	UN18 (-)
Construction and capital repairs						
Construction output						
Construction put in place						
Construction, total	Residential, non-residential, activity (value added in civil engineering constant prices)	index	Yes	A	World	UN18 (-)
Fixed assets, gross additions to		nat curr	Yes	A	World	UN18 (-)
Fixed assets, buildings		nat curr	Yes	A	World	UN18 (-)
Fixed assets, cost of new		nat curr	Yes	A	World	UN18 (-)
Fixed assets, cost of new buildings		nat curr	Yes	A	World	UN18 (-)
Gross fixed capital formation	Total, in construction and residential buildings as a percentage of GDP, as a percentage of total fixed capital formation and as a percentage of gross fixed capital formation in construction	%	Yes	A	World	UN10 (2)
Investments	Total and in construction	%	Yes	A	EC	UN10 (3)
Non-residential buildings completed - floor area	Industrial, commercial, educational, health, other	sq m	Yes	A	World	UN18 (-)
Non-residential buildings completed - number	Industrial, commercial, educational, health, other	nos	Yes	A	World	UN18 (-)
Non-residential buildings completed - tender value	Industrial, commercial, educational, health, other	nat curr	Yes	A	World	UN18 (-)
Output		nat curr	Yes	A	World	UN18 (-)
Output	Seasonally adjusted	indices	Yes	A, M	EC	EC53 (6.24)
Output	Total value of	nat curr	Yes	A	World	UN18 (-)
Production by the EC construction industry	By type of construction	%	No		EC	EC35 (-)
Production indices	Per working day, seasonally adjusted, building and civil engineering, construction of buildings, civil engineering	indices	Yes	A, M	EC	EC52 (-)
Residential buildings completed - floor area		sq m	Yes	A	World	UN18 (-)

Subject	Categories	Units	Time series Yes/No Frequency		Territorial coverage	Source (Table no.)
Residential buildings completed - number	One- or two-dwelling buildings, multi-dwelling buildings	nos	Yes	A	World	UN18 (-)
Residential buildings completed - tender value		nat curr	Yes	A	World	UN18 (-)
Value	By type of building	indices	Yes	A, M	OECD	OECD22
		ECUs	No		EC	EC76 (-)
Value added		nat curr	Yes	A	World	UN18 (-)
Value added		nat curr	Yes	A	World	UN18 (-)
Value of buildings, new completed	By type of building	nat curr	Yes	A	World	UN18 (-)
Value of construction		nat curr	Yes	A	World	UN10 (10)
Value of construction	New construction and capital repairs, current repairs and maintenance	nat curr	Yes	A	World	UN18 (-)
Value of output		nat curr	Yes	A	World	UN10 (12)
Work, put in place	Total, residential, private sector,	nat curr	Yes	A, M	OECD	OECD22
Work, in progress	Total, dwellings	nat curr, sq m, nos	Yes	A, Q	OECD	OECD22
7.6.7 Starts – see also Section 23						
Buildings started	Total	nat curr cu m	Yes	A, M	OECD	OECD22
Housing starts	Construction index	nos, indices	Yes	A, Q, M	OECD	OECD21

8 CONSUMPTION

Subject	Categories	Units	Time series Yes/No Frequency		Territorial coverage	Source (Table no.)
8.1 AGRICULTURE AND AGRICULTURAL PRODUCTS - see also Section 2						
8.1.1 Crops						
Cereals		kg/capita	No		EC, USA, USSR, Canada, Japan	EC9 (5.9)
Cocoa	By country, per caput	kg/head	Yes	A	World	ICC02 (19)
Cocoa	By final consumer, by country	tonnes	Yes	A	World	ICC02 (18)
Coffee, apparent consumption per head		tonnes, kg, per capita	Yes	A	World	UN50 (24)
Coffee, tea, cocoa and tobacco		tonnes/ capita	Yes	A	Nordic countries	NCM1 (166)
Crops	By use, consumer, by product	tonnes	Yes	A	EC	EC19 (V)
Grape products	Wine, grape juice, and regions fresh grapes, raisins	hl, q	No		World	OIVV1 (G)
Grapes	Pressings, fruit consumption of raisins, table grapes,	q	No		World	OIVV1 (E)
Potatoes		kg/capita	No		EC, USA, USSR, Canada, Japan	EC9 (5.9)
Rice		kg/capita	No		EC, USA, USSR, Canada, Japan	EC9 (5.9)
Tea, apparent consumption per head	By country	tonnes, kg, per capita	Yes	6 M	Selected countries	ITC1 (G2)
Tea, consumption in producing countries		tonnes	Yes	A	Selected countries	ITC1 (D44)
Tobacco	By country, by product	nos	No		EC	EM1 (1408)
Vegetables		kg/capita	No		EC, USA, USSR, Canada, Japan	EC9 (5.9)
Wheat		tonnes	Yes	A	World	IWhC3 (A.3)
Wine		hl	Yes	4 yr	World	OIVV1 (H)
Wine		kg/capita	No		EC, USA, USSR, Canada, Japan	EC9 (5.9)
Wine		l/capita	No		World	OIVV1 (I)
Wine	By consumer, domestic use wine grapes	hl	No		World	OIVV1 (K)
8.1.2 Dairy Products						
Butter		kg/capita	No		EC, USA, USSR, Canada, Japan	EC9 (5.10)
Butter and margarine		kg/head	Yes	A	EC	MMB1 (119)
Cheese	By cheese, fresh cheese	kg/head	Yes	A	EC	MMB1 (120)
Cream and dairy ice cream		kg/head	Yes	A	EC	MMB1 (118)
Dairy products	By country, by product	kg, l, nos	No		EC	EM1 (1403)
Eggs		kg/capita	No		EC, USA, USSR, Canada, Japan	EC9 (5.10)
Milk		kg/capita	No		EC, USA, USSR, Canada, Japan	EC9 (5.10)
Milk fat, protein		kg/head	Yes	A	EC	MMB1 (121)
Milk, intermediate	By size of herd	%	Yes	A	EC	EC58 (5.1)
Milk, liquid	By type	kg/head	Yes	A	EC	MMB1 (116)
Yogurt and condensed milk	Total	kg/head	Yes	A	EC	MMB1 (117)
8.1.3 Fertilisers						
Fertiliser	By type	tonnes	Yes	A	World	FAO5 (1)
Fertiliser per hectare	By agricultural area, arable land and permanent crops, and per caput	kg	Yes	A	World	FAO5 (10)

8 CONSUMPTION

Subject	Categories	Units	Time series Yes/No Frequency		Territorial coverage	Source (Table no.)
Nitrogenous fertiliser		tonnes	Yes	A	World	FAO5 (20)
Nitrogenous fertiliser	By economic class	tonnes	Yes	A	World	FAO5 (2)
Nitrogenous, phosphate and potash fertiliser	Total	tonnes	Yes	A	World	FAO5 (32)
Phosphate fertiliser		tonnes	Yes	A	World	FAO5 (24)
Phosphate fertiliser	By economic class	tonnes	Yes	A	World	FAO5 (3)
Potash fertiliser		tonnes	Yes	A	World	FAO5 (28)
Potash fertiliser	By economic class	tonnes	Yes	A	World	FAO5 (4)
8.1.4 Rubber						
Rubber	By country	tonnes	Yes	A	Selected countries	IRSG1 (16-20)
Rubber	By major sector	tonnes	Yes	A	World	IRSG2 (5)
Rubber	By major sectors	tonnes	Yes	A, Q	World	IRSG1 (37)
Rubber	By type of rubber	tonnes	No		Selected countries	IRSG1 (29-36)
Rubber	By type of rubber	tonnes	No		USA	IRSG1 (29)
					Brazil	IRSG1 (30)
					France	IRSG1 (31)
					Germany	IRSG1 (32)
					UK	IRSG1 (33)
					Australia	IRSG1 (34)
					India	IRSG1 (35)
					Japan	IRSG1 (36)
Rubber	Latex, total	tonnes	Yes	A	Malaysia, peninsular	IRSG1 (16)
					Indonesia	IRSG1 (18)
					Thailand	IRSG1 (19)
					Sri Lanka	IRSG1 (20)
Rubber	Natural, synthetic	tonnes, kilos, per capita	Yes	A	World	UN50 (120)
Rubber goods, indices of production		ind	Yes	A, M	USA, France, UK Germany, Japan, Italy	IRSG1 (42)
Rubber latex, natural		tonnes	Yes	A, M	World	IRSG1 (23)
Rubber, apparent consumption	By non-reporting countries	tonnes	Yes	A	World	IRSG2 (6)
Rubber, area under plantation	Estates, smallholdings	ha	No		World	IRSG1 (46)
Rubber, natural		tonnes	Yes	A	World	IRSG2 (10)
Rubber, natural		tonnes	Yes	A, M	World	IRSG1 (13)
Rubber, natural		tonnes	Yes	A, M	World	IRSG1 (7)
Rubber, natural	By country	tonnes	Yes	A	World	IRSG2 (7)
Rubber, natural	By producing countries	tonnes	Yes	A	World	IRSG2 (11)
Rubber, natural	By producing countries	tonnes	Yes	A, M	World	IRSG1 (14)
Rubber, natural	Consumption, production, stocks	tonnes	Yes	A, M	World	IRSG1 (1)
Rubber, natural	Consumption, production, stocks	tonnes	Yes	A	World	IRSG2 (25)
Rubber, natural and synthetic		tonnes	Yes	A, M	World	IRSG1 (3)
Rubber, synthetic		%	Yes	A, M	World	IRSG1 (4)
Rubber, synthetic		tonnes	Yes	A	World	IRSG2 (15)
Rubber, synthetic		tonnes	Yes	A	World	IRSG2(18)
Rubber, synthetic		tonnes	Yes	A, M	World	IRSG1 (24)
Rubber, synthetic		tonnes	Yes	A, M	World	IRSG1(28)
Rubber, synthetic	Consumption, production, stocks	tonnes	Yes	A, M	World	IRSG2 (2)
Rubber, technically specified		tonnes	Yes	A, M	World	IRSG1 (8)
Tyres	Car commercial vehicle	nos	Yes	A	World	IRSG2(22)
Tyres	Car, truck	nos	Yes	A, Q	World	IRSG1 (38)
Tyres	Car, truck	nos	Yes	A, Q	World	IRSG1 (39)

Subject	Categories	Units	Time series Yes/No Frequency		Territorial coverage	Source (Table no.)
8.1.5 Sugar						
Consumption	By country	tonnes	Yes	A	World	ISO3 (-)
Consumption	By country	tonnes	Yes	A, M	World	ISO2 (-)
Consumption	Total, per capita	tonnes, # kilos	Yes	A	World	UN50 (23)
World consumption	By country, per capita	kgs	Yes	A	World	ISO3 (-)
		kg/capita	No		EC, USA, USSR, Canada, Japan	EC9 (5.9)
World sugar balance	By countries, stocks, imports, exports, production consumption	tonnes	Yes	A	World	FOL3 (15-23)
8.2 CHEMICALS - see also Section 25.3						
Consumption	By country	US$	Yes	A	Western World	CIA1 (16)
Fluorine		tonnes	Yes	A	EC	EC68 (-)
Fluorine	Fluorspar, hydrofluoric acid and aluminium fluoride	tonnes	No		EC	EC68 (-)
Home demand	By country	nat curr	Yes	A	Selected countries	CIA1 (5)
Home sales	By country	nat curr	Yes	A	Selected countries	CIA1 (4)
Home sales	By country	US$	Yes	A	Western World	CIA1 (15)
Phosphates		tonnes	Yes	A	EC	EC68 (-)
Phosphates	Natural phosphates, phosphoric acid, slag and fertilizers	tonnes	No		EC	EC68 (-)
Sales	By country	nat curr	Yes	A	Selected countries	CIA1 (1)
Sales	By country	US$	Yes	A	Western World	CIA1 (12)
Urea	Home deliveries	tonnes, %	Yes	A	World	IFA1 (-)
8.3 DRUGS - see also Section 14						
8.3.1 Narcotics						
Consumption , principal narcotic drugs	By type of narcotic and country	kg	Yes	A	World	UN29 (XI)
Consumption, defined daily doses per million inhabitants	By type of narcotic and country	nos	No		World	UN29 (XIII)
Consumption, other narcotic drugs	Derivatives of opium alkaloids, synthetic narcotic drugs	kg	Yes	A	World	UN30(XII)
8.3.2 Psychotropic Substances						
Consumption, defined daily doses per thousand inhabitants per day	By country and group of psychotropic substance	nos	No		World	UN30 (IV)
8.4 ENERGY - see also Section 17						
8.4.1 Coal						
Coal		toe % share % change	Yes	A		BP1 (p29)
Coal	By final use	tonnes	Yes	A	World	IEA7
Coal	By fuel type	tce, tonnes	Yes	I	OECD	IEA2 (-)
Coal and lignite		toe	Yes	A	World, EC, USA, USSR, Canada, Japan	EC9 (4.19)
Coal balance	Supply and consumption	tce	Yes	A	Selected Non-OECD countries	IEA2 (III.11-III.20)
Coal balance	Supply and consumption	tce	Yes	I	OECD	IEA2 (-)

8 CONSUMPTION

Subject	Categories	Units	Time series Yes/No Frequency		Territorial coverage	Source (Table no.)
Coal, hard		tonnes	No		World	IEA2 (III.1-III.10)
Coal, hard	By country	tonnes	Yes	A	ESCAP countries	UN44
Coal, hard	By steel industry, power stations and households	tonnes	No		World	IEA2 (III.1-III.10)
8.4.2 Electrical						
Electric energy	Average annual rates of growth	ind	Yes	A	Latin American and Caribbean countries	UN45 (56)
Electric energy	Energy available for consumption and supplied to consumers, average consumption per inhabitant, by country	GWh, kWh	Yes	A	EC, USA	UN7 (1)
Electric energy	Per capita	kWh	Yes	A	Latin American and Caribbean countries	UN45 (55)
Electric energy, fuel consumption	Consumption of fuel and net electricity, production, by fuel type, by type of producer, by country	tonnes, TJ, GWh	Yes	A	EC, USA	UN7 (4)
Electric energy, supplied to consumers	Energy producing industries by type, other consumers by type, by country	GWh	Yes	A	EC, USA	UN7 (2)
Electric generating capacity	By type	kWh	Yes	A	World	UN21 (33)
Electricity		kWh, kWh per capita	Yes	A	World	UN21 (35)
Electricity	By country	kWh	Yes	A	ESCAP countries	UN44
Electricity	By final use	GWh	Yes	A	World	IEA7
Electricity	By fuel type	TWh	Yes	I	OECD	IEA2 (-)
Electricity	By country	kwh	No		EC	EC18 (8.8)
Electricity demand	By type of industry, type of transport, agriculture, commerce and public service, and residential users	TWh	Yes	I	OECD	IEA3 (-)
Electricity, changes in projections	By fuel	TWh	No		OECD	IEA2 (-)
Electricity, fuel inputs	By fuel type	tce	Yes	I	OECD	IEA2 (-)
Electricity, primary		toe	Yes	A	World, EC, USA, USSR, Canada, Japan	EC9 (4.19)
Electricity, share of total final consumption		%	Yes	I	OECD	IEA3 (-)
Electricity, voltage applied	Industrial standard consumers	kv	No		EC	EC28
Hydro-electricity		toe	Yes		World % share % change	BP1 (p32)
8.4.3 Gas						
Gas consumption	By country	cu m, % change, % share	Yes	A	World	BP2 (-)
Gas demand by sector	By country, end user	cu m	No		OECD	BP2 (-)
Gas, by energy producing industries	By type of gas, by country	TJ	Yes	A	EC, USA	UN8 (1)
Gas, gross	By type of gas, by country	TJ	Yes	A	EC, USA	UN8 (1)

Subject	Categories	Units	Time series Yes/No	Frequency	Territorial coverage	Source (Table no.)
Gas, household consumers	By type of gas	nos	Yes	A	EC, USA	UN8 (4)
Gas, non-energy use	By type of gas, by country	TJ	Yes	A	EC, USA	UN8 (1)
Gas, unaccounted losses	By type of gas, by country	TJ	Yes	A	EC, USA	UN8 (1)
Gases		TJ, mj per capita	Yes	A	World	UN21 (31)
Liquids and condensates	By OPEC and non OPEC	tonnes	Yes	A, M	World	DSC2 (3.1)
LPG consumption	By country	tonnes, % change, % share	Yes	A	World	BP2 (-)
Natural gas		TJ	No		EC	EC9 (4.30)
Natural gas		TJ	Yes	A	OECD	IEA10 (II.9)
Natural gas		TJ	Yes	A	World, OECD, non-OECD	IEA10 (I.20)
Natural gas		TJ, mj per capita	Yes	A	World	UN21 (28)
Natural gas		toe	Yes	A	World, EC, USA, USSR, Canada, Japan	EC9 (4.19)
Natural gas		toe, % share	Yes	A	World	BP1 (p22)
Natural gas	By final use	toe	Yes	A	World	IEA7
Refinery gas		tonnes	Yes	A	OECD	IEA10(II.6A)
Stock levels, OECD	By crude, products	tonnes	Yes	A, M	World	DSC2 (3.3)
8.4.4 General						
Bitumen		tonnes	Yes	A	OECD	IEA10 (II.6B)
		capita				
Consumer industry		toe per capita	Yes	A	EC	EC9 (4.21)
Consumption	By product, country	tonnes oil equivalent, % change	No		World	BP2 (-)
Consumption	Coal, oil, gas, total, per capita	toe	No		VICES countries and Yugoslavia	VICES1 (V/1)
Consumption and supply	Type of fuel and sector	tonnes, TJ, GWh	Yes	A	OECD	IEA8&9
Consumption, final		toe	Yes	I	OECD	IEA3 (-)
Consumption, final	By form of energy and major consumers	TJ	Yes	A	EC, USA, Canada	UN9 (2)
Consumption, final	By sector and type of primary energy per capita	toe	No		VICES countries	VICES1 (V/1)
Consumption, growth rates	Total, per capita	%	Yes	I	World	UNCTAD1 (6.9)
Consumption, total		toe	Yes	A	EC	EC9 (4.18)
Energy consumption	Forms of energy	terajoules	Yes	A	EC, USA Canada	UN13 (5)
Energy consumption, pipeline	Forms of energy	terajoules	Yes	A	EC, USA, Canada	UN13 (5)
Energy consumption, rail	Forms of energy	terajoules	Yes	A	EC, USA Canada	UN13 (5)
Energy consumption, road	Forms of energy	terajoules	Yes	A	EC, USA Canada	UN13 (5)
Energy consumption, shipping	By oil and non-oil	toe	Yes	A/Q	OECD and regions	DSC2 (1.11)
Energy consumption, transport	Forms of energy and mode of transport	terajoules	Yes	A	EC, USA Canada	UN13 (5)
Energy producing industries	By form of energy	TJ	Yes	A	EC, USA, Canada	UN9 (2)
Energy production, consumption and trade	By high, middle, low income	tonnes, kg, %	No		World	CS1 (16)
Energy requirements (conventional fuel equivalent)	By type	TJ, gj per capita	Yes	A	World	UN21 (4)

8 CONSUMPTION

Subject	Categories	Units	Time series Yes/No Frequency		Territorial coverage	Source (Table no.)
Energy, commercial		tce	Yes	A	World, ESCAP countries, developing ESCAP countries	UN44 (p3)
Energy, commercial	Total and by type	j, j per	Yes	A	World	UN21 (3)
Energy, commercial	Total, per capita, share of liquid fuel in total consumption economic regions	tce %	Yes	I	World	UNCTAD1 (6.9)
Energy, commercial (coal equivalent)	Total and by type	tonnes, kg per capita	Yes	A	World	UN21(1)
Energy, commercial (oil equivalent)	Total and by type	tonnes, kg per capita	Yes	A	World	UN21 (2)
Energy, final	By fuel type	tce, %	Yes	I	OECD	IEA2 (-)
Energy, primary		toe % share % change	Yes	A	World	BP1 (p33)
Energy, primary		toe	Yes	A	World, EC, USA, USSR, Canada Japan	EC9 (4.19)
Energy, primary	By fuel type	toe	Yes	A	World	BP1 (p34)
Energy, primary	Coal, lignite, oil, natural gas, nuclear energy, electricity	%	No		EC	EC9 (4.20)
Energy, primary	Coal, lignite, oil, natural gas, nuclear energy, electricity	%	Yes	A	EC	EC9 (4.20)
Energy, primary and equivalents	By form of energy	TJ	Yes	A	EC, USA, Canada	UN9 (2)
Fuel, changes in projections	By fuel type	tce	No		OECD	IEA2 (-)
Fuels, liquid	By type	tonnes, kg per capita	Yes	A	World	UN21 (14, 7-24)
Fuels, solid	By type	tonnes, kg per capita	Yes	A	World	UN21 (5-6, 8-13)
Heat		tce	Yes	I	OECD	IEA2 (-)
Households, commerce,		toe per capita services, etc.	Yes	A	EC	EC9 (4.21)
Hydrocarbons	Average annual rates of growth	indices	Yes	A	Latin American and Caribbean countries	UN45 (54)
Hydrocarbons	Per capita	kg.p.e	Yes	A	Latin American and Caribbean countries	UN45 (53)
Marine bunkering	By form of energy	TJ	Yes	A	EC, USA, Canada	UN9 (2)
Naphtha		tonnes	Yes	A	OECD	IEA10 (II.6A)
Non-oil		%	Yes	I	OECD	IEA10 (I.1)
Oil		km, tonnes, tonne-kms	Yes	A	EC, USA	UN13 (28)
Solid fuels, by energy producing industries	By fuel type, by country	tonnes	Yes	I	EC, USA	UN6 (1)
Solid fuels, calorific value	By fuel type, by country	kJ, kg	Yes	I	EC, USA	UN6 (1)
Solid fuels, gross	By fuel type, by country	tonnes	Yes	I	EC, USA	UN6 (1)
Solid fuels, non-energy use	By fuel type, by country	tonnes	Yes	I	EC , USA	UN6 (1)
Solid fuels, total	By fuel type, by final consumer, by country	tonnes	Yes	I	EC, USA	UN6 (1)
Transfers	By form of energy	TJ	Yes	A	EC, USA, Canada	UN9 (2)
Transport		toe per capita	Yes	A	EC	EC9 (4.21)

Subject	Categories	Units	Time series Yes/No	Frequency	Territorial coverage	Source (Table no.)
8.4.5 Nuclear						
Nuclear energy		toe % share % change	Yes	A	World	BP1 (p30)
Nuclear energy		toe	Yes	A	World, EC, USA, USSR, Canada, Japan	EC9 (4.19)
8.4.6 Oil						
Crude oil		toe	Yes	A	World, EC, USA, USSR, Canada Japan	EC9 (4.19)
Crude petroleum	By country	tonnes % change	Yes	A	ESCAP countries	UN44
Gas, diesel oil		tonnes	Yes	A	OECD	IEA10 (II.5A)
Heavy fuel oil		tonnes	Yes	A	OECD	IEA10 (II.5B)
Kerosene		tonnes	Yes	A	OECD	IEA10 (II.6A)
Liquefied petroleum gases		tonnes	Yes	A	OECD	IEA10 (II.6A)
Lubricants		tonnes	Yes	A	OECD	IEA10 (II.6A)
Oil		%	Yes	I	OECD	IEA10 (I.1)
Oil		barrels/day, % share % change	Yes	A	World	BP1 (p8)
Oil		tonnes	Yes	A	World, OECD and non-OECD	IEA10 (I.3)
Oil		tonnes, % share % change	Yes	A	World	BP1 (p7)
Oil	By consumers	tonnes	Yes	A	OECD	IEA10 (II.1)
Oil	By product groups, by region	tonnes % share	Yes	A	World	BP1 (p10)
Oil balance	Supply, demand	barrels/day	Yes	A/Q	World	OPEC2
Oil Products	By type	tonnes, barrels/day	Yes	A	World, OECD and non-OECD	IEA7
Paraffin waxes		tonnes	Yes	A	OECD	IEA10 (II.6B)
Petroleum coke		tonnes	Yes	A	OECD	IEA10 (II.6B)
Petroleum products		tonnes	Yes	A	OECD	IEA10 (II.5C)
Petroleum products	By country	tonnes	Yes	A	World	IP1 (-)
Petroleum products	By OECD area	barrels/day	Yes	Q	N. America, OECD EC, OECD Pacific	OECD26 (XIV)
Refined products		barrels/day	Yes	A	OPEC countries	OPEC1 (21)
Refined products	By country	barrels/day	Yes	A	World	OPEC1 (50)
Refined products	By region	barrels/day	Yes	A	World	OPEC1(22)
Refined products	By type	barrels/day	Yes	A	OPEC countries	OPEC1 (49)
White spirit and SBP		tonnes	Yes	A	OECD	IEA10 (II.6A)
8.5 EXPENDITURE - see also Section 34						
Consumer expenditure		indices	Yes	A, M	Netherlands	OECD22
Consumer expenditure	Average annual rates of growth	indices	Yes	A	Latin American and Caribbean countries	UN45 (23)
Consumer expenditure	By country	nat curr	No		EC	EM1 (1101)

8 CONSUMPTION

Subject	Categories	Units	Time series Yes/No Frequency	Territorial coverage	Source (Table no.)
Consumer expenditure	By country, by object	%	No	EC	EM1 (1103)
Consumer expenditure	By country, by object	US$	No	EC	EM1 (1102)
Consumer expenditure	By household, food, drink and tobacco	%	No	EC	WC1 (-)
Consumer expenditure, alcoholic drinks	By country, by growth	nat curr, %	No	EC	EM1 (1105)
Consumer expenditure, clothing	By country, by growth	nat curr, %	No	EC	EM1 (1108)
Consumer expenditure, communications	By country, by growth	nat curr, %	No	EC	EM1 (1115)
Consumer expenditure, food	By country, by growth	nat curr, %	No	EC	EM1 (1104)
Consumer expenditure, footwear	By country, by growth	nat curr, %	No	EC	EM1 (1109)
Consumer expenditure, fuel	By country, by growth	nat curr, %	No	EC	EM1 (1111)
Consumer expenditure, health goods and medical services	By country, by growth	nat curr, %	No	EC	EM1 (1113)
Consumer expenditure, hotels and restaurants	By country, by growth	nat curr, %	No	EC	EM1 (1117)
Consumer expenditure, household goods and services	By country, by growth	nat curr, %	No	EC	EM1 (1112)
Consumer expenditure, housing	By country, by growth	nat curr, %	No	EC	EM1 (1110)
Consumer expenditure, leisure and education	By country, by growth	nat curr, %	No	EC	EM1 (1116)
Consumer expenditure, non-alcoholic drinks	By country, by growth	nat curr, %	No	EC	EM1 (1106)
Consumer expenditure, tobacco	By country, by growth	nat curr, %	No	EC	EM1 (1107)
Consumer expenditure, transport	By country, by growth	nat curr, %	No	EC	EM1 (1114)
Consumption	At current prices, average annual growth rate at constant prices, % of distributeed national product (net) at current prices	nat curr, %	Yes A	VICES countries and Yugoslavia	VICES1 (I.1)
Consumption patterns	By country, by item	%	No	EC	EC35 (-)
Consumption, average annual per head	By selected item, according to socio-economic category of head of household, type of household, income category,	kg, l, nos, kWh, tonnes, cu m	No	EC	EC42 (3/1-3/5)
Consumption, households	Food, beverages, tobacco clothing and footwear, rent, fuel and power, furniture, furnishings, household equipment and operation, medical care and health expenses, transport and communication recreation, education, entertainment, and cultural services, etc	ECU/head	No	EC, USA, USSR, Canada, Japan	EC9 (2.8)
Consumption, private, percentage GDP	By percentage points	%	Yes A	World	WB6 (15)
Consumption, private, net	At current prices, average annual growth rate at constant prices, % of distributed national product (net) at current prices	nat curr,	Yes A	VICES countries and Yugoslavia	VICES1 (II/1)
Consumption, private, per capita	By country and region	US$	Yes A	World	WB6 (3)

Subject	Categories	Units	Time series Yes/No Frequency		Territorial coverage	Source (Table no.)
Consumption, public, net	At current prices, average annual growth rate at constant prices, % of distributed national product (net) at current prices	nat curr, %	Yes	A	VICES countries and Yugoslavia	VICES1 (II/1)
Expenditure structure, average annual	By individual expenses, according to socio-economic category of head of household, type of household, income category, region and urban, rural environment, by country		No		EC	EC42 (2/1-2/5)
Expenditure, absolute	By main groups, according to socio-economic category of head of household, type of household, income category, region and urban, rural environment, by country	nat curr	No		EC	EC42 (2)
Expenditure, real	By country, annual rates of change	%	No		EC	EC35 (-)
Intermediate, technical	By user, branch and country region and urban, rural environment, by country		No		EC	EC63
Structure of demand	By high, middle, low income	%	No		World	CS1 (5)

8.6 FISH - see also Section 20

Consumption		kg/capita	No		World, EC, USA, USSR, Canada, Japan	EC9 (5.27)
Fresh produce consumption	By country, by product	kg	No		EC	EM1 (1402)
Meat and fish consumption	By country	kg	No		EC	EM1 (1401)

8.7 FOOD AND DRINK

Alcoholic beverages	Total	litres	Yes	A	Nordic countries	NCM1 (167)
Bakery products consumption	By country, by product	kg	No		EC	EM1 (1404)
Convenience and miscellaneous foods	By country	kg, l	No		EC	EM1 (1405)
Dairy products consumption	By country, by product	kg, l, nos	No		EC	EM1 (1403)
Drinks consumption	By country, by type	l	No		EC	EM1 (1407)
Food consumption	By food type	kg/head, nos/head	Yes	A	VICES countries and Yugoslavia	VICES1 (II/3)
Food consumption	Per capita	volume index, price index	No		Africa	EC1 (V2)
Food consumption	Per person by major foodstuffs, by country	kg/year, g/day, calories/day	Yes	A	OECD	OECD12
Food utilisation, feed	By major foodstuffs, by country	tonnes	Yes	A	OECD	OECD12
Food utilisation, processing	By major foodstuffs, food, industrial products, by country	tonnes	Yes	A	OECD	OECD12

8 CONSUMPTION

Subject	Categories	Units	Time series Yes/No Frequency		Territorial coverage	Source (Table no.)
Food utilisation, seed	By major foodstuffs, by country	tonnes	Yes	A	OECD	OECD12
Food utilisation, total	By major foodstuffs, by country	tonnes	Yes	A	OECD	OECD12
Food utilisation, waste	By major foodstuffs, by country	tonnes	Yes	A	OECD	OECD12
Fresh produce consumption	By country, by product	kg	No		EC	EM1 (1402)
Meat and fish consumption	By country	kg	No		EC	EM1 (1401)
Snack food and hot beverages	By country, by confectionery, savoury	kg	No		EC	EM1 (1406)
Tobacco consumption	By country, by product	nos	No		EC	EM1 (1408)

8.8 GENERAL - see also Section 2

Subject	Categories	Units	Time series	Frequency	Territorial coverage	Source (Table no.)
Cement		tonnes	Yes	A	World	UN10 (16)
Commodities, selected	By commodity, by country	tonnes, kg/capita	Yes	A	ESCAP countries	UN44
Consumption	Total, at constant market prices	US$	Yes	A	Latin American and Caribbean countries	UN45 (118)
Consumption, footwear	By production, imports, exports, country	pairs	Yes	A	World	SATRA1(-)
Consumption, households	By type	kg/capita	Yes	A	EC, World	EC6 (IA 6)
Consumption, households	Total at current prices, volume index numbers, per inhabitant, expenditure for food	ECU, indices ECU, %	Yes	A	EC	EC6 (IA 9)
Fats and oils		kg/capita	No		EC, USA, USSR, Canada, Japan	EC9 (5.10)
Industrial products	Households	indices	Yes	A/M	France	OECD22
Water consumption from public water works	Total	cu m	Yes	A	Nordic countries	NCM1 (85)

8.9 MEAT AND LIVESTOCK PRODUCTS - see also Section 2

Subject	Categories	Units	Time series	Frequency	Territorial coverage	Source (Table no.)
Animals and animals' products	By animal, by product, by consumer	tonnes	Yes	A	EC	EC7 (IV)
Animal products, human consumption	By product	kg/head/yr	Yes	A	EC	EC7 (IV)
Beef and veal	Consumption, consumption per capita, self-sufficiency	tonnes, kg, %	Yes	A	EC	MLC1 (-)
Beef and veal	Total and per head	tonnes, kg/head	Yes	A	OECD	OECD26
Beef and veal	Total, per capita	tonnes, %, kg/capita	Yes	A	World	GATT2 (5)
Beef and veal, apparent consumption	Per head	kg,%	Yes	A	EC	UN34 (V)
Beef, veal, mutton, lamb, goat and pig meat	Consumption, consumption per capita, self-sufficiency	tonnes kg, %	Yes	A	EC	MLC1 (-)
Edible offal	Total and per head	tonnes, kg/head	Yes	A	OECD	OECD26
Fresh produce consumption	By country, by product	kg	No		EC	EM1 (1402)
Horse meat	Total and per head	tonnes, kg/head	Yes	A	OECD	OECD26
Meat		kg/capita	No		EEC, USA, USSR, Canada, Japan	EC9 (5.10)
Meat	By meat type and by country, consumption	tonnes, kg/year/ head	Yes	A	OECD	OECD26

Subject	Categories	Units	Time series Yes/No	Frequency	Territorial coverage	Source (Table no.)
Meat	Total and per head	tonnes, kg/year	Yes	A	OECD	OECD26
Meat and fish consumption	By country	kg	No		EC	EM1 (1401)
Meat, other	Total and per head	tonnes, kg/head	Yes	A	OECD	OECD26
Mutton, lamb and goat meat	Total and per head	tonnes, kg/head	Yes	A	OECD	OECD26
Pig meat	Total and per head	tonnes, kg/head	Yes	A	OECD	OECD26
Pig meat, apparent consumption	Per head	kg, %	Yes	A	EC	UN34(XX)
Pigmeat	Total, per capita	tonnes, % kg/capita	Yes	A	World	GATT2 (16)
Poultry meat	Ready to cook basis total, per capita	tonnes, % kg/capita	Yes	A	World	GATT2 (20)
Poultry meat	Total and per head	tonnes, kg/head	Yes	A	OECD	OECD26
Poultry meat, apparent consumption	Per head	kg, %	Yes	A	EC	UN34 (XLIX)
Poultry meat, offal and all meat and offal	Consumption, consumption per capita, self-sufficiency	tonnes kg, %	Yes	A	EC	MLC1 (-)
			Yes	A	EC	MLC1 (-)
Sheep meat, apparent consumption	Per head	kg, %	Yes	A	Selected European countries	UN34 (XXXV)
Sheepmeat	Total, per capita	tonnes, cwe, kg/capita, %	Yes	A	World	GATT2 (24)

8.10 MINERALS, METALS AND ORES - see also Sections 25, 32 and 33

Subject	Categories	Units	Time series Yes/No	Frequency	Territorial coverage	Source (Table no.)
Aluminium dispatches	By end-use, by country	tonnes, %	Yes	A	EC	EAA1 (-)
Aluminium, per capita	Home market	kg/capita	Yes	A	EC, USA, Japan	EAA1 (-)
Aluminium, primary		tonnes	Yes	A	World	IBA1 (4)
Aluminium, primary and secondary		tonnes	Yes	A	EC	EAA1 (-)
Coke, oven coke	Total and blast furnaces	tonnes	No		OECD EC	OECD18 (12)
Consumption, estimated	By micrgrits, powders, fibres, whiskers	tonnes	No		World	EAT1(6.4)
Consumption, estimates	By country	tonnes	Yes	A	World	MJ1 (-)
Consumption, refined	By country	tonnes	Yes	A	World	MJ1 (IV)
Crude steel, apparent consumption per capita	By country, region	kg	Yes	A	World	IISI4 (11)
Crude steel, apparent consumption	Final consumption	tonnes, kg/capita	Yes	A	EC	EC55 (6.3)
Crude steel, apparent consumption	By country, region	tonnes	Yes	A	World	IISI4 (10)
ECSC steel and non-ECSC steel, apparent consumption	In crude steel equivalent	tonnes kg/capita	Yes	A	EC	EC55 (6.2)
ECSC steel, apparent consumption	In crude steel equivalent	tonnes kg/capita	Yes	A	EC	EC55 (6.1)
Finished steel, apparent consumption	By country, region	tonnes	Yes	A	World	IISI4 (12)
	industrial process	MWh, GJ			Japan	
Iron and major alloying metals	By metal type	tonnes	No		EC, USA, USSR	EC68 (-)
steel		kg/capita	Yes	A		EC9 (4.35)
Iron and steel industry	Total/per capita	tonnes	Yes	A	World	UN50 (121)
Iron ore	Apparent consumption	tonnes	No		World	IISI5 (-)
Iron ore	Total and by percentage iron content	tonnes	No		OECD	OECD18 (9)
Lead		tonnes	Yes	A	EC, USA, Japan	EC34 (5.1)
Lead		tonnes	Yes	A, M	Peru	ILZSG1 (22)
Lead	By principal uses	tonnes	Yes	A, M	Germany	ILZSG1 (18)
Lead	By principal uses	tonnes	Yes	A, M	Italy	ILZSG1 (19)
Lead	By principal uses	tonnes	Yes	A, M	Japan	ILZSG1 (20)
Lead	By principal uses	tonnes	Yes	A, M	UK	ILZSG1 (23)
Lead	By principal uses	tonnes	Yes	A, M	US	ILZSG1 (24)

8 CONSUMPTION

Subject	Categories	Units	Time series Yes/No Frequency	Territorial coverage	Source (Table no.)
Lead	Metal consumption	tonnes	Yes A	Eastern Europe Socialist countries	ILZSG1 (9)
Lead	By principal uses	tonnes	Yes A, M	Australia	ILZSG1 (15)
Lead	By principal uses	tonnes	Yes A, M	Canada	ILZSG1 (16)
Lead	By principal uses	tonnes	Yes A, M	France	ILZSG1 (17)
Lead, recovery of secondary lead	Refined lead and lead alloys, remelted lead and lead alloys	tonnes	Yes A, Q	World	ILZSG1 (11)
Lead, refined		tonnes	Yes A	EC, US, Japan	ILZSG1 (2)
Lead, refined		tonnes	Yes A, M	World	ILZSG1 (7)
Lead, refined		tonnes	Yes A, Q	Western World	ILZSG1 (1)
Lead, refined		tonnes, %	Yes A	Western World	ILZSG1 (25)
Lead, refined		tonnes, %	Yes A	World	ILZSG1 (25)
Lead, refined	By principal uses	tonnes	Yes A, M	Mexico	ILZSG1 (21)
Manganese ore	Total	tonnes	No	OECD EC	OECD18 (10)
Mercury		tonnes	Yes A	EC, USA, Japan	EC34 (5.2)
Metals	By type	tonnes	Yes A	EC	EC68 (-)
Metals	Mercury, Antimony, Titanium and Zirconium	tonnes	No	EC	EC68 (-)
Non-ferrous metals	By metal type	tonnes	No	EC	EC68 (-)
Pig iron	Apparent consumption	tonnes	Yes A	World	ISII1 (-)
Refined consumption	By metal	tonnes	Yes A	World	WBMS3 (-)
Refined consumption	By metal type	tonnes	Yes A	World	WBMS1(-)
Rolled products, apparent home	By type	tonnes	No	OECD EC	OECD18 (22)
Scrap		tonnes	No	OECD, EC	OECD18 (13)
Scrap	Apparent domestic supply	tonnes	No	World	IISI5 (-)
Scrap	Consumption by country, region	tonnes	Yes A	World	IISI4 (23)
Silicon carbide grain trade	By end use	tonnes	No	World	EAT1(6.3)
Silicon carbide grain trade	By production, exports, imports, apparent consumption	tonnes	Yes A	World	EAT1(6.2)
Silicon carbide grain, apparent consumption	By geographic area	tonnes	Yes A	World	EAT1(6.1)
Steel	Total/per capita	tonnes, kilos	Yes A	Nordic countries	NCM1 (168)
Steel consumption	By branch and ECSC product	tonnes, % of total consumption, % of all products	Yes A	EC	EC74 (1.1-1.13)
Steel consumption	By branch and non-ECSC product	tonnes, % of total consumption, % of all products	Yes A	EC	EC74 (2.1-2.11)
Steel industry	By fuel type and by	tonnes, cu m,	No	EC, USA, Canada,	UN11 (7)
Steel industry raw materials	By type	tonnes	No	EC, USA, Canada Japan	UN11 (5)
Steel products, total deliveries	By grade, by type by country	tonnes	Yes A	World	IISI4 (6, 6a)
Steel, apparent consumption	Estimated change	tonnes, %	No	Developing countries	IISI3 (3)
Steel, apparent consumption	Estimated change	tonnes, %	No	World	IISI3 (4)
Steel, apparent consumption	Estimated change	tonnes, %	No	Industrialised countries	IISI3 (2)
Steel, apparent consumption	Estimated change	tonnes, %	No	Developing countries	IISI1 (6, 9)
Steel, apparent consumption	Estimated change	tonnes, %	No	World	IISI1(7,10)

Subject	Categories	Units	Time series Yes/No Frequency		Territorial coverage	Source (Table no.)
Steel, apparent consumption	Estimated change	tonnes, %	No		Industrialised countries	IISI1 (5, 8)
Steel, apparent home	Percentage imports	tonnes, %	No		OECD EC	OECD18 (21)
Steel, real consumption	By consuming branch	tonnes, %	Yes	A	EC	EC55 (6.5)
Steel, real consumption	By product category	tonnes	Yes	A	EC	EC55 (6.4)
Tin, industrial		tonnes	Yes	A	World	UN50 (122)
Tungsten products	By product consumed, by end use	tonnes	Yes	A	World	UNCTAD 3 (3.2)
Tungsten, ores and concentrates		tonnes	Yes	A	World	UNCTAD 3 (3.1)
Unrefined consumption	By metal	tonnes	Yes	A	World	WBMS3 (-)
Zinc		tonnes	Yes	A	Western World	ILZSG1 (26)
Zinc		tonnes	Yes	A, M	Peru	ILZSG1 (47)
Zinc	By principal uses	tonnes	Yes	A, M	Australia	ILZSG1 (40)
Zinc	By principal uses	tonnes	Yes	A, M	Canada	ILZSG1 (41)
Zinc	By principal uses	tonnes	Yes	A, M	France	ILZSG1 (42)
Zinc	By principal uses	tonnes	Yes	A, M	Germany	ILZSG1 (43)
Zinc	By principal uses	tonnes	Yes	A, M	Italy	ILZSG1 (44)
Zinc	By principal uses	tonnes	Yes	A, M	Japan	ILZSG1 (45)
Zinc	By principal uses	tonnes	Yes	A, M	Mexico	ILZSG1 (46)
Zinc	By principal uses	tonnes	Yes	A, M	UK	ILZSG1 (48)
Zinc	By principal uses	tonnes	Yes	A, M	US	ILZSG1 (49)
Zinc, metal		tonnes	Yes	A	Eastern Europe Socialist countries	ILZSG1 (34)
Zinc, recovery of secondary zinc	Refined zinc metal, remelted zinc and direct use of secondary materials	tonnes	Yes	A, Q	World	ILZSG1 (36)
Zinc, refined		tonnes	Yes	A	Western world	ILZSG1 (50)
Zinc, refined		tonnes	Yes	A	World	ILZSG1 (50)
Zinc, refined		tonnes	Yes	A, M	EC, US, Japan	ILZSG1 (27)
Zinc, refined		tonnes	Yes	A, M	World	ILZSG1 (32)

8.11 TEXTILES - see also Section 25

Subject	Categories	Units	Time series Yes/No Frequency		Territorial coverage	Source (Table no.)
Adults' knitwear	By wool type	kg, %	Yes	A	World	IWS1 (42)
Carpets	By wool type	kg, %	Yes	A	World	IWS1 (45)
Carpets, tufted	By wool type	sq m, %	Yes	A	World	IWS1 (47)
Carpets, woven	By wool type	sq m, %	Yes	A	World	IWS1 (46)
Chemical Fibres	By country	tonnes, %	Yes	A	World	ICAC2 (p81-100)
Consumption	By fibre type	tonnes	No		Selected countries	ITMF2 (3.2-3.5)
Consumption, summary	By fibre type	tonnes	No		Selected countries	ITMF2 (3.1)
Cotton		bales	Yes	A	World	ICAC2 (p18-19)
Cotton		tonnes	Yes	A	China, E. Europe, CIS, India, US, EC, Pakistan, E. Asia	ICAC2
Cotton	By calender year	bales	Yes	A	World	ICAC2 (p20-21)
Cotton	Distribution	bales	Yes	A	World	ICAC2 (p1)
Cotton	Use	acre, bales	Yes	A	World	ICAC2 (p2)
Cotton	Use, by country	acres, bales lbs/acre	No		World	ICAC2 (p4-5)
Cotton	Use, by country	acres, bales lbs/acre	No		World	ICAC2 (p6-7)
Cotton	Use, by country	acres, bales lbs/acre	No		World	ICAC2 (p8-9)
Cotton	Use, by country	acres, bales lbs/acre	No		World	ICAC2 (p10-11)

8 CONSUMPTION

Subject	Categories	Units	Time series Yes/No Frequency		Territorial coverage	Source (Table no.)
Cotton	Use, by country	ha, tonnes Kg/ha	No		World	ICAC1 (p13-14)
Cotton	Use, by country	ha, tonnes Kg/ha	No		World	ICAC1 (p15-16)
Cotton	Use,by major	tonnes	Yes	A	World	ICAC1 (p2)
Cotton	By country, mill use	tonnes, %	Yes	A	World	ICAC2 (pp81-100)
Cotton (extra-fine)		bales	Yes	A	World	ICAC2 (p3)
Cotton (extra-fine)		tonnes	Yes	A	World	ICAC1 (p12)
Cotton, industrial		tonnes	Yes	A	World	UN50 (118)
Fibre consumption	By fibre type	tonnes	Yes	A	World	TMF1 (3.1)
Fibre consumption in domestic production of textile articles	By fibre type, article produced	nos, tonnes	No		EC	CIRFS1 (-)
Fibre consumption in main end-uses	By fibre, end-use	tonnes	Yes	A	EC6, USA	CIRFS1 (-)
Fibre consumption, non-wovens	By type, end-use	tonnes	Yes	A	EC6, UK	CIRFS1 (-)
Fibre consumption, textile floor coverings	By fibre type, pile	tonnes	Yes	A	EC	CIRFS1 (-)
Hand knitting yarn	By wool type	kg, %	Yes	A	World	IWS1 (48)
Men's coats	By wool type	garments, %	Yes	A	World	IWS1 (34)
Men's jackets	By wool type	garments, %	Yes	A	World	IWS1 (33)
Men's outerwear	By wool type	kg	Yes	A	World	IWS1 (30)
Men's suits	By wool type	garments, %	Yes	A	World	IWS1 (31)
Men's sweaters	By wool type	garments, %	Yes	A	World	IWS1 (43)
Men's trousers	By wool type	garments, %	Yes	A	World	IWS1 (32)
Textile fibres, mill consumption	By fibre type	tonnes	Yes	A	EC	CIRFS1 (-)
Textured filament yarns (excluding carpets), consumption	By type, weaving, knitting, others	tonnes	Yes	A	EC	CIRFS1 (-)
Women's coats	By wool type	garments, %	Yes	A	World	IWS1 (40)
Women's dresses	By wool type	garments, %	Yes	A	World	IWS1 (36)
Women's jackets	By wool type	garments, %	Yes	A	World	IWS1 (41)
Women's outerwear	By wool type	kg, %	Yes	A	World	IWS1 (35)
Women's skirts	By wool type	garments, %	Yes	A	World	IWS1 (37)
Women's sweaters	By wool type	garments, %	Yes	A	World	IWS1 (44)
Women's trousers	By wool type	garments, %	Yes	A	World	IWS1 (39)
Women's suits	By wool type	garments, %	Yes	A	World	IWS1 (38)
Wool	By country	tonnes, %	Yes	A	World	ICAC2 (pp81-100)
Wool, industrial		tonnes	Yes	A	World	UN50 (119)

8.12 WOOD AND FORESTRY PRODUCTS - see also Sections 21 and 25

Subject	Categories	Units	Time series Yes/No	Frequency	Territorial coverage	Source (Table no.)
Newsprint	Total, per capita	tons/kilos	Yes	5 yrly	World	UN50 (25)
Newsprint	Total, per capita	tons/kilos	Yes	A	Nordic countries	NCM1 (169)
Paper and board	By country	tonnes	Yes	A	World	BPB1 (-)
Paper and board	By country, per capita	kg	Yes	A	OECD	OECD38 (VII)
Paper and board	By country, total and annual variations	tonnes, %	Yes	A	OECD	OECD38 (V)
Paper consumption		kg per 1000	No		World population	UN16 (14A)
Timber, tropical	By product, by ITTC producer	cu m	Yes	A	ITTC producing countries worldwide	ITTO1 (App 1)
Woodpulp	By country, total and annual variations	tonnes, %	Yes	A	OECD	OECD38 (IV)

9 CRIME AND JUSTICE

Subject	Categories	Units	Time series Yes/No Frequency		Territorial coverage	Source (Table No.)
Cases brought before the Court of Justice	By category	nos	No		EC	EC72 (12.11)
Crimes recorded	Number, per 100,000 population % in largest city	nos rate %	Yes	Selected years	World	UN16 (34)
Criminal justice occupations	By police, prosecutors	nos, %	No		World	UN17 (33B)
Criminal justice occupations	By police, prosecutors	nos, %	No		Africa	UN46 (30B)
Homicides, intentional	Number, per 100,000 population	nos rate	Yes	Selected years	World	UN16 (34)
Infringement procedures	By country, by stage of procedure	nos	No		EC	EC72 (12.12)
Judgments pronounced	By type	nos	No		EC	EC35
Offences registered by the police	By kind, age	nos, per capita	Yes	A	Nordic countries	NCM1 (235)
Persons apprehended	Number, per 100,000 population years per 100 crimes recorded	nos, rate	Yes	Selected	World	UN16 (34)
Persons apprehended and prison population	By sex	nos	No		Africa	UN46 (30A)
Persons apprehended and prison population	By sex	nos	No		World	UN17 (33A)
Persons found guilty of offences against the Penal Code	By sanction, age	nos, per capita	Yes	A	Nordic countries	NCM1 (236)
Police personnel	Number, per 1000 population per 100 crimes recorded	nos rate rate	Yes	Selected years	World	UN16 (34)
Prison population	Number, by sex, per 100,000 population by sex	nos rate	Yes	Selected years	World	UN16 (34)
Prisoners	By age	nos, per capita	Yes	A	Nordic countries	NCM1 (237)
Seizures of cocaine and psychotropic substances reported to the United Nations	Number, quantity cocaine, opiates	nos, kg	Yes	Selected	World	UN16 (35)

10 CULTURE

Subject	Categories	Units	Time series Yes/No Frequency		Territorial coverage	Source (Table no.)
10.1 BOOKS AND PAMPHLETS PUBLISHED						
10.1.1 Language of Publications						
Book titles published	By country	nos	No		EC	EM1 (2402)
Children's Books	Titles, copies	nos	No	I	World	UNESCO1 (7.10)
National language	Foreign, two or more	nos	No	I	World	UNESCO1 (7.6)
School textbooks	Titles, copies	nos	No		World	UNESCO1 (7.9)
Subject groups	UDC classes	nos	No	I	World	UNESCO1 (7.5)
Subject groups	UDC classes	nos	No	I	World	UNESCO1 (7.8)
Total		nos	No	I	World	UNESCO1 (7.6)
Total	UDC classes	nos	No	I	World	UNESCO1 (7.7)
10.1.2 Production and Trade						
Book titles published		nos	No		World	UN16 (14A)
Books, production (no of titles)	Fiction, non fiction	nos	Yes	A	Nordic countries	NCM1 (254)
Books, production (no of titles)	By subject group	nos	No		Nordic countries	NCM1 (255)
Books, production (no of titles)	Subjects, language	nos	No		World	UN50 (43,44)
Books, production (no of titles published)	Total, per capita, % production, population	nos, %	Yes	5 A	World	UNESCO1 (6.1)
Books published	By country, by subject	nos, %	No		EC	EM1 (2403)
Importation and exportation	Balance	US$	No	I	World	UNESCO1 (11.1)
Total	UDC classes	nos	No	I	World	UNESCO1 (7.4)
10.1.3 Translations						
Book production translations	By language, books	nos	Yes	A	World	NCM1 (257)
Intra-Nordic translations of literature	Into overseas	nos	No		World	NCM1 (256)
Number, authors most frequently translsated		nos	Yes	A	World	UNESCO1 (7.15)
Original language, and UDC classes	Other, two or more	nos	Yes	A	World	UNESCO1 (7.12)
Original language and selected languages into which translated		nos	No	I	World	UNESCO1 (7.14)
Total		nos	Yes	A	World	UNESCO1 (7.11)
Total		nos	No	I	World	UNESCO1 (7.13)
10.2 CINEMAS AND THEATRES						
Cinemas	Attendance, annual	nos	Yes	5 A	Continents, major areas and groups of countries	UNESCO1 (6.7)
Cinemas	By country, by screens, attendances, revenue	nos, nat curr	No		EC	EM1 (1307)
Cinemas	By country, by attendance	nos	No		EC	EM1 (2406)
Cinemas	By type, capacity, attendance	nos	Yes	A	Nordic countries	NCM1 (263)

10 CULTURE

Subject	Categories	Units	Time series Yes/No Frequency		Territorial coverage	Source (Table no.)
Cinemas	By type, capacity,	nos	No		World	UNESCO1 (9.3)
Cinemas	Fixed, seating capacity	nos, per capita	No	I	Continents, major areas and groups of countries	UNESCO1 (6.6)
Cinemas	Seating capacity	nos	Yes	A	ASEAN	ASEANS1 (9.3.2)
Theatres	Performances, visitors, persons engaged	nos	Yes	A	Nordic countries	NCM1 (264)

10.3 FILMS

Subject	Categories	Units	Time series Yes/No Frequency		Territorial coverage	Source (Table no.)
Films, long		nos	No		World	UN16 (14B)
Imported	Definition of data, by country of origin	nos	No	I	World	UNESCO1 (9.2)
Imported	First showing, by country of origin	nos	Yes	A	World	NCM1 (262)
Long films	Length in metres	nos	Yes	A	Nordic countries	NCM1 (261)
Production	Length, definition of data	nos	Yes	5 A	World	UNESCO1 (9.1)
Production (estimated)		nos	Yes	5 A	Continents, major areas and groups of countries	UNESCO1 (6.5)

10.4 LIBRARIES

Subject	Categories	Units	Time series Yes/No Frequency		Territorial coverage	Source (Table no.)
Administrative units		nos	No	I	World	UNESCO1 (7.3)
Annual additions	Volumes, other materials	nos	No	I	World	UNESCO1 (7.3)
Audio visual documents		nos	No	I	World	UNESCO1 (7.3)
Current expenditure	Total, staff	nos, %	No	I	World	UNESCO1 (7.3)
Libraries, schools	By category, volumes, %	nos, %	No		World	UNESCO1 (7.3)
Libraries	By category, volumes	nos	No		World	UNESCO1 (7.1)
Libraries	By category	nos	No		Nordic countries	NCM1 (258)
Libraries	Number of libraries number of volumes, by category	nos	No		ASEAN	ASEANS1 (9.2.1)
Libraries of institutions of higher education	By category, volumes, %	nos, %	No		World	UNESCO1 (7.2)
Library employees		nos	No	I	World	UNESCO1 (7.3)
Library membership and book collections	Membership by age, book collections, loans of	nos, per thou	Yes	A	ASEAN	ASEANS1 (9.2.2)
Library statistics	By country, by stocks, borrowers, type	nos	No		EC	EM1 (2401)
Loans to users		nos	No	I	World	UNESCO1 (7.3)
Other library materials		nos	No	I	World	UNESCO1 (7.3)
Population served		nos	No	I	World	UNESCO1 (7.3)
Registered users		nos	No	I	World	UNESCO1 (7.3)
Service points		nos	No	I	World	UNESCO1 (7.3)

Subject	Categories	Units	Time series Yes/No Frequency		Territorial coverage	Source (Table no.)
10.5 LITERACY - see also Section 42						
Literacy rates	By sex	nos, %	No		ASEAN	ASEANS1 (1.5)
10.6 MUSEUMS						
Archival institutions	Holdings, accessions, reference service, expenditure	nos	No	I	World	UNESCO1 (8.2)
Museums	By country, by type,	nos	No		EC	EM1 (2405)
Museums	By visitors		Yes	A	Nordic countries	NCM1 (260)
Museums	Subject of collection, personnel, total personnel and current visitors	nos, nat curr	No		World	UNESCO1 (8.1)
10.7 NEWSPAPERS AND PERIODICALS						
Importation and exportation	Balance	US$	No	I	World	UNESCO1 (11.2)
Newspapers, circulation		nos	Yes	A	ASEAN	ASEANS1 (9.3.1)
Newspapers, daily	Number, circulation	nos	No	I	World, continents major areas and groups of countries	UNESCO1 (6.2)
Newspapers, daily	Circulation, per capita	nos	Yes	A	Nordic countries	NCM1 (250)
Newspapers, non-daily	Circulation, per capita	nos	Yes	A	Nordic countries	NCM1 (251)
Newspapers, daily	Numbers	nos	No		World	UN16 (14A)
Newspapers, daily	Circulation	per 100	No		World	UN16 (14A)
Newspapers	By country, by daily newspapers published, circulation	nos	No		EC	EC72 (11.16)
Newspapers	Daily, non daily newspapers, circulation	nos, per capita	No		World	UN50 (45,46)
Newspapers	Number, circulation total, daily, non daily	nos, per capita	No	I	World	UNESCO1 (7.16,17)
Newspapers daily	Issuing locality, political tendency, by net circulation	nos	No		Nordic countries	NCM1 (252)
Newsprint	Production, consumption, per capita	tonnes, kg	Yes	5 A	World, continents major areas and groups of countries	UNESCO1 (6.3)
Newsprint	Production, consumption, per capita, imports, exports	tonnes, kg	Yes	5 A	World	UNESCO1 (7.18)
Periodicals, other	Number, circulation	nos, per capita	No		World	UN50 (46)
Periodicals, other	Number, circulation	nos, per capita	No		World	UNESCO1 (7.17)
Printing and writing paper, other	Production, consumption, per capita	tonnes, kg	Yes	5 A	World	UNESCO1 (6.4)
Printing and writing paper, other	Production, consumption, per capita imports, exports	tonnes, kg	Yes	5 A	World	UNESCO1 (7.18)
Weeklies, magazines, trade and technical papers	Number, circulation, frequency	nos	No		Nordic countries	NCM1 (253)

Subject	Categories	Units	Time series Yes/No Frequency		Territorial coverage	Source (Table no.)
10.8 RADIO AND TELEVISION - see also Sections 6 and 42						
Radio and television	Licences, broadcasting time	nos, per capita, hours	Yes	A	Nordic countries	NCM1 (266)
Radio and television sets in use	By countries	nos	No		The Americas and Australasia	MAC2 (G10)
Radio programmes	By category	%, hours	No		Nordic countries	NCM1 (267)
Radio programmes	By function, by type of institution	hours, %	No	I	World	UNESCO1 (10.3)
Radio receivers		nos, per capita	Yes	5 A	World	UN50 (48)
Radio receivers	In use, licences issued	nos, per capita	Yes	5 A	World	UNESCO1 (10.1)
Radio receivers	Total	nos, per capita	Yes	5 A	Continents, major areas and groups of countries	UNESCO1 (6.9)
Radio transmitters		nos	Yes	5 A	Continents, major areas and groups of countries	UNESCO1 (6.8)
Sound and television transmitters	In use for receiving	nos, %	No		Nordic countries	NCM1 265)
Television and radio stations	By country, by commercial-non-commercial	nos	No		EC	EM1 (1306)
Television programmes	By category	%, hours week	No		Nordic countries	NCM1 (268)
Television programmes	By function and by type of institution	hours, %	No	I	World	UNESCO1 (10.4)
Television receivers		nos, per capita	Yes	5 A	World	UN50 (47)
Television receivers	In use, licences issued, per capita	nos	Yes	5 A	World	UNESCO1 (10.2)
Television receivers	Total	nos, per capita	Yes	5 A	Continents, major areas and groups of countries	UNESCO1 (6.11)
Television sets	By country	nos	No		EC	EC72 (11.14)
Television transmitters		nos	Yes	5 A	Continents, major areas and groups of countries	UNESCO1 (6.10)

11 DEFENCE

Subject	Categories	Units	Time series Yes/No	Frequency	Territorial coverage	Source (Table no.)
11.1 EQUIPMENT						
Defence equipment	By country	nos	No		EC	EM1 (0902)
11.2 EXPENDITURE						
Defence expenditure and personnel	By country, by category	US$, %	No		EC	EM1 (0901)
Defence expenditure of NATO countries	1980 prices and exchange rates	nat curr, US$	Yes	A	NATO Europe North America NATO total	NATO1 (II.2)
Defence expenditures as percentage of gross domestic product	Based on constant prices	%	Yes	A	NATO Europe Canada, United States, North America NATO total	NATO1 (III.2)
Defence expenditures as percentage of gross domestic product	Based on current prices	%	Yes	A	NATO Europe Canada, United States, North America NATO total	NATO1 (III.1)
Defence expenditures of NATO countries	Current prices and exchange rates	nat curr, US$	Yes	A	NATO Europe North America NATO total	NATO1 (II.1)
Defence expenditures per capita	1980 prices and exchange rates	US$	Yes	A	NATO Europe Canada, United States, North America NATO total	NATO1 (V)
Distribution of total defence expenditures by category	Equipment and infrastructure expenditures	%	Yes	A	Selected NATO countries	NATO1 (VI.1)
Distribution of total defence expenditures by category	Personnel and operating expenditures	%	Yes	A	Selected NATO countries	NATO1 (VI.2)
Military and resource use imbalances	Military expenditure, arms imports, armed forces	%, US$, per thou, ratio	No		Developing countries	UN25 (19)
Military and resource use imbalances	Military expenditure, arms exports, armed forces	%, US$, per thou, ratio	No		Industrial countries	UN25 (40)
11.3 GENERAL						
NATO countries	By area, population and density of population	sq mile, sq km, nos	Yes	5 yrly	NATO total EC - Total Canada and United States, North America	NATO1 (I)
11.4 PERSONNEL – see also Sections 16 and 36						
Military		nos	Yes	5A	NATO countries	NATO1 (6)
Military and civilian		%	Yes	A	NATO Europe Canada, United States, North America NATO total	NATO1 (VII.2)
Military and civilian		% labour force	Yes	5A	NATO countries	NATO1 (6)
Military strengths		nos	Yes	A	NATO Europe Canada, United States, North America NATO total	NATO1 (VII.1)
Personnel	By category	%	No		EC	EM1 (0901)
Personnel as percentage of labour force					NATO Europe Canada, United States, North America NATO total	NATO1 (V11.2)

12 DEVELOPMENT AND AID

Subject	Categories	Units	Time series Yes/No Frequency		Territorial coverage	Source (Table no.)
12.1 DEBT						
12.1.1 Debt Restructuring						
Agreements of middle income countries with official creditors	By debts consolidated, period, repayment terms	US$	No		Selected countries	WB3 (A.II.2)
Agreements with official creditors	By agreements, amounts rescheduled	nos	Yes	A	Selected countries	WB3 (A.II.1)
Buybacks financed by IDA debt	By resource, country	US$	No		Selected countries	WB3 (A.III.7)
Concluded DDSR agreements	By DDSR instruments, new money	US$, %	No		Developing countries	WB3 (A.III.3)
Concluded DDSR agreements	By finance (commitment)	US$	No		Developing countries	WB3 (A.III.4)
Debt conversion programmes	By country	US$	Yes	A	Selected countries	WB3 (A.III.9)
Debt conversion programmes	By type	US$	Yes	A	Developing countries	WB3 (A.III.8)
Debt restructuring agreements with commercial banks	By country, consolidation period, amount assistance, repayment terms	US$,	No		Developing countries	WB3 (AIII.1)
Debt-for-nature swaps	By country, cost, value, funds, price, leverage	US$	No		Developing countries	WB3 (A.III.10)
Multi-year debt restructuring agreements with commercial banks	By country, date, consolidation period terms of repayment	US$,	No		Developing countries	WB3 (A.III.2)
Multilateral debt relief agreements	By country, date, amount consolidated, type of creditor	%	No		Developing countries	WB3 (A.III.13)
Multilateral debt relief agreements with offical creditors	By consolidation period, proportion and amount consolidated, repayment terms	US$, %	No		Selected countries	WB3 (A.II.5)
Multilateral debt relief agreements with commercial banks	By country, consolidation period, amount, other assistance, repayment terms	US$,	No		Developing countries	WB3 (A.III.12)
Paris club agreements for highly indebted lower-middle-income countries	By amount consolidated, period, repayment terms, swap ceilings	US$, %	No		Selected countries	WB3 (A.II.4)
Paris club enhanced Toronto terms	By first, second and final stage agreements	US$	No		Selected countries	WB3 (A.II.3)
12.1.2 Debt Stocks and Flows						
Arrears, stock of	By official, private, by interest	US$	Yes	A	Developing countries	WB3 (1.3)
Assistance, special programme of	By debt data, by new commitments	US$, %	Yes	A	All countries reporting to World Bank	WB3 (-)
Average terms of new commitments	By creditors, by region by category	%	Yes	A	All countries reporting to World Bank	WB3 (-)
Debt and liabilities outstanding at year end	OECD countries and capital markets, multilateral	US$	No		World	OECD9 (1,2)
Debt distribution of long-term	By type of debtor	US$	Yes	A	World	WB4 (-)
Debt indicators		%	Yes	A	World	WB4 (-)
Debt indicators	By debt-to-exports ratio, debt-to-exports service ratio, country group	%	Yes	A	Developing countries	WB3 (1.4)

12 DEVELOPMENT AND AID

Subject	Categories	Units	Time series Yes/No Frequency		Territorial coverage	Source (Table no.)
Debt outstanding	Includes undisbursed, disbursed only, by source of lending	US$	Yes	A	World economic regions. Developing countries and territories	UNCTAD1 (5.13)
Debt outstanding at year end	ODA, export credits, financial markets, multilateral	US$	No		World	OECD9
Debt outstanding, as share of developing countries debt	ODA, export credits, financial markets, multilateral	%	No		World	OECD9 (D)
Debt outstanding, composition at year end	ODA, export credits, financial markets, multilateral	%	No		World	OECD9 (C)
Debt outstanding, long-term	Total amount, % of GDP	US$, %	Yes	A	Developing countries and territories	UNCTAD1 (5.14)
Debt reduction of officially supported commercial bank DDSR operations in SIMICs	By face value, debt reduction equivalent	US$, %	No		Developing countries	WB3 (1.14)
Debt reduction, officially-supported financing packages involving	By timing, exit, new money instruments	various	No		Developing countries	WB3 (1.13)
Debt restructuring	By amount rescheduled by region, by category	US$	Yes	A	All countries reporting to World Bank	WB3 (-)
Debt restructurings		US$	Yes	A	World	WB4 (-)
Debt service	Total amount, % of exports of goods and services	US$, %	Yes	A	Developing countries and territories	UNCTAD1 (5.14)
Debt service projections	By projected non-guaranteed debt service	US$	Yes	A	Selected countries	WB4 (-)
Debt service, total	Amortization, interest by source of lending	US$	Yes	A	World economic regions. Developing countries and territories	UNCTAD1 (5.13)
Debt stocks and debt flows	By region by category	US$	Yes	A	All countries reporting to World Bank	WB3 (-)
Debt stocks and flows		US$	Yes	A	World	WB4 (-)
Debt, contractual obligations on outstanding long-term	By total long-term	US$	Yes	A	World	WB4 (-)
Debt, long term	By debt outstanding, undisturbed debt, commitments, disbursments, principal repayments, net flows and transfers on debt, interest payments, debt service	US$	Yes	A	World	WB4 (-)
Debt, long-term	By debt outstanding, undisbursed debt, commitments, disburse-ments, repayments net flows, interest transfers, debt service by region, by category	US$	Yes	A	All countries reporting to World Bank	WB3 (-)
Debt, private non-guaranteed	By debt outstanding and disbursed, disbursements principal repayments, net flows, interest payments, net transfers total debt service	US$	Yes	A	Selected countries	WB4 (-)
Debt, sources of change in	By source	US$	Yes	A	Developing countries	WB3 (1.2)

Subject	Categories	Units	Time series Yes/No Frequency		Territorial coverage	Source (Table no.)
Debt, sources of change in	By source, middle, low income countries	US$	No		Developing countries	WB3 (A.I.2)
Dedt indicators	By type, by region by category	%	Yes	A	All countries reporting to World Bank	WB3 (-)
Disbursement	By source of lending	US$	Yes	A	World economic regions. Developing countries and territories	UNCTAD1 (5.13)
Disbursements sectoral allocation of, on long term debt		US$	Yes	A	World	WB4 (-)
Discounted bank debt reduction and trading volume	By total debt reduction, secondary market trading	US$	Yes	A	Developing countries	WB3 (A.IV.I)
External debt	By long-term, short-term debt, IMF credit use, export credit	US$	Yes	A	Developing countries	WB3 (1.1)
External debt, nominal and currency-adjusted rates of growth of	By total debt, growth of debt	US$	Yes	A	Developing countries	WB3 (A.I.1)
External debts, official	By country	ECU	No		Developing countries	EC35 (-)
FSU, allocation of debt to republics	By estimated shares in exports, income	%	No		FSU	WB3 (2.6)
FSU, average terms of new borrowing	By interest rates, maturity, grace period	%,	No		FSU	WB3 (2.2)
FSU, convertible currency debt service	By credits, bonds, debt	US$	Yes	A	FSU	WB3 (2.4)
FSU, debt arrears	By debt type	US$	Yes	A	FSU	WB3 (2.3)
FSU, debt indicators	By indicator	US$	Yes	A	FSU	WB3 (2.1)
FSU, external debt	By long-term, short-term debt	US$	No		FSU	WB3 (2.5)
Indebtedness ratios	By country	%	No		Developing countries	WB3 (A.VI.4)
Net debt-related flows and transfers	By official, private creditors	US$	Yes	A	SIMICs	WB3 (A.I.3)
Net debt-related flows and transfers	By official, private creditors	US$	Yes	A	SILICs	WB3 (A.I.4)
Net debt-related flows and transfers	By official, private creditors	US$	Yes	A	Non-restructuring countries	WB3 (A.I.5)
Net disbursement and debt outstanding and disbursed	By country, by external capital flows, debt and debt burden ratios, bank and IDA ratios	US$	Yes	A	Developing countries	WB2 (-)
Net flow and net transfer	By region, flows, loans, grants, FDI	US$	No		Developing countries	WB3 (A.I.6)
New commitments, average terms of	By all creditors	%,	Yes	A	World	WB4 (-)
Transfer, net	By source of lending	US$	Yes	A	World economic regions. Developing countries and territories	UNCTAD1 (5.13)

12.2 ECONOMIC AND SOCIAL INDICATORS

Subject	Categories	Units	Time series Yes/No Frequency		Territorial coverage	Source (Table no.)
ACP countries	By country, by capital, area, population	sq km, nos	No		Africa, Caribbean and Pacific	EC35 (-)
Demographic balance sheet	Vital demographic factors	nos, %, per thou, per ha, ratio	No		Developing countries	UN25 (21)
Economic aggregates, major	By country	US$	No		Developing countries	WB3 (A.VI.3)

12 DEVELOPMENT AND AID

Subject	Categories	Units	Time series Yes/No Frequency		Territorial coverage	Source (Table no.)
Economic aggregates, major	By GNP, exports, imports, reserves, current account balance by region, by category	US$	Yes	A	All countries reporting to World Bank	WB3 (-)
Economic and social indicators for least developed countries and the rest of the world	GDP per capita	US$	Yes	Selected years	World, by development groups	UNCTAD5 (5.3)
	Ratio of long-term external debt to GDP	%				
	Ratio of long-term debt service to exports	%				
	Exports per capita	US$				
	Share of primary commodities in total exports	%				
	Share of manufacturing in GDP	%				
	Energy consumption per capita	kg of coal equiv				
	Population with access to safe water	%				
	Primary school enrolment ratios (percentage of age group)	%				
Economic development indicators	By high, middle, low income, by PQLI	US$, %, index	Yes	A	World	CS1 (2)
Economic performance indicators	GDP, agricultural production, export volume, import volume	%	Yes	Selected years	World, by development groups	UNCTAD5 (5.1)
Education	By enrolment rates, pupil-teacher ratio, pupils reaching grade 6	rates, ratio %	No		Developing countries	WB1 (-)
External factors influencing economic performance	Export unit prices, terms of trade, total financial flows	%	Yes	Selected years	World, by development groups	UNCTAD5 (5.2)
Female-male gaps	Indicators of human development	%	No		Developing countries	UN25 (10)
Female-male gaps	Indicators of human development	%	No		Industrial countries	UN25 (31)
Food, health and nutrition	Food production, calories and proteins population per physician, nurse and hospital bed access to safe water	indices grammes nos %	No		Developing countries	WB1 (-)
Food security	Indicators of food security	indices, US$, tonnes, %	No		Developing countries	UN25 (13)
GDP, share of	By country, by memorandum, items, government finance	%	Yes	A	Developing countries	WB2 (-)
GDP shares and growth rates	By country, by taxes, agriculture, industry, services, resource balance, expenditures	%	Yes	A	Developing countries	WB2 (-)
GNP		US$	Yes	A	Developing countries	OECD14 (-)
GNP per capita		US$ and index	Yes	A	Developing countries	OECD14 (-)
Growth rates	By country, by population, labor force, gross national income, private consumption, import elasticity, savings, ICOR	%	No		Developing countries	WB2 (-)

Subject	Categories	Units	Time series Yes/No Frequency	Territorial coverage	Source (Table no.)
Growth rates	Population, GNP, private consumption, labour force in agriculture, infant mortality, calorie supply, primary school enrolment	per capita %	No	Developing countries	WB1 (2)
Housing	By size of household, with electricity	nos, %	No	Developing countries	WB1 (-)
Human deprivation	Indicators of deprivation	nos	No	Developing countries	UN25 (3)
Human development, trends	Indicators of human development	years, %, US$, PPP$	No	Industrial countries	UN25 (29)
Human development, trends	Indicators of human development	years, nos, %, PPP$	No	Developing countries	UN25 (4)
Human development index	Indicators of human development	years, %, PPP$, ind	No	World	UN25 (1)
Human development profile	Indicators of human development	years, %, US$, PPP$	No	Developing countries	UN25 (2)
Human development profile	Indicators of human development	years, %, per thou, nos, US$, PPP$	No	Industrial countries	UN25 (26)
Income, consumption and poverty	By energy consumption, private income, absolute poverty income and population below, passenger cars, newspaper circulation	kg of oil equivalent, %, US$ per capita, nos	No	Developing countries	WB1 (-)
Labour force, share of	By country, by employment	%	Yes A	Developing countries	WB2 (-)
Labour force	By sex, agriculture, industry, participation rate, age dependency	%	No	Developing countries	WB1 (-)
Labour force in agriculture					
Land area	Total, agricultural	sq km, %	No	Developing countries	WB1 (-)
Macroeconomic environment	By growth rate, investment, domestic savings, resource balance, GDP	%	No	Developing countries	WB3 (3.3)
Major economic aggregates	GNP, exports, imports, international reserves current account balance	US$	Yes A	World	WB4 (-)
North-south human gaps, basic	Indicators of human development	indices	No	Developing countries	UN25 (7)
North-south human gaps, trends	Indicators of human development	indices	No	Developing countries	UN25 (6)
Population		Nos	Yes A	Developing countries	OECD14 (-)
Population		per capita,	No	Selected countries	WB1 (1)
Population and vital statistics	By urban, growth rate, life expectancy, projections, density age structure crude birth, death fertility,infant mortality, child death rates, family planning	nos, %, sq km	No	Developing countries	WB1 (-)
Price indices	By country, by consumer prices, wholesale prices, GDP deflator, expenditures deflator	index	Yes A	Developing countries	WB2 (-)

12 DEVELOPMENT AND AID

Subject	Categories	Units	Time series Yes/No Frequency	Territorial coverage	Source (Table no.)
Rural-urban gaps	Population, access to services	%, indices	No	Developing countries	UN25 (9)
South-north, real expenditure	Food, health, education	indices	No	Developing countries	UN25 (8)
12.3 EMPLOYMENT AND WAGES					
Female employees, total employment	By ISIC group	%	No	World	UNIDO1 (2.13)
Wages	By ISIC group	US$	Yes I	World	UNIDO1 (1.12, 2.5)
Wages per employee	By ISIC group	US$	No	World	UNIDO1 (2.6)
Wages, value added		%	Yes I	World	UNIDO1 (1.12, 2.5)
Wages, value added	By ISIC group	%	No	World	UNIDO1 (2.6)
12.4 FINANCIAL AID					
Aid	By economic sector and beneficiary country by type	ECU	No	ACP states	EC1 (III3-4)
Aid by type and beneficiary country		ECU	No	ACP states	EC1 (III5)
Aid-the cumulative payments	By beneficiary country	ECU	Yes	ACP states	EC1 (III6)
Balance sheet aggregate	By ACP state	ECU	Yes	ACP states	EC1 (III7)
Assistance, bilateral flow, official	By region and main recipient countries	US$	No	All countries	NCM1 (211)
Assistance, official	Bilateral and multilateral flows	US$	Yes A	Nordic countries	NCM1 (210)
Assistance, official	Percentage of GNP	%	Yes A	Nordic countries	NCM1 (212)
Assistance, total		US$	Yes A	World	UN50 (51)
Assistance, total per capita		US$	Yes A	World	UN50 (51)
Balance sheet aggregate	By product	ECU	Yes	ACP states	EC1 (III8)
Bilateral assistance, commitments, official	By sector of destination	US$	No	Nordic countries	NCM1 (209)
Bilateral concessional flows, total, net	From OPEC member countries to developing countries and territories	US$	Yes A	Developing countries and territories	UNCTAD1 (5.7)
Bilateral flows, total, net	Total official and private flows. ODA, other official flows and official and private export credits. From DAC member countries to developing countries and territories	US$	Yes A	Developing countries and territories	UNCTAD1 (5.6)
Bilateral official development assistance from developed market economies		US$	Yes A	World	UN50 (51)
Commitments of concessional asssistance by DAC countries combined, to individual recipients		US$	Yes A	Developing countries	OECD14 (-)
Commitments of concessional asssistance from all sources combined, to individual recipients		US$	Yes A	Developing countries	OECD14 (-)
Community development co-operation with the ACP countries	By convention, by date of entry, population, financial total, number of countries	nos, ECU	No	Selected countries	EC35(-)

Subject	Categories	Units	Time series Yes/No Frequency		Territorial coverage	Source (Table no.)
Development assistance commitments' official	By high, middle, low income, by source	US$	No		World	CS1 (23)
Disbursement and debt outstanding and disbursed, net	By country, by external capital flows, debt and debt burden ratios, bank and IDA ratios	US$	Yes	A	Developing countries	WB2 (-)
Disbursements by multilateral agencies combined, to individual recipients, total net		US$	Yes	A	Developing countries	OECD14 (-)
Disbursements from multilateral institutions		US$	Yes	A	World	UN50 (51)
Disbursements of concessional assistance by multilateral agencies combined, to individual recipients, net		US$	Yes	A	Developing countries	OECD14 (-)
Disbursements of concessional assistance from all sources combined, to individual recipients, net		US$	Yes	A	Developing countries	OECD14 (-)
Disbursements of financial flows by DAC countries combined, to individual recipients, total net		US$	Yes	A	Developing countries	OECD14 (-)
Disbursements of financial flows from all sources combined, to individual recipients, total net		US$	Yes	A	Developing countries	OECD14 (-)
Disbursements of ODA by DAC countries to individual recipients, net		US$	Yes	A	Developing countries	OECD14 (-)
EIB loans (LOME II and III)		ECU, %	No		ACP states	EC1 (III9-10)
Eurocurrency credits (gross commitments)		US$	Yes	A	Developing countries and territories	UNCTAD1 (5.12)
Expenditure, extra budgetary funds		US$	No		Selected countries	UN50 (52)
Expenditure, IBRD		US$	No		Selected countries	UN50 (52)
Expenditure, IBRD/IDA technical co-operation		US$	No		Selected countries	UN50 (52)
Expenditure, IDA		US$	No		Selected countries	UN50 (52)
Expenditure, IFAD		US$	No		Selected countries	UN50 (52)
Expenditure, IFC		US$	No		Selected countries	UN50 (52)
Expenditure, regular budgetary funds		US$	No		Selected countries	UN50 (52)
Expenditure, relief and related grants		US$	No		Selected countries	UN50 (52)
Expenditure, self-supporting		US$	No		Selected countries	UN50 (52)
Expenditure, total		US$	No		Selected countries	UN50 (52)
Expenditure, UNDP		US$	No		Selected countries	UN50 (52)
Expenditure, UNDP administered funds		US$	No		Selected countries	UN50 (52)
Expenditure, UNFPA		US$	No		Selected countries	UN50 (52)
Expenditure, UNICEF		US$	No		Selected countries	UN50 (52)
Expenditure, WFP		US$	No		Selected countries	UN50 (52)
Financial aid, distribution of	By country, by fund	ECU	No		EC	EC72 (12.13)
Financial flows and net transfers, net long-term	Current prices, average annual increment	US$	Yes	Selected year	Developing countries, least developed countries	UNCTAD5 (3.15)
Financial flows, structure	ODA, non-concessional, from DAC member countries, OPEC member countries, and multilateral agencies to developing countries and territories	%	Yes	A	Developing countries and territories	UNCTAD1 (5.4)

12 DEVELOPMENT AND AID

Subject	Categories	Units	Time series Yes/No Frequency		Territorial coverage	Source (Table no.)
Financial flows, total	Concessional, non-concessional, from OPEC member countries to developing countries and territories and multilateral agencies	US$	Yes	A	OPEC	UNCTAD1 (5.11)
Financial flows, total, net	Total, concessional, from multilateral agencies largely financed by DAC member countries to developing countries and territories	US$	Yes	A	Developing countries and territories	UNCTAD1 (5.8A)
Financial flows, total, net	Total, concessional, from multilateral agencies largely financed by OPEC member countries to developing countries and territories	US$	Yes	A	Developing countries and territories	UNCTAD1 (5.8B)
Financial flows, total, net	Total, concessional, from DAC member countries, OPEC member countries and multilateral agencies to developing countries and territories	US$	Yes	A	Developing countries and territories	UNCTAD1 (5.5)
Financial resources, flows,	As % of GNP	%	Yes	A	DAC countries	UNCTAD1 (5.9B)
Financial resources, flows,	At current prices, at 1970 prices	US$	Yes	A	DAC countries	UNCTAD1 (5.9A)
Financing situation	By method of financing and by administrative body EDF resources, total	ECU	No		ACP states	EC1 (III1-2)
IMF lending to capital-importing developing countries, net flows of	By conditionality	US$	Yes	A	Developing countries	UNCTAD5 (3.17A)
Loans, grants					Countries	
Net official aid from DAC members		US$, %	No		ACP states	EC1 (122)
Net official aid per capita		US$	No		ACP states	EC1 (123)
Net resource flows (long-term)	By type of resource	US$	Yes	A	Developing countries	WB3 (1.5)
Net resource flows and net transfers, long term		US$	Yes	A	World	WB4 (-)
ODA disbursements	By country, % of GNP	%, US$	Yes	A	World	WB3 (1.8)
ODA forgiveness	By donor country	US$	Yes	A	World	WB3 (1.9)
ODA performance of DAC and OPEC countries		US$, %, ratio	Yes	2 yrly	DAC and OPEC countries	UNCTAD5) (3.16)
ODF commitments	Purpose, sector	%	Yes	A	Developing countries	OECD14 (-)
Of direct investment, major destination	By low-income, middle income countries	US$	Yes	A	Developing countries	WB3 (1.10)
Official aid of the main donors	By country	ECU	No		Selected countries	EC35 (-)
Official aid to development	By country	ECU	No		Developing countries	EC35 (-)

Subject	Categories	Units	Time series Yes/No Frequency		Territorial coverage	Source (Table no.)
Official development assistance	Commitments to developing countries and territories and multilateral agencies. Bilateral commitments to least developed countries	US$, %	Yes	A	DAC countries	UNCTAD1 (5.10)
Official development assistance	As % of GNP	%	Yes	A	DAC countries	UNCTAD1 (5.9B)
Official development assistance	By country, region	US$, %	No		UNICEF assisted countries	UNICEF2 (-)
Official development assistance,	At current prices, at 1970 prices	US$	Yes	A	DAC countries	UNCTAD1 (5.9A)
Personnel, official assistance		nos	Yes	A	Nordic countries	NCM1 (213)
Receipts	Net, gross	US$	Yes	A	Developing	OECD14 (-)
Resource flow imbalances	Official development assistance given, current account balance, trade dependency, terms of trade, exports, imports	US$, %, indices, ratio	No		Industrial countries	UN25 (39)
Resource flow imbalances	Official development assistance, debt, reserves, trade, current account balance	US$, %, indices	No		Developing countries	UN25 (18)
Resource flows and net transfers on long-term debt, net	By low, middle income severely indebted countries	US$	Yes	A	Developing countries	WB3 (1.7)
Resource flows and transfers, net	By net resource flows, net transfers by region, category	US$	Yes	A	All countries reporting to World Bank	WB3 (-)
Shares of GSP of main beneficiary countries	By country	%	No		Selected countries	EC35 (-)
Transfers (long-term), net	By type of transfer	US$	Yes	A	Developing countries	WB3 (1.6)
Utilization of aid	By economic sector	ECU, %	No		EC	EC35(-)
World Bank lending commitments and disbursements by type	By IBRD, IDA	US$, %	Yes	A	Developing countries	UNCTAD5 (3.17B)
12.5 FOOD AID						
12.5.1 General Food Aid						
Delivery schedules	Donor, commodity, quantity, beneficiary	tonnes	No		Selected recipient countries	WFP1 (6A-M)
Distribution of shipments and local purchases	By donor and source, region, category, beneficiaries, commodity, delivery mode	tonnes	Yes	A	Donor countries	WFPI (7)
Distribution of shipments and local purchases	By source, channel, commodity	tonnes	Yes	A	Source countries	WFP1 (12)
Imports and local purchases	Actual and projected deliveries of cereals and non-cereals	tonnes	Yes	M	Africa, Asia, L America,Carib EC	WFP1 (5)
Imports and local purchases	By donor, category and beneficiary type	tonnes	Yes	A	Africa, Asia, L America,Carib EC	WFP1 (2)
Imports and local purchases	By donor, category and beneficiary type	tonnes	Yes	A	Donor countries	WFP1 (9)
Imports and local purchases	Cereals, non-cereals	tonnes	Yes	A	Africa, Asia, L America,Carib EC	WFP1 (3)

12 DEVELOPMENT AND AID

Subject	Categories	Units	Time series Yes/No Frequency		Territorial coverage	Source (Table no.)
Imports and local purchases	Donor, cereals, non-cereals	tonnes	Yes	A	Donor countries	WFP1 (10)
Total		tonnes, US$	No		ACP states	EC1 (II-)
Total		tonnes, US$	No		Mediterranean countries	EC1 (IV-)
Total	By donor and recipient	tonnes	Yes	A	Africa, Asia, L America,Carib EC	WFP1 (8)
Total	By donor and source	tonnes	Yes	A	Donor countries	WFP1 (7)
Total	By donor, cereals	tonnes	Yes	A	Africa, Asia, L America,Carib EC	WFP1 (4)
Total	Cereal, non-cereal	tonnes	Yes	A	Africa, Asia, L America,Carib EC	WFP1 (1)
Transactions and triangular local purchases	Donor, commodity, recipient country, quantity, country of supply	tonnes	No		Donor countries	WFP1 (11)
12.5.2 Grain						
All grains	Recipient country	tonnes	No		Donor country	IWhC1 (4e)
Cash contributions for the purchase of grain	Recipient year of obligation channel type of grain product cash contribution actual tonnage shipped purchased from month of shipment	tonnes	No		Donor country	IWhC1 (3)
Coarse grains and products	Recipient country, total and multilateral	tonnes	No		Donor country	IWhC1 (4c)
Food aid, production ratio		ratio	Yes	Selected years	World	UN16 (19B)
Food aid received in cereals		tonnes	Yes	Selected years	World	UN16 (19B
Rice	By donor	tonnes	Yes	A	Various countries	IRRI1 (98)
Rice and products	Recipient country	tonnes	No		Donor country	IWhC1 (4d)
Shipments	Minimum contribution	tonnes	Yes	A	Donor country	IWhC1 (1)
Shipments	Recipient year of obligation channel type of grain or product rate of equivalent amount shipped transport paid month of shipment	tonnes	No		Donor country	IWhC1 (2)
Shipments total		tonnes	No		Donor country	IWhC1 (2)
Wheat and flour	Recipient country, total and multilateral	tonnes	No		Donor country	IWhC1 (4a)
Wheat products other than flour	Recipient country, total and multilateral	tonnes	No		Donor country	IWhC1 (4b)
12.5.3 Transport and Logistics						
Contributions involving the purchase by donors of grain from other countries (except cash contributions)	Recipient channel type of grain or product actual tonnage wheat equivalent month of shipment source	tonnes	No		Donor country	IWhC1 (Annex 2)
Ocean freight rates by commodity	Major load,discharge areas	US$	No		World	WFP1 (15)

Subject	Categories	Units	Time series Yes/No Frequency		Territorial coverage	Source (Table no.)
Overland transport	Location served, port of discharge, mode of transport, cost, distance, transit time	US$, kms	No		Africa, South America, Asia	WFP1 (14)
Port accommodation, discharge and handling		tonnes, sq m	No		Africa, Pakistan, South Africa	WFP1 (13)
Shipment costs		tonnes	No		Donor country	IWhC1 (Annex 1)
Shipment costs beyond f.o.b. stage		US$	No		Donor country	IWhC1 (Annex 1)
12.6 INDUSTRY						
Demand-supply by industry	Selected indicators	%	No		World	UNIDO1 (2.10)
Intensities	Industrial, chemical and basic metal	%	Yes	I	World	UNIDO1 (2.11)
Manufactures	By origin, destination and country group	%, US$	Yes	I	World	UNIDO1 (1.17)
Manufactures, commodity trade share		%	Yes	I	World	UNIDO1 (1.16)
Manufactures, selected indicators	By end-use	indices	No		World	UNIDO1 (1.19)
Manufactures, selected indicators	By end-use and R&D intensity	indices	Yes	I	World	UNIDO1 (2.8)
Manufactures, selected indicators	By group	%	No		World	UNIDO1 (2.9)
Manufactures, selected indicators	By R&D intensity	indices	No		World	UNIDO1 (1.18)
Merchandise, selected indicators		indices	Yes	I	World	UNIDO1 (2.7)
MVA		%	Yes	A	China	UNIDO1 (1.2)
MVA	By ISIC group	%	No		World	UNIDO1 (2.6)
MVA	Economic groups and developing countries	%	Yes	A	World	UNIDO1 (1.1)
MVA in output		%	Yes	I	World	UNIDO1 (1.12, 2.5)
MVA per employee	By ISIC group	US$	No		World	UNIDO1 (2.6)
MVA per employee	By ISIC group	US$	Yes	I	World	UNIDO1 (1.12, 2.5)
MVA, annual growth		%, indices	Yes	A	World, individual countries	UNIDO1 (1.4, 2.1)
MVA, annual growth	By ISIC group	%	Yes	I	World	UNIDO1 (1.11)
MVA, developing regions' share	By selected ISIC group	%	No		Developing countries	UNIDO1 (1.7)
MVA, ISIC groups distribution among economic groupings		%	Yes	I	World	UNIDO1 (1.6)
MVA, least-developed share in developing countries	By selected ISIC group	%	Yes	I	Least developed countries	UNIDO1 (1.8)
MVA, ratio of purchased fuels to value added	By ISIC group	%	Yes	I	World	UNIDO1 (2.12)
MVA, share in GDP		%	Yes	I	World, individual countries	UNIDO1 (1.5, 2.2)
MVA, structure	By economic grouping	%	Yes	I	Developing countries	UNIDO1 (1.10)
MVA, structure	By economic grouping	%	Yes	I	World	UNIDO1 (1.9)
Output, value added	By ISIC group	%	No		World	UNIDO1 (2.6)

12 DEVELOPMENT AND AID

Subject	Categories	Units	Time series Yes/No Frequency		Territorial coverage	Source (Table no.)
Processing of selected agricultural commodities in principal developing producing countries.	By commodity	tonnes, units, pairs, cu metres	No		Principal developing countries	UNCTAD3 (A.4)
Production, annual growth	By ISIC group	%, indices	Yes	A	World	UNIDO1 (2.4)
Raw materials output processed in principal developing countries for selected mineral commodities.	By commodity	tonnes	No		Principal developing countries	UNCTAD3 (A.5)
Structure of industry	By ISIC group	%	Yes	I	World	UNIDO1 (2.3)
12.7 PORTFOLIO INVESTMENTS						
Bond issues, international	By country, coupon, yield, maturity	nos	Yes	A	Developing countries	WB3 (A.V.3)
Certificates of deposit issued	By amount, issue date	US$	No		Developing countries	WB3(A.V.5)
Commercial paper issued	By issue date, type	US$	No		Developing countries	WB3 (A.V.4)
Emerging market closed-end country funds	By region, initial capital, net assets, market capitalization	US$	Yes	A	Developing countries	WB3 (A.V.6)
Equity issues, international	By issuer, launch, amount, where offered	nat curr	No		Developing countries	WB3 (A.V.7)
Foreign portfolio investment flows	By region	US$	Yes	A	Developing countries	WB3 (1.11)
Gross portfolio equity flows	By analytical group	US$	Yes	A	Developing countries	WB3 (A.V.2)
Gross portfolio equity flows	By region	US$	Yes	A	Developing countries	WB3 (A.V.1)
Portfolio investment	By type	US$	Yes	A	Latin America	WB3 (1.12)
12.8 REFUGEES						
Aid Programmes	Source of funds, type of assistance	US$	No		Africa, Asia and Oceania, EC and N. America Latin America	UN51
Contributions to UNHCR assistance programmes	Governments, intergovernmental organizations, united nations system, others.	US$	No		World	UN41 (3)
Expenditure	By country or regional bureau, source of funds	US$	No		World	UN41 (1)
Expenditure	By country or regional bureau, main types of assistance activities	US$	No		World	UN41 (2)
12.9 TRADE						
Agricultural raw materials	Value of exports, imports	US$	Yes	A	World	UNCTAD3 (1.8, 1.9)

Subject	Categories	Units	Time series Yes/No Frequency		Territorial coverage	Source (Table no.)
Balance of payments	By country, by exports, imports, resource balance, net factor income, net current transfers, current account balance, long-term capital inflow, other items, change in net reserves	US$	Yes	A	Developing countries	WB2 (-)
Balance of payments, current account		US$	Yes	A	Developing countries	OECD14 (-)
Commodities	Exports, imports	US$	Yes	A	World	UNCTAD3 (1.15, 1.16)
Commodities	Principal exporters, importers	US$	Yes	A	World	UNCTAD3 (1.17,1.18)
Commodities	Value of exports, imports	US$	Yes	A	World	UNCTAD3 (1.13, 1.14)
Dependence of developing countries on non-oil primary commodity exports	Total	%	No		Developing countries	UNCTAD5 (4.10)
Developing countries as suppliers of basic commodities to DMECs	By commodity	US$, %	Yes	Selected years	DMECs	UNCTAD5 (4.8)
Direction of commodity exports	By origin and destination, all food items	%	Yes	2 A	World	UNCTAD3 (1.26)
Direction of commodity exports	By origin and destination, total agricultural raw materials	%	Yes	2 A	World	UNCTAD3 (1.27)
Direction of commodity exports	By origin and destination, total minerals and ores	%	Yes	2 A	World	UNCTAD3 (1.28)
Direction of commodity exports	By origin and destination, total mineral fuels	%	Yes	2 A	World	UNCTAD3 (1.29)
Exports to OECD		US$	Yes	A	Developing countries	OECD14 (-)
Exports, economic groupings share		%	Yes	A	World	UNIDO1 (1.13)
Exports, primary commodities	Fuels including and excluding	%	Yes	2 A	World	UNCTAD3 (1.24, 1.25)
Exports, selected countries share		%	Yes	I	Developing countries	UNIDO1 (1.14)
Food	Value of exports, imports	US$	Yes	A	World	UNCTAD3 (1.6, 1.7)
Imports by developed-market-economy countries from developing countries	By commodity, as a proportion of total import values of the commodity group	$; %	No		Developed and developing countries	UNCTAD3 (A.6)
Imports from OECD		US$	Yes	A	Developing countries	OECD14 (-)
Intra-trade of economic co-operation and integration groupings of developing countries	Value and % of total exports	US$, %	Yes	Selected years	World, by development groups	UNCTAD5 (5.5)
Merchandise exports	By country, by food, manufactures, residual	index, US$	Yes	A	Developing countries	WB2 (-)
Merchandise imports	By country, by food,index, fuel and energy, other consumer goods, other intermediate goods, capital goods	US$	Yes	A	Developing countries	WB2 (-)
Merchandise terms of trade	By country, by export price index, import price index, terms of trade	index	Yes	A	Developing countries	WB2 (-)

12 DEVELOPMENT AND AID

Subject	Categories	Units	Time series Yes/No Frequency		Territorial coverage	Source (Table no.)
Merchandise trade, total	Value of exports, imports	US$	Yes	A	World	UNCTAD3 (1.1, 1.2)
Mineral fuels	Value of exports	US$	Yes	A	World	UNCTAD3 (1.12)
Minerals, ores and metals	Value of exports, imports	US$	Yes	A	World	UNCTAD3 (1.10, 1.11)
Network of intra-trade and inter-trade of developing countries	By commodity group	US$, %	No		World, by development groups	UNCTAD5 (5.8)
Primary commodities	Value of exports including, excluding fuels	US$	Yes	A	World	UNCTAD3 (1.3, 1.4)
Primary commodities	Value of imports excluding fuels	US$	Yes	A	World	UNCTAD3 (1.5)
Share of primary commodities in developing country exports	By commodity	US$, %	Yes	Selected years	Developing countries	UNCTAD5 (4.9)
Share of primary commodities in all merchandise trade	By region, exports, imports	%	Yes	A	World	UNCTAD3 (1.19)
Share of primary commodity exports in GDP	By country	%	Yes	A	World	UNCTAD3 (1.22)
Share of regions in world total primary commodity trade values	Exports, imports	%	Yes	A	World	UNCTAD3 (1.21)
Share of three leading commodities in total exports	By commodity, by developing country	%	No		Developing countries	UNCTAD3 (A.7)
Structure of intra-developing and inter-developing country trade	Product group	US$, %	Yes	Selected years	World, by development groups	UNCTAD5 (5.6)
Structure of intra-trade and inter-trade of developing countries	By commodity group	US$, %	No		World, by development groups	UNCTAD5 (5.7)
Trade among developing countries, relative importance of percentage	All commodities, manufactures, world trade, export, imports	%	Yes	Selected years	World, by development groups	UNCTAD5 (5.4)

13 DISTRIBUTION

Subject	Categories	Units	Time series Yes/No Frequency	Territorial coverage	Source (Table no.)
13.1 CONSUMPTION					
Household consumption	Private national consumption, per inhabitant, tradeable consumption	ECU, indices, %	No	EUR12	EC71 (EUR4)
Household consumption	Private national consumption, per inhabitant, tradeable consumption	ECU, indices, %	No	EUR12	EC71 (EUR4)
Penetration rates of selected durable goods	By type of goods	%	No	EC	EC71 (EUR5)
13.2 DUTY FREE					
13.2.1 Cigarettes, Cigars and Tobacco					
Cigarettes	By brand, by price, rate, ranking	US$, %, nos	No	World	GP1 (S1)
Cigars	By brand, by price, rate, ranking	US$, %, nos	No	World	GP1 (S2)
Tobacco	By brand, by price, rate, ranking	US$, %, nos	No	World	GP1 (S3)
13.2.2 Miscellaneous Goods					
Audiovisual and electronic equipment	By product, by price, rate, ranking	US$, %, nos	No	World	GP1 (M5)
Cameras and optics	By product, by price, rate, ranking	US$, %, nos	No	World	GP1 (M6)
Confectionery and foodstuffs	By product, by price,	US$, %, nos	No	World	GP1 (M9)
Fashion, accessories and leather goods	By product, by price, rate, ranking	US$, %, nos	No	World	GP1 (M4)
Gift items	By product, by price, rate, ranking	US$, %, nos	No	World	GP1 (M8)
Jewellery	By product, by price, rate, ranking	US$, %, nos	No	World	GP1 (M7)
Lighters and smokers' requisites	By product, by price, rate, ranking	US$, %, nos	No	World	GP1 (M2)
Miscellaneous products	By product, by price, rate, ranking	US$, %, nos	No	World	GP1 (M10)
Watches and clocks	By product, by price, rate, ranking	US$, %, nos	No	World	GP1 (M3)
Writing instruments	By product, by price, rate, ranking	US$, %, nos	No	World	GP1 (M1)
13.2.3 Perfumes and Cosmetics					
Men's fragrances	By product, by price, rate, ranking	US$, %, nos	No	World	GP1 (F3)
Men's toiletries	By product, by price, rate, ranking	US$, %, nos	No	World	GP1 (F4)
Women's cosmetics and toiletries	By product, by price, rate, ranking	US$, %, nos	No	World	GP1 (F2)
Women's fragrances	By product, by price, rate, ranking	US$, %, nos	No	World	GP1 (F1)
13.2.4 Wines and Spirits					
Aperitif, cocktail and vermouth	By brand, by price, rate, ranking	US$, %, nos	No	World	GP1 (D5)
Armagnac and brandy	By brand, by price, rate, ranking	US$, %, nos	No	World	GO1 (D3)
Beer	By brand, by price, rate, ranking	US$, %, nos	No	World	GP1 (D10)
Champagne and sparkling wine	By brand, by price, rate, ranking	US$, %, nos	No	World	GP1 (D8)

13 DISTRIBUTION

Subject	Categories	Units	Time series Yes/No Frequency		Territorial coverage	Source (Table no.)
Cognac	By brand, by price, rate, ranking	US$, %, nos	No		World	GP1 (D2)
Liqueur	By brand, by price, rate, ranking	US$, %, nos	No		World	GP1 (D7)
Sherry, port and madeira	By brand, by price, rate, ranking	US$, %, nos	No		World	GP1 (D6)
Whisky and whiskey	By brand, by price, rate, ranking	US$, %, nos	No		World	GP1 (D1)
White spirits	By brand, by price, rate, ranking	US$, %, nos	No		World	GP1 (D4)
Wines and spirits, miscellaneous	By product, by price, rate, ranking	US$, %, nos	No		World	GP1 (D9)
13.3 RETAIL DISTRIBUTION						
13.3.1 Employment						
Employment		nos	No		EFTA	EC71 (EUR21)
Employment	By country	nos	No		EC	EM1 (1203)
Employment	By main activity	%	No		EC	EC71 (EUR10)
Employment characteristics in retailing	Low and high share of employees; by employment category	nos, %	No		EUR12	EC71 (EUR9)
Female employment		%	No		EFTA	EC71 (EUR21)
Part-time workers		%	No		EFTA	EC71 (EUR21)
Persons, turnover		%	No		EUR12	EC71 (EUR1b)
Sales establishments	By size, persons engaged, product	nos	Yes		Nordic Countries	NCM1 (114)
Self-employment		%	No		EFTA	EC71 (EUR21)
Wage and salary earners		%	No		EFTA	EC71 (EUR21)
13.3.2 Sales and Turnover						
Direct selling	By country, by company, salesperson, sales value	nat curr	No		EC	EM1 (1218)
Franchising	By country, by franchisors, franchisees, sales value	nos, ECU	No		EC	EM1 (1221)
Internal trade	Retail trade	nat curr	Yes	M M	Asia and Pacific	UN43(-)
Persons, turnover		%	No		EUR12	EC71 (EUR1b)
Quantities of tea sold (London)	By country	tonnes per kg	Yes	A	Selected countries	ITC1 (F6-F8)
Quantities of tea sold (producing countries)	By type	tonnes	Yes	A	Selected countries	ITC1 (F9- F10)
Retail trade volume	index-gross, index-seasonally adjusted, change	indices, %	Yes	A, M	EC, USA, Japan	EC36
Sales		indices	Yes	A, Q,	OECD,	OECD20 (-)
Sales	By country, by growth	nat curr, %	No		EC	EM1 (1201)
Sales	By type of goods	indices	Yes	A, M	OECD	OECD22
Sales	Total, recreational and motor dealers	nat curr	Yes	A, Q, M	OECD	OECD22
Sales	Value, volume, motor dealers, durable goods major outlets	nat curr, indices	Yes	A, M	OECD	OECD22
Sales	Volume	indices	Yes	A, M	OECD, EC, OECD Major Seven OECD EC	OECD22
Sales	By main activity	indices	No		EC EUR9, USA, Japan	EC71 (EUR13)
Sales	Total, durable goods, passenger cars	US$, nos	Yes	A, M	OECD	OECD22
Sales area	Per capita	sq m	No		Central and Eastern EC	EC71 (EUR23)

Subject	Categories	Units	Time series Yes/No Frequency		Territorial coverage	Source (Table no.)
Sales area	Per outlet	sq m	No		Central and Eastern EC	EC71 (EUR23)
Sales through department and variety stores	By country	nat curr, US$	No		EC	EM1 (1211)
Sales through mail order groups	By country	nat curr	No		EC	EM1 (1214)
Sales volume		indices	Yes	A	EUR 9, EC, USA,Japan	EC9 (7.2)
Sales volume	By country	index	No		EC	EM1 (1202)
Share of commerce and main branches in the value added	By branch	%, ECU	Yes	10 yrly	EUR12	EC71 (EUR2)
Turnover	At current prices, average annual growth rate at constant prices	nat curr, %	Yes	A	VICES countries and Yugoslavia	VICES1 (II/1)
Turnover	By enterprise	ECU	No		EFTA	EC71 (EUR21)
Turnover	By type of organization state, co-operatives, private	%	No		Central and Eastern EC	EC71 (EUR23)
Turnover	Excluding VAT	nat curr, ECU	No		EFTA	EC71 (EUR21)
Turnover	Share in food, non-food	%	No		Central and Eastern EC	EC71 (EUR23)
Turnover	By main activity	%	No		EC	EC71 (EUR12)
Turnover	Per enterprise, per capita	ECU	No		EUR12	EC71 (EUR11)
Value added		nat curr	No		EFTA	EC71 (EUR21)
Value index	General, food, apparel	indices	Yes	A	Nordic countries	NCM1 (115)
13.3.3 Structure						
Buying and sales organizations, major	By outlets, organization, turnover, market share	nos, ECU, %	No		Selected countries	EC71 (EUR18)
Co-operatives	By country, by members, market shares	nos, %	No		EC	EM1 (1213)
Department and variety stores	By country	nos	No		EC	EM1 (1212)
Discount enterprises, main	By enterprise	% shares	No		EC EFTA	EC71 (EUR14)
EC retail sector, share of retail enterprises	Main activity by countries with high share and low share of food retailers	%	No		EUR12	EC71 (EUR7)
EC retail sector , number of retail outlets	High, low outlet density, by sector	nos, % share	No		EUR12	EC71 (EUR8)
EC retail sector	By enterprises, employment, share of proprietorships, limited companies by countries with high density, low density	nos, %	No		EUR12	EC71 (EUR6)
Enterprises, number	Wholesale, retail	nos, ECU	No		EUR12, USA, Japan, EFTA	EC71 (EUR1a)
Enterprises, outlets		nos, per capita	No		EFTA	EC71 (EUR21)
Food distribution	By country, by form of organization	%	No		EC	EM1 (1208)
Food outlets	By country, by type	nos	No		EC	EM1 (1206)
Franchising	By country, by franchisors, franchisees, sales value	nos, ECU	No		EC	EM1 (1221)
Hypermarkets and supermarkets		nos	Yes		AEC countries	EC71 (EUR16)
Hypermarkets and superstores	By country, by market share, sales area, turnover	%, sq m, nat curr	No		EC	EM1 (1210)
Hypermarkets and superstores	By country	nos	No		EC	EM1 (1209)
Mail order market share	By country, by sales	%	No		EC	EM1 (1215)
Non-food specialists	By country, by type	nos	No		EC	EM1 (1207)
Own brands	By country	%	No		EC	EM1 (1220)
Persons, turnover		%	No		EUR12	EC71 (EUR1b)
Retail groupings, top 20	By enterprise, activity, turnover	ECU	No		Selected countries	EC71 (EUR15)

13 DISTRIBUTION

Subject	Categories	Units	Time series Yes/No Frequency		Territorial coverage	Source (Table no.)
Retail outlets	By type of organization, state, co-operatives, private, local, itinerary trade,	nos, per capita %	No		Central and Eastern EC	EC71 (EUR23)
Retail sales	By country, by form of outlet	%	No		EC	EM1 (1205)
Retail trade	By country, by form of organization	%	No		EC	EM1 (1204)
Retailers, international activities of	By company turnover, activity	ECU, %	No		Selected countries	EC71 (EUR17)
Sales establishments	By size, persons engaged, product	nos	Yes		Nordic countries	NCM1 (114)
Scanning stores	By country, by type	nos	No		EC	EM1 (1217)
Service stations	By country, by outlets, fuel sales	nos, %	No		EC	EM1 (1219)
Value added	Share of commerce and main branches	%, ECU	Yes	10 yrly	EUR12	EC71 (EUR2)
13.3.4 Taxation – see also Section 43						
VAT rates	By member states	%	No		EC	EC71 (EUR19)
13.4 WHOLESALE DISTRIBUTION						
Enterprises	Wholesale, retail	nos, ECU	No		EUR12, USA, Japan, EFTA	EC71 (EUR1a)
Persons, turnover		%	No		EUR12	EC71 (EUR1b)
Value added	Share of commerce and main branches	%, ECU	Yes	10 yrly	EUR12	EC71 (EUR2)
Wholesale distribution	Value, volume	nat curr	Yes	A, M	OECD	OECD22

14 DRUGS

14.1 NARCOTICS

14.2 PSYCHOTROPIC SUBSTANCES

Subject	Categories	Units	Time series Yes/No Frequency		Territorial coverage	Source (Table no.)
14.1 NARCOTICS						
Alkaloids, extraction from opium	Opium used, alkaloids extracted	kg, %	Yes	A	World	UN29 (V)
Alkaloids, extraction from poppy straw	Poppy straw used, concentrate of poppy straw, morphine manufactured	kg, %	Yes	A	World	UN29 (VI)
Cocaine	Production, utilisation, imports, exports of coca leaves, manufacture of cocaine	kg, % US$	Yes	A	Bolivia, Peru	UN29 (X)
Consumption , principal narcotic drugs	By type of narcotic and country	kg	Yes	A	World	UN29 (XI)
Consumption, narcotic drugs	By type of narcotic and country	rate	No		World	UN29 (XIII)
Consumption, other narcotic drugs	Derivatives of opium alkaloids, synthetic narcotic drugs	kg	Yes	A	World	UN29 (XII)
Cultivation of papaver somniferum for opium production	Area, opium, yield, exports	ha, kg	Yes	A	China, India Rep. of Korea Japan	UN29 (III)
Cultivation of papaver somniferum for purpose other than opium production	Area, poppy straw harvested, yield per hectare	ha, kg	Yes	A	World	UN29 (IV)
Manufacture, other narcotic drugs	Derivatives of opium alkaloids, synthetic narcotic drugs	kg	Yes	A	World	UN29 (IX)
Manufacture, principal narcotic drugs	Opium alkaloids, derivatives, synthetic narcotic drugs	kg	Yes	A	World	UN29 (VIII)
Morphine, conversion	Morphine manufactured morphine used for conversion, total morphine used	kg, %	Yes	A	World	UN29 (VII)
Requirements , estimated	By type of narcotic	kg	Yes	A	World	UN29 (II)
Requirements, estimated	By country and type of narcotic	g	No		World	UN29 (I)
Seizures of cocaine and psychotropic substances reported to the United Nations	Cocaine, opiates	nos, kg	Yes	Selected years	World	UN16 (35)
Seizures of drugs	By drug seized	nos, kg	Yes	A	ASEAN	ASEANS1 (9.7)
Seizures of narcotics	By country and type of narcotic	kg	No		World	UN29 (XVI)
Stocks of narcotics	By type of narcotic	kg	Yes	A	World	UN29 (XIV)
Supply and consumption	By country and amounts available or utilised	kg	No		World	UN29 (XVII)
Trade	Importers, exporters opium, poppy straw, concentrate of poppy straw, morphine, codeine, ethylmorphine, dihydrocodeine, pholcodine, cocaine, dextropropoxyphene, pethidine, tilidine, methadone, diphenoxylate	kg	No		World	UN29 (XV)

Subject	Categories	Units	Time series Yes/No Frequency		Territorial coverage	Source (Table no.)
14.2 PSYCHOTROPIC SUBSTANCES						
Benzodiazepines: hypnotics and clonazepam	By country, manufacture, exports, imports	kg	Yes	A	World	UN29
Central nervous system stimulants	By country, manufacture, imports, exports	kg	Yes	A	World	UN29
Consumption	By country and group of psychotropic substance	nos	No		World	UN29 (IV)
Exports	By country and group of psychotropic substance	kg	Yes	A	World	UN29
Imports	By country and group of psychotropic substance	kg	Yes	A	World	UN29
Manufacture	By country and group of psychotropic substance	kg	Yes	A	World	UN29
Requirements, domestic, medical scientific	By country and group of psychotropic substance	kg	No		World	UN29
Sedative hypnotics, barbiturate type anti-epileptics	By country, manufacture, imports, exports	kg	Yes	A	World	UN29
Seizures of cocaine and psychotropic substances reported to the United Nations	Cocaine, opiates	nos, kg	Yes	Selected years	World	UN16 (35)
Tranquilizers, benzodiazepines and meprobamate	By country and type of tranquillizer, imports, exports	kg	Yes	A	World	UN29

15 EDUCATION AND TRAINING

15.1 ENROLMENT

15.2 EXPENDITURE

15.3 GENERAL

15.4 LITERACY/ILLITERACY

15.5 OUTCOMES OF EDUCATION

15.6 PRIMARY EDUCATION

15.7 PUPILS/STUDENTS – GENERAL

15.8 SECONDARY EDUCATION

15.9 SCHOOLS AND OTHER EDUCATIONAL ESTABLISHMENTS

15.10 TEACHERS/STAFF – GENERAL
15.10.1 Emoluments
15.10.2 Numbers

15.11 TERTIARY EDUCATION

15.12 VOCATIONAL EDUCATION AND TRAINING

Subject	Categories	Units	Time series Yes/No	Frequency	Territorial coverage	Source (Table no.)

15.1 ENROLMENT – see also under Primary Education (15.6), pupils/students - General (15.7) Secondary Education (15.8) and Tertiary Education (15.11)

Subject	Categories	Units	Time series Yes/No	Frequency	Territorial coverage	Source (Table no.)
Enrolment	First, second and third levels, and primary, secondary enrolment ratio, by sex	nos, %	Yes	Selected years	World	UN16 (13)
Enrolment rates	By age, full and part-time	%	Yes	I	OECD	OECD7 (IV)
Enrolment ratios		%	Yes	A	World	UN55
Enrolment ratios for primary schools, gross	Both sexes, by sex	%	Yes	A	African countries	UN1(13)
Enrolment ratios, estimated	Age group, sex	nos	Yes	5 yrly	World	UNESCO1 (2.11)
Enrolment ratios, gross	Higher education	%	Yes	A	African countries	UN1(14)
Enrolment ratios, gross	Secondary schools	%	Yes	A	African countries	UN1(14)
Enrolments		%	Yes	I	OECD	OECD7 (III)
Enrolments, private	By level	%	Yes	I	OECD	OECD7 (VI)
Pupils enrolled		nos	No		World	UN50 (37,38)
School enrolment	By sex, annual growth rate, first, second and third levels, and primary, secondary enrolment ratio combined primary, secondary enrolment ratio	nos, %	No		Africa	UN46 (20)
School enrolment	By sex, annual growth, first, second and third levels, and primary, secondary enrolment ratio	nos, % rate	No		World	UN17 (21)
Students enrolled	Pre-school, first level,	nos second level, third level	Yes	A	ASEAN (9.1.3)	ASEANS1

15.2 EXPENDITURE - see also Section 34

Subject	Categories	Units	Time series Yes/No	Frequency	Territorial coverage	Source (Table no.)
Capital expenditure		nat curr	No	I	World	UNESCO1 (4.1)
Capital expenditure	Amount, % GNP, % of Government expenditure	nat curr, %	No		World	UN50 (41)
Current expenditure	% current government expenditure	%	No	I	World	UNESCO1 (4.1)
Current expenditure	% total government expenditure	%	No	I	World	UNESCO1 (4.1)
Current expenditure	Total % GNP	nat curr, %	No	I	World	UNESCO1 (4.1)
Education expenditure	As % of GNP, per inhabitant	$	No	I	World	UNESCO1 (2.12)
Education expenditure	By level, total, general, teacher training, vocational	nos	No	I	World	UNESCO1 (4.3, 4.4)
Educational expenditure	As proportion of GDP	%	Yes		ASEAN	ASEANS1 (10.2.1)
Educational expenditure	As proportion of total government expenditure	%	Yes		ASEAN	ASEANS1 (10.2.2)
Educational expenditure	Illiterates	% GDP	Yes	A	World	UN55
Educational expenditure, shares of	By country,by public sources, private sources	%	No		OECD	OECD6 (P3)

15 EDUCATION AND TRAINING

Subject	Categories	Units	Time series Yes/No Frequency		Territorial coverage	Source (Table no.)
Expenditure of households on education-	By country	%	No		EC	EC72 (3.13)
Expenditure on education	By country, by public expenditure, private expenditure	%	No		OECD	OECD6 (P1)
Expenditure per pupil, public	By educational level	%	Yes	I	OECD	OECD7 (X.4)
Expenditure per student	By country, by public source, private source	US$	No		OECD	OECD6 (P6)
Expenditure per student, relative	By country, by source, education level	%	No		OECD	OECD6 (P8)
Expenditure, current and capital	By country, by total educational expenditure, distribution, resource category	%	No		OECD	OECD6 (P5)
Expenditure, public	% of total public expenditure	%	Yes	I	OECD	OECD7 (X.2)
Expenditure, public	By educational level	%	Yes	I	OECD	OECD7 (X.3)
Expenditure, public	Current and capital expenditure, as a % of GDP and total public expenditure	%, nat curr	No		OECD	OECD7 (6.2)
Expenditure, public as	% of G.D.P.	%	Yes	I	OECD	OECD7 (X.1)
Expenditure, public current	By purpose	%	No		OECD	OECD7 (6.3)
Expenditure, total	From public and private sources, as a % of GDP	%, nat curr	No		OECD	OECD7 (6.1)
Government expenditure on education	By agency	US$	No		Saudi Arabia	CH1 (10.20)
Higher education expenditure	By field of science and source of funds, by country	nat curr	Yes	A	OECD	OECD3 (16)
Higher education intramural expenditure	By field of science, and type of costs, by country	nat curr	Yes	A	OECD	OECD3 (15)
Higher education intramural expenditure	By field of science, by country constant	nat curr US$	Yes	A	OECD	OECD3 (14)
Public expenditure	By country, by GDP, general government expenditure	%	No		EC	EC72 (3.12)
Public expenditure on education	% of GDP at current prices	%	Yes	A	Latin American and Caribbean countries	UN45 (35)
Public expenditure on education	By country	%	No		OECD	OECD6 (P2)
15.3 GENERAL						
Adult education, population having participated in	By selected characteristic	%	No		OECD	OECD20 (6.1)
Compulsory education		years	Yes	A	World	UNESCO1 (2.1)
Compulsory education	Age group, years	nos	No	I	World	UNESCO1 (3.1)
Decision-making by schools	By country, by education level	%	No		OECD	OECD6 (P18e)

15 EDUCATION AND TRAINING

Subject	Categories	Units	Time series Yes/No Frequency		Territorial coverage	Source (Table no.)
Decision-making, domains of	By country, by resources, personnel, structures, organisation	%	No		OECD	OECD6 (P19e)
Decision-making, locus of	By country, by level of governance	%	No		OECD	OECD6 (P17e)
Decision-making, modes of	By country, by mode	%	No		OECD	OECD6 (P20e)
Decision-making, school autonomy in	By country, by public, private	%	No		OECD	OECD6 (P21e)
Education		nos	Yes	A	World	UNESCO1 (2.1)
Education	By enrolment rates, pupil-teacher ratio, pupils reaching grade 6	rates, ratio %	No		Developing countries	WB1 (-)
Education	By high, middle, low income, by type	%	No		World	CS1 (31)
Education attainment and illiteracy, urban and rural	By total, by age group and sex	%	No		Africa	UN46 (19)
Education attainment and illiteracy, urban and rural	By total, by age group and sex	%	No		World	UN17 (20)
Education imbalances	Indicators of education of a population	%	No		Developing countries	UN25 (15)
Education profile	Indicators of education of a population	%, per thou	No		Developing countries	UN25 (14)
Education profile	Indicators of education of a population	%, ratio	No		Industrial countries	UN25 (33)
Education summary,	By country	nos	Yes	A	ESCAP countries	UN44
Education, regular, average years of	By characteristic	years	Yes	10 yrly	OECD	OECD20 (5.1-5.2)
Educational attainment and illiteracy	By age group and sex, urban and rural areas	%	No		World	UN16 (12)
Formal education, participation in	By country, by private, public	%	No		OECD	OECD6 (P10)
Gender differences in education	By country, by type	nos	No		OECD	OECD6 (C2)
National effort in education	By country, by source, education level	%	No		OECD	OECD6 (P7)
No compulsory education		nos	Yes	A	World	UNESCO1 (2.1)
No schooling	Sex, age group	%	No		World	UNESCO1 (1.4)
Other education structures	Age group, years	nos	No	I	World	UNESCO1 (3.1A)
Population with a level of education below "ISCED 2 completed"	By selected characteristic	%	No		OECD	OECD20 (5.4)
Population with a level of education at least "ISCED 3 completed"	By selected characteristic	%	No		OECD	OECD20 (5.5)
Population with at least some university or equivalent level	By selected characteristic (ISCED 6 and 7)	%	No		OECD	OECD20 (5.6)
Population, distribution of	By highest ISCED level	%	Yes	10 yrly	OECD	OECD20 (5.3)
Pre-compulsory effort	By country, by starting age, ending age, private, public	years, %	No		OECD	OECD6 (P11)
Qualifications	By country	%	No		EC	EM1 (1806)
Scholarships		%	No	I	World	UNESCO1 (4.2)
School pupils, general	By country	nos	No		EC	EC18 (5.5)
School teachers, general	By country	nos	No		EC	EC18 (5.11)

15 EDUCATION AND TRAINING

Subject	Categories	Units	Time series Yes/No Frequency		Territorial coverage	Source (Table no.)
Schooling	Sex, age group	nos	No		World	UNESCO1 (1.4)
Structural changes		nos	No		World	UNESCO1 (3.1B)
Subsidies not distributed		%	No	I	World	UNESCO1 (4.2)
Teaching materials		nos	No	I	World	UNESCO1 (4.2)
Welfare services	Total, meals and board	%	No	I	World	UNESCO1 (4.2)
15.4 LITERACY/ILLITERACY						
Adult literacy rates	By country, by gender	nos	No		SEAR countries	WHO1(19)
Adult rate, 15 years plus	Total, male, female, by country, region	%	No		UNICEF assisted countries	UNICEF2
Education attainment and illiteracy, urban and rural	By total, by age group and sex	%	No		Africa	UN46 (19)
Education attainment and illiteracy, urban and rural	By total, by age group and sex	%	No		World	UN17 (20)
Education indicators	By country, by adult literacy rate, school leaving age	%, years	No		EC	EM1 (1801)
Educational attainment and illiteracy	By age group and sex, urban and rural areas	%	No		World	UN16 (12)
Illiteracy	% of population aged 15 and over	%	Yes	5yr	Latin American and Caribbean countries	UN45 (30)
Illiteracy rate		%	No		Developing countries	UNCTAD5 (1.4)
Illiterate		%	Yes		World	UN55
Illiterate population	Age group	%	No		World	UN50 (42)
Illiterate population	Sex	nos	No		World	UN50 (42)
Literacy rates	By sex	nos, %	No		ASEAN	ASEANS1 (1.5)
15.5 OUTCOMES OF EDUCATION						
Educational attainment of the adult population	By country, by type	%	No		OECD	OECD6 (C1)
Higher education graduation	By country, by degree type, age, gender	years, %	No		OECD	OECD6 (R2)
Higher education survival	By country, by degree type, age, gender	years, %	No		OECD	OECD6 (R3e)
Human capital formation	Indicators of human capital formation	%, nos	No		Developing countries	UN25 (5)
Human capital formation	Indicators of human capital formation	%, per thou	No		Industrial countries	UN25 (30)
Mathematical achievement	By country	%	No		OECD	OECD6 (R8e)
School differences in achievement	By country, by variance, schools, students	%, nos	No		OECD	OECD6 (R9e)
Science and engineering degrees	By country, by type, gender	%	No		OECD	OECD6 (R4)
Science and engineering effort	By country	%, nos	No		OECD	OECD6 (R5e)
Scientific and engineering workforce potential	By sex, annual rate of growth	nos, %	No		Africa	UN46 (21B)
Scientific and engineering workforce potential	By sex, annual rate of growth	nos, %	No		World	UN17 (22B)

Subject	Categories	Units	Time series Yes/No Frequency	Territorial coverage	Source (Table no.)
Student differences in achievement	By country, by students with mathematics scores	%, nos	No	OECD	OECD6 (R10e)
Unemployment and education	By country, by education level, gender	%	No	OECD	OECD6 (R6)
Upper secondary completion	By country by age, duration, gender	years, %	No	OECD	OECD6 (R1)

15.6 PRIMARY EDUCATION – see also under Enrolment (15.1), Pupils/Students (15.7), Schools (15.9) and Teachers/Staff (15.10)

Subject	Categories	Units	Time series Yes/No Frequency	Territorial coverage	Source (Table no.)
Age – year of change	Duration	nos	No	World	UNESCO1 (3.1B)
Age of entrance	Duration	nos	No I	World	UNESCO1 (3.1A)
Age of entrance	Duration of education	nos	No I	World	UNESCO1 (3.1)
Children reaching final grade	% of first grade, by country, region	%	No	UNICEF assisted countries	UNICEF2 (-)
Enrolment	Gross, net, by sex by country, region	ratio	No	UNICEF assisted countries	UNICEF2 (-)
Enrolment	Sex, grade	%	No I	World	UNESCO1 (3.5)
Enrolment in primary school	By country, by gender	%	No	SEAR countries	WHO1(20)
Enrolment rate	By age group	%	No	OECD	OECD7 (4.1)
Enrolment ratios	Sex, gross, net	nos	No I	World	UNESCO1 (3.2)
Enrolment ratios, estimated gross	Sex	nos	Yes 5 yrly	World	UNESCO1 (2.10)
Enrolment, gross rates		rate	Yes A	Latin American and Caribbean countries	UN45 (31a)
Enrolments		nos	Yes A	Latin American and Caribbean countries	UN45 (368)
Enrolments, changes in		indices	Yes I	OECD	OECD7 (I.1)
Entrance age		nos	No I	World	UNESCO1 (3.1)
Females per 100 males in primary education	Per 100 males		No	Developing countries	UNCTAD5 (1.4)
First level	Sex, age group, incompl, completed	%	No	World	UNESCO1 (1.4)
Pre-primary education	By country, by schools, pupils, staff	nos	No	EC	EM1 (1802)
Primary education	By country	nos	No	EC	EM1 (1803)
Primary education,	% of age group in		% No	Developing countries	UNCTAD5 (1.4)
Pupil-teacher ratio		ratio	No I	World	UNESCO1 (2.7, 3.4)
Pupils		nos	No I	World	UNESCO1 (2.2)
Pupils	Girls in private education	%	No	OECD	OECD7 (1.1)
Pupils enrolled		nos	No I	World	UNESCO1 (2.2)
Pupils enrolled	Total, female, % female, % private	nos, %	No I	World	UNESCO1 (3.3)
Pupils enrolled	Total, female, % female, % private	nos, %	No I	World	UNESCO1 (3.4)
Pupils enrolled (females)		indices	No I	World	UNESCO1 (2.6)

15 EDUCATION AND TRAINING

Subject	Categories	Units	Time series Yes/No	Frequency	Territorial coverage	Source (Table no.)
Pupils enrolled (females)		nos, %	No	I	World	UNESCO1 (2.4)
Pupils in school	Per ten thousand inhabitants	nos	Yes	A	VICES region, VICES countries and Yugoslavia	VICES1 (II/4)
Pupils, primary and secondary school		nos	No		ACP state	EC1 (II-)
Pupils, primary and secondary school		nos	No		Mediterranean countries	EC1 (IV-)
Pupils, total		nos	No		OECD	OECD7 (1.1)
Repeaters	Sex, total, grade	%	No	I	World	UNESCO1 (3.6)
Schools		nos	No	I	World	UNESCO1 (3.3)
Schools		nos	No	I	World	UNESCO1 (3.4)
Students completing preparatory and secondary school	By type of school	nos	No		Qatar	CH1 (10.13)
Teachers		nos	Yes	A	Latin American and Caribbean countries	UN45 (369)
Teachers	Pupils per teacher	nos	Yes	A	Latin American and Caribbean countries	UN45 (32a)
Teachers	Total	nos	No		OECD	OECD7 (2.1-2.2)
Teachers, full-time equivalents		nos	No		OECD	OECD7 (2.1-2.2)
Teachers, part-time	% women	%	No		OECD	OECD7 (2.1-2.2)
Teachers, total	% part-time	ind, %	Yes	I	OECD	OECD7 (IX.1-IX.2)
Teachers, women	Women part-time	%	Yes	I	OECD	OECD7 (IX.1-IX.2)
Teaching staff		indices	No	I	World	UNESCO1 (2.6)
Teaching staff		nos	No	I	World	UNESCO1 (2.2)
Teaching staff	Total, female, % female	nos, %	No	I	World	UNESCO1 (3.3)
Teaching staff	Total, female, % female	nos, %	No	I	World	UNESCO1 (3.4)
Teaching staff	Sex	nos, %	No	I	World	UNESCO1 (2.8)
Teaching staff, female		nos, %	No	I	World	UNESCO1 (2.5)

15.7 PUPIL/STUDENTS-GENERAL – see also under Enrolment (15.7)

Subject	Categories	Units	Time series Yes/No	Frequency	Territorial coverage	Source (Table no.)
Children and teachers in schools	By countries	nos	Yes	A	EC	MAC3 (I1)
Economically active	Over minimum school leaving age, total, attainment	nos	No		EC	EC11 (13)
Economically active population	By number of years of schooling completed	nos	No		Latin American and Caribbean countries	UN45(374)
Economically active population	Number of years of education completed	%	Yes	10yr	Latin American and Caribbean countries	UN45 (33)
Economically inactive not in full time education	Over minimum school leaving age, total,	nos	No		EC	EC11 (13)
Foreigners		%	Yes	I	EC	EC9 (3.14)

Subject	Categories	Units	Time series Yes/No Frequency		Territorial coverage	Source (Table no.)
Full time pupils	All levels	nos	Yes	A	EC	EC69 (VII.3)
Full-time pupils and students in EC	By education level	nos	No		EC	EC35 (-)
Opinions of young people	By age, by reason for subject choice	%	No		EC	EC72 (3.15)
Opinions of young people	By country, by reason for subject choice	%	No		EC	EC72 (3.14)
Persons by highest educational level (second and third)	30-64 years of age	%, sex	Yes		Nordic countries	NCM1 (242)
Pupil:teacher ratio	By country, by education level, public, private	%	No		OECD	OECD6 (P16)
Pupils	By school type, sex	nos	No		EC by region	EC65 (-)
Pupils	Total	nos	No		OECD	OECD7 (1.5)
Pupils and students	By country, by level of education	nos	No		EC	EC72 (3.2)
Pupils and students aged 5 to 24	By country	%	No		EC	EC72 (3.4)
Pupils and teachers in schools	By countries	nos	No		The Americas and Australasia	MAC2 (J1)
Pupils and teachers in schools	By country, school type	nos	Yes	A	Africa and Asia	MAC1 (J1)
Pupils in regular-normal education second level, second stage	By field of study	nos	No		Nordic countries	NCM1 (239)
Pupils in regular-normal education third level	By field of study	nos, sex	Yes		Nordic countries	NCM1 (241)
Pupils, girls	Private education	%	No		OECD	OECD7 (1.5)
Pupils, students in regular-normal education	All levels	age, sex	No		Nordic countries	NCM1 (240)
Pupils, students in regular-normal education	All levels	nos	Yes	A	Nordic countries	NCM1 (238)
Still in full time education	Over minimum school leaving age, total, attainment	nos	No		EC	EC11 (13)
Students	% of population educational level	nos, %	Yes	I	EC	EC9 (3.14)
Students abroad	By country, by subject, gender	nos	No		Selected countries	CH1 (10.3)
Students in government schools	By country, by subject, gender	nos	No		Selected countries	CH1 (10.4)
Students, distribution of	By type of education, teachers, classrooms, schools, gender	nos	No		United Arab Emirates	CH1 (10.21)
Teachers and students		nos	Yes	A	Central Africa	UN5 (10-1-1)
Teachers and students		nos	Yes	A	East and Southern Africa	UN4 (10-1-1)
Teachers and students		nos	Yes	A	North Africa	UN2 (10-1-1)
Teachers and students		nos	Yes	A	West Africa	UN3 (10-1-1)
Teaching staff, students		nos	Yes	A	Central Africa	UN5(47)
Teaching staff, students		nos	Yes	A	East and Southern Africa	UN4(47)
Teaching staff, students		nos	Yes	A	North Africa	UN2(47)
Teaching staff, students		nos	Yes	A	West Africa	UN3(47)
Trend in number of full-time pupils	By education level and students in EC	nos	No		EC	EC35 (-)
Trends in females	By country, by level of education	%	No		EC	EC72 (3.7)

15.8 SECONDARY EDUCATION

Age – year of change	Duration	nos	No		World	UNESCO1 (3.1B)
Age of entrance	Duration	nos	No	I	World	UNESCO1 (3.1A)

15 EDUCATION AND TRAINING

Subject	Categories	Units	Time series Yes/No Frequency		Territorial coverage	Source (Table no.)
Age of entrance	Duration of education	nos	No	I	World	UNESCO1 (3.1)
Enrolment	General, teacher		No	I	World	UNESCO1 (2.9)
Enrolment	Gross enrolment rates	nos	Yes	A	Latin American and Caribbean countries	UN45(31b)
Enrolment	Gross, net, by sex By country, region	ratio	No		UNICEF assisted countries	UNICEF2
Enrolment	Sex, grade	%	No	I	World	UNESCO1 (3.8)
Enrolment rate	By age group	%	No		OECD	OECD7 (4.2)
Enrolment ratios	Sex, gross, net	nos	No	I	World	UNESCO1 (3.2)
Enrolment ratios, estimated gross	Sex	ratios	Yes	5 yrly	World	UNESCO1 (2.10)
Enrolments	By education type	%	Yes	I	OECD	OECD7 (I.4)
Enrolments, changes in		indices	Yes	I	OECD	OECD7 (I.3)
Female participation		%	Yes	I	OECD	OECD7 (V.1)
General and teacher training	Teachers, pupils	nos	No	I	World	UNESCO1 (3.7)
Graduates		indices	Yes	I	OECD	OECD7 (VII.1)
Graduates, age group proportion		indices	Yes	I	OECD	OECD7 (VII.2)
Participation rates		%	Yes	I	OECD	OECD7 (I.3)
Pupils enrolled		nos	No	I	World	UNESCO1 (2.2)
Pupils enrolled, females		indices	No	I	World	UNESCO1 (2.6)
Pupils enrolled, females		nos, %	No	I	World	UNESCO1 (2.4)
Pupils in school	Per ten thousand inhabitants	nos	Yes	A	VICES region, VICES countries and Yugoslavia	VICES1 (II/4)
Pupils, girls	Private education	%	No		OECD	OECD7 (1.2-1.3)
Pupils, part-time	By type and sex	nos, %	No		OECD	OECD7 (1.4)
Pupils, total	By type	nos	No		OECD	OECD7 (1.2-1.3)
Pupils, total female	%, 1975-80, 1980-88	nos, %	No	I	World	UNESCO1 (2.4)
Qualifications		nos	No		OECD	OECD7 (5.1-5.2)
Qualifications, for higher education		nos	No		OECD	OECD7 (5.3)
Qualifications, women		%	No		OECD	OECD7 (5.1-5.2)
Repeaters	Sex, total, grade	%	No	I	World	UNESCO1 (3.9)
Second level	Sex, age group	%	No		World	UNESCO1 (1.4)
Secondary education	By country	nos	No		EC	EM1 (1804)
Students enrolled		nos	Yes	A	Latin American and Caribbean countries	UN45(370)

Subject	Categories	Units	Time series Yes/No Frequency		Territorial coverage	Source (Table no.)
Teachers		nos	No		OECD	OECD7 (2.3-2.5)
Teachers		nos	Yes	A	Latin American and Caribbean countries	UN45(371)
Teachers	% part-time	indices, %	Yes	I	OECD	OECD7 (IX.3)
Teachers	Pupils per teacher	nos	Yes	A	Latin American and Caribbean countries	UN45(32b)
Teachers, full-time equivalents		nos	No		OECD	OECD7 (2.3-2.5)
Teachers, part-time	% women	%	No		OECD	OECD7 (2.3-2.5)
Teachers, pupils		nos	No	I	World	UNESCO1 (3.7)
Teachers, women	Women part-time	%	Yes	I	OECD	OECD7 (IX.3)
Teaching staff		indices	No	I	World	UNESCO1 (2.6)
Teaching staff		nos	No	I	World	UNESCO1 (2.2)
Teaching staff	General, teacher		No	I	World	UNESCO1 (2.9)
Teaching staff, female		nos, %	No	I	World	UNESCO1 (2.5)
Teaching staff, training, vocational		%	No	I	World	UNESCO1 (2.9)
Upper secondary education	By country, by age, gender, type	years, nos	No		OECD	OECD6 (P12)

15.9 SCHOOLS AND OTHER EDUCATIONAL ESTABLISHMENTS

All institutions, universities and equivalent institutions	Teachers, pupils	nos	No		World	UN50 (40)
General and teacher training	Teachers, pupils	nos	No		World	UN50 (39)
General schools	By country	nos	No		EC	EC18 (5.1)
Other	Teachers, pupils	nos	No		World	UN50 (39)
Schools		nos	No		World	UN50 (37,38)
Schools, number	Pre-school, first level, second level, third level	nos	Yes	A	ASEAN	ASEANS1 (9.1.1)
Total	Teachers, pupils	nos	No		World	UN50 (39)

15.10 TEACHERS/STAFF - see also under Primary Education (15.6), Secondary Education (15.8) and Tertiary Education (15.11)

15.10.1 Emoluments

Earnings and education	By country, by education level, gender	index	No		OECD	OECD6 (R7)
Emoluments	Administrative, teaching, other personnel	%	No	I	World	UNESCO1 (4.2)

15.10.2 Numbers

Personnel		%	No	I	World	UNESCO1 (4.2)
Staff employed in education	By country, by teaching staff, other staff	%	No		OECD	OECD6 (P9e)
Teachers and students		nos	Yes	A	Central Africa	UN5 (10-1-1)
Teachers and students		nos	Yes	A	East and Southern Africa	UN4 (10-1-1)
Teachers and students		nos	Yes	A	North Africa	UN2 (10-1-1)
Teachers and students		nos	Yes	A	West Africa	UN3 (10-1-1)

15 EDUCATION AND TRAINING

Subject	Categories	Units	Time series Yes/No Frequency		Territorial coverage	Source (Table no.)
Teachers at first and second levels	By sex, annual rate of growth	nos, %	No		World	UN17 (22A)
Teachers at first and second levels	By sex, annual rate of growth	nos, %	No		Africa	UN46 (21A)
Teachers in schools	By countries	nos	Yes	A	EC	MAC3 (I1)
Teachers, full-time equivalents		nos	No		OECD	OECD7 (2.6)
Teachers, part-time	% women	%	No		OECD	OECD7 (2.6)
Teachers, total		nos	No		OECD	OECD7 (2.6)
Teaching staff	Sex	nos	No		World	UN50 (37,38)
Teaching staff and students		nos	Yes	A	Central Africa	UN5(47)
Teaching staff and students		nos	Yes	A	East and Southern Africa	UN4(47)
Teaching staff and students		nos	Yes	A	North Africa	UN2(47)
Teaching staff and students		nos	Yes	A	West Africa	UN3(47)
Teaching staff, number	Pre-school, first level, second level, third level	nos	Yes	A	ASEAN	ASEANS1 (9.1.1)

15.11 TERTIARY EDUCATION

Subject	Categories	Units	Time series Yes/No Frequency		Territorial coverage	Source (Table no.)
Enrolment		nos	No		World	UNESCO1 (3.13)
Enrolment rate	By age group	%	No		OECD	OECD7 (4.3)
Enrolment ratios	Sex, gross, net	nos	No	I	World	UNESCO1 (3.2)
Enrolment ratios, estimated gross	Sex	nos	Yes	5 yrly	World	UNESCO1 (2.10)
Enrolment, gross rates		nos	Yes	A	Latin American and Caribbean countries	UN45(31c)
Enrolments, changes in		indices	Yes	I	OECD	OECD7 (II.1)
Entry ratio to tertiary education	By country, by starting age, gender, type	years, %	No		OECD	OECD6 (P13)
Female participation	By level	%	Yes	I	OECD	OECD7 (V.2)
Graduates of universities and higher institutions	By field of study	nos	No		ASEAN	ASEANS1 (10.1.1)
Graduates, total	As a proportion of age group	indices	Yes	I	OECD	OECD7 (VIII.1 VIII.3)
Higher education	By country, by age, duration, gender, full-time, part-time	years, %	No		OECD	OECD6 (P15)
Higher education	By country, by establishments, staff, students	nos, %	No		EC	EM1 (1805)
New entrants		indices	Yes	I	OECD	OECD7 (VII.1)
New entrants, age group-proportion		indices	Yes	I	OECD	OECD7 (VII.2)
New entrants, age-group proportion		nos	No		OECD	OECD7 (3.2)
Non-university tertiary education	By country, by age, duration, gender, full-time, part-time	years, %	No		OECD	OECD6 (P14)
Number of students in universities	By countries	nos	Yes	A	EC	MAC3 (I2)
Participation rates		%	Yes	I	OECD	OECD7 (II.1)

Subject	Categories	Units	Time series Yes/No Frequency	Territorial coverage	Source (Table no.)
Personnel, higher education	By field of science and occupation, by country	fte	Yes A	OECD	OECD3 (17)
Population, changes in		indices	Yes I	OECD	OECD7 (II.1)
Pupils		nos	No	OECD	OECD7 (3.3)
Pupils	% women, % in private sector	%	No	OECD	OECD7 (3.3)
Pupils enrolled		nos	No I	World	UNESCO1 (2.2)
Pupils enrolled	Field of study, ISCED level	nos	No	World	UNESCO1 (3.13)
Pupils enrolled	Sex	nos	No I	World	UNESCO1 (3.14)
Pupils enrolled	Sex, field of study	nos	No I	World	UNESCO1 (3.12)
Pupils enrolled (females)		indices	No I	World	UNESCO1 (2.6)
Pupils enrolled, female		nos, %	No I	World	UNESCO1 (2.4)
Pupils, distribution among levels		%	Yes I	OECD	OECD7 (II.2)
Pupils, distribution among levels	% women in each level	nos	No	OECD	OECD7 (3.4)
Pupils, female	%, 1975-80, 1980-88	nos, %	No I	World	UNESCO1 (2.4)
Pupils, new entrant total	% women	nos, %	No	OECD	OECD7 (3.1)
Pupils, part-time	By level	%	Yes I	OECD	OECD7 (II.3)
Qualifications, age-group proportion	By type	nos	No	OECD	OECD7 (5.5)
Qualifications, total obtained	By type	nos	No	OECD	OECD7 (5.4)
Qualifications, women	By type	%	No	OECD	OECD7 (5.4)
Student/staff ratio		%	No I	World	UNESCO1 (2.3)
Students		nos	No I	Selected countries	UNESCO1 (3.15)
Students		nos	No I	World	UNESCO1 (2.2)
Students	Country of origin	nos	No I	Selected countries	UNESCO1 (3.15)
Students enrolled		nos	Yes A	Latin American and Caribbean countries	UN45(372)
Students in universities	By countries	nos	No	The Americas and Australasia	MAC2 (J2)
Students in universities	By country	nos	Yes A	Africa and Asia	MAC1 (J2)
Students per 100,000 inhabitants	Sex	nos	No I	World	UNESCO1 (3.10)
Students, post-secondary	Sex, age group	%	No	World	UNESCO1 (1.4)
Students, universities and colleges	Including, excluding night courses, per ten thousand inhabitants	nos	Yes A	VICES region, VICES countries and Yugoslavia	VICES1 (II/4)
Teachers		nos	Yes A	Latin American and Caribbean countries	UN45(373)

Subject	Categories	Units	Time series Yes/No Frequency		Territorial coverage	Source (Table no.)
Teachers	Pupils per teacher	nos	Yes	A	Latin American and Caribbean countries	UN45(32c)
Teachers and students	All institutions, universities and equivalent institutions	nos	No	I	World	UNESCO1 (3.11)
Teaching staff		%	No	I	World	UNESCO1 (2.3)
Teaching staff		indices	No	I	World	UNESCO1 (2.6)
Teaching staff		nos	No	I	World	UNESCO1 (2.2)
Technical college graduates	By country	nos	No		EC	EC18 (5.8)
Technical college lectures	By country	nos	No		EC	EC18 (5.12)
Technical college students	By country	nos	No		EC	EC18 (5.7)
Technical colleges	By country	nos	No		EC	EC18 (5.3)
Universities	By country	nos	No		EC	EC18 (5.4)
University academic staff	By country	nos	No		EC	EC18 (5.13)
University graduates	By country	nos	No		EC	EC18 (5.10)
University undergraduates	By country	nos	No		EC	EC18 (5.9)

15.12 VOCATIONAL EDUCATION AND TRAINING

Subject	Categories	Units	Time series Yes/No Frequency		Territorial coverage	Source (Table no.)
Pupils in vocational schools	Including night courses, per ten thousand inhabitants	nos	Yes	A	VICES region, VICES countries and Yugoslavia	VICES1 (II/4)
Students in vocational training institutes	By education level, by gender	nos	No		Oman	CH1 (10.12)
Vocational school pupils	By country	nos	No		EC	EC18 (5.6)
Vocational schools	By country	nos	No		EC	EC18 (5.2)

16 EMPLOYMENT AND UNEMPLOYMENT

16.1 EMPLOYMENT – GENERAL

16.2 EMPLOYMENT BY INDUSTRY OR SECTOR

- 16.2.1 Agriculture
- 16.2.2 Chemicals
- 16.2.3 Construction
- 16.2.4 Education
- 16.2.5 Finance
- 16.2.6 Forestry
- 16.2.7 General
- 16.2.8 Health
- 16.2.9 Iron and Steel
- 16.2.10 Manufacturing
- 16.2.11 Mining and Quarrying
- 16.2.12 Retail Distribution
- 16.2.13 Science and Technology
- 16.2.14 Textiles
- 16.2.15 Tourism
- 16.2.16 Transport

16.3 LABOUR FORCE

16.4 UNEMPLOYMENT

16.5 VACANCIES

Subject	Categories	Units	Time series Yes/No Frequency		Territorial coverage	Source (Table no.)

16.1 EMPLOYMENT - GENERAL – see also under Labour Force (16.3) and Section 36

Active population, trend of	Observations, projections	nos, indices	Yes	5 yrly	OECD	OECD4 (II.3.)
Active population, age distribution	Observations, projections	%	Yes	5 yrly	OECD	OECD4
Active population	By country, by gender	nos	No		EC	EC72 (4.7)
Active population	Sex, age		No		OECD	OECD4 (A-K,1,2)
Active population	By country, by gender	nos	No		EC	EC35 (-)
Active population and total population, trend of		nos	Yes	5 yrly	OECD	OECD4 (II.4.)
Activity rate, crude	Total, male, female	%	Yes	A	North Africa	UN2 (5)
Activity rate, crude	Total, male, female	%	Yes	A	West Africa	UN3 (5)
Activity rate, crude	Total, male, female	%	Yes	A	East & Southern Africa	UN4 (5)
Activity rate, crude	Total, male, female	%	Yes	A	Central Africa	UN5 (5)
Activity rate		%	Yes	A	EC by region	EC65 (-)
Activity rate	By age, by marital status, gender	%	No		EC	EC72 (4.12)
Activity rate	By country, by gender	%	No		EC	EC35 (-)
Activity rate in the EC	By marital status, age, gender	%	No		EC	EC35 (-)
Activity rates	By country, by gender	%	No		EC	EC72 (4.6)
Activity rates	By sex and age, marital status, nationality,	%	No		EC	EC56 (3,4,5)
Activity rates	Sex, age group	%	No		Asian countries	ILO2 (2)
Activity rates	Sex, age group	%	No		African countries	ILO3 (2)
Activity rates	Sex, age group	%	No		Africa	ILO3 (2)
Activity rates	Sex, age group	%	No		Northern America EC, Oceania and USSR	ILO5 (2)
Activity rates	Sex, age group	%	No		World	ILO6 (2)
Activity rates	Sex, age	%	No		EC	EC69 (II.3)
Activity rates	Total, 15-24 years, by sex	%	Yes	A	EC	EC29 (II/1)
Activity rates	Observations, projections	nos, indices	Yes	5 yrly	OECD	OECD4 (II.7.)
Activity rates by major age-groups	Observations, projections	nos, indices	Yes	5 yrly	OECD	OECD4 (II.8.)
Age of unemployed and of the active population, average	By country, by gender	years	No		EC	EC72 (4.26)
Characteristics of activity, principal	Sex, age	nos	No		EC	EC69 (II.1)
Characteristics of resident employment	By sex, age, employees full time, part-time, temporary	%	No		EC by region	EC65 (-)
Characteristics of the population, changes in principal	By gender, by population age, persons in employment persons seeking employment, job training	nos	No		EC	EC72 (4.3)
Civilian		indices	Yes	A, M	OECD	OECD22
Civilian employees	Percentage change	%	Yes	A	OECD, EC	OECD32 (1.12)
Civilian employment	By type for total, male and female population	nos	Yes	A	OECD	OECD19 (III (A-C))
Civilian employment	Percentage change	%	Yes	A	OECD, EC	OECD32 (1.7)
Civilian employment	Total, male, female and married by country	nos, %	Yes	A	OECD	OECD19 (II)
Civilian employment	Total	indices	Yes	M, Q, A	OECD	OECD23 (-)
Civilian employment in services	Percentage change	%	Yes	A	OECD, EC	OECD32 (1.11)

16 EMPLOYMENT AND UNEMPLOYMENT

Subject	Categories	Units	Time series Yes/No Frequency		Territorial coverage	Source (Table no.)
Economic activity, participation in	By sex, by sex and age	%	Yes	I	Latin American and Caribbean countries	UN45 (13-16)
Economically active and not economically active population	By sex and age	nos, %	No		World	UN16 (22, 23)
Economically active and not economically active populations,	By total, by age, by sex, of total population urban and rural	nos, years, %	No		World	UN17 (10)
Economically active and not economically active populations,	By total, by age, by sex, % of total population urban and rural	nos, years, %	No		Africa	UN46 (10)
Economically active foreign-born population	Occupation, sex	nos	No		World	UN19 (35)
Economically active persons aged 15 years or over by sex, age group and occupational status	Males, females	nos	No		EC	EC11 (9)
Economically active population, structure of	By country, by gender	nos, %	No		EC	EM1 (0607)
Economically active population		nos	Yes	5yr	Latin American and Caribbean countries	UN45 (359)
Economically active population	By country, by age	nos	No		EC	EM1 (0609)
Economically active population	By country, by age	%	No		EC	EM1 (0610)
Economically active population	By country, by status	nos	No		EC	EM1 (0611)
Economically active population	By country, by status	%	No		EC	EM1 (0612)
Economically active population	By major activity group, country, gender	nos	Yes	10 yr	Africa and Asia	MAC1 (C1)
Economically active population	By occupation	nos	No		Latin American and Caribbean countries	UN45 (363)
Economically active population	By sex and age group	nos, %	No		World	UN17 (8)
Economically active population	By sex and occupation	nos, %	No		World groups	UN16 (24)
Economically active, population	By total, sex and occupational groups	nos, %	No		World	UN17 (12)
Economically active, population	By total, sex and occupational groups	nos, %	No		Africa	UN46 (12)
Economically active population	Wage earners, self-employed, unremunerated family members, total	nos	No		Latin American and Caribbean countries	UN45 (364)
Economically active population by major industrial groups	By countries	nos	Yes	A	EC	MAC3 (B1)
Economically active population by sex and occupational status	Persons, males, females	nos	No		EC	EC11 (8)
Employed	Labour force rate, age, sex	nos, rate	Yes	A	Nordic countries	NCM1 (47/51)
Employees, foreign	By country	%	No		EC	EC35 (-)
Employees, foreign	By country, by community-non-community	nos	No		EC	EC72 (4.33)
Employees		nos, %	No		EC, USA, USSR, Canada, Japan	EC9 (3.16)
Employees		nos	Yes	Q	OECD	OECD40 (-)
Employees	By country, by selected areas of the economy	nos	No		EC	EC18 (6.1)
Employees	By country, by nationality	%	No		EC	EC72 (4.35)
Employees	Wage earners	nos, 1000	Yes	A	North Africa	UN2 (2-1)
Employees	Wage earners	nos, 1000	Yes	A	West Africa	UN3 (2-1)
Employees	Wage earners	nos, 1000	Yes	A	East & Southern Africa	UN4 (2-1)
Employees	Wage earners	nos, 1000	Yes	A	Central Africa	UN5 (2-1)
Employers, self-employed and family workers		nos, %	No		EC, USA, USSR, Canada, Japan	EC9 (3.16)
Employment, general level of	By country, by growth	nos, %	No		EC	EM1 (0601)
Employment, total		indices	Yes	A, Q, M	OECD	OECD22

Subject	Categories	Units	Time series Yes/No	Frequency	Territorial coverage	Source (Table no.)
Employment, total		nos, indices	Yes	A	OECD, EC	OECD19 (4.0)
Employment, total		indices	Yes	A, M	OECD total, EC total Major Seven total OECD, EC	OECD22
Employment, foreign workers		nos	Yes	A, M	OECD	OECD22
Employment, total	Percentage change	%	Yes	A	OECD, EC	OECD32 (1.6)
Employment, total	Percentage of population from 15-64	%	Yes	A	OECD, EC	OECD32 (2.14)
Employment, total	By activity	nos	Yes	A	OECD	OECD29
Employment, sectoral growth of	By sex	%	No		American and Caribbean countries	UN45 (20)
Employment, population ratios	By sex and age, marital status	%	No		EC	EC56 (6,7)
Employment, total		indices	Yes	M, Q, A	OECD - total Major seven EC	OECD23 (-)
Employment, summary	Indicators of employment	%	No		Developing countries	UN25 (16)
Employment, summary	Indicators of employment	%	No		Industrial countries	UN25 (35)
Employment, rates of growth	Sex, age group	%	No		Asian countries	ILO2 (1,2)
Employment, rates of growth	Sex, age group	%	No		African countries	ILO3 (1,2)
Employment, rates of growth	Sex,age group	%	No		Northern America EC, Oceania and USSR	ILO5 (1,2)
Employment, rates of growth	Sex, age group	%	No		Northern America EC, Oceania and USSR	ILO5 (1,2)
Employment, rates of growth	Sex, age group	%	No		World	ILO6 (1,2)
Employment, rate of change		%			Africa	UN46 (9)
Employment	in agriculture, industry and services	nos, %	No		EC, USA, USSR, Canada, Japan	EC9 (3.17-3.18)
Employment	By broad sector	%	Yes	A	EC by region	EC65 (-)
Employment	By country, by gender	nos	No		EC	EC72 (4.22)
Employment	By occupation: Professional Technical and related workers Administrative and managerial workers Clerical and related workers Sales workers Service workers	nos	No	I	World	ILO7 (3C)
Employment	By occupational status, by gender	%	No		EC	EC72 (4.18)
Employment	By professional status, sex	nos, %	No		EC	EC56 (25,27)
	By professional status, sector of activity, sex	nos, %	No		EC	EC56 (29,30)
	By professional status, and full-time, part-time sex	nos, %	No		EC	EC56 (33,34)
Employment	By sectors of economic activity in employment	%	Yes	A	EC	EC29 (II/8)
Employment	By sex	nos	Yes	Q	OECD	OECD38 (-)
Employment	By sex and age	nos, %	No		EC	EC56 (18,19)
Employment	Sex, age group	nos	No		Asian countries	ILO2 (1,2)
Employment	Sex, age group	nos	No		African countries	ILO3 (1,2)
Employment	Sex, age group	nos	No		Latin American countries	ILO4 (1,2)

16 EMPLOYMENT AND UNEMPLOYMENT

Subject	Categories	Units	Time series Yes/No	Frequency	Territorial coverage	Source (Table no.)
Employment	Sex, age group	nos	No		Northern America EC, Oceania and USSR	ILO5 (1,2)
Employment	Sex, age group	nos	No		World	ILO6 (1,2)
Employment	Sex	nos	Yes	A	World	ILO7 (3A)
Employment	Sex	nos	Yes	A	World	ILO7 (4)
Employment	Sex	nos	Yes	A	World	ILO7 (5A)
Employment	Sex	nos	Yes	A	World	ILO7 (5B)
Employment	Sex and industry: Electricity, gas and water Trade, restaurants and hotels Financing, insurance, real estate,business services Community, social and personal services	nos	Yes	A	World	ILO7 (3B)
Employment as a share of total employment		%	Yes	A	EC	EC2 (A2)
Employment by sex and occupational status	Males, females	%				EC11 (1) EC11 (1)
Employment of women and young people	By country	nos, %	No		EC	EC35 (-)
Employment. civilian	By sex, proportion of females in total	nos, %	Yes	A	EC	EC29 (II/3)
Employment. civilian	By sex	nos	Yes	Q	OECD	OECD40 (-)
Female economically active population,	By marital status and age group	by years, total, %, nos	No		World	UN17 (13)
Female economically active population	By marital status and age group	years, total, %, nos	No		Africa	UN46 (13)
Females, proportion of in the active population	Observations, projections	nos, indices	Yes	5 yrly	OECD	OECD4 (II.10.)
Full-time employees, industry and services	By hours worked and by sex	%	Yes	A	EC	EC29 (VI/6)
Government employees	By nationals, expatriates	nos, %	No		Arabian Gulf	CH1 (5.12)
Government employment	Percentage change	%	Yes	A	OECD, EC	OECD32 (1.13)
Household membership	By country, by household, relationship with employment market	%	No		EC	EC72 (4.31)
Labour distribution	By country, by sector	nos	No		Selected countries	CH1 (7.4)
Labour force	Agriculture, industry, services	%	No		World	UNCTAD1 (6.10B)
Manual and non-manual staff	By country	nos	No		EC	EC18 (6.2)
Non-agricultural activities		nos	Yes	A, M	World, Latin	UN35 (5)
Part-time employees, industry and services	By hours worked and by sex	%	Yes	A	EC	EC29 (VI/7)
Part-time employees	By country, by % of all employees, all female employees, female employees in services	nos, %	No		EC	EC35 (-)
Part-time work	By country, by gender	%	No		EC	EC72 (5,7)
Part-time work	By country, by sector	%	No		EC	EC72 (5.9)
Part-time work	By country, by gender % of total employment	%	No		EC	EC35 (-)
Participation rates	By country and age range	nos	Yes	A	OECD	OECD19
Persons in employment by sex and occupational group	By type of employment persons, males, females	nos	No		EC	EC11 (11)
Population of working age (15-64), trend of	Observations, projections	nos, indices	Yes	5 yrly	OECD	OECD4 (II.5.)
Population of working age without migration		nos	Yes	5 yrly	OECD	OECD4 (II.6.)
Populations economically active and not economically active, rates of change	By sex	% %	Yes	15 yrly	World	UN17 (11)

Subject	Categories	Units	Time series Yes/No	Frequency	Territorial coverage	Source (Table no.)
Qualified personnel	By country	nos	No		EC	EC18 (6.3)
Rate of change, employment		%	Yes	10 yrly	World	UN17 (9)
Rates of change in populations economically active and not economically active	By sex	%	No		Africa	UN46 (11)
Temporary contracts	By country, by gender	%	No		EC	EC72 (5.13)
Temporary contracts	By country, by age	%	No		EC	EC72 (5.14)
Wage earners and paid employees	By activity for total, male and female population	nos, %	Yes	A	OECD	OECD19 (IV (A-C))
Working week in non-agricultural activities	By country, by growth	hours, %	No		EC	EM1 (0605)

16.2 EMPLOYMENT BY INDUSTRY OR SECTOR

16.2.1 Agriculture – see also under Employment – General (16.1), under General (16.2.7) and Section 2

Subject	Categories	Units	Time series Yes/No	Frequency	Territorial coverage	Source (Table no.)
Activity rates	Sex, age group	%	No		Latin American countries	ILO4 (2)
Agricultural holders	By sex	nos, %	No		World	UN16 (25B)
Agricultural population	Total, in agriculture	nos, %	Yes	A	ASEAN	ASEANS1 (3.1)
Agricultural population		nos, %	Yes	A	World	FAO1 (3)
Agriculture, animal husbandry and forestry workers, fishermen and hunters		nos	No	I	World	ILO7 (3C)
Agriculture, hunting, forestry and fishing	Sex	nos	Yes	A	World	ILO7 (3B)
Civilian employment in agriculture	Percentage change	%	Yes	A	OECD, EC	OECD32 (1.8)
Dual activity, farming	Of holder who is also manager, of members of holder's family	nos	No		EC	EC45 (AX)
Economically active population in agriculture	By % of total, by sex; by % of population by sex	nos, %	Yes	10 yrly	World	UN17 (9)
Economically active population in agriculture	By % of total, by sex; by % of population by sex	nos, %	No		Africa	UN46 (9)
Economically active population by sector, distribution of	Agriculture, male, female	%	Yes	A	African countries	UN1 (7)
Economically active population in agriculture	By sex	nos, %	No		World	UN16 (25A)
Employees	Agriculture, by industry,	indices, nos	Yes	A, Q	EC, USA, Japan	EC36
Employment, female	Percentage of females	nos	No		EC, USA, USSR, Canada, Japan	EC9 (3.15)
Employment, rates of growth	Sex, age group	%	No		Latin American countries	ILO4 (1,2)
Employment	By sector	'000, %	No		EC	WC1 (-)
Employment	Sex, age group	nos	No		Northern America EC, Oceania and USSR	ILO5 (1,2)
Employment in agriculture	% of civilian employment	%	Yes	A	OECD, EC	OECD32 (2.9)
Employment in agriculture	Civilian labour	%	Yes	A	EC	MMB1 (11)
Employment in agriculture as percentage of civilian employment		%	Yes	A	OECD	OECD5 (II.2)
Labour force, farm	By workers, work time, annual work units, age classes of holder	nos	No		EC	EC45 (AIX)

16 EMPLOYMENT AND UNEMPLOYMENT

Subject	Categories	Units	Time series Yes/No	Frequency	Territorial coverage	Source (Table no.)
Labour force, farm holdings	By worker, by age class of holder, by work-time of holder, by size class of holding, by country	nos	No		EC	EC45 (B)
Labour force, farm holdings	AWU, number of persons, distribution of the holders-by work time, per age, OGA, by type of farming by country	nos, %	No		EC	EC45 (C)
Labour force, farm holdings	By worker, by age class of holder, by work time of holder, by country, region	nos	No		EC	EC45 (D)
Labour force, agricultural	By holders, family workers, non-family workers	nos	No		EC	EC9 (5.17)
Labour force	By sex, agriculture, industry, participation rate, age dependency	%	No		Developing countries	WB1 (-)
Manual workers, full-time		nos	No		EC	EC23 (I.1)
Manual workers	By country, provision of benefits in kind and work type	nos	No		EC	EC23 (-)
Manual workers	By country, provision of benefits in kind, by sex and age group	nos, %	No		EC	EC23 (-)
Manual workers	By country and region	nos	No		EC	EC23 (III.1-III.7)
Manual workers	By farm size and sex	nos	No		EC	EC23 (I.2)
Manual workers	By provision of benefits in kind and by sex	nos	No		EC	EC23 (I.4)
Manual workers	By sex and age group	nos	No		EC	EC23 (I.5)
Manual workers	By work type and sex	nos	No		EC	EC23 (I.3)
Professional qualifications	By country and type	nos	No		EC	EC23 (-)
Total, family members,	Agricultural holdings, AWU	nos	Yes	A	EC, EC non-family members	EC29 (II/14)
16.2.2 Chemicals						
Employees	By country	nos	Yes	A	Western world	CIA1 (7)
16.2.3 Construction – see also under General (16.2.7) and Section 7						
Employees		nos	Yes	A	World	UN18 (-)
Employees	By firm size	nos	Yes	A	World	UN10 (12)
Employees	By country	nos	No		EC	EC18 (8.11)
Employment		nos	No		EC by region	EC76 (-)
Employment	Sex	nos	Yes	A	World	ILO7 (3B)
Employment	Sex	nos	Yes	A	World	ILO7 (7)
Expectations	Construction as a whole, building, housing, other buildings, public works (civil engineering)	indices	Yes	M	EC	EC70
16.2.4 Education – see also under General (16.2.7) and Section 15						
Labour force participation and unemployment	By country, by rate, gender	nos	No		OECD	OECD6 (C3)
Staff employed in education	By country, by teaching staff, other staff	%	No		OECD	OECD6 (P9e)

Subject	Categories	Units	Time series Yes/No	Frequency	Territorial coverage	Source (Table no.)
16.2.5 Finance – see also under General (16.2.7)						
Employment	By country (details given for each country vary)	indices	Yes	A, M	World	IMF6 (-)
Employment	Indices		Yes	A, M	World	IMF7 (-)
Labour force, share of	By country, by employment	%	Yes	A	Developing countries	WB2 (-)
16.2.6 Forestry – see also Section 21						
Employment, total, tropical timber		nos	No		World tropical timber producing countries	ITTO1 (5)
16.2.7 General						
Branch of activity		indices	Yes	A	World	UN27 (-)
Branch of activity		indices	Yes	A	World excluding Eastern EC and USSR	UN27 (-)
Branch of activity	By region	indices	Yes	A	World excluding Eastern EC and USSR	UN27 (-)
Branch of activity	Developed countries	indices	Yes	A	World excluding Eastern EC and USSR	UN27 (-)
Branch of activity	Developing countries	indices	Yes	A	World excluding Eastern EC and USSR	UN27 (-)
Civilian employment, female	Services	indices, nos, %	Yes	A	EC, USA, Japan	EC36
Civilian employment	By sector	nos, indices, %	Yes	A	OECD	OECD19 (7.0)
Civilian employment	By sex, proportion of females in total	nos, %	Yes	A	EC	EC29 (II/5)
Civilian employment in industry	Percentage change	%	Yes	A	OECD, EC,	OECD32 (1.9)
Economic activity	All activities	nos	No		EC, USA and Japan	EC53 (1.1)
Economically active population by sector	Industry, male, female	%	Yes	A	African countries	UN1 (7)
Economically active population by sector	Services, male, female	%	Yes	A	African countries	UN1 (7)
Economically active population	By country, by industry	%	No		EC	EM1 (0608)
Economically active population	By sex and sector of economic activity	%	Yes	10yr	Latin American and Caribbean countries	UN45 (17-19)
Economically active population	By sex and sector of economic activity	nos	Yes	10yr	Latin American and Caribbean countries	UN45 (362)
Economically active population	Industry and sex	nos 1000	No		Central Africa	UN5 (3)
Economically active population	Industry and sex	nos 1000	No		North Africa	UN2 (3)
Economically active population	Industry and sex	nos 1000	No		West Africa	UN3 (3)
Economically active population	Industry and sex	nos 1000	No		East & Southern Africa	UN4 (3)
Economically active population by major industrial groups	Cities	nos	No		The Americas and Australasia	MAC2 (C1)
Employed persons	By economic activity and country	nos	Yes	A	Asian Countries	APO1
Employed persons	By economic sectors, by country	nos	Yes	A	VICES countries and Yugoslavia	VICES1 (I/2)
Employed persons	By main industry	nos	Yes	A	ASEAN	ASEANS1 (1.8)
Employed persons	By NACE by size of enterprise	nos	Yes	A	EC	EC77 (-)
Employed Persons	By selected branches of industry, annual average, by country	nos	Yes	A	VICES countries and Yugoslavia	VICES1 (I/4)
Employees, number	Seasonally adjusted, by NACE sector,	indices	Yes	A, Q	EC	EC52 (-)
Employees, foreign	By NACE division	nos	Yes	A	EC	EC29 (III/8)

16 EMPLOYMENT AND UNEMPLOYMENT

Subject	Categories	Units	Time series Yes/No Frequency		Territorial coverage	Source (Table no.)
Employees, foreign		nos	Yes	A	EC	EC29 (III/6)
Employees, foreign	By nationality, by sex	nos	No		EC	EC29 (III/7)
Employees, female	By NACE class	%	No		EC	EC29 (III/3)
Employees, female , total employment share	By ISIC group	%	No		World	UNIDO1 (2.13)
Employees	Average number	nos	Yes	A	World	UN27 (-)
Employees	By economic activity	nos	No		EC	EC9 (3.19)
Employees	By economic activity, sex	nos, %	No		EC	EC56 (45,46)
Employees	By industry	Indices	No		EC	EC53 (2.2)
Employees	By industry	nos	No		EC	EC53 (2.1)
Employees	By ISIC economic activity, by country	nos	Yes	A	EC	EC29 (III/5)
Employees	By NACE class	%	No		EC	EC29 (III/2)
Employees	By NACE division, by country	nos	Yes	A	EC	EC29 (III/1)
Employees	By sector of activity, and full-time, part-time	nos, % sex	No		EC	EC56 (37,38)
Employees	By sector of economic activity	%	Yes	A	EC	EC29 (II/14)
Employees	By sex, by NACE class	nos	Yes	A	EC	EC29 (III/4)
Employees	By industry, region	nos	No		EC	EC53 (7.1)
Employees	By ISIC division	nos	Yes	A	OECD	OECD16
Employees	By NACE	nos	No		EC	EC75 (2), (3.2)
Employees in employment, females	By sector of economic activity	nos	Yes	A	EC	EC29 (II/13)
Employees in employment	By sector of economic activity	nos	Yes	A	EC	EC29 (II/12)
Employers, self-employed and family workers	By sector of economic activity	nos	Yes	A	EC	EC29 (II/10)
Employers, self-employed and family workers, female	By sector of economic activity	nos	Yes	A	EC	EC29 (II/11)
Employment, share of industry in	Manufacturing, building and civil engineering	%	No		EC, USA and Japan	EC53 (1.2)
Employment, total	Total by sex, changes in total working population	nos, %	Yes	A	EC	EC29 (II/4)
Employment, share of each economic sector in	By country, by sector	nos, %	No		EC	EC72 (4.15)
Employment, civilian	By sex by industrial sector	nos	Yes	Q	OECD	OECD40 (-)
Employment, civilian	Industrial sector	index, % of total	Yes	Q	OECD	OECD40 (-)
Employment, female	Proportion of women employed in each sector of economic activity	%	Yes	A	EC	EC29 (II/9)
Employment, female	By sector of economic activity	nos	Yes	A	EC	EC29 (II/7)

Subject	Categories	Units	Time series Yes/No Frequency		Territorial coverage	Source (Table no.)
Employment	Agriculture, hunting, forestry, fishing	nos	No		World	UN50 (16)
	Mining and quarrying	nos	No		World	UN50 (16)
	Manufacturing industries	nos	No		World	UN50 (16)
	Electricity, gas, water	nos	No		World	UN50 (16)
	Construction	nos	No		World	UN50 (16)
	Trade, restaurants and hotels	nos	No		World	UN50 (16)
	Transport, storage and	nos	No		World	UN50 (16)
	communication	nos	No		World	UN50 (16)
	Financing, insurance, real estate and business services	nos	No		World	UN50 (16)
	Community, social and personal	nos	No		World	UN50 (16)
Employment	By branch	nos	No		EC	EC69 (III.6)
Employment	By branch of economic activity, by country	nos	Yes	A	EC	EC78 (VI.2.1)
Employment	By broad sector	%	Yes	A	EC	EC65 (-)
Employment	By industry	nos	No		EC	EC53 (3.1)
Employment	By ISIC division	nos	Yes	A	OECD	OECD16
Employment	By NACE	nos	Yes	A	EC	EC75 (1), (3.1)
Employment	By sector	indices	Yes	Q, M	OECD	OECD15
Employment	By sector of economic activity	nos	Yes	A	EC	EC29 (II/6)
Employment	By sector of activity, gender, nationality	%	No		EC	EC35 (-)
Employment	By type, age and sex	nos	No		Nordic countries	NCM1 (22)
Employment	By type	nos	No		Nordic countries	NCM1 (20)
Employment	Industry group	nos, %	No		African countries	ILO3 (3)
Employment	Industry group	nos, %	No		Latin American countries	ILO4 (3)
Employment	Industry group	nos, %	No		Northern America EC, Oceania and USSR	ILO5 (3)
Employment	Industry group	nos, %	No		World	ILO6 (3)
Employment	Sector and selected industries	indices	Yes	A	World,	UN50 (9)
Employment	Sex	nos, rate	Yes	Q	World	ILO1 (4)
Employment	Sex	nos	Yes	Q	World	ILO1 (1)
Employment	Sex	nos	Yes	Q	World	ILO1 (2)
Employment	Sex	nos	Yes	Q	World	ILO1 (3)
Employment	Total, by industry	indices	Yes	A, M	OECD	OECD22
Employment - share of different industries	By NACE	%	No		EC	EC75 (3.1)
Employment by kind of activity	All persons, employees	nos	Yes	A	OECD	OECD29 (15)
Employment distribution	By type	nos	No		Nordic countries	NCM1 (21)
Employment, industrial	By selected industries	indices	Yes	A	World	UNCTAD1 (6.7)
Employment in industrial production	By country	nos	No		EC	EC18 (8.3)
Employment in industry	By type, sex	nos	Yes	A	Nordic countries	NCM1 (49/50)
Employment in industry	Percentage of civilian employment	%	Yes	A	OECD, EC,	OECD32 (2.10)
Employment in services	Percentage of civilian employment	%	Yes	A	OECD, EC	OECD32 (2.12)
Employment in the EC	By population aged 14-64	nos	No		EC	EC35 (-)
Expectations	By industry sector	indices	No		EC	EC70
Foreign workers in the GCC region	By nationality	nos	No		Arabian Gulf	CH1 (5.23)
Government employment	Percentage of total employment	%	Yes	A	OECD, EC	OECD32 (2.13)

16 EMPLOYMENT AND UNEMPLOYMENT

Subject	Categories	Units	Time series Yes/No Frequency		Territorial coverage	Source (Table no.)
Labour force, distribution of	By sector	% DMECs	Yes	Selected years	Developing countries,	UNCTAD5 (1.2)
Labour force	By high, middle, low income, by sector	%	No		World	CS1 (25)
Manpower	Persons employed by industry, unemployed by country	nos	Yes	A	ESCAP	UN44
Non-employees	By sector of activity and full-time, part-time employers and self-employed, family workers,	nos, % sex	No		EC	EC56 (39,40)
Numbers	Industry group	nos, %	No		Asian countries	ILO2 (3)
Occupied population	By country, by sector of activity	nos, %	No		Selected countries	EC35 (-)
Occupied population, share of economic sectors in	By country, by sector	nos, %	No		EC	EC35 (-)
Occupied population	By branch	%	No		EC	EC61 (2)
Occupied population: average annual	By branch	%	No		EC	EC61 (6)
Operatives	Number of	average	Yes	A	World	UN27 (-)
Part-time employees	By sector of economic activity, by sex	%	Yes	A	EC	EC29 (VI/2)
Persons engaged	Average number	nos	Yes	A	World	UN27 (-)
Persons in employment	By economic activity, sex	nos, %	No		EC	EC56 (43,44)
Persons in employment	By sector of activity, sex	nos, %	No		EC	EC56 (26,28)
Persons in employment	By sector of activity and professional status,	nos, % sex	No		EC	EC56 (31,32)
Persons in employment	By sector of activity and full-time, part-time	nos, % sex	No		EC	EC56 (35,36)
Persons in employment	By sector	nos, %				EC11 (1)
Persons in employment	By sex and branch of economic activity	nos	No		EC	EC11 (10)
Persons working full-time, part-time	By age and sex	nos, %	No		EC	EC56 (41,42)
Wage and salary earners	By industry	nos	No		EC	EC69 (III.7)
Wage and salary earners	By NACE class, sex, age	nos	No		EC	EC69 (V.1)
Wage and salary earners	By NACE class, females, age	nos	No		EC	EC69 (V.2)
Wage employees	Industry	nos 1000	Yes	A	Central Africa	UN5 (4)
Wage employees	Industry	nos 1000	Yes	A	East & Southern Africa	UN4 (4)
Wage employees	Industry	nos 1000	Yes	A	North Africa	UN2 (4)
Wage employees	Industry	nos 1000	Yes	A	West Africa	UN3 (4)
Wage or salary earners in each economic activity	By country, by sector	%	No		EC	EC72 4.19)
Workers in industrial production	By country	nos	No		EC	EC18 (8.4)
Working population		nos, %	No		EC, USA, USSR, Canada, Japan	EC9 (3.15)
16.2.8 Health – see also Section 22						
Economically active population employed	By country, by major industry divisions	%	No		SEAR countries	WHO1 (63)
16.2.9 Iron and Steel - see also Section 25						
Employees, steel industry		nos	Yes	A	World	IISI5 (-)
Employees		nos	Yes	A	EC	EC55 (2.2)
Employees	Manual, non-manual	nos	Yes	A	EC	EC29 (III/9)
Manpower	Total and process workers	tonnes	No		OECD, EC	OECD18 (18)

Subject	Categories	Units	Time series Yes/No Frequency		Territorial coverage	Source (Table no.)
Workforce changes in	Entrants, leavers by reason	nos	Yes	A	EC	EC29 (III/10)
16.2.10 Manufacturing						
Civilian employment in manufacturing	Percentage change	%	Yes	A	OECD, EC, OECD, EC	OECD32 (1.10)
Employees		indices	Yes	A, M	OECD	OECD22
Employees		nos	No		World	UN50 (90)
Employees	Sex	nos	Yes	A	World	ILO7 (3B)
Employment		indices	Yes	A, Q, M	OECD	OECD22 (-)
Employment		indices	Yes	A, Q, M	OECD	OECD22
Employment		indices	Yes	M, Q, A	OECD	OECD23 (-)
Employment		nos	Yes	A, M	World	UN35 (6)
Employment	By type of industry: solid fuels; coke ovens; petroleum and natural gas; mineral oil refining; nuclear fuels industry; production and distribution of electricity, gas, steam, hot water; water supply, collection purification and distribution; metalliferous ores, extraction and preparation; metals, production and preliminary processing; extraction of minerals, peat; non-metallic mineral products; chemical industry; man-made fibres, industry; metal articles; mechanical engineering; office, data processing machinery, manufacture of; electrical engineering; motor vehicles, parts, accessories, manufacture of; other means of transport, manufacture of; instrument engineering; food, drink, tobacco industry; textile industry; leather, leather goods; footwear, clothing; timber, wooden furniture; paper, paper products, manufacture of, printing, publishing; rubber, plastics, processing of; other manufacturing industries	nos	No		EC by region	EC76 (-)
Employment	By country, by growth	nos, %	No		EC	EM1 (0604)
Employment in manufacturing	Percentage of civilian employment	%	Yes	A	OECD EC, OECD, EC	OECD32 (2.11)
Persons engaged		nos	No		World	UN50 (90)

16 EMPLOYMENT AND UNEMPLOYMENT

Subject	Categories	Units	Time series Yes/No	Frequency	Territorial coverage	Source (Table no.)
Production and related workers, transport equipment operators and labourers		nos	No	I	World	ILO7 (3C)
Wage earners and paid employees	By activity in manufacturing	nos, %	Yes	A	OECD	OECD19 (V)
16.2.11 Mining and Quarrying – see also Section 33						
Brown coal mines, employment structure	Workers, shifts, output	nos, hours, tonnes	Yes	A	EC , USA	UN6 (3)
Coal, total		nos	No		EC	EC33 (-)
Coal mining	Employees by type, including apprentices	nos	Yes	A	EC	EC29 (III/11)
Employment	Sex	nos	Yes	A	World	ILO7 (6)
Hard coal mines, employment structure	Workers, shifts, output	nos, hours, tonnes	Yes	A	EC, USA	UN6 (2)
Mining, quarrying	Sex	nos	Yes	A	World	ILO7 (3B)
Persons engaged	By industry	nos	No		Nordic countries	NCM1 (78)
Persons engaged and wage earners	By industry	nos	No		Nordic countries	NCM1 (77)
16.2.12 Retail Distribution – see also Section 13						
Employment characteristics in retailing	By total workforce, employees, self-employed country	nos, %	No		EC	B7, DK7, D7, GR7, E7, F7, IRL7, I7, L7, NL7, P7, UK7
Employment in retailing	By sectors of activity, employees,	nos, %	Yes	1/4	EC	B6, DK6, D6, GR6, E6, F6, IRL6, I6, L6, NL6, P6, UK6
16.2.13 Science and Technology - see also Section 40						
Economically active, stock of qualified manpower			No	I	Countries and territories	UNESCO1 (5.2)
Employees	Full and part time, sex		No	I	World	UNESCO1 (5.4)
Employment, higher education and the general service sectors	By discipline: natural sciences engineering and technology medical sciences agricultural sciences other	nos, %	No	I	World	UNESCO1 (5.7)
Employment		nos	No	I	Countries and territories	UNESCO1 (5.2)
Employment		nos	No	I	World	UNESCO1 (5.3)
Employment	By industry: agriculture, forestry, hunting and fishing extracting industries manufacturing industries utilities construction transport and communication other activities	nos, %	No	I	World	UNESCO1 (5.6)
Employment	By type: scientists and engineers technicians auxiliary personnel	per capita	No	I	World	UNESCO1 (5.15)

Subject	Categories	Units	Time series Yes/No Frequency		Territorial coverage	Source (Table no.)
Employment by field	Natural sciences engineering and technology, medical sciences, agricultural sciences social sciences and humanities other fields	nos	No	I	World	UNESCO1 (5.4)
Employment in R&D	By type and sector: scientists and engineers technicians auxiliary personnel all sectors productive sector (integrated, non integrated) higher education general service	nos, %	No	I	World	UNESCO1 (5.5)
Man-years and total man-years in relation to total manpower		nos, %	Yes	2 yrly	Nordic countries	NCM1 (248)
Personnel, higher education	By field of science and occupation, by country	fte	Yes	A	OECD	OECD3 (17)
Personnel, business enterprise	R&D scientists engineers and researchers, by industry, by country	fte	Yes	A	OECD	OECD3 (13)
Personnel, total business enterprise R&D	By industry, by country	fte	Yes	A	OECD	OECD3 (12)
Personnel, total	By sector of employment and main scientific field, by country	fte	Yes	A	OECD	OECD3 (8)
Personnel, total	By sector of employment and formal qualification, by country	fte	Yes	A	OECD	OECD3 (6)
Personnel, total	By sector of employment and occupation, by country	fte	Yes	A	OECD	OECD3 (5)
Personnel engaged and number of man-years	By sector of performance	nos	Yes		Nordic countries	NCM1 (249)
Scientific and technical manpower	Total manpower, potential scientist and engineer, potential technicians	nos	No		ASEAN	ASEANS1 (10.3.1)
Scientific and technical manpower potential: estimates for 1980 and 1985	Estimated number, per million population	nos	Yes		Continents, major areas and groups of countries	UNESCO1 (5.1)
Scientists and technicians engaged in research and development activities	Total manpower, scientists, potential technicians	nos	No		ASEAN	ASEANS1 (10.3.2)
Scientists and engineers, potential	Total, female	nos	No	I	Countries and territories	UNESCO1 (5.2)
Scientists and engineers		per million population	No	I	World	UNESCO1 (5.17)
Scientists and engineers	Total, female	nos	No	I	World	UNESCO1 (5.3)
Scientists and engineers in R&D	As % of potential scientists and engineers	%	No	I	World	UNESCO1 (5.17)
Scientists and technicians	Personnel, funding, by country	nat curr, nos	No		ESCAP	UN44
Technicians, potential	Total, female	nos	No	I	Countries and territories	UNESCO1 (5.2)

16 EMPLOYMENT AND UNEMPLOYMENT

Subject	Categories	Units	Time series Yes/No Frequency		Territorial coverage	Source (Table no.)
Technicians		per million population	No	I	World	UNESCO1 (5.17)
Technicians		per scientist or engineer	No	I	World	UNESCO1 (5.17)
Technicians	Total, female	nos	No	I	World	UNESCO1 (5.3)
16.2.14 Textiles						
Employees		nos,	Yes	A	World	ITMF1 (2.2)
Employment in man-made fibre industry	By workers, administrative and technical departments	nos	Yes	A	World	CIRFS1 (-)
16.2.15 Tourism - see also Section 44						
Employment	Self-employed, employees, total by type of establishment, accommodation establishments and other tourist facilities	nos	Yes	A	EC	EC78 (VI.1.1) EC78 (VI.1.2)
16.2.16 Transport - see also Section 45						
Employment	By sector of transport industry, by country	nos	Yes	A	World	IRTU1
Employment	By transport type	nos	Yes	A	ECMT countries	ECMT2 (1-0-5)
Employment	Sex	nos	Yes	A	World	ILO7 (8)
Networks, staff strength	By occupation	nos	No		EC	EC80 (2.21)
Other rail networks, staff strength		nos	Yes	A	EC	EC80 (2.23)
Paid employment in transport, storage and communication	Sex	nos	Yes	A	World	ILO7 (3B)
Rail, staff	By railway, by general management, railway operations, other operations, total staff strength, permanent staff, supplied by contractors	nos	No		World	IUR1 (31)
Shipping employment	By ship type, trade,	grt, gt, nos, dwt, %, years	Yes	A	World	ISL2 (6.2.1.1-6.2.4.4.6)
Shipping employment	By cargo	dwt, %	Yes	A, M	World	DSC1 (16)
Shipping personnel	Flag, type, age, size class, personnel employed	grt, gt, nos, %, TEU, years, dwt	Yes	A	OECD	ISL2 (6.1.1.1-5)
Shipping personnel (merchant marines)	By nationality	nos	No		OECD	OECD25 (XXXIV)
Shipping personnel (merchant marines)	By occupation	nos	No		OECD	OECD25 (XXXIII)
Staff		nos	Yes	A	EC, USA, Canada	UN13 (10)
Transport, storage, communication	Sex	nos	Yes	A	World	ILO7 (3B)
16.3 LABOUR FORCE						
Active population, migration, incidence of		nos	Yes	5 yrly	OECD	OECD4 (II.9.2.)
Active population migration, incidence of		nos	Yes	5 yrly	OECD	OECD4 (II.9.1.)
Activity rate, women	By country, by marital status, age	%	No		EC	EC72 (4.13)

Subject	Categories	Units	Time series Yes/No Frequency		Territorial coverage	Source (Table no.)
Armed forces	Total, male and female by country	nos, %	Yes	A	OECD	OECD19 (II)
Armed forces	Total and as a percentage of total labour force	nos, %	Yes	A	OECD, EC	OECD19 (4.1)
Characteristics of activity of population, principal	By labour force, non-active, by sex and age	nos, %	No		EC	EC56 (1,2)
Civilian		nos, indices	Yes	A	OECD, EC	OECD19 (6.0)
Civilian labour force		nos, indices	Yes	A	OECD, EC	OECD19 (5.0)
Civilian labour force	Total, male and female by country	nos, %	Yes	A	OECD	OECD19 (II)
Economically active population	By sex and age group	nos, %	Yes	15 yrly	Africa	UN46 (8)
Labour force, female	Percentage of population from 15-64	%	Yes	A	OECD, EC	OECD32 (2.8)
Labour force, female	Percentage of total labour force	%	Yes	A	OECD, EC	OECD32 (2.3)
Labour force, female	Percentage of total female population	%	Yes	A	OECD, EC	OECD32 (2.5)
Labour force, female	Percentage change	%	Yes	A	OECD, EC	OECD32 (1.5)
Labour force, female	Age, female	age, years	Yes	A	Nordic countries	NCM1 (46)
Labour force, civilian	By classification, by Omanis, expatriates	nos	No		Arabian Gulf	CH1 (5.11)
Labour force, structure of	By economic activity, by nationality	nos, %	No		Arabian Gulf	CH1 (5.14)
Labour force, total	Total and as a percentage of total population	nos, indices, %	Yes	A	OECD, EC	OECD19 (3.0)
Labour force, total	Male, female and married by country	nos, %	Yes	A	OECD	OECD19 (II)
Labour force	Age, sex	age, years	Yes	A	Nordic countries	NCM1 (44)
Labour force	By gender, by economic activity, Kuwaiti, non-Kuwaiti	nos	No		Arabian Gulf	CH1 (5.10)
Labour force	By sex and age,	nos, %	No		EC	EC56 (14-15)
Labour force	By sex and age, nationality	nos, %	No		EC and non-EC countries	EC56 (16-17)
Labour force	Labour force, total employed, unemployed, unemployment rates				ASEAN	ASEANS1 (1.7)
Labour force	Sex, age	nos	No		EC	EC69 (II.1,2)
Labour force	Total by sex, changes in total working population	nos, %	Yes	A	EC	EC29 (II/2)
Labour force and its distribution	By sector, by nationality	nos, %	No		Arabian Gulf	CH1 (5.13)
Labour force and participation rates	By gender, by age	nos, %	No		Arabian Gulf	CH1 (5.3)
Male labour force	Age, male	age, years	Yes	A	Nordic countries	NCM1 (45)
Male labour force	Percentage change	%	Yes	A	OECD, EC,	OECD32 (1.4)
Male labour force	Percentage of population from 15-64	%	Yes	A	OECD, EC,	OECD32 (2.7)
Male labour force	Percentage of total male population	%	Yes	A	OECD, EC,	OECD32 (2.4)
Population aged between 15-16 years and 64-74 years	Employed, unemployed, other	nos	Yes	A	Nordic countries	NCM1 (43)
Total labour force	Percentage change	%	Yes	A	OECD, EC	OECD32 (1.3)
Total labour force	Percentage of population from 15-64	%	Yes	A	OECD, EC	OECD32 (2.6)

Subject	Categories	Units	Time series Yes/No	Frequency	Territorial coverage	Source (Table no.)
Total labour force	Percentage of total population	%	Yes	A	OECD, EC	OECD32 (2.2)
Young persons in education	By main population, sex and age	nos	No		EC	EC56 (24)

16.4 UNEMPLOYMENT

Subject	Categories	Units	Time series Yes/No	Frequency	Territorial coverage	Source (Table no.)
Discouraged workers rates	Selected characteristics	rate	No		OECD	OECD20 (9.1)
Duration of unemployment	By sex	nos, %	No		EC	EC56 (83,84)
Inactive persons	By sex and age	nos, %	No		EC	EC56 (22,23)
Job search – duration of search for unemployed job-seekers	By age and sex, by relationship to head of household	%	No		EC	EC56 (72,73)
Job search – duration of search for the main groups of unemployed job-seekers	By sex	nos, %	No		EC	EC56 (70,71)
Job search – duration of search for unemployed jobseekers	By sex	nos, %	No		EC	EC56 (68,69)
Job search – persons having a job and seeking another	By age and sex	nos, % and reasons	No		EC	EC56 (81,82)
Job search – unemployed and other persons seeking employment	By sex	nos, %	No		EC	EC56 (62,63)
Job search – unemployed seeking or having found job to start later	By age and sex and type of employment sought	nos, %	No		EC	EC56 (77,78)
Job search – unemployed seeking paid employment	By method of job search,	nos, % sex	No		EC	EC56 (79,80)
Job search – unemployed seeking or having found job to start later	By type of employment sought, sex	nos, %	No		EC	EC56 (75,76)
Job search – young unemployed and other young persons seeking employment	By sex	nos, %	No		EC	EC56 (64,65)
Non-active population	Sex, age group	nos	No		EC	EC69 (II.1)
Persons in part-time employment who would prefer full-time status	Age, socio-economic status	%	No		OECD	OECD20 (8.1)
Unemployed, registered		%	Yes	A, Q, M	OECD	OECD22 (-)
Unemployed, registered	By previous economic activity. by country	nos	Yes	A	EC	EC29 (IV/9)
Unemployed, registered	By profession, by country	nos	Yes	A	EC	EC29 (IV/10)
Unemployed, registered	By age and sex	nos, %	No		EC	EC29 (IV/6-IV/7)
Unemployed, registered	Annual average, under 25 years, by sex	nos	Yes	A	EC	EC29 (IV/5)
Unemployed, registered	Annual average, all age groups, by sex	nos	Yes	A	EC	EC29 (IV/4)
Unemployed, registered	Total, women, < 25 years of age	nos	Yes	A, M	EC, USA, Japan	EC36
Unemployed, registered	By sex	nos	Yes	A, M	EC	EC81 (-)
Unemployed, unemployment rates					ASEAN	ASEANS1 (1.7)
Unemployed		nos, %	Yes	A, M	World	UN35 (8)
Unemployed	Age, sex	rate	Yes	A, M	Nordic countries	NCM1 (47)
Unemployed	By duration of registration, by sex, by country	nos, %	Yes	A	EC	EC29 (IV/8)
Unemployed	By relationship to head of household	nos, %	No		EC	EC56 (66,67)

Subject	Categories	Units	Time series Yes/No Frequency	Territorial coverage	Source (Table no.)
Unemployed	By sex	nos	Yes A	EC	EC81 (-)
Unemployed	Sex, age	nos, %	Yes A	EC	EC69 (II.4)
Unemployed having lost, left job as employee due to economic reasons	By previous economic activity, sex	nos	No	EC	EC56 (74)
Unemployed persons	By sex and age	nos, %	No	EC	EC56 (20,21)
Unemployed who are new entrants on the labour market involuntary part-time work	Sex	%	No	OECD	OECD20 (7.2)
Unemployment, summary	Indicators of unemployment	%, ratio	No	Industrial countries	UN25 (36)
Unemployment, male	Percentage of male labour force	%	Yes A	OECD, EC	OECD32 (2.16)
Unemployment, female	Percentage of female labour force	%	Yes A	OECD, EC	OECD32 (2.17)
Unemployment, male	Percentage of total unemployment	%	Yes A	OECD, EC	OECD32 (2.18)
Unemployment, youth	Percentage of total unemployment	%	Yes A	OECD, EC	OECD32 (2.19)
Unemployment, total	Total and as a percentage of total labour force	nos, %	Yes A	OECD, EC	OECD19 (5.1)
Unemployment, long-term	By country, by gender	%	No	EC	EC35 (-)
Unemployment, rates	Seasonally adjusted, not seasonally adjusted, by age class, by sex	%	Yes M	EC	EC81 (-)
Unemployment, rates	By age class, by sex	%	Yes A	EC	EC81 (-)
Unemployment, trends	By country, by growth	nos, %	No	EC	EM1 (0602)
Unemployment, trends	By country, by growth	%	No	EC	EM1 (0603)
Unemployment, urban	Average annual rates	%	Yes A	Latin American and Caribbean countries	UN45 (21)
Unemployment, fluctuations in long-term	By country, by gender	%	No	EC	EC72 (4.28)
Unemployment, rates, civilian labour force		%	Yes M, Q, A	OECD - total Major Seven, EC	OECD23 (-)
Unemployment, youth	By sex	% of total	Yes Q	OECD	OECD40 (-)
Unemployment, urban	By sex	nos, %	No	World	UN17 (15)
Unemployment		%	No	EC	WC1 (-)
Unemployment		%	Yes A	EC, USA, Canada, Japan	EC9 (3.22)
Unemployment		%	Yes A	EC by region	EC65 (-)
Unemployment		%	Yes A	World	UN50 (17)
Unemployment		no, %	Yes A	Nordic countries	NCM1 (48)
Unemployment		nos, %	Yes A, Q, M	OECD	OECD22 (-)
Unemployment	By countries	nos	No	The Americas and Australasia	MAC2 (C2)
Unemployment	By country, by gender	nos, %	No	EC	EC35 (-)
Unemployment	By country, appropriate workforce	nos, %	Yes A	Africa and Asia	MAC1 (C2)
Unemployment	By sex by age group	nos	Yes Q	OECD	OECD40 (-)
Unemployment	Employed, unemployed, other	nos	Yes A	Nordic countries	NCM1 (43)
Unemployment	Percentage of total labour force	%	Yes A	OECD, EC	OECD32 (2.15)
Unemployment	Registered, insured	nos, %	Yes A, M	OECD	OECD22
Unemployment	Sex, age <25, age >25	%	No	EC EC regions and administrative units	EC9 (3.23-3.30)

16 EMPLOYMENT AND UNEMPLOYMENT

Subject	Categories	Units	Time series Yes/No Frequency	Territorial coverage	Source (Table no.)
Unemployment	Total, male and female by country	nos, %	Yes A	OECD	OECD19 (II)
Unemployment	Total, by gender	%	Yes A	Western World	MLC1 (-)
Unemployment	Women, age <25	nos, %	Yes A	EC	EC9 (3.21)
Unemployment		nos	Yes M, Q, A	OECD - Total Major Seven, EC	OECD23 (-)
Unemployment rate, standardized		%	Yes A, Q, M	OECD	OECD22 (-)
Unemployment rate, standardized		%	Yes A, Q, M	OECD	OECD22 (-)
Unemployment rate, standardised		%	Yes M, Q, A	OECD - Total Major Seven, EC	OECD23 (-)
Unemployment rate, standardised		%	Yes A	Selected OECD countries	OECD40 (-)
Unemployment rate	By sex	%	Yes Q	OECD	OECD40 (-)
Unemployment rates, standardized		%	Yes A	OECD, EC	OECD32 (2.20)
Unemployment rates	Age, sex	age, years	Yes A	Nordic countries	NCM1 (44)
Unemployment rates	Age, male	age, years	Yes A	Nordic countries	NCM1 (45)
Unemployment rates	Age, female	age, years	Yes A	Nordic countries	NCM1 (46)
Unemployment rates	By country, by gender age	%	No	EC	EC25 (4.21)
Unemployment rates	By country	%	No	Selected countries	EC35 (-)
Unemployment rates	By country and age range	nos	Yes A	OECD	OECD19
Unemployment rates	By sex and age, marital status	%	No	EC	EC56 (8,9)
Unemployment rates	Sex and age, specific groups of population, household type and sex, by duration	%	Yes 5 yrly	OECD	OECD20 (7.1)
Unemployment rates	Total, by age group, by sex, annual averages	%	Yes A	EC	EC29 (IV/2)
Unemployment rates	Total, by age group, by sex, seasonally adjusted	%	Yes A	EC	EC29 (IV/1)
Unemployment rates	Total, men, women, <25 years of age, seasonally adjusted	%	Yes A, M	EC, USA, Japan	EC36
Unemployment. structure of	Share of females by age group, share of under 25's by sex, annual averages	%	Yes A	EC	EC29 (IV/3)
16.5 VACANCIES					
Job advertisements		indices	Yes A, M	OECD	OECD22
Jobs vacant, unfilled vacancies		nos	Yes A, Q	OECD	OECD22
Jobs vacant, new vacancies		nos	Yes A, M	OECD	OECD22
Vacancies offered, vacancies filled	Public employment offices	nos	Yes A	EC	EC29 (IV/11)

17 ENERGY

17.12 PRODUCTION

17.13 STOCKS AND RESERVES

17.14 TAXATION

17.15 TRANSPORT

Subject	Categories	Units	Time series Yes/No Frequency		Territorial coverage	Source (Table no.)
17.1 BALANCE SHEETS						
Balance sheet of energy sources	By individual Nordic country, energy sources	tonnes, cu m	No		Nordic countries	NCM1 (93-97)
Balance sheets	production, consumption, transformation, imports exports, bunkers, stock change, by fuel type	tonnes	No		EC, USA, Japan	EC54 (-)
Balance sheets	Energy requirements and generation by type (total and per capita)	toe, US$, kWh	Yes	A	World	IEA7
Balance sheets, raw material	By metal content	tonnes	No		EC	EC53 (8.10)
Consumption	Industry, households, other	TJ	No		Developing countries	UN20 (-)
Consumption	Type of fuel and sector	toe	Yes	A	OECD	IEA4&5 (-)
Consumption	Type of fuel and source	toe	Yes	A	World	IEA12 (-)
Electric energy, balance sheet of transformation in conventional power stations	Public supply, self-producers, total, by country	tonnes, TJ, gWh	No		EC	EC31 (5)
Electricity, generation	By source	toe	Yes	A	OECD	IEA4&5 (-)
Energy balance sheets		toe	No		World	IEA7
Energy balances	Imports, exports, stocks, solids, liquids, gases, electricity, biomass, total energy requirements	TJ, bunker, unallocated,	Yes	A	African countries	UN1 (24)
Energy balances, overall	By individual Nordic country type of energy	TJ	No		Nordic countries	NCM1 (98-102)
Energy conversion	By sector, product	TJ	No		Developing countries	UN20 (-)
Energy requirements	Production, by energy source and product; imports, by energy source and product; exports, by energy source and product; marine, aviation bunkers, by energy source and product; stock change, by energy source and product	TJ	No		Developing countries	UN20 (-)
Energy, final	Production, consumption, imports, exports, transformation, by energy type, by country	tonnes, TJ, GWh toe	No		EC	EC31 (5)
Final	By fuel, energy type, by country	tonnes, TJ, toe, gWh	No		EC	EC30 (-)
Imports	Type of fuel	toe	Yes	A	OECD	IEA4&5 (-)
Production	Type of fuel	toe	Yes	A	OECD	IEA4&5 (-)
Supply	Type of fuel and source	toe	Yes	A	OECD	IEA4&5 (-)
Supply	Type of fuel and source	toe	Yes	A	World	IEA12
Supply balance	By fuel type	toe	Yes	Q	OECD	IEA11

17 ENERGY

Subject	Categories	Units	Time series Yes/No Frequency		Territorial coverage	Source (Table no.)
Supply, aviation kerosene	Indigenous production, imports, exports, gross and net consumption and stock levels	tonnes	Yes	Q	OECD	IEA11
Supply, gas, diesel oil	Indigenous production, imports, exports, gross and net consumption and stock levels	tonnes	Yes	Q	OECD	IEA11
Supply, gasoline	Indigenous production, imports, exports, gross and net consumption and stock levels	tonnes	Yes	Q	OECD	IEA11
Supply, heavy fuel oil	Indigenous production, imports, exports, gross and net consumption and stock levels	tonnes	Yes	Q	OECD	IEA11
Supply, kerosene	Indigenous production, imports, exports, gross and net consumption and stock levels	tonnes	Yes	Q	OECD	IEA11
Supply, LPG	Indigenous production, imports, exports, gross and net consumption and stock levels	tonnes	Yes	Q	OECD	IEA11
Supply, naphtha	Indigenous production, imports, exports, gross and net consumption and stock levels	tonnes	Yes	Q	OECD	IEA11
Supply, natural gas	Indigenous production, imports, exports, consumption and stock levels	cu m	Yes	Q	OECD	IEA11
Supply, NGL	Indigenous production, imports, exports, refinery intake and losses and stock levels	tonnes	Yes	Q	OECD	IEA11
Supply, other origins	Indigenous production, imports, exports, refinery intake and losses and stock levels	tonnes	Yes	Q	OECD	IEA11
Supply, other products	Indigenous production, imports, exports, gross and net consumption and stock levels	tonnes	Yes	Q	OECD	IEA11
Supply, refinery feedstocks	Indigenous production, imports, exports, refinery intake and losses and stock levels	tonnes	Yes	Q	OECD	IEA11
Supply, total products	Indigenous production, imports,exports, gross and net consumption and stock levels	tonnes	Yes	Q	OECD	IEA11
17.2 COAL AND COAL PRODUCTS						
17.2.1 Capacity						
Coal, mine capacity		tonnes	No		EC	EC33 (-)
17.2.2 Labour						
Brown coal mines, employment structure	Workers, shifts, output	nos, hours, tonnes	Yes	A	EC	UN6 (3)
Coal, productivity		man-hrs	No		EC	EC33 (-)
Coal, total		nos	No		EC	EC33 (-)

Subject	Categories	Units	Time series Yes/No Frequency		Territorial coverage	Source (Table no.)
Hard coal mines, employment structure	Workers, shifts, output	nos, hours, tonnes	Yes	A	EC, USA	UN6 (2)
17.2.3 Production and Consumption - see also under Consumption (17.3) and Section 38						
Brown coal mines, production structure	By country	tonnes	Yes	A	EC, USA	UN6 (3)
Coal		toe, % share % change	Yes	A	World	BP1 (p28)
Coal		toe % share % change	Yes	A	World	BP1 (p29)
Coal		tonnes	Yes	A	World, ASEAN	ASEANS1 (4.2.3)
Coal		tonnes	Yes	A	World, OECD	IEA7
Coal		tonnes, indices	Yes	A, M	EC, USA Japan	EC36
Coal	By country	toe, tonnes	Yes	A	World	ISL2 (2.3.3.1-2)
Coal	By country and type	tonnes	Yes	A	Africa and Asia	MAC1 (E2)
Coal	By final use	tonnes	Yes	A	World	IEA7
Coal	By fuel type	tce, tonnes	Yes	I	OECD	IEA2 (-)
Coal	By type of coal	tonnes	Yes	A	World	BP1 (p28)
Coal and lignite		toe	No		World, EC, USA, USSR, Canada, Japan	EC9 (4.15)
Coal and lignite	Total	tonnes	Yes	A	World	BB1 (6-1-6.2)
Coal and lignite production	By country	tonnes	Yes	A, M	World	BB2 (6-1-6.2)
Coal balance	Supply and consumption	tce	Yes	I	OECD	IEA2
Coal balance	Supply and consumption	tce	Yes	A	Selected non-OECD countries	IEA2 (III.11-III.20)
Coal mines		nos	No		EC	EC33 (-)
Coal transformation, principal aggregates	By type	tonnes	No		EC	EC33 (-)
Coal, economy indicators		indices	No		EC	EC33 (-)
Coal, hard		tonnes of coal equivalent	Yes	A	World	UN50 (125)
Coal, hard		tonnes	No		World	IEA2 (III.1-III.10)
Coal, hard		tonnes	No		World	IEA2 (III.1-III.10)
Coal, hard	By country	tonnes	Yes	A	ESCAP	UN44
Coal, hard	By country	tonnes	Yes	A	ESCAP	UN44
Coal, hard	By sector	tonnes	No		EC	EC33 (-)
Coal, hard	By steel industry, power stations and households	tonnes	No		World	IEA2 (III.1-III.10)
Coal, hard, mines, production structure	By country	tonnes	Yes	A	EC, USA	UN6 (2)
Coal, hard, principal aggregates	By type	tonnes	Yes	M	EC	EC31 (1)
coal		tonnes	Yes	A	World	EC9 (4.23)
Coal, hard, principal aggregates	By type	tonnes	Yes	M	EC	EC31 (1)
Coal, hard, principal aggregates	By type	tonnes	Yes	M	EC	EC31 (1)
Coal, hard, principal aggregates	By type	tonnes	Yes	M	EC	EC31 (1)
Coal, lignite, coke-oven		tonnes	No		World, EC	EC9 (4.24)
Coal, mine output		tonnes	No		EC	EC33 (-)
Coal, output	By countries	nos	No		The Americas and Australasia	MAC2 (E2)
Coal, principal aggregates	By type	tonnes	No		EC	EC33 (-)

17 ENERGY

Subject	Categories	Units	Time series Yes/No Frequency		Territorial coverage	Source (Table no.)
Coke		tonnes of coal equivalent	Yes	A	World	UN50 (125)
Consumption, energy branch	By fuel, energy type, by country	tonnes, TJ, toe, gWh	No		EC	EC30 (-)
Energy, availability for final consumption	By fuel, energy type, by country	tonnes, TJ,toe, gWh	No		EC	EC30 (-)
Energy final	By end user by fuel, energy type,	tonnes TJ, toe, gWh	No		EC	EC30 (-)
Fuel projections, changes in	By fuel	tce	No		OECD	IEA2 (-)
Inland energy production gross	By fuel, energy type, by country	tonnes, TJ, toe, gWh	No		EC	EC30 (-)
Lignite		tonnes	Yes	A	World, OECD	IEA7
Lignite	Total	tonnes	Yes	A	World	BB1 (6.3)
Lignite brown coal		tonnes of coal equivalent	Yes	A	World	UN50 (125)
Non-energy, final	Chemical industry, other sectors, by fuel, energy type, by country	tonnes, TJ, toe, gWh	No		EC	EC30 (-)
Other solid fuels		TJ	Yes	A	OECD	IEA8&9 (–)
Solid fuel	By type	tonnes	Yes	A	World	UN21 (5-6, 8-13)
Solid fuels	By country, by production, final consumption	tonnes	No		EC	EM1 (0808)
Solid fuels	By fuel type, by country	tonnes	Yes	I	EC, USA	UN6 (1)
Solid fuels	Production, consumption, imports, exports	1000 tonne of coal equiv	Yes	A	African countries	UN1(27)
Solid fuels, bunkering	By fuel type, by country	tonnes	Yes	I	EC, USA	UN6 (1)
Solid fuels, by energy-producing industries	By fuel type, by country	tonnes	Yes	I	EC, USA	UN6 (1)
Solid fuels, calorific value	By fuel type, by country	kJ/kg	Yes	I	EC, USA	UN6 (1)
Solid fuels, derivative energy	Patent fuel coke total, coke-oven coke, gas coke, brown coal coke, brown coal briquettes	tonnes	Yes	A	EC, USA, Canada	UN9 (1)
Solid fuels, energy converted	By fuel type, by type of plant, by country	tonnes	Yes	I	EC, USA	UN6 (1)
Solid fuels, gross	By fuel type, by country	tonnes	Yes	I	EC, USA	UN6 (1)
Solid fuels, non-energy use	By fuel type, by country	tonnes	Yes	I	EC, USA	UN6 (1)
Solid fuels, recovered slurry	By fuel type, by country	tonnes	Yes	I	EC. USA	UN6 (1)
Solid fuels, total	By fuel type, by final consumer, by country	tonnes	Yes	I	EC, USA	UN6 (1)
17.2.4 Stocks and Reserves						
Coal reserves	By type of coal	tonnes, % share R/P ratio	No		World	BP1 (p26)

Subject	Categories	Units	Time series Yes/No Frequency		Territorial coverage	Source (Table no.)
Coal, mine stocks		tonnes	No		EC	EC33 (-)
Coal, stocks	By type	tonnes	No		EC	EC33 (-)
Solid fuels, changes in stocks	By fuel type, by country	tonnes	Yes	I	EC, USA	UN6 (1)

17.3 CONSUMPTION - see also under Balance Sheets (17.1) and Section 8

Subject	Categories	Units	Time series Yes/No Frequency		Territorial coverage	Source (Table no.)
Coal and lignite		toe	Yes	A	World, EC, USSR USA, Japan, Canada	EC9 (4.19)
Commercial energy		tce	Yes	A	World,	UN44 (p3)
Commercial energy	Total and by type	J, J per capita	Yes	A	World	UN21 (3)
Commercial energy	Total and by type	TJ	Yes	A	World	UN21 (3)
Commercial energy	Total, per capita, share of liquid fuel in total consumption	tce %	Yes	I	World, ESCAP, developing ESCAP countries	UNCTAD1 (6.9)
Commercial energy (coal equivalent)	Total and by type	tonnes	Yes	A	World	UN21 (1)
Commercial energy (coal equivalent)	Total and by type	tonnes, kg per capita	Yes	A	World	UN21 (1)
Commercial energy (oil equivalent)	Total and by type	tonnes	Yes	A	World	UN21 (2)
Commercial energy (oil equivalent)	Total and by type	tonnes, kg per capita	Yes	A	World	UN21 (2)
Consumers	Industry, households, commerce, services, etc.	toe, capita	Yes	A	EC	EC9 (4.21)
Consumption	By country	tonnes, % change, % share	Yes	A	World	BP2 (-)
Consumption	Coal, oil, gas, total, per capita	toe	No		VICES and Yugoslavia	VICES1 (V/1)
Consumption	Type	tonnes of coal equiv	Yes	A	World	UN50 (11)
Consumption by energy producing industries	By form of energy	TJ	Yes	A	EC, USA, Canada	UN9 (2)
Consumption by households	Total and % of total by energy type	J, %	Yes	A	World	UN10 (7)
Consumption per capita		kg	Yes	A	World	UN50 (11)
Consumption ratios		ratio	No		EC	EC33 (-)
Consumption share of	By fuel type and sector	toe, %	No		EC	EC33 (-)
Consumption, final	By sector and type of primary energy per capita	toe	No		VICES	VICES1 (V/1)
Consumption, growth rates	Total, per capita	%	Yes	I	World	UNCTAD1 (6.9)
Consumption, per capita	By fuel type and sector	toe	No		EC	EC33 (-)
Consumption, per capita	Solids liquids, gas, electricity	kg	Yes	A	World	UN50 (124)
Consumption, total	By fuel type and sector	toe	No		EC	EC33 (-)
Crude oil		toe	Yes	A	World, EC, USSR USA, Japan, Canada	EC9 (4.19)
Demand by major product	By product	b/doe	Yes	A	OECD	BB1 (16.1-16.6)
Distribution losses	By fuel/energy type, by country	tonnes, TJ, toe, gWh	No		EC	EC30 (-)
Electricity		kWh, kWh per capita	Yes	A	World	UN21 (35)
Electricity	By sector, total	toe	No		EC	UN22 (I-1.5.6
Electricity, primary		toe	Yes	A	World , EC, USSR, USA, Japan, Canada	EC9 (4.19)
Energy	By final consumer as proportion of total	toe, %	Yes	A	EC	EC34 (3.17-3.26)

17 ENERGY

Subject	Categories	Units	Time series Yes/No	Frequency	Territorial coverage	Source (Table no.)
Energy	By type	toe	Yes	M	EC	EC31 (4)
Energy	By type	toe	Yes	M	EC	EC31 (4)
Energy consumption	By agriculture	tpe, % change	No		Selected countries	UN22 (II-3.2.4a)
Energy consumption	By oil and non-oil	toe	Yes	A, Q	OECD	DSC2 (1.11)
Energy consumption	Forms of energy and mode of transport	TJ	Yes	A	EC, USA, Canada	UN13 (5)
Energy consumption, agricultural	By energy input, hectare, and production and the efficiency of mj-person-day, by energy output/hectare, seven agricultural systems yield, productivity, surplus energy income, energy ratio	mj, %, mj/ha-yr	No		Selected countries	UN22 (II-3.2.4b)
Energy production, consumption and trade	By high, middle, low income	tonnes, kg, %	No		World	CS1 (16)
Energy requirements (conventional fuel equivalent)	By type	TJ, MJ per capita	Yes	A	World	UN21 (4)
Energy, final consumption of		%	Yes	A	OECD	OECD33 (9.5C)
Energy, final consumption of	By source	toe	Yes	A	World, OECD	OECD33 (9.5A)
Energy, final consumption of	By type by sector	indices,toe, US$	Yes	A	OECD	OECD33 (9.5D)
Energy, final consumption of	Total	%	Yes	A	OECD	OECD33 (9.5B)
Energy, gross		toe, koe per capita, toe per million $ GDP	No		EC	UN22 (I.1.5.4)
Energy, gross		toe, toe per capita, toe per million $ GDP	No		EC	UN22 (I.1.5.4)
Energy, gross inland	By type	toe	Yes	M	EC	EC31 (4)
Final consumption, total	By form of energy and major consumers	TJ	Yes	A	EC, USA, Canada	UN9 (2)
Final energy	By fuel type	tce, %	Yes	I	OECD	IEA2 (-)
Final energy	By sector, total	toe	No		EC	UN22 (I-1.5.5)
Final energy	By sector, total	toe kW	No		EC	UN22 (I-1.5.5)
Gas, natural		TJ	No		EC	EC9 (4.30)
Gas, natural		toe	Yes	A	World, EC, USSR, USA, Japan, Canada	EC9 (4.19)
Gases		TJ, MJ per capita	Yes	A	World	UN21 (31)
Inland energy consumption	Final, by energy sources	tonnes, cu m, gWh	Yes	A	Nordic countris	NCM1(92)
Inland energy consumption	Final, %	TJ	Yes	A	Nordic countries	NCM1(91)
Liquid fuels	By type	tonnes, kg per capita	Yes	A	World	UN21 (14, 7-24)
Losses in transport and distribution	By form of energy	TJ	Yes	A	EC, USA, Canada	UN9 (2)
Motor gasoline	By country	tonnes	No		EC	EM1 (0805)
Natural gas		TJ, MJ per capita	Yes	A	World	UN21 (28)
Nuclear energy		toe	Yes	A	World, EC, USSR, USA, Japan, Canada	EC9 (4.19)
Nuclear energy consumption	By country	toe	No		EC	EM1 (0813)
Oil		km, tonnes,	Yes	A	EC, USA, tonne-kms	UN13 (28)
Petroleum products consumption	By country,	tonnes	Yes	A	World	IP1 (-)
Pipelines energy consumption	Forms of energy	TJ	Yes	A	EC, USA, Canada	UN13 (5)
Power stations fuel consumption,		TJ	No		EC	EC33 (-)
Primary energy		toe	Yes	A	World	EC9 (4.19)

Subject	Categories	Units	Time series Yes/No Frequency		Territorial coverage	Source (Table no.)
Primary energy	By type by country	toe	Yes	I	VICES and Yugoslavia	VICES1 (V/2)
Primary energy	Coal, lignite, oil, natural gas, nuclear energy, electricity	%	No		EC	EC9 (4.20)
Primary energy	Coal, lignite, oil, natural gas, nuclear energy, electricity	%	Yes	A	EC	EC9 (4.20)
Primary energy and equivalents	By form of energy	TJ	Yes	A	EC, USA Canada	UN9 (2)
Primary energy consumption	By country, by selected	toe	No		EC	EM1 (0801)
Rail energy consumption	Forms of energy	TJ	Yes	A	EC, USA, Canada	UN13 (5)
Raw material consumption		per capita	No		EC	EC53 (8.9)
Refined products	By country, by product	tonnes	No		EC	EM1 (0804)
Road energy consumption	Forms of energy	TJ	Yes	A	EC, USA, Canada	UN13 (5)
Road transport, energy consumption		toe,%, tonnes,TJ	Yes	A	EC	EC80 (3.11)
Sea energy consumption	Forms of energy	TJ	Yes	A	EC, USA, Canada	UN13 (5)
Self-reliance, degree	Total energy consumption	%	No		VICES and Yugoslavia	VICES1 (V/1)
Solid fuel	By type	tonnes, kg per capita	Yes	A	World	UN21 (5-6, 8-13)
Solid fuels, household consumption	By country	tonnes	No		EC	EM1 (0809)
Steel industry	By fuel type and by industrial process	tonnes, cu m, mWh, GJ	No		EC, USA, Canada, Japan	UN11 (7)
Supply and consumption	Type of fuel suppliers, consumers industry	tonnes, TJ, gWh	Yes	A	OECD	IEA8&9 (–)
Total		toe	Yes	A	EC	EC9 (4.18)
Total by type	Solids, liquids, gas, electricity	tonnes of coal equivalent	Yes	A	World	UN50 (124)
Total energy		toe	Yes	I	OECD	IEA10 (I-I)
Total final		toe	Yes	I	OECD	IEA3 (-)
Tractive stock, energy consumption	By type total and unit consumption per 1000 tonne-kms	tonnes, kWh	No		EC	EC80 (2.20)
Transformation	Input and output	tonnes	No		EC	EC33 (-)
Transport		toe, capita	Yes	A	EC	EC9 (4.21)

17.4 ELECTRICITY

17.4.1 Capacity

Subject	Categories	Units	Time series Yes/No Frequency		Territorial coverage	Source (Table no.)
Capacity, electricity generation projections	By fuel type	gW	No		OECD	IEA2 (-)
Capacity, net installed	By source	kW	Yes	A	Developing countries	UN20 (-)
Capacity, net maximum	Public utilities, autoproducers, by type of fuel, type of generation	mW	Yes	A	OECD	IEA8&9 (–)
Capacity, power stations	By type	mW	Yes	A	OECD,	IEA2 (-)
Capacity, power station	For single-fired and multi-fired stations by fuel type	gW	Yes	I	OECD	IEA3 (-)
Electric energy, maximum net capacity	By type of plant in continuous operation, by country	mW	Yes	A	EC, USA	UN7 (3)
Electric generating capacity	By type	kWh	Yes	A	World	UN21 (33)
Electric generating plants net installed capacity	By type	kW	Yes	A	World	UN21 (32)
Electrical equipment capacity		W	No		EC	EC33 (-)
Electricity capacity, estimated	Total, nuclear	gWh, %	Yes	I	OECD	OECD31 (2)

Subject	Categories	Units	Time series Yes/No Frequency		Territorial coverage	Source (Table no.)
Electricity, installed capacity		kWh	Yes	A	Latin American and Caribbean countries	UN45 (352)
Installed capacity	By unit and installed hydro and wind power	mW, gWh	No		Nordic countries	(103)
Power station capacity	By country	mW	No		EC	EC18 (8.6)
Transformation	Electricity, installed capacity, per thousand inhabitants; petroleum, refinery capacity as % of liquid fuel consumption	kW, %	Yes	I	World	UNCTAD1 (6.9)
17.4.2 Hydro-Electricity						
Electric energy	Produced by public power plants, self-producers	gWh	Yes	A	EC, USA, Canada	UN9 (1)
Electric energy, derivative energy by source	Gross production, thermo electric energy, hydro-electric energy resulting from pumping	gWh	Yes	A	EC, USA, Canada	UN9 (1)
Electrical energy by source	Total, hydro, geothermal, nuclear, conventional thermal	gWh	No		World	EC9 (4.32)
Electricity	Hydro, thermal, by country	kWh	Yes	A	ESCAP	UN44
Electricity generation by source	Total generation, proportion derived from nuclear energy, proportion derived from fossil fuels, proportion derived from hydro-electric and geothermal sources	toe, %	Yes	A	EC	EC34 (3.29-3.32)
Hydro, other electricity		gWh	Yes	A	World	IEA7
Hydro-electric potential, estimates		mW	Yes	I	Latin American and Caribbean countries	UN45 (353)
Hydro-electric power	Share in generation of electricity	%	Yes	A	Latin American and Caribbean countries	UN45 (57)
Hydro-electricity		toe % share % change	Yes		World	BP1 (p32)
Installed capacity and corresponding production by installed hydro and wind power	By unit	mW/gWh	No		Nordic countries	NCM1 (103)
17.4.3 Production and Consumption						
Consumption	By sectors	kWh	Yes	A	Developing countries	UN20
Efficiency (output, input)		%	Yes	A	Developing countries	UN20
Electric energy	By country	kWh	Yes	A	Africa and Asia	MAC1 (E28)
Electric energy	Energy available for consumption and supplied to consumers, average consumption per inhabitant, by country	gWh, kWh	Yes	A	EC, USA	UN7R (1)
Electric energy	Per capita	kWh	Yes	A	Latin American and Caribbean countries	UN45 (55)

Subject	Categories	Units	Time series Yes/No Frequency		Territorial coverage	Source (Table no.)
Electric energy	Produced by, public power plants, self-producers	gWh	Yes	A	EC, USA Canada	UN9 (1)
Electric energy, balance sheet of transformation in conventional power stations	Public supply, self-producers, total, by country	tonnes, TJ, gWh	No		EC	EC31 (5)
Electric energy, consumption of fuel	By fuel type	tonnes, TJ	Yes	M	EC	EC31 (3)
Electric energy, derivative energy	Gross production, thermo electric energy, hydro-electric energy resulting from pumping,	gWh	Yes	A	EC, USA, Canada	UN9 (1)
Electric energy, fuel consumption	Consumption of fuel and net electricity production, by fuel type, by type of producer, by country	tonnes, TJ, gWh	Yes	A	EC, USA	UN7 (4)
Electric energy, gross	By type of producer, by type of plant, by country	gWh	Yes	A	EC, USA	UN7 (1)
Electric energy, growth	Average annual rates	indices	Yes	A	Latin American and Caribbean countries	UN45 (56)
Electric energy, net	By type of producer, by type of plant, by country	gWh	Yes	A	EC, USA	UN7 (1)
Electric energy, supplied to consumers	Energy producing industries by type, other consumers by type, by country	gWh	Yes	A	EC, USA	UN7 (2)
Electrical energy		gWh	Yes	A	EC	EC9 (4.31)
Electrical energy		kWh	Yes	M	EC	EC31 (3)
Electrical energy		kWh	Yes	M	EC	EC31 (3)
Electrical energy	By country, by supply, production	gWh, %	No		EC	EM1 (0806)
Electrical energy	By source	indices	No		EC	EC33 (-)
Electrical energy	By type of production	kWh	Yes	M	EC	EC31 (3)
Electrical energy	Capacity, production	1000/million	Yes	A	Central Africa	UN5 (22)
Electrical energy	Capacity, production	1000/million kW	Yes	A	North Africa	UN2 (22)
Electrical energy	Capacity, production	1000/million kW	Yes	A	East and Southern Africa	UN4 (22)
Electrical energy	Capacity, production	1000/million kW	Yes	A	West Africa	UN3 (22)
Electrical energy	Gross inland, absorbed by storage pumping, available for internal market	kWh, %	Yes	M	EC	EC31 (3)
Electrical energy	Total generation	gWh	Yes	A	EC	EC53 (8.6)
Electrical energy	Total generation	gWh	Yes	A	EC, USA and Japan	EC53 (1.18)
Electrical energy	Total, hydro, geothermal, nuclear, conventional thermal	gWh	No		World EC, USSR, USA, Canada, Japan	EC9 (4.32)
Electrical energy, economy indicators	By type, sector and fuel type	%, indices	No		EC	EC33 (-)
Electrical energy, principal aggregates		kWh	No		EC	EC33 (-)
Electrical energy, principal aggregates	By source	gWh	No		EC	EC33 (-)
Electrical energy, total, principal aggregates	By sector	kWh	No		EC	EC33 (-)
Electricity		gWh	Yes	A	World, OECD	IEA7

17 ENERGY

Subject	Categories	Units	Time series Yes/No Frequency		Territorial coverage	Source (Table no.)
Electricity		gWh, indices	Yes	A, M	EC, USA, Japan	EC36
Electricity		kWh	Yes	A	Latin American and Caribbean countries	UN45 (350)
Electricity		tonnes of coal equivalent	Yes	A	World	UN50 (125)
Electricity	By country	kWh	Yes	A	ESCAP	UN44
Electricity	By country, by supplies to households	gWh	No		EC	EM1 (0807)
Electricity	By final use	gWh	Yes	A	World	IEA7
Electricity	By fuel type	tWh	Yes	I	OECD	IEA2
Electricity	By product, total	kWh	Yes	A	World	UN28
Electricity	By sector, total	toe	No		EC	UN22 (I-1.5.6)
Electricity	By type	kW	Yes	A	World	UN21 (34)
Electricity	By type of plant	kWh	Yes	I	Latin American and Caribbean countries	UN45 (351)
Electricity	Hydro, thermal, by country	kWh	Yes	A	ESCAP	UN44
Electricity	Production & consumption	%	Yes	A	African countries	UN1 (26)
Electricity	Production, production index	kWh, indices	Yes	A	World, ASEAN	ASEANS1 (4.3)
Electricity	Public, industrial	kWh	Yes	A, M	World	UN35R (44)
Electricity	Total	kWh	Yes	A	World	UN21 (35)
Electricity	Total consumption, as proportion of total final energy consumption	toe, %	Yes	A	EC	EC34 (3.27-3.28)
Electricity	Total, by type	gWh, %	No		EC	UN22 (I-1.5.2)
Electricity	Total, by type	gWh, %	No		EC	UN22 (I-1.5.2)
Electricity	Type of power	gWh	Yes	A	Nordic countries	NCM1 (104)
Electricity consumed	Quantity	kWh	Yes	A	World	UN27 (-)
Electricity consumption	By country	kwh	No		EC	EC18 (8.8)
Electricity demand	By type of industry, type of transport, agriculture, commerce and public service, and residential users	tWh	Yes	I	OECD	IEA3 (-)
Electricity generated		tWh	Yes	A	World, OECD	OECD33 (9.4A)
Electricity generated	Total	%	Yes	A	OECD	OECD33 (9.4B)
Electricity generation	Total generation, proportion derived from nuclear energy, proportion derived from fossil fuels, proportion derived from hydro-electric and geothermal sources	toe, %	Yes	A	EC	EC34 (3.29-3.32)
Electricity generation, estimated	Total, nuclear	tWh, %	Yes	I	OECD	OECD31 (1)
Electricity input	By fuel type	toe	Yes	I	OECD	IEA3 (-)
Electricity output	By fuel type	tWh	Yes	I	OECD	IEA3 (-)
Electricity output, share of each fuel	By fuel type	%	Yes	I	OECD	IEA3 (-)
Electricity primary	Total	kWh	Yes	A	World	BB1 (7.1-7.2)
Electricity production	By country, by thermal, nuclear, hydro-electric	kwh	No		EC	EC18 (8.7)
Electricity production	By country;	kWh	Yes	A, M	World	BB2 (7.1-7.2)
Electricity, changes in projections	By fuel	tWh	No		OECD	IEA2 (-)

Subject	Categories	Units	Time series Yes/No Frequency		Territorial coverage	Source (Table no.)
Electricity, conventional thermal		gWh, indices	Yes	A, M	EC, USA, Japan	EC36
Electricity, primary		toe	No		World, EC, USSR, USA, Canada, Japan	EC9 (4.15)
Electricity, share of each fuel	By fuel type	%	Yes	I	OECD	IEA3 (-)
Electricity, share of total final consumption		%	Yes	I	OECD	IEA3 (-)
Electricity, voltage applied	Industrial standard consumers	kV	No		EC	EC28
Energy supply		toe	Yes	A	OECD	OECD33 (9.3A)
Energy supply	By source		No		World	OECD33 (9.3B)
Energy supply	By unit of GDP	indices, toe, US$	Yes	A	OECD	OECD33 (9.3C)
Energy supply	Per capita	indices, toe, capita	Yes	A	OECD	OECD33 (9.3D)
Energy supply	Total	toe	No		OECD	OECD33 (9.3B)
Final consumption of energy	By industry, by type	tonnes	No		EC	EC35 (-)
Fossil fuels inputs, for electricity and steam generation	By type	toe	No		EC	UN22 (I-1.5.3)
Fossil fuels inputs, for electricity and steam generation	By type	toe	No		EC	UN22 (I-1.5.3)
Fuel inputs to electricity	By fuel type	tce	Yes	I	OECD	IEA2 (-)
Hydro, other electricity		gWh	Yes	A	World, OECD	IEA7
Inland supply of energy	Gross, %, annual growth	TJ	Yes	A	Nordic countries	NCM1(90)
Installed capacity and corresponding production by installed hydro and wind power	By unit	mW/gWh	No		Nordic countries	NCM1 (103)
Power stations fuel consumption, electric	By fuel type	%	No		EC	EC33 (-)
Production	By source	kWh	Yes	A	Developing countries	UN20 (-)
Production	Gross, net, by source	gWh	Yes	A	OECD	IEA8&9 (–)
Steam and hot water	From geothermal and thermal sources	TJ	Yes	A	World	UN21 (36)
Steam and hot water	From geothermal sources, from public thermal power plants for combined generation of electric energy and heat	TJ	Yes	A	EC, USA, Canada	UN9(1)
Thermal electricity		gWh	Yes	A	World, OECD	IEA7
Thermal power plant input	By energy source	TJ	Yes	A	Developing countries	UN20 (-)
Thermal power plant production		TJ	Yes	A	Developing countries	UN20 (-)
Trade	Imports, exports	kWh	Yes	A	Developing countries	UN20 (-)

17.5 GAS - see also under Oil and Natural Gas (17.9)

17.5.1 Production and Consumption

Subject	Categories	Units	Time series Yes/No Frequency		Territorial coverage	Source (Table no.)
Average annual growth by sector	By country, end user	%	No		OECD	BP2 (-)
Gas	By country, by production, gross consumption	TJ	No		EC	EM1 (0810)
Gas	By type	indices	No		EC	EC33 (-)
Gas	Primary production, associated-dissolved and non-associated gases, derived production, by type of gas, by country	TJ	Yes	A	EC, USA	UN8 (1)
Gas produced by gas works	By product, total	TJ				
Gas, production	By country	cu m	Yes	A, Q, M	Selected countries	DSC2 (3.6)

17 ENERGY

Subject	Categories	Units	Time series Yes/No Frequency		Territorial coverage	Source (Table no.)
Gas supplies to households	By country	TJ	No		EC	EM1 (0811)
Gas, by energy producing industries	By type of gas, by country	TJ	Yes	A	EC, USA	UN8 (1)
Gas, consumption	By country	cu m, % change, % share	Yes	A	World	BP2 (-)
Gas, consumption	By product, country	tonnes oil equivalent, % change	No		World	BP2 (-)
Gas, converted	By type of conversion and type of gas, by country	TJ	Yes	A	EC, USA	UN8 (1)
Gas, deliveries for final consumption	By industry, by type of gas, by country	TJ	Yes	A	EC, USA	UN8 (1)
Gas, demand by sector	By country, end user	cu m	No		OECD	BP2 (-)
Gas, economy indicators	By sector	%	No		EC	EC33 (-)
Gas, gross	By type of gas, by country	TJ	Yes	A	EC	UN8 (1)
Gas, household consumers	By type of gas	nos	Yes	A	EC, USA	UN8 (4)
Gas, manufactured	Heat value	TJ	Yes	A, M	World	UN35 (45)
Gas, manufactured		TJ	Yes	A	ASEAN	ASEANS1 (4.1.1)
Gas, non-energy use	By type of gas, by country	TJ	Yes	A	EC, USA	UN8 (1)
Gas, unaccounted losses	By type of gas, by country	TJ	Yes	A	EC, USA	UN8 (1)
Gases		TJ	Yes	A	World	UN21 (31)
Gases, other		tonnes of coal equivalent	Yes	A	World	UN50 (125)
Gases, other	By type	TJ	Yes	A	World	UN21 (30)
Natural gas	By final use	toe	Yes	A	World	IEA7
17.5.2 Stocks						
Gas, changes in stocks by country	By type of gas,	TJ	Yes	A	EC, USA	UN8 (1)
17.5.3 Transmission						
Gas, length of mains for transport	Pipeline transmission system, distribution system	km	Yes	A	EC, USA	UN8 (5)
Gas, transfers	By type of gas, by country	TJ	Yes	A	EC, USA	UN8 (1)
17.6 INTERNATIONAL TRADE						
Coal	By type	tce	Yes	A	OECD	IEA2 (-)
Coal	By type	tce	Yes	A	OECD	IEA2 (-)
Coal	Production	tonnes	No		EC	EC9 (4.24)
Coal, exporting ports	By country	nos	No		World	IEA2 (-)
Coal, importing ports	By country	nos	No		World	IEA2 (-)
Coal, coking	By destination	tonnes	Yes	A	OECD	IEA2 (-)
Coal, coking: from non-EC countries to the EC	By country	tonnes, %	Yes	A, Q	Selected non-EC countries	IEA6(I.14)
Coal, coking to Japan	By country	tonnes, %	Yes	A, Q	World	IEA6(I.16)
Coal, economy indicators	Intra and extra EC	indices	No		EC	EC33 (-)
Coal, hard	By destination	tonnes	Yes	A	OECD	IEA2 (-)
Coal, hard	By origin	tonnes	Yes	A	OECD	IEA2 (-)
Coal, hard	By principal importers and exporters	tonnes	No		World	UN21 (7)

Subject	Categories	Units	Time series Yes/No Frequency		Territorial coverage	Source (Table no.)
Coal, hard	Imports by origin and exports by destination for major non-OECD traders	tonnes	Yes	A	Selected non-OECD countries	IEA2 (III.21-III.30)
Coal, hard	Imports, exports	tonnes	Yes	A	EC	EC53 (8.2)
Coal, hard	Imports, exports, by country	tonnes	Yes	A	ESCAP	UN44
Coal, hard	Intra and extra EC	tonnes	No		EC	EC33 (-)
Coal, principal aggregates	By type	tonnes	No		EC	EC33 (-)
Coal, steam	By destination	tonnes	Yes	A	OECD	IEA2 (-)
Coal, steam :from non-EC countries to the EC	By country	tonnes, %	Yes	A, Q	Selected non-EC countries	IEA6 (I.8)
Coal, steam to Japan	By country	tonnes, %	Yes	A, Q	World	IEA6(I.10)
Commercial energy	Total and by type	TJ	Yes	A	World	UN21 (3)
Commercial energy (coal equivalent)	Total and by type	tonnes	Yes	A	World	UN21 (1)
Commercial energy (oil equivalent)	Total and by type	tonnes	Yes	A	World	UN21 (2)
Crude and products	By importers, exporters	b/d	Yes	A	World	BB4 (2.4, 2.6-2.8)
Crude oil		tonnes	No		World	EC9 (4.25)
Crude oil	By country	b/d	Yes	A	World	OPEC1 (56)
Crude oil	By country of destination	tonnes	Yes	A	World, OECD non-OECD	IEA10 (II.8A)
Crude oil	By country of origin	tonnes	Yes	A	World, OECD non-OECD	IEA10 (II.7A)
Crude oil	By destination	b/d	Yes	A	OPEC	OPEC1 (51)
Crude oil	By importers, exporters	b/d	Yes	A	World	BB4 (3.1-4.8)
Crude oil	Share of total OPEC crude oil exports, by region	%	Yes	A	World	OPEC1 (25)
Crude oil and natural gas liquids		tonnes	Yes	A	World, OECD non-OECD	IEA10 (I.9)
Crude oil and natural gas liquids		tonnes	Yes	A	World, OECD non-OECD	IEA10 (I.7)
Crude oil and NGL exports		tonnes	Yes	A	World, OECD, non-OECD	IEA7
Crude oil and products, net imports	By country	b/d	Yes	A, M	World	BB2 (17)
Crude oil and products, net imports	Total	b/d	Yes	A	World excluding EC, ISC	BB1 (20.1-20.2)
Crude oil and refined products	By importers, exporters	b/d	Yes	A	World	BB4 (1-1-2.3, 2.5)
Crude oil exports, GCC	By country	b/d	No		Arabian Gulf	CH1 (3.3)
Crude oil, gross imports by country of origin	By country, importer	b/d	Yes	A	World	BB2 (18)
Crude petroleum	By principal importers and exporters	tonnes	No		World	UN21 (15)
Crude petroleum	Imports, exports, by country	tonnes	Yes	A	ESCAP	UN44
Electric energy	By country	gWh	Yes	A	EC, USA	UN7 (1)
Electric energy	By country	gWh	Yes	A	EC, USA	UN7 (1)
Electric energy	Partner countries	gWh	Yes	A	EC, USA	UN7 (5)
Electric energy	Partner countries	gWh	Yes	A	EC, USA	UN7 (5)
Electric energy, international exchanges	By importing country	gWh	Yes	A	EC, USA	UN7 (6)
Electricity		kWh	Yes	A	World	UN21 (35)
Electricity	Imports, exports, by country	kWh	Yes	A	ESCAP	UN44
Electricity	Net imports, net imports as a proportion of total primary energy requirement	toe, %	Yes	A	EC	EC34 (3.15-3.16)
Electricity exports		tWh	Yes	I	OECD	IEA3 (-)

17 ENERGY

Subject	Categories	Units	Time series Yes/No Frequency		Territorial coverage	Source (Table no.)
Electricity imports	Total and net	tWh	Yes	I	OECD	IEA3 (-)
Energy	By form of energy	TJ	Yes	A	EC, USA, Canada	UN9 (2)
Energy	By form of energy	TJ	Yes	A	EC, USA, Canada	UN9 (2)
Energy, total	Net exports of total energy as % of total energy production, net imports of total energy as % of total energy consumption	%	Yes	I	World	UNCTAD1 (6.9)
Energy trade	By high, middle, low income countries	tonnes, kg, %	No		World	CS1 (16)
Exporters	Total	b/d, %	Yes	A	World	BB4 (1V)
Exporters	Total	b/d, %	Yes	A	World	BB4 (V1)
Exports		tonnes of coal equivalent	Yes	A	World	UN50 (124)
Exports		toe	Yes	A	EC	EC9 (4.17)
Exports	By fuel type	toe	No		EC	EC33 (-)
Exports	By fuel, energy type, by country	tonnes, TJ, toe, gWh	No		EC	EC30 (-)
Exports	Type	tonnes of coal equiv	Yes	A	World	UN50 (11)
Exports estimated seaborne	By country	tonnes	Yes	A, Q, M	World	DSC2(2.10)
Exports, eastern energy	To VICES area by type	US$	No		VICES	VICES1 (V/4)
Exports, imports		b/d, %	Yes	A	World	BB4 (V)
Exports, non-petroleum	Value	US$	Yes	A	OPEC	OPEC1 (6)
Exports, petroleum	Value	US$	Yes	A	OPEC	OPEC1 (5)
Exports, western energy	To VICES area by SITC, at current prices	US$	No		VICES	VICES1 (V/4)
Feedstocks	By country of destination	tonnes	Yes	A	World, OECD non-OECD	IEA10 (II.8A)
Feedstocks	By country of origin	tonnes	Yes	A	World, OECD non-OECD	IEA10 (II.7A)
Fuel	By region, country or area	US$, indices, % of total	Yes	A	Developed economies	UN32 (D,E)
Gas	By country of origin, destination, by type of gas	TJ	Yes	A	EC, USA	UN8 (2)
Gas	By country of origin, destination, by type of gas	TJ	Yes	A	EC, USA	UN8 (3)
Gas	By type of gas, by country	TJ	Yes	A	EC , USA	UN8 (1)
Gas	By type of gas, by country	TJ	Yes	A	EC, USA	UN8 (1)
Gas, diesel oil	By country of destination	tonnes	Yes	A	World, OECD non-OECD	IEA10 (II.8B)
Gas, diesel oil	By country of origin	tonnes	Yes	A	World, OECD non-OECD	IEA10 (II.7C)
Gas, economy indicators	Intra and extra EC	indices	No		EC	EC33 (-)
Gas, natural		TJ	No		EC	EC9 (4.30)
Gas, natural	Production, imports	TJ	Yes	A	EC	EC53 (8.5)
Gases		TJ	Yes	A	World	UN21 (31)
Gasoline (total)	By country of destination	tonnes	Yes	A	World, OECD non-OECD	IEA10 (II.8B)
Gasoline (total)	By country of origin	tonnes	Yes	A	World, OECD non-OECD	IEA10 (II.7C)
Heavy fuel oil (residual)	By country of destination	tonnes	Yes	A	World, OECD non-OECD	IEA10 (II.8B)

Subject	Categories	Units	Time series Yes/No Frequency		Territorial coverage	Source (Table no.)
Heavy fuel oil (residual)	By country of origin	tonnes	Yes	A	World, OECD non-OECD	IEA10 (II.7D)
Hydrocarbons, principal aggregates	By type	tonnes	No		EC	EC33 (-)
Hydrocarbons, principal aggregates	By type	tonnes	No		EC	EC33 (-)
Importers	Total	b/d, %	Yes	A	World	BB4 (V11)
Imports		%	Yes	A	EC	EC9 (4.22)
Imports		tonnes of coal equivalent	Yes	A	World	UN50 (124)
Imports		toe	Yes	A	EC	EC9 (4.17)
Imports	By exporter, importer, region	tonnes	Yes	A	USA, OECD, Japan	BP2 (-)
Imports	By fuel type	toe	No		EC	EC33 (-)
Imports	By fuel/energy type, by country	tonnes, TJ, toe, gWh	No		EC	EC30 (-)
Imports	By importers and exporters	cu m nge	Yes	A, M	World	DSC2 (3.7-3.8)
Imports	Type	tonnes of coal equiv	Yes	A	World	UN50 (11)
Imports, exports		b/d	No		World	BB4 (1-111)
Imports, exports		gWh	Yes	A	OECD	IEA8&9 (–)
Imports, exports	Selected energy commodities	tonnes	Yes	A	EC	EC53 (8.1)
Imports, OECD	By major source country and regions	tonnes	Yes	A, Q, M	World	DSC2 (2.13-2.14)
Imports, raw material	By main origins, metal content	tonnes/%	No		EC	EC53 (8.11)
Imports, western energy	From VICES area by SITC, at current prices	US$	No		VICES	VICES1 (V/4)
Kerosene (total)	By country of destination	tonnes	Yes	A	World, OECD non-OECD	IEA10 (II.8B)
Kerosene (total)	By country of origin	tonnes	Yes	A	World, OECD non-OECD	IEA10 (II.7C)
Liquefied petroleum gases	By country of destination	tonnes	Yes	A	World, OECD non-OECD	IEA10 (II.8A)
Liquefied petroleum products	By country of origin	tonnes	Yes	A	World, OECD non-OECD	IEA10 (II.7B)
Liquid fuels	By type	tonnes	Yes	A	World	UN21 (14, 17-24)
LNG project and contract summary	By exporter, importer, contract, duration, cif price	years, $ per Btu	No		Western Europe and American markets, Far East markets	BP2 (-)
Naphtha	By country of destination	tonnes	Yes	A	World, OECD non-OECD	IEA10 (II.8A)
Naphtha	By country of origin	tonnes	Yes	A	World, OECD non-OECD	IEA10 (II.7B)
Natural gas		TJ	Yes	A	World	UN21 (28)
Natural gas		TJ	Yes	A	World, OECD non-OECD	IEA10 (I.22)
Natural gas		TJ	Yes	A	World, OECD non-OECD	IEA10 (I.23)
Natural gas	By country	cu m	Yes	A	World	OPEC1 (55)
Natural gas	By country	cu m	Yes	A	World	OPEC1 (58)
Natural gas	By country of destination	TJ, cu m	Yes	A	World, OECD non-OECD	IEA10 (II.11)
Natural gas	By country of origin	TJ, cu m	Yes	A	World, OECD non-OECD	IEA10 (II.10)
Natural gas	By principal importers and exporters	TJ	No		World	UN21 (29)

17 ENERGY

Subject	Categories	Units	Time series Yes/No Frequency		Territorial coverage	Source (Table no.)
Natural gas	Origin to destination	cu m	No		World	BP1 (p24)
Natural gas	Origin to destination	cu m	No		World	BP1 (p24)
Natural gas liquids	By country of destination	tonnes	Yes	A	World, OECD non-OECD	IEA10 (II.8A)
Natural gas liquids	By country of origin	tonnes	Yes	A	World, OECD non-OECD	IEA10 (II.7A)
Natural gas, trade movements	Origin to destination	cu m	No		World	BP1 (p24)
Oil, net, imports, value of	Total	$, nat curr	Yes	A	Selected countries	BB1 (21)
Oil		b/d % share % change	Yes	A	World	BP1 (p16)
Oil		b/d % share % change	Yes	A	World	BP1 (p16)
Oil	% of total exports	%	Yes	A	OPEC	OPEC1 (7)
Oil	Crude, product imports and exports	tonnes b/d	No		World	BP1 (p17)
Oil	Crude, product imports and exports	tonnes b/d	No		World	BP1 (p17)
Oil and balance of trade	By oil, all goods	$, nat curr	Yes	A	World	BB1 (22.1-22.2)
Oil and the balance of trade	By country	nat curr	Yes	A, M	World	BB2 (16)
Oil export value		US$, fob	Yes	A	OPEC	OPEC1 (4)
Oil import value		US$, cif	Yes	A	OPEC	OPEC1 (8)
Oil imports, net		toe	Yes	A	OECD	OECD33 (9.2)
Oil trade	By imports, exports, total	b/d	Yes	A	Selected countries	BB4 (7-154)
Oil trade, international	By imports, exports	tonnes	No		World, OECD	IP1 (-)
Oil, crude	Imports, exports	tonnes	Yes	A	EC	EC53 (8.3)
Oil, imports/exports		b/d % share % change	Yes	A	World	BP1 (p16)
Oil, inter-area movements	Origin to destination	tonnes b/d	No		World	BP1 (p16)
Petrolem products	By type	tonnes	No		EC	EC33 (-)
Petroleum (crude oil and products)		tonnes	Yes	A	EC	EC9 (4.28)
Petroleum coke	By country of destination	tonnes	Yes	A	World, OECD non-OECD	IEA10 (II.8B)
Petroleum coke	By country of origin	tonnes	Yes	A	World, OECD non-OECD	IEA10 (II.7D)
Petroleum products		tonnes	Yes	A	World, OECD non-OECD	IEA10 (I.10)
Petroleum products		tonnes	Yes	A	World, OECD non-OECD	IEA10 (I.8)
Petroleum products	By country of destination	tonnes	Yes	A	World, OECD non-OECD	IEA10 (II.8A)
Petroleum products	By country of origin	tonnes	Yes	A	World, OECD non-OECD	IEA10 (II.7B)
Petroleum products	By type	tonnes	No		EC	EC33 (-)
Petroleum products, derived	Imports, exports	tonnes	Yes	A	EC	EC53 (8.4)
Petroleum, economy indicators	By type	indices	No		EC	EC33 (-)
Petroleum, economy indicators	By type	indices	No		EC	EC33 (-)
Primary energy, net	By type by country	toe	Yes	I	VICES and Yugoslavia	VICES1 (V/2)
Principal international movements of natural gas	By country; total	cu m	Yes	A, M	World	BB2 (19.1-19.2)
Refined oil products	By importers, exporters	b/d	Yes	A	World	BB4 (5.4, 5.5)
Refined products	By country	b/d	Yes	A	World	OPEC1 (54)
Refined products	By country	b/d	Yes	A	World	OPEC1 (57)

Subject	Categories	Units	Time series Yes/No Frequency		Territorial coverage	Source (Table no.)
Refined products	By destination	b/d	Yes	A	OPEC	OPEC1 (53)
Refined products	By importers, exporters	b/d	Yes	A	World	BB4 (5.1-5.3, 5.6-6.8)
Refined products	By OPEC country	b/d	Yes	A	OPEC	OPEC1 (27)
Refined products	By region	b/d	Yes	A	World	OPEC1 (28)
Solid fuel	By type	tonnes	Yes	A	World	UN21 (5-6,8-13)
Solid fuels	By country of origin, by fuel type, by country	tonnes	No		EC , USA	UN6 (5)
Solid fuels	By country of origin, by fuel type, by country	tonnes	No		EC, USA	UN6 (4)
Solid fuels	By fuel type, by country	tonnes	Yes	I	EC , USA	UN6 (1)
Solid fuels	By fuel type, by country	tonnes	Yes	I	EC, USA	UN6 (1)
17.7 LABOUR						
Employees		nos	Yes	A	World	UN50 (123)
Persons engaged		nos	Yes	A	World	UN50 (123)
Wages and salaries		nat curr	Yes	A	World	UN50 (123)
17.8 NUCLEAR ENERGY						
17.8.1 Capacity and Related Data						
Capacity, nuclear generating, long-term	Low, high demand scenarios	gWe	Yes	A	Areas	OECD47 (18)
Fuel fabrication, nuclear energy	Capacities and requirements, by fuel type, actual, forecast	tonnes/year	Yes	5yr	OECD	OECD31 (8A, 8B)
Fuel spent, nuclear energy	Storage capacities and arisings, actual, forecast	tonnes	Yes	5yr	OECD	OECD31 (9A, 9B)
Nuclear electricity generating capacity, installed		mWe	Yes	A	Various countries	OECD47(16)
Nuclear energy capacity	By country, by stations	nos, mWe	No		EC	EM1 (0812)
Nuclear power plants, connected to the grid	Units and capacity, by type of power plant	gWe	No		OECD	OECD31 (3B)
Nuclear power plants, status	Units and capacity of power plants: connected to the grid, under construction, firmly committed, planned	gWe	No		OECD	OECD31 (3A)
Reprocessing capacities, nuclear energy	By fuel type, actual, forecast	tonnes/year	Yes	5yr	OECD	OECD31 (10)
Requirements, uranium reactor-related		tonnes	Yes	A	OECD	OECD47 (17)
long-term	by reactor strategy	tonnes	Yes	A	OECD	OECD47 (19,20)
Uranium resources		tonnes	No		World, OECD	OECD31 (5A)
Uranium stocks, reported	By type	tonnes	No		Various countries	OECD47 (21)
Uranium, conversion	Capacities and requirements, actual, forecast	tonnes/year	Yes	5yr	OECD	OECD31 (6A, 6B)

Subject	Categories	Units	Time series Yes/No Frequency		Territorial coverage	Source (Table no.)
Uranium, enrichment	Capacities and requirements, actual, forecast	tonnes/year	Yes	5yr	OECD	OECD31 (7A, 7B)
17.8.2 Industry						
Nuclear power plants, firmly committed and planned	Units and capacity, by type of power plant	gWe	No		OECD	OECD31 (3D)
Nuclear power plants, to be taken out of service	Units, capacity and lifetime, by country and type of power plant	nos, gWe, years	Yes	I	OECD	OECD31 (4A, 4B)
Nuclear power plants, under construction	Units and capacity, by type of power plant	gWe	No		OECD	OECD31 (3C)
Nuclear power stations	Production and performance data for individual power stations	mW,gWh hours, %	Yes	A, M	World	IAEA1 (-)
Nuclear power, equipment	Commissioned, decommissioned, rerated, situation, end of year by type of reactor	mW	No		EC	EC64 (-)
Nuclear power, operating data	Summary of operating factors, by country and nuclear power station	gWh, %, hours, mW	Yes	A, M	EC	EC64 (-)
Nuclear power, performance	Mean energy availability factor, load factor by type of reactor	%	No		EC	EC64 (-)
17.8.3 Production and Consumption						
Electrical energy	Total, hydro, geothermal, nuclear, conventional thermal	gWh	No		World , EC, USSR USA, Canada, Japan	EC9 (4.32)
Electricity generation	Total generation, proportion derived from nuclear energy, proportion derived from fossil fuels, proportion derived from hydro-electric and geothermal sources	toe, %	Yes	A	EC	EC34 (3.29-3.32)
Nuclear electricity		gWh	Yes	A	World, OECD, non-OECD	IEA7
Nuclear electricity	Total	kWh	Yes	A	World	BB1 (7.3)
Nuclear energy		toe	No		World, EC, USSR USA, Canada, Japan	EC9 (4.15)
Nuclear energy		toe % share % change	Yes	A	World	BP1 (p30)
Nuclear heat		kWh,	Yes	M	EC	EC31 (3)
Nuclear power, generation		gWh	No		EC	EC64 (-)
Nuclear power, net production	By type of reactor	gWh	No		EC	EC64 (-)
Nuclear power, thermal production		gWh	No		EC	EC64 (-)
Nuclear share of total electricity production		%	No		EC	EC64 (-)
Nuclear share of total energy, heat generation	Total primary energy production, total energy consumption	%	No		EC	EC64 (-)
Plutonium, annual requirements	By fuel type, actual, forecast	tonnes	Yes	5yr	OECD	OECD31 (11)
Uranium		tonnes	Yes	A	World	UN21 (37)
Uranium missions from electricity generation	By type	rate	No		World	OECD47 (22)

Subject	Categories	Units	Time series Yes/No Frequency		Territorial coverage	Source (Table no.)
Uranium production, natural	Actual, forecast	tonnes/year	Yes	5yr	World	OECD31 (5B)
Uranium requirements, natural	Actual, forecast	tonnes/year	Yes	5yr	OECD	OECD31 (5C)

17.9 OIL, OIL PRODUCTS AND NATURAL GAS

17.9.1 Capacity

Capacity of crude oil refineries		tonnes	Yes	A	Nordic countries	NCM1 (105)
Crude oil	Refinery input, refining capacity	tonnes	No		World, EC, USSR, USA, Canada, Japan	EC9 (4.25)
Crude oil refineries, throughput and capacity		tonnes	No		EC	EC33 (-)
Natural gas liquid plants	Production and capacity by type	tonnes	Yes	A	World	UN21 (27)
Oil refineries in the GCC region	By country, by location, type	b/d	No		Arabian Gulf	CH1 (3.8)
Oil refining capacity	By country, by all capacity, export capacity	b/cd	No		Arabian Gulf	CH1 (3.7)
Oil, refinery capacities		b/d % share % change	Yes	A	World	BP1 (p14)
Petroleum, refinery capacity		indices	No		EC	EC33 (-)
Refineries, capacity utilization		%	No		EC	EC33 (-)
Refinery capacities	By country	tonnes	No		EC	EM1 (0803)
Refinery capacity		b/d	Yes	A	OPEC	OPEC1 (17)
Refinery capacity	By country	b/d	Yes	A	World	OPEC1 (46)
Refinery capacity	By location	b/d	Yes	A	OPEC	OPEC1 (45)
Refinery capacity	By region	b/d	Yes	A	World	OPEC1 (18)
Refinery capacity, growth rates		%	Yes	I	World	UNCTAD1 (6.9)
Refinery crude distillation capacity	Total	b/d	Yes	A	World	BB1 (11.1-11.2)
Refinery distillation	Capacity, throughput and output	tonnes	Yes	A	World	UN21 (16)
Refinery projects, crude processing units under construction or planned	By capacity projects, completion date, projects capacity	bd, nos	No		World	BB2 (10)
Refinery runs	By country	b/d	Yes	A, M	World	BB2 (9)
Refinery runs	Total	b/d	Yes	A	World	BB1 (12.1-12.2)
Refining capacity		b/d	Yes	A	OECD	IEA1(A10)
Refining capacity	By country	tonnes, nos b/cd	Yes	A	World	IP1 (-)
Transformation	Electricity, installed capacity, per thousand inhabitants; petroleum, refinery capacity as a percent of liquid fuel consumption	kW, %	Yes	I	World	UNCTAD1 (6.9)

17.9.2 Exploration, Development and Reserves

Crude oil, proved reserves	Total	bl	Yes	A	World	BB1 (1.1-1.2)
Gas producing countries and reserves		cu m	Yes	A	World	ISL2 (2.3.2.2.1-2)

Subject	Categories	Units	Time series Yes/No Frequency		Territorial coverage	Source (Table no.)
Gas, proved natural gas reserves	Total	cu m	Yes	A	World	BB1 (2.1-2.2)
Gas, proved reserves crude oil and natural gas liquids	By country, by % world total	tonnes, %	Yes	A	World	IP1 (-)
Gas, proved reserves gas	By share of total, country	cu ft, cu m, R/P ratio	No		World	BP2 (-)
GCC proven crude oil reserves	By country	bl	No		Arabian Gulf	CH1(3.1)
GCC proven natural gas reserves	By country	cu m	No		Arabian Gulf	CH1 (3.6)
Liquid natural gas projects in the GCC region	By country, by location, status, feedstock products	cu f/d	No		Arabian Gulf	CH1 (3.9)
Natural gas	Production and	cu m	Yes	A	World	ISL2 (2.3.2.1)
Natural gas reserves, proved		cu m, cu ft % share R/P ratio	No		World	BP1 (p18)
New exploration and production	By company, designation, agreements	%, sq kms	No		World	BB2 (1)
Oil and gas discoveries	By company, designation; by location, test flows, type	%, b/d, mncfd	No		World	BB2 (2)
Oil reserves, proved		barrels, tonnes, % R/P ratio	No		World	BP1 (p2)
Oil reserves, proven	By country	barrels	Yes	A	World	OPEC1 (33)
Oil reserves, proven	By region	barrels	Yes	A	OPEC countries	OPEC1 (11)
Reserves, comparison with oil gas	By product, country	cu m, toe, tonnes, R/P ratio	No		World	BP2 (-)
Rigs active	By land, offshore	nos	Yes	A	World	BB1 (9.1-9.3)
Rigs active, estimated number	By land, offshore, total	nos.	Yes	A	World	BB2 (3.1-3.3)
Rigs, active	OPEC member	nos	Yes	A	World	OPEC1 (35)
Wells completed	By OPEC country	nos	Yes	A	OPEC	OPEC1 (36)
Wells drilled	Total	nos	Yes	A	World excluding EC	BB1 (10.1-10.2)
17.9.3 Financial Accounts						
Capital expenditures	For major oil companies	US$	Yes	A	World	IEA1(A16)
Cashflow	For major oil companies	US$	Yes	A	World	IEA1(A16)
Costs, deductions, net income revenue	Oil companies, major	%	Yes	A	World	OPEC1 (74)
Debt to capital ratio	For major oil companies	US$	Yes	A	World	IEA1(A16)
Earnings	By company section for major oil companies	US$	Yes	A	World	IEA1(A15)
Long-term debt	For major oil companies	US$	Yes	A	World	IEA1(A16)
Net income	For major oil companies	US$	Yes	A	World	IEA1(A15)
Netbacks and refiners margins		US$/barrel	No		World	OPEC2
Oil companies, major	Capital expenditure	US$	Yes	A	World	OPEC1 (75)
Oil company earnings and share prices	By company; closing prices	US$	Yes	A, M, W	World	BB2 (25.1-25.2)
Operating costs, deductions, taxation, net income	Oil companies, major	US$	Yes	A	World	OPEC1 (73)
Parent companys', percentage equity	In companies holding producing rights	%	No		OPEC	OPEC1 (43)

Subject	Categories	Units	Time series Yes/No Frequency		Territorial coverage	Source (Table no.)
17.9.4 Industry						
Natural gas reserves, proven	By country	cu m	Yes	A	World	OPEC1 (34)
Natural gas reserves, proven	By region	cu m	Yes	A	OPEC	OPEC1 (12)
Oil companies, major	Principal operations	b/d	Yes	A	World	OPEC1 (72)
Oil wells, producing	Flowing, artificial lift	nos	Yes	A	OPEC	OPEC1 (37)
Producing, reserves, refining, consuming	By country	tonnes/%	Yes	A	World	ISL2 (2.3.1.3.1-4)
17.9.5 Production, Consumption and Deliveries						
Aviation fuels		tonnes	Yes	A	OECD	IEA10 (II.4)
Aviation gasoline		tonnes of coal equivalent	Yes	A	World	UN50 (125)
Balance, supply, demand		b/d	Yes	A, Q	World	OPEC2
Balance, supply, demand		b/d	Yes	A, Q	World	OPEC2
Bitumen		tonnes	Yes	A	OECD	IEA10 (II.6B)
Bitumen		tonnes	Yes	A	OECD	IEA10 (II.6B)
Condensate		tonnes of coal equivalent	Yes	A	World	UN50 (125)
Crude oil		b/d	Yes	Q, M	OPEC	OPEC2
Crude oil		toe	No		World, EC, USSR, USA, Canada, Japan	EC9 (4.15)
Crude oil		tonnes	Yes	A	OECD	IEA10 (II.2)
Crude oil		tonnes, indices	Yes	A, M	EC, USA, Japan	EC36
Crude oil	By companies	b/d	Yes	A	OPEC	OPEC1 (42)
Crude oil	By country	b/d	Yes	A	World	OPEC1 (39)
Crude oil	By country	b/d	Yes	A	World	OPEC1 (52)
Crude oil	By country, since commencement	barrels	Yes	A	OPEC	OPEC1 (38)
Crude oil	By OPEC country	b/d	Yes	A	OPEC	OPEC1 (23)
Crude oil	By region	b/d	Yes	A	World	OPEC1 (14)
Crude oil	By region	b/d	Yes	A	World	OPEC1 (26)
Crude oil	Treated in refineries	tonnes, indices	Yes	A, M	EC, USA, Japan	EC36
Crude oil and feedstocks		tonnes	Yes	M	EC	EC31 (2)
Crude oil and feedstocks	By origin worldwide	tonnes	Yes	M	EC	EC31 (2)
Crude oil and natural gas liquid	Total	b/d	Yes	A	World	BB1 (3.1-3.3)
Crude oil and natural gas liquids		tonnes	Yes	A	World	IEA10 (I.18)
Crude oil and NGL		tonnes, b/d	Yes	A	World , OECD and non-OECD	IEA7
Crude oil and NGLs production		b/d	Yes	A	World	BB2 (4.1-4.6)
Crude oil and refined products	By OPEC country	b/d	Yes	A	OPEC	OPEC1 (29)

17 ENERGY

Subject	Categories	Units	Time series Yes/No Frequency		Territorial coverage	Source (Table no.)
Crude oil and refined products	By region	b/d	Yes	A	World	OPEC1 (30)
Crude oil reserves		barrels	Yes	A	World	IEA10 (I.19)
Crude oil,	Parent companies estimated gross share	b/d	Yes	A	OPEC	OPEC1 (44)
Crude oil, NGL and refinery stocks		tonnes	Yes	Q	OECD	IEA11
Crude oil, OPEC	By region	b/d	Yes	A	World	OPEC1 (24)
Crude petroleum		tonnes	Yes	A	World, ASEAN	ASEANS1 (4.2.1)
Crude petroleum		tonnes	Yes	A, M	OECD	OECD22
Crude petroleum	By country	tonnes	Yes	A	Africa and Asia	MAC1 (E3)
Crude petroleum	By country	tonnes	Yes	A	ESCAP	UN44
Crude petroleum	By country	tonnes	Yes	A	ESCAP	UN44
Crude petroleum	By production	tonnes	Yes	A	World	UNCTAD4 (3.11.1)
Crude petroleum	By production, exports, imports	tonnes	Yes	A	World	BGS2(-)
Crude petroleum. output	By countries	nos	No		The Americas and Australasia	MAC2 (E3)
Distillation and conversion		b/d	Yes	A	World	IEA1 (A9)
Energy products from refineries	By type	tonnes	Yes	A	World	UN21 (26)
Fuel oil, residual		tonnes	Yes	Q	OECD	IEA11
Fuel, residual		tonnes of coal equivalent	Yes	A	World	UN50 (125)
Gas, diesel oil		tonnes of coal equivalent	Yes	A	World	UN50 (125)
Gas, diesel oil		tonnes	Yes	A	OECD	IEA10 (II.5A)
Gas, diesel oil		tonnes	Yes	A	OECD	IEA10 (II.5A)
Gas, diesel oil		tonnes	Yes	Q	OECD	IEA11
Gas, natural		cu m TJ	No		World, EC, USSR, USA, Canada, Japan	EC9 (4.30)
Gas, natural		TJ	Yes	A	EC, W Germany France, Ireland, Italy, Netherlands, UK	EC9 (4.29)
Gas, natural		toe	No		World, EC, USSR, USA, Canada, Japan	EC9 (4.15)
Gas, natural		tonnes of coal equivalent	Yes	A	World	UN50 (125)
Gas, natural	Production, imports	TJ	Yes	A	EC	EC53 (8.5)
Gasoline		cu m	Yes	A	Latin American and Caribbean countries	UN45 (341)
Gasoline, natural		tonnes of coal equivalent	Yes	A	World	UN50 (125)
Gasoline, total		tonnes	Yes	Q	OECD	IEA11
GCC crude oil production	By country	b/d	No		Arabian Gulf	CH1 (3.2)
Heavy fuel oil		tonnes	Yes	A	OECD	IEA10 (II.5B)
Heavy fuel oil (residual)		tonnes	Yes	A	OECD	IEA10 (II.5B)
Hydrocarbon refinery inputs, principal aggregates	By type	tonnes	No		EC	EC33 (-)
Hydrocarbons	Per capita	kg	Yes	A	Latin American and Caribbean countries	UN45 (53)

Subject	Categories	Units	Time series Yes/No Frequency		Territorial coverage	Source (Table no.)
Hydrocarbons available, principal aggregates	By type	tonnes	No		EC	EC33 (-)
Hydrocarbons, growth	Average annual rates	indices	Yes	A	Latin American and Caribbean countries	UN45 (54)
Hydrocarbons, principal aggregates	By type	tonnes	No		EC	EC33 (-)
Hydrocarbons, principal aggregates	By type	tonnes	No		EC	EC33 (-)
Hydrocarbons, principal aggregates	By type	tonnes	No		EC	EC33 (-)
Jet fuels		tonnes of coal equivalent	Yes	A	World	UN50 (125)
Kerosene		tonnes	Yes	A	OECD	IEA10 (II.6A)
Kerosene		tonnes	Yes	A	OECD	IEA10 (II.6A)
Kerosene		tonnes of coal equivalent	Yes	A	World	UN50 (125)
Liquefied petroleum gases		tonnes	Yes	A	OECD	IEA10 (II.6A)
Liquefied petroleum gases		tonnes	Yes	A	OECD	IEA10 (II.6A)
Liquid fuels	By type	tonnes	Yes	A	World	UN21 (14, 17-24)
Liquid fuels, derivative energy	Light products: aviation and motor gasoline, jet fuel, kerosene, naphthas, heavy products: gas (diesel) oil, residual fuel oil	tonnes	Yes	A	EC, USA, Canada	UN9 (1)
LPG		tonnes of coal equivalent	Yes	A	World	UN50 (125)
Lubricants		tonnes	Yes	A	OECD	IEA10 (II.6A)
Lubricants		tonnes	Yes	A	OECD	IEA10 (II.6A)
Lubricants		tonnes of coal equivalent	Yes	A	World	UN50 (125)
Motor gasoline		tonnes	Yes	A	OECD	IEA10 (II.3)
Motor gasoline		tonnes of coal equivalent	Yes	A	World	UN50 (125)
Naphtha		tonnes	Yes	A	OECD	IEA10 (II.6A)
Naphtha		tonnes	Yes	A	OECD	IEA10 (II.6A)
Naphtha		tonnes	Yes	Q	OECD	IEA11
Natural gas		cu m	Yes	A, M	OECD	OECD22
Natural gas		cu m	Yes	A, Q, M	OECD	OECD22
Natural gas		TJ	Yes	A	OECD	IEA10 (II.9)
Natural gas		TJ	Yes	A	OECD	IEA10 (II.9)
Natural gas		TJ	Yes	A	World	IEA10 (I.21)
Natural gas		TJ	Yes	A	World	UN21 (28)
Natural gas		TJ	Yes	A	World, ASEAN	ASEANS1 (4.2.2)
Natural gas		TJ	Yes	A	World, OECD, non-OECD	IEA10 (I.20)

17 ENERGY

Subject	Categories	Units	Time series Yes/No Frequency		Territorial coverage	Source (Table no.)
Natural gas		TJ, indices	Yes	A, M	EC, USA, Japan	EC36
Natural gas		toe	Yes	A	World, OECD and non-OECD	IEA7
Natural gas		toe, % share % change	Yes	A	World	BP1 (p20)
Natural gas		toe, % share % change	Yes	A	World	BP1 (p22)
Natural gas	By country	cu m	Yes	A	Africa and Asia	MAC1 (E4)
Natural gas	By OPEC country	cu m	Yes	A	OPEC	OPEC1 (31)
Natural gas	By production	cu m	Yes	A	World	BGS2(-)
Natural gas	By region	cu m	Yes	A	World	OPEC1 (32)
Natural gas	Marketed	cu m	Yes	A	OPEC	OPEC1 (15)
Natural gas	Marketed, by region	cu m	Yes	A	World	OPEC1 (16)
Natural gas	Production and reserves	cu m	Yes	A	World	ISL2 (2.3.2.1)
Natural gas	Total	cu m	Yes	A	World	BB1 (5.1-5.2)
Natural gas liquid plants	Production and capacity by type	tonnes	Yes	A	World	UN21 (27)
Natural gas liquids		tonnes	Yes	A	OECD	IEA10 (II.2)
Natural gas liquids	Total	b/d	Yes	A	World	BB1 (4.1-4.2)
Natural gas production	By country	cu m	Yes	A, M	World	BB2 (5.1-5.3)
Natural gas, GCC gross production	By country	cu m	No		Arabian Gulf	CH1 (3.5)
Natural gas, gross and marketed	Re-injected, flared, shrinkage	cu m	Yes	A	OPEC	OPEC1 (40)
Natural gas, marketed	By country	cu m	Yes	A	World	OPEC1 (41)
Natural gas, output	By countries	nos	No		The Americas and Australasia	MAC2 (E4)
Natural gas, principal aggregates		TJ	Yes	M	EC	EC31 (2)
Natural gas, principal aggregates	By origin worldwide	TJ	Yes	M	EC	EC31 (2)
Natural gas, principal aggregates	Gross inland	TJ	Yes	M	EC	EC31 (2)
Natural gas, production and utilization in the GCC region	By country, by production, flared, waste	cu m	No		Arabian Gulf	CH1 (3.4)
Non-energy product from refineries	By type	tonnes	Yes	A	World	UN21 (25)
Non-oil		%	Yes	I	OECD	IEA10 (I.1)
Offshore gas production	By country	cu ft/day	Yes	A	World	ISL2 (2.3.2.3)
Offshore production gas	By country	cu m, % share	Yes	A	World	BP2 (-)
Oil		b/d, % share % change	Yes	A	World	BP1 (p8)
Oil		%	Yes	I	OECD	IEA10 (I.1)
Oil		b/d % share % change	Yes	A	World	BP1 (p5)
Oil		tonnes	Yes	A	World, OECD, non-OECD	IEA10 (I.3)
Oil		tonnes, % share % change	Yes	A	World	BP1 (p4)
Oil		tonnes, % share % change	Yes	A	World	BP1 (p7)

Subject	Categories	Units	Time series Yes/No Frequency		Territorial coverage	Source (Table no.)
Oil	By consumers	tonnes	Yes	A	OECD	IEA10 (II.1)
Oil	By origin of oil	tonnes	Yes	A	OECD	IEA10 (II.1)
Oil	GDP,industrial production index, passenger cars	tonnes	Yes	A	OECD	IEA10 (I.2)
Oil (inter-regional movements)	Origin and destination	tonnes	No		World	OECD25 (XVI)
Oil and gas	By consumption sector	tonnes	Yes	A	World, OECD, non-OECD	IEA10 (I.5)
Oil demand		b/d	Yes	A	OECD , non-OECD	IEA1 (A5-A6)
Oil demand	By country	b/d	Yes	A, M	World	BB2 (11.1-11.2)
Oil demand	Total	b/d	Yes	A	World	BB1 (14.1-14.3)
Oil demand by products	By country and product	b/d	Yes	A, M	Selected countries	BB2 (12.1-12.4)
Oil output		b/d	Yes	Q	World	OECD25 (XIII)
Oil products	By product type	tonnes	Yes	A	World, OECD, non-OECD	IEA10 (I.4)
Oil products	By type	tonnes, b/d	Yes	A	World, OECD non-OECD	IEA7
Oil, refinery throughputs		b/d % share % change	Yes	A	World	BP1 (p15)
Oil, regional consumption	By product groups	tonnes % share % change	Yes	A	World	BP1 (p10)
Oil, supply and demand		b/d	Yes	A, Q	World	IEA1 (A1-A2)
Oil, total products		tonnes	Yes	Q	OECD	IEA11
Paraffin waxes		tonnes	Yes	A	OECD	IEA10 (II.6B)
Paraffin waxes		tonnes	Yes	A	OECD	IEA10 (II.6B)
Petrol		tonnes, indices	Yes	A, M	EC, USA, Japan	EC36
Petroleum		cu m	Yes	A	Latin American and Caribbean countries	UN45 (333)
Petroleum coke		tonnes	Yes	A	OECD	IEA10 (II.6B)
Petroleum coke		tonnes	Yes	A	OECD	IEA10 (II.6B)
Petroleum production	By country	tonnes, b/d	Yes	A	World	IP1 (-)
Petroleum products		tonnes	Yes	A	OECD	IEA10 (II.5C)
Petroleum products		tonnes	Yes	A	OECD	IEA10 (II.5C)
Petroleum products		tonnes	Yes	A	World, ASEAN	ASEANS1 (4.1.4)
Petroleum products	By origin worldwide	tonnes	Yes	M	EC	EC31 (2)
Petroleum products	By origin worldwide	tonnes	Yes	M	EC	EC31 (2)
Petroleum products	By type	tonnes	No		EC	EC33 (-)
Petroleum products	By type	tonnes	No		EC	EC33 (-)
Petroleum products	By type	tonnes	No		World, EC, USSR USA, Canada, Japan	EC9 (4.26)
Petroleum products	By type	tonnes	Yes	M	EC	EC31 (2)

17 ENERGY

Subject	Categories	Units	Time series Yes/No Frequency		Territorial coverage	Source (Table no.)
Petroleum products	Total production	tonnes	Yes	A	EC	EC9 (4.27)
Petroleum products demand		b/d	Yes	A, Q	OECD	IEA1 (A3-A4)
Petroleum products, deliveries	For inland consumption, by type of product	TJ, tonnes	Yes	A	EC, USA, Canada	UN9 (3)
Petroleum products, refineries	By type	tonnes	Yes	M	EC	EC31 (2)
Petroleum refinery inputs, economy indicators	By type	indices	No		EC	EC33 (-)
Petroleum, crude		tonnes	Yes	A, Q, M	OECD	OECD22
Petroleum, crude		tonnes of coal equivalent	Yes	A	World	UN50 (125)
Petroleum, economy indicators	By sector	%	No		EC	EC33 (-)
Petroleum, economy indicators	By type	indices	No		EC	EC33 (-)
Primary supply, trends in		toe	Yes	A	OECD	IEA1 (A7)
Production		b/d	Yes	A	World	IEA1 (A8)
Production	Net addition to reserves, cumulative	b/d	Yes	A	OPEC	OPEC1 (p43)
Production from refineries	By product	b/d	No		OECD	BB1 (13.1-13.6)
Production from refineries	By product, country	b/d	Yes	A	World	BB2 (8.1-8.2)
Production gas	By country	cu m, % change, % share	Yes	A	World	BP2 (-)
Refined products		b/d	Yes	A	OPEC	OPEC1 (19)
Refined products		b/d	Yes	A	OPEC	OPEC1 (21)
Refined products	By country	b/d	Yes	A	World	OPEC1 (50)
Refined products	By country	b/d	Yes	A	World	OPEC1 (48)
Refined products	By region	b/d	Yes	A	World	OPEC1 (22)
Refined products	By region	b/d	Yes	A	World	OPEC1 (20)
Refined products	By type	b/d	Yes	A	OPEC	OPEC1 (47)
Refined products	By type	b/d	Yes	A	OPEC	OPEC1 (49)
Refinery feedstocks		tonnes	Yes	A	OECD	IEA10 (II.2)
Refinery gas		tonnes	Yes	A	OECD	IEA10 (II.6A)
Refinery gas		tonnes	Yes	A	OECD	IEA10 (II.6A)
Refinery output		tonnes	Yes	A	World	IEA10 (I.6)
Refinery utilization		%	Yes	A, Q	Selected OECD countries	OPEC2
Supply, crude, NGL, refinery	Indigenous production	tonnes	Yes	Q	OECD	IEA11
Trends in oil-refining	By input, primary capacity, optimum capacity	tonnes	No		EC	EC35 (-)
White spirit and SBP		tonnes	Yes	A	OECD	IEA10 (II.6A)
White spirit and SBP		tonnes	Yes	A	OECD	IEA10 (II.6A)
17.9.6 Stocks						
Crude oil and refined product stocks	By country	bl	Yes	A, M, Q	OECD	BB2 (13.1)
Crude oil and refined products stocks	Total	bl	Yes	A	OECD	BB1 (23.2)

Subject	Categories	Units	Time series Yes/No Frequency		Territorial coverage	Source (Table no.)
Crude oil prices	By API, M average	$ per bl fob	Yes	A	OPEC	BB1 (17.1, 17.3)
Crude oil stocks	Total	bl	Yes	A, Q	OECD	BB1 (23.1)
Gas, natural		cu m	No		World, EC	EC9 (4.30)
Hydrocarbons, stock changes, principal aggregates	By type	tonnes	No		EC	EC33 (-)
Hydrocarbons, stock levels principal aggregates	By type	tonnes	No		EC	EC33 (-)
Industry stocks on land (product components)		tonnes, days demand	Yes	A	OECD	IEA1 (A12)
Land stocks		tonnes, days demand	Yes	A	OECD	IEA1 (A11)
Liquids and condensates	By OPEC and non OPEC	tonnes	Yes	A, M	World	DSC2 (3.1)
Petroleum products	By origin worldwide	tonnes	Yes	M	EC	EC31 (2)
Refined product stocks	By product	bl	Yes	A, M, Q	OECD	BB2 (13.2)
Stock change	Type	tonnes of coal equiv	Yes	A	World	UN50 (11)
Stock levels, OECD	By crude, products	tonnes	Yes	A, M	World	DSC2 (3.3)
17.9.7 Transport - see also Section 41						
Principal international gas movements	Total	cu m	Yes	A	OECD	BB1 (24)
Tanker fleet	Total	nos, dwt	Yes	A	World	BB1 (25)
Tanker market indicators		dwt	Yes	M	World	OPEC2
17.10 PRICES - see also Sections 37 and 41						
17.10.1 Coal and Coal Products						
Coal export	By destination	US$	Yes	A	OECD	IEA2 (II.17)
Coal import	By origin	US$	Yes	A	OECD	IEA2 (-)
Coal, coking	By country	nat curr per tonne	Yes	A, Q	OECD	IEA6 (IIB.1)
Coal, coking	By country	nat curr per tonne	Yes	A, Q	Non-OECD countries	IEA6 (IIIA.1)
Coal, coking	For industrial use	US$ per tonne, toe	Yes	A	OECD	IEA6 (IID.15)
Coal, coking	For industrial use by country	US$ per tonne/ toe	Yes	A	Non-OECD countries	IEA6 (IIIB.15)
Coal, coking, import	By country	indices	Yes	A, Q	OECD, EC	IEA6 (I.12)
Coal, coking, import	By country	US$ per tonne	Yes	A, Q	OECD, EC	IEA6 (I.11)
Coal, coking, import prices from non-EC countries to the EC	By country	US$ per tonne	Yes	A, Q	Selected non-EC countries	IEA6 (I.13)
Coal, coking, import prices to Japan	By country	US$ per tonne	Yes	A, Q	World	IEA6 (I.15)
Coal, export prices	Steam and coking coal	US$ per tonne indices	Yes	A, Q	Australia and USA	IEA6 (1.17-I.18)
Coal, steam	By country incl. and excl. tax	nat curr per toe	Yes	A, Q	OECD	IEA6 (IIB.2)
Coal, steam	For industry and electricity generation	US$ per tonne, toe	Yes	A	OECD	IEA6((IID.13- D.14)
Coal, steam	For industry and electricity generation by country	US$ per tonne/ toe	Yes	A	Non-OECD countries	IEA6 (IIIB.13-B.14)
Coal, steam	For industry, electricity generation and households by country	nat curr per tonne	Yes	A, Q	OECD	IEA6 (IIB.1)
Coal, steam	For industry, electricity generation and household use by country	nat curr per tonne	Yes	A, Q	Non-OECD countries	IEA6 (IIIA.1)
Coal, steam	Incl. and excl. tax by country	nat curr per toe	Yes	A, Q	Non-OECD countries	IEA6 (IIIA.2)
Coal, steam, import	By country	indices	Yes	A, Q	OECD	IEA6 (I.6)

17 ENERGY

Subject	Categories	Units	Time series Yes/No Frequency	Territorial coverage	Source (Table no.)
Coal, steam, import	By country	US$ per tonne	Yes A, Q	OECD	IEA6 (I.5)
Coal, steam, import prices from non-EC countries to the EC	By country	US$ per tonne	Yes A, Q	Selected non-EC countries	IEA6 (I.7)
Coal, steam, import prices to Japan	By country	US$ per tonne	Yes A, Q	World	IEA6 (I.9)
17.10.2 Electricity					
Electricity	For industry and household use by country	nat curr per kWh	Yes A, Q	Non-OECD countries	IEA6 (IIIA.1)
Electricity	For industry and household use by country	US$ per kWh/ toe	Yes A	Non-OECD countries	IEA6 (IIIB.8-B.9)
Electricity	For industry and households by country	nat curr per kWh	Yes A, Q	OECD	IEA6 (IIB.1)
Electricity	For industry and household use	US$ per kWh/ toe	Yes A	OECD	IEA6 (IID.8-D.9)
Electricity for households	Using exchange rates and PPPs	US$ per kWh	Yes A	OECD	IEA6 (IIE.4)
Electricity generation	By fuel type and by country incl. and excl. tax	nat curr per toe	Yes A, Q	Non-OECD countries	IEA6 (IIIA.2)
Electricity generation	By fuel type and by country incl. and excl. tax	nat curr per toe	Yes A, Q	OECD	IEA6 (IIB.2)
Electricity, domestic	Net of tax, VAT excluded, selling price, by country	nat curr/kWh PPS/kWh ECU/kWh	Yes A	EC, selected cities	EC28
Electricity, industry	Net of tax, VAT excluded, selling price, by country	nat curr/kWh PPS/kWh ECU/kWh	Yes A	EC, Selected cities	EC28
17.10.3 Gas					
Gasworks gas prices for households	By region, by price net of tax, price excluding VAT, selling price	nat curr	Yes A	EC	EC48 (-)
Gasworks gas prices for industry	By region, by price net of tax, price excluding VAT, selling price	nat curr	Yes A	EC	EC48 (-)
17.10.4 General					
Energy	By fuel type wholesale and retail by country	indices	Yes A, Q	Non-OECD countries	IEA6 (IIIA.3)
Energy prices	By fuel type wholesale and retail by country	indices	Yes A, Q	OECD	IEA6 (IIB.3)
Energy prices for end-users	By country	indices	Yes A, Q	OECD	IEA6 (IIA.5)
Energy prices, for end-users	By energy type for industry and households	indices	Yes A, Q	OECD, OECD-EC, USA and Japan	IEA6 (II(A.1-A.4)
Fuel and power		indices	Yes A	EC,USA, Japan	EC9 (2.43)
Fuel to end users	Electricity generation and industrial use by fuel type	US$ nat curr	Yes A	OECD	IEA2 (-)
Household consumer	By energy type, by country	nat curr, PPS, ECU	Yes 2/yr	EC	EC32 (-)
Household fuel	By fuel type and by country incl. and excl. tax	nat curr per toe	Yes A, Q	Non-OECD countries	IEA6 (IIIA.2)
Household fuel	By type and by country incl. and excl. tax	nat curr per toe	Yes A, Q	OECD	IEA6 (IIB.2)
Industrial consumer	By energy type, by country	nat curr, PPS, ECU	Yes 2/yr	EC	EC32 (-)

Subject	Categories	Units	Time series Yes/No Frequency	Territorial coverage	Source (Table no.)
Supplied energy prices	Price comparison; household sector (all taxes included), industrial sector (VAT and deductible specific taxes excluded), by energy type	ECU, GJ	Yes 2/yr	EC	EC32 (-)
Unit, value	By fuel type	ECU	No	EC	EC33 (-)
Useful energy prices	Price comparison; household sector (all taxes included), industrial sector (VAT and deductible specific taxes excluded), by energy type	ECU, GJ	Yes 2/yr	EC	EC32 (-)
Useful energy prices	Price comparison; household sector (all taxes included), industrial sector (VAT and deductible specific taxes excluded), by energy type	indices	Yes 2/yr	EC	EC32 (-)
17.10.5 Oil, Oil Products and Natural Gas					
Average spot freight rates (27)	Total	%, US$ per long ton, $ per tonnes	Yes	A, M	World BB1
Crude oil	By type of product and market, fob	US$,barrel	Yes M	EC, USA, Caribbean, Middle East, Singapore	OPEC2
Crude oil	Dubai, Brent, WTI	US$, barrel	Yes A, M	Rotterdam	IEA10 (I.13)
Crude oil imports	By country	indices	Yes A, Q, M	OECD	IEA6 (I.3)
Crude oil imports	By country	US$, bbl	Yes A, Q, M	OECD	IEA6 (I.2)
Crude oil imports	By type of crude	US$, bbl	Yes A, Q, M	World	IEA6 (I.4)
Crude oil imports	By country	US$, barrel	Yes A	IBA	IEA10 (I.12)
Crude oil imports	By type of crude	US$, barrel	Yes A, M	World, OECD, non-OECD	IEA10 (I.11)
Crude oil netback values	By API	US$/bl per fob	Yes A, M	UK, M East, Africa	BB1 (19.1)
Crude oil netback values monthly averages and values	By country by product, API	US$ per bl fob	Yes A, M	World	BB2 (14.1)
Crude oil prices, OPEC	By country and product	US$ per bl fob	Yes A, M	OPEC	BB2 (14.3)
Crude oil prices, Saudi Arabian	By M average	US$ per bl fob	Yes A	Selected countries	BB1 (17.2)
Crude oil sales prices, non-OPEC	By country and product	US$, bl	Yes A, M	Non-OPEC	BB2 (14.4)
Crude oil, FOB loading ports	By type of crude and gravity API	US$, barrel	Yes A	OPEC	OPEC1 (71)
Crude oil, spot		US$, barrel	Yes M	OPEC countries	OECD2
Crude oil, spot	By country, type of crude	US$, barrel	Yes M	Selected non-OPEC countries	OPEC2
Crude oil, spot	By type of crude	US$,bbl	Yes A, Q, M	World	IEA6 (I.1)

17 ENERGY

Subject	Categories	Units	Time series Yes/No Frequency		Territorial coverage	Source (Table no.)
Crude oil, spot	OPEC basket and selected crudes	US$, barrel	No		World	OPEC2
Crude sales prices	By API	US$ per bl fob	Yes	A, M	Non-OPEC	BB1 (17.4)
Crudes (CIF)		US$, barrel	Yes	Q	World	IEA1 (A13)
Crude (CIF)		US$, barrel	Yes	A	World	IEA1 (A14)
Diesel oil, automotive		US$ per litre, toe	Yes	A	OECD	IEA6 (IID.3)
Diesel oil, automotive	By country	US$ per litre, toe	Yes	A	Non-OECD countries	IEA6 (IIIB.3)
Dirty tonnage spot chartered	By all hauls, all tankers	tonnes	Yes	A, M	World	BB1 (28)
Freight costs	Crude oil and products	US$, barrel, worldscale points	Yes	M	World	OPEC2
Fuel oil	By type and country incl. and excl. tax	nat curr per toe	Yes	A, Q	OECD	IEA6 (IIB.2)
Fuel oil	By type incl. and excl. tax by country	nat curr per toe	Yes	A, Q	Non-OECD countries	IEA6 (IIIA.2)
Fuel oil, heavy	For industry and electricity generation by country	nat curr per tonne	Yes	A, Q	Non-OECD countries	IEA6 (IIIA.1)
Fuel oil, heavy	For industry and electricity generation by country	US$ per tonne, toe	Yes	A	Non-OECD countries	IEA6 (IIIB.6-B.7)
Fuel oil, heavy	For industry and electricity generation	US$ per tonne, toe	Yes	A	OECD	IEA6 (IID.6-D.7)
Fuel oil, light	For industry and household use by country	nat curr per per 'ooo litres	Yes	A, Q	Non-OECD countries	IEA6 (IIIA.1)
Fuel oil, light	For industry and household use by country	US$ per 'ooo litres, toe	Yes	A	Non-OECD countries	IEA6 (IIIB.4-B.5)
Fuel oil, light	For industry and household use	US$ per litre, toe	Yes	A	OECD	IEA6 (IID.4-D.5)
Fuel oil, light for households	Using exchangerRates and PPPs	US$ per '000 litres	Yes	A	OECD	IEA6 (IIE.3)
Fuel oils	By type and country	nat curr per litre,tonne	Yes	A, Q	OECD	IEA6 (IIB.1)
Fuels, automotive	By type and by country	nat curr per per litre	Yes	A, Q	Non-OECD countries	IEA6 (IIIA.1)
Fuels, automotive	By type and country	nat curr per litre	Yes	A, Q	OECD	IEA6 (IIB.1)
Gas	By source delivered	US$ per mm Btu	Yes	A, M	World	DSC2 (3.4)
Gas and oil prices	By country, product	US$ per Btu	Yes	A	Japan, OECD, USA	BP2 (-)
Gas, liquefied natural: imports		US$ per toe	Yes	A, Q	France and Japan	IEA6 (I.20)
Gas, natural	By country incl. and excl. tax	nat curr per toe	Yes	A, Q	OECD	IEA6 (IIB.2)
Gas, natural	For industry, electricity generation and household use by country	nat curr per 107 kCal	Yes	A, Q	Non-OECD countries	IEA6 (IIIA.1)
Gas, natural	For industry, electricity generation and households by country	nat curr per 107 Kcal	Yes	A, Q	OECD	IEA6 (IIB.1)
Gas, natural	For industry, electricity generation and household use	US$ per 107kcal toe	Yes	A	OECD	IEA6 (IID.10-D.12)
Gas, natural	For industry, electricity generation and household use by country	US$ per 107kCal, toe	Yes	A	Non-OECD countries	IEA6 (IIIB.10-B.12)
Gas, natural	Incl. and excl. tax by country	nat curr per toe	Yes	A, Q	Non-OECD countries	IEA6 (IIIA.2)
Gas, natural for households	Using exchange rates and PPPs	US$ per Yes 107kcal	A		OECD	IEA6 (IIE.5)

Subject	Categories	Units	Time series Yes/No	Frequency	Territorial coverage	Source (Table no.)
Gas, natural, exported by pipeline		US$ per toe	Yes	A, Q	Netherlands and Norway	IEA6 (I.21)
Gas, natural, imports by pipeline	By country	US$ per toe	Yes	A, Q	Selected OECD countries	IEA6 (I.19)
Gasoline		US$ per litre. toe	Yes	A	OECD	IEA6 (IID.2)
Gasoline	By country	US$ per litre, toe	Yes	A	Non-OECD countries	IEA6 (IIIB.2)
Gasoline	Using exchange rates and PPPs	US$ per litre	Yes	A	OECD	IEA6 (IIE.2)
Heavy fuel oil for industry	By country	nat curr, t	Yes	A, Q	France, Germany, Italy, Spain, UK, Japan, USA	IEA10 (I.17)
Light fuel oil for households	By country	nat curr, litre	Yes	A	France, Germany, Italy, Spain, UK, Japan, USA	IEA10 (I.16)
Motor fuels	By fuel type	nat curr	No		EC	EC33 (-)
Natural gas		US$, btu	Yes	A	EC, Western Europe USA	BP1 (p25)
Natural gas prices for households	By region, by price net of tax, price excluding VAT, selling price	nat curr	Yes	A	EC	EC48 (-)
Natural gas prices for industry	By region, by price net of tax, price excluding VAT, selling price	nat curr	Yes	A	EC	EC48 (-)
Oil, crude spot	By type of crude	US$, barrel	Yes	A	USA	BP1 (p12)
Petroleum products	Premium gasoline	US$/tonne US$/barrel	Yes	A, Q	Rotterdam	IEA10 (I.14)
Petroleum products, spot	November average	US$, barrel	No		World	OPEC2
Prices	By product	US$ per bl	Yes	A, M	World	DSC2 (2.7)
Prices in major markets	By product, market	US$ per tonne	Yes	A, Q	Major markets	BP2 (-)
Refined product prices, spot, monthly averages 15.2)	By product, futures	US$, tonne; US$/bl;c/gal; %	Yes	A, M,	World W	BB2 (15.1-
Retail motor gasoline	By country	nat curr,litre	Yes	A, Q	France, Germany, Italy, Spain, UK, Japan, USA	IEA10 (I.15)
Road transport, retail fuel prices	By fuel type	nat curr, ECU	Yes	A	EC	EC80 (3.12)
Spot (dirty) freight rates	By major haul	US$ per tonnes	Yes	A, M	World	BB1 (26)
Spot crude oil prices	By API	US$ per bl fob	Yes	A, M	World	BB1 (18)
Spot crude oil prices monthly averages	Price by country and product, API	US$ per bl fob	Yes	A, M, W	World	BB2 (14.2)
Spot refined product prices	By M average, product	US$/tonnes, US$/bl, c/gl	Yes	A, M	World	BB1 (19.2-19.3)

17.11 PRIMARY ENERGY - see also under headings for specific sources of energy (17.2.3, 17.4.3, 17.5.1, 17.8.3, 17.9.5)

Subject	Categories	Units	Time series Yes/No	Frequency	Territorial coverage	Source (Table no.)
Electric energy, primary energy	Gross production: geothermal electric energy, hydro-electric energy, nuclear electric energy	gWh	Yes	A	EC, USA, Canada	UN9R (1)
Energy, primary production	By type	toe	Yes	M	EC	EC31 (4)
Gaseous fuels, primary energy	Gasworks gas, coke-oven gas, blast furnace gas, substitute natural gas, LPG	TJ	Yes	A	EC, USA, Canada	UN9 (1)
Gaseous fuels, primary energy	Total, natural gas, LPG`	TJ	Yes	A	EC, USA, Canada	UN9 (1)
Liquid fuels, primary energy	Crude petroleum, total	tonnes	Yes	A	EC, USA, Canada	UN9 (1)

17 ENERGY

Subject	Categories	Units	Time series Yes/No Frequency		Territorial coverage	Source (Table no.)
Primary	By fuel, energy type, by country	tonnes, TJ, toe, gWh	No		EC	EC30 (-)
Primary energy		tce	Yes	A	World, ESCAP	UN44R (p3)
Primary energy		TJ	Yes	A	EC, USA, Canada	UN9 (2)
Primary energy		toe	Yes	A	EC	EC9 (4.16)
Primary energy		toe % share % change	Yes	A	World	BP1 (p33)
Primary energy	By fuel type	toe	Yes	A	World	BP1 (p34)
Primary energy	By type	tce, %	Yes	I	World	UNCTAD1 (6)
Primary energy	By type, by country	toe	Yes	I	VICES and Yugoslavia	VICES1 (V/2)
Primary energy	Coal and lignite, crude oil, gas, nuclear energy, primary electricity	toe	No		World, EC, USA USSR, Canada, Japan	EC9 (4.15)
Primary energy	Primary energy, requirement by type of energy, as proportion of total requirement	toe, %	Yes	A	EC	EC34 (3.3-3.14)
Primary energy	Total	b/doe	Yes	A	World	BB1
Primary energy	Total requirement, total per capita	toe, toe,capita	Yes	A	EC	EC34 (3.1, 3.2)
Primary energy	Total, total per capita,	toe, koe	No		EC	UN22 (I-
Primary energy	Total, total, per capita by type by type	toe, koe	No		EC	UN22 (I-1.5.1)
Primary energy demand	Total	b/d	Yes	A	World	BB1 (15.1-15.3)
Primary energy production		toe	Yes	A	EC	EC53 (8.1)
Primary energy production	By country, by hydro-carbon	toe	No		EC	EM1 (0802)
Primary energy production	Total solids, liquids, gas, electricity	tonnes of coal equivalent	Yes	A	World	UN50 (124)
Primary energy supply		toe	Yes	A	World, OECD	IEA7
Primary energy supply, changes in projections	By fuel type	tce	No		OECD	IEA2
Primary energy supply, total	By fuel type	tce, %	Yes	I	OECD	IEA2
Primary energy supply, total	By fuel type	toe	Yes	I	OECD	IEA3
Solid fuels, primary energy	Hard coal, brown coal and lignite, other	tonnes	Yes	A	EC, USA, Canada	UN9

17.12 PRODUCTION see also under Balance Sheets (17.1), specific energy sources (17.2.3, 17.4.3, 17.5.1, 17.8.3, 17.9.5), Primary Energy (17.11) and Section 38

Coal, gas, crude oil and net electricity output		TJ, tonnes cu m, kWh	No		EC	EC69 (V.3)
Coal production	Production, consumption,	tons	Yes	A	World	IEA12 (-)
Commercial energy	Total and by type	TJ	Yes	A	World	UN21 (3)
Commercial energy (coal equivalent)	Total and by type	tonnes	Yes	A	World	UN21 (1)
Commercial energy (oil equivalent)	Total and by type	tonnes	Yes	A	World	UN21 (2)
Consumption	Type of fuel and sector	tonnes, TJ, gWh	Yes	A	OECD	IEA8&9 (-)
Electricity	Production, source	gWh	Yes	A	World	IEA12 (-)

Subject	Categories	Units	Time series Yes/No	Frequency	Territorial coverage	Source (Table no.)
Electricity, capacity, net maximum	Public utilities, autoproducers, by type of fuel, type of generation	mW	Yes	A	OECD	IEA8&9 (-)
Energy converted, total	By form of energy and method of conversion	TJ	Yes	A	EC, USA, Canada	UN9 (2)
Energy production, consumption and trade	By high, middle, low income	tonnes, kg, %	No		World	CS1 (16)
Exchanges and transfers	By fuel, energy type, by country	tonnes, TJ, toe, gWh	No		EC	EC30 (-)
Fuel, changes in projections	By fuel type	tce	No		OECD	IEA2 (-)
Fuelwood		tonnes of coal equivalent	Yes	A	World	UN50 (125)
Heat		tce	Yes	I	OECD	IEA2 (-)
Heat		TJ	Yes	A	OECD	IEA8&9 (–)
International trade	Imports, exports	gWh	Yes	A	OECD	IEA8&9 (-)
Natural gas	Production, consumption	toe	Yes	A	World	IEA12 (-)
Oil	Production ,consumption, exports	tons	Yes	A	World	IEA12(-)
Production	By country	tonnes, % change, % share	Yes	A	World	BP2 (-)
Production	By fuel type	toe	No		World	EC33 (-)
Production	Coal, oil, gas, total, per capita	toe	No		VICES and Yugoslavia	VICES1 (V/1)
Production	Gross, net, by source	gWh	Yes	A	OECD	IEA8&9 (-)
Production	Other solid fuels	TJ	Yes	A	OECD	IEA8&9(-)
	heat	TJ	Yes	A	OECD	IEA8&9 (-)
Production	Total	toe	Yes	A	OECD	OECD33
Production	Type	tonnes of coal equiv	Yes	A	World	UN50 (11)
Production of selected energy commodities	Imports, exports	tonnes	Yes	A	EC	EC53 (8.1)
Production, growth rates	Total, main sources, type	%	Yes	I	World	UNCTAD1 (6.9)
Recovered products	By fuel, energy type, by country	tonnes, TJ, toe, gWh	No		EC	EC30 (-)
Share of energy sources in primary energy	By production and consumption	%	No		EC	EC53 (8.7)
Supply	Type of fuel and source	tonnes, TJ, gWh	Yes	A	OECD	IEA8&9 (-)
Transformation input	By producer, by fuel, energy type, by country	tonnes, TJ, toe, gWh	No		EC	EC30 (-)
Transformation output	By producer, by fuel, energy type, by country	tonnes, TJ, toe, gWh	No		EC	EC30 (-)
Vegetable fuels		toe	Yes	A	Non-OECD	IEA7
Vegetable fuels		toe	Yes	A	World	IEA12 (-)

17.13 STOCKS AND RESERVES - see also under headings for specific energy sources (17.2.4, 17.5.2, 17.9.6)

Bunkers	Air, sea	tonnes of coal equivalent	Yes	A	World	UN50 (124)
Bunkers	By fuel, energy type, by country	tonnes, TJ, toe, gWh	No		EC	EC30 (-)

17 ENERGY

Subject	Categories	Units	Time series Yes/No Frequency		Territorial coverage	Source (Table no.)
Bunkers	Type	tonnes of coal equiv	Yes	A	World	UN50 (11)
Electric energy, stocks of fuel at thermal power stations	By fuel type	tonnes	Yes	M	EC	EC31 (3)
Marine bunkering	By form of energy	TJ	Yes	A	EC, USA, Canada	UN9 (2)
Reserves	By energy resource	tonnes	No		World	UN21 (38)
Reserves	By fuel type	Physical units	No		EC	EC33 (-)
Reserves	Coal, oil, gas, total, per capita	toe	No		VICES and Yugoslavia	VICES1 (V/1)
Stock change	By fuel, energy type, by country	tonnes, TJ, toe, gWh	No		EC	EC30 (-)
Transfers	By form of energy	TJ	Yes	A	EC, USA, Canada	UN9 (2)

17.14 TAXATION - see also Section 43

Subject	Categories	Units	Time series Yes/No Frequency		Territorial coverage	Source (Table no.)
Change in stocks	By form of energy	TJ	Yes	A	EC, USA, Canada	UN9 (2)
Coal, steam, percentage taxation	In industry	%	Yes	A	OECD	IEA6 (IIC.12)
Diesel, automotive, percentage taxation		%	Yes	A	OECD	IEA6 (IIC.2)
Electricity sales	VAT	% of price before VAT	Yes	A	EC	EC28
Electricity, percentage taxation	In industry and households	%	Yes	A	OECD	IEA6 (IIC.7-C.8)
Fuel oil, heavy, percentage taxation	In industry and households	%	Yes	A	OECD	IEA6 (IIC.5-C.6)
Fuel oil, light, percentage taxation	In industry and households	%	Yes	A	OECD	IEA6 (IIC.3-C.4)
Gas, natural, percentage taxation	In industry, electricity generation and households	%	Yes	A	OECD	IEA6 (IIC.9-C.11)
Gasoline, percentage taxation		%	Yes	A	OECD	IEA6 (IIC.1)
Taxation, incidence	Household sector (as % of price all taxes included), industry sector (as % of price VAT and deductible specific taxes excluded), by energy type	%	Yes	2/yr	EC	EC32 (-)

17.15 TRANSPORT - see also under Prices (17.10) and Sections 37 and 45

Subject	Categories	Units	Time series Yes/No Frequency		Territorial coverage	Source (Table no.)
Carrier fleet, combined	By size, 10,000 dwt and over	dwt	Yes	A	World	OPEC1 (63)
Crude oil and petroleum products	By traffic type	tonne-kms	Yes	A	EC	EC80 (7.3)
Crude oil and petroleum products	By traffic type	tonnes	Yes	A	EC	EC80 (7.2)
Energy consumption	By mode	toe	Yes	I	OECD	OECD33 (10.4)
Energy consumption	Diesel, electricity and coal	tonnes, kWh	Yes	I	ECMT	ECMT2 (2-4-1)
Freight rate index, general	% of worldscale	ind	Yes	A	World	OPEC1 (66)
Freight rates, average spot	% of worldscale	dwt	Yes	A	World	
Liquid gas carrier fleet	By size and type	cu m	No		OPEC	OPEC1 (62)
Liquid gas carrier fleet	By size and type	cu m	No		World	OPEC1 (61)
LNG trade, main international movements by pipeline	By exporter, importer, product	cu m	No		World	BP2 (-)

Subject	Categories	Units	Time series Yes/No Frequency		Territorial coverage	Source (Table no.)
Oil pipeline length		kms	Yes	A	EC	EC80 (7.1)
Pipelines, crude oil	Length, diameter, operator	miles, inches	No		OPEC	OPEC1 (68)
Pipelines, gas	Length, diameter, operator	miles, inches	No		OPEC	OPEC1 (69)
Pipelines, product	Length, diameter, operator	miles, inches	No		OPEC	OPEC1 (70)
Prices, spot (dirty) freight rates	By haul	tonnes, % of WS, US$ per tonne	Yes	A, M	Selected countries	BB2 (23)
Prices, spot (dirty) tanker fixtures and freight rates	By haul and company	nos, tonnes, % of WS, US$ per tonne	No		World	BB2 (20)
Prices, spot freight rates by tanker size	By ASFR, spot(dirty),	tonnes, % of WS, US$ per tonne	Yes	A, M	World	BB2 (22)
Prices, tanker freight rates, spot	By route	%, $/LT	Yes	A	World	OPEC1 (67)
Solid fuels, losses in transport and distribution	By fuel type, by country	tonnes	Yes	A	EC, USA	UN6 (1)
Tanker fleet	By age, 10,000 dwt and over	dwt	Yes	5yr	World	OPEC1 (60)
Tanker fleet	By dwt	dwt, %	Yes	A	World	IP1 (-)
Tanker fleet	Development	dwt	Yes	A	OPEC	OPEC1 (59)
Tanker time charters fixed	By charterer, vessel, period, rate, delivery	dwt, US$	No		World	BB2 (21)
Tanker tonnage	By country, by %	dwt, %	Yes	A	World	IP1 (-)
Tankers	By type of tanker	nos, dwt	Yes	A	World	IP1 (-)
Tonnage, world laid-up tanker and combined carrier tonnage	By size	dwt	Yes	A	World	OPEC1 (64)

18 ENVIRONMENT

18 AGRICULTURE AND THE ENVIRONMENT
- 18.1.1 Air
- 18.1.2 Fertilizers and Pesticides
- 18.1.3 Foodstuffs and Human Health
- 18.1.4 General
- 18.1.5 Irrigation and Drainage
- 18.1.6 Livestock
- 18.1.7 Soil
- 18.1.8 Water

18.2 AIR
- 18.2.1 Concentrations Data
- 18.2.2 Pollutants
- 18.2.3 Quality

18.3 CHEMICALS AND METALS
- 18.3.1 Consumption
- 18.3.2 Production

18.4 ENERGY
- 18.4.1 Consumption
- 18.4.2 Imports
- 18.4.3 Production
- 18.4.4 Requirements

18.5 ENVIRONMENTAL MANAGEMENT
- 18.5.1 Investment
- 18.5.2 Pollution Abatement and Control
- 18.5.3 Protection Expenditures and Facilities

18.6 FAUNA AND FLORA

18.7 FORESTS
- 18.7.1 Damage
- 18.7.2 Forest Cover
- 18.7.3 Ownership
- 18.7.4 Production and Trade in Forest Industry Products
- 18.7.5 Wooded Area

18.8 LAND
- 18.8.1 Conservation
- 18.8.2 Land Area and Use
- 18.8.3 Protected Areas

18.9 NOISE

18.10 RISKS
- 18.10.1 Floods and Related Losses
- 18.10.2 Hazardous Substances

18.11 WASTE
- 18.11.1 Generation of Waste
- 18.11.2 Hazardous and Special Waste
- 18.11.3 Waste Management
- 18.11.4 Municipal Waste
- 18.11.5 Recycling of Waste
- 18.11.6 Solid Waste
- 18.11.7 Treatment and Disposal of Waste

18.12 WATER
- 18.12.1 Quality Indicators
- 18.12.2 Inland Water
- 18.12.3 Resources and Use
- 18.12.4 Waste

18.13 WILDLIFE

18.14 WORK
- 18.14.1 Work Environment Nuisances

Subject	Categories	Units	Time series Yes/No Frequency	Territorial coverage	Source (Table No.)
18.1 AGRICULTURE AND THE ENVIRONMENT					
18.1.1 Air					
Ammonia emissions, theoretical,	Calculated on the basis of head of cattle and NH_3 emission coefficients	tonnes	No	Selected countries	UN22 (4.4.2c)
Animal excreta production	By animal	tonnes	No	Selected countries	UN22 (4.4.1)
Fertilizing elements, amounts of, corresponding to animal excreta		tonnes	No	Selected countries	UN22 (4.4.2b)
Fertilizing matter in excreta, coefficients of content		% of dry matter	No	Selected countries	UN22 (4.4.2a)
Livestock emissions					
Methane into the air		tonnes	No	Selected countries	UN22 (II-4.4.2d)
	N_2O to the air	tonnes	No	Selected countries	UN22 (II-4.4.2e)
18.1.2 Fertilizers and Pesticides					
Fertilizing and plant protection practices on: wheat cultivation	By use of chemicals	ha, nos	No	Selected countries	UN22 (II-3.2.8c)
Fertilizing and plant protection pratices on: fruit trees	By use of chemicals	ha, nos	No	Selected countries	UN22 (II-3.2.8d)
Fertilizing practices, wheat cultivation	By application of fertilizers, by type of fertilizer	kg, ha, tonnes, ha	No	Selected countries	UN22 (II-3.2.7d)
Fruit trees	By application of fertilizers, by type of fertilizer	kg, ha, tonnes, ha	No	Selected countries	UN22 (II-3.2.7e)
Mineral fertilizers consumption per hectare	By type	kg/ha	No	Selected countries	UN22 (II-3.2.7c)
Mineral fertilizers, consumption	By type	tonnes, % change	No	Selected countries	UN22 (II-3.2.7b)
Pest control, use of alternative methods	By pest control measure, treated area, quantity sold, total expenditure	ha, nos	No	Selected countries	UN22 (II-3.2.8e)
Pesticides, consumption of	By type	kg, % change	No	Selected countries	UN22 (II-3.2.8a,b)
18.1.3 Foodstuffs and Human Health					
Heavy metals, residues, in foodstuffs	By plant origin, vegetables and fruit, citrus, eggs, meat, milk	nos, %	No	Selected countries	UN22 (II-4.5.2)
Pesticide residues in foodstuffs	By plant origin, vegetables and fruit, citrus	nos, %	No	Selected countries	UN22 (II-4.5.1)
Radioactivity in foodstuffs	By plant origin, vegetables and fruit, citrus, eggs, meat, milk	nos, %	No	Selected countries	UN22 (II-4.5.3)
18.1.4 General					
Agricultural land , used for greenhouses		ha, % change	No	Selected countries	UN22 (II-3.2.12)
Arable and permanent meadows, net change in area of	By combined land, non-combined land	ha	No	EC	UN22 (II-3.1.2)
Crop rotations, change	By type of crop past 30 years	nos	No	Selected countries	UN22 (II-3.2.10)
Genetic diversity in wheat	By principal variety, % of total area	nos, %	No	Selected countries	UN22 (II-3.2.1d)
Genetic diversity in agriculture	By variety	nos	No	Selected countries	UN22 (II-3.2.1c)
Genetic diversity in agriculture	By number of banks,	nos	No	Selected countries	UN22
Land use	By arable, permanent crops, permanent pasture	ha	No	Selected countries	UN22 (II-3.1.1)
Nitrogen balance in agricultural land	By input, by output	kg N/ha	No	Selected countries	UN22 (II-4.6.2)
Nitrogen cycle, guideline values of, in agricultural land	By input, by output	kg N/ha	No	Selected countries	UN22 (II-4.6.1)

18 ENVIRONMENT

Subject	Categories	Units	Time series Yes/No Frequency	Territorial coverage	Source (Table No.)
Wheat crop	species, cultivars				(II-2.6.1)
18.1.5 Irrigation and Drainage					
Drainage		ha, % change	No	Selected countries	UN22 (II-3.2.6a)
Irrigated area		ha, % change	No	Selected countries	UN22 (II-3.2.6b)
Irrigation techniques	By surface and localised techniques	%	No	Selected countries	UN22 (II-3.2.6d)
Utilization of water for irrigation	By area, quantity used, source, quality	ha, cu m, yr	No	Selected countries	UN22 (II-3.2.6c)
18.1.6 Livestock					
Breeds, number of	By breeds used	nos	No	Selected countries	UN22 (II-3.2.2b)
Cattle and horses		head, % change	No	Selected countries	UN22 (II-3.2.2e)
Endangered and extinct breeds	By domestic animals only	nos	No	Selected countries	UN22 (II-3.2.2c)
Poultry and pigs		head, % change	No	Selected countries	UN22 (II-3.2.2f)
Sheep and goats		head, % change	No	Selected countries	UN22 (II-3.2.2d)
18.1.7 Soil					
Area of holdings and number of	By area, as % of total	ha, %	No	EC	UN22 (II-5.5.1)
Chemical deterioration	By loss of nutrients,and or organic matter, soil pollution, acidification, salinization, alkalinization	ha	No	Selected countries	UN22 (II-4.2.2e)
Natural phosphates	By phosphorus and cadmium content	%, cd/kg, cd/kg p	No	Selected countries	UN22 (II-4.2.2g)
Physical deterioration	By soil compaction, by water logging	ha	No	Selected countries	UN22 (II-4.2.2d)
Physical deterioration	By water erosion, by wind erosion	ha	No	Selected countries	UN22 (II-4.2.2c)
Producers who went over to organic pesticide levels in human milk	Farming methods	mg, kg	Yes Selected years	Various countries	UNCTAD5 (4.44)
Sewage sludge production of and proportion used for agriculture	By production, by disposal	tonnes, %	No	Selected countries	UN22 (II-4.2.2i)
Soil degradation	By type, by degree	sq m	No	Europe, and North America	UN22 (II-4.2.2a,b)
Soil suitability and topography	By suitability for type of	ha	No	Selected countries	UN22 (II-3.1.3)
18.1.8 Water					
Agricultural water pollution through nitrates	By samples, samples with nitrate concentration, national limit	nos, %	No	Selected countries	UN22 (II-4.3.1c)
Agricultural water pollution through pesticides	Pesticides in ground water	nos, %	No	Selected countries	UN22 (II-4.3.1f)
Concentrations and fumigants and their admixtures measured in shallow and deep groundwater	By compound, area, sample, depth, concentration	m, nos, mg	No	Selected countries	UN22 (II-4.3.1n)
Herbicide, concentrations of, (other than triazines) measured in shallow and deep groundwater	By compound, area, sample, depth, concentration	m, nos, mg	No	Selected countries	UN22 (II-4.3.1m)
Insecticides and nematicides, concentrations of, in groundwater	By compound, area, sample, depth, concentration	m, nos, mg	No	Selected countries	UN22 (II-4.3.1i)
Summary data from pesticide monitoring of US and Canada surface waters used for public drinking-water supplies	By raw water, furnished water	nos, mg, %	No	Selected countries	UN22 (II-4.3.1u)

Subject	Categories	Units	Time series Yes/No Frequency		Territorial coverage	Source (Table No.)
Triazine herbicides, concentrations of, and their transformation products in water	By compound, area, sample, concentration	nos, mg	No		Selected countries	UN22 (II-4.3.1l)
Triazine herbicides, residues of, measured in the upper groundwater of treated fields	By compound, area, sample, depth, concentration	m, nos, mg	No		Selected countries	UN22 (II-4.3.1k)
18.2 AIR						
18.2.1 Concentrations Data						
Acid		pH mg/l - sulphur oxide mg/l - nitrogen oxide	Yes	A	Selected areas	OECD33 (2.4)
Climatological data, changes in data	By country	nos, mm, ^{o}C	No		EC	EC35 (-)
Nitrogen dioxide		index (%)	Yes	A	Selected cities	OECD33 (2.3B)
Particulates		index (%)	Yes	A	Selected cities	OECD33 (2.3C)
Sulphur dioxide		index (%)	Yes	A	Selected cities	OECD33 (2.3A)
Sulphur dioxide concentration in air	Large cities	mg per cu	No		Nordic countries	NCM1 (6)
Sulphur oxides and nitogen oxides, emissions	By country	tonnes	No		EC	EC35 (-)
carbon dioxide, emissions	By country	tonnes	No		EC	EC35 (-)
18.2.2 Pollutants						
Acid precipitation, concentration	By country, by acidity of rainwater, sulphates, nitrates	%, mg/l	No		EC	EM1 (1002)
Air pollutants, emissions	By type of pollutant	tonnes	No		OECD	OECD20 (26.1)
Air pollutants, emissions	By country, by pollutant	tonnes	No		EC	EM1 (1001)
Atmospheric emissions, estimated	By type	tonnes	No		Global, North America, EC Canada, Japan	UN22 (I-2.1.1)
Carbon dioxide	By source	tonnes	No		OECD	OECD33 (2.2B)
Carbon dioxide	By source	tonnes	Yes	A	OECD, World	OECD33 (2.2A)
Carbon dioxide emissions from fossil fuels		tonnes, tonnes per capita	Yes	A	World, EC, USA, USSR, Canada, Japan	EC9 (8.2-8.3)
Carbon dioxide, emissions	Total emissions and emissions per capita of: all fossil fuels, natural gas, liquid fuels, solid fuels	tonnes, tonnes, capita	Yes	A	EC, USA, Japan	EC34 (4.1-4.8)
Carbon monoxide	Source (mobile, stationary), total	tonnes	Yes	A	Selected countries	OECD33 (2.1D)
Carbon monoxide, emissions	Mobile sources, stationary sources	tonnes	Yes	A	EC, USA, Japan	EC34 (7.15-7.16)
Carbon monoxide, emissions	Total emissions, emissions per capita	tonnes, kg, capita	Yes	A	EC, USA, Japan	EC34 (7.13-7.14)
CO emissions by source	From stationary, mobile	tonnes	No		Selected countries	UN22 (I-2.1.11)
CO_2 emissions by source	From stationary, mobile	tonnes of CO_2	No		Selected countries	UN22 (I-2.1.12)

18 ENVIRONMENT

Subject	Categories	Units	Time series Yes/No	Frequency	Territorial coverage	Source (Table No.)
Emissions of carbon dioxide	Biotic, industrial in the world by region	tonnes, %	Yes	Selected years	Developing countries	UNCTAD5 (4.43)
Hydrocarbons	Sources (mobile, stationary), total	tonnes	Yes	A	Selected countries	OECD33 (2.1E)
Hydrocarbons, emissions	Mobile sources, stationary sources	tonnes	Yes	A	EC, USA, Japan	EC34 (7.19-7.20)
Hydrocarbons, emissions	Total emissions, emissions per capita	tonnes, kg, capita	Yes	A	EC, USA, Japan	EC34 (7.17-7.18)
Nitrogen oxides	Source (mobile, stationary), total	tonnes	Yes	A	Selected countries North America, OECD, EC,	OECD33 (2.1B)
Nitrogen oxides, emissions	Mobile sources, stationary sources	tonnes	Yes	A	EC, USA, Japan	EC34 (7.7, 7.8)
Nitrogen oxides, emissions	Total emissions, emissions per capita	tonnes, kg, capita	Yes	A	EC, USA, Japan	EC34 (7.5, 7.6)
Nitrous oxide emissions		per capita	Yes	5 yrly	EC, USA,	EC9 (8.4)
Nitrous oxide emissions	By sector	%	No		EC	EC9 (8.5)
NO_2 emissions and depositions		tonnes NO_2, tonnes N, %, gN, sq m	No		Selected countries	UN22 (I-2.1.4)
NO_2 emissions by source	From stationary, mobile	tonnes of NO_2	No		Selected countries	UN22 (I-2.1.8)
Particle emissions	Mobile sources, stationary sources	tonnes	Yes	A	EC, USA, Japan	EC34 (7.11-7.12)
Particle emissions	Total emissions, emissions per capita	tonnes, kg, capita	Yes	A	EC, USA, Japan	EC34 (7.9-7.10)
Particulates	Source (mobile, stationary), total	tonnes	Yes	A	Selected countries	OECD33 (2.1C)
SO_2 and NO_2 emissions	Per capita, unit of GDP and energy consumption	kg, capita, tonnes $ GDP kg, toe	No		Selected countries	UN22 (I-2.1.2)
SO_2 emissions and depositions		tonnes S, %, gS, sq m	No		Selected countries	UN22 (I-2.1.3)
SO_2 emissions by source	From stationary, mobile	tonnes of S	No		Selected countries	UN22 (I-2.1.7)
Sulphur dioxide emissions		per capita	Yes	5 yrly	EC, USA, Canada, Japan	EC9 (8.4)
Sulphur dioxide emissions	By sector	%	No		EC,	EC9 (8.5)
Sulphur oxides	Source (mobile, stationary), total	tonnes	Yes	A	Selected countries North America, OECD, EC,	OECD33 (2.1A)
Sulphur oxides, emissions	Mobile sources, stationary sources	tonnes	Yes	A	EC, USA, Japan	EC34 (7.3, 7.4)
Sulphur oxides, emissions	Total emissions, emissions per capita	tonnes, kg, capita	Yes	A	EC, USA, Japan	EC34 (7.1, 7.2)
Suspended particulates, carbon monoxide and ammonia emissions		tonnes	No		Selected countries	UN22 (I-2.1.5)
TSP emissions by source	From stationary, mobile	tonnes	No		Selected countries	UN22 (I-2.1.10)
VOC emissions by source	From stationary, mobile	tonnes	No		Selected countries	UN22 (I-2.1.9)
Volatile organic compounds, lead and carbon dioxide, emissions		tonnes	No		Selected countries	UN22 (I-2.1.6)
18.2.3 Quality						
Aerosol concentrations	By substance	mg, cu m	No		Selected EMEP stations	UN22 (I-3.2.1) (I-3.2.2)
Air quality at CAPMoN stations		kg, ha	No		CAPMoN stations	UN22 (I-3.2.6)
Depositions of selected substances at EMEP stations		g, sq m	No		EMEP stations	UN22 (I-3.2.7)
Ozone: cumulative production and release into the atmosphere of CFC-11 and CFC-12		tonnes	Yes	5 yrly	Atmosphere	UN22 (I-3.3.3)

Subject	Categories	Units	Time series Yes/No Frequency		Territorial coverage	Source (Table No.)
Ozone: trends in total ozone derived by region based data	By number of stations, season	% per decade	No		North America, EC, Japan	UN22 (I-3.3.1)
Precipitation quality	By substance	pH, mg/l			Selected EMEP stations	UN22 (I-3.2.3)
	By substance	pH, mg/l	No		Selected CAPMoN stations	UN22 (I-3.2.4)
18.3 CHEMICALS AND METALS						
18.3.1 Consumption						
Chlorofluorocarbons	Sales by type, exports, stock change	tonnes	Yes	A	EC	EC34 (6.1)
Lead		tonnes	Yes	A	EC, USA, Japan	EC34 (5.1)
Mercury		tonnes	Yes	A	EC, USA, Japan	EC34 (5.2)
Nitrogen fertilizers applied to arable land	By country	tonnes	No		EC	EC35 (-)
18.3.2 Production						
Chlorofluorocarbons	EC production, world production, EC production as % of world production	tonnes, %	Yes	A	World, EC	EC34 (6.1)
Chlorofluorocarbons, production and consumption	By sales, exports	kg	No		EC	EC35 (-)
18.4 ENERGY - see also Section 17						
18.4.1 Consumption						
Electricity	By sector, total	toe	No		EC	UN22 (I-1.5.6)
Electricity	Total consumption, as proportion of total final energy consumption	toe, %	Yes	A	EC	EC34 (3.27-3.28)
Energy	By final consumer as proportion of total	toe, %	Yes	A	EC	EC34 (3.17-3.26)
Energy, final	By sector, total	toe	No		EC	UN22 (I-1.5.5)
Energy, gross consumption		toe, koe per capita, toe per million $ GDP	No		EC	UN22 (I.1.5.4)
Energy, household consumption	By country, by fuel per capita	kgoe	No		EC	EC72 (9.13)
Fossil fuels inputs, for electricity and steam generation	By type	toe	No		EC	UN22 (I-1.5.3)
18.4.2 Imports						
Electricity	Net imports, net imports as a proportion of total primary energy requirement	toe, %	Yes	A	EC	EC34 (3.15-3.16)
18.4.3 Production						
Electricity generation	Total generation, proportion derived from nuclear energy, proportion derived from fossil fuels, proportion derived from hydro-electric and geothermal sources	toe, %	Yes	A	EC	EC34 (3.29-3.32)
Electricity, production	Total, by type	gWh, %	No		EC	UN22 (I-1.5.2)

18 ENVIRONMENT

Subject	Categories	Units	Time series Yes/No	Frequency	Territorial coverage	Source (Table No.)
Primary energy, production	Total, total, per capita by type	toe, koe	No		EC	UN22 (I-1.5.1)
18.4.4 Requirements						
Primary energy	Primary energy, requirement by type of energy, as proportion of total requirement	toe, %	Yes	A	EC	EC34 (3.3-3.14)
Primary energy	Total requirement, total per capita	toe, toe, capita	Yes	A	EC	EC34 (3.1-3.2)
18.5 ENVIRONMENTAL MANAGEMENT						
18.5.1 Investment						
Investments	Public, private	% of national total	No		Selected countries	OECD33 (13.2A)
R&D for environmental protection, public		US$/%	Yes	A	Selected countries	OECD33 (13.3)
18.5.2 Pollution Abatement and Control						
Environment, dissatisfaction	By quality of water, noise, air pollution, waste disposal, access to open spaces, loss of farmland, damage to landscape	index	No		EC	EC72 (9.7)
Environment, local	Drinking water quality, noise air pollution, rubbish disposal, access to countryside, loss of good farmland, damage to landscape	indices	Yes	I	EC	EC34 (11.1)
Environment, national and world	Freshwater pollution, marine pollution, air pollution, industrial waste disposal, extinction of world species, loss of natural resources, CO_2 emissions	indices	Yes	I	EC	EC34 (11.2)
Environment, public opinion	Very concerned about national environmental problems, type of problem	%	No		Selected countries	OECD3 (13.1C)
Environment, public opinion	Very concerned about international environmental problems, type of problem	%	No		Selected countries	OECD33 (13.1D)
Environment, public opinion	Very concerned about local environment problems	%	No		Selected countries	OECD33 (13.1B)
Environment, public perception	By quality of water, noise, air pollution, waste disposal, access to open spaces, loss of farmland, damage to landscape	%	No		EC	EC72 (9.6)
Environmentally significant industries	Selected industries	indices	Yes	A	Selected countries	OECD33 (11.2B)
Expenditure		% of GDP	No		Selected countries	OECD33 (13.2A)
Pollution control	Public, private	indices	Yes	A	Selected countries	OECD33 (13.2B)

Subject	Categories	Units	Time series Yes/No Frequency	Territorial coverage	Source (Table No.)
18.5.3 Protection Expenditures and Facilities					
Expenditure on protective activities, total	By central, state and local government, manufacturing industries, other	nat curr	No	Selected countries	UN22 (I-4.1.5)
Expenditure on technical operations at constant prices, current	By cleaning of exhaust gases, waste water treatment, waste collection, transport, treatment and disposal	nat curr	No	Selected countries	UN22 (I-4.1.2)
Expenditure on technical operations: gross fixed capital formation	By cleaning of exhaust gases, waste water treatment, waste collection, transport, treatment and disposal	nat curr	No	Selected countries	UN22 (I-4.1.1)
Monitoring, facilities for	By number of measurement sites, number of measurements	nos	No	Selected countries	UN22 (I-4.2.4)
Protection of ambient air	Collection, transport, treatment and disposal of waste, nature and landscape, protection noise abatement other protective activities	nat curr	No	Selected countries	UN22 (I-4.1.3)
Protection of ambient air	Collection, transport. treatment and disposal of waste, nature and landscape, protection noise abatement and other protective activities	nat curr	No	Selected countries	UN22 (I-4.1.4)
Waste treatment, installation	Hazardous, non-hazardous by type	nos	No	Selected countries	UN22 (I-4.2.1)
Waste water treatment plants	By mechanical, biological, advanced treatment, households connected	nos, %	No	Selected countries	UN22 (I-4.2.2)
Wastes, disposal of, number of installations	By hazardous, other than hazardous	nos	No	Selected countries	UN22 (I-4.2.3)
18.6 FAUNA AND FLORA					
Areas, protected		nos, ha	No	EC	UN22 (I-1.4.19)
Birds of the EC	Share of world population and global status	nos, %	No	EC	UN22 (I-1.4.5)
Birds, breeding populations	Selected birds share of EC and world population	pairs, %	No	EC, World	UN22 (I-1.4.3)
Corncrake, nesting pairs	Number and percent	nos, %	No	EC	UN22 (I-1.4.8)
Fish catch, nominal	Total and % of inland fishing	tonnes, %	No	EC	UN22 (I-1.4.18)
Green turtle, nesting population		nos	No	EC	UN22 (I-1.4.10)
Green turtle, nominal catch		tonnes	Yes A	Selected countries	UN22 (I-1.4.11)
Hunting of selected species	By numbers killed	nos	No	Selected countries	UN22 (I-1.4.17)
Orchids, distribution of	In climatic regions	nos	No	EC	UN22 (I-1.4.15)
Population of selected hunted species	By type	nos	No	Selected countries	UN22 (I-1.4.16)
Sea otter populations	Size and status	nos	No	Selected countries	UN22 (I-1.4.7)
Species, endangered and vulnerable	By group	nos	No	Selected countries	UN22 (I-1.4.2)
Species, number of	By group	nos	No	Selected countries	UN22 (I-1.4.1)
Species, threatened, number of	By species group in the EC Red List	nos	No	EC	UN22 (I-1.4.4)

Subject	Categories	Units	Time series Yes/No Frequency	Territorial coverage	Source (Table No.)
Wetlands of international importance		nos, ha	No	EC	UN22 (I-1.4.20)
Wolf	Number, % of former range, population and legal status	nos, %	No	EC and North America	UN22 (I-1.4.6)
18.7 FORESTS - see also Section 21					
18.7.1 Damage					
Area burned		hectares	Yes A	Selected countries	OECD33 (5.7)
Area surveyed and samples		ha, nos	No	Selected countries	UN22 (I-3.4.2)
Biomass, above-ground	Growing stock, net annual increment, fellings and harvesting intensity	cu m, %	No	Selected countries	UN22 (I-3.4.1)
Defoliation	By species	%	No	Selected countries	UN22 (I-3.4.4)
Depletion	Harvest, losses, total	cu m	No	Selected countries	OECD33 (5.2B)
Fires on forest and other wooded land	By number, area and size	nos, ha	Yes A	Selected countries	UN22 (I-3.4.5)
Forest damage survey results	By all age classes, conifers and broadleaves	%	Yes A	Selected countries	UN22 (I-3.4.3)
Losses		US$	Yes A	Selected countries	OECD33 (5.7)
18.7.2 Forest Cover					
Forest	Type of wood	sq km, %	No	OECD	OECD33 (5.1B)
Volume of standing wood		cu m	No	OECD, World	OECD33 (5.2A)
18.7.3 Ownership					
Private	Farms and other, industry, total	% of area covered	No	OECD, World	OECD33 (5.6)
Public	National, other, total	% of area covered	No	OECD, World	OECD33 (5.6)
18.7.4 Production and Trade in Forest Industry Products - see also Sections 21 and 27					
Exports	Total, per capita	US$	No	OECD, World	OECD33 (5.4A)
Exports, imports balance	Total, per capita	US$	No	OECD, World	OECD33 (5.4A)
Forestry, growth		cu m	No	Selected countries	OECD33 (5.2B)
Forestry, intensity of use, growth ratio	Harvested	ratio	No	Selected countries	OECD33 (5.2B)
Forestry, total	By source, per capita, % of total imports	US$ %	No	OECD	OECD33 (5.5)
Fuelwood and charcoal, production		cu m	No	OECD, World	OECD33 (5.2A)
Imports	Total, per capita	US$	No	OECD,World	OECD33 (5.4A)
Industrial roundwood		cu m, % world	No	OECD, World	OECD33 (5.3)
Industrial roundwood	Product category		No	OECD, World	OECD33 (5.4B)
	Import, export		No	World	OECD33 (5.4C)
Paper and paperboard		cu m, % world	No	OECD, World	OECD33 (5.3)
Roundwood production		cu m	No	OECD, World	OECD33 (5.2A)
Sawnwood and sleepers		cu m, % world	No	OECD, World	OECD33 (5.3)

Subject	Categories	Units	Time series Yes/No Frequency		Territorial coverage	Source (Table No.)
Tropical hardwoods, trade	Net imports, by quantity, by value	tonnes, ecu	Yes	A	EC	EC34 (10.1-10.2)
Wood based panels		cu m, % world	No		OECD, World	OECD33 (5.3)
Wood pulp		cu m, % world	No		OECD, World	OECD33 (5.3)
18.7.5 Wooded Area						
Forest and other wooded land,	By major recognized	%	No		Selected countries	UN22 (I-1.2.3)
Forest land	By type, % of total land	sq m, %	No		Selected countries	UN22 (I-1.2.2)
Open lands	By type	sq m	No		Selected countries	UN22 (I-1.2.4)
Wooded area	Per 1000 capita, % of land area	sq km	No, %		OECD, World	OECD33 (5.1A)
18.8 LAND						
18.8.1 Conservation						
Conservation and protection	Parks, reserves, other	nos, hectares	Yes	A	Nordic countries	NCM1(70)
Internationally designated sites	By country, by area	sq km, nos	No		EC	EC35 (-)
18.8.2 Land Area and Use - see also Section 29						
Arable and crop land		indices	Yes	5 yrly	OECD	OECD33 (4.1B)
Arable and permanent cropland		sq km, %	No		OECD	OECD33 (4.1A)
Arable land	Total arable land, area as proportion of total land area	sq m, %	Yes	A	EC	EC34 (2.5-2.6)
Balance sheet	Land area, arable land, livestock, fuelwood, water resources, greenhouse index, deforestation	ha, %, cu m, nos, capita, cu m, capita, tonnes, capita	No		Developing countries	UN25(22)
Built-up area	As per cent of total land and as surface per inhabitant	%, sq m per 1000 inhabitants	No		Selected countries	UN22 (I-1.2.5)
Change of land use	By type of land	%	No		Selected countries	UN22 (I-1.2.6)
Forest and other wooded land		sq km, %	No		OECD	OECD33 (4.1A)
Forest and other wooded land	By country, total	indices	Yes	5 yrly	OECD, World	OECD33 (4.1B)
Land area, other areas		sq km, %	No		OECD	OECD33 (4.1A)
Land area, total		sq km, %	No		World	OECD33 (4.1A)
Land area, total		sq m	Yes	A	EC	EC34 (2.4)
Land use, current estimates	By broad category functions	sq m	No		Selected countries	UN22 (I-1.2.1)
National Parks: number of sites		nos	No		OECD	OECD33 (4.3C)
National parks: per cent of territory		%	No		OECD	OECD33 (4.3C)
National parks: protected area		per capita	No		OECD	OECD33 (4.3C)
National parks: total size		sq km	No		OECD	OECD33 (4.3C)
National parks: world, total		nos, sq km, %, per capita	No		World	OECD33 (4.3C)
Perennial crops	Total perennial crops, area as proportion of total land area	sq m, %	Yes	A	EC	EC34 (2.9-2.10)

18 ENVIRONMENT

Subject	Categories	Units	Time series Yes/No Frequency		Territorial coverage	Source (Table No.)
Permanent grassland		indices	Yes	5 yrly	OECD	OECD33 (4.1B)
Permanent grassland		sq km, %	No		OECD	OECD33 (4.1A)
Permanent grassland	Total permanent, grassland, area as proportion of total land area	sq m, %	Yes	A	EC	EC34 (2.7-2.8)
Wetlands, state and changes	Losses	sq km, %	No		Selected countries	OECD33 (4.2)
Woodland	Total woodland, area as proportion of total land area	sq m, %	Yes	A	EC	EC34 (2.11-2.12)
18.8.3 Protected Areas						
Biosphere reserves	Sites, area	nos, sq km	No		Selected countries	OECD33 (6.3)
Landscapes, protected areas, total		no of sites	No		OECD, World	OECD33 (6.4)
National monuments		no of sites	No		OECD, World	OECD33 (6.4)
National parks		no of sites	No		OECD, World	OECD33 (6.4)
Nature reserves		no of sites	No		OECD, World	OECD33 (6.4)
Protected areas		per capita	No		OECD	OECD33 (4.3A)
Protected areas	By country	sq km	No		EC	EM1 (1006)
Protected areas, major		no of sites	No		OECD, World	OECD33 (6.4)
Protected areas, total		no of sites	No		OECD, World	OECD33 (6.4)
Sites	Per cent territory	%	No		OECD	OECD33 (4.3A)
Sites, changes		nos, sq km	No		OECD	OECD33 (4.3B)
Sites, number		nos	No		OECD	OECD33 (4.3A)
Sites, world, total		nos, sq km	No		World	OECD33 (4.3B)
Sites, world, total		nos, sq km	No		World	OECD33 (4.3A)
Size, total		sq km	No		OECD	OECD33 (4.3A)
Wetlands of international importance	Sites, area	sq km	No		Selected countries	OECD33 (6.5)
18.9 NOISE						
Population exposure to transport noise	By source	%	No		OECD	OECD20 (27.1)
18.10 RISKS						
18.10.1 Floods and Related Losses						
Damage, extent of		nos	Yes	I	OECD	OECD33 (8.1C)
Damage, extent of	Deaths, monetary, type	nos, US$	Yes	I	OECD	OECD33 (8.1A)
Damage, extent of	Human deaths, injured, homeless	nos US$	Yes	I	OECD	OECD33 (8.1B)

Subject	Categories	Units	Time series Yes/No Frequency		Territorial coverage	Source (Table No.)
Disasters, major	Type		Yes	I	OECD	OECD33 (8.1C)
Houses damaged, destroyed	Type	nos	Yes	I	OECD	OECD33 (8.1B)
Natural disasters, major, geological	Type		Yes	I	OECD	OECD33 (8.1B)
Oil spills from tankers, accidental	Deaths, insured name of ship flag country affected quantity spilled	US$, tonnes	Yes	I	World	OECD33 (8.2)
18.10.2 Hazardous Substances						
Deaths		nos	Yes	I	World	OECD33 (8.3)
Evacuated		nos	Yes	I	World	OECD33 (8.3)
Injured		nos	Yes	I	World	OECD33 (8.3)
Origin of accident			Yes	I	World	OECD33 (8.3)
Products involved			Yes	I	World	OECD33 (8.3)
18.11 WASTE						
18.11.1 Generation of Waste						
Generation of waste	By activity	tonnes	No		Selected EC countries	UN22 (I-2.3.2)
Generation of waste	By household and similar	tonnes	No		Selected countries	UN22 (I-2.3.3)
Generation of waste	By material	tonnes	No		Selected EC countries	UN22 (I-2.3.1)
18.11.2 Hazardous and Special Waste						
Dumping at sea		tonnes, /%	No		Selected countries	OECD33 (7.3C)
Imports, exports		tonnes, %	No		Selected countries	OECD33 (7.3C)
Incineration at sea		tonnes, %	No		Selected countries	OECD33 (7.3C)
Production and movement of		tonnes, %	No		Selected countries	OECD33 (7.3C)
Radioactive waste and stocks of hazardous wastes	Exports, imports	tonnes	No		Selected countries	UN22 (I-2.3.6)
Treatment and disposal of hazardous wastes		tonnes	No		Selected countries	UN22 (I-2.3.7)
18.11.3 Waste Management						
Natural resources balance sheet	Water resources and treatment, nuclear fuel inventories, hazardous waste generation, emission of air pollutants, greenhouse index	ha, per ha cu m/yr, kg/ha, %, kg, nos, tonnes, capita, tonnes, sq m	No		Industrial countries	UN25(43)
Quantity of waste produced	By country, by source	tonnes	No		EC	EC35 (-)
18.11.4 Municipal Waste						
Municipal waste	% increase	tons, %	Yes	5 yrly	Selected countries	OECD33 (7.2A)
Municipal waste, amounts	Amounts, amounts per capita, % increase	tonnes, kg, capita, %	Yes	I	EC, USA, Japan	EC34 (9.2)

18 ENVIRONMENT

Subject	Categories	Units	Time series Yes/No Frequency		Territorial coverage	Source (Table No.)
Municipal waste, composition	Paper and cardboard, plastics, glass metals, others	%	Yes	5yrly	EC, USA, Japan	EC34 (9.3)
Municipal waste, disposal	Mechanical sorting, composting, incineration, landfill, other	%	No		EC, USA, Japan	EC34 (9.4)
Population served by municipal waste services	(% energy)	%	Yes	5 yrly	Selected countries	OECD33 (7.2C)
Urban waste	By country	kg	No		EC	EC35 (-)
Waste generated	By country, by municipal waste, industrial waste	tonnes, kg	No		EC	EM1 (1003)
Waste generated	By source	tonnes	No		EC, USA, Japan	EC34 (9.1)
Waste indicators	Municipal waste	tonnes kg, capita	Yes	5 yrly	EC, USA, USSR, Canada, Japan	EC9 (8.6)
18.11.5 Recycling of Waste						
Recycling	Paper, board, glass	%	No		EC, USA, USSR, Canada, Japan	EC9 (8.6)
Recycling activities, recovery rates	Paper and cardboard, glass	%	Yes	5 yrly	Selected countries	OECD33 (7.5)
Recycling and re-use of materials	By type	tonnes	No		Selected EC countries	UN22 (I-2.3.4)
Recycling of packaging waste	By country, by type of packaging	%	No		EC	EM1 (1004)
Waste recycling activities	Recovery rates for paper and cardboard, glass	%	Yes	5yrly	EC , USA, Japan	EC34 (9.5)
18.11.6 Solid Waste						
Amounts of solid waste	% increase	kg per capita	Yes	5 yrly	Selected countries	OECD33 (7.2A)
Amounts of solid waste	By type	tonnes	No		Selected countries	OECD33 (7.3A-7.3B)
Composition of solid waste	By type	%	Yes	5 yrly	Selected countries	OECD33 (7.2B)
Disposal of solid waste	By method incineration	tonnes	No		Selected countries	OECD33 (7.4)
Waste generated	By source	tonnes	No		Selected countris	OECD33 (7.1)
18.11.7 Treatment and Disposal of Waste						
Treatment and disposal	By type	tonnes	No		Selected EC countries	UN22 (I-2.3.5)
18.12 WATER						
18.12.1 Quality Indicators						
Ammonium		mgN/litre	Yes	5 yrly	Selected rivers, countries	OECD33 (3.3C)
Biological oxygen demand		mg/litres	Yes	5 yrly	Selected rivers, countries	OECD33 (3.3A)
Cadmium		μg/litre	Yes	5 yrly	Selected rivers, countries	OECD33 (3.3D)
Chromium		μg/litre	Yes	5 yrly	Selected rivers, countries	OECD33 (3.3E)
Copper		μg/litre	Yes	5 yrly	Selected rivers, countries	OECD33 (3.3E)
Dissolved oxygen		mg/litres	Yes	5 yrly	Selected rivers, countries	OECD33 (3.3A)
Lead		μg/litre	Yes	5 yrly	Selected rivers, countries	OECD33 (3.3D)

Subject	Categories	Units	Time series Yes/No	Frequency	Territorial coverage	Source (Table No.)
Nitrate		mgN/litre	Yes	5 yrly	Selected rivers, countries	OECD33 (3.3B)
Nitrogen	Water quality of lakes, annual mean concentration	mgN/litre	Yes	5 yrly	Selected lakes, countries	OECD33 (3.4)
Phosphorous		mgP/litre	Yes	5 yrly	Selected rivers, countries	OECD33 (3.3B)
Phosphorous	Water quality of lakes, annual mean concentration	mgP/litre	Yes	5 yrly	Selected lakes, countries	OECD33 (3.4)
Quality of bathing water	By country	nos	No		EC	EC35 (-)
Water quality indicators	By chemical indicators, for selected rivers and lakes	mg/l, μg/l	Yes	I	EC, USA,Japan	EC34 (8.4-8.5)
Water quality indicators	By country, by river, dissolved oxygen, biological oxygen demand	mg/l	No		EC	EC72 (9.23)
Water quality indicators	By selected river, by country, indicator	%, mg/l	No		EC	EC35 (-)
Water quality indicators	Water supply, population served by sewage treatment plant	cu m, %	No		EC, USA, Canada, Japan	EC9 (8.1)
18.12.2 Inland Water						
Ground water withdrawal		cu m, %	Yes	5yrly	EC, USA, Japan	EC34 (8.2)
Renewable resources and total water abstraction	By country	cu m, %	No		EC	EC35 (-)
Surface water withdrawal		cu m, %	Yes	5yrly	EC, USA, Japan	EC34 (8.2)
Water resources	Development and expenditure, by country	nos, ha, US$, km, cu m	Yes	A	ESCAP countries	UN44
Water withdrawal	Surface, ground, total	cu m	Yes	5 yrly	Selected countries	OECD33 (3.1A)
Water withdrawal	% of annual availability	%, cu m per capita	Yes	5 yrly	OECD	OECD33 (3.1B)
Water withdrawal	Total withdrawal, withdrawal per capita	cu m, cu m, capita	Yes	5yrly	EC, USA, Japan	EC34 (8.1)
Water withdrawal	By major users	cu m, %	No		Selected countries	OECD33 (3.1C)
18.12.3 Resources and Use						
Agricultural and industrial use of water		cu m	No		Selected countries	UN22 (I-1.3.7)
Water abstraction	By source	cu m	No		Selected countries	UN22 (I-1.3.2)
	by activity	cu m	No		Selected countries	UN22 (I-1.3.3)
Water resources		cu m	No		Selected countries	UN22 (I-1.3.1)
Water supply	By activity	cu m	No		Selected countries	UN22 (I-1.3.5)
Water supply, total	By type	cu m	No		Selected countries	UN22 (I-1.3.4)
Water use, industrial	By sector	cu m	No		Selected countries	UN22 (I-1.3.6)
18.12.4 Waste						
Discharge, without and after treatment	By type, total	cu m	No		Selected countries	UN22 (I-2.2.3)
Discharges, of polluting substances	By type of pollutant	tonnes	No		Selected countries	UN22 (I-2.2.4)
Industrial treatment plants	By generation, use, disposal	cu m	No		Selected countries	UN22 (I-2.2.6)
Oxidisable matter discharged into inland waters	Total, per capita, per unit of GDP	tonnes kg, inhabitant tonnes, US$	No		Selected countries	OECD33 (3.2B)
Population served by sewage treatment plants	By country	%	No		EC	EC35 (-)
Population served by waste water treatment plants	By country	%	No		EC	EM1 (1005)
Population served by waste water treatment plants	Degree of treatment	% population	Yes	5 yrly	Selected countries	OECD33 (3.2A)

18 ENVIRONMENT

Subject	Categories	Units	Time series Yes/No Frequency	Territorial coverage	Source (Table No.)
Public sewerage, collection and generation in type of industry		cu m	No	Selected countries	UN22 (I-2.2.1)
Public treatment plants	By generation, use, disposal	cu m	No	Selected countries	UN22 (I-2.2.5)
Public wastewater treatment works	Serving 200 persons, type, total	nos	No	Nordic countries	NCM1(86)
Sludge, treatment, total volume	By type, total, BOD influents and effluents	cu m	No	Selected countries	UN22 (I-2.2.2)
Waste water treatment plants	Total population served, population served by primary only, primary and secondary and/or tertiary	%	Yes I	EC, USA, Japan	EC34 (8.3)
18.13 WILDLIFE					
Algae	Species known	nos	No	OECD	OECD33 (6.1C)
Amphibians	Species known, threatened decreasing	nos, %	No	OECD	OECD33 (6.1B)
Biosphere reserves	Sites, area	nos, sq km	No	Selected countries	OECD33 (6.3)
Birds	Species known, threatened, decreasing	nos, %	No	OECD	OECD33 (6.1A)
Extinction of certain plant species, factors responsible	By factor	nos	No	Germany	EC35 (-)
Fish	Species known, threatened, decreasing	nos, %	No	OECD	OECD33 (6.1A)
Fish production	Food, industrial quantity, value	tonnes US$	No	OECD	OECD33 (6.2)
Fungi	Species known	nos	No	OECD	OECD33 (6.1C) (6.5)
Invertebrates	Species known, threatened, decreasing	nos, %	No	OECD	OECD33 (6.1B)
Landscapes, protected areas, total		no of sites	No	OECD, World	OECD33 (6.4)
Lichens	Species known	nos	No	OECD	OECD33 (6.1C)
Mosses	Species known	nos	No	OECD	OECD33 (6.1C)
National parks		no of sites	No	OECD, World	OECD33 (6.4)
National monuments		no of sites	No	OECD, World	OECD33 (6.4)
Nature reserves		no of sites	No	OECD, World	OECD33 (6.4)
Protected areas, major	Scientific	no of sites	No	OECD, World	OECD33 (6.4)
Reptiles	Species known, threatened, decreasing	nos, %	No	OECD	OECD33 (6.1B)
Species reported as being under threat during the 1980s	By country	%	No	EC	EC35 (-)
State of mammals	Species known, threatened, decreasing	nos, %	No	OECD	OECD33 (6.1A)

Subject	Categories	Units	Time series Yes/No Frequency	Territorial coverage	Source (Table No.)
Vascular plants	Species known, threatened, decreasing	nos, %	No	OECD	OECD33 (6.1C)
Wetlands of international importance	Sites, area	sq km	No	Selected countries	OECD33
18.14 WORK					
18.14.1 Work Environment Nuisances					
Persons employed reporting exposure to specific nuisances in their work environment	By selected characteristics	%	No	OECD	OECD20 (16.1)

19 FINANCE

19.1 FINANCIAL SYSTEM - STRUCTURE

19.2 FINANCIAL MARKETS
- 19.2.1 Assets and Liabilities
- 19.2.2 Banking Industry
- 19.2.3 Capital Market
- 19.2.4 Corporate Finance
- 19.2.5 Credit
- 19.2.6 Deposits and Savings
- 19.2.7 Exchange Rates
- 19.2.8 Insurance
- 19.2.9 Interest Rates
- 19.2.10 International Finance
- 19.2.11 Money Supply
- 19.2.12 Personal Finance
- 19.2.13 Stock Exchange

19.3 INVESTMENT
- 9.3.1 Domestic Investment
- 19.3.2 Foreign Investment

19.4 PUBLIC FINANCE
- 19.4.1 Central Government
- 19.4.2 Local Government

Subject	Categories	Units	Time series Yes/No Frequency		Territorial coverage	Source (Table No.)
19.1 FINANCIAL SYSTEM - STRUCTURE						
Capital operations and financial transactions, other sectors	Receipts, expenditure, lending, borrowing by type by sector	nat curr	Yes	A	OECD	OECD36 (33F)
Capital operations and financial transactions of financial institutions	Assets, liabilities, by type and sector	nat curr	Yes	A	OECD	OECD36 (31F)
Capital operations and financial transactions of the central bank	By type and sector	nat curr	Yes	A	OECD	OECD36 (311F)
Capital operations and financial transactions of other monetary institutions	By type and sector	nat curr	Yes	A	OECD	OECD36 (312F)
Capital operations and financial transactions of insurance companies and pension funds	By type and sector	nat curr	Yes	A	OECD	OECD36 (313F)
Capital operations and financial transactions of other financial institutions	By type and sector	nat curr	Yes	A	OECD	OECD36 (314F)
Capital operations and financial transactions with the rest of the world	Receipts, expenditure, lending,borrowing by type by sector	nat curr	Yes	A	OECD	OECD36 (34F)
Financial flows, summary - structure of, supply of, and demand for, funds	By debtor, creditor, sector by financial instrument	nat curr	Yes	A	OECD	OECD36 (21F)
Financial flows, state and local government	Receipts, expenditure, lending, borrowing by type	nat curr	Yes	A	OECD	OECD36 (322F)
Financial flows, central government	Receipts, expenditure, lending, borrowing by type	nat curr	Yes	A	OECD	OECD36 (321F)
Oustanding financial assets and liabilities of insurance companies and pension funds	By type and sector	nat curr	Yes	A	OECD	OECD36 (313B)
Outstanding external financial assets, rest of the world	By type and liabilities	nat curr	Yes	A	OECD	OECD36 (34B)
Outstanding financial assets and liabilities of financial institutions	By type and sector	nat curr	Yes	A	OECD	OECD36 (31B)
Outstanding financial assets and liabilities of the central bank	By type and sector	nat curr	Yes	A	OECD	OECD36 (311B)
Outstanding financial assets and liabilities of other monetary institutions	By type and sector	nat curr	Yes	A	OECD	OECD36 (312B)
Outstanding financial assets and liabilities, other sectors	By type	nat curr	Yes	A	OECD	OECD36 (33B)
Outstanding financial assets and liabilities of central government	By type	nat curr	Yes	A	OECD	OECD36 (321B)
Outstanding financial assets and liabilities	By type	nat curr	Yes	A	OECD	OECD36 (322B)
Outstanding financial assets and liabilities of other financial institutions	By type and sector	nat curr	Yes	A	OECD	OECD36 (314B)
Saving, investment and financial transactions, structure of	Sector by type of transaction	nat curr	Yes	Selected years	OECD	OECD36 (1F)
19.2 FINANCIAL MARKETS						
19.2.1 Assets and Liabilities						
Assets, liabilities and net position	EC position (compared to rest of the world)	%	Yes	A	EC	EC59 (I.6)
Assets and liabilities of the monetary authority and the chartered banks	By country, by category	US$	No		GCC region	CH1 (9.1)

19 FINANCE

Subject	Categories	Units	Time series Yes/No	Frequency	Territorial coverage	Source (Table No.)
Balance sheet, assets and liabilities	Non-financial assets, short-term financial assets, long-term financial assets, other assets, equity, accumulated depreciation reserves, short-term liabilities, long-term liabilities, other liabilities, by country	nat curr	Yes	A	OECD	OECD37
Balance sheet, integrated	By credit institution	ECU	Yes	Q	EC	EC5 (III.1)
Bank reserves	By country	nat curr	No		EC	EM1 (0402)
Corporate and quasi-corporate enterprises, non-financial	Change in financial assets, liabilities, loans and shares	ECU, %	Yes	A	EC	EC59 (I.1.4)
Credit institutions	Assets, liabilities and net position	ECU	Yes	A	EC	EC59 (III.7.3)
Credit institutions	Change in financial assets, loans, bonds and liabilities	ECU, %	Yes	A	EC	EC59 (I.1.6)
Credit institutions: main financial transactions	By type change in assets and liabilities	nat curr	Yes	A	EC	EC62 (6.3)
External position	VICES assets held in western banks, liabilities vis a vis western banks, net position	US$	Yes	I	VICES countries and Yugoslavia	VICES1 (III/6)
Financial assets and liabilities net change	By sector	ECU	Yes	A	EC	EC62 (0.1)
Financial assets and liabilities	By sector	nat curr	No		EC	EC62 (3)
Financial intermediaries	By type change in assets and liabilities	nat curr	Yes	A	EC	EC62 (6.1)
Fixed assets	Acquisitions, all industries, manufacturing industries	Norwegian kroner	Yes	A,Q	Norway	OECD22
Foreign assets	By country	US$	No		EC	EM1 (0403)
Foreign assets	Total excl. gold, end of period, gross	ECU	Yes	A, M	EC, USA, Japan	EC36
Foreign liabilities	By country	US$	No		EC	EM1 (0404)
Households and private non-profit institutions	Change in financial assets, loans, securities and liabilities	ECU, %	Yes	A	EC	EC59 (I.1.3)
Insurance enterprises	Change in financial assets, loans and liabilities	ECU, %	Yes	A	EC	EC59 (I.1.7)
Liabilities, maturity distribution	Amounts outstanding vis a vis western banks	US$	No		VICES countries and Yugoslavia	VICES1 (III/6)
Liabilities, external	Excluding international organizations, monetary authorities	£	Yes	A, M	United Kingdom	OECD22
Liabilities to foreigners		US$	Yes	A, M	USA	OECD22
National economy	Assets, liabilities and net position	ECU	Yes	A	EC	EC59 (III.7.1)
National economy	Change in financial assets, loans and liabilities	ECU, %	Yes	A	EC	EC59 (I.1.2)
Non-financial corporate and quasi-corporate enterprises: main financial transactions	By type change in assets and liabilities	nat curr	Yes	A	EC	EC62 (6.5)
Non-financial resident units	By type change in assets and liabilities	nat curr	Yes	A	EC	EC62 (6.2)
Private lending	By country	nat curr	No		EC	EM1 (0405)

Subject	Categories	Units	Time series Yes/No Frequency		Territorial coverage	Source (Table No.)
Private non-banking sector	Assets, liabilities and net position	ECU	Yes	A	EC	EC59 (III.7.4)
World, rest of: main financial transactions	By type change in assets and liabilities	nat curr	Yes	A	EC	EC62 (6.6)
19.2.2 Banking Industry						
Balance sheet, assets	By type of bank, by category	nat curr	Yes	A	OECD	OECD2 (-)
Income statement	By type of bank, by category	nat curr	Yes	A	OECD	OECD2 (-)
Income statement	By type of bank, by category	%	Yes	A	OECD	OECD2 (-)
Liabilities	By type of bank, by category	nat curr	Yes	A	OECD	OECD2 (-)
Memoranda	By type of bank, by category	nat curr	Yes	A	OECD	OECD2 (-)
Number of branches		nos	Yes	A	OECD	OECD2 (-)
Number of employees		nos	Yes	A	OECD	OECD2 (-)
Number of institutions		nos	Yes	A	OECD	OECD2 (-)
19.2.3 Capital Market						
Financial market rates	Share price index yields on shares, yields on securities		Yes	A	EC, USA, USSR, Canada, Japan	EC9 (2.33)
Industrial shares, market prices		indices	Yes	A, M	World	UN35 (57)
Industrial shares, market prices		indices	Yes	A	World	UN50 (33)
Market prices of industrial shares		indices	Yes	A, M	World	UN35 (57)
Money market instruments, issue on domestic market		nat curr	Yes	Q	OECD	OECD35 (D4/01-D4/22)
Money market rates			No		EC, USA, USSR, Canada, Japan	EC9 (2.28)
Oil company earnings and share prices	By company, closing prices	US$	Yes	A, M, W	World	BB2 (25.1-25.2)
Securities: net issues	By sector	ECU	Yes	A	EC	EC62 (0.1)
Securities: net purchases	By sector	ECU	Yes	A	EC	EC62 (0.1)
Security issues	Shares, bonds and debt certificates	nat curr	Yes	A, Q	OECD	OECD35 (D1/01-D1/22)
Share issues, new		Swedish kroner	Yes	A, M	Sweden	OECD22
Share price		index	Yes	A	EC	EC9 (2.34)
Share price index	At constant prices and in ECU	ECU, indices	Yes	A, Q, M	EC	EC59 (III.5)
Share prices		indices	Yes	A, Q, M	OECD	OECD22 (-)
Share prices	Industrials, all shares	indices	Yes	A, M	OECD	OECD22
Share prices share	By type	indices	Yes	A, M	Nordic countries	NCM1 (185)
Stock exchange capitalisation	For all shares, bonds and securities	nat curr, US$	No		OECD	OECD35 (D.3)
19.2.4 Corporate Finance						
Bond issues, net, new	Corporations	nat curr	Yes	A, M	OECD	OECD22
Capital expenditures	For major oil companies	US$	Yes	A	World	IEA1 (A16)
Capital issues, net, new		nat curr	Yes	A, Q	OECD	OECD22
Capital issues, net, new	Corporations	nat curr	Yes	A, M	OECD	OECD22
Cash flow	For major oil companies	US$	Yes	A	World	IEA1 (A16)
Corporate profits, after tax		US$	Yes	A, M	OECD	OECD22
Debt to capital ratio	For major oil companies	US$	Yes	A	World	IEA1 (A16)
Earnings	By company section for major oil companies	US$	Yes	A	World	IEA1 (A15)
Insurance enterprises	By transaction	nat curr	Yes	A	EC	EC62 (4.7)

Subject	Categories	Units	Time series Yes/No	Frequency	Territorial coverage	Source (Table No.)
Long-term debt	For major oil companies	US$	Yes	A, M	World	IEA1 (A16) (-)
Net income	For major oil companies	US$	Yes	A	World	IEA1 (A15)
Non-financial corporate and quasi-corporate enterprises and households	By transaction	nat curr	Yes	A	EC	EC62 (4.1)
Non-financial corporate and quasi-corporate enterprises	By transaction	nat curr	Yes	A	EC	EC62 (4.2)
Operating surplus, net	Percentage of net value added in manufacturing	%	Yes	A	OECD	OECD32 (7.1)
Operating surplus, gross	Percentage of gross value added in manufacturing	%	Yes	A	OECD	OECD32 (7.2)
Operating surplus, net	Percentage of net value added in industry plus transport and communication	%	Yes	A	OECD	OECD32 (7.3)
Operating surplus, gross	Percentage of gross value added in industry plus transport and communication	%	Yes	A	OECD	OECD32 (7.4)
Operating surplus, gross	By sector	ECU	Yes	A	EC	EC62 (0.1)
Securities: net issues	By sector	ECU	Yes	A	EC	EC62 (0.1)
Securities: net purchases	By sector	ECU	Yes	A	EC	EC62 (0.1)
World, rest of transactions	By type	nat curr	Yes	A	EC	EC62 (4.9)
World, rest of subsectors: principal transactions	By type	nat curr	Yes	A	EC	EC62 (4.10)
19.2.5 Credit						
Borrowing and lending flows	By user	nat curr	Yes	A, 6m	OECD	OECD35 (D5/01-D5/22)
Consumer credit	Outstanding, new	nat curr	Yes	A, M	OECD	OECD22
Consumer credit outstanding		nat curr	Yes	A, Q	OECD	OECD22
Consumer credit outstanding	By lending institution	nat curr, US$	No		OECD	OECD35 (D.6)
Credit, commercial banks, other credit institutions	To private sector industry, non-industry, to domestic sector, long, short-term	nat curr	Yes	A, M	OECD	OECD22
Credit, unused	Commercial and savings banks	Norwegian kroner	Yes	A, M	Norway	OECD22
Credit, domestic	Public sector, private sector	% GDP	Yes	A	Central and South American countries	IADB1
Credit cards – Eurocard, Mastercard holders	By country	nos	No		EC	EM1 (0407)
Credit cards – Visa cardholders	By country	nos	No		EC	EM1 (0408)
Credit institutions, sub-sectors	By transaction type changes in assets and liabilities	nat curr	Yes	A	EC	EC62 (4.6)
Credit institutions	By transaction	nat curr	Yes	A	EC	EC62 (4.5)
Credit to economy, bank	Short-term, medium ,long-term	DM	Yes	A, M	Germany	OECD22
Credit to economy	Commercial banks, monetary institutions non-monetary institutions	nat curr	Yes	A, M	OECD	OECD22
Credit to economy	Percentage change	%	Yes	A	OECD Europe, OECD, EC	OECD32 (10.5)
Credit to economy: commercial banks		nat curr	Yes	A, Q	OECD	OECD22
Debt, external	Total	US$	Yes	A	Central and South American countries	IADB1
Debt, service	Total	US$	Yes	A	Central and South American countries	IADB1
Instalment credit outstanding	Other credit institutions	nat curr	Yes	A, Q	OECD	OECD22
Lending or borrowing, net	By sector	ECU	Yes	A	EC	EC62 (0.1)
Loans, to domestic sector, change	Private, public sector	£	Yes	A, M	United Kingdom	OECD22
Loans, new, for equipment	Commercial banks	yen	Yes	A, M	Japan	OECD22
Loans	Commercial banks	US$	Yes	A, M	United States	OECD22

Subject	Categories	Units	Time series Yes/No Frequency	Territorial coverage	Source (Table No.)
Loans and discounts	Commercial banks	yen	Yes A, M	Japan	OECD22
Loans and investments	Commercial banks	US$	Yes A, M	United States	OECD22
Loans: net borrowing	By sector	ECU	Yes A	EC	EC62 (0.1)
Loans: net lending	By sector	ECU	Yes A	EC	EC62 (0.1)
19.2.6 Deposits and Savings					
Bank deposits, domestic	Public sector	£	Yes A, M	United Kingdom	OECD22
Bank deposits, change	Domestic	£	Yes A, M	United Kingdom	OECD22
Commercial banks	Assets, liabilities	nat curr	Yes A	Nordic countries	NCM1 (182)
Currency and deposits: assets	By sector	ECU	Yes A	EC	EC62 (0.1)
Deposits, blocked		dinars	Yes A, M	Yugoslavia	OECD22
Deposits by the public, advances and bonds of credit institutions	By institutions	nat curr	No	Nordic countries	NCM1 (181)
Deposits in commercial banks	By countries	nat curr	Yes A	EC	MAC3 (G2)
Deposits in commercial banks	By countries	nos	No	The Americas and Australasia	MAC2 (H2)
Deposits in commercial banks	By country	nat curr	Yes A	Africa and Asia	MAC1 (H2)
Deposits in savings banks	By countries	nat curr	Yes A M	EC	MAC3 (G3)
Ownership of savings and investment	By country, by type of savings and investment	%	No	EC	EM1 (0409)
Postal and bank giro services	Total	nos	Yes A	Nordic countries	NCM1 (184)
Saving, gross domestic		US$	Yes A	Latin American and Caribbean countries	UN45 (123)
Saving, gross national		US$	Yes A	Latin American and Caribbean countries	UN45 (124)
Saving, gross national, share in investment financing	% gross domestic investment at constant prices	%	Yes A	Latin American and Caribbean countries	UN45 (69)
Saving, gross domestic, share in investment financing	% gross domestic investment at constant prices	%	Yes A	Latin American and Caribbean countries	UN45 (67)
Saving, net	Percentage of GDP	%	Yes A	OECD Europe, OECD, EC	OECD32 (6.16)
Saving, gross	Percentage of GDP	%	Yes A	OECD Europe, OECD, EC	OECD32 (6.17)
Saving, net household	Percentage of disposable household income	%	Yes A	OECD Europe, OECD, EC	OECD32 (6.18)
Saving, gross	By sector	ECU	Yes A	EC	EC62 (0.1)
Saving, domestic	Percentage of GDP	%	Yes A	ASEAN	ASEANS (2.1.8)
Saving coefficients, gross national	% real gross national disposable income at constant prices	%	Yes A	Latin American and Caribbean countries	UN45 (68)
Saving coefficients, gross domestic	% real gross domestic income at constant prices	%	Yes A	Latin American and Caribbean countries	UN45 (66)
Savings	By country	nat curr	No	EC	EC18 (12.3)
Savings bank deposit	By country	nos	No	The Americas and Australasia	MAC2 (H3)
Savings bank deposit	By country	nat curr	Yes A	Africa and Asia	MAC1 (H3)
Savings banks position	Assets	nat curr	Yes A	Nordic countries	NCM1 (183)
Savings deposits, private		nat curr	Yes A	VICES countries and Yugoslavia	VICES1 (IV/2)
Savings deposits, commercial banks		nat curr	Yes A, Q	OECD	OECD22
Savings deposits	Commercial banks, personal savings	nat curr	Yes A, M	OECD	OECD22
Sight deposits		Luxembourg francs	Yes A, M	Luxembourg	OECD22

Subject	Categories	Units	Time series Yes/No	Frequency	Territorial coverage	Source (Table No.)
19.2.7 Exchange Rates						
Conversion rates		ECU	Yes	A	EC, USA USSR, Canada, Japan	EC9 (2.29)
Exchange rate, SDR		SDRs,US$	Yes	A, M	United States	OECD22
Exchange rates, mean		ECU	Yes	A, M	EC, USA, Japan	EC36
Exchange rates, mean		1 SDR=	Yes	A, M	EC,	EC36
Exchange rates, mean		1 US$=			USA, Japan	EC36
Exchange rates	Average and period end figures, indexes by country	ECU, US$	Yes	A, Q, M	EC	EC59 (III.6)
Exchange rates	By country, by rate	nat curr, US$	No		EC	EC18 (12.1)
Exchange rates	By rate	US$	Yes	A, M	Nordic countries	NCM1 (180)
Exchange rates	GDP PPPs and internal purchasing power of currency	PPPs, %	Yes	A	EC	EC59 (I.5)
Exchange rates	Mid-point rates	nat curr per US$	Yes	A, M	World	UN35 (52)
US dollar exchange rate	Spot, forward (90 days)	nat curr	Yes	A, M	OECD	OECD22
19.2.8 Insurance						
Insurance, distribution of world insurance premium volume	By volume, world share	US$, %	Yes	Selected years	World, by development groups	UNCTAD5 (4.36)
Insurance, non-life insurance premiums paid as a percentage of GDP	% range	nos	No		World, by development groups	UNCTAD5 (4.38)
Reinsurance, dependence of developing countries on foreign reinsurance markets	Reinsurance ratio, line of business	nos	No		Developing countries	UNCTAD5 (4.37)
19.2.9 Interest Rates						
Base rate	London clearing banks	% per annum	Yes	A, M	United Kingdom	OECD22
Bond yields	when issued guaranteed, not guaranteed by the government	% per annum	Yes	A, M	France	OECD22
Bonds, yields	Credit institutions	% per annum	Yes	A, M	Italy	OECD22
Bonds, long-term	Yield	% per annum	Yes	A, M	Denmark	OECD22
Call money rate		% per annum	Yes	A, M	OECD	OECD22
Central bank discount rate	By rate		Yes	A	Nordic countries	NCM1 (177)
Commercial bills	90 days	% per annum	Yes	A, M	Australia	OECD22
Confederation bonds	Yield	% per annum	Yes	A, M	Switzerland	OECD22
Country tables	By country (details given for each country vary)					
Discount rate, official		% per annum	Yes	A, M	OECD	OECD22
Gensaki rate	3 months	% per annum	Yes	A, M	Japan	OECD22
Government bonds, long-term	Yield	% per annum	Yes	A, M	OECD	OECD22
Government bonds	Yields of long-term bonds	% per annum	Yes	A, M	World	UN35 (56)
Government bonds	Yields of long-term bonds	% per annum	Yes	A, M	World	UN35 (56)
Government bonds	Yields of long-term bonds	% per annum	Yes	A	World	UN50 (32)
Interest rates, typical short-term	By country	%	Yes	M	OECD	OECD35 (S.4)
Interest rates, typical long-term	By country	%	Yes	M	OECD	OECD35 (S.5)
Interest rates, short-term		%	Yes	A, Q, M	OECD	OECD22 (-)
Interest rates, long-term		%	Yes	A, Q, M	OECD	OECD22 (-)
Interest rates, national		%	Yes	A, M	World	IMF7 (-)
Interest rates, national		%	Yes	A, M	World	IMF6 (-)
Interest rates		nat curr	Yes	A, M	World	IMF6 (-)
Interest rates		nat curr	Yes	A, M	World	IMF7 (-)
Interest rates		nat curr	Yes	A, M	World	IMF7 (-)

Subject	Categories	Units	Time series Yes/No Frequency		Territorial coverage	Source (Table No.)
Interest rates		nat curr	Yes	A, M	World	IMF6 (-)
Interest rates	By country	%	No		Europe	EM1 (0401)
Interest rates	By type	%	Yes	A, Q, M	OECD	OECD22 (-)
Interest rates	Official discount, short-term and long-term rates	%	Yes	A	EC	EC59 (I.4)
Interest rates	Short-term,long term	% per annum	Yes	A, M	OECD	OECD22
Interest rates and share yields	By type	%	Yes	A, Q, M	EC	EC59 (III.4)
Interest rates on bonds	By rate		Yes	A	Nordic countries	NCM1 (178)
Interest rates on international market	Euro-currency and international bond market	%	Yes	M	World	OECD35 (R.1)
Interest rates, official discount	By country	%	Yes	I	OECD	OECD35 (S.3)
Lending and borrowing rates	Money, security and other markets	%	Yes	M	OECD	OECD35 (R2/01-R2/23)
Long-term interest rates, nominal		%	Yes	A	OECD	OECD32 (10.9)
Long-term interest rates, real		%	Yes	A	OECD	OECD32 (10.10)
Money market rates	By rate		Yes	A	Nordic countries	NCM1 (179)
Money market rates	Treasury bill rate, call money rate	% per annum	Yes	A	World	UN35 (59)
Money market rates	Treasury bill rate, call money rate	% per annum	Yes	A	World	UN50 (34)
Money rate, day-to-day		%	Yes	A, M	EC, USA, Japan	EC36
Money rates, day-to-day	By country	%	No		EC	EC35 (-)
National interest rates		%	Yes	A, M	World	IMF6 (-)
National interest rates		%	Yes	A, M	World	IMF7 (-)
Prime corporate paper	90 days	% per annum	Yes	A, M	OECD	OECD22
Prime interest rate	Commercial banks	% per annum	Yes	A, M	OECD	OECD22
Rate, on 3-month loans		% per annum	Yes	A, M	OECD	OECD22
Rate, on 3-month deposits	Major banks	% per annum	Yes	A, M	Switzerland	OECD22
Rates of discount of central banks		% per annum	Yes	A, M	World	UN35 (58)
Rates of discount of central banks		% per annum	Yes	A, M	World	UN35 (58)
Short-term interest rates, nominal		%	Yes	A	OECD	OECD32 (10.7)
Short-term interest rates, real		%	Yes	A	OECD	OECD32 (10.8)
Treasury bill rate	3 months	% per annum	Yes	A, M	OECD	OECD22
Yields of government bonds	By country, by nominal, real	%	No		Selected countries	EC35 (-)
19.2.10 International Finance						
Bank loans, international medium and long-term	By borrowing country or institution	US$	Yes	Q, M	World	OECD34 (I.31)
Bank loans, foreign medium and long-term	By borrowing country or institution	US$	Yes	Q, M	World	OECD34 (I.33)
Bonds, international issues of	By borrowing country or institution	US$	Yes	Q, M	World	OECD34 (I.11)
Bonds, traditional foreign issues of	By borrowing country or institution	US$	Yes	Q, M	World	OECD34 (I.21)
Bonds, international issues of	By currency of issue	US$	Yes	Q, M	World	OECD34 (I.12)
Bonds, traditional foreign issues of	By country of issue	US$	Yes	Q, M	World	OECD34 (I.22)
EAGGF expenditure		ECU	Yes	A	EC	WC1 (-)
EAGGF guarantee expenditure	By product	ECU, %	Yes	A	EC	WC1 (-)
EAGGF guidance and guarantee expenditure by member state	Total	ECU	No		EC	WC1 (-)
EC budget revenue, structure of	Total	ECU, %	Yes	A	EC	WC1 (-)

19 FINANCE

Subject	Categories	Units	Time series Yes/No Frequency		Territorial coverage	Source (Table No.)
EC finance	By priority objective	ECU	No		EC	EC35 (-)
EC financial perspectives	Total	ECU	No		EC	WC1 (-)
EC financing	By country	ECU, %	No		EC	EC35 (-)
EC structural funds, appropriations of	By objective	ECU	No		EC	EC35 (-)
EC structural funds	Budget	ECU, %	Yes	A	EC	WC1 (-)
		ECU			EC, USA, USSR, Canada, Japan	EC9 (2.36)
ECU conversion rate		ECU	Yes	A	EC	EC73 (12)
EIB financing	By objective	ECU	No		EC	EC35 (-)
European Community	Grants,loans	ECU	No		EC	EC69 (VIII.0)
Facilities, other international medium and long-term	By borrowing country or institution	US$	Yes	Q, M	World	OECD34 (I.32)
Financial indicators	Balance of payments, international reserves, external public debt, debt service, exports	US$, SDR, %	No		Mediterranean countries	EC1 (IV-)
Foreign exchange reserves		US$	Yes	A	Nordic countries	NCM1 (175)
Foreign official reserves (excl. gold)	Annual variation, monthly imports and world reserves	%	Yes	A	EC	EC59 (I.7)
Foreign official reserves	Total incl. and excl. of monetary gold, foreign exchange, special drawing rights, position in IMF and monetary gold	ECU, ounces	Yes	A, Q, M	EC	EC59 (III.8)
Foreign position	Commercial banks	nat curr	Yes	A, M	OECD	OECD22
Funds raised on international markets	By borrowing country or institution	US$	Yes	Q, M	World	OECD34 (S.2)
Funds raised on international markets	By type of instrument	US$	Yes	Q, M	World	OECD34 (S.1)
Gold reserves		ounces	Yes	A, M	World	UN35 (55)
International Monetary Fund (IMF)	Quota, SDR allocations, reserve position	ECU	No		EC, USA, USSR, Canada, Japan	EC9 (2.37)
International reserves, minus gold	Reserve position in IMF + Foreign exchange + SDR	US$	Yes	A, M	World	UN35 (54)
Official reserves	Excluding gold	nos SDRs	Yes	A, M	OECD	OECD22
PPS conversion rate		PPS	Yes	A	EC	EC73 (12)
Reserves of convertible currencies		ECU	Yes	A	EC,	EC9 (2.35)
Resources raised by the EIB	By country	ECU, %	No		EC	EC35 (-)
Special drawing rights		ECU	Yes	A	EC, USA, USSR, Canada, Japan	EC9 (2.36)
19.2.11 Money Supply						
Banknote circulation	By countries	nat curr	Yes	A	EC	MAC3 (G1)
Currency and banking	End of period, assets	million CFA frs US$	Yes	A	North Africa	UN2 (41)
Currency and banking	End of period, assets	million CFA frs US$	Yes	A	West Africa	UN3 (41)
Currency and banking	End of period, assets	million CFA frs US$	Yes	A	East and Southern Africa	UN4 (41)
Currency and banking	End of period, assets	million CFA frs US$	Yes	A	Central Africa	UN5 (41)
Currency in circulation	By countries	nos	No		The Americas and Australasia	MAC2 (H1)
Currency in circulation	By country	nat curr	Yes	A	Africa and Asia EC Total	MAC1 (H1)
Income velocity of money plus quasi-money		indices	Yes	A	World	IMF7 (-)
Liquidity, total		nat curr	Yes	A, M	OECD Major Seven Total	OECD22
Monetary holdings	By country	nat curr	Yes	A	World	WB6 (-)
Money		%	Yes	M	World	IMF6 (-)

Subject	Categories	Units	Time series Yes/No Frequency		Territorial coverage	Source (Table No.)
Money		indices, %	Yes	A	World	IMF7 (-)
Money and banking	Money supply (M1), quasi money, money supply (M2), deposit money banks,	nat curr	Yes	A	ASEAN	ASEANS1 (7.6)
Money in circulation		nat curr	Yes	A	VICES countries and Yugoslavia	VICES1 (IV/3)
Money in circulation	By country	nat curr	No		EC	EC18 (12.2)
Money plus quasi-money		indices, %	Yes	A	World	IMF7 (-)
Money stock, central bank		DM	Yes	A, M	Germany	OECD22
Money supply, real	Percentage change	%	Yes	A	OECD Europe,	OECD32
Money supply		indices	Yes	A, Q	OECD,	OECD22
Money supply		nat curr	Yes	A, Q	OECD	OECD22
Money supply		nat curr	Yes	A	EC	EC9 (2.32)
Money supply		nat curr	Yes	A	World	UN50 (28)
Money supply	By countries	nat curr	Yes	A	EC	MAC3 (G4)
Money supply	By country	nat curr	No		EC	EM1 (0305)
Money supply	By type	ECU	Yes	A, Q	EC	EC59 (III.2)
Money supply	Exchange rate	nat curr	Yes	M	Asia and Pacific	UN43 (-)
Money supply	Money, reserve money	nat curr	Yes	A, M	World	UN35 (53)
Money supply	Money, reserve money	nat curr	Yes	A, M	World	UN35 (53)
Money supply	Notes and coins in circulation, scriptural money	ECU	Yes	A	EC, USA, USSR, Canada, Japan	EC9 (2.31)
Money supply	Percentage annual change	%	Yes	A	Nordic countries	NCM1 (176)
Money supply	Percentage change	%	Yes	A	OECD Europe,	OECD32
Money supply	Velocity of circulation, currency and liquidity ratios	%	Yes	A	EC	EC59 (I.2)
Money supply (M1)		indices	Yes	A, M	OECD total, EC total, Major Seven total, OECD Europe,	OECD22
Money supply (M1)		nat curr	Yes	A, M	OECD	OECD22
Money supply (M1)	% GDP		Yes	A	Central and South American countries	IADB1
Money supply (M1) plus quasi-money		indices, nat curr	Yes	A, M	OECD Total	OECD22
Money supply plus quasi-money, real	Percentage change	%	Yes	A	OECD, EC	OECD32 (10.4)
Money supply plus quasi-money		indices, nat curr	Yes	A, Q	OECD,	OECD22
Money supply plus quasi-money	Percentage change	%	Yes	A	OECD, EC	OECD32 (10.1-10.3)
Quasi-money		schilling	Yes	A, M	Austria	OECD22
Ratio of reserve money to money plus quasi-money		%	Yes	A	World	IMF7 (-)
Reserve money		%	Yes	A	World	IMF7 (-)
Velocity of circulation of money	Percentage change	%	Yes	A	OECD Europe, OECD, EC	OECD32 (10.6)
19.2.12 Personal Finance						
Compensation of employees	By component	nat curr	Yes	A	EC	EC62 (5.2)
Households	By transaction	nat curr	Yes	A	EC	EC62 (4.3)
Life insurance	By country	nat curr	Yes	A	ESCAP countries	UN44
Personal finance	By country, by bank account, cheque book, cash dispenser card	%	No		EC	EM1 (0406)
Personal income	Total, non-agricultural	nat curr	Yes	A, M	OECD	OECD22
Private non-profit institutions	By transaction	nat curr	Yes	A	EC	EC62 (4.4)
Social benefits	By type and providing sector	nat curr	Yes	A	EC	EC62 (5.4)

Subject	Categories	Units	Time series Yes/No Frequency		Territorial coverage	Source (Table No.)
Social contributions	By type and receiving sector	nat curr	Yes	A	EC	EC62 (5.3)
19.2.13 Stock Exchange						
Stock exchange turnover	All shares, bonds and securities	nat curr	Yes	Q, M	OECD	OECD35 (D2/01-D2/23)
19.3 INVESTMENT						
19.3.1 Domestic Investment						
Construction	% of gross fixed investment at constant 1980 prices	%	Yes	A	Latin American and Caribbean countries	UN45 (64)
Construction	At constant market prices	US$	Yes	A	Latin American and Caribbean countries	UN45 (120)
Funds, uses	Investment in non-financial assets, investment in financial assets, by country	nat curr	Yes	A	OECD	OECD37
Gross domestic investment, contribution of net external financing	% of gross domestic investment at constant 1980 prices	%	Yes	A	Latin American and Caribbean countries	UN45 (100)
Gross fixed capital formation	By sector	ECU	Yes	A	EC	EC62 (0.1)
Gross fixed capital formation	Machinery and equipment	nat curr	Yes	A	World	UN27 (-)
Gross fixed capital formation	Total	nat curr	Yes	A	World	UN27 (-)
Gross investment, domestic, coefficients	% GDP at constant 1980 prices	%	Yes	A	Latin American and Caribbean countries	UN45 (45)
Gross investment	By economic sectors, by country	nat curr	Yes	A	VICES countries and Yugoslavia	VICES1 (I.3)
Gross investment	By selected branches of industry, by country	nat curr	Yes	A	VICES countries	VICES1 (I/4)
Industrial investments	By industry	nat curr	Yes	A	Nordic countries	NCM1 (81)
Investment	As % of turnover	%	Yes	A	Western World	CIA1 (28)
Investment	By country	nat curr	Yes	A	Selected countries	CIA1 (8)
Investment	By country	US$	Yes	A	Western World	CIA1 (18)
Investment	By industrial sector	US$	No		United Arab Emirates	CH1 (8.16)
Investment	By industry	ECU	No		EC	EC53 (3.5)
Investment	By industry (NACE): building,civil engineering, chemical industry, coke ovens, electrical engineering, electricity,gas, steam,hot water, extraction of minerals, peat, food,drink,tobacco, footwear,clothing, leather,leather goods man-made fibres mechanical engineering metal articles metalliferous ores metals mineral oil refining	ECUs	No		EC	EC76 (-)

Subject	Categories	Units	Time series Yes/No Frequency		Territorial coverage	Source (Table No.)
Investment *(cont)*	By industry (NACE): motor vehicles,parts, accessories non-metallic mineral products nuclear fuels industry office,data processing machinery other manufacturing industries other means of transport paper,paper products, printing,publishing petroleum and natural gas rubber,plastics solid fuels water supply	ECUs	No		EC	EC76 (-)
Investment	By ISIC division	nat curr	Yes	A	OECD	OECD16
Investment expenditure	By sector	US$, %	No		OECD	OECD18 (23)
Investment expenditure	In relation to crude steel production in main OECD producing countries	US$,tonne	No		OECD	OECD18 (24)
Investment per capita	By country	nat curr	Yes	A	Selected countries	CIA1 (10)
Investment per head	By country	US$	Yes	A	Western World	CIA1 (20)
Investment rates	By industry (investment as a percentage of gross value-added at factor cost)	%	No	1985	EC	EC53 (3.9)
Machinery and equipment	% of gross fixed investment at constant 1980 prices	%	Yes	A	Latin American and Caribbean countries	UN45 (65)
Machinery and equipment	At constant market prices	US$	Yes	A	Latin American and Caribbean countries	UN45 (121)
Machinery and equipment	By ISIC division	nat curr	Yes	A	OECD	OECD16
Stocks	Total Textile industry Timber,wooden furniture	nat curr	Yes	A	World	UN27 (-)
Turnover	By country	per capita, nat curr	Yes	A	Selected countries	CIA1 (9)
Turnover per capita	By country	US$	Yes	A	Western World	CIA1 (19)
19.3.2 Foreign Investment						
Foreign owned industrial enterprises	By industry	nos	No		Nordic countries	NCM1 (82)
Kuwait foreign investments	By allocations	US$	No		Kuwait	CH1 (6.5)
Share of foreign capital in non-oil manufacturing investment	By subsectors	nat curr, %	No		Saudi Arabia	CH1 (8.9)
Total investment of foreign capital	By activity	US$	No		Saudi Arabia	CH1 (8.14)
Value of inputs and gross output	By industrial sector	US$	No		United Arab	CH1 (8.15)
19.4 PUBLIC FINANCE						
19.4.1 Central Government						
Actual expenditure on investment	By Ministry	US$	No		United Arab Emirates	CH1 (6.18)
Agriculture	Central government	% total	Yes	A	World	IMF5 (pp 66-67)

19 FINANCE

Subject	Categories	Units	Time series Yes/No Frequency		Territorial coverage	Source (Table No.)
Agriculture	General government	% GDP	Yes	A	World	IMF5 (pp 111)
Budget	Revenue, expenditure, by sector, by country	nat curr	Yes	A	VICES countries and Yugoslavia	VICES1 (IV/1)
Budget	Revenue, expenditure, by sector, by country	nat curr	Yes	A	VICES countries and Yugoslavia	VICES1 (IV/1)
Capital	Central government	% total	Yes	A	World	IMF5 (pp 76-77)
Central	Type	nat curr	Yes	A	OECD	OECD42 (pp 153-176)
Central government, consolidated	By type of debt holder, by country	nat curr	Yes	A	World	IMF5 (pp 114-622)
Central government, consolidated	By type of debt instrument, by country,	nat curr	Yes	A	World	IMF5 (pp 114-622)
Central government, overall	Surplus, without grants	% GDP	Yes	A	World	IMF5 (pp 80-81)
Central government, overall	Surplus	% GDP	Yes	A	World	IMF5 (pp 78-79)
Central government, overall	Surplus	% total	Yes	A	World	IMF5 (pp 44-45)
Central government, budgetary	Summary of finance, by country	nat curr	Yes	A	World	IMF5 (pp 114-622)
Central government, consolidated	Summary of finance by country	nat curr	Yes	A	World	IMF5 (pp 114-622)
Central government, consolidated	By country by type of debt instrument	nat curr	Yes	A	World	IMF5 (pp 114-622)
Central government, overall	Deficit	% GDP	Yes	A	World	IMF5 (pp 78-79)
Central government, overall	Deficit, without grants	% GDP	Yes	A	World	IMF5 (pp 80-81)
Central government	By economic type	% total	No		World	IMF5 (pp 42-43)
Central government	By function	% total	No		World	IMF5 (pp 40-41)
Central government	By major components	% total	No		World	IMF5 (pp 36-37)
Central government	By type of revenue	% total	No		World	IMF5 (pp 38-39)
Central government	Domestic, foreign	% total	Yes	A	World	IMF5 (pp 46-47)
Central government	Domestic debt, foreign debt	% total	Yes	A	World	IMF5 (pp 50-51)
Central government	Monetary authorities, deposit money banks	% total	Yes	A	World	IMF5 (pp 48-49)
Central government	Non-tax revenue, grants	% total	Yes	A	World	IMF5 (pp 56-57)
Central government	Taxes on domestic goods and services, taxes on international trade and transactions	% total	Yes	A	World	IMF5 (pp 54-55)
Central government	Taxes on incomes and profits, social security contributions	% total	Yes	A	World	IMF5 (pp 52-53)
Central government budget and debt		%	Yes	A	EC	EC59 (I.3)
Central government budget and debt	By type	ECU	Yes	A	EC	EC59 (III.3)
Central government expenditure	By countries	nat curr	Yes	A	EC	MAC3 (G5)

Subject	Categories	Units	Time series Yes/No	Frequency	Territorial coverage	Source (Table No.)
Central government expenditure	By countries	nos	No		The Americas and Australasia	MAC2 (H4)
Central government expenditure	Consolidated central government, by function	nat curr	Yes	A	World	IMF5 (pp 114-622)
Central government revenue, with some main tax yields	By countries	nos	No		The Americas and Australasia	MAC2 (H5)
Consumption, final	By functions	nat curr	Yes	A	Nordic countries	NCM1 (203)
Convertible currency debt	Gross debt, net debt, assets	US$	Yes	A	VICES region, VICES countries and Yugoslavia	VICES1 (III/6)
Current account, central government	With,without grants	% GDP	Yes	A	World	IMF5 (pp 82-85)
Current account, general government	Without grants	% GDP	Yes	A	World	IMF5 (pp 98-99)
Debt, central government	Total, domestic, foreign	ECU	Yes	A	EC, USA, USSR, Canada, Japan	EC9 (2.30)
Debt - public	Gross, internal, external	million CFA frs	Yes	A	North Africa	UN2 (46)
Debt - public	Gross, internal, external	million CFA frs	Yes	A	West Africa	UN3 (46)
Debt - public	Gross, internal, external	million CFA frs	Yes	A	East and Southern Africa	UN4 (46)
Debt - public	Gross, internal, external	million CFA frs	Yes	A	Central Africa	UN5 (46)
Debt service	% of goods and services exports, by country, region	%	No		UNICEF assisted countries	UNICEF2 (-)
Defence	Central government	% GDP	Yes	A	World	IMF5 (pp 90-91)
Defence	Central government	% total	Yes	A	World	IMF5 (pp 58-59)
EC expenditure in relation to GDP	By type of expenditure	ECU, %	No		EC	EC35 (-)
EC staff shown in the 1991 budget	By department, by permanent, temporary	nos	No		EC	EC35 (-)
Economic affairs and services	Central government	% total	Yes	A	World	IMF5 (pp 62-63)
Education	Central government	% total	Yes	A	World	IMF5 (pp 60-61)
Education	General government	% GDP	Yes	A	World	IMF5 (pp 110)
Expenditure	Government	million US$	Yes	A	Central Africa	UN5 (9-1-2)
Expenditure	Government	million US$	Yes	A	East and Southern Africa	UN4 (9-1-2)
Expenditure	Government	million US$	Yes	A	North Africa	UN2 (9-1-2)
Expenditure	Government	million US$	Yes	A	West Africa	UN3 (9-1-2)
Expenditure and lending minus repayments	Consolidated general government, by country, by economic type	nat curr	Yes	A	World	IMF5 (pp 114-622)
Expenditure and lending minus repayments	General government	% GDP	Yes	A	World	IMF5 (pp 108-109)
Expenditure and revenue	By type	nat curr	Yes	A	Nordic countries	NCM1 (202)
Extra budgetary accounts	Summary of finance, by country	nat curr	Yes	A	World	IMF5 (pp 114-622)
Federal government actual budget	By ministry, by current and capital expenditure, fixed investments and finance	US$	No		United Arab Emirates	CH1 (6.17)
Foreign debt	By country, by gross, net	US$	No		EC	EC18 (13.2)
Fuel and energy	Central government	% total	Yes	A	World	IMF5 (pp 66-67)
General	Type	nat curr	Yes	A	OECD	OECD42 (pp 153-176)
General goverment: main financial transactions	By type change in assets and liabilities	nat curr	Yes	A	EC	EC62 (6.4)

19 FINANCE

Subject	Categories	Units	Time series Yes/No Frequency		Territorial coverage	Source (Table No.)
General government, overall	Surplus, without grants	% GDP	Yes	A	World	IMF 5 (pp 96-97)
General government, overall	Surplus	% GDP	Yes	A	World	IMF5 (pp 94-95)
General government, overall	Deficit	% total	Yes	A	World	IMF5 (pp 44-45)
General government, overall	Deficit, without grants	% GDP	Yes	A	World	IMF5 (pp 96-97)
General government, overall	Deficit	% GDP	Yes	A	World	IMF5 (pp 94-95)
General government	Assets, liabilities and net position	ECU	Yes	A	EC	EC59 (III.7.2)
General government	By transaction	nat curr	Yes	A	EC	EC62 (4.8)
General government	Change in financial assets, liabilities, bonds and loans	ECU, %	Yes	A	EC	EC59 (I.1.5)
General government expenditures	By current expenditures, investment, by estimate, actual	US$, %	No		United Arab Emirates	CH1 (6.19)
Goods and services	Central government	% total	Yes	A	World	IMF5 (pp 70-71)
Government	Health, education, defence, by country, region	%	No		UNICEF assisted countries	UNICEF2
Government debt and budget surplus,deficit	By country	%	No		EC	EC35 (-)
Government deficit or surplus	By country	nat curr	Yes	A	World	WB6 (-)
Government expenditure	By high, middle, low income, by sector	%	No		World	CS1 (27)
Government expenditure	Economic classification	million CFA frs	Yes	A	North Africa	UN2 (45)
Government expenditure	Economic classification	million CFA frs	Yes	A	West Africa	UN3 (45)
Government expenditure	Economic classification	million CFA frs	Yes	A	East and Southern Africa	UN4 (45)
Government expenditure	Economic classification	million CFA frs	Yes	A	Central Africa	UN5 (45)
Government expenditure	Functional classification	million CFA frs	Yes	A	North Africa	UN2 (44)
Government expenditure	Functional classification	million CFA frs	Yes	A	West Africa	UN3 (44)
Government expenditure	Functional classification	million CFA frs	Yes	A	East and Southern Africa	UN4 (44)
Government expenditure	Functional classification	million CFA frs	Yes	A	Central Africa	UN5 (44)
Government finance	By country, revenue and expenditure	nat curr	Yes	A	Africa and Asia	MAC1 (H4)
Government receipts		million CFA frs	Yes	A	Central Africa	UN5 (43)
Government receipts		million CFA frs	Yes	A	East and Southern Africa	UN4 (43)
Government receipts		million CFA frs	Yes	A	North Africa	UN2 (43)
Government receipts		million CFA frs	Yes	A	West Africa	UN3 (43)
Government revenue	By countries and main tax yields	nat curr	Yes	A	EC	MAC3 (G6)
Grants received	Type	nat curr	Yes	A	OECD	OECD42 (pp 153-176)
Health	Central government	% total	Yes	A	World	IMF5 (pp 60-61)
Health	General government	% GDP	Yes	A	World	IMF5 (pp 110)
Household	Health, education, by country, region	%	No		UNICEF assisted countries	UNICEF2 (-)
Housing and community amenities	Central government	% total	Yes	A	World	IMF5 (pp 62-63))
Inter-governmental	By function, by country	nat curr	Yes	A	World	IMF5 (pp 114-622)
Interest payments	Central government	% total	Yes	A	World	IMF5 (pp 74-75)
Lending minus repayments	Central government	% total	Yes	A	World	IMF5 (pp 76-77)

Subject	Categories	Units	Time series Yes/No Frequency		Territorial coverage	Source (Table No.)
Lending minus repayments and expenditure	Consolidated central government, by country, by economic type	nat curr	Yes	A	World	IMF5 (pp 114-622)
Military expenditure	Constant price figures, % of GDP	US$	Yes	A	Nordic countries	NCM1 (204)
Mining, manufacturing and construction	Central government	% total	Yes	A	World	IMF5 (pp 64-65)
Net foreign liabilities	Current prices, % of GDP	nat curr, %	Yes	A	Nordic countries	NCM1 (205)
Non-tax revenue	General government	% GDP	Yes	a	World	IMF5 (pp 106-107)
Revenue	Government	million US$	Yes	A	Central Africa	UN5 (9-1-1)
Revenue	Government	million US$	Yes	A	East and Southern Africa	UN4 (9-1-1)
Revenue	Government	million US$	Yes	A	North Africa	UN2 (9-1-1)
Revenue	Government	million US$	Yes	A	West Africa	UN3 (9-1-1)
Revenue and expenditure in the state budget	By country, by item	nat curr	No		EC	EC18 (13.1)
Revenue and grants	Consolidated central government, by country	nat curr	Yes	A	World	IMF5 (pp 114-622)
Revenue and grants	Consolidated general government, by country	nat curr	Yes	A	World	IMF5 (pp 114-622)
Road transport	Central government	% total	Yes	A	World	IMF5 (pp 68-69)
Social security, welfare, housing	General government	% GDP	Yes	A	World	IMF5 (pp 111)
Social security and welfare	Central government	% total	Yes	A	World	IMF5 (pp 58-59)
Social security funds	Summary of finance, by country	nat curr	Yes	A	World	IMF5 (pp 114-622)
State	Type	nat curr	Yes	A	OECD	OECD42 (pp 153-176)
State debt	By type	nat curr, US$	Yes	A	Nordic countries	NCM1 (208)
Subsidies and other current transfers	Central government	% total	Yes	A	World	IMF5 (pp 70-71)
Tax revenue	General government	% GDP	Yes	A	World	IMF5 (pp 102-103)
Taxes, income, profits and capital gains	General government	% GDP	Yes	A	World	IMF5 (pp 104)
Taxes, domestic goods and services	General government	% GDP	Yes	A	World	IMF5 (pp 105)
Taxes and contributions	By type, % GDP	nat curr,	Yes	A	Nordic countries	NCM1 (207)
Taxes and contributions	Per capita	nat curr, US$	Yes	A	Nordic countries	NCM1 (206)
Total expenditure	Central government	% GDP	Yes	A	World	IMF5 (pp 88-89)
Total expenditure and lending minus repayments	Central government	% GDP	Yes	A	World	IMF5 (pp 92-93)
Total revenue	Central government	% GDP	Yes	A	World	IMF5 (pp 86-87)
Total revenue	General government	% GDP	Yes	A	World	IMF5 (pp 100-101)
Transfers to other levels of national government	Central government	% total	Yes	A	World	IMF5 (pp 74-75)
Transportation and communication	Central government	% total	Yes	A	World	IMF5 (pp 68-69)
Wages and salaries	Central government	% total	Yes	A	World	IMF5 (pp 72-73)
19.4.2 Local Government						
Expenditure and lending minus repayments	By economic type, by country	nat curr	Yes	A	World	IMF5 (pp 114-622)
Revenue and grants	By country	nat curr	Yes	A	World	IMF5 (pp 114-622)

19 FINANCE

Subject	Categories	Units	Time series Yes/No Frequency		Territorial coverage	Source (Table No.)
Type of debt		nat curr	Yes	A	OECD	OECD42 (pp 153-176)
Type of debt	Instrument, by country	nat curr	Yes	A	World	IMF5 (pp 114-622)
Type of debt holder	By country	nat curr	Yes	A	World	IMF5 (pp 114-622)
Type of debt holder	By country	nat curr	Yes	A	World	IMF5 (pp 114-622)
Type of debt instrument	By country	nat curr	Yes	A	World	IMF5 (pp 114-622)

20 FISHING

Subject	Categories	Units	Time series Yes/No Frequency		Territorial coverage	Source (Table no.)
20.1 CONSUMPTION						
Catch, utilisation	By uses	tonnes, %	Yes	A	OECD	OECD43
Consumption		kg/capita	No		World	EC9 (5.27)
Utilisation	By country, fish type	tonnes, % change	Yes	A	EC	SFIA1 (-)
20.2 FISH						
20.2.1 Catch						
Abalones, winkles, conchs etc	Nominal catch	tonnes	Yes	A	World	FAO3 (B52)
Aquatic bird guano, eggs, etc	Nominal catch	tonnes	Yes	A	World	FAO3 (B84)
Aquatic invertebrates (misc)	Nominal catch	tonnes	Yes	A	World	FAO3 (B76)
Aquatic mammals (misc)	Nominal catch	tonnes	Yes	A	World	FAO3 (B65)
Aquatic plants (misc)	Nominal catch	tonnes	Yes	A	World	FAO3 (B94)
Billfish catch, atlantic and mediterranean	By species, region, country and gear	nos	Yes	A	World	ICCAT1 (5)
Brown seaweeds	Nominal catch	tonnes	Yes	A	World	FAO3 (B91)
Carps, babels and other cyprinds	Nominal catch	tonnes	Yes	A	World	FAO3 (B11)
Clams, cockles, arkshells etc	Nominal catch	tonnes	Yes	A	World	FAO3 (B56)
Cods, hakes, haddocks	Nominal catch	tonnes	Yes	A	World	FAO3 (B32)
Corals	Nominal catch	tonnes	Yes	A	World	FAO3 (B82)
Crab (United States)	By species	nos	No		Bering Sea	INPFC1 (56-59)
Diadromous fish (misc)	Nominal catch	tonnes	Yes	A	World	FAO3 (B25)
Eared Seals, hair seals, walruses etc	Nominal catch	tonnes	Yes	A	World	FAO3 (B64)
Fish, crustaceans, molluscs etc.	Inland, marine nominal catch, by country	tonnes	Yes	A	ESCAP countries	UN44
Fish, crustaceans, molluscs etc	Total nominal catch, in inland waters by type, in marine fishing areas by area	tonnes	Yes	A	World, continents	FAO3 (A1(a))
Fish, crustaceans, molluscs etc	Nominal catches by fishing area, principal producers	tonnes	Yes	A	World, marine area	FAO3 (A1(b-c))
Fish, crustaceans, molluscs etc	Nominal catch by groups of species and principal species	tonnes	Yes	A	World	FAO3 (A1(d-e))
Fish, crustaceans, molluscs etc	Nominal catch by producer for all areas, for inland waters, marine waters	tonnes	Yes	A	World	FAO3 (A2-A4)
Fish, crustaceans, molluscs etc	Nominal catch by economic region	tonnes	Yes	A	World	FAO3 (A5)
Fish, crustaceans, molluscs etc	Nominal catch by species groups and major fishing areas	tonnes	Yes	A	World	FAO3 (B(a))
Fish, crustaceans, molluscs etc	Nominal catch by species item	tonnes	Yes	A	World	FAO3 (B(b))
Fish, crustaceans, molluscs etc	Nominal catch by species and individual fishing area	tonnes	Yes	A	World	FAO3 (C(1-88))
Fish, crustaceans, molluscs etc	Nominal catch by continent	tonnes	Yes	A	World	FAO3 (D(1-7))
Fish, crustaceans, molluscs etc	Nominal catch by species in each continent	tonnes	Yes	A	World	FAO3 (E(1-7))
Fish, production		tonnes, indices	Yes	A	OECD	OECD43
Fishery catch, nominal	All species	tonnes	Yes	A	Northwest Atlantic	NWAFO1 (I.A)
Fishery catch, nominal	By selected species	tonnes	Yes	A	Northwest Atlantic	NWAFO1 (I.B)

20 FISHING

Subject	Categories	Units	Time series Yes/No Frequency		Territorial coverage	Source (Table no.)
Fishery catch, nominal	By species group, by division, by country	tonnes	No		Northwest Atlantic	NWAFO1 (II.2)
Fishery catch, nominal	By individual species, by division, by country	tonnes	No		Northwest Atlantic	NWAFO1 (II.3)
Fishery catch, nominal	By selected species, by division, by country	tonnes	Yes	M	Northwest Atlantic	NWAFO1 (II.4)
Fishery catch, nominal	By division, gear, tonnage class, and main species	tonnes	Yes	M	Northwest Atlantic	NWAFO1 (II.5)
Fishery catch, nominal	For countries whose vessels fished under co-operative arrangements with coastal states	tonnes	Yes	M	Northwest Atlantic	NWAFO1 (II.6)
Fishery catch, nominal	By species and subarea	tonnes	No		Northwest Atlantic	NWAFO1 (II.1)
Fishery catch, total allowable	Allocations and catches, by country	nos	Yes	A	OECD	OECD43
Fishery catch, joint-venture	By species and area	tonnes	No		Northeast Pacific	INPFC1 (51-55)
Fishery catch, world		tonnes, %	Yes	A	World	FAO4 (A1)
Fishery catch, general		tonnes ECU, kg, grt	Yes	A	World	EC6 (III 1)
Fishery catch		1000 tons	Yes	A	Central Africa	UN5(18)
Fishery catch		1000 tons	Yes	A	East and Southern Africa	UN4(18)
Fishery catch		1000 tons	Yes	A	North Africa	UN2(18)
Fishery catch		tonnes	Yes	A, M	Iceland	OECD22
Fishery catch		tonnes	Yes	A	World	UN50 (1)
Fishery catch		tonnes	Yes	A	World	UN50 (80)
Fishery catch	By country	nos	No		EC	EC18 (7.14)
Fishery catch	By main species value, species	tonnes	Yes	A	EC	EC6 (III 3)
Fishery catch	By region	tonnes	Yes	A	Fishing region	EC6 (III 2)
Fishery catch	By regions	tonnes	No		World	EC9 (5.26)
Fishery catch	Total, marine, freshwater	tonnes	Yes	A	ASEAN	ASEANS1 (3.6)
Fishery catch	By species	tonnes	Yes	A	World	EC46 (B)
Fishery catch	Sea fishing, quantity	tonnes	Yes	A	Nordic countries	NCM1(72)
Fishery catch	Sea fishing, value	nat curr	Yes	A	Nordic countries	NCM1(73)
Fishery catch	Sea fishing, quantity, value, species	nat curr	No		Nordic countries	NCM1(74)
Flounders, halibuts, soles	Nominal catch	tonnes	Yes	A	World	FAO3 (B31)
Freshwater crustaceans	Nominal catch	tonnes	Yes	A	World	FAO3 (B41)
Freshwater fish (misc)	Nominal catch	tonnes	Yes	A	World	FAO3 (B13)
Freshwater molluscs	Nominal catch	tonnes	Yes	A	World	FAO3 (B51)
Frogs and amphibians	Nominal catch	tonnes	Yes	A	World	FAO3 (B71)
Fshery catch	By fishing region	tonnes	Yes	A	World	EC46 (A)
Green seaweed and algae	Nominal catch	tonnes	Yes	A	World	FAO3 (B93)
Groundfish, shrimp, herring, halibut	By country, area, gear, vessel type	nos, tonnes,	Yes	A	Northeast Pacific	INPFC1 (35-50)
Halibut, commercial catch	By regulatory area	lbs	No		Pacific Ocean	IPHC1 (4)
Halibut, commercial landings	By port and country	lbs	No		Pacific Ocean	IPHC1 (5)
Halibut, commercial landings	By ports	lbs	Yes	10 yr	Canada, US	IPHC1 (2)
Halibut, commercial fishery	Regulatory area fishing period	lbs, days	No		Pacific Ocean	IPHC1 (1)
Halibut, commercial fishery	Regulatory area fishing period	lbs, days	No		Pacific Ocean	IPHC1 (2)
Halibut	average halibut catch landed value	lbs, US$	Yes	5 yr	Canada, US	IPHC1 (3)

Subject	Categories	Units	Time series Yes/No Frequency		Territorial coverage	Source (Table no.)
Herrings, sardines, anchovies	Nominal catch	tonnes	Yes	A	World	FAO3 (B35)
Horseshoe crabs and arachnoids	Nominal catch	tonnes	Yes	A	World	FAO3 (B74)
Jacks, mullets, sauries	Nominal catch	tonnes	Yes	A	World	FAO3 (B34)
Krill, planktonic crustaceans etc	Nominal catch	tonnes	Yes	A	World	FAO3 (B46)
Landings, catches average price	By country, fish type	% change, tonnes,	Yes	A	EC	SFIA1 (-)
Landings, catch and values	By method of production, product and port of landing, by country	tonnes nat curr	Yes	A	OECD	OECD43
Landings of fish	By countries	nos	No		The Americas and Australasia	MAC2 (D13)
Landings of fish	By countries	tonnes	Yes	A	EC	MAC3 (C9)
Landings of fish	By country	tonnes	Yes	A	Africa and Asia	MAC1 (D13)
Lobsters, spiny-rock lobsters	Nominal catch	tonnes	Yes	A	World	FAO3 (B43)
Mackerels, snoeks, cutlassfish etc	Nominal catch	tonnes	Yes	A	World	FAO3 (B37)
Marine crustaceans (misc)	Nominal catch	tonnes	Yes	A	World	FAO3 (B47)
Marine fish (misc)	Nominal catch	tonnes	Yes	A	World	FAO3 (B39)
Marine molluscs (misc)	Nominal catch	tonnes	Yes	A	World	FAO3 (B58)
Mussels	Nominal catch	tonnes nat curr	Yes	A	World	FAO3 (B54)
Oysters	Nominal catch	tonnes	Yes	A	World	FAO3 (B53)
Pearls, mother-of-pearl, shells etc	Nominal catch	tonnes	Yes	A	World	FAO3 (B81)
Porpoises, dolphins, etc	Nominal catch	tonnes	Yes	A	World	FAO3 (B63)
Porpoises catch, harbour	By grounds	nos	Yes	A, M	World	IWC1(z10)
Red seaweeds	Nominal catch	tonnes	Yes	A	World	FAO3 (B92)
Redfishes, basses, congers	Nominal catch	tonnes	Yes	A	World	FAO3 (B33)
River eels	Nominal catch	tonnes	Yes	A	World	FAO3 (B22)
Salmon	By species, area region, gear	nos, tonnes, tans	Yes	M, 10days	Northeast Pacific	INPFC1 (1-34)
Salmons, trouts, smelts	Nominal catch	tonnes	Yes	A	World	FAO3 (B23)
Scallops, pectens	Nominal catch	tonnes	Yes	A	World	FAO3 (B55)
Sea-spiders, crabs, etc	Nominal catch	tonnes	Yes	A	World	FAO3 (B42)
Sea-squirts and tunicates	Nominal catch	tonnes	Yes	A	World	FAO3 (B73)
Sea-urchins and echinoderms	Nominal catch	tonnes	Yes	A	World	FAO3 (B75)
Seal catches	Harp and hooded seals	nos	No		Northwest Atlantic	NWAFO1 (III.1)
Seaweeds and aquatic plants	Nominal catch by country for all fishing areas	tonnes	Yes	A	World	FAO3 (A6)
Shads	Nominal catch	tonnes	Yes	A	World	FAO3 (B24)
Sharks, rays, chimaeras	Nominal catch	tonnes	Yes	A	World	FAO3 (B38)
Shrimps, prawns etc	Nominal catch	tonnes	Yes	A	World	FAO3 (B45)
Sponges	Nominal catch	tonnes	Yes	A	World	FAO3 (B83)
Squat-lobsters	Nominal catch	tonnes	Yes	A	World	FAO3 (B44)
Squids, cuttlefishes, octopuses etc	Nominal catch	tonnes	Yes	A	World	FAO3 (B57)
Sturgeons, paddlefish	Nominal catch	tonnes	Yes	A	World	FAO3 (B21)
Tilapias and other cichlids	Nominal catch	tonnes	Yes	A	World	FAO3 (B12)
Tuna, national catches	By country, gear, area and species	nos	Yes	A	World	ICCAT1 (4)
Tuna catch, atlantic and mediterranean	By species, gear, area and country	nos	Yes	A	World	ICCAT1 (2)
Tuna catch	By ocean and species, by country	nos	Yes	A	World	ICCAT1 (1)
Tunas, bonitos, billfishes	Nominal catch	tonnes	Yes	A	World	FAO3 (B36)
Turtles and reptiles	Nominal catch	tonnes	Yes	A	World	FAO3 (B72)
Whale size on capture	By type, sex and country	feet	No		World	IWC1 (5, 11)
Whale size on killing	By type and region	feet	Yes	A	World	IWC1 (h)
Whales – blue-whales, fin-whales, etc	Nominal catch	tonnes	Yes	A	World	FAO3 (B61)
Whales – sperm-whales, pilot-whales, etc	Nominal catch	tonnes	Yes	A	World	FAO3 (B62)
Whales - bottlenosed whale catch	By grounds	nos	Yes	A, M	World	IWC1 (z4)
Whales - minke whale catch	By grounds	nos	Yes	A, M	World	IWC1 (z3)
Whales - small whale catch	By type and country	nos	Yes	A	World	IWC1 (z2)

20 FISHING

Subject	Categories	Units	Time series Yes/No Frequency		Territorial coverage	Source (Table no.)
Whales -Baird's beaked whales	By grounds	nos	Yes	A, M	World	IWC1 (z8)
Whales -killer whale catch	By grounds	nos	Yes	A, M	World	IWC1 (z6)
Whales -Narwhal catch	By grounds	nos	Yes	A, M	World	IWC1 (z9)
Whales -pilot whale catch	By grounds	nos	Yes	A, M	World	IWC1 (z5)
Whales -small whale catch, other	By grounds	nos	Yes	A, M	World	IWC1(z11)
Whales -white whale catch	By grounds	nos	Yes	A	World	IWC1 (z7)
Whales caught	By type, sex and size	nos, feet	No		World	IWC1 (6, 12)
Whales caught	By type and area	nos	Yes	A	World	IWC1 (i-
Whales killed	By area	nos	Yes	A	World	IWC1 (c)
Whales killed	By country	nos	Yes	A	World	IWC1 (e)
Whales killed	By species	nos	Yes	A	World	IWC1 (b)
Whaling in antarctic season	By country and type	nos	No		World	IWC1 (1-4 and 7-10) (y1)
20.2.2 Processed						
Abalones fresh, chilled or frozen		US$, tonnes	Yes	A	World	FAO4(J24)
Clams fresh, chilled or frozen		US$, tonnes	Yes	A	World	FAO4(J28)
Cod (not in fillets), dried		tonnes	Yes	A	World	FAO4 (C1.3)
Cods, hakes, haddock fresh, chilled or frozen		US$, tonnes	Yes	A	World	FAO4 (J6)
Cods, hakes, haddocks dried, salted or in brine		US$, tonnes	Yes	A	World	FAO4 (J13)
Crabs fresh, chilled or frozen		US$, tonnes	Yes	A	World	FAO4(J22)
Crustacean and mollusc products and preparations		tonnes	Yes	A	World	FAO4 (F1.1)
Crustacean and molluscs preparations not in airtight containers		tonnes	Yes	A	World	FAO4 (F1.5)
Crustacean and molluscs products and preparations		US$, tonnes	Yes	A	World	FAO4 (F2.1)
Crustacean products, canned		tonnes	Yes	A	World	FAO4 (F1.2)
Crustaceans, fresh, frozen, salted in brine or dried		tonnes	Yes	A	World	FAO4 (D1.2)
Crustaceans and molluscs, fresh, frozen, dried, salted		tonnes	Yes	A	World	FAO4 (D1.1)
Crustaceans and molluscs, prepared or preserved		tonnes	Yes	A	World	FAO4 (F1.4)
Crustaceans and molluscs, fresh, frozen, dried, salted		US$, tonnes	Yes	A	World	FAO4 (D2.1)
Eels, fresh, chilled or frozen		US$, tonnes	Yes	A	World	FAO4 (J2)
Fish, fresh, chilled or frozen		tonnes	Yes	A	World	FAO4 (B1.1)
Fish, frozen (excl fillets)		tonnes	Yes	A	World	FAO4 (B1.4)
Fish, dried, salted or smoked		tonnes	Yes	A	World	FAO4 (C1.1)
Fish, dried, salted or in brine		tonnes	Yes	A	World	FAO4 (C1.4)
Fish, fresh, chilled or frozen		US$, tonnes	Yes	A	World	FAO4 (B2.1)
Fish, dried, salted or smoked		US$, tonnes	Yes	A	World	FAO4 (C2.1)
Fish by-products	By grounds and type of product	tonnes	Yes	A	World	IWC1 (z1)
Fish fillets, fresh or chilled		tonnes	Yes	A	World	FAO4 (B1.2)
Fish fillets, frozen		tonnes	Yes	A	World	FAO4 (B1.3)
Fish fillets fresh, chilled or frozen		US$, tonnes	Yes	A	World	FAO4 (J12)
Fish liver oils		tonnes	Yes	A	World	FAO4 (G1.2)
Fish meal fit for human consumption		tonnes	Yes	A	World	FAO4 (C1.2)
Fish meal from oily fish		tonnes	Yes	A	World	FAO4 (H1.3)
Fish meal from white fish		tonnes	Yes	A	World	FAO4 (H1.2)
Fish oils and fats (other)		tonnes	Yes	A	World	FAO4 (G1.3)
Fish preparations not in airtight containers		tonnes	Yes	A	World	FAO4 (E1.7)
Fish products (airtight containers)		tonnes	Yes	A	World	FAO4 (E1.6)
Fish products and preparations		tonnes	Yes	A	World	FAO4 (E1.1)
Fish products and preparations		US$, tonnes	Yes	A	World	FAO4 (E2.1)
Fish products canned, misc		tonnes	Yes	A	World	FAO4 (E1.5)
Fish roes dried, salted or in brine		US$, tonnes	Yes	A	World	FAO4(J16)

Subject	Categories	Units	Time series Yes/No Frequency		Territorial coverage	Source (Table no.)
Fish roes fresh, chilled or frozen		US$, tonnes	Yes	A	World	FAO4 (J11)
Fish smoked		tonnes	Yes	A	World	FAO4 (C1.5)
Flatfishes fresh, chilled or frozen		US$, tonnes	Yes	A	World	FAO4 (J5)
Herrings, sardines, anchovies etc canned		tonnes	Yes	A	World	FAO4 (E1.3)
Herrings, sardines, anchovies fresh, chilled or frozen		US$, tonnes	Yes	A	World	FAO4 (J8)
Herrings, sardines, anchovies dried, salted or in brine		US$, tonnes	Yes	A	World	FAO4(J14)
Lobsters fresh, chilled or frozen		US$, tonnes	Yes	A	World	FAO4(J21)
Mackerals, canned		US$, tonnes	Yes	A	World	FAO4(J20)
Mackerels fresh, chilled or frozen		US$, tonnes	Yes	A	World	FAO4 (J10)
Meals and animal feeding stuffs of aquatic animal origin		tonnes	Yes	A	World	FAO4 (H1.1)
Mollusc products, canned		tonnes	Yes	A	World	FAO4 (F1.3)
Molluscs, fresh, frozen, salted in brine or dried		tonnes	Yes	A	World	FAO4 (D1.3)
Mussels fresh, chilled or frozen		US$, tonnes	Yes	A	World	FAO4(J26)
Oils and fats, crude or refined of aquatic animal origin		tonnes	Yes	A	World	FAO4 (G1.1)
Oils and fats, crude or refined of aquatic animal origin		US$, tonnes	Yes	A	World	FAO4 (G2.1)
Oils and fats of aquatic animals		tonnes	Yes	A	World	FAO4 (G1.5)
Oils and fats of marine mammals		tonnes	Yes	A	World	FAO4 (G1.4)
Oysters fresh, chilled or frozen		US$, tonnes	Yes	A	World	FAO4(J25)
Preserved and processed fishery commodities	By product	tonnes	Yes	A	World	FAO4 (A4)
Production of fishery products	By country, by product	tonnes	No		EC	EM1 (1910)
Redfishes, basses, congers fresh, chilled or frozen		US$, tonnes	Yes	A	World	FAO4 (J7)
Salmon, canned		US$, tonnes	Yes	A	World	FAO4(J18)
Salmons canned		tonnes	Yes	A	World	FAO4 (E1.2)
Salmons fresh, chilled or frozen		US$, tonnes	Yes	A	World	FAO4 (J3)
Sardines, canned		US$, tonnes	Yes	A	World	FAO4(J17)
Scallops fresh, chilled or frozen		US$, tonnes	Yes	A	World	FAO4(J27)
Sharks fins dried, salted		US$, tonnes	Yes	A	World	FAO4(J15)
Shrimps and prawns fresh, chilled or frozen		US$, tonnes	Yes	A	World	FAO4(J23)
Solubles from fish and marine mammals		tonnes	Yes	A	World	FAO4 (H1.5)
Sperm oil	By country	barrels	Yes	A	World	IWC1 (g)
Squids, cuttlefish and octopuses fresh, chilled or frozen		US$, tonnes	Yes	A	World	FAO4(J29)
Trout and bonitos, canned		US$, tonnes	Yes	A	World	FAO4(J19)
Trouts fresh, chilled or frozen		US$, tonnes	Yes	A	World	FAO4 (J4)
Tunas, bonitos, billfishes etc canned		tonnes	Yes	A	World	FAO4 (E1.4)
Tunas fresh, chilled or frozen		US$, tonnes	Yes	A	World	FAO4 (J9)
Whaling oil	By area	barrels	Yes	A	World	IWC1 (d)
Whaling oil	By country	barrels	Yes	A	World	IWC1 (f)
20.2.3 Products – see also under Processed (20.2.2)						
Production of fishery products	By country, by product	tonnes	No		EC	EM1 (1910)
20.3 FISH FARMING						
Fish-farming output	By country, by fish, molluscs and shellfish	tonnes	No		EC	EC35 (-)

20 FISHING

Subject	Categories	Units	Time series Yes/No	Frequency	Territorial coverage	Source (Table no.)
20.4 INDUSTRY						
Fishing effort	By division, gear, tonnage class, and main species	tonnes	Yes	M	Northwest Atlantic	NWAFO1 (II.5)
Seal-hunting effort	Catching method, no. of vessels, tonnage, engine, no. of crew, days absent	nos, HP, tonnes	No		Northwest Atlantic	NWAFO1 (III.2)
Whaling material in operation	For shore stations, floating factories and catchers	nos	Yes	A	World	IWC1 (a)
20.5 INTERNATIONAL TRADE						
Exports		tonnes, ECU	No		World, EC, USA, USSR, Canada, Japan	EC9 (5.27)
Exports	By country of destination	% change, tonnes,	Yes	A	North America	SFIA1 (-)
Exports	By country of origin and destination, fish type	tonnes, nat curr, % change	Yes	A	EC	SFIA1 (-)
Exports of agricultural, fishing and forestry products	By countries	tonnes, score, hl, cu m, nos	Yes	A	EC	MAC3 (C11)
Fish, crustaceans, molluscs, and preparations thereof	By country, region of destination	US$	No		OECD	OECD43
Fish, food	By major product groups and major world regions	US$	No		OECD and non-OECD regions	OECD43
Fish and fish products, total	By major products and country, quantity value	tonnes	Yes	A	OECD	OECD43
Fish and fish products, total	By major products and country, quantity, value	tonnes	Yes	A	OECD	OECD43
Fish and fish products	Imports, exports, quantity, value	tonnes	Yes	A	OECD	OECD43
Fish for ornamental purposes		US$, tonnes	Yes	A	World	FAO4 (J1)
Imports		tonnes, ECU	No		World, EC, USA, USSR, Canada, Japan	EC9 (5.27)
Imports	By country of origin, fish type,	nat curr, tonnes, % change	Yes	A	EC	SFIA1 (-)
Imports	By country of origin	% change tonnes	Yes	A	North America	SFIA1 (-)
Meals and animal feedingstuffs of aquatic animal origin		US$, tonnes	Yes	A	World	FAO4 (H2.1)
		nat curr nat curr				
Trade, fish products	Total, intra-EC, extra-EC, by type	tonnes, ECU	Yes	A	EC	EC46 (D)
Trade	By principal importers and exporters	US$	Yes	A	World	FAO4(A5)
Trade	Total	tonnes	Yes	A	World	FAO4(A3)

Subject	Categories	Units	Time series Yes/No Frequency		Territorial coverage	Source (Table no.)
20.6 LABOUR						
Fishermen	Sea fishing, professional, part time, all	nos	Yes	A	Nordic countries	NCM1(75)
Fishermen	Total, full-time, part-time	nos	Yes	A	OECD	OECD43
20.7 VESSELS						
Fishing fleets		grt	Yes	A	EC	EC6 (III 4)
Fishing fleets		nos, grt	Yes	I	OECD	OECD43
Fishing fleets	By country, by vessels	nos, tonnes tonnage	No		EC	EC35 (-)
Fishing fleets	Tonnage, length, age, power, by country	nos	Yes	A	EC	EC46 (C)
Fishing vessels, stock	By country	nos, tonnes	No		EC	EC18 (7.13)
Fishing vessels	Type of boat	Gross tonnage	No		Nordic countries	NCM1(76)
Fishing vessels by major flags	Total, type of vessel	nos, grt-gt, %			World	ISL2 (1.5.10.2)
Fishing vessels development	Total, type of vessel	nos, grt-gt, %	Yes	A	World	ISL2 (1.5.10.1)
Halibut, vessels licensed, unlicensed	By area and nationality	nos	No		Canada, US	IPHC1 (1)
Halibut, vessels and catch	By vessel length	nos, lbs	No		Pacific Ocean	IPHC1 (3)
Tuna, number of boats	By year, country, type and size	nos	Yes	A	World	ICCAT1 (3)

21 FORESTRY

Subject	Categories	Units	Time series Yes/No Frequency		Territorial coverage	Source (Table no.)
21.1 CONSUMPTION - see also Section 8						
Apparent domestic consumption	By product type, total all	cu m	Yes	A	Selected countries	ITTO1 (1-1)
Apparent domestic consumption	By product type, total all	cu m	Yes	A	Selected countries	ITTO1 (1-2)
Pulpwood	By type of industrial product	cu m	Yes	A	EC	EC47 (7)
Timber, tropical	By product, by ITTC producer	cu m	Yes	A	ITTC producing countries worldwide	ITTO1 (App 1)
21.2 DAMAGE						
Area burned		ha	Yes	A	Selected countries	OECD33 (5.7)
Area surveyed and samples		ha, nos	No		Selected countries	UN22 (I-3.4.2)
Biomass	Above ground, growing stock, net annual increment, fellings and harvesting intensity	cu m, %	No		Selected countries	UN22 (I-3.4.1)
Defoliation	By species	%	No		Selected countries	UN22 (I-3.4.4)
Fires on forest and other wooded land	By number, area and size	nos, ha	Yes	A	Selected countries	UN22 (I-3.4.5)
Forest damage survey results	By all age classes, conifers and broadleaves	%	Yes	A	Selected countries	UN22 (I-3.4.3)
Forest fire damage		ECU, nos, ha	Yes	A	EC	EC47 (8)
Losses		US$	Yes	A	Selected countries	OECD33 (5.7)
21.3 EMPLOYMENT - see also Section 16						
Tropical timber	Logging companies, sawmills, veneer mills, ply mills, total employment	nos	No		World tropical timber-producing countries	ITTO1 (5)
21.4 FINANCIAL ACCOUNTS - see also Section 34						
Accounts, forestry		ECU	Yes	A	EC	EC9 (5.24)
Accounts, forestry		volume indices	Yes	A	EC	EC9 (5.25)
Fixed capital formation, gross forestry	At current prices and exchange rates	ECU	Yes	A	EC	EC26 (B.1.1-B.1.12)
Fixed capital formation, gross forestry	At current prices	nat curr	Yes	A	EC	EC26 (B.2.1-B.2.12)
Fixed capital formation, net forestry	At current prices and exchange rates	ECU	Yes	A	EC	EC26 (B.1.1-B.1.12)
Fixed capital formation, net forestry	At current prices	nat curr	Yes	A	EC	EC26 (B.2.1-B.2.12)
Income, net of family forestry labour	At current prices and exchange rates	ECU	Yes	A	EC	EC26 (B.1.1-B.1.12)
Income, net of forestry family labour	At current prices	nat curr	Yes	A	EC	EC26 (B.2.1-B.2.12)
Income, net of total forestry labour	At current prices	nat curr	Yes	A	EC	EC26 (B.2.1-B.2.12)
Income, net of total forestry labour	At current prices and exchange rates	ECU	Yes	A	EC	EC26 (B.1.1-.1.12)
Operating surplus, net forestry	At current prices and exchange rates	ECU	Yes	A	EC	EC26 (B.1.1-B.1.12)
Operating surplus, net forestry	At current prices	nat curr	Yes	A	EC	EC26 (B.2.1-B.2.12)
Value added, gross forestry (at market prices)	At current prices and exchange rates	ECU	Yes	A	EC	EC26 (B.1.1-B.1.12)
Value added, gross forestry (at factor cost)	At current prices and exchange rates	ECU	Yes	A	EC	EC26 (B.1.1-B.1.12)

21 FORESTRY

Subject	Categories	Units	Time series Yes/No Frequency		Territorial coverage	Source (Table no.)
Value added, gross forestry (at market prices)	At current prices	nat curr	Yes	A	EC	EC26 (B.2.1-B.2.12)
Value added, gross forestry (at factor cost)	At current prices	nat curr	Yes	A	EC	EC26 (B.2.1-B.2.12)
Value added, net forestry (at factor cost)	At current prices and exchange rates	ECU	Yes	A	EC	EC26 (B.1.1-B.1.12)
Value added, net forestry (at factor cost)	At current prices	nat curr	Yes	A	EC	EC26 (B.2.1-B.2.12)

21.5 HOLDINGS AND WOODED AREA

Subject	Categories	Units	Time series	Territorial coverage	Source
Agricultural holdings with wooded areas	By size, %	nos	No	EC	EC6(IIA 2)
Forest	Type of wood	sq km, %	No	OECD	OECD33 (5.1B)
Forest area ownership Forest cover		%	No	EC	EC47 (1.3)
Forest holdings, average size	State and private forests	ha	No	EC	EC47 (1.2)
Forest holdings, number	By type of ownership and holding size category	nos	No	EC	EC47 (2.5)
Forestry holdings, area	By type of ownership and holding size category	ha	No	EC	EC47 (2.6)
High forest, area	By tree species and age group	ha	No	EC	EC47 (2.7)
Land area, total		ha	No	Selected countries	ITTO1 (3)
Natural closed broadleaved forest	Productive, total, unproductive, total	ha	No	Selected countries	ITTO1 (3)
Ownership of forests	By country, by private, state, other	%	No	EC	EC35 (-)
Plantations and natural coniferous forest	By hardwood, softwood	ha	No	Selected countries	ITTO1 (3)
Private	Farms and other, industry, total	% of area covered	No	OECD, World	OECD33 (5.6)
Public	National, other, total	% of area covered	No	OECD, World	OECD33 (5.6)
Standing wood, volume		cu m	No	OECD, World	OECD33 (5.2A)
Standing wood, volume	Increment, allowable cut, planned cut by type of ownership and tree species	cu m	No	EC	EC47 (2.8)
Tropical forest area, total		ha	No	Selected countries	ITTO1 (3)
Wooded area		ha	No	EC	EC47 (1.1)
Wooded area	By forest type	ha, %	No	EC	EC47 (1.8)
Wooded area	Timber production	ha	No	World, EC, USA, USSR, Canada, Japan	EC9 (5.19)
Wooded area	Total, per 1000 capita per cent of land area	sq km	No	OECD, World	OECD33 (5.1A)
Wooded area, distribution		%, ha	No	EC	EC47 (2.1)
Wooded area, distribution	By ownership type	ha, %	No	EC	EC47 (2.2)
Wooded area, distribution	By sylvicultural treatment	ha, %	No	EC	EC47 (2.3)
Wooded area, distribution	By type of ownership and sylvicultural treatment	ha	No	EC	EC47 (2.4)
Wooded areas of agricultural holdings	By area, %	ha	No	EC	EC6(IIA 3)

Subject	Categories	Units	Time series Yes/No Frequency		Territorial coverage	Source (Table no.)
21.6 INTERNATIONAL TRADE - see also Section 27						
21.6.1 Direction of trade						
Chips and particles	Major importers and exporters	cu m	No		World	FAO8
Fibreboard	Major importers and exporters	cu m	No		World	FAO8
Newsprint	Major importers and exporters	tonnes	No		World	FAO8
Paper and paperboard	Major importers and exporters	tonnes	No		World	FAO8
Particle board	Major importers and exporters	cu m	No		World	FAO8
Plywood	Major importers and exporters	cu m	No		World	FAO8
Pulpwood round and split	Major importers and exporters	cu m	No		World	FAO8
Sawlogs and veneer logs (C)	Major importers and exporters	tonnes	No		World	FAO8
Sawlogs and veneer logs (NC)	Major importers and exporters	cu m	No		World	FAO8
Sawnwood (C)	Major importers and exporters	cu m	No		World	FAO8
Sawnwood (NC)	Major importers and exporters	cu m	No		World	FAO8
Veneer sheet	Major importers and exporters	cu m	No		World	FAO8
Wood pulp	Major importers and exporters	tonnes	No		World	FAO8
21.6.2 Exports and Imports						
Agricultural, fishing and forestry products	Exports by countries	tonnes, score, hl, cu m, nos	Yes	A	EC	MAC3 (C11)
Bleached sulphate pulp	By quantity and value	tonnes, US$	Yes	A	World	FAO8
Bleached sulphite pulp	By quantity and value	tonnes, US$	Yes	A	World	FAO8
Charcoal	By quantity and value	tonnes, US$	Yes	A	World	FAO8
Chemical wood pulp	By quantity and value	tonnes, US$	Yes	A	World	FAO8
Chips and particles	By quantity and value	cu m, US$	Yes	A	World	FAO8
Dissolving wood pulp	By quantity and value	tonnes, US$	Yes	A	World	FAO8
Fibre pulp (other)	By quantity and value	tonnes, US$	Yes	A	World	FAO8
Fibreboard	By quantity and value	cu m, US$	Yes	A	World	FAO8
Fibreboard, compressed	By quantity and value	cu m, US$	Yes	A	World	FAO8
Fibreboard, non-compressed	By quantity and value	cu m, US$	Yes	A	World	FAO8
Forest products	By value	US$	Yes	A	World	FAO8
Forest products, tropical	Imports by product, by ITTC consumers	cu m	Yes	A	ITTC consuming countries worldwide	ITTO1 (App 2)
Fuelwood	By quantity and value	cu m, US$	Yes	A	World	FAO8
Fuelwood and charcoal	By quantity and value	cu m, US$	Yes	A	World	FAO8
Household and sanitary paper	By quantity and value	tonnes, US$	Yes	A	World	FAO8
Imports cork and wood, total	Imports by source per capita, % of total imports	US$	No		OECD	OECD33 (5.5)
Industrial roundwood	By quantity and value	cu m, US$	Yes	A	World	FAO8
Industrial roundwood	Product category		No		OECD and world	OECD33 (5.4B)
Industrial roundwood (other)	By quantity and value	cu m, US$	Yes	A	World	FAO8
Longwood	Exports, imports	cu m	Yes	A	EC	EC47 (5.1.2)
Mechanical wood pulp	By quantity and value	tonnes, US$	Yes	A	World	FAO8
Newsprint	By quantity and value	tonnes, US$	Yes	A	World	FAO8
Newsprint	Unit value	US$ per tonne	Yes	A	World	FAO8
Paper and paperboard	By quantity and value	tonnes, US$	Yes	A	World	FAO8
Paper and paperboard (not	By quantity and value	tonnes, US$	Yes	A	World	FAO8
Paper and paperboard (other)	By quantity and value	tonnes, US$	Yes	A	World	FAO8
Paper and paperboard (other)	Unit value	US$ per tonne	Yes	A	World	FAO8

21 FORESTRY

Subject	Categories	Units	Time series Yes/No Frequency		Territorial coverage	Source (Table no.)
Paper, board and pulp	By production, imports, exports	tonnes	Yes	A	World	PPI1 (-)
Particle board	By quantity and value	cu m, US$	Yes	A	World	FAO8
Particle board	Unit value	US$ per cu m	Yes	A	World	FAO8
Plywood	By importing, exporting	cu m	No		World	ITTO1 (App 3)
Plywood	By quantity and value	cu m, US$	Yes	A	World	FAO8
Plywood	Unit value	US$ per cu m	Yes	A	World	FAO8
Printing and writing paper	By quantity and value	tonnes, US$	Yes	A	World	FAO8
Printing and writing paper	Unit value	US$ per tonne	Yes	A	World	FAO8
Pulpwood	By quantity and value	cu m, US$	Yes	A	World	FAO8
Pulpwood	Unit value	US$ per cu m	Yes	A	World	FAO8
Pulpwood and particles	By quantity and value	cu m, US$	Yes	A	World	FAO8
Pulpwood supply balance sheet	Production, imports and exports	cu m	Yes	A	EC	EC47 (4.4)
Raw wood supply balances	Production, imports and exports	cu m	Yes	A	EC	EC47 (4.1)
Raw wood, total (excl. wood chips, particles and wood residues)	Exports, imports	cu m	Yes	A	EC	EC47 (5.1.1)
Roundwood	By quantity and value	cu m, US$	Yes	A	World	FAO8
Sawlogs and veneer logs	By quantity and value	cu m, US$	Yes	A	World	FAO8
Sawlogs and veneer logs (C)	By quantity and value	cu m, US$	Yes	A	World	FAO8
Sawlogs and veneer logs (C)	Unit value	US$ per tonne	Yes	A	World	FAO8
Sawlogs and veneer logs (NC)	By quantity and value	cu m, US$	Yes	A	World	FAO8
Sawlogs and veneer logs (NC)	Unit value	US$ per tonne	Yes	A	World	FAO8
Sawlogs, veneer logs	By importing, exporting	cu m	No		World	ITTO1 (App 3)
Sawnwood	By importing, exporting	cu m	No		World	ITTO1 (App 3)
Sawnwood (C)	By quantity and value	cu m, US$	Yes	A	World	FAO8
Sawnwood (C)	Unit value	US$ per cu m	Yes	A	World	FAO8
Sawnwood (NC)	By quantity and value	cu m, US$	Yes	A	World	FAO8
Sawnwood (NC)	Unit value	US$ per cu m	Yes	A	World	FAO8
Sawnwood and railway sleepers	Imports	cu m	Yes	A	EC	EC47 (1.7)
Sawnwood and sleepers	By quantity and value	cu m, US$	Yes	A	World	FAO8
Semi-chemical wood pulp	By quantity and value	tonnes, US$	Yes	A	World	FAO8
SPWP imports	By category	US$	Yes	A	Selected countries	ITTO1 (8)
SPWP major exporters	By value and %	US$, %	Yes	A	Selected countries	ITTO1 (9)
SPWP major importers	By total	US$	Yes	A	Selected countries	ITTO1 (7)
Stackwood	Exports, imports	cu m	Yes	A	EC	EC47 (5.1.3)
Timber	By countries, exports, by main trading countries	nos	No		The Americas and Australasia	MAC2 (D18)
Timber	By product type, total all consumers, imports, exports	cu m	Yes	A	Selected countries	ITTO1 (1-1)
Timber	By product type, total all consumers, imports, exports	cu m	Yes	A	Selected countries	ITTO1 (1-2)
Timber	Exports, by products	cu m, US$	No		World, tropical countries	ITTO1 (1)
Timber	Exports, imports, total per capita	US$	No		OECD, World	OECD33 (5.4A)
Timber, composition of exports	By region	cu m	Yes	A	Selected countries	ITTO1 (6)
Timber, tropical	By product by ITTC producer	cu m	Yes	A	ITTC producing countries worldwide	ITTO1 (App 1)
Timber, tropical	ITTC share in global exports, by product	%	No		World	ITTO1 (2)

Subject	Categories	Units	Time series Yes/No Frequency		Territorial coverage	Source (Table no.)
Timber, tropical	Log production, log exports, processed exports, total exports, by region	cu m	No		World tropical timber producing regions	ITTO1 (10)
Timber, tropical	World and ITTC, by product	cu m	No		World	ITTO1 (1)
Tropical timber products, value of trade	By ITTO producers	$US	No		Selected countries	ITTO1 (3-2)
Tropical logs exported from Asia-Pacific	By total imports, total exports	cu m	No		Selected countries	ITTO1 (2-1-3)
Tropical logs exported from Africa	By total imports, total exports	cu m	No		Selected countries	ITTO1 (2-1-1)
Tropical logs exported from Africa	By total imports, total exports	cu m	No		EC	ITTO1 (2-1-2)
Tropical logs re-exported from Europe, exported from Latin America, Caribbean	By total imports, total exports	cu m	No		EC	ITTO1 (2-1-4)
Tropical plywood exported from Asia-Pacific	By total imports, total exports	cu m	No		EC	ITTO1 (2-4-3)
Tropical plywood exported from Asia-Pacific	By total imports, total exports	cu m	No		Selected countries	ITTO1 (2-4-2)
Tropical plywood exported from Latin America, Caribbean and North America	By total imports, total exports	cu m	No		Selected countries	ITTO1 (2-4-4)
Tropical plywood exported from Europe	By total imports, total exports	cu m	No		Selected countries	ITTO1 (2-4-5)
Tropical plywood exported from Africa	By total imports, total exports	cu m	No		Selected countries	ITTO1 (2-4-1)
Tropical sawnwood exported from Africa	By total imports, total exports	cu m	No		Selected countries	ITTO1 (2-2-2)
Tropical sawnwood exported from Asia-Pacific	By total imports, total exports	cu m	No		Selected countries	ITTO1 (2-2-3)
Tropical sawnwood exported from Asia-Pacific	By total imports, total exports	cu m	No		EC	ITTO1 (2-2-4)
Tropical sawnwood exported from Latin America, Caribbean and North America	By total imports, total exports	cu m	No		Selected countries	ITTO1 (2-2-5)
Tropical sawnwood exported from Africa	By total imports, total exports	cu m	No		Selected countries	ITTO1 (2-2-1)
Tropical sawnwood exported from Europe	By total imports, total exports	cu m	No		Selected countries	ITTO1 (2-2-6)
Tropical timber products, value of trade	By ITTO consumers	$US	No		Selected countries	ITTO1 (3-1)
Tropical timber, ITTO's share	Production and exports	%	No		Selected countries	ITTO1 (2)
Tropical veneer exported from Asia-Pacific	By total imports, total exports	cu m	No		EC	ITTO1 (2-3-3)
Tropical veneer exported from Asia-Pacific	By total imports, total exports	cu m	No		Selected countries	ITTO1 (2-3-2)
Tropical veneer exported from Latin America, Caribbean and North America	By total imports, total exports	cu m	No		Selected countries	ITTO1 (2-3-4)
Tropical veneer exported from Africa	By total imports, total exports	cu m	No		Selected countries	ITTO1 (2-3-1)
Tropical veneer exported from Europe	By total imports, total exports	cu m	No		Selected countries	ITTO1 (2-3-5)
Unbleached sulphate pulp	By quantity and value	tonnes, US$	Yes	A	World	FAO8
Unbleached sulphite pulp	By quantity and value	tonnes, US$	Yes	A	World	FAO8
Veneer	By importing, exporting	cu m	No		World	ITTO1 (App 3)
Veneer sheets	By quantity and value	cu m, US$	Yes	A	World	FAO8
Wood chips, particles and wood residues	Exports, imports	cu m	Yes	A	EC	EC47 (5.1.4)
Wood pulp	By quantity and value	tonnes, US$	Yes	A	World	FAO8

21 FORESTRY

Subject	Categories	Units	Time series Yes/No Frequency		Territorial coverage	Source (Table no.)
Wood pulp	Unit value	US$ per tonne	Yes	A	World	FAO8
Wood residues	By quantity and value	cu m, US$	Yes	A	World	FAO8
Wood-based panels	By quantity and value	cu m, US$	Yes	A	World	FAO8
Wrapping and packaging paper	By quantity and value	tonnes, US$	Yes	A	World	FAO8
21.7 INDUSTRY						
Conversion rate, average	By type of activity	%	No		Selected countries	ITTO1 (5)
Employees, number	By type of activity	nos	No		Selected countries	ITTO1 (5)
Enterprises, number	By type of activity	nos	No		Selected countries	ITTO1 (5)
Installed capacity	By type of activity	cu m	No		Selected countries	ITTO1 (5)
21.8 INVESTMENT - see also Section 34						
Fixed capital formation, gross forestry	At current prices and exchange rates	ECU	Yes	A	EC	EC26 (B.1.1-B.1.12)
Fixed capital formation, gross forestry	At current prices	nat curr	Yes	A	EC	EC26 (B.2.1-B.2.12)
Fixed capital formation, net forestry	At current prices and exchange rates	ECU	Yes	A	EC	EC26 (B.1.1-B.1.12)
Fixed capital formation, net forestry	At current prices	nat curr	Yes	A	EC	EC26 (B.2.1-B.2.12)
21.9 PRICES - see also Section 37						
Forestry, final	At current prices and exchange rates	ECU	Yes	A	EC	EC26 (B.1.1-B.1.12)
Forestry, final	At current prices	nat curr	Yes	A	EC	EC26 (B.2.1-B.2.12)
Intermediate forestry	By type at current prices	ECU	Yes	A	EC	EC26 (B.2.1-B.2.12)
Intermediate forestry	By type at current prices	nat curr	Yes	A	EC	EC26 (B.2.1-B.2.12)
Intermediate forestry, final	At current prices and exchange rates	ECU	Yes	A	EC	EC26 (B.1.1-B.1.12)
Intermediate forestry, final	At current prices and exchange rates	nat curr	Yes	A	EC	EC26 (B.1.1-B.1.12)
Market pulp prices	By type, period	tonnes, nat curr, c.i.f.	No		Western EC, North America	JP1 (-)
Raw wood	By type at current prices and exchange rates	ECU	Yes	A	EC	EC26 (B.1.1-B.1.12)
Raw wood	By type at current prices	nat curr	Yes	A	EC	EC26 (B.2.1-B.2.12)
Raw wood, total	At current prices and exchange rates	ECU	Yes	A	EC	EC26 (B.1.1-B.1.12)
Raw wood, total	At current prices	nat curr	Yes	A	EC	EC26 (B.2.1-B.2.12)
21.10 PRODUCTION - see also Section 38						
Afforestation and new plantations, state	By country	ha	No		EC	EC18 (7.11)
Bleached sulphate pulp	By product	tonnes	Yes	A	World	FAO8
Capacity utilization ratios	By country, period	tonnes	No		Selected countries	JP1 (-)
Charcoal		tonnes	Yes	A	World	FAO8
Dissolving wood pulp		tonnes	Yes	A	World	FAO8
Fellings	By country	cu m	No		EC	EC18 (7.12)
Fellings per hectare		nos	Yes	A	EC	EC47 (1.5)
Fellings, EC		%	Yes	A	EC	EC47 (1.4)
Fibre pulp (other)		tonnes	Yes	A	World	FAO8
Fibreboard		cu m	Yes	A	World	FAO8

Subject	Categories	Units	Time series Yes/No Frequency		Territorial coverage	Source (Table no.)
Fibreboard compressed		cu m	Yes	A	World	FAO8
Fibreboard, non-compressed		tonnes	Yes	A	World	FAO8
Forest area	By owner groups	ha	No		Nordic countries	NCM1(67)
Forestry, depletion	Harvest, losses, total	cu m	No		Selected countries	OECD33 (5.2B)
Forestry, growth		cu m	No		Selected countries	OECD33 (5.2B)
Fuelwood (C)		cu m	Yes	A	World	FAO8
Fuelwood (NC)		cu m	Yes	A	World	FAO8
Fuelwood and charcoal		cu m	Yes	A	World	FAO8
Fuelwood and charcoal	Global production	cu m	No		OECD	OECD33 (5.2A)
Household and sanitary paper		tonnes	Yes	A	World	FAO8
Industrial roundwood		cu m	Yes	A	World	FAO8
Industrial roundwood		cu m, % world	No		OECD, World	OECD33 (5.3)
Industrial roundwood (C)		cu m	Yes	A	World	FAO8
Industrial roundwood (C) (other)		cu m	Yes	A	World	FAO8
Industrial roundwood (NC)		cu m	Yes	A	World	FAO8
Industrial roundwood (NC) (other)		cu m	Yes	A	World	FAO8
Industrial roundwood (other)		cu m	Yes	A	World	FAO8
Intensity of use	Harvested, annual growth ratio	ratio	No		Selected countries	OECD33 (5.2B)
Newsprint		tonnes	Yes	A	World	FAO8
Paper and board production	By grade, country	tonnes	Yes	A	World	PPI1 (-)
Paper and paperboard		cu m, % world	No		OECD, World	OECD33 (5.3)
Paper and paperboard		tonnes	Yes	A	World	FAO8
Paper and paperboard (not elsewhere specified)		tonnes	Yes	A	World	FAO8
Paper and paperboard (other)		tonnes	Yes	A	World	FAO8
Paper, board and pulp	By production, imports, exports	tonnes	Yes	A	World	PPI1 (-)
Particle board		cu m	Yes	A	World	FAO8
Plywood		cu m	Yes	A	World	FAO8
Plywood	By region	cu m	Yes	A	World tropical timber-producing regions	ITTO1 (9)
Printing and writing paper		tonnes	Yes	A	World	FAO8
Production of forestry, paper products	By country, by product	tonnes, m	No		EC	EM1 (1909)
Pulp production	By grade, country	tonnes	Yes	A	World	PPI1 (-)
Pulp, paper and board production and trade	By country, consumption	tonnes, nos mills	Yes	A	World	PPI1 (-)
Pulpwood (C)		cu m	Yes	A	World	FAO8
Pulpwood (NC)		cu m	Yes	A	World	FAO8
Pulpwood and particles		cu m	Yes	A	World	FAO8
Raw wood removals	By forest type	cu m, %	No		EC	EC47 (1.8)
Raw wood supply	Home production, imports	cu m	Yes	A	EC	EC47 (1.6)
Raw wood, removals	By category	cu m	Yes	A	EC	EC47 (3.4)
Raw wood, removals	By ownership type	cu m	Yes	A	EC	EC47 (3.3)
Raw wood, removals	By type	cu m	Yes	A	EC	EC47(3.5.1 -3.5.8)
Raw wood, total	By type	cu m	Yes	A	EC	EC47 (3.1)
Removals, estimated	By type solid volume without bark		Yes	A	Nordic countries	NCM1(69)
Roundwood		cu m	Yes	A	World	FAO8
Roundwood		cu m	Yes	A	World	UN50 (78)
Roundwood		tonnes	Yes	A	World	UN50 (1)
Roundwood (C)		cu m	Yes	A	World	FAO8
Roundwood (NC)		cu m	Yes	A	World	FAO8

21 FORESTRY

Subject	Categories	Units	Time series Yes/No Frequency		Territorial coverage	Source (Table no.)
Roundwood production		cu m	No		OECD	OECD33 (5.2A)
Roundwood removals	By type of forest, plantation, and forest management	cu m	No		World tropical timber-producing countries	ITTO1 (4)
Roundwood removals	Coniferous, broad leaves	1000 cu m	Yes	A	North Africa	UN2 (19)
Roundwood removals	Coniferous, broad leaves	1000 cu m	Yes	A	Central Africa	UN5 (19)
Roundwood removals	Coniferous, broad leaves	1000 cu m	Yes	A	East & Southern Africa	UN4 (19)
Roundwood removals	Coniferous, broad leaves	1000 cu m	Yes	A	West Africa	UN3 (19)
Roundwood removals	Total, industrial, fuel woods	tonnes	Yes	A	ASEAN	ASEANS1 (3.7)
Roundwood removals: coniferous and broadleaved	Industrial, fuel wood by country	cu m	Yes	A	ESCAP	UN44
Rubber, natural		tonnes	Yes	A	World	UN50 (79)
Rubber, natural		tonnes	Yes	A, M	World	UN35 (9)
Saw, veneer logs	By region	cu m	Yes	A	World tropical timber-producing regions	ITTO1 (6)
Sawlogs and veneer logs		cu m	Yes	A	World	FAO8
Sawlogs and veneer logs (C)		cu m	Yes	A	World	FAO8
Sawlogs and veneer logs (NC)		cu m	Yes	A	World	FAO8
Sawnwood	By region	cu m	Yes	A	World tropical timber-producing regions	ITTO1 (7)
Sawnwood (C)		cu m	Yes	A	World	FAO8
Sawnwood (NC)		cu m	Yes	A	World	FAO8
Sawnwood and sleepers		cu m	Yes	A	World	FAO8
Sawnwood and sleepers		cu m, % world	No		OECD, World	OECD33 (5.3)
Start-ups and expected near-term start-ups, shut downs	By mill, total and market capacity, grades, period	tonnes	No		World	JP1 (-)
Sulphate pulp, unbleached		tonnes	Yes	A	World	FAO8
Sulphite pulp, bleached		tonnes	Yes	A	World	FAO8
Sulphite pulp, unbleached		tonnes	Yes	A	World	FAO8
Timber	Roundwood, softwood	cu m	No		World, EC, USA, USSR, Canada, Japan	EC9 (5.19)
Timber production	By country, by conifers, non-conifers	nos, %	No		World	EC35 (-)
Timber, tropical	By product, by ITTC producer	cu m	Yes	A	ITTC producing countries worldwide	ITTO1 (App 1)
Timber, tropical	ITTC share in	%	No		World	ITTO1 (2)
Timber, tropical	World and ITTC, by product	cu m	No		World	ITTO1 (1)
Timber, tropical (forest, harvest and reforestation areas)	Area by status of forest cover, area by status of management, harvested, reforested areas	ha	No		World tropical timber-producing countries	ITTO1 (3)
Timber, tropical (industrial structure and capacity)	Number and capacity of logging companies, sawmills, veneer mills, ply mills	nos, cu m	No		World tropical timber-producing countries	ITTO1 (5)
Tree species	By growing stock, annual growth	cu m	No		Nordic countries	NCM1(68)
Tropical roundwood removals	By type of removal, total	cu m	No		Selected countries	ITTO1 (4)
Tropical timber, ITTO's share	Production and exports	%	No		Selected countries	ITTO1 (2)
Veneer	By region	cu m	Yes	A	World tropical timber-producing regions	ITTO1 (8)
Veneer sheets		cu m	Yes	A	World	FAO8

Subject	Categories	Units	Time series Yes/No Frequency		Territorial coverage	Source (Table no.)
Wood based panels		cu m, % world	No		OECD, World	OECD33 (5.3)
Wood fellings		cu m	Yes	A, M	OECD	OECD22
Wood in the rough, supplies of	By production	metres (length)	Yes	A	EC	EC6(IIC 3)
Wood production	By product type, total all consumers	cu m	Yes	A	Selected countries	ITTO1 (1-1)
Wood production	By product type, total all	cu m	Yes	A	Selected countries	ITTO1 (1-2)
Wood Production	By wood type	cu m, tonnes	No		World, tropical countries	ITTO1 (1)
Wood production	Total, by type	metres (length)	Yes	A	EC	EC6 (IIC1)
Wood production, general review	By production	indices	Yes	A	EC	EC6 (IIC2)
Wood products supply balance sheet	Production, imports and exports by product type	cu m	Yes	A	EC	EC47 (6)
Wood pulp		cu m, % world	No		OECD, World	OECD33 (5.3)
Wood pulp		tonnes	Yes	A	World	FAO8
Wood pulp		tonnes	Yes	A, Q	OECD	OECD22
Wood pulp, chemical		tonnes	Yes	A	World	FAO8
Wood pulp, mechanical		tonnes	Yes	A	World	FAO8
Wood pulp, semi-mechanical		tonnes	Yes	A	World	FAO8
Wood, development	Production per hectare, member states share in production	indices, cu m %	Yes	A	EC	EC47 (3.2)
Wood-based panels		cu m	Yes	A	World	FAO8
Wooded area, breakdown of	By type, production	ha	No		EC	EC6 (IIA1)
Woodpulp production	By region, and period indices, average	%	Yes	A, Q	Selected countries	JP1 (-)
Wrapping and packaging paper and board		tonnes	Yes	A	World	FAO8

22 HEALTH

Subject	Categories	Units	Time series Yes/No Frequency	Territorial coverage	Source (Table no.)
22.1 ALCOHOLIC BEVERAGES CONSUMPTION					
Alcohol per capita		litres	Yes Selected	World	UN16 (20)
Beer per capita		litres	Yes Selected	World	UN16 (20)
Expenditure on alcohol	By country	%	No	EC	EC72 (8.9)
Wine per capita		litres	Yes Selected	World	UN16 (20)
22.2 CHILD HEALTH					
Babies, low birth-weight	By country, region	%	No	UNICEF assisted countries	UNICEF2
Children having acceptable weight-for-age	By country	%	No	SEAR	WHO1 (53)
Corneal xerophthalmia and blindness due to vitamin A deficiency in children under-six	By country	nos, %	No	SEAR	WHO1 (52)
Diarrhoea morbidity rates in children less than five years of age	By country	nos	No	SEAR	WHO1 (41)
Oral rehydration solution and therapy, availability and use of	By under-5 population, diarrhoea episodes, ORS used, ORS access ORS and ORT use rates	nos, l	No	Developing countries	PC1 (38)
Respiratory infection situation in children, acute	By country	nos, %	No	SEAR	WHO1 (44)
Survival and development	Indicators of survival and development	%, per thou	No	Developing countries	UN25 (11)
Under-five mortality rate very high, high, middle, low	By % with access to safe water, % with access to health service, % immunized, ORT use rate	%, nos	No	World	UNICEF1 (3)
Underweight children, under 5	Weight for age, by country, region	%	No	UNICEF assisted countries	UNICEF2
Vital Statistics	Proportion of infants immunized, access to water, expenditure on health as % of GNP, population per physician	%, nos, per thou	No	World	UNCTAD1 (6.10A)
22.3 DISABILITY					
	Age group, by sex	%	No	World	UN16 (21)
Bed days	By selected characteristics	nos	No	OECD	OECD20 (3.2)
Causes of disability	By country, by gender	%	No	SEAR	WHO1 (68)
Disability days	By selected characteristics	nos	No	OECD	OECD20 (3.1)
Disability prevalence	By sex, male, female per 100,000 population	rate	No	World	UN16 (21)
Disability, prevalence of	By sex	nos	No	Africa	UN46 (25)
Disability, prevalence of	By sex	nos	No	World	UN17 (27)
Disability, selected characteristics of	By urban and rural, disabled population	%, years by age and sex	No	World	UN17 (27)
Disabled persons	Urban, rural areas by sex	%	No	World	UN16 (21)
Disabled population, selected characteristics of	By urban and rural, by age and sex	%, years	No	Africa	UN46 (25)
Illiterate persons	By sex	%	No	World	UN16 (21)
Population restricted in daily activities because of long-standing health conditions	By selected characteristics	%	No	OECD	OECD20 (4.1)
Population with certain types of functional disability	By age and sex	%	No	OECD	OECD20 (4.2)

22 HEALTH

Subject	Categories	Units	Time series Yes/No Frequency		Territorial coverage	Source (Table no.)
22.4 EXPENDITURE						
Central government, per capita expenditure on health	GNP per capita, % GNP spent on health, health expenditure per capita	US$, %	Yes	I	World	WHO2 (7)
Estimated costs of antihypertensive drug treatment related to total health care expenditure	By country, by cost	US$, %	No		Selected countries	WHO1 (55)
Expenditure on health	By country	%	No		EC	EC72 (8.4)
Health expenditure	By country	US$, %	No		EC	EM1 (1704)
Public expenditure	% GDP at current prices	%	Yes	A	Latin American and Caribbean countries	UN45 (29)
Sales of medical products	By product, dose per capita	nos	Yes	A	Nordic countries	NCM1 (234)
22.5 GENERAL STATISTICS – see also under Vital Statistics (22.12) and Section 36						
AIDS	By transmission group, by gender	%	No		EC	EC72 (8.22)
AIDS and HIV infection	By country	nos, date	No		SEAR	WHO1 (49)
AIDS cases and infected persons, current assessment						
AIDS cases, symptomatic	Reported, estimated actual,	nos	No		World	UN16 (18B)
AIDS, cumulative cases	By age, by gender	nos	No		EC	EC72 (8.19)
AIDS, registered cases	Notified, deaths	nos	Yes	A	Nordic counties	NCM1 (230)
AIDS, reported cases	By country, by date of report	nos	No		EC	EM1 (1703)
AIDS, reported cases	New, cumulative total	nos	No		World	UN16 (18C)
Cancer - incidence	By age, by sex, by site of cancer	rate	No		World	IARC1(8)
Cancer - incidence and mortality	Indices of reliability registration	indices	No		World	IARC1 (7.6)
Cancer - incidence rates	Age-standardized and cumulative rates, by sex, by site of cancer	standard unit	No		World	IARC1 (12.2)
Cancer - incidence rates	Age-standardized rates, by sex, by site of cancer	standard unit	No		World	IARC1 (12.1)
Cancer, new cases	Primary site, sex	nos	Yes	A	Nordic countries	NCM1 (229)
Death rates from cardiovascular disease	By sex, age	nos	Yes	A	Nordic countries	NCM1 (232)
Death rates from neoplasms	By sex, age	nos	Yes	A	Nordic countries	NCM1 (233)
Deaths analysed	By cause	nos	No		Nordic countries	NCM1 (231)
Deaths by motor-vehicle accident	By age, by gender	nos	No		EC	EC72 (8.30)
Deaths, percentage of distribution of causes, where registered	By sex	%	No		World	UN17 (24)
Deaths, percentage of distribution of causes, where registered	Classified according to abbreviated international list by sex	%	No		Africa	UN46 (23A,B)
Dengue haemorrhagic fever situation	By country, by incidence rate, deaths, fatality rate	nos, %	No		SEAR	WHO1 (39)
Diarrhoa diseases programme and targets, status of control	By number of programmes	nos	No		SEAR	WHO1 (43)
EPI diseases, reported incidence	By country, by disease	nos	No		SEAR	WHO1 (37)
EPI target diseases, fatality rates	By country, by disease	nos	No		SEAR	WHO1 (36)
EPI target diseases, reported cases	By country, by disease	nos	No		SEAR	WHO1 (35)

Subject	Categories	Units	Time series Yes/No Frequency	Territorial coverage	Source (Table no.)
Estimates of ORS access and ORS	By country ORT use rates	nos	No	SEAR	WHO1 (42)
Fatalities	By country, by cause of death	nos	No	EC	EC18 (4.2)
Health profile	Indicators of human health	%, nos, indices, per 100,000	No	Industrial countries	UN25 (32)
Health profile	Indicators of human health	%, per 1000	No	Developing countries	UN25 (12)
Health-related indicators	By high, middle, low income	nos, %	No	World	CS1 (30)
Hepatitis B virus carrier status among healthy populations and frequency of hepatocellular carcinoma	By country	nos	No	SEAR	WHO1 (51)
Illness, registered	By country, by illness	nos	No	EC	EC18 (4.1)
Illnesses, major	By country, by illness	nos	No	EC	EM1 (1702)
Infected persons, estimated number of	Female, male ratio,	nos, ratio	No	World, type of area	UN16 (18A)
Injured and killed	By country, by victims, killed, injured	nos	No	EC	EC72 (8.32)
Japanese encephalitis	By country, by incidence rate, deaths, fatality rate	nos, %	No	SEAR	WHO1 (40)
Killed and injured in road accidents	By country	nos	No	EC	EC35 (-)
Leprosy situation	By country	nos, %	No	SEAR	WHO1 (48)
Life expectancy and life expectancy without disability	By country, by gender, at birth, at 65	years	No	EC	EC72 (8.8)
Life expectancy at 40	By country, by gender	years	No	EC	EC72 (8.7)
Malaria situation	By country, by annual blood slide examination rate, parasite incidence, slide positivity rate	nos, %	No	SEAR	WHO1 (38)
Meningococcal meningitis cases and deaths	By population	nos, %	No	Selected countries	WHO1 (50)
Mortality	By major cause of death	%	No	EC	EC72 (8.12)
Mortality rate for death by cancer, standardized	By country, by gender	nos	No	EC	EC72 (8.16)
Mortality rate for some avoidable causes of death, standardized	By country, by cause	nos	No	EC	EC72 (8.14)
Mortality rate, excess	By country, by gender	%	No	EC	EC72 (8.15)
Mortality rate, standardized	By country, by gender	nos	No	EC	EC72 (8.11)
Mortality rate, standardized, trends in the	By country, by gender	nos	No	EC	EC35 (-)
Mortality, rate from cancer, standardized, trends in the	By country, by gender	nos	No	EC	EC35 (-)
Motor-vehicle accidents in total deaths	By age, by gender	%	No	EC	EC72 (8.31)
Multidrug therapy implementation	By country	%, nos	No	SEAR	WHO1 (47)
Periodontal diseases	By country, by CPITN method	nos	No	SEAR	WHO1 (62)
Persons injured	By country, by major industry divisions, lost work	nos	No	SEAR	WHO1 (64)
Respiratory infection control plans status, national acute	By country		No	SEAR	WHO1 (45)
Suicide	By age, by gender	nos	No	EC	EC72 (8.25)
Suicides in total deaths	By age, by gender	%	No	EC	EC72 (8.26)
Teeth, decayed, missing and filled permanent teeth per person	By country	nos	No	SEAR	WHO1 (61)

22 HEALTH

Subject	Categories	Units	Time series Yes/No Frequency		Territorial coverage	Source (Table no.)
Tuberculosis cases and rates	By country	nos	No		SEAR	WHO1 (46)
22.6 HOSPITALS, SERVICES						
22.6.1 Beds						
Beds in medical institutions	By country	nos	No		EC	EC18 (4.3)
Beds in sanatoria	By country	nos	No		EC	EC18 (4.4)
Beds, hospital	By speciality	nos	No		Nordic countries	NCM1 (223)
Beds, hospital	Discharges, bed days	nos, %	Yes	A	Nordic countries	NCM1 (222)
Beds, hospital	Of which psychiatric	nos, per capita	No		EC	EC69 (VII.1)
Beds, hospital		nos	Yes	A	ASEAN	ASEANS1 (9.4.2)
Beds, hospital		nos	Yes	A	Latin American and Caribbean countries	UN45 (365)
Beds, hospital	% AGR	nos, %	Yes	10 yrs	World	UN26
Beds, hospital	Beds per thousand inhabitants	nos	Yes	A	Latin American and Caribbean countries	UN45 (28)
Beds, hospital	Per ten thousand inhabitants	nos	Yes	A	VICES countries and Yugoslavia	VICES1 (II/4)
Beds, nursing and old-age homes	By type	nos	No		Nordic countries	NCM1 (224)
22.6.2 General						
Abortions, legal	By age of female	nos, age	Yes	A	Nordic countries	NCM1 (228)
Births attended by trained personnel	By country, region	%	No		UNICEF assisted countries	UNICEF2
Contraceptive coverage by trained staff	By country	nos, %	No		SEAR	WHO1 (58)
Coverage of maternal and child health services by trained personnel	By country	%	No		SEAR	WHO1 (56)
Essential drugs programmes, comparative development of	By country	%, nos	No		SEAR	WHO1 (71)
Estimated maternal and child health services by trained personnel	By country	nos, %	No		SEAR	WHO1 (57)
Health services, access	By country, region	%	No		UNICEF assisted countries	UNICEF2
Hospital admissions for acute pesticide poisoning	By admissions, deaths	nos	No		Sri Lanka	WHO1 (66)
Hospitals, activity		nos, nat curr, per capita	No		Nordic countries	NCM1 (227)
Hospitals, number		nos	Yes	A	ASEAN	ASEANS1 (9.4.1)
Local health care, access to	Total, urban, rural	%	Yes	I	World	WHO2 (5)
Local health services, population covered by	By country	%	No		SEAR	WHO1 (72)
Medical facilities	Summary, by country	nos	Yes	A	ESCAP countries	UN44
Medical services, provision	By country, by beds, doctors, dentists, nurses, pharmacists	nos	No		EC	EM1 (1701)
Pesticide users among agricultural workers	By country	nos, %	No		SEAR	WHO1 (65)
Pregnancy, care	Pre-natal care, delivery care, infant care	%	Yes	I	World	WHO2 (6)

Subject	Categories	Units	Time series Yes/No Frequency		Territorial coverage	Source (Table no.)
22.7 IMMUNIZATION						
Coverage	Infants immunized, by type of vaccine	%	Yes	I	World	WHO2 (4)
Immunization coverage	By newborns, infant mortality, type of vaccination	nos, %	No		Developing countries	PC1 (36)
Immunization coverage	By vaccine, % of children aged 12-23 months immunized with specific vaccines	%	No		Developing countries	PC1 (37)
One year olds	Tuberculosis, diphtheria, polio, measles by country, region	%	Yes	I	UNICEF assisted countries	UNICEF2
Pregnant women, tetanus	By country, region	%	Yes	I	UNICEF assisted countries	UNICEF2
Women immunized with tetanus toxoid	By residence, by education	nos, %	No		Developing countries	PC1 (33)
22.8 NUTRITION						
Breast feeding mothers	3, 6, 12 months, by country, region	%	No		UNICEF assisted countries	UNICEF2
Calorie intake	Per capita as % of requirements, by country, region	%	No		UNICEF assisted countries	UNICEF2
Calorie supply	As % of requirements	%	Yes		World	UN16 (19A)
Calories and proteins available	Per day, per capita, three-year averages	calories, g	Yes	I	Latin American and Caribbean countries	UN45 (24)
Calories per capita per day	Numbers	nos	No		World	UN16 (19A)
	Growth rate	%	No		World	UN16 (19A)
Daily calorie supply		per capita	No		Developing countries	UNCTAD5 (1.4)
Food production	Per capita, by country, region	indices	No		UNICEF assisted countries	UNICEF2
Food, health and nutrition	Food production, calories and proteins population per physician, nurse and hospital bed access to safe water	indices grammes nos %	No		Developing countries	WB1 (-)
Household expenditure on food	By country, region	%	No		UNICEF assisted countries	UNICEF2
Infants and pregnant women	By country	%	No		SEAR	WHO1 (34)
Nutrition	Average food supplies per day	calories per capita	Yes		World	UN55
Protein per capita per day	Numbers	nos	No		World	UN16 (19A)
	Growth rate	%	No		World	UN16 (19A)
Stunting, prevalence	By country, region	%	No		UNICEF assisted countries	UNICEF2
Wasting, prevalence	By country, region	%	No		UNICEF assisted countries	UNICEF2
22.9 PERSONNEL						
Cancers, incidence rates	By country, by gender	nos	No		Selected countries	WHO1 (54)
Dentists		nos	No		World	UN50 (36)
Dentists		nos	Yes	A	ASEAN	ASEANS1 (9.4.3)
Dentists	By country	nos	No		EC	EC18 (4.6)

22 HEALTH

Subject	Categories	Units	Time series Yes/No Frequency		Territorial coverage	Source (Table no.)
Doctors	By country	nos	No		EC	EC18 (4.5)
Doctors, pharmacists, dentists		nos, per capita	No		EC	EC69
Health personnel coverage	By population per physician, nurse	nos	No		Developing countries	PC1 (31)
Health personnel, active	By profession	nos	No		Nordic countries	NCM1 (225)
Health professions	By country, by doctors, dentists, pharmacists	nos	No		EC	EC72 (8.2)
Medical and dental practitioners and facilities	By country, by doctors, dentists, hospital beds, beds in psychiatric hospitals	nos	No		EC	EC35 (-)
Medical assistants		nos	Yes	A	Latin American and Caribbean countries	UN45 (367)
Medical assistants	Inhabitants per medical assistant	nos	Yes	A	Latin American and Caribbean countries	UN45 (27)
Medical practitioners	Physicians, surgeons and dental surgeons per ten thousand inhabitants	nos	Yes	A	VICES region, VICES countries and Yugoslavia	VICES1 (II/4)
Midwifery personnel		nos	No		World	UN50 (36)
Midwives		nos	Yes	A	ASEAN	ASEANS1 (9.4.3)
Nurses		nos	Yes	A	ASEAN	ASEANS1 (9.4.3)
Nursing personnel		nos	No		World	UN50 (36)
Persons by doctor		nos	No		ACP states	EC1 (II-)
Persons by doctor		nos	No		Mediterranean countries	EC1 (IV-)
Persons by hospital bed		nos	No		ACP states	EC1 (II-)
Persons by hospital bed		nos	No		Mediterranean countries	EC1 (IV-)
Pharmacists		nos	No		World	UN50 (36)
Pharmacists		nos	Yes	A	ASEAN	ASEANS1 (9.4.3)
Pharmacists	By country	nos	No		EC	EC18 (4.7)
Physicians		nos	No		World	UN50 (36)
Physicians		nos	Yes	A	ASEAN	ASEANS1 (9.4.3)
Physicians		nos	Yes	A	East and Southern Africa	UN4 (10-2)
Physicians		nos	Yes	A	East and Southern Africa	UN4 (48)
Physicians		nos	Yes	A	Latin American and Caribbean countries	UN45 (366)
Physicians		nos	Yes	A	North Africa	UN2 (10-2)
Physicians		nos	Yes	A	North Africa	UN2 (48)
Physicians		nos	Yes	A	West Africa	UN3 (10-2)
Physicians		nos	Yes	A	West Africa	UN3 (48)
Physicians		per 10 000	No		World	UN50 (36)
Physicians	% AGR	nos, %	Yes	10 yrs	World	UN26
Physicians	Inhabitants per physician	nos	Yes	A	Latin American and Caribbean countries	UN45 (25)
Physicians, active	By occupational group	nos	No		Nordic countries	NCM1 (226) (VII.1)
Physicians, total		nos	Yes	A	Central Africa	UN5 (10-2)
Physicians, total		nos	Yes	A	Central Africa	UN5 (48)

Subject	Categories	Units	Time series Yes/No Frequency		Territorial coverage	Source (Table no.)
22.10 RESOURCES						
Health resources	Physicians, total establishments, beds	nos	Yes	A	Central Africa	UN5 (10-2)
Health resources	Physicians, total establishments, beds	nos	Yes	A	Central Africa	UN5 (48)
Health resources	Physicians, total establishments, beds	nos	Yes	A	Central Africa	UN5 (10-2)
Health resources	Physicians, total establishments, beds	nos	Yes	A	Central Africa	UN5(48)
Health resources	Physicians, total establishments, beds	nos	Yes	A	East and Southern Africa	UN4 (10-2)
Health resources	Physicians, total establishments, beds	nos	Yes	A	East and Southern Africa	UN4 (48)
Health resources	Physicians, total establishments, beds	nos	Yes	A	East and Southern Africa	UN4 (10-2)
Health resources	Physicians, total establishments, beds	nos	Yes	A	East and Southern Africa	UN4(48)
Health resources	Physicians, total establishments, beds	nos	Yes	A	North Africa	UN2 (10-2)
Health resources	Physicians, total establishments, beds	nos	Yes	A	North Africa	UN2 (10-2)
Health resources	Physicians, total establishments, beds	nos	Yes	A	North Africa	UN2 (48)
Health resources	Physicians, total establishments, beds	nos	Yes	A	North Africa	UN2 (48)
Health resources	Physicians, total establishments, beds	nos	Yes	A	West Africa	UN3 (10-2)
Health resources	Physicians, total establishments, beds	nos	Yes	A	West Africa	UN3 (10-2)
Health resources	Physicians, total establishments, beds	nos	Yes	A	West Africa	UN3 (48)
Health resources	Physicians, total establishments, beds	nos	Yes	A	West Africa	UN3 (48)
Human resources for health	By country, by major category	nos	No		SEAR	WHO1 (69)
Medical services, provision of	By country, by beds, doctors, dentists, nurses, pharmacists	nos	No		EC	EM1 (1701)
Resources for health, availability of	By country, by internal resources, external resources, local health care, equitable distribution	%, US$	No		SEAR	WHO1 (70)
22.11 SMOKING						
Adults who smoke	By sex	%	No		World	UN16 (20)
Cigarette consumption and percentage of adults who smoke		%, nos	No		Africa	UN46 (26)
Cigarette consumption and percentage of adults who smoke	By sex	%	Yes	15 yrly	World	UN17 (26)
Cigarettes per adult		nos	Yes	Selected years	World	UN16 (20)
22.12 VITAL STATISTICS - see also Section 36						
Death, causes of, percentage distribution	By cause	%	No		World	UN16 (16A, B)
Infant mortality, health personnel	Births, per 10,000 population					

22 HEALTH

Subject	Categories	Units	Time series Yes/No	Frequency	Territorial coverage	Source (Table no.)
Life expectancy	At birth and various ages	years	Yes	10 yrly	OECD	OECD20 (1.1-1.5)
Life expectancy and mortality	By sex and age	years, rate	No		Africa	UN46 (22)
Life expectancy and mortality	By sex and age	years, rate	No		World	UN17 (23)
Life expectancy at birth		years	No		Developing countries	UNCTAD5 (1.4)
Life expectancy at birth,		years, per 1000	Yes		World	UN55
Life expectancy at birth,	By sex	years	Yes	Selected years	World	UN16 (15)
Mortality rates, child	By sex	rate	Yes	Selected years	World	UN16 (15)
Mortality rates, infants		rate	Yes	Selected years	World	UN16 (15)
Mortality rates, perinatal	By age of mother, by marital status of mother	rate	Yes	10 yrly	OECD	OECD20 (2.1-2.3)
Mortality, infant		rate per 1000	No		Developing countries	UNCTAD5 (1.4)
Survival rates	Age group	rate	Yes	Selected years	World	UN16 (15)

22.13 WATER, SANITATION

Subject	Categories	Units	Time series Yes/No	Frequency	Territorial coverage	Source (Table no.)
Access to safe drinking water and sanitation, percentage of population with	By urban, rural area	%	No		Developing countries	PC1 (39)
Safe water, access to	By country, region	%	No		UNICEF assisted countries	UNICEF2
Safe water, access to		% of population	No		Developing countries	UNCTAD5 (1.4)
Safe water, access to	Total, urban, rural	%	Yes	I	World	WHO2 (2)
Sanitation adequate , access to	By country, region	%	No		UNICEF assisted countries	UNICEF2
Sanitation, access to	Total, urban, rural	%	Yes	I	World	WHO2 (3)
Water supply and sanitation problems and issues	By country, by institut-ional item, financial item, operational item		No		SEAR	WHO1 (60)
Water supply and sanitation coverage	By country	nos, %	No		SEAR	WHO1 (59)

22.14 WOMEN'S HEALTH AND HEALTH SERVICES

Subject	Categories	Units	Time series Yes/No	Frequency	Territorial coverage	Source (Table no.)
Anaemia, women aged 15-49 with		%	No		World	UN16 (17)
Births attended by trained personnel		%	No		World	UN16 (17)
Breast-feeding	By prevalence and duration	%	No		Developing countries	PC1 (35)
Contraceptives, currently married women using	Age group	%	No		World	UN16 (17)
Estimates of maternal mortality and nos of live births	By mortality ratio, live births, maternal deaths	nos	No		World	PC1 (30)
Female health and health services, selected indicators of		%, nos	No		World	UN17 (25)
Female health and health services, selected indicators of		%, rate	No		Africa	UN46 (24)
Maternal care	% of women receiving by prenatal care, attended births, low birthweight babies	%	No		Developing countries	PC1 (32)
Maternal mortality		100,000 live births	No		Developing countries	UNCTAD5 (1.4)

Subject	Categories	Units	Time series Yes/No Frequency	Territorial coverage	Source (Table no.)
Maternal mortality		rate	No	World	UN16 (17)
Pregnancy, care	Pre-natal care, delivery care, infant care	%	Yes I	World	WHO2 (6)
Women immunized with tetanus toxoid	By residence, by education	nos, %	No	Developing countries	PC1 (33)

23 HOUSING

23 HOUSING

Subject	Categories	Units	Time series Yes/No Frequency		Territorial coverage	Source (Table no.)
23.1 CONSTRUCTION						
23.1.1 Authorised, Permits Issued						
Authorized	By location and investor	nos	Yes	A	World	UN18 (-)
Authorized	By type	nos, cu m	Yes	A	World	UN18 (-)
Dwelling construction authorised, by type of investor	State and local governments,	nos	Yes	A	World	UN18 (-)
	other public bodies		Yes	A	World	UN18 (-)
	co-operatives, private	nos	Yes	A	World	UN18 (-)
Dwellings - floor area		sq m	Yes	A	World	UN18 (-)
Dwellings - number		nos	Yes	A	World	UN18 (-)
Dwellings construction authorised	Urban, rural by location	nos	Yes	A	World	UN18 (-)
Dwellings created by restoration and conversion (authorised)	Number, floor area	nos	Yes	A	World	UN18 (-)
		sq m	Yes	A	World	UN18 (-)
New construction authorised in residential buildings	Number, % one- or two-dwelling	nos	Yes	A	World	UN18 (-)
	buildings, multi-dwelling, floor area	sq m	Yes	A	World	UN18 (-)
New construction authorised in non-residential buildings	Number, floor area	nos	Yes	A	World	UN18 (-)
		sq m	Yes	A	World	UN18 (-)
Permits issued	Total, residential	nat curr cu m, nos	Yes	A, M	OECD	OECD22
Permits issued	Total and residential	nat curr	Yes	A, Q, M	OECD	OECD22
Rooms, authorized dwelling construction		nos	Yes	A	World	UN18 (-)
Rooms in all dwellings authorised		nos	Yes	A	World	UN18 (-)
Tender value		nat curr	Yes	A	World	UN18 (-)
23.1.2 Completions - see also under Investment Expenditure (23.1.3)						
Dwelling construction	Authorised, completed, started	nos	Yes	A	World	UN18 (-)
Dwelling construction in residential buildings	Number, floor area, one- or two-dwelling buildings, multi-dwelling buildings	nos, sq m	Yes	A	World	UN18 (-)
Dwellings - created by restoration and conversion (completed)	Number, floor area	nos sq m	Yes	A	World	UN18 (-)
Dwellings completed		nos, tonnes	Yes	M	Asia and Pacific	UN43 (-)
Dwellings completed	By country, by habitable area	nos, sq m	No		EC	EC18(8.12)
Dwellings completed	By country	nos	No		EC	EM1 (1602)
Dwellings completed	By location and investor	nos	Yes	A	World	UN18 (-)
Dwellings completed	By number of rooms	nos, %	Yes	A	World	UN10 (4)
Dwellings completed	By type	nos, cu m	Yes	A	World	UN18 (-)
Dwellings completed	By type	nos	Yes	A	Nordic countries	NCM1 (106)
Dwellings completed	By type of investor	nos	Yes	A	World	UN10 (6)
Dwellings completed	Flats per thousand inhabitants	nos	Yes	A	VICES region, VICES countries and Yugoslavia	VICES1 (II/4)
Dwellings completed	In ground and high-rise residential buildings	nos, %	No		World	UN10 (5)
Dwellings completed	Total, urban and rural and % AGR	nos, %	Yes	10 yrs	World	UN26
Dwellings completed	Total and percentage of which with amenities, in urban areas and in rural areas	nos, %	Yes	A	World	UN10 (4)
Dwellings completed - floor area		sq m	Yes	A	World	UN18 (-)
Dwellings completed - number		nos	Yes	A	World	UN18 (-)
Dwellings completed by location	Urban, rural	nos	Yes	A	World	UN18 (-)
Dwellings completed by type of investor	State and local governments, other public bodies	nos	Yes	A	World	UN18 (-)
	co-operatives, privates	nos	Yes	A	World	UN18 (-)
Housing	Summary, by country	nos, %,	Yes	A	ESCAP countries	UN44

23 HOUSING

Subject	Categories	Units	Time series Yes/No Frequency		Territorial coverage	Source (Table no.)
Index numbers of construction activity (value added in constant prices)	Residential, non-residential, civil engineering	index	Yes	A	World	UN18 (-)
New dwelling construction in non-residential buildings	Number, floor area	nos, sq m	Yes	A	World	UN18 (-)
Rooms, dwellings completed		nos	Yes	A	World	UN18 (-)
Rooms in all dwellings completed		nos	Yes	A	World	UN18 (-)
23.1.3 Expenditure and Output						
Gross fixed capital formation	Total, in construction and residential buildings as a percentage of GDP, as a percentage of total fixed capital formation and as a percentage of gross fixed capital formation in construction	%	Yes	A	World	UN10 (2)
Housing investment	Gross fixed capital formation in residential building construction as % of total and GDP and % AGR	%	Yes	10 yrs	World	UN26
Investments	Total and in construction	%	Yes	A	Eastern EC	UN10 (3)
Residential construction	Percentage of GDP	%	Yes	A	OECD, EC	OECD32 (6.9)
Value of construction		nat curr	Yes	A	World	UN10 (10)
Value of output		nat curr	Yes	A	World	UN10 (12)
Values at constant prices	% of total, % of GDP	nat curr, %	No		World	UN16 (6)
23.1.4 Starts						
Housing started		nos, indices	Yes	A, M	EC USA, Japan	EC36
Housing starts		nos	Yes	A, M	OECD	OECD22
Housing starts		nos	Yes	A, M	OECD, EC Major Seven Total	OECD22
Housing starts	Construction index	nos, indices	Yes	A, Q, M	OECD	OECD22
23.2 ENERGY CONSUMPTION - see also Section 17						
Consumption by households	Total and percentage of total by energy type	joules, %	Yes	A	World	UN10 (7)
Housing expenditure	Private final consumption expenditure on rent, fuel and power as % of total and % AGR	%	Yes	10 yrs	World	UN26
Rent, fuel and power (private final consumption) at constant prices		nat curr	No		World	UN16 (6)
23.3 FINANCE						
Mortgages, owner-occupied dwellings with		%	No		EC	MHPPE1 (-)
Mortgages, duration of, average		years	No		EC	MHPPE1 (-)
Mortgages, interest rate		%	Yes	Selected years	EC	MHPPE1 (-)
Taxes levied on housing	By type	%	No		EC	MHPPE1 (-)

Subject	Categories	Units	Time series Yes/No Frequency	Territorial coverage	Source (Table no.)
23.4 HOUSEHOLDS - see also Section 36					
Dwelling households	By number of children	nos, age, years	No	Nordic countries	NCM1 (113)
Dwelling households	By number of members	nos	No	Nordic countries	NCM1 (112)
Dwelling households	By number of occupants, size of dwelling	nos	No	Nordic countries	NCM1 (110)
Dwelling households and occupants	By size of dwelling	nos	No	Nordic countries	NCM1 (111)
Dwelling units occupied	By number of occupants	nos	No	Latin American and Caribbean countries	UN45 (377)
Dwelling units occupied	By type of occupation in urban and rural areas	nos	No	Latin American and Caribbean countries	UN45 (375)
Family nuclei	By type and by number of children in family nucleus	nos	No	EC	EC11 (18)
Household numbers	By country	nos	No	EC	EM1 (1605)
Household numbers	By type	nos, %	No	World	UN10 (17)
Household numbers	Total, urban and rural and % AGR	nos, %	Yes 10 yrs	World	UN26
Household size, average		nos	No	World	UN16 (5)
Household size	By country, by number of persons	%	No	EC	EM1 (1606)
Household size	By country	nos	No	EC	EM1 (1607)
Household size	Total, urban and rural and % AGR	nos, %	Yes 10 yrs	World	UN26
Households, persons in private	Total, private, not in private, % in private	nos, %	No	EC	EC11 (14)
Households, private	Size of household, members, total	nos	No	EC	EC11 (15)
Households, private members of private households and numbers of children by type of household	Type of household, total private households	nos	No	EC	EC11 (16)
Households, private	By total number of persons and number of economically active persons in household	nos	No	EC	EC11 (17)
Households, private	By total number of persons and number of persons aged under 15 years	nos	No	EC	EC11 (17.1)
Households, private	By total number of persons and number aged 65 years and over	nos	No	EC	EC11 (17.2)
Households, private	Housing units, living quarters other than housing units, total	nos	No	EC	EC11 (19)
Households	By size of household, with electricity	nos, %	No	Developing countries	WB1 (-)
Households equipped with household appliances	By country, by appliance	%	No	EC	EC72 (10.11)
Households having access to an area of open space within a 20 minute walking time	By characteristics of head	%	No	OECD	OECD20 (23.2)
Households lacking some of the basic amenities in the dwelling	Amenities by characteristic by head	%	No	OECD	OECD20 (24.2)
Households with access to an outdoor space adjacent to the dwelling	By characteristic of head	%	No	OECD	OECD20 (23.1)
Households with electrical appliances	By country, by appliance	%	No	EC	EC35 (-)
households, private	Persons, total households	nos			EC11 (1)
Owner occupancy ratio	Total, urban and rural and % AGR	%	Yes 10 yrs	World	UN26
Ownership of consumer electronics	By country, by item	%	No	EC	EM1 (1608)
Ownership of major appliances	By country, by appliance	%	No	EC	EM1 (1609)

23 HOUSING

Subject	Categories	Units	Time series Yes/No Frequency		Territorial coverage	Source (Table no.)
Persons, per room	Urban area	nos	Yes	I	Latin American and Caribbean countries	UN45 (36)
Population with basic amenities inside the dwelling		%	Yes	10 yrly	OECD	OECD20 (24.1)
23.5 HOUSING STOCK						
23.5.1 Characteristics						
Accommodation	By title, type, year of construction, and number of rooms, according to the socio-economic category of the head of household, the type of household, the income category, the region and the urban, rural environment, by country	%	No		EC	EC42 (1/1-1/5)
Amenities	Bath or shower, central heating	%	No		EC	MHPPE1 (-)
Amenities	By country, by amenity	%	No		EC	EM1 (1604)
Amenities	By country, by amenity	%	No		EC	EC35 (-)
Amenities	By country	%	No		EC	EC72 (10.10)
Amenities of occupied conventional dwellings by principal amenities	Total	nos, %	No		EC	EC11 (24)
Amenities-dwellings without electricity		%	No		World	UN16 (5)
Amenities-dwellings without piped water		%	No		World	UN16 (5)
Amenities-dwellings without toilet		%	No		World	UN16 (5)
Amenities-housing units, water supply	Total, urban and rural and % AGR	%	Yes	10 yrs	World	UN26
Amenities-housing units, toilet facility	Total, urban and rural and % AGR	%	Yes	10 yrs	World	UN26
Amenities-housing units, electric lighting	Total, urban and rural and % AGR	%	Yes	10 yrs	World	UN26
Amenities-occupied dwelling units	By type of services available in urban and rural areas	nos	No		Latin American and Caribbean countries	UN45 (378)
Amenities-occupied private dwelling units	By type of services available	%	No		Latin American and Caribbean countries	UN45 (37)
Condition of housing stock	Good, lacking basic amenities, unfit, serious disrepair	%	No		EC	MHPPE1 (-)
Dwelling by construction period		%	No		EC	MHPPE1 (-)
Dwellings	By period of construction, type	nos	No		Nordic countries	NCM1 (108)
Dwellings by construction period	By country, by period of construction	%	No		EC	EC72 (10.7)
Dwellings by construction period	By country	%	No		EC	EC35 (-)
Dwellings by type	By quantity, type, amenities	nos, %	No		EC	EC69 (VII.4)
Dwellings by type	By type of house, convenience	nos, %	No		Nordic countries	NCM1 (109)
Dwellings by type and size	By type of house, size	nos	No		Nordic countries	NCM1 (107)
Floor space, average useful	Total stock, newly-built	sq m	No		EC	MHPPE1 (-)
Floor space per dwelling	Average useful and average living	sq m	Yes	A	World	UN10 (4)
Heating	Type of fuel	%	No		EC	MHPPE1 (-)
Households with more than one person per room	By characteristics of head	%	No		OECD	OECD20 (22.3)
Housing units	By country, by type	nos	No		EC	EC72 (10.2)

Subject	Categories	Units	Time series Yes/No Frequency		Territorial coverage	Source (Table no.)
Multi-dwelling buildings		%	Yes	Selected years	EC	MHPPE1 (-)
New dwellings, minimum officially required size		sq m, rooms	No		EC	MHPPE1 (-)
Owner-occupied, subsidised		%	Yes	Selected years	EC	MHPPE1 (-)
Person per room, average		nos	No		World	UN16 (5)
Persons per dwelling, average		nos	Yes	Selected years	EC	MHPPE1 (-)
Persons per room		nos	Yes	10 yrly	OECD	OECD20 (22.1)
Persons per room	By country	nos	No		EC	EC72 (10.9)
Population, by density of occupation of dwellings		%	Yes	Various	OECD	OECD20 (22.2)
Population, without safe water		%	No		World	UN16 (5)
Population, without sanitation facilities		%	No		World	UN16 (5)
Rental dwellings, social		%	Yes	Selected years	EC	MHPPE1 (-)
Rental dwellings	Social, private	%	Yes	Selected years	EC	MHPPE1 (-)
Rooms, average number		nos	No		World	UN16 (5)
Rooms per dwelling		nos	Yes	A	World	UN10 (4)
Rooms per dwelling	% distribution	%	No		EC	MHPPE1 (-)
Rooms per dwelling	average number of rooms Total, urban and rural and % AGR	nos, %	Yes	10 yrs	World	UN26
Selected indicators of housing and human settlements conditions	By population, housing characteristics, housing units	%, nos	No		World	UN17 (28)
Selected indicators of housing and human settlements conditions	By population, housing characteristics, housing units	%, nos	No		Africa	UN46 (27)
Tenure	Rental, owner-occupation, other	%	Yes	Selected years	EC	MHPPE1 (-)
23.5.2 Size of Stock						
Decreases in		nos	Yes	Selected years	EC	MHPPE1 (-)
Dwellings		nos	No		EC, USA, USSR, Canada, Japan	EC9 (4.14)
Dwellings	By country, by number of rooms	%	No		EC	EM1 (1603)
Dwellings	By country, by number of rooms	%	No		EC	EC35 (-)
Dwellings	By country	nos	No		EC	EM1 (1601)
Dwellings	By date of construction	nos	No		World	UN10 (18)
Dwellings	Increases and decreases	nos	No		World	UN10 (18)
Dwellings	Summary, by country	nos, %,	Yes	A	ESCAP countries	UN44
Dwellings	Total, urban and rural and % AGR	nos, %	Yes	10 yrs	World	UN26
Dwellings occupied	By number of rooms	nos	No		Latin American and Caribbean countries	UN45 (376)
Dwellings occupied	By numbers of inhabitants	nos	No		World	UN10 (19)
Dwellings occupied	Persons in owner-occupied, other dwellings					
Dwellings occupied	Total dwellings, total rooms	nos	No		EC	EC11 (20)
Dwellings occupied	By tenure status	nos, %	No		EC	EC11 (21)
Dwellings occupied	By tenure status and period of construction	nos	No		EC	EC11 (23)

23 HOUSING

Subject	Categories	Units	Time series Yes/No Frequency		Territorial coverage	Source (Table no.)
Dwellings occupied	By tenure status, total dwellings, persons, rooms, persons per dwelling, average number of persons per room	nos	No		EC	EC11 (22)
Dwellings per 1000 inhabitants		nos	Yes	Selected years	EC	MHPPE1 (-)
Dwellings per inhabitant	Total, in urban and rural areas	nos	Yes	A	World	UN10 (4)
Floor space, average useful	Total stock, newly-built	sq m	No		EC	MHPPE1 (-)
Multi-dwelling buildings		%	Yes	Selected	EC	MHPPE1 (-)
Residential buildings - floor area		sq m	Yes	A	World	UN18 (-)
Residential buildings - number	One- or two-dwelling buildings, multi-dwelling buildings	nos	Yes	A	World	UN18 (-)
23.6 PRICES - see also under Rents (23.7)						
Input and output price indices		indices	Yes	A	World	UN10 (13)
Residential construction	Implicit price index	%	Yes	A	OECD, EC	OECD32 (8.6)
23.7 RENTS						
Housing expenditure	Private final consumption expenditure on rent, fuel and power as % of total and % AGR	%	Yes	10 yrs	World	UN26
Rent, fuel and power (private final consumption) at constant prices		nat curr	No		World	UN16 (6)
Rents	By country	index	No		EC	EC72 (10.15)

24 INCOME AND WEALTH

Subject	Categories	Units	Time series Yes/No	Frequency	Territorial coverage	Source (Table no.)
24.1 EARNINGS						
24.1.1 All Workers						
Compensation of employees		% (value)	Yes	A	OECD, EC	OECD28
Compensation of employees	By component	nat curr	Yes	A	EC	EC62 (5.2)
Compensation of employees	Per wage and salary earner at current and 1985 prices, PPPs and exchange rates	PPPs, ECU	Yes	A	EC, USA and Japan	EC60 (J.2)
Compensation of employees	Share of compensation of employees in VAFC by branch	ECU, %	Yes	A	EC	EC61 (-)
Compensation of employees	Total at current and 1985 prices, PPPs and exchange rates	PPPs, ECU	Yes	A	EC, USA and Japan	EC60 (J.1)
Earnings, all industries	Earnings per hour	nat curr, sex	Yes	A	Nordic countries	NCM1 (162)
Earnings, all industries	Hour, day, month, year per worker	nat curr	Yes	A	World	ILO7 (22A)
Earnings, average monthly	By country, by economic sector	nat curr	No		EC	EC18 (14.1)
Earnings, total	Earnings per hour, day week, month, sex	nat curr	Yes	Q	World	ILO1 (8)
Employees	Wages and salaries	nat curr	Yes	A	World	UN27 (-)
Income, real per head	Average annual growth rate	%	Yes	A	VICES countries and Yugoslavia	VICES1 (II/2)
Income earners, incomes and taxes		nat curr	No		Nordic countries	NCM1 (1700
Income earners and average income	By sex, age	nat curr	No		Nordic countries	NCM1 (172)
Manual and non-manual workers	By country, by sector	PPPs	No		EC	EC35 (-)
Manual and non-manual workers	Hourly labour costs	nat curr	Yes	A	EC	EC55 (8.18)
Manual and non-manual workers in industry	Hourly labour costs	nat curr ECU, PPPs	Yes	A	EC	EC9 (3.42)
Manual workers in industry	Hourly earnings, gross	indices,	Yes	A	EC, USA, Sweden, Japan	EC9 (3.38)
		nat curr, PPPs,	Yes	A	EC	EC9 (3.40)
	by sex	indices	Yes	A	EC	EC9 (3.39)
	by sector	nat curr	No		EC	EC9 (3.41)
Money wages in industry	Industry A	EC	MAC3			(B4,A-D)
Non-agricultural activities	Earnings, per hour, day, week, month, sex	nat curr	Yes	A	World	ILO7 (16)
Non-agricultural activities	Earnings per hour, day, week, month, sex	nat curr	Yes	Q	World	ILO1 (7)
Operatives	Wages and salaries	nat curr	Yes	A	World	UN27 (-)
Supplements	Wages and salaries	nat curr	Yes	A	World	UN27 (-)
Tax payers	Total	nos	Yes	5 yrly	Nordic countries	NCM1 (171)
Wage and salary earners		nos	Yes	A	EC, USA and Japan	EC60 (O)
Wage and salary earners	By branch and yearly change of compensation of employees per employee	nos, %	Yes	A	EC	EC61 (-)
Workers, total	Earnings per hour, day, week, month, sex	nat curr	Yes	A	World	ILO7 (17A)
Workers, total	Earnings per hour, day, week, month, sex	nat curr	Yes	A	World	ILO7 (17B)
24.1.2 By Industry						
Agriculture						
Earnings	Earnings per hour, day, week, month, sex	nat curr	Yes	A	World	ILO7 (21)
Manual workers, full-time	Hourly earnings and number of hours paid	nat curr, hrs	No		EC	EC23 (I.1)
Manual workers, gross hourly earnings		indices	No		EC	EC23 (I.2)

24 INCOME AND WEALTH

Subject	Categories	Units	Time series Yes/No Frequency	Territorial coverage	Source (Table no.)
Manual workers, gross hourly earnings	By work type and sex	indices	No	EC	EC23 (I.3)
Manual workers, gross hourly earnings	By provision of benefits in kind and by sex	indices	No	EC	EC23 (I.4)
Manual workers, gross hourly earnings	By sex and age group	indices	No	EC	EC23 (I.5)
Manual workers, hours paid per month	By country, provision of benefits in kind and work type	hrs	No	EC	EC23 (-)
Manual workers, gross hourly earnings	By country, provision of benefits in kind and work type	nat curr	No	EC	EC23 (-)
Manual workers, gross hourly earnings	By country, provision of benefits in kind, by sex and age group	nat curr, indices	No	EC	EC23 (-)
Manual workers, hours paid	By country and region	hrs	No	EC	EC23 (III.1-III.7)
Manual workers, gross hourly earnings	By country and region	nat curr	No	EC	EC23 (III.1-III.7)
Manual workers in agriculture	By nature of work, by size of farm, by receipt of benefits in kind	indices nat curr	Yes BA No	EC EC	EC9 (3.44) EC9 (3.44)
Professional qualification, gross hourly earnings	By country and type	nat curr	No	EC	EC23
Seasonal workers, gross daily earnings		nat curr, ECU	No	EC	EC23 (IV.1-IV.2)
Seasonal workers, number hours worked		hrs	No	EC	EC23 (IV.1-IV.2)
Wages in agriculture	By countries	indices	Yes A	EC	MAC3 (B5,A-D)
Wages in agriculture	By countries	nos	No	The Americas and Australasia	MAC2 (C5)
Automobile Industry					
Net hourly earnings		dm PPP	No	World	IMWF1 (-)
Social security		%	Swiss francs	World	IMWF1 (-)
Construction Industry					
Building, civil engineering		ECUs	No	EC by region	EC76 (-)
Construction	Earnings per hour, day week, month, sex	nat curr	Yes A	World	ILO7 (19)
Manufacturing and construction by branches of industry	Earnings per hour, adults	nat curr, sex	Yes A	Nordic countries	NCM1 (161)
Wages and Salaries		nat curr	Yes A	World	UN18 (-)
Electrical Engineering					
Net hourly earnings		dm PPP	No	World	IMWF1 (-)
Social security		%	Swiss francs	World	IMWF1 (-)
General					
Earnings, hourly, daily, weekly, monthly	By industry	indices	Yes A, M	OECD	OECD22
Earnings, hourly	Manufacturing	indices	Yes M, Q, A	OECD, EC	OECD23 (-)
Earnings	By industry, by hour, day, month, year per worker	nat curr	Yes A	World	ILO7 (22B)
Gross wages and salaries	Monthly average per employed person by economic sectors, by country	nat curr	Yes A	VICES countries and Yugoslavia	VICES1 (I/2)
Hourly wages, industry	Nominal, real	indices	Yes A, M	EC, USA, Japan	EC36
Index of hourly earnings in industry	Nominal, real	indices	No	EC countries, USA and Japan	EC53 (1.3)

Subject	Categories	Units	Time series Yes/No	Frequency	Territorial coverage	Source (Table no.)
Manual workers, average gross hourly	By NACE sector and region, by country	nat curr	Yes	2x yr	EC	EC24 (I/4)
Manual workers, average gross hourly	By NACE sector, by country	nat curr	Yes	2x yr	EC	EC24 (I/3)
Manual workers, average gross hourly	Trends, by NACE sector	indices	No		EC	EC24 (I/2)
Manual workers, average gross hourly	By major industrial groups	nat curr, indices, ECU, current PPPs	Yes	2x yr	EC	EC24 (I/1)
Manual workers	Major industrial groups, hourly earnings	PPPs	Yes	A	EC	EC53 (2.4)
Nominal and real trends		indices				
Non-manual workers, average gross monthly	Trends, by NACE sector	indices	No		EC	EC24 (III/2)
Non-manual workers, average gross monthly	By groups of activity (NACE), by country	nat curr	Yes	2x yr	EC	EC24 (III/3)
Non-manual workers, average gross monthly	By major groups of activity	nat curr, indices, ECU, PPPs	Yes	2x yr	EC	EC24 (III/1)
Non-manual workers, average gross monthly	By major industrial groups	nat curr, indices, ECU, current PPPs	Yes	2x yr	EC	EC24 (II/1)
Non-manual workers, average gross monthly	Trends, by NACE sector	indices	No		EC	EC24 (II/2)
Non-manual workers, average gross monthly	By NACE sector, by country	nat curr	Yes	2x yr	EC	EC24 (II/3)
Non-manual workers	Major industrial groups, earnings	monthly	Yes	A	EC	EC53 (2.5)
Total	By ISIC group	%	No		World	UNIDO1 (2.6)
Wages, value added		%	Yes	I	World	UNIDO1 (1.12, 2.5)
Wages, value added	By ISIC group	%	No		World	UNIDO1 (2.6)
Wages	By industrial sector, by country	indices, nat curr	Yes	A	ESCAP	UN44
Wages	By ISIC group	US$	Yes	I	World	UNIDO1 (1.12, 2.5)
Wages and earnings, indices of	By country, indices	indices	Yes	A	Africa and Asia	MAC1 (C4)
Wages and salaries, supplements	By ISIC division	nat curr	Yes	A	OECD	OECD16
Wages and salaries	By industry	nat curr	No		Nordic countries	NCM1 (77)
Wages and salaries	By ISIC division	nat curr	Yes	A	OECD	OECD16
Wages and salaries (gross)	Solid fuels coke ovens petroleum and natural gas mineral oil refining) nuclear fuels indices electricity, gas, steam, hot water, production and distribution of water supply, collection, purification and distribution metalliferous ores extraction and preparation metals, production and preliminary processing extraction of minerals, peat non-metallic mineral products, manufacture of chemical indices man-made fibres, industry metal articles mechanical engineering office, data processing	ECUs	No		EC by region	EC76 (-)

24 INCOME AND WEALTH

Subject	Categories	Units	Time series Yes/No Frequency		Territorial coverage	Source (Table no.)
Wages and salaries (gross) *cont*	machinery, manufacture of electrical engineering motor vehicles, parts, accessories, manufacture of other means of transport instrument engineering food, drink, tobacco indices textile industry leather, leather goods industry footwear and clothing industry timber, wooden furniture industry paper, paper products, printing, publishing, manufacture of rubber, plastics, processing of other manufacturing industries	ECUs	No		EC by region	EC76 (-)
Wages in industry	By countries	nos	No		The Americas and Australasia	MAC2 (C4)
Wages in non-agricultural activities	Earnings per hour, day week, month, sex	nat curr	Yes	Q	World	ILO1 (7)
Wages per employee	By ISIC group	US$	No		World	UNIDO1 (2.6)
Manufacturing						
Earnings	Earnings per hour, day, week, month, sex	nat curr	Yes	Q	World	ILO1 (8)
Earnings	Indices		Yes	M, Q, A	OECD - total	OECD23 (-)
Earnings	Sex	nat curr	Yes	A	World	UN50 (20)
Earnings, hourly		indices	Yes	A, Q	OECD	OECD22
Earnings, hourly	Manufacturing	indices	Yes	A, M	OECD, EC Major Seven Total	OECD22
Earnings, hourly	Manufacturing	indices	Yes	M, Q, A	OECD	OECD23 (-)
Earnings, hourly	Percentage change	%	Yes	A	OECD, EC Major seven	OECD32 (9.1)
Earnings, hourly, adults	Manufacturing and construction by branches of industry, by sex	nat curr	Yes	A	Nordic countries	NCM1 (161)
Earnings, hourly, real	Percentage change	%	Yes	A	OECD, EC	OECD32 (9.2)
Wage rates, hourly	Percentage change	%	Yes	A	OECD, EC	OECD32 (9.3)
Wage rates, real hourly	Percentage change	%	Yes	A	OECD, EC	OECD32 (9.4)
Wages: manufacturing		indices	Yes	A, Q	OECD	OECD22
Wages and salaries		nat curr	No		World	UN50 (90)
Mechanical engineering						
Hourly earnings, net		dm PPP	No		World	IMWF1 (-)
Social security		%	Swiss francs		World	IMWF1 (-)
Mining and Quarrying						
Earnings	Earnings per hour, day, week, month, sex	nat curr	Yes	A	World	ILO7 (18)
Shipbuilding						
Hourly earnings, net		dm PPP	No		World	IMWF1 (-)
Social security		%	Swiss francs		World	IMWF1 (-)
Steel Industry						
Hourly earnings, net		dm PPP	No		World	IMWF1 (-)
Social security		%	Swiss francs		World	IMWF1 (-)
Transportation and Communication						
Transport, storage and communication	Earnings per hour, day, week, month, sex	nat curr	Yes	A	World	ILO7 (20)

Subject	Categories	Units	Time series Yes/No Frequency		Territorial coverage	Source (Table no.)
24.1.3 Distribution						
Annual earnings of full-time adult employees	Deciles	%	No		OECD	OECD20 (14.1)
Deciles for income earners	By sex, total	nos	No		Nordic countries	NCM1 (173)
Frequency of low earnings among employees	By selected characteristics	%	No		OECD	OECD20
Income shares in decile groups	By sex, total	nos, %	No		Nordic countries	NCM1 (174)
Relative median earnings of full-time employees	By selected characteristics	%	No		OECD	OECD20 (14.2)
24.1.4 Manual Workers						
Major industrial groups	Manual workers earnings hourly	PPPs	Yes	A	EC	EC53 (2.4)
Manual workers, average gross hourly	By NACE sector and region, by country	nat curr	Yes	2x yr	EC	EC24 (I/4)
Manual workers, average gross hourly	By NACE sector, by country	nat curr	Yes	2x yr	EC	EC24 (I/3)
Manual workers, average gross hourly	Trends, by NACE sector	indices	No		EC	EC24 (I/2)
Manual workers, average gross hourly	By major industrial groups	nat curr, indices, ECU, current PPPs	Yes	2x yr	EC	EC24 (I/1)
Manual workers, gross hourly wage		nat curr	Yes	A	EC	EC55 (8.17)
24.1.5 Non-manual Workers						
Major industry groups	Non-manual workers monthly earnings	indices	Yes	A	EC	EC53 (2.5)
Non-manual workers, average gross monthly	Trends, by NACE sector	indices	No		EC	EC24 (III/2)
Non-manual workers, average gross monthly	By groups of activity (NACE), by country	nat curr	Yes	2x yr	EC	EC24 (III/3)
Non-manual workers, average gross monthly	By major groups of activity	nat curr, indices, ECU, PPPs	Yes	2x yr	EC	EC24 (III/1)
Non-manual workers, average gross monthly	By major indices groups	nat curr, indices, ECU, current PPPs	Yes	2x yr	EC	EC24 (II/1)
Non-manual workers, average gross monthly	Trends, by NACE sector	indices	No		EC	EC24 (II/2)
Non-manual workers, average gross monthly	By NACE sector, by country	nat curr	Yes	2x yr	EC	EC24 (II/3)
24.2 INCOME DISTRIBUTION						
Distribution of disposable income of private households	Deciles	%	No		OECD	OECD20 (19.1)
Household income share	Top 20%, bottom 40%, by country, region	ratio	No		UNICEF assisted countries	UNICEF2 (-)
Households in each income decile with a number of income earners		%	No		OECD	OECD20 (19.2)
Income characteristics of households of head of household	By characteristics	index, nos	No		OECD	OECD20 (19.3)
Population in each decile of the income distribution		%	No		OECD	OECD20 (19.2)
Low Incomes						
Components of income by decile groups of households	By urban, rural areas and per capita income	nat curr	No		Various countries	UN37 (7)
Components of income by income size groups by	By urban, rural areas and per capita income	nat curr	No		Various countries	UN37 (8)
Households by income size group	Age group of household	nos, head	No		Various countries	UN37 (2)

24 INCOME AND WEALTH

Subject	Categories	Units	Time series Yes/No Frequency		Territorial coverage	Source (Table no.)
Households classified by characteristics of head in the lowest quintile of the equivalent income distribution		%	No		OECD	OECD20 (20.1)
Income	Components of income by socio-economic status of head of household	nat curr	No		Various countries	UN37 (6)
Percentage distribution of income by percentile groups of households		%,	Yes	Selected years	World	UN16 (30)
24.3 LABOUR COSTS						
Labour costs, structure of	Direct costs, indirect costs	% of total	No		EC	EC9 (3.43)
Labour costs	By NACE, by size of enterprise	ECU	Yes	A	EC	EC77 (-)
Labour costs	By NACE	ECU	No		EC	EC75(2), (3.1)
24.4 PURCHASING POWER						
Working time required for purchases	By consumer items	hours	No		World	IMWF1 (-)
24.5 WEALTH						
Distribution of total personal net worth of households	Quintiles	%	No		OECD	OECD20 (21.1)
Rate of household ownership of selected wealth items	By age of head of household	%	No		OECD	OECD20 (21.2)
Wealth	By socio-economic status of head of household	%	No		OECD	OECD20 (21.2)
Wealth, poverty and social investment	Indicators of population wealth, poverty	PPPs, %, US$, ratio	No		Industrial countries	UN25 (38)
Wealth, poverty and social investment	Indicators of population wealth, poverty	PPPs, %, US$, ratio	No		Developing countries	UN25 (17)
24.6 WAGES RATES						
24.6.1 Chemical Industry						
Hourly wage rate	Percentage change	%	Yes	A	OECD, EC	OECD32 (9.6)
24.6.2 Food, Beverages and Tobacco Industry						
Hourly wage rate	Percentage change	%	Yes	A	OECD, EC	OECD32 (9.5)
24.6.3 Metal Industry						
Hourly wage rate: basic metals	Percentage change	%	Yes	A	OECD, EC	OECD32 (9.7)
Hourly wage rate: metal products, machinery and equipment	Percentage change	%	Yes	A	OECD, EC	OECD32 (9.8)
24.6.4 Textile Industry						
Hourly wage rate	Percentage change	%	Yes	A	OECD, EC	OECD32 (9.9)

APPENDIX A

INDEX OF PUBLICATIONS

ARRANGED BY *instat* CODE

FULL BIBLIOGRAPHICAL DETAILS

INTRODUCTION TO APPENDIX A

Publications are referred to by code only throughout the main body of this book. The titles of the publications and other bibliographical details are presented in this Appendix arranged by ***instat*** code. Notes on the information provided are given below.

***instat* codes**

The ***instat*** codes consist of two parts:

- an alphabetical prefix which denotes the organization responsible for compiling the publication
- a numerical suffix which distinguishes different publications of the same organization

Arrangement

All publications are listed here in alphanumeric order according to the ***instat*** codes referred to above.

Information provided

In addition to the ***instat*** code, the title of the publication and the full name of the organization responsible, the following information is provided:

- **Edition indexed**

  This indicates, as appropriate, the edition date and/or the volume number of the edition examined when compiling this book. Note that the edition date is *not* necessarily the same as the publication date (given separately)

- **Publisher**

  Name of the publisher. This is generally, but not necessarily, the same as the name of the sponsoring body for the publication

- **Frequency**

  This is the frequency of publication for serial publications

- **Date**

  This is the date of publication of the edition indexed when compiling this book

- **Place**

  Place of publication: town or city and country

- **ISBN** and **ISSN**

  International Standard Book Number and/or International Standard Serial Number, where applicable, of the edition indexed when compiling this book. A dash in this column indicates that the edition has neither an ISBN nor ISSN

***instat* code**	**Title**	**Edition indexed**	**Publisher Frequency Date Place**	**ISBN ISSN**
AEA: ASSOCIATION OF EUROPEAN AIRLINES				
AEA1	Association of European Airlines Yearbook	1992	AEA Annually 1992 Brussels, Belgium	—
AEA2	Statistical Appendices to AEA Yearbook	1992	AEA Annually 1992 Brussels, Belgium	—
AEA3	Intra-European Country to Country Traffic	1990 October	AEA Monthly 1991 Brussels, Belgium	—
AEA4	Medium-Term Forecast of European Scheduled Passenger Traffic	1992–96	AEA Irregular 1992 Brussels, Belgium	—
APO: ASIAN PRODUCTIVITY ORGANISATION				
APO1	Comparative Information on Productivity Levels and Changes in APO Member Countries	1991	APO Irregular 1991 Tokyo, Japan	ISBN 9 2 833 1 613 4
ASEANS: ASSOCIATION OF SOUTH-EAST ASIAN NATIONS SECRETARIAT				
ASEANS1	ASEAN Selected Statistics	1982–88	ASEANS Occasional 1990 Jakarta, Indonesia	—
BB: BASIL BLACKWELL LTD				
BB1	Oil and Energy Trends, Annual Statistical Review	1992	Energy Economics Research/ Blackwell Annually 1992 Oxford, UK	ISSN 0953 1033
BB2	Oil and Energy Trends	1992 December	Blackwell Monthly 1992 Oxford, UK	ISSN 0950 1045
BB3	Tanker Charter Record	1993 January	Blackwell Monthly 1993 Oxford, UK	ISSN 0958 8787
BB4	World Oil Trade Review of International Oil Movements	1992 Vol 14	Blackwell Biannual 1992 Oxford, UK	ISSN 0950 1029

***instat* code**	**Title**	**Edition indexed**	**Publisher Frequency Date Place**	**ISBN ISSN**
BGS: BRITISH GEOLOGICAL SURVEY				
BGS1	World Mineral Statistics Vol 1 Metals and Energy	1986–90	BGS Annually 1992 Keyworth, UK	ISBN 0 85272 210 9
BGS2	World Mineral Statistics Vol 2 Industrial Minerals	1986–90	BGS Annually 1992 Keyworth, UK	ISBN 0 85272 211 7
BP: BRITISH PETROLEUM COMPANY PLC				
BP1	BP Statistical Review of World Energy	1990	BP Annually 1990 London, UK	ISBN 0 86165 184 7
BP2	BP Review of World Gas	1992	BP Annually 1992 London, UK	—
BPB: BRITISH PAPER AND BOARD INDUSTRY FEDERATION				
BPB1	Reference Tables	1991	BPB Annually 1991 Swindon, UK	—
CAA: CIVIL AVIATION AUTHORITY				
CAA1	Fatal Accident Statistics for Passenger Air Transport Services CAA Paper 83014	1964–81	CAA Occasional 1983 London, UK	ISBN 0 86039 190 6
CBI: CONFEDERATION OF BRITISH INDUSTRY				
CBI1	West European Living Costs	1991	CBI Annually 1991 London, UK	ISBN 0 85201 2829
CCS: CARIBBEAN COMMUNITY SECRETARIAT				
CCS1	Caricom's Trade	1985–1990	CCS Irregular January 1993 Georgetown, Guyana	—
CCS2	A Digest of Trade Statistics	1970–80	CCS Irregular 1983 Georgetown, Guyana	—

instat code	Title	Edition indexed	Publisher Frequency Date Place	ISBN ISSN

CE: COUNCIL OF EUROPE

CE1	Recent Demographic Developments in Europe	1991	Council of Europe Press Annually 1991 Strasbourg, France	ISBN 92 871 1989 9

CH: CROOM HELM LIMITED

CH1	The Economies of the Arabian Gulf: A Statistical Source Book	1984	Croom Helm Irregular 1984 London, UK	ISBN 0 7099 1543 8

CIA: CHEMICAL INDUSTRIES ASSOCIATION

CIA1	Basic International Chemical Industry Statistics	1963–90	CIA Irregular 1991 London, UK	ISBN 0 900 623 640 ISSN 0961 7531

CIRFS: COMITE INTERNATIONAL DE LA RAYONNE ET DES FIBRES SYNTHETIQUES

CIRFS1	Information on Man-made Fibres	1986	CIRFS Annually 1986 Paris, France	—

COS: CHAMBER OF SHIPPING

COS1	Statistical Brief	1992 (4)	COS Quarterly 1992 London, UK	—

CS: COMMONWEALTH SECRETARIAT

CS1	Basic Statistical Data on Selected Countries	1992	Commonwealth Secretariat Annually 1992 London, UK	—

DSC: DREWRY SHIPPING CONSULTANTS LIMITED

DSC1	Shipping Statistics and Economics	1993 March	Drewry Monthly 1993 London, UK	ISSN 0306 1817
DSC2	Shipping Trade, Trends and Statistics	1992 December	Drewry Monthly 1992 London, UK	ISSN 0966 7032

instat code	Title	Edition indexed	Publisher Frequency Date Place	ISBN ISSN
EAA: EUROPEAN ALUMINIUM ASSOCIATION				
EAA1	European Aluminium Statistics	1991	EAA Annually 1991 Brussels, Belgium	—
EAT: ELSEVIER ADVANCED TECHNOLOGY				
EAT1	Silicon Carbide	1992 Vol 1	EAT Irregular 1992 Oxford, UK	ISBN 1 85617 151 5
EAT2	Telecommunications: Profile of the Worldwide Telecommunications Industry	1990	EAT Irregular 1990 Oxford, UK	ISBN 0946 395 594
EC: EUROPEAN COMMUNITY (EUROSTAT)[1]				
EC1	ACP Basic Statistics	1988	SOEC Annually 1989 Luxembourg	ISBN 92 825 8867 X
EC2	Agricultural Income	1991	SOEC Irregular 1992 Luxembourg	ISBN 92 826 4005 1
EC3	Agricultural Markets: Prices	1991 (4)	SOEC 5 per year 1991 Luxembourg	ISSN 1014 8159
EC4	Agricultural Prices: Price Indices and Absolute Prices	1980–89	SOEC Annually 1990 Luxembourg	ISBN 92 826 1721 1

1 In addition to the publications listed here, the EC (Eurostat) also publish a series entitled *Rapid Reports*, the purpose of which is to summarize the main results of surveys, studies or publications. These have not been indexed in this volume because their content varies from one report to another. Details of the series are as follows:

Rapid Reports – Agriculture, Forestry and Fisheries. ISSN 1017–5776.
Rapid Reports – Economy and Finance. ISSN 1016–0213.
Rapid Reports – Energy and Industry. ISSN 1016–0191.
Rapid Reports – Environment. ISSN 1017–5849.
Rapid Reports – External Trade and Balance of Payments. ISSN 1017–5792.
Rapid Reports – Population and Social Conditions. ISSN 1013–0535.
Rapid Reports – Regions. ISSN 1013– 0535.

instat code	Title	Edition indexed	Publisher Frequency Date Place	ISBN ISSN
EC5	Agricultural Prices: Price Indices and Absolute Prices	1990 (2)	SOEC Quarterly 1990 Luxembourg	ISSN 1015 9924
EC6	Agriculture Statistical Yearbook	1990	SOEC Annually 1991 Luxembourg	ISBN 92 826 2596 6
EC7	Animal Production, Quarterly Statistics	1990	SOEC Quarterly 1990 Luxembourg	ISSN 0250 6580
EC8	Areas Under Vines, Results of the Annual Surveys	1979–89	SOEC Annually 1991 Luxembourg	ISBN 92 826 2965 1
EC9	Basic Statistics of the Community	1990	SOEC Annually 1990 Luxembourg	ISBN 92 826 1497 2
EC10	Balance of Payments: Geographical Breakdown	1980–84	SOEC Annually 1986 Luxembourg	ISBN 92 825 6382 0
EC11	Censuses of Population in the Community Countries 1981– 82	1981–82	SOEC Irregular 1988 Luxembourg	ISBN 92 825 7609 4
EC12	Carriage of Goods – Inland Waterways	1987	SOEC Annually 1989 Luxembourg	ISBN 92 825 9879 9
EC13	Carriage of Goods – Railways	1987	SOEC Annually 1989 Luxembourg	ISBN 92 825 9880 2
EC14	Carriage of Goods – Road	1987	SOEC Annually 1989 Luxembourg	ISBN 92 826 0690 2
EC15	Community Survey of Orchard Fruit Trees	1987	SOEC Irregular 1990 Luxembourg	ISBN 92 826 0782 8
EC16	Consumer Price Index	1992 (1)	SOEC Monthly 1992 Luxembourg	ISSN 1010 2779

instat code	Title	Edition indexed	Publisher Frequency Date Place	ISBN ISSN
EC17	Consumer Prices in the EEC	1988	SOEC Irregular 1990 Luxembourg	ISBN 92 826 1321 6
EC18	Country Reports, Central and Eastern Europe	1991	SOEC Irregular 1991 Luxembourg	ISBN 92 826 2371 8
EC19	Crop Production, Quarterly Statistics	1991 (4)	SOEC Quarterly 1992 Luxembourg	ISSN 0378 3588
EC20	Demographic Statistics	1990	SOEC Annually 1990 Luxembourg	ISBN 92 826 1481 6
EC21	Digest of Statistics on Social Protection in Europe Vol 1 Old Age	1980–88	SOEC Irregular 1992 Luxembourg	ISBN 92 826 3719 0
EC22	Digest of Statistics on Social Protection in Europe Vol 2 Invalidity/Disability	1980–88	SOEC Irregular 1992 Luxembourg	ISBN 92 826 3720 4
EC23	Earnings in Agriculture	1988	SOEC Annually 1990 Luxembourg	ISBN 92 826 1689 4
EC24	Earnings, Industry and Services	1991	SOEC Annually 1991 Luxembourg	ISBN 92 826 3355 1
EC25	EC External Trade Indices	1980–86	SOEC Irregular 1988 Luxembourg	ISBN 92 825 7787 2
EC26	Economic Accounts for Agriculture and Forestry	1984–89	SOEC Annually 1991 Luxembourg	ISBN 92 826 2401 3
EC27	ECU– EMS Information	1991 (11–12)	SOEC Monthly 1991 Luxembourg	ISSN 1011 0844
EC28	Electricity Prices	1985–91	SOEC Annually 1991 Luxembourg	ISBN 92 826 3068 4

instat code	Title	Edition indexed	Publisher Frequency Date Place	ISBN ISSN
EC29	Employment and Unemployment	1989	SOEC Annually 1989 Luxembourg	ISBN 92 825 9734 2
EC30	Energy Balance Sheets	1988–89	SOEC Annually 1991 Luxembourg	ISBN 92 826 2244 4
EC31	Energy, Monthly Statistics	1991 (12)	SOEC Monthly 1991 Luxembourg	ISSN 0258 3569
EC32	Energy Prices	1978–90	SOEC 2 per year 1991 Luxembourg	ISBN 92 826 2354 8
EC33	Energy Yearly Statistics	1990	SOEC Annually 1992 Luxembourg	ISBN 92 826 3947 9
EC34	Environment Statistics	1989	SOEC Irregular 1990 Luxembourg	ISBN 92 826 1108 6
EC35	Europe in Figures	1992	SOEC Irregular 1992 Luxembourg	ISBN 92 826 3372 1
EC36	Eurostatistics – Data for Short-term Economic Analysis No 5	1992	SOEC Monthly 1992 Luxembourg	ISSN 0252 8266
EC37	External Trade: Analytical Tables A– L, Imports and Exports	1990	SOEC Annually 1991 Luxembourg	ISBN 92 826 2613 X
EC38	External Trade and Balance of Payments	1992	SOEC Monthly 1992 Luxembourg	ISSN 1017 6004
EC39	External Trade Statistical Yearbook	1958–89	SOEC Annually 1990 Luxembourg	ISBN 92 826 1666 5
EC40	External Trade, System of Generalized Tariff Preferences Imports 1988 Vol I	1988	SOEC Annually 1990 Luxembourg	ISBN 92 826 1110 8

instat code	Title	Edition indexed	Publisher Frequency Date Place	ISBN ISSN
EC41	External Trade, System of Generalized Tariff Preferences Imports 1988 Vol II	1988	SOEC Annually 1990 Luxembourg	ISBN 92 826 1110 8
EC42	Family Budgets: Comparative Tables Vols I and II	1990	SOEC Irregular 1990 Luxembourg	ISBN 92 826 1568 5
EC43	Farm Structure: 1985 Survey Analysis of Results. Economic Size and Other Gainful Activities	1985	SOEC Irregular 1988 Luxembourg	ISBN 92 825 7706 6
EC44	Farm Structure: 1985 Survey Analysis of Results. Regional Structure of Agricultural Production	1985	SOEC Irregular 1991 Luxembourg	ISBN 92 826 1970 2
EC45	Farm Structure: 1985 Survey Main Results	1985	SOEC Irregular 1987 Luxembourg	ISBN 92 825 7626 4
EC46	Fisheries, Yearly Statistics	1990	SOEC Annually 1990 Luxembourg	ISBN 92 826 1914 1
EC47	Forestry Statistics	1980–84	SOEC Irregular 1987 Luxembourg	ISBN 92 825 6943 8
EC48	Gas Prices	1985–90	SOEC Annually 1990 Luxembourg	ISBN 92 826 1679 7
EC49	General Government Accounts and Statistics	1970–87	SOEC Annually 1990 Luxembourg	ISBN 92 826 1570 7
EC50	Government Financing of Research and Development	1980–90	SOEC Annually 1991 Luxembourg	ISBN 92 826 2885 X
EC51	Industrial Production Quarterly Statistics	1991 (2)	SOEC Quarterly 1991 Luxembourg	ISSN 0254 0649
EC52	Industrial Trends Monthly Statistics	1992 December	SOEC Monthly 1992 Luxembourg	ISSN 0258 1922

instat code	Title	Edition indexed	Publisher Frequency Date Place	ISBN ISSN
EC53	Industry Statistical Yearbook	1988	SOEC Annually 1989 Luxembourg	ISBN 92 825 9038 0
EC54	International Comparisons of Energy Data	1988	SOEC Irregular 1991 Luxembourg	ISBN 92 826 2156 1
EC55	Iron and Steel, Yearly Statistics	1991	SOEC Annually 1991 Luxembourg	ISBN 92 826 3261 X
EC56	Labour Force Survey Results 1991	1991	SOEC Annually 1993 Luxembourg	ISBN 92 826 5414 1
EC57	Milk Quotas – their Effects on Agriculture in the European Community, Vol 1 Main Report	1990	SOEC Irregular 1990 Luxembourg	ISBN 92 826 1245 7
EC58	Milk Quotas – their Effects on Agriculture in the European Community, Vol 2 Annex	1990	SOEC Irregular 1990 Luxembourg	ISBN 92 826 1246 5
EC59	Money and Finance	1990 (4)	SOEC Quarterly 1991 Luxembourg	ISSN 0255 6510
EC60	National Accounts ESA Aggregates	1970–89	SOEC Annually 1991 Luxembourg	ISBN 92 826 2099 9
EC61	National Accounts ESA Detailed Tables by Branch	1989	SOEC Annually 1990 Luxembourg	ISBN 92 826 1001 2
EC62	National Accounts ESA Detailed Tables by Sector	1970–87	SOEC Annually 1990 Luxembourg	ISBN 92 826 1431 X
EC63	National Accounts ESA Input-Output Tables	1980	SOEC 5 yearly 1986 Luxembourg	ISBN 92 825 6539 4
EC64	Operation of Nuclear Power Stations	1989	SOEC Annually 1990 Luxembourg	ISBN 92 826 1531 6

instat code	Title	Edition indexed	Publisher Frequency Date Place	ISBN ISSN
EC65	Portrait of the Regions: Vol I Germany Benelux Denmark Vol II France United Kingdom Ireland Vol III Portugal Spain Italy Greece	1993	SOEC Irregular 1993 Luxembourg	ISBN 92 826 3222 9 ISBN 92 826 3223 7 ISBN 92 826 3224 5
EC66	Price Structure of the Community Countries in 1985	1985	SOEC Irregular 1988 Luxembourg	ISBN 92 825 7715 5
EC67	Quarterly National Accounts ESA	1990 (4)	SOEC Quarterly 1990 Luxembourg	ISSN 1010 1764
EC68	Raw Material EC Supply	1975–83	SOEC Irregular 1986 Luxembourg	ISBN 92 825 5837 1
EC69	Regions Statistical Yearbook	1989	SOEC Annually 1990 Luxembourg	ISBN 92 826 1198 1
EC70	Results of the Business Survey Carried Out Among Managements in the Community	1992 January	SOEC Monthly 1992 Luxembourg	ISSN 0378 4479
EC71	Retailing in the European Single Market 1993	1993	SOEC Irregular 1993 Luxembourg	ISBN 92 826 54583
EC72	A Social Portrait of Europe	1991	SOEC Irregular 1991 Luxembourg	ISBN 92 826 1747 5
EC73	Social Protection Expenditure and Receipts	1980–89	SOEC Irregular 1991 Luxembourg	ISBN 92 826 3251 2
EC74	Steel Consumption by User Branch	1970–84	SOEC Irregular 1986 Luxembourg	ISBN 92 825 6813 X
EC75	Structure and Activity of Industry: Annual Enquiry Main Results	1987–88	SOEC Annually 1991 Luxembourg	ISBN 92 826 3254 7
EC76	Structure and Activity of Industry: Data by Regions	1986–87	SOEC Annually 1991 Luxembourg	ISBN 92 826 2157 X

instat code	Title	Edition indexed	Publisher Frequency Date Place	ISBN ISSN
EC77	Structure and Activity of Industry: Data by Size of Enterprises	1986–88	SOEC Irregular 1991 Luxembourg	ISBN 92 826 2759 4
EC78	Tourism Annual Statistics	1988–89	SOEC Annually 1991 Luxembourg	ISBN 92 826 0530 2
EC79	Tourism in Europe, Trends	1989	SOEC Annually 1990 Luxembourg	ISBN 92 826 1581 2
EC80	Transport and Communications Annual Statistics	1970–87	SOEC Annually 1990 Luxembourg	ISBN 92 826 1564 2
EC81	Unemployment	1991 (1)	SOEC Monthly 1991 Luxembourg	ISSN 0252 9920

ECMT: EUROPEAN CONFERENCE OF MINISTERS OF TRANSPORT

ECMT1	Statistical Report on Road Accidents	1990	ECMT Annually 1992 Paris, France	ISBN 92 821 0174 6 ISSN 1012 9898
ECMT2	Statistical Trends in Transport	1965–88	ECMT Annually 1992 Paris, France	ISBN 92 821 0173 8
ECMT3	Trends in the Transport Sector	1970–90	ECMT Annually 1991 Paris, France	—

EDFM: E D & F MAN COCOA LIMITED

EDFM1	Cocoa Market Report	1993 No 347	EDFM 3 per year 1993 London, UK	—

EFTA: EUROPEAN FREE TRADE ASSOCIATION

EFTA1	EFTA Trade	1990	EFTA Economic Affairs Department Annually 1991 Geneva, Switzerland	ISSN 0531 4119

***instat* code**	**Title**	**Edition indexed**	**Publisher Frequency Date Place**	**ISBN ISSN**
EM: EUROMONITOR				
EM1	European Marketing Data and Statistics	1993	Euromonitor Annually 1993 London, UK	ISBN 0 86338 457 9 ISSN 0071 2930
EPI: EUROPEAN PAPER INSTITUTE				
EPI1	European Paper Institute Annual Statistics	1983–90	EPI Annually 1991 Paris, France	—
EPO: EUROPEAN PATENT OFFICE				
EPO1	Facts and Figures	1991	EPO Annually 1992 Munich, Germany	—
F: FEARNLEYS				
F1	Fearnley's Review	1987	Fearnleys Annually 1988 Oslo, Norway	ISSN 0801 5589
F2	World Bulk Fleet	1988	Fearnleys Half-yearly August 1988 Oslo, Norway	ISSN 0801 5007
F3	World Bulk Trades	1986	Fearnleys Annually 1987 Oslo, Norway	ISSN 0801 4086
FAO: FOOD AND AGRICULTURE ORGANISATION				
FAO1	FAO Production Yearbook	1990 Vol 44	FAO Annually 1991 Rome, Italy	ISBN 92 5 003067 3 ISSN 0071 7118
FAO2	FAO Trade Yearbook	1986 Vol 40	FAO Annually 1987 Rome, Italy	ISBN 92 5 002596 3
FAO3	FAO Yearbook of Fishery Statistics: Catches and Landings	1986 Vol 62	FAO Annually 1988 Rome, Italy	ISBN 92 5 002627 7 ISSN 02515679

instat code	Title	Edition indexed	Publisher Frequency Date Place	ISBN ISSN
FAO4	FAO Yearbook of Fishery Statistics: Commodities	1986 Vol 68	FAO Annually 1988 Rome, Italy	ISBN 92 5 002628 5 ISSN 02515687
FAO5	Fertiliser Yearbook	1989 Vol 39	FAO Annually 1990 Rome, Italy	ISBN 92 5 002964 0
FAO6	Quarterly Bulletin of Statistics	1993 Vol 6 (3)	FAO Quarterly 1993 Rome, Italy	ISSN 1011 8780
FAO7	World Crop and Livestock Statistics	1948–85	FAO Irregular 1987 Rome, Italy	ISBN 92 5 002530 0
FAO8	Yearbook of Forest Products	1976–87	FAO Annually 1989 Rome, Italy	ISBN 92 5 002727 3

FNOCL: FEDERATION NATIONALE DES ORGANISMES DE CONTROLE LAITIER

FNOCL1	Situation de la Production Laitière et du Contrôle Laitier dans les Pays Members	1991	FNOCL Annually 1992 Paris, France	—

FOL: F O LICHT

FOL1	International Molasses and Alcohol Report	1992 Vol 29 No 17	F O Licht Bi-monthly 1992 Ratzeburg, Germany	—
FOL2	International Sugar and Sweetener Report	1993 14 April Vol 125	F O Licht Weekly 1993 Ratzeburg, Germany	—
FOL3	World Sugar and Sweetener Yearbook	1989	F O Licht Annually 1989 Ratzeburg, Germany	ISBN 3 9801139 0 6

G: E A GIBSON SHIPBROKERS LIMITED

G1	Oil, Chemical and Combined Carriers	1993 March	Gibsons Irregular 1993 London, UK	—

instat code	Title	Edition indexed	Publisher Frequency Date Place	ISBN ISSN
G2	Register of Liquified Gas Carriers	1993	Gibsons Annually 1993 London, UK	—

GATT: GENERAL AGREEMENT ON TARIFFS AND TRADE

instat code	Title	Edition indexed	Publisher Frequency Date Place	ISBN ISSN
GATT1	The International Markets for Meat	1991–92	GATT Annually 1992 Geneva, Switzerland	ISBN 92 870 1053 6 ISSN 0259 8213
GATT2	The International Markets for Meat. Arrangement Regarding Bovine Meat 12th Annual Report	1991–92	GATT Annually 1992 Geneva, Switzerland	ISBN 92 870 1066 8 ISSN 0259 8213
GATT3	International Trade Statistics Vol I	1989–90	GATT Annually 1990 Geneva, Switzerland	ISBN 92 870 1057 9 ISSN 0072 064X
GATT4	International Trade Statistics Vol II	1989–90	GATT Annually 1990 Geneva, Switzerland	ISBN 92 870 1058 7 ISSN 0072 064X
GATT5	The World Market for Dairy Products	1991	GATT Annually 1991 Geneva, Switzerland	ISBN 92 870 1065 X ISSN 0259 8213

GP: GENERATION PUBLICATIONS

instat code	Title	Edition indexed	Publisher Frequency Date Place	ISBN ISSN
GP1	The Best 'N' Most in DFS	1992–93	General Publications Annually 1992 Örnsköldsvik, Sweden	ISBN 91 86166 15 8 ISSN 1100 3006

HI: HORWATH INTERNATIONAL

instat code	Title	Edition indexed	Publisher Frequency Date Place	ISBN ISSN
HI1	Worldwide Hotel Industry	1992	Horwath International Annually 1992 New York, USA	—

IADB: INTER-AMERICAN DEVELOPMENT BANK

instat code	Title	Edition indexed	Publisher Frequency Date Place	ISBN ISSN
IADB1	Pocket Profiles	1991	IADB Irregular 1991 Washington DC, USA	—

instat code	Title	Edition indexed	Publisher Frequency Date Place	ISBN ISSN

IAEA: INTERNATIONAL ATOMIC ENERGY AGENCY

IAEA1	Operating Experience with Nuclear Power Stations in Member States in 1990	1990	IAEA Annually 1991 Vienna, Austria	ISBN 92 0 159391 0 ISSN 1011 2634

IAHP: INTERNATIONAL ASSOCIATION OF HORTICULTURAL PRODUCERS

IAHP1	Yearbook of International Horticultural Statistics	1992 Vol 40	IAHP Annually 1992 The Hague, Netherlands	ISBN 90 74486 01 0

IARC: INTERNATIONAL AGENCY FOR RESEARCH ON CANCER

IARC1	Cancer Incidence in Five Continents	1987 Vol V	IARC 5 yearly 1987 Lyon, France	ISBN 92 832 1188X ISSN 0300 5085

IATA: INTERNATIONAL AIR TRANSPORT ASSOCIATION

IATA1	World Air Transport Statistics	1991 No 36	IATA Annually 1992 London, UK	ISBN 92 9035 454 2

IBA: INTERNATIONAL BAUXITE ASSOCIATION

IBA1	IBA Quarterly Review	1991 Vol 17	IBA Quarterly 1991 Jamaica	—

ICAC: INTERNATIONAL COTTON ADVISORY COMMITTEE

ICAC1	Cotton: Review of the World Situation	1992 Vol 45 No 3	ICAC 2 monthly 1992 Washington DC, USA	ISSN 0010 9754
ICAC2	Cotton: World Statistics, Bulletin of the International Cotton Advisory Committee	1991 Vol 45 No 1	ICAC Annually 1991 Washington DC, USA	—

ICAO: INTERNATIONAL CIVIL AVIATION ORGANIZATION

ICAO1	Accident/Incident Reporting (ADREP) Annual Statistics	1987	ICAO Annually 1991 Montreal, Canada	—

instat code	Title	Edition indexed	Publisher Frequency Date Place	ISBN ISSN
ICAO2	Civil Aviation Statistics of the World Doc 9180	1990	ICAO Annually 1991 Montreal, Canada	—
ICAO3	Digest of Statistics Series AF Airport and Route Facilities, Financial Data and Summary Traffic Data	Digest No 399 Series AF No 9 1991	ICAO Annually 1993 Montreal, Canada	—
ICAO4	Digest of Statistics Series AT Airport Traffic	Digest No 383 Series AT No 31 1990	ICAO Annually 1991 Montreal, Canada	—
ICAO5	Digest of Statistics Series F Financial Data, Commercial Air Carriers	Digest No 397 Series F No 45 1991	ICAO Annually 1993 Montreal, Canada	—
ICAO6	Digest of Statistics Series FP Fleet – Personnel, Commercial Air Carriers	Digest No 385 Series FP No 44 1990	ICAO Annually 1991 Montreal, Canada	—
ICAO7	Digest of Statistics Series OFOD On Flight Origin and Destination	Digest No 381 Series OFOD No 44 1990	ICAO Quarterly 1990 Montreal, Canada	—
ICAO8	Digest of Statistics Series R Civil Aircraft on Register	Digest No 382 Series R No 30 1990	ICAO Annually 1991 Montreal, Canada	—
ICAO9	Digest of Statistics Series T Traffic – Commercial Air Carriers	Digest No 379 Series T No 50 1986–90	ICAO Annually 1991 Montreal, Canada	—
ICAO10	Digest of Statistics Series TF Traffic By Flight Stage	Digest No 398 Series TF No 106 1991	ICAO Annually 1991 Montreal, Canada	—

ICCAT: INTERNATIONAL COMMISSION FOR THE CONSERVATION OF ATLANTIC TUNAS

ICCAT1	Statistical Bulletin	1989 Vol 20	ICCAT Annually 1989 Madrid, Spain	—

instat code	Title	Edition indexed	Publisher Frequency Date Place	ISBN ISSN
ICCO: INTERNATIONAL COCOA COUNCIL ORGANIZATION				
ICCO1	International Cocoa Organization Annual Report	1991–92	ICCO Annually 1992 London, UK	—
ICCO2	Quarterly Bulletin of Cocoa Statistics	1991 Vol XVIII No 1	ICCO Quarterly 1991 London, UK	ISSN 0308 4469
ICCO3	The World Cocoa Market: An Analysis of Recent Trends and of Prospects to the Year 2000	1993	ICCO Irregular 1993 London, UK	ISBN 1 85670 0054
IDF: INTERNATIONAL DAIRY FEDERATION				
IDF1	Bulletin–Consumption Statistics for Milk and Milk Products	1991 No 282	IDF Annually 1993 Brussels, Belgium	ISSN 0250 5118
IEA: INTERNATIONAL ENERGY AGENCY				
IEA1	Annual Oil Market Report	1990	OECD/IEA Annually 1991 Paris, France	ISBN 92 64 13550 2
IEA2	Coal Information	1991	OECD/IEA Annually 1991 Paris, France	ISBN 92 64 13536 7
IEA3	Electricity Supply in the OECD	1992	OECD/IEA Irregular 1992 Paris, France	ISBN 92 64 13599 5
IEA4	Energy Balances of OECD Countries 1980–89	1980–89	OECD/IEA Irregular 1991 Paris, France	ISBN 92 64 03500 1
IEA5	Energy Balances of OECD Countries 1990–91	1990–91	OECD/IEA Annually 1993 Paris, France	ISBN 92 64 03860 4
IEA6	Energy Prices and Taxes	1991 (4)	OECD/IEA Quarterly 1991 Paris, France	ISBN 92 64 13644 4

instat code	Title	Edition indexed	Publisher Frequency Date Place	ISBN ISSN
IEA7	Energy Statistics and Balances of Non-OECD Countries	1988–89	OECD/IEA Annually 1991 Paris, France	ISBN 92 64 03511 7
IEA8	Energy Statistics of OECD Countries 1980– 89	1980–89	OECD/IEA Irregular 1991 Paris, France	ISBN 92 64 03299 1
IEA9	Energy Statistics of OECD Countries 1989– 90	1989–90	OECD/IEA Annually 1992 Paris, France	ISBN 92 64 03534 6
IEA10	Oil and Gas Information	1988–90	OECD/IEA Annually 1991 Paris, France	ISBN 92 64 03507 9
IEA11	Quarterly Oil Statistics and Energy Balances	1991 (3)	OECD/IEA Quarterly 1991 Paris, France	ISSN 0378 6536
IEA12	World Energy Statistics and Balances	1985–88	OECD/IEA Irregular 1990 Paris, France	ISBN 92 64 03335 1
IFA: INTERNATIONAL FERTILIZER INDUSTRY ASSOCIATION				
IFA1	Urea Statistics	1991	IFA Annually 1992 Paris, France	—
IISI: INTERNATIONAL IRON AND STEEL INSTITUTE				
IISI1	Annual Report of the International Iron and Steel Institute	1992	IISI Annually 1992 Brussels, Belgium	—
IISI2	Monthly Crude Iron and Steel Production	1993 May	IISI Monthly 1993 Brussels, Belgium	—
IISI3	Steel Statistics of Developing Countries	1992	IISI Annually 1992 Brussels, Belgium	—
IISI4	Steel Statistical Yearbook	1992	IISI Annually 1992 Brussels, Belgium	—

instat code	Title	Edition indexed	Publisher Frequency Date Place	ISBN ISSN
IISI5	World Steel in Figures	1991	IISI Annually 1991 Brussels, Belgium	—

IISRP: INTERNATIONAL INSTITUTE OF SYNTHETIC RUBBER PRODUCERS

IISRP1	Worldwide Rubber Statistics	1993	IISRP Annually 1993 Houston, USA	—

ILO: INTERNATIONAL LABOUR ORGANIZATION

ILO1	Bulletin of Labour Statistics	1991 (4)	ILO Quarterly 1991 Geneva, Switzerland	ISSN 0007 4950
ILO2	Economically Active Population 1950– 2025 Vol I Asia	1986	ILO Irregular 1986 Geneva, Switzerland	ISBN 92 2 005345 4 ISSN 0258 0489
ILO3	Economically Active Population 1950– 2025 Vol II Africa	1986	ILO Irregular 1986 Geneva, Switzerland	ISBN 92 2 005346 2 ISSN 0258 0489
ILO4	Economically Active Population 1950– 2025 Vol III Latin America	1986	ILO Irregular 1986 Geneva, Switzerland	ISBN 92 2 005347 0 ISSN 0258 0489
ILO5	Economically Active Population 1950– 2025 Vol IV Northern America, Europe, Oceania and USSR	1986	ILO Irregular 1986 Geneva, Switzerland	ISBN 92 2 005348 9 ISSN 0258 0489
ILO6	Economically Active Population 1950– 2025 Vol V World	1986	ILO Irregular 1986 Geneva, Switzerland	ISBN 92 2 005349 7 ISSN 0258 0489
ILO7	Yearbook of Labour Statistics	1991	ILO Annually 1991 Geneva, Switzerland	ISBN 92 2 007339 0 ISSN 0084 3857

ILZSG: INTERNATIONAL LEAD AND ZINC STUDY GROUP

ILZSG1	Bulletin of the Lead and Zinc Study Group: Lead and Zinc Statistics	1992 Vol 32 No 2	ILZSG Monthly 1992 London, UK	—

instat code	Title	Edition indexed	Publisher Frequency Date Place	ISBN ISSN
ILZSG2	Joint Production of Lead and Zinc	1957–81	ILZSG Irregular 1983 London, UK	—

IMF: INTERNATIONAL MONETARY FUND

instat code	Title	Edition indexed	Publisher Frequency Date Place	ISBN ISSN
IMF1	Balance of Payments Statistical Yearbook Part I	1990 Vol 41	IMF Annually 1990 Washington DC, USA	ISBN 1 55775 157 9 ISSN 0252 3035
IMF2	Balance of Payments Statistical Yearbook Part II	1990 Vol 41	IMF Annually 1990 Washington DC, USA	ISBN 1 55775 157 9 ISSN 0252 3035
IMF3	Direction of Trade Statistics Yearbook	1991	IMF Annually 1991 Washington DC, USA	ISBN 1 55775 1773 ISSN 0252 306X
IMF4	Direction of Trade Statistics	1992 March	IMF Quarterly 1992 Washington DC, USA	ISSN 0252 306X
IMF5	Government Finance Statistics Yearbook	1991	IMF Annually 1991 Washington DC, USA	ISBN 1 5577 5178 1 ISSN 0250 7374
IMF6	International Financial Statistics	1992 Vol XLV No 2	IMF Monthly 1992 Washington DC, USA	ISSN 0020 6725
IMF7	International Financial Statistics Yearbook	1991 Vol XLIV	IMF Annually 1991 Washington DC, USA	ISBN 1 55775 223 0 ISSN 0250 7463

IMWF: INTERNATIONAL METALWORKERS' FEDERATION

instat code	Title	Edition indexed	Publisher Frequency Date Place	ISBN ISSN
IMWF1	The Purchasing Power of Working Time. An International Comparison	1989	IMWF Irregular 1990 Geneva, Switzerland	—

INPFC: INTERNATIONAL NORTH PACIFIC FISHERIES COMMISSION

instat code	Title	Edition indexed	Publisher Frequency Date Place	ISBN ISSN
INPFC1	International North Pacific Fisheries Commission Statistical Yearbook	1988	INPFC Annually 1991 Vancouver, Canada	ISSN 0535 1588

instat code	Title	Edition indexed	Publisher Frequency Date Place	ISBN ISSN

IP: INSTITUTE OF PETROLEUM

IP1	Know More About Oil, World Statistics	1992	IP Annually 1992 London, UK	ISSN 0141 4305

IPHC: INTERNATIONAL PACIFIC HALIBUT COMMISSION

IPHC1	International Pacific Halibut Commission, Annual Report	1990	IPHC Winterholm Press Annually Seattle, USA	ISSN 0074 7238

IPU: INTER-PARLIAMENTARY UNION

IPU1	Distribution of Seats Between Men and Women in National Parliaments. Statistical Data from 1945 to 30 June 1991	1991	IPU Irregular 1991 Geneva, Switzerland	—
IPU2	Women and Political Power Survey carried out among the 150 National Parliaments existing as from 31.10.91	1991	IPU Irregular 1991 Geneva, Switzerland	—

IRF: INTERNATIONAL ROAD FEDERATION

IRF1	World Road Statistics, 1986–90	1991	IRF Annually 1991 Geneva, Switzerland	ISSN 0444 1419

IRRI: INTERNATIONAL RICE RESEARCH INSTITUTE

IRRI1	World Rice Statistics, 1987	1987	IRRI Annually 1988 Manilla, Philippines	ISBN 971 104 204 5

IRSG: INTERNATIONAL RUBBER STUDY GROUP

IRSG1	Rubber Statistical Bulletin	1993 Vol 47 No 11	IRSG Monthly 1993 London, UK	ISSN 0035 9548
IRSG2	World Rubber Statistics Handbook	1960–90 Vol 4	IRSG Irregular 1992 London, UK	—

***instat* code**	**Title**	**Edition indexed**	**Publisher Frequency Date Place**	**ISBN ISSN**
IRTU: INTERNATIONAL ROAD TRANSPORT UNION				
IRTU1	World Transport Data	1990	IRTU Annually 1990 Geneva, Switzerland	—
ISL: INSTITUTE OF SHIPPING ECONOMICS AND LOGISTICS				
ISL1	Shipping Statistics	1993 April	ISL 10– 12 per year 1993 Bremen, Germany	ISSN 0721 3751
ISL2	Shipping Statistics Yearbook	1991	ISL Annually 1991 Bremen, Germany	ISSN 0721 3220
ISO: INTERNATIONAL SUGAR ORGANIZATION				
ISO1	Quarterly Market Review	1993	ISO Quarterly 1993 London, UK	—
ISO2	Statistical Bulletin	1993 Vol 51 No 4	ISO Monthly 1993 London, UK	—
ISO3	Sugar Yearbook	1991	ISO Annually 1992 London, UK	—
ISSB: IRON AND STEEL STATISTICS BUREAU				
ISSB1	International Steel Statistics Summary Tables	1988	ISSB Annually 1991 Croydon, UK	ISSN 0952 6803
ISSB2	World Trade Stainless, High Speed and Other Alloy Steel	1988	ISSB Bi-annually 1988 Croydon, UK	ISSN 0952 5742
ISSB3	World Trade Steel	1988	ISSB Quarterly 1988 Croydon, UK	—

instat code	Title	Edition indexed	Publisher Frequency Date Place	ISBN ISSN

ISTA: ISTA MIELK GmbH

ISTA1	Oil World	1992 31 January	ISTA Mielke Weekly 1992 Hamburg, Germany	—
ISTA2	Oil World Annual	1992	ISTA Mielke Annually 1992 Hamburg, Germany	—

ITC: INTERNATIONAL TEA COMMITTEE

ITC1	Annual Bulletin of Statistics	1992	ITC Annually 1992 London, UK	ISSN 0305 2370

ITMF: INTERNATIONAL TEXTILE MANUFACTURERS FEDERATION

ITMF1	Country Statements	1992	ITMF Annually 1992 Zurich, Switzerland	—
ITMF2	International Cotton Industry Statistics	1991 Vol 34	ITMF Annually 1992 Zurich, Switzerland	—
ITMF3	International Textile Machinery Shipment Statistics	1991 Vol 14	ITMF Annually 1992 Zurich, Switzerland	—

ITTO: INTERNATIONAL TROPICAL TIMBER ORGANIZATION

ITTO1	Annual Review and Assessment of the World Tropical Timber Situation	1992	ITTO Annually 1993 Yokohama, Japan	—

ITU: INTERNATIONAL TELECOMMUNICATION UNION

ITU1	Yearbook of Common Carrier Telecommunications Statistics	1981–90	ITU Annually 1992 Geneva, Switzerland	ISBN 92 71 1706 X

IUR: INTERNATIONAL UNION OF RAILWAYS

IUR1	International Railway Statistics Statistics of Individual Railways	1991	IUR Annually 1993 Paris, France	—

instat code	Title	Edition indexed	Publisher Frequency Date Place	ISBN ISSN
IWC: INTERNATIONAL WHALING COMMISSION				
IWC1	International Whaling Statistics	1988	IWC Irregular 1988 Cambridge, UK	ISSN 0020 9090
IWhC: INTERNATIONAL WHEAT COUNCIL				
IWhC1	Food Aid Shipments	1987–88	IWhC Annually 1989 London, UK	—
IWhC2	Grain Market Report	1993	IWhC Monthly 1993 London, UK	—
IWhC3	Report for the Crop Year	1989–90	IWhC Annually 1991 London, UK	—
IWS: INTERNATIONAL WOOL SECRETARIAT				
IWS1	Wool Facts 1991– 92	1992	IWS Annually 1992 London, UK	—
JM: JOHNSON MATTHEY				
JM1	Platinum	1993	Johnson Matthey Bi-annually 1993 London, UK	ISSN 0268 7305
JP: JAAKKO PÖYRY				
JP1	Short-term Review of International Pulp and Paper Markets	1992 No 58	Jaakko Pöyry 3– 4 times yearly 1992 Vantaa, Finland	ISSN 0784 7289
LRS: LLOYDS REGISTER OF SHIPPING				
LRS1	Annual Summary of Merchant Ships Completed	1992	Lloyd's Register Annually 1993 London, UK	ISSN 0261 1848

instat code	Title	Edition indexed	Publisher Frequency Date Place	ISBN ISSN
LRS2	Casualty Return	1991	Lloyd's Register Annually 1992 London, UK	ISSN 0268 0815
LRS3	Merchant Shipbuilding Return	1993 March	Lloyd's Register Quarterly 1993 London, UK	ISSN 0261 0848
LRS4	World Fleet Statistics	1992 December	Lloyd's Register Annually 1993 London, UK	ISSN 0076 0234
MAC: MACMILLAN				
MAC1	International Historical Statistics, Africa and Asia	1982	Macmillan Irregular 1982 London, UK	ISBN 0 333 31630
MAC2	International Historical Statistics, The Americas and Australasia	1983	Macmillan Irregular 1983 London, UK	ISBN 0 333 31629 0
MAC3	International Historical Statistics, Europe 1750– 1988	1992 3rd edn	Macmillan[1] Irregular 1992 Basingstoke, UK	ISBN 0 333 56872 9
MB: METAL BULLETIN BOOKS LIMITED				
MB1	Iron and Manganese Ore Databook	1992	Metal Bulletin Irregular 1992 Worcester Park, UK	ISBN 0 947671 62 5 ISSN 0967 7925
MB2	Metal Bulletin's Prices and Data	1992	Metal Bulletin Annual 1992 Worcester Park, UK	ISBN 0 947671 58 7 ISSN 0269 1698
MHPPE: MINISTRY OF HOUSING, PHYSICAL PLANNING AND THE ENVIRONMENT (NETHERLANDS)				
MHPPE1	Statistics on Housing in the European Community	1992	MHPPE Annually 1992 The Hague, The Netherlands	—

1 Published in the United States and Canada by Stockton Press, 1992. ISBN 1 56159 038 X

instat code	Title	Edition indexed	Publisher Frequency Date Place	ISBN ISSN

MJ: MINING JOURNAL

MJ1	Metals and Minerals The Safer World of SGS	1992	Mining Journal Annually 1992 London, UK	ISBN 0 900117 58 3

MLC: MEAT AND LIVESTOCK COMMISSION

MLC1	European Handbook, EEC and International Statistics	1992 Vol II	Meat and Livestock Commission Irregular 1992 Milton Keynes, UK	—

MMB: MILK MARKETING BOARD

MMB1	EC Dairy Facts and Figures	1992	MMB Annually 1992 Thames Ditton, Surrey	—

NATO: NORTH ATLANTIC TREATY ORGANIZATION

NATO1	The North Atlantic Treaty Organization 1949– 89, Facts and Figures	1949–89	NATO Irregular 1989 Brussels, Belgium	ISBN 92 845 0041 9

NCM: NORDIC COUNCIL OF MINISTERS AND THE NORDIC STATISTICAL SECRETARIAT

NCM1	Yearbook of Nordic Statistics	1991	Nordic Council of Ministers and the Nordic Statistical Secretariat Annually 1991 Copenhagen, Denmark	ISBN (Denmark) 87 7303 529 7) ISBN (Sweden) 91 7996 303 X ISSN 0078 1088

NWAFO: NORTH WEST ATLANTIC FISHERIES ORGANIZATION

NWAFO1	Statistical Bulletin, Fishery Statistics for 1988	1988 Vol 38	NWAFO Annually 1991 Dartmouth, Nova Scotia, Canada	ISSN 0250 6394

instat code	Title	Edition indexed	Publisher Frequency Date Place	ISBN ISSN

OECD: ORGANIZATION FOR ECONOMIC CO-OPERATION AND DEVELOPMENT [1]

instat code	Title	Edition indexed	Publisher Frequency Date Place	ISBN ISSN
OECD1	Balances of Payments of OECD Countries	1965–84	OECD Irregular 1986 Paris, France	ISBN 92 64 02836 6
OECD2	Bank Profitability: Statistical Supplement – Financial Statements of Banks	1981–89	OECD Irregular 1991 Paris, France	ISBN 92 64 03518 4
OECD3	Basic Science and Technology Statistics	1991	OECD Biennially 1991 Paris, France	ISBN 92 64 03501 X
OECD4	Demographic Trends in OECD Member Countries	1970–85	OECD Irregular 1974 Paris, France	ISBN 92 64 01262 1
OECD5	Economic Accounts for Agriculture	1976–89	OECD Irregular 1991 Paris, France	ISBN 92 64 03521 4
OECD6	Education at a Glance	1992	OECD Irregular 1992 Paris, France	ISBN 92 64 03692 X
OECD7	Education in OECD Countries	1987–88	OECD Annually 1990 Paris, France	ISBN 92 64 13425 5
OECD8	External Debt Statistics: The Debt and Other External Liabilities of Developing, CMEA and Certain Other Countries and Territories at end December 1987 and end December 1988	1989	OECD Annually 1989 Paris, France	ISBN 92 54 13305 4
OECD9	External Debt Statistics: The Debt and Other External Liabilities of Developing, Central and Eastern European and Certain Other Countries and Territories at end December 1988 and end December 1989	1989	OECD Annually 1990 Paris, France	ISBN 92 64 13427 1
OECD10	Financial Market Trends	1993 No 56	OECD 3 per year 1993 Paris, France	ISSN 0378 651X

1 Publications of the International Energy Agency and the European Conference of Ministers of Transport are listed separately under IEA and ECMT respectively.

instat **code**	**Title**	**Edition indexed**	**Publisher Frequency Date Place**	**ISBN ISSN**
OECD11	Flows and Stocks of Fixed Capital: 1964– 89	1964–89	OECD Irregular 1991 Paris, France	ISBN 92 64 03514 1
OECD12	Food Consumption Statistics	1979–88	OECD Irregular 1991 Paris, France	ISBN 92 64 03513 3
OECD13	Foreign Trade by Commodities Vols I to V Series C	1990	OECD Annually 1992 Paris, France	ISSN 0474 540X
OECD14	Geographical Distribution of Financial Flows to Developing Countries, Disbursements, Commitments, Economic Indicators: 1986– 89	1991	OECD Irregular 1991 Paris, France	ISBN 92 64 03345 9 ISSN 1015 3934
OECD15	Indicators of Industrial Activity	1991 (4)	OECD Quarterly 1991 Paris, France	ISSN 0250 4278
OECD16	Industrial Structure Statistics	1989–90	OECD Irregular 1992 Paris, France	ISBN 92 64 03528 1
OECD17	International Direct Investment Statistics Yearbook	1993	OECD Annually 1993 Paris, France	ISBN 92 64 03887 6
OECD18	The Iron and Steel Industry	1990	OECD Annually 1992 Paris, France	ISBN 92 64 03530 3
OECD19	Labour Force Statistics	1969–89	OECD Annually 1991 Paris, France	ISBN 92 64 03510 9
OECD20	Living Conditions in OECD Countries: Compendium of Social Indicators	1986	OECD Irregular 1986 Paris, France	ISBN 92 64 12734 8
OECD21	Main Economic Indicators	1992 June	OECD Monthly 1992 Paris, France	ISSN 0474 5523
OECD22	Main Economic Indicators, Historical Statistics	1969–1988	OECD Irregular 1990 Paris, France	ISBN 92 64 03296 70

instat code	Title	Edition indexed	Publisher Frequency Date Place	ISBN ISSN
OECD23	Main Economic Indicators, Historical Statistics: Prices Labour and Wages 1962– 91	1962–91	OECD Irregular 1993 Paris, France	ISBN 92 64 03873 6
OECD24	Main Science and Technology Indicators	1993 (1)	OECD Biannually 1993 Paris, France	ISSN 1011 792X
OECD25	Maritime Transport	1990	OECD Annually 1991 Paris, France	ISBN 92 64 13587 1 ISSN 0474 5884
OECD26	Meat Balances in OECD Countries	1982–88	OECD Irregular 1990 Paris, France	ISBN 92 64 03374 2
OECD27	Monthly Statistics of Foreign Trade, Series A	1992 May	OECD Monthly 1992 Paris, France	ISSN 0474 5388
OECD28	National Accounts Vol I Main Aggregates	1960–90	OECD Annually 1992 Paris, France	ISBN 92 64 03522 2 ISSN 0256 758X
OECD29	National Accounts Vol II Detailed Tables	1978–90	OECD Annually 1992 Paris, France	ISBN 92 64 03683 0 ISSN 0256 7571
OECD30	National and International Tourism Statistics	1974–85	OECD Irregular 1989 Paris, France	ISBN 92 64 03221 5
OECD31	Nuclear Energy Data	1991	OECD Nuclear Energy Agency Annually 1991 Paris, France	ISBN 92 64 03297 5 ISSN 1017 9402
OECD32	OECD Economic Outlook Historical Statistics	1960–89	OECD Annually 1991 Paris, France	ISBN 92 64 03348 3
OECD33	OECD Environmental Data Compendium	1991	OECD 2 yearly 1991 Paris, France	ISBN 92 64 03512 5
OECD34	OECD Financial Statistics Part 1, Section 1 International Markets	1992	OECD Monthly 1992 Paris, France	ISSN 0304 3371

***instat* code**	**Title**	**Edition indexed**	**Publisher Frequency Date Place**	**ISBN ISSN**
OECD35	OECD Financial Statistics Part 1, Section 2 Domestic Markets – Interest Rates	1992	OECD Monthly 1992 Paris, France	ISSN 0304 3371
OECD36	OECD Financial Statistics Part 2, Financial Accounts of OECD Countries (series of booklets – one for each country)	1976–91	OECD Annually 1993 Paris, France	ISSN 0304 3371
OECD37	OECD Financial Statistics Part 3 Non-Financial Enterprises Financial Statements	1991	OECD Annually 1992 Paris, France	ISSN 0304 3371
OECD38	The Pulp and Paper Industry	1988	OECD Annually 1991 Paris, France	ISBN 92 64 03509 5
OECD39	Purchasing Power Parities and Real Expenditures	1990	OECD Irregular 1992 Paris, France	ISBN 92 64 03686 5
OECD40	Quarterly Labour Force Statistics	1993 (2)	OECD Quarterly 1993 Paris, France	ISSN 0255 3627
OECD41	Quarterly National Accounts	1992 (4)	OECD Quarterly 1992 Paris, France	ISSN 0304 3738
OECD42	Revenue Statistics of OECD Member Countries	1965–90	OECD Annually 1991 Paris, France	ISBN 92 64 03504 4
OECD43	Review of Fisheries in OECD Member Countries	1989	OECD Annually 1991 Paris, France	ISBN 92 64 13541 3 ISSN 0078 6241
OECD44	Services: Statistics on International Transactions	1970–89	OECD Irregular 1992 Paris, France	ISBN 92 64 03681 4
OECD45	Steel Market in 1991 and the Outlook for 1992	1992	OECD Annually 1992 Paris, France	ISBN 92 64 13677 0
OECD46	Tourism Policy and International Tourism in OECD Member Countries	1989	OECD Annually 1990 Paris, France	ISBN 92 64 13424 7 ISSN 0256 7598

***instat* code**	**Title**	**Edition indexed**	**Publisher Frequency Date Place**	**ISBN ISSN**
OECD47	Uranium – Resources, Production and Demand	1989	OECD Irregular 1990 Paris, France	ISBN 92 64 13364 X

OIVV: OFFICE INTERNATIONAL DE LA VIGNE ET DU VIN

OIVV1	Bulletin de IOIV	1991 November– December	Office International de la Vigne et du Vin Bi-monthly 1991 Paris, France	ISSN 0029 7127

OPEC: ORGANIZATION OF PETROLEUM EXPORTING COUNTRIES

OPEC1	OPEC Annual Statistical Bulletin	1989	OPEC Annually 1990 Vienna, Austria	ISSN 0475 0608
OPEC2	OPEC Bulletin	1992 January	OPEC 10 issues per year 1992 Vienna, Austria	ISSN 0474 6279

PC: THE POPULATION COUNCIL

PC1	Family Planning and Child Survival Programs as Assessed in 1991	1991	The Population Council Irregular 1992 New York, USA	ISBN 0 87834 066 1

PKF: PANNELL KERR FORSTER

PKF1	Euro Trends Survey	1992	Panell Kerr Forster Annually 1992 London, UK	—
PKF2	Trends in the Hotel Industry	1989	Panell Kerr Forster Annually 1989 Houston, USA	—

PPI: PULP AND PAPER INTERNATIONAL

PPI1	Pulp and Paper International Annual Review	1992	PPI Annually 1992 Brussels, Belgium	—

instat code	Title	Edition indexed	Publisher Frequency Date Place	ISBN ISSN
SATRA: SATRA FOOTWEAR TECHNOLOGY CENTRE				
SATRA1	World Footwear Markets	1992	SATRA Annually 1992 Kettering, UK	ISSN 0266 0709
SFIA: SEA FISH INDUSTRY AUTHORITY				
SFIA1	European Supplies Bulletin	1989 December	SFIA Annually 1989 Edinburgh, UK	ISSN 0142 973X
SMMT: SOCIETY OF MOTOR MANUFACTURERS AND TRADERS LIMITED				
SMMT1	Monthly Statistical Review	1993 April	SMMT Monthly 1993 London, UK	—
SMMT2	Motor Industry of Great Britain: World Automotive Statistics	1992	SMMT Annually 1992 London, UK	—
SPC: SOUTH PACIFIC COMMISSION				
SPC1	Retail Price Indices, Statistical Bulletin of the South Pacific	1992 No 44	SPC Annually 1993 Noumea, New Caledonia	ISSN 1018 0958
SPC2	South Pacific Economies	1992	SPC Irregular 1992 Noumea, New Caledonia	ISBN 982 203 246 3
UN: UNITED NATIONS[1]				
UN1	African Socio-economic Indicators 1990–91	1990–91	UN Irregular 1992 Addis Ababa, Ethiopia	ISBN 92 1 025034 6
UN2	African Statistical Yearbook 1988–89 Vol I, Part 1 North Africa	1988–89	UN Annually 1992 New York, USA	—

[1] Publications of the International Civil Aviation Organization, International Telecommunication Union, the United Nations Conference on Trade and Development, the United Nations Educational, Scientific and Cultural Organization, the United Nations Children's Fund, the United Nations Industrial Development Organization, World Health Organization and the World Meteorological Organization are listed separately under ICAO, ITU, UNCTAD, UNESCO, UNICEF, UNIDO, WHO and WMO respectively.

***instat* code**	**Title**	**Edition indexed**	**Publisher Frequency Date Place**	**ISBN ISSN**
UN3	African Statistical Yearbook 1988– 89 Vol I, Part 2 West Africa	1988–89	UN Annually 1992 New York, USA	—
UN4	African Statistical Yearbook 1988– 89 Vol II, Part 3 East and Southern Africa	1988–89	UN Annually 1992 Addis Ababa, Ethiopia	ISBN 92 1 025 030 3
UN5	African Statistical Yearbook 1988– 89 Vol II, Part 4 Central Africa, Others in Africa	1988–89	UN Annually 1992 Addis Ababa, Ethiopia	ISBN 92 1 025031 1
UN6	Annual Bulletin of Coal Statistics for Europe	1991	UN, ECE Annually 1991 Geneva, Switzerland	ISBN 92 1 016260 9 ISSN 0066 3808
UN7	Annual Bulletin of Electric Energy Statistics for Europe	1990	UN, ECE Annually 1991 Geneva, Switzerland	ISBN 92 1 016244 7 ISSN 0066 3816
UN8	Annual Bulletin of Gas Statistics for Europe	1991	UN, ECE Annually 1991 New York, USA	ISBN 92 1 016239 0 ISSN 0066 3824
UN9	Annual Bulletin of General Energy Statistics for Europe	1989 Vol 22	UN, ECE Annually 1991 New York, USA	ISBN 92 1 016259 5 ISSN 0377 9165
UN10	Annual Bulletin of Housing and Building Statistics for Europe	1980, 1986–89 Vol 33	UN, ECE Annually 1991 Geneva, Switzerland	ISBN 92 1 016243 9 ISSN 0066 3840
UN11	Annual Bulletin of Steel Statistics for Europe	1989 Vol 17	UN, ECE Annually 1990 New York, USA	ISBN 92 1 016241 2
UN12	Annual Bulletin of Trade in Chemical Products	1989 Vol 16	UN Annually 1991 New York, USA	ISBN 92 1 016262 5 ISSN 0250 9911
UN13	Annual Bulletin of Transport Statistics for Europe	1990 Vol 40	UN, ECE Annually 1990 Geneva, Switzerland	ISBN 92 1 016228 5 ISSN 0250 9911
UN14	Bulletin of Statistics on World Trade in Engineering Products	1988	UN Annually 1990 New York, USA	ISBN 92 1 016245 5 ISSN 0084 8174

instat code	Title	Edition indexed	Publisher Frequency Date Place	ISBN ISSN
UN15	Commodity Trade Statistics	1990 Vol XL	UN Approximately 28 issues per year 1990 New York, USA	—
UN16	Compendium of Social Statistics and Indicators	1988	UN Irregular 1988 New York, USA	ISBN 92 1 061145 4
UN17	Compendium of Statistics and Indicators on the Situation of Women	1986	UN Irregular 1989 New York	ISBN 92 1 061130 6
UN18	Construction Statistics Yearbook	1985	UN Annually 1988 New York, USA	ISBN 92 1 061126 8
UN19	Demographic Yearbook	1989	UN Annually 1991 New York, USA	ISBN 92 1 051074 7
UN20	Energy Balances and Electricity Profiles	1990	UN Irregular 1992 New York	ISBN 92 1 061147 0
UN21	Energy Statistics Yearbook	1989	UN Annually 1991 New York, USA	ISBN 92 1 061143 8
UN22	The Environment in Europe and North America: Annotated Statistics 1992	1992	UN Irregular 1992 New York, USA	ISBN 92 1 116537 7
UN23	Foreign Trade Statistics for Africa, Direction of Trade Series A	1990	UN Annually 1990 Addis Ababa, Ethiopia	ISBN 92 1 125058 7
UN24	Foreign Trade Statistics of Asia and the Pacific	1984–88	UN Irregular 1990 New York, USA	ISBN 92 1 119548 9 ISSN 1011 4858
UN25	Human Development Report	1991	Oxford University Press for the UN Development Programme Irregular 1991 Oxford, UK	ISBN 0 19 507147 6
UN26	Human Settlements Basic Statistics	1990	UN Irregular 1990 Nairobi, Kenya	ISBN 92 1 131098 9

instat code	Title	Edition indexed	Publisher Frequency Date Place	ISBN ISSN
UN27	Industrial Statistics Yearbook, Vol I General Industrial Statistics	1989	UN Annually 1991 New York, USA	ISBN 92 1 161338 8
UN28	Industrial Statistics Yearbook, Vol II Commodity Production Statistics	1980–89	UN Annually 1991 New York, USA	ISBN 92 1 061146 2
UN29	International Narcotics Control Board – Narcotic Drugs, Estimated World Requirement Statistics for 1990	1990	UN Annually 1991 Geneva, Switzerland	ISBN 92 1 048050 3 ISSN 1013 3453
UN30	International Narcotics Control Board – Psychotropic Substances, Statistics for 1990	1990	UN Annually 1991 Geneva, Switzerland	ISBN 92 1 048051 1
UN31	International Sea-borne Trade Statistics: Yearbook 1984– 85	1984–85	UN Annually 1988 New York	ISBN 92 1 161285 3
UN32	International Trade Statistics Yearbook, Vol I Trade by Country	1989	UN Annually 1991 New York, USA	ISBN 92 1 061140 3
UN33	International Trade Statistics Yearbook, Vol II Trade by Commodity	1989	UN Annually 1991 New York, USA	ISBN 92 1 061140 3
UN34	The Livestock and Meat Market	1988 and 1989 Vol IV	UN Biennial 1990 New York, USA	ISBN 92 1 116483 4 ISSN 1011 3363
UN35	Monthly Bulletin of Statistics	1992 April	UN Monthly 1992 New York, USA	—
UN36	National Accounts Statistics: Analysis of Main Aggregates 1988– 89	1988–89	UN Annually 1991 New York	ISBN 92 1 161341 8
UN37	National Accounts Statistics: Compendium of Income Distribution Statistics	Series M No 79	UN Irregular 1985 New York, USA	ISBN 92 1 161253 5
UN38	National Accounts Statistics: Main Aggregates and Detailed Tables Parts I and II	1989	UN Annually 1991 New York, USA	ISBN 92 1 161339 6

instat code	Title	Edition indexed	Publisher Frequency Date Place	ISBN ISSN
UN39	Population and Vital Statistics Report	XLV No 1	UN Quarterly 1993 New York, USA	—
UN40	Prices of Agricultural Products and Selected Inputs in Europe and North America	1990–91	UN Annual 1992 New York, USA	ISBN 92 1 116538 5 ISSN 0251 3986
UN41	Report of the UN High Commissioner for Refugees. General Assembly Official Records: 46th Session, Supplement No 12	1991	UN High Commission for Refugees Annually 1991 New York, USA	ISSN 0251 8023
UN42	Standardized Input-Output Tables of ECE Countries for Years Around 1975	1982	UN Irregular 1982 New York, USA	ISBN 011 907 7493
UN43	Statistical Indicators for Asia and the Pacific	1992 Vol XXII	UN Quarterly 1992 New York, USA	ISBN 92 1 119604 3 ISSN 0252 4457
UN44	Statistical Yearbook for Asia and the Pacific	1986–87	UN Economic and Social Commission for Asia and the Pacific Annually Bangkok, Thailand	ISBN 92 1 119447 4 ISSN 0252 3655
UN45	Statistical Yearbook for Latin America and the Caribbean	1990	UN Economic Commission for Latin America and the Caribbean Annually 1991 Santiago, Chile	ISSN 92 1 021029 8 ISBN 0251 9445
UN46	Statistics and Indicators on Women in Africa	1986	UN Irregular 1989 New York, USA	ISBN 92 1 061133 0
UN47	Statistics of Road Traffic Accidents in Europe	1991	UN, ECE Annually 1991 Geneva, Switzerland	ISBN 92 1 016261 7
UN48	Statistics of World Trade in Steel	1989	UN, ECE Annually 1990 New York, USA	ISBN 92 1 016242 0 ISSN 0501 3062
UN49	The Steel Market in 1991	1992	UN Annually 1992 Geneva, Switzerland	ISBN 92 1 116551 2 ISSN 0497 9478

instat code	Title	Edition indexed	Publisher Frequency Date Place	ISBN ISSN
UN50	UN Statistical Yearbook	1987	UN Annually 1990 New York, USA	ISBN 92 1 061131 4
UN51	UNHCR Activities Financed by Voluntary Funds. Report for 1990– 91 and Proposed Programmes and Budget for 1992. Part 1: Africa Part 2: Asia and Oceania Part 3: Europe and North America Part 4: Latin America Part 5: South West Asia, North Africa and the Middle East Part 6: Overall Allocations	1990–91	UNHCR Annually 1991 Geneva, Switzerland	—
UN52	World Investment Directory Vol I Asia and the Pacific	1992	UN Irregular 1992 New York, USA	ISBN 92 1 104389 1
UN53	World Investment Directory Vol II Central and Eastern Europe	1992	UN Annually 1992 New York, USA	ISBN 92 1 104402 2
UN54	World Population Prospects	1990	UN Bi-ennially 1991 New York, USA	ISBN 92 1 151223 9
UN55	World Statistics in Brief, United Nations Statistical Pocketbook	14th edn	UN Annually 1992 New York	ISBN 92 1 161344 2

UNCTAD: UNITED NATIONS CONFERENCE ON TRADE AND DEVELOPMENT

UNCTAD1	Handbook of International Trade and Development Statistics	1988	UNCTAD Irregular 1989 New York, USA	ISBN 92 1 012025 6 ISSN 0251 9461
UNCTAD2	Review of Maritime Transport	1989	UNCTAD Annually 1990 New York, USA	ISBN 92 1 112292 9 ISSN 0566 7682
UNCTAD3	Tungsten Statistics	1990	UNCTAD Annually 1991 New York, USA	ISBN 92 1 112298 8 ISSN 0049 4828
UNCTAD4	UNCTAD Commodity Yearbook	1992	UNCTAD Annually 1992 New York, USA	ISBN 92 1 012030 2 ISSN 1012 0793

instat code	Title	Edition indexed	Publisher Frequency Date Place	ISBN ISSN
UNCTAD5	UNCTAD Statistical Pocket Book	1989	UNCTAD Irregular 1989 New York, USA	ISBN 92 1 112281 3

UNESCO: UNITED NATIONS EDUCATIONAL, SCIENTIFIC, AND CULTURAL ORGANIZATION

UNESCO1	Statistical Yearbook	1990	UNESCO Annually 1990 Paris, France	ISBN 92 3 0027008 1

UNICEF: UNITED NATIONS CHILDREN'S FUND

UNICEF1	The State of the World's Children	1992	Oxford University Press Annually 1992 Oxford, UK	ISBN 0 19 262228 5 ISSN 0265 718X
UNICEF2	Statistics on Children in UNICEF Assisted Countries	1992	UNICEF Annually 1992 New York, USA	ISBN 92 806 1084 8

UNIDO: UNITED NATIONS INDUSTRIAL DEVELOPMENT ORGANIZATION

UNIDO1	Handbook of Industrial Statistics	1990	Edward Elgar Publishing Ltd for UNIDO Annually 1991 Aldershot, UK	ISBN 1 85278 440 7

VICES: VIENNA INSTITUTE FOR COMPARATIVE ECONOMIC STUDIES

VICES1	Comecon Data	1988	Macmillan Irregular 1989 Basingstoke, UK	ISBN 0 333 51798 9 ISSN 0263 3701

WB: THE WORLD BANK

WB1	Social Indicators of Development	1988	World Bank Irregular 1988 Washington DC, USA	ISBN 0 8018 3831 2 ISSN 1012 8026
WB2	Trends in Developing Economies	1992	World Bank Annually 1992 Washington DC, USA	ISBN 0 8213 2234 6
WB3	World Debt Tables, Vol 1 Analysis and Summary Tables	1992–93	World Bank Annually 1992 Washington DC, USA	ISBN 0 8213 2226 5

instat code	Title	Edition indexed	Publisher Frequency Date Place	ISBN ISSN
WB4	World Debt Tables Vol 2 External Finance for Developing Countries, Country Tables	1992–93	World Bank Annually 1992 Washington, USA	ISBN 0 8213 2227 3
WB5	World Population Projections	1989–90	John Hopkins University Press Irregular 1990 Maryland, USA	ISBN 0 8018 4094 5
WB6	World Tables	1991	John Hopkins University Press Annually 1991 Washington DC, USA	ISBN 0 8018 4252 2 ISSN 1043 5573

WBMS: WORLD BUREAU OF METAL STATISTICS

WBMS1	World Metal Statistics	1993	WBMS and Inco Europe Limited Monthly 1993 Ware, UK	ISSN 0043 8758
WBMS2	World Metal Statistics Quarterly Summary	1993 January	WBMS Quarterly 1993 Ware, UK	—
WBMS3	World Metal Statistics Yearbook	1991	WBMS Annually 1991 Ware, UK	—
WBMS4	World Stainless Steel Statistics	1990	WBMS and Inco Europe Limited Annually 1990 Ware, UK	ISSN 0141 0806

WC: WYE COLLEGE

WC1	Agrifacts: A Handbook of UK and EEC Agricultural and Food Statistics	1990	Harvester Wheatsheaf 1990 Hemel Hempstead, UK	ISBN 0 7450 0756 2

WFP: WORLD FOOD PROGRAMME

WFP1	The Food Aid Monitor: World Food Aid Flows, Transport and Logistics	1992	WFP Quarterly 1992 Rome, Italy	—

instat code	Title	Edition indexed	Publisher Frequency Date Place	ISBN ISSN
WHO: WORLD HEALTH ORGANISATION				
WHO1	Bulletin of Regional Health Information	1988–90	WHO 3 yearly 1992 New Delhi, India	—
WHO2	World Health Statistics Annual	1991	WHO Annually 1992 Geneva, Switzerland	ISBN 92 4 067910 3 ISSN 0250 3794
WIPO: WORLD INTELLECTUAL PROPERTY ORGANIZATION				
WIPO1	Industrial Property Statistics, Part I, Patents	1990 Part I	WIPO Annually 1992 Geneva, Switzerland	ISBN 92 805 0393 6
WIPO2	Industrial Property Statistics, Part II Trademarks and Service Marks, Utility Models, Industrial Designs, Varieties of Plants, Micro-organisms	1990	WIPO Annually 1992 Geneva, Switzerland	—
WIPO3	Industrial Property Statistics, Publication A (Supplement to Industrial Property) No 11	1990	WIPO Annually 1991 Geneva, Switzerland	—
WMO: WORLD METEOROLOGICAL ORGANIZATION				
WMO1	Climatological Normals (CLINO) for CLIMAT and CLIMAT Ship Stations	1931–60	WMO Irregular 1971 Geneva, Switzerland	—
WTO: WORLD TOURISM ORGANIZATION				
WTO1	Compendium of Tourism Statistics	1986–90	WTO Annually 1992 Madrid, Spain	ISBN 92 844 0016 3 ISSN 1014 1744
WTO2	Travel and Tourism Barometer	1992	WTO Monthly 1992 Madrid, Spain	ISSN 1014 7306
WTO3	Yearbook of Tourism Statistics Vol 1	1990	WTO Annually 1991 Madrid, Spain	ISBN 92 844 0014 7 ISSN 1011 8977
WTO4	Yearbook of Tourism Statistics Vol 2	1990	WTO Annually 1991 Madrid, Spain	ISBN 92 844 0014 7 ISSN 1011 8977

APPENDIX B

INDEX OF PUBLICATIONS

ARRANGED BY TITLE OF PUBLICATION

Title of publication	*instat* code	Name of organization
Accident/Incident Reporting (ADREP) Annual Statistics	ICAO1	International Civil Aviation Organization
ACP Basic Statistics	EC1	European Community
African Socio-economic Indicators 1990–91	UN1	United Nations
African Statistical Yearbook 1988–89 Vol I, Part 1 North Africa	UN2	United Nations
African Statistical Yearbook 1988–89 Vol I, Part 2 West Africa	UN3	United Nations
African Statistical Yearbook 1988–89 Vol II, Part 3 East and Southern Africa	UN4	United Nations
African Statistical Yearbook 1988–89 Vol II, Part 4 Central Africa, Others in Africa	UN5	United Nations
Agricultural Income	EC2	European Community
Agricultural Markets: Prices	EC3	European Community
Agricultural Prices: Price Indices and Absolute Prices	EC4	European Community
Agricultural Prices: Price Indices and Absolute Prices	EC5	European Community
Agriculture Statistical Yearbook	EC6	European Community
Agrifacts: A Handbook of UK and EEC Agricultural and Food Statistics	WC1	Wye College
Animal Production, Quarterly Statistics	EC7	European Community
Annual Bulletin of Coal Statistics for Europe	UN6	United Nations
Annual Bulletin of Electric Energy Statistics for Europe	UN7	United Nations
Annual Bulletin of Gas Statistics for Europe	UN8	United Nations
Annual Bulletin of General Energy Statistics for Europe	UN9	United Nations
Annual Bulletin of Housing and Building Statistics for Europe	UN10	United Nations
Annual Bulletin of Statistics	ITC1	International Tea Committee
Annual Bulletin of Steel Statistics for Europe	UN11	United Nations
Annual Bulletin of Trade in Chemical Products	UN12	United Nations
Annual Bulletin of Transport Statistics for Europe	UN13	United Nations
Annual Oil Market Report	IEA1	International Energy Agency
Annual Report of the International Iron and Steel Institute	IISI1	International Iron and Steel Institute

Title of publication	*instat* code	Name of organization
Annual Review and Assessment of the World Tropical Timber Situation	ITTO1	International Tropical Timber Organization
Annual Summary of Merchant Ships Completed	LRS1	Lloyds Register of Shipping
Areas Under Vines, Results of the Annual Surveys	EC8	European Community
ASEAN Selected Statistics	ASEANS1	Association of South-East Asian Nations Secretariat
Association of European Airlines Yearbook	AEA1	Association of European Airlines
Balance of Payments Statistical Yearbook, Part I	IMF1	International Monetary Fund
Balance of Payments Statistical Yearbook, Part II	IMF2	International Monetary Fund
Balance of Payments: Geographical Breakdown	EC10	European Community
Balances of Payments of OECD Countries	OECD1	Organization for Economic Co-operation and Development
Bank Profitability: Statistical Supplement - Financial Statements of Banks	OECD2	Organization for Economic Co-operation and Development
Basic International Chemical Industry Statistics	CIA1	Chemical Industries Association
Basic Science and Technology	OECD3	Organization for Economic Co-operation and Development
Basic Statistical Data on Selected Countries	CS1	Commonwealth Secretariat
Basic Statistics of the Community	EC9	European Community
The Best 'N' Most in DFS	GP1	Generation Publications
BP Review of World Gas	BP2	British Petroleum Company Plc
BP Statistical Review of World Energy	BP1	British Petroleum Company Plc
Bulletin–Consumption Statistics for Milk and Milk Products	IDF1	International Dairy Federation
Bulletin de IOIV	OIVY1	Bulletin de IOIV
Bulletin of Labour Statistics	ILO1	International Labour Organization
Bulletin of Regional Health Information	WHO1	World Health Organization
Bulletin of Statistics on World Trade in Engineering Products	UN14	United Nations
Bulletin of the Lead and Zinc Study Group: Lead and Zinc Statistics	ILZSG1	International Lead and Zinc Study Group
Cancer Incidence in Five Continents on	IARC1	International Agency for Research Cancer

Title of publication	*instat* code	Name of organization
Caricom's Trade	CCS1	Caribbean Community Secretariat
Carriage of Goods – Inland Waterways	EC12	European Community
Carriage of Goods – Railways	EC13	European Community
Carriage of Goods – Road	EC14	European Community
Casualty Return	LRS2	Lloyds Register of Shipping
Censuses of Population in the Community Countries 1981–82	EC11	European Community
Civil Aviation Statistics of the World, Doc 9180	ICAO2	International Civil Aviation Organization
Climatological Normals (CLINO) for CLIMAT and CLIMAT Ship Stations	WMO1	World Meteorological Organization
Coal Information	IEA2	International Energy Agency
Cocoa Market Report	EDFM1	E D & F Man Cocoa Limited
Comecon Data	VICES1	Vienna Institute for Comparative Economic Studies
Commodity Trade Statistics	UN15	United Nations
Community Survey of Orchard Fruit Trees	EC15	European Community
Comparative Information on Productivity Levels and Changes in APO Member Countries	APO1	Asian Productivity Organization
Compendium of Social Statistics and Indicators	UN16	United Nations
Compendium of Statistics and Indicators on the Situation of Women	UN17	United Nations
Compendium of Tourism Statistics	WTO1	World Tourism Organization
Construction Statistics Yearbook	UN18	United Nations
Consumer Price Index	EC16	European Community
Consumer Prices in the EEC	EC17	European Community
Cotton: Review of the World Situation	ICAC1	International Cotton Advisory Committee
Cotton: World Statistics, Bulletin of the International Cotton Advisory Committee	ICAC2	International Cotton Advisory Committee
Country Reports, Central and Eastern Europe	EC18	European Community
Country Statements	ITMF1	International Textile Manufacturers Federation

Title of publication	*instat* code	Name of organization
Economic Accounts for Agriculture	OECD5	Organization for Economic Co-operation and Development
Economic Accounts for Agriculture and Forestry	EC26	European Community
Economically Active Population 1950–2025, Vol I Asia	ILO2	International Labour Organization
Economically Active Population 1950–2025, Vol II Africa	ILO3	International Labour Organization
Economically Active Population 1950–2025, Vol III Latin America	ILO4	International Labour Organization
Economically Active Population 1950–2025, Vol IV Northern America, Europe, Oceania and USSR	ILO5	International Labour Organization
Economically Active Population 1950–2025, Vol V World	ILO6	International Labour Organization
The Economies of the Arabian Gulf: A Statistical Source Book	CH1	Croom Helm Limited
ECU-EMS Information	EC27	European Community
Education at a Glance	OECD6	Organization for Economic Co-operation and Development
Education in OECD Countries	OECD7	Organization for Economic Co-operation and Development
EFTA Trade	EFTA1	European Free Trade Association
Electricity Prices	EC28	European Community
Electricity Supply in the OECD	IEA3	International Energy Agency
Employment and Unemployment	EC29	European Community
Energy Balance Sheets	EC30	European Community
Energy Balances and Electricity Profiles	UN20	United Nations
Energy Balances of OECD Countries 1980–89	IEA4	International Energy Agency
Energy Balances of OECD Countries 1990–91	IEA5	International Energy Agency
Energy, Monthly Statistics	EC31	European Community
Energy Prices	EC32	European Community
Energy Prices and Taxes	IEA6	International Energy Agency
Energy Statistics and Balances of Non-OECD Countries	IEA7	International Energy Agency
Energy Statistics of OECD Countries 1980–89	IEA8	International Energy Agency
Energy Statistics of OECD Countries 1989–90	IEA9	International Energy Agency
Energy Statistics Yearbook	UN21	United Nations

Title of publication	*instat* code	Name of organization
The Environment in Europe and North America: Annotated Statistics 1992	UN22	United Nations
Energy Yearly Statistics	EC33	European Community
Environment Statistics	EC34	European Community
Euro Trends Survey	PKF1	Pannell Kerr Forster
Europe in Figures	EC35	European Community
European Aluminium Statistics	EAA1	European Aluminium Association
European Handbook, EEC and International Statistics	MLC1	Meat and Livestock Commission
European Marketing Data and Statistics	EM1	Euromonitor
European Paper Institute Annual Statistics	EPI1	European Paper Institute
European Supplies Bulletin	SFIA1	Sea Fish Industry Authority
Eurostatistics – Data for Short-term Economic Analysis, No 5	EC36	European Community
External Debt Statistics: The Debt and Other External Liabilities of Developing, Central and Eastern European and Certain Other Countries and Territories at end December 1988 and end December 1989	OECD9	Organization for Economic Co-operation and Development
External Debt Statistics: The Debt and Other External Liabilities of Developing, CMEA and Certain Other Countries and Territories at end December 1987 and end December 1988	OECD8	Organization for Economic Co-operation and Development
External Trade: Analytical Tables A–L, Imports and Exports	EC37	European Community
External Trade and Balance of Payments	EC38	European Community
External Trade Statistical Yearbook	EC39	European Community
External Trade, System of Generalized Tariff Preferences, Imports 1988, Vol I	EC40	European Community
External Trade, System of Generalized Tariff Preferences, Imports 1988, Vol II	EC41	European Community
Facts and Figures	EPO1	European Patent Office
Family Budgets: Comparative Tables, Vols I and II	EC42	European Community
Family Planning and Child Survival Programs as Assessed in 1991	PC1	The Population Council
FAO Production Yearbook	FAO1	Food and Agriculture Organization
FAO Trade Yearbook	FAO2	Food and Agriculture Organization
FAO Yearbook of Fishery Statistics: Catches and Landings	FAO3	Food and Agriculture Organization

Title of publication	*instat* code	Name of organization
FAO Yearbook of Fishery Statistics: Commodities	FAO4	Food and Agriculture Organization
Farm Structure 1985 Survey: Main Results	EC45	European Community
Farm Structure: 1985 Survey Analysis of Results. Economic Size and Other Gainful Activities	EC43	European Community
Farm Structure: 1985 Survey Analysis of Results. Regional Structure of Agricultural Production	EC44	European Community
Fatal Accident Statistics for Passenger Air Transport Services CAA Paper 83014	CAA1	Civil Aviation Authority
Fearnley's Review	F1	Fearnleys Review
Fertiliser Yearbook	FAO5	Food and Agriculture Organization
Financial Market Trends	OECD10	Organization for Economic Co-operation and Development
Fisheries, Yearly Statistics	EC46	European Community
Flows and Stocks of Fixed Capital: 1964–89	OECD11	Organization for Economic Co-operation and Development
The Food Aid Monitor: World Food Aid Flows, Transport and Logistics	WFP1	World Food Programme
Food Aid Shipments	IWhC1	International Wheat Council
Food Consumption Statistics	OECD12	Organization for Economic Co-operation and Development
Foreign Trade by Commodities, Vols I to V, Series C	OECD13	Organization for Economic Co-operation and Development
Foreign Trade Statistics for Africa, Direction of Trade Series A	UN23	United Nations
Foreign Trade Statistics of Asia and the Pacific	UN24	United Nations
Forestry Statistics	EC47	European Community
Gas Prices	EC48	European Community
General Government Accounts and Statistics	EC49	European Community
Geographical Distribution of Financial Flows to Developing Countries, Disbursements, Commitments, Economic Indicators: 1986–89	OECD14	Organization for Economic Co-operation and Development
Government Finance Statistics Yearbook	IMF5	International Monetary Fund
Government Financing of Research and Development	EC50	European Community

Title of publication	*instat* code	Name of organization
Grain Market Report	IWhC2	International Wheat Council
Handbook of Industrial Statistics	UNIDO1	United Nations Industrial Development Organization
Handbook of International Trade and Development Statistics	UNCTAD1	United Nations Conference on Trade and Development
Human Development Report	UN25	United Nations
Human Settlements Basic Statistics	UN26	United Nations
IBA Quarterly Review	IBA1	International Bauxite Association
Indicators of Industrial Activity	OECD15	Organization for Economic Co-operation and Development
Industrial Production Quarterly Statistics	EC51	European Community
Industrial Property Statistics, Part I, Patents	WIPO1	World Intellectual Property Organization
Industrial Property Statistics, Part II Trademarks and Service Marks, Utility Models, Industrial Designs, Varieties of Plants, Micro-organisms	WIPO2	World Intellectual Property Organization
Industrial Property Statistics, Publication A (Supplement to Industrial Property) No 11	WIPO3	World Intellectual Property Organization
Industrial Statistics Yearbook, Vol I General Industrial Statistics	UN27	United Nations
Industrial Statistics Yearbook, Vol II Commodity Production Statistics	UN28	United Nations
Industrial Structure Statistics	OECD16	Organization for Economic Co-operation and Development
Industrial Trends Monthly Statistics	EC52	European Community
Industry Statistical Yearbook	EC53	European Community
Information on Man-made Fibres	CIRFS1	Comité International de la Rayonne et des Fibres Synthétiques
International Cocoa Organization Annual Report	ICCO1	International Cocoa Council Organization
International Comparisons of Energy Data	EC54	European Community
International Cotton Industry Statistics	ITMF2	International Textile Manufacturers Federation
International Direct Investment Statistics Yearbook	OECD17	Organization for Economic Co-operation and Development

Title of publication	*instat* code	Name of organization
International Financial Statistics	IMF6	International Monetary Fund
International Financial Statistics Yearbook	IMF7	International Monetary Fund
International Historical Statistics, Africa and Asia	MAC1	Macmillan Press Limited
International Historical Statistics, The Americas and Australasia	MAC2	Macmillan Press Limited
International Historical Statistics, Europe 1750–1988	MAC3	Macmillan Press Limited
The International Markets for Meat	GATT1	General Agreement on Tariffs and Trade
The International Markets for Meat. Arrangement Regarding Bovine Meat 12th Annual Report	GATT2	General Agreement on Tariffs and Trade
International Molasses and Alcohol Report	FOL1	F O Licht
International Narcotics Control Board – Narcotic Drugs, Estimated World Requirement Statistics for 1990	UN29	United Nations
International North Pacific Fisheries Commission Statistical Yearbook	INPFC1	International North Pacific Fisheries Commission
International Narcotics Control Board – Psychotropic Substances, Statistics for 1990	UN30	United Nations
International Pacific Halibut Commission, Annual Report	IPHC1	International Pacific Halibut Commission
International Sea-borne Trade Statistics: Yearbook 1984–85	UN31	United Nations
International Railway Statistics, Statistics of Individual Railways	IUR1	International Union of Railways
International Steel Statistics Summary Tables	ISSB1	Iron and Steel Statistics Bureau
International Sugar and Sweetener Report	FOL2	F O Licht
International Textile Machinery Shipment Statistics	ITMF3	International Textile Manufacturers Federation
International Trade Statistics Vol I	GATT3	General Agreement on Tariffs and Trade
International Trade Statistics Vol II	GATT4	General Agreement on Tariffs and Trade
International Trade Statistics Yearbook, Vol I Trade by Country	UN32	United Nations
International Trade Statistics Yearbook, Vol II Trade by Commodity	UN33	United Nations
International Whaling Statistics	IWC1	International Whaling Commission
Intra-European Country to Country Traffic	AEA3	Association of European Airlines

Title of publication	*instat* code	Name of organization
Iron and Manganese Ore Databook	MB1	Metal Bulletin Books Limited
The Iron and Steel Industry	OECD18	Organization for Economic Co-operation and Development
Iron and Steel, Yearly Statistics	EC55	European Community
Joint Production of Lead and Zinc	ILZSG2	International Lead and Zinc Study Group
Know More About Oil, World Statistics	IP1	Institute of Petroleum
Labour Force Survey, Results 1991	EC56	European Community
Labour Force Statistics	OECD19	Organization for Economic Co-operation and Development
The Livestock and Meat Market	UN34	United Nations
Living Conditions in OECD Countries: Compendium of Social Indicators	OECD20	Organization for Economic Co-operation and Development
Main Economic Indicators	OECD21	Organization for Economic Co-operation and Development
Main Economic Indicators, Historical Statistics	OECD22	Organization for Economic Co-operation and Development
Main Economic Indicators, Historical Statistics: Prices Labour and Wages 1962–91	OECD23	Organization for Economic Co-operation and Development
Main Science and Technology Indicators	OECD24	Organization for Economic Co-operation and Development
Maritime Transport	OECD25	Organization for Economic Co-operation and Development
Meat Balances in OECD Countries	OECD26	Organization for Economic Co-operation and Development
Medium-Term Forecast of European Scheduled Passenger Traffic	AEA4	Association of European Airlines
Merchant Shipbuilding Return	LRS3	Lloyds Register of Shipping
Metal Bulletin's Prices and Data	MB2	Metal Bulletin Books Limited
Metals and Minerals, The Safer World of SGS	MJ1	Mining Journal
Milk Quotas – their Effects on Agriculture in the European Community, Vol 1 Main Report	EC57	European Community
Milk Quotas – their Effects on Agriculture in the European Community, Vol 2 Annex	EC58	European Community
Money and Finance	EC59	European Community

Title of publication	*instat* code	Name of organization
Monthly Bulletin of Statistics	UN35	United Nations
Monthly Crude Iron and Steel Production	IISI2	International Iron and Steel Institute
Monthly Statistical Review	SMMT1	Society of Motor Manufacturers and Traders Limited
Monthly Statistics of Foreign Trade, Series A	OECD27	Organization for Economic Co-operation and Development
Motor Industry of Great Britain: World Automotive Statistics	SMMT2	Society of Motor Manufacturers and Traders Limited
National Accounts ESA Aggregates	EC60	European Community
National Accounts ESA Detailed Tables by Branch	EC61	European Community
National Accounts ESA Detailed Tables by Sector	EC62	European Community
National Accounts ESA Input-Output Tables	EC63	European Community
National Accounts Statistics: Analysis of Main Aggregates 1988–89	UN36	United Nations
National Accounts Statistics: Compendium of Income Distribution Statistics	UN37	United Nations
National Accounts Statistics: Main Aggregates and Detailed Tables Parts I and II	UN38	United Nations
National Accounts, Vol I Main Aggregates	OECD28	Organization for Economic Co-operation and Development
National Accounts, Vol II Detailed Tables	OECD29	Organization for Economic Co-operation and Development
National and International Tourism Statistics	OECD30	Organization for Economic Co-operation and Development
The North Atlantic Treaty Organization 1949–89, Facts and Figures	NATO1	North Atlantic Treaty Organization
Nuclear Energy Data	OECD31	Organization for Economic Co-operation and Development
OECD Economic Outlook Historical Statistics	OECD32	Organization for Economic Co-operation and Development
OECD Environmental Data Compendium	OECD33	Organization for Economic Co-operation and Development
OECD Financial Statistics Part 1 Section 1 International Markets	OECD34	Organization for Economic Co-operation and Development
OECD Financial Statistics Part 1 Section 2 Domestic Markets – Interest Rates	OECD35	Organization for Economic Co-operation and Development

Title of publication	*instat* code	Name of organization
OECD Financial Statistics Part 2 Financial Accounts of OECD Countries	OECD36	Organization for Economic Co-operation and Development
OECD Financial Statistics Part 3 Non-Financial Enterprises Financial Statements	OECD37	Organization for Economic Co-operation and Development
Oil and Energy Trends	BB2	Basil Blackwell Limited
Oil and Energy Trends, Annual Statistical Review	BB1	Basil Blackwell Limited
Oil and Gas Information	IEA10	International Energy Agency
Oil World	ISTA1	Ista Mielk Gmbh
Oil World Annual	ISTA2	Ista Mielk Gmbh
Oil, Chemical and Combined Carriers	G1	E A Gibson Shipbrokers Limited
OPEC Annual Statistical Bulletin	OPEC1	Organization of Petroleum Exporting Countries
OPEC Bulletin	OPEC2	Organization of Petroleum Exporting Countries
Operating Experience with Nuclear Power Stations in Member States in 1990	IAEA1	International Atomic Energy Agency
Operation of Nuclear Power Stations	EC64	European Community
Platinum	JM1	Johnson Matthey
Pocket Profiles	IADB1	Inter-American Development Bank
Population and Vital Statistics Report	UN39	United Nations
Portrait of the Regions: Vol I Germany Benelux Denmark, Vol II France, United Kingdom, Ireland, Vol III Portugal, Spain, Italy	EC65	European Community
Price Structure of the Community Countries in 1985	EC66	European Community
Prices of Agricultural Products and Selected Inputs in Europe and North America	UN40	United Nations
The Pulp and Paper Industry	OECD38	Organization for Economic Co-operation and Development
Pulp and Paper International Annual Review	PPI1	Pulp and Paper International
The Purchasing Power of Working Time. An International Comparison	IMWF1	International Metalworkers' Federation
Purchasing Power Parities and Real Expenditures	OECD39	Organization for Economic Co-operation and Development

Title of publication	*instat* code	Name of organization
Quarterly Bulletin of Cocoa Statistics	ICCO2	International Cocoa Council Organization
Quarterly Bulletin of Statistics	FAO6	Food and Agriculture Organization
Quarterly Labour Force Statistics	OECD40	Organization for Economic Co-operation and Development
Quarterly Market Review	ISO1	International Sugar Organization
Quarterly National Accounts	OECD41	Organization for Economic Co-operation and Development
Quarterly National Accounts ESA	EC67	European Community
Quarterly Oil Statistics and Energy Balances	IEA11	International Energy Agency
Raw Material EC Supply	EC68	European Community
Recent Demographic Developments in Europe	CE1	Council of Europe
Reference Tables	BPB1	British Paper and Board Industry Federation
Regions Statistical Yearbook	EC69	European Community
Register of Liquified Gas Carriers	G2	E A Gibson Shipbrokers Limited
Report of the UN High Commissioner for Refugees. General Assembly Official Records: 46th Session, Supplement No 12	UN41	United Nations
Report for the Crop Year	IWhC3	International Wheat Council
Results of the Business Survey Carried Out Among Managements in the Community	EC70	European Community
Retail Price Indices, Statistical Bulletin of the South Pacific	SPC1	South Pacific Commission
Retailing in the European Single Market 1993	EC71	European Community
Revenue Statistics of OECD Member Countries	OECD42	Organization for Economic Co-operation and Development
Review of Fisheries in OECD Member Countries	OECD43	Organization for Economic Co-operation and Development
Review of Maritime Transport	UNCTAD2	United Nations Conference on Trade and Development
Rubber Statistical Bulletin	IRSG1	International Rubber Study Group
Services: Statistics on International Transactions	OECD44	Organization for Economic Co-operation and Development

Title of publication	*instat* code	Name of organization
Shipping Statistics	ISL1	Institute of Shipping Economics and Logistics
Shipping Statistics and Economics	DSC1	Drewry Shipping Consultants Limited
Shipping Statistics Yearbook	ISL2	Institute of Shipping Economics and Logistics
Shipping Trade, Trends and Statistics	DSC2	Drewry Shipping Consultants Limited
Short-term Review of International Pulp and Paper Markets	JP1	Jaakko Pöyry
Silicon Carbide	EAT1	Elsevier Advanced Technology
Situation de la Production Laitière et du Contrôle Laitier dans les Organismes Pays Members	FNOCL1	Federation Nationale des de Contrôle Laitier
Social Indicators of Development	WB1	The World Bank
A Social Portrait of Europe	EC72	European Community
Social Protection Expenditure and Receipts	EC73	European Community
South Pacific Economies	SPC2	South Pacific Commission
Standardized Input–Output Tables of ECE Countries for Years Around 1975	UN42	United Nations
The State of the World's Children	UNICEF1	United Nations Children's Fund
Statistical Appendices to AEA Yearbook	AEA2	Association of European Airlines
Statistical Brief	COS1	Chamber of Shipping
Statistical Bulletin	ICCAT1	International Commission for the Conservation of Atlantic Tunas
Statistical Bulletin	ISO2	International Sugar Organization
Statistical Bulletin, Fishery Statistics for 1988	NWAFO1	North West Atlantic Fisheries Organization
Statistical Indicators for Asia and the Pacific	UN43	United Nations
Statistical Report on Road Accidents	ECMT1	European Conference of Ministers of Transport
Statistical Trends in Transport	ECMT2	European Conference of Ministers of Transport

Title of publication	*instat* code	Name of organization
Statistical Yearbook for Asia and the Pacific	UN44	United Nations
Statistical Yearbook for Latin America and the Caribbean	UN45	United Nations
Statistics and Indicators on Women in Africa	UN46	United Nations
Statistics of Road Traffic Accidents in Europe	UN47	United Nations
Statistics of World Trade in Steel	UN48	United Nations
Statistics on Children in UNICEF Assisted Countries	UNICEF2	United Nations Children's Fund
Statistics on Housing in the European Community	MHPPE1	Ministry of Housing, Physical Planning and the Environment (Netherlands)
Steel Consumption by User Branch	EC74	European Community
The Steel Market in 1991	UN49	United Nations
Steel Market in 1991 and the Outlook for 1992	OECD45	Organization for Economic Co-operation and Development
Steel Statistical Yearbook	IISI4	International Iron and Steel Institute
Steel Statistics of Developing Countries	IISI3	International Iron and Steel Institute
Structure and Activity of Industry: Annual Enquiry Main Results	EC75	European Community
Structure and Activity of Industry: Data by Regions	EC76	European Community
Structure and Activity of Industry: Data by Size of Enterprises	EC77	European Community
Sugar Yearbook	ISO3	International Sugar Organization
Tanker Charter Record	BB3	Basil Blackwell Limited
Telecommunications: Profile of the Worldwide Telecommunications Industry	EAT2	Elsevier Advanced Technology
Tourism Annual Statistics	EC78	European Community
Tourism in Europe, Trends	EC79	European Community
Tourism Policy and International Tourism in OECD Member Countries	OECD46	Organization for Economic Co-operation and Development
Transport and Communications Annual Statistics	EC80	European Community
Travel and Tourism Barometer	WTO2	World Tourism Organization
Trends in Developing Economies	WB2	The World Bank

Title of publication	*instat* code	Name of organization
Trends in the Hotel Industry	PKF2	Pannell Kerr Forster
Trends in the Transport Sector	ECMT3	European Conference of Ministers of Transport
Tungsten Statistics	UNCTAD3	United Nations Conference on Trade and Development
UN Statistical Yearbook	UN50	United Nations
UNCTAD Commodity Yearbook	UNCTAD4	United Nations Conference on Trade and Development
UNCTAD Statistical Pocket Book	UNCTAD5	United Nations Conference on Trade and Development
Unemployment	EC81	European Community
UNHCR Activities Financed by Voluntary Funds. Report for 1990–91 and Proposed Programmes and Budget for 1992. Part 1: Africa Part 2: Asia and Oceania Part 3: Europe and North America Part 4: Latin America Part 5: South West Asia, North Africa and the Middle East Part 6: Overall Allocations	UN51	United Nations
Uranium – Resources, Production and Demand	OECD47	Organization for Economic Co-operation and Development
Urea Statistics	IFA1	International Fertilizer Industry Association
Western European Living Costs	CBI1	Confederation of British Industry
Women and Political Power Survey carried out among the National Parliaments existing as from 31.10.91	IPU2	Inter-Parliamentary Union
Wool Facts 1991–92	IWS1	International Wool Secretariat
World Air Transport Statistics	IATA1	International Air Transport Association
World Bulk Fleet	F2	Fearnleys
World Bulk Trades	F3	Fearnleys
The World Cocoa Market: An Analysis of Recent Trends and of Prospects to the Year 2000	ICCO3	International Cocoa Council Organization
World Crop and Livestock Statistics	FAO7	Food and Agriculture Organization
World Debt Tables, Vol 1, Analysis and Summary Tables	WB3	The World Bank
World Debt Tables, Vol 2, External Finance for Developing Countries, Country Tables	WB4	The World Bank

Title of publication	*instat* code	Name of organization
World Energy Statistics and Balances	IEA12	International Energy Agency
World Fleet Statistics	LRS4	Lloyds Register of Shipping
World Footwear Markets	SATRA1	Satra Footwear Technology Centre
World Health Statistics Annual	WHO2	World Health Organization
World Investment Directory Vol I Asia and the Pacific	UN52	United Nations
World Investment Directory Vol II Central and Eastern Europe	UN53	United Nations
The World Market for Dairy Products	GATT5	General Agreement on Tariffs and Trade
World Metal Statistics	WBMS1	World Bureau of Metal Statistics
World Metal Statistics Quarterly Summary	WBMS2	World Bureau of Metal Statistics
World Metal Statistics Yearbook	WBMS3	World Bureau of Metal Statistics
World Mineral Statistics Vol 1 Metals and Energy	BGS1	British Geological Survey
World Mineral Statistics Vol 2 Industrial Minerals	BGS2	British Geological Survey
World Oil Trade Review of International Oil Movements	BB4	Basil Blackwell Limited
World Population Projections	WB5	The World Bank
World Population Prospects	UN54	United Nations
World Rice Statistics, 1987	IRRI1	International Rice Research Institute
World Road Statistics, 1986–90	IRF1	World Road Federation
Worldwide Rubber Statistics	IISRP1	International Institute of Synthetic Rubber Producers
World Rubber Statistics Handbook	IRSG2	International Rubber Study Group
World Stainless Steel Statistics	WBMS4	World Bureau of Metal Statistics
World Statistics in Brief, United Nations Statistical Pocketbook	UN55	United Nations
World Steel in Figures	IISI5	International Iron and Steel Institute
World Sugar and Sweetener Yearbook	FOL3	F O Licht
World Tables	WB6	The World Bank
World Trade Stainless, High Speed and Other Alloy Steel	ISSB2	Iron and Steel Statistics Bureau
World Trade Steel	ISSB3	Iron and Steel Statistics Bureau

Title of publication	*instat* code	Name of organization
World Transport Data	IRTU1	International Road Transport Union
Worldwide Hotel Industry	HI1	Horwath International
Yearbook of Common Carrier Telecommunications Statistics	ITU1	International Telecommunication Union
Yearbook of Forest Products	FAO8	Food and Agriculture Organization
Yearbook of International Horticultural Statistics	IAHP1	International Association of Horticultural Statistics
Yearbook of Labour Statistics	ILO7	International Labour Organization
Yearbook of Nordic Statistics	NCM1	Nordic Council of Ministers and the Nordic Statistical Secretariat
Yearbook of Tourism Statistics, Vol 1	WTO3	World Tourism Organization
Yearbook of Tourism Statistics, Vol 2	WTO4	World Tourism Organization

APPENDIX C

INDEX OF PUBLICATIONS

ARRANGED BY NAME OF ORGANIZATION

Name of organization	*instat* code	Title of publication
Asian Productivity Organization	APO1	Comparative Information on Productivity Levels and Changes in APO Member Countries
Association of European Airlines	AEA1	Association of European Airlines Yearbook
	AEA2	Statistical Appendices to AEA Yearbook
	AEA3	Intra-European Country to Country Traffic
	AEA4	Medium-Term Forecast of European Scheduled Passenger Traffic
Association of South-East Asian Nations Secretariat	ASEANS1	ASEAN Selected Statistics
Basil Blackwell Limited	BB1	Oil and Energy Trends, Annual Statistical Review
	BB2	Oil and Energy Trends
	BB3	Tanker Charter Record
	BB4	World Oil Trade Review of International Oil Movements
British Geological Survey	BGS1	World Mineral Statistics Vol 1 Metals and Energy
	BGS2	World Mineral Statistics Vol 2 Industrial Minerals
British Paper and Board Industry Federation	BPB1	Reference Tables
British Petroleum Company Plc	BP1	BP Statistical Review of World Energy
	BP2	BP Review of World Gas
Caribbean Community Secretariat	CCS1	Caricom's Trade
	CCS2	A Digest of Trade Statistics
Chamber of Shipping	COS1	Statistical Brief
Chemical Industries Association	CIA1	Basic International Chemical Industry Statistics
Civil Aviation Authority	CAA1	Fatal Accident Statistics for Passenger Air Transport Services
		CAA Paper 83014
Comité International de la Rayonne et des Fibres Synthétiques	CIRFS1	Information on Man-made Fibres
Commonwealth Secretariat	CS1	Basic Statistical Data on Selected Countries
Confederation of British Industry	CBI1	Western European Living Costs
Council of Europe	CE1	Recent Demographic Developments in Europe
Croom Helm Limited	CH1	The Economies of the Arabian Gulf: A Statistical Source Book

Name of organization	*instat* code	Title of publication
Drewry Shipping Consultants Limited	DSC1	Shipping Statistics and Economics
	DSC2	Shipping Trade, Trends and Statistics
E D & F Man Cocoa Limited	EDFM1	Cocoa Market Report
Elsevier Advanced Technology	EAT1	Silicon Carbide
	EAT2	Telecommunications: Profile of the Worldwide Telecommunications Industry
Euromonitor	EM1	European Marketing Data and Statistics
European Aluminium Association	EAA1	European Aluminium Statistics
European Community	EC1	ACP Basic Statistics
	EC2	Agricultural Income
	EC3	Agricultural Markets: Prices
	EC4	Agricultural Prices: Price Indices and Absolute Prices
	EC5	Agricultural Prices: Price Indices and Absolute Prices
	EC6	Agriculture Statistical Yearbook
	EC7	Animal Production, Quarterly Statistics
	EC8	Areas Under Vines, Results of the Annual Surveys
	EC9	Basic Statistics of the Community
	EC10	Balance of Payments: Geographical Breakdown
	EC11	Censuses of Population in the Community Countries 1981–82
	EC12	Carriage of Goods – Inland Waterways
	EC13	Carriage of Goods – Railways
	EC14	Carriage of Goods – Road
	EC15	Community Survey of Orchard Fruit Trees
	EC16	Consumer Price Index
	EC17	Consumer Prices in the EEC
	EC18	Country Reports, Central and Eastern Europe
	EC19	Crop Production, Quarterly Statistics
	EC20	Demographic Statistics

Name of organization	*instat* code	Title of publication
European Community	EC21	Digest of Statistics on Social Protection in Europe, Vol 1 Old Age
	EC22	Digest of Statistics on Social Protection in Europe, Vol 2 Invalidity/Disability
	EC23	Earnings in Agriculture
	EC24	Earnings, Industry and Services
	EC25	EC External Trade Indices
	EC26	Economic Accounts for Agriculture and Forestry
	EC27	ECU–EMS Information
	EC28	Electricity Prices
	EC29	Employment and Unemployment
	EC30	Energy Balance Sheets
	EC31	Energy, Monthly Statistics
	EC32	Energy Prices
	EC33	Energy Yearly Statistics
	EC34	Environment Statistics
	EC35	Europe in Figures
	EC36	Eurostatistics – Data for Short-term Economic Analysis, No 5
	EC37	External Trade: Analytical Tables A–L, Imports and Exports
	EC38	External Trade and Balance of Payments
	EC39	External Trade Statistical Yearbook
	EC40	External Trade, System of Generalized Tariff Preferences, Imports 1988, Vol I
	EC41	External Trade, System of Generalized Tariff Preferences, Imports 1988, Vol II
	EC42	Family Budgets: Comparative Tables, Vols I and II
	EC43	Farm Structure: 1985 Survey Analysis of Results. Economic Size and Other Gainful Activities
	EC44	Farm Structure: 1985 Survey Analysis of Results. Regional Structure of Agricultural Production
	EC45	Farm Structure 1985 Survey: Main Results

Name of organization	*instat* code	Title of publication
European Community	EC46	Fisheries, Yearly Statistics
	EC47	Forestry Statistics
	EC48	Gas Prices
	EC49	General Government Accounts and Statistics
	EC50	Government Financing of Research and Development
	EC51	Industrial Production Quarterly Statistics
	EC52	Industrial Trends Monthly Statistics
	EC53	Industry Statistical Yearbook
	EC54	International Comparisons of Energy Data
	EC55	Iron and Steel, Yearly Statistics
	EC56	Labour Force Survey, Results 1991
	EC57	Milk Quotas – Their Effects on Agriculture in the European Community, Vol 1 Main Report
	EC58	Milk Quotas – Their Effects on Agriculture in the European Community, Vol 2 Annex
	EC59	Money and Finance
	EC60	National Accounts ESA Aggregates
	EC61	National Accounts ESA Detailed Tables by Branch
	EC62	National Accounts ESA Detailed Tables by Sector
	EC63	National Accounts ESA Input-Output Tables
	EC64	Operation of Nuclear Power Stations
	EC65	Portrait of the Regions: Vol I Germany, Benelux, Denmark,, Vol II France ,United Kingdom, Ireland, Vol III Portugal, Spain, Italy
	EC66	Price Structure of the Community Countries in 1985
	EC67	Quarterly National Accounts ESA
	EC68	Raw Material EC Supply
	EC69	Regions Statistical Yearbook
	EC70	Results of the Business Survey Carried Out Among Managements in the Community

Name of organization	*instat* code	Title of publication
European Community	EC71	Retailing in the European Single Market 1993
	EC72	A Social Portrait of Europe
	EC73	Social Protection Expenditure and Receipts
	EC74	Steel Consumption by User Branch
	EC75	Structure and Activity of Industry: Annual Enquiry Main Results
	EC76	Structure and Activity of Industry: Data by Regions
	EC77	Structure and Activity of Industry: Data by Size of Enterprises
	EC78	Tourism Annual Statistics
	EC79	Tourism in Europe, Trends
	EC80	Transport and Communications Annual Statistics
	EC81	Unemployment
European Conference of Ministers of Transport	ECMT1	Statistical Report on Road Accidents
	ECMT2	Statistical Trends in Transport
	ECMT3	Trends in the Transport Sector
European Free Trade Association	EFTA1	EFTA Trade
European Paper Institute	EPI1	European Paper Institute Annual Statistics
European Patent Office	EPO1	Facts and Figures
Fearnleys	F1	Fearnley's Review
	F2	World Bulk Fleet
	F3	World Bulk Trades
Federation Nationale des Organismes de Contrôle Laitier	FNOCL1	Situation de la Production Laitière et du Contrôle Laitier dans les Pays Members
F O Licht	FOL1	International Molasses and Alcohol Report
	FOL2	International Sugar and Sweetener Report
	FOL3	World Sugar and Sweetener Yearbook
Food and Agriculture Organization	FAO1	FAO Production Yearbook
	FAO2	FAO Trade Yearbook
	FAO3	FAO Yearbook of Fishery Statistics: Catches and Landings

Name of organization	*instat* code	Title of publication
Food and Agriculture Organization	FAO4	FAO Yearbook of Fishery Statistics: Commodities
	FAO5	Fertiliser Yearbook
	FAO6	Quarterly Bulletin of Statistics
	FAO7	World Crop and Livestock Statistics
	FAO8	Yearbook of Forest Products
General Agreement on Tariffs and Trade	GATT1	The International Markets for Meat
	GATT2	The International Markets for Meat. Arrangement Regarding Bovine Meat 12th Annual Report
	GATT3	International Trade Statistics Vol I
	GATT4	International Trade Statistics Vol II
	GATT5	The World Market for Dairy Products
Generation Publications	GP1	The Best 'N' Most in DFS
E A Gibson Shipbrokers Limited	G1	Oil, Chemical and Combined Carriers
	G2	Register of Liquified Gas Carriers
Horwath International	HI1	Worldwide Hotel Industry
Institute of Petroleum	IP1	Know More About Oil, World Statistics
Institute of Shipping Economics and Logistics	ISL1	Shipping Statistics
	ISL2	Shipping Statistics Yearbook
Inter-American Development Bank	IADB1	Pocket Profiles
International Agency for Research on Cancer	IARC1	Cancer Incidence in Five Continents
International Air Transport Association	IATA1	World Air Transport Statistics
International Association of Horticultural Producers	IAHP1	Yearbook of International Horticultural Statistics
International Atomic Energy Agency	IAEA1	Operating Experience with Nuclear Power Stations in Member States in 1990
International Bauxite Association	IBA1	IBA Quarterly Review
International Civil Aviation Organization	ICAO1	Accident/Incident Reporting (ADREP) Annual Statistics
	ICAO2	Civil Aviation Statistics of the World, Doc 9180

Name of organization	*instat* code	Title of publication
International Civil Aviation Organization	ICAO3	Digest of Statistics No 399, Series AF – No 9, Airport and Route Facilities, Financial Data and Summary Traffic Data
	ICAO4	Digest of Statistics No 383, Series AT–No 31, Airport Traffic
	ICAO5	Digest of Statistics No 397, Series F – No 45, Financial Data, Commercial Air Carriers
	ICAO6	Digest of Statistics No 385, Series FP – No 44, Fleet – Personnel, Commercial Air Carriers
	ICAO7	Digest of Statistics No 381, Series OFOD – No 44, On Flight Origin and Destination
	ICAO8	Digest of Statistics No 382, Series R – No 30, Civil Aircraft on Register
	ICAO9	Digest of Statistics No 379, Series T – No 50, Traffic – Commercial Air Carriers
	ICAO10	Digest of Statistics No 398, Series TF – No 10, Traffic By Flight Stage
International Cocoa Council Organization	ICCO1	International Cocoa Organization Annual Report
	ICCO2	Quarterly Bulletin of Cocoa Statistics
	ICCO3	The World Cocoa Market: An Analysis of Recent Trends and of Prospects to the Year 2000
International Commission for the Conservation of Atlantic Tunas	ICCAT1	Statistical Bulletin
International Cotton Advisory Committee	ICAC1	Cotton: Review of the World Situation
	ICAC2	Cotton: World Statistics, Bulletin of the International Cotton Advisory Committee
International Dairy Federation	IDF1	Bulletin–Consumption Statistics for Milk and Milk Products
International Energy Agency	IEA1	Annual Oil Market Report
	IEA2	Coal Information
	IEA3	Electricity Supply in the OECD
	IEA4	Energy Balances of OECD Countries 1980–89
	IEA5	Energy Balances of OECD Countries1990–91
	IEA6	Energy Prices and Taxes
	IEA7	Energy Statistics and Balances of Non-OECD Countries

Name of organization	*instat* code	Title of publication
International Energy Agency	IEA8	Energy Statistics of OECD Countries 1980–89
	IEA9	Energy Statistics of OECD Countries 1989–90
	IEA10	Oil and Gas Information
	IEA11	Quarterly Oil Statistics and Energy Balances
	IEA12	World Energy Statistics and Balances
International Fertilizer Industry Association	IFA1	Urea Statistics
International Institute of Synthetic Rubber Producers	IISRP1	Worldwide Rubber Statistics
International Iron and Steel Institute	IISI1	Annual Report of the International Iron and Steel Institute
	IISI2	Monthly Crude Iron and Steel Production
	IISI3	Steel Statistics of Developing Countries
	IISI4	Steel Statistical Yearbook
	IISI5	World Steel in Figures
International Labour Organization	ILO1	Bulletin of Labour Statistics
	ILO2	Economically Active Population 1950–2025 Asia, Vol I
	ILO3	Economically Active Population 1950–2025 Africa, Vol II
	ILO4	Economically Active Population 1950–2025 Latin America, Vol III
	ILO5	Economically Active Population 1950–2025 Northern America Europe Oceania and USSR, Vol IV
	ILO6	Economically Active Population 1950–2025 World, Vol V
	ILO7	Yearbook of Labour Statistics
International Lead and Zinc Study Group	ILZSG1	Bulletin of the Lead and Zinc Study Group: Lead and Zinc Statistics
	ILZSG2	Joint Production of Lead and Zinc
International Metalworkers' Federation	IMWF1	The Purchasing Power of Working Time. An International Comparison
International Monetary Fund	IMF1	Balance of Payments Statistical Yearbook, Part I
	IMF2	Balance of Payments Statistical Yearbook, Part II
	IMF3	Direction of Trade Statistics Yearbook

Name of organization	*instat* code	Title of publication
International Monetary Fund	IMF4	Direction of Trade Statistics
	IMF5	Government Finance Statistics Yearbook
	IMF6	International Financial Statistics
	IMF7	International Financial Statistics Yearbook
International North Pacific Fisheries Commission	INPFC1	International North Pacific Fisheries Commission Statistical Yearbook
International Pacific Halibut Commission	IPHC1	International Pacific Halibut Commission, Annual Report
International Rice Research Institute	IRRI1	World Rice Statistics, 1987
International Road Federation	IRF1	World Road Statistics, 1986–90
International Road Transport Union	IRTU1	World Transport Data
International Rubber Study Group	IRSG1	Rubber Statistical Bulletin
	IRSG2	World Rubber Statistics Handbook
International Sugar Organization	ISO1	Quarterly Market Review
	ISO2	Statistical Bulletin
	ISO3	Sugar Yearbook
International Tea Committee	ITC1	International Tea Committee Annual Bulletin of Statistics
International Telecommunication Union	ITU1	Yearbook of Common Carrier Telecommunications Statistics
International Textile Manufacturers Federation	ITMF1	Country Statements
	ITMF2	International Cotton Industry Statistics
	ITMF3	International Textile Machinery Shipment Statistics
International Tropical Timber Organization	ITTO1	Annual Review and Assessment of the World Tropical Timber Situation
International Union of Railways	IUR1	International Railway Statistics, Statistics of Individual Railways
International Whaling Commission	IWC1	International Whaling Statistics
International Wheat Council	IWhC1	Food Aid Shipments
	IWhC2	Grain Market Report
	IWhC3	Report for the Crop Year
International Wool Secretariat	IWS1	Wool Facts 1991–92

Name of organization	*instat* code	Title of publication
Inter-Parliamentary Union	IPU1	Distribution of Seats Between Men and Women in National Parliaments. Statistical Data from 1945 to 30 June 1991
	IPU2	Women and Political Power Survey carried out among the National Parliaments existing as from 31.10.91
Iron and Steel Statistics Bureau	ISSB1	International Steel Statistics Summary Tables
	ISSB2	World Trade Stainless, High Speed and Other Alloy Steel
	ISSB3	World Trade Steel
Ista Mielk Gmbh	ISTA1	Oil World
	ISTA2	Oil World Annual
Jaakko Pöyry	JP1	Short-term Review of International Pulp and Paper Markets
Johnson Matthey	JM1	Platinum
Lloyds Register of Shipping	LRS1	Annual Summary of Merchant Ships Completed
	LRS2	Casualty Return
	LRS3	Merchant Shipbuilding Return
	LRS4	World Fleet Statistics
Macmillan Press Limited	MAC1	International Historical Statistics, Africa and Asia
	MAC2	International Historical Statistics, The Americas and Australasia
	MAC3	International Historical Statistics Europe, 1750–1988
Meat and Livestock Commission	MLC1	European Handbook, EEC and International Statistics
Metal Bulletin Books Limited	MB1	Iron and Manganese Ore Databook
	MB2	Metal Bulletin's Prices and Data
Milk Marketing Board	MMB1	EC Dairy Facts and Figures
Mining Journal	MJ1	Metals and Minerals, The Safer World of SGS
Ministry of Housing, Physical Planning and the Environment (Netherlands)	MHPPE1	Statistics on Housing in the European Community
Nordic Council of Ministers and the Nordic Statistical Secretariat	NCM1	Yearbook of Nordic Statistics
North Atlantic Treaty Organization	NATO1	The North Atlantic Treaty Organization 1949–89, Facts and Figures

Name of organization	*instat* code	Title of publication
North West Atlantic Fisheries Organization	NWAFO1	Statistical Bulletin, Fishery Statistics for 1988
Office International de la Vigne et du Vin	OIVV1	Bulletin de IOIV
Organization for Economic Co-operation and Development	OECD1	Balances of Payments of OECD Countries
	OECD2	Bank Profitability: Statistical Supplement – Financial Statements of Banks
	OECD3	Basic Science and Technology
	OECD4	Demographic Trends in OECD Member Countries
	OECD5	Economic Accounts for Agriculture
	OECD6	Education at a Glance
	OECD7	Education in OECD Countries
	OECD8	External Debt Statistics: The Debt and Other External Liabilities of Developing, CMEA and Certain Other Countries and Territories at end December 1987 and end December 1988
	OECD9	External Debt Statistics: The Debt and Other External Liabilities of Developing, Central and Eastern European and Certain Other Countries and Territories at end December 1988 and end December 1989
	OECD10	Financial Market Trends
	OECD11	Flows and Stocks of Fixed Capital: 1964–89
	OECD12	Food Consumption Statistics
	OECD13	Foreign Trade by Commodities, Vols I to V, Series C
	OECD14	Geographical Distribution of Financial Flows to Developing Countries, Disbursements, Commitments, Economic Indicators: 1986–89
	OECD15	Indicators of Industrial Activity
	OECD16	Industrial Structure Statistics
	OECD17	International Direct Investment Statistics Yearbook
	OECD18	The Iron and Steel Industry
	OECD19	Labour Force Statistics
	OECD20	Living Conditions in OECD Countries: Compendium of Social Indicators

Name of organization	*instat* code	Title of publication
Organization for Economic Co-operation and Development	OECD21	Main Economic Indicators
	OECD22	Main Economic Indicators, Historical Statistics
	OECD23	Main Economic Indicators, Historical Statistics: Prices Labour and Wages 1962–91
	OECD24	Main Science and Technology Indicators
	OECD25	Maritime Transport
	OECD26	Meat Balances in OECD Countries
	OECD27	Monthly Statistics of Foreign Trade, Series A
	OECD28	National Accounts, Vol I Main Aggregates
	OECD29	National Accounts, Vol II Detailed Tables
	OECD30	National and International Tourism Statistics
	OECD31	Nuclear Energy Data
	OECD32	OECD Economic Outlook Historical Statistics
	OECD33	OECD Environmental Data Compendium
	OECD34	OECD Financial Statistics Part 1 Section 1 International Markets
	OECD35	OECD Financial Statistics Part 1 Section 2 Domestic Markets – Interest Rates
	OECD36	OECD Financial Statistics Part 2 Financial Accounts of OECD Countries
	OECD37	OECD Financial Statistics Part 3 Non–Financial Enterprises Financial Statements
	OECD38	The Pulp and Paper Industry
	OECD39	Purchasing Power Parities and Real Expenditures
	OECD40	Quarterly Labour Force Statistics
	OECD41	Quarterly National Accounts
	OECD42	Revenue Statistics of OECD Member Countries
	OECD43	Review of Fisheries in OECD Member Countries
	OECD44	Services: Statistics on International Transactions
	OECD45	Steel Market in 1991 and the Outlook for 1992

Name of organization	*instat* code	Title of publication
Organization of Petroleum Exporting Countries	OECD46	Tourism Policy and International Tourism in OECD Member Countries
	OECD47	Uranium – Resources, Production and Demand
Organization of Petroleum Exporting Countries	OPEC1	OPEC Annual Statistical Bulletin
	OPEC2	OPEC Bulletin
Pannell Kerr Forster	PKF1	Euro Trends Survey
	PKF2	Trends in the Hotel Industry
The Population Council	PC1	Family Planning and Child Survival Programs as Assessed in 1991
Pulp and Paper International	PPI1	Pulp and Paper International Annual Review
Satra Footwear Technology Centre	SATRA1	World Footwear Markets
Sea Fish Industry Authority	SFIA1	European Supplies Bulletin
Society of Motor Manufacturers and Traders Limited	SMMT1	Monthly Statistical Review
	SMMT2	Motor Industry of Great Britain: World Automotive Statistics
South Pacific Commission	SPC1	Retail Price Indices, Statistical Bulletin of the South Pacific
	SPC2	South Pacific Economies
United Nations	UN1	African Socio-economic Indicators 1990–91
	UN2	African Statistical Yearbook 1988–89 Vol I, Part 1 North Africa
	UN3	African Statistical Yearbook 1988–89 Vol I, Part 2 West Africa
	UN4	African Statistical Yearbook 1988–89 Vol II, Part 3 East and Southern Africa
	UN5	African Statistical Yearbook 1988–89 Vol II, Part 4 Central Africa, Others in Africa
	UN6	Annual Bulletin of Coal Statistics for Europe
	UN7	Annual Bulletin of Electric Energy Statistics for Europe
	UN8	Annual Bulletin of Gas Statistics for Europe
	UN9	Annual Bulletin of General Energy Statistics for Europe
	UN10	Annual Bulletin of Housing and Building Statistics for Europe
	UN11	Annual Bulletin of Steel Statistics for Europe

Name of organization	*instat* code	Title of publication
United Nations	UN12	Annual Bulletin of Trade in Chemical Products
	UN13	Annual Bulletin of Transport Statistics for Europe
	UN14	Bulletin of Statistics on World Trade in Engineering Products
	UN15	Commodity Trade Statistics
	UN16	Compendium of Social Statistics and Indicators
	UN17	Compendium of Statistics and Indicators on the Situation of Women
	UN18	Construction Statistics Yearbook
	UN19	Demographic Ycarbook
	UN20	Energy Balances and Electricity Profiles
	UN21	Energy Statistics Yearbook
	UN22	The Environment in Europe and North America: Annotated Statistics 1992
	UN23	Foreign Trade Statistics for Africa, Direction of Trade Series A
	UN24	Foreign Trade Statistics of Asia and the Pacific
	UN25	Human Development Report
	UN26	Human Settlements Basic Statistics
	UN27	Industrial Statistics Yearbook, Vol I General Industrial Statistics
	UN28	Industrial Statistics Yearbook, Vol II Commodity Production Statistics
	UN29	International Narcotics Control Board – Narcotic Drugs, Estimated World Requirement Statistics for 1990
	UN30	International Narcotics Control Board – Psychotropic Substances, Statistics for 1990
	UN31	International Sea-borne Trade Statistics: Yearbook 1984–85
	UN32	International Trade Statistics Yearbook, Vol I Trade by Country
	UN33	International Trade Statistics Yearbook, Vol II Trade by Commodity
	UN34	The Livestock and Meat Market
	UN35	Monthly Bulletin of Statistics

Name of organization	*instat* code	Title of publication
United Nations	UN36	National Accounts Statistics: Analysis of Main Aggregates 1988–89
	UN37	National Accounts Statistics: Compendium of Income Distribution Statistics
	UN38	National Accounts Statistics: Main Aggregates and Detailed Tables Parts I and II
	UN39	Population and Vital Statistics Report
	UN40	Prices of Agricultural Products and Selected Inputs in Europe and North America
	UN41	Report of the UN High Commissioner for Refugees. General Assembly Official Records: 46th Session, Supplement No 12
	UN42	Standardized Input-Output Tables of ECE Countries for Years Around 1975
	UN43	Statistical Indicators for Asia and the Pacific
	UN44	Statistical Yearbook for Asia and the Pacific
	UN45	Statistical Yearbook for Latin America and the Caribbean
	UN46	Statistics and Indicators on Women in Africa
	UN47	Statistics of Road Traffic Accidents in Europe
	UN48	Statistics of World Trade in Steel
	UN49	The Steel Market in 1991
	UN50	UN Statistical Yearbook
	UN51	UNHCR Activities Financed by Voluntary Funds. Report for 1990–91 and Proposed Programmes and Budget for 1992. Part 1: Africa Part 2: Asia and Oceania Part 3: Europe and North America Part 4: Latin America Part 5: South-West Asia, North Africa and the Middle East Part 6: Overall Allocations
	UN52	World Investment Directory Vol I Asia and the Pacific
	UN53	World Investment Directory Vol II Central and Eastern Europe
	UN54	World Population Prospects
	UN55	World Statistics in Brief, United Nations Statistical Pocketbook
United Nations Children's Fund	UNICEF1	The State of the World's Children

Name of organization	*instat* code	Title of publication
United Nations Children's Fund	UNICEF2	Statistics on Children in UNICEF Assisted Countries
United Nations Conference on Trade and Development	UNCTAD1	Handbook of International Trade and Development Statistics
	UNCTAD2	Review of Maritime Transport
United Nations Conference on Trade and Development	UNCTAD3	Tungsten Statistics
	UNCTAD4	UNCTAD Commodity Yearbook
	UNCTAD5	UNCTAD Statistical Pocket Book
United Nations Educational, Scientific, and Cultural Organization	UNESCO1	Statistical Yearbook
United Nations Industrial Development Organization	UNIDO1	Handbook of Industrial Statistics
Vienna Institute for Comparative Economic Studies	VICES1	Comecon Data
The World Bank	WB1	Social Indicators of Development
	WB2	Trends in Developing Economies
	WB3	World Debt Tables, Vol 1, Analysis and Summary Tables
	WB4	World Debt Tables, Vol 2, External Finance for Developing Countries, Country Tables
	WB5	World Population Projections
	WB6	World Tables
World Bureau of Metal Statistics	WBMS1	World Metal Statistics
	WBMS2	World Metal Statistics Quarterly Summary
	WBMS3	World Metal Statistics Yearbook
	WBMS4	World Stainless Steel Statistics
World Food Programme	WFP1	The Food Aid Monitor: World Food Aid Flows, Transport and Logistics
World Health Organization	WHO1	Bulletin of Regional Health Information
	WHO2	World Health Statistics Annual
World Intellectual Property Organization	WIPO1	Industrial Property Statistics, Patents, Part I

Name of organization	*instat* code	Title of publication
World Intellectual Property Organization	WIPO2	Industrial Property Statistics, Part II Trademarks and Service Marks, Utility Models, Industrial Designs, Varieties of Plants, Micro-organisms
	WIPO3	Industrial Property Statistics, Publication A (Supplement to Industrial Property) No 11
World Meteorological Organization	WMO1	Climatological Normals (CLINO) for CLIMAT and CLIMAT Ship Stations
World Tourism Organization	WTO1	Compendium of Tourism Statistics
	WTO2	Travel and Tourism Barometer
	WTO3	Yearbook of Tourism Statistics, Vol 1
	WTO4	Yearbook of Tourism Statistics, Vol 2
Wye College	WC1	Agrifacts: A Handbook of UK and EEC Agricultural and Food Statistics

APPENDIX D

NAMES AND ADDRESSES OF ORGANIZATIONS

ALPHABETICAL LISTING

ASIAN PRODUCTIVITY ORGANIZATION (APO)
4–14 Akasaka 8–Chome, Minato-ku, Tokyo 107, Japan

ASSOCIATION OF EUROPEAN AIRLINES (AEA)
Publications Department, Association of European Airlines, 350 Avenue Louise, Bte 4, 1050 Brussels, Belgium

ASSOCIATION OF SOUTH-EAST ASIAN NATIONS SECRETARIAT (ASEANS)
70A Kebayoran Baru, PO Box 2072, Jakarta 12110, Indonesia

BASIL BLACKWELL LTD (BB)
108 Cowley Road, Oxford, OX4 1JF, UK

BRITISH GEOLOGICAL SURVEY (BGS)
Keyworth, Nottingham, NG12 5GG, UK

BRITISH PAPER AND BOARD INDUSTRY FEDERATION (BPB)
Papermakers House, Rivenhall Road, Westlea, Swindon, SN5 7BE, UK

BRITISH PETROLEUM COMPANY PLC (BP)
Britannic House, 1 Finsbury Circus, London, EC2M 7BA, UK

CARIBBEAN COMMUNITY SECRETARIAT (CCS)
PO Box 10827, Bank of Guyana Building 3rd Floor, Avenue of the Republic, Georgetown, Guyana

CHAMBER OF SHIPPING (COS)
30–32 St Mary Axe, London, EC3A 8ET, UK

CHEMICAL INDUSTRIES ASSOCIATION (CIA)
King's Building, Smiths Square, London, SW1P 3JJ, UK

CIVIL AVIATION AUTHORITY (CAA)
Greville House, 37 Gratton Road, Cheltenham, Gloucestershire, GL50 2BN, UK

COMITE INTERNATIONAL DE LA RAYONNE ET DES FIBRES SYNTHETIQUES (CIRFS)
29 rue de Courcelles, 75008, Paris, France

COMMONWEALTH SECRETARIAT (CS)
Marlborough House, Pall Mall, London, SW1Y 5HX, UK

CONFEDERATION OF BRITISH INDUSTRY (CBI)
Centre Point, 103 New Oxford Street, London, WC1A 1DU, UK

COUNCIL OF EUROPE (CE)
Strasbourg, France

CROOM HELM LIMITED (CH)
c/o Routledge, 11 New Fetter Lane, London, EC4P 4EE

DREWRY SHIPPING CONSULTANTS LIMITED (DSC)
11 Heron Quay, London, E14 4JF, UK

E A GIBSON SHIPBROKERS LIMITED (G)
PO Box 278, Audrey House, 16–20 Ely Place, London, EC1P 1HP, UK

E D & F MAN COCOA LIMITED (EDFM)
Sugar Quay, Lower Thames Street, London, EC3R 6DU, UK

ELSEVIER ADVANCED TECHNOLOGY (EAT)
Mayfield House, 256 Banbury Road, Oxford, OX2 7DH, UK

EUROMONITOR (EM)
87–88 Turnmill Street, London, EC1M 5QU, UK

EUROPEAN ALUMINIUM ASSOCIATION (EAA)
Avenue de Broqueville, 12, B–1150 Brussels, Belgium

EUROPEAN COMMUNITY (EUROSTAT) (EC)
Bâtiment Jean Monnet, L–2920, Luxembourg

EUROPEAN CONFERENCE OF MINISTERS OF TRANSPORT (ECMT)
19 rue de Franqueville F–75775, Paris, Cedex 16, France

EUROPEAN FREE TRADE ASSOCIATION (EFTA)
9–11 rue de Varembé, CH–1211 Geneva 20, Switzerland

EUROPEAN PAPER INSTITUTE (EPI)
42 rue Galilé, 75116 Paris, France

EUROPEAN PATENT OFFICE (EPO)
Erhardtstrasse 27, D–800, Munich 2, Germany

FEARNLEYS (F)
PO Box 1158 Sentrum, 0107 Oslo 1, Norway

FEDERATION NATIONALE DES ORGANISMES DE CONTROLE LAITIER (FNOCL)
149 rue de Bercy, 75595 Paris, Cedex 12, France

F O LICHT (FOL)
PO Box 1220, D–2418 Ratzeburg, Germany

FOOD AND AGRICULTURE ORGANIZATION (FAO)
Via Deile Terme Di Caracella, 00100 Rome, Italy

GENERAL AGREEMENT ON TARIFFS AND TRADE (GATT)
Centre William Rappard, rue de Lausanne 154, CH–1211 Geneva 21, Switzerland

GENERATION PUBLICATIONS (GP)
PO Box 234, S–891 25 Örnsköldsvik, Sweden

HORWATH INTERNATIONAL (HI)
Headquarters, 415 Madison Avenue, New York, NY10017, USA

INSTITUTE OF PETROLEUM (IP)
61 New Cavendish Street, London, W1M 8AR, UK

INSTITUTE OF SHIPPING ECONOMICS AND LOGISTICS (ISL)
Universitätsallee GW1, Block A, D–2800, Bremen 33, Germany

INTER-AMERICAN DEVELOPMENT BANK (IADB)
Headquarters, 13000 New York Avenue, Washington DC, 20577, USA

INTERNATIONAL AGENCY FOR RESEARCH ON CANCER (IARC)
150 Cours Albert Thomas, F–69372 Lyon, Cedex 08, France

INTERNATIONAL AIR TRANSPORT ASSOCIATION (IATA)
3rd Floor, Sceptre House, 75–81 Staines Road, Hounslow, TW3 3HW, UK

INTERNATIONAL ASSOCIATION OF HORTICULTURAL PRODUCERS (IAHP)
Bezuidenhoutseweg 153, Postbus 93099, NL–2509 AB's–Gravenhage, Netherlands

INTERNATIONAL ATOMIC ENERGY AGENCY (IAEA)
Wagramerstrasse 5, PO Box 100, A–1400 Vienna, Austria

INTERNATIONAL BAUXITE ASSOCIATION (IBA)
36 Trafalgar Road, PO Box 551, Kingston 5, Jamaica

INTERNATIONAL CIVIL AVIATION ORGANIZATION (ICAO)
1000 Sherbrook Street W, Montreal PQ, H3A 2RZ, Canada

INTERNATIONAL COCOA COUNCIL ORGANIZATION (ICCO)
22 Berners Street, London, W1P 3DB, UK

INTERNATIONAL COMMISSION FOR THE CONSERVATION OF ATLANTIC TUNAS (ICCAT)
Calle Principe de Vergara 17–7, 28001 Madrid, Spain

INTERNATIONAL COTTON ADVISORY COMMITTEE (ICAC)
1901 Pennsylvania Av NW, Suite 201, Washington DC 20006, USA

INTERNATIONAL DAIRY FEDERATION (IDF)
41 Square Vergote, B–1040 Brussels, Belgium

INTERNATIONAL ENERGY AGENCY (IEA)
IEA 2 rue André Pascal, F–75775 Paris Cedex 16, France

INTERNATIONAL FERTILIZER INDUSTRY ASSOCIATION (IFA)
28 rue Marbeuf, 75008 Paris, France

INTERNATIONAL INSTITUTE OF SYNTHETIC RUBBER PRODUCERS (IISRP)
2077 South Gessner Road Suite 133, Houston, Texas 77063, USA

INTERNATIONAL IRON AND STEEL INSTITUTE (IISI)
rue Colonel Bourg, 120 B–11140 Brussels, Belgium

INTERNATIONAL LABOUR ORGANIZATION (ILO)
4 Route des Murillons, Ch–1211, Geneva 22, Switzerland

INTERNATIONAL LEAD AND ZINC STUDY GROUP (ILZSG)
Metro House, 58 St James Street, London, SW1A 1LD, UK

INTERNATIONAL METALWORKERS' FEDERATION (IMWF)
54 bis route des Acacias, Care Postale, 563, CH–1227 Geneva, Switzerland

INTERNATIONAL MONETARY FUND (IMF)
700 19th Street NW, Washington DC 20431, USA

INTERNATIONAL NORTH PACIFIC FISHERIES COMMISSION (INPFC)[1]
6640 Northwest Marine Drive, Vancouver, V6T 1X2, Canada

INTERNATIONAL PACIFIC HALIBUT COMMISSION (IPHC)
PO Box 5009, University Station, Seattle, WA 98145, USA

INTERNATIONAL RICE RESEARCH INSTITUTE (IRRI)
Headquarters, PO Box 933, 1099 Manila, Philippines

INTERNATIONAL ROAD FEDERATION (IRF)
CH–1202, 63 rue de Lausanne, Geneva, Switzerland

INTERNATIONAL ROAD TRANSPORT UNION (IRTU)
Centre International, BP 44, 3 rue de Varembé, CH–1211 Geneva 20, Switzerland

INTERNATIONAL RUBBER STUDY GROUP (IRSG)
York House, Empire Way, Wembley, HA9 0PA, UK

INTERNATIONAL SUGAR ORGANIZATION (ISO)
1 Canada Square, Canary Wharf, London, E14 5AA, UK

INTERNATIONAL TEA COMMITTEE (ITC)
Sir John Lyon House, 5 High Timber Street, London, EC4V 3NH, UK

INTERNATIONAL TELECOMMUNICATION UNION (ITU)
Head Office, Place des Nations, CH–1211 Geneva 20, Switzerland

INTERNATIONAL TEXTILE MANUFACTURERS FEDERATION (ITMF)
Am Schanzengraben 29, Postfach, 8039 Zurich, Switzerland

---

1 To be replaced by the North Pacific Anadromous Fish Commission after 1993.

INTERNATIONAL TROPICAL TIMBER ORGANIZATION (ITTO)
International Organization Centre, SF/Pacifico–Yokohama, H–1 Minato-Mirai, Nishi-ku, Yokohama 220, Japan

INTERNATIONAL UNION OF RAILWAYS (IUR)
16 rue Jean-Rey, 75015 Paris, France

INTERNATIONAL WHALING COMMISSION (IWC)
The Red House, Station Road, Histon, Cambridge CB4 4NP, UK

INTERNATIONAL WHEAT COUNCIL (IWhC)
Haymarket House, 28 Haymarket, London, SW1Y 4SS, UK

INTERNATIONAL WOOL SECRETARIAT (IWS)
Development Centre, Valley Drive, Ilkley, West Yorkshire, LS29 8PB, UK

INTER-PARLIAMENTARY UNION (IPU)
Place du petit-saconnex, CP–438, CH–1211, Geneva 19, Switzerland

IRON AND STEEL STATISTICS BUREAU (ISSB)
Canterbury House, 2 Sydenham Road, Croydon, CR9 2LZ, UK

ISTA MIELK GmbH (ISTA)
2100 Hamburg 90, Langenberg 25, Germany

JAAKKO PÖYRY (JP)
Third Floor, Century House, Station Way, Cheam, Surrey, SM3 8SW, UK

JOHNSON MATTHEY (JM)
Blounts Court, Sonning Common, Reading, RG4 9NH, UK

LLOYDS REGISTER OF SHIPPING (LRS)
71 Fenchurch Street, London, EC3M 4BS, UK

MACMILLAN PRESS LIMITED (MAC)
Houndmills, Basingstoke, Hampshire, RG21 2XS, UK

MEAT AND LIVESTOCK COMMISSION (MLC)
PO Box 44, Winterhill House, Snowdon Drive, Milton Keynes, MK6 1AX, UK

METAL BULLETIN BOOKS LIMITED (MB)
Park House, Park Terrace, Worcester Park, Surrey, KT4 7HY, UK

MILK MARKETING BOARD (MMB)
Portsmouth Road, Thames Ditton, Surrey, KT7 OEL, UK

MINING JOURNAL (MJ)
60 Worship Street, London, EC2A 2HD, UK

MINISTRY OF HOUSING, PHYSICAL PLANNING AND THE ENVIRONMENT (MHPPE)
PO Box 20951, 2500 EZ The Hague, The Netherlands

NORDIC COUNCIL OF MINISTERS AND THE NORDIC STATISTICAL SECRETARIAT (NCM)
Store Strandstraede 18, DK–1255 Copenhagen K, Denmark, and
Nordic Statistical Secretariat, Sejøgade 11, DK–2100 Copenhagen Ø, Denmark

NORTH ATLANTIC TREATY ORGANIZATION (NATO)
Headquarters, B–1110, Brussels, Belgium

NORTH WEST ATLANTIC FISHERIES ORGANIZATION (NWAFO)
PO Box 638, Dartmouth BZY, 3Y9, Canada

OFFICE INTERNATIONAL DE LA VIGNE ET DU VIN (OIVV)
Paris 8e, 11 rue Roquepine, Paris, France

ORGANIZATION FOR ECONOMIC CO-OPERATION AND DEVELOPMENT (OECD)
2 rue André Pascal, F–75775, Paris, Cedex 16, France

ORGANIZATION OF PETROLEUM EXPORTING COUNTRIES (OPEC)
Obere Donaustrasse 93, A–1020 Vienna 11, Austria

PANNELL KERR FORSTER (PKF)
262 North Belt East, Suite 300, Houston, TX 77060, USA

THE POPULATION COUNCIL (PC)
1 Dag Hammarskjold Plaza, New York, NY 1007, USA

PULP AND PAPER INTERNATIONAL (PPI)
123a Chaussee de Charleroi, B–1060 Brussels, Belgium

SATRA FOOTWEAR TECHNOLOGY CENTRE (SATRA)
SATRA House, Rockingham Road, Kettering, Northamptonshire, NN16 9JH, UK

SEA FISH INDUSTRY AUTHORITY (SFIA)
Fishery Economics Research Unit, Sea Fisheries House, 10 Young Street, Edinburgh, EH2 4JQ, UK

SOCIETY OF MOTOR MANUFACTURERS AND TRADERS LIMITED (SMMT)
Forbes House, Halkin Street, London, SW1X 7DS, UK

SOUTH PACIFIC COMMISSION (SPC)
Anse Vata, BPD5, Noumea Cedex, New Caledonia

UNITED NATIONS (UN)
New York, NY 10017, USA
Economic and Social Commission for Asia and the Pacific, United Nations Building, Rajadamern Avenue, Bangkok 10200, Thailand
Economic Commission for Africa, PO Box 3001, Addis Ababa, Ethiopia
Economic Commission for Europe, Palais des Nations, Ch–1211, Geneva 10, Switzerland
Office of the UN Disaster Relief Coordinator, Palais des Nations, CH–1211, Geneva, Switzerland
United Nations Centre for Human Settlements, Habitat, PO Box 30030 Nairobi, Kenya
United Nations Centre for Regional Development, Nagono 1–41–1, Nakamura-Ku, Nagoya 450, Japan
United Nations Environment Programme, PO Box 30552, Nairobi, Kenya
United Nations Conference on Trade and Development, Palais des Nations, CH–1211 Geneva 10, Switzerland
United Nations Educational, Scientific, and Cultural Organization, 7 Place de Fontenoy, F–75700, Paris, France

UNITED NATIONS CHILDREN'S FUND (UNICEF)
Unicef House 3 United Nations Plaza, New York NY10017, USA

UNITED NATIONS CONFERENCE ON TRADE AND DEVELOPMENT (UNCTAD)
Palais des Nations, CH–1211, Geneva 10, Switzerland

UNITED NATIONS EDUCATIONAL, SCIENTIFIC, AND CULTURAL ORGANIZATION (UNESCO)
7 Place de Fontenoy, F–75700, Paris, France

UNITED NATIONS INDUSTRIAL DEVELOPMENT ORGANIZATION (UNIDO)
Vienna International Centre, PO Box 300, A–1400 Vienna, Austria

VIENNA INSTITUTE FOR COMPARATIVE ECONOMIC STUDIES (VICES)
Postfach 87, A–1103 Wein, Austria

THE WORLD BANK (WB)
Head Office, 1818 H Street, NW, Washington DC 2043, USA

WORLD BUREAU OF METAL STATISTICS (WBMS)
27 High Street, Ware, Hertfordshire, SG12 9BQ, UK

WORLD FOOD PROGRAMME (WFP)
426, Via Cristoford Colombo, I–00145 Rome, Italy

WORLD HEALTH ORGANIZATION (WHO)
CH–1211, Geneva 27, Switzerland

WORLD INTELLECTUAL PROPERTY ORGANIZATION (WIPO)
Case Postale 2300, 41 AV Giuseppe-Motta, CH–1211 Geneva 2, Switzerland

WORLD METEOROLOGICAL ORGANIZATION (WMO)
Case Postale 2300, 41 Av Giuseppe-Motta, CH–1211 Geneva 2, Switzerland

WORLD TOURISM ORGANIZATION (WTO)
Calle Capitan Haya 42, Madrid 28020, Spain

WYE COLLEGE (WC)
Wye College, University of London, Wye, Ashford, Kent, TN25 5AH, UK

Subject index

(*Note*: bold headings denote main subject sections)

Subject index

instat

INTERNATIONAL STATISTICS SOURCES

Subject Guide to Sources of International Comparative Statistics

MICHAEL C. FLEMING
Professor of Economics
Department of Economics
Loughborough University

and

JOSEPH G. NELLIS
Professor of International Management Economics
School of Management
Cranfield University

Volume 2

ROUTLEDGE
London and New York

First published in 1995
by Routledge
11 New Fetter Lane, London EC4P 4EE
29 West 35th Street, New York, NY 10001

Printed in Great Britain by TJ Press (Padstow), Cornwall

Printed on acid-free paper

British Library Cataloguing in Publication Data
A catalogue record for this book is available from the British Library.

Library of Congress Cataloging-in-Publication Data
A catalog record for this book has been requested.

ISBN 0-415-08634-5 (set)
0-415-11358-X (Volume 1)
0-415-11359-8 (Volume 2)

Contents

Volume 2

For contents of Volume 1, see overleaf

Contents

Volume 1

How to use *instat*

Organization of *instat*

Instat is published in two volumes and organized in three main parts as follows:

- An analysis of broad subject areas and sources – given in the **Overview of subjects and sources** section
- Detailed sub-classifications of subjects and their sources – given in 46 subject sections in Volumes 1 and 2
- A set of four Appendices containing information on publications and organizations as follows:

Appendix A	Index of publications arranged by ***instat*** code: full bibliographical details
Appendix B	Index of publications arranged by title of publication
Appendix C	Index of sources arranged by name of organization
Appendix D	Names and addresses of organizations

To trace sources of statistical data on a particular subject, users should consult either the **Overview** section, or the relevant **Subject Section** or the **Subject Index**, depending on whether the nature of the topic in which they are interested is general, specific or very specific. The use and structure of the book is described in more detail below.

The overview of subjects and sources

This part of ***instat*** is solely concerned with broad subject areas – 46 broad subject areas in all. These are cross-referenced to the publication sources in which the relevant data are published. The **Overview** is, therefore, structured as a matrix with a row for each main subject and a column for each publication source. Hence, this allows the user to see at a glance both the range of sources in which a particular subject is covered and, conversely, the range of subjects covered in any one source. Thus the **Overview** serves a dual purpose depending on whether the subject or the publication source is of primary interest.

Each cell of the **Overview** matrix indicates whether or not a publication source contains data on a particular subject and, if so, whether it is a major or a minor source using the following key:

■ Major source indexed in the subject chapters
● Minor source indexed in the subject chapters
○ Minor source not indexed in the subject chapters, but cross-referenced to other subject chapters

Minor sources are defined as those which contain data that are subsidiary to the main subject. For example, many international volumes contain information about the size of the population in each country but are not the primary source of population statistics.

Publication codes in *instat*

All publication sources are assigned an alphanumeric code: an alphabetic prefix denotes the organization responsible for the publication(s) and a numerical suffix defines a particular publication. For example, publications of the United Nations are coded UN1, UN2, etc. Full bibliographical information is given in Appendix A.

Detailed sub-classifications of subjects

This part of ***instat*** represents the core of the book. It consists of 46 chapters, one for each broad subject area, providing much more detailed subject breakdowns than those given in the **Overview** matrix described above. Each chapter is arranged according to a common format (explained in more detail below).

The information in each subject chapter is organized under successively more detailed sub-headings, cross-referenced once again to publication sources, and arranged in alphabetical order. Information is then given about each statistical category as follows:

- Sub-categories of the data available
- Units of measurement
- Whether or not the publication contains time series data and, if so, the frequency
- Territorial coverage
- Source – gives ***instat*** publication code and table identifier

A full cross-referencing system is adopted for subjects which appear under alternative headings.

The terms used to refer to sub-categories of data in different publications vary from one source to another. From the point of view of classification in ***instat*** this presents a dilemma. On the one hand, it would be helpful to have a standardized set of terms. On the other hand, to use terms which are not used in the source publications themselves would not be helpful to users in tracing the data in the original sources. On balance, it is important to retain the use of the terms used in the original sources in so far as possible, and, in the main, this is the approach adopted in ***instat***.

Details of publications and organizations

Throughout ***instat,*** publication references are given by means of the coding system described above. Full bibliographical information about each publication, including details of the particular volume indexed, are given in **Appendix A**, arranged in alphanumeric order according to the ***instat*** coding system. The publication details given in **Appendix A** follow a common format as follows:

- Title
- Publisher
- Place of publication
- Edition and date of publication of the volume indexed
- Frequency of publication
- ISBN and/or ISSN numbers

An important reason for specifying the edition and date of publication of the volume indexed is to permit the data to be readily located. Thus, where appropriate, table numbers referring to these volumes are given in the 46 individual subject chapters. It also provides, of course, a point of reference indicating how up to date the information about a particular source is and is also useful as a benchmark when publications are discontinued or change their names.

Two further appendices, **Appendix B** and **Appendix C**, provide additional classifications of publications and the organizations responsible for them. **Appendix B** is arranged alphabetically according to the *titles* of publications while **Appendix C** is arranged alphabetically according to the *names* of the organizations. The names and addresses of the organizations covered by ***instat*** are listed in **Appendix D.**

Abbreviations and acronyms

Many abbreviations and acronyms are used in the published sources covered by ***instat***. These, and others used in this book, are listed at the front of Volumes 1 and 2.

Definitions of country groupings

Details of countries covered within particular geographical groupings and their appropriate abbreviations or acronyms are also listed at the front of Volumes 1 and 2; for example, the countries within the OECD (Organization for Economic Co-operation and Development).

Subject index

Finally, a **Subject Index** provides a further alternative means of locating information about a particular topic. It acts as a conventional means of reference and includes synonyms cross-referenced to the broad and detailed subject headings used in the subject chapters. In the main, it provides a guide to the subject information classified in the main body of ***instat***. It is thus a means of pinpointing quickly the subject information given there.

Summary

In summary, ***instat*** provides three options to the user for locating statistical information about particular topics. These vary according to the degree of detail in the information required. The options are as follows:

- For broad subject information, consult the **Overview of subjects and sources** section
- For information within the broad subject areas, consult the subject chapters 1 to 46
- For references to specific topics, consult the **Subject index**

Finally, for details concerning publication sources and the organizations responsible, consult Appendices A to D.

Abbreviations and acronyms

A	annually
AA	agricultural area
ACP	African, Caribbean and Pacific
AEA	Association of European Airlines
AGR	average growth rate
agric	agricultural
AIDS	acquired immuno-deficiency syndrome
alh	average length of haul
API	American Petroleum Institute
APO	Asian Productivity Organization
App	appendix
ARA	Amsterdam, Rotterdam, Antwerp
ASEAN	Association of South-East Asian Nations
ASEANS	Association of South-East Asian Nations Secretariat
ASFR	average spot freight rates
avlble	available
AWU	annual worker unit
Bags	60 kilograms
BB	Basil Blackwell Limited
b/cd	barrels per calendar day
b/d	barrels per day
BERD	expenditure on research and development in the business enterprise sector
BFI	Baltic Freight Index
BGS	British Geological Survey
bl	barrel
BOD	biochemical oxygen demand
BOF	basic oxygen furnace

BP	British Petroleum plc
BPB	British Paper and Board Industry Federation
BSU	British size unit
Btu	British thermal units
C	coniferous
CAA	Civil Aviation Authority
CAPMoN	Canadian Air and Precipitation Monitoring Network
Carib	Caribbean
CARICOM	Caribbean Community
CBE	cocoa butter equivalent
CBI	Confederation of British Industry
CCS	Caribbean Community Secretariat
cd	cadmium
CE	Council of Europe
CEEC	Central and Eastern European countries
CF	capital formation
CFA Franc	Franc of the "Communauté Financière Africaine"
CFC	chlorofluorocarbons
cgal	cents gallon
CH	Croom Helm Limited
CIA	Chemical Industries Association
CICPE	Comité International pour le Contrôle des Performances en Élevage
c.i.f.	cost insurance freight
CIRFS	Comité International de La Rayonne et des Fibres Synthétiques
CIS	Commonwealth of Independent States–see EECISC
CMEA	Council for Mutual Economic Assistance
CO	carbon monoxide
CO_2	carbon dioxide
cons	consumption

COS	Chamber of Shipping
CPITN	Community periodontal index of treatment needs
CS	Commonwealth Secretariat
CSFR	Czech and Slovak Federal Republics
CSR	thousand cubic metres
ctry	country
CTQ	sum of the guaranteed quantities (milk) for deliveries and direct sales
Cu	cubic
Cuf/d	cubic feet per day
Curr exp	current expenditure
cwe	carcass weight equivalent
D	daily
DAC	Development Assistance Committee (OECD)
DAE	dynamic Asian economies
defs	definitions
DDSR	debt and debt service reduction
DFS	duty-free shops
DM	Deutschmarks
DMEC	developed market-economy country
dmt	dry metric tonne
doz	dozen
DPI	domestic product of industry
DR	direct-reduced
DSC	Drewry Shipping Consultants Limited
dt	quintal
dwct	dead-weight cargo tonnes
dwt	dead-weight tons
E	European
EAA	European Aluminium Association

EAF	electric arc furnace
EAGGF	European Agricultural Guidance and Guarantee Fund
EAT	Elsevier Advanced Technology
EC	European Community
ECE	Economic Commission for Europe (UN)
ECMT	European Conference of Ministers of Transport
ECU	European currency unit
ECSC	European Coal and Steel Community
EDF	European Development Fund
EEC	European Economic Community
EECISC	Eastern Europe, CIS area and China
EFTA	European Free Trade Association
EIB	European Investment Bank
EKS	Elteto-Köves-Szule
elec	electricity or electrical
EM	Euromonitor
EMCF	European Monetary Co-operation Fund
EMEP	Co-operative programme on monitoring and evaluation of the long range transmission of air pollutants in Europe
EPI	European Paper Institute *or* expanded programme on immunization
EPO	European Patent Office
equiv	equivalent
ESA	European system of integrated economic accounts (EC)
ESCAP	Economic and Social Commission for Asia and the Pacific
est	estimate or estimated
ESU	European size unit
EUR 9	Total of 9 member states of the EEC (Definitions of Country Groupings)
EUR 10	Total of 10 member states of the EEC (Definitions of Country Groupings)
EUR 11	Total of 11 member states of the EEC (Definitions of Country Groupings)

EUR 12	Total of 12 member states of the EEC (Definitions of Country Groupings)
F	Fearnleys
FAO	Food and Agriculture Organization
FDI	foreign direct investment
FEOGA	Fonds Européen d'Orientation et de Garantie Agricole (European Agricultural Guidance and Guarantee Fund)
FNOCL	Fédération Nationale des Organismes de Contrôle Laitier
FF	French francs
f.o.b.	free on board
FOL	F O Licht
FSU	former Soviet Union
fte	full-time equivalents
G	E A Gibson Shipbrokers Limited
g	gram
GAP	gross agricultural product
GATT	General Agreement on Tariffs and Trade
GBAORD	government budget appropriations for outlays for research and development
GCC	Gulf Co-operation Council
GD	Gill and Duffus Group Limited
GDP	gross domestic product
GERD	gross domestic expenditure on research and development
GFCF	gross fixed capital formation
GNP	gross national product
govt	government
GP	General Publications
GRA	general resources account
grt	gross registered tonnage
gsp	generalized system of preferences
gt	gross tonnage

GVA	gross value added
GWe	gigawatt equivalent
GWh	gigawatt hour
h	hour
ha	hectare
HERD	higher education expenditure on research and development
HI	Horwath International
hl	hectolitre
hun	hundred
HIV	human immuno-deficiency virus
HWU	million kilowatt hours
I	irregular
IADB	Inter-American Development Bank
IAEA	International Atomic Energy Agency
IAHP	International Association of Horticultural Producers
IARC	International Agency for Research on Cancer
IATA	International Air Transport Association
IBA	International Bauxite Association
IBRD	International Bank for Reconstruction and Development (World Bank)
ICAC	International Cotton Advisory Committee
ICAO	International Civil Aviation Organization
ICCAT	International Commission for the Conservation of Atlantic Tunas
ICCO	International Cocoa Council Organization
ICOR	incremental capital-output ratios
ICP	International Comparison Project (UN)
IDA	International Development Association
IDF	International Dairy Federation
IEA	International Energy Agency
IFAD	International Fund for Agricultural Development

IFC	International Finance Corporation
IFIA	International Fertilizer Industry Association
IISI	International Iron and Steel Institute
ILO	International Labour Organization
ILZSG	International Lead and Zinc Study Group
IMF	International Monetary Fund
IMWF	International Metalworkers' Federation
ind	industry *or* index
INPFC	International North Pacific Fisheries Commission
INRO	International Natural Rubber Organization
int	international
IP	Institute of Petroleum
IPC	International Patent Classification
IPHC	International Pacific Halibut Commission
IPU	Inter-Parliamentary Union
IRF	International Road Federation
IRTU	International Road Transport Union
IRSG	International Rubber Study Group
ISA	International Sugar Agreement
ISBN	International Standard Book Number
ISCED	International Standard Classification of Education
ISIC	International Standard Industrial Classification of all Economic Activities
ISL	Institute of Shipping Economics and Logistics
ISO	International Sugar Organization
ISSB	Iron and Steel Statistics Bureau
ISSN	International Standard Serial Number
ISTA	ISTA Mielk GmbH
ITC	International Tea Committee
ITMF	International Textile Manufacturers Federation

ITTC	International Tropical Timber Council
ITTO	International Tropical Timber Organization
ITU	International Telecommunication Union
IUR	International Union of Railways
IWC	International Whaling Commission
IWhC	International Wheat Council
IWS	International Wool Secretariat
JM	Johnson Matthey
JP	Jaakko Pöyry
kcal	kilocalorie
kg	kilogram
kg/an	kilograms per animal
kg/c	kilograms per capita
kgoe	kilogram oil equivalent
km	kilometre
km^2	square kilometre
km/h	kilometres per hour
KOE	kilograms of oil equivalent
kVa	kilovolt-ampere
KW	kilowatt
kWh	kilowatt hours
l	litre
LDCs	less-developed countries
ldt	light deadweight tonnes
LIBOR	London interbank offered rate
LNG	liquefied natural gas
LRS	Lloyds Register of Shipping
ltd	light displacement weight
LPG	liquefied petroleum gas

LU	livestock units
LME	London Metal Exchange
m	metre
M	monthly
MAC	Macmillan Press Limited
MB	Metal Bulletin Books Limited
m^2	square metre
MDCs	more-developed countries
mg/l	milligrams per litre
MHPPE	Ministry of Housing, Physical Planning and the Environment (Netherlands)
MJ	mega joules *or* Mining Journal
MLC	Meat and Livestock Commission
mm	millimetre
MPS	System of Material Product Balances
MVA	manufacturing value added
MW	megawatt
MWe	megawatt equivalent
µg	microgram
N	nitrogen
NABS	Nomenclature for Analysis and Comparison of Scientific Programmes and Budgets
NACE/CLIO	Classification of goods derived from NACE for use in ESA and input-output tables
NACE	Nomenclature Générale des Activités dans les Communautés Européennes (General Industrial Classification of Economic Activities in the European Communities)
nat curr	national currency
NATO	North Atlantic Treaty Organization
NC	non-coniferous
NCM	Nordic Council of Ministers and the Nordic Statistical Secretariat
nge	natural gas equivalent
ngl	natural gas liquids

NH_3	ammonia
nes	not elsewhere specified
NMP	net material product
NNP	net national product
nos	numbers
NO_2	nitrogen dioxide
NO_X	nitrogen oxides
nrt	net registered tonnage
NST	Nomenclature Uniforme des Marchandises pour les Statistiques des Transport
NTM	non-tariff measures
N_2O	nitrous oxide
NWAFO	North West Atlantic Fisheries Organization
NWE	North West Europe
NWE/ARA	North West Europe/Amsterdam Rotterdam Antwerp
OCBN	Organization Commune Benin Niger des Chemins de Fer et des Transports
OCTG	oil-country tubular goods
ODA	Overseas Development Administration *or* Official Development Assistance
ODF	official development financing
OECD	Organization for Economic Co-operation and Development
OGA	other gainful activity
OHF	open hearth furnace
OIVV	Office International de la Vigne et du Vin
ONATRA	Office National des Transports
OPEC	Organization of Petroleum Exporting Countries
ORS	oral rehydration solution
ORT	oral rehydration therapy
oz	ounces troy
p	piece
PAX	passengers

PC	The Population Council
PCE	private consumption expenditure
PKF	Pannel Kerr Forster
PPI	Pulp and Paper International
ppl	pence per litre
ppm	parts per million
PPP	purchasing power parity
PPS	purchasing power standard
PQLI	physical quality of life index
pse	producer subsidy equivalents
q	quintal
Q	quarterly
Recip	recipient
Reg	region
R & D	research and development
Ro/Ro	roll-on/roll-off
R/P	reserves/production
RSE	research and development scientists and engineers
S	sulphur
s.a.	seasonally adjusted
SATRA	SATRA (Shoe and Allied Trades Research Association) Footwear Technology Centre
SBP	special boiling point spirit (industrial spirit)
SDR	special drawing rights
SEAR	South East Asia Region
SFIA	Sea Fish Industry Authority
SGM	standard gross margin
SIDF	Saudi Industrial Development Fund
SILICs	severely-indebted lower income countries
SIMICs	severely-indebted middle income countries

SITC	Standard International Trade Classification
SMMT	Society of Motor Manufacturers and Traders Limited
SNA	System of National Accounts (UN)
SNCZ	Société National des Chemins de Fer Zairois
SOEC	Statistical Office of the European Communities (Eurostat)
SO_2	sulphur dioxide
SPC	South Pacific Commission
S'pore	Singapore
SPWP	secondary-processed wood products
sq km	square kilometre
sq m	square metre
TEU	20 feet equivalent unit
TFS	tin-free steel
thou	thousand
TJ	terajoule
toe	ton of oil equivalent
tpe	tons products equivalent
TPER	total primary energy requirements
TPES	total primary energy supply
TSP	total suspended particulates
TWh	terawatt hour
UAA	utilized agricultural area
UDC	Universal Decimal Classification
UN	United Nations
UNCTAD	United Nations Conference on Trade and Development
UNDP	United Nations Development Programme
UNESCO	United Nations Educational, Scientific and Cultural Organization
UNFPA	United Nations Fund for Population
UNHCR	United Nations High Commission for Refugees

UNICEF	United Nations Children's Fund
UNIDO	United Nations Industrial Development Organization
USA	United States of America
USG	United States Gulf
USSR	Union of Soviet Socialist Republics
veh-km	vehicle-kilometre
VICES	Vienna Institute for Comparative Economic Studies
VOC	volatile organic compounds
WB	World Bank
WBMS	World Bureau of Metal Statistics
WC	Wye College
WFP	World Food Programme
WHO	World Health Organization
WIPO	World Intellectual Property Organization
WMO	World Meteorological Organization
WOCA	world-outside-centrally-planned-economies areas
WS	worldscale
WSR	thousand metric tons
WTI	West Texas intermediate
WTO	World Tourism Organization
yr	year
yrly	yearly

Definitions of country groupings

ACP	African, Caribbean and Pacific countries (signatories to the LOMÉ Convention)
APO	Asian Productivity Organization Bangladesh, Fiji, Hong Kong, India, Indonesia, Iran (Islamic Republic of), Japan, Korea, Malaysia, Mongolia, Nepal, Pakistan, Philippines, Singapore, Sri Lanka, Taiwan (Republic of China), Thailand, Vietnam
ASEAN	Association of South-East Asian Nations Brunei, Malaysia, Singapore, Indonesia, Philippines, Thailand
CARICOM	Caribbean Community countries Antigua-Barbuda, Bahamas, Barbados, Belize, Dominica, Grenada, Guyana, Jamaica, Montserrat, St Kitts-Nevis, St Lucia, St Vincent-Grenadines, Trinidad and Tobago
CEEC	Central and Eastern European countries Albania, Bulgaria, Czechoslovakia, Hungary, Poland, Romania, USSR, Yugoslavia
CICPE	Members of Comité International pour le Contrôle des Performances en Élevage. As at 1991 the member countries were: Austria, Belgium, Canada, Czechoslovakia, Denmark, England and Wales, Federal Republic of Germany, Finland, France, Greece, Ireland, Israel, Italy, Japan, Jersey, Luxembourg, Netherlands, New Zealand, Northern Ireland, Norway, Portugal, Scotland, Slovenia, South Africa, Spain, Sweden, Switzerland, Tunisia, United States of America, Zimbabwe, Australia
CIS	Commonwealth of Independent States – see EECISC
EC	European Community Coverage defined as EC9, EC12, EUR9, EUR10, EUR11 or EUR12 (*qv*)
EC9	Total of 9 member states of the former EEC West Germany, France, Italy, Netherlands, Belgium, Luxembourg, United Kingdom, Ireland, Denmark
EC12	Total of 12 member countries of the EC Germany, France, Italy, Netherlands, Belgium, Luxembourg, United Kingdom, Ireland, Denmark, Greece, Spain, Portugal
ECMT	European Conference of Ministers of Transport Austria, Belgium, Czech and Slovak Federal Republics, Denmark, Finland, France, Germany, Greece, Hungary, Ireland, Italy, Luxembourg, Netherlands, Norway, Poland, Portugal, Spain, Sweden, Switzerland, Turkey, and United Kingdom. (Associate Member countries: Australia, Canada, Japan, New Zealand, the United States. Observer country: Morocco)
EEC	European Economic Community – see EC

EECISC	Eastern Europe, the Commonwealth of Independent States (CIS area), and China. *Eastern Europe*: Albania, Bulgaria, Czechoslovakia, Hungary, Poland, Romania, Yugoslavia and the Baltic Republics of Estonia, Latvia and Lithuania *Commonwealth of Independent States (CIS)*: Russia, Armenia, Azerbaijan, Belorussia, Kazakhstan, Kirgizia, Moldova, Tajikstan, Turkmenistan, Ukraine and Uzbekistan. For the sake of convenience, non-members Georgia and Mongolia are also included
EFTA	European Free Trade Association Austria, Finland, Iceland, Norway, Sweden, Switzerland (and Liechtenstein)
ESCAP	Economic and Social Commission for Asia and the Pacific Afghanistan, Australia, Bangladesh, Cook Islands, Fiji, Hong Kong, India, Indonesia, Iran (Islamic Republic of), Japan, Korea (Republic of), Malaysia, Myanmar, Nepal, New Zealand, Niue, Pakistan, Papua New Guinea, Philippines, Samoa, Singapore, Solomon Islands, Sri Lanka, Thailand, Tonga, Vanuatu
EUR9	Total of 9 member states of the EEC – see EC9
EUR10	EUR9 plus Greece
EUR11	EUR10 plus Spain
EUR12	EUR11 plus Portugal
ICCO	Members of International Cocoa Organization. As at 30 June 1992 the member countries were: *Exporting members*: Brazil, Cameroon, Côte d'Ivoire, Ecuador, Gabon, Ghana, Grenada, Guatemala, Haiti, Jamaica, Mexico, Nigeria, Papua New Guinea, Samoa, Sierra Leone, Togo, Trinidad and Tobago, Venezuela *Importing members*: Belgium/Luxembourg, Bulgaria, Czechoslovakia, Denmark, Finland, France, Germany, Greece, Hungary, Ireland, Italy, Japan, Netherlands, Norway, Portugal, Russian Federation, Spain, Sweden, Switzerland, United Kingdom, Yugoslavia
MPS countries	Afghanistan, Albania, Bulgaria, China, Cuba, Czechoslovakia, Germany – former German Democratic Republic, Hungary, Korea (Democratic People's Republic), Mongolia, Poland, USSR, Vietnam
NATO	North Atlantic Treaty Organization Belgium, Denmark, France, Germany, Greece, Iceland, Italy, Luxembourg, Netherlands, Norway, Portugal, Spain, Turkey, United Kingdom, Canada, United States of America
NORDIC countries	Denmark, Finland, Iceland, Norway, Sweden
OECD	Organization for Economic Co-operation and Development Austria, Belgium, Canada, Denmark, France, Germany, Greece, Iceland, Ireland, Italy, Luxembourg, Netherlands, Norway, Portugal, Spain, Sweden, Switzerland, Turkey, United Kingdom, United States, Japan, Finland, Australia, New Zealand The former Yugoslavia took part in some of the work of the OECD (agreement of 28 October 1961)
OECD – Europe	All European member countries of OECD, i.e. EC countries plus Austria, Finland, Iceland, Norway, Sweden, Switzerland, Turkey

OECD Major Seven	Canada, France, Germany, Italy, Japan, United Kingdom, United States of America
OECD Total	All member countries of OECD, i.e. countries of OECD-Europe plus Canada, United States of America, Japan, Australia and New Zealand
OPEC	Organization of Petroleum Exporting Countries The members at 1991 were: Abu Dhabi, Algeria, Dubai, Ecuador, Gabon, Indonesia, Iran, Iraq, Kuwait, Libya, Neutral (Divided) Zone, Nigeria, Qatar, Ras al Khaimah, Saudi Arabia, Sharjah, Venezuela
SEAR	South-East Asia Region Bangladesh, Bhutan, DPR Korea, India, Indonesia, Maldives, Mongolia, Myanmar, Nepal, Sri Lanka, Thailand
SNA countries	Countries in North America and Western Europe (except Yugoslavia) together with Australia, Israel, Japan, New Zealand and South Africa

Overview of subjects and sources

The **Overview of subjects and sources** is a matrix in which each column denotes one of 399 ***instat*** publication codes and each row denotes one of the 46 subject categories. Full bibliographical details of the publications denoted by the ***instat*** codes are given in Appendix A.

Major and minor sources

A distinction is made in the matrix between *major* and *minor* publication sources which are indexed in the relevant subject chapters. In addition, some publications also contain statistical information which is merely incidental in nature. For example, many international volumes contain details about size in terms of population, national income, land area, etc. but such details may not be the primary focus of the publication concerned. In such cases, therefore, the publication is not indexed as a source of such data in the relevant subject chapters but simply cross-referenced as appropriate. Such cases, however, are indicated in the matrix. Major and minor publication sources are denoted in the matrix by use of the following symbols:

■	Major source indexed in the subject chapters
●	Minor source indexed in the subject chapters
○	Minor source not indexed in the subject chapters, but cross-referenced to other subject chapters

Thus, to illustrate the use of the three classificatory symbols, it will be seen, for example, that *Oil and Energy Trends*, coded BB1 on page 3 of the matrix, is denoted as a major source of energy statistics (Subject 17), a minor source for industries (Subject 25), international trade and finance (Subject 27), prices (Subject 37) and shipping (Subject 41) but as a non-indexed minor source for production (Subject 38).

General sources

Some statistical publications are collections of data covering a wide range of different subjects. The *UN Statistical Yearbook* (***instat*** code UN50) is one such example. While such sources are important, they do not cover any one subject in great detail, and thus we do not treat them as major sources for any particular subject. Such sources can be identified in the **Overview of subjects and sources** matrix by the large number of subjects covered, showing the relevant publication as a minor source only.

Use of the overview matrix

The **Overview** matrix can be used in one of two ways:

(a) to locate major and minor publication sources which cover a particular subject area by reading along the relevant row

(b) to identify the range of subject areas covered in any one publication source by reading down the relevant column

SUBJECT	PUBLICATION CODE				
	AEA1	AEA2	AEA3	AEA4	APO1
1. ACCIDENTS					
2. AGRICULTURE					
3. CIVIL AVIATION	■	■	■	■	
4. CLIMATE					
5. COMMODITIES					
6. COMMUNICATIONS					
7. CONSTRUCTION					
8. CONSUMPTION					
9. CRIME AND JUSTICE					
10. CULTURE					
11. DEFENCE					
12. DEVELOPMENT AND AID					
13. DISTRIBUTION					
14. DRUGS					
15. EDUCATION AND TRAINING					
16. EMPLOYMENT AND UNEMPLOYMENT					●
17. ENERGY					
18. ENVIRONMENT					
19. FINANCE					
20. FISHING					
21. FORESTRY					
22. HEALTH					
23. HOUSING					
24. INCOME AND WEALTH					
25. INDUSTRIES	●	●	●	●	
26. INTELLECTUAL PROPERTY					
27. INTERNATIONAL TRADE AND FINANCE					
28. LABOUR					■
29. LAND					
30. LIVING COSTS AND STANDARDS					
31. MIGRATION					
32. MINERALS					
33. MINING AND QUARRYING					
34. NATIONAL ACCOUNTS					●
35. PARLIAMENT AND PUBLIC AFFAIRS					
36. POPULATION AND VITAL STATISTICS					
37. PRICES					
38. PRODUCTION					
39. REFUGEES					
40. SCIENCE AND TECHNOLOGY					
41. SHIPPING					
42. SOCIAL INDICATORS					
43. TAXATION					
44. TOURISM					
45. TRANSPORT	●	●	●	●	
46. WELFARE					

PUBLICATION CODE								
ASEANS1	BB1	BB2	BB3	BB4	BGS1	BGS2	BP1	BP2
●								
●								
●								
●					■	■	●	○
●								
							○	●
●								
●								
●								
●								
●	■	■		■	○		■	■
●		●						
●								
●								
●								
	●	●	○	○	○	○	○	○
●	●	●		●	○	○	●	●
●								
●					■	■	○	
●								
●								
●								
●	●	●	●				●	●
●	○	●			○	○	●	●
●								
●	●	●	■					
●								
●								
●								

SUBJECT	PUBLICATION CODE				
	BPB1	CAA1	CBI1	CCS1	CCS2
1. ACCIDENTS		■			
2. AGRICULTURE					
3. CIVIL AVIATION		■			
4. CLIMATE					
5. COMMODITIES	○				
6. COMMUNICATIONS					
7. CONSTRUCTION					
8. CONSUMPTION	●				
9. CRIME AND JUSTICE					
10. CULTURE					
11. DEFENCE					
12. DEVELOPMENT AND AID					
13. DISTRIBUTION					
14. DRUGS					
15. EDUCATION AND TRAINING					
16. EMPLOYMENT AND UNEMPLOYMENT					
17. ENERGY					
18. ENVIRONMENT					
19. FINANCE					
20. FISHING					
21. FORESTRY					
22. HEALTH					
23. HOUSING					
24. INCOME AND WEALTH					
25. INDUSTRIES	■				
26. INTELLECTUAL PROPERTY					
27. INTERNATIONAL TRADE AND FINANCE				■	■
28. LABOUR					
29. LAND					
30. LIVING COSTS AND STANDARDS			■		
31. MIGRATION					
32. MINERALS					
33. MINING AND QUARRYING					
34. NATIONAL ACCOUNTS					
35. PARLIAMENT AND PUBLIC AFFAIRS					
36. POPULATION AND VITAL STATISTICS					
37. PRICES					
38. PRODUCTION	●				
39. REFUGEES					
40. SCIENCE AND TECHNOLOGY					
41. SHIPPING					
42. SOCIAL INDICATORS					
43. TAXATION					
44. TOURISM					
45. TRANSPORT		○			
46. WELFARE					

PUBLICATION CODE								
CE1	CH1	CIA1	CIRFS1	COS1	CS1	DSC1	DSC2	EAA1
	●				●			
			●				○	○
					●			
		●	●		●		●	●
					●			
	●				●			
	●	●	●		●	●		
	●				●		●	
	●	●			●	●		
					●			
	●	■	■	○		○	○	●
	●	●	●	●	●	●	●	●
	●				●			
					●			
●								
								■
	●						●	
■	●				●			
		●		●	●	●	●	
	●	●	●		●	●	●	●
				■		■	■	
					●			
				○	●	○		
					●			

SUBJECT	PUBLICATION CODE				
	EAT1	EAT2	EC1	EC2	EC3
1. ACCIDENTS					
2. AGRICULTURE			●	■	■
3. CIVIL AVIATION					
4. CLIMATE					
5. COMMODITIES	○				●
6. COMMUNICATIONS		■			
7. CONSTRUCTION					
8. CONSUMPTION	●		●		
9. CRIME AND JUSTICE					
10. CULTURE					
11. DEFENCE					
12. DEVELOPMENT AND AID			●		
13. DISTRIBUTION					
14. DRUGS					
15. EDUCATION AND TRAINING			●		
16. EMPLOYMENT AND UNEMPLOYMENT				●	
17. ENERGY					
18. ENVIRONMENT					
19. FINANCE			●		
20. FISHING					
21. FORESTRY					
22. HEALTH			●		
23. HOUSING					
24. INCOME AND WEALTH			●	●	
25. INDUSTRIES	○		○		○
26. INTELLECTUAL PROPERTY					
27. INTERNATIONAL TRADE AND FINANCE	●	●	●		
28. LABOUR					
29. LAND					
30. LIVING COSTS AND STANDARDS					
31. MIGRATION					
32. MINERALS	■				
33. MINING AND QUARRYING					
34. NATIONAL ACCOUNTS			●		
35. PARLIAMENT AND PUBLIC AFFAIRS					
36. POPULATION AND VITAL STATISTICS			●		
37. PRICES				●	●
38. PRODUCTION	●	●	●	●	
39. REFUGEES					
40. SCIENCE AND TECHNOLOGY					
41. SHIPPING					
42. SOCIAL INDICATORS					
43. TAXATION					
44. TOURISM					
45. TRANSPORT					
46. WELFARE					

PUBLICATION CODE								
EC4	EC5	EC6	EC7	EC8	EC9	EC10	EC11	EC12
					●			
■	■	■	■	■	●			
					●			
		●						
		●	○		●			
					●			
		●	●		●			
					●			
					●		●	
					●		●	
					●			
					●			
		●			●			
		■			●			
		■			●			
					●		■	
		●			●			
○	○	○	○	○	●			○
		●	●		●	■		
					●			
		●		●	●		●	
					●			
					●			
		●			●			
		●			●		■	
●	●	●			●			
		●	●	○	●			
					●			
					●			
					●			■
					●			

SUBJECT	PUBLICATION CODE				
	EC13	EC14	EC15	EC16	EC17
1. ACCIDENTS					
2. AGRICULTURE			■		
3. CIVIL AVIATION					
4. CLIMATE					
5. COMMODITIES					
6. COMMUNICATIONS					
7. CONSTRUCTION					
8. CONSUMPTION					
9. CRIME AND JUSTICE					
10. CULTURE					
11. DEFENCE					
12. DEVELOPMENT AND AID					
13. DISTRIBUTION					
14. DRUGS					
15. EDUCATION AND TRAINING					
16. EMPLOYMENT AND UNEMPLOYMENT					
17. ENERGY					
18. ENVIRONMENT					
19. FINANCE					
20. FISHING					
21. FORESTRY					
22. HEALTH					
23. HOUSING					
24. INCOME AND WEALTH					
25. INDUSTRIES	○	○	○		
26. INTELLECTUAL PROPERTY					
27. INTERNATIONAL TRADE AND FINANCE					
28. LABOUR					
29. LAND					
30. LIVING COSTS AND STANDARDS				●	●
31. MIGRATION					
32. MINERALS					
33. MINING AND QUARRYING					
34. NATIONAL ACCOUNTS					
35. PARLIAMENT AND PUBLIC AFFAIRS					
36. POPULATION AND VITAL STATISTICS					
37. PRICES				■	■
38. PRODUCTION			●		
39. REFUGEES					
40. SCIENCE AND TECHNOLOGY					
41. SHIPPING					
42. SOCIAL INDICATORS					
43. TAXATION					
44. TOURISM					
45. TRANSPORT	■	■			
46. WELFARE					

PUBLICATION CODE								
EC18	EC19	EC20	EC21	EC22	EC23	EC24	EC25	EC26
●								
●	■				■			■
●								
●	■							
	●							○
●								
●								
●	●							○
●								
●					●			
●								
●								○
●								
●								■
●								
●								
●					●	■		○
●	○							●
●	●						■	
●								
●	●							
●								
		●						
●								
●								●
●		■						
●								○
●	●							○
●								
●								
●								
●								
			■	■				

SUBJECT	PUBLICATION CODE				
	EC27	EC28	EC29	EC30	EC31
1. ACCIDENTS					
2. AGRICULTURE			●		
3. CIVIL AVIATION					
4. CLIMATE					
5. COMMODITIES					
6. COMMUNICATIONS					
7. CONSTRUCTION					
8. CONSUMPTION		●		○	○
9. CRIME AND JUSTICE					
10. CULTURE					
11. DEFENCE					
12. DEVELOPMENT AND AID					
13. DISTRIBUTION					
14. DRUGS					
15. EDUCATION AND TRAINING					
16. EMPLOYMENT AND UNEMPLOYMENT			■		
17. ENERGY		■		■	■
18. ENVIRONMENT					
19. FINANCE					
20. FISHING					
21. FORESTRY					
22. HEALTH					
23. HOUSING					
24. INCOME AND WEALTH					
25. INDUSTRIES		○	■	○	○
26. INTELLECTUAL PROPERTY					
27. INTERNATIONAL TRADE AND FINANCE	■			○	○
28. LABOUR			■		
29. LAND					
30. LIVING COSTS AND STANDARDS					
31. MIGRATION					
32. MINERALS					
33. MINING AND QUARRYING					
34. NATIONAL ACCOUNTS					
35. PARLIAMENT AND PUBLIC AFFAIRS					
36. POPULATION AND VITAL STATISTICS			●		
37. PRICES	●	●			
38. PRODUCTION				○	○
39. REFUGEES					
40. SCIENCE AND TECHNOLOGY					
41. SHIPPING					
42. SOCIAL INDICATORS					
43. TAXATION		●			
44. TOURISM					
45. TRANSPORT					
46. WELFARE					

PUBLICATION CODE								
EC32	EC33	EC34	EC35	EC36	EC37	EC38	EC39	EC40
			●					
			●	●				
		○		●	○	○	○	○
	○	●	●					
			●					
			●					
				●				
			●					
	●		●	●				
■	■	■	●	●				
		■	●					
			●	●				
			●					
			●					
			●					
			●	●				
	○		●	●				
○	○	○	●	●				
	○		●	●	■	■	■	■
	●		●	●				
		■	●					
		●						
			●	●				
			●					
		●	●	●				
●	●		●	●				
	○	○	○	●				
			●					
●								
			●					
			●					

SUBJECT	PUBLICATION CODE				
	EC41	EC42	EC43	EC44	EC45
1. ACCIDENTS					
2. AGRICULTURE			■	■	■
3. CIVIL AVIATION					
4. CLIMATE					
5. COMMODITIES	○				
6. COMMUNICATIONS					
7. CONSTRUCTION					
8. CONSUMPTION		●			
9. CRIME AND JUSTICE					
10. CULTURE					
11. DEFENCE					
12. DEVELOPMENT AND AID					
13. DISTRIBUTION					
14. DRUGS					
15. EDUCATION AND TRAINING					
16. EMPLOYMENT AND UNEMPLOYMENT					●
17. ENERGY					
18. ENVIRONMENT					
19. FINANCE					
20. FISHING					
21. FORESTRY					
22. HEALTH					
23. HOUSING		●			
24. INCOME AND WEALTH					
25. INDUSTRIES			○	○	○
26. INTELLECTUAL PROPERTY					
27. INTERNATIONAL TRADE AND FINANCE	■				
28. LABOUR			○		
29. LAND					●
30. LIVING COSTS AND STANDARDS		■			
31. MIGRATION					
32. MINERALS					
33. MINING AND QUARRYING					
34. NATIONAL ACCOUNTS					
35. PARLIAMENT AND PUBLIC AFFAIRS					
36. POPULATION AND VITAL STATISTICS		●			
37. PRICES					
38. PRODUCTION				○	○
39. REFUGEES					
40. SCIENCE AND TECHNOLOGY					
41. SHIPPING					
42. SOCIAL INDICATORS		●			
43. TAXATION					
44. TOURISM					
45. TRANSPORT					
46. WELFARE					

PUBLICATION CODE								
EC46	EC47	EC48	EC49	EC50	EC51	EC52	EC53	EC54
							○	
	○						●	
						●	●	
	○						●	○
						●	■	
		■					●	■
			○				●	
■								
	■							
							■	
○	○	○			■	■	■	
○	○						●	○
							■	
	●							
							●	
			■				●	
		●				●		
○	○				■	■	■	○
				■				
			●					

SUBJECT	PUBLICATION CODE				
	EC55	EC56	EC57	EC58	EC59
1. ACCIDENTS					
2. AGRICULTURE			■	■	
3. CIVIL AVIATION					
4. CLIMATE					
5. COMMODITIES			○	○	
6. COMMUNICATIONS					
7. CONSTRUCTION					
8. CONSUMPTION	●		○	●	
9. CRIME AND JUSTICE					
10. CULTURE					
11. DEFENCE					
12. DEVELOPMENT AND AID					
13. DISTRIBUTION					
14. DRUGS					
15. EDUCATION AND TRAINING		○			
16. EMPLOYMENT AND UNEMPLOYMENT	●	■			
17. ENERGY					
18. ENVIRONMENT					
19. FINANCE			○	○	■
20. FISHING					
21. FORESTRY					
22. HEALTH					
23. HOUSING					
24. INCOME AND WEALTH	●		●	●	
25. INDUSTRIES	■	○	○	●	
26. INTELLECTUAL PROPERTY					
27. INTERNATIONAL TRADE AND FINANCE	●				●
28. LABOUR		○			
29. LAND			●	●	
30. LIVING COSTS AND STANDARDS					
31. MIGRATION					
32. MINERALS					
33. MINING AND QUARRYING					
34. NATIONAL ACCOUNTS					
35. PARLIAMENT AND PUBLIC AFFAIRS					
36. POPULATION AND VITAL STATISTICS		○	○		
37. PRICES	○		●	●	●
38. PRODUCTION	○		○		
39. REFUGEES					
40. SCIENCE AND TECHNOLOGY					
41. SHIPPING					
42. SOCIAL INDICATORS					
43. TAXATION	●				
44. TOURISM					
45. TRANSPORT					
46. WELFARE					

PUBLICATION CODE								
EC60	EC61	EC62	EC63	EC64	EC65	EC66	EC67	EC68
						○		
○			●					●
					●			
○	○				●			
				■				
		■						●
●	●	●						
				○				●
●			●					●
	●							
					●			
								■
■	■	■	■		●		■	
●					●			
	○		●			■	○	
			○	○				●
		●						

SUBJECT	PUBLICATION CODE				
	EC69	EC70	EC71	EC72	EC73
1. ACCIDENTS				●	
2. AGRICULTURE	●				
3. CIVIL AVIATION	●				
4. CLIMATE					
5. COMMODITIES					
6. COMMUNICATIONS					
7. CONSTRUCTION		●			
8. CONSUMPTION			○	●	
9. CRIME AND JUSTICE				●	
10. CULTURE				●	
11. DEFENCE					
12. DEVELOPMENT AND AID				●	
13. DISTRIBUTION			■		
14. DRUGS					
15. EDUCATION AND TRAINING	●			●	
16. EMPLOYMENT AND UNEMPLOYMENT	●	●	○	●	
17. ENERGY	●				
18. ENVIRONMENT				●	
19. FINANCE	●		○		●
20. FISHING					
21. FORESTRY					
22. HEALTH	●			●	
23. HOUSING	●	○		●	
24. INCOME AND WEALTH	●				
25. INDUSTRIES	●	■	■		
26. INTELLECTUAL PROPERTY					
27. INTERNATIONAL TRADE AND FINANCE		●			
28. LABOUR				●	
29. LAND	●				
30. LIVING COSTS AND STANDARDS				●	
31. MIGRATION	●				
32. MINERALS					
33. MINING AND QUARRYING					
34. NATIONAL ACCOUNTS	●				●
35. PARLIAMENT AND PUBLIC AFFAIRS				●	
36. POPULATION AND VITAL STATISTICS	●			●	●
37. PRICES		○			●
38. PRODUCTION	○	●			
39. REFUGEES			○		
40. SCIENCE AND TECHNOLOGY					
41. SHIPPING	●				
42. SOCIAL INDICATORS	●			■	
43. TAXATION			●		
44. TOURISM				●	
45. TRANSPORT	●			●	
46. WELFARE				●	■

PUBLICATION CODE

EC74	EC75	EC76	EC77	EC78	EC79	EC80	EC81	ECMT1
						●		■
						■		
○								
						■		
	○	●						
■						○		
	●	■	■	●		●	■	
						●		
	○	●						
	●	■	■					
●	■	■	■	○		○		
				●	○			
	●							
								●
				●	○			
								●
				○				
	●		○					
						■		
				■	■			
				○		■		■

SUBJECT	PUBLICATION CODE				
	ECMT2	ECMT3	EDFM1	EFTA1	EM1
1. ACCIDENTS		●			
2. AGRICULTURE			■		●
3. CIVIL AVIATION					●
4. CLIMATE					
5. COMMODITIES			○		○
6. COMMUNICATIONS					●
7. CONSTRUCTION					○
8. CONSUMPTION			○		●
9. CRIME AND JUSTICE					
10. CULTURE					●
11. DEFENCE					●
12. DEVELOPMENT AND AID					
13. DISTRIBUTION					●
14. DRUGS					
15. EDUCATION AND TRAINING					●
16. EMPLOYMENT AND UNEMPLOYMENT	●				●
17. ENERGY	●				●
18. ENVIRONMENT					●
19. FINANCE					●
20. FISHING					●
21. FORESTRY					●
22. HEALTH					●
23. HOUSING					●
24. INCOME AND WEALTH					
25. INDUSTRIES	○	○			●
26. INTELLECTUAL PROPERTY					
27. INTERNATIONAL TRADE AND FINANCE			○	■	●
28. LABOUR					○
29. LAND					●
30. LIVING COSTS AND STANDARDS					●
31. MIGRATION					
32. MINERALS					○
33. MINING AND QUARRYING					○
34. NATIONAL ACCOUNTS					●
35. PARLIAMENT AND PUBLIC AFFAIRS					
36. POPULATION AND VITAL STATISTICS					●
37. PRICES			○		●
38. PRODUCTION			○		●
39. REFUGEES					
40. SCIENCE AND TECHNOLOGY					
41. SHIPPING	●				●
42. SOCIAL INDICATORS					○
43. TAXATION					
44. TOURISM					●
45. TRANSPORT	■	■			●
46. WELFARE					○

PUBLICATION CODE								
EPI1	EPO1	F1	F2	F3	FAO1	FAO2	FAO3	FAO4
					■	■		
○				○	○	○	○	○
○								
					●			
							■	■
■		○	○	○	○		○	○
	■							
○		○		○		■		●
					●			
				○				
					○			
		●			●			
○					●		○	○
		■	■	■				
		○	○	○				

SUBJECT	PUBLICATION CODE				
	FAO5	FAO6	FAO7	FAO8	FNOCL1
1. ACCIDENTS					
2. AGRICULTURE	■	■	■		■
3. CIVIL AVIATION					
4. CLIMATE					
5. COMMODITIES	○	○	○	○	○
6. COMMUNICATIONS					
7. CONSTRUCTION					
8. CONSUMPTION	●				
9. CRIME AND JUSTICE					
10. CULTURE					
11. DEFENCE					
12. DEVELOPMENT AND AID					
13. DISTRIBUTION					
14. DRUGS					
15. EDUCATION AND TRAINING					
16. EMPLOYMENT AND UNEMPLOYMENT					
17. ENERGY					
18. ENVIRONMENT					
19. FINANCE	●				
20. FISHING					
21. FORESTRY				■	
22. HEALTH					
23. HOUSING					
24. INCOME AND WEALTH					
25. INDUSTRIES	●		○	○	○
26. INTELLECTUAL PROPERTY					
27. INTERNATIONAL TRADE AND FINANCE	●			●	
28. LABOUR					
29. LAND					
30. LIVING COSTS AND STANDARDS					
31. MIGRATION					
32. MINERALS					
33. MINING AND QUARRYING					
34. NATIONAL ACCOUNTS					
35. PARLIAMENT AND PUBLIC AFFAIRS					
36. POPULATION AND VITAL STATISTICS					
37. PRICES	●	●			
38. PRODUCTION	○	○	○	○	○
39. REFUGEES					
40. SCIENCE AND TECHNOLOGY					
41. SHIPPING					
42. SOCIAL INDICATORS					
43. TAXATION					
44. TOURISM					
45. TRANSPORT					
46. WELFARE					

PUBLICATION CODE								
FOL1	FOL2	FOL3	G1	G2	GATT1	GATT2	GATT3	GATT4
■	■	■			■	■		
○	○	○			○	○	○	○
							■	
	○				○	○		
○	○	○	○	○				
●	●	●			■	■	■	■
	●				●	●	●	●
○	○	○				○	●	
			■	■				

SUBJECT	PUBLICATION CODE				
	GATT5	GP1	HI1	IADB1	IAEA1
1. ACCIDENTS					
2. AGRICULTURE	■				
3. CIVIL AVIATION					
4. CLIMATE					
5. COMMODITIES	○				
6. COMMUNICATIONS					
7. CONSTRUCTION					
8. CONSUMPTION	○				
9. CRIME AND JUSTICE					
10. CULTURE					
11. DEFENCE					
12. DEVELOPMENT AND AID					
13. DISTRIBUTION		●			
14. DRUGS					
15. EDUCATION AND TRAINING					
16. EMPLOYMENT AND UNEMPLOYMENT			○		
17. ENERGY					■
18. ENVIRONMENT					
19. FINANCE			○	●	
20. FISHING					
21. FORESTRY					
22. HEALTH					
23. HOUSING					
24. INCOME AND WEALTH					
25. INDUSTRIES			○		○
26. INTELLECTUAL PROPERTY					
27. INTERNATIONAL TRADE AND FINANCE	○			■	
28. LABOUR					
29. LAND					
30. LIVING COSTS AND STANDARDS					
31. MIGRATION					
32. MINERALS					
33. MINING AND QUARRYING					
34. NATIONAL ACCOUNTS				●	
35. PARLIAMENT AND PUBLIC AFFAIRS					
36. POPULATION AND VITAL STATISTICS				●	
37. PRICES		○		●	
38. PRODUCTION	○				●
39. REFUGEES					
40. SCIENCE AND TECHNOLOGY					
41. SHIPPING					
42. SOCIAL INDICATORS					
43. TAXATION					
44. TOURISM			■		
45. TRANSPORT					
46. WELFARE					

PUBLICATION CODE								
IAHP1	IARC1	IATA1	IBA1	ICAC1	ICAC2	ICAO1	ICAO2	ICAO3
		●				■	●	
■				○	○			
		■				■	■	■
				■	■			
○			●	●	●			
				●	●			
		○						
		○	●				○	○
	■							
○		○	○			○	○	○
●				●	●			
○								
			■					
○		○	●		●			
○		○	●	●	●			
		●				○	○	○

SUBJECT	PUBLICATION CODE				
	ICAO4	ICAO5	ICAO6	ICAO7	ICAO8
1. ACCIDENTS					
2. AGRICULTURE					
3. CIVIL AVIATION	■	■	■	■	■
4. CLIMATE					
5. COMMODITIES					
6. COMMUNICATIONS					
7. CONSTRUCTION					
8. CONSUMPTION					
9. CRIME AND JUSTICE					
10. CULTURE					
11. DEFENCE					
12. DEVELOPMENT AND AID					
13. DISTRIBUTION					
14. DRUGS					
15. EDUCATION AND TRAINING					
16. EMPLOYMENT AND UNEMPLOYMENT					
17. ENERGY					
18. ENVIRONMENT					
19. FINANCE					
20. FISHING					
21. FORESTRY					
22. HEALTH					
23. HOUSING					
24. INCOME AND WEALTH					
25. INDUSTRIES	○	○	○	○	○
26. INTELLECTUAL PROPERTY					
27. INTERNATIONAL TRADE AND FINANCE					
28. LABOUR					
29. LAND					
30. LIVING COSTS AND STANDARDS					
31. MIGRATION					
32. MINERALS					
33. MINING AND QUARRYING					
34. NATIONAL ACCOUNTS					
35. PARLIAMENT AND PUBLIC AFFAIRS					
36. POPULATION AND VITAL STATISTICS					
37. PRICES					
38. PRODUCTION					
39. REFUGEES					
40. SCIENCE AND TECHNOLOGY					
41. SHIPPING					
42. SOCIAL INDICATORS					
43. TAXATION					
44. TOURISM					
45. TRANSPORT	○	○	○	○	○
46. WELFARE					

PUBLICATION CODE

ICAO9	ICAO10	ICCAT1	ICCO1	ICCO2	ICCO3	IDF1	IEA1	IEA2
			■	■	■	■		
■	■							
			●	●	●	○		
				●	○	○	○	●
								●
							■	■
							●	
		■						
○	○	○					○	○
			○	●			●	●
			○	●	○		○	●
			○	●	○		○	○
○	○							

SUBJECT	PUBLICATION CODE				
	IEA3	IEA4	IEA5	IEA6	IEA7
1. ACCIDENTS					
2. AGRICULTURE					
3. CIVIL AVIATION					
4. CLIMATE					
5. COMMODITIES					
6. COMMUNICATIONS					
7. CONSTRUCTION					
8. CONSUMPTION	●	○	○		●
9. CRIME AND JUSTICE					
10. CULTURE					
11. DEFENCE					
12. DEVELOPMENT AND AID					
13. DISTRIBUTION					
14. DRUGS					
15. EDUCATION AND TRAINING					
16. EMPLOYMENT AND UNEMPLOYMENT					
17. ENERGY	■	■	■	■	■
18. ENVIRONMENT					
19. FINANCE					
20. FISHING					
21. FORESTRY					
22. HEALTH					
23. HOUSING					
24. INCOME AND WEALTH					
25. INDUSTRIES	○	○	○	○	○
26. INTELLECTUAL PROPERTY					
27. INTERNATIONAL TRADE AND FINANCE	●	○	○	●	●
28. LABOUR					
29. LAND					
30. LIVING COSTS AND STANDARDS					
31. MIGRATION					
32. MINERALS					
33. MINING AND QUARRYING					
34. NATIONAL ACCOUNTS					
35. PARLIAMENT AND PUBLIC AFFAIRS					
36. POPULATION AND VITAL STATISTICS					
37. PRICES				●	
38. PRODUCTION	●	○	○		●
39. REFUGEES					
40. SCIENCE AND TECHNOLOGY					
41. SHIPPING					
42. SOCIAL INDICATORS					
43. TAXATION				●	
44. TOURISM					
45. TRANSPORT					
46. WELFARE					

PUBLICATION CODE								
IEA8	IEA9	IEA10	IEA11	IEA12	IFA1	IISI1	IISI2	IISI3
					■			
		○			○	■	■	■
●	●	●		○	●	●		●
●	●							
■	■	■	■	■				
○	○	○	○	○	●	○	○	○
●	●	●	●	○	●			●
		●						
●	●	●	●	○	●		●	●

Overview of subjects and sources

SUBJECT	PUBLICATION CODE				
	IISI4	IISI5	IISRP1	ILO1	ILO2
1. ACCIDENTS					
2. AGRICULTURE					
3. CIVIL AVIATION					
4. CLIMATE					
5. COMMODITIES	■	■	■		
6. COMMUNICATIONS					
7. CONSTRUCTION					
8. CONSUMPTION	●	●			
9. CRIME AND JUSTICE					
10. CULTURE					
11. DEFENCE					
12. DEVELOPMENT AND AID					
13. DISTRIBUTION					
14. DRUGS					
15. EDUCATION AND TRAINING					
16. EMPLOYMENT AND UNEMPLOYMENT		●		■	■
17. ENERGY					
18. ENVIRONMENT					
19. FINANCE					
20. FISHING					
21. FORESTRY					
22. HEALTH					
23. HOUSING					
24. INCOME AND WEALTH				■	
25. INDUSTRIES	○	○	○	○	○
26. INTELLECTUAL PROPERTY					
27. INTERNATIONAL TRADE AND FINANCE	●	●			
28. LABOUR				■	
29. LAND					
30. LIVING COSTS AND STANDARDS					
31. MIGRATION					
32. MINERALS					
33. MINING AND QUARRYING					
34. NATIONAL ACCOUNTS					
35. PARLIAMENT AND PUBLIC AFFAIRS					
36. POPULATION AND VITAL STATISTICS					■
37. PRICES					
38. PRODUCTION	●	●			
39. REFUGEES					
40. SCIENCE AND TECHNOLOGY					
41. SHIPPING					
42. SOCIAL INDICATORS					
43. TAXATION					
44. TOURISM					
45. TRANSPORT					
46. WELFARE					

PUBLICATION CODE								
ILO3	ILO4	ILO5	ILO6	ILO7	ILZSG1	ILZSG2	IMF1	IMF2
				■				
				○				
					■	○		
				○				
					●			
■	■	■	■	■				
				○				
				○				
				○				
				■				
○	○	○	○	○	○	○		
					●		■	■
				■				
					■	■		
				○	■	■		
■	■	■	■					
					●	●		
					●	●		
				○				

SUBJECT	PUBLICATION CODE				
	IMF3	IMF4	IMF5	IMF6	IMF7
1. ACCIDENTS					
2. AGRICULTURE			○		
3. CIVIL AVIATION					
4. CLIMATE					
5. COMMODITIES					
6. COMMUNICATIONS			○		
7. CONSTRUCTION			○		
8. CONSUMPTION					
9. CRIME AND JUSTICE					
10. CULTURE					
11. DEFENCE			○		
12. DEVELOPMENT AND AID					
13. DISTRIBUTION					
14. DRUGS					
15. EDUCATION AND TRAINING			○		
16. EMPLOYMENT AND UNEMPLOYMENT				●	●
17. ENERGY			○		
18. ENVIRONMENT					
19. FINANCE			■	■	■
20. FISHING					
21. FORESTRY					
22. HEALTH			○		
23. HOUSING			○		
24. INCOME AND WEALTH			○		
25. INDUSTRIES					
26. INTELLECTUAL PROPERTY					
27. INTERNATIONAL TRADE AND FINANCE	■	■		■	■
28. LABOUR					
29. LAND					
30. LIVING COSTS AND STANDARDS					
31. MIGRATION					
32. MINERALS					
33. MINING AND QUARRYING			○		
34. NATIONAL ACCOUNTS			■	●	●
35. PARLIAMENT AND PUBLIC AFFAIRS					
36. POPULATION AND VITAL STATISTICS				●	●
37. PRICES				●	●
38. PRODUCTION				●	●
39. REFUGEES					
40. SCIENCE AND TECHNOLOGY					
41. SHIPPING					
42. SOCIAL INDICATORS					
43. TAXATION			●		
44. TOURISM					
45. TRANSPORT			○		
46. WELFARE			○		

PUBLICATION CODE								
IMWF1	INPFC1	IP1	IPHC1	IPU1	IPU2	IRF1	IRRI1	IRSG1
						●		
							■	
		○					○	■
		●					○	●
							●	
							○	
		■						
	■		■					
■							○	
●	○		○				○	○
		●				●	○	●
○								
							○	
●								
				■	■			
							○	●
		●				●	○	●
		●						
						●		
						■		

SUBJECT	PUBLICATION CODE				
	IRSG2	IRTU1	ISL1	ISL2	ISO1
1. ACCIDENTS			●	●	
2. AGRICULTURE					■
3. CIVIL AVIATION		●			
4. CLIMATE					
5. COMMODITIES	■			●	●
6. COMMUNICATIONS					
7. CONSTRUCTION					
8. CONSUMPTION	●				○
9. CRIME AND JUSTICE					
10. CULTURE					
11. DEFENCE					
12. DEVELOPMENT AND AID					
13. DISTRIBUTION					
14. DRUGS					
15. EDUCATION AND TRAINING					
16. EMPLOYMENT AND UNEMPLOYMENT		●		●	
17. ENERGY					
18. ENVIRONMENT					
19. FINANCE					
20. FISHING				●	
21. FORESTRY					
22. HEALTH					
23. HOUSING					
24. INCOME AND WEALTH					
25. INDUSTRIES	○	○	○	○	
26. INTELLECTUAL PROPERTY					
27. INTERNATIONAL TRADE AND FINANCE	●			●	○
28. LABOUR					
29. LAND					
30. LIVING COSTS AND STANDARDS					
31. MIGRATION					
32. MINERALS					
33. MINING AND QUARRYING					
34. NATIONAL ACCOUNTS					
35. PARLIAMENT AND PUBLIC AFFAIRS					
36. POPULATION AND VITAL STATISTICS					
37. PRICES	●		●	●	●
38. PRODUCTION	●		●		○
39. REFUGEES					
40. SCIENCE AND TECHNOLOGY					
41. SHIPPING		●	■	■	
42. SOCIAL INDICATORS					
43. TAXATION					
44. TOURISM					
45. TRANSPORT	●	■			
46. WELFARE					

PUBLICATION CODE								
ISO2	ISO3	ISSB1	ISSB2	ISSB3	ISTA1	ISTA2	ITC1	ITMF1
■	■				■	■	■	
●	●	■	■	■	○	○	○	○
●	●					○	●	●
							●	
								●
								●
		○	○	○	○	○	○	■
●	●	●	○	●	●	●	●	●
								●
						●	●	
●	●					●	●	
●	●	●			○	○	○	○

SUBJECT	PUBLICATION CODE				
	ITMF2	ITMF3	ITTO1	ITU1	IUR1
1. ACCIDENTS					
2. AGRICULTURE					
3. CIVIL AVIATION					
4. CLIMATE					
5. COMMODITIES	●	○	○		
6. COMMUNICATIONS				■	
7. CONSTRUCTION					
8. CONSUMPTION	●				
9. CRIME AND JUSTICE					
10. CULTURE					
11. DEFENCE					
12. DEVELOPMENT AND AID					
13. DISTRIBUTION					
14. DRUGS					
15. EDUCATION AND TRAINING					
16. EMPLOYMENT AND UNEMPLOYMENT			○	○	●
17. ENERGY					
18. ENVIRONMENT					
19. FINANCE				○	○
20. FISHING					
21. FORESTRY			■		
22. HEALTH					
23. HOUSING					
24. INCOME AND WEALTH					
25. INDUSTRIES	■	■	○	○	○
26. INTELLECTUAL PROPERTY					
27. INTERNATIONAL TRADE AND FINANCE			○		
28. LABOUR					
29. LAND			●		
30. LIVING COSTS AND STANDARDS					
31. MIGRATION					
32. MINERALS					
33. MINING AND QUARRYING					
34. NATIONAL ACCOUNTS					
35. PARLIAMENT AND PUBLIC AFFAIRS					
36. POPULATION AND VITAL STATISTICS					
37. PRICES					
38. PRODUCTION			○		
39. REFUGEES					
40. SCIENCE AND TECHNOLOGY					
41. SHIPPING					
42. SOCIAL INDICATORS					
43. TAXATION					
44. TOURISM					
45. TRANSPORT					■
46. WELFARE					

PUBLICATION CODE								
IWC1	IWhC1	IWhC2	IWhC3	IWS1	JM1	JP1	LRS1	LRS2
								■
	○	■	■	●				
○		○	○	■	○	○		
		○	●	●	○			
	■							
■								
						●		
○				○		■	○	○
		○	●	●				
					■			
		○	●			●		
○		○	○	○	○	○	○	
							■	■

SUBJECT	PUBLICATION CODE				
	LRS3	LRS4	MAC1	MAC2	MAC3
1. ACCIDENTS					
2. AGRICULTURE			●	●	●
3. CIVIL AVIATION			●	●	●
4. CLIMATE			●	●	
5. COMMODITIES			●	●	○
6. COMMUNICATIONS			●	●	●
7. CONSTRUCTION					
8. CONSUMPTION					
9. CRIME AND JUSTICE					
10. CULTURE				●	
11. DEFENCE					
12. DEVELOPMENT AND AID					
13. DISTRIBUTION					
14. DRUGS					
15. EDUCATION AND TRAINING			●	●	●
16. EMPLOYMENT AND UNEMPLOYMENT			●	●	●
17. ENERGY			●	●	
18. ENVIRONMENT					
19. FINANCE			●	●	●
20. FISHING		○	●	●	
21. FORESTRY				●	
22. HEALTH					
23. HOUSING					
24. INCOME AND WEALTH			●	●	●
25. INDUSTRIES	■	○	○	○	
26. INTELLECTUAL PROPERTY					
27. INTERNATIONAL TRADE AND FINANCE			●	●	●
28. LABOUR			●	●	●
29. LAND					
30. LIVING COSTS AND STANDARDS					
31. MIGRATION				●	●
32. MINERALS			○	○	○
33. MINING AND QUARRYING					
34. NATIONAL ACCOUNTS			●	●	●
35. PARLIAMENT AND PUBLIC AFFAIRS					
36. POPULATION AND VITAL STATISTICS			●	●	●
37. PRICES			●	●	●
38. PRODUCTION	○	○	●	●	●
39. REFUGEES					
40. SCIENCE AND TECHNOLOGY					
41. SHIPPING	○	■	●	●	●
42. SOCIAL INDICATORS					
43. TAXATION					
44. TOURISM					
45. TRANSPORT		○	●	●	●
46. WELFARE					

PUBLICATION CODE								
MB1	MB2	MHPPE1	MJ1	MLC1	MMB1	NATO1	NCM1	NWAFO1
							●	
				■	■		●	
							●	
							●	
○	■		○	○	○		○	
							●	
							●	
○	○	●	●	●	●		●	
							●	
							●	
						■		
							●	
							●	
							●	
				●	●	○	●	
							●	
							●	
		●	●		●	○	●	
							●	■
							●	
							●	
		■					●	
		●					●	
○	○		○	○	○		●	○
							●	
●		○	●	●	●		●	
							●	
		●		●			●	
		●						
		●					●	
○	○		■					
■			■				●	
		●			●		●	
							●	
		●		●	●		●	
●	●	●	●	●	●		●	
○	○		●	○	○		●	
							●	
							●	
		●						
		●					●	
							●	
							●	
		●					●	

SUBJECT	PUBLICATION CODE				
	OECD1	OECD2	OECD3	OECD4	OECD5
1. ACCIDENTS					
2. AGRICULTURE					■
3. CIVIL AVIATION					
4. CLIMATE					
5. COMMODITIES					○
6. COMMUNICATIONS					
7. CONSTRUCTION					
8. CONSUMPTION					
9. CRIME AND JUSTICE					
10. CULTURE					
11. DEFENCE					
12. DEVELOPMENT AND AID					
13. DISTRIBUTION					
14. DRUGS					
15. EDUCATION AND TRAINING			●		
16. EMPLOYMENT AND UNEMPLOYMENT		○	●	●	●
17. ENERGY					
18. ENVIRONMENT					
19. FINANCE		■			○
20. FISHING					
21. FORESTRY					
22. HEALTH					
23. HOUSING					
24. INCOME AND WEALTH					○
25. INDUSTRIES		○	○		○
26. INTELLECTUAL PROPERTY			●		
27. INTERNATIONAL TRADE AND FINANCE	■		●		●
28. LABOUR					
29. LAND					
30. LIVING COSTS AND STANDARDS					
31. MIGRATION				■	
32. MINERALS					
33. MINING AND QUARRYING					
34. NATIONAL ACCOUNTS					
35. PARLIAMENT AND PUBLIC AFFAIRS					
36. POPULATION AND VITAL STATISTICS				■	
37. PRICES					
38. PRODUCTION					○
39. REFUGEES					
40. SCIENCE AND TECHNOLOGY			■		
41. SHIPPING					
42. SOCIAL INDICATORS					
43. TAXATION					
44. TOURISM					
45. TRANSPORT					
46. WELFARE					

PUBLICATION CODE								
OECD6	OECD7	OECD8	OECD9	OECD10	OECD11	OECD12	OECD13	OECD14
						○		
						○		
						■		
			■					■
■	■							
●	○							
○	○		○	○				
○								
						○		
		■	■	■		●	■	○
					■			
●								
						●		
○								

PUBLICATION CODE								
OECD6	OECD7	OECD8	OECD9	OECD10	OECD11	OECD12	OECD13	OECD14
						○		
						○		
						■		
			■					■
■	■							
●	○							
○	○		○	○				
○								
						○		
		■	■	■		●	■	○
					■			
●								
						●		
○								

PUBLICATION CODE								
OECD20	OECD21	OECD22	OECD23	OECD24	OECD25	OECD26	OECD27	OECD28
●								
						■		
					○	○		
	●	●						
		●			●	●		
	●	●						
●								
●	●	●	■		●			
	●	●			●			
●								
	●	●						
		●						
		●						
●								
●	●	●						
●	●	●	■					○
					○	○		
	●	●		●	●	●	■	●
●		●	■					
	●	●						■
●								
	●	●	■		●			
	●	●			●	●		
				■				
		●			■			
■								
	●	●			○			

SUBJECT	PUBLICATION CODE				
	OECD29	OECD30	OECD31	OECD32	OECD33
1. ACCIDENTS					■
2. AGRICULTURE				○	●
3. CIVIL AVIATION					
4. CLIMATE					
5. COMMODITIES					○
6. COMMUNICATIONS					
7. CONSTRUCTION				●	
8. CONSUMPTION				○	○
9. CRIME AND JUSTICE					
10. CULTURE					
11. DEFENCE					
12. DEVELOPMENT AND AID					
13. DISTRIBUTION					
14. DRUGS					
15. EDUCATION AND TRAINING					
16. EMPLOYMENT AND UNEMPLOYMENT	●			■	
17. ENERGY			■		●
18. ENVIRONMENT					■
19. FINANCE				●	
20. FISHING					
21. FORESTRY					■
22. HEALTH					
23. HOUSING				●	
24. INCOME AND WEALTH	○			■	
25. INDUSTRIES			○	○	●
26. INTELLECTUAL PROPERTY					
27. INTERNATIONAL TRADE AND FINANCE				●	●
28. LABOUR				●	
29. LAND					■
30. LIVING COSTS AND STANDARDS					
31. MIGRATION					
32. MINERALS					○
33. MINING AND QUARRYING					
34. NATIONAL ACCOUNTS	■			■	●
35. PARLIAMENT AND PUBLIC AFFAIRS					
36. POPULATION AND VITAL STATISTICS				●	●
37. PRICES				■	
38. PRODUCTION			●		○
39. REFUGEES					
40. SCIENCE AND TECHNOLOGY					●
41. SHIPPING					
42. SOCIAL INDICATORS					
43. TAXATION					
44. TOURISM		■			●
45. TRANSPORT		○			●
46. WELFARE	○			○	

PUBLICATION CODE								
OECD34	OECD35	OECD36	OECD37	OECD38	OECD39	OECD40	OECD41	OECD42
				○				
				●			○	○
						■		
●	■	■	■					●
								○
				■				
■	●			●			○	●
					■		■	●
							○	
				●				
								■
								●

SUBJECT	PUBLICATION CODE				
	OECD43	OECD44	OECD45	OECD46	OECD47
1. ACCIDENTS					
2. AGRICULTURE					
3. CIVIL AVIATION					
4. CLIMATE					
5. COMMODITIES			○		○
6. COMMUNICATIONS		○			
7. CONSTRUCTION					
8. CONSUMPTION			○		
9. CRIME AND JUSTICE					
10. CULTURE					
11. DEFENCE					
12. DEVELOPMENT AND AID					
13. DISTRIBUTION					
14. DRUGS					
15. EDUCATION AND TRAINING					
16. EMPLOYMENT AND UNEMPLOYMENT			○	○	○
17. ENERGY					●
18. ENVIRONMENT					
19. FINANCE				○	
20. FISHING	■				
21. FORESTRY					
22. HEALTH					
23. HOUSING					
24. INCOME AND WEALTH					
25. INDUSTRIES	○	○	■	○	○
26. INTELLECTUAL PROPERTY					
27. INTERNATIONAL TRADE AND FINANCE	●	■	○	●	
28. LABOUR					
29. LAND					
30. LIVING COSTS AND STANDARDS					
31. MIGRATION					
32. MINERALS					■
33. MINING AND QUARRYING					
34. NATIONAL ACCOUNTS					
35. PARLIAMENT AND PUBLIC AFFAIRS					
36. POPULATION AND VITAL STATISTICS					
37. PRICES				○	
38. PRODUCTION	●		○		○
39. REFUGEES					
40. SCIENCE AND TECHNOLOGY					
41. SHIPPING					
42. SOCIAL INDICATORS					
43. TAXATION					
44. TOURISM		○		■	
45. TRANSPORT		○			
46. WELFARE					

PUBLICATION CODE								
OIVV1	OPEC1	OPEC2	PC1	PKF1	PKF2	PPI1	SATRA1	SFIA1
■								
○	○	○				●	○	
●	●	●				○	●	
							○	
	■	■						
	○	○	○	○	○			
								■
						●		
			○					
○	○	○		○	○	■	■	○
●	●		○			○	●	●
○								
	●							
	●		■					
	●	●						○
●	●	●				○	●	
	●	●						
			●					
				■	■			
	●							
			○					

SUBJECT	PUBLICATION CODE				
	SMMT1	SMMT2	SPC1	SPC2	UN1
1. ACCIDENTS					
2. AGRICULTURE					○
3. CIVIL AVIATION					●
4. CLIMATE					
5. COMMODITIES			○		○
6. COMMUNICATIONS					
7. CONSTRUCTION					
8. CONSUMPTION					○
9. CRIME AND JUSTICE					
10. CULTURE					
11. DEFENCE					
12. DEVELOPMENT AND AID				●	
13. DISTRIBUTION					
14. DRUGS					
15. EDUCATION AND TRAINING					●
16. EMPLOYMENT AND UNEMPLOYMENT					●
17. ENERGY					●
18. ENVIRONMENT					
19. FINANCE					
20. FISHING					
21. FORESTRY					
22. HEALTH					
23. HOUSING					
24. INCOME AND WEALTH					
25. INDUSTRIES	■	■			
26. INTELLECTUAL PROPERTY					
27. INTERNATIONAL TRADE AND FINANCE		●		●	●
28. LABOUR					
29. LAND					●
30. LIVING COSTS AND STANDARDS			■	●	
31. MIGRATION					
32. MINERALS					
33. MINING AND QUARRYING					
34. NATIONAL ACCOUNTS				●	●
35. PARLIAMENT AND PUBLIC AFFAIRS					
36. POPULATION AND VITAL STATISTICS				●	●
37. PRICES			■	●	●
38. PRODUCTION	●	●			●
39. REFUGEES					
40. SCIENCE AND TECHNOLOGY					
41. SHIPPING					●
42. SOCIAL INDICATORS					■
43. TAXATION					
44. TOURISM				●	
45. TRANSPORT	○	○			●
46. WELFARE					

PUBLICATION CODE								
UN2	UN3	UN4	UN5	UN6	UN7	UN8	UN9	UN10
●	●	●	●					
●	●	●	●					
				○			○	●
●	●	●	●					
●	●	●	●					■
				●	●	●	●	●
							●	
●	●	●	●					
●	●	●	●	●				●
●	●	●	●	■	■	■	■	●
●	●	●	●					
●	●	●	●					
●	●	●	●					
●	●	●	●					
								■
				○	○	○	○	■
●	●	●	●	●	●	●	●	●
				○				
				■				
●	●	●	●					
●	●	●	●					●
●	●	●	●					●
●	●	●	●	●	●	●	●	●
●	●	●	●					
●	●	●	●					
●	●	●	●					

SUBJECT	PUBLICATION CODE				
	UN11	UN12	UN13	UN14	UN15
1. ACCIDENTS					
2. AGRICULTURE					
3. CIVIL AVIATION			●		
4. CLIMATE					
5. COMMODITIES	■	●		●	●
6. COMMUNICATIONS					
7. CONSTRUCTION					
8. CONSUMPTION	●		●		
9. CRIME AND JUSTICE					
10. CULTURE					
11. DEFENCE					
12. DEVELOPMENT AND AID					
13. DISTRIBUTION					
14. DRUGS					
15. EDUCATION AND TRAINING					
16. EMPLOYMENT AND UNEMPLOYMENT			●		
17. ENERGY	●		●		
18. ENVIRONMENT					
19. FINANCE					
20. FISHING					
21. FORESTRY					
22. HEALTH					
23. HOUSING					
24. INCOME AND WEALTH					
25. INDUSTRIES	■		●	○	
26. INTELLECTUAL PROPERTY					
27. INTERNATIONAL TRADE AND FINANCE	●	■		■	■
28. LABOUR					
29. LAND			●		
30. LIVING COSTS AND STANDARDS					
31. MIGRATION					
32. MINERALS					
33. MINING AND QUARRYING					
34. NATIONAL ACCOUNTS			●		
35. PARLIAMENT AND PUBLIC AFFAIRS					
36. POPULATION AND VITAL STATISTICS					
37. PRICES					
38. PRODUCTION	●				
39. REFUGEES					
40. SCIENCE AND TECHNOLOGY					
41. SHIPPING			●		
42. SOCIAL INDICATORS					
43. TAXATION					
44. TOURISM					
45. TRANSPORT			■		
46. WELFARE					

PUBLICATION CODE								
UN16	UN17	UN18	UN19	UN20	UN21	UN22	UN23	UN24
○						●		
●						●		
					○	○		●
●								
		■						
○	○			○	●			
●	●							
●								
●								
●								
●	●					○		
●	●	●	●					
				■	■	●		
●						■		
						○		
						●		
●	●							
●	●	●						
●		●						
○		○		○	○	●		
○				○	●	○	■	■
●			●			●		
			■					
●	●							
●	●							
●	●		■			●		
○	○	●		○	●			
■	■		●					
●						●		
●								

SUBJECT	PUBLICATION CODE				
	UN25	UN26	UN27	UN28	UN29
1. ACCIDENTS					
2. AGRICULTURE	○				
3. CIVIL AVIATION					
4. CLIMATE					
5. COMMODITIES				■	
6. COMMUNICATIONS	●				
7. CONSTRUCTION		●			
8. CONSUMPTION		○			●
9. CRIME AND JUSTICE					
10. CULTURE					
11. DEFENCE	●				
12. DEVELOPMENT AND AID	●				
13. DISTRIBUTION					
14. DRUGS					■
15. EDUCATION AND TRAINING	●				
16. EMPLOYMENT AND UNEMPLOYMENT	●		■		
17. ENERGY			●	●	
18. ENVIRONMENT	●				
19. FINANCE			●		
20. FISHING					
21. FORESTRY					
22. HEALTH	●	●			
23. HOUSING		■			
24. INCOME AND WEALTH	●		●		
25. INDUSTRIES	○		■		
26. INTELLECTUAL PROPERTY					
27. INTERNATIONAL TRADE AND FINANCE					●
28. LABOUR	○		●		
29. LAND	●	■			
30. LIVING COSTS AND STANDARDS	●	○			
31. MIGRATION					
32. MINERALS				○	
33. MINING AND QUARRYING				●	
34. NATIONAL ACCOUNTS	●				
35. PARLIAMENT AND PUBLIC AFFAIRS					
36. POPULATION AND VITAL STATISTICS	●	●			
37. PRICES	○				
38. PRODUCTION			●	■	○
39. REFUGEES					
40. SCIENCE AND TECHNOLOGY					
41. SHIPPING					
42. SOCIAL INDICATORS	●	●			
43. TAXATION	●				
44. TOURISM					
45. TRANSPORT		●			
46. WELFARE	●				

PUBLICATION CODE								
UN30	UN31	UN32	UN33	UN34	UN35	UN36	UN37	UN38
				■				
	○	○	○		●			
●				●				
■								
					●			
		●			●			
					●			
					●			
							■	
				○	○			
●	○	■	■	●	●			●
					●			
	○				●			
					●			
						■	■	■
					●			
		●		●	●	○		
○				○	●			
	■	●			●			
	○	○			●			

SUBJECT	PUBLICATION CODE				
	UN39	UN40	UN41	UN42	UN43
1. ACCIDENTS					
2. AGRICULTURE		■			●
3. CIVIL AVIATION					●
4. CLIMATE					
5. COMMODITIES		○			●
6. COMMUNICATIONS					
7. CONSTRUCTION					●
8. CONSUMPTION					
9. CRIME AND JUSTICE					
10. CULTURE					
11. DEFENCE					
12. DEVELOPMENT AND AID			■		
13. DISTRIBUTION					●
14. DRUGS					
15. EDUCATION AND TRAINING					
16. EMPLOYMENT AND UNEMPLOYMENT					
17. ENERGY					○
18. ENVIRONMENT					
19. FINANCE					●
20. FISHING					
21. FORESTRY					
22. HEALTH					
23. HOUSING					●
24. INCOME AND WEALTH					
25. INDUSTRIES		○			
26. INTELLECTUAL PROPERTY					
27. INTERNATIONAL TRADE AND FINANCE					●
28. LABOUR		●			
29. LAND					
30. LIVING COSTS AND STANDARDS					
31. MIGRATION					●
32. MINERALS					○
33. MINING AND QUARRYING					○
34. NATIONAL ACCOUNTS				■	●
35. PARLIAMENT AND PUBLIC AFFAIRS					
36. POPULATION AND VITAL STATISTICS	■				●
37. PRICES		●			●
38. PRODUCTION					●
39. REFUGEES			■		
40. SCIENCE AND TECHNOLOGY					
41. SHIPPING					
42. SOCIAL INDICATORS					
43. TAXATION					
44. TOURISM					
45. TRANSPORT					●
46. WELFARE					

PUBLICATION CODE								
UN44	UN45	UN46	UN47	UN48	UN49	UN50	UN51	UN52
●			■					
●	●					●		
●	●					●		
○	○			■	■	○		
●						●		
	●							
●	●				○	●		
		●						
						●		
						●	●	
●	●	●				●		
●	●	●				●		
●	●					●		
●								
●	●					●		
●						●		
●						●		
●	●	●				●		
●	●	●						
●						●		
○	○				○	●		
						●		
●	●			○	○	●		■
	○					○		
●	●					●		
●	●					○		
	●					○		
●	○					●		
●	●	●				●		
●	●	●				●		
●	●					●		
●	●				○	●		
							■	
●						●		
●	●					●		
		■				○		
						●		
●						●		
●	●		●			●		
	●							

SUBJECT	PUBLICATION CODE				
	UN53	UN54	UN55	UNCTAD1	UNCTAD2
1. ACCIDENTS					
2. AGRICULTURE			●	●	
3. CIVIL AVIATION					
4. CLIMATE					
5. COMMODITIES					
6. COMMUNICATIONS			●		
7. CONSTRUCTION					
8. CONSUMPTION				●	
9. CRIME AND JUSTICE					
10. CULTURE					
11. DEFENCE					
12. DEVELOPMENT AND AID				●	
13. DISTRIBUTION					
14. DRUGS					
15. EDUCATION AND TRAINING			●	●	
16. EMPLOYMENT AND UNEMPLOYMENT			●	●	
17. ENERGY			●	●	
18. ENVIRONMENT					
19. FINANCE					
20. FISHING					
21. FORESTRY					
22. HEALTH			●	●	
23. HOUSING					
24. INCOME AND WEALTH					
25. INDUSTRIES					○
26. INTELLECTUAL PROPERTY					
27. INTERNATIONAL TRADE AND FINANCE	■		●	●	●
28. LABOUR				●	
29. LAND				●	
30. LIVING COSTS AND STANDARDS					
31. MIGRATION					
32. MINERALS					
33. MINING AND QUARRYING					
34. NATIONAL ACCOUNTS				●	
35. PARLIAMENT AND PUBLIC AFFAIRS					
36. POPULATION AND VITAL STATISTICS		■	●	●	
37. PRICES				●	●
38. PRODUCTION			●	●	
39. REFUGEES					
40. SCIENCE AND TECHNOLOGY					
41. SHIPPING				○	■
42. SOCIAL INDICATORS				●	
43. TAXATION					
44. TOURISM			●		
45. TRANSPORT			●	●	●
46. WELFARE					

PUBLICATION CODE								
UNCTAD3	UNCTAD4	UNCTAD5	UNESCO1	UNICEF1	UNICEF2	UNIDO1	VICES1	WB1
		●					●	●
○	■						○	
			■		●		●	
							●	
●							●	○
			■					○
		●			●	●		■
							●	
		●	■	●	■		●	●
		●	●			●	●	●
							●	○
		●						
		●			●		●	
		●		●	■		●	●
							●	●
					●	●	●	○
○						■	●	
●	■	●				●	●	
						●		○
		●	●					●
							●	
■	○							
○								
		●			●		●	●
		●	●	●	●		●	●
●	●	●			●		●	
●		●				●	●	
		●	■			●		
		●						
		●			●		○	■
		●						
							●	
				■	■		●	●

SUBJECT	PUBLICATION CODE				
	WB2	WB3	WB4	WB5	WB6
1. ACCIDENTS					
2. AGRICULTURE					○
3. CIVIL AVIATION					
4. CLIMATE					
5. COMMODITIES					
6. COMMUNICATIONS					
7. CONSTRUCTION					
8. CONSUMPTION					●
9. CRIME AND JUSTICE					
10. CULTURE					
11. DEFENCE					
12. DEVELOPMENT AND AID	■	■	■		
13. DISTRIBUTION					
14. DRUGS					
15. EDUCATION AND TRAINING					
16. EMPLOYMENT AND UNEMPLOYMENT	●				
17. ENERGY					
18. ENVIRONMENT					
19. FINANCE					●
20. FISHING					
21. FORESTRY					
22. HEALTH					
23. HOUSING					
24. INCOME AND WEALTH					
25. INDUSTRIES					○
26. INTELLECTUAL PROPERTY					
27. INTERNATIONAL TRADE AND FINANCE	●	■	■		●
28. LABOUR					
29. LAND					
30. LIVING COSTS AND STANDARDS					
31. MIGRATION				■	
32. MINERALS					
33. MINING AND QUARRYING					
34. NATIONAL ACCOUNTS	●				●
35. PARLIAMENT AND PUBLIC AFFAIRS					
36. POPULATION AND VITAL STATISTICS				■	
37. PRICES	●				●
38. PRODUCTION					
39. REFUGEES					
40. SCIENCE AND TECHNOLOGY					
41. SHIPPING					
42. SOCIAL INDICATORS					
43. TAXATION					
44. TOURISM					
45. TRANSPORT					
46. WELFARE					

PUBLICATION CODE								
WBMS1	WBMS2	WBMS3	WBMS4	WC1	WFP1	WHO1	WHO2	WIPO1
						●		
				■				
○	○	○	■		○			
●	○	●	○	●	○			
					■			
						●		
				●		●		
				●				
						■	■	
○	○	○	○	○				
								■
●		●	●	●	○			
				●				
				●				
■	■	■	●					
●								
				●				
				●		●	●	
●	●	●		●	●			
●	○	●	●					
						●	●	
					○			
				●		●		

SUBJECT	PUBLICATION CODE				
	WIPO2	WIPO3	WMO1	WTO1	WTO2
1. ACCIDENTS					
2. AGRICULTURE					
3. CIVIL AVIATION					
4. CLIMATE			■		
5. COMMODITIES					
6. COMMUNICATIONS					
7. CONSTRUCTION					
8. CONSUMPTION					
9. CRIME AND JUSTICE					
10. CULTURE					
11. DEFENCE					
12. DEVELOPMENT AND AID					
13. DISTRIBUTION					
14. DRUGS					
15. EDUCATION AND TRAINING					
16. EMPLOYMENT AND UNEMPLOYMENT					
17. ENERGY					
18. ENVIRONMENT					
19. FINANCE					
20. FISHING					
21. FORESTRY					
22. HEALTH					
23. HOUSING					
24. INCOME AND WEALTH					
25. INDUSTRIES					
26. INTELLECTUAL PROPERTY	■	■			
27. INTERNATIONAL TRADE AND FINANCE					
28. LABOUR					
29. LAND					
30. LIVING COSTS AND STANDARDS					
31. MIGRATION					
32. MINERALS					
33. MINING AND QUARRYING					
34. NATIONAL ACCOUNTS					
35. PARLIAMENT AND PUBLIC AFFAIRS					
36. POPULATION AND VITAL STATISTICS					
37. PRICES					
38. PRODUCTION					
39. REFUGEES					
40. SCIENCE AND TECHNOLOGY					
41. SHIPPING					
42. SOCIAL INDICATORS					
43. TAXATION					
44. TOURISM				■	■
45. TRANSPORT				○	
46. WELFARE					

PUBLICATION CODE								
WTO3	WTO4							
○	○							
○								
	○							
■	■							
○	○							

instat

GUIDE TO SUBJECTS AND SOURCES

Sections 25 - 46

25 INDUSTRIES

***Note**. Some industries are covered in separate Subject Sections. A list of these is given at the end of the Introduction to this chapter below.*

INTRODUCTION TO SECTION 25 – CONTENT AND COVERAGE

INTRODUCTION TO SECTION 25 – CONTENT AND COVERAGE

This section covers information about the organization and structure of particular industries including such data as:

- the number of enterprises
- the sizes of enterprises
- the types of enterprises
- analyses of production, employment, investment etc. according to size and type of enterprise

It also covers related information such as:

- capacity and capacity utilization
- business expectations

For information about more general industrial subjects such as production, employment, earnings etc., reference should also be made to the appropriate Subject Sections. In addition, a number of industries are also covered individually in separate Sections. These are as follows:

Agriculture (Section 2)
Civil Aviation (Section 3)
Communications (Section 6)
Construction (Section 7)
Distribution (Section 13)
Energy (Section 17)
Fishing (Section 20)
Forestry (Section 21)
Mining and Quarrying (Section 33)
Shipping (Section 41)
Tourism (Section 44)
Transport (Section 45)

Subject	Categories	Units	Time series Yes/No Frequency		Territorial coverage	Source (Table No.)
25.1 AGRICULTURE - see also under General (25.9) and Section 2						
25.1.1 Milk and Dairy Products						
Average intake	Per enterprise	tonnes	Yes	A	EC	MMB1 (45)
Butter producing enterprises	By annual output	tonnes, %	No		EC	MMB1 (48)
Cheese enterprises	By type of manufacture	tonnes, nos	No		EC	MMB1 (50)
Cheese producing enterprises	By annual output	tonnes, %	No		EC	MMB1 (49)
Condensed milk enterprises	By annual output	tonnes, %	No		EC	MMB1 (51)
Dairy co-operatives	By organisations, market share	nos, %	No		EC	MMB1 (53)
Major dairy companies	By turnover, intake	nat curr, %	No		EC	MMB1 (54)
Milk powder enterprises	By annual output	tonnes, %	No		EC	MMB1 (52)
Number of enterprises	Total	nos	Yes	A	EC	MMB1 (44)
Size structure of enterprises	By annual milk intake	tonnes, %	No		EC	MMB1 (46)
Size structure of enterprises	By output of liquid milk and products	tonnes, %	No		EC	MMB1 (47)
25.1.2 General						
Agricultural holdings	By size group	nos	No		EC	EC9 (5.15)
Agricultural holdings, economic size,	By size group	nos	No		EC	EC9 (5.18)
Agricultural land tenure and number of enterprises	By type of land tenure	ha, nos	No		Selected countries	UN22 (II-3.1.6)
Farm population, ratio to cultivated land	By ratio and % change	ha per farm	No		Selected countries	UN22 (II-3.1.7)
Farm specialization	By speciality crop, animal production, field crops	nos	No		Selected countries	UN22 (II-3.1.5b)
Farming, type of	Specialized, mixed	nos	No		EC	EC9 (5.18)
Farms, number of	By area category	ha	No		Selected countries	UN22 (II-3.1.4)
Legal personality and holding management		nos	Yes	2A	EC	EC6 (IC 2)
Number and area of holdings	By AA size category	nos, total	Yes	2 A	EC	EC6 (IC 4)
Types of tenure		nos	Yes	2 A	EC	EC6 (IC 3)
25.2 ALUMINIUM						
Aluminium companies, financial performance	Return on funds employed, net income (loss), net margin on sales, sales, by company	%, US$	Yes	A	World	IBA1 (7)
Aluminium, primary, capacity	Major interests	tonnes	No		EC	EAA1 (-)
25.3 CHEMICALS AND FERTILISERS - see also under General (25.9)						
25.3.1 Consumption						
Ammonia production capacity		tonnes	No		World	FAO5 (13)
Consumption	By country	US$	Yes	A	Western World	CIA1 (16)
Fluorine		tonnes	Yes	A	EC	EC68 (-)
Fluorine	Fluorspar, hydrofluoric acid and aluminium fluoride	tonnes	No		EC	EC68 (-)
Nitrogenous fertiliser		tonnes	Yes	A	World	FAO5 (17)
Nitrogenous, phosphate and potash fertiliser	Total	tonnes	Yes	A	World	FAO5 (29)
Phosphate fertiliser		tonnes	Yes	A	World	FAO5 (21)
Phosphates		tonnes	Yes	A	EC	EC68 (-)
Phosphates	Natural phosphates, phosphoric acid, slag and fertilizers	tonnes	No		EC	EC68 (-)
Potash (technical grade)		tonnes	Yes	A	World	FAO5 (7)

25 INDUSTRIES

Subject	Categories	Units	Time series Yes/No Frequency		Territorial coverage	Source (Table No.)
Potash fertiliser		tonnes	Yes	A	World	FAO5 (25)
Rock phosphate		tonnes	Yes	A	World	FAO5 (11)
Urea, home deliveries		tonnes, %	Yes	A	World	IFA1R (-)
25.3.2 Demand						
Home demand	By country	nat curr	Yes	A	Selected countries	CIA1 (5)
25.3.3 Employment						
Chemical industry		nos	No		EC	EC76 (-)
Employees	By country	nos	Yes	A	Western world	CIA1 (7)
Extraction of minerals/peat		nos	No		EC	EC76 (-)
Non-metallic mineral products, manufacture of		nos	No		EC	EC76 (-)
25.3.4 Investments						
Chemical industry		ECU	No		EC	EC76 (-)
Existing and planned fertilizer industries in the GCC region	By country, by location, products, capacity, status	tonnes	No		Arabian Gulf	CH1 (3.10)
Existing and planned petrochemical projects in the GCC region	By country, by location, products, capacity, status	tonnes	No		Arabian Gulf	CH1 (3.11)
Investment	As % of turnover	%	Yes	A	Western World	CIA1 (28)
Investment	By country	nat curr	Yes	A	Selected countries	CIA1 (8)
Investment	By country	US$	Yes	A	Western World	CIA1 (18)
Investment per capita	By country	nat curr	Yes	A	Selected countries	CIA1 (10)
Investment per head	By country	US$	Yes	A	Western World	CIA1 (20)
25.3.5 Prices						
Consumer price indices	By country	indices	Yes	A	Selected countries	CIA1 (30)
Prices	Home sales	indices	Yes	A	Western World	CIA1 (29)
Real prices	Annual % change	%	Yes	A	Western World	CIA1 (31)
25.3.6 Production						
Chemical industry	By NACE	tonnes, hl	Yes	A, Q	EC	EC51 (B)
Chemical industry, including man-made fibres industry	Seasonally adjusted	indices	Yes	A, M	EC	EC53 (6.8)
EC chemical industry	By indicator	ECU, nos	No		EC	EC35 (-)
Fertiliser	By type	tonnes	Yes	A	World	FAO5 (1)
Fluorine		tonnes	Yes	A	EC	EC68 (-)
Fluorine	Fluorspar, hydrofluoric acid and aluminium fluoride	tonnes	No		EC	EC68 (-)
Nitrogenous fertiliser	By economic class	tonnes	Yes	A	World	FAO5 (2)
Output, per capita	World index	indices	Yes	A	Western World	CIA1 (22)
Phosphate fertiliser	By economic class	tonnes	Yes	A	World	FAO5 (3)
Phosphates		tonnes	Yes	A	EC	EC68 (-)
Phosphates	Natural phosphates, phosphoric acid, slag and fertilizers	tonnes	No		EC	EC68 (-)
Phosphoric acid production capacity		tonnes	No		World	FAO5 (14)
Potash fertiliser	By economic class	tonnes	Yes	A	World	FAO5 (4)
Production	World index	indices	Yes	A	Western World	CIA1 (21)
Urea		tonnes, %	Yes	A	World	IFA1R (-)
Urea, granular	Share of production	%	No		World	IFA1R (-)
25.3.7 Sales						
Home sales	By country	nat curr	Yes	A	Selected countries	CIA1 (4)
Home sales	By country	US$	Yes	A	Western World	CIA1 (15)
Sales	By country	nat curr	Yes	A	Selected countries	CIA1 (1)
Sales	By country	US$	Yes	A	Western World	CIA1 (12)
Turnover	By country	per capita, nat curr	Yes	A	Selected countries	CIA1 (9)
Turnover per capita	By country	US$	Yes	A	Western World	CIA1 (19)

Subject	Categories	Units	Time series Yes/No Frequency		Territorial coverage	Source (Table No.)
25.3.8 Trade						
Ammonia		tonnes	Yes	A	World	FAO5 (15)
EC chemical industry	By country, by imports, exports, balance of trade	ECU	No		Selected countries	EC35 (-)
Economic classes and regions		%	Yes	A	World	FAO5 (6)
Exchange rates	By country	US$	Yes	A	Selected countries	CIA1 (11)
Exports	As % of sales	%	Yes	A	Western World	CIA1 (23)
Exports	By country	nat curr	Yes	A	Selected countries	CIA1 (2)
Exports	By country	US$	Yes	A	Western World	CIA1 (13)
Exports and imports	Exports, imports	%	Yes	A	Western World	CIA1 (25-27)
Fertiliser	By type	tonnes	Yes	A	World	FAO5 (1)
Fluorine		tonnes	Yes	A	EC	EC68 (-)
Fluorine	Fluorspar, hydrofluoric acid and aluminium fluoride	tonnes	No		EC	EC68 (-)
Imports	As % of home demand	%	Yes	A	Western World	CIA1 (24)
Imports	By country	nat curr	Yes	A	Selected countries	CIA1 (3)
Imports	By country	US$	Yes	A	Western World	CIA1 (14)
Nitrogenous fertiliser		tonnes	Yes	A	World	FAO5 (18-19)
Nitrogenous fertiliser	By economic class	tonnes	Yes	A	World	FAO5 (2)
Nitrogenous, phosphate and potash fertiliser		tonnes	Yes	A	World	FAO5 (30-31)
Phosphate fertiliser		tonnes	Yes	A	World	FAO5 (22-23)
Phosphate fertiliser	By economic class	tonnes	Yes	A	World	FAO5 (3)
Phosphates		tonnes	Yes	A	EC	EC68 (-)
Phosphates	Fatural phosphates, phosphoric acid, slag and fertilizers	tonnes	No		EC	EC68 (-)
Phosphoric acid		tonnes	Yes	A	World	FAO5 (16)
Potash fertiliser		tonnes	Yes	A	World	FAO5 (26-27)
Potash fertiliser	By economic class	tonnes	Yes	A	World	FAO5 (4)
Potash re-exports (complex fertiliser)		tonnes	Yes	A	World	FAO5 (8)
Rock phosphate		tonnes	Yes	A	World	FAO5 (12)
Trade balance	By country	nat curr	Yes	A	Selected countries	CIA1 (6)
Trade balance	By country	US$	Yes	A	Western World	CIA1 (17)
Urea		tonnes, %	Yes	A	World	IFA1R (-)
Urea	Origin, destination	tonnes	No		World	IFA1R (-)
25.4 CONSUMER GOODS - see also under General (25.9)						
Household cleaning products	By country, by product	kg	No		EC	EM1 (1409)
Market sizes, clothing and footwear	By country, by item	US$, nos	No		EC	EM1 (1413)
Market sizes, consumer electronics	By country, by product	nos	No		EC	EM1 (1416)
Market sizes, cosmetics and toiletries	By country, by product	US$	No		EC	EM1 (1411)
Market sizes, healthcare	By country, by product	US$	No		EC	EM1 (1412)
Market sizes, home furnishings and housewares	By country, by product	US$	No		EC	EM1 (1414)
Market sizes, paper products	By country, by disposable paper products	US$	No		EC	EM1 (1410)
Market sizes, personal and leisure goods	By country, by product	nos, US$	No		EC	EM1 (1417)
Market sizes, small electrical appliances	By country, by appliance	nos	No		EC	EM1 (1418)
Markets sizes, white goods	By country, by refrigerators, freezers, cookers, microwaves, washing machines, dishwashers	nos	No		EC	EM1 (1415)

25 INDUSTRIES

25.5 DISTRIBUTION

25.5.1 Employment and Activity

Subject	Categories	Units	Time series Yes/No	Frequency	Territorial coverage	Source (Table No.)
Commerce and main branches in the value added, share of	By branch	%, ECU	Yes	10 yrly	EUR12	EC71 (EUR2)
Consumption, household	Private national consumption, per inhabitant, tradeable consumption	ECU, indices, %	No		EUR12	EC71 (EUR4)
Demographic and commercial indicators, main	By population, area, density, age groups GDP, distributive trade sector	nos, sq km, %, ECU	No		Central and Eastern EC	EC71 (EUR22)
Demographic and commercial indicators, main	By population, area, density, living standards, distributive trade sector	nos, sq km GDP, PPS, %	No		EFTA	EC71 (EUR20)
Durable goods, penetration rates of selected	By type of good	%	No		EC	EC71 (EUR5)
EC retail sector, contrasting structures within the EC retail sector						
Employment		nos	No		EFTA	EC71 (EUR21)
Employment characteristics in retailing	Low and high share of employees; by employment category	nos, %	No		EUR12	EC71 (EUR9)
Employment, retail	By main activity	%	No		EC	EC71 (EUR10)
Female employment		%	No		EFTA	EC71 (EUR21)
Geographic and socio-economic density, age groups	By population, area, living standard indicators	nos, sq km, %	No		EUR12, USA Japan, EFTA	EC71 (EUR3)
Itinerary trade, share of		%	No		Central and Eastern Europe	EC71 (EUR23)
Part-time workers		%	No		EFTA	EC71 (EUR21)
Persons, turnover		%	No		EUR12	EC71 (EUR1b)
Retail trade turnover	At current prices, average annual growth rate at constant prices	nat curr, %	Yes	A	VICES countries and Yugoslavia	VICES1 (II/1)
Sales area per capita		sq m	No		Central and Eastern Europe	EC71 (EUR23)
Sales area per outlet, average		sq m	No		Central and Eastern Europe	EC71 (EUR23)
Sales retail, change in	By main activity	indices	No		EC EUR9, USA, Japan	EC71 (EUR13)
Self-employed		%	No		EFTA	EC71 (EUR21)
Turnover by type of organization	State, co-operatives, private	%	No		Central and Eastern Europe	EC71 (EUR23)
Turnover retail, breakdown of	By main activity	%	No		EC	EC71 (EUR12)
Turnover retail, characteristics of	Per enterprise, per capita	ECU	No		EUR12	EC71 (EUR11)
Turnover, by enterprise		ECU	No		EFTA	EC71 (EUR21)
Turnover, excluding VAT		nat curr, ECU	No		EFTA	EC71 (EUR21)
Turnover, share in	Food, non-food	%	No		Central and Eastern Europe	EC71 (EUR23)
VAT rates in the Member States		%	No		EC	EC71 (EUR19)
Wage and salary earners		%	No		EFTA	EC71 (EUR21)

25.5.2 Enterprises

Subject	Categories	Units	Time series Yes/No	Frequency	Territorial coverage	Source (Table No.)
Buying and sales organizations, major	By outlets, organization, turnover, market share	nos, ECU, %	No		Selected countries	EC71 (EUR18)
Discount enterprises, main	By enterprise	% shares	No		EC, EFTA	EC71 (EUR14)
Enterprises, enterprises per capita		nos	No		EFTA	EC71 (EUR21)
Enterprises, number of	Wholesale, retail	nos, ECU	No		EUR12, USA, Japan, EFTA	EC71 (EUR1a)

Subject	Categories	Units	Time series Yes/No	Frequency	Territorial coverage	Source (Table No.)
Enterprises, type of	Employment, share of proprietorships, limited companies by countries with high density, low density	nos, %	No		EUR12	EC71 (EUR6)
Outlets by type of organization	State, co-operatives, private	%	No		Central and Eastern Europe	EC71 (EUR23)
Outlets, outlets per capita		nos	No		EFTA	EC71 (EUR21)
Retail enterprises according to main activity	By countries with high share and low share of food retailers	%	No		EUR12	EC71 (EUR7)
Retail groupings, top 20	By enterprise, activity, turnover	ECU	No		Selected countries	EC71 (EUR15)
Retail outlets, no of	High, low outlet density, by sector	nos, % share	No		EUR12	EC71 (EUR8)
Retail, outlets		nos	No		Central and Eastern EC	EC71 (EUR23)
Retail, outlets, local		per capita	No		Central and Eastern Europe	EC71 (EUR23)
Retail trade,value added		nat curr	No		EFTA	EC71 (EUR21)
Retailers, international activities of	By company turnover, activity	ECU, %	No		Selected countries	EC71 (EUR17)
Supermarkets and hypermarkets	Supermarkets, hypermarkets	nos	Yes	A	EC	EC71 (EUR16)
25.6 ELECTRICAL AND ELECTRONIC ENGINEERING - see also under General (25.9)						
Data processing equipment production	By NACE	ECU, nos	Yes	A, Q	EC	EC51 (A)
Domestic electrical appliances	By NACE	ECU, nos	Yes	A, Q	EC	EC51 (A)
EC electrical and electronics industry, main indicators for	By indicator	ECU, nos	No		EC	EC35 (-)
Electric and electronic construction	By NACE	ECU, nos	Yes	A	EC	EC51 (A)
Electrical engineering production	Seasonally adjusted	indices	Yes	A, M	EC	EC53 (6.12)
Production and employment	By product	%	No		EC	EC35 (-)
Trade figures for the EC electrical and electronics industry	By country, by imports, exports, balance of trade	ECU	No		Selected countries	EC35 (-)
25.7 ENERGY AND OIL - see also under General (25.9) and Section 17						
25.7.1 Consumption						
Electricity consumed	Quantity	kwh	Yes	A	World, EC, USA,	UN27 (-)
Steel industry	By fuel type and by industrial process	tonnes,cu m, mwh, GJ	No		Canada and Japan	UN11 (7)
25.7.2 Employment						
Coke ovens		nos	No		EC	EC76 (-)
Electricity, gas, steam, hot water, production and distribution of		nos	No		EC	EC76 (-)
Mineral oil refining		nos	No		EC	EC76 (-)
Nucelar fuels industry		nos	No		EC	EC76 (-)
Petroleum and natural gas		nos	No		EC	EC76 (-)
Solid fuels		nos	No		EC	EC76 (-)
25.7.3 Investments						
Coke ovens		ECU	No		EC	EC76 (-)
Electricity, gas, steam, hot water		ECU	No		EC	EC76 (-)
Mineral oil refining		ECU	No		EC	EC76 (-)
Nuclear fuels industry		ECU	No		EC	EC76 (-)
Petroleum and natural gas		ECU	No		EC	EC76 (-)

Subject	Categories	Units	Time series Yes/No Frequency		Territorial coverage	Source (Table No.)
Solid fuels		ECU	No		EC	EC76 (-)
25.7.4 Production						
Electrical energy	Total generation	gwh	Yes	A	EC	EC53 (8.6)
Electrical energy	Total generation	gwh	Yes	A	EC, USA and Japan	EC53 (1.18)
Gas, natural	Production, imports	TJ	Yes	A	EC	EC53 (8.5)
Mineral oil refining	Seasonally adjusted	indices	Yes	A, M	EC	EC53 (6.5)
Primary energy production		toe	Yes	A	EC	EC53 (8.1)
Production of selected energy, commodities	Imports, exports	tonnes	Yes	A	EC	EC53 (8.1)
Refinery crude distillation capacity	Total	b/d	Yes	A	World	BB1 (11.1-11.2)
Refinery runs	Total	b/d	Yes	A	World	BB1 (12.1-12.2)
Rigs active	By change	nos, %	Yes	A	World	BB1 (-)
Rigs active	By change	nos, %	Yes	A, M	World	BB2 (-)
Rigs active	By land, offshore	nos	Yes	A	World	BB1 (9.1- 9.3)
Rigs active, estimated number of	By land, offshore, total	nos	Yes	A	World	BB2 (3.1-3.3)
Share of energy sources in primary energy	By production and consumption	%	No		EC	EC53 (8.7)
Wells drilled	Total	nos	Yes	A	World excluding EECISC	BB1 (10.1-10.2)
25.7.5 Trade						
Hard coal	Imports, exports	tonnes	Yes	A	EC	EC53 (8.2)
Imports, raw material	By main origins, metal content	tonnes/%	No		EC	EC53 (8.11)
Oil, crude	Imports, exports	tonnes	Yes	A	EC	EC53 (8.3)
Petroleum products, derived	Imports, exports	tonnes	Yes	A	EC	EC53 (8.4)
25.8 FOOD - see also under General (25.9)						
EC food industry main indicators for	By indicator	ECU, nos	No			EC35 (-)
Food, drink and tobacco industry	Seasonally adjusted	indices	Yes	A, M	EC	EC53 (6.14)
Food, edible oils and fats	Seasonally adjusted	indices	Yes	A, M	EC	EC53 (6.15)
Trade figures for the EC food industry	By country, by imports, exports, balance of trade	ECU	No		Selected countries	EC35 (-)
25.9 GENERAL						
25.9.1 Capacity						
Capacity utilisation	By industry sector	%	No		EC	EC70
Capacity, adequacy	By industry sector	indices	No		EC	EC70
Limits to production	None, demand, labour, equipment, other, by industry sector	indices	No		EC	EC70
Power station capacity	By country	MW	No		EC	EC18 (8.6)
Earnings - see Labour Costs and Hours (25.9.7)						
25.9.2 Employment						
Employees	Average number	nos	Yes	A	World	UN27 (-)
Employees	By industry	indices	No		EC	EC53 (2.2)
Employees	By industry	nos	No		EC	EC53 (2.1)
Employees	By ISIC division	nos	Yes	A	OECD	OECD16

Subject	Categories	Units	Time series Yes/No Frequency		Territorial coverage	Source (Table No.)
Employees	Total industry, intermediate goods, capital goods, consumer goods, industry	indices	Yes	M	EC, USA, Japan	EC52
Employees	By industry, region	nos	No		EC	EC53 (7.1)
Employees, number	By NACE	nos	No		EC	EC75 (2), (3.2)
Employees, number	Seasonally adjusted, by NACE sector,	indices	Yes	A, Q	EC	EC52 (-)
Employment	By identity (NACE): Water supply Extraction of minerals, peat Non-metallic mineral products Office, data processing machinery Timber, wooden furniture Paper, paper products, printing, publishing Rubber, plastics Other manufacturing industries Building, civil engineering	nos	No		EC	EC76 (-)
Employment	By NACE	nos	Yes	A	EC,	EC75 (1), (3.1)
Employment in industrial production	By country	nos	No		EC	EC18 (8.3)
Employment, share of different industries	By NACE	%	No		EC	EC75 (3.1)
Employment, share of workers	Manufacturing, building and civil engineering	%	No		EC, USA and Japan	EC53 (1.2)
	by country	nos	No		EC	EC18 (8.2)
Female employees, total employment	By ISIC group	%	No		World	UNIDO1 (2.13)
Operatives		nos	Yes	A	World	UN27 (-)
Persons employed	By industry (NACE)	nos	No		EC	EC76
Persons employed	By industry,	nos	No		EC	EC53 (3.1)
	by economic activity	nos	No		EC, USA and Japan	EC53 (1.1)
Persons employed	By NACE by size of enterprise	nos	Yes	A	EC	EC77 (-)
Persons employed per production unit	By industry (NACE)	nos	No		EC	EC76
Persons engaged	Average number	nos	Yes	A	World	UN27 (-)
Total	By ISIC division	nos	Yes	A	OECD	OECD16
Workers in industrial production	By country	nos	No		EC	EC18 (8.4)
25.9.3 Enterprises						
Employing 20 or more persons	By industry	nos	No		EC	EC53 (4.1)
Enterprises	By ISIC division	nos	Yes	A	OECD	OECD16
Enterprises, number of	By NACE	nos	No		EC	EC75 (2)
Enterprises, number of	By NACE by size of enterprise	nos	Yes	A	EC	EC77 (-)
Establishments	By size, persons engaged	nos,%	No		Nordic countries	NCM1 (80)
Establishments, number		nos	Yes	A	World	UN27 (-)
Foreign-owned industrial enterprises	By industry	nos	No		Nordic countries	NCM1 (82)
Importance of, employing less than 20 persons	By industry, turnover	nos,%, ECU	No		EC	EC53 (4.2)

Subject	Categories	Units	Time series Yes/No	Frequency	Territorial coverage	Source (Table No.)
Importance of, employing between 20-99 persons	By industry, gross value added at factor cost	nos,%	No		EC	EC53 (4.3)
Industrial undertakings and workers	By country	nos	No		EC	EC18 (8.2)
Large licensed industrial establishments	By product, by production capacity	tonnes, nat curr	No		Bahrain Emirates	CH1 (8.1)
Production Units	By industry (NACE)	nos	No		EC	EC76
Statistical units		nos	No		World	UN50 (90)
Undertakings	By country, by sector	nos	No		EC	EC18 (8.1)
25.9.4 Expectations						
Capacity utilization	By industry	nos	Yes	A	EC	EC70
Duration of assured production	By industry	nos	Yes	A	EC	EC70
Employment expectations	By industry	nos	Yes	A	EC	EC70
Estimates and Forecasts		indices	Yes	6 M	EC	EC70
Export expectations	By industry	nos	Yes	A	EC	EC70
Export order books	By industry	nos	Yes	M	EC	EC70
Industry survey	By industry	indices	No		EC	EC70
Investment trents and prospects	By industry	nos	Yes	6 M	EC	EC70
Limits to production	By industry	nos	Yes	A	EC	EC70
New orders, recent	By industry	nos	Yes	A	EC	EC70
Order books	By industry	nos	Yes	M	EC	EC70
Order books	By industry	indices	Yes	M	EC	EC70
Orders, expectations	By industry	indices	No		EC	EC70
Production capacity	By industry	nos	Yes	A	EC	EC70
Production expectations	By industry	nos	Yes	M	EC	EC70
Production trend	By industry	nos	Yes	M	EC	EC70
Selling price expectations	By industry	nos	Yes	M	EC	EC70
Stocks of finished products	By industry	nos	Yes	M	EC	EC70
Stocks of raw materials	By industry	nos	Yes	A	EC	EC70
25.9.5 Investments - see also Section 34						
Gross fixed capital formation	Machinery and equipment	nat curr	Yes	A	World	UN27 (-)
Gross fixed capital formation	Total	nat curr	Yes	A	World	UN27 (-)
Gross investment	By selected branches of industry, by country	nat curr	Yes	A	VICES countries	VICES1 (I/4)
Industrial investments	By industry	Nat curr	Yes	A	Nordic countries	NCM1 (81)
Investment	By industrial sector	US$	No		United Arab Emirates	CH1 (8.16)
Investment	By industry	ECU	No		EC	EC53 (3.5)
Investment	By ISIC division	nat curr	Yes	A	OECD	OECD16
Investment of foreign capital	By activity	US$	No		Saudi Arabia	CH1 (8.14)
Investment per person employed	By industry (NACE)	ECU	No		EC	EC76
Investment rates	Investment as a percentage of gross value-added at factor cost, by industry	%	No		EC	EC53 (3.9)
Investment, industrial		indices	Yes	A	OECD	OECD33 (11.3)
Investment, machinery and equipment	By ISIC division	nat curr	Yes	A	OECD	OECD16
Investments	By industry (NACE)	ECU	No		EC	EC76
Investments	By industry: Investment as a percentage of gross value-added at factor cost; Water supply; Extraction of minerals, peat; Non-metallic mineral products					

Subject	Categories	Units	Time series Yes/No Frequency		Territorial coverage	Source (Table No.)
	Office, data processing machinery					
	Timber, wooden furniture					
	Paper, paper products, printing, publishing					
	Rubber, plastics					
	other manufacturing industries					
	Building, civil engineering					
	Man-made fibres					
	Mechanical engineering					
	Electrical engineering					
	Food, drink, tobacco					
	Textile industry					
	Leather, leather goods					
	Footwear, clothing					
Investments	By NACE	ECU	No		EC	EC75 (2)
25.9.6 Labour Costs and Hours						
Compensation of employees	By industry	ECU	No		EC	EC69 (III.4)
Hours or days worked, operatives		nos	Yes	A	World	UN27 (-)
Labour costs	By industry	ECU	No		EC	EC53 (3.4)
Labour costs	By NACE	ECU	No		EC	EC75 (2), (3.1)
Labour costs	By NACE by size of enterprise	ECU	Yes	A	EC	EC77 (-)
Labour costs per person employed	By industry	ECU	No		EC	EC53 (3.8)
Manhours	By ISIC division	nos	Yes	A	OECD	OECD16
Total	By ISIC group	%	No		World	UNIDO1 (2.6)
Wages	By ISIC group	US$	Yes	I	World	UNIDO1 (1.12, 2.5)
Wages and salaries		nat curr	Yes	A	World	UN27 (-)
Wages and salaries	By industry (NACE):	ECU	No		EC	EC76 (-)
	Water supply, collection, purification and distribution					
	Paper, paper products, printing, publishing, manufacture of					
	Mechanical engineering					
	Office, data processing machinery, manufacture of					
	Electrical engineering					
	Motor vehicles, parts, accessories, manufacture of					
	Other means of transport					
	Food, drink, tobacco industry					
	Instrument engineering					
	Timber, wooden furniture industry					
	Rubber, plastics, processing of					
	Other manufacturing industries					
	Building, civil engineering					
Wages and salaries	By ISIC division	nat curr	Yes	A	OECD	OECD16
Wages and salaries, operatives		nat curr	Yes	A	World	UN27 (-)
Wages and salaries, supplements	By ISIC division	nat curr	Yes	A	OECD	OECD16
Wages per employee	By ISIC group	US$	No		World	UNIDO1 (2.6)

25 INDUSTRIES

Subject	Categories	Units	Time series Yes/No Frequency		Territorial coverage	Source (Table No.)
Wages, value added		%	Yes	I	World	UNIDO1 (1.12, 2.5)
Wages, value added	By ISIC group	%	No		World	UNIDO1 (2.6)
25.9.7 Prices						
Indices	Total industry NACE 1-4, intermediate goods, capital goods industries, consumer goods, total NACE 1, NACE 2-4	indices	Yes	A, M	EC	EC52
Price indices	Total industry (intermediate goods capital goods consumer goods)	indices (nat curr, ECU)	Yes	M	EC, USA, Japan	EC52
Producer price indices	By NACE sector	indices	Yes	A, M	EC	EC52
Producer price indices	By industry groups	indices (nat curr, ECU)	Yes	M	EC, USA, Japan	EC52
Producer price indices	Total industry, intermediate goods, capital goods, consumer goods, industry	indices	Yes	M	EC, USA, Japan	EC52
Selling price, expectations	By industry sector	indices	Yes	M	EC	EC70
Producers - see Enterprises (25.9.3)						
25.9.8 Production and Stocks - see also Sections 34 and 38						
Assured production	By industry sector	months	No		EC	EC70
Building and civil engineering	Seasonally adjusted	indices	Yes	A, M	EC	EC53 (6.24)
Capital goods	Seasonally adjusted	indices	Yes	A, M	EC	EC53 (6.3)
Cement		tonnes	Yes	A	EC, USA and Japan	EC53 (1.14)
Changes in production and productivity	By industry	%	No		EC	EC35
Construction industry, EC	By type of construction	%	No		EC	EC35
Construction output	By country	index	No		EC	EM1 (0704)
Consumer goods	Seasonally adjusted	indices	Yes	A, M	EC	EC53 (6.4)
Demand-supply by industry	Selected indicators	%	No		World	UNIDO1 (2.10)
General industrial output	By country	index	No		EC	EM1 (0701)
Gross domestic product	By economic activity	ECU	No		EC, USA and Japan	EC53 (1.5)
Gross domestic product, index	By economic activity	indices	No		EC, USA and Japan	EC53 (1.6)
Gross industrial production	By country	index	No		EC	EC18 (8.5)
Gross production	By selected branches of industry, by country	nat curr	Yes	A	VICES countries and Yugoslavia	VICES1 (I/4)
Gross value added (factor cost)	By industry	ECU	No		EC	EC53 (3.2)
Gross value added per person employed (factor cost)	By industry	ECU	No		EC	EC53 (3.7)
Gross value added	By NACE by size of enterprise	ECU	Yes	A	EC	EC77
Gross value-added at market prices	By region	ECU,%	No		EC	EC53 (7.2)
Industrial production	Branch of activity	indices	Yes	A	World	UN27
Industrial production	Branch of activity developed countries	indices	Yes	A	World excluding Eastern Europe and USSR	UN27

Subject	Categories	Units	Time series Yes/No Frequency		Territorial coverage	Source (Table No.)
Industrial production	Branch of activity developing countries	indices	Yes	A	World excluding Eastern Europe and USSR	UN27
Industrial production	Branch of activity by region mechanical engineering, electrical engineering, automobile industry, by consumer item	indices	Yes	A	World excluding Eastern Europe and USSR	UN27
Industrial production,		indices	Yes	A	World	UN27
Intermediate products industry	Seasonally adjusted	indices	Yes	A, M	EC	EC53 (6.2)
Manufacture of metal articles	Seasonally adjusted	indices	Yes	A, M	EC	EC53 (6.9)
Manufacture of office and data processing machinery	Seasonally adjusted	indices	Yes	A, M	EC	EC53 (6.11)
Manufacturing	Seasonally adjusted	indices	Yes	A, M	EC	EC53 (6.1)
Manufacturing industries	By country, by product	tonnes, nos	No		EC	EC18 (8.10)
Manufacturing production	By country	index	No		EC	EM1 (0703)
Minerals, production of selected	By country, by mineral	tonnes	No		EC	EM1 (0705)
Mining and quarrying	By industry, establishments	nos	No		Nordic countries	NCM1(77)
Mining and quarrying	By industry, establishments	nos	No		Nordic countries	NCM1(78)
Mining production	By country	index	No		EC	EM1 (0702)
MVA	By ISIC group	%	No		World	UNIDO1 (2.6)
MVA	ISIC groups distribution	%	Yes	I	World	UNIDO1 (1.6)
MVA in output		%	Yes	I	World	UNIDO1 (1.12, 2.5)
MVA per employee	By ISIC group	US$	No		World	UNIDO1 (2.6)
MVA per employee	By ISIC group	US$	Yes	I	World	UNIDO1 (1.12, 2.5)
MVA, annual growth		%, indices	Yes	A	World	UNIDO1 (1.4, 2.1)
MVA, annual growth	By ISIC group	%	Yes	I	World	UNIDO1 (1.11)
MVA, developing regions share	By selected ISIC group	%	No		Developing countries	UNIDO1 (1.7)
MVA, economic groups and developing countries		%	Yes	A	World	UNIDO1 (1.1)
MVA, least developed share in developing countries	By selected ISIC group	%	Yes	I	Least developed countries	UNIDO1 (1.8)
MVA, ratio of purchased fuels to value added	By ISIC group	%	Yes	I	World	UNIDO1 (2.12)
MVA, share in GDP		%	Yes	I	World	UNIDO1 (1.5, 2.2)
MVA, structure	By economic grouping	%	Yes	I	Developing countries	UNIDO1 (1.10)
MVA, structure	By economic grouping	%	Yes	I	World	UNIDO1 (1.9)
Non-metallic mineral products	Seasonally adjusted	indices	Yes	A, M	EC	EC53 (6.7)
Ores, metals and non-metallic minerals	By NACE	tonnes, cu m, sq m, nos	Yes	A, Q	EC	EC51 (B)
Output	In producers' prices	nat curr	Yes	A	World	UN27 (-)
Output	Selected industrial products, by country	kWh, cu m, tonnes, nos, sq m, hl	Yes	A	VICES region, VICES countries and Yugoslavia	VICES1 (I/4)
Output, value added	By ISIC group	%	No		World	UNIDO1 (2.6)
Processing of plastics	Seasonally adjusted	indices	Yes	A, M	EC	EC53 (6.23)
Production		indices	Yes	A	OECD	OECD33 (11.1)

25 INDUSTRIES

Subject	Categories	Units	Time series Yes/No Frequency		Territorial coverage	Source (Table No.)
Production	By industry	ECU	No		EC	EC53 (3.3)
Production	By industry	indices	No		EC, USA and Japan	EC53 (1.8)
Production	By NACE	ECU	Yes	A	EC	EC75 (1)
Production	Total	by ISIC division nat curr	Yes	A	OECD	OECD16
Production at current prices and employment	By industry	ECU, nos	No		EC	EC35 (-)
Production expectations	By industry sector	indices	Yes	M	EC	EC70
Production indices	Total industry intermediate goods, capital goods industries, consumer goods	indices	No		EC, USA, Japan	EC52 (-)
Production indices	Total industry intermediate goods, capital goods, consumer goods, industry	indices	Yes	M	EC, USA, Japan	EC52
Production indices per working day	NACE 1-4	indices	Yes	M	EC, USA, Japan	EC52
Production value	By NACE	ECU	No		EC	EC75 (3.1)
Production, annual growth	By ISIC group	%, indices	Yes	A	World	UNIDO1 (2.4)
Production, intensities	Industrial, Chemical and basic metal	%	Yes	I	World	UNIDO1 (2.11)
Productivity	By NACE	ECU/capita	Yes	A	EC	EC75 (1)
Raw material stocks	By industry sector	indices	No		EC	EC70
Rubber manufacture	Seasonally adjusted	indices	Yes	A, M	EC	EC53 (6.22)
Share of individual industries in gross value added (factor cost)	By manufacturing industries	%	No		EC	EC53 (3.6)
Share of industry in gross value-added	Current prices and exchange rates	%	No		EC, USA and Japan	EC53 (1.7)
Soaps and detergents, production of selected	By country, by product	tonnes	No		EC	EM1 (0707)
Stocks, finished products	By industry sector	indices	Yes	M	EC	EC70
Stocks, value of	Total	nat curr	Yes	A	World	UN27 (-)
Timber and wooden furniture	Seasonally adjusted	indices	Yes	A, M	EC	EC53 (6.19)
Value added	By ISIC division	nat curr	Yes	A	OECD	OECD16
Value added	By NACE	ECU, %	Yes	A	EC	EC75 (1), (3.1)
Value added	In producers' prices	nat curr	Yes	A	World	UN27 (-)
Value of inputs and gross output	By industrial sector	US$	No		United Arab Emirates	CH1 (8.15)
25.9.9 Raw Materials						
Balance sheets, raw material consumption	By metal content	tonnes	No		EC	EC53 (8.10)
Degree of raw material dependence (technical)	By ores	imports and exports over consumnption	No		EC, USA and Japan	EC53 (1.19)
Degree of raw material dependence (technical)	By ores	imports and exports over consumption	No		EC	EC53 (8.8)
Raw material consumption		per capita	No		EC	EC53 (8.9)
Raw material consumption	By ores	per capita	No		EC, USA and Japan	EC53 (1.20)
25.9.10 Trade						
Balance of trade for manufacturing industry, EC	By country, by industry consumer goods, industry	ECU	No		Selected countries	EC35
Export volume	Total industry, intermediate goods,	indices	Yes	M	EC, USA, Japan	EC52

Subject	Categories	Units	Time series Yes/No Frequency		Territorial coverage	Source (Table No.)
Export volume	Total industry, intermediate goods, capital goods, consumer goods, industry	indices	Yes	M	EC, USA, Japan	EC52
Exports, economic groupings share		%	Yes	A	World	UNIDO1 (1.13)
Exports, selected countries share		%	Yes	I	Developing countries	UNIDO1 (1.14)
Import volume	Total industry, intermediate goods, capital goods,	indices	Yes	M	EC, USA, Japan	EC52
Manufactures	By origin, destination and country group	%, US$	Yes	I	World	UNIDO1 (1.17)
Manufactures, annual growth		%	Yes	A	World	UNIDO1 (1.15)
Manufactures, commodity trade share		%	Yes	I	World	UNIDO1 (1.16)
Manufactures, selected indicators	By end-use	indices	No		World	UNIDO1 (1.19)
Manufactures, selected indicators	By end-use and R&D intensity	indices	Yes	I	World	UNIDO1 (2.8)
Manufactures, selected indicators	By group	%	No		World	UNIDO1 (2.9)
Manufactures, selected indicators	By R&D intensity	indices	No		World	UNIDO1 (1.18)
Merchandise, selected indicators		indices	Yes	I	World	UNIDO1 (2.7)
Raw materials	By country of origin and raw material type	tonnes, %	Yes	I	EC	EC68 (-)
Structure of trade	By ISIC group	%	Yes	I	World	UNIDO1 (2.3)
25.9.11 Trends						
Employees	Total industry, intermediate goods, capital goods, consumer goods, industry	indices	Yes	M	EC, USA, Japan	EC52
Export volume	Total industry, intermediate goods, capital goods, consumer goods, industry	indices	Yes	M	EC, USA, Japan	EC52
Import volume	Total industry, intermediate goods, capital goods, consumer goods, industry	indices	Yes	M	EC, USA, Japan	EC52
New orders	By industry sector	indices	No		EC	EC70
Order books	By industry sector	indices	Yes	M	EC	EC70
Price indices	Total industry (intermediate goods capital goods consumer goods)	indices nat curr, ECU	Yes	M	EC, USA, Japan	EC52
Producer price indices	By industry groups	indices nat curr, ECU	Yes	M	EC, USA, Japan	EC52
Producer price indices	Total industry, intermediate goods, capital goods, consumer goods, industry	indices	Yes	M	EC, USA, Japan	EC52

25 INDUSTRIES

Subject	Categories	Units	Time series Yes/No Frequency		Territorial coverage	Source (Table No.)
Production indices	Total industry intermediate goods, capital goods industries, consumer goods	indices	No		EC, USA, Japan	EC52
Production indices	Total industry intermediate goods, capital goods, consumer goods, industry	indices	Yes	M	EC, USA, Japan	EC52
Production indices per working day	NACE 1-4	indices	Yes	M	EC, USA, Japan	EC52
Trends	By industry sector	indices	Yes	M	EC	EC70
Turnover indices	Total industry, intermediate goods, capital goods, consumer goods, industry	indices	Yes	M	EC, USA, Japan	EC52
25.9.12 Turnover						
Capital goods	Seasonally adjusted	indices	Yes	A, M	EC	EC53 (6.27)
Chemical industry, including including man-made fibres	Seasonally adjusted	indices	Yes	A, M	EC	EC53 (6.30)
Consumer goods	Seasonally adjusted	indices	Yes	A, M	EC	EC53 (6.28)
Electrical engineering	Seasonally adjusted	indices	Yes	A, M	EC	EC53 (6.33)
Food, drink and tobacco industry	Seasonally adjusted	indices	Yes	A, M	EC	EC53 (6.35)
Intermediate products	Seasonally adjusted	indices	Yes	A, M	EC	EC53 (6.26)
Manufacture of metal articles	Seasonally adjusted	indices	Yes	A, M	EC	EC53 (6.31)
Manufacturing	Seasonally adjusted	indices	Yes	A, M	EC	EC53 (6.25)
Mechanical engineering	Seasonally adjusted	indices	Yes	A, M	EC	EC53 (6.32)
Motor vehicles, parts and accessories	Seasonally adjusted	indices	Yes	A, M	EC	EC53 (6.34)
Production and preliminary processing of metals	Seasonally adjusted	indices	Yes	A, M	EC	EC53 (6.29)
Textile industry	Seasonally adjusted	indices	Yes	A, M	EC	EC53 (6.36)
Turnover	By NACE	ECU	No		EC	EC75 (2)
Turnover	By NACE by size of enterprise	ECU	Yes	A	EC	EC77
Turnover indices	Total industry, intermediate goods, capital goods, consumer goods, industry	indices	Yes	M	EC, USA, Japan	EC52
25.10 IRON, STEEL AND OTHER METALS - see also under General (25.9) and Section 32						
25.10.1 Capacity						
Blast furnaces - dimensions		cm	Yes	5 yr	EC	EC55 (2.6)
Blast furnaces in use	By number lined with silicon carbide	nos	No		Western World	EAT1 (7.5)
Capacity for crude steel		tonnes	No		OECD, EC	OECD18 (30)
Capacity for pig iron		tonnes	No		OECD, EC	OECD18 (29)
Crude iron - capacity and capacity utilization in production plants		tonnes, %	Yes	A	EC	EC55 (3.4)
Crude steel - capacity and capacity utilization in production plants	By member country, by process	tonnes, %	Yes	A	EC	EC55 (3.13)
Refractories installed in blast furnaces	By bond system application	tonnes, nos,	No		Western World	EAT1 (7.6)
Silicon carbide, production facilities	By location, capacity	tonnes	No		World	EAT1 (4.2)
Steel capacity		tonnes	Yes	A	USA, EC and Japan	OECD45 (7)
Steel capacity		tpe	Yes	A	EC	OECD45 (8)
Steel capacity		tpe	Yes	A	Other Western Europe and Mexico	OECD45 (9)

Subject	Categories	Units	Time series Yes/No Frequency		Territorial coverage	Source (Table No.)
Steel capacity utilisation		%	Yes	A	EC	OECD45 (8)
Steel capacity utilisation		%	Yes	A	Other Western Europe and Mexico	OECD45 (9)
Steel capacity utilisation		%	Yes	A	USA, EC and Japan	OECD45 (7)
Steelmaking plants	By capacity class	nos	Yes	5 yr	EC	EC55 (2.7)
Tungsten, mine production capacity		tonnes	Yes	I	World	UNCTAD3 (2.4)

25.10.2 Consumption - see also under Steel Market Balance Sheets (25.10.9)

Subject	Categories	Units	Time series Yes/No Frequency		Territorial coverage	Source (Table No.)
Coke - consumption by department	Sinter plants, blast furnaces,	tonnes	Yes	A	EC	EC55 (2.22)
Coke-oven coke	Total and blast furnaces	tonnes	No		OECD, EC	OECD18 (12)
Consumption, estimated	By microgrits, powders, fibres, whiskers	tonnes	No		World	EAT1 (6.4)
Crude steel - apparent consumption	Final consumption	tonnes, kg per capita	Yes	A	EC	EC55 (6.3)
ECSC steel - apparent consumption	In crude steel equivalent	tonnes kg per capita	Yes	A	EC	EC55 (6.1)
ECSC steel and non-ECSC steel - apparent consumption	In crude steel equivalent	tonnes kg per capita	Yes	A	EC	EC55 (6.2)
Energy - consumption and delivery	By fuel type	tonnes, GJ kWh	Yes	A	EC	EC55 (2.23)
Iron and major alloying metals	By metal type	tonnes	No		EC	EC68 (-)
Iron ore	Total and by percentage iron content	tonnes	No		OECD	OECD18 (9)
Iron ore - sinter consumption		tonnes, kg/t	Yes	A	EC	EC55 (2.11)
Iron ore consumption by department	Sinter plants, blast furnaces, steelworks	tonnes	Yes	A	EC	EC55 (2.12)
Manganese ore consumption by department	Sinter plants, blast furnaces, melting shops	tonnes	Yes	A	EC	EC55 (2.13)
Manganese ore, total		tonnes	No		OECD, EC	OECD18 (10)
Metals	By type	tonnes	Yes	A	EC	EC68 (-)
Metals	Mercury, antimony, titanium and zirconium	tonnes	No		EC	EC68 (-)
Non-ferrous metals	By metal type	tonnes	No		EC	EC68 (-)
Pig-iron, spiegel and high-carbon ferromanganese - consumption	Independent steel foundries, melting shops,	tonnes	Yes	A	EC	EC55 (2.16)
Pyrite residues consumption	Sinter plants	tonnes	Yes	A	EC	EC55 (2.14)
Raw materials consumption in in independent steel foundries	By type	tonnes	Yes	A	EC	EC55 (2.25)
Rolled products, apparent home consumption	By type	tonnes	No		OECD, EC	OECD18 (22)
Scrap		tonnes	No		OECD, EC	OECD18 (13)
Scrap consumption by department	Blast furnaces, melting shops, rolling mills, independent steel foundries	tonnes	Yes	A	EC	EC55 (2.18)

25 INDUSTRIES

Subject	Categories	Units	Time series Yes/No Frequency		Territorial coverage	Source (Table No.)
Scrap consumption by steel categories		tonnes	Yes	A	EC	EC55 (2.19)
Silicon carbide grain consumption, apparent	By geographic area	tonnes	Yes	A	World	EAT1 (6.1)
Steel consumption, real	By consuming branch	tonnes, %	Yes	A	EC	EC55 (6.5)
Steel consumption, real	By product category	tonnes	Yes	A	EC	EC55 (6.4)
Steel consumption	By branch and ECSC product, % of total consumption, % of all products	tonnes	Yes	A	EC	EC74 (1.1-1.13)
Steel consumption	By branch and non-ECSC product, % of total consumption, % of all products	tonnes	Yes	A	EC	EC74 (2.1- 2.11)
Steel consumption, apparent		tpe, %	Yes	A	World	OECD45 (1)
Steel industry raw materials	By type	tonnes	No		EC, USA, Canada and Japan	UN11 (5)
Steel production, crude		tonnes, %	Yes	A	World	OECD45 (3)
Steel, apparent home consumption	Percentage imports, share in	tonnes, %	No		OECD, EC	OECD18 (21)
Works deliveries of ECSC steel products	By type of product	tonnes, %	Yes	A	EC	EC55 (4.4)
Works deliveries of ordinary steel ingots and semis	By country of origin, By country of destination	tonnes	Yes	A	EC	EC55 (4.2)
Works deliveries of steel	Ordinary steel, special steel, market inter-penetration	tonnes, %	Yes	A	EC	EC55 (4.5)
Works home market deliveries of ordinary steel	By consuming industry	tonnes	Yes	A	EC	EC55 (4.3)
25.10.3 Employment and Hours Worked						
Employees in industry	Yearly average	nos	Yes	A	EC	EC55 (2.2)
Employees in iron and steel industry	Total employees, total registered workers, total foreign workers, workers from third countries	nos	Yes	A	EC	EC55 (2.1)
Employment, metal articles		nos	No		EC	EC76
Employment, metalliferous ores extraction and preparation		nos	No		EC	EC76
Employment, metals, production and preliminary processing		nos	No		EC	EC76
Hourly wage, gross, manual workers		nat curr	Yes	A	EC	EC55 (8.17)
Hours worked		hours	No		OECD	OECD18 (19)
Labour costs, hourly, manual and non-manual workers		nat curr	Yes	A	EC	EC55 (8.18)
Manpower	By numbers employed	nos, % change	Yes	A	OECD	OECD45 (10)
Manpower	Total and process workers	tonnes	No		OECD, EC	OECD18 (18)
25.10.4 Enterprises						
Crude steel producers	The 30 most important organisations	tonnes	Yes	A	World	EC55 (3.12)
Size of iron and steel enterprises	Crude steel production	tonnes/year	Yes	A	EC	EC55 (2.3)
Size of iron and steelworks	Crude steel production	tonnes/year	Yes	A	EC	EC55 (2.4)
Tungsten	By type of mine, number of mines operating	tonnes, nos	Yes	A	World	UNCTAD3 (2.2)

Subject	Categories	Units	Time series Yes/No Frequency		Territorial coverage	Source (Table No.)
25.10.5 General						
EC iron and steel industry, main indicators for	By indicator	tonnes, nos	No		EC	EC35 (-)
25.10.6 Investments						
ECSC iron and steel industry	By production sectors	ECU	Yes	A	EC	EC55 (7.4)
ECSC iron and steel industry and iron ore mining industry		ECU	Yes	A	EC	EC55 (7.2)
Gross investments in fixed assets	All industries, iron and steel industry	ECU	Yes	A	EC	EC55 (7.1)
Investment expenditure, actual	In relation to crude steel production	US$ /tonne	No		OECD	OECD18 (24)
Investment expenditure, annual	Percentage breakdown by sector	US$, %	No		OECD	OECD18 (23)
Investments per tonne produced and production capacity	Iron and steel industry, Iron ore mining industry	ECU	Yes	A	EC	EC55 (7.3)
Metal articles		ECU	No		EC	EC76 (-)
Metalliferous ores		ECU	No		EC	EC76 (-)
Metals		ECU	No		EC	EC76 (-)
Tungsten, investment in new mining and processing capacities	Project, company, capacity, completion date	tonnes	No		World	UNCTAD3 (2.5)
25.10.7 Prices						
ECSC basic prices	By product	nat curr/tonne	Yes	A	EC	EC55 (8.2-8.13)
Scrap foreign trade-average values		ECU/tonne	Yes	A	EC	EC55 (8.14)
Iron and steel foreign trade - average values	By type of product	ECU/tonne	Yes	A	EC	EC55 (8.16)
Iron ore imports - average values	By country or origin	ECU/tonne	Yes	A	EC	EC55 (8.15)
Levy rate	By type of product	levy/tonne	Yes	A	EC	EC55 (9.1)
Prices home, iron and steel products	By type	US$, nat curr	No		OECD	OECD18 (27)
Prices, continental producers for iron and steel products	By type	US$ /tonne	Yes	I	OECD	OECD18 (28)
Prices, iron-ore		nat curr ind	Yes	M	OECD	OECD18 (25)
Prices, scrap		ind	Yes	A	OECD	OECD18 (26)
Share of ECSC levy	By country	%	Yes	A	EC	EC55 (9.2)
producer prices		nat curr, ECU	Yes	A	EC	EC55 (8.1)
Producers - see Enterprises (25.10.4)						
25.10.8 Production and Stocks - see also under Steel Market Balance Sheets (25.10.9)						
Alloy steel, total		tonnes	No		OECD, EC	OECD18 (6)
By-products of blast furnace and steel furnace	By by-product	tonnes	Yes	A	EC	EC55 (3.26)
Coils - products obtained		tonnes	Yes	A	EC	EC55 (3.19)
Coke - production		tonnes, %	Yes	A	EC	EC55 (2.21)
Coke-oven coke, national output		tonnes	No		OECD, EC	OECD18 (11)
Crude iron		tonnes, %	Yes	A	World	EC55 (3.3)
Crude iron	By country	tonnes	Yes	A	EC	EC55 (3.5)
Crude iron	By grade	tonnes, %	Yes	A	EC	EC55 (3.6)
Crude iron - foundry	Phosphoric non-phosphoric	tonnes, %	Yes	A	EC	EC55 (3.8)
Crude iron - special		tonnes, %	Yes	A	EC	EC55 (3.10)
Crude iron for steelmaking	Phosphoric, non-phosphoric	tonnes, %	Yes	A	EC	EC55 (3.7)
Crude steel		tonnes, %	Yes	A	World	EC55 (3.11)
Crude steel	By member countries	tonnes	Yes	A	EC	EC55 (3.14)
Crude steel	By process	tonnes, %	Yes	A	EC	EC55 (3.16)
Crude steel	Ingots, continuously cast, liquid steel for casting	tonnes	Yes	A	EC	EC55 (3.15)
Crude steel	Total, percentage variation and amount of cast	tonnes, %	No		OECD	OECD18 (4)

25 INDUSTRIES

Subject	Categories	Units	Time series Yes/No Frequency		Territorial coverage	Source (Table No.)
Crude steel	Total, percentage variation and percentage of world total	tonnes, %	No		World, OECD	OECD18 (2)
Crude steel balance	ECSC steel non-ECSC steel and steel products	tonnes	Yes	A	EC	EC55 (1.3)
Crude steel output	By process, total and percentage of steel output	tonnes, %	No		OECD	OECD18 (5)
Crude steel output per worker		indices	No		OECD	OECD18 (20)
Energy - solid fuel receipts	By type, by origin	tonnes	Yes	A	EC	EC55 (2.24)
Industrial activity	In iron ore mining, iron and steel industry first transformatin of iron and steel	various	Yes	A	EC	EC55 (1.4)
Industrial production, indices of	NACE	indices	Yes	A	EC	EC55 (1.2)
Iron and major alloying metals	By metal type	tonnes	No		EC	EC68 (-)
Iron or, merchantable	Total and by percentage iron content	tonnes	No		OECD, EC	OECD18 (8)
Iron ore, commercial production		tonnes	Yes	A	EC	EC55 (2.10)
Iron ore, production and stocks		tonnes	Yes	A	EC	EC55 (2.9)
Iron products of the steel industry	By type	tonnes	Yes	A, Q	EC, USA, Canada and Japan	UN11 (1)
Liquid steel for castings from independent steel foundries	By process	tonnes, %	Yes	A	EC	EC55 (3.24)
Metals	By type	tonnes	Yes	A	EC	EC68 (-)
Metals	Mercury, antimony, titanium and zirconium	tonnes	No		EC	EC68 (-)
Metals, selected	By country, by metal	tonnes	No		EC	EM1 (0706)
Non-ferrous metals	By metal type	tonnes	No		EC	EC68 (-)
Pig-iron and ferro-alloys	Total and percentage variation	tonnes, %	No		OECD	OECD18 (3)
Pig-iron and ferro-alloys	Total, percentage variation and percentage of world total	tonnes, %	No		World, OECD	OECD18 (1)
Pig-iron, spiegel and high-carbon ferromanganese	By steel category	tonnes	Yes	A	EC	EC55 (2.15)
Primary iron and steel processing	By process	tonnes	Yes	A	EC	EC55 (3.25)
Production and preliminary processing of metals	Seasonally adjusted	indices	Yes	A, M	EC	EC53 (6.6)
Production ratios	By product type	%-kg/t	Yes	A	EC	EC55 (3.1)
Production share	By product type	%	Yes	A	EC	EC55 (3.2)
Rolled steel products	By product group	tonnes, %	Yes	A	EC	EC55 (3.18)
Scrap production, consumption and supply	Supply, use	tonnes	Yes	A	EC	EC55 (2.20)
Share of crude steel production	By the largest works	%, tonnes	Yes	A	EC	EC55 (2.5)
Silicon carbide grain production	By major producing countries	tonnes	Yes	A	Selected countries	EAT1 (4.1)
Silicon carbide production	By microgrits, powders, fibres, whiskers	tonnes/US$	Yes	A	World	EAT1 (4.3)
Sound steel castings		tonnes, %	Yes	A	EC	EC55 (3.23)
Special steels	By type	tonnes	Yes	A	EC	EC55 (3.17)
Spiegel and high-carbon ferromanganese		tonnes, %	Yes	A	EC	EC55 (3.9)
Stainless steel	Total, in ingot and liquid forms for casting	tonnes	No		OECD	OECD18 (7)
Steel industry raw materials	By type	tonnes	Yes	A, Q	EC, USA, Canada and Japan	UN11 (1)
Steel products, finished and semi-finished	By type	tonnes	Yes	A, Q	EC, USA, Canada and Japan	UN11 (2)
Steel scrap balance	Supply, use	tonnes	Yes	A	EC	EC55 (2.17)
Steel, end products	By type of product	tonnes	Yes	A	EC	EC55 (3.20)
Steel, finished	By type of product	tonnes	Yes	A	EC	EC55 (3.21)
Steel, finished and end products	By type of product	tonnes	Yes	A	EC	EC55 (3.22)

Subject	Categories	Units	Time series Yes/No Frequency		Territorial coverage	Source (Table No.)
Steel, high speed	Total, in ingot and liquid forms for casting	tonnes	No		OECD	OECD18 (7)
Tungsten	By type of mine, number of mines operating	tonnes, nos	Yes	A	World	UNCTAD3 (2.2)
Tungsten products	By type	tonnes	Yes	A	World	UNCTAD3 (2.6)
Tungsten, co-production of other metals from mines	Tin, copper, bismuth, molybdenum sulphide	tonnes	Yes	A	World	UNCTAD3 (2.3)
Tungsten, ores and concentrates		tonnes	Yes	A	World	UNCTAD3 (2.1)
Works deliveries of steel	For home market, other ECSC countries third countries	tonnes, indices	Yes	A	EC	EC55 (4.1)
25.10.9 Steel Market Balance Sheets - see also under Consumption (25.10.2), Production and Stocks (25.10.8) and Trade (25.10.10)						
Apparent consumption		tpe	Yes	A	EC	OECD45 (8)
Apparent consumption		tpe	Yes	A	Other Western Europe and Mexico	OECD45 (9)
Crude steel production		tonnes	Yes	A	USA, EC and Japan	OECD45 (7)
Crude steel production		tpe	Yes	A	EC	OECD45 (8)
Crude steel production		tpe	Yes	A	Other Western Europe and Mexico	OECD45 (9)
Deliveries		tonnes	Yes	A	USA, EC and Japan	OECD45 (7)
Exports		tonnes	Yes	A	USA, EC and Japan	OECD45 (7)
Exports		tpe	Yes	A	EC	OECD45 (8)
Exports		tpe	Yes	A	Other Western Europe and Mexico	OECD45 (9)
Imports		tonnes	Yes	A	USA, EC and Japan	OECD45 (7)
Imports		tpe	Yes	A	EC	OECD45 (8)
Imports		tpe	Yes	A	Other Western Europe and Mexico	OECD45 (9)
Markets		tonnes	Yes	A	USA, EC and Japan	OECD45 (7)
Production		tonnes	Yes	A	USA, EC and Japan	OECD45 (7)
Production		tpe	Yes	A	EC	OECD45 (8)
Production		tpe	Yes	A	Other Western Europe and Mexico	OECD45 (9)
Production, imports, exports, balance, consumption		tonnes	Yes	A	World	OECD45 (4,5,6)
Real consumption		tonnes	Yes	A	USA, EC and Japan	OECD45 (7)
Real consumption		tpe	Yes	A	EC	OECD45 (8)
Stocks		tonnes	Yes	A	USA, EC and Japan	OECD45 (7)
Stocks		tpe	Yes	A	EC	OECD45 (8)
Stocks producers		tonnes	Yes	A	USA, EC and Japan	OECD45 (7)
25.10.10 Trade - see also under Steel Market Balance Sheets (25.10.9)						
Alloy steels	By products and steel type	tonnes	No		OECD	OECD18 (16,17)
ECSC	By product groups	tonnes	Yes	A	EC, Africa, America, Asia, Oceania	EC55 (5.6)
ECSC and non-ECSC steel		tonnes	Yes	A	EC	EC55 (5.8)
ECSC products in total foreign trade	By type of product	ECU, %	Yes	A	EC	EC55 (5.3)
ECSC steel products	Internal trade, imports, exports	tonnes, %	Yes	A	EC	EC55 (5.5)
Exports from Japan	By product type	tonnes, %	Yes	A	World	EC55 (5.10)
Foreign trade - indirect	In crude steel equivalent	tonnes	Yes	A	EC	EC55 (5.11)
Foreign trade by markets	Pig-iron, ECSC steel, alloy steels	tonnes, %	Yes	A	EC, Africa, America, Asia, Oceania	EC55 (5.7)
Foreign trade of USA	By product type	tonnes	Yes	A	World	EC55 (5.9)
Foreign trade ratios	Import and export shares, net exports	tonnes, %	Yes	A	EC	EC55 (5.1)

Subject	Categories	Units	Time series Yes/No Frequency		Territorial coverage	Source (Table No.)
Import share		%	Yes	A	USA, EC and Japan	OECD45 (7)
Iron and major alloying metals	By metal type	tonnes	No		EC	EC68 (-)
Iron and steel scrap, movements	By type of movement	tonnes	No		EC, USA, Canada and Japan	UN11 (6)
Metals	By type	tonnes	Yes	A	EC	EC68 (-)
Metals	Mercury, antimony, titanium and zirconium	tonnes	No		EC	EC68 (-)
Non-ferrous metals	By metal type	tonnes	No		EC	EC68 (-)
Raw material supplies dependence		%	No		EC, USA, Japan	EC55 (5.2)
Scrap		tonnes	No		OECD, EC	OECD18 (13)
Scrap - internal and foreign trade	By type of scrap	tonnes, %	Yes	A	EC	EC55 (5.12)
Silicion carbide, exports	By exporting country	tonnes	Yes	A	World	EAT1 (5.3a)
Silicion carbide, exports	By exporting country	US$	Yes	A	World	EAT1 (5.3b)
Silicion carbide, exports, recorded	By country, type	tonnes/US$	Yes	A	World	EAT1 (5.5)
Silicion carbide, imports	By country	tonnes	Yes	A	World	EAT1 (5.4a)
Silicion carbide, imports	By country	US$	Yes	A	World	EAT1 (5.4b)
Silicion carbide, imports	By geographic area, quantity, value, average value	tonnes/US$ US$/tonne	Yes	A	World	EAT1 (5.2)
Silicion carbide, imports, recorded	By country, type	tonnes/US$	Yes	A	World	EAT1 (5.6)
Silicon carbide grain trade	By end use	tonnes	No		World	EAT1 (6.3)
Silicon carbide grain trade	By production, exports, imports, apparent consumption	tonnes	Yes	A	World	EAT1 (6.2)
Silicon carbide, exports	By geographic area, quantity, value, average value	tonnes/US$, US$/tonne	Yes	A	World	EAT1 (5.1)
Steel		tonnes	No		OECD, EC	OECD18 (14,15)
Steel	Direct and indirect	crude equiv.	Yes	A	EC	EC55 (5.4)
Steel industry deliveries and receipts	By product type	tonnes	No		EC, USA, Canada and Japan	UN11 (3)
Steel industry raw materials	By type	tonnes	Yes	A, Q	EC, USA, Canada and Japan	UN11 (4)
Steel products	By type	tonnes	Yes	A, Q	EC, USA, Canada and Japan	UN11 (4)
Trade balance, imports and exports		tonnes	Yes	A	Selected countries	OECD45 (2)

25.11 MECHANICAL ENGINEERING - see also under General (25.9)

EC mechanical engineering industry, trade	By country, by imports, exports, balance of trade	ECU	No		Selected countries	EC35 (-)
Mechanical engineering in the EC, main indicators	By indicator	ECU, nos	No		EC	EC35 (-)
Production	Seasonally adjusted	indices	Yes	A, M	EC	EC53 (6.10)
Products	By NACE	ECU, nos	Yes	A	EC	EC51 (A)

25.12 PAPER and BOARD - see also under General (25.9)

25.12.1 Capacity

Capacity utilization ratios	By country, period	tonnes	No		Seleted countries	JP1 (-)
Major changes in newsprint capacity, shut downs	By mill, total capacity, grades	tonnes	No		North America	JP1 (-)
Making, production capacity						(VI)
Paper and paperboard, production capacity	By country	tonnes	No		OECD	OECD38 (VI)
Paper and paperboard, production capacity	By country	tonnes	Yes	A	OECD	OECD38 (XI)

Subject	Categories	Units	Time series Yes/No Frequency	Territorial coverage	Source (Table No.)
Recent start-ups and expected near-term, start-ups, shut downs	By mill, total and market capacity, grades, period	tonnes	No	World	JP1 (-)
Recent start-ups and expected near-term start-ups	By mill, total capacity, grades	tonnes	No	Selected countries	JP1 (-)
Woodpulp for paper and paperboard	By country	tonnes	No	OECD	OECD38
Woodpulp for paper and paperboard making, production capacity	By country	tonnes	Yes A	OECD	OECD38 (VIII)
25.12.2 Consumption					
Chemical		tonnes; %	Yes A	EFTA and EC	EPI1 (-)
Consumption	By country	tonnes	Yes A	World	BPB1 (-)
Consumption	Total	tonnes; %	Yes A	EFTA and EC	EPI1 (-)
Consumption, apparent	Total	tonnes; %	Yes A	EFTA and EC	EPI1 (-)
Mechanical		tonnes; %	Yes A	EFTA and EC	EPI1 (-)
Paper and board	By country, total and annual variations	tonnes, %	Yes A	OECD	OECD38 (V)
Paper and board, per capita	By country	kg	Yes A	OECD	OECD38 (VII)
Use of waste paper	Total	tonnes; %	Yes A	EFTA and EC	EPI1 (-)
Woodpulp	By country, total and annual variations	tonnes, %	Yes A	OECD	OECD38 (IV)
25.12.3 Enterprises					
Producers	By country	tonnes	Yes 5 A	World	BPB1 (-)
25.12.4 Prices					
Linerboard	By country,	nat curr/tonnes	No	Selected countries	JP1 (-)
Market pulp	By type, period	nat curr/tonnes, c.i.f,	No	Western Europe, North America	JP1 (-)
Newsprint	By market, grades	nat curr/tonnes, lb, grammes/ sq m	No	Selected countries	JP1 (-)
Prices	By market, grades	nat curr/tonnes	No	USA, Germany	JP1 (-)
Printing and writings	By market, grades	nat curr/tonnes	No	Selected countries	JP1 (-)
Sack and other kraft papers	By market, grades	nat curr/tonnes	No	Germany, USA	JP1 (-)
Producers - see Enterprises (25.12.3)					
25.12.5 Production					
Case materials	By production	tonnes; %	Yes A	EFTA and EC	EPI1 (-)
Chemical	By production	tonnes; %	Yes A	EFTA and EC	EPI1 (-)
Coated graphic paper	By production, coated mechanical, coated woodfree	tonnes; %	Yes A	EFTA and EC	EPI1 (-)
Coated graphic paper	By production, total	tonnes; %	Yes A	EFTA and EC	EPI1 (-)
Folding boxboard	By production	tonnes; %	Yes A	EFTA and EC	EPI1 (-)
Kraft paper production, index of	By region, country	indices	Yes A, Q	North America, Scandinavia	JP1 (-)
Kraftliner production, index of	By region	indices	Yes A, Q	North America, Scandinavia	JP1 (-)
Mechanical	By production	tonnes; %	Yes A	EFTA and EC	EPI1 (-)
Newsprint	By production, total	tonnes; %	Yes A	EFTA and EC	EPI1 (-)
Newsprint production, index of	By region	indices	No	Selected countries	JP1 (-)
Other boards	By production	tonnes; %	Yes A	EFTA and EC	EPI1 (-)
Other papers	By production	tonnes; %	Yes A	EFTA and EC	EPI1 (-)
Paper and board	By country, total and annual variations	tonnes, %	Yes A	OECD	OECD38 (V)
Paper and board production	By grade, country	tonnes	Yes A	World	PPI1 (-)
Paper and paperboard, total	By type and by country	tonnes	No	OECD	OECD38 (II)
Paper, board and pulp	By production, imports, exports	tonnes	Yes A	World	PPI1 (-)
Printing and writing paper production, index of	By region	indices	Yes A, Q	EC, Scandinavia	JP1 (-)

Subject	Categories	Units	Time series Yes/No Frequency		Territorial coverage	Source (Table No.)
Printing industries	Seasonally adjusted	indices	Yes	A, M	EC	EC53 (6.21)
Production	By country	tonnes	Yes	A	World	BPB1 (-)
Production, total,		tonnes; %	Yes	A	EFTA and EC	EPI1 (-)
Production, total,	By grade	tonnes; %	Yes	A	EFTA and EC	EPI1 (-)
Pulp and paperboard, comparison to industrial production	By country	%	Yes	A	OECD	OECD38 (III)
Pulp production	By grade, country	tonnes	Yes	A	World	PPI1 (-)
Pulp, paper and board	By NACE	tonnes	Yes	A, Q	EC	EC51 (A)
Pulp, paper and board production and trade	By country, consumption	tonnes, nos mills	Yes	A	World	PPI1 (-)
Pulp, paper and paperboard	Seasonally adjusted	indices	Yes	A, M	EC	EC53 (6.20)
Pulp, total	By type and by country	tonnes	No		OECD	OECD38 (I)
Sanitary and household	By production	tonnes; %	Yes	A	EFTA and EC	EPI1 (-)
Summary, industry	Paper and board; pulp	tonnes; %	Yes	A	EFTA and EC	EPI1 (-)
Uncoated mechanical	By production, total	tonnes; %	Yes	A	EFTA and EC	EPI1 (-)
Uncoated woodfree	By production, total	tonnes; %	Yes	A	EFTA and EC	EPI1 (-)
Woodpulp	By country, total and annual variations	tonnes, %	Yes	A	OECD	OECD38 (IV)
Woodpulp production	By region	indices	Yes	A, Q	Selected countries	JP1 (-)
Wrappings	By production	tonnes; %	Yes	A	EFTA and EC	EPI1 (-)
25.12.6 Trade						
Chemical	Exports, imports	tonnes; %	Yes	A	EFTA and EC	EPI1 (-)
Exports	Total	tonnes; %	Yes	A	EFTA and EC	EPI1 (-)
Imports	Total	tonnes; %	Yes	A	EFTA and EC	EPI1 (-)
Mechanical	Exports, imports	tonnes; %	Yes	A	EFTA and EC	EPI1 (-)
Paper and paperboard	By type and by trading countries	tonnes	No		OECD	OECD38 (13- 33)
Pulp, total	By type and by trading countries	tonnes	No		OECD	OECD38 (1-11)
Waste paper	By trading countries	tonnes	No		OECD	OECD38 (12)

25.13 TEXTILES - see also under General (25.9)

Subject	Categories	Units	Time series Yes/No Frequency		Territorial coverage	Source (Table No.)
25.13.1 Capacity						
Capacity utilization	By hours worked per year	spindle/hours,	Yes	A	World	ITMF1 (2.1)
Installed capacities	By machine type	nos	Yes	A	World	ITMF1
Loom type	By number installed	nos	No		Selected countries	ITMF2 (1.1)
Loom type	By number installed	nos	No		Selected countries	ITMF2 (2.1)
Loom type	By number installed and active looms, hours worked on active machine	nos, hours	No		Selected countries	ITMF2 (1.2-1.5)
Loom type	By number installed and activelooms, hours worked on active machine	nos, hours	No		Selected countries	ITMF2 (2.2-2.5)
25.13.2 Consumption						
Consumption	By fibre type,	tonnes	No		Selected countries	ITMF2 (3.2-3.5)
Consumption	By production, imports, exports, country	pairs	Yes	A	World	SATRA1
Consumption of textured filament yarns (excluding carpets)	By type, weaving, knitting, others	tonnes	Yes	A	EC	CIRFS1
Consumption summary	By fibre type	tonnes	No		Selected countries	ITMF2 (3.1)

Subject	Categories	Units	Time series Yes/No Frequency		Territorial coverage	Source (Table No.)
Fibre consumption	By fibre type	tonnes	Yes	A	World	ITMF1 (3.1)
Fibre consumption in textile floor coverings	By fibre type, pile	tonnes	Yes	A	EC	CIRFS1 (-)
Fibre consumption in domestic production of textile articles	By fibre type, article produced	nos, tonnes	No		EC	CIRFS1 (-)
Fibre consumption in main end-uses	By fibre, end-use	tonnes	Yes	A	EEC6, USA	CIRFS1 (-)
Fibre consumption in non-wovens	By type, end-use	tonnes	Yes	A	EEC6 + UK	CIRFS1 (-)
Mill consumption of textile fibres	By fibre type	tonnes	Yes	A	Western Europe	CIRFS1 (-)
Mill consumption of textile fibres	By fibre type, end-use	tonnes	Yes	A	EEC6 + UK	CIRFS1 (-)
25.13.3 Employment						
Employment in man-made fibre industry	By workers, administrative and technical departments	nos	Yes	A	World	CIRFS1 (-)
Manpower	By employees, hours worked average cost of labour per hour	nos, nat curr, US$	Yes	A	World	ITMF1 (2.2)
25.13.4 General						
EC textile industry, main indicators	By indicator	ECU, nos	No		EC	EC35 (-)
Producers - see Structure of Industry (25.13.6)						
25.13.5 Production						
Cellulosic, filament and staple	By country	tonnes	Yes	A	World	CIRFS1 (-)
Clothing industry	Seasonally adjusted	indices	Yes	A, M	EC	EC53 (6.18)
Cotton, wool and man-made fibres	By fibre type, yarn	tonnes, %	Yes	A	World	CIRFS1 (-)
Cotton, wool and man-made fibres by country	By fibre type, yarn,	tonnes	Yes	A	World	CIRFS1 (-)
Fabric production	By type of loom	tonnes	Yes	A	World	ITMF1 (3.3) (3.4)
Footwear manufacture	Seasonally adjusted	indices	Yes	A, M	EC	EC53 (6.17)
Leather and footwear	By NACE	tonnes, sq m, nos	Yes	A, Q	EC	EC51 (A)
Man-made fibres, textiles, clothing	By NACE	tonnes, sq m, nos	Yes	A, Q	EC	EC51 (A)
Production	By leather, non-leather, country	pairs	Yes	A	World	SATRA1
Production of selected textiles	By country, by textile	tonnes	No		EC	EM1 (0708)
Synthetic filament and staple yarn	By country	tonnes	Yes	A	World	CIRFS1 (-)
Synthetics, detailed production of	By yarn, staple	tonnes	Yes	A	Selected countries	CIRFS1 (-)
Textile industry	Seasonally adjusted	indices	Yes	A, M	EC	EC53 (6.16)
Yarn production	By type	tonnes	Yes	A	World	ITMF1 (3.2)
25.13.6 Structure of Industry						
Geographic structure	By area, employment, production, country	%	No		World	SATRA1
Industry structure	By firms and employees, country	nos	No		World	SATRA1
25.13.7 Trade						
Cellulosic filament yarn	By country of import, export	tonnes	No		EC EFTA others	CIRFS1 (-)
Cellulosic filament yarn	By import, country by export, country	tonnes	Yes	A	World	CIRFS1 (-)
Cellulosic knitted fabrics	By import, country by export, country	tonnes	Yes	A	World	CIRFS1 (-)
Cellulosic spun yarn	By country of import, export	tonnes	No		EC EFTA others	CIRFS1 (-)
Cellulosic spun yarn	By import, country by export, country	tonnes	Yes	A	World	CIRFS1 (-)

25 INDUSTRIES

Subject	Categories	Units	Time series Yes/No Frequency		Territorial coverage	Source (Table No.)
Cellulosic staple	By import, country by export, country	tonnes	Yes	A	World	CIRFS1 (-)
Cellulosic staple, carded and combed	By country of import, export	tonnes	No		EC EFTA others	CIRFS1 (-)
Cellulosic woven pure and blended filament fabrics	By country of import, export	tonnes	No		EC EFTA others	CIRFS1 (-)
Cellulosic woven pure and blended spun yarn fabrics	By country of import, export	tonnes	No		EC EFTA others	CIRFS1 (-)
Cellulosic woven pure and blended fabrics	By import, country by export, country	tonnes	Yes	A	World	CIRFS1 (-)
Cellulosic woven pure and blended spun yarn fabrics	By import, country by export, country	tonnes	Yes	A	World	CIRFS1 (-)
Cellulosic staple	By country of import, export	tonnes	No		EC EFTA others	CIRFS1 (-)
Destinations	By type installed capacity	nos	No		World	ITMF3 (1.1)
Destinations	By type of loom, installed capacity	nos	No		World	ITMF3 (2.10)
EC textile industry	By country, by imports, exports, balance of trade	ECU	No		Selected countries	EC35 (-)
Export destinations, major	By value, country pairs	nat curr	No		World	SATRA1
Import origins, major	By value, country pairs	nat curr	No		World	SATRA1
Imports and exports	By leather, textile, synthetic, rubber, clogs, other, country	pairs	Yes	A	World	SATRA1
Imports and exports in value terms	By type	US$	Yes	A	World	ITMF1 (4.1, 5.1)
Imports and exports in volume terms	By type	tonnes	Yes	A	World	ITMF1 (4.3, 5.3)
Shipments	By type installed capacity	nos	No		World	ITMF3 (1.1)
Shipments	By type of loom, installed capacity	nos	No		World	ITMF3 (2.1)
Shipments, cumulative	By type installed capacity	nos	No		World	ITMF3 (1.1)
Shipments, cumulative	By type of loom, installed capacity	nos	No		World	ITMF3 (2.1)
Synthetic filament yarn	By country of import, export	tonnes	No		EC EFTA others	CIRFS1 (-)
Synthetic filament yarn	By import, country by export, country	tonnes	Yes	A	World	CIRFS1 (-)
Synthetic knitted fabrics	By import, country by export, country	tonnes	Yes	A	World	CIRFS1 (-)
Synthetic spun yarn	By country of import, export	tonnes	No		EC EFTA others	CIRFS1 (-)
Synthetic spun yarn	By import, country by export, country	tonnes	Yes	A	World	CIRFS1 (-)
Synthetic staple	By country of import, export	tonnes	No		EC EFTA other	CIRFS1 (-)
Synthetic staple	By import, country by export, country	tonnes	Yes	A	World	CIRFS1 (-)
Synthetic staple, carded and combed	By country of import, export	tonnes	No		EC EFTA others	CIRFS1 (-)
Synthetic woven pure and blended spun yarn fabrics	By country of import, export	tonnes	No		EC EFTA others	CIRFS1 (-)
Synthetic-woven pure and blended filament fabrics	By import, country by export, country	tonnes	Yes	A	World	CIRFS1 (-)
Synthetic-woven pure and blended spun yarn fabrics	By import, country by export, country	tonnes	Yes	A	World	CIRFS1 (-)
Value of all imports and exports	By type	US$, nat curr	Yes	A	World	ITMF1 (4.2, 5.2)

Subject	Categories	Units	Time series Yes/No	Frequency	Territorial coverage	Source (Table No.)
25.14 TRANSPORT EQUIPMENT - see also under General (25.9)						
25.14.1 Motor Vehicles – see also Section 45						
Car models, top ten	Total	nos; %	No		Selected European countries	SMMT2 (35)
Cars in use, passenger	By country, by growth	nos, %	No		EC	EM1 (2105)
Cars, commercial vehicles, production of	By manufacturer; total	nos	No		Selected countries	SMMT2 (34, 36, 37,38)
Cars, production of		nos	Yes	A	Selected countries	SMMT2 (10)
Cars, production of	By country	nos	No		EC	EM1 (2103)
Cars, production of	By model	nos	Yes	A	Selected countries	SMMT2(-)
Commercial vehicles in use	By country, by growth	nos, %	No		EC	EM1 (2106)
Commercial vehicles, production of		nos	Yes	A	Selected countries	SMMT2 (11)
Diesel cars, production		nos	Yes	A	Selected countries	SMMT2 (39)
Exporters, principal	By cars and commercial vehicles	nos	Yes	A	Selected countries	SMMT2 (88)
Exports of cars and commercial vehicles	Manufacturers	nos	Yes	A	Selected countries	SMMT2 (81, 82, 83, 84, 85, 86, 87)
Exports of motor vehicles	By cars and commercial vehicles; total	nos	No		World	SMMT2 (79)
Exports, summary	By cars and commercial vehicles; total	nos;US$	Yes	A	Selected countries	SMMT2 (80)
Gross capital formation	% of total gross fixed capital formation	nat curr, %	Yes	A	EC, Canada, USA	UN13 (2)
Investments	% of total investment	indices, %	Yes	A	EC, Canada, USA	UN13 (2)
Manufacture of motor vehicles parts and accessories	Seasonally adjusted	indices	Yes	A, M	EC	EC53 (6.13)
Net material product	% of total net material product	indices, %	Yes	A	EC, Canada, USA	UN13 (2)
New registrations of commercial vehicles	By country	nos	No		EC	EM1 (2102)
New registrations of diesel cars	By country	nos	No		EC	EM1 (2107)
New registrations of new cars	By manufacturer	nos	No		Selected European countries	SMMT1(-)
New registrations of passenger cars	By country	nos	No		EC	EM1 (2101)
New registrations of two-wheelers	By country	nos	No		EC	EM1 (2110)
Penetration of unleaded petrol	By country	nos	No		EC	EM1 (2111)
Production of commercial vehicles	By country	nos	No		EC	EM1 (2104)
Production, summary	By cars and commercial vehicles; total	nos	Yes	A	Selected countries	SMMT2 (52)
Two-wheeler production	By country	nos	No		EC	EM1 (2108)
Two-wheelers in use	By country	nos	No		EC	EM1 (2109)
Value added	% of GDP	nat curr, %	Yes	A	EC, Canada, USA	UN13 (2)
Vehicles in use	By persons per car; total vehicles	nos	No		World	SMMT2 (53)
Vehicles, production of	By vehicle type; total	nos	Yes	A	Selected countries	SMMT2 (12)
25.14.2 Ships						
Commenced	Where building, by ship type	nos, GT	No		World	LRS3 (7)
Completed	Where building, by ship type	nos, GT	No		World	LRS3 (9)
Completed	Where built, by ship type	nos, tonnes dwt	No		World	LRS3 (11)
Launched	Where building, by ship type	nos, GT	No		World	LRS3 (8)
Launched ships	Where building	nos, GT	Yes	A, Q	World	LRS3 (14A)

25 INDUSTRIES

Subject	Categories	Units	Time series Yes/No Frequency		Territorial coverage	Source (Table No.)
Not commenced	Country to be built in	nos, GT	Yes	A, Q	World	LRS3 (13B)
Not commenced	Where building, by ship type	nos, GT	No		World	LRS3 (3)
Order book	Where building, under construction, not commenced, by ship type	nos, tonnes dwt	No		World	LRS3 (10)
Order book ships	Where building	nos, GT	Yes	A, Q	World	LRS3 (12)
Order book ships	Where building, under construction, not commenced	nos, GT, % of world tonnage, dwt	No		World	LRS3 (1)
Registration in the world order book ships	Where building and registration countries	nos, GT	No		World	LRS3 (6)
Ships completed	Where built	nos, GT	Yes	A, Q	World	LRS3 (14B)
Size not commenced	Country to be built in	GT	No		World	LRS3 (5)
Size under construction ships	Where building	GT	No		World	LRS3 (4)
Under construction	Where building	nos, GT	Yes	A, Q	World	LRS3 (13A)
Under construction	Where building, by ship type	nos, GT	No		World	LRS3 (2)
25.14.3 General						
EC transport equipment industry, average annual growth rate	By country	%	No		EC	EC35 (-)
EC transport equipment industry, trade	By country, by imports, exports, balance of trade	ECU	No		EC	EC35 (-)
EC transport equipment industry, main indicators	By indicator	ECU, nos	No		EC	EC35 (-)
EC's largest transport equipment companies	By company, by country, turnover, employees, net profits	ECU, nos	No		EC	EC35 (-)
Transport equipment, manufacture	By NACE	tonnes, nos	Yes	A, Q	EC	EC51 (B)
25.15 URANIUM - see also under General (25.9)						
25.15.1 Capacity						
Capability, long-term	Existing and committed centres; existing, committed, planned and prospective centres	tonnes	Yes	5 yrly	Various countries	OECD47 (15)
Capability, short-term	Existing and committed centres; existing, committed, planned and prospective centres	tonnes	Yes	5 yrly	Various countries	OECD47 (14)
Capacity, nuclear generating, long-term	Low, high demand scenarios	GWe	Yes	A	Various countries	OECD47 (18)
Nuclear electricity generating capacity, installed		MWe	Yes	A	Various countries	OECD47 (16)
25.15.2 Employment						
Employment	Person years		Yes	A	Various countries	OECD47 (13)
25.15.3 Production and Stocks						
Emissions from electricity generation	By type	rate	No		World	OECD47 (22)
Ownership	Domestic, foreign, government, private	tonnes, %	No		OECD, WOCA	OECD47 (12)
Production		tonnes	Yes	A	Various countries	OECD47 (11)
Stocks, reported	By type	tonnes	No		Various countries	OECD47 (21)

Subject	Categories	Units	Time series Yes/No Frequency		Territorial coverage	Source (Table No.)
25.15.4 Requirements						
Uranium, reactor-related		tonnes	Yes	A	Various countries	OECD47 (17)
Uranium, long-term	By reactor strategy	tonnes	Yes	A	Various countries	OECD47 (19,20)
25.15.5 Resources and Exploration						
Estimated additional	By category, by cost range	tonnes	No		Various countries	OECD47 (2,4)
Exploration expenditure		US$	Yes	A	Various countries	OECD47 (8,9)
Reasonably assured	By cost range	tonnes	No		Various countries	OECD47 (1,3)
Speculative	By cost range	tonnes	No		Various countries	OECD47 (5,6)
Unconventional and by-product	By source	tonnes	No		Various countries	OECD47 (7)

26 INTELLECTUAL PROPERTY

Subject	Categories	Units	Time series Yes/No Frequency		Territorial coverage	Source (Table no.)
26.1 INDUSTRIAL DESIGNS						
Industrial designs	Applications, deposits registered, priority claims, by country	nos	No		World	WIPO2
Industrial designs	Applications filed, deposits registered	nos	No		World	WIPO3
Industrial designs	Applications, registrations granted, in force	nos	Yes	A	World	UN50 (54)
26.2 MICRO-ORGANISMS						
Micro-organisms		nos	Yes	A	World	WIPO3
Micro-organisms	Deposits furnished during 1990 under Rule 11 of the regulations of the Budapest treaty	nos	No		World	WIPO3
Micro-organisms	Deposits made, deposits furnished, by authority	nos	No		World	WIPO2
26.3 PATENTS						
Autosufficiency ratio, resident, national patent applications	By country	nos	Yes	A	OECD	OECD24 (76)
Dependancy ratio, non-resident, resident patent applications	By country	nos	Yes	A	OECD	OECD24 (75)
Inventiveness coefficient, resident patent applications per10,000 population	By country	nos	Yes	A	OECD	OECD24 (77)
Patent applications	According to the relationship of patentee to patent office, by country	nos	Yes	A	OECD	OECD3 (20)
Patent applications	By country	nos	No		Selected countries	EC35 (-)
Patent applications	By country of origin and designated contracting states	nos	No		EC, USA, Japan	EPO1
Patent applications	By residence of applicants	nos, %	No		EC, USA, Japan	EPO1
Patent applications	Country of origin	nos	No		World	NCM1 (88)
Patent applications	Filed by, granted to	nos	No		Reporting countries	WIPO1 (I)
Patent applications	Filed by non–residents	nos	No		Reporting countries	WIPO1 (IIA)
Patent applications	Pending, according to year of filing	nos	No		Reporting countries	WIPO1 (V)
Patent applications	Priority claims according to country where first filing made	nos	No		Reporting countries	WIPO1 (IIIA)
Patent applications, external	By country of application,	nos	Yes	A	OECD	OECD3 (22)
Patent applications, external	By country	nos	Yes	A	OECD	OECD24 (74)
Patent applications, foreign	By country of origin,	nos	Yes	A	OECD	OECD3 (21)
Patent applications, national	By country	nos	Yes	A	OECD	OECD24 (71)
Patent applications, non-resident	By country	nos	Yes	A	OECD	OECD24 (73)
Patent applications, resident	By country	nos	Yes	A	OECD	OECD24 (72)
Patent applications and patents granted		nos	No		World	WIPO3

26 INTELLECTUAL PROPERTY

Subject	Categories	Units	Time series Yes/No Frequency		Territorial coverage	Source (Table No.)
Patent applications and patents granted	According to country of residence of applicant	nos	No		Reporting countries	WIPO1 (IVA)
Patent applications and patents granted	In certain countries according to technical units of IPC	technical units	No		Reporting countries	WIPO1 (IVB)
Patents	Applications, grants in force	nos	Yes	A	World	UN50 (53)
Patents granted	According to year of filing of application	nos	No		Reporting countries	WIPO1 (VII)
Patents granted	Country of origin	nos	No		World	NCM1 (89)
Patents granted	Priority claims according to country where first filing made	nos	No		Reporting countries	WIPO1 (IIIB)
Patents granted to non–residents	According to country of residence of applicant	nos	No		Reporting countries	WIPO1 (IIB)
Patents in force	According to year of granting	nos	No		Reporting countries	WIPO1 (VI)
Patents valid		nos	Yes	A	Nordic countries	NCM1 (87)
Rate of diffusion	By country	%	Yes	A	OECD	OECD24 (78)

26.4 PATENT CO-OPERATION TREATY APPLICATIONS

Designations of states	According to receiving offices	nos	No		Designated states	WIPO1 (VIIID)
Record copies received	According to receiving offices and languages of filing	nos	No		Receiving countries	WIPO1 (VIIIC)
Time limits		nos	No		Reporting countries	WIPO1 (VIIIA, B)

26.5 TRADEMARKS

Trademarks and servicemarks	Applications, registrations effected, priority claims, by class of goods, by Nice classification, by country	nos	No		World	WIPO2
Trademarks and servicemarks	Applications, registrations effected	nos	No		World	WIPO3
Trademarks and servicemarks	Applications, registrations granted, in force	nos	Yes	A	World	UN50 (55)

26.6 UTILITY MODELS

Utility models	Applications, registrations effected, priority claims, by country	nos	No		World	WIPO2
Utility models	Applications filed, registrations effected	nos	No		World	WIPO3

26.7 VARIETIES OF PLANTS

Varieties of plants	Applications filed, registrations effected	nos	No		World	WIPO3
Varieties of plants	Applications, registrations, by country	nos	No		World	WIPO2

27 INTERNATIONAL TRADE AND FINANCE

27.6 PRICES AND UNIT VALUES

27.7 TERMS OF TRADE

Subject	Categories	Units	Time series Yes/No	Frequency	Territorial coverage	Source (Table No.)

27.1 BALANCE OF PAYMENTS

27.1.1 Capital Account

Subject	Categories	Units	Time series Yes/No	Frequency	Territorial coverage	Source (Table No.)
Accounts of financial institutions		nat curr	Yes	A, M	World	IMF7 (-)
Accounts of financial institutions		nat curr	Yes	A, M	World	IMF6 (-)
Balance, overall (excl. exceptional financing and liabilities)	By country group and country	US$	Yes	A	World	IMF2 (A-8)
Capital account		US$	Yes	A	World	IMF7 (-)
Capital account	Assets and liabilities by country and country group	US$	Yes	A	World	IMF2(C-13)
Capital account balance		US$	Yes	A	Central and South American countries	IADB1
Capital accumulation account	By category	nat curr	Yes	A	World	UN38 (3.52)
Capital finance account	By category	nat curr	Yes	A	World	UN38 (3.53)
Capital movements, net		nat curr	Yes	A, Q, M	OECD	OECD22 (-)
Coefficients of net external financing	% of real gross national disposable income at constant 1980 prices	%	Yes	A	Latin American and Caribbean countries	UN45 (101)
Counterpart items	By country group and country	US$	Yes	A	World	IMF2 (A-7)
Credit from the international monetary fund	By country and country group	US$	Yes	A	World	IMF2(C-34)
Direct investment flows	By country, by investments made, investments received	ECU	No		Selected countries	EC35 (-)
Exceptional financing	by country group and country	US$	Yes	A	World	IMF2 (A-9)
Exceptional financing	Aggregated and detailed presentations containing transactions data	US$	Yes	A, Q	World	IMF1 (-)
Exceptional financing and liabilities	By country and country group	US$	Yes	A	World	IMF2(C-32)
Facilities, other international medium and long-term	By borrowing country or institution	US$	Yes	Q, M	World	OECD34 (I.32)
Financial flows	By high, middle, low income, by source	US$	No		World	CS1 (22)
Foreign exchange assets	By country and country group	US$	Yes	A	World	IMF2(C-35)
Funds raised on international markets	By borrowing country or institution	US$	Yes	Q, M	World	OECD34 (S.2)
Funds raised on international markets	By type of instrument	US$	Yes	Q, M	World	OECD34 (S.1)
International liquidity		US$	Yes	A, M	World	IMF7 (-)
International liquidity		US$	Yes	A, M	World	IMF6 (-)
International transactions		US$	Yes	A, M	World	IMF7 (-)
International transactions		US$	Yes	A, M	World	IMF6 (-)
International transactions	Credit and debit figures by country group and transaction type	US$	Yes	A	World	IMF2 (B-1)
Monetary gold and special drawing rights	By country and country group	US$	Yes	A	World	IMF2(C-33)
Net resource flows and net transfers	By net resource flows, net transfers by region, category	US$	Yes	A	World reporting to World Bank	WB3 (-)
Official settlements balance		ECU	Yes	A, Q	EC, USA, Japan	EC36
Reserve position in international monetary fund	By country and country group	US$	Yes	A	World	IMF2(C-34)
SDRs: department		SDRs	Yes	A	World	IMF6 (-)
SDRs: all purchases		SDRs	Yes	A, M	World	IMF7 (-)
SDRs: all purchases		SDRs	Yes	A, M	World	IMF6 (-)

Subject	Categories	Units	Time series Yes/No	Frequency	Territorial coverage	Source (Table No.)
SDRs: arrangements	Date, amount	SDRs	Yes	A, M	World	IMF6 (-)
SDRs: borrowing agreements	Amounts	SDRs	Yes	A	World	IMF6 (-)
SDRs: financing components of members' outstanding obligations to the fund	Outstanding purchases, loans	SDRs	Yes	A	World	IMF6 (-)
SDRs: fund holdings of currency		SDRs	Yes	A	World	IMF6 (-)
SDRs: IMF position		SDRs	Yes	A, M	World	IMF7 (-)
SDRs: IMF position		SDRs	Yes	A, M	World	IMF6 (-)
SDRs: quota		SDRs	Yes	A	World	IMF6 (-)
SDRS: repurchases of purchases		SDRs	Yes	A, M	World	IMF7 (-)
SDRs: repurchases of purchases		SDRs	Yes	A, M	World	IMF6 (-)
SDRs: reserve position		SDRs	Yes	A	World	IMF6 (-)
SDRs: use of fund credit (GRA)		SDRs	Yes	A, M	World	IMF7 (-)
SDRs: use of fund credit (GRA)		SDRs	Yes	A, M	World	IMF6 (-)
27.1.2 Current Account						
Advertising	By country, net, credits, debits	US$	Yes	A	OECD	OECD44 (A.20)
Commissions and brokerage	By country, net, credits, debits	US$	Yes	A	OECD	OECD44 (A.15)
Communications	By type, country, net, credits, debits	US$	Yes	A	OECD	OECD44 (A.10)
Computer related services	By country, net, credits, debits	US$	Yes	A	OECD	OECD44 (A.14)
Consultancy and technical co-operation	By country, type, net credits, debits	US$	Yes	A	OECD	OECD44 (A.17)
Current account		ECU	Yes	A	EC, USA USSR, Canada, Japan	EC9 (2.40)
Current account	% f.o.b value of total exports of goods and services	%	Yes	A	Latin American and Caribbean countries	UN45 (98)
Current account	Aggregated and detailed presentations containing transactions data	US$	Yes	A, Q	World	IMF1 (-)
Current account	As a % of GDP	%	Yes	A, Q	EC, USA, Japan	EC36
Current account	Detailed transactions	nat curr	Yes	A	World	UN38 (3.51)
Current account	By country group and country	US$	Yes	A	World	IMF2 (A-1)
Current account	By reporting country, by geographical zone	ECU	Yes	A	EC	EC10 (2C)
Current account : financing	By source deficits	$US	Yes	Selected years	Developing countries	UNCTAD5 (3.13)
Current account balance		ECU	Yes	A, Q	EC, USA, Japan	EC36
Current account balance		US$	Yes	A	Central and South American countries	IADB1
Current account balance		US$	Yes	A	World	IMF7 (-)
Current account balance	% of GDP	%	Yes	A	World	IMF7 (-)
Current account balance	By exporters - oil, summary of manufacturing	US$	Yes	Selected years	DMECs, developing countries, Least developed countries	UNCTAD5 (3.12)
Current account balances	% value of total imports of goods and services	%	Yes	A	Latin American and Caribbean countries	UN45 (99)
Current account balances	Estimated	US$	Yes	A	OPEC countries	OPEC1 (9)
Current account, adjusted aalances		US$	Yes	A	World	IMF2 (3)
Current account, summary of balances	By component	US$	Yes	A	World	IMF2 (2)
Earnings from work	By reporting country, by geographical zone	ECU	Yes	A	EC	EC10 (2A2.5)
EC trade	By product, by imports, exports	ECU, %	No		EC	EC35 (-)
EC trade	By country, by imports, exports	ECU, %	No		World	EC35 (-)
EC trade balance	By partner country	ECU	No		World	EC3 (-)
EC trade balance	By service	ECU	No		EC	EC35 (-)

Subject	Categories	Units	Time series Yes/No Frequency		Territorial coverage	Source (Table No.)
EC trade: member states' share of extra-community trade	By country, by imports, exports, balance	%	No		EC	EC35 (-)
Engineering, construction, architectural and mining	By country, net, credits, debits	US$	Yes	A	OECD	OECD44 (A.11)
Equipment leasing, rentals	By country, net, credits, debits	US$	Yes	A	OECD	OECD44 (A.16)
Films and television	By country, net, credits, debits	US$	Yes	A	OECD	OECD44 (A.21)
Financial services	By country, net, credits, debits	US$	Yes	A	OECD	OECD44 (A.13)
Freight	By country, net, credits, debits	US$	Yes	A	OECD	OECD44 (A.4)
Goods and services	By reporting country, by geographical zone	ECU	Yes	A	EC	EC10 (2A)
Goods, services and income	Credit and debit figures by country and country group	US$	Yes	A	World	IMF2 (C-2)
Goods, services and income, official	Credit and debit figures by country and country group	US$	Yes	A	World	IMF2 (C-9)
Goods, services and income, private	Credit and debit figures by country and country group	US$	Yes	A	World	IMF2(C-10)
Goods, sevices and income	Credit and debit figures by country group and transaction type	US$	Yes	A	World	IMF2 (B-2)
Government services	By goods, services, transactions, by country, net, credits, debits	US$	Yes	A	OECD	OECD44 (A.6)
Insurance	By type, country, net, credits, debits	US$	Yes	A	OECD	OECD44 (A.12)
Insurance on transport	By reporting country, by geographical zone	ECU	Yes	A	EC	EC10 (2A2.2)
Invisible trade balance		ECU	Yes	A, Q	EC USA, Japan	EC36
Legal services	By country, net, credits, debits	US$	Yes	A	OECD	OECD44 (A.18)
Management services	By country, net, credits, debits	US$	Yes	A	OECD	OECD44 (A.19)
Merchandise (f.o.b.)	By reporting country, by geographical zone	ECU	Yes	A	EC	EC10 (2A.1)
Merchandise f.o.b. (incl. gold)	Credit and debit figures by country and country group	US$	Yes	A	World	IMF2 (C-1)
Merchanting	By country, net, credits, debits	US$	Yes	A	OECD	OECD44 (A.8)
Passenger fares	By country, net, credits, debits	US$	Yes	A	OECD	OECD44 (A.5)
Payments of profits and interest, remittances	% of f.o.b value of total exports of goods and services	%	Yes	A	Latin American and Caribbean countries	UN45 (102)
Private services, other	By country, net, credits, debits	US$	Yes	A	OECD	OECD44 (A.7)
Processing and repair	By processing, refining, installation, repair, by country, net, credits, debits	US$	Yes	A	OECD	OECD44 (A.9)
Profits paid		US$	Yes	A	Latin American and Caribbean countries	UN45 (267)
Service balance		US$	Yes	A	Central and South American countries	IADB1
Services	By reporting country, by geographical zone	ECU	Yes	A	EC	EC10 (2A.2)

27 INTERNATIONAL TRADE AND FINANCE

Subject	Categories	Units	Time series Yes/No	Frequency	Territorial coverage	Source (Table No.)
Services and other current account transactions of developing countries	Exports, imports by type of transaction by region, shares and growth rate	%	No		Developing countries	UNCTAD5 (4.28)
Shipment	Credit and debit figures by country and country group	US$	Yes	A	World	IMF2 (C-3)
Surplus on current transactions	Percentage of GDP	%	Yes	A	OECD Europe, OECD, EC	OECD32 (6.15)
Trade		ECU	Yes	A	EC USA, USSR, Canada, Japan	EC9 (2.39)
Trade balance		US$	Yes	A	Wold	IMF7 (-)
Trade balance	f.o.b.	ECU	Yes	A, Q	EC, USA, Japan	EC36
Trade in services	By country	US$	Yes	A	OECD	OECD44 (B.1-23)
Trade in services	By service, by country	US$	No		OECD	OECD44 (B.24)
Transfers, official unrequited	Credit and debit figures by country and country group	US$	Yes	A	World	IMF2(C-12)
Transfers, private unrequited	Credit and debit figures by country and country group	US$	Yes	A	World	IMF2(C-11)
Transportation	By country, net, credits, debits	US$	Yes	A	OECD	OECD44 (A.3)
Transportation	Credit and debit figures by country and country group	US$	Yes	A	World	IMF2 (C-4)
Travel	By country, net, credits, debits	US$	Yes	A	OECD	OECD44 (A.2)
Travel	Credit and debit figures by country and country group	US$	Yes	A	World	IMF2 (C-5)
27.1.3 General						
Balance, overall (incl. exceptional financing but excl. liabilities)	By country group and country	US$	Yes	A	World	IMF2(A-10)
Balance, overall (incl. exceptional financing and liabilities)	By country group and country	US$	Yes	A	World	IMF2(A-12)
Balance of payments	Breakdown by country	US$	Yes	A	ASEAN	ASEANS1 (7.4)
Balance of payments, international reserves and IMF credit	By high, middle, low income	US$, nos	No		World	CS1 (18)
Balance of payments, summary	Main components	US$	Yes	A	World	UN50 (26)
Balance of payments, trends	By country, by item, account	US$	No		Europe	EC18 (17.1)
Balance of payments		US$	Yes	A	Nordic countries	NCM1 (201)
Balance of payments	Breakdown by country	US$	Yes	A	ASEAN	ASEANS1 (7.4)
Balance of payments	By category	US$	Yes	A	OECD-total	OECD1 (-)
Balance of payments	By countries	nat curr and nat defs, IMF defs in US$	Yes	A	EC	MAC3 (J3,A,B)
Balance of payments	By countries	nat curr and nat defs, IMF defs in US$	Yes	A	Europe	MAC3 (J3,A,B)
Balance of payments	By countries	nos	No		The Americas and Australasia	MAC2 (K3)
Balance of payments	By country, by item	US$	No		Selected countries	CH1 (4.18)

Subject	Categories	Units	Time series Yes/No Frequency		Territorial coverage	Source (Table No.)
Balance of payments	By country, by exports, imports, resource balance, net factor income, net current transfers, current account balance, long-term capital inflow, other items, change in net reserves	US$	Yes	A	Developing countries	WB2 (-)
Balance of payments	By country	nat curr	Yes	A	Africa and Asia	MAC1 (K3)
Balance of payments	By country	US$	Yes	A	ESCAP coutnries	UN44
Balance of payments	By country/, region	US$	Yes	A	Latin American and Caribbean countries	UN45 - (237265)
Balance of payments	By reporting country, by geographical zone, for goods and services, unrequited transfers, portfolio investment long-term capital	ECU	Yes	A	EC	EC10 (1)
Balance of payments	By type	ECU	Yes	A, Q	EC	EC38 (II)
Balance of payments	Goods, services, unrequited transfers, current, basic, long-term and short-term capital, reserves	ECU	No		EC, USA, USSR, Canada, Japan	EC9 (2.38)
Balance of payments	Goods, services, income unrequited transfers (net), capital flows including reserves	US$	Yes	A	African countries	UN1(34)
Balance of payments	In convertible or non-convertible currencies, or all currencies, by country	US$	Yes	A	VICES countries and Yugoslavia	VICES1 (III/6)
Balance of payments	Income, capital, reserves	SDRs	Yes	A	West Africa	UN3(42)
Balance of payments	Income, capital, reserves	SDRs	Yes	A	East & Southern Africa	UN4(42)
Balance of payments	Income, capital, reserves	SDRs	Yes	A	Central Africa	UN5(42)
Balance of payments	Net trade, curr. balance, net capital movements	nat curr	Yes	A/M	OECD	OECD22
Balance of payments	By country, by current account, capital account	US$	No		Selected countries	CH1 (4.19)
Balance of payments: international comparisons	By country	ECU	Yes	A, Q	World	EC38 (I)
Balance on goods and services	By category	US$	Yes	A	OECD	OECD1 (-)
Balance on non-monetary transactions	By category	US$	Yes	A	OECD	OECD1 (-)
Balance on official settlements	By category	US$	Yes	A	OECD	OECD1 (-)
Balances on non-monetary transactions		US$	Yes	A	OECD-total	OECD1 (-)
Balances on official settlements		US$	Yes	A	OECD-total	OECD1 (-)
Basic balances		ECU	Yes	A, Q	EC, USA, Japan	EC36
Basic balances		ECU	Yes	A	EC, USA, USSR, Canada, Japan	EC9 (2.41)
Basic balances	By reporting country, by geographical zone	ECU	Yes	A	EC	EC10 (2E3)
Basic balances		US$	Yes	A	OECD-total	OECD1 (-)
Basic balances	By category	US$	Yes	A	OECD	OECD1 (-)
Capital movements	By category	US$	Yes	A	OECD	OECD1 (-)
Counterpart items	Aggregated and Detailed Presentations containing transactions data	US$	Yes	A, Q	World	IMF1 (-)

27 INTERNATIONAL TRADE AND FINANCE

Subject	Categories	Units	Time series Yes/No Frequency		Territorial coverage	Source (Table No.)
Current account, capital account and net errors and omissions	By country group and country	US$	Yes	A	World	IMF2 (A-6)
Current account and long-term capital	By country group and country	US$	Yes	A	World	IMF2 (A-3)
Current and capital accounts	By country	ECU	Yes	A, Q	EC	EC38 (III)
Current balances		US$	Yes	A	OECD-total	OECD1 (-)
Current balances	By category	US$	Yes	A	OECD	OECD1 (-)
Current invisibles	By category	US$	Yes	A	OECD	OECD1 (-)
Current invisibles	By category	US$	Yes	A	OECD-total	OECD1 (-)
Errors and omissions, net	Aggregated and Detailed pesentations containing transactions data	US$	Yes	A, Q	World	IMF1 (-)
Errors and omissions, net	By country group and country	US$	Yes	A	World	IMF2 (A-5)
International transactions, summary of balances		US$	Yes	A	World	IMF2 (1)
International transactions	Balance on goods, services and private transfers, capital account, overall balance, SDR allocations, change in reserves and related items, by country or economic region	US$	Yes	A	World and economic groups	UNCTAD1 (5.1)
Major economic aggregates	By GNP, exports, imports, reserves, current account balance by region, by category	US$	Yes	A	World reporting to World Bank	WB3 (-)
Overall balance		US$	Yes	A	World	IMF7 (-)
Reserves, changes in	By category	US$	Yes	A	OECD	OECD1 (-)
Technology balance of payments, receipts	By country	nat curr	Yes	A	OECD	OECD28 (79)
Technology balance of payments, payments	By country	nat curr	Yes	A	OECD	OECD28 (80)
Technology balance of payments, balance	By country	nat curr	Yes	A	OECD	OECD28 (81)
Technology balance of payments, coverage ratio	By country	nos	Yes	A	OECD	OECD28 (82)
Technology balance of payments, total transactions	By country	nat curr	Yes	A	OECD	OECD28 (83)
Trade balances	By category	US$	Yes	A	OECD	OECD1 (-)
27.2 BARRIERS TO TRADE						
Anti-dumping, incidence of	Cases initiated	nos, %	Yes	A	DMECs	UNCTAD5 (4.24)
Export restraints, voluntary	By exporter, product group	$US	No		EC, USA, Canada	UNCTAD5 (4.25)
Protectionism in agriculture: percentage of imports covered by NTMs	By product group	%	No		EEC, EFTA, Japan, USA	UNCTAD5 (4.26)
Tariff and non-tariff measures facing imports in DMECs	By product group	%	No		DMECs	UNCTAD5 (4.22)
Tariffs on tropical products by degree of processing in principal markets	By product group	%	No		EC, Japan, USA	UNCTAD5 (4.27)
Trade coverage ratio of NTMs on DMEC imports	By product group	%	Yes	Selected years	DMECs	UNCTAD5 (4.23)
27.3 EXCHANGE RATES						
Bilateral central rates in force since April 1992	By currency, by city	nat curr	No		EC	EC35 (-)
Composition of the ECU basket	By currency	nat curr	No		EC	EC35 (-)
Currency exchange rates		nat curr	Yes	A/M	World	BB2 (24)

Subject	Categories	Units	Time series Yes/No Frequency		Territorial coverage	Source (Table No.)
ECU exchange rates	By currency	nat curr	No		Selected countries	EC35 (-)
ERM currencies, bilateral fluctuations	Central rates and intervention limit rates, in force since 8 October 1990	nat curr per SDR	No		EC participating in the EMS exchange mechanism	EC27 (1)
Exchange rates	Yearly averages	nat curr/US$	Yes	A	OPEC countries	OPEC1(10)
Exchange rates		1 SDR= 1 US$=	Yes	A, M	EC, USA, Japan	EC36
Exchange rates		1pps= nat curr	Yes	A	EC, USA, Japan	EC36
Exchange rates		by rate/US$	Yes	A, M	Nordic countries	NCM1 (180)
Exchange rates		indicies	Yes	A, Q, M	OECD	OECD22 (-)
Exchange rates		nat curr/US$	Yes	A	ASEAN	ASEANS1 (7.2)
Exchange rates		nat curr/US$	Yes	A	ASEAN	ASEANS1 (7.2)
Exchange rates		nat.curr. per SDR	Yes	M	World	IMF6 (-)
Exchange rates		Per US$	Yes	A	World	UN50 (27)
Exchange rates		SDR	Yes	A, M	World	IMF6 (-)
Exchange rates		SDR	Yes	A, M	World	IMF7 (-)
exchange rates		US$ per SDR	Yes	M	World	IMF6 (-)
Exchange rates	Against ECU, by country	nat curr	No		EC participating	EM1 (0316)
Exchange rates	Against US$, by country	nat curr	No		EC	EM1 (0315)
Exchange rates	Average and period end figures, indexes by country	ECU, US$,	Yes	A, Q, M	EC	EC59 (III.6)
Exchange rates	By producers, importers, exporters	Per US$, nat currency	Yes	A	Selected countries	ITC1 (-)
Exchange rates	Daily	nat curr	Yes	M	World	IMF6 (-)
Exchange rates	ECU	US$	yes	A	EFTA countries	EFTA1 (1.17)
Exchange rates	GDP PPPs and internal purchasing power of currency	PPPs, %	Yes	A	EC	EC59 (I.5)
Exchange rates	Mid-point rates	nat curr per US$	Yes	A/M	World	UN35 (52)
Exchange rates	National currencies against the dollar	units/US$, %	Yes	A	OECD	OECD46 (17)
Exchange rates	US$ spot, forward (90 days)	nat curr	Yes	A, M	OECD	OECD22
Exchange rates	US$, by average of daily spot rates	nat curr	Yes	A, M	World	DSC2 (1.8)
Exchange rates	US$, by country, by rate	nat curr, US$	No		EC	EC18 (12.1)
Exchange rates		nat curr	Yes	A	OECD	OECD42 (37)
Exchange rates	By country	ECU	Yes	A, Q	World	EC38 (I)
Exchange rates	By country	US$	No		Arabian Gulf	CH1 (1.1)
Exchange rates	By type	ECU	Yes	A, Q	EC	EC38 (II)
Exchange rates, official		nat curr/US$	Yes	A	Central and South American countries	IADB1
Local currency units per US $	Monthly averages, start of month	Nat curr	Yes	A, M	Selected countries	DSC1 (-)
Purchasing power indices		indcies	Yes	A	World economic regions	UNCTAD1 (2.6)
Purchasing power of exports	Imports, exports	Index	Yes	A	World	UN50 (129)
Purchasing power of exports of goods		indices	Yes	A	Latin American and Caribbean countries	UN45 (277)
Purchasing power parities (PPP) conversion rates(agriculture)		US$	Yes	A	OECD	OECD5 (II.11)
Real effective exchange rate		indices	Yes	A, M	Industrial countries	IMF7 (-)
Real effective exchange rates		indices	Yes	A, M	Industrial countries	IMF6 (-)

Subject	Categories	Units	Time series Yes/No	Frequency	Territorial coverage	Source (Table No.)
Real exchange rates, changes in		%	Yes	Selected years	Developing countries	UNCTAD5 (3.8)
SDRs : rates, daily		US$	Yes	M	World	IMF6 (-)
SDRs: exchange rate,		SDR's/US$	Yes	A, M	United States	OECD22
Trade structure of countries	Exports, imports of Eastern Europe by destination/origin	%	Yes	Selected years	Socialist countries of Eastern Europe	UNCTAD5 (3.10)
World trade indicators - changes in trade	Categories, region volumes, terms of trade and purchasing power of exports	%	Yes	Selected years	DMECs, developing countries, least developed countries	UNCTAD5 (3.11)

27.4 EXPORTS AND IMPORTS

27.4.1 Agricultural Products - see also Section 2

Subject	Categories	Units	Time series Yes/No	Frequency	Territorial coverage	Source (Table No.)
Agricultural	% of the f.o.b value of total exports of goods	%	Yes	A	Latin American and Caribbean countries	UN45 (51)
Agricultural products by import, EC	By country	ECU	Yes	A	EUR 12	EC6 (IA12)
Agricultural products quantities and values	By product by country	kg, ECU	No		EC, World	EC37 Vol A
Agricultural products	Import volume, import unit value and import value	indices	Yes	A	World, economic regions and classes	FAO2 (1)
Agricultural raw materials	Price index	indces	Yes	A	World	UN32 (K)
Agricultural trade, value	By country, by product	US$	Yes	A	World	FAO2 (133-196)
Agriculture, imports		tonnes, ECU	No		World, EC, USA, USSR, Canada, Japan	EC9 (5.27)
Agriculure trade, EC	By commodity, import, export	ECU	Yes	A	EC	EC6 (IA11)
Agriculure trade, EC	Extra EC imports	ECU	No		EC	EC6 (IA14)
Agriculure trade, EC	Extra EC exports	ECU	No		EC	EC6 (IA15)
Agricutural products	Export volume, export unit value and export value	indices	Yes	A	World, economic regions and classes	FAO2 (3)
Animal feed, EC imports	By product	tonnes	Yes	A	EC	WC1 (-)
Bananas	By production	tonnes	Yes	A	World	UNCTAD4 (2.8.1)
Bananas	Consumption, apparent	tonnes	Yes	A	World	UNCTAD4 (2.8.4)
Bananas	Quantity and value of exports and imports	tonnes; US$	Yes	A	World	UNCTAD4 (2.8.2, 2.8.3)
Beverages, tropical	Value of exports and imports	US$	Yes	A	World	UNCTAD4 (2.10.1,2.10.2)
Butter, destination of exports	From, to country	tonnes	Yes	A	EC	MMB1 (99)
Butter, source of imports	To, from country	tonnes	Yes	A	EC	MMB1 (98)
Casein, destination of exports	From, to country	tonnes	Yes	A	EC	MMB1 (113)
Casein, source of imports	To, from country	tonnes	Yes	A	EC	MMB1 (112)
Cereal Crops : canadian exports	By destination	tonnes	Yes	A, M	World	DSC2(7.13)
Cereal Crops : exports	By exporter	tonnes	Yes	A, M	Selected countries	DSC2 (7.9)
Cereal Crops : major exporters	By crop shipments and country	US$	Yes	A	Selected countries	DSC2 (7.5)
Cereals and cereal preparations	Value of exports and imports	US$	Yes	A	World	UNCTAD4 (2.4.1, 2.4.2)
Cheese, destination of exports	From, to country	tonnes	Yes	A	EC	MMB1 (101)
Cheese, source of imports	To, from country	tonnes	Yes	A	EC	MMB1 (100)
Chocolate and chocolate products	By country	tonnes	Yes	A, Q	World	ICC02 (9)
Chocolate and chocolate products	By country	tonnes	Yes	A, Q	World	ICC02 (14)
Coarse grains, production and trade	By country/destination	tonnes	Yes	A	World	ISL2 (2.3.17.3-4)

Subject	Categories	Units	Time series Yes/No Frequency		Territorial coverage	Source (Table No.)
Coarse grains, import and export	By destination	tonnes	Yes	A	World	ISL2 (2.3.17.4.1-2)
Cocoa, powder and cake	By country	tonnes	Yes	A/Q	World	ICC02 (7)
Cocoa, production and trade	By country	tonnes, %	Yes	A	World	ISL2 (2.3.23)
Cocoa	By consumption	tonnes	Yes	A	World	UNCTAD4 (2.12.6)
Cocoa beans	By country	tonnes	Yes	A,Q	World	ICC02 (4)
Cocoa and cocoa products	Destination of exports, by cocoa product, by country	tonnes	Yes	A, Q	World	ICC02 (20-29)
Cocoa and cocoa products	Origin of imports, by cocoa product, by country	tonnes	Yes	A, Q	World	ICC02 (20-30)
Cocoa beans, re-exports	By country	tonnes	Yes	A, Q	World	ICC02 (5)
Cocoa beans	By country	tonnes	Yes	A, Q	World	ICC02 (10)
Cocoa beans	By production	tonnes	Yes	A	World	UNCTAD4 (2.12.1)
Cocoa beans	Quantity and value of exports and imports	tonnes; US$	Yes	A	World	UNCTAD4 (2.12.2,2.12.3)
Cocoa butter	By country	tonnes	Yes	A, Q	World	ICC02 (6)
Cocoa butter	By country	tonnes	Yes	A, Q	World	ICC02 (11)
Cocoa paste, liquor	By country	tonnes	Yes	A, Q	World	ICC02 (8)
Cocoa paste, liquor	By country	tonnes	Yes	A, Q	World	ICC02 (13)
Cocoa powder and cake	By country	tonnes	Yes	A, Q	World	ICC02 (12)
Cocoa products	Quantity and value of exports and imports	tonnes; US$	Yes	A	World	UNCTAD4 (2.12.4,2.12.5)
Coffee, production and trade	By country	tonnes, %	Yes	A	World	ISL2 (2.3.21)
Coffee	By consumption	bags	Yes	A	World	UNCTAD4 (2.11.4)
Coffee	By production	tonnes	Yes	A	World	UNCTAD4 (2.11.1)
Coffee	Quantity and value of exports and imports	tonnes; US$	Yes	A	World	UNCTAD4 (2.11.2,2.11.3)
Copra	By production	tonnes	Yes	A	World	UNCTAD4 (2.21.1)
Copra	Quantity and value of exports and imports	tonnes; US$	Yes	A	World	UNCTAD4 (2.21.2,2.21.3)
Cotton, percentage, production, trade and consumption		bales/%	Yes	A	World	ISL2 (2.3.13.1-2)
Cotton	By consumption	tonnes	Yes	A	World	UNCTAD4 (2.31.9)
Cotton	By production	tonnes	Yes	A	World	UNCTAD4 (2.31.3)
Cotton	Quantity and value of exports and imports	tonnes; US$	Yes	A	World	UNCTAD4 (2.31.4,2.31.5)
Cotton and cotton yarn	Value of exports and imports	US$	Yes	A	World	UNCTAD4 (2.31.1,2.31.2)
Cotton yarn	By production	tonnes	Yes	A	World	UNCTAD4 (2.31.6)
Cotton yarn	Quantity of exports and imports	tonnes	Yes	A	World	UNCTAD4 (2.31.7,2.31.8)
Cream, source of imports	To, from country	tonnes	Yes	A	EC	MMB1 (92)
Cream	From, to country	tonnes	Yes	A	EC	MMB1 (93)
Crops	Total, intra-EUR12, by product	tonnes	Yes	A	EC	EC19 (V)
Crops	Total, intra-EUR12, resources, by product	tonnes	Yes	A	EC	EC19 (V)
Dairy ice, destination of exports of cream	From, to country	tonnes	Yes	A	EC	MMB1 (97)
Dairy ice cream, source of imports	To, from country	tonnes	Yes	A	EC	MMB1 (96)

27 INTERNATIONAL TRADE AND FINANCE

Subject	Categories	Units	Time series Yes/No Frequency		Territorial coverage	Source (Table No.)
EC external trade, agricultural products by export	By country	ECU	Yes	A	EUR 12	EC6 (IA13)
Exports, principal	Meat, wheat flour, wool, iron ore, coal	tonnes	Yes	M	Asia and Pacific	UN43 (-)
Exports of various agricultural products by main trading countries	By countries	nos	No		The Americas and Australasia	MAC2 (D17)
Fish, crustaceans, molluscs, and products thereof	By country, region of origin	US$	No		OECD	OECD43
Fish, food	By major product groups and major world regions	US$	No		OECD and non-OECD regions	OECD43
Fish, mports	By country of origin, fish type,	nat curr, tonnes, % change	Yes	A	EC	SFIA1 (-)
Fish, imports	By country of origin	% change tonnes nat curr	Yes	A	North America	SFIA1 (-)
Fish and fish products, total	By major products and country, quantity, value	tonnes	Yes	A	OECD	OECD43
Fish and fish products	Imports/exports, quantity/value, by country	tonnes	Yes	A	OECD	OECD43
Food (excl fish)	Export volume, export unit value and export value	indices	Yes	A	World, economic regions and classes	FAO2 (4)
Food (excl fish)	Import volume, import unit value and import value	indices	Yes	A	World, economic regions and classes	FAO2 (2)
Food and beverages	Price index	indices	Yes	A	World	UN32 (K)
Food exports	By major foodstuffs, by country	tonnes	Yes	A	OECD	OECD12
Food imports	By major foodstuffs, by country	tonnes	Yes	A	OECD	OECD12
Fresh milk products, other, source of imports	To, from country	tonnes	Yes	A	EC	MMB1 (94)
Grain imports	By country and region	tonnes	Yes	A	World	DSC2(7.16)
Grains, coarse	Quantity and value of exports and imports	tonnes; US$	Yes	A	World	UNCTAD4 (2.7.1, 2.7.2)
Grapes, table, exports		q	Yes	4 yr	World and regions	OIVV1 (Q)
Grapes, table, imports		q	Yes	4 yr	World and regions	OIVV1 (P)
Groundnuts	Quantity and value of exports and imports	tonnes; US$	Yes	A	World	UNCTAD4 (2.17.2,2.17.3)
Groundnuts	By production	tonnes	Yes	A	World	UNCTAD4 (2.17.1)
Milk, unsweetened condensed, destination of of exports	From, to country	tonnes	Yes	A	EC	MMB1 (105)
Milk, liquid milk, source of imports	To, from country	tonnes	Yes	A	EC	MMB1 (90)
Milk, sweetened condensed source of imports	To, from country	tonnes	Yes	A	EC	MMB1 (102)
Milk, unsweetened condensed, source of imports	To, from country	tonnes	Yes	A	EC	MMB1 (104)
Milk liquid, destination of exports	From, to country	tonnes	Yes	A	EC	MMB1 (91)
Milk powder, skimmed sources of imports	To, from country	tonnes	Yes	A	EC	MMB1 (108)
Milk powder, skimmed	By production, balance,	tonnes	Yes	A	Selected countries	ISTA2(-)
Milk powder, destination of exports	From, to country	tonnes	Yes	A	EC	MMB1(107)
Milk powder, whole source of imports of	To, from country	tonnes	Yes	A	EC	MMB1 (106)
Milk products, other, fresh destination of exports	From, to country	tonnes	Yes	A	EC	MMB1 (95)
Molasses	By imports and exports	tonnes	Yes	A	World	FOL3 (72-77)

Subject	Categories	Units	Time series Yes/No	Frequency	Territorial coverage	Source (Table No.)
Molasses	By production and harvest	tonnes	Yes	A	World	FOL3 (78-80)
Palm kernels	By production	tonnes	Yes	A	World	UNCTAD4 (2.23.1)
Palm nuts and kernels	Quantity and value of exports and imports	tonnes; US$	Yes	A	World	UNCTAD4 (2.23.2,2.23.3)
Peppers	Quantity and value of exports and imports	tonnes; US$	Yes	A	World	UNCTAD4 (2.14.3,2.14.4)
Raisins, imports		q	Yes	4 yr	World and regions	OIVV1 (S)
Raisins, exports		q	Yes	4 yr	World and regions	OIVV1 (T)
Rice, paddy	By production	tonnes	Yes	A	World	UNCTAD4 (2.6.1)
Rice	Quantity and value of exports and imports	tonnes; US$	Yes	A	World	UNCTAD4 (2.6.2, 2.6.3)
Rice, production and trade	By country	tonnes	Yes	A	World	ISL2 (2.3.18)
Rubber, natural	By production	tonnes	Yes	A	World	UNCTAD4 (2.28.1)
Rubber, natural	Quantity and value of exports and imports	tonnes; US$	Yes	A	World	UNCTAD4 (2.28.2,2.28.3)
Rubber, natural	By consumption	tonnes	Yes	A	World	UNCTAD4 (2.28.4)
Safflowerseed	By imports, exports	tonnes	Yes	A	Selected countries	ISTA2(-)
Share of exports of food and agricultural products in exports of all products		%	No		EC	WC1 (-)
Skimmed milk powder, destination of exports	From, to country	tonnes	Yes	A	EC	MMB1 (109)
Soybean oil, import and export	By country	tonnes, %	Yes	A	World	ISL2 (2.3.19.2)
Soybeans, production and trade	By country	tonnes, %	Yes	A	World	ISL2 (2.3.19.1)
Soybeans	By production	tonnes	Yes	A	World	UNCTAD4 (2.19.1)
Soybeans	Quantity and value of exports and imports	tonnes; US$	Yes	A	World	UNCTAD4 (2.19.2,2.19.3)
Spices	Quantity and value of exports and imports	tonnes; US$	Yes	A	World	UNCTAD4 (2.14.1,2.14.2)
Sugar, centrifugal: exports	By country	tonnes	Yes	A	World	ISO3(-)
Sugar, centrifugal: net exports	By country	tonnes	Yes	A	World	ISO3(-)
Sugar, raw and white	By imports and exports	tonnes, %	Yes	A	World	FOL3 (34-39)
Sugar, surplus, deficit stocks	Above and below normal working stocks	tonnes, %	Yes	A	World	FOL3 (40,41)
Sugar, consumption	Per capita	kg, %	Yes	A	World	FOL3 (70,71)
Sugar, gross exports and imports	By country of origin, sugar type	tonnes	Yes	A	World	ISO3 (-)
Sugar, raw	By production	tonnes	Yes	A	World	UNCTAD4 (2.9.1)
Sugar, raw and refined	Total, value of exports and imports	US$	Yes	A	World	UNCTAD4 (2.9.2, 2.9.3)
Sugar, raw and refined	Quantity of exports and imports	tonnes	Yes	A	World	UNCTAD4 (2.9.4, 2.9.5)
Sugar, production and trade	By country	tonnes, %	Yes	A	World	ISL2 (2.3.20)
Sugar, net imports from the free market	By country	tonnes	Yes	A	World	ISO3 (-)
Sugar	By consumption	tonnes	Yes	A	World	UNCTAD4 (2.9.6)
Sugar	By country	tonnes	Yes	A	World	FOL3 (32,33)
Sugar	Origin and destination	tonnes	No		World	OECD28 (XI)
Sugar centrifugal, net imports	By country	tonnes	Yes	A	World	ISO3 (-)
Sugar centrifugal, imports	By country	tonnes	Yes	A	World	ISO3 (-)
Sugar centrifugal, imports	By country	tonnes	Yes	A, M	World	ISO2 (-)
Sugar centrifugal, net imports to free market	By country	tonnes	Yes	A, M	World	ISO2 (-)

27 INTERNATIONAL TRADE AND FINANCE

Subject	Categories	Units	Time series Yes/No Frequency		Territorial coverage	Source (Table No.)
Sugar centrifugal: exports	By country	tonnes	Yes	A, M	World	ISO2(-)
Sugar centrifugal: net exports to free market	By country	tonnes	Yes	A, M	World	ISO2(-)
Sugar: net exports to the free market	By country	tonnes	Yes	A	World	ISO3 (-)
Suger: exports by main trading countries	By countries	nos	No		The Americas and Australasia	MAC2 (D15)
Sweetened condensed milk, destination of exports	From, to country	tonnes	Yes	A	EC	MMB1(103)
Tea, production and trade	By country	tonnes/%	Yes	A	World	ISL2 (2.3.22)
Tea, imports, re-exports	By country of origin	tonnes, US$	Yes	A	World	ITC1 (D2, D6-15,D17-D25,D27-D43)
Tea, imports, re-exports, net imports, apparent consumption per head		tonnes, kg	Yes	A		ITC1 (D5)
Tea, instant, exports	By origin, destination	kg	Yes	A	Selected countries	ITC1 (H1-H3, H5)
Tea, instant, imports	By origin, destination	Kg	Yes	A	Selected countries	ITC1 (H4)
Tea	By consumption	tonnes	Yes	A	World	UNCTAD4 (2.13.4)
Tea	By production	tonnes	Yes	A	World	UNCTAD4 (2.13.1)
Tea	Quantity and value of exports and imports	tonnes; US$	Yes	A	World	UNCTAD4 (2.13.2,2.13.3)
Tea, re-exports	By country of destination	tonnes, US$	Yes	A	World	ITC1 (D4,D16)
Tea exports	By destination	tonnes, US$	Yes	A	World	ITC1 (C2-C20)
Tea exports including green tea	By produce	tonnes	Yes	A	World	ITC1 (C)
Tea imports for consumption	By country	tonnes	Yes	A	World	ITC1 (D1)
Tea imports in packages	By country of origin	tonnes, US$	Yes	A	Selected countries	ITC1 (D3)
Tea retained for consumption	By imports	%	Yes	A	World	ITC1 (D1A)
Tea supply and absorption	By exporters, importers, production, exports	tonnes	Yes	A	World	ITC1 (G1)
Textile fibres, natural	Value of exports and imports	US$	Yes	A	World	UNCTAD4 (2.30.1,2.30.2)
Tobacco	By consumption	tonnes	Yes	A	World	UNCTAD4 (2.26.4)
Tobacco	Quantity and value of exports and imports	tonnes; US$	Yes	A	World	UNCTAD4 (2.26.2,2.26.3)
Tobacco leaves	By production	tonnes	Yes	A	World	UNCTAD4 (2.26.1)
Tobaco, production and trade	By country	tonnes, %	Yes	A	World	ISL2 (2.3.24)
Trade balance	Value, and as % of imports	US$, %	Yes	A	World and regions	UNCTAD1 (1.11)
Wheat and wheat flour	Quantity and value of exports and imports	tonnes; US$	Yes	A	World	UNCTAD4 (2.5.2, 2.5.3)
Whey, preserved, destination of exports	From, to country	tonnes	Yes	A	EC	MMB1 (111)
Whey preserved, source of imports	To/from country	tonnes	Yes	A	EC	MMB1 (110)
Wine, imports		hl	Yes	4 yr	World and regions	OIVV1 (L)
Wine, imports	Total, appellation and regions	hl	No		World	OIVV1 (N)
Wine exports		hl	Yes	4 yr	World and regions	OIVV1 (M)
Wine exports	Total, appellation	hl	No		World and regions	OIVV1 (N)
Wool, greasy	By production	tonnes	Yes	A	World	UNCTAD4 (2.34.1)
Wool, total	Value of exports and imports	US$	Yes	A	World	UNCTAD4 (2.34.2,2.34.3)
Wool, greasy and degreased	Quantity of exports and imports	tonnes	Yes	A	World	UNCTAD4 (2.34.4,.34.5)

Subject	Categories	Units	Time series Yes/No Frequency		Territorial coverage	Source (Table No.)
Wool	By consumption	tonnes	Yes	A	World	UNCTAD4 (2.34.6)
World sugar balance	By stocks, imports production, exports	tonnes, %	Yes	A	World	FOL3 (14)
World sugar balance by countries	By stocks, imports exports, production, consumption	tonnes	Yes	A	World	FOL3 (15-23)
27.4.2 Chemicals						
Ammonia		tonnes	Yes	A	World	FAO5 (15)
Chemical, imports	By country	nat curr	Yes	A	Selected countries	CIA1(3)
Chemical, imports	By country	US$	Yes	A	Western World	CIA1(14)
Chemical, imports	As % of home demand	%	Yes	A	Western World	CIA1(24)
Chemical products, total	By countries of origin, destination with world countries	US$	No		World	UN12
Chemical products	By SITC section, by countries of origin, destination with world countries	US$	No		World	UN12
Chemical products	By SITC section, by countries of origin, destination with world countries	tonnes, cu m	No		World	UN12
Chemicals, trade balance	By country	nat curr	Yes	A	Selected countries	CIA1(6)
Chemicals, trade balance	By country	US$	Yes	A	Western World	CIA1(17)
Chemicals, trade figures	Exports/imports	%	Yes	A	Western World	CIA1(25-27)
Chemicals quantities and values	By product by country	kg, ECU	No		EC, World	EC37 Vol C
Chemicals: exports	As % of sales	%	Yes	A	Western World	CIA1(23)
Chemicals: exports	By country	nat curr	Yes	A	Selected countries	CIA1(2)
Chemicals: exports	By country	US$	Yes	A	Western World	CIA1(13)
Current account balance before official transfers	By percentage of GDP	%	Yes	A	World	WB6 (16)
Exports recorded	By country, type	tonnes/US$	Yes	A	World	EAT1(5.5)
Fertiliser	By type	tonnes	Yes	A	World	FAO5 (1)
Fluorine, exports		tonnes	Yes	A	EC	EC68 (-)
Fluorine, exports	Fluorspar, hydrofluoric acid and aluminium fluoride	tonnes	No		EC	EC68 (-)
Fluorine, imports		tonnes	Yes	A	EC	EC68 (-)
Fluorine, imports	Fuorspar, hydrofluoric acid and aluminium fluoride	tonnes	No		EC	EC68 (-)
Imports recorded	By country, type	tonnes/US$	Yes	A	World	EAT1(5.6)
Moroccan exports of phosphate rock	By importer	tonnes	Yes	A, Q	World	DSC2 (9.3)
Nitrogenous, phosphate and potash fertiliser	total	tonnes	Yes	A	World	FAO5 (30-31)
Nitrogenous fertiliser		tonnes	Yes	A	World	FAO5 (18-19)
Nitrogenous fertiliser	By economic class	tonnes	Yes	A	World	FAO5 (2)
Phosphate fertiliser		tonnes	Yes	A	World	FAO5 (22-23)
Phosphate fertiliser	By economic class	tonnes	Yes	A	World	FAO5 (3)
Phosphates, exports		tonnes	Yes	A	EC	EC68 (-)
Phosphates, exports	Natural phosphates, phosphoric acid, slag and fertilizers	tonnes	No		EC	EC68 (-)
Phosphates, imports		tonnes	Yes	A	EC	EC68 (-)
Phosphates, imports	Natural phosphates, phosphoric acid, slag and fertilizers	tonnes	No		EC	EC68 (-)
Phosphoric acid		tonnes	Yes	A	World	FAO5 (16)
Potash, phosphate, nitrogenous	Production and trade	tonnes/%	Yes	A	World	ISL2 (2.3.11.1-3)
Potash fertiliser		tonnes	Yes	A	World	FAO5 (26-27)
Potash fertiliser	By economic class	tonnes	Yes	A	World	FAO5 (4)
Potash re-exports (complex fertiliser)		tonnes	Yes	A	World	FAO5 (8)

Subject	Categories	Units	Time series Yes/No	Frequency	Territorial coverage	Source (Table No.)
Rock phosphate		tonnes	Yes	A	World	FAO5 (12)
Silicon carbide, exports	By geographic area, quantity, value, average value	tonnes, US$, US$, tonne	Yes	A	World	EAT1(5.1)
Silicon carbide, exports	By exporting country	tonnes	Yes	A	World	EAT1(5.3a)
Silicon carbide, exports	By exporting country	US$	Yes	A	World	EAT1(5.3b)
Silicon carbide, imports	By geographic area, quantity, value, average value	tonnes/US$ US$/tonne	Yes	A	World	EAT1(5.2)
Silicon carbide, imports	By country	tonnes	Yes	A	World	EAT1(5.4a)
Silicon carbide, imports	By country	US$	Yes	A	World	EAT1(5.4b)
Urea		tonnes, %	Yes	A	World	IFA1 (-)
Urea	Origin, destination	tonnes	No		World	IFA1 (-)
27.4.3 Commodities						
Agricultural commodities processed in principal developing producing countries	By commodity	tonnes; units; pairs; cu m	No		Principal developing countries	UNCTAD4 (A.4)
Alcohol	By imports, exports, country	hl	Yes	A	World	FOL1 (144-145)
Bleached sulphate pulp	By quantity and value	tonnes, US$	Yes	A	World	FAO8
Charcoal	By quantity and value	tonnes, US$	Yes	A	World	FAO8
Chemical wood pulp	By quantity and value	tonnes, US$	Yes	A	World	FAO8
Chips and particles	By quantity and value	cu m, US$	Yes	A	World	FAO8
Chips and particles	Major importers and exporters	cu m	No		World	FAO8
Commercial services trade	Leading exporters leading importers	US$	Yes	10yr	World	GATT3 (12)
Commodity imports and exports	Selected commodities	Million CFA frs 1000 tons	Yes	A	East & Southern Africa	UN4(38)
Commodities, bulk	By major commodities	tonnes	Yes	A	World	OECD28 (XII)
Commoditiy imports from VICES	Imports of eight industrialized countries and industrialized west from VICES countries. value, share of commodity groups, average annual growth rate, by commodity groups, by country	US$, %	Yes	A	VICES countries and Yugoslavia	VICES1 (III/4)
Commodity, exports	Price quotations, by country	US$	Yes	A	ESCAP countries	UN44
Commodity class, imports	By SITC	ECU	No		EC, USA, USSR, Canada, Japan	EC9 (6.11)
Commodity class, imports	By SITC	%	No		EC, USA, USSR, Canada, Japan	EC9 (6.12)
Commodity class	Exports to/from regions, areas	US$	Yes	A	World	UN50 (128)
Commodity class exports	By SITC	%	No		EC, USA, USSR, Canada, Japan	EC9 (6.14)
Commodity class exports	By SITC	ECU	No		EC, USA USSR, Canada, Japan	EC9 (6.13)
Commodity export principal	Relative importance	% of total	Yes	A	African countries	UN1(33)
Commodity exports	By country, by SITC classification	%	No		EC	EM1 (0510)
Commodity exports	By country, by SITC classification	US$	No		EC	EM1 (0509)
Commodity imports	By commodity groups, by selected commodities, at current prices by country	nat curr, nos, tonnes, kWh, kg, l, cu m, sq m	Yes	A	VICES countries	VICES1 (III/2)
Commodity imports	By country, by SITC classification	US$	No		EC	EM1 (0507)

Subject	Categories	Units	Time series Yes/No Frequency		Territorial coverage	Source (Table No.)
Commodity imports	By country, by SITC classification	%	No		EC	EM1 (0508)
Commodity imports and exports	Goods, services, by category	nat curr	Yes	A	World	UN38 (2.17)
Commodity imports and exports	Selected commodities	Million CFA frs 1000 tons	Yes	A	West Africa	UN3(38, 39)
Commodity imports and exports	Selected commodities	Million CFA frs 1000 tons	Yes	A	Central Africa	UN5(38, 39)
Commodity imports to GCC from other Arab countries	By country of origin, by destination country	US$	No		Arabian Gulf	CH1 (4.8)
Commodity imports to the GCC region from the rest of the world,	By country, by commodity group	US$	No		Arabian Gulf	CH1 (4.12)
Commodity trade, developing countries as suppliers	By commodity of basic commodities to DMECs	$US, %	Yes	Selected years	DMECs	UNCTAD5 (4.8)
Community imports by developed market economy countries from developing countries	By selected commodity	$; %	No		Developed and developing countries	UNCTAD4 (A.6)
Dependence of developing countries on non-oil primary commodity exports	Total	%	No		Developing countries	UNCTAD5 (4.10)
Dissolving wood pulp	By quantity and value	tonnes, US$	Yes	A	World	FAO8
DMEC imports of locally-processed commodities from developing countries	By commodity	$US, %	Yes	Selected years	DMEC countries	UNCTAD5 (4.14)
Exports, imports balance	Total, per capita		No		OECD and world regions	OECD33 (5.4A)
		US$	No		OECD and world regions	OECD33 (5.4A)
			No		OECD and world regions	OECD33 (5.4A)
			No		OECD and world regions	OECD33 (5.4A)
Fibre pulp (other)	By quantity and value	tonnes, US$	Yes	A	World	FAO8
Fibreboard, compressed	By quantity and value	cu m, US$	Yes	A	World	FAO8
Fibreboard, non-compressed	By quantity and value	cu m, US$	Yes	A	World	FAO8
Fibreboard	By quantity and value	cu m, US$	Yes	A	World	FAO8
Fibreboard	Major importers and exporters	cu m	No		World	FAO8
Forest products	By value	US$	Yes	A	World	FAO8
Fuelwood	By quantity and value	cu m, US$	Yes	A	World	FAO8
Fuelwood and charcoal	By quantity and value	cu m, US$	Yes	A	World	FAO8
Glucose, isoglucose and dextrose trade	By imports, exports, by country	tonnes	Yes	A	EC	FOL2 (196)
Household and sanitary paper	By quantity and value	tonnes, US$	Yes	A	World	FAO8
	Import, export		No		World regions	OECD33 (5.4C)
Industrial roundwood	By quantity and value	cu m, US$	Yes	A	World	FAO8
Industrial roundwood	Product category		No		OECD and world regions	OECD33 (5.4B)
Industrial roundwood (other)	By quantity and value	cu m, US$	Yes	A	World	FAO8
Local processing of selected primary commodities	By commodity	%	Yes	Selected years	Developing countries	UNCTAD5 (4.13)
Manufactures, commodity trade share		%	Yes	I	World	UNIDO1 (1.16)
Manufactures	By origin, destination and country group	%, US$	Yes	I	World	UNIDO1 (1.17)
Mechanical wood pulp	By quantity and value	tonnes, US$	Yes	A	World	FAO8
Merchandise imports, sources	By high, middle, low income	%	No		World	CS1 (9)
Merchandise imports	By country, by food, consumer goods, other intermediate goods, capital goods	index, US$	Yes	A	Developing fuel and energy, other countries	WB2 (-)
Merchandise trade	By broad economic categories	US$	Yes	A	Latin American and Caribbean	UN45 (281)

27 INTERNATIONAL TRADE AND FINANCE

Subject	Categories	Units	Time series Yes/No Frequency		Territorial coverage	Source (Table No.)
Merchandise trade	Leading exporters, leading importers	US$	Yes	10yr	World	GATT3 (11)
Molasses	By imports, exports, country	tonnes	Yes	A	World	FOL1 (137-143)
Molasses import levy		ECU, kg	No		EC	FOL1 (-)
Molasses production	By exporter	tonnes	Yes	A	World	FOL1 (-)
Newsprint	By quantity and value	tonnes, US$	Yes	A	World	FAO8
Newsprint	Major importers and exporters	tonnes	No		World	FAO8
Newsprint	Unit value	US$ per tonne	Yes	A	World	FAO8
Paper and paperboard	By quantity and value	tonnes, US$	Yes	A	World	FAO8
Paper and paperboard	By type and by trading countries	tonnes	No		OECD	OECD38 (13-33)
Paper and paperboard	Major importers and exporters	tonnes	No		World	FAO8
Paper and paperboard (not elsewhere specified)	By quantity and value	tonnes, US$	Yes	A	World	FAO8
Paper and paperboard (other)	By quantity and value	tonnes, US$	Yes	A	World	FAO8
Paper and paperboard (other)	Unit value	US$ per tonne	Yes	A	World	FAO8
Particle board	By quantity and value	cu m, US$	Yes	A	World	FAO8
Particle board	Major importers and exporters	cu m	No		World	FAO8
Particle board	Unit value	US$ per cu m	Yes	A	World	FAO8
Plywood	By importing, exporting	cu m	No		World	ITTO1 (App 3)
Plywood	By quantity and value	cu m, US$	Yes	A	World	FAO8
Plywood	Major importers and exporters	cu m	No		World	FAO8
Plywood	Unit value	US$ per cu m	Yes	A	World	FAO8
Printing and writing paper	By quantity and value	tonnes, US$	Yes	A	World	FAO8
Printing and writing paper	Unit value	US$ per tonne	Yes	A	World	FAO8
Pulp, total	By type and by trading countries	tonnes	No		OECD	OECD38 (1-11)
Pulpwood	By quantity and value	cu m, US$	Yes	A	World	FAO8
Pulpwood	Unit value	US$ per cu m	Yes	A	World	FAO8
Pulpwood and particles	By quantity and value	cu m, US$	Yes	A	World	FAO8
Pulpwood round and split	Major importers and exporters	cu m	No		World	FAO8
Raw Materials	By country of origin and raw material type	tonnes, %	Yes	I	EC	EC68 (-)
Roundwood	By quantity and value	cu m, US$	Yes	A	World	FAO8
Sandwood (C)	Major importers and exporters	cu m	No		World	FAO8
Sandwood (NC)	Major importers and exporters	cu m	No		World	FAO8
Sawlogs, veneer logs	By importing, exporting	cu m	No		World	ITTO1 (App 3)
Sawlogs and veneer logs	By quantity and value	cu m, US$	Yes	A	World	FAO8
Sawlogs and veneer logs (C)	By quantity and value	cu m, US$	Yes	A	World	FAO8
Sawlogs and veneer logs (C)	Major importers and exporters	tonnes	No		World	FAO8
Sawlogs and veneer logs (C)	Unit value	US$ per tonne	Yes	A	World	FAO8
Sawlogs and veneer logs (NC)	By quantity and value	cu m, US$	Yes	A	World	FAO8
Sawlogs and veneer logs (NC)	Major importers and exporters	cu m	No		World	FAO8
Sawlogs and veneer logs (NC)	Unit value	US$ per tonne	Yes	A	World	FAO8
Sawnwood	By importing, exporting	cu m	No		World	ITTO1 (App 3)
Sawnwood (C)	By quantity and value	cu m, US$	Yes	A	World	FAO8
Sawnwood (C)	Unit value	US$ per cu m	Yes	A	World	FAO8
Sawnwood (NC)	By quantity and value	cu m, US$	Yes	A	World	FAO8
Sawnwood (NC)	Unit value	US$ per cu m	Yes	A	World	FAO8
Sawnwood and sleepers	By quantity and value	cu m, US$	Yes	A	World	FAO8
Semi-chemical wood pulp	By quantity and value	tonnes, US$	Yes	A	World	FAO8

Subject	Categories	Units	Time series Yes/No Frequency		Territorial coverage	Source (Table No.)
Share of primary commodities in developing country exports	By commodity	%, $US	Yes	Selected years	Developing countries	UNCTAD5 (4.9)
Unbleached sulphate pulp	By quantity and value	tonnes, US$	Yes	A	World	FAO8
Veneer	By importing, exporting	cu m	No		World	ITTO1 (App 3)
Veneer sheet	Major importers and exporters	cu m	No		World	FAO8
Veneer sheets	By quantity and value	cu m, US$	Yes	A	World	FAO8
Waste paper	By trading countries	tonnes	No		OECD	OECD38 (12)
Wood pulp	By quantity and value	tonnes, US$	Yes	A	World	FAO8
Wood pulp	Major importers and exporters	tonnes	No		World	FAO8
Wood pulp	Unit value	US$ per tonne	Yes	A	World	FAO8
Wood residues	By quantity and value	cu m, US$	Yes	A	World	FAO8
Wood-based panels	By quantity and value	cu m, US$	Yes	A	World	FAO8
Wrapping and packaging paper	By quantity and value	tonnes, US$	Yes	A	World	FAO8
27.4.4 Direction of Trade						
Agricultural raw materials	Value of exports; imports	US$	Yes	A	World	UNCTAD4 (1.8, 1.9)
Commodities, primary	Value of exports including; excluding fuels	US$	Yes	A	World	UNCTAD4 (1.3, 1.4)
Commodities, primary	Value of imports excluding fuels	US$	Yes	A	World	UNCTAD4 (1.5)
Commodities, primary	Fuels including and excluding	%	Yes	2 yrly	World	UNCTAD4 (1.24, 1.25)
Commodity, trade	Value of exports; imports	US$	Yes	A	World	UNCTAD4 (1.13, 1.14)
Commodity, trade	Exports; imports	US$	Yes	A	World	UNCTAD4 (1.15, 1.16)
Commodity, trade	Principal exporters; importers	US$	Yes	A	World	UNCTAD4 (1.17, 1.18)
Commodity exports, direction	By origin and destination; all food items	%	Yes	2 yrly	World	UNCTAD4 (1.26)
Commodity exports, direction	By origin and destination; total agricultural raw materials	%	Yes	2 yrly	World	UNCTAD4 (1.27)
Commodity exports, direction	By origin and destination; total minerals and ores	%	Yes	2 yrly	World	UNCTAD4 (1.28)
Commodity exports, direction	By origin and destination; total mineral fuels	%	Yes	2 yrly	World	UNCTAD4 (1.29)
DMEC imports of manufactures	By exports from by origin by exports to	%	Yes	Selected years	DMEC countries	UNCTAD5 (4.17)
EC and world trade	By country	US$, %	Yes	A	World	EC38 (A)
EC trade	By partner countries with world countries	ECU	No		World	EC38 (9)
EEC - extra-community trade	EEC % of non-EEC countries' total trade	%	Yes	A	EC	EC9 (6.15)
EEC - intra-community trade		ECU	Yes	A	EC	EC9 (6.10)
EFTA trade	With EC by SITC section	%	Yes	A	EFTA countries	EFTA1 (2.19)
Exports, VICES to the West	Value of top 25 commodities; exports, shares, cumulated shares, by country	US$, %	No		VICES countries and Yugoslavia	VICES1 (III/4)
Exports, VICES	To industrialized west, at current prices	US$	Yes	A	VICES region, VICES countries and Yugoslavia	VICES1 (III, 1)

Subject	Categories	Units	Time series Yes/No Frequency		Territorial coverage	Source (Table No.)
Exports	By country of destination	US$	No		EC	EM1 (0505)
Exports	By country of destination	US$	No		EC	EM1 (0506)
Exports	By country of destination: USA. Japan, ACP, rest of world	%	No		EC, USA, USSR, Canada, Japan	EC9 (6.9)
Exports	By country of destination:- USA, Japan, ACP, rest of world	ECU	No		EC, USA, USSR Canada, Japan	EC9 (6.8)
Exports	By country of origin:- USA, ACP, Japan, rest of world	ECU	No		EC USA, USSR, Canada, Japan	EC9 (6.6)
Exports of manufactures to third countries	Total	ECU	No		EC	EC53 (5.3)
External trade, evolution	By country	nat curr, US$	No		EC	EC18 (9.1)
Food items, all	Value of exports; imports	US$	Yes	A	World	UNCTAD4 (1.6, 1.7)
GCC commodity exports to other Arab countries	By country of origin, by destination country, year	US$	No		Arabian Gulf	CH1 (4.9)
GCC commodity exports to the rest of the world	By country of origin, by destination country, year	US$	No		Arabian Gulf	CH1 (4.16)
Geographic pattern of merchandise trade	Change in no. of trading partners, trading partners in 1988	nos	No		France, UK, US, Germany, Fed. Rep., Japan	GATT3 (15)
German trade	By SITC section	ECU	Yes	A, M	World	EC38 (C)
German trade	With world countries	ECU	Yes	A, M	World	EC38 (B)
Imports, the West to VICES	Value of top 25 commodities; imports, shares, cumulated shares, by country	US$, %	No		VICES countries and Yugoslavia	VICES1 (III/4)
Imports, VICES	From industrialized west, at current prices	US$	Yes	A	VICES region, VICES countries	VICES1 (III/1)
Imports, intra-regional	% of intra-regional imports with respect to total imports calculated on the basis of f.o.b exports	%	Yes	A	Latin American and Caribbean countries	UN45 (93)
Imports	By country of origin, USA Japan, ACP, rest of world	%	No		EC, USA, USSR, Canada, Japan	EC9 (6.7)
Imports	By country of origin	%	No		EC	EM1 (0504)
Imports	By country of origin	US$	No		EC	EM1 (0503)
Imports	By country of origin:-, USA Japan, ACP, rest of world	ECU	No		EC, USA, USSR, Canada, Japan	EC9 (6.6)
Imports	From developing countries, from ACP	indices, ECU	Yes	A, M	EC	EC36
Imports	From western industrialised third countries, from, USA, from Japan	indices, ECU	Yes	A, M	EC	EC36
Imports of manufactures from third countries	Total	ECU	No		EC	EC53 (5.2)
Intra-caricom trade	By country; imports; exports	%	Yes	A	Intra-Caricom countries	CCS1 (8.5)
Intra-caricom trade	By SITC sections; imports; exports	%	Yes	A	Intra-Caricom countries	CCS1 (8.6)
Intra-CARICOM Trade	Imports/exports and balance of trade, by SITC section, by country	US$, %	Yes	A	CARICOM region, and countries	CCS2

Subject	Categories	Units	Time series Yes/No Frequency		Territorial coverage	Source (Table No.)
Merchandise exports, destination	By high, middle, low income	%	No		World	CS1 (8)
Merchandise trade	Value of exports; imports	US$	Yes	A	World	UNCTAD4 (1.1, 1.2)
Mineral fuels	Value of exports	US$	Yes	A	World	UNCTAD4 (1.12)
Minerals, ores and metals	Value of exports; imports	US$	Yes	A	World	UNCTAD4 (1.10, 1.11)
Trade, EC		US$	Yes	A	EC	IMF3 (-)
Trade, oil exporting		US$	Yes	A, M	Oil exporting countries	IMF3,4 (-)
Trade, non-oil developing		US$	Yes	A, M	Non-oil developing countries	IMF3,4 (-)
Trade, developing countries	To and from countries listed, to and from developingcountries	US$	Yes	A, M	World	IMF3,4 (-)
Trade, geographic composition	Net increase/ net decrease of trading partners	nos.	No		World	GATT3 (14)
Trade, direction	Exports, imports	%	Yes	Selected years	World, by development groups	UNCTAD5 (2.3)
Trade	Percentage distribution, percentage change	%	Yes	A	World	IMF3 (-)
Trade between Germany and central and eastern European countries	By country, by imports	US$, nat curr	No		EC	EC18 (9.7)
27.4.5 Drugs and Medical Supplies						
Benzodiazepines: hypnotics and clonazepam	By country, manufacture exports, imports,	kg	Yes	A	World	UN30
Central nervous system stimulants	By country, manufacture imports, exports	kg	Yes	A	World	UN30
Cultivation of papaver somniferum for opium production	Area, opium, yield/ha exports	ha, kg	Yes	A	China, India Rep. of Korea Japan	UN29 (III)
Exports	By country and group of psychotropic substance	kg	Yes	A	World	UN30
Imports	By country and group of psychotropic substance	kg	Yes	A	World	UN30
Sedative hypnotics, barbiturate type anti-epileptics	By country, manufacture, imports, exports	kg	Yes	A	World	UN30
Trade, imports, exports	Importers/exporters opium, poppy straw, concentrate of poppy straw, morphine, codeine, ethylmorphine, dihydrocodeine, pholcodine, cocaine, dextropropoxyphene, pethidine, tilidine, methadone, diphenoxylate	kg	No		World	UN29 (XV)
Tranquilizers, benzodiazepines and meprobamate,	By country and type of tranquillizer exports/imports	kg	Yes	A	World	UN30
27.4.6 Energy - see also Section 17						
Coal, coking to Japan	By country	tonnes, %	Yes	A, Q	World	IEA6 (I.16)
Coal	By type	tce	Yes	A	OECD and Regions	IEA2 (-)
Coal	Production	tonnes	No		EC	EC9 (4.24)
Coal, Australian exports	By product and destination	tonnes	Yes	A, M	Selected countries	DSC2 (6.6)
Coal, US exports	By product and destination	tonnes	Yes	A, M	Selected countries	DSC2 (6.7-6.8)
Coal, Japanese and EC-12 deliveries	By country, destination exports, imports	tonnes	Yes	A, M	World, EC	DSC2(6.15)
		toe	Yes	A		EC9 (4.17)

27 INTERNATIONAL TRADE AND FINANCE

Subject	Categories	Units	Time series Yes/No	Frequency	Territorial coverage	Source (Table No.)
Coal, Japanese and EC-12 imports	By exporter and product	tonnes	Yes	A, M	World	DSC2(6.14)
Coal, coking	By destination	tonnes	Yes	A	OECD and OECD Regions	IEA2 (-)
Coal, coking: from non-EC Countries to the EC	By country	tonnes, %	Yes	A, Q	Selected Non-EC Countries	IEA6 (I.14)
Coal, hard		tonnes	No		World	IEA2 (III.1- III.10)
Coal, hard	By origin	tonnes	Yes	A	OECD and Regions	IEA2 (-)
Coal, hard	By principal importers and exporters	tonnes	No		World	UN21 (7)
Coal, hard	Imports by origin and exports by destination for major non-OECD traders	tonnes	Yes	A	Selected Non-OECD	IEA2 (III.21- III.30)
Coal, hard	Imports/exports, by country	tonnes	Yes	A	ESCAP countries	UN44
Coal, hard	Imports, exports	tonnes	Yes	A	EC, USA and Japan	EC53 (1.15)
Coal, steam	By destination	tonnes	Yes	A	OECD, and OECD Regions	IEA2 (-)
Coal, steam: from non-EC Countries to the EC	By country	tonnes, %	Yes	A, Q	Selected Non-EC Countries	IEA6 (I.8)
Coal, steam to Japan	By country	tonnes, %	Yes	A, Q	World	IEA6 (I.10)
Coal exporting ports	By country	nos	No		World	IEA2 (-)
Coal hard	By exporter	tonnes	Yes	A, M	Selected countries	DSC2 (6.1)
Coal imports, Japanese	By product and country of origin	tonnes	Yes	A, M	World	DSC2 (6.12- 6.13)
Coal imports, Korean	By exporter	tonnes	Yes	A, M	Selected countries	DSC2(6.10)
Coal, imports and exports	By countries	tonnes	Yes	A	EC	MAC3 (D11)
Coal, imports and exports	By countries	nos	No		The Americas and Australasia	MAC2 (E23)
Commercial energy	Total and by type	TJ	Yes	A	World	UN21 (3)
Commercial energy (coal equivalent)	Total and by type	tonnes	Yes	A	World	UN21 (1)
Commercial energy (oil equivalent)	Total and by type	tonnes	Yes	A	World	UN21 (2)
Crude oil		tonnes	No		World, EC, USA, USSR, Canada, Japan	EC9 (4.25)
Crude oil	By country	barrels/day	Yes	A	World	OPEC1 (52)
Crude oil	By country	barrels/day	Yes	A	World	OPEC1 (56)
Crude oil	By country of origin	tonnes	Yes	A	World,	IEA10
Crude oil	By destination	barrels/day	Yes	A	OPEC	OPEC1 (51)
Crude oil	By importers, exporters	barrels/day	Yes	A	World	BB4 (3.1- 4.8)
Crude Oil	By OPEC country	barrels/day	Yes	A	OPEC	OPEC1 (23)
Crude oil	By region	barrels/day	Yes	A	World	OPEC1 (26)
Crude oil	Share of total OPEC crude oil exports, by region	%	Yes	A	World	OPEC1 (25)
Crude oil	By country of destination	tonnes	Yes	A	World, OECD, non-OECD	IEA10 (II.8A)
Crude oil, NGL and refinery stocks		tonnes	Yes	Q	OECD	IEA11
Crude oil, OPEC	By region	barrels/day	Yes	A	World	OPEC1 (24)
Crude oil and natural gas liquids		tonnes	Yes	A	World, OECD, non-OECD	IEA10 (I.7)
Crude oil and natural gas liquids		tonnes	Yes	A	World, OECD, non-OECD	IEA10 (I.9)
Crude oil by country of origin, gross imports	By country, importer	barrels/day	Yes	A	World	BB2 (18)
Crude oil exports by GCC	By country	barrels/day	No		Arabian Gulf	CH1 (3.3)
Crude oil exports estimated seaborne	By country	tonnes	Yes	A, Q, M	World	DSC2(2.10)
Crude oil and NGL exports		tonnes	Yes	A	World, OECD and non-OECD	IEA7
Crude oil and products, net imports	By country	barrels/day	Yes	A, M	World	BB2 (17)
Crude oil and products	By importers, exporters	barrels/day	Yes	A	World	BB4 (2.4, 2.6-2.8)

Subject	Categories	Units	Time series Yes/No	Frequency	Territorial coverage	Source (Table No.)
Crude oil and refined products	By importers, exporters	barrels/day	Yes	A	World	BB4 (1.1-2.3, 2.5)
Crude oil and refined products	By OPEC country	barrels/day	Yes	A	OPEC	OPEC1 (29)
Crude oil and refined products	By region	barrels/day	Yes	A	World	OPEC1 (30)
Crude oil imports, OECD	By major source country and regions	tonnes	Yes	A, Q, M	World	DSC2 (2.13 -2.14)
Crude oil stocks	Total	Bl	Yes	A, Q	OECD	BB1 (23.1)
Crude petroleum	By principal importers and exporters	tonnes		No	World	UN21 (15)
Crude petroleum	Imports/exports, by country	tonnes	Yes	A	ESCAP countries	UN44
Crude petroleum	Quantity and value of exports and imports	tonnes; US$	Yes	A	World	UNCTAD4 (3.11.2, 3.11.3)
Eastern energy, exports	To VICES area by type, region,	US$	No		VICES countries	VICES1 (V/4)
Electric energy	By country	GWh	Yes	A	EC, USA	UN7 (1)
Electric energy	Partner countries	GWh	Yes	A	EC, USA	UN7 (5)
Electric energy, international exchanges	By importing country	GWh	Yes	A	EC, USA	UN7 (6)
Electricity		kWh	Yes	A	World	UN21 (35)
Electricity	Imports/exports, by country	kWh	Yes	A	ESCAP countries	UN44
Electricity	Total and net	TWh	Yes	I	OECD, Selected OECD Countries and Regions	IEA3 (-)
Energy	By form of energy	TJ	Yes	A	EC, USA, Canada	UN9 (2)
Energy	Exports, imports	toe, %	Yes	A	EC	EC9 (4.17,4.22)
Energy, imports	From VICES area by SITC, at current prices	US$	No		VICES countries	VICES1 (V/4)
Energy, total	Net exports of total energy as % of total energy production, net imports of total energy as % of total energy consumption	%	Yes	I	World and economic regions	UNCTAD1 (6.9)
Energy international trade	Imports; exports	GWh	Yes	A	OECD	IEA8&9 (–)
Energy, primary	By type by country	toe	Yes	I	VICES countries and Yugoslavia	VICES1 (V/2)
Energy production, consumption and trade	By high, middle, low income	tonnes, kg, %	No		World	CS1 (16)
Exports, non-petroleum	Value	US$	Yes	A	OPEC	OPEC1 (6)
Feedstocks	By country of origin	tonnes	Yes	A	World, OECD, non-OECD	IEA10 (II.7A)
Feedstocks	By country of destination	tonnes	Yes	A	World, OECD, non-OECD	IEA10 (II.8A)
Fuel	By region, country or area	US$, indices, % of total	Yes	A	Developed economies	UN32(D,E)
Fuel projections, changes in	By fuel	tce	No		OECD and regions	IEA2 (-)
Gas	By country of origin/destination, by type of gas	TJ	Yes	A	EC USA	UN8 (2)
Gas	By country of origin, destination, by type of gas	TJ	Yes	A	EC, USA	UN8 (3)
Gas	By type of gas, by country	TJ	Yes	A	EC, USA	UN8 (1)
Gas, diesel oil	By country of origin	tonnes	Yes	A	World, OECD, non-OECD	IEA10 (II.7C)
Gas, diesel oil	By country of destination	tonnes	Yes	A	World, OECD, non-OECD	IEA10 (II.8B)
Gas, diesel oil		tonnes	Yes	Q	OECD and regions	IEA11

27 INTERNATIONAL TRADE AND FINANCE

Subject	Categories	Units	Time series Yes/No Frequency		Territorial coverage	Source (Table No.)
Gas, natural		TJ	No		EC	EC9 (4.30)
Gas, natural	Imports, exports	terajoules	Yes	A	EC, USA and Japan	EC53 (1.17)
Gases		TJ	Yes	A	World	UN21 (31)
Gasoline (total)	By country of origin	tonnes	Yes	A	World, OECD, non-OECD	IEA10 (II.7C)
Gasoline (total)	By country of destination	tonnes	Yes	A	World, OECD, non-OECD	IEA10 (II.8B)
Gasoline, total		tonnes	Yes	Q	OECD and regions	IEA11
Heavy fuel oil (residual)	By country of origin	tonnes	Yes	A	World OECD, non-OECD	IEA10 (II.7D)
Heavy fuel oil (residual)	By country of destination	tonnes	Yes	A	World, OECD, non-OECD	IEA10 (II.8B)
Kerosene (total)	By country of origin	tonnes	Yes	A	World, OECD, non-OECD	IEA10 (II.7C)
Kerosene (total)	By country of destination	tonnes	Yes	A	World, OECD, non-OECD	IEA10 (II.8B)
LG trade min international movements by pipeline	By exporter, importer, product	cu m	No		World	BP2 (-)
Liquefied petroleum products	By country of origin	tonnes	Yes	A	World, OECD, non-OECD	IEA10 (II.7B)
Liquefied petroleum gases	By country of destination	tonnes	Yes	A	World, OECD, non-OECD	IEA10 (II.8A)
Liquid fuels	By type	tonnes	Yes	A	World,	UN21 (14, 17-24)
LPG imports	By exporter, importer, region	tonnes	Yes	A	USA, OECD, Japan	BP2 (-)
Naphtha	By country of destination	tonnes	Yes	A	World, OECD, non-OECD	IEA10 (II.8A)
Naphtha	By country of origin	tonnes	Yes	A	World, OECD, non-OECD	IEA10 (II.7B)
Naphtha		tonnes	Yes	Q	OECD and regions	IEA11
Natural gas	By country of origin	TJ, cu m	Yes	A	World, OECD, non-OECD	IEA10 (II.10)
Natural gas		TJ	Yes	A	World, OECD, non-OECD	IEA10 (I.22)
Natural gas		TJ	Yes	A	World,OECD, non-OECD	IEA10 (I.23)
Natural gas	By country	cu m	Yes	A	World	OPEC1 (55)
Natural gas	By country	cu m	Yes	A	World	OPEC1 (58)
Natural gas	By OPEC country	cu m	Yes	A	OPEC	OPEC1 (31)
Natural gas	By region	cu m	Yes	A	World	OPEC1 (32)
Natural gas	By country of destination	TJ, cu m	Yes	A	World, OECD, non-OECD	IEA10 (II.11)
Natural gas	By principal importers and exporters	TJ	No		World	UN21 (29)
Natural gas	Origin to destination	cu m	No		World	BP1 (p24)
Natural gas		TJ	Yes	A	World	UN21 (28)
Natural gas, oil	Origin to destination	cu m	No		World	BP1 (p24)
	imports, exports	barrels/day % share % change	Yes	A	World	BP1 (p16)
Natural gas, principal international movements of	By country; total	cu m	Yes	A, M	World	BB2 (19.1- 9.2)
Natural gas imports	By importers and exporters	cu m %	Yes	A, M	World	DSC2 (3.7-3.8)
Natural gas liquids	By country of origin	tonnes	Yes	A	World, OECD, non-OECD	IEA10 (II.7A)
Natural gas liquids	By country of destination	tonnes	Yes	A	World, OECD, non-OECD	IEA10 (II.8A)
Net imports of crude and products	Total	barrels/day	Yes	A	World excluding EC, ISC	BB1 (20.1-20.2)
Oil	% of total exports	%	Yes	A	OPEC	OPEC1 (7)

Subject	Categories	Units	Time series Yes/No	Frequency	Territorial coverage	Source (Table No.)
Oil		barrels/day % share % change	Yes	A	World	BP1 (p16)
Oil	Crude/product imports and exports	tonnes barrels/day	No		World	BP1 (p17)
Oil	f.o.b.	US$	Yes	A	OPEC	OPEC1 (4)
Oil	Origin to destination	tonnes barrels/day	No		World	BP1 (p16)
Oil	Value, % net imports	$, nat curr	Yes	A	Selected countries	BB1 (21)
Oil, crude	Imports, exports	tonnes	Yes	A	EC, USA and Japan	EC53 (1.16)
Oil, total products		tonnes	Yes	Q	OECD	IEA11
Oil and balance of trade	By oil, all goods	$, nat curr	Yes	A	World	BB1 (22.1-22.2)
Oil and the balance of trade	By country	nat curr	Yes	A, M	World	BB2 (16)
Oil exporters	Total	barrels/day, %	Yes	A	World and regions	BB4 (1V)
Oil exports, imports		barrels/day, %	Yes	A	World	BB4 (V)
Oil: importers	Total	barrels/day, %	Yes	A	World	BB4 (V11)
Oil: summary, exporters	Total	barrels/day, %	Yes	A	World	BB4 (V1)
Oil summary, importers	Total	barrels/day, %	Yes	A	World	BB4 (V1)
Oil trade	By imports, exports, total	barrels/day	Yes	A	Selected countries	BB4 (7-154)
Oil trade	Total imports, exports	barrels/day	No		World	BB4 (1-111)
Oil trade, international	By imports, exports	tonnes	No		World	IP1 (-)
Petroleum, exports	Value	US$	Yes	A	OPEC	OPEC1 (5)
Petroleum, imports and exports	By countries, imports, exports	nos	No		The Americas and Australasia	MAC2 (E24)
Petroleum, imports and exports	By countries	tonnes	Yes	A	EC	MAC3 (D12)
Petroleum coke	By country of origin	tonnes	Yes	A	World OECD, non-OECD	IEA10 (II.7D)
Petroleum coke		tonnes	Yes	A	World, OECD, non-OECD	IEA10 (II.8B)
Petroleum (crude oil and products)		tonnes	Yes	A	EC	EC9 (4.28)
Petroleum products	By country of origin	tonnes	Yes	A	World, OECD, non-OECD	IEA10 (II.7B)
Petroleum products		tonnes	Yes	A	World, OECD, non-OECD	IEA10 (I.8)
Petroleum products	By country of destination	tonnes	Yes	A	World, OECD, non-OECD	IEA10 (I.10)
	By country of destination	tonnes	Yes	A	World, OECD, non-OECD	IEA10 (II.8A)
Refined oil products	By importers, exporters	barrels/day	Yes	A	World	BB4 (5.4, 5.5)
Refined products	By region	barrels/day	Yes	A	World	OPEC1 (28)
Refined products	By country	barrels/day	Yes	A	World	OPEC1 (54)
Refined products	By country	barrels, day	Yes	A	World	OPEC1 (57)
Refined poducts	By destination	barrels/day	Yes	A	OPEC	OPEC1 (53)
Refined products	By importers, exporters	barrels/day	Yes	A	World	BB4 (5.1-5.3, 5.6-6.8)
Refined products	By OPEC country	barrels/day	Yes	A	OPEC	OPEC1 (27)
Residual fuel oil		tonnes	Yes	Q	OECD and regions	IEA11
Solid fuel	By type	tonnes	Yes	A	World	UN21 (5-6,8-13)
Solid fuels	By fuel type, by country	tonnes	Yes	I	EC, USA	UN6 (1)
Solid fuels	By country of origin, by fuel type, by country	tonnes	No		EC, USA	UN6 (4)
Solid fuels	By country of origin, by fuel type, by country	tonnes	No		EC, USA	UN6 (5)
Solid fuels	By fuel type, By country	tonnes	Yes	I	EC, USA	UN6 (1)

Subject	Categories	Units	Time series Yes/No Frequency		Territorial coverage	Source (Table No.)
Western energy, exports	To VICES area by SITC, at current region, prices	US$	No		VICES countries VICES countries	VICES (V/4)
24.4.7 Engineering Products						
Engineering poducts	Between countries in the EEC region (total)	US$	No		EC	UN14 (3)
Engineering poducts	Between geographical and/or economic regions (total)	US$	No		World	UN14 (2)
Engineering products, exports		US$/%	No		World	UN14 (1)
Engineering products, exports	By region and country of destination (total)	US$/%	No		World	UN14 (4)
Engineering products, exports	Main exporter and by commodity group (total)	US$	No		World	UN14 (5a)
Engineering products, exports	Main exporter (total)	US$	No		Selected countries	UN14 (5b)
Engineering products, exports	Exports by region and country of destination	US$	No		World	UN14 (7)
Engineering products, exports	Manufactures of metal (nes) by region and country of destination	US$	No		World	UN14 (8)
	by region and country of destination	US$	No		World	UN14 (9)
Professional scientific and controlling instruments and apparatus; photographic apparatus and equipment; optical goods; watches and clocks, exports	By destination	US$	No		World	UN14 (6a,b)
27.4.8 Export Share						
Exports, economic groupings share		%	Yes	A	World	UNIDO1 (1.13)
Exports, selected countries share		%	Yes	I	Developing countries	UNIDO1 (1.14)
Exports, share of manufactures in total exports by country group	By exports from by exports to	%	Yes	Selected years	World, by development groups	UNCTAD5 (4.16)
Share, exports	Share by country of total exports and exports of manufactures of selected industrialized countries and the industrialized West	%	No		VICES countries and Yugoslavia	VICES1 (III/5)
Share of primary commodities in all merchandise trade values	By region; exports; imports	%	Yes	A	World	UNCTAD4 (1.19)
Share of primary commodity exports in GDP	By country	%	Yes	A	World	UNCTAD4 (1.22)
Share of regions in world total primary commodity trade values	Exports; imports	%	Yes	A	World	UNCTAD4 (1.21)
Share of three leading commodities in total exports by developing country	By commodity	%	No		Developing countries	UNCTAD4 (A.7)
Share of world exports		%	Yes	A	World	UNCTAD1 (1.9)
Shares of world exports	By region	%	No		World	GATT3 (A.3)
Trade, EC and main-EC Partners	By reporting country	US$, %	No		World	EC39 (E)
27.4.9 Export Structure						
Export structure	By commodity class and region	%	Yes	A	World	UN32 (I)
Export structure	By main categories and selected commodity groups, by country	%	Yes	I	World	UNCTAD1 (4.1)

Subject	Categories	Units	Time series Yes/No	Frequency	Territorial coverage	Source (Table No.)
Export structure	By main regions destination, by country of origin	%	Yes	I	World	UNCTAD1 of (3.4)
Export structure	By SITC group (ranked by average 1984-1985 values), by country, economic region	US$, %	No		World	UNCTAD1 (4.3)
Export structure	Share, annual average growth rates, by destination and major commodity groups	US$, %	Yes	I	World	UNCTAD1 (3.2)
Export structure	Exports by commodity classes and by regions commodity composition	%	Yes	A	World	UN50 (131)
Export structure and markets		$US, %	Yes	Selected years	World, by development groups	UNCTAD5 (4.19)
Exports f.o.b.	Type of trade	US$	Yes	A, M	World	UN35R (46)
Exports structure	Primary commodities, manufacturers, other	%	Yes	A	African countries	UN1(31)
Imports structure	Food items, fuel, machinery and transport equipment, other manufactured goods, other	%	Yes	A	African countries	UN1(32)
Merchandise exports. structure	By high, middle, low income	%	No		World	CS1 (10)
Merchandise trade, structure of	Exports, imports by sector	%, $US	Yes	Selected years	World, least developed countries	UNCTAD5 (2.4)
Trade in services,	By sector structure	$US	Yes	Selected years	DMECs, developing countries, least developed countries	UNCTAD5 (2.6)
Trade structure of countries	Exports, imports of Eastern Europe by destination/origin	%	Yes	Selected years	Socialist countries of Eastern Europe	UNCTAD5 (3.10)

27.4.10 Export and Import Trends - see also Sections 5 and 25

Subject	Categories	Units	Time series Yes/No	Frequency	Territorial coverage	Source (Table No.)
Commodity trade, growth	By commodity class	%	Yes	A	World	UN32 (H)
EC Trade, trends in	By SITC section with world, intra-EC and extra-EC	ECU, %	Yes	A, M	World	EC38 (8)
EC trade, trends	By country	ECU, %	Yes	A	World	EC39 (2)
EC trade, trends in	World, intra- and extra-EC by country	ECU	Yes	A, M	World	EC38 (5)
EC trade, trends in	Intra-EC by member countries	ECU	Yes	A, M	EC	EC38 (6)
EC trade, trends in	With major world areas by EC country	ECU, %	Yes	A, M	World	EC38 (7)
Exports, annual growth rates	To selected countries worldwide	%	Yes	A	ASEAN	ASEANS1 (6.3.5)
Exports of goods and services : volume	Percentage change	%	Yes	A	OECD Europe, OECD, EC	OECD32 (4.8)
Imports, annual growth rates	From selected countries worldwide	%	Yes	A	ASEAN	ASEANS1 (6.3.2)
Imports of goods and services	average annual rates of growth	indices	Yes	A	Latin American and Caribbean countries	UN45 (41)
Imports of goods and services : volume	Percentage change	%	Yes	A	OECD Europe, OECD, EC	OECD32 (4.9)
Merchandise and commercial products, trends	By rate of expansion of selected product groups	%	No		World	GATT3 (9)
Merchandise exports and output growth	By major product group	%	Yes	A	World	GATT3 (2)
Merchandise trade, value	By imports and exports	US$	Yes	A	World	WB6 (17-18)

27 INTERNATIONAL TRADE AND FINANCE

Subject	Categories	Units	Time series Yes/No Frequency		Territorial coverage	Source (Table No.)
Merchandise trade, growth	By imports and exports, average annual growth	%	Yes	A	World	WB6 (19- 20)
Trade, trends of non-EC countries	By country	US$	Yes	A	World	EC39 (D)
Trade, trends in EC	By member countries	ECU	Yes	A	World with major world areas	EC39 (6)
Trade, trends in EC	By SITC section for	ECU	Yes	A	World, Intra-EC and Extra-EC Trade	EC39 (7)
Trade, growth rates		%	Yes	A	World and economic regions	UNCTAD1 (1.6)
Trade, growth rates	By economic grouping	%	Yes	A	Developing countries	UNCTAD1 (1.8)
Trade, trends in EC	By member countries	ECU	Yes	A	EC for World, Intra-EC Countries and Extra-EC trade	EC39 (4)
Trade, trends in intra-EC	By member countries	ECU	Yes	A	EC	EC39 (5)
Trade, growth of markets	All products by destination	%	Yes	Selected years	World, DMECs, development groups	UNCTAD5 (3.9)
Trade	Growth rates, annual average	%	Yes	A	World, and economic regions	UNCTAD1 (1.5)
Trade	Growth rates, annual average by economic grouping	%	Yes	A	Developing countries and territories	UNCTAD1 (1.7)
Trade in manufactures	By export from, by exports to	Rate of growth	Yes	Selected years	World, by development groups	UNCTAD5 (4.15)
Trends in trade	By country	ECU	Yes	A, M	Non-EC countries	EC38 (12)
World merchandise exports	By value of exports, volume of exports, export unit value	% rates	Yes	A	Least developed countries	UNCTAD5 (2.5)
27.4.11 Exporters and Importers						
Abalones fresh, chilled or frozen		US$, tonnes	Yes	A	World	FAO4 (J24)
Clams fresh, chilled or frozen		US$, tonnes	Yes	A	World	FAO4 (J28)
Coarse grains		tonnes	Yes	A	World	IWhC3 (A.7)
Cods, hakes, haddock fresh, chilled or frozen		US$, tonnes	Yes	A	World	FAO4 (J6)
Cods, kakes, haddocks dried, salted or in brine		US$, tonnes	Yes	A	World	FAO4 (J13)
Crabs fresh, chilled or frozen		US$, tonnes	Yes	A	World	FAO4 (J22)
Crustacean and molluscs products and preparations		US$, tonnes	Yes	A	World	FAO4 (F2.1)
Crustaceans and molluscs, fresh, frozen, dried, salted		US$, tonnes	Yes	A	World	FAO4 (D2.1)
Eels, fresh, chilled or frozen		US$, tonnes	Yes	A	World	FAO4 (J2)
Exporters, major	Leading commodity exports of developing countries and territories, by SITC group, (ranked by average 1984-1985 values)	US$, %	No		Developing countries, world economic groups	UNCTAD1 (4.4)
Exporters, top 20 developing-country	By main category, value exporters of services	US$, % share	No		World	UNCTAD5 (4.31)
Fish, fresh, chilled or frozen		US$,tonnes	Yes	A	World	FAO4 (B2.1)
Fish, dried, salted or smoked		US$, tonnes	Yes	A	World	FAO4 (C2.1)
Fish fillets fresh, chilled or frozen		US$, tonnes	Yes	A	World	FAO4 (J12)
Fish for ornamental purposes		US$, tonnes	Yes	A	World	FAO4 (J1)
Fish products and preparations		US$, tonnes	Yes	A	World	FAO4 (E2.1)
Fish roes dried, salted or in brine		US$, tonnes	Yes	A	World	FAO4 (J16)

Subject	Categories	Units	Time series Yes/No Frequency		Territorial coverage	Source (Table No.)
Fish roes fresh, chilled or frozen		US$, tonnes	Yes	A	World	FAO4 (J11)
Fishery commodities, preserved and processed	By product	tonnes	Yes	A	World	FAO4 (A4)
Flatfishes fresh, chilled or frozen		US$, tonnes	Yes	A	World	FAO4 (J5)
Herrings, sardines, anchovies fresh, chilled or frozen		US$, tonnes	Yes	A	World	FAO4 (J8)
Herrings, sardines, anchovies dried, salted or in brine		US$, tonnes	Yes	A	World	FAO4 (J14)
Importers, top 20 developing-country importers of services	By main category, value	US$, % share	No		World	UNCTAD5 (4.32)
Lobsters fresh, chilled or frozen		US$, tonnes	Yes	A	World,	FAO4 (J21)
Mackerals, canned		US$, tonnes	Yes	A	World	FAO4 (J20)
Mackerels fresh, chilled or frozen		US$, tonnes	Yes	A	World	FAO4 (J10)
Meals and animal feedingstuffs of aquatic animal origin		US$, tonnes	Yes	A	World	FAO4 (H2.1)
Mussels fresh, chilled or frozen		US$, tonnes	Yes	A	World	FAO4 (J26)
Oils and fats, crude or refined of aquatic animal origin		US$, tonnes	Yes	A	World	FAO4 (G2.1)
Oysters fresh, chilled or frozen		US$, tonnes	Yes	A	World	FAO4 (J25)
Redfishes, basses, congers fresh, chilled or frozen		US$, tonnes	Yes	A	World	FAO4 (J7)
Salmon, canned		US$, tonnes	Yes	A	World	FAO4 (J18)
Salmons fresh, chilled or frozen		US$, tonnes	Yes	A	World	FAO4 (J3)
Sardines, canned		US$, tonnes	Yes	A	World	FAO4 (J17)
Scallops fresh, chilled or frozen		US$, tonnes	Yes	A	World	FAO4 (J27)
Services, top 20 exporters	Service category	US$, % share	No		World	UNCTAD5 (4.29)
Services, top 20 importers	Service category	US$, % share	No		World	UNCTAD5 (4.30)
Sharks fins dried, salted		US$, tonnes	Yes	A	World	FAO4 (J15)
Shrimps and prawns fresh, chilled or frozen		US$, tonnes	Yes	A	World	FAO4 (J23)
Squids, cuttlefish and octopuses fresh, chilled or frozen		US$, tonnes	Yes	A	World	FAO4 (J29)
Trade	By principal importers and exporters	US$	Yes	A	World	FAO4 (A5)
Trade	Total	tonnes	Yes	A	World	FAO4 (A3)
Trout and bonitos, canned		US$, tonnes	Yes	A	World,	FAO4 (J19)
Trouts fresh, chilled or frozen		US$, tonnes	Yes	A	World	FAO4 (J4)
Tunas fresh, chilled or frozen		US$, tonnes	Yes	A	World	FAO4 (J9)
Wheat and flour	Imports, exports	tonnes	Yes	A	World	IWhC3 (A.2)
27.4.12 Fish - see also Section 22 and under Exporters and Importers (27.4.11)						
Fish and fish products	Imports, exports, quantity, value by country	tonnes	Yes	A	OECD	OECD43
Fish and fish products, total	By major products and country, quantity, value	tonnes	Yes	A	OECD	OECD43
Fish catches, nominal and trade	By country	tonnes, %, US$	Yes	A	World	ISL2 (2.3.25.1-2)
Fish exports		tonnes, ECU	No		World, EC	EC9 (5.27)
Fish exports	By country of destination	% change, tonnes, nat curr	Yes	A	North America	SFIA1 (-)
Fish exports	By country of origin and destination, fish type	tonnes, nat curr, % change	Yes	A	EC	SFIA1 (-)
Fish, crustaceans, molluscs, and preparations thereof	By country, region of destination	US$	No		OECD	OECD43

27 INTERNATIONAL TRADE AND FINANCE

Subject	Categories	Units	Time series Yes/No Frequency		Territorial coverage	Source (Table No.)
Fishery commodities	Value of exports and imports	US$	Yes	A	World	UNCTAD4 (2.3.1, 2.3.2)
27.4.13 General and Miscellaneous						
Apparent consumption	Trade as % of apparent consumption, by sector of industry	US$	Yes	A	EC, US, Canada, Japan	UNCTAD1 (7.1)
Balance of trade	by type of import, intra, extra EC	million US$	Yes	A	African countries countries	UN1(29) (4.1-4.74)
Caricom imports	By principal sources of origin	EC$, %	No		Caricom countries	CCS1 (I)
Caricom trade, trade balance		EC$	Yes	A	Caricom countries	CCS1 (1.5, 2.5, 3.5, 4.5, 5.5, 6.5, 7.5)
Caricom trade, value of domestic exports	Annual changes and as percentages of total domestic exports and domestice exports to extra-regional destinations	EC$, %	Yes	A	Caricom countries	CCS1 (1.3, 2.3, 3.3, 4.3, 5.3, 6.3, 7.3)
Caricom trade, value of domestic exports	By SITC sections and annual changes	EC$, %	Yes	A	Caricom countries	CCS1 (1.4, 2.4, 3.4, 4.4, 5.4)
Caricom trade, value of imports	By SITC sections and annual changes	EC$, %			Caricom countries	CCS1 (1.2, 2.2, 3.2, 4.2, 5.2)
Caricom trade, value of imports	Annual changes and as percentages of total imports and imports from extra-regional sources	US$, %	Yes	A	Caricom countries	CCS1 (1.1,2.1,3.1, 4.1, 5.1, 6.1, 7.1)
Caricom trade, value of intra-regional imports	Annual changes and as percentages of total imports	EC$, %	Yes	A	Intra-Caricom countries	CCS1 (8.1)
Caricom trade, value of intra-regional domestic exports	Annual changes and as percentage of total total domestic exports	EC$, %	Yes	A	Intra-Caricom countries	CCS1 (8.3)
Caricom trade, value of intra-regional domestic exports	By SITC sections and annual changes	EC$, %	Yes	A	Intra-Caricom countries	CCS1 (8.4)
Caricom trade, value of intra-regional imports	By SITC sections and annual changes	EC$, %	Yes	A	Intra-Caricom countries	CCS1 (8.2)
Caricom trade: destinations of the LDCs	Intra-regional domestic exports	EC$	Yes	A	Intra-Caricom countries	CCS1 (8.8)
Caricom trade: LDCs balance of trade with the MDCs		EC$	Yes	A	Intra-Caricom countries	CCS1 (8.11)
Caricom trade: origins of the LDCs	Intra-regional imports	EC$	Yes	A	Intra-Caricom countries	CCS1 (8.7)
Caricom trade: percentage distribution of the LDCs	Intra-regional domestic exports	%	Yes	A	Intra-Caricom countries	CCS1 (8.10)
Caricom trade: percentage distribution of the LDCs	Intra-regional imports	%	Yes	A	Intra-Caricom countries	CCS1 (8.9)
Cars	Imports intra, exports extra	nos	No		EC	EC53 (5.7)
Cars	Imports, exports	nos	No		EC, USA and Japan	EC53 (1.11)
Coefficients of imports of goods and services	% GDP at constant 1980 prices	%	Yes	A	Latin America and Caribbean countries	UN45 (42)
Commercial motor vehicles	Imports intra, exports extra	nos	No		EC	EC53 (5.8)
Commercial motor vehicles	Imports, exports	nos	No		EC, USA and Japan	EC53 (1.12)
Commercial services	Leading exporters leading importers	US$	Yes	10yr	World	GATT3 (12)

Subject	Categories	Units	Time series Yes/No Frequency		Territorial coverage	Source (Table No.)
Commercial services trade	Leading exporters leading importers	US$	Yes	10yr	World	GATT3 (12)
Commercial services, product composition	Imports, exports by region	%	No		World	GATT3 (A.5)
Commodities	By commodity groups, by selected commodities, at current prices by country	nat curr, nos, tonnes, kWh, kg, l, cu m, sq m	Yes	A	VICES countries	VICES1 (III/2)
Commodities, exports to VICES	Exports of eight industrialized countries and industrialized west to VICES countries. value, share of commodity groups, average annual growth rate, by commodity groups, by country	US$, %	Yes	A	VICES countries and Yugoslavia	VICES1 (III/4)
Commodity export concentration, diversification and instability indices	By high, middle, low income	nos, index	No		World	CS1 (13)
Commodity exports	By countries	nos	No		The Americas and Australasia	MAC2 (F3)
Commodity exports	By country, product, type	nat curr	Yes	A	Africa and Asia	MAC1 (F3)
Commodity exports	By commodity	value by weight	Yes	A	ASEAN	ASEANS1 (8.3)
Commodity trade as a proportion of total value of merchandise exports	By high, middle, low income	%	No		World	CS1 (12)
Commodity trade within the GCC and with the rest of the world	By country of origin, by destination country, year	US$	No		Arabian Gulf	CH1 (4.1)
Concentration and "diversification" indices	Number of commodities exported, " diversification index", concentration economic regions index	nos, indices	No		World	UNCTAD1 (4.5)
Countries of provenance and destination	By imports, exports, country	US$	Yes	A	World	UN24 (1)
Developed countries, trade with Central and Eastern Europe, USSR.	Imports, exports	US$	No		World	GATT3 (A.1)
EC export indices	By type of export, intra, extra EC	indices	Yes	A, M	EC and third countries	EC25 (1.68-1.131)
EC export indices	By type of export, intra, extra EC	indices	Yes	A, M	EC and third countries	EC25 (2.29-2.56)
EC export indices	By type of export, intra, extra EC	indices	Yes	A, M	EC and third countries	EC25 (3.18-3.34)
EC export indices	By type of export, intra, extra EC	indices	Yes	A, M	EC and third countries	EC25 (4.75-4.143)
EC import indices	Indices by NACE-CLIO (R44) branch, by type of import, intra, extra EC	indices	Yes	A, M	EC and third countries	EC25 (3.1-3.17)
EC import indices	Indices by Nimexe chapter,	indices	Yes	A, M	EC and third	EC25
EC import indices	Indices by SITC revision 2 sections and divisions, by type of import, intra, extra EC	indices	Yes	A, M	EC and third countries	EC25 (1.1-1.67)
EC import indices	Indices by UN broad economic category, by type of import, intra, extra EC	indices	Yes	A, M	EC and third countries	EC25 (2.1-2.28)
EC trade, total	By commodities	ECU	Yes	A, Q, M	World	EC38 (3-4)
EC trade, total	By country	ECU	Yes	A, Q, M	World	EC38 (1-2)
EFTA trade	with DAE's and other selected countries	US$	Yes	A	EFTA	EFTA1 (2.28)

27 INTERNATIONAL TRADE AND FINANCE

Subject	Categories	Units	Time series Yes/No	Frequency	Territorial coverage	Source (Table No.)
EFTA trade	By SITC section	US$	Yes	A	EFTA	EFTA1 (2.10)
EFTA trade	Imports, exports	% change	Yes	A	EFTA	EFTA1 (2.3)
EFTA trade	Main areas worldwide, imports, exports	% share	No		World	EFTA1 (2.8)
EFTA trade	Share of CEEC	%	Yes	A	EFTA	EFTA1 (2.27)
EFTA trade	With EC countries imports, exports	US$, % share	Yes	A	EFTA	EFTA1 (2.14-2.16)
EFTA trade	With EC, manufactured and non-manufactured goods	US$	Yes	A	EFTA	EFTA1 (2.17)
EFTA trade	With the EC by SITC section	US$	Yes	A	EFTA	EFTA1 (2.18)
EFTA trade	With USA, Japan, Czechoslovakia, Yugoslavia, CEEC, Poland, Hungary, by SITC section	US$	Yes	A	EFTA	EFTA1 (2.20-2.26)
EFTA trade, distribution	By partner countries, imports, exports	%	Yes	A	EFTA	EFTA1 (2.12)
EFTA trade, intra		US$	Yes	A	EFTA	EFTA1 (2.11)
EFTA trade, intra	By SITC section	US$	Yes	A	EFTA	EFTA1 (2.13)
EFTA trade, value	Imports, exports, trade balances	US$	Yes	A	EFTA	EFTA1 (2.2)
Export goods and categories to central and eastern European countries	By country, by SITC headings	US$, nat curr	No		EC	EC18 (9.9)
Export of goods and services	At current prices and 1985 exchange rates, price levels and exchange rates of 1985, current prices and current exchange rates, volume and price indices	US$, indices	Yes	A	OECD and EC	OECD28 (part 6)
Export orders, new	Net, by type of goods	nat curr	Yes	A, M	OECD	OECD22
Export value of Caricom's domestic exports	By principal areas of destination	EC$, %	No		Caricom countries	CCS1 (II)
Export/import ratio, aerospace industry	By country	nos	Yes	A	OECD	OECD28 (84)
Export/import ratio, drug industry	By country	nos	Yes	A	OECD	OECD28 (87)
Export/import ratio, electrical/ electronic industry	By country	nos	Yes	A	OECD	OECD28 (85)
Export/import ratio, office machinery and computer industry	By country	nos	Yes	A	OECD	OECD28 (86)
Export/import ratio, other manufacturing industries	By country	nos	Yes	A	OECD	OECD28 (88)
Export/import ratio, total manufacturing	By country	nos	Yes	A	OECD	OECD28 (89)
Exports		ECU, %	Yes	A	World, EC	EC9 (6.3)
Exports		ECU, %, ECU per capita	No		EC, USA USSR, Canada, Japan	EC9 (6.1)
Exports		nat curr	Yes	A, M	OECD	OECD22
Exports		US$	Yes	A, M	OECD Total EC Total Major Seven Total OECD Europe	OECD22
Exports		US$	Yes	A, M	World	IMF6 (-)
Exports		US$	Yes	A, M	World	IMF7 (-)
Exports		US$ per nat curr	Yes	A	World	UN50 (126)
Exports		volume indices	Yes	A	EC	EC9 (6.5)
Exports	At current and 1985 prices, PPPs and exchange rates	PPPs, ECU	Yes	A	EC, USA and Japan	EC60 (G)

Subject	Categories	Units	Time series Yes/No Frequency		Territorial coverage	Source (Table No.)
Exports	By branch and country for total imports and imports to EC and third countries		No		EC	EC63
Exports	By commodities (SITC) and country	US$	Yes	A	World	UN32 (5)
Exports	By commodity	US$	Yes	A	World	UN33
Exports	By country (incl gold)	nat curr US$	Yes	A	World	UN32 (1)
Exports	By country and industrial origin	% of total	Yes	A	World	UN32 (2)
Exports	By country with principal countries	US$ % of total	Yes	A	World	UN32 (3)
Exports	By country, by category of goods	%	No		EC	EC18 (9.4)
Exports	By region and country	indices	Yes	A	World	UN32(F-G)
Exports	By regions and countries or area	US$	Yes	A	World	UN32 (A)
Exports	By selected commodities, by country	US$	Yes	A	ASEAN	ASEANS1 (6.6)
Exports	By SITC section and trading partners, by country or area	tonnes, US$	No		World	UN15
Exports	By SITC section and countries of origin and destination	US$	Yes	A	OECD	OECD13 (-)
Exports	Direction of trade and export by SITC section and selected commodity group	US$	Yes	A	ESCAP region, developing ESCAP region	UN44 (7, 12)
Exports	Extra EC, intra EC, by SITC section	indices, ECU	Yes	A, M	EC	EC36
Exports	From developing countries, from ACP	indices, ECU	Yes	A, M	EC	EC36
Exports	From western industrialised third countries, from USA, from Japan	indices, ECU	Yes	A, M	EC	EC36
	Exports	nat cur	Yes	A	Nordic countries	NCM1 (116)
Exports	To selected countries worldwide	%	Yes	A	ASEAN	ASEANS1 (6.3.5)
Exports	To selected countries worldwide	US$	Yes	A	ASEAN	ASEANS1 (6.3.4)
Exports	Total value	US$	Yes	A	World, ESCAP countries, developing ESCAP countries	UN44 (p4)
Exports	Total, extra EC	ECU	Yes	A, M	EC	EC36
	Exports	US$	Yes	A	Nordic countries	NCM1 (117)
Exports	Volume	indices, %	Yes	A, Q	EC, USA, Japan	EC36
Exports	Volume and price growth	indices	Yes	A	EC, USA and Japan	EC60 (R.7)
Exports	World by commodity class and region	US$	Yes	A	World	UN32 (B)
Exports	Selected commodities	million CFA frs 1000 tons	Yes	A	North Africa	UN2(39)
Exports (EC)		%, ECU	No		World, Developing OPEC, Non-OPEC, ACP	EC1 (I21)
Exports and imports		US$	No		ACP states	EC1 (II-)
Exports and imports		US$	No		Mediterranean countries	EC1 (IV-)

27 INTERNATIONAL TRADE AND FINANCE

Subject	Categories	Units	Time series Yes/No Frequency		Territorial coverage	Source (Table No.)
Exports and imports	Imports, exports, balance of trade	US$	Yes	A	World, ASEAN	ASEANS1 (6.1)
Exports and imports	Intra, extra country	ECU, % GDP	No		EC, USA and Japan	EC53 (1.9)
Exports and imports	Of the 18 and 10 core commodities covered by the IPC	%	No		World	UNCTAD1 (4.11)
Exports and imports	To and from EC	US$	No		ACP states	EC1 (II-)
Exports and imports	To and from EC	US$	No		Mediterranean countries	EC1 (IV-)
Exports and imports, balance	At current prices, PPPs and exchange rates	PPPs, ECU	Yes	A	EC, USA and Japan	EC60 (I)
Exports and imports, world	To and from countries listed, to and from the world	US$	Yes	A, M	World	IMF3,4 (-)
Exports by countries and regions of consumption/ consignment, value	To and from countries listed	US$	No		World	NCM1 (121)
Exports by partner countries	By exporting country	US$	No		EC	EC18 (9.6)
Exports by SITC sections	Sections 0-9	million CFA frs	Yes	A	Central Africa	UN5(37)
Exports by SITC sections	Sections 0-9	million CFA frs	Yes	A	East & Southern Africa	UN4(37)
Exports by SITC sections	Sections 0-9	million CFA frs	Yes	A	North Africa	UN2(37)
Exports by SITC sections	Sections 0-9	million CFA frs	Yes	A	West Africa	UN3(37)
Exports f.o.b.		nat curr	Yes	A, Q, M	OECD	OECD22 (-)
Exports f.o.b.		US$	Yes	A	World	UN50 (127)
Exports f.o.b.	Type of trade	US$	Yes	A, M	World	UN35 (46)
Exports of goods and non-factor services	% of GDP	%	Yes	A	World	IMF7 (-)
Exports of goods and services	At current prices and 1985 exchange rates	US$	Yes	A	OECD, EC	OECD28 (-)
Exports of goods and services	At current prices and current exchange rates	US$	Yes	A	OECD, EC	OECD28 (-)
Exports of goods and services	Percentage of GDP	%	Yes	A	OECD, EC	OECD32 (6.12)
Exports of goods and services	Price indices	indices	Yes	A	OECD, EC	OECD28 (-)
Exports of goods and services	Volume indices	indices	Yes	A	OECD, EC	OECD28 (-)
Exports of motor vehicles	By cars and commercial vehicles, total	nos	No		World	SMMT2 (79)
Exports to world		%, US$	No		World, Developing, OPEC, Non-OPEC, ACP, EC	EC1 (I18)
Exports, all commodities quantum and unit value		indices	Yes	A	World	UN50 (1)
Exports, coefficients of exports of goods and services	% of GDP at constant 1980 prices	%	Yes	A	Latin American and Caribbean countries	UN45 (44)
Exports, f.o.b.		US$	Yes	A	World	UN50 (1)
Exports, goods and services	Average annual rates	indices	Yes	A	Latin American and Caribbean	UN45 (43)
Exports, intra-ASEAN	By origin and destination	US$	No		ASEAN	ASEANS1 (6.4.2)
Exports, intra-regional	% intra-regional exports with respect to total exports calculated on the basis of f.o.b exports	%	Yes	A	Latin American and Caribbean countries	UN45 (92)
Exports, leading products	By SITC section, by % share	%	Yes	A	Latin American and Caribbean countries	UN45 (72-91)

Subject	Categories	Units	Time series Yes/No Frequency		Territorial coverage	Source (Table No.)
Exports, manufactured goods	By region, country or area	US$	Yes	A	World	UN32 (C)
Exports, manufactures	% f.o.b value of total exports of goods	%	Yes	A	Latin American and Caribbean countries	UN45 (71)
Exports, manufactures quantum and unit value		indices	Yes	A	World	UN50 (1)
Exports, OECD total	OECD total, OECD EC, to VICES countries, at current prices	US$	Yes	A	VICES countries and Yugoslavia	VICES1 (III/3)
Exports, primary products	% f.o.b value of total exports of goods	%	Yes	A	Latin American and Caribbean countries	UN45 (70)
Exports, total	By country	nat curr	No		EC	EM1 (0502)
Exports, total	By region, by important trading partners, at current prices by country	nat curr	Yes	A	VICES countries and Yugoslavia	VICES1 (III/1)
Exports, total	Primary products, manufactured products, f.o.b	US$	Yes	A	Latin American and Caribbean countries	UN45 (279)
Exports, value		US$	Yes	A	World	UNCTAD1 (1.1)
Exports, value	By economic grouping	US$	Yes	A	Developing countries and territories	UNCTAD1 (1.3)
Exports, value	By type of export	US$, %	Yes	A	World	GATT3 (1)
Exports, value and volume	For 18 individual commodities covered by the IPC	tonnes, US$	Yes	A	Developing countries	UNCTAD1 (4.10)
Exports, value of goods	At current prices, at constant 1980 prices, f.o.b	US$	Yes	A	Latin American and Caribbean countries	UN45 (278)
Exports, value of goods	Percentage change	%	Yes	A	OECD, EC	OECD32 (11.4)
Exports, volume indices		indices	Yes	A	World	UNCTAD1 (2.1)
Exports, volume of goods	Percentage change	%	Yes	A	OECD EC, OECD	OECD32 (11.2)
Exports, world network	By selected commodity classes (SITC) and region of origin and destination	US$ f.o.b.	Yes	A	World, EC	UNCTAD1 (A.1-11)
External trade	Total value of imports and exports	nat curr	Yes	M	Asia and Pacific	UN43(-)
Generalized tariff preferences, EC (GSP)	Countries by product	ECU	No		World	EC41
Generalized tariff preferences, EC (GSP)	Products by country	ECU	No		World	EC40
Goods exports	By sector of economic activity	US$	Yes	A	Latin American	UN45 (282)
Goods exports	Indices		Yes	A	Latin American and Caribbean countries	UN45 (272)
High-technology products	Export, import	ratio	Yes	A	EFTA	EFTA1 (2.29)
Import goods and categories from central and eastern european countries	By country, by SITC headings	US$, nat curr	No		EC	EC18 (9.8)
Import, export ratio	Of current values	%	Yes	A, M	EC, USA, Japan	EC36

27 INTERNATIONAL TRADE AND FINANCE

Subject	Categories	Units	Time series Yes/No	Frequency	Territorial coverage	Source (Table No.)
Imports		%, ECU	No		World, Developing OPEC, Non-OPEC, ACP	EC1 (I20)
Imports		ECU, %	Yes	A	World, EC	EC9 (6.2)
Imports		ECU, %, ECU per capita	No		EC, USA, USSR, Canada, Japan	EC9 (6.1)
Imports		nat curr	Yes	A, M	OECD	OECD22
Imports		US$	Yes	A, M	OECD Total EC Total Major Seven Total	OECD22
Imports		US$	Yes	A, M	World	IMF6 (-)
Imports		US$	Yes	A, M	World	IMF7 (-)
Imports		US$ per nat curr	Yes	A	World	UN50 (126)
Imports		volume indices	Yes	A	EC	EC9 (6.5)
Imports	At current and 1985 prices, PPPs and exchange rates	PPPs, ECU	Yes	A	EC, USA and Japan	EC60 (H)
Imports	By branch and country for total imports, imports from EC and third countries		No		EC	EC63
Imports	By commodities (SITC) and country	US$	Yes	A	World	UN32 (4)
Imports	By commodity	US$	Yes	A	World	UN33
Imports	By country (incl gold) US$	nat curr	Yes	A	World	UN32 (1)
Imports	By country and economic category	% of total	Yes	A	World	UN32 (2)
Imports	By country with principal countries	US$ % of total	Yes	A	World	UN32 (3)
Imports	By country, by category of goods	%	No		EC	EC18 (9.3)
Imports	By partner countries, by importing country	US$	No		EC	EC18 (9.5)
Imports	By region and country	indices	Yes	A	World	UN32(F-G)
Imports	By regions and countries or area	US$	Yes	A	World	UN32 (A)
Imports	By selected commodities, by country	US$	Yes	A	ASEAN	ASEANS1 (6.6)
Imports	By SITC section and countries of origin and destination	US$	Yes	A	OECD	OECD13 (-)
Imports	By SITC section and trading partners, by country or area	tonnes, US$	No		World	UN15
Imports	c.i.f.	US$	Yes	A	World	UN50 (1)
Imports	c.i.f.	US$	Yes	A	World	UN50 (127)
Imports	Direction of trade and composition of imports	US$	Yes	A	ESCAP region, developing ESCAP region	UN44 (7, 12)
Imports	Extra EC, intra EC, by SITC section	indices, ECU	Yes	A, M	EC	EC36
Imports	From selected countries worldwide	US$	Yes	A	ASEAN	ASEANS1 (6.3.7-6.3.19)
Imports	From selected countries worldwide	US$	Yes	A	ASEAN	ASEANS1 (6.3.1)
Imports	From world	% US$	No		World, Developing, OPEC, Non-OPEC, ACP, ECQ	EC1 (I19)

Subject	Categories	Units	Time series Yes/No Frequency		Territorial coverage	Source (Table No.)
Imports	Total value	US$	Yes	A	World, ESCAP countries, developing ESCAP countries	UN44 (p4)
Imports	Total, extra EC, intra EC	ECU	Yes	A, M	EC	EC36
Imports	Type of trade, c.i.f.	US$	Yes	A, M	World	UN35 (46)
	Imports	US$	Yes	A	Nordic countries	NCM1 (117)
Imports	Volume	indices, %	Yes	A, Q	EC, USA, Japan	EC36
Imports	Volume and price growth	indices	Yes	A	EC, USA and Japan	EC60 (R.8)
Imports	By end use	million CFA frs	Yes	A	Central Africa	UN5(36)
Imports	By end use	million CFA frs	Yes	A	East & Southern Africa	UN4(36)
Imports	By end use	million CFA frs	Yes	A	North Africa	UN2(36)
Imports	By end use	million CFA frs	Yes	A	West Africa	UN3(36)
Imports	Selected commodities	million CFA frs 1000 tons	Yes	A	North Africa	UN2(38)
Imports	Type of trade, f.o.b.	nat curr	Yes	A, Q, M	OECD	OECD22
Imports and exports	By destination	tonnes	Yes	A	World	ISL2 (2.3.17.2.1-2)
Imports and exports	Index numbers	nos	Yes	A	Central Africa	UN5(33)
Imports and exports	Index numbers	nos	Yes	A	East & Southern Africa	UN4(33)
Imports and exports	Index numbers	nos	Yes	A	West Africa	UN3(33)
Imports and exports	Value	million CFA frs million US$	Yes	A	Central Africa	UN5(32)
Imports and exports	Value	million CFA frs million US$	Yes	A	East & Southern Africa	UN4(32)
Imports and exports	Value	million CFA frs million US$	Yes	A	North Africa	UN2(32)
Imports and exports	Value	million CFA frs million US$	Yes	A	West Africa	UN3(32)
Imports and exports, trade destination	Index numbers	nos	Yes	A	North Africa, World	UN2(33)
Imports and exports, total	Imports c.i.f., exports f.o.b.	million US$	Yes	A	African countries	UN1(28)
Imports by countries and regions of origin, value	From and to countries listed	US$	No		World	NCM1 (120)
Imports by SITC sections	Sections 0-9	million CFA frs	Yes	A	Central Africa	UN5(35)
Imports by SITC sections	Sections 0-9	million CFA frs	Yes	A	East & Southern Africa	UN4(35)
Imports by SITC sections	Sections 0-9	million CFA frs	Yes	A	North Africa	UN2(35)
Imports by SITC sections	Sections 0-9	million CFA frs	Yes	A	West Africa	UN3(35)
Imports of goods and non-factor services	% of GDP	%	Yes	A	World	IMF7 (-)
Imports of goods and services	At current prices and current exchange rates	US$	Yes	A	OECD, EC	OECD28
Imports of goods and services	At current prices and 1985 exchange rates, price levels and exchange rates of 1985, current prices and current exchange rates, volume and price indices	US$, indices	Yes	A	OECD, EC	OECD28 (part 6)
Imports of goods and services	At current prices and 1985 exchange rates	US$	Yes	A	OECD, EC	OECD28
Imports of goods and services	At the price levels and 1985 exchange rates	US$	Yes	A	OECD, EC	OECD28
Imports of goods and services	Percentage of GDP	%	Yes	A	OECD, EC	OECD32 (6.13)
Imports of goods and services	Price indices	indices	Yes	A	OECD, EC	OECD28 (-)
Imports of goods and services	Volume indices	indices	Yes	A	OECD, EC	OECD28 (-)

27 INTERNATIONAL TRADE AND FINANCE

Subject	Categories	Units	Time series Yes/No Frequency		Territorial coverage	Source (Table No.)
Imports of goods, volume	f.o.b	indices	Yes	A	Latin American and Caribbean countries	UN45 (275)
Imports, average value of goods	Percentage change	%	Yes	A	OECD, EC	OECD32 (11.3)
Imports, intra-ASEAN	By origin and destination	US$	No		ASEAN	ASEANS1 (6.4.1)
Imports, OECD	OECD total, OECD Europe, from VICES countries, at current prices	US$	Yes	A	VICES countries and Yugoslavia	VICES1 (III/3)
Imports, per cent distribution	From selected countries worldwide	%	Yes	A	ASEAN	ASEANS1 (6.3.3)
Imports, share	Share by country of total imports and imports of manufactures of selected industrialized countries and the industrialized West	%	No		VICES countries and Yugoslavia	VICES1 (III/5)
Imports, total	By country	nat curr	No		EC	EM1 (0501)
Imports, total	By regions, by important trading partners, at current prices	nat curr	Yes	A	VICES countries and Yugoslavia	VICES1 (III/1)
Imports, unit value of goods	f.o.b	indices	Yes	A	Latin American and Caribbean countries	UN45 (276)
Imports, value and volume						
Imports, value of goods	At current prices, at constant 1980 prices, f.o.b	US$	Yes	A	Latin American and Caribbean countries	UN45 (280)
Imports, volume of goods	Percentage change	%	Yes	A	OECD, EC	OECD32 (11.1)
Intra-trade	Value of intra-trade, share of intra trade in: world exports, total group exports, by region	US$, %	Yes	A	Developed regions	UNCTAD1 (1.12)
Intra-trade	Value of intra-trade, exports to developing countries as % of total group exports, intra-trade of group as % of total exports of each group, by region	US$, %	Yes	A	Developing countries and territories	UNCTAD1 (1.15)
Machinery and equipment quantities and values	By product by country	kg, ECU	No		EC, World	EC37 Vol J
Merchandise exports	By country, by food, man-ufactures, residual	index, US$	Yes	A	Developing countries	WB2 (-)
Merchandise exports	Commodity output, real GDP	US$, indices	Yes	A	World	GATT4 (A.1)
Merchandise trade	By areas and commodity groups	US$	Yes	I	US and selected countries	GATT4 (A.6)
Merchandise trade	By country group: major country groups highly indebted countries,least developed countries	US$, %	Yes	I	World	GATT4 (II)

Subject	Categories	Units	Time series Yes/No Frequency		Territorial coverage	Source (Table No.)
Merchandise trade	By product: food, raw materials, ores, minerals and non-ferrous metals, fuels, iron and steel, chemicals, machinery and transport materials, textiles,clothing	US$, %	Yes	I	World	GATT4 (IV)
Merchandise trade	By region: N. America Latin America Western Europe Central and Eastern Europe and USSR, Africa, Asia, Middle East	US$, %	Yes	I	World	GATT4 (III)
Merchandise trade	By selected economy	US$, %	No		World	GATT4 (A.2)
Merchandise trade	GATT contracting parties	US$, %	No		World	GATT4 (A.19)
Merchandise trade	Imports, exports with CMEA, with developed countries	%	Yes	A	Central and Eastern Europe, USSR	GATT3 (6)
Merchandise trade	Leading exporters leading importers	US$	Yes	10yr	World	GATT3 (11)
Merchandise trade	Leading exporters leading importers	US$	Yes	10yr	World	GATT3 (11)
Merchandise trade	Population, GDP, share of merchandise trade in GDP of GATT contracting parties	US$, %	Yes		World	GATT4 (A.20)
Merchandise trade network	By major country group and region	US$	Yes	A	World	GATT4 (A.3)
Merchandise trade network	By major country group and product	US$	Yes	A	World	GATT4 (A.4)
Merchandise trade, product composition	Imports, exports by region	%	No		World	GATT3 (A.4)
Merchandise trade, product composition	Imports, exports by product group	%	No		Western Europe's trade with USSR, Central and Eastern Europe	GATT3 (7)
Merchandise trade, value	Imports, exports by region	US$, %	No		World	GATT3 (5)
Merchandise trade, value	Imports, exports by major country group	US$, %	Yes	A	World	GATT3 (3)
Merchandise trade, volumes	Imports, exports	%	Yes	A	Selected countries and country groups	GATT3 (4)
Merchandise, growth	By imports and exports, average annual growth	%	Yes	A	World	WB6 (19-20)
Merchandise, value	By imports and exports	US$	Yes	A	World	WB6 (17-18)
		million CFA frs	Yes	A	North Africa	UN2(34)
Motor vehicles, first registration and import of	By country, vehicle type	nos	Yes	A	World	IRF1 (III)
Motor vehicles, production and export of	By country, vehicle type	nos	Yes	A	World	IRF1 (II)
Plastics, leather quantities and values	By product by country	kg, ECU	No		EC, World	EC37 Vol D
Precision and optical instruments quantities and values	By product by country	kg, ECU	No		EC, World	EC37 Vol L
Preferential imports under the GSP		US$	Yes	Selected years	World, by development groups	UNCTAD5 (4.21)
Trade balance	With main areas	US$	No		EFTA, EC, USA, Japan, OECD, CEEC, OPEC, DAE	EFTA1 (2.7)

27 INTERNATIONAL TRADE AND FINANCE

Subject	Categories	Units	Time series Yes/No	Frequency	Territorial coverage	Source (Table No.)
Production and trade	By region and country	tonnes	Yes	A	World	ISL2 (2.3.17.1-2)
Share of trade		%	Yes	A	World	UNCTAD1 (1.10)
SITC sections and groups	By country, commodities by imports, exports	US$	Yes	A	World	UN24 (2-3)
Summary, exports	By cars and commercial vehicles, total	nos, $	Yes	A	Selected countries	SMMT2 (80)
Summary, manufacturers	Exports of cars and commercial vehicles	nos	Yes	A	Selected countries	SMMT2 (81, 82, 83, 84, 85, 86, 87)
Summary, principal exporters	By cars and commercial vehicles	nos	Yes	A	Selected countries	SMMT2 (88)
Trade		indices	No		ACP states	EC1 (II-)
Trade		indices	No		Mediterranean countries	EC1 (IV-)
Trade		US$, %	Yes	I	World	GATT4 (I)
Trade	Balance	million US$	Yes	A	Central Africa	UN5(7-3)
Trade	Balance	million US$	Yes	A	East & Southern Africa	UN4(7-3)
Trade	Balance	million US$	Yes	A	North Africa	UN2(7-3)
Trade	Balance	million US$	Yes	A	West Africa	UN3(7-3)
Trade	By area, imports, exports	% change	Yes	A	World	EFTA1 (2.9)
Trade	By country	US$	Yes	A	Africa	UN23 (-)
Trade	By OECD member countries with world countries for imports and exports	US$	Yes	Q, M	OECD	OECD28 (IV)
Trade	By sections and divisions of the SITC	US$	No		Nordic countries	NCM1 (119)
Trade	Exports f.o.b.	million US$	Yes	A	Central Africa	UN5(7-2)
Trade	Exports f.o.b.	million US$	Yes	A	East & Southern Africa	UN4(7-2)
Trade	Exports f.o.b.	million US$	Yes	A	North Africa	UN2(7-2)
Trade	Exports f.o.b.	million US$	Yes	A	West Africa	UN3(7-2)
Trade	Exports, imports, terms of trade, purchasing power of exports, by country, territory	indices	Yes	A	Developing countries and territories	UNCTAD1 (7.2)
Trade	Imports and exports, by SITC section	US$	Yes	A	ASEAN	ASEANS1 (6.5.1)
Trade	Imports c.i.f.	million US$	Yes	A	Central Africa	UN5(7-1)
Trade	Imports c.i.f.	million US$	Yes	A	East & Southern Africa	UN4(7-1)
Trade	Imports c.i.f.	million US$	Yes	A	North Africa	UN2(7-1)
Trade	Imports c.i.f.	million US$	Yes	A	West Africa	UN3(7-1)
Trade	Imports, exports	US$	Yes	A	Africa	UN23 (1)
Trade	Imports, exports, value by SITC section, composition, selected commodities, direction of trade, by country	tonnes, nat curr	Yes	A	ESCAP countries	UN44
Trade	Imports, exports, by main areas	US$	No		EFTA	EFTA1 (2.6)
Trade	Percentage distribution by partner country group	%	Yes	A	USA, Japan, EC, EFTA, OECD	OECD32 (13.1-13.10)
Trade	Percentage distribution by SITC section	%	Yes	A	USA, Japan, EC, EFTA, OECD	OECD32 (14.1-14.10)
Trade (by value) with main trading partners	By countries	nat curr	Yes	A	EC	MAC3 (E2)

27 INTERNATIONAL TRADE AND FINANCE

Subject	Categories	Units	Time series Yes/No Frequency		Territorial coverage	Source (Table No.)
Trade aggregates	By countries current value	nat curr	Yes	A	EC	MAC3 (E1)
Trade balance		ECU	No		EC, USA, USSR, Canada, Japan	EC9 (6.1)
Trade balance		ECU	Yes	A	EC, USA, USSR, Canada, Japan	EC9 (6.4)
Trade balance		nat curr	Yes	A, M	OECD	OECD22
Trade balance		nat curr	Yes	A, Q, M	OECD	OECD22 (-)
Trade balance		US$	Yes	A, M	OECD, EC Major Seven	OECD22
Trade balance	By regions, at current prices	nat curr	Yes	A	VICES countries and Yugoslavia	VICES1 (III/1)
Trade balance	Exports, imports	US$	Yes	A	Central and South American countries	IADB1
Trade balance	Imports, exports and exports less imports	US$	Yes	A, Q, M	OECD	OECD22 (-)
Trade balance	Percentage of GDP	%	Yes	A	OECD, EC	OECD32 (6.14)
Trade balance	Total, extra EC, intra EC, (f.o.b.)	ECU	Yes	A, M	EC, USA Japan	EC36
Trade balance	With industrialized west, at current	US$	Yes	A	VICES countries and Yugoslavia	VICES1 (III/1)
Trade balance, external	Food and agricultural products	ECU	No		EC	WC1 (-)
Trade balance, OECD	OECD total, OECD Europe, trade balances with VICES countries, at current prices	US$	Yes	A	VICES countries and Yugoslavia	VICES1 (III/3)
Trade destination	Worldwide	million CFA frs	Yes	A	Central Africa	UN5(34)
Trade destination	Worldwide	million CFA frs	Yes	A	East & Southern Africa	UN4(34)
Trade destination	Worldwide	million CFA frs	Yes	A	West Africa	UN3(34)
Trade flows (regional), developments	Share of world merchandise trade, average annual change	%	Yes	10yr	World	GATT3 (10)
Trade in manufacture trends	Imports, exports, intra, extra EC	ECU	No		EC, USA and Japan	EC53 (1.10)
Trade in manufacture, scale	Imports extra, exports intra	ECU, %, GDP	No		EC	EC53 (5.1)
Trade in manufactures	By industry	ECU	No		EC	EC53 (5.4)
Trade in manufactures trends	By industry, intra community imports	indices	Yes	A	EC	EC53 (5.5)
Trade in manufactures, share in industrial branches	By industry, extra community	%	No		EC	EC53 (5.6)
Trade indicators, changes in trade	Categories, region volumes, terms of trade and purchasing power of exports	%	Yes	Selected years	DMECs, developing countries, least developed countries	UNCTAD5 (3.11)
Trade indices	By country for imports and exports	indices	Yes	Q, M	OECD	OECD28 (II)
Trade network	Average value of exports, average growth rates of exports, share of world exports by origin, share of world exports by destination, imports as % of exports	US$, %	Yes	I	World economic groups	UNCTAD1 (3.1)
Trade network, merchandise	By region	US$	Yes	A	World	GATT4 (A.5)
Trade of developing countries	Exports, imports by main product category	%	Yes	Selected years	Developing countries, least developed countries	UNCTAD5 (1.3A,B)

27 INTERNATIONAL TRADE AND FINANCE

Subject	Categories	Units	Time series Yes/No	Frequency	Territorial coverage	Source (Table No.)
Trade of OECD	By main region imports and exports	US$	Yes	Q, M	OECD	OECD28 (I)
Trade of OECD countries	By country and SITC section for imports and exports	US$	Yes	Q, M	OECD	OECD28 (III)
Trade of OECD countries	By region and country imports and exports	US$	Yes	Q, M	OECD	OECD28 (I)
Trade structure of countries	Exports, imports of Eastern Europe by destination, origin	%	Yes	Selected years	Socialist countries of Eastern Europe	UNCTAD5 (3.10)
Trade with main trading partners	By country, imports, exports	nat curr	Yes	A	Africa and Asia	MAC1 (F2)
Trade, annual growth rates	Imports, exports	%	Yes	A	World, ASEAN	ASEANS1 (6.2)
Trade, classification by broad economic categories	By imports and exports, by commodities	US$	Yes	A	Asia and Pacific	UN24 (4)
Trade, EC		indices, ECU	Yes	A, M	EC	EC36
Trade, EC and main-EC partners	By reporting country	US$, %	No		World	EC39 (E)
Trade, EC and world	By country and region	US$	Yes	A	World	EC39 (A)
Trade, EC and world	By SITC section	US$	Yes	A	World	EC39 (B)
Trade, external aggregates in current values	By countries, imports, exports	nos	No		The Americas and Australasia	MAC2 (F1)
Trade, external aggregates in current values	By country, imports, exports	nat curr	Yes	A	Africa and Asia	MAC1 (F1)
Trade, external with main trading partners	By countries, imports, exports	nos	No		The Americas and Australasia	MAC2 (F2)
Trade, Faroe Islands	By commodities, exports, analysis by SITC	US$	No		Nordic countries	NCM1 (129)
Trade, Faroe Islands	By commodities, imports, analysis by SITC	US$	No		Nordic countries	NCM1 (128)
Trade, Greenland	By commodities, exports, analysis by SITC	US$	No		Nordic countries	NCM1 (131)
Trade, Greenland	By commodities, imports, analysis by SITC	US$	No		Nordic countries	NCM1 (130)
Trade, growth rates	Imports c.i.f., exports f.o.b.	%	Yes	A	African countries	UN1(30)
Trade, indexes		indices	Yes	A	World	IMF7
Trade, intra-regional	Destination, origin, based on exports, f.o.b	US$	Yes	A	Latin American and Caribbean countries	UN45 (283-295)
Trade, net		nat curr	Yes	A, Q, M	OECD	OECD22
Trade, Nordic countries	By sections and divisions of the SITC	US$	No		Nordic countries	NCM1 (122)
Trade, Nordic countries	Imports from and exports to Nordic countries	US$	No		Nordic countries	NCM1 (127)
Trade, Nordic countries	Value of exports to and from Nordic countries	US$	No		Nordic countries	NCM1 (126)
Trade, Nordic countries	Value of exports to and from Nordic countries	US$	Yes	A	Nordic countries	NCM1 (124)
Trade, Nordic countries	Value of imports from and to Nordic countries	US$	No		Nordic countries	NCM1 (125)
Trade, Nordic countries	Value of imports from and to Nordic countries	US$	Yes	A	Nordic countries	NCM1 (123)
Trade, quantity	Imports, exports	tonnes	Yes	A	Nordic countries	NCM1 (118)
Trade, quantum indices			Yes	A	World	UN50 (130)
Trade, quantum indices	Exports and imports	indices	Yes	A	Market economies by regions	UN50 (12)
Trade, quantum indices	Exports and imports	indices	Yes	A	World	UN35 (47)
Trade, quantum indices	Imports, exports, by country	indices	Yes	A	ESCAP countries	UN44
Trade, services						
Trade, services	By service categories	US$	Yes	A	OECD	OECD44 (A1.2)

Subject	Categories	Units	Time series Yes/No	Frequency	Territorial coverage	Source (Table No.)
Trade, services	Total by countries, net, credits %, debits %	US$, %	Yes	A	OECD	OECD44 (A1.1)
Trade, summary of EC	By commodity for intra	ECU	Yes	A	EC and extra-EC	EC39 (3)
Trade, summary of EC	By country	ECU	Yes	A	World	EC39 (1)
Trade, total	Imports, exports and balance of trade, by SITC section, by trading areas, by country	EC$, %	Yes	A	CARICOM	CCS2
Trade, total	Imports, exports and exports less imports	US$	Yes	Q, M	OECD	OECD28 (I)
Trade, trends of non-EC countries	By country	US$	Yes	A	World	EC39 (D)
Trade, value						
Trade, value		US$	Yes	A	World	UN50 (130)
Trade, value		US$	Yes	A	World	UNCTAD1 (1.2)
Trade, value	By economic grouping	US$	Yes	A	Developing countries and territories	UNCTAD1 (1.4)
Trade, value	By SITC section	US$	Yes	A	USA, Japan, EFTA, OECD EC	OECD32 (12.1-12.6)
Trade, value	Imports	nat curr	Yes	A	Nordic countries	NCM1 (116)
Trade, volume	Imports, exports	indices, %	Yes	I	EFTA	EFTA1 (2.4)
Trade, volume and unit value indices	Intra- and extra-EC trade	indices	Yes	A	EC	EC39 (8)
Trade, volume and unit value indices	Intra- and extra-EC	indices	Yes	A, M	EC	EC38 (11)
Trade, volume index	Total imports, total exports, ratios	indices	Yes	A, M	EC, USA Japan	EC36
Trade, volume indices		indices	Yes	A	World economic regions	UNCTAD1 (2.2)
World exports and EC external trade		US$	Yes	A	EC, Caribbean countries	WC1 (-)
World trade	By provenance and destination	US$	Yes	A	World	EC39 (C)
27.4.14 Horticulture						
External trade for important groups	By imports, exports, kind	nat curr, kg	No		West Europe	IAHP1 (1-6)
External trade of individual countries important positions	By imports, exports, kind	nat curr, kg	No		EC	IAHP1 (-)
External trade of some non-European countries	By imports, exports, kind	nat curr	Yes	A	Selected countries	IAHP1 (1, 2, 3, 5.2,6)
External trade total	By selected groups	nat curr, %, tonnes	Yes	A	West Europe	IAHP1 (1, 2, 3, 6, 6.1, 6.3)
Quantum index	Imports, exports	index	Yes	A	World	UN50R (129)
Summary tables of West-Europe	External trade, kind	nat curr, %	Yes	A	West Europe	IAHP1 (1, 2, 3)
27.4.15 Import Penetration						
Import penetration ratios for manufactures in DMECs	By product group and importer, exporter	%	Yes	Selected years	World, by development groups	UNCTAD5 (4.20)
27.4.16 Import Structure						
Import structure	By main categories and selected commodity groups, by country	%	Yes	I	World	UNCTAD1R (4.2)
Import structure	By main regions of origin, by country of destination	%	Yes	I	World	UNCTAD1 (3.5)

27 INTERNATIONAL TRADE AND FINANCE

Subject	Categories	Units	Time series Yes/No	Frequency	Territorial coverage	Source (Table No.)
Import structure	Share, annual average growth rates, by origin and major commodity groups	US$, %	Yes	I	World	UNCTAD1 (3.3)
Imports c.i.f.	Type of trade	US$	Yes	A, M	World	UN35 (46)
Imports, product composition of DMEC imports of manufactures from developing countries, growth rate	By product group	US$	Yes	Selected years	World, by development groups	UNCTAD5 (4.18)
Imports, product composition of DMEC imports of manufactures from developing countries, value	By product group	US$	Yes	Selected years	World, by development groups	UNCTAD5 (4.18)
Imports, product composition of DMEC imports of manufactures from developing countries, share in total imports of manufactures	By product group	US$	Yes	Selected years	World, by development groups	UNCTAD5 (4.18)
Merchandise trade, structure of	Exports, imports by sector	%, US$	Yes	Selected years	World, Least developed countries	UNCTAD5 (2.4)
Structure of merchandise imports	By high, middle, low income	%	No		World	CS1 (11)
Trade in services, structure of	By sector	US$	Yes	Selected years	DMECs, Developing countries, Least developed countries	UNCTAD5 (2.6)
Trade structure of countries	Exports, imports of Eastern Europe by destination, origin	%	Yes	Selected years	Socialist countries of Eastern Europe	UNCTAD5 (3.10)
27.4.17 Meat and Livestock - see also Section 2						
Animals and animal products exports	Total, intra-EC, by animal, product	tonnes	Yes	A	EC	EC7 (IV)
Animals and animal products imports	Total, intra-EC, resources, by animal, product	tonnes	Yes	A	EC	EC7 (IV)
Animals, live exports	By type	tonnes	Yes	M	EC	EC7 (I)
Animals, live imports	By type	tonnes	Yes	M	EC	EC7 (I)
Beef and veal exports	Destination	tonnes, %	Yes	A	Seven Major exporting countries	GATT1 (II)
Beef and veal exports	Estimates, change, forecast	tonnes, %	Yes	A	Selected countries	GATTI (1)
Beef and veal exports	By type, country of destination	tonnes, cwe	Yes	A	Selected countries	MLC1 (-)
Beef and veal exports, fresh, chilled or frozen		tonnes cwe, %	Yes	A	World	GATT2 (10)
Beef and veal exports, fresh, chilled and/or frozen	Carcass weight	tonnes, % equivalent	Yes	A	World	GATT1 (10)
Beef and veal exports, other than fresh, chilled and/or frozen	Canned, cooked etc	tonnes, %	Yes	A	World	GATT1 (11)
Beef and veal exports, other than fresh, chilled or frozen		tonnes cwe, %	Yes	A	World	GATT2 (11)
Beef and veal imports	By type, country of origin	tonnes, cwe	Yes	A	Selected countries	MLC1 (-)
Beef and veal imports, fresh, chilled or frozen		tonnes, cwe, %	Yes	A	World	GATT2 (7)
Beef and veal imports, other than fresh, chilled and/or frozen	Canned, cooked etc	tonnes, %	Yes	A	World	GATT1 (8)
Beef and veal imports, other than fresh, chilled or frozen		tonnes, cwe, %	Yes	A	World	GATT2 (8)
Beef and veal trade with third countries	By exports, imports, type, total weight	tonnes, cwe tonnes product	Yes	A	EC	MLC1 (-)
Beef and veal, fresh, chilled and/or frozen	Carcass weight	tonnes, % equivalent	Yes	A	World	GATT1 (7)
Bovine meat trade	By exports and imports, quantity and value	tonnes, US$	Yes	A	World	UNCTAD4 (2.2.2, 2.2.3)

Subject	Categories	Units	Time series Yes/No Frequency		Territorial coverage	Source (Table No.)
Cattle and calves, live exports		nos, % tonnes cwe	Yes	A	World	GATT2 (9)
Cattle and calves, live exports	Carcass weight	tonnes, % equivalent	Yes	A	Selected countries	GATT1 (9)
Cattle and calves, live imports		nos, %	Yes	A	World	GATT2 (6)
Cattle and calves, live imports	Carcass weight	tonnes, % equivalent	Yes	A	Selected countries	GATT1 (6)
Exports of beef and veal	By principal regions of destination	tonnes	Yes	A	Western Europe and Hungary	UN34 (XVI)
Exports of meat by main trading countries	By countries	nos	No		The Americas and Australasia	MAC2 (D14)
Exports of poultry meat	By principal regions of destination	tonnes	Yes	A	Western Europe, Bulgaria and Hungary	UN34 (LIV)
Exports of principal livestock products by main trading countries	By countries	nos	No		The Americas and Australasia	MAC2 (D16)
Imports of live cattle, beef and veal	By principal regions of origin	tonnes	Yes	A	Western Europe	UN34 (XV)
Imports of live pigs, pork, bacon and ham	By principal regions of origin	tonnes	Yes	A	Western Europe	UN34 (XXXI)
Imports of live sheep and sheep meat	By principal regions of origin, gross volume	tonnes	Yes	A	Western Europe	UN34 (XLV)
Live animals trade, meat and meat preparation	Value of exports and imports	US$	Yes	A	World	UNCTAD4 (2.1.1, 2.1.2)
Live exports	Total	tonnes	Yes	A	EC	MLC1 (-)
Live imports	Total	tonnes	Yes	A	EC	MLC1 (-)
Meat and livestock imports	Estimates, change, forecast	tonnes, %	Yes	A	Selected countries	GATTI (1)
Pig meat trade with third countries	By exports, imports, type, total	tonnes, cwe	Yes	A	EC	MLC1 (-)
Pigmeat exports		tonnes, cwe, %	Yes	A	World	GATT2 (18)
Pigmeat exports	Carcass weight	tonnes, %	Yes	A	Selected countries	GATT1 (-)
Pigmeat exports	Carcass weight	tonnes, %	Yes	A	World	GATT1 (18)
Pigmeat imports		tonnes, cwe, %	Yes	A	World	GATT2 (17)
Pigmeat imports	Carcass weight	tonnes, %	Yes	A	Selected countries	GATT1 (-)
Pigmeat imports	Carcass weight	tonnes, %	Yes	A	World	GATT1 (17)
Poultry meat exports		tonnes, %	Yes	A	Selected countries	GATT1 (-)
Poultry meat exports		tonnes, cwe, %	Yes	A	World	GATT2 (22)
Poultry meat exports	Carcass weight	tonnes, %	Yes	A	World	GATT1 (22)
Poultry meat imports		tonnes, %	Yes	A	Selected countries	GATT1 (-)
Poultry meat imports		tonnes, cwe, %	Yes	A	World	GATT2 (21)
Poultry meat imports	Carcass weight	tonnes, %	Yes	A	World	GATT1 (21)
Poultry meat, offal and all meat and offal, exports	Total	tonnes	Yes	A	EC	MLC1 (-)
Poultry meat, offal and all meat and offal, imports	Total	tonnes	Yes	A	EC	MLC1 (-)
Poultry, chicks exports	By type of poultry, by type of stock	nos	Yes	M	EC	EC7 (II)
Poultry, chicks imports	By type of poultry, by type of stock	nos	Yes	M	EC	EC7 (II)
Sheep meat exports		tonnes, cwe, %	Yes	A	World	GATT2 (26)
Sheep meat exports	Carcass weight	tonnes, %	Yes	A	Selected countries	GATT1 (-)
Sheep meat exports	Carcass weight	tonnes, %	Yes	A	World	GATT1 (26)
Sheep meat trade with third countries	By exports, imports, type, total	tonnes, cwe	Yes	A	EC	MLC1 (-)
Sheepmeat imports		tonnes, cwe, %	Yes	A	World	GATT2 (25)

Subject	Categories	Units	Time series Yes/No Frequency		Territorial coverage	Source (Table No.)
Sheepmeat imports	By type, country of origin	tonnes	Yes	A	Selected countries	MLC1 (-)
Sheepmeat imports	Carcass weight	tonnes, %	Yes	A	Selected countries	GATT1 (-)
Sheepmeat imports	Carcass weight	tonnes, %	Yes	A	World	GATT1 (25)
Trade in bacon, ham and other dried, salted or smoked pig meat	Exports, imports	tonnes, %	Yes	A	Selected European countries	UN34R (XXVI)
Trade in bacon, ham, salted and dried pig meat	By exports, imports	tonnes	Yes	A	World	MLC1 (-)
Trade in beef and veal	By exports, imports	tonnes	Yes	A	World	MLC1 (-)
Trade in beef and veal	Carcass weight	tonnes	Yes	A	World	GATT1 (4)
Trade in beef and veal	Exports, imports	tonnes	Yes	A	Selected European countries	UN34 (X)
Trade in beef and veal	Imports and exports	tonnes	Yes	A	OECD	OECD28
Trade in beef and veal	Imports, exports	tonnes	Yes	A	Selected European countries	UN34 (XI)
Trade in canned pig meat	By exports, imports	tonnes	Yes	A	World	MLC1 (-)
Trade in edible offal		tonnes	Yes	A	OECD	OECD28
Trade in horse meat		tonnes	Yes	A	OECD	OECD28
Trade in live cattle and calves	Exports, imports	head, %	Yes	A	Selected European countries	UN34(VIII)
Trade in live cattle and calves	Imports, exports	head	Yes	A	Selected European countries	UN34 (IX)
Trade in live cattle, beef and veal	Value of imports and exports	tonnes, %	Yes	A	Western Europe	UN34 (XIII)
Trade in live cattle, beef and veal	Value of imports	US$	Yes	A	Western Europe	UN34 (XII)
Trade in live cattle, beef and veal	Volume	tonnes	Yes	A	Western Europe	UN34 (XIV)
Trade in live pigs	Exports, imports	head, %	Yes	A	Selected European countries	UN34 (XXIII)
Trade in live pigs	Imports, exports	head, %	Yes	A	Selected European countries	UN34 (XXIV)
Trade in live pigs, pork, bacon and ham	Volume	tonnes	Yes	A	Western Europe	UN34 (XXIX)
Trade in live pigs, pork, bacon and ham	Volume (net)	tonnes	Yes	A	Western Europe	UN34 (XXX)
Trade in live pigs, pork, bacon and ham	Value	US$, %	Yes	A	Western Europe	UN34 (XXVIII)
Trade in live sheep	Imports, exports	head, %	Yes	A	Selected European countries	UN34 (XXXIX)
Trade in live sheep and lambs	Exports, imports	head, %	Yes	A	Selected European countries	UN34 (XXXVIII)
Trade in live sheep and sheep meat	Value	US$, %	Yes	A	Western Europe	UN34 (XLII)
Trade in live sheep and sheep meat	Volume	tonnes, %	Yes	A	Western Europe	UN34 (XLIII)
Trade in live sheep and sheep meat	Volume (net)	tonnes	Yes	A	Western Europe	UN34 (XLIV)
Trade in livestock	By exports, imports	head	Yes	A	World	MLC1 (-)
Trade in meat and livestock	By imports, exports	ECU	No		EC	MLC1 (-)
Trade in meat and meat products of the USSR	Imports, exports	tonnes	Yes	A	USSR	UN34 (LV)
Trade in meat, total	Imports and exports	tonnes	Yes	A	OECD	OECD28
Trade in mutton, lamb and goat meat		tonnes	Yes	A	OECD	OECD28
Trade in other meat		tonnes	Yes	A	OECD	OECD28
Trade in pig meat	By type, country of destination	tonnes, cwe	No		Selected countries	MLC1 (-)
Trade in pig meat	Imports and exports	tonnes	Yes	A	OECD	OECD28
Trade in pig meat	Imports, exports	tonnes, %	Yes	A	Selected European countries	UN34R (XXVII)
Trade in pork	By exports, imports	tonnes	Yes	A	World	MLC1 (-)
Trade in pork	Exports, imports	tonnes, %	Yes	A	Selected European countries	UN34 (XXV)
Trade in poultry meat		tonnes	Yes	A	OECD	OECD28
Trade in poultry meat	Exports, imports	tonnes, %	Yes	A	Selected European countries	UN34 (LII)
Trade in poultry meat	Imports, exports	tonnes	Yes	A	Selected European countries	UN34 (LIII)

Subject	Categories	Units	Time series Yes/No Frequency		Territorial coverage	Source (Table No.)
Trade in prepared, preserved and sausages	By exports, imports	tonnes	Yes	A	World	MLC1 (-)
Trade in sheep meat	By imports	tonnes	Yes	A	World	MLC1 (-)
Trade in sheep meat	Exports, imports	tonnes, %	Yes	A	Selected European countries	UN34 (XL)
Trade in sheep meat	Imports, exports	tonnes, %	Yes	A	Selected European countries	UN34 (XLI)
27.4.18 Metals, Ores and Minerals - see also Sections 32 and 33						
Alloy steel, exports	By country, by product	tonnes	No		Selected countries	ISSB2 (-)
Alloy steels	By products and steel type	tonnes	No		OECD	OECD18 (16, 17)
Alumina	By production	tonnes	Yes	A	World	UNCTAD4 (3.1.6)
Alumina	Quantity and value of exports and imports	tonnes, US$	Yes	A	World	UNCTAD4 (3.1.7, 3.1.8)
Aluminium	By production	tonnes	Yes	A	World	UNCTAD4 (3.1.9)
Aluminium	Quantity and value of exports and imports	tonnes, US$	Yes	A	World	UNCTAD4 (3.1.10, 3.1.11)
Aluminium production and exports	By volume, by value	tonnes, nat curr	No		Bahrain	CH1 (8.2)
Aluminium, primary	By consumption	tonnes	Yes	A	World	UNCTAD4 (3.1.12)
Aluminium, primary and secondary	By consumption	tonnes	Yes	A	World	UNCTAD4 (3.1.13)
Aluminium, production	By country	tonnes	Yes	A	World	ISL2 (2.3.7)
Aluminium, semi-fabricated products	By type	tonnes, %	No		EC	EAA1 (-)
Aluminium, unwrought	Primary, total unwrought	tonnes	Yes	A	EC	EAA1 (-)
Bars and flats	By country, by product	tonnes	No		World	ISSB1 (-)
Bauxite	By production, quantity	tonnes	Yes	A	World	UNCTAD4 (3.1.1)
Bauxite	Quantity of exports and imports	tonnes	Yes	A	World	UNCTAD4 (3.1.3, 3.1.5)
Bauxite	Value of exports and imports	US$	Yes	A	World	UNCTAD4 (3.1.2, 3.1.4)
Cement		tonnes	Yes	A	World	UN10 (16)
Cold finished bars	By country, by destination	tonnes	No		World	ISSB3 (5)
Cold finished/cold formed and forged sections	By country, by destination	tonnes	No		World	ISSB3 (8)
Cold reduced plate and sheet in coil and lengths	By country, by destination	tonnes	No		World	ISSB3 (13)
Cold rolled strip	By country, by destination	tonnes	No		World	ISSB3 (15)
Copper ore	By production	tonnes	Yes	A	World	UNCTAD4 (3.2.1)
Copper ore	Quantity and value of exports and imports	tonnes, US$	Yes	A	World	UNCTAD4 (3.2.2, 3.2.3)
Copper production	By country	tonnes	Yes	A	World	ISL2 (2.3.8)
Copper, refined	By consumption	tonnes	Yes	A	World	UNCTAD4 (3.2.11)
Copper, refined	By production	tonnes	Yes	A	World	UNCTAD4 (3.2.7)
Copper, refined	By production, secondary	tonnes	Yes	A	World	UNCTAD4 (3.2.8)
Copper, refined	Quantity and value of exports and imports	tonnes, US$	Yes	A	World	UNCTAD4 (3.2.9, 3.2.10)
Copper, unrefined	By production	tonnes	Yes	A	World	UNCTAD4 (3.2.4)

27 INTERNATIONAL TRADE AND FINANCE

Subject	Categories	Units	Time series Yes/No	Frequency	Territorial coverage	Source (Table No.)
Copper, unrefined	Quantity and value of exports and imports	tonnes, US$	Yes	A	World	UNCTAD4 (3.2.50, 3.2.6)
Crude steel	By production	tonnes	Yes	A	World	UNCTAD4 (3.3.9)
Crude steel production, trade in steel products, trade by area	By country, exports, destination	tonnes, %	Yes	A	World	ISL2 (2.3.5.1-3)
Deformed reinforcing bars and rods	By country, by destination	tonnes	No		World	ISSB3 (2)
ECSC products	By country, by destination	tonnes	No		World	ISSB3 (30)
ECSC products foreign trade	By product groups	tonnes	Yes	A	EC, Africa, America, Asia, Oceania	EC55(5.6)
ECSC products in total foreign trade	By type of product	ECU, %	Yes	A	EC	EC55(5.3)
ECSC steel products	By country, by year	tonnes	Yes	A	Selected countries	ISSB1 (-)
ECSC steel products summary	By country, by product	tonnes	No		World	ISSB1 (-)
Ferromanganese	By production	tonnes	Yes	A	World	UNCTAD4 (3.5.4)
Ferromanganese	Quantity and value of exports and imports	tonnes, US$	Yes	A	World	UNCTAD4 (3.5.5, 3.5.6)
Heavy sections 80mm and over	By country, by destination	tonnes	No		World	ISSB3 (7)
Hot rolled bars and flats in lengths	By country, by destination	tonnes	No		Selected countries	ISSB3 (4)
Hot rolled light sections	By country, by destination	tonnes	No		World	ISSB3 (6)
Hot rolled plate 3mm thick or more	By country, by destination	tonnes	No		World	ISSB3 (11)
Hot rolled sheet up to 3mm thick	By country, by destination	tonnes	No		World	ISSB3 (12)
Hot rolled strip	By country, by destination	tonnes	No		World	ISSB3 (14)
Hot rolled wide strip	By country, by destination	tonnes	No		World	ISSB3 (10)
Imported industrial machinery and raw materials	By activity	US$	No		Saudi Arabia	CH1 (8.13)
Ingots and semis	By country, by product	tonnes	No		World	ISSB1 (-)
Ingots, blooms, billets and slabs	By country, by destination	tonnes	No		World	ISSB3 (1)
Iron and major alloying metals	By exporter and importer	tonnes	Yes	A, M	Selected countries	DSC2 (5.6, 5.7)
Iron and major alloying metals	By metal type	tonnes	No		EC	EC68 (-)
Iron and steel						
Iron and steel foreign trade - average values	By type of product	ECU, tonne	Yes	A	EC	EC55(8.16)
Iron ore	By countries by main trading countries	nos	No		The Americas and Australasia	MAC2 (E25)
Iron ore	By production, quantity	tonnes	Yes	A	World	UNCTAD4 (3.3.1)
Iron ore	Quantity of exports and imports	tonnes	Yes	A	World	UNCTAD4 (3.3.5, 3.3.7)
Iron ore	Value of exports and imports	US$	Yes	A	World	UNCTAD4 (3.3.4, 3.3.6)
Iron ore exports	By country	tonnes	No		World	MB2 (-)
Iron ore exports	By country, region	tonnes	Yes	A	World	IISI4(21)
Iron ore imports	By country	tonnes	No		World	MB2 (-)
Iron ore imports	By country, region	tonnes	Yes	A	World	IISI4(22)
Iron ore imports - average values	By country or origin	ECU, tonne	Yes	A	EC	EC55(8.15)
Iron ore pellets	By production	tonnes	Yes	A	World	UNCTAD4 (3.3.2)
Iron ore sinter	By production	tonnes	Yes	A	World	UNCTAD4 (3.3.3)
Iron ore trade, world	By destination, by area	tonnes	No		World	MB2 (-)

Subject	Categories	Units	Time series Yes/No Frequency		Territorial coverage	Source (Table No.)
Iron ore, exports, imports	By countries	tonnes	Yes	A	EC	MAC3 (D13)
Iron ore, production	By country	tonnes, %	Yes	A	World	ISL2 (2.3.4)
Iron, scrap, ore and ferro alloys	By country, by product	tonnes	No		World	ISSB1 (-)
Lead	Antimonial lead	tonnes	Yes	A, M	Japan	ILZSG1 (20)
Lead	Concentrates refined lead	tonnes	Yes	A, Q	USSR	ILZSG1 (10)
Lead	Ores and concentrates lead bullion refined lead	tonnes	Yes	A, Q	Eastern Europe Socialist countries	ILZSG1 (14)
Lead	Ores, concentrates lead bullion refined lead	tonnes	Yes	A, M	Australia	ILZSG1 (15)
Lead	Ores, concentrates refined lead	tonnes	Yes	A, M	Canada	ILZSG1 (16)
Lead	Ores, concentrates refined lead	tonnes	Yes	A, M	Italy	ILZSG1 (19)
Lead	Ores, concentrates refined lead	tonnes	Yes	A, M	Peru	ILZSG1 (22)
Lead	Ores, concentrates refined lead	tonnes	Yes	A, M	US	ILZSG1 (24)
Lead	Refined lead lead bullion	tonnes	Yes	A, M	France	ILZSG1 (17)
Lead	Refined lead lead bullion	tonnes	Yes	A, M	UK	ILZSG1 (23)
Lead	Refined lead	tonnes	Yes	A, M	Mexico	ILZSG1 (21)
Lead metal	Quantity and value of exports and imports	tonnes, US$	Yes	A	World	UNCTAD4 (3.4.5, 3.4.6)
Lead metal, primary	By consumption	tonnes	Yes	A	World	UNCTAD4 (3.4.7)
Lead metal, primary	By production	tonnes	Yes	A	World	UNCTAD4 (3.4.4)
Lead ore	By production	tonnes	Yes	A	World	UNCTAD4 (3.4.1)
Lead ore	Quantity and value of exports and imports	tonnes, US$	Yes	A	World	UNCTAD4 (3.4.2, 3.4.3)
Lead refined, production, consumption and trade		tonnes	Yes	A	World	ISL2 (2.3.10)
Lead, exports, imports	Ores and concentrates lead bullion, refined lead	tonnes	Yes	A, Q	Eastern Europe, Socialist countries	ILZSG1(14)
Lead, metal		tonnes	Yes	A, M	EC, America, Africa, Oceania	ILZSG1 (13)
Lead, ores and concentrates		tonnes	Yes	A, M	EC, Africa America, Oceania	ILZSG1 (12)
Lead, refined		tonnes	Yes	A, M	Germany	ILZSG1 (18)
Manganese exports	By country	tonnes	No		World	MB2 (-)
Manganese imports	By country	tonnes	No		World	MB2 (-)
Manganese ore	By production	tonnes	Yes	A	World	UNCTAD4 (3.5.1)
Manganese ore	Quantity and value of exports and imports	tonnes, US$	Yes	A	World	UNCTAD4 (3.5.2, 3.5.3)
Metals	By type	tonnes	Yes	A	EC	EC68 (-)
Metals	Mercury, antimony, titanium and zirconium	tonnes	No		EC	EC68 (-)
Metals (non-ferrous)	Price index	indices	Yes	A	World	UN32 (K)
Nickel ore	By production	tonnes	Yes	A	World	UNCTAD4 (3.6.1)
Nickel ore	Quantity and value of exports and imports	tonnes, US$	Yes	A	World	UNCTAD4 (3.6.2, 3.6.3)
Nickel, intermediate products	Quantity and value of exports and imports	tonnes, US$	Yes	A	World	UNCTAD4 (3.6.5, 3.6.6)
Nickel, unwrought	By consumption	tonnes	Yes	A	World	UNCTAD4 (3.6.9)
Nickel, unwrought	By production	tonnes	Yes	A	World	UNCTAD4 (3.6.4)

27 INTERNATIONAL TRADE AND FINANCE

Subject	Categories	Units	Time series Yes/No Frequency		Territorial coverage	Source (Table No.)
Nickel, unwrought	Quantity and value of exports and imports	tonnes, US$	Yes	A	World	UNCTAD4 (3.6.7, 3.6.8)
Non-ferrous metals	By metal type	tonnes	No		EC	EC68 (-)
Ores and concentrates quantities and values	By product by country	kg, ECU	No		EC, World	EC37 Vol B
Other base metals quantities and values	By product by country	kg, ECU	No		EC, World	EC37 Vol I
Phosphate rock	By production	tonnes	Yes	A	World	UNCTAD4 (3.7.1)
Phosphate rock	Quantity and value of exports and imports	tonnes, US$	Yes	A	World	UNCTAD4 (3.7.2, 3.7.3)
Pig iron	By production	tonnes	Yes	A	World	UNCTAD4 (3.3.8)
Pig iron exports	By country, region	tonnes	Yes	A	World	IISI4(18)
Pig iron imports	By country, region	tonnes	Yes	A	World	IISI4(19)
Pig iron, iron and steel quantities and values	By product by country	kg, ECU	No		EC, World	EC37 Vol H
Rails, sleepers, fishplates, sole-plates, points, switches, crossings etc	By country, by destin-ation	tonnes	No		World	ISSB3 (9)
Refined trade	By metal type	tonnes	Yes	A	World	WBMS1(-)
Refined trade, East West	By metal type	tonnes	Yes	A	World	WBMS1(-)
Scrap		tonnes	No		OECD, EC	OECD18 (13)
Scrap - average values in foreign trade		ECU, tonne	Yes	A	EC	EC55(8.14)
Scrap - internal and foreign trade	By type of scrap	tonnes, %	Yes	A	EC	EC55(5.12)
Scrap exports	By country, region	tonnes	Yes	A	World	IISI4(24)
Scrap imports	By country, region	tonnes	Yes	A	World	IISI4(25)
Stainless steel, bars, rods and sections	By export, import	tonnes	Yes	A	World	WBMS4(-)
Stainless steel, cold rolled sheet	By export, import, thickness, type	tonnes	Yes	A	World	WBMS4(-)
Stainless steel, cold rolled strip	By export, import thickness, type	tonnes	Yes	A	World	WBMS4(-)
Stainless steel, consumption	By product group	tonnes	No		Western world	WBMS4(-)
Stainless steel, consumption	Total	tonnes	Yes	A	Western world	WBMS4(-)
Stainless steel, exports	By country of origin, steel type	tonnes	No		World	WBMS4(-)
Stainless steel, hot rolled coils	By export, import, thickness	tonnes	Yes	A	World	WBMS4(-)
Stainless steel, hot rolled plate	By export, import, thickness	tonnes	Yes	A	World	WBMS4 (-)
Stainless steel, hot rolled strip	By export, import	tonnes	Yes	A	World	WBMS4(-)
Stainless steel, imports	By country of origin	tonnes	No		World	WBMS4(-)
Stainless steel, ingots, blooms and billets	By export, import	tonnes	Yes	A	World	WBMS4(-)
Stainless steel, net trade and apparent consumption	By slab production, estimated deliveries imports, exports	tonnes	No		Western world	WBMS4(-)
Stainless steel, otherwise worked	By export, import, type	tonnes	Yes	A	World	WBMS4(-)
Stainless steel, trade	By exports, imports	tonnes	Yes	A	Western world	WBMS4(-)
Stainless steel, tubes and pipes	By export, import, type	tonnes	Yes	A	World	WBMS4(-)
Stainless steel, wire	By export, import	tonnes	Yes	A	World	WBMS4(-)
Stainless steel, wire rod	By export, import	tonnes	Yes	A	World	WBMS4(-)
Steel		tonnes	No		OECD, EC	OECD18 (14, 15)
Steel castings -unworked	By country, by destin-ation	tonnes	No		World	ISSB3 (28)
Steel forgings - unworked	By country, by destin-ation	tonnes	No		World	ISSB3 (27)
Steel industry raw materials	By type	tonnes	Yes	A, Q	EC, USA, Canada and Japan	UN11 (4)

Subject	Categories	Units	Time series Yes/No Frequency		Territorial coverage	Source (Table No.)
Steel products	By country, by destination	tonnes	No		World	ISSB3 (29)
Steel products	By type	tonnes	Yes	A, Q	EC, USA Canada and Japan	UN11 (4)
Steel products summary	By country, by product	tonnes	No		World	ISSB1 (-)
Steel products, total	By country, by year	tonnes	Yes	A	Selected countries	ISSB1 (-)
Steel products, world exports	By country	tonnes	Yes	A	World	MJ1 (II)
Steel sections	By country, by product	tonnes	No		World	ISSB1 (-)
Steel sheet and strip, other coated	By country, by destination	tonnes	No		World	ISSB3 (18)
Steel sheet and strip, zinc coated	By country, by destination	tonnes	No		World	ISSB3 (17)
Steel tube and pipe fittings	By country, by destination	tonnes	No		World	ISSB3 (23)
Steel tubes and pipes - seamless	By country, by destination	tonnes	No		World	ISSB3 (21)
Steel tubes and pipes - welded	By country, by destination	tonnes	No		World	ISSB3 (22)
Steel, cold formed sections, wire, narrow strip	By country, by product	tonnes	No		World	ISSB1 (-)
Steel, crude		tonnes	Yes	A	EC	EC53 (5.9)
Steel, crude	Imports, exports	tonnes	Yes	A	EC, USA and Japan	EC53 (1.13)
Steel, destinations	By country, by product	tonnes	No		World	ISSB3 (-)
Steel, drawn line, single	By country, by destination	tonnes	No		World	ISSB3 (24)
Steel, electrical sheet and strip	By country, by destination	tonnes	No		World	ISSB3 (19)
Steel, exporting countries	By country, by product	tonnes	No		Selected countries	ISSB3 (-)
Steel, exports from Japan	By product type	tonnes, %	Yes	A	World	EC55(5.10)
Steel, exports of semi-finished and finished steel product	By country	tonnes	Yes	A	World	IISI4(7)
Steel, exports, analysis	By product	tonnes	Yes	A	World	IISI5 (-)
Steel, finished rolled	By type	tonnes	No		EC	EC53 (5.11)
Steel, foreign trade - indirect	In crude steel equivalent	tonnes	Yes	A	EC	EC55(5.11)
Steel, foreign trade by markets	Pig-iron, ECSC steel, alloy steels	tonnes, %	Yes	A	EC, Africa, America, Asia, Oceania	EC55(5.7)
Steel, foreign trade of USA	By product type	tonnes	Yes	A	World	EC55(5.9)
Steel, foreign trade ratios	Import and export shares, net exports	tonnes, %	Yes	A	EC	EC55(5.1)
Steel, foreign trade	ECSC and non-ECSC steel	tonnes	Yes	A	EC	EC55(5.8)
Steel, forged blooms, billets, slabs and bars	By country, by destination	tonnes	No		World	ISSB3 (25)
Steel, further worked flat products	By country, by destination	tonnes	No		World	ISSB3 (20)
Steel, high speed flat products, coated sheet and strip	By country, by product	tonnes	No		World	ISSB1(-)
Steel, hot rolled and cold rolled plate and sheet	By country, by product	tonnes	No		World	ISSB1(-)
Steel, hot rolled wide strip and plate	By country, by product	tonnes	No		World	ISSB1 (-)
Steel, importers and exporters, major	Net	tonnes	No		World	IISI5 (-)
Steel, imports of semi-finished and finished steel products	By country	tonnes	Yes	A	World	IISI4(8)
Steel, products	Exports, production	tonnes, %	Yes	A	World	IISI5 (-)
Steel, railway tyres, wheels and axles	By country, by destination	tonnes	No		World	ISSB3 (26)
Steel, raw material supplies dependence		%	No		EC, USA, Japan	EC55(5.2)
Steel, special	Non-alloy steel ingots, alloy steel ingots	tonnes	No		EC	EC53 (5.10)

Subject	Categories	Units	Time series Yes/No Frequency		Territorial coverage	Source (Table No.)
Steel, trade by area	Exports, imports	tonnes	No		World	IISI5 (-)
Steel, tubes	By country, by product	tonnes	No		World	ISSB1 (-)
Steel, tubes, forgings and cast products	By country, by product	tonnes	No		World	ISSB1 (-)
Stone, plaster, ceramincs, glass quantities and values	By product by country	kg, ECU	No		EC, World	EC37 Vol G
Sulphur	By production	tonnes	Yes	A	World	UNCTAD4 (3.8.1)
Sulphur	Quantity and value of exports and imports	tonnes, US$	Yes	A	World	UNCTAD4 (3.8.2, 3.8.3)
Tin metal	Quantity and value of exports and imports	tonnes, US$	Yes	A	World	UNCTAD4 (3.9.6, 3.9.7)
Tin metal, primary	By consumption	tonnes	Yes	A	World	UNCTAD4 (3.9.8)
Tin metal, primary	By production	tonnes	Yes	A	World	UNCTAD4 (3.9.4)
Tin metal, secondary	By consumption	tonnes	Yes	A	World	UNCTAD4 (3.9.9)
Tin metal, secondary	By production	tonnes	Yes	A	World	UNCTAD4 (3.9.5)
Tin ore	By production	tonnes	Yes	A	World	UNCTAD4 (3.9.1)
Tin ore	Quantity and value of exports and imports	tonnes, US$	Yes	A	World	UNCTAD4 (3.9.2, 3.9.3)
Tinplate and TFS sheet and strip	By country, by destin-ation	tonnes	No		World	ISSB3 (16)
Trade in ECSC steel products	Internal trade, imports, exports	tonnes, %	Yes	A	EC	EC55(5.5)
Trade in metals	By metal	tonnes	Yes	A	World	WBMS3 (-)
Trade in metals, East-West	By exports from western countries, imports from eastern countries	tonnes	Yes	A	World	MJ1 (VI)
Trade in metals, East-West	By metal, by type	tonnes	Yes	A	World	WBMS3 (-)
Trade in ores	By metal type	tonnes	Yes	A	World	WBMS1(-)
Trade in ores, East-West	By metal type	tonnes	Yes	A	World	WBMS1(-)
Trade in steel	Direct and indirect	crude equiv	Yes	A	EC	EC55(5.4)
Tungsten ore	By consumption	tonnes	Yes	A	World	UNCTAD4 (3.10.4)
Tungsten ore	By production	tonnes	Yes	A	World	UNCTAD4 (3.10.1)
Tungsten ore	Quantity and value of exports and imports	tonnes, US$	Yes	A	World	UNCTAD4 (3.10.2, 3.10.3)
Tungsten products	Quantity, value, by product	tonnes US$	Yes	A	World	UNCTAD3 (5.3)
Tungsten products	Quantity, value, by country	tonnes, US$	Yes	A	World	UNCTAD3 (5.1)
Tungsten, ores and concentrates		tonnes	Yes	A	World	UNCTAD3 (4.4)
Tungsten, ores and concentrates	By country of destination	tonnes	Yes	A	World	UNCTAD3 (4.2)
Tungsten, ores and concentrates, value	f.o.b	US$	Yes	A	World	UNCTAD3 (4.6)
Wire rod and other hot rolled bars in coil	By country, by destin-ation	tonnes	No		World	ISSB3 (3)
Wire rods, reinforcement, rails	By country, by product	tonnes	No		World	ISSB1 (-)
Zinc	Concentrates slab zinc	tonnes	Yes	A, Q	Eastern Europe Socialist countries	
Zinc	Ores and concentrates refined zinc	tonnes	Yes	A, Q	Eastern Europe Socialist countries	ILZSG1 (39)
Zinc	Ores, concentrates refined zinc	tonnes	Yes	A, M	Australia	ILZSG1 (40)
Zinc	Ores, concentrates refined zinc	tonnes	Yes	A, M	Canada	ILZSG1 (41)

Subject	Categories	Units	Time series Yes/No Frequency		Territorial coverage	Source (Table No.)
Zinc	Ores, concentrates refined zinc	tonnes	Yes	A, M	France	ILZSG1 (42)
Zinc	Ores, concentrates refined zinc	tonnes	Yes	A, M	Germany	ILZSG1 (43)
Zinc	Ores, concentrates refined zinc	tonnes	Yes	A, M	Mexico	ILZSG1 (46)
Zinc	Ores, concentrates refined zinc	tonnes	Yes	A, M	Peru	ILZSG1 (47)
Zinc	Ores, concentrates refined zinc	tonnes	Yes	A, M	US	ILZSG1 (49)
Zinc	Refined zinc	tonnes	Yes	A, M	Italy	ILZSG1 (44)
Zinc	Refined zinc	tonnes	Yes	A, M	Japan	ILZSG1 (45)
Zinc	Zinc alloys refined zinc	tonnes	Yes	A, M	UK	ILZSG1 (48)
Zinc refined, production, consumption and trade		tonnes	Yes	A	World	ISL2 (2.3.9)
Zinc, exports, imports	Ores and concentrates refined zinc	tonnes	Yes	A, Q	Eastern Europe, Socialist countries	ILZSG1(39)
Zinc, metal		tonnes	Yes	A, M	World	ILZSG1 (38)
Zinc, ores and concentrates		tonnes	Yes	A, M	World	ILZSG1 (37)
Zinc, refined		tonnes	Yes	A, Q	USSR	ILZSG1 (35)
27.4.19 Oils, Fats and Oilmeals						
Coconut oil	Quantity and value of exports and imports	tonnes, US$	Yes	A	World	UNCTAD4 (2.22.1,2.22.2)
Groundnut oil	Quantity and value of exports and imports	tonnes, US$	Yes	A	World	UNCTAD4 (2.18.1,2.18.2)
Groundnuts, crushings and trade	Crushings, exports, imports	tonnes	Yes	A	World	ISTA1 (-)
Oilmeals	By country, by product imports, exports	tonnes	Yes	A	EC, World	ISTA2(-)
Oilmeals	By product, country imports and exports	tonnes	Yes	A	World	ISTA1 (-)
Oilmeals, new supplies	By production, imports exports, new supplies	tonnes	Yes	A	World	ISTA1 (-)
Oils and fats, world summary balance	Opening stocks, production, imports, exports, disappearance, ending stocks	tonnes	Yes	A	World	ISTA2(-)
Oils, balance	By oil type, stocks, production, imports, exports, disappearance	tonnes	Yes	A	World	ISTA1 (-)
Oilseed crop balance	By stocks, imports, crushings, other use	tonnes	Yes	A	EC, World	ISTA2(-)
Oilseeds	By type, crushings, exports, imports	tonnes	Yes	A	World	ISTA2(-)
Oilseeds, fats, oils, oil cakes and meals	Value of exports and imports	US$	Yes	A	World	UNCTAD4 (2.15.1,2.15.2)
Oilseeds, imports	By crops, imports, crushings, share	tonnes, %	Yes	A	EC	ISTA2(-)
Palm kernel oil	Quantity and value of exports and imports	tonnes, US$	Yes	A	World	UNCTAD4 (2.24.1,2.24.2)
Palm oil	By production	tonnes	Yes	A	World	UNCTAD4 (2.25.1)
Palm oil	Quantity and value of exports and imports	tonnes, US$	Yes	A	World	UNCTAD4 (2.25.2,2.25.3)
Safflower oil	By imports, exports	tonnes	Yes	A	Selected countries	ISTA2(-)
Soybean oil	Quantity and value of exports and imports	tonnes, US$	Yes	A	World	UNCTAD4 (2.20.1,2.20.2)
Vegetable oilseeds	By production	tonnes	Yes	A	World	UNCTAD4 (2.16.1)
Vegetable oilseeds, oleaginous fruits and oils	Value of exports and imports	US$	Yes	A	World	UNCTAD4 (2.16.2,2.16.3)

Subject	Categories	Units	Time series Yes/No Frequency		Territorial coverage	Source (Table No.)
27.4.20 Rubber						
Rubber	By type of rubber	tonnes	No		USA Brazil France Germany UK Australia India Japan	IRSG1 (29-36)
Rubber	Latex, total	tonnes	Yes	A	Malaysia, peninsular Singapore Indonesia Thailand Sri Lanka	IRSG1 (16-20)
Rubber latex, natural, net imports		tonnes	Yes	A, M	World	IRSG1 (22)
Rubber tyres	Car, truck	tonnes	Yes	A, Q	Major exporting countries worldwide	IRSG1 (40)
Rubber tyres	Car, truck	tonnes	Yes	A, Q	Major importing countries worldwide	IRSG1 (41)
Rubber, natural		tonnes	Yes	A	World	IRSG2 (8)
Rubber, natural		tonnes	Yes	A	World	IRSG2 (9)
Rubber, natural , gross imports to major non-producing countries		tonnes	No		World	IRSG1 (21)
Rubber, natural and synthetic	By production	tonnes	Yes	A	World	ISL2 (2.3.12.1-2)
Rubber, natural,		tonnes	Yes	A, M	World	IRSG1 (9)
Rubber, natural, net		tonnes	Yes	A, M	World	IRSG1 (8,9)
Rubber, SBR values		nat curr /tonne	Yes	A	World	IRSG2 (21)
Rubber, sheet, gross exports	By grade	tonnes	Yes	M	World	IRSG1 (10)
Rubber, sheet, gross	By grade	tonnes	Yes	A	World	IRSG2 (9)
Rubber, sheet, gross exports	By grade	tonnes	Yes	A, M	Malaysia, Indonesia Thailand	IRSG1 (10)
Rubber, synthetic		tonnes	Yes	A	World	IRSG2 (16)
Rubber, synthetic		tonnes	Yes	A	World	IRSG2 (17)
Rubber, synthetic		tonnes	Yes	A, M	World	IRSG1 (20,25)
Rubber, synthetic	By destination	tonnes	Yes	A	World	IRSG1 (26)
Rubber, synthetic	By destination	tonnes	Yes	M	World	IRSG2 (26)
Rubber, synthetic, gross exports		tonnes	Yes	A, M	World	IRSG1 (25)
Rubber, synthetic, net imports		tonnes	Yes	A, M	World	IRSG1 (27)
Rubber, technically specified	By grade	tonnes	Yes	A, M	Malaysia Indonesia Thailand	IRSG1 (11)
Rubber, technically-specified	By grade	tonnes	Yes	A, M	World	IRSG1 (10,11)
27.4.21 Textiles, Clothing and Footwear						
Cellulosic filament yarn	By country of import, export	tonnes	No		EC, EFTA others	CIRFS1 (-)
Cellulosic filament yarn	By import, country by export, country	tonnes	Yes	A	World	CIRFS1 (-)
Cellulosic knitted fabrics	By import, country by export, country	tonnes	Yes	A	World	CIRFS1 (-)
Cellulosic spun yarn	By country of import, export	tonnes	No		EC, EFTA others	CIRFS1 (-)
Cellulosic spun yarn	By import, country by export, country	tonnes	Yes	A	World	CIRFS1 (-)
Cellulosic staple	By import, country by export, country	tonnes	Yes	A	World	CIRFS1 (-)
Cellulosic staple, carded and combed	By country of import, export	tonnes	No		EC, EFTA	CIRFS1 (-)
Cellulosic woven pure and blended filament fabrics	By country of import, export	tonnes	No		EC, EFTA others	CIRFS1 (-)

Subject	Categories	Units	Time series Yes/No Frequency		Territorial coverage	Source (Table No.)
Cellulosic woven pure and blended spun yarn fabrics	By country of import, export	tonnes	No		EC, EFTA others	CIRFS1 (-)
Cellulosic woven pure and blended fabrics	By import, country by export, country	tonnes	Yes	A	World	CIRFS1 (-)
Cellulosic woven pure and blended spun yarn fabrics	By import, country by export, country	tonnes	Yes	A	World	CIRFS1 (-)
Celulosic staple	By country of import, export	tonnes	No		EC, EFTA others	CIRFS1 (-)
Cotton		bales	Yes	A	World	ICAC2 (pp22-23)
Cotton		bales	Yes	A	World	ICAC2 (pp24-25)
Cotton	By country	tonnes	Yes	A	World	ICAC2 (pp101 -156)
Cotton	By country	tonnes	Yes	A	World	ICAC2 (pp101-156)
Cotton	Commitments	tonnes	No		World	ICAC1 (p6)
Cotton (total)		tonnes	Yes	A	E. Asia, EC, China, E.Europe, CIS	ICAC1 (p2)
Cotton (total)		tonnes	Yes	A	US, CIS, India Francophone Africa, Australia, China, Pakistan	ICAC1 (p2)
Cotton fabric		tonnes	Yes	A	World	ICAC2 (pp74-75)
Cotton fabric		tonnes	Yes	A	World	ICAC2 (pp76-77)
Cotton yarn		tonnes	Yes	A	World	ICAC2 (pp68-69)
Cotton yarn		tonnes	Yes	A	World	ICAC2 (pp70-71)
Footwear, imports and exports	By leather, textile, synthetic, rubber, clogs, other, country	pairs	Yes	A	World	SATRA1(-)
Footwear, major export destinations	By value, country	pairs, nat curr	No		World	SATRA1(-)
Footwear, major import origins	By value, country	pairs, nat curr	No		World	SATRA1(-)
Hides, skins and furskins, undressed	Value of exports and imports	US$	Yes	A	World	UNCTAD4 (2.27.1,2.27.2)
Raw wool fibres, grower country	By wool type, raw wool destination	kg	No		World	IWS1 (6)
Raw wool, clean, dry-combed	Monthly average prices	UK pence/kg	Yes	A	World	IWS1 (12)
Raw wool, greasy	By average price	nat curr per kg	Yes	A	Australia, New Zealand, South Africa	IWS1 (11)
Synthetic filament yarn	By country of import, export	tonnes	No		EC, EFTA others	CIRFS1 (-)
Synthetic filament yarn	By import, country by export, country	tonnes	Yes	A	World	CIRFS1 (-)
Synthetic knitted fabrics	By import, country by export, country	tonnes	Yes	A	World	CIRFS1 (-)
Synthetic spun yarn	By country of import, export	tonnes	No		EC, EFTA others	CIRFS1 (-)
Synthetic spun yarn	By import, country by export, country	tonnes	Yes	A	World	CIRFS1 (-)
Synthetic staple	By country of import, export	tonnes	No		EC, EFTA others	CIRFS1 (-)
Synthetic staple	By import, country by export, country	tonnes	Yes	A	World	CIRFS1 (-)
Synthetic staple, carded and combed	By country of import, export	tonnes	No		EC, EFTA others	CIRFS1 (-)

Subject	Categories	Units	Time series Yes/No	Frequency	Territorial coverage	Source (Table No.)
Synthetic woven pure and blended spun yarn fabrics	By country of import, export	tonnes	No		EC, EFTA others	CIRFS1 (-)
Synthetic-woven pure and blended filament fabrics	By import, country by export, country	tonnes	Yes	A	World	CIRFS1 (-)
Synthetic-woven pure and blended spun yarn fabrics	By import, country by export, country	tonnes	Yes	A	World	CIRFS1 (-)
Textile and apparel trade	By type, imports and exports in value terms	US$	Yes	A	World	ITMF1 (4.1, 5.1)
Textile and apparel trade	By type, imports and exports in volume terms	tonnes	Yes	A	World	ITMF1 (4.3, 5.3)
Textile and apparel trade	By type, value of all imports and exports	US$, nat curr	Yes	A	World	ITMF1 (4.2, 5.2)
Textiles footwear quantities and values	By product by country	kg, ECU	No		EC, World	EC37 Vol F
Virgin wool	By actual weight	kg	Yes	A	World	IWS1 (7)
Virgin wool	By actual weight	kg	Yes	A	World	IWS1 (9)
Virgin wool	Share held by main producers	%	Yes	A	World	IWS1 (10)
Virgin wool	Share held by main producers	%	Yes	A	World	IWS1 (8)
27.4.22 Transportation - see also Section 41						
Freight costs in world trade, total	Estimate of total freight costs of imports, value of imports, freight costs as % of import value	US$	Yes	I	World	UNCTAD2 (31)
Sea trade, goods unloaded, loaded	By world, region, country or area	tonnes	Yes	A	World	UN32 (L)
Transport equipment quantities and values	By product by country	kg, ECU	No		EC, World	EC37 Vol K
UK seaborne trade	By tanker, cargo type, exports, imports	%, tonnes, tonne-km	Yes	A	World	COS1 (11.1-11.2)
World fleet and trade	By dry cargo tanker	dwt, tonnes, indices	Yes	A	World	COS1 (9)
World seaborne trade	By cargo	tonnes, %	No		World	COS1 (10)
27.4.23 Wood and Forestry Products						
Abaca	By production	tonnes	Yes	A	World	UNCTAD4 (2.33.8)
Abaca	Quantity and value of exports and imports	tonnes, US$	Yes	A	World	UNCTAD4 (2.33.9, 2.33.10)
Forest industry products, exports	Total, per capita	US$	No		OECD and world regions	OECD33 (5.4A)
Forest industry products, imports	Total, per capita	US$	No		OECD and world regions	OECD33 (5.4A)
Forest products, tropical	By product, by ITTC1 consumers	cu m	Yes	A	ITTC consuming countries worldwide	ITTO1 (App 2)
Hard fibres and hard fibres manufactures	Value of exports and imports	US$	Yes	A	World	UNCTAD4 (2.33.1,2.33.2)
Hard fibres manufactures	Quantity of exports and imports	tonnes	Yes	A	World	UNCTAD4 (2.33.3,2.33.4)
Jute	By consumption	tonnes	Yes	A	World	UNCTAD4 (2.32.9)
Jute	By production	tonnes	Yes	A	World	UNCTAD4 (2.32.6)
Jute	Quantity and value of exports and imports	tonnes, US$	Yes	A	World	UNCTAD4 (2.32.4,2.32.5)
Jute and jute products	Value of exports and imports	US$	Yes	A	World	UNCTAD4 (2.32.1,2.32.2)
Jute and jute-like fibres	By production	tonnes	Yes	A	World	UNCTAD4 (2.32.3)

Subject	Categories	Units	Time series Yes/No Frequency		Territorial coverage	Source (Table No.)
Jute products	Quantity of exports and imports	tonnes	Yes	A	World	UNCTAD4 (2.32.7,2.32.8)
Roundwood, non-coniferous industrial	By production	cu m	Yes	A	World	UNCTAD4 (2.29.1)
Sisal	By production	tonnes	Yes	A	World	UNCTAD4 (2.33.5)
Sisal	Quantity and value of exports and imports	tonnes, US$	Yes	A	World	UNCTAD4 (2.33.6,2.33.7)
Timber exports by main trading countries	By countries	nos	No		The Americas and Australasia	MAC2 (D18)
Timber, tropical	By product by ITTC1 producer	cu m	Yes	A	ITTC producing countries worldwide	ITTO1 (App 1)
Timber, tropical	ITTC1 share in global imports, by product	%	No		World	ITTO1 (2)
Timber, tropical	Log production, log exports, processed exports, total exports, by region	cu m	No		World tropical timber producing regions	ITTO1 (10)
Timber, tropical	World and ITTC1, by product	cu m	No		World	ITTO1 (1)
Tropical wood-imports of cork and wood	By source countries per capita, % of total imports	US$, %	No		OECD	OECD33 (5.5)
Wood and forestry products, imports						
Wood, non-coniferous	Quantity and value of exports and imports	cu m, US$	Yes	A	World	UNCTAD4 (2.29.2,2.29.3)
Wood, paper, cork quantities and values	By product by country	kg, ECU	No		EC, World	EC37 (Vol E)
27.5 INTERNATIONAL FINANCE						
27.5.1 Assets and Liabilities						
Bank loans, international medium and long-term	By borrowing country or institution	US$	Yes	Q, M	World	OECD34 (I.31)
Capital, long-term	By country group and country	US$	Yes	A	World	IMF2 (A-2)
Capital, short-term	By country group and country	US$	Yes	A	World	IMF2 (A-4)
Capital, other	Long-term and short-term by country and country group	US$	Yes	A	World	IMF2 (C-16)
Capital, other of resident official sector	Long-term and short-term by country and country group	US$	Yes	A	World	IMF2 (C-17)
Capital, other of deposit money banks	Long-term and short-term by country and country group	US$	Yes	A	World	IMF2 (C-18)
Capital, other of other sectors	Long-term and short-term by country and country group	US$	Yes	A	World	IMF2 (C-19)
Capital, long-term of resident official sector	Drawings and repayments on loans extended, by country and country group	US$	Yes	A	World	IMF2 (C-20)
Capital, long-term of resident official sector	Drawings and repayments on loans received, by country and country group	US$	Yes	A	World	IMF2 (C-21)
Capital, long-term of resident official sector	Assets and liabilities by country and country group	US$	Yes	A	World	IMF2 (C-22)

Subject	Categories	Units	Time series Yes/No Frequency		Territorial coverage	Source (Table No.)
Capital, long-term of deposit money banks	Drawings and repayments on loans extended, by country and country group	US$	Yes	A	World	IMF2 (C-23)
Capital, long-term of deposit money banks	Drawings and repayments on loans received, by country and country group	US$	Yes	A	World	IMF2 (C-24)
Capital, long-term of deposit money banks	Assets and liabilities by country and country group	US$	Yes	A	World	IMF2 (C-25)
Capital, long-term of other sectors	Drawings and repayments on loans extended by country and country group	US$	Yes	A	World	IMF2 (C-26)
Capital, long-term of other sectors	Drawings and repayments on loans received, by country and country group	US$	Yes	A	World	IMF2 (C-27)
Capital, long-term of other sectors	Assets and liabilities by country and country group	US$	Yes	A	World	IMF2 (C-28)
Capital, short-term of resident official sector	Assets and liabilities by country and country group	US$	Yes	A	World	IMF2 (C-29)
Capital, short-term of deposit	Assets and liabilities	US$	Yes	A	World	IMF2 (C-30)
Capital, short-term of other sectors	Assets and liabilities by country and country group	US$	Yes	A	World	IMF2 (C-31)
Capital, short-term	Aggregated and detailed presentations containing transactions data	US$	Yes	A, Q	World	IMF1 (-)
Capital	Long-term and short-term by country group and transaction type	US$	Yes	A	World	IMF2 (B-3)
Capital operations and financial transactions with the rest of the world	Receipts, expenditure, lending, borrowing by type by sector	nat curr	Yes	A	OECD	OECD36 (34F)
Commercial banks assets and liabilities	By assets, by deposits	ECU	No		Europe	EC35 (-)
Credit and loans outstanding		SDRs	Yes	A	World	IMF6 (-)
Debt and liabilities outstanding	By category	US$	Yes	A	Developing, CMEA and certain other countries	OECD8 (1, 2)
EC position (compared to rest of the world)	Assets, liabilities and net position	%	Yes	A	EC	EC59 (I.6)
Foreign assets	Total excl. gold, end of period, gross	ECU	Yes	A, M	EC, USA, Japan	EC36
Fund credit and loans outstanding		SDRs	Yes	A, M	World	IMF7 (-)
Fund credit and loans outstanding		SDRs	Yes	A, M	World	IMF6 (-)
Loan disbursements		SDRs	Yes	A, M	World	IMF7 (-)
Loan disbursements		SDRs	Yes	A, M	World	IMF6 (-)
Outstanding external financial assets	By type and liabilities	nat curr	Yes	A	OECD	OECD36 (34B)
Repayments of loans		SDRs	Yes	A, M	World	IMF7 (-)
Repayments of loans		SDRs	Yes	A, M	World	IMF6 (-)
27.5.2 Banking						
Cross-border bank credit to non-banks by residence of borrower		US$	Yes	A, M	World	IMF6 (-)
Cross-border bank credit to non-banks by residence of lending bank		US$	Yes	A, M	World	IMF6 (-)

Subject	Categories	Units	Time series Yes/No Frequency		Territorial coverage	Source (Table No.)
Cross-border bank credit to non-banks by residence of borrower		US$	Yes	A, M	World	IMF7 (-)
Cross-border bank credit to non-banks by residence of lending bank		US$	Yes	A, M	World	IMF7 (-)
Cross-border bank deposits of non-banks by residence of borrowing bank		US$	Yes	A, M	World	IMF6 (-)
Cross-border bank deposits of non-banks by residence of depositor		US$	Yes	A, M	World	IMF6 (-)
Cross-border bank deposits of non-banks by residence of borrowing bank		US$	Yes	A, M	World	IMF7 (-)
Cross-border bank deposits of non-banks by residence of depositor		US$	Yes	A, M	World	IMF7 (-)
Cross-border interbank claims by residence of lending bank		US$	Yes	A, M	World	IMF6 (-)
Cross-border interbank claims by residence of lending bank		US$	Yes	A, M	World	IMF7 (-)
Cross-border interbank liabilities by residence of borrowing bank		US$	Yes	A, M	World	IMF6 (-)
Cross-border interbank liabilities by residence of borrowing bank		US$	Yes	A, M	World	IMF7 (-)
Deposit banks' foreign assets		US$	Yes	A, M	World	IMF6 (-)
Deposit banks' foreign assets		US$	Yes	A, M	World	IMF7 (-)
Deposit banks' foreign liabilities		US$	Yes	A, M	World	IMF6 (-)
Deposit banks' foreign liabilities		US$	Yes	A, M	World	IMF7 (-)
27.5.3 Bonds and Bond Issues						
All issues		US$	Yes	A, Q	World	OECD10 (5)
Bond issues	By currency	US$, %	No		Selected countries	EC35 (-)
Bond issues in sterling, external	By borrower, by quarterly data	sterling	Yes	A, Q	World	OECD10 (10)
Bond offerings, international and foreign	All issues	US$	Yes	A	OECD	OECD10 (1)
Bond offerings, external	By borrower	US$	Yes	A	World	OECD10 (2)
Bonds, international issues of	By borrowing country or institution	US$	Yes	Q, M	World	OECD34 (I.11)
Bonds, traditional foreign issues of	By borrowing country or institution	US$	Yes	Q, M	World	OECD34 (I.21)
Bonds, international issues of	By currency of issue	US$	Yes	Q, M	World	OECD34 (I.12)
Bonds, traditional foreign issues of	By country of issue	US$	Yes	Q, M	World	OECD34 (I.22)
Bonds with equity warrants attached	By borrower	US$	Yes	A	World	OECD10 (5)
Committed borrowing facilities	By borrower, by quarterly data	US$	Yes	A, Q	World	OECD10 (14)
Convertible bonds	By borrower	US$	Yes	A	World	OECD10 (5)
DM bond issues, external	By borrower, by quarterly data	DM	Yes	A, Q	World	OECD10 (9)
ECU bond issues	Business sector, governments, institutions, total	ECU	Yes	A, Q	EC, non-EC	EC27 (II)
ECU bond issues	Previous month, issued, issue price, term, yields	ECU, %	No		World	EC27 (IV)
Euro-commercial paper	By borrower,	US$	Yes	A, Q	World	OECD10 (15)
External bond issues, in French francs	By borrower, by quarterly data	Ff	Yes	A, Q	World	OECD10 (12)

Subject	Categories	Units	Time series Yes/No	Frequency	Territorial coverage	Source (Table No.)
External bond issues in yen	By borrower, by quarterly data	yen	Yes	A, Q	World	OECD10 (7)
External dollar bond issues	By borrower, by quarterly data	US$	Yes	A, Q	World	OECD10 (6)
Floating-rate issues	By borrower,	US$	Yes	A	World	OECD10 (4)
	by currency,	US$	Yes	A	World	OECD10 (4)
	by quarterly data	US$	Yes	A, Q	World	OECD10 (4)
Foreign bond issues	By borrower, in Switzerland	Swiss francs	Yes	A, Q	World	OECD10 (8)
Foreign issues	By market	US$	Yes	A	OECD	OECD10 (1)
	quarterly data	US$	Yes	A, Q	OECD	OECD10 (1)
International bond issues in ECU	By borrower, by quarterly data	ECU	Yes	A, Q	World	OECD10 (11)
International bond issues	By country, coupon, yield, maturity	nos	Yes	A	Developing countries	WB3 (A.V.3)
International issues	By currency	US$	Yes	A	OECD	OECD10 (1)
Non-underwritten facilities, other	By borrower by quarterly data	US$	Yes	A, Q	World	OECD10 (16)
programmes	by quarterly data					
Straight bonds, market	By borrower,	US$	Yes	A	World	OECD10 (3)
	by currency,	US$	Yes	A	World	OECD10 (3)
	by quarterly data	US$	Yes	A, Q	World	OECD10 (3)
Syndicated credits	By borrower	US$	Yes	A	World	OECD10 (13)
27.5.4 Debt						
Aggregate net resource flows and net transfers, long term		US$	Yes	A	World	WB4 (-)
Agreements of middle income countries with official creditors	By debts consolidated, period, repayment terms	US$	No		Selected countries	WB3 (A.II.2)
Agreements with official creditors	By agreements, amounts rescheduled	nos	Yes	A	Selected countries	WB3 (A.II.1)
Buy-backs financed by IDA debt	By resource, country	US$	No		Selected countries	WB3 (A.III.7)
DDSR agreements concluded	By DDSR instruments, new money	US$, %	No		Developing countries	WB3 (A.III.3)
DDSR agreements concluded	By finance (commitment)	US$	No		Developing countries	WB3 (A.III.4)
Debt, external net resource flows per capita and net transfers	By high, middle, low income	US$	No		World	CS1 (19)
Debt, composition of	By high, middle, low income, by type of debt	%	No		World	CS1 (21)
Debt and liabilities outstanding	By category and certain other	US$	Yes	A	Developing, CMEA countries	OECD8 (1, 2)
Debt and liabilities outstanding	OECD countries and capital markets, multilateral	US$	No		World	OECD9 (1, 2)
Debt arrears, stock	By official, private, by interest	US$	Yes	A	Developing countries	WB3 (1.3)
Debt burden ratios		%	Yes	2 yrly	Developing countries	UNCTAD5 (4.5)
Debt conversion programmes	By country	US$	Yes	A	Selected countries	WB3 (A.III.9)
Debt conversion programmes	By type	US$	Yes	A	Developing countries	WB3 (A.III.8)
Debt data, summary	By total debt stocks and flows,	US$	Yes	A	World	WB4 (-)
Debt data, summary	By total debt stocks, total debt flows by region, by category	US$	Yes	A	All countries reporting to World Bank	WB3 (-)
Debt indicators		%	Yes	A	World	WB4 (-)
Debt indicators	By debt-to-exports ratio, debt-to-exports service ratio, country group	%	Yes	A	Developing countries	WB3 (1.4)
Debt indicators	By high, middle, low income	%	No		World	CS1 (20)

Subject	Categories	Units	Time series Yes/No Frequency		Territorial coverage	Source (Table No.)
Debt outstanding, composition at year end	ODA, export credits, financial markets, multilateral	%	No		World	OECD9 (C)
Debt outstanding, as share of developing countries debt	ODA, export credits, financial markets, multilateral	%	No		World	OECD9 (D)
Debt outstanding	ODA, export credits, financial markets, multilateral	US$	No		World	OECD9 (A, B)
Debt restructuring, official creditors, agreements		nos	Yes	A	Developing countries	UNCTAD5 (4.6)
Debt restructuring, official creditors, amounts rescheduled		US$	Yes	A	Developing countries	UNCTAD5 (4.6)
Debt restructuring, official creditors,consolidation period		years	Yes	A	Developing countries	UNCTAD5 (4.6)
Debt restructuring, official creditors, maturity		years	Yes	A	Developing countries	UNCTAD5 (4.6)
Debt restructuring, commercial banks, number of agreements		nos	Yes	A	Developing countries	UNCTAD5 (4.7)
Debt restructuring, official creditors, amounts rescheduled		US$	Yes	A	Developing countries	UNCTAD5 (4.7)
Debt restructuring, official creditors, consolidation period		years	Yes	A	Developing countries	UNCTAD5 (4.7)
Debt restructuring, commercial banks, repayment terms	By maturity, grace, spread over LIBOR	%	Yes	A	Developing countries	UNCTAD5 (4.7)
Debt restructuring	By amount rescheduled by region, by category	US$	Yes	A	All countries reporting to World Bank	WB3 (-)
Debt restructuring agreements with commercial banks, multi-year	By country, date, consolidation period terms of repayment	US$	No		Developing countries	WB3 (A.III.2)
Debt restructuring agreements with commercial banks	By country, consolidation period, amount assistance, repayment terms	US$	No		Developing countries	WB3 (AIII.1)
Debt restructurings		US$	Yes	A	World	WB4 (-)
Debt service projections	By projected nonguaranteed debt service	US$	Yes	A	Selected countries	WB4 (-)
Debt-for-nature swaps	By country, cost, value, funds, price, leverage	US$	No		Developing countries	WB3 (A.III.10)
Dedt indicators	By type, by region by category	%	Yes	A	All countries reporting to World Bank	WB3 (-)
Disbursed external debt	Balance at end of year	US$	Yes	A	Latin American and Caribbean countries	UN45 (271)
Discounted bank debt reduction and trading volume	By total debt reduction, secondary market trading	US$	Yes	A	Developing countries	WB3 (A.IV.1)
External debt, growth rate	By total debt, growth of debt	US$	Yes	A	Developing countries	WB3 (A.I.1)
External debt, maturity structure	By source of lending	US$, %	Yes	A	Developing countries	UNCTAD5 (4.3)
External debt, interest rates on,	By type of debt	%	Yes	A	Developing countries	UNCTAD5 (4.4)
External debt	By long-term, short-term debt, IMF credit use, export credit	US$	Yes	A	Developing countries	WB3 (1.1)
External debt of developing countries		US$	Yes	A	Developing	UN50 (35)
External indebtedness of developing countries	By debt, debt services	%	Yes	Selected years	Developing countries, least developed countries	UNCTAD5 (4.1)
Foreign debt	By country, by gross, net	US$	No		Europe	EC18 (13.2)

27 INTERNATIONAL TRADE AND FINANCE

Subject	Categories	Units	Time series Yes/No Frequency		Territorial coverage	Source (Table No.)
FSU, debt indicators	By indicator	US$	Yes	A	FSU	WB3 (2.1)
FSU, average terms of new borrowing	By interest rates, maturity, grace period	%, years	No		FSU	WB3 (2.2)
FSU, debt arrears	By debt type	US$	Yes	A	FSU	WB3 (2.3)
FSU, convertible currency debt service	By credits, bonds, debt	US$	Yes	A	FSU	WB3 (2.4)
FSU, external debt	By long-term, short term debt	-US$	No		FSU	WB3 (2.5)
FSU, allocation of debt to republics	By estimated shares in exports, income	%	No		FSU	WB3 (2.6)
Indebtedness, key ratios	By country	%	No		Developing countries	WB3 (A.VI.4)
Long-term debt, sectoral allocation of disbursements		US$	Yes	A	World	WB4 (-)
Long-term debt, distribution of	By type of debtor	US$	Yes	A	World	WB4 (-)
Long-term debt, contractual obligations	By total long-term	US$	Yes	A	World	WB4 (-)
Long-term debt, composition of	By type	US$	Yes	2 yearly	Developing countries, least developed countries	UNCTAD5 (4.2)
Long-term debt	By debt outstanding, undisbursed debt, commitments, disburse-ments, repayments net flows, interest transfers, debt service by region, by category	US$	Yes	A	All countries reporting to World Bank	WB3 (-)
Long-term debt	By debt outstanding, undisturbed debt, commitments, disbursments, principal repayments, net flows and transfers on debt, interest payments, debt service	US$	Yes	A	World	WB4 (-)
Multilateral debt relief agreements, summary	By country, date, amount consolidated, type of creditor	%	No		Developing countries	WB3 (A.III.13)
Multilateral debt relief agreements with offical creditors	By consolidation period, proportion and amount consolidated, repayment terms	%, US$	No		Selected countries	WB3 (A.II.5)
Multilateral debt relief agreements with commercial banks	By country, consolidation period, amount, other assistance, repayment terms	US$	No		Developing countries	WB3 (A.III.12)
Net debt-related flows and transfers	By official, private creditors	US$	Yes	A	SIMICs	WB3 (A.I.3)
Net debt-related flows and transfers	By official, private creditors	US$	Yes	A	SILICs	WB3 (A.I.4)
Net debt-related flows and transfers	By official, private creditors	US$	Yes	A	Non-restructuring countries	WB3 (A.I.5)
Net disbursement and debt outstanding and disbursed	By country, by external capital flows, debt and debt burden ratios, bank and IDA ratios	US$	Yes	A	Developing countries	WB2 (-)
Net flow and net transfer	By region, flows, loans, grants, FDI	US$	No		Developing countries	WB3 (A.I.6)
Net resource flows (long- term)	By type of resource	US$	Yes	A	Developing countries	WB3 (1.5)
New commitments, average terms	By all creditors	%, years	Yes	A	World	WB4 (-)
New commitments, average terms	By creditors, by region by category	%	Yes	A	All countries reporting to World Bank	WB3 (-)
Paris club agreements for highly indebted lower-middle-income countries	By amount consolidated, period, repayment terms, swap ceilings	US$, %	No		Selected countries	WB3 (A.II.4)

Subject	Categories	Units	Time series Yes/No Frequency		Territorial coverage	Source (Table No.)
Paris club enhanced Toronto terms	By first, second and final stage agreements	US$	No		Selected countries	WB3 (A.II.3)
Private non-guaranteed debt	By debt outstanding and disbursed, disbursement principal repayments, net flows, interest payments, net transfers total debt service	US$	Yes	A	Selected countries	WB4 (-)
Special programme of assistance	By debt data, by new commitments	US$, %	Yes	A	All countries reporting to World Bank	WB3 (-)
Total debt, sources of change	By source, middle, low income countries	US$	No		Developing countries	WB3 (A.I.2)
Total debt, sources of change	By source	US$	Yes	A	Developing countries	WB3 (1.2)
27.5.5 Interest Rates						
ECU interest rates	By rate, by deposit length, yields	nos	No		Europe	EC35 (-)
Interest paid and outstanding		US$	Yes	A	Latin American and Caribbean countries	UN45 (266)
Interest rates on international market	Euro-currency and International bond market	%	Yes	M	World	OECD35 (R.1)
International interest rates			Yes	A, M	World	IMF6 (-)
International interest rates		%	Yes	A, M	World	IMF7 (-)
International interest rates	By country	% p.a.	Yes	A, M	Selected countries	DSC2 (1.7)
Rates of discount of central banks		% p.a.	Yes	A	World	UN50 (31)
27.5.6 Investments						
Certificates of deposit issued	By amount, issue date	US$	No		Developing countries	WB3 (A.V.5)
Commercial paper issued	By issue date, type	US$	No		Developing countries	WB3 (A.V.4)
Direct investment	Abroad and in reporting economy by country and country group	US$	Yes	A	World	IMF2 (C-14)
Direct investment abroad	By reporting country, by geographical zone	ECU	Yes	A	EC	EC10 (2D1.1)
Direct investment abroad from foreign direct investment flows in OECD countries, outflows		US$	Yes	A	OECD	OECD17 (II)
Direct investment abroad from foreign direct investment flows		US$	Yes	A	OECD	OECD17 (III)
Direct investment and long-term capital	Aggregated and detailed presentations containing transactions data	US$	Yes	A, Q	World	IMF1 (-)
Direct investment flows	Inflows, outflows	US$	Yes	A	OECD	OECD17 (I)
Direct investment in reporting country	By reporting country, by geographical zone	ECU	Yes	A	EC	EC10 (2D1.2)
Direct investment position abroad of OECD countries	By sector by country	US$ nat curr	Yes	A	OECD	OECD17 (4,8,V)
Direct investment, major destination	By low-income, middle income countries	US$	Yes	A	Developing countries	WB3 (1.10)
ECU investments, interest rates and yields	deposits, bonds	%	Yes	A, M	EC	EC27 (III)
EMCF, operations rates		%	Yes	A, M	EC	EC27 (III)
Emerging market closed-end country funds	By region, initial capital, net assets, market capitalization	US$	Yes	A	Developing countries	WB3 (A.V.6)
Equity issues, international	By issuer, launch, amount, where offered	nat curr	No		Developing countries	WB3 (A.V.7)
Foreign affiliates in host economy, largest	By home economy partner; industry; % of foreign equity; total invested in foreign affiliates	nat curr	No		Central and Eastern Europe	UN53 (17)

Subject	Categories	Units	Time series Yes/No Frequency		Territorial coverage	Source (Table No.)
Foreign affiliates in host economy, largest	Home economy, industry, sales	nat curr	No		Asia and the Pacific by country	UN52 (III.17)
Foreign affiliates in host economy, indicators of significance	Sector and industry	nat curr	No		Asia and the Pacific by country	UN52 (III.11)
Foreign affiliates in host economy	Developed, developing	nat curr	Yes	A	Asia and the Pacific by country	UN52 (III.14)
Foreign affiliates in host economy, indicators of significance	By republic, sales, value added employment, exports; imports	nat curr	No		Central and Eastern Europe	UN53 (11)
Foreign direct investment stock, sectoral distribution	By inward, outward investment	US$	Yes	A	Central and Eastern Europe	UN53 (6)
Foreign direct investment stock, geographical distribution	By inward, outward investment	US$	Yes	A	Central and Eastern Europe	UN53 (9)
Foreign direct investment stock, distribution of foreign affiliates	By inward; outwards investmeny by % of ownership company	US$	No		Central and Eastern Europe	UN53 (13)
Foreign direct investment affiliates, sectoral and regional distribution	By region,inward, outward investment	US$	No		Central and Eastern Europe	UN53 (10)
Foreign direct investment stock, geographical distribution	By republic	US$	No		Central and Eastern Europe	UN53 (9a)
Foreign direct investment position of OECD countries	By sector, by country	US$ nat curr	Yes	A	OECD	OECD17 (3,7,VI)
Foreign direct investment stock, industrial distribution	By sector, inward, outward investment	US$	Yes	A	Central and Eastern Europe	UN53 (7)
Foreign direct investment stock, industrial distribution	Inward, outward	nat curr	No		Asia and the Pacific by country	UN52 (III.7)
Foreign direct investment stock, geographical distribution	Inward, outward	nat curr	No		Asia and the Pacific by country	UN52 (III.9)
Foreign direct investment flows, industrial distribution	Inward, outward	nat curr	Yes	A	Asia and the Pacific	UN52 (III.3)
Foreign direct investment stock, sectoral distribution	Inward, outward	nat curr	Yes	A	Asia and the Pacific by country	UN52 (III.6)
Foreign direct investment stock, regional distribution	Inward, outward	nat curr	Yes	A	Asia and the Pacific by country	UN52 (III.8)
Foreign direct investment flows, geographical distribution by country	Inward, outward	nat curr	Yes	A	Asia and the Pacific	UN52 (III.4)
Foreign direct investment flows	By inward, outward investment	US$	Yes	A	Central and Eastern Europe	UN53 (2)
Foreign direct investment stock and distribution of foreign affiliates	Inward, outward ownership of parent companies	nat curr %	No		Asia and the Pacific by country	UN52 (III.13)
Foreign investment inflows, share of, in gross domestic capital formation	Annual averages	%	No		Asia and the Pacific	UN52 (6)
Foreign investment	By type, by field of activity or industry by country	US$	Yes	A	ASEAN	ASEANS1 (7.5)
Foreign investment flows	By sector	nat curr	Yes	A	OECD	OECD17 (2)
	by country	nat curr	Yes	A	OECD	OECD17 (6)
Foreign investment inflows	Annual averages	domestic currency unit	No		Asia and the Pacific	UN52 (5)
Foreign investment, distribution of	Inward stock by home country, region developed, developing	%	No		Asia and the Pacific	UN52 (8)
Foreign investment, flows	Inward, outward	nat curr	Yes	A	Asia and the Pacific	UN52 (III.2)
Foreign investment, outflows	Annual averages	domestic currency units	No		Asia and the Pacific	UN52 (13)

Subject	Categories	Units	Time series Yes/No Frequency		Territorial coverage	Source (Table No.)
Foreign investment, outward stock, regional distribution	Developed, developing areas	%	No		Asia and the Pacific	UN52 (14)
Foreign investment, stock, sectoral distribution of	Inward, outward stock	%	No		Asia and the Pacific	UN52 (9)
Foreign investment, stock, within the secondary sector	Manufacturing industries of foreign direct investment stock	%	No		Asia and the Pacific	UN52 (10)
Foreign investment, stock, inward within the tertiary sector	Service industries of foreign direct investment stock	%	No		Asia and the Pacific	UN52 (11)
Foreign portfolio investment flows in OECD countries, inflows	By region	US$	Yes	A	Developing countries	WB3 (1.11)
Income, direct investment	Credit and debit figures by country and country group	US$	Yes	A	World	IMF2 (C-7)
Income, other investment	Credit and debit figures by country and country group	US$	Yes	A	World	IMF2 (C-8)
International direct investment	Inward, outward position of selected OECD countries	US$	Yes	A	OECD	OECD17 (IV)
	by sector	nat curr	Yes	A	OECD	OECD17 (1)
	by country	nat curr	Yes	A	OECD	OECD17 (5)
International investment position	By variable, inward outward investment	US$	No		Central and Eastern Europe	UN53 (1)
International investment position, summary	Inward, outward	nat curr	No		Asia and the Pacific	UN52 (III.1)
Investment income	By reporting country, by geographical zone	ECU	Yes	A	EC	EC10 (2A2.4)
Investment of foreign capital, total	By activity	US$	No		Saudi Arabia	CH1 (8.14)
Inward investment flows, EFTA-6's, net	By region	US$	Yes	A	EFTA, EC, N. America	EFTA1 (1.4)
Inward investment flows, net		US$	Yes	A	Austria	EFTA1 (1.6)
Inward investment flows, net		US$	Yes	A	Finland	EFTA1 (1.8)
Inward investment flows, net		US$	Yes	A	Iceland	EFTA1 (1.10)
Inward investment flows, net		US$	Yes	A	Norway	EFTA1 (1.12)
Inward investment flows, net		US$	Yes	A	Sweden	EFTA1 (1.14)
Inward investment flows, net		US$	Yes	A	Switzerland	EFTA1 (1.16)
Inward investment flows, net	By country, region	US$	Yes	A	EFTA	EFTA1 (1.2)
Largest transnational corporation abroad	By industry; by foreign affiliates	nos	No		Central and Eastern Europe	UN53 (18)
Long-term capital	By reporting country, by geographical zone	ECU	Yes	A	EC	EC10 (2D)
Long-term capital	Net	ECU	Yes	A, Q	EC, USA, Japan	EC36
Long-term capital - deposit money sectors	By reporting country, by geographical zone	ECU	Yes	A	EC	EC10 (2D3.1)
Long-term capital - official sector	By reporting country, by geographical zone	ECU	Yes	A	EC	EC10 (2D3)
Net direct investment		US$	Yes	A	Latin American and Caribbean countries	UN45 (269)
Outward investment flows, EFTA-6's, net	By region	US$	Yes	A	EFTA, EC, N. America	EFTA1 (1.3)
Outward investment flows, net		US$	Yes	A	Austria	EFTA1 (1.5)
Outward investment flows, net		US$	Yes	A	Finland	EFTA1 (1.7)
Outward investment flows, net		US$	Yes	A	Iceland	EFTA1 (1.9)
Outward investment flows, net		US$	Yes	A	Norway	EFTA1 (1.11)
Outward investment flows, net		US$	Yes	A	Sweden	EFTA1 (1.13)
Outward investment flows, net		US$	Yes	A	Switzerland	EFTA1 (1.15)
Outward investment flows, net	By country, region	US$	Yes	A	EFTA	EFTA1 (1.1)
Outward stock of FDI	By sector	%	Yes	I	Selected countries	GATT3 (A.6)
Portfolio equity flows, gross	By analytical group	US$	Yes	A	Developing countries	WB3 (A.V.2)
Portfolio equity flows, gross	By region	US$	Yes	A	Developing countries	WB3 (A.V.1)

Subject	Categories	Units	Time series Yes/No Frequency		Territorial coverage	Source (Table No.)
Portfolio investment	By reporting country, by geographical zone	ECU	Yes	A	EC	EC10 (2D2)
Portfolio investment	By type	US$	Yes	A	Latin America	WB3 (1.12)
Portfolio Investment	Assets and liabilities by country and country group	US$	Yes	A	World	IMF2 (C-15)
Reinvested earnings on direct investment	Credit and debit figures by country and country group	US$	Yes	A	World	IMF2 (C-6)
Transnational corporations abroad, largest	Industry, assets	nat curr	No		Asia and the Pacific by country	UN52 (III.18)
Transnational corporations, indicators of significance for the home economy	By sector and industry, exports	%	No		Central and Eastern Europe	UN53 (12)
Transnational corporations, royalty payments by domestic firms and foreign affiliates	Domestic currency Units		No		Asia and the Pacific	UN52 (12)
Transnational corporations, indicators of significance for activities of the host economy	Primary, secondary, tertiary	%	No		Asia and the Pacific	UN52 (7)
27.5.7 Reserves						
Currency and banking	Summary, by country	nat curr	Yes	A	ESCAP country	UN44
Foreign exchange		SDRs	Yes	A, M	World	IMF7 (-)
Foreign exchange		SDRs	Yes	A, M	World	IMF6 (-)
Foreign exchange reserves		US$	Yes	A	Nordic countries	NCM1 (175)
Foreign official reserves (excl. gold)	Annual variation, monthly imports and world reserves	%	Yes	A	EC	EC59 (I.7)
Foreign official reserves	Total incl. and excl. of monetary gold, Foreign Exchange, special drawing rights, position in IMF and monetary gold	ECU, ounces	Yes	A, Q, M	EC	EC59 (III.8)
Gold		SDRs/million ounces	Yes	A	World	IMF7 (-)
Gold (million fine troy ounces)		SDRs	Yes	M	World	IMF6 (-)
Gold holdings		SDR at US$ 35 per ounce	Yes	A	World	IMF7 (-)
Gold holdings		SDRs	Yes	M	World	IMF6 (-)
Gold holdings		SDRs/market prices	Yes	A	World	IMF7 (-)
Gold holdings at market prices		SDRs	Yes	M	World	IMF6 (-)
Gold prices and SDR rates		SDRs	Yes	A, M	World	IMF7 (-)
Gold prices and SDR rates		SDRs	Yes	A, M	World	IMF6 (-)
Gold reserves		ounces	Yes	A, M	World	UN35 (55)
Gold reserves		ounces	Yes	A	World	UN50 (1)
Gold reserves		ounces	Yes	A	World	UN50 (30)
IMF gold transactions			Yes	A	World	IMF7 (-)
International reserves, all countries		SDR	Yes	A	World	UN50 (1)
International reserves, position in IMF		SDR	Yes	A	World	UN50 (1)
International reserves, foreign exchange		SDR	Yes	A	World	UN50 (1)
International reserves, excluding gold		US$	Yes	A	World	UN50 (29)
International reserves, minus gold	Reserve position in IMF, Foreign exchange, SDR	US$	Yes	A, M	World	UN35 (54)
International reserves		US$	Yes	A	Developing ESCAP region	UN44 (13)
International reserves	Incl. gold	US$	Yes	A	ASEAN	ASEANS1 (7.3)

Subject	Categories	Units	Time series Yes/No	Frequency	Territorial coverage	Source (Table No.)
International reserves	SDR, IMF reserve position, foreign exchange assets, gold, total, months of imports	US$, months	Yes	A	Latin American and Caribbean countries	UN45 (270)
International reserves and imports	Official reserve holdings, cover of reserves months of imports covered by total reserves	$US	Yes	A	Developing countries, least developed countries	UNCTAD5 (3.14)
Liabilities constituting foreign authorities' reserves	Aggregated and detailed presentations containing transactions data	US$	Yes	A, Q	World	IMF1 (-)
Liabilities constituting foreign authorities' reserves	By country group and country	US$	Yes	A	World	IMF2 (A-11)
Non-gold reserves			Yes	A	World	IMF7 (-)
Official reserves	Excluding gold	SDRs	Yes	A, M	OECD	OECD22
Ratio of official reserves to imports		nos	Yes	A	OECD, EC	OECD32 (11.6)
Reserve claims	By country and country group	US$	Yes	A	World	IMF2 (C-35)
Reserve position in IMF		SDRs	Yes	A, M	World	IMF7 (-)
Reserve position in IMF		SDRs	Yes	A, M	World	IMF6 (-)
Reserves, total change	By country group and country	US$	Yes	A	World	IMF2 (A-13)
Reserves, total change in authorities' reserves	Aggregated and detailed presentations containing transactions data	US$	Yes	A, Q	World	IMF1 (-)
Reserves, annual changes		US$	Yes	A	Latin American and Caribbean countries	UN45 (103)
Reserves		ECU	Yes	A, Q	EC, USA, Japan	EC36
Reserves		ECU	Yes	A	EC, Eur Countries, USA, USSR, Canada, Japan	EC9 (2.42)
Reserves		US$	Yes	A	Central and South American countries	IADB1
Reserves	Reserves total, average annual change months in reserves, number of months of imports	US$	Yes	A	Developing countries and territories	UNCTAD1 (5.2)
Reserves (counterpart items plus total change in reserves)	By country group and country	US$	Yes	A	World	IMF2 (A-14)
SDR holdings		SDRs	Yes	M	World	IMF6 (-)
SDR holdings		SDRs	Yes	A	World	IMF7 (-)
Total reserves		SDRs	Yes	M	World	IMF6 (-)
Total reserves		SDRs at US$ 35 per ounce	Yes	A	World	IMF7 (-)
Total reserves minus gold		SDRs	Yes	A	World	IMF7 (-)
Total reserves minus gold		SDRs	Yes	M	World	IMF6 (-)
27.5.8 Transfers						
Aggregate net transfers (long-term)	By type of transfer	US$	Yes	A	Developing countries	WB3 (1.6)
Debt reduction of officially supported commercial bank DDSR operations in SIMICs	By face value, debt reduction equivalent	US$, %	No		Developing countries	WB3 (1.14)
Government transactions	By reporting country, by geographical zone	ECU	Yes	A	EC	EC10 (2A2.6)
Net resource flows, net transfers on long-term debt	By low, middle income severely indebted	US$	Yes	A	Developing countries	WB3 (1.7)
Net transfer of resources		US$, %	Yes	A	Latin American and Caribbean countries	UN45 (268)
ODA disbursements	By country, % of GNP	US$ %	Yes	A	World	WB3 (1.8)
ODA forgiveness	By donor country	US$	Yes	A	World	WB3 (1.9)

Subject	Categories	Units	Time series Yes/No Frequency		Territorial coverage	Source (Table No.)
Official transfers	By reporting country, by geographical zone	ECU	Yes	A	EC	EC10 (2B2)
Officially supported financing packages involving debt reduction	By timing, exit, new money instruments	various	No		Developing countries	WB3 (1.13)
Private transfers	By reporting country, by geographical zone	ECU	Yes	A	EC	EC10 (2B1)
Unrequited transfers		US$	Yes	A	Central and South American countries	IADB1
Unrequited transfers	By reporting country, by geographical zone	ECU	Yes	A	EC	EC10 (2B)
27.5.9 Transport and Travel						
Transport, passenger	Credit, debit, net by country	ECU	Yes	A	EC	EC78 (X.3.1)
Transport, passenger	Credit, debit, net by country	ECU	Yes	A, Q	EC	EC78 (X.3.2)
Transport, passenger	Credit, debit, net by country	ECU	Yes	A, M	EC	EC78 (X.3.3)
Transport, passenger	Credit, debit, net geographical breakdown of payments by country or region, by country	ECU	Yes	A	EC	EC78 (X.4.1)
Transport	By reporting country, by geographical zone	ECU	Yes	A	EC	EC10 (2A2.1)
Travel	By reporting country, by geographical zone	ECU	Yes	A	EC	EC10 (2A2.3)
Travel	Credit, debits, net	ECU	Yes	A	EC	EC78 (X.1.1)
Travel	Credit, debits, net	ECU	Yes	A, Q	EC	EC78 (X.1.2)
Travel	Credit, debits, net	ECU	Yes	A, M	EC	EC78 (X.1.3)
Travel	Credit, debits, net, geographical breakdown of payments by country or region, by country	ECU	Yes	A	EC	EC78 (X.2.1)
27.6 PRICES AND UNIT VALUES – see also Section 37						
Export price index numbers of primary commodities and non-ferrous base metals	By type	indices	Yes	A	Market economies	UN50 (13)
Export price index numbers	Primary commodities, non-ferrous base metals	indices	Yes	A, M	World	UN35 (50)
Export unit values		indices/ US$	Yes	A, M	World	IMF7 (-)
Export unit values		indices/ US$	Yes	A, M	World	IMF6 (-)
Import unit values		indices/ US$	Yes	A, M	World	IMF7 (-)
Import unit values		indices/ US$	Yes	A, M	World	IMF6 (-)
Price factor	c.i.f., f.o.b.	US$	Yes	A	World	IMF7 (-)
Price indices	Selected manufactured goods, by SITC group	indices	Yes	A	World	UNCTAD1 (2.8)
Prices, international trade	Imports, exports, exchange rate, balance of payments	million US$ nat curr/US$	Yes		World	UN55
Prices	By country, import prices, export prices, terms of trade,	indices	No		Europe	EC18 (15.2)

Subject	Categories	Units	Time series Yes/No Frequency		Territorial coverage	Source (Table No.)
Prices	Import prices, export prices, terms of trade, by country	indices	Yes	A	VICES countries and Yugoslavia	VICES1 (III/1)
Prices	Import prices, export prices, terms of trade, by country	indices	Yes	A	VICES countries and Yugoslavia	VICES1 (III/1)
Prices – free market prices and price indices of selected primary commodities		indices; US$ per metric ton	Yes	A	World	UNCTAD4 (A.1)
Prices – instability indices and trends in monthly market prices	By selected primary commodity	%	No		World	UNCTAD4 (A.2)
Unit value and quantum indices	Imports and exports and terms of trade	indices	Yes	A	Nordic countries	NCM1 (132)
Unit value indices	Imports, exports	indices	Yes	A	World	UN50 (129)
Unit value indices		indices	Yes	A	World economic regions	UNCTAD1 (2.3)
Unit value indices		indices	Yes	A	World economic regions	UNCTAD1 (2.4)
Unit value indices		indices in US$, indices in nat curr	Yes	A	World	UN50 (130)
Unit value indices	Exports and Imports	indices	Yes	A	World	UN35 (47)
Unit value indices	Terms of trade, imports, exports	indices, %	Yes	A	EFTA	EFTA1 (2.5)
Unit value indices	Total exports	indices	Yes	A, M	EC	EC36
Unit value indices	Total imports	indices	Yes	A, M	EC, Market	EC36
Units value of exports of goods	f.o.b	indices	Yes	A	Latin American and Caribbean countries	UN45 (273)
Volume and unit value indices	Intra- and extra-EC trade	indices	Yes	A	EC	EC39 (8)

27.7 TERMS OF TRADE

Subject	Categories	Units	Time series Yes/No Frequency		Territorial coverage	Source (Table No.)
External trade and terms of trade	By country, by volume of imports, exports, value imports, exports	indices	No		Europe	EC18 (9.2)
Merchandise, terms and growth rates of trade	By high, middle, low income	US$, %	No		World	CS1 (7)
Merchandise terms of trade	By country, by export price index, import price index, terms of trade	index	Yes	A	Developing countries	WB2 (-)
Terms of trade, goods	f.o.b, c.i.f	indices	Yes	A	Latin American and Caribbean countries	UN45 (274)
Terms of trade, effect of	At constant 1980 prices	US$	Yes	A	Latin American and Caribbean countries	UN45 (125)
Terms of trade		%	Yes	A	World	IMF7 (-)
Terms of trade		indices	Yes	A, M	EC	EC36
Terms of trade		indices	Yes	A	Market economies by regions	UN50 (12)
Terms of trade	For 18 individual commodities covered by the IPC	indices	Yes	A	Developing countries	UNCTAD1 (4.10)
Terms of trade	Imports, exports	indices	Yes	A	World	UN50 (129)
Terms of trade	Percentage change	%	Yes	A	OECD, EC	OECD32 (11.5)
Terms of trade indices		indices	Yes	A	World economic regions	UNCTAD1 (2.5)

27 INTERNATIONAL TRADE AND FINANCE

Subject	Categories	Units	Time series Yes/No Frequency		Territorial coverage	Source (Table No.)
Trade structure of countries	Exports, imports of Eastern Europe by destination, origin	%	Yes	Selected years	Socialist countries of Eastern Europe	UNCTAD5 (3.10)
World trade indicators	Categories, region volumes, terms of trade and purchasing power of exports	%	Yes	Selected years	DMECs, developing countries, least developed countries	UNCTAD5 (3.11)

28 LABOUR

Subject	Categories	Units	Time series Yes/No	Frequency	Territorial coverage	Source (Table no.)

28.1 DISPUTES

Subject	Categories	Units	Time series Yes/No	Frequency	Territorial coverage	Source (Table no.)
Industrial disputes	By countries, workers involved, days lost	nos	Yes	A	EC	MAC3 (B3)
Industrial disputes	By country	nos	No		The Americas and Australasia	MAC2 (C3)
Industrial disputes	By dispute, workers involved, working days lost	nos,	Yes	A	Africa and Asia	MAC1 (C3)
Industrial stoppages	Working days lost, by economic activity, by country	nos	Yes	A	EC	EC29 (V/2)
Industrial stoppages	Working days lost employees, by sector of economic activity	per thou per thou	Yes	A	EC	EC29 (V/1)
Labour disputes, time lost		person days	Yes	M, Q, A	OECD	OECD23
Labour disputes	Time lost	person-days	Yes	A, M	OECD	OECD22
Stoppages of work	Employees affected days lost	nos, days	Yes	A	Nordic countries	NCM1 (53)

28.2 HOURS OF WORK – see also Working Conditions (28.6)

Subject	Categories	Units	Time series Yes/No	Frequency	Territorial coverage	Source (Table no.)
Average number of hours actually worked in a week	By selected characteristics	hours	No		OECD	OECD20 (10.3)
Construction	Sex, hours worked, hours paid for	hours	Yes	A	World	ILO7 (14)
Distribution of employed	By actual hours worked per week	%	No		OECD	OECD20 (10.2)
Full-time employees, industry and services	By hours worked and by sex	%	Yes	A	EC	EC29 (VI/6)
Hours of work		hours per week	Yes	M, Q, A	OECD	OECD23 (-)
Hours worked, industry	Hours per employee during a reference week, full-time by NACE division, part-time by sex	hours	Yes	A	EC	EC29 (VI/4)
Hours worked, services	Hours per employee during a reference week, full-time by NACE division, part-time by sex	hours	Yes	A	EC	EC29 (VI/5)
Hours worked, trends		hours per week	Yes	10 yrly	OECD	OECD20 (10.1)
Hours worked	By industry	hours per week	No		EC	EC9 (3.20)
Hours worked	By industry	indices	Yes	A, M	EC, USA, Japan	EC36
Hours worked	Hours per employee during a reference week, full-time, part-time, by sex	hours	Yes	A	EC	EC29 (VI/3)
Hours worked	Hours worked during the year per employee, by sector	hours	Yes	I	EC	EC29 (VI/8)
Iron and steel	Per manual worker, per employee	hours	Yes	A	EC	EC29 (VI/9)
Man hours	By ISIC division	nos	Yes	A	OECD	OECD16
Manpower, textile industry	By employees, hours worked, average cost of labour	nos, nat curr, US$ per hour	Yes	A	World	ITMF1 (2.2)
Manual workers, weekly work offered	By NACE class	hours	Yes	A	EC	EC29 (VI/1)
Manufacturing	Hours, week		Yes	A, M	World	UN35 (7)
Manufacturing	Hours		Yes	A	World	UN50 (18)

28 LABOUR

Subject	Categories	Units	Time series Yes/No	Frequency	Territorial coverage	Source (Table no.)
Manufacturing	Sex, hours worked, hours paid for by industry	hours	Yes	Q	World	ILO1 (6)
Manufacturing and mining	Weekly, monthly,	hours	Yes	A, M	OECD	OECD22
Mining and quarrying	Sex, hours worked, hours paid for	hours	Yes	A	World	ILO7 (13)
Non-agricultural activities	Sex, hours worked, hours paid for	hours	Yes	A	World	ILO7 (11)
Non-agricultural activities	Sex, hours worked, hours paid for	hours	Yes	Q	World	ILO1 (5)
Operatives	Hours or days worked	nos	Yes	A	World	UN27 (-)
Part-time employees, industry and services	By hours worked and by sex	%	Yes	A	EC	EC29 (VI/7)
Percentage of employed having worked 45 hours or more during the reference week	By selected characteristics	%	No		OECD	OECD20 (10.4)
Percentage of employed having worked long hours during the characteristics. reference week	By selected	%	No		OECD	OECD20 (10.4bis)
Total	Sex, hours worked, hours paid for	hours	Yes	A	World	ILO7 (12A)
Total	Sex, hours worked, hours paid for	hours	Yes	A	World	ILO7 (12B)
Transport, storage and communication	Sex, hours worked, hours paid for	hours	Yes	A	World	ILO7 (15)
Working hours for wage earners	By industry	hours	No		Nordic countries	NCM1 (77)

28.3 LABOUR COSTS

Subject	Categories	Units	Time series Yes/No	Frequency	Territorial coverage	Source (Table no.)
Annual average increase in hourly earnings	Nominal, real	%	No		EC, USA, Japan	EC53 (1.4)
Hourly, real	By industry	indices	No		EC	EC53 (2.3)
Index of hourly earnings in industry	Nominal, real	indices	No		EC, USA, Japan	EC53 (1.3)
Labour costs	By industry	ECU	No		EC	EC53 (3.4)
Labour costs per hour of a permanent adult agricultural worker	By type of job	nat curr, US$	Yes	A	EC and North America	UN40 (XXII)
Labour costs per person employed	By industry	ECU	No		EC	EC53 (3.8)
Manpower, textile industry	By employees, hours worked, average cost of labour	nos, nat curr, US$ per hour	Yes	A	World	ITMF1 (2.2)
Unit labour costs	Manufacturing	%	Yes	A	OECD, EC	OECD32 (9.10)
Unit labour costs	Manufacturing industry	indices	Yes	A, M	OECD	OECD22
Unit labour costs	Manufacturing industry	indices	Yes	M, Q, A	OECD	OECD23 (-)

28.4 LABOUR PRODUCTIVITY

Subject	Categories	Units	Time series Yes/No	Frequency	Territorial coverage	Source (Table no.)
Coal, productivity	Man hours		No		EC	EC33 (-)
Labour productivity	Apparent productivity by branch	%	No		EC	EC61 (11)
Labour productivity	By economic activity and country	indices	Yes	A	Asian Countries	APO1
Labour productivity	By selected industries. economic regions	indices	Yes	A	World	UNCTAD1 (6.8)

Subject	Categories	Units	Time series Yes/No Frequency		Territorial coverage	Source (Table no.)
Labour productivity	National, agriculture, manufacturing, electricity gas and water, construction, trade, transport and communication and finance	indices	Yes	A	Asian Countries	APO1 (A.1-A.8)
Labour productivity	Sector and selected industries and regions	indices	Yes	A	World	UN50 (10)
Labour productivity level (current prices)	By economic activity and country	US$	Yes	A	Asian Countries	APO1
Labour productivity level (constant prices)	By economic activity and country	US$	Yes	A	Asian Countries	APO1
Labour productivity ratio	Apparent productivity of labour of each branch to apparent productivity of the total	nos	No		EC	EC61 (10)
Production value	By industry	ECU	No		EC	EC53 (3.3)
Productivity	By NACE	ECU, capita	Yes	A	EC	EC75 (1)
Productivity levels (current prices)	National, agriculture, manufacturing, electricity gas and water, construction, trade, transport and communication and finance	US$	Yes	A	Asian Countries	APO1 (B.1-B.8)
Productivity levels (constant prices)	National, agriculture, manufacturing, electricity gas and water, construction, trade, transport and communication and finance	US$	Yes	A	Asian Countries	APO1 (C.1-C.8)
Productivity of intermediate consumption, trends in		indices	Yes	A	EC	EC2 (A34)
28.5 VACANCIES						
Help-wanted advertising		indices	Yes	M, Q, A	OECD	OECD23 (-)
Public employment offices	Vacancies offered, vacancies filled	nos	Yes	A	EC,	EC29 (IV/11)
28.6 WORKING CONDITIONS						
28.6.1 Hours Lost						
Hours lost by sickness	By gender, by sector	%	No		EC	EC35 (-)
28.6.2 Leave Entitlement						
Public holidays and leave entitlement per year		nos	No		OECD	OECD20 (12.1)
28.6.3 Length of Working Week						
Hours usually worked during the reference week and hours lost	By country	nos, %	No		EC	EC72 (5.16)
Hours usually worked per week	By country, full-time self-employed persons	nos	No		EC	EC72 (5.3)
Hours usually worked per week	By country, full-time employees, sector, gender	nos	No		EC	EC72 (5.4)
Hours usually worked per week	By economic activity, sex	hours	No		EC	EC56 (54)
Hours usually worked per week	By type of employment, sector, gender	nos	No		EC	EC72 (5.2)

28 LABOUR

Subject	Categories	Units	Time series Yes/No Frequency	Territorial coverage	Source (Table no.)
Length of working week	By country, full-time employees, sector, gender	hours	No	EC	EC35 (-)
Length of working week	By country, part-time employees, gender	hours	No	EC	EC35 (-)
Persons in employment	Hours, week, by sector of activity, sex	hours	No	EC	EC56 (47,48)
Working hours for full-time self-employed	By country, gender	hours	No	EC	EC35 (-)
28.6.4 Part-time Work					
Hours worked part-time per week	By country, gender	nos	No	EC	EC72 (5.12)
Part-time employees	By country, % of all employees, all female employees, female employees in services	nos, %	No	EC	EC35 (-)
Part-time work	By country, gender	%	No	EC	EC72 (5,7)
Part-time work	By country, sector	%	No	EC	EC72 (5.9)
Part-time work	By country, gender	%	No	EC	EC72 (5.11)
Part-time work	By country, gender, as a % of total employment	%	No	EC	EC35 (-)
28.6.5 Shift-work, Night-work, etc.					
Employed working at night	By selected characteristics	%	No	OECD	OECD20 (13.2)
Employed working on Sundays and public holidays	By selected characteristics	%	No	OECD	OECD20 (13.3)
Employees working in shifts	By selected characteristics	%	No	OECD	OECD20 (13.1)
28.6.6 Temporary Contracts					
Temporary contracts	By country, gender	%	No	EC	EC72 (5.13)
Temporary contracts	By country, age	%	No	EC	EC72 (5.14)
28.6.7 Travel-to-work Time					
Daily commuters	By travel time to work	%	No	OECD	OECD20 (11.1)
Full-time and part-time employment	Difference between usual and actual hours, sex	nos	No	EC	EC56 (53)
Full-time and part-time employment	Hours, week, sex	%	No	EC	EC56 (49-52)
Full-time and part-time employment	Hours worked per week by economic activity, sex	hours	No	EC	EC56 (55,56)
Full-time employment	Hours worked per week, sex	%	No	EC	EC56 (60,61)
Full-time employment industry	Hours worked per week by economic activity, sex	%	No	EC	EC56 (57)
Full-time employment services	Hours worked per week by economic activity, sex	%	No	EC	EC56 (58)
Mode of transport		%	No	OECD	OECD20 (11.2)
Mode of transport with more than one hour of travel time to work	By selected	%	No	OECD	OECD20 (11.4)
Mode of transport with travel time to work up to 15 minutes	By selected characteristics	%	No	OECD	OECD20 (11.3)
Part-time employment	Hours worked per week by economic activity, sex	%	No	EC	EC56 (59)

29 LAND

Subject	Categories	Units	Time series Yes/No Frequency		Territorial coverage	Source (Table no.)
29.1 AGRICULTURE – see also Section 2						
29.1.1 Holdings						
Arable land, distribution of holdings	By area under selected arable land crops	%	No		EC	EC45 (A IIIB)
Arable land, holdings	Holdings with arable land and area under arable land, by type	nos	No		EC	EC45 (A IIIA)
Holdings	Total, in less favoured areas, in mountain areas, agricultural area, by country, region	nos	No		EC	EC45 (D)
Holdings	With and without cattle	ha, nos	No		Nordic countries	NCM1 (60)
Holdings	By size of arable land	nos, %	No		Nordic countries	NCM1 (56)
Land use	By crops	nos	Yes	2 yrly	EC	EC6 (IC 8)
Land Use	Number of holdings, area, by type of farming, by country	nos	No		EC	EC45 (C)
Land use	Number of holdings, area under crops, by type of crop, by size class of holding, by country	nos	No		EC	EC45 (B)
Land use	Number of holdings, area under crop, by type of crop, by country, region	nos	No		EC	EC45 (D)
29.1.2 Land Use						
Agricultural area	Arable land, permanent crops, permanent pasture, forest area, irrigated land	ha	Yes	A	Latin American and Caribbean countries	UN45 (301)
Agricultural area	Utilised	ha	No		EC	WC1 (-)
Arable and permanent meadows, net change in area	By combined land, non-combined land	ha	No		EC	UN22 (II-3.1.2)
Arable land, use of	By crops, fallow	ha	No		Nordic countries	NCM1 (55)
Arable land	Total arable land, area as proportion of total land area	sq km, %	Yes	A	EC	EC34 (2.5, 2.6)
Arable land and gardens		ha	No		Nordic countries	NCM1 (54)
Area, population, agriculture	By population, agriculture	ha, per capita, nos	Yes	A	EC	EC6 (IA2.2)
Area	Total	sq km	No		EC	WC1 (-)
Area of crops and grass, arable, cereals and sugar beet	Per dairy cow and head of cattle, type 41 holdings	area, %	Yes	2 yrly	EUR9	EC57 (6.26)
Area of crops and grass, arable, cereals and sugar beet	Per dairy cow and head of cattle, type 41 holdings	area, %	Yes	2 yrly	EC	EC58 (6.21)
Area used for production of cereals, dried pulses, industrial crops, oilseeds, fresh vegetables, and fodder	From arable land	ha, indices	Yes	A	EUR10	EC57 (6.27)
Area used for production of cereals, dried pulses, industrial crops, oilseeds, fresh vegetables, and fodder	From arable land	ha, indices	Yes	A	EC	EC58 (6.20)
Broad areas	Main crops	ha	Yes	A	EC	EC6 (IB 1)
Broad areas	Total, by type	ha	Yes	A	EC	EC6 (IA2.1)
Broad areas	Total, land, arable, permanent, forest, other	ha	Yes	5 yrly	World	FAO1 (1)
Crop, land use	By product	ha	Yes	A	EC	EC19 (I)

29 LAND

Subject	Categories	Units	Time series Yes/No Frequency		Territorial coverage	Source (Table no.)
Drainage		ha, % change	No		Selected countries	UN22 (II-3.2.6a)
Holdings, number and area of	Farm size class	ha UAA, nos, %, ha	No		EC	WC1 (-)
Irrigated area		ha, % change	No		Selected countries	UN22 (II-3.2.6b)
Irrigation		ha	Yes	5 yrly	World	FAO1 (2)
Land area, total		sq km	No		OECD	OECD33 (4.1A)
Land area	By country, by arable crops, permanent crops, irrigated, non-irrigated	ha	No		GCC region	CH1 (7.1)
Land use, arable and permanent cropland, permanent grassland, other		sq km, %	No		OECD	OECD33 (4.1A)
Land use, agriculture	By type of land use	ha, %	Yes	A	ASEAN	ASEANS1 (3.2)
Land use	Arable, pastoral, irrigated, unirrigated, forest and woodland, by country	ha	Yes	A	ESCAP countries	UN44
Land use	Arable, crops, grassland wooded	ha	No		World, EC, USA, USSR, Canada, Japan	EC9 (5.1)
Land use	Arable, by crop, permanent grassland, permanent crops - by crop kitchen gardens	ha	No		EC	EC9 (5.2)
Land use	By arable, permanent crops permanent pasture	ha	No		Selected countries	UN22 (II-3.1.1)
Land use	By type of crop, type of animal	holdings	No		EC	EC9 (5.17)
Land use and irrigation	By country, by use	ha	No		EC	EM1 (1903)
Land utilization	By country, by use	%	No		GCC region	CH1 (7.2)
Perennial crops	Total perennial crops, area as proportion of total land area	sq km, %	Yes	A	EC	EC34 (2.9, 2.10)
Permanent grassland	Total permanent, grassland, area as proportion of total land area	sq km, %	Yes	A	EC	EC34 (2.7, 2.8)
Soil suitability and topography	By suitability for type of crop, by land slope	ha	No		Selected countries	UN22 (II-3.1.3)
Use of agricultural land						
Utilised agricultural area, woods and forests		ha, % of UAA,	No		EC	WC1 (-)
Utilised agricultural area	Total % change, % of EC	ha, %	No		EC	MLC1 (-)
Utilized agricultural area	By size group of holding	ha	No		EC	EC9 (5.16)
Utilized agricultural area	Type 41 holdings	nos	Yes	2 yrly	EC	EC57 (6.12)
Wooded and utilized agricultural area	By grassland, crop, arable	ha	No		EC	EC69 (IV.1)
World, total area,		sq km, %	No		World	OECD33 (4.1A)
29.1.3 Wine-grape Areas						
Areas grubbed or no longer cultivated	By production, class potential yield, by region	ha	No		EC	EC8 (6.0P)
Areas grubbed or no longer cultivated	By production, class actual yield, by region	ha	No		EC	EC8 (6.1A)
Planted wine-grape vine areas	By production, class, actual yield, by region	ha	No		EC	EC8 (5.1)

Subject	Categories	Units	Time series Yes/No Frequency		Territorial coverage	Source (Table no.)
Planted wine-grape vine areas	By production, yield class, by region	ha	No		EC	EC8 (6.-P)
Production of grape-must or wine	By production, potential yield, alcoholic strength %, by region	hl	No		EC	EC8 (7.0)
Production of grape-must or wine	By production, actual yield, alcoholic strength %, by region	hl	No		EC	EC8 (7.1)
Replanted wine-grape vine areas	By production, class potential yield, by region	ha	No		EC	EC8 (6.0R)
Wine-grape vine areas production	By production, class, potential yield, by region	ha	No		EC	EC8 (5.0)
29.2 FORESTRY – see also Section 21						
29.2.1 Holdings						
Agricultural holdings with wooded areas	By size, %	nos	No		EC	EC6 (IIA 2)
Forest area ownership		%	No		EC	EC47 (1.3)
Forest holdings, number	By type of ownership and holding size category	nos	No		EC	EC47 (2.5)
Forest holdings, average size	State and private forests	ha	No		EC	EC47 (1.2)
Forestry holdings, area	By type of ownership and holding size category	ha	No		EC	EC47 (2.6)
Wooded areas of agricultural holdings	By area, %	ha	No		EC	EC6 (IIA 3)
29.2.2 Land Use						
Forest and other wooded		sq km, %	No		OECD	OECD33 (4.1A)
Forest and other wooded land, estimates	By major recognized functions	%	No		Selected countries	UN22 (I-1.2.3)
Forest land	By type, % of total land	sq km, %	No		Selected countries	UN22 (I-1.2.2)
High forest, area	By tree species and age group	ha	No		EC	EC47 (2.7)
Land area, total		ha	No		Selected Countries	ITTO1 (3)
Land use in developing Africa	Arable land, land under permanent crops, permanent meadows and pastures, forest and woodland, other land, total agricultural and irrigated land	1000 ha, %	Yes	A	African Countries	UN1 (19a)
Land use in developing Africa	Arable land, land under permanent crops, permanent meadows and pastures, forest and woodland, other land, total agricultural and irrigated land	1000 ha, per capita	Yes	A	African countries	UN1 (19b)
Land use selected indicators	Total agricultural land use, arable land	% of total land, irrigated land area	Yes	A	African countries	UN1 (20)
Land use selected indicators	Change in forest and woodland	%	Yes	A	African countries	UN1 (20)
Natural closed broadleaved forest	Productive, total, unproductive, total	ha	No		Selected Countries	ITTO1 (3)
Plantations and natural coniferous forest	By hardwood, softwood	ha	No		Selected Countries	ITTO1 (3)
Tropical forest area, total		ha	No		Selected Countries	ITTO1 (3)
Wooded area, distribution		%, ha	No		EC	EC47 (2.1)

29 LAND

Subject	Categories	Units	Time series Yes/No	Frequency	Territorial coverage	Source (Table no.)
Wooded area, distribution	By ownership type	ha, %	No		EC	EC47 (2.2)
Wooded area, distribution	By sylvicultural treatment	ha, %	No		EC	EC47 (2.3)
Wooded area, distribution	By type of ownership and slvicultural treatment	ha	No		EC	EC47 (2.4)
Wooded area		ha	No		EC	EC47 (1.1)
Wooded area	By forest type	ha, %	No		EC	EC47 (1.8)
Woodland	Total woodland, area as proportion of total land area	sq km, %	Yes	A	EC	EC34 (2.11 2.12)

29.3 LAND AREA

29.3.1 Population Density

Subject	Categories	Units	Time series Yes/No	Frequency	Territorial coverage	Source (Table no.)
Density	Area, density	sq km, nos	No		World, economic regions	UNCTAD1R (6.1)
Density	Inhabitants	sq km	No		World	UNCTAD5 (-)
Land area		sq km	No		ECMT countries	ECMT1 (2)
Population		nos	No		ECMT countries	ECMT1 (2
Population density	By country, by area	sq km, nos	No		EC	EC35 (-)
Population density	Inhabitants	per sq km	Yes	A	OECD, World	OECD33 (14.3)
Surface area density		per sq km	No		World	UN19 (3)
Surface area density		per sq km	No		World, macro regions	UN50 (2)
Surface area density		per sq km	No		World	UN50 (14)
Surface area density	Mid-year estimates	per sq km, per capita	No		World	NCM1 (1)
Surface area density	Mid-year estimates	per sq km	Yes	5 yrly	World	UNESCO1 (1.1)

29.3.2 Surface Area

Subject	Categories	Units	Time series Yes/No	Frequency	Territorial coverage	Source (Table no.)
Area	By administrative unit	sq km	No		EC	EC18 (2.1)
Land area, total		sq km	No	1989	OECD, World	OECD33 (14.2)
Land area, total		sq km	Yes	A	EC	EC34 (2.4)
Land area, total	Agricultural	sq km, %	No		Developing countries	WB1 (-)
Land area		sq km	Yes	A	EC by region	EC65 (-)
Land area	Total, arable, meadows and pastures, forests and woodlands, other land and % AGR	ha, %	Yes	10 yrs	World	UN26
Residential area		%	No		EC	MHPPE1 (-)
Size indicators and other characteristics	By high, middle, low income	sq km, nos, US$	Yes	A	World	CS1 (1)
Surface and land area		ha	Yes	Selected years	World	UN16 (8)
Surface area, total	By country	nos	Yes	A	EC, Canada, USA	UN13 (1)
Surface area		sq km	No		EC	EC11 (1)
Surface area		sq km	No		EC	MHPPE1 (-)

29.4 LAND USE – see also under Agriculture (29.1) and Forestry (29.2)

29.4.1 Changes in Land Use

Subject	Categories	Units	Time series Yes/No	Frequency	Territorial coverage	Source (Table no.)
Arable and crop land		indices	Yes	5 yrly	OECD	OECD33 (4.1B)
Forest and other wooded land		indices	Yes	5 yrly	OECD	OECD33 (4.1B)
Land use, changes in	By type of land	%	No		Selected countries	UN22 (I-1.2.6)

Subject	Categories	Units	Time series Yes/No Frequency		Territorial coverage	Source (Table no.)
Permanent grassland		indices	Yes	5 yrly	OECD	OECD33 (4.1B)
Wetlands, state and changes	Losses	sq km, %	No		Selected countries	OECD33 (4.2)
World, total		indices	Yes	5 yrly	World	OECD33 (4.1B)
29.4.2 Land Use – General						
Built-up area	As per cent of total land and as surface per inhabitant	%, sq km per 1000 inhabitants	No		Selected countries	UN22 (I-1.2.5)
Land use	Agricultural, forest, other	ha, %	Yes	Selected years	World	UN16 (8)
Land use	By broad category	sq km	No		Selected countries	UN22 (I-1.2.1)
Land use	By country, by use	sq km, %	No		EC	EC35 (-)
Land use	By country	ha	No		EC	EC18 (7.1)
Land use	Total, area	sq km	No		World	NCM1 (1)
Land use	Total, Land area , water, above sea level	sq km	No		Nordic countries	NCM1 (2)
Open lands	By type	sq km	No		Selected countries	UN22 (I-1.2.4)
Urbanization	By country, by conurbations, population	nos, %	No		EC	EC35 (-)
29.4.3 National Parks						
Number of sites		nos	No		OECD	OECD33 (4.3C)
Percentage of territory		%	No		OECD	OECD33 (4.3C)
Protected area		per capita	No		OECD	OECD33 (4.3C)
Total, world		nos, sq km, %, per capita	No		World	OECD33 (4.3C)
Total size		sq km	No		OECD	OECD33 (4.3C)
29.4.4 Protected Areas, Major						
Changes	Sites	nos, sq km	No		OECD	OECD33 (4.3B)
Number of sites		nos	No		OECD	OECD33 (4.3A)
Percentage of territory		%	No		OECD	OECD33 (4.3A)
Protected area		per capita	No		OECD	OECD33 (4.3A)
Total, world		nos, sq km	No		World	OECD33 (4.3A)
Total, world	Sites	nos, sq km	No		World	OECD33 (4.3B)
Total size		sq km	No		OECD	OECD33 (4.3A)
29.4.5 Soils						
Chemical deterioration	By loss of nutrients, and or organic matter, soil pollution, acidification, salinization, alkalinization	ha	No		Selected countries	UN22 (II-4.2.2e)
Physical deterioration	By soil compaction, by water logging	ha	No		Selected countries	UN22 (II-4.2.2d)
Physical deterioration	By water erosion, by wind erosion	ha	No		Selected countries	UN22 (II-4.2.2c)
Soil degradation	By type, by degree	sq km	No		EC, and North America	UN22 (II-4.2.2a,b)

30 LIVING COSTS AND STANDARDS

Subject	Categories	Units	Time series Yes/No Frequency		Territorial coverage	Source (Table no.)

30.1 CONSUMER PRICES - see also Section 42

Consumer prices	All items, food	indices	Yes	A, M	World	UN35 (51)
Consumer prices	By type of goods, by country	indices	Yes	A	ESCAP countries	UN44
Consumer prices	General	indices	Yes	A	EC, USA, Japan	EC9 (2.43)
Consumer prices	General level, food, annual rates	indices	Yes	A	Latin American and Caribbean countries	UN45 (236)
Consumer prices	Growth rate, annual	%	Yes	A	VICES countries, and Yugoslavia	VICES1 (II/2)
Consumer prices, index numbers	All groups, food groups	indices nos	Yes	Q	South Pacific	SPC1 (1,2)
Consumer prices, index numbers	By group	indices	Yes	Q	South Pacific	SPC1 (4)
Consumer prices, percentage changes	All groups food groups	%	Yes	Q	South Pacific	SPC1 (3)
Consumer prices, variations in	By high, middle, low income	%	Yes	A	World	CS1 (6)
Consumer prices, variations in	General level, food, average annual rates	indices	Yes	A	Latin American and Caribbean countries	UN45 (63)
Cost-of-living price index	By country, by index group	indices	No		EC	EC18 (15.1)
Durable goods	By type	nat curr, ECU	No		EC	EC16
Expenditure, real per capita	By type of expense	indices	No		Industrial countries	UN25 (37)
Food, beverages and tobacco	By type	nat curr, ECU	No		EC	EC16
	Food, excl drinks and meals out, drinks (home consumption), tobacco, clothing, footwear, inc repairs, rent, fuel, power, household goods and services, transport, communications recreation, education, culture, fuel and power, goods and services, inc meals and drinks out	indices	Yes	A	EC, USA, Japan	EC9 (2.43)
General index	Price indices, rate of increase over one month, rate of increase over 12 months	indices, %	Yes	A, M	EC	EC17 (1)
General index	Price indices, rate of increase over one month, rate of increase over 12 months	indices, %	Yes	A, M	USA, Japan, Switzerland, Austria, Norway, Sweden, Finland, Canada	EC17 (2)
Inflation		GDP	No		EC	WC1 (-)
Retail price indices, weighting patterns	By group	per 1000	No		South Pacific	SPC1 (5)
Retail prices	Selected commodities	$A	No		South Pacific	SPC1 (6)

30 LIVING COSTS AND STANDARDS

Subject	Categories	Units	Time series Yes/No Frequency	Territorial coverage	Source (Table no.)
30.2 LIVING COSTS - see also Section 37					
Accommodation	By type and country	nat curr	No	West Europe	CBI1
Clothes and personal care	By selected item and country	nat curr	No	West Europe	CBI1
Consumer goods	By selected item and country	nat curr	No	West Europe	CBI1
Education	By level, type and country	nat curr	No	West Europe	CBI1
Entertainment	By item and country	nat curr	No	West Europe	CBI1
Family budgets, expenditure structure average annual	By individual expenses, according to socio-economic category of head of household, type of household, income category, region and urban/rural environment, by country		No	EC	EC42 (2/1-2/5)
Family budgets, expenditure structure, absolute	By main groups, according to socio-economic category of the head of household, type of household, income category, region and urban/rural environment, by country	nat curr	No	EC	EC42 (2)
Family budgets, consumption, average annual per head	By selected item, according to socio-economic category of head of household type of household, income category, region and urban/rural environment, by country	kg, l, nos, kWh, tonnes, cu m	No	EC	EC42 (3/1-3/5)
Food	By selected item and country	nat curr	No	West Europe	CBI1
Gross salaries	By occupation and country	nat curr	No	West Europe	CBI1
Inflation	Consumer prices	%	Yes A	West Europe	CBI1
Office services	By service and country	nat curr	No	West Europe	CBI1
Social security	By country	%	No	West Europe	CBI1
Sports facilities	By type and country	nat curr	No	West Europe	CBI1
Tax	By rate, type, and country	nat curr, %	No	West Europe	CBI1
Transport	By type and country	nat curr	No	West Europe	CBI1
Utilities	By type and country	nat curr	No	West Europe	CBI1
30.3 PURCHASING POWER					
30.3.1 Steel Industry					
Net hourly earnings		DM PPP	No	World	IMWF1 (-)
Social security		%, Swiss francs	No	World	IMWF1 (-)
Working time required for purchases	By consumer items	hours	No	World	IMWF1 (-)
30.3.2 Shipbuilding Industry					
Net hourly earnings		DM PPP	No	World	IMWF1 (-)

Subject	Categories	Units	Time series Yes/No Frequency	Territorial coverage	Source (Table no.)
Social security		%, Swiss francs	No	World	IMWF1 (-)
Working time required for purchases	By consumer items	hours	No	World	IMWF1 (-)
30.3.3 Mechanical Engineering Indsutry					
Net hourly earnings		DM PPP	No	World	IMWF1 (-)
Social security		%, Swiss francs	No	World	IMWF1 (-)
Working time required for purchases	By consumer items	hours	No	World	IMWF1 (-)
30.3.4 Electrical Engineering Industry					
Net hourly earnings		DM PPP	No	World	IMWF1 (-)
Social security		%, Swiss francs	No	World	IMWF1 (-)
Working time required for purchases	By consumer items	hours	No	World	IMWF1 (-)
30.3.5 Automobile Industry					
Social security		DM PPP %, Swiss/francs, hours	No	World	IMWF1 (-)
Working time required for purchases	By consumer items, net hourly earnings	DM PPP %, Swiss francs, hours	No	World	IMWF1 (-)
30.4 STANDARD OF LIVING - see also Section 37					
Accommodation, households	By title, type, year of construction, and number of rooms, according to socio-economic category of head of household, type of household, income category, region and urban/rural environment, by country	%	No	EC	EC42 (1/1-1/5)
Amenities, households	By type, according to socio-economic category of head of household, type of household, income category, region and urban/rural environment, by country	%	No	EC	EC42 (1/1-1/5)
Consumer durables	By type, according to socio-economic category of head of household, type of household, income category, region and urban/rural environment, by country	%	No	EC	EC42 (1/1-1/5)
Effective change in gross hourly earnings of industrial employees	By country	indices	No	EC	EC72 (6.14)
Final consumption of households per head	By country, by food, clothing, furnishing, medical care, transport, recreation, other goods and services, housing	nat curr	No	EC	EC72 (6.23)

30 LIVING COSTS AND STANDARDS

Subject	Categories	Units	Time series Yes/No Frequency	Territorial coverage	Source (Table no.)
Final consumption of households per head	By country, by food, clothing, furnishing, medical care, transport, recreation, other goods and services, housing	PPS	No	EC	EC72 (6.24)
Final consumption of households, change in pattern	By country, by food, clothing, furnishing, medical care, transport, recreation, other goods and services, housing	%	No	EC	EC72 (6.25)
Households	By type, composition, and economic situation, according to socio-economic category of head of household, type of household, income category, region and urban/rural environment, by country	%	No	EC	EC42 (1/1-1/5)
Members of households	By sex and age, according to socio-economic category of head of household, type of household, income category, region and urban/rural environment, by country	%	No	EC	EC42 (1/1-1/5)
Net national income per head	By country, by use	PPS	No	EC	EC72 (6.19)
Savings and consumption in net national income	By country	%	No	EC	EC72 (6.20)
Volume change in earnings per employee	By country	indices	No	EC	EC72 (6.12)
Volume change in GDP	By country	indices	No	EC	EC72 (6.4)
Volume change in national final consumption per head	By country	indices	No	EC	EC72 (6.22)
Volume change in national income	By country	indices	No	EC	EC72 (6.9)

31 MIGRATION

Subject	Categories	Units	Time series Yes/No Frequency		Territorial coverage	Source (Table no.)
31.1 EMIGRATION						
Departures to another country or area	Major categories	nos	Yes	A	World	UN19 (26)
Emigrants		nos, years	Yes		Selected EC	MHPPE1 (-)
Emigrants	Age, sex	age, years	Yes	A	World	UN19 (29)
Emigrants	Mean population	nos	Yes	A	Nordic countries	NCM1 (23, 24)
Emigration from EC	By decades	nos	Yes	10 yrly	EC	MAC3 (A8)
Inter-regional migration		nos	No		EC	EC69 (I.4)
Internal migrations	Cities	nos	No		The Americas and Australasia	MAC2 (B7)
International migration	By country, by year	nos	No		EC	CE1 (5)
31.2 IMMIGRATION						
Arrival from another country or area	Major categories	nos	Yes	A	World	UN19 (27)
Immigrants		nos	Yes		Selected EC	MHPPE1 (-)
Immigrants	Age, sex	age, years	Yes	A	World	UN19 (30)
Immigrants	Continent of origin	%,	No		EC	MHPPE1 (-)
Immigrants	Mean population	nos	Yes	A	Nordic Countries	NCM1 (23, 24)
Inter-regional migration		nos	No		EC	EC69 (I.4)
Internal migrations	Cities	nos	No		The Americas and Australasia	MAC2 (B7)
International migration	By country, by year	nos	No		EC	CE1 (5)
Migration statistics	Cities	nos	Yes	A	EC	MAC3 (A9)
31.3 NET MIGRATION						
Inter-regional migration		nos	No		EC	EC69 (I.4)
Internal migrations	Cities	nos	No		The Americas and Australasia	MAC2 (B7)
International migration	By country, by year	nos	No		EC	CE1 (5)
Net migration		nos	Yes		Selected EC	MHPPE1 (-)
Net migration		nos, %	No		EC	EC69 (I.2)
Net migration		per thou	Yes	A	EC	EC20 (A-3)
Net migration	By country, by year	%	Yes	A	EC	CE1 (1.4)
Net migration	Mean population	nos	Yes	A	Nordic Countries	NCM1 (23, 24)
Net migration	Relative variation in total population, variation in the dependency rate of inactive population	%	No		OECD	OECD4 (II.14.)
31.4 POPULATION - see also Section 36						
31.4.1 Foreign Born						
Aliens	By sex and marital status	nos	No		Nordic countries	NCM1 (16)
Aliens naturalized		nos	No		Nordic countries	NCM1 (41)
Asylum applicants, quota refugees	Residence permits granted for refugees	nos	Yes	A	Nordic countries	NCM1 (42)
Emigrants	Age, sex	age, years	Yes	A	World	UN19 (29)
Emigrants and immigrants by country or area	Last or intended permanent residence	nos	No		World	UN19 (28)
Foreign born population by country or area of birth	Age, sex	age, years	No		World	UN19 (32)
Foreign born population in country or area for less than five years	Country of birth, age, sex	age, years	No		World	UN19 (33)
Foreign residents	EC, non-EC	nos years	Yes		Selected EC	MHPPE1 (-)

31 MIGRATION

Subject	Categories	Units	Time series Yes/No Frequency		Territorial coverage	Source (Table no.)
Immigrants	Age, sex	age, years	Yes	A	World	UN19 (30)
Immigrants and emigrants	Total, sex by	nos	No		Nordic countries	NCM1 (40)
Native and foreign-born	Age, sex	age, years	No		Nordic countries	NCM1 (13)
Native and foreign-born population	Age, sex, urban, rural residence	age, years	No		World	UN19 (31)
Population	Sex, urban, rural by citizenship	nos	No		World	UN19 (34)
Residents, aliens	By sex, citizenship and age	nos	No		Nordic countries	NCM1 (15)
31.4.2 Incidence of Migration						
Incidence of active population migration		nos, rate	Yes	5 yrly	OECD	OECD4 (II.9.1.)
Incidence of active population migration		nos, rate	Yes	5 yrly	OECD	OECD4 (II.9.2.)
Migration rate		per thousand	No		EC regions and basic administrative units	EC9 (3.2-3.9)
31.4.3 Projections						
Projections	Rate, net income groups	%	Yes	5yr, 25yr	World	WB5 (-)
With migration	Sex; age		No		OECD	OECD4 (A-K,1,2)
Without migration	Sex; age		No		OECD	OECD4 (A-K,1,2)

32 MINERALS, ORES AND METALS

32.6 MINING AND QUARRYING

32.7 PRICES

32.8 PRODUCTION
- 32.8.1 Aluminium and Alumina
- 32.8.2 Industrial Minerals
- 32.8.3 Lead
- 32.8.4 Mineral Energy
- 32.8.5 Miscellaneous Minerals, Ores and Metals by Type
- 32.8.6 Zinc

32.9 SCRAP

32.10 STOCKS

32.11 SUPPLY

32 MINERALS, ORES AND METALS

Subject	Categories	Units	Time series Yes/No Frequency		Territorial coverage	Source (Table no.)
32.1 BALANCE SHEETS – see also under Consumption(32.2), Production (32.8) and Supply (32.11) and Section 25						
32.1.1. Availability						
Production, domestic recovery, imports, stock change	Metals by type, non-metals (flourine, phosphates)	tonnes	Yes	A	EC	EC68
	tungsten ores and concentrates	tonnes	Yes	A	World	UNCTAD3 (7)
32.1.2 Utilization						
Consumption, exports, stock change	Metals by type, non-metals (flourine, phosphates)	tonnes	Yes	A	EC	EC68
	tungsten ores and concentrates	tonnes	Yes	A	World	UNCTAD3 (7)
32.2 CONSUMPTION - see also under Balance Sheets (32.1) and Sections 8 and 25						
32.2.1 Aluminium						
Dispatches	By end-use, by country	tonnes, %	Yes	A	EC	EAA1 (-)
Per capita	Home market	kg/capita	Yes	A	EC, USA, Japan	EAA1 (-)
Primary		tonnes	Yes	A	World	IBA1 (4)
Primary and secondary		tonnes	Yes	A	EC	EAA1 (-)
32.2.2 General						
Refined consumption	By country	tonnes	Yes	A	World	MJ1 (IV)
Smelter, refinery, summary	By production, deliveries, stock	tonnes	Yes	A	Western world	WBMS3 (-)
32.2.3 Lead						
Lead		tonnes	Yes	A	EC, USA, Japan	EC34 (5.1)
Lead		tonnes	Yes	A, M	Peru	ILZSG1 (22)
Lead	By principal uses	tonnes	Yes	A, M	Australia	ILZSG1 (15)
Lead	By principal uses	tonnes	Yes	A, M	Canada	ILZSG1 (16)
Lead	By principal uses	tonnes	Yes	A, M	France	ILZSG1 (17)
Lead	By principal uses	tonnes	Yes	A, M	Germany	ILZSG1 (18)
Lead	By principal uses	tonnes	Yes	A, M	Italy	ILZSG1 (19)
Lead	By principal uses	tonnes	Yes	A, M	Japan	ILZSG1 (20)
Lead	By principal uses	tonnes	Yes	A, M	UK	ILZSG1 (23)
Lead	By principal uses	tonnes	Yes	A, M	US	ILZSG1 (24)
Lead	Metal consumption	tonnes	Yes	A	Eastern Europe Socialist countries	ILZSG1 (9)
Lead, refined	By principal uses	tonnes	Yes	A, M	Mexico	ILZSG1 (21)
32.2.4 Miscellaneous Minerals, Ores and Metals - see also under Balance Sheets (32.1) and Sections 8 and 25						
Mercury		tonnes	Yes	A	EC, USA, Japan	EC34 (5.2)
Principal end uses	By metal type	tonnes	Yes	A	World	WBMS1 (-)
Refined consumption	By metal	tonnes	Yes	A	World	WBMS3 (-)
Refined consumption	By metal type	tonnes	Yes	A	World	WBMS1 (-)
Tungsten products	By product consumed, by end use	tonnes	Yes	A	World	UNCTAD3 (3.2)
Tungsten, ores and concentrates		tonnes, ‰	Yes	A	World and economic regions	UNCTAD3 (3.1)
Unrefined consumption	By metal	tonnes	Yes	A	World	WBMS3 (-)
32.2.5 Silicon Carbide						
Consumption	By microgrits, powders, fibres, whiskers	tonnes	No		World	EAT1 (6.4)
Grain consumption	By geographic area	tonnes	Yes	A	World	EAT1 (6.1)
Grain trade	By end use	tonnes	No		World	EAT1 (6.3)

32 MINERALS, ORES AND METALS

Subject	Categories	Units	Time series Yes/No	Frequency	Territorial coverage	Source (Table no.)
Grain trade	By production, exports, imports, apparent consumption	tonnes	Yes	A	World	EAT1 (6.2)
32.2.6 Speciality Metals						
Consumption estimates	By country	tonnes	Yes	A	World	MJ1 (-)
32.2.7 Zinc						
Zinc		tonnes	Yes	A	Western World	ILZSG1 (26)
Zinc		tonnes	Yes	A, M	Peru	ILZSG1 (47)
Zinc	By principal uses	tonnes	Yes	A, M	Australia	ILZSG1 (40)
Zinc	By principal uses	tonnes	Yes	A, M	Canada	ILZSG1 (41)
Zinc	By principal uses	tonnes	Yes	A, M	France	ILZSG1 (42)
Zinc	By principal uses	tonnes	Yes	A, M	Germany	ILZSG1 (43)
Zinc	By principal uses	tonnes	Yes	A, M	Italy	ILZSG1 (44)
Zinc	By principal uses	tonnes	Yes	A, M	Japan	ILZSG1 (45)
Zinc	By principal uses	tonnes	Yes	A, M	Mexico	ILZSG1 (46)
Zinc	By principal uses	tonnes	Yes	A, M	UK	ILZSG1 (48)
Zinc	By principal uses	tonnes	Yes	A, M	US	ILZSG1 (49)
Zinc, metal		tonnes	Yes	A	Eastern Europe Socialist countries	ILZSG1 (34)

32.3 INTERNATIONAL TRADE - see also under Minerals, Ores and Metals (32.5) and Sections 25 and 27

Subject	Categories	Units	Time series Yes/No	Frequency	Territorial coverage	Source (Table no.)
32.3.1 Exports						
Aluminium, semi-fabricated products	By type	tonnes, %	No		EC	EAA1 (-)
Aluminium, unwrought	Primary, total unwrought	tonnes	Yes	A	EC	EAA1 (-)
Fluorine		tonnes	Yes	A	EC	EC68 (-)
Fluorine	Fluorspar, hydrofluoric acid and aluminium fluoride	tonnes	No		EC	EC68 (-)
Iron and major alloying metals	By metal type	tonnes	No		EC	EC68 (-)
Lead	Antimonial lead	tonnes	Yes	A, M	Japan	ILZSG1 (20)
Lead	By country	tonnes	Yes	A	World	MJ1 (II)
Lead	Concentrates	tonnes	Yes	A, Q	USSR	ILZSG1 (10)
Lead	Ores and concentrates	tonnes	Yes	A, M	EC, Africa America, Oceania	ILZSG1 (12)
Lead	Ores and concentrates lead bullion refined lead	tonnes	Yes	A, Q	Eastern Europe, Socialist countries	ILZSG1 (14)
Lead	Ores, concentrates lead bullion refined lead	tonnes	Yes	A, M	Australia	ILZSG1 (15)
Lead	Ores, concentrates refined lead	tonnes	Yes	A, M	Canada	ILZSG1 (16)
Lead	Ores, concentrates refined lead	tonnes	Yes	A, M	Italy	ILZSG1 (19)
Lead	Ores, concentrates refined lead	tonnes	Yes	A, M	Peru	ILZSG1 (22)
Lead	Ores, concentrates refined lead	tonnes	Yes	A, M	US	ILZSG1 (24)
Lead	Refined lead	tonnes	Yes	A, M	EC, America, Africa, Oceania	ILZSG1 (13)
Lead	Refined lead lead bullion	tonnes	Yes	A, M	France	ILZSG1 (17)
Lead	Refined lead lead bullion	tonnes	Yes	A, M	UK	ILZSG1 (23)
Lead	Refined lead	tonnes	Yes	A, M	Mexico	ILZSG1 (21)
Lead, refined		tonnes	Yes	A, M	Germany	ILZSG1 (18)
Metals	By type	tonnes	Yes	A	EC	EC68 (-)
Metals	Mercury, antimony, titanium and zirconium	tonnes	No		EC	EC68 (-)

Subject	Categories	Units	Time series Yes/No Frequency		Territorial coverage	Source (Table no.)
Metals, non-ferrous	By metal type	tonnes	No		EC	EC68 (-)
Phosphates		tonnes	Yes	A	EC	EC68 (-)
Phosphates	Natural phosphates, phosphoric acid, slag and fertilizers	tonnes	No		EC	EC68 (-)
Silicon carbide	By country, type	tonnes/US$	Yes	A	World	EAT1 (5.5)
Silicon carbide	By exporting country	tonnes	Yes	A	World	EAT1 (5.3a)
Silicon carbide	By exporting country	US$	Yes	A	World	EAT1 (5.3b)
Silicon carbide	By geographic area, quantity, value, average value	tonnes/US$, US$/tonne	Yes	A	World	EAT1 (5.1)
Tungsten	By country of destination, ores and concentrates	tonnes	Yes	A	World	UNCTAD3 (4.2)
Tungsten	Ores and concentrates	tonnes	Yes	A	World and economic regions	UNCTAD3 4.4)
Tungsten	Ores and concentrates, value	US$	Yes	A	World and economic regions	UNCTAD3 (4.6)
Tungsten products	Quantity, value, by product	tonnes US$	‰Yes	A	World	UNCTAD3 (5.3)
Tungsten products	Quantity, value, by country	tonnes, US$	Yes	A	World	UNCTAD3 (5.1)
Zinc		tonnes	Yes	A, M	World	ILZSG1 (38)
Zinc	Concentrates slab zinc	tonnes	Yes	A, Q	Eastern Europe Socialist countries	
Zinc	Ores , concentrates refined zinc	tonnes	Yes	A, M	Mexico	ILZSG1 (46)
Zinc	Ores and concentrates	tonnes	Yes	A, M	World	ILZSG1 (37)
Zinc	Ores and concentrates refined zinc	tonnes	Yes	A, Q	Eastern Europe, Socialist countries	ILZSG1 (39)
Zinc	Ores, concentrates refined zinc	tonnes	Yes	A, M	Australia	ILZSG1 (40)
Zinc	Ores, concentrates refined zinc	tonnes	Yes	A, M	Canada	ILZSG1 (41)
Zinc	Ores, concentrates refined zinc	tonnes	Yes	A, M	France	ILZSG1 (42)
Zinc	Ores, concentrates refined zinc	tonnes	Yes	A, M	Germany	ILZSG1 (43)
Zinc	Ores, concentrates refined zinc	tonnes	Yes	A, M	Peru	ILZSG1 (47)
Zinc	Ores, concentrates refined zinc	tonnes	Yes	A, M	US	ILZSG1 (49)
Zinc	Refined zinc	tonnes	Yes	A, M	Italy	ILZSG1 (44)
Zinc	Refined zinc	tonnes	Yes	A, M	Japan	ILZSG1 (45)
Zinc	Zinc alloys refined zinc	tonnes	Yes	A, M	UK	ILZSG1 (48)
Zinc, refined		tonnes	Yes	A, Q	USSR	ILZSG1 (35)
32.3.2 General						
East-West trade	By exports from western countries, imports from eastern countries	tonnes	Yes	A	World	MJ1 (VI)
East-West trade	By metal type	tonnes	Yes	A	World	WBMS1 (-)
East-West trade	By metal, by type	tonnes	Yes	A	World	WBMS3 (-)
East-West trade in ores	By metal type	tonnes	Yes	A	World	WBMS1 (-)
Lead, exports/imports	Ores and concentrates lead bullion refined lead	tonnes	Yes	A, Q	Eastern Europe, Socialist countries	ILZSG1 (14)
Refined trade	By metal type	tonnes	Yes	A	World	WBMS1 (-)
Trade in ores	By metal type	tonnes	Yes	A	World	WBMS1 (-)
World trade	By metal	tonnes	Yes	A	World	WBMS3 (-)
Zinc, exports/imports	Ores and concentrates refined zinc	tonnes	Yes	A, Q	Eastern Europe, Socialist countries	ILZSG1 (39)

Subject	Categories	Units	Time series Yes/No Frequency		Territorial coverage	Source (Table no.)
32.3.3 Imports						
Aluminium, semi-fabricated products	By type	tonnes, %	No		EC	EAA1 (-)
Aluminium, unwrought	Primary, total unwrought	tonnes	Yes	A	EC	EAA1 (-)
Fluorine		tonnes	Yes	A	EC	EC68 (-)
Fluorine	Fluorspar, hydrofluoric acid and aluminium fluoride	tonnes	No		EC	EC68 (-)
Iron and major alloying metals	By metal type	tonnes	No		EC	EC68 (-)
Lead		tonnes	Yes	A, M	EC, Asia, America	ILZSG1 (13)
Lead	Concentrates refined lead	tonnes	Yes	A, Q	USSR	ILZSG1 (10)
Lead	Ores and concentrates	tonnes	Yes	A, M	EC, Asia, America	ILZSG1 (12)
Lead	Ores and concentrates refined lead	tonnes	Yes	A, Q	Eastern Europe, Socialist countries	ILZSG1 (14)
Lead	Ores, concentrates refined lead	tonnes	Yes	A, M	Canada	ILZSG1 (16)
Lead	Ores, concentrates lead bullion refined lead	tonnes	Yes	A, M	France	ILZSG1 (17)
Lead	Ores, concentrates lead bullion refined lead	tonnes	Yes	A, M	Germany	ILZSG1 (18)
Lead	Ores, concentrates lead bullion refined lead	tonnes	Yes	A, M	Italy	ILZSG1 (19)
Lead	Ores, concentrates lead bullion refined lead	tonnes	Yes	A, M	Japan	ILZSG1 (20)
Lead	Ores, concentrates lead bullion refined lead	tonnes	Yes	A, M	UK	ILZSG1 (23)
Lead	Ores, concentrates refined lead lead bulion	tonnes	Yes	A, M	US	ILZSG1 (24)
Metals	By type	tonnes	Yes	A	EC	EC68 (-)
Metals	Mercury, antimony, titanium and zirconium	tonnes	No		EC	EC68 (-)
Metals, non-ferrous	By metal type	tonnes	No		EC	EC68 (-)
Phosphates		tonnes	Yes	A	EC	EC68 (-)
Phosphates	Natural phosphates, phosphoric acid, slag and fertilizers	tonnes	No		EC	EC68 (-)
Raw materials	By country of origin and raw material type	tonnes, %	Yes	I	EC	EC68 (-)
Silicon carbide	By country	tonnes	Yes	A	World	EAT1 (5.4a)
Silicon carbide	By country	US$	Yes	A	World	EAT1 (5.4b)
Silicon carbide	By country, type	tonnes/US$	Yes	A	World	EAT1 (5.6)
Silicon carbide	By geographic area, quantity, value, average value	tonnes/US$ US$/tonne	Yes	A	World	EAT1 (5.2)
Tungsten	By country of origin, ores and concentrates	tonnes	Yes	A	World	UNCTAD3 (4.1)
Tungsten	Ores and concentrates	tonnes	Yes	A	World and economic regions	UNCTAD3 (4.3)
Tungsten	Ores and concentrates, c.i.f.	US$	Yes	A	World and economic regions	UNCTAD3 (4.5)
Tungsten products	Quantity, value, by product	tonnes US$	Yes	A	World	UNCTAD3 (5.2)

Subject	Categories	Units	Time series Yes/No Frequency		Territorial coverage	Source (Table no.)
Tungsten products	Quantity, value, by country	tonnes, US$	Yes	A	World	UNCTAD3 (5.1)
Zinc		tonnes	Yes	A, M	World	ILZSG1 (38)
Zinc	Concentrates refined zinc	tonnes	Yes	A, Q	USSR	ILZSG1 (34)
Zinc	Ores and concentrates	tonnes	Yes	A, M	World	ILZSG1 (37)
Zinc	Ores and concentrates refined zinc	tonnes	Yes	A, Q	Eastern Europe, Socialist countries	ILZSG1 (39)
Zinc	Ores, concentrates refined zinc	tonnes	Yes	A, M	Canada	ILZSG1 (41)
Zinc	Ores, concentrates refined zinc	tonnes	Yes	A, M	France	ILZSG1 (42)
Zinc	Ores, concentrates refined zinc	tonnes	Yes	A, M	Germany	ILZSG1 (43)
Zinc	Ores, concentrates refined zinc	tonnes	Yes	A, M	Italy	ILZSG1 (44)
Zinc	Ores, concentrates refined zinc zinc alloys	tonnes	Yes	A, M	UK	ILZSG1 (48)
Zinc	Ores, concentrates refined zinc	tonnes	Yes	A, M	US	ILZSG1 (49)
Zinc	Refined zinc ores, concentrates	tonnes	Yes	A, M	Japan	ILZSG1 (45)

32.4 LONDON METAL EXCHANGE STATISTICS

Subject	Categories	Units	Time series Yes/No	Frequency	Territorial coverage	Source (Table no.)
Metal exchange stocks	Aluminium, by country	tonnes	Yes	A, Q, M	World	WBMS2 (-)
	Copper, by country	tonnes	Yes	A, Q, M	World	WBMS2 (-)
	Lead, by country	tonnes	Yes	A, Q, M	World	WBMS2 (-)
	Nickel, by country	tonnes	Yes	A, Q, M	World	WBMS2 (-)
	Tin, by country	tonnes	Yes	A, Q, M	World	WBMS2 (-)
	Zinc, by country	tonnes	Yes	A, Q, M	World	WBMS2 (-)
Official turnover	By metal	oz, tonnes	Yes	A	World	MJ1 (1)
Officially quoted prices	By metal	US$/tonne	No		World	MJ1 (2)
Stock movements	By metal	nos	No		World	MJ1 (3)

32.5 MINERALS, ORES AND METALS BY TYPE - see also under Consumption (32.2), International Trade (32.3), Production (32.8) and Sections 8, 25 and 38

32.5.1 Alumina, Bauxite and Aluminium

Subject	Categories	Units	Time series Yes/No	Frequency	Territorial coverage	Source (Table no.)
Alumina	By production, exports, imports	tonnes	Yes	A	World	BGS2 (-)
Alumina, bauxite and aluminium	By production, exports, imports, type, country	tonnes	Yes	A	World	BGS1 (-)
Aluminium	By metal balance	tonnes	Yes	A	World	WBMS2 (-)
Aluminium	By production, exports, imports	tonnes	Yes	A	World	BGS2 (-)
Aluminium	By production, consumption, stocks, metal balance	tonnes	Yes	A, Q, M	World	WBMS2 (-)
Bauxite	By production exports, imports	tonnes	Yes	A	World	BGS2 (-)

32.5.2 Antimony

Subject	Categories	Units	Time series Yes/No	Frequency	Territorial coverage	Source (Table no.)
Antimony	By production, exports, imports	tonnes	Yes	A	World	BGS2 (-)

32.5.3 Arsenic

Subject	Categories	Units	Time series Yes/No	Frequency	Territorial coverage	Source (Table no.)
Arsenic	By production, exports, imports	tonnes	Yes	A	World	BGS2 (-)

Subject	Categories	Units	Time series Yes/No Frequency		Territorial coverage	Source (Table no.)
32.5.4 Asbestos						
Asbestos	By production, exports, imports of unmanufactured asbestos by country	tonnes	Yes	A	World	BGS1 (-)
32.5.5 Barytes						
Barytes	By production, exports, imports, by country	tonnes	Yes	A	World	BGS1 (-)
32.5.6 Bentonite and Fullers Earth						
Bentonite and Fullers earth	By production, exports, imports, type, country	tonnes	Yes	A	World	BGS1 (-)
32.5.7 Beryl						
Beryl	By production, country	tonnes	Yes	A	World	BGS1 (-)
32.5.8 Bismuth						
Bismuth	By production exports, imports	tonnes	Yes	A	World	BGS2 (-)
32.5.9 Borates						
Borates	By production, country	tonnes	Yes	A	World	BGS1 (-)
32.5.10 Bromine						
Bromine	By production, exports, imports, country	kg	Yes	A	World	BGS1 (-)
32.5.11 Cadmium						
Cadmium	By production exports, imports	tonnes	Yes	A	World	BGS2 (-)
32.5.12 Chromium Ores and Concentrates						
Chromium	By production exports, imports	tonnes	Yes	A	World	BGS2 (-)
Chromium ores and concentrates	By production, exports, imports, by country, by type	tonnes	Yes	A	World	BGS1 (-)
32.5.13 Coal						
Coal	By production exports, imports	tonnes	Yes	A	World	BGS2 (-)
32.5.14 Cobalt						
Cobalt	By production exports, imports	tonnes	Yes	A‰	World	BGS2 (-)
32.5.15 Copper						
Copper	By metal balance	tonnes	Yes	A	World	WBMS2 (-)
Copper	By production exports, imports	‰tonnes	Yes	A	World	BGS2 (-)
Copper	By production, consumption, stocks, metal balance	tonnes	Yes	A, Q, M	World	WBMS2 (-)
32.5.16 Diamond						
Diamond	By production, exports, imports, by type, country	carats	Yes	A	World	BGS1 (-)
32.5.17 Diatomite						
Diatomite	By production, exports, imports, country	tonnes	Yes	A	World	BGS1 (-)

Subject	Categories	Units	Time series Yes/No Frequency		Territorial coverage	Source (Table no.)
32.5.18 Feldspar						
Feldspar	By production, exports, imports, country	tonnes	Yes	A	World	BGS1 (-)
32.5.19 Ferro-alloys						
Ferro-alloys	By production, exports, imports	tonnes	Yes	A	World	BGS2 (-)
32.5.20 Fluorspar						
Fluorspar	By production, exports, imports, country	tonnes	Yes	A	World	BGS1 (-)
32.5.21 Germanium						
Germanium	By production exports, imports	tonnes	Yes	A	World	BGS2 (-)
32.5.22 Gold						
Gold	By production, exports, imports	kg	Yes	A	World	BGS2 (-)
Gold	By total production	tonnes	Yes	A, Q, M	World	WBMS2 (-)
32.5.23 Graphite						
Graphite	By production, exports, imports, country	tonnes	Yes	A	World	BGS1 (-)
32.5.24 Gypsum						
Gypsum	By production, exports, imports, type, country	tonnes	Yes	A	World	BGS1 (-)
32.5.25 Iodine						
Iodine	By production, exports, imports, country	kg	Yes	A	World	BGS1 (-)
32.5.26 Iron and Steel						
Iron and steel	By production, exports, imports	tonnes	Yes	A	World	BGS2 (-)
32.5.27 Iron Ore						
Iron Ore	By production exports, imports	tonnes	Yes	A	World	BGS2 (-)
32.5.28 Kaolin						
Kaolin	By production, exports, imports, country	tonnes	Yes	A	World	BGS1 (-)
32.5.29 Lead						
Lead	By metal balance	tonnes	Yes	A	World	WBMS2 (-)
Lead	By production, consumption, stocks, metal balance	tonnes	Yes	A, Q, M	World	WBMS2 (-)
Lead	By production, exports, imports	tonnes, %	Yes	A	World	BGS2 (-)
32.5.30 Lithium						
Lithium	By production, exports, imports	tonnes	Yes	A	World	BGS2 (-)
32.5.31 Lithium Minerals						
Lithium minerals	By production, exports, imports, type, country	tonnes	Yes	A	World	BGS1 (-)

Subject	Categories	Units	Time series Yes/No Frequency		Territorial coverage	Source (Table no.)
32.5.32 Magnesite						
Magnesite	By production	tonnes	Yes	A	World	BGS1 (-)
32.5.33 Magnesite and Magnesia						
Magnesite and magnesia	By exports, imports, by type, by country	tonnes	Yes	A	World	BGS1 (-)
32.5.34 Magnesium						
Magnesium	By production, exports, imports	tonnes	Yes	A	World	BGS2 (-)
32.5.35 Mercury						
Mercury	By production, exports, imports	kg	Yes	A	World	BGS2 (-)
32.5.36 Mica						
Mica	By production, imports, exports, type, country	tonnes	Yes	A	World	BGS1 (-)
32.5.37 Molybdenum						
Molybdenum	By production, exports, imports	tonnes	Yes	A	World	BGS2 (-)
32.5.38 Nepheline Syenite						
Nepheline syenite	By production, country	tonnes	Yes	A	World	BGS1 (-)
32.5.39 Nickel						
Nickel	By metal balance	tonnes	Yes	A	World	WBMS2 (-)
Nickel	By production, exports, imports	tonnes	Yes	A	World	BGS2 (-)
Nickel	By production, consumption, stocks, metal balance	tonnes	Yes	A, Q, M	World	WBMS2 (-)
32.5.40 Niobium						
Niobium	By production, exports, imports	tonnes	Yes	A	World	BGS2 (-)
32.5.41 Palladium						
Palladium demand	By country, by application	oz	Yes	A	Western World	JM1 (-)
Palladium supply and demand	By country, by application	oz	Yes	A	Western World	JM1 (-)
32.5.42 Perlite						
Perlite	By production, country	tonnes	Yes	A	World	BGS1 (-)
32.5.43 Phosphate Rock						
Phosphate rock	By production, exports, imports, country	tonnes	Yes	A	World	BGS1 (-)
32.5.44 Platinum						
Platinum	By production, exports, imports	kg	Yes	A	World	BGS2 (-)
Platinum demand	By country, by application	oz	Yes	A	Western World	JM1 (-)
Platinum supply and demand	By country, by application	oz	Yes	A	Western World	JM1 (-)
32.5.45 Potash						
Potash	By production, exports, imports, type, country	tonnes	Yes	A	World	BGS1 (-)
32.5.46 Precious Metals and Minerals						
Mine production	By country, by metal	tonnes	Yes	A	World	MJ1 (-)
Production costs	By country, by metal	US$/oz	Yes	A	World	MJ1 (-)
Supply and demand	By metal, by end use	tonnes	Yes	A	Western World	MJ1 (-)

Subject	Categories	Units	Time series Yes/No Frequency		Territorial coverage	Source (Table no.)
32.5.47 Rare Earth Mineral						
Rare earth minerals	By production, type, exports, imports, country	tonnes	Yes	A	World	BGS1 (-)
Rare earths	By production, exports, imports	tonnes	Yes	A	World	BGS2 (-)
32.5.48 Rhodium						
Rhodium supply and demand	By country, by application	oz	Yes	A	Western World	JM1 (-)
32.5.49 Salt						
Salt	By production, type, exports, imports, country	tonnes	Yes	A	World	BGS1 (-)
32.5.50 Selenium						
Selenium	By production, exports, imports	tonnes	Yes	A	World	BGS2 (-)
32.5.51 Silicon Carbide						
Estimated production	By microgrits, powders, fibres, whiskers	tonnes/US$	Yes	A	World	EAT1 (4.3)
Silicon carbide grain production	By major producing countries	tonnes	Yes	A	Selected countries	EAT1 (4.1)
32.5.52 Sillimanite						
Sillimanite	By production, exports, imports, type, country	tonnes	Yes	A	World	BGS1 (-)
32.5.53 Silver						
Silver	By production, exports, imports	kg	Yes	A	World	BGS2 (-)
Silver	By total production	tonnes	Yes	A, Q, M	World	WBMS2 (-)
32.5.54 Speciality metals						
Consumption estimates	By country	tonnes	Yes	A	World	MJ1 (-)
Principal end-uses	By product	tonnes	Yes	A	World	WBMS3 (-)
Production capacity	By country	tonnes	Yes	A	World	MJ1 (-)
32.5.55 Strontium Minerals						
Strontium minerals	By production, country	tonnes	Yes	A	World	BGS1 (-)
32.5.56 Sulphur and Pyrites						
Sulphur and pyrites	By production, type, exports, imports, country	tonnes	Yes	A	World	BGS1 (-)
32.5.57 Talc						
Talc	By production, type, exports, imports, country	tonnes	Yes	A	World	BGS1 (-)
32.5.58 Tantalum						
Tantalum	By production, exports, imports	tonnes	Yes	A	World	BGS2 (-)
32.5.59 Tellurium						
Tellurium	By production, exports, imports	tonnes	Yes	A	World	BGS2 (-)
32.5.60 Tin						
Tin	By metal balance	tonnes	Yes	A	World	WBMS2 (-)
Tin	By production, exports, imports	tonnes	Yes	A	World	BGS2 (-)

32 MINERALS, ORES AND METALS

Subject	Categories	Units	Time series Yes/No Frequency		Territorial coverage	Source (Table no.)
Tin	By production, consumption, stocks, metal balance	tonnes	Yes	A, Q, M	World	WBMS2 (-)
32.5.61 Titanium Minerals						
Titanium	By production, exports, imports	tonnes	Yes	A	World	BGS2 (-)
Titanium materials	By production, type, exports, imports, country	tonnes	Yes	A	World	BGS1 (-)
32.5.62 Tungsten						
Tungsten	By production, exports, imports	tonnes	Yes	A	World	BGS2 (-)
32.5.63 Uranium - see also Sections 17 and 25						
Production		tonnes	Yes	A	Various countries	OECD47 (11)
Uranium	By production, exports, imports	tonnes	Yes	A	World	BGS2 (-)
32.5.64 Vanadium						
Vanadium	By production, exports, imports	tonnes	Yes	A	World	BGS2 (-)
32.5.65 Vermiculite						
Vermiculite	By production, country	tonnes	Yes	A	World	BGS1 (-)
32.5.66 Wollastonite						
Wollastonite	By production, country	tonnes	Yes	A	World	BGS1 (-)
32.5.67 Zinc						
Zinc	By metal balance	tonnes	Yes	A	World	WBMS2 (-)
Zinc	By production, exports, imports	tonnes	Yes	A	World	BGS2 (-)
Zinc	By production, consumption, stocks, metal balance	tonnes	Yes	A, Q, M	World	WBMS2 (-)
32.5.68 Zirconium Minerals						
Zirconium minerals	By production, type, exports, imports, country	tonnes	Yes	A	World	BGS1 (-)
32.6 MINING AND QUARRYING - see also under Minerals, Ores and Metals by Type (32.5) and Sections 25 and 33						
Bauxite		tonnes	Yes	A	World	UN35 (16)
Coal		tonnes	Yes	A, M	World	UN35 (11)
Copper						
Copper ore		tonnes	Yes	A, M	World	UN35 (17)
Copper, joint production with lead and zinc	By production, by joint production	tonnes, %	No		World	ILZSG2 (10)
Copper, mine production	By ore type	%	No		World	ILZSG2 (11)
Copper, mine production, survey totals	By ore type	tonnes	No		World	ILZSG2 (12)
Crude petroleum	Specific gravity	tonnes	Yes	A, M	World	UN35 (14)
Growth in mining production	Including, excluding petroleum, average annual rates	indices	Yes	A	Latin American and Caribbean countries	UN45 (52)
Iron-ore	Metal content	tonnes	Yes	A, M	World	UN35 (15)
Lead						
Lead	Mine production refined metal production	tonnes, %	Yes	A	Western World	ILZSG1 (25)

Subject	Categories	Units	Time series Yes/No Frequency		Territorial coverage	Source (Table no.)
Lead	Mine production refined metal production	tonnes, %	Yes	A	World	ILZSG1 (25)
Lead	Mine production, metal production	tonnes	Yes	A	Eastern Europe. Socialist countries	ILZSG1 (9)
Lead ore		tonnes	Yes	A, M	World	UN35 (18)
Lead, mine production		tonnes	Yes	A	EC, US, Australia	ILZSG1 (2)
Lead, mine production		tonnes	Yes	A, M	World	ILZSG1 (5)
Lead, mine production	By ore type	%	No		World	ILZSG2 (7)
Lead, mine production	By survey coverage	tonnes, %	No		World	ILZSG2 (8)
Lead, mine production, survey totals	By ore type	tonnes	No		World	ILZSG2 (9)
Lignite and brown coal		tonnes	Yes	A, M	World	UN35 (12)
Mine production	By country	tonnes	Yes	A	World	MJ1 (I)
Mine production	By metal type	tonnes	Yes	A	World	WBMS1 (-)
Mining		indices	Yes	A	World	UN50 (1)
Mining production	Including, excluding petroleum	indices	Yes	A	Latin American and Caribbean countries	UN45 (327)
Natural gas	Heat value	TJ	Yes	A, M	World	UN35 (13)
Precious metals and minerals, mine production	By country, by metal	tonnes	Yes	A	World	MJ1 (-)
Silver						
Silver, joint production with lead and zinc	By production, by joint production	tonnes, %	No		World	ILZSG2 (13)
Silver, mine production	By ore type	%	No		World	ILZSG2 (14)
Silver, mine production, survey totals	By ore type	tonnes	No		World	ILZSG2 (15)
Silver, production	By ore type	g/tonne	No		World	ILZSG2 (16)
Tin concentrates		tonnes	Yes	A, M	World	UN35 (19)
Zinc						
Zinc		tonnes, %	Yes	A, M	World	ILZSG1 (31)
Zinc	Mine production refined zinc	tonnes	Yes	A, M	EC, Canada, Australia, Japan	ILZSG1 (27)
Zinc	Mine production, refined metal production	tonnes	Yes	A	Western world	ILZSG1 (50)
Zinc	Mine production, refined metal production	tonnes	Yes	A	World	ILZSG1 (50)
Zinc	Mine production, metal production	tonnes, %	Yes	A	Eastern European Socialist countries	
Zinc	Ore	tonnes	Yes	A, M	World	UN35 (20)
Zinc	Mine production	tonnes	Yes	A, M	World	ILZSG1 (30)
Zinc, mine production	By ore type	%	No		World	ILZSG2 (4)
Zinc, mine production	By survey coverage	tonnes, %	No		World	ILZSG2 (5)
Zinc, mine production, survey totals	By ore type	tonnes	No		World	ILZSG2 (6)

32.7 PRICES - see also Section 37

Subject	Categories	Units	Time series Yes/No Frequency		Territorial coverage	Source (Table no.)
Aluminium	By London Exchange cash settlement	$ per tonne	Yes	A, M	World	WBMS2 (-)
Aluminium	By settlement, by 3 months	$ per tonne	Yes	D	World	WBMS2 (-)
Aluminium alloy	By settlement, by 3 months	$ per tonne	Yes	D	World	WBMS2 (-)
Aluminium, primary ingot	London Metal Exchange cash price	USc/lb	Yes	A	World	IBA1 (5)
Ammonium paratungstate	Low, high, average	US$/mtu	Yes	I	USA, EC	UNCTAD3 (1.4)
Copper	By London Exchange cash settlement, US producer price	£ per tonne, cents per lb	Yes	A, M	World	WBMS2 (-)
Copper	By settlement, by 3 months, by producer price	£ per tonne, cents per lb	Yes	D	World	WBMS2 (-)

32 MINERALS, ORES AND METALS

Subject	Categories	Units	Time series Yes/No Frequency		Territorial coverage	Source (Table no.)
Ferro-tungsten	Low, high, average	US$/kg	Yes	I	World	UNCTAD3 (1.3)
Gold	By London bullion dealers fixed price	$ per troy oz	Yes	A, M	World	WBMS2 (-)
Gold	By spot price	$ per troy oz	Yes	D	World	WBMS2 (-)
Lead	By London Exchange cash settlement, US producer price	£ per tonne, cents per lb	Yes	A, M	World	WBMS2 (-)
Lead	By settlement, by 3 months, by producer price	£ per tonne, cents per lb	Yes	D	World	WBMS2 (-)
Lead, refined	London Metal Exchange United States	£ per tonne, USc/lb	Yes	A, M	London, US	ILZSG1 (4)
Metal prices, average	By metal type	£ and $	Yes	A, M	World	WBMS1 (-)
Metal prices, average	By type	US$ tonnes, cents per lb, £ tonnes, pence troy ounce, US$ troy ounce	Yes	A	World	WBMS3 (-)
Nickel	By London exchange cash settlement, producer price	$ per tonne, $ per lb	Yes	A, M	World	WBMS2 (-)
Nickel	By settlement, by 3 months	$ per tonne	Yes	D	World	WBMS2 (-)
Silver	By London bullion dealers fixed price, by US producer price	pence per troy oz, cents per troy oz	Yes	A, M	World	WBMS2 (-)
Silver	By spot price, 3, 6,12 months, producer price	pence per troy oz, cents per troy oz	Yes	D	World	WBMS2 (-)
Tin	By London Exchange cash settlement, US producer price	$ per tonne, cents per lb	Yes	A, M	World	WBMS2 (-)
Tin	By settlement, by 3 months, by Kuala Lumpur	$ per tonne, cents per lb	Yes	D	World	WBMS2 (-)
Tungsten carbide powder	Low, high, average	£/kg	Yes	I	World	UNCTAD3 (1.3)
Tungsten concentrates	Price and quantity	US$/mtu, tonnes, %, mtu	Yes	A, M	World	UNCTAD3 (1.2)
Tungsten concentrates	Wolframite, scheelite	US$/mtu, tonnes	Yes	A, M	World	UNCTAD3 (1.1)
Tungsten powder	Low, high, average	£/kg	Yes	I	World	UNCTAD3 (1.3)
Zinc	By London Exchange cash settlement, US producer price	$ per tonne, cents per lb	Yes	A, M	World	WBMS2 (-)
Zinc	By settlement, by 3 months, by producer price	$ per tonne, cents per lb	Yes	D	World	WBMS2 (-)
Zinc	London Metal Exchange United States	US$/ tonne, USc/lb	Yes	A, M	London, US	ILZSG1 (29)

32.8 PRODUCTION - see also under Minerals, Ores and Metals by Type (32.5) and Sections 33 and 38

32.8.1 Aluminium and Alumina

Alumina		tonnes	Yes	A	World and regions	IBA1 (2)
Aluminium	By type	tonnes	Yes	A	World	WBMS1 (-)
Aluminium	By type	tonnes	Yes	A	World	WBMS3 (-)
Aluminium castings		tonnes	Yes	A	EC	EAA1 (-)

Subject	Categories	Units	Time series Yes/No Frequency		Territorial coverage	Source (Table no.)
Aluminium extrusions		tonnes	Yes	A	EC	EAA1 (-)
Aluminium products, semi-fabricated		tonnes	Yes	A	EC	EAA1 (-)
Aluminium rolled products		tonnes	Yes	A	EC	EAA1 (-)
Aluminium, primary		tonnes	Yes	A	EC	EAA1 (-)
Aluminium, primary		tonnes	Yes	A	World and regions	IBA1 (3)
Aluminium, secondary		tonnes	Yes	A	EC	EAA1 (-)
Aluminium, secondary recovery		tonnes, %	Yes	A	Western world, western countries and regions	IBA1 (6)
32.8.2 Industrial Minerals						
Mine-refinery gap	By production, losses, exports, change in stocks, output	tonnes	Yes	A	World	MJ1 (III)
Production	By country	tonnes	Yes	A	World	MJ1 (-)
Refined primary and secondary production	By country	tonnes	Yes	A	World	MJ1 (II)
32.8.3 Lead						
Lead	By type	tonnes	Yes	A	World	WBMS1 (-)
Lead	By type	tonnes	Yes	A	World	WBMS3 (-)
Lead	Concentrates	tonnes	Yes	A, Q	Western world	ILZSG1 (1)
Lead	Mine production	tonnes	Yes	A	EC, US, Australia	ILZSG1 (2)
Lead	Mine production	tonnes	Yes	A, M	World	ILZSG1 (5)
Lead	Mine production, metal production	tonnes	Yes	A	Eastern Europe. Socialist countries	ILZSG1 (9)
Lead	Ores and concentrates refined lead	tonnes	Yes	A, M	Mexico	ILZSG1 (21)
Lead	Ores, concentrates lead bullion refined lead	tonnes	Yes	A, M	Australia	ILZSG1 (15)
Lead	Ores, concentrates refined lead	tonnes	Yes	A, M	Canada	ILZSG1 (16)
Lead	Ores, concentrates refined lead	tonnes	Yes	A, M	France	ILZSG1 (17)
Lead	Ores, concentrates lead bullion refined lead	tonnes	Yes	A, M	Germany	ILZSG1 (18)
Lead	Ores, concentrates refined lead	tonnes	Yes	A, M	Italy	ILZSG1 (19)
Lead	Ores, concentrates refined lead	tonnes	Yes	A, M	Peru	ILZSG1 (22)
Lead	Ores, concentrates lead bullion refined lead	tonnes	Yes	A, M	UK	ILZSG1 (23)
Lead	Ores, concentrates refined lead	tonnes	Yes	A, M	US	ILZSG1 (24)
Lead	Ores, concentrates, lead bullion, refined lead, antimonial lead	tonnes	Yes	A, M	Japan	ILZSG1 (20)
Lead, recovery of secondary lead	Refined lead and lead alloys, remelted lead and lead alloys	tonnes %	Yes	A, Q	World	ILZSG1 (11)
Lead, refined		tonnes,%	Yes	A, Q	Western world	ILZSG1 (1)
Lead, refined		tonnes	Yes	A	EC, US, Japan	ILZSG1 (2)
Lead, refined		tonnes	Yes	A	EC, US, Japan	ILZSG1 (2)
Lead, refined		tonnes	Yes	A, M	World	ILZSG1 (6)
Lead, refined		tonnes	Yes	A, M	World	ILZSG1 (7)
Lead, refined		tonnes	Yes	A, Q	Western world	ILZSG1 (1)
Lead, total refined		tonnes, %	Yes	A	Western world	ILZSG1 (25)
Lead, total refined		tonnes, %	Yes	A	World	ILZSG1 (25)

32 MINERALS, ORES AND METALS

Subject	Categories	Units	Time series Yes/No Frequency		Territorial coverage	Source (Table no.)
Lead, totals	Mine production refined metal production	tonnes, % %	Yes	A	Western world	ILZSG1 (25)
Lead, totals	Mine production refined metal production	tonnes, % %	Yes	A	World	ILZSG1 (25)
32.8.4 Mineral Energy - see also Section 17						
Developments in demand	By country	tonnes	Yes	A	World	MJ1 (-)
Production	By country	tonnes	Yes	A	World	MJ1 (-)
32.8.5 Miscellaneous Minerals, Ores and Metals by Type						
Antimony	By type	tonnes	Yes	A	World	WBMS1 (-)
Antimony	Total	tonnes	Yes	A	World	WBMS3 (-)
Bauxite		tonnes	Yes	A	Latin American and Caribbean countries	UN45 (328)
Bauxite		tonnes	Yes	A	World and regions	IBA1 (1)
Bauxite		tonnes, %	Yes	A	World, ASEAN member countries	ASEANS1 (4.1.8)
Bismuth	Total	tonnes	Yes	A	World	WBMS3 (-)
Cadmium	By type	tonnes	Yes	A	World	WBMS1 (-)
Cadmium	Total	tonnes	Yes	A	World	WBMS3 (-)
Chromium	Total	tonnes	Yes	A	World	WBMS3 (-)
Coal		tonnes, %	Yes	A	Latin American and Caribbean countries	UN45 (329)
Cobalt	Total	tonnes	Yes	A	World	WBMS3 (-)
Copper		tonne, %	Yes	A	Latin American and Caribbean countries	UN45 (330)
Copper	By type	tonnes	Yes	A	World	WBMS1 (-)
Copper	By type	tonnes	Yes	A	World	WBMS3 (-)
Copper ore		tonnes	Yes	A	World, ASEAN member countries	ASEANS1 (4.1.6)
Fluorine		tonnes	Yes	A	EC	EC68 (-)
Fluorine	Fluorspar, hydrofluoric acid and aluminium fluoride	tonnes	No		EC	EC68 (-)
Gold	By content	tonnes	Yes	A	World	WBMS1 (-)
Gold	Total	tonnes	Yes	A	World	WBMS3 (-)
Iron		tonnes	Yes	A	Latin American and Caribbean countries	UN45 (332)
Iron and major alloying metals	By metal type	tonnes	No		EC	EC68 (-)
Iron ore		tonnes, %	Yes	A	World, ASEAN member countries	ASEANS1 (4.1.5)
Magnesium	Total	tonnes	Yes	A	World	WBMS3 (-)
Manganese	Total	tonnes	Yes	A	World	WBMS3 (-)
Manganese ore		tonnes	Yes	A	World, ASEAN member countries	ASEANS1 (4.1.7)
Mercury	Total	tonnes	Yes	A	World	WBMS3 (-)
Metals	By type	tonnes	Yes	A	EC	EC68 (-)
Metals	Mercury, antimony, titanium and zirconium	tonnes	No		EC	EC68 (-)
Metals, non-ferrous	By metal type	tonnes	No		EC	EC68 (-)
Molybdenum	By type	tonnes	Yes	A	World	WBMS1 (-)
Molybdenum	Total	tonnes	Yes	A	World	WBMS3 (-)
Nickel	By type	tonnes	Yes	A	World	WBMS1 (-)
Nickel	By type	tonnes	Yes	A	World	WBMS3 (-)
Non-metallic mineral products		indices	Yes	A, M	EC	EC53 (6.7)
Phosphates		tonnes	Yes	A	EC	EC68 (-)
Phosphates	Natural phosphates, phosphoric acid, slag and fertilizers	tonnes	No		EC	EC68 (-)

Subject	Categories	Units	Time series Yes/No Frequency		Territorial coverage	Source (Table no.)
Pig iron		tonnes	Yes	A	Latin American and Caribbean countries	UN45 (346)
Platinum	Total	tonnes	Yes	A	World	WBMS3 (-)
Production of semi-manufactures	By metal type	tonnes	Yes	A	World	WBMS1 (-)
Refined production	By metal type	tonnes	Yes	A	World	WBMS1 (-)
Salt		tonnes	Yes	A	World, ASEAN member countries	ASEANS1 (4.1.9)
Secondary production	By metal	tonnes	Yes	A	World	WBMS3 (-)
Silver	By content	tonnes	Yes	A	World	WBMS1 (-)
Silver	Total	tonnes	Yes	A	World	WBMS3 (-)
Smelter production	By metal type	tonnes	Yes	A	World	WBMS1 (-)
Smelter, refinery, summary	By production, deliveries, stock	tonnes	Yes	A	Western world	WBMS3 (-)
Speciality metals	Consumption estimates, production capacity, by country	tonnes	Yes	A	World	MJ1 (-)
Steel		tonnes, %	Yes	A	LatinAmerican and Caribbean countries	UN45 (347)
Steel industry metals	By country	tonnes	Yes	A	World	MJ1 (I)
Tin		tonnes	Yes	A	Latin American and Caribbean countries	UN45 (331)
Tin	By content	tonnes	Yes	A	World	WBMS1 (-)
Tin	By type	tonnes	Yes	A	World	WBMS3 (-)
Tin in concentrates		tonnes, %	Yes	A	World, ASEAN member countries	ASEANS1 (4.1.4)
Tin metal		tonnes	Yes	A	World, ASEAN member countries	ASEANS1 (4.1.2)
Titanium	By type	tonnes	Yes	A	World	WBMS3 (-)
Tungsten	By type of mine, number of mines operating	tonnes, nos	Yes	A	World	UNCTAD3 (2.2)
Tungsten	Total	tonnes	Yes	A	World	WBMS3 (-)
Tungsten products	By type	tonnes	Yes	A	World	UNCTAD3 (2.6)
Tungsten, co-production of other metals from mines	Tin, copper, bismuth, molybdenum sulphide	tonnes	Yes	A	World	UNCTAD3 (2.3)
Tungsten, investment in new mining and processing capacities	Project, company, capacity, completion date	tonnes		No	World	UNCTAD3 (2.5)
Tungsten, mine production capacity		tonnes	Yes	I	World and economic regions	UNCTAD3 (2.4)
Tungsten, ores and concentrates		tonnes	Yes	A	World and economic regions	UNCTAD3 (2.1)
Uranium	Total	tonnes	Yes	A	World	WBMS3 (-)
32.8.6 Zinc						
Zinc		tonnes	Yes	A	LatinAmerican and Caribbean countries	UN45 (334)
Zinc		tonnes, %	Yes	A, M	World	ILZSG1 (31)
Zinc	By content	tonnes	Yes	A	World	WBMS1 (-)
Zinc	By type	tonnes	Yes	A	World	WBMS3 (-)
Zinc	Concentrates slab zinc	tonnes, %	Yes	A, Q	Western world	ILZSG1 (26)
Zinc	Mine production refined metal production	tonnes	Yes	A	Western world	ILZSG1 (50)
Zinc	Mine production refined metal production	tonnes	Yes	A	World	ILZSG1 (50)
Zinc	Mine production refined zinc	tonnes	Yes	A, M	EC, Canada, Australia, Japan	ILZSG1 (27)
Zinc	Mine production	tonnes	Yes	A, M	World	ILZSG1 (30)

32 MINERALS, ORES AND METALS

Subject	Categories	Units	Time series Yes/No Frequency		Territorial coverage	Source (Table no.)
Zinc	Mine production metal production	tonnes, %	Yes	A	Eastern European Socialist countries	
Zinc	Ores , concentrates refined zinc	tonnes	Yes	A, M	Mexico	ILZSG1 (46)
Zinc	Ores, concentrates refined zinc	tonnes	Yes	A, M	Australia	ILZSG1 (40)
Zinc	Ores, concentrates refined zinc	tonnes	Yes	A, M	Canada	ILZSG1 (41)
Zinc	Ores, concentrates refined zinc	tonnes	Yes	A, M	France	ILZSG1 (42)
Zinc	Ores, concentrates refined zinc	tonnes	Yes	A, M	Germany	ILZSG1 (43)
Zinc	Ores, concentrates refined zinc	tonnes	Yes	A, M	Italy	ILZSG1 (44)
Zinc	Ores, concentrates refined zinc	tonnes	Yes	A, M	Peru	ILZSG1 (47)
Zinc	Ores, concentrates refined zinc	tonnes	Yes	A, M	US	ILZSG1 (49)
Zinc	Refined zinc ore, concentrates	tonnes, %	Yes	A, M	Japan	ILZSG1 (45)
Zinc, recovery of secondary zinc	Refined zinc metal, remelted zinc and direct use of secondary materials	tonnes	Yes	A, Q	World	ILZSG1 (36)
Zinc, refined		tonnes	Yes	A, M	EC, US, Japan	ILZSG1 (27)
Zinc, refined		tonnes	Yes	A, M	World	ILZSG1 (32)
Zinc, total refined		tonnes	Yes	A	Western world	ILZSG1 (50)
Zinc, total refined		tonnes	Yes	A	World	ILZSG1 (50)

32.9 SCRAP

Subject	Categories	Units	Time series Yes/No Frequency		Territorial coverage	Source (Table no.)
Lead, recovery of secondary lead	Refined lead and lead alloys, remelted lead and lead alloys	tonnes, %	Yes	A, Q	World	ILZSG1 (11)
Lead, recovery of secondary lead	Refined lead and lead alloys, remelted lead and lead alloys	tonnes	Yes	A, Q	World	ILZSG1 (11)
Scrap recovery	By manufacturers	tonnes	Yes	A	World	WBMS3 (-)
Scrap recovery	By metal type	tonnes	Yes	A	World	WBMS1 (-)
Zinc, recovery of secondary zinc	Refined zinc metal, Remelted zinc and direct use of secondary materials	tonnes	Yes	A, Q	World	ILZSG1 (36)
Zinc, recovery of secondary zinc	Refined zinc metal, remelted zinc and direct use of secondary materials	tonnes	Yes	A, Q	World	ILZSG1 (36)

32.10 STOCKS

Subject	Categories	Units	Time series Yes/No Frequency		Territorial coverage	Source (Table no.)
Aluminium, London Metal Exchange	By country	tonnes	Yes	A, Q, M	World	WBMS2 (-)
Copper, London Metal Exchange	By country	tonnes	Yes	A, Q, M	World	WBMS2 (-)
Lead, London Metal Exchange	By country	tonnes	Yes	A, Q, M	World	WBMS2 (-)
Lead, refined metal stocks	Commercial stocks, (producers, consumers, merchants, London Metal Exchange) non-commercial stocks	tonnes	Yes	A, M	World	ILZSG1 (8)
Lead, reported metal stocks		tonnes	Yes	A, Q	Western Europe	ILZSG1 (1)
Lead, stocks		tonnes	Yes	A, M	Australia	ILZSG1 (15)
Lead, stocks		tonnes	Yes	A, M	Canada	ILZSG1 (16)

Subject	Categories	Units	Time series Yes/No Frequency		Territorial coverage	Source (Table no.)
Lead, stocks		tonnes	Yes	A, M	UK	ILZSG1 (23)
Lead, stocks	Consumers merchants	tonnes	Yes	A, M	Germany	ILZSG1 (18)
Lead, stocks	Primary secondary	tonnes	Yes	A, M	Japan	ILZSG1 (20)
Lead, stocks	Producer consumer London Metal Exchange	tonnes	Yes	A	EC, US, Japan	ILZSG1 (3)
Lead, stocks	Producers consumers stockpile	tonnes	Yes	A, M	US	ILZSG1 (24)
Nickel, London Metal Exchange	By country	tonnes	Yes	A, Q, M	World	WBMS2 (-)
Smelter, refinery, summary	By production, deliveries, stock	tonnes	Yes	A	Western world	WBMS3 (-)
Stocks	By metal	tonnes	Yes	A	World	WBMS3 (-)
Stocks	By metal type	tonnes	Yes	A	World	WBMS1 (-)
Stocks, identified	By Metal Exchanges, producers, consumers, merchants	tonnes	Yes	A	World	MJ1 (V)
Tin, London Metal Exchange	By country	tonnes	Yes	A, Q, M	World	WBMS2 (-)
Tungsten	Ores and concentrates, producer's stocks, consumer's stocks, dealer's stocks, government's stocks	tonnes	Yes	A	World	UNCTAD3 (6.1)
Tungsten products	By product and country	tonnes	Yes	A	World	UNCTAD3 (6.2)
Zinc, London Metal Exchange	By country	tonnes	Yes	A, Q, M	World	WBMS2 (-)
Zinc, metal stocks	Commercial stocks non-commercial stocks	tonnes	Yes	A, M	World	ILZSG1 (33)
Zinc, stocks		tonnes	Yes	A, M	Australia	ILZSG1 (40)
Zinc, stocks		tonnes	Yes	A, M	Canada	ILZSG1 (41)
Zinc, stocks	Consumers	tonnes	Yes	A, M	UK	ILZSG1 (48)
Zinc, stocks	Consumers, merchants	tonnes	Yes	A, M	Germany	ILZSG1 (43)
Zinc, stocks	Consumers, producers merchants	tonnes	Yes	A, M	Japan	ILZSG1 (45)
Zinc, stocks	Producers, consumers merchants London Metal Exchange	tonnes	Yes	A, M	EC, US, Japan	ILZSG1 (28)
Zinc, stocks	Producers, consumers merchants	tonnes	Yes	A, M	US	ILZSG1 (49)
Zinc, stocks	Producers, consumers merchants London Metal Exchange	tonnes	Yes	A, M	Western world	ILZSG1 (26)

32.11 SUPPLY - See also under Balance Sheets (32.1) and Production (32.8)

Fluorine		indices	Yes	A	EC	EC68 (-)
Fluorine	Fluorspar, hydrofluoric acid and aluminium fluoride	indices	No		EC	EC68 (-)
Iron and major alloying metals	By metal type	indices	No		EC	EC68 (-)
Metals	Mercury, antimony, titanium and zirconium	indices	No		EC	EC68 (-)
Metals, non-ferrous	By metal type	indices	No		EC	EC68 (-)
Metals, stock variations	By type	indices	Yes	A	EC	EC68 (-)
Phosphates		indices	Yes	A	EC	EC68 (-)
Phosphates	Natural phosphates, phosphoric acid, slag and fertilizers	indices	No		EC	EC68 (-)

33 MINING AND QUARRYING

Subject	Categories	Units	Time series Yes/No Frequency		Territorial coverage	Source (Table no.)
33.1 EARNINGS AND HOURS OF WORK - see also Section 24						
Employment structure, hard coal mines	Workers, shifts, output	nos, hours, tonnes	Yes	A	EC, USA	UN6 (2)
Employment structure, brown coal mines	Workers, shifts, output	nos, hours, tonnes	Yes	A	EC, USA	UN6 (3)
Wages and salaries		nat curr	No		World	UN50 (82)
Wages and salaries	By industry	nat curr	No		Nordic countries	NCM1 (77)
Working hours for wage earners	By industry	hours	No		Nordic countries	NCM1 (77)
33.2 EMPLOYMENT - see also Section 16						
Employees		nos	No		World	UN50 (82)
Employment structure, hard coal mines	Workers, shifts, output	nos, hours, tonnes	Yes	A	EC, USA	UN6 (2)
Employment structure, brown coal mines	Workers, shifts, output	nos, hours, tonnes	Yes	A	EC, USA	UN6 (3)
Persons engaged		nos	No		World	UN50 (82)
Persons engaged	By industry	nos	No		Nordic countries	NCM1 (78)
Persons engaged and wage earners	By industry	nos	No		Nordic countries	NCM1 (77)
33.3 INDUSTRY - see also Section 25						
Mining and quarrying	By industry, establishments	nos	No		Nordic countries	NCM1 (77)
Mining and quarrying	By industry, establishments	nos	No		Nordic countries	NCM1 (78)
Report coverage	By country		No		World	ILZSG2 (1)
Scheduled mine closures and reductions	By country, company, mine, withdrawn capacity	tonnes	No		World	MJ1 (VII)
Scheduled new mines and extensions	By country, company, mine, withdrawn capacity	tonnes	No		World	MJ1 (VIII)
Statistical units		nos	No		World	UN50 (82)
World pelletizing capacity	By country, by sites, plants, units	nos, tonnes	No		World	MB2 (-)
33.4 INTERNATIONAL TRADE - see also Section 27						
33.4.1 Iron Ore						
Exports	By country	tonnes	No		World	MB2 (-)
Imports	By country	tonnes	No		World	MB2 (-)
Principal world iron ore loading and discharging ports	By port	nautical miles	No		World	MB2 (-)
World iron ore trade	By destination, by area	tonnes	No		World	MB2 (-)
33.4.2 Manganese Ore						
Exports	By country	tonnes	No		World	MB2 (-)
Imports	By country	tonnes	No		World	MB2 (-)
33.5 PRICES - see also Section 37						
European iron ore prices	By country, by type	US cents per tonne	No		Selected countries	MB2 (-)
Japan iron ore prices	By country, by type	US cents per tonne	No		Selected countries	MB2 (-)
Price ratio of silver to base-metals	By base metal	US cents	No		World	ILZSG2 (3)
Relative metal prices	By selected metal, by ratio relative to zinc	US cents	No		World	ILZSG2 (2)

33 MINING AND QUARRYING

Subject	Categories	Units	Time series Yes/No Frequency		Territorial coverage	Source (Table no.)
33.6 PRODUCTION - see also Section 38						
Bauxite		tonnes	Yes	A	World	UN35 (16)
Bauxite		tonnes	Yes	A	World	UN50 (86)
Bauxite		tonnes	Yes	A	World, ASEAN	ASEANS1 (4.2.8)
Coal		tonnes	Yes	A	World, ASEAN	ASEANS1 (4.2.3)
Coal		tonnes	Yes	A, M	World	UN35 (11)
Coal	By type, total	tonnes	Yes	A	World	UN28 (-)
Copper ore		tonnes	Yes	A	World, ASEAN	ASEANS1 (4.2.6)
Copper ore		tonnes	Yes	A, M	World	UN35 (17)
Copper, joint production with lead and zinc	By production, by joint production	tonnes, %	No		World	ILZSG2 (10)
Copper, mine production	By ore type	%	No		World	ILZSG2 (11)
Copper, mine production, survey totals	By ore type	tonnes	No		World	ILZSG2 (12)
Copper, mining		indices	Yes	A	World	UN50R (1)
Crude petrolelum and natural gas	Total	tonnes	Yes	A	World	UN28 (-)
Crude petroleum		tonnes	Yes	A	World, ASEAN	ASEANS1 (4.2.1)
Crude petroleum	Specific gravity	tonnes	Yes	A, M	World	UN35 (14)
Diamonds, output		carats	Yes	A	World	UN50 (83)
Ferrous and non-ferrous metal ores	By type, total	tonnes, kilograms	Yes	A	World	UN28 (-)
Gold		kilograms	Yes	A	World	UN50 (89)
Iron ore		tonnes	Yes	A	World, ASEAN	ASEANS1 (4.2.5)
Iron ore	Metal content	tonnes	Yes	A, M	World	UN35 (15)
Iron ore, pellet production	By country	tonnes	Yes	A	World	MB2 (-)
Iron ore, production	By country	tonnes	Yes	A	World	MB2 (-)
Iron ore, production	By country, by product	tonnes	No		Selected countries	MB2 (-)
Iron ore, production, trade and apparent consumption	By country, by exports	tonnes	No		World	MB2 (-)
Iron-bearing ores		tonnes	Yes	A	World	UN50 (85)
Lead ore		tonnes	Yes	A, M	World	UN35 (18)
Lead, mine production	By ore type	%	No		World	ILZSG2 (7)
Lead, mine production	By survey coverage	tonnes, %	No		World	ILZSG2 (8)
Lead, mine production, survey totals	By ore type	tonnes	No		World	ILZSG2 (9)
Lignite and brown coal		tonnes	Yes	A, M	World	UN35 (12)
Manganese ore		tonnes	Yes	A	World, ASEAN	ASEANS1 (4.2.7)
Manganese ore, production	By country	tonnes	Yes	A	World	MB2 (-)
Mining	By country, by product	tonnes, cu m	No		EC	EC18 (8.9)
Mining	By product, by country	tonnes	Yes	A	ESCAP countries	UN44
Mining production index		indices	Yes	A	World, ASEAN	ASEANS1 (4.2)
Natural gas		TJ	Yes	A	World, ASEAN	ASEANS1 (4.2.2)
Natural gas	Heat value	terajoules	Yes	A, M	World	UN35 (13)
Non-metallic minerals and fertilizers	By type, total	tonnes, cu m, carats	Yes	A	World	UN28 (-)
Phosphate rock		tonnes	Yes	A	World	UN50 (87)
Pig iron, production	By country	tonnes	Yes	A	World	MB2 (-)
Production structure, hard coal mines	By country	tonnes	Yes	A	EC, USA	UN6 (2)
Production structure, brown coal mines	By country	tonnes	Yes	A	EC, USA	UN6 (3)
Production, industrial			Yes	A	World	UN50 (1)
Raw steel, production	By country	tonnes	Yes	A	World	MB2 (-)
Salt		tonnes	Yes	A	World, ASEAN	ASEANS1 (4.2.9)
Silver		tonnes	Yes	A	World	UN50 (88)

Subject	Categories	Units	Time series Yes/No	Frequency	Territorial coverage	Source (Table no.)
Silver, joint production with lead and zinc	By production, by joint production	tonnes, %	No		World	ILZSG2 (13)
Silver, mine production	By ore type	%	No		World	ILZSG2 (14)
Silver, mine production, survey totals	By ore type	tonnes	No		World	ILZSG2 (15)
Silver, production	By ore type	g/tonne	No		World	ILZSG2 (16)
Tin concentrates		tonnes	Yes	A, M	World	UN35 (19)
Tin in concentrates		tonnes	Yes	A	World, ASEAN	ASEANS1 (4.2.4)
Uranium	Reserves, and production	tonnes	Yes	A	World	UN50 (84)
Value added		nat curr	No		World	UN50 (82)
Value added	By industry	nat curr	No		Nordic countries	NCM1 (77)
Value of gross output	By industry	nat curr	No		Nordic countries	NCM1 (77)
Value of output		nat curr	No		World	UN50 (82)
Value of raw materials	By industry	nat curr	No		Nordic countries	NCM1 (77)
Zinc ore		tonnes	Yes	A, M	World	UN35 (20)
Zinc, mine production	By ore type	%	No		World	ILZSG2 (4)
Zinc, mine production	By survey coverage	tonnes, %	No		World	ILZSG2 (5)
Zinc, mine production, survey totals	By ore type	tonnes	No		World	ILZSG2 (6)
Zinc, production	By metal type	tonnes	Yes	A	World	WBMS1 (-)

34 NATIONAL ACCOUNTS

34.1 CAPITAL ACCOUNTS
- 34.1.1 Capital Consumption
- 34.1.2 Capital Formation
- 34.1.3 Capital Stock
- 34.1.4 Finance of Capital Formation
- 34.1.5 Stocks and Work in Progress

34.2 COSTS AND PRICES

34.3 EXPENDITURE
- 34.3.1 Consumption
- 34.3.2 Expenditure on GDP According to ICP and SNA Classifications
- 34.3.3 General

34.4 FINANCIAL ACCOUNTS
- 34.4.1 Government Accounts
- 34.4.2 Non-Government Accounts

34.5 INCOME
- 34.5.1 Corporate Sector
- 34.5.2 Personal Sector

34.6 INTERNATIONAL TRANSACTIONS
- 34.6.1 Trade
- 34.6.2 External Debt
- 34.6.3 Foreign Investment
- 34.6.4 International Finance

34.7 INPUT-OUTPUT TABLES

34.8 PRODUCTION – AGGREGATES
- 34.8.1 Main Aggregates
- 34.8.2 Growth Rates
- 34.8.3 Productivity

34.9 PRODUCTION – INDUSTRIAL AND SECTORAL ACCOUNTS
- 34.9.1 Industrial Accounts
- 34.9.2 Sectoral Accounts

34.1 CAPITAL ACCOUNTS

34.1.1 Capital Consumption

Subject	Categories	Units	Time series Yes/No	Frequency	Territorial coverage	Source (Table no.)
Consumption of fixed capital	At current prices and exchange rates	PPPs, ECU	Yes	A	EC, USA and Japan	EC60 (K)

34.1.2 Capital Formation

Subject	Categories	Units	Time series Yes/No	Frequency	Territorial coverage	Source (Table no.)
Capital formation, residential	Percentage of GDP	%	Yes	A	OECD, EC	OECD32 (6.9)
Capital formation, non-residential	Percentage of GDP	%	Yes	A	OECD, EC	OECD32 (6.10)
Capital formation, machinery and equipment	Percentage of GDP	%	Yes	A	OECD, EC	OECD32 (6.11)
Capital formation, gross	By type of goods and owner at current and constant prices	nat curr	Yes	A	World	UN38 (2.7, 2.8)
	By kind of activity of owner, ISIC major divisions at current and constant prices	nat curr	Yes	A	World	UN38 (2.9, 2.10)
Capital formation, material product balances	By kind of activity at constant market prices	nat curr using MPS	Yes	A	World	UN38 (6a, 6b)
Capital formation	As % of GDP	%	Yes	A	ASEAN	ASEANS1 (2.1.8)
Coefficients of gross domestic investment	% GDP at constant 1980 prices	%	Yes	A	Latin American and Caribbean countries	UN45 (45)
Construction	% of gross fixed investment at constant 1980 prices	%	Yes	A	Latin American and Caribbean countries	UN45 (64)
Construction	At constant market prices	US$	Yes	A	Latin American and Caribbean countries	UN45 (120)
Expenditure, government, capital		% GDP	Yes	A	Central and South American countries	IADB1
Fixed capital formation, average annual growth rate	At constant prices, by product	%	No		EC	EC61 (8)
Fixed capital formation		indices	Yes	A	Nordic countries	NCM1 (195)
Fixed capital formation	By branch	%	No		EC	EC61 (4)
Gross capital formation	By good type and owner	nat curr	Yes	A	OECD	OECD29
Gross capital formation	By type	nat curr	Yes	A	OECD	OECD29
Gross capital formation	By type and based on exchange rates and PPPs	US$, nat curr	Yes	A	OECD, EC	OECD28 (part 2-3)
Gross capital formation	By type of goods and owner, by country	nat curr	Yes	A	ESCAP countries	UN44
Gross capital formation - composition at current purchasers values	Type of capital goods, by kind of economic activity	million CFA frs	Yes	A	North Africa	UN2 (12)
Gross capital formation - composition at current purchasers values	Type of capital goods, by kind of economic activity	million CFA frs	Yes	A	West Africa	UN3 (12)
Gross capital formation - composition at current purchasers values	Type of capital goods, by kind of economic activity	million CFA frs	Yes	A	East and Southern Africa	UN4 (12)
Gross capital formation - composition at current purchasers values	Type of capital goods, by kind of economic activity	million CFA frs	Yes	A	Central Africa	UN5 (12)
Gross capital formation at current prices and current exchange rates		US$	Yes	A	OECD, EC OECD-Total	OECD28 (-)

Subject	Categories	Units	Time series Yes/No Frequency		Territorial coverage	Source (Table no.)
Gross capital formation at the price levels and exchange rates of 1985		US$	Yes	A	OECD, EC OECD-Total	OECD28 (-)
Gross capital formation at current prices and 1985 exchange rates	By component	US$, nat curr	Yes	A	OECD, EC OECD-Total	OECD28 (-)
Gross capital formation at current prices and current PPPs	By component	US$, nat curr	Yes	A	OECD, EC OECD-Total	OECD28 (-)
Gross capital formation at current prices	By institutional sector, by type of capital goods	nat curr	Yes	Q	OECD	OECD41 (5a)
Gross capital formation at constant prices	By institutional sector, by type of capital goods	nat curr	Yes	Q	OECD	OECD41 (5b)
Gross domestic investment	By percentage points	%	Yes	A	World	WB6 (11)
Gross domestic investment	By percentage points	%	Yes	A	World	WB6 (13)
Gross domestic investment per capita	By country and region	US$	Yes	A	World	WB6 (4)
Gross fixed capital formation, composition of	By type	nat curr	Yes	A	Nordic countries	NCM1 (194)
Gross fixed capital formation (real)	Percentage change	%	Yes	A	OECD, EC	OECD32 (4.3)
Gross fixed capital formation, average annual growth rate	At constant prices, by ownership branch	%	No		EC	EC61 (9)
Gross fixed capital formation, agriculture	At current prices and exchange rates and at investment rate	ECU, %	Yes	A	EC	EC26 (A.0.11)
Gross fixed capital formation, agriculture	At current prices and exchange rates	ECU	Yes	A	EC	EC26 (A.1-A.1.12)
Gross fixed capital formation, agriculture	At current prices	nat curr	Yes	A	EC	EC26 (A.2.1-A.2.12)
Gross fixed capital formation, forestry	At current prices and exchange rates	ECU	Yes	A	EC	EC26 (B.1.1-B.1.12)
Gross fixed capital formation, forestry	At current prices	nat curr	Yes	A	EC	EC26 (B.2.1-B.2.12)
Gross fixed capital formation, agriculture	By region	ECU	Yes	A	EC	EC26 (C.0.3)
Gross fixed capital formation,	By kind of activity of owner, ISIC major divisions at current and constant prices	nat curr	Yes	A	World	UN38 (2.11, 2.12)
Gross fixed capital formation	At constant market prices	US$	Yes	A	Latin American and Caribbean countries	UN45 (119)
Gross fixed capital formation	At constant market prices	US$	Yes	A	Latin American and Caribbean countries	UN45 (119)
Gross fixed capital formation	At current and 1985 prices, PPPs and exchange rates	PPPs, ECU	Yes	A	EC, USA and Japan	EC60 (F)
Gross fixed capital formation	At current prices and 1985 exchange rates, price levels and exchange rates of 1985, current prices and current exchange rates, volume and price indices	US$, indices	Yes	A	OECD, EC	OECD28 (part 6)
Gross fixed capital formation	At current prices and current PPPs, per head at current prices and current PPPs, per head indices using current PPPs	US$, indices	Yes	A	OECD, EC	OECD28 (part 7)
Gross fixed capital formation	By activity of owner	nat curr	Yes	A	OECD	OECD29
Gross fixed capital formation	By branch and country		No		EC	EC63
Gross fixed capital formation	By industry	ECU	No		EC	EC69 (III.5)

Subject	Categories	Units	Time series Yes/No Frequency		Territorial coverage	Source (Table no.)
Gross fixed capital formation	By kind of activity of owner, current and constant prices	nat curr	Yes	A	OECD	OECD29 (3)
Gross fixed capital formation	By kind of economc activity	nat curr	Yes	A	Nordic countries	NCM1 (196)
Gross fixed capital formation	By kind of economic activity	indices	Yes	A	Nordic countries	NCM1 (197)
Gross fixed capital formation	By ownership branch	ECU, indices	Yes	A	EC	EC61 (-)
Gross fixed capital formation	By ownership branch	nat curr, indices	Yes	A	EC	EC61 (-)
Gross fixed capital formation	By product	%	No		EC	EC61 (3)Gross
Gross fixed capital formation	By product	ECU, indices	Yes	A	EC	EC61 (-)
Gross fixed capital formation	By product	nat curr, indices	Yes	A	EC	EC61 (-)
Gross fixed capital formation	By sector	ECU	Yes	A	EC	EC62 (0.1)
Gross fixed capital formation	Dwellings, non-residential buildings, equipment	%	No		EC, USA, USSR, Canada, Japan	EC9 (2.9)
Gross fixed capital formation	Percentage of GDP	%	Yes	A	OECD, EC	OECD32 (6.8)
Gross fixed capital formation	Total and per head of total population	indices	Yes	A	EC, USA and Japan	EC60 (Q.3)
Gross fixed capital formation	Volume, change in price	indices, %	Yes	A/Q	EC, USA, Japan	EC36
Gross fixed capital formation	Volume and price growth	indices	Yes	A	EC, USA and Japan	EC60 (R.6)
Gross fixed capital formation : residential construction, real	Percentage change	%	Yes	A	OECD, EC	OECD32 (4.4)
Gross fixed capital formation : non-residential construction, real	Percentage change	%	Yes	A	OECD, EC	OECD32 (4.5)
Gross fixed capital formation : machinery and equipment, real	Percentage change	%	Yes	A	OECD, EC	OECD32 (4.6)
Gross fixed capital formation at current prices and exchange rates		ECU	Yes	A	EC	EC6 (IG 7)
Gross fixed capital formation at 1980 prices and exchange rates		ECU	Yes	A	EC	EC6 (IG 8)
Gross fixed capital formation at current prices and 1985 exchange rates		US$	Yes	A	OECD, EC OECD-Total	OECD28 (-)
Gross fixed capital formation growth	Based on exchange rates and PPPs	%	Yes	A	OECD, EC	OECD28 (part 4-5)
Gross investment	By economic sectors, by country	nat curr	Yes	A	VICES countries and Yugoslavia	VICES1 (I.3)
Investment, rate of	By branch	%	No		EC	EC61 (12)
Investment	By industry	ECU	No	1985	EC	EC53 (3.5)
Investment	% of GDP	%	Yes	A	World	IMF7 (-)
Investment as percentage of GDP		%	Yes	A	World	IMF7 (-)
Investment in dwellings as percentage of total investment		%	Yes	Selected years	EC	MHPPE1 (-)
Investment rates (investment as a percentage of gross value-added at factor cost)	By industry	%	No	1985	EC	EC53 (3.9)
Machinery and equipment	% of gross fixed investment at constant 1980 prices	%	Yes	A	Latin American and Caribbean countries	UN45 (65)
Machinery and equipment	At constant market prices	US$	Yes	A	Latin American and Caribbean countries	UN45 (121)
Net capital formation		nat curr	No		OECD	OECD32 (A)
Net capital formation		nat curr	Yes	A	OECD	OECD29
Net capital formation		US$	No		OECD, EC	OECD32 (B)

34 NATIONAL ACCOUNTS

Subject	Categories	Units	Time series Yes/No Frequency	Territorial coverage	Source (Table no.)
Net capital formation	At current prices and PPPs	US$	No	OECD, EC	OECD32 (C)
Net capital formation	Based on exchange rates and PPPs	US$, nat curr	Yes A	OECD, EC	OECD28 (part 2-3)
Net fixed capital formation, agriculture	At current prices and exchange rates	ECU	Yes A	EC	EC26 (A.1-A.1.12)
Net fixed capital formation, agriculture	At current prices	nat curr	Yes A	EC	EC26 (A.2.1-A.2.12)
Net fixed capital formation, forestry	At current prices and exchange rates	ECU	Yes A	EC	EC26 (B.1.1-B.1.12)
Netfixed capital formation, forestry	At current prices	nat curr	Yes A	EC	EC26 (B.2.1-B.2.12)
Price indices		indices	Yes A	OECD, EC OECD-Total	OECD28 (-)
Resources gap	As % of GDP	%	Yes A	ASEAN	ASEANS1 (2.1.8)
Volume indices		indices	Yes A	OECD, EC OECD-Total	OECD28 (-)
34.1.3 Capital Stock					
Stocks of reproducible fixed assets	By type of goods and owner at current and constant prices	nat curr	Yes A	World	UN38 (2.13, 2.14)
Stocks of reproducible fixed assets	By kind of activity at current and constant prices	nat curr	Yes A	World	UN38 (2.15, 2.16)
34.1.4 Finance of Capital Formation					
Capital finance accounts	By sector	nat curr	Yes A	OECD	OECD29
Capital finance accounts	By sector	nat curr	Yes A	OECD	OECD29 (11)
Capital Transactions	Finance of gross accumulation, gross accumulation, by country	nat curr	Yes A	ESCAP countries	UN44
Finance of capital transactions	By type	nat curr	Yes A	OECD	OECD29 (1)
Finance of gross capital formation at current prices and 1985 exchange rates	By component	US$, nat curr	Yes A	OECD, EC OECD-Total	OECD28 (-)
Finance of gross capital formation at current prices and current PPPs	By component	US$, nat curr	Yes A	OECD, EC OECD-Total	OECD28 (-)
Finance of Gross capital formation	By type	nat curr	No	OECD	OECD32 (A)
Finance of Gross capital formation	By type	US$	No	OECD, EC	OECD32 (B)
Finance of Gross capital formation	By type at current prices and PPPs	US$	No	OECD, EC	OECD32 (C)
Financing capital transactions	By source	nat curr	Yes Q	OECD	OECD41 (4)
Gross Accumulation and its Financing	By sector	nat curr	Yes A	EC	EC62 (5.1)
Gross capital formation	By type	nat curr	Yes A	OECD	OECD29 (1)
Gross domestic investment, contribution of net external financing	% of gross domestic investment at constant 1980 prices	%	Yes A	Latin American and Caribbean countries	UN45 (100)
34.1.5 Stocks and Work in Progress					
Values at constant prices		nat curr	Yes Q	OECD	OECD41 (5b)
Values at current prices		nat curr	Yes Q	OECD	OECD41 (5a)
34.2 COSTS AND PRICES - see also Section 37					
Commodity price index	Indices		Yes A	World	IMF7 (-)
Commodity prices	55 commodities	US$/cents	Yes A, M		IMF7 (-)
Compensation of employees (value)		%	Yes A	OECD, EC OECD-Total	OECD28 (-)
Domestic prices, deflators	By country	indices	Yes A	World	WB6 (-)

Subject	Categories	Units	Time series Yes/No Frequency		Territorial coverage	Source (Table no.)
Fixed capital formation, Growth rate of implicit prices	By ownership branch	%	No		EC	EC61 (16)
Fixed capital formation, Growth rate of implicit prices	By product	%	No		EC	EC61 (15)
GDP	volume, change in price	indices, %	Yes	A, Q	EC, USA, Japan	EC36
GDP	Volume and price growth	%, indices	Yes	A	EC	EC60 (R.1)
GDP deflators		%	Yes	A	World	IMF7 (-)
GDP deflators		%	Yes	A	World	IMF7 (-)
GDP Price Change	By component	%	Yes	A, Q	EC, USA and Japan	EC67 (-)
Government final consumption expenditure (implicit price deflator)		%	Yes	A	OECD, EC OECD-Total	OECD28 (-)
Gross domestic product (implicit price deflator)		%	Yes	A	OECD, EC OECD-Total	OECD28 (-)
Gross domestic/national product		index	Yes	Q	OECD	OECD41 (-)
Gross fixed capital formation (implicit price deflator)		%	Yes	A	OECD, EC OECD-Total	OECD28 (-)
Gross value added, implicit prices:	By branch	%	No		EC	EC61 (13)
Households, implicit prices of final Consumption :average annual growth rate	By purpose	%	No		EC	EC61 (14)
Inflation rates	By country	%	No		EC	EM1 (0306)
Price indices		indices	Yes	A	OECD, EC OECD-Total	OECD28 (-)
Price indices		indices	Yes	A	World	IMF7 (-)
Private consumption		index	Yes	Q	OECD	OECD41 (-)
Implicit price deflators of GDP	In US$, national currency, exchange rates	index nos	Yes	A	World	UN36 (7)
Private final consumption expenditure (implicit price deflator)		%	Yes	A	OECD, EC OECD-Total	OECD28 (-)

34.3 EXPENDITURE - see also under Capital Formation (34.1.2)

34.3.1 Consumption

Subject	Categories	Units	Time series Yes/No Frequency		Territorial coverage	Source (Table no.)
Consumption	By type, % of total By type, % of GDP	%	No		World	UN16 (26B)
	Per capita, by type	$US, $int	No		World	UN16 (26B)
Consumption	% of GDP	%	Yes	A	World	IMF7 (-)
Consumption of the population		%	No		MPS countries	UN16 (27B)
Final consumption (MPS)	By category at current and constant market prices	nat curr using MPS	Yes	A	World	UN38 (7a, 7b)
GDP or net material product, and selected measures of consumption expenditure,	GDP per capita, government, and private, final consumption expenditure, total and per capita	nat curr, per capita, %, $US, $int	No		Africa	UN46 (15)
Government final consumption expenditure		%	Yes		Selected SNA countries	UN16 (27A)
Government final consumption	% of GDP	% years	Yes		World Selected countries	UN16 (26A)
	Per capita	$US, $int years	Yes		World Selected countries	UN16 (26A)
Government final consumption expenditure	At current prices and 1985 exchange rates	US$	Yes	A	OECD, EC OECD-Total	OECD28 (-)
	At the price levels and exchange rates of 1985	US$	Yes	A		OECD28 (-)
	At current prices and current exchange rates	US$	Yes	A		OECD28 (-)
Government final consumption expenditure	By function at current constant prices	nat curr	Yes	A	World	UN38 (2.1, 2.2)

Subject	Categories	Units	Time series Yes/No	Frequency	Territorial coverage	Source (Table no.)
Government final consumption expenditure on selected categories of goods and services	Total, % of GDP	nat curr, %	No		World	UN16 (26B)
Households, consumption	By branch and country		No		EC	EC63
Households, final consumption : growth rate	At constant prices, by purpose	%	No		EC	EC61 (7)
Households, final consumption on the economic territory	By purpose	ECU, indices	Yes	A	EC	EC61 (-)
Households, final consumption on the Economic Territory	By purpose	nat curr, indices	Yes	A	EC	EC61 (-)
Households' consumption	Food, beverages, tobacco clothing and footwear; rent, fuel and power; furniture, furnishings, household equipment and operation; medical care and health expenses; transport and communication recreation, education, entertainment, and cultural services	ECU/head	No		EC, USA, USSR, Canada, Japan	EC9 (2.8)
Households' consumption	Volume, change in price	indices, %	Yes	A, Q	EC, USA, Japan	EC36
Material consumption		%	No		MPS countries	UN16 (27B)
National consumption, final	At current and 1985 prices, PPPs and exchange rates	PPPs, ECU	Yes	A	EC, USA and Japan	EC60 (C)
National consumption, final	Volume and price growth	indices	Yes	A	EC, USA and Japan	EC60 (R.3)
National consumption, final	By sector	ECU	Yes	A	EC	EC62 (0.1)
National consumption as percentage of GDP		%	Yes	A	World	IMF7 (-)
National consumption		%	Yes	A	World	WB6 (10)
National consumption	At current prices, average annual growth rate at constant prices, % of distributed national product (net) at current prices	nat curr, %	Yes	A	VICES countries and Yugoslavia	VICES (I.1)
Personal consumption (MPS)	By source of goods and material services at current market prices	nat curr using MPS	Yes	A	World	UN38 (8)
Price indices		indices	Yes	A	OECD, EC OECD-Total	OECD28 (-)
Price indices		indices	Yes	A	OECD, EC OECD-Total	OECD28 (-)
Private consumption, net	At current prices, average annual growth rate at constant prices, % of distributed national product (net) at current prices	nat curr, %	Yes	A	VICES countries and Yugoslavia	VICES1 (II/1)
Private consumption	At current and 1985 prices, PPPs and exchange rates	PPPs, ECU	Yes	A	EC, USA and Japan	EC60 (D)
Private consumption	At current prices and 1985 exchange rates, price levels and exchange rates of 1985, current prices and current exchange rates, volume and price indices	US$, indices	Yes	A	OECD, EC	OECD28 (part 6)

Subject	Categories	Units	Time series Yes/No Frequency		Territorial coverage	Source (Table no.)
Private consumption	At current prices and current PPPs, per head at current prices and current PPPs, per head indices using current PPPs	US$, indices	Yes	A	OECD, EC	OECD28 (part 7)
Private consumption	Based on exchange rates and PPPs	%	Yes	A	OECD, EC	OECD28 (part 4-5)
Private consumption	By country	nat curr	No		EC	EM1 (0308)
Private consumption expenditure	By food and non-alcoholic beverages	%, per capita	No		Africa	UN46 (17)
Private consumption	By percentage points	%	Yes	A	World	WB6 (15)
Private consumption	By type	nat curr	Yes	A	Nordic countries	NCM1 (198)
Private consumption	By type and purpose	nat curr	Yes	A	OECD	OECD29
Private consumption expenditure per capita, real	Percentage change	%	Yes	A	OECD, EC	OECD32 (4.2)
Private consumption expenditure	Percentage of GDP	%	Yes	A	OECD, EC	OECD32 (6.1)
Private consumption	Total and per head of total population	indices	Yes	A	EC, USA and Japan	EC60(Q.1)
Private consumption	Volume and price growth	indices	Yes	A	EC, USA and Japan	EC60 (R.4)
Private consumption	At current prices and 1985 exchange rates,	US$	Yes	A	OECD, EC OECD-Total	OECD28 (-)
	at the price levels and exchange rates of 1985,	US$	Yes	A	OECD, EC OECD-Total	OECD28 (-)
	at current prices and current exchange rates	US$	Yes	A		OECD28 (-)
Private consumption per head	At current prices and 1985 exchange rates, price levels and exchange rates of 1985, current prices and current exchange rates	US$	Yes	A	OECD, EC	OECD28 (part 6)
Private consumption expenditure on selected categories of goods and services	Total,	nat curr	No		World	UN16 (26C)
	% of GDP	%	No		World	UN16 (26C)
	% of total, by category	%	No		World	UN16 (26C)
	% of GDP, by category	%	No		World	UN16 (26C)
	Per capita, by category	$US	No		World	UN16 (26C)
Private consumption per capita	By country and region	US$	Yes	A	World	WB6 (3)
Private consumption per head	At current prices and 1985 exchange rates,	US$	Yes	A	OECD, EC OECD-Total	OECD28 (-)
	At the price levels and exchange rates of 1985,	US$	Yes	A	OECD, EC OECD-Total	OECD28 (-)
	At current prices and current exchange rates	US$	Yes	A	OECD, EC OECD-Total	OECD28 (-)
Private final consumption expenditure		%	Yes		Selected SNA countries	UN16 (27A)
Private final consumption expenditure, Real	percentage change	%	Yes	A	OECD, EC	OECD32 (4.1)
Private final consumption	% of GDP	% years	Yes		World Selected countries	UN16 (26A)
	Per capita	$US, $int years	Yes		World Selected countries	UN16 (26A)
Private final consumption expenditure	By food and non-alcoholic beverages	%, per capita $ int	No		World	UN17 (18)
Private final consumption expenditure	By type and purpose at current and constant prices	nat curr	Yes	A	World	UN38 (2.5, 2.6)
Total consumption (MPS)	At current and constant market prices	nat curr using MPS	Yes	A	World	UN38 (9a, 9b)

34 NATIONAL ACCOUNTS

Subject	Categories	Units	Time series Yes/No Frequency		Territorial coverage	Source (Table no.)
Volume indices		indices	Yes	A	OECD, EC OECD -Total	OECD28 (-)
Volume indices		indices	Yes	A	OECD, EC OECD-Total	OECD28 (-)
34.3.2 Expenditure on GDP according to ICP and SNA classifications						
Comparative dollar price levels (PPPs)	By category	indices	No		OECD	OECD39 (1.6, 2.6)
Domestic resources per capita distribution of	By type of expenditure	$US	Yes	Selected years	Developing countries DMECs	UNCTAD5 (3.3)
Expenditure	By category	indices	No		OECD	OECD39 (1.2, 2.2)
Expenditure	By category	indices per capita	No		OECD	OECD39 (1.4, 2.4)
Expenditure on GDP, per capita	By country, by public consumption, private consumption, gross fixed capital formation	ECU	No		Selected countries	EC35 (-)
Expenditure on GDP, distribution of	By type of expenditure	%	Yes	Selected years	Developing countries DMECs	UNCTAD5 (3.1)
Expenditure on GDP	By country, by consumption, SNA market prices	nat curr, %	No		EC	EC18 (16.8)
Expenditure on GDP	Private, government consumption, gross fixed capital formation, change in stocks export, import	%	No		EC, USA, USSR, Canada, Japan	EC9 (2.7)
Expenditure per capita	By category	No			OECD	OECD39 (1.3, 2.3)
Expenditure per capita (PPPs) by category		US$	No		OECD	OECD39 (1.8, 2.8)
Expenditure per capita (PPPs) by category	Value indices	indices	No		OECD	OECD39 (1.9, 2.9)
Expenditure per capita (PPPs) by category	Value per capita indices	PPP	No		OECD	OECD39 (1.10, 2.10)
Exports of goods and services		index	Yes	Q	OECD	OECD41 (-)
GDP by type of expenditure	Values at current prices and 1985 PPPs, sa, by type of expenditure	US$	Yes	Q	OECD-Total OECD EC, Major Seven	OECD41 (1a)
	Values at PPPs and price levels of 1985, sa, by type of expenditure	US$	Yes	Q	OECD-Total OECD, EC, Major Seven	OECD41 (1b)
	Values at current prices by type of expenditure	nat curr	Yes	Q	OECD	OECD41 (1a)
	Values at constant prices by type of expenditure	nat curr	Yes	Q	OECD	OECD41 (1b)
	Implicit price indices by type of expenditure	index	Yes	Q	OECD	OECD41 (2)
Government consumption		index	Yes	Q	OECD	OECD41 (-)
Government social benefit expenditure		%			Africa	UN46 (17)
Government social security benefit expenditure, and private final consumption expenditure, current prices	GDP	nat curr, per capita, %	No		Africa	UN46 (18)
Gross domestic/national product		index	Yes	Q	OECD	OECD41 (-)
Gross fixed capital formation		index	Yes	Q	OECD	OECD41 (-)
Imports of goods and services		index	Yes	Q	OECD	OECD41 (-)
Nominal values at national prices	By category	US$	No		OECD	OECD39 (1.7, 2.7)
Private consumption		index	Yes	Q	OECD	OECD41 (-)

Subject	Categories	Units	Time series Yes/No Frequency		Territorial coverage	Source (Table no.)
Private consumption expenditure	Values at current prices by type of expenditure	nat curr	Yes	Q	OECD	OECD41 (6a)
	Values at constant prices by type of expenditure	nat curr	Yes	Q	OECD	OECD41 (6b)
	Values at current prices by object of expenditure	nat curr	Yes	Q	OECD	OECD41 (7a)
	Values at constant prices by object of expenditure	nat curr	Yes	Q	OECD	OECD41 (7b)
Purchasing power parities for final expenditure on GDP at international prices	By category	nat curr per US$	No		OECD	OECD39 (1.5, 2.5)
Real values at international prices	By category	US$	No		OECD	OECD39 (1.1, 2.1)
Savings, income from abroad and exports, ratio of to GDP	By type of expenditure	%	Yes	Selected years	Developing countries DMECs	UNCTAD5 (3.2)
Use and origins of resources	By country	nat curr	Yes	A	World	WB6 (-)
34.3.3 General						
Central government,	Lending minus repayments and expenditure by economic type	nat curr	Yes	A	World	IMF5 (p114-622)
Central government	Agriculture	% total	Yes	A	World	IMF5 (p66-67)
Central government	By economic type	% total	No		World	IMF5 (p42-43)
Central government	By function	% total	No		World	IMF5 (p40-41)
Central government	By major components	% total	No		World	IMF5 (p36-37)
Central government	Capital	% total	Yes	A	World	IMF5 (p76-77)
Central government	Defence	% GDP	Yes	A	World	IMF5 (p90-91)
Central government	Defence	% total	Yes	A	World	IMF5 (p58-59)
Central government	Economic affairs and services	% total	Yes	A	World	IMF5 (p62-63)
Central government	Education	% total	Yes	A	World	IMF5 (p60-61)
Central government	Fuel and energy	% total	Yes	A	World	IMF5 (p66-67)
Central government	Goods and services	% total	Yes	A	World	IMF5 (p70-71)
Central government	Health	% total	Yes	A	World	IMF5 (p60-61)
Central government	Housing and amenities	% total	Yes	A	World	IMF5 (p62-63))
Central government	Interest payments	% total	Yes	A	World	IMF5 (p74-75)
Central government	Lending minus repayments	% total	Yes	A	World	IMF5 (p76-77)
Central government	Mining, manufacturing and construction	% total	Yes	A	World	IMF5 (p64-65)
Central government	Road transport	% total	Yes	A	World	IMF5 (p68-69)
Central government	Social security and welfare	% total	Yes	A	World	IMF5 (p58-59)
Central government	Subsidies and other current transfers	% total	Yes	A	World	IMF5 (p70-71)
Central government	Total expenditure	% GDP	Yes	A	World	IMF5 (p88-89)
Central government	Total expenditure and lending minus repayments	% GDP	Yes	A	World	IMF5 (p92-93)

Subject	Categories	Units	Time series Yes/No Frequency		Territorial coverage	Source (Table no.)
Central government	Transfers to other levels of national government	% total	Yes	A	World	IMF5 (p74-75)
Central government	Transportation and communication	% total	Yes	A	World	IMF5 (p68-69)
Central government	Wages and Salaries	% total	Yes	A	World	IMF5 (p72-73)
Consolidated central government,	Expenditure by function	nat curr	Yes	A	World	IMF5 (p114-622)
Expenditure, current and capital	General government sector, central and local government and social security fundsSub-sectors	%	Yes	A	EC	EC49 (A)
Expenditure, subsidies and transfers	By type	nat curr	Yes	A	EC	EC49 (4)
Expenditure of real GDP, growth rates	Private consumption, government consumption, gross capital formation	%	Yes	A	ASEAN	ASEANS1 (2.1.6)
Expenditure on GDP	By type	nat curr	No		OECD	OECD32 (A)
Expenditure on GDP	By type	nat curr	Yes	A	OECD	OECD29
Expenditure on GDP	By type	US$	No		OECD, EC	OECD32 (B)
Expenditure on GDP	By type and based on exchange rates and PPPs	US$, nat curr	Yes	A	OECD, EC	OECD28 (part 2-3)
Expenditure on GDP	By type at current prices and PPPs	US$	No		OECD, EC	OECD32 (C)
Expenditure on GDP	Consumer, Government, gross private domestic fixed investment, stock change, exports of goods and services	nat curr	Yes	A, Q, M	OECD	OECD22 (-)
Expenditure on GDP at 1980 constant market prices	Government expenditure, Private expenditure, gross capital formation, exports of goods and services, imports of goods and services, total	millions US$	Yes	A	African countries	UN1 (18)
Expenditure on GDP per head		nat curr	No		OECD	OECD32 (A)
Expenditure on GDP per head	At current prices and PPPs	US$	No		OECD, EC	OECD32 (C)
Expenditure on GDP per head	By type	US$	No		OECD, EC	OECD32 (B)
Expenditure shares of real GDP		%	Yes	A	ASEAN	ASEANS1 (2.1.7)
Expenditures on GDP	By country, by item	US$	No		Arabian Gulf	CH1 (2.2)
GDP, expenditure on	By category at current and constant prices,	nat curr	Yes	A	World	UN38 (1.1, 1.2)
	by cost components	nat curr	Yes	A	World	UN38 (1.3)
GDP	By type of expenditure,	%	Yes	A	World	UN36 (2)
	by kind of economic activity	%	Yes	A	World	UN36 (3)
General government,	Expenditure and lending minus repayments by economic type	nat curr	Yes	A	World	IMF5 (p114-622)
General government, collective consumption	At current and 1985 prices, PPPs and exchange rates	PPPs, ECU	Yes	A	EC, USA and Japan	EC60 (E)
General government, collective consumption	Total and per head of total population	indices	Yes	A	EC, USA and Japan	EC60 (Q.2)
General government, collective consumption	Volume and price growth	indices	Yes	A	EC, USA and Japan	EC60 (R.5)
General government	Agriculture	% GDP	Yes	A	World	IMF5 (p111)

Subject	Categories	Units	Time series Yes/No Frequency		Territorial coverage	Source (Table no.)
General government	By main economic category	%	Yes	A	EC	EC49 (B)
General government	By main economic categories	nat curr	Yes	A	EC	EC49 (2)
General government	By purpose	%	Yes	A	EC	EC49 (C)
General government	By purpose and transaction type	nat curr	Yes	A	EC	EC49 (5)
General government	Education	% GDP	Yes	A	World	IMF5 (p110)
General government	Expenditure and lending minus repayments	% GDP	Yes	A	World	IMF5 (p108-109)
General government	Health	% GDP	Yes	A	World	IMF5 (p110)
General government	Social security, welfare, housing	% GDP	Yes	A	World	IMF5 (p111)
General government transactions	By type and country	nat curr	Yes	A	EC	EC49 (1)
Government, final consumption	Percentage of GDP	%	Yes	A	OECD, EC	OECD32 (6.2)
Government, current disbursements	Percentage of GDP	%	Yes	A	OECD, EC	OECD32 (6.4)
Government, total outlays	Percentage of GDP	%	Yes	A	OECD, EC	OECD32 (6.5)
Government, current expenditure		% GDP	Yes	A	Central and South American countries	IADB1
Government final consumption, expenditure growth	Based on exchange rates and PPPs	%	Yes	A	OECD, EC	OECD28 (part 4-5)
Government final consumption	At current prices and 1985 exchange rates, price levels and exchange rates of 1985, current prices and current exchange rates, volume and price indices	US$, indices	Yes	A	OECD, EC	OECD28 (part 6)
Government final consumption	At current prices and current PPPs, per head at current prices and current PPPs, per head indices using current PPPs	US$, indices	Yes	A	OECD, EC	OECD28 (part 7)
Government expenditure	By country, by service	nat curr	No		EC	EM1 (0310)
Government expenditure	Health, unemployment, pensions, family allowance	%	Yes	Selected	World	UN16 (28)
Government expenditure	Summary, by country	nat curr	Yes	A	ESCAP countries	UN44
Government final consumption	Percentage change	%	Yes	A	OECD, EC	OECD32 (4.7)
Government outlay	By function and type	nat curr	Yes	A	OECD	OECD29
Government social benefit expenditure	% of GDP	%	No		World	UN17 (18)
Government social security benefit expenditure, and private final consumption expenditure	per capita	nat curr, %	No		World	UN17 (19)
Government social security benefit expenditure	Total	nat curr	Yes	Selected	World	UN16 (28)
	% of GDP	%	Yes	Selected years	World	UN16 (28)
	Per capita	nat curr, $US	Yes	Selected	World	UN16 (28)
Government social security benefits and social assistance to households	By type	nat curr	Yes	A	World	UN38 (2.4)
Local government	Expenditure and lending minus repayments by economic type	nat curr	Yes	A	World	IMF5 (p114-622)

Subject	Categories	Units	Time series Yes/No Frequency		Territorial coverage	Source (Table no.)
Public consumption, net	at current prices, average annual growth rate at constant prices, % of distributed national product (net) at current prices	nat curr, %	Yes	A	VICES countries and Yugoslavia	VICES1 (II/1)
Public consumption	By country	nat curr	No		EC	EM1 (0307)
Total government outlays	By function and type	nat curr	Yes	A	World	UN38 (2.3)
Volume index numbers, private final consumption expenditure	By type by expenditure	indices, nat curr	Yes	A	Nordic countries	NCM1 (199,192,193)
34.4 FINANCIAL ACCOUNTS						
34.4.1 Government Accounts						
Budget	Revenue, expenditure, by sector, by country	nat curr	Yes	A	VICES countries and Yugoslavia	VICES1 (IV/1)
Capital transactions	By category	nat curr	Yes	A	World	UN38 (1.8)
Central government, consolidated	By type of debt holder, by country	nat curr	Yes	A	World	IMF5 (p114-622)
Central government, consolidated	By type of debt instrument, by country	nat curr	Yes	A	World	IMF5 (p114-662)
Central government, budgetary	Summary of finance, by country	nat curr	Yes	A	World	IMF5 (p114-622)
Central government, consolidated	Summary of finance by country	nat curr	Yes	A	World	IMF5 (p114-622)
Central government, consolidated	By country by type of debt instrument	nat curr	Yes	A	World	IMF5 (p114-622)
Central government, consolidated	By type of debt holder by country	nat curr	Yes	A	World	IMF5 (p114-622)
Central government, revenue and grants	By country	nat curr	Yes	A	World	IMF5 (p114-622)
Central government, total revenue		% GDP	Yes	A	World	IMF5 (p86-87)
Central government, current account	With, without grants	% GDP	Yes	A	World	IMF5 (p82-85)
Central government deficit, surplus	% of GDP	%	Yes	A	World	IMF7 (-)
Central government revenue and grants	% of GDP	%	Yes	A	World	IMF7 (-)
Central government	By major components	% total	No		World	IMF5 (p36-37)
Central government	By type of revenue	% total	No		World	IMF5 (p38-39)
Central government	Deficit, without grants	% GDP	Yes	A	World	IMF5 (p80-81)
Central government	Deficit	% GDP	Yes	A	World	IMF5 (p78-79)
Central government	Domestic, foreign	% total	Yes	A	World	IMF5 (p46-47)
Central government	Domestic debt, foreign debt	% total	Yes	A	World	IMF5 (p50-51)
Central government	Monetary authorities, deposit money banks	% total	Yes	A	World	IMF5 (p48-49)
Central government	Non-tax revenue, grants	% total	Yes	A	World	IMF5 (p56-57)
Central government social security funds	Summary of finance, by country	nat curr	Yes	A	World	IMF5 (p114-622)
Central government	Surplus, without grants	% GDP	Yes	A	World	IMF5 (p80-81)

Subject	Categories	Units	Time series Yes/No Frequency		Territorial coverage	Source (Table no.)
Central government	Surplus	% GDP	Yes	A	World	IMF5 (p78-79)
Central government	Taxes on domestic goods and services, taxes on international trade and transactions	% total	Yes	A	World	IMF5 (p54-55)
Central government	Taxes on incomes and profits, social security contributions	% total	Yes	A	World	IMF5 (p52-53)
Central government accounts		nat curr	Yes	A	OECD	OECD29
Central government deficit, surplus as a percentage of GDP		%	Yes	Selected years	World	UNCTAD5 (3.4)
Central government expenditure and lending minus repayments	% of GDP	%	Yes	A	World	IMF7 (-)
Central government expenditure	By function	% of total	Yes	A	African countries	UN1 (37)
Central government receipts and expenditures	Average annual change	%	Yes	A	African countries	UN1 (35)
Central government revenue and expenditures	Revenue, expenditure by type	%	Yes	Selected years	World	UNCTAD5 (3.5)
Central government Spending, allocation of	By selected categories	%	Yes	Selected years	World	UNCTAD5 (3.6)
Central government tax revenue and expenditure as percentage of GDP	Tax, total, current	%	Yes	A	African countries	UN1 (36)
External transactions, current and capital accumulation accounts		nat curr	Yes	A	OECD	OECD29
Extrabudgetary accounts	Summary of finance, by country	nat curr	Yes	A	World	IMF5 (p114-622)
General government, revenue and grants		nat curr	Yes	A	World	IMF5 (p114-622)
General government, non-tax revenue		% GDP	Yes	a	World	IMF5 (p106-107)
General government, total revenue		% GDP	Yes	A	World	IMF5 (p100-101)
General government, balances	By main economic categories	nat curr	Yes	A	EC	EC49 (2)
General government, receipts	By main economic categories	nat curr	Yes	A	EC	EC49 (2)
General government	By transaction	nat curr	Yes	A	EC	EC62 (4.8)
General government	Deficit, without grants	% GDP	Yes	A	World	IMF5 (p96-97)
General government	Deficit	% GDP	Yes	A	World	IMF5 (p94-95)
General government	Deficit	% total	Yes	A	World	IMF5 (p44-45)
General government receipts, total	General government sector, central and local government and social security fund sub-sectors	%	Yes	A	EC	EC49 (A)
General government	Surplus, without grants	% GDP	Yes	A	World	IMF5 (p96-97)
General government	Surplus	% GDP	Yes	A	World	IMF5 (p94-95)
General government	Tax revenue	% GDP	Yes	A	World	IMF5 (p102-103)
General government	Taxes, income, profits and capital gains	% GDP	Yes	A	World	IMF5 (p104)
General government	Taxes, domestic goods and services	% GDP	Yes	A	World	IMF5 (p105)
General government current account,	Without grants	% GDP	Yes	A	World	IMF5 (p98-99)
General government accounts		nat curr	Yes	A	OECD	OECD29
General government: main financial transactions	By type change in assets and liabilities	nat curr	Yes	A	EC	EC62 (6.4)

Subject	Categories	Units	Time series Yes/No	Frequency	Territorial coverage	Source (Table no.)
Government, current savings		% GDP	Yes	A	Central and South American countries	IADB1
Government, net lending	Percentage of GDP	%	Yes	A	OECD, EC	OECD32 (6.7)
Government, current receipts	Percentage of GDP	%	Yes	A	OECD, EC	OECD32 (6.6)
Government, current revenue		% GDP	Yes	A	Central and South American countries	IADB1
Government deficit	Surplus	% GDP	Yes	A	Central and South American countries	IADB1
Government deficit-or surplus	By country	nat curr	Yes	A	World	WB6 (-)
Government domestic finance		% GDP	Yes	A	Central and South American countries	IADB1
Government finance	By country, by revenue, expenditure, surplus, deficit, foreign debt, gold reserves, foreign exchange reserves	nat curr	No		EC	EM1 (0309)
Government revenue, budget	Summary, by country	nat curr	Yes	A	ESCAP country	UN44
	revenue, expenditure, by sector, by country	nat curr	Yes	A	VICES countries and Yugoslavia	VICES1 (IV/1)
Government revenue and expenditure	Deficit, revenue, grant received, expenditure, lending minus repayment	nat curr	Yes	A	ASEAN	ASEANS1 (7.1.1)
Government surplus	Deficit	% GDP	Yes	A	Central and South American countries	IADB1
Income and outlay of the general government	By country	nat curr	Yes	A	Latin American and Caribbean countries	UN45 (127-233)
Intergovernmental	By function, by country	nat curr	Yes	A	World	IMF5 (p114-622)
Local government, revenue and grants		nat curr	Yes	A	World	IMF5 (p114-622)
Local government	By country, by type of debt instrument	nat curr	Yes	A	World	IMF5 (p114-622)
Local government	By type of debt instrument, by country	nat curr	Yes	A	World	IMF5 (p114-622)
Local government	By type of debt holder by country	nat curr	Yes	A	World	IMF5 (p114-622)
Local government	By type of debt holder by country	nat curr	Yes	A	World	IMF5 (p114-622)
Local government accounts		nat curr	Yes	A	OECD	OECD29
Net factor income paid to the rest of the world	At constant 1980 prices	US$	Yes	A	Latin American and Caribbean countries	UN45 (126)
Overall central government	Surplus	% total	Yes	A	World	IMF5 (p44-45)
Profit shares and rates of return on capital		nat curr, %	Yes	A	OECD	OECD29 (14)
Profit shares and tates of return on capital	By type	nat curr	Yes	A	OECD	OECD29
Receipts, total from taxes and social security contributions	By category	%	Yes	A	EC	EC49 (D)
Receipts, total from taxes and social security contributions	By receiving sub-sector	%	Yes	A	EC	EC49 (E)
Receipts, total from taxes and social contributions	By type	nat curr	Yes	A	EC	EC49 (8)
Social benefits	By type and providing sector	nat curr	Yes	A	EC	EC62 (5.4)

Subject	Categories	Units	Time series Yes/No Frequency	Territorial coverage	Source (Table no.)
Social contributions	By type and receiving sector	nat curr	Yes A	EC	EC62 (5.3)
Social security fund accounts		nat curr	Yes A	OECD	OECD29
Social security transfers	Percentage of GDP	%	Yes A	OECD, EC	OECD32 (6.3)
State or provincial government accounts		nat curr	Yes A	OECD	OECD29
Subsidies, agriculture	At current prices and exchange rates and as % of final agricultural output	ECU, %	Yes A	EC	EC26 (A.0.4)
Tax receipts	By type and receiving sub-sector	nat curr	Yes A	EC	EC49 (-)
Taxes, agriculture linked to production (excl VAT)	At current prices and exchange rates and as % of final agricultural output	ECU, %	Yes A	EC	EC26 (A.0.5)
Taxes	Taxes, GDP, taxes as % of GDP	nat curr	Yes A	ASEAN	ASEANS1 (7.1.2)
Taxes	Total production and imports, income and wealth, capital tax, social contributions	ECU, %	No	EC,	EC9 (2.10)
Taxes and social contributions	By category and receiving sub-sector	nat curr	Yes A	EC	EC49 (6)
Taxes linked to production	Imports paid to EC	nat curr	Yes A	EC	EC49 (7)
34.4.2 Non-Government Accounts					
Assets and Liabilities					
Credit institutions, sub-sectors	By transaction type changes in assets and liabilities	nat curr	Yes A	EC	EC62 (4.6)
Credit institutions	By transaction	nat curr	Yes A	EC	EC62 (4.5)
Credit institutions: main financial transactions	By type change in assets and liabilities	nat curr	Yes A	EC	EC62 (6.3)
Financial assets and liabilities net change	By sector	ECU	Yes A	EC	EC62 (0.1)
Financial assets and liabilities	By sector	nat curr	No	EC	EC62 (3)
Financial institutions accounts		nat curr	Yes A	OECD	OECD29
Financial intermediaries	By type change in assets and liabilities	nat curr	Yes A	EC	EC62 (6.1)
Gross accumulation and its financing	By sector	nat curr	Yes A	EC	EC62 (5.1)
Households	By transaction	nat curr	Yes A	EC	EC62 (4.3)
Households and private unincorporated enterprises accounts		nat curr	Yes A	OECD	OECD29
Income and outlay of households, including private unincorporated non-financial enterprises	By country	nat curr	Yes A	Latin American and Caribbean countries	UN45 (127-233)
Insurance enterprises	By transaction	nat curr	Yes A	EC	EC62 (4.7)
Loans: net borrowing	By sector	ECU	Yes A	EC	EC62 (0.1)
Loans: net lending	By sector	ECU	Yes A	EC	EC62 (0.1)
Non-financial and financial corporate and quasi-corporate enterprises accounts		nat curr	Yes A	OECD	OECD29
Non-financial corporate and quasi-corporate enterprises accounts		nat curr	Yes A	OECD	OECD29
Non-financial corporate and quasi-corporate enterprises and households	By transaction	nat curr	Yes A	EC	EC62 (4.1)
Non-financial corporate and quasi-corporate enterprises	By transaction	nat curr	Yes A	EC	EC62 (4.2)

Subject	Categories	Units	Time series Yes/No Frequency		Territorial coverage	Source (Table no.)
Non-financial corporate and quasi-corporate enterprises: main financial transactions	By type change in assets and liabilities	nat curr	Yes	A	EC	EC62 (6.5)
Non-financial resident units	By type change in assets and liabilities	nat curr	Yes	A	EC	EC62 (6.2)
Private non-profit institutions serving households accounts		nat curr	Yes	A	OECD	OECD29
Private non-profit institutions	By transaction	nat curr	Yes	A	EC	EC62 (4.4)
Deposits and Savings						
Currency and deposits : assets	By sector	ECU	Yes	A	EC	EC62 (0.1)
Domestic saving	As % of GDP	%	Yes	A	ASEAN	ASEANS1 (2.1.8)
Gross domestic savings	By percentage points	%	Yes	A	World	WB6 (14)
Gross saving	By sector	ECU	Yes	A	EC	EC62 (0.1)
Net saving		nat curr	No		OECD	OECD32 (A)
Net saving		nat curr	Yes	A	OECD	OECD29
Net saving		US$	No		OECD, EC	OECD32 (B)
Net saving	based on exchange rates and PPPs	US$, nat curr	Yes	A	OECD, EC	OECD28 (part 2-3)
Net saving	At current prices and PPPs	US$	No		OECD, EC	OECD32 (C)
Lending and Borrowing						
Credit, domestic	Public sector, private sector	% GDP	Yes	A	Central and South American countries	IADB1
Debt, service	Total	US$	Yes	A	Central and South American countries	IADB1
Lending or borrowing, net	By sector	ECU	Yes	A	EC	EC62 (0.1)
Net lending or net borrowing	General government sector, central and local government and social security and sub-sectors	%	Yes	A	EC	EC49 (A)
34.5 INCOME						
34.5.1 Corporate Sector						
Compensation of agricultural employees	By region	ECU	Yes	A	EC	EC26 (C.0.3)
Income, net of total agricultural labour	At current prices and exchange rates and as % of net value added at factor cost	ECU, %	Yes	A	EC	EC26 (A.0.9)
Income, net of agricultural family labour	At current prices and exchange rates and as % of net value added at factor cost	ECU, %	Yes	A	EC	EC26 (A.0.10)
Income, net of total agricultural labour	At current prices and exchange rates	ECU	Yes	A	EC	EC26 (A.1-A.1.12)
Income, net of agricultural family labour	At current prices and exchange rates	ECU	Yes	A	EC	EC26 (A.1-A.1.12)
Income, net of total agricultural labour	At current prices	nat curr	Yes	A	EC	EC26 (A.2.1-A.2.12)
Income, net of family agricultural labour	At current prices	nat curr	Yes	A	EC	EC26 (A.2.1-A.2.12)
Income, net of total forestry labour	At current prices and exchange rates	ECU	Yes	A	EC	EC26 (B.1.1-B.1.12)
Income, net of family forestry labour	At current prices and exchange rates	ECU	Yes	A	EC	EC26 (B.1.1-B.1.12)
Income, net of total forestry labour	At current prices	nat curr	Yes	A	EC	EC26 (B.2.1-B.2.12)

Subject	Categories	Units	Time series Yes/No Frequency		Territorial coverage	Source (Table no.)
Income, net of forestry Family labour	At current prices	nat curr	Yes	A	EC	EC26 (B.2.1-B.2.12)
Interest, agricultural	By region	ECU	Yes	A	EC	EC26 (C.0.3)
Operating surplus, gross	By sector	ECU	Yes	A	EC	EC62 (0.1)
Operating surplus, net agricultural	At current prices and exchange rates and as % of net value added at factor cost	ECU, %	Yes	A	EC	EC26 (A.0.8)
Operating surplus, net agricultural	At current prices and exchange rates	ECU	Yes	A	EC	EC26 (A.1-A.1.12)
Operating surplus, net agricultural	At current prices	nat curr	Yes	A	EC	EC26 (A.2.1-A.2.12)
Operating surplus, net forestry	At current prices and exchange rates	ECU	Yes	A	EC	EC26 (B.1.1-B.1.12)
Operating surplus, net forestry	At current prices	nat curr	Yes	A	EC	EC26 (B.2.1-B.2.12)
Operating surplus, net agricultural	By region	ECU	Yes	A	EC	EC26 (C.0.1)
Operating surplus of economy, net	At current prices and exchange rates	PPPs, ECU	Yes	A	EC, USA and Japan	EC60 (L)
Payments agricultural e.g. rent	By region	ECU	Yes	A	EC	EC26 (C.0.3)
34.5.2 Personal Sector						
Compensation of employees, growth	Based on exchange rates and PPPs	%	Yes	A	OECD, EC	OECD28 (part 4-5)
Compensation of employees	By branch and share of compensation of employees in VAFC by branch	nat curr, %	Yes	A	EC	EC61 (-)
Compensation of employees	By component	nat curr	Yes	A	EC	EC62 (5.2)
Compensation of employees	Per wage and salary earner at current and 1985 prices, PPPs and exchange rates	PPPs, ECU	Yes	A	EC, USA and Japan	EC60 (J.2)
Compensation of employees	Share of compensation of employees in VAFC by branch	ECU, %	Yes	A	EC	EC61 (-)
Compensation of employees	Total at current and 1985 prices, PPPs and exchange rates	PPPs, ECU	Yes	A	EC, USA and Japan	EC60 (J.1)
Compensation of employees from agriculture	At current prices and exchange rates and as % of net value added at factor cost	ECU, %	Yes	A	EC	EC26 (A.0.7)
Income components	By decile groups of households By urban, rural areas and per capita income	nat curr	No		Various countries	UN37 (7)
Income components	By income size groups, By urban, rural areas and per capita income	nat curr	No		Various countries	UN37 (8)
Income components	By socio-economic status of head of household	nat curr	No		Various countries	UN37 (6)
Number of households by income size group	Age group of household head	nos	No		Various countries	UN37 (2)
	Household size	nos	No		Various countries	UN37 (3)
	Educational attainment of household head	nos	No		Various countries	UN37 (4)
	Socio-economic status of head of household	nos	No		Various countries	UN37 (5)

Subject	Categories	Units	Time series Yes/No	Frequency	Territorial coverage	Source (Table no.)
Wage and salary earners	By branch and yearly change of compensation of	nos, %	Yes	A	EC	EC61 (-)

34.6 INTERNATIONAL TRANSACTIONS - See also Section 27

34.6.1 Trade

Subject	Categories	Units	Time series Yes/No	Frequency	Territorial coverage	Source (Table no.)
Balance of exports and imports	At current prices, PPPs and exchange rates	PPPs, ECU	Yes	A	EC, USA and Japan	EC60 (I)
Current account	Detailed transactions	nat curr	Yes	A	World	UN38 (3.51)
Export of goods and services	At current prices and 1985 exchange rates, price levels and exchange rates of 1985, current prices and current exchange rates, volume and price indices	US$, indices	Yes	A	OECD, EC	OECD28 (part 6)
Exports		%	No		MPS countries	UN16 (27B)
Exports		%	Yes	Selected years	SNA countries	UN16 (27A)
Exports	At current and 1985 prices, PPPs and exchange rates	PPPs, ECU	Yes	A	EC, USA and Japan	EC60 (G)
Exports	By branch and country for total imports and imports to EC and third countries		No		EC	EC63
Exports	Volume and price growth	indices	Yes	A	EC, USA and Japan	EC60 (R.7)
Exports and imports	Goods, services, by category	nat curr	Yes	A	World	UN38 (2.17)
Exports of goods and services	At current prices and 1985 exchange rates	US$	Yes	A	OECD, EC OECD-Total	OECD28 (-)
	At the price levels and exchange rates of 1985	US$	Yes	A	OECD, EC OECD-Total	OECD28 (-)
	At current prices and current exchange rates	US$	Yes	A	OECD, EC OECD-Total	OECD28 (-)
	Volume indices	indices	Yes	A	OECD, EC OECD-Total	OECD28 (-)
	Price indices	indices	Yes	A	OECD, EC OECD-Total	OECD28 (-)
External transactions, current account	Payments, receipts, by type	nat curr	Yes	A	World	UN38 (1.7)
Imports		%	No		MPS countries	UN16 (27B)
Imports		%	Yes	Selected years	SNA countries	UN16 (27A)
Imports	At current and 1985 prices, PPPs and exchange rates	PPPs, ECU	Yes	A	EC, USA and Japan	EC60 (hl)
Imports	By branch and country for total imports, imports from EC and third countries		No		EC	EC63
Imports	Volume and price growth	indices	Yes	A	EC, USA and Japan	EC60 (R.8)
Imports of goods and services	At current prices and 1985 exchange rates, price levels and exchange rates of 1985, current prices and current exchange rates, volume and price indices	US$, indices	Yes	A	OECD, EC	OECD28 (part 6)

Subject	Categories	Units	Time series Yes/No Frequency	Territorial coverage	Source (Table no.)
Imports of goods and services	At current prices and 1985 exchange rates	US$	Yes A	OECD, EC OECD-Total	OECD28 (-)
	At the price levels and exchange rates of 1985	US$	Yes A	OECD, EC OECD-Total	OECD28 (-)
	At current prices and current exchange rates	US$	Yes A	OECD, EC OECD-Total	OECD28 (-)
	Volume indices	indices	Yes A	OECD, EC OECD-Total	OECD28 (-)
	Price indices	indices	Yes A	OECD, EC OECD-Total	OECD28 (-)
34.6.2 External Debt					
Convertible currency debt	Gross debt, net debt, assets	US$	Yes A	VICES region, VICES countries and Yugoslavia	VICES1 (III/6)
Debt, external	Total	US$	Yes A	Central and South American countries	IADB1
External position, VICES	Assets held in Western banks, liabilities vis a vis Western banks, net position	US$	Yes I	VICES countries and Yugoslavia	VICES1 (III/6)
Liabilities, maturity distribution	Amounts outstanding vis a vis Western banks	US$	No	VICES countries and Yugoslavia	VICES1 (III/6)
34.6.3 Foreign Investment					
Foreign investment	By type, by field of activity or industry, by country	US$	Yes A	ASEAN	ASEANS1 (7.5)
34.6.4 International Finance					
Capital accumulation account	By category	nat curr	Yes A	World	UN38 (3.52)
Capital finance account	By category	nat curr	Yes A	World	UN38 (3.53)
Current account, source of financing	Current account deficit, long-term financing, short-term-financing and errors and omissions, reserves and related items	US$	Yes A	Developing countries and territories, major exporters of manufactures, least developed countries	UNCTAD1 (5.3)
External transactions, current and capital accumulation accounts	Exports, imports; current account, capital account	nat curr	Yes A	OECD	OECD29 (10)
International reserves	Incl. gold	US$	Yes A	ASEAN	ASEANS1 (7.3)
Transactions	External	million CFA frs	Yes A	Central Africa	UN5 (13)
Transactions	External	million CFA frs	Yes A	East and Southern Africa	UN4 (13)
Transactions	External	million CFA frs	Yes A	North Africa	UN2 (13)
Transactions	External	million CFA frs	Yes A	West Africa	UN3 (13)
World, rest of: principal transactions	By type	nat curr	Yes A	EC	EC62 (4.9)
World, rest of subsectors: principal transactions	By type	nat curr	Yes A	EC	EC62 (4.10)
World rest of: main financial transactions	By type change in assets and liabilities	nat curr	Yes A	EC	EC62 (6.6)

Subject	Categories	Units	Time series Yes/No Frequency		Territorial coverage	Source (Table no.)
34.7 INPUT-OUTPUT TABLES						
Consumption						
Consumption, intermediate	Industry or service	nat curr	No		EC	UN42 (-)
Final uses, domestic origin: producers' prices	By country, NACE classification and final use	nat curr	No		EC	EC63
Final uses, imports: producers' prices	By country, NACE classification and final use	nat curr	No		EC	EC63
Final uses	By type	nat curr	No		EC	UN42 (-)
Inputs, primary: producers' prices	By country,type and NACE classification	nat curr	No		EC	EC63
Inputs, intermediate: producers' prices	By country and NACE classification	nat curr	No		EC	EC63
Inputs, intermediate of domestic origin: producers' prices	By country and NACE classification	nat curr	No		EC	EC63
Inputs, intermediate, imports: producers' prices	By country and NACE classification	nat curr	No		EC	EC63
Inputs, intermediate, technical	By user, branch and country		No		EC	EC63
Inputs	Goods and services, primary inputs, resources, all by type	nat curr	No		EC	UN42 (-)
Output, actual	By branch and country		No		EC	EC63
Output, total intermediate	By branch and country		No		EC	EC63
final uses	by country, NACE classification and final uses	nat curr	No		EC	EC63
34.8 PRODUCTION - AGGREGATES						
34.8.1 - Main Aggregates						
a) Gross Domestic Product (GDP)						
GDP, EC, member states real share in	Total	%	Yes	A	Western World	MLC1 (-)
GDP, real	Total, agriculture, industry, manufacturing, durable manufacturing, non-durable manufactures, construction, services	indices	Yes	A, M	OECD	OECD22
GDP, EC	At current prices, PPPs and exchange rates % of each country with respect to community	%	Yes	A	EC, USA and Japan	EC60 (R.2)
GDP, value of		nat curr	Yes	Selected	World	UN16 (26A)
GDP		%	Yes	A	World	UN50 (3)
GDP		%	Yes	Selected	SNA countries	UN16 (27A)
GDP		ECU	Yes	A	EC, USA, USSR, Canada, Japan	EC9 (2.1)
GDP		indices	Yes	A, Q	OECD	OECD22 (-)
GDP		indices	Yes	A	EC, USA, USSR, Canada, Japan	EC9 (2.3)
GDP		nat curr	No		OECD	OECD32 (A)
GDP		nat curr	Yes	A, Q, M	OECD	OECD22 (-)
GDP		nat curr	Yes	A	OECD	OECD29
GDP		nat curr	Yes	M	Asia and Pacific	UN43 (-)
GDP		PPS	Yes	A	EC, USA, USSR, Canada, Japan	EC9 (2.2)
GDP		US$	No		OECD, EC,	OECD32 (B)

Subject	Categories	Units	Time series Yes/No Frequency	Territorial coverage	Source (Table no.)
GDP		US$	Yes A	Central and South American countries	IADB1
GDP		US$	Yes A	ESCAP region, developing ESCAP region	UN44 (p5, 10)
GDP		US$ per Capita US$	Yes A	Canada, USA	UN13 (2)
GDP	by type of expenditure, by kind of economic activity, by individual country and territory	%	Yes I	World	UNCTAD1 (6.4)
GDP	volume, change in price	indices, %	Yes A, Q	EC, USA, Japan	EC36
GDP	Agriculture, industrial activities, basic services, other services, at constant market prices	US$	Yes A	Latin American and Caribbean countries	UN45 (114-117)
GDP	At constant market prices, 1980	US$	Yes A	Latin American and Caribbean countries	UN45 (112)
GDP	At constant prices	% indices	Yes A	World	IMF7 (-)
GDP	At constant prices	nat curr	Yes A	ASEAN	ASEANS1 (2.1.1)
GDP	At current and constant prices by country	nat curr, indices	Yes A, Q, M	OECD	OECD22 (-)
GDP	At current market prices, implicit price level	nat curr, indices	Yes A, Q	OECD, EC OECD Total EC Total Major Seven Total	OECD22
GDP	At current prices and PPPs	US$	No	OECD, EC	OECD32 (C)
GDP	At current prices and 1985 exchange rates, price levels and exchange rates of 1985, current prices and current exchange rates, volume and price indices	US$, indices	Yes A	OECD, EC	OECD28 (part 6)
GDP	At current prices and current PPPs, per head at current prices and current PPPs, per head indices using current PPPs	US$, indices	Yes A	OECD, EC	OECD28 (part 7)
GDP	At current prices and 1985 exchange rates	US$	Yes A	OECD, EC OECD-Total	OECD28 (-)
GDP	At current prices and current exchange rates	US$	Yes A	OECD, EC OECD-Total	OECD28 (-)
GDP	At market price	ECU	Yes A	EC	EC73 (12)
GDP	At the price levels and exchange rates of 1985	US$	Yes A	OECD, EC OECD-Total	OECD28 (-)
	At current prices and current exchange rates	US$	Yes A	OECD, EC OECD-Total	OECD28 (-)
GDP	At the price levels and exchange rates of 1985	US$	Yes A	OECD, EC OECD-Total	OECD28 (-)
GDP	Based on exchange rates and PPPs	US$, nat curr	Yes A	OECD, EC	OECD28 (part 2-3)
GDP	By activity	nat curr	Yes A	OECD	OECD29
GDP	By country	ECU, %	No	Selected countries	EC35 (-)
GDP	By country	nat curr	No	EC	EM1 (0301)

34 NATIONAL ACCOUNTS

Subject	Categories	Units	Time series Yes/No Frequency		Territorial coverage	Source (Table no.)
GDP	By kind of economic activity	nat curr	Yes	A	ESCAP countries	UN44
GDP	By kind of economic activity, at factor cost	nat curr	Yes	A	Latin American and Caribbean	UN45 (127-233)
GDP	By kind of economic activity	nat curr	Yes	A	Nordic countries	NCM1 (191)
GDP	By kind of economic activity, at constant market prices	US$	Yes	A	Latin America and the Caribbean	UN45 (110)
GDP	By type of expenditure, at market prices	nat curr	Yes	A	Latin American and Caribbean countries	UN45 (127-233)
GDP	By type of expenditure, at constant market prices	US$	Yes	A	Latin America and the Caribbean	UN45 (108)
GDP	By type of expenditure, by kind of economic activity, by major economic grouping	%	Yes	5yr	World economic regions	UNCTAD1 (6.3)
GDP	Current purchasers value	million US$	Yes	A	Central Africa	UN5 (3-1)
GDP	Current purchasers value	million US$	Yes	A	East and Southern Africa	UN4 (3-1)
GDP	Current purchasers value	million US$	Yes	A	North Africa	UN2 (3-1)
GDP	Current purchasers value	million US$	Yes	A	West Africa	UN3 (3-1)
GDP	Per capita, using current exchange rate	US$	Yes	A	Nordic countries	NCM1 (189)
GDP	Per capita, using current PPPs	US$	Yes	A	Nordic countries	NCM1 (190)
GDP	PPPs and exchange rates	ECU, % PPPs	Yes	A	EC. USA and Japan	EC60 (P)
GDP	Current and constant at market prices price values at current and 1985 prices and exchange rates	PPPs, ECU	Yes	A	EC USA and Japan	EC60 (B.1)
GDP	Current market prices	millions US$	Yes	A	African countries	UN1 (15)
GDP	Per head of total population at current and 1985 prices, PPPs and exchange rates	PPPs, ECU	Yes	A	EC, USA and Japan	EC60 (B.2)
GDP	Volume and price growth	%, indices	Yes	A	EC, USA and Japan	EC60 (R.1)
GDP and net material product		nat curr US$	Yes	A	World	UN50 (19)
GDP at constant prices		%	Yes	A	World	IMF7 (-)
GDP at current prices	Total, per head	$US	Yes	Selected years	World	UN36 (1)
GDP at market prices		nat curr	Yes	A	OECD	OECD42 (36)
GDP at market prices	Total at current prices, volume index numbers, per inhabitant, per civilian active person	ECU, indices, per capita,	Yes	A	EC	EC6 (IA 8)
GDP in purchasers' values	Current prices	nat curr	Yes	A	Nordic countries	NCM1 (186)
GDP indexes	Indices		Yes	A	World	IMF7 (-)
GDP or net material product, current and constant prices, and selected measures of consumption expenditure	By total and per capita % GDP, per capita	nat curr	No		World	UN17 (16)
GDP per capita		%	Yes	A	World	UN50 (3)
GDP per capita		%	Yes	Selected	SNA countries	UN16 (27A)
GDP per capita		nat curr, US, mint	Yes	Selected	World	UN16 (26A)

Subject	Categories	Units	Time series Yes/No	Frequency	Territorial coverage	Source (Table no.)
GDP per capita		PPS	No		EC	WC1 (-)
GDP per capita		US$	No		OECD	OECD6 (C5)
GDP per capita		US$	No		World and economic regions	UNCTAD1 (6.1)
GDP per capita		US$/capita	Yes	A	Central and South American countries	IADB1
GDP per capita	$US	$US	No		World	UNCTAD5 (-)
GDP per capita	At constant market prices	US$	Yes	A	Latin American and Caribbean countries	UN45 (113)
GDP per capita	At current prices and 1985 exchange rates	US$	Yes	A	OECD, EC OECD-Total	OECD28 (-)
GDP per capita	Growth based on exchange rates and PPPs	%	Yes	A	OECD, EC	OECD28 (part 4-5)
GDP per capita	By country	ECU, PPS	No		Selected countries	EC35 (-)
GDP per head	At current prices and 1985 exchange rates, price levels and exchange rates of 1985, current prices and current exchange rates	US$	Yes	A	OECD, EC	OECD28 (part 6)
GDP per inhabitant	EUR (PPS) index	Yes	A		EC by region	EC65 (-)
GDP value index		Official exchange rate	No		Africa	EC1 (V1)
GDP volume in purchasers' value		indices, US$	Yes	A	OECD	OECD33 (14.4)
Growth of GDP	Annual percentage change in volume	%	Yes	A	Nordic countries	NCM1 (187)
National Accounts totals	By country, current and constant price, GFCF, stocks	nat curr	Yes	A	Africa and Asia	MAC1 (K1)
Share of GDP	By country, by memorandum, items, government finance	%	Yes	A	Developing countries	WB2 (-)
Volume index		PPP	No		Africa	EC1 (V1)
Volume index numbers	Total, per capita	indices	Yes	A	Nordic countries	NCM1 (188)
Volume indices		indices	Yes	A	OECD, EC OECD-Total	OECD28 (-)
b) GDP, Cost Components of						
Cost components of GDP	By type	nat curr	Yes	A	OECD	OECD29 (1)
Cost components of value added	By activity	nat curr	Yes	A	OECD	OECD29
GDP, cost components	By type	nat curr	Yes	A	OECD	OECD29
GDP, cost components	By type and based on exchange rates and PPPs	US$, nat curr	Yes	A	OECD, EC	OECD28 (part 2-3)
GDP, cost components	By type	nat curr	No	A	OECD	OECD32 (A)
GDP, cost components	By type	US$	No		OECD, EC	OECD32 (B)
GDP, cost components	By type at current prices and PPPs	US$	No		OECD, EC	OECD32 (C)
GDP	Cost components	nat curr	Yes	Q	OECD	OECD41 (2)
GDP	Cost structure at current purchasers values	million CFA frs	Yes	A	East and Southern Africa	UN4(7)
GDP	Cost structure at current purchasers values	million CFA frs	Yes	A	Central Africa	UN5(7)
GDP	Cost structure at current purchasers values	million CFA frs	Yes	A	North Africa	UN2(7)
GDP	Cost structure at current purchasers values	million CFA frs	Yes	A	West Africa	UN3(7)

Subject	Categories	Units	Time series Yes/No	Frequency	Territorial coverage	Source (Table no.)
Values at current prices and current PPPs	By component	US$, nat curr	Yes	A	OECD, EC OECD-Total	OECD28 (-)
Values at current prices and 1985 exchange rates	By component	US$, nat curr	Yes	A	OECD, EC OECD-Total	OECD28 (-)
c) GDP, Expenditure on						
Expenditure on GDP	Current and constant prices, by type	nat curr	Yes	A	OECD	OECD29 (1)
GDP	Expenditure at 1970/1980 purchasers values	million CFA frs	Yes	A	Central Africa	UN5 (8)
GDP	Expenditure at 1970/1980 purchasers values	million CFA frs	Yes	A	East and Southern Africa	UN4 (8)
GDP	Expenditure at 1970/1980 purchasers values	million CFA frs	Yes	A	North Africa	UN2 (8)
GDP	Expenditure at current purchasers values	million CFA frs	Yes	A	Central Africa	UN5 (6)
GDP	Expenditure at current purchasers values	million CFA frs	Yes	A	East and Southern Africa	UN4 (6)
GDP	Expenditure at current purchasers values	million CFA frs	Yes	A	North Africa	UN2 (6)
GDP	Expenditure at current purchasers values	million CFA frs	Yes	A	West Africa	UN3 (6)
Usage of GDP	By country, government expenditure, private expenditure, stocks, capital formation, exports, imports	nat curr	No		EC	EM1 (0313)
Usage of GDP	By country, government expenditure, private expenditure, stocks, capital formation, exports, imports	%	No		EC	EM1 (0314)
Values at current prices and 1985 exchange rates	By component	US$, nat curr	Yes	A	OECD, EC OECD-Total	OECD28 (-)
Values at current prices and and current PPPs	By component	US$, nat curr	Yes	A	OECD, EC OECD-Total	OECD28 (-)
Values at prices levels and exchange rates of 1985	By component	US$, nat curr	Yes	A	OECD, EC, OECD-total	OECD28 (-)
Values at the price levels and PPPs of 1985	By component	US$, nat curr	Yes	A	OECD, EC OECD-Total	OECD28 (-)
d) Gross National Product (GNP)						
Current GNP per capita	By country	US$, nos	Yes	A	World	WB6 (-)
GNP, current prices		ECU	Yes	Selected years	EC	MHPPE1 (-)
GNP	By country	nat curr	No		EC	EM1 (0302)
GNP	Per capita, per capita annual growth rate	US$, %	No		UNICEF assisted countries	UNICEF2 (-)
GNP per capita		US$				WB1 (-)
GNP per capita		US$	No		ACP states	EC1 (II-)
GNP per capita		US$	No		Mediterranean countries	EC1 (IV-)
GNP per capita		US$	No		World developing countries OPEC, non-OPEC, ACP, EC	EC1 (I2)
GNP per capita		US$/capita	Yes	A	ASEAN	ASEANS1 (2.2)
Gross national product		nat curr	No		OECD	OECD32 (A)
Gross national product		nat curr	Yes	A	OECD	OECD29

Subject	Categories	Units	Time series Yes/No Frequency	Territorial coverage	Source (Table no.)
Gross national product		US$	No	OECD, EC	OECD32 (B)
Gross national product	At current market prices	US$	Yes A	OPEC	OPEC1 (3)
Gross national product	At current market prices	nat curr, indices	Yes A, Q	OECD	OECD22
Gross national product	Based on exchange rates and PPPs	US$, nat curr	Yes A	OECD, EC	OECD28 (part 2-3)
Gross national product and income per capita	By country and region	US$	Yes A	World	WB6 (1-2)
Grossn national product	At current prices and PPPs	US$	No	OECD, EC	OECD32 (C)
e) Material Product Balances					
Accumulation	At current prices, average annual growth rate at constant prices, % of distributed national product (net) at current prices	nat curr, %	Yes A	VICES countries and Yugoslavia	VICES1 (I.1)
Distributed national product	At current prices, average annual growth rate at constant prices	nat curr, %	Yes A	VICES region, VICES countries and Yugoslavia	VICES1 (I/1)
GDP or net material product, current and constant prices, and selected measures of consumption expenditure, total and per capita	GDP per capita, government, and private, final consumption expenditure	nat curr, per capita, %, $US, $ int	No	Africa	UN46 (15)
Net material product		%	No	VICES region, VICES countries and Yugoslavia	VICES1 (0/1)
Net material product		indices	Yes A	Canada, USA	UN13 (2)
Net material product	At current prices, average annual growth rate at constant prices	nat curr, %	Yes A	VICES region, VICES countries and Yugoslavia	VICES1 (I/1)
Net material product	By use at current and constant market prices	nat curr using MPS	Yes A	World	UN38 (1a, 1b)
Net material product	Per capitaIndices		Yes A	Canada, USA	UN13 (2)
NMP		%	No	MPS countries	UN16 (27B)
NMP per capita		%	No	MPS countries	UN16 (27B)
Primary incomes (MPS)	By kind of activity at constant prices	nat curr using MPS	Yes A	World	UN38 (3)
Primary incomes (MPS)	From net material product, population, enterprises	nat curr using MPS	Yes A	World	UN38 (4)
Supply and disposition of goods and material services	Current and constant market prices	nat curr using MPS	Yes A	World	UN38 (5a, 5b)
f) National Income					
Gross national income	By average national growth	%	Yes A	World	WB6 (5)
Growth of real gross national disposable income	Average annual rates, constant market prices	indices	Yes A	Latin American and Caribbean countries	UN45 (40)
Income	Gross national and disposable	million CFA frs	Yes A	Central Africa	UN5 (11)
Income	Gross national and disposable	million CFA frs	Yes A	East and Southern Africa	UN4 (11)
Income	Gross national and disposable	million CFA frs	Yes A	North Africa	UN2 (11)
Income	Gross national and disposable	million CFA frs	Yes A	West Africa	UN3 (11)
National disposable income, net	At current prices and exchange rates	PPPs, ECU	Yes A	EC, USA and Japan	EC60 (M)
National disposable income		nat curr	No	OECD	OECD32 (A)
National disposable income		nat curr	Yes A	OECD	OECD29

Subject	Categories	Units	Time series Yes/No	Frequency	Territorial coverage	Source (Table no.)
National disposable income	At current prices and PPPs	US$	No		OECD, EC	OECD32R (C)
National disposable income	Based on exchange rates and PPPs	US$, nat curr	Yes	A	OECD, EC	OECD28 (part 2-3)
National income		nat curr	No		OECD	OECD32 (A)
National income		nat curr	Yes	A, M	World	IMF6 (-)
National income		nat curr	Yes	A, M	World	IMF7 (-)
National income		nat curr	Yes	A	OECD	OECD29
National income		US$	No		OECD, EC	OECD32 (B)
National income	At current prices and PPPs	US$	No		OECD, EC	OECD32 (C)
National income	Based on exchange rates and PPPs	US$, nat curr	Yes	A	OECD, EC	OECD28 (part 2-3)
National income	By country, by growth of produced national income, per capita national income, national income by selected economic sectors	index, %	No		Central and Eastern EC	EC18 (16.1)
National income	National income and disposible income, by country	nat curr	Yes	A	ESCAP countries	UN44
National income and national disposable income	Total	nat curr	Yes	A	Nordic countries	NCM1 (200)
Real gross national disposable income	At constant market prices	US$	Yes	A	Latin American and Caribbean countries	UN45 (122)
Real gross national disposable income	At constant market prices	US$	Yes	A	Latin American and Caribbean countries	UN45 (122)
Use of national income	By country, by consumption	nat curr, %	No		Central and Eastern EC	EC18 (16.7)
g) Principal Aggregates - see also under GDP, GNP, Material Product Balances and National Income						
Aggregates, principal	By type at current prices and PPPs	PPPs	No		EC, USA and Japan	EC60 (A.1)
Aggregates, related to population and employment	At current and 1985 prices and PPPs	PPPs	No		EC, USA and Japan	EC60 (A.2)
Aggregates, use and supply of goods and services	By type at current prices and PPPs	PPPs	No		EC, USA and Japan	EC60 (A.3)
Aggregates, principal	At current prices and exchange rates	ECU	No		EC, USA and Japan	EC60 (A.4)
Aggregates, use and supply of goods and services	At current prices and exchange rates	ECU	No		EC, USA and Japan	EC60 (A.5)
Aggregates, use and supply of goods and services	Volume and price changes	%	No		EC, USA and Japan	EC60 (A.6)
Aggregates, principal	At current prices and PPPs	PPPs	Yes	A	EC	EC60 (-)
Aggregates, related to population and employment	At current and 1985 prices and PPPs	PPPS	Yes	A	EC	EC60 (-)
Aggregates, use and supply of goods and services	At current and 1985 prices and PPPs	PPPs	Yes	A	EC	EC60 (-)
Aggregates, principal	At current prices and	ECU	Yes	A	EC	EC60 (-)
Aggregates, use and supply of goods and services	PPPs at current prices and exchange rates	ECU	Yes	A	EC	EC60 (-)
Aggregates, use and supply of goods and services	Volume and price indices	indices	Yes	A	EC	EC60 (-)
Aggregates, principal	At current prices by country	nat curr	Yes	A	EC, USA and Japan	EC60 (-)
Aggregates, related to population and employment	At current and 1985 prices by country	nat curr	Yes	A	EC, USA and Japan	EC60 (-)
Aggregates, use and supply of goods and services	At current and 1985 prices by country	nat curr	Yes	A	EC, USA and Japan	EC60 (-)

Subject	Categories	Units	Time series Yes/No Frequency		Territorial coverage	Source (Table no.)
Aggregates, use and supply of goods and services	Volume and price indices	indices	Yes	A	EC, USA and Japan	EC60 (-)
Aggregates, principal	By type and sector	ECU	No		EC	EC62 (0.2)
Aggregates, principal	By type	nat curr	Yes	A	EC	EC62 (1)
Cost structure	Net operating surplus, compensation of employees, taxes-production, imports, consumption of fixed capital	%	No		EC, USA, USSR, Canada, Japan	EC9 (2.6)
National accounting aggregates, relations among	GDP, GNP, national income, national disposable income, net saving, net capital formation	nat curr	Yes	A	OECD	OECD29 (1)
National accounting aggregates, relations among		nat curr	Yes	A	World	UN38 (1.12)
National accounts	GDP, GNP, inflation, tax revenue, surplus, deficit, investment, savings	US$, %	No		Industrial countries	UN25 (44)
National accounts	GDP, GNP, inflation, tax revenue, surplus, deficit, investment, savings	US$, %	No		Developing countries	UN25 (23)
National accounts	nat curr.		Yes	A, M	World	IMF7 (-)
National accounts	nat curr.		Yes	A, M	World	IMF6 (-)
National accounts totals	By countries, CP, GDP, GNP, NMP, NNP	nat curr	Yes	A	EC	MAC3 (J1)
National accounts totals	By countries	nos	No		The Americas and Australasia	MAC2 (K1)
National product, proportions of	By countries by sector of origin	%	Yes	A	EC	MAC3 (J2)
Regional indicators	% EC, indices per capita	ECU, PPS	No		EC , EC regions and administrative units	EC9 (2.12-2.19)
Relations among main national accounts aggregates	At constant prices	US$	Yes	A	Latin America and the Caribbean	UN45 (111)
Relations among main national accounts aggregates	At current prices, by country	nat curr	Yes	A	Latin American and Caribbean countries	UN45 (127-233)
Resources, total	By branch and country	ECU, PPPs	No		EC	EC63
Values at current prices and 1985 exchange rates	By main category: GDP, GNP, national income, national disposable income, net saving, net capital formation	US$, nat curr	Yes	A	OECD OECD, EC OECD-Total	OECD28 (-)
Values at current prices and current PPPs	By main category: GDP, GNP, national income, national disposable income, net saving, net capital formation	US$, nat curr	Yes	A	OECD, EC OECD-Total	OECD28 (-)
34.8.2 Growth Rates						
Agriculture	By percentage points	%	Yes	A	World	WB6 (7)
Annual growth rates of GDP	Per capita at 1980 constant market prices	%	Yes	A	African countries	UN1 (16)

34 NATIONAL ACCOUNTS

Subject	Categories	Units	Time series Yes/No Frequency	Territorial coverage	Source (Table no.)
Annual rates of growth, average, selected economic accounts aggregates developed SNA countries					
Contribution to growth of GDP resource balance	By percentage points	%	Yes A	World	WB6 (12)
Economic growth annual rates of growth	By country total population; occupied population	GDP/GNP index total %, % per capita	Yes A No	World EC, USA, USSR, Canada, Japan	DSC2 (1.4) EC9 (2.4)
GDP, trends in GDP	By country	US$	No	EC	EM1 (0303)
GDP		%	Yes A	World	UN36 (4)
GDP		in national currency index nos	Yes A	World	UN36 (7)
GDP	By kind of economic activity	%	Yes A	World	UN36 (6)
GDP	By total, per capita	%	Yes Selected years	World, by	UNCTAD5 (2.1, 2.2)
GDP	By type of expenditure	%	Yes A	World	UN36 (5)
GDP	Share in world	%	Yes Selected years	World, by development groups least developed countries	UNCTAD5 (2.1)
GDP (volume)		%	Yes A	OECD, EC OECD-Total	OECD28 (-)
GDP at current prices		in $US index nos	Yes A	World	UN36 (7)
GDP growth	Based on exchange rates and PPPs	%	Yes A	OECD, EC	OECD28 (part 4-5)
GDP growth	By component	%	Yes A, Q	EC, USA and Japan	EC67 (-)
GDP in purchasers' values	Current prices	nat curr	Yes A	Nordic countries	NCM1 (186)
GDP per head		%	Yes A	OECD, EC OECD-Total	OECD28 (-)
Generation of national income	By country, by agriculture, industry, construction, distribution trades, transport, other sectors	nat curr, %	No	Central and Eastern EC	EC18 (16.5)
GNP, trends in GNP	By country	US$	No	EC	EM1 (0304)
Government final consumption expenditure (volume)		%	Yes A	OECD, EC OECD-Total	OECD28 (-)
Gross domestic product	By average national growth	%	Yes A	World	WB6 (6)
Gross fixed capital formation (volume)		%	Yes A	OECD, EC OECD-Total	OECD28 (-)
Growth, per capita	Average annual rates, constant market prices	indices	Yes A	Latin American and Caribbean countries	UN45 (39)
Growth	Average annual rates constant market prices	indices	Yes A	Latin American and Caribbean countries	UN45 (38)
Growth of GDP	By country, by SNA market prices	nat curr index	No	EC	EC18 (16.3)
Growth of GDP by kind of economic activity		%	Yes A	SNA countries by regions	UN50 (4)
Growth of GDP by type of expenditure		%	Yes A	SNA countries by regions	UN50 (5)
Growth of GNP	By country, by actual prices, constant prices	nat curr index	No	Soviet Union	EC18 (16.4)
Growth of produced national income	By country, by actual index	nat curr,	No	Central and Eastern EC	EC18 (16.2)

Subject	Categories	Units	Time series Yes/No Frequency		Territorial coverage	Source (Table no.)
Growth of real gross national disposable income	Average annual rates, constant market prices	indices	Yes	A	Latin American and Caribbean countries	UN45 (40)
Growth rates, annual average	Total, per capita real gross domestic product at market prices	%	Yes	A	World economic regions	UNCTAD1 (6.2)
Growth rates	By country, by population, labor force, gross national income, private consumption, import elasticity, savings, ICOR	%	No		Developing countries	WB2 (-)
Growth rates of main national accounting aggregates at constant prices						
Industry	By percentage points	%	Yes	A	World	WB6 (8)
National disposable income (value)		%	Yes	A	OECD, EC OECD-Total	OECD28 (-)
National disposable income growth	Based on exchange rates and PPPs	%	Yes	A	OECD, EC	OECD28 (part 4-5)
Private final consumption expenditure (volume)		%	Yes	A	OECD, EC OECD-Total	OECD28 (-)
Private final consumption expenditure per head (volume)		%	Yes	A	OECD, EC OECD-Total	OECD28 (-)
Rates of growth, average, selected economic accounts aggregates	By market economies By centrally planned economies	rate	Yes	5 yrly	World	UN17 (17 A, B)
Rates of growth, average, selected economic accounts aggregates		rate	Yes	5 yrly	Africa	UN46 (16)
Real GDP, growth rates		%	Yes	A	ASEAN	ASEANS1 (2.1.2)
Real GDP, growth rates	By economic sector, by country	%	Yes	A	ASEAN	ASEANS1 (2.1.5)
Real GDP	Percentage change	%	Yes	A	OECD, EC	OECD32 (3.1)
Real GDP per capita	Percentage change	%	Yes	A	OECD, EC	OECD32 (3.2)
Real GDP per person employed	Percentage change	%	Yes	A	OECD, EC	OECD32 (3.7)
Services	By percentage points	%	Yes	A	World	WB6 (9)
Share of GDP and growth rates	By country, by taxes, agriculture, industry, services, resource balance, expenditures	%	Yes	A	Developing countries	WB2 (-)
34.8.3 Productivity						
Average annual growth rate						
Index of real net value-added at factor cost and per work unit		indices	Yes	A	EC	EC6 (IG 9)
Labour index	By economic activity and country	indices	Yes	A	Asian countries	APO1
Labour productivity, apparent:	By branch	%	No		EC	EC61 (11)
Labour productivity index	By economic activity and country	indices	Yes	A	Asian countries	APO1
Labour productivity index	National, agriculture, manufacturing, electricity gas and water, construction, trade, transport and communication and finance	indices	Yes	A	Asian countries	APO1 (A.1-A.8)
Labour productivity level (current prices)	By economic activity and country	US$	Yes	A	Asian countries	APO1

Subject	Categories	Units	Time series Yes/No	Frequency	Territorial coverage	Source (Table no.)
Labour productivity level (constant prices)	By economic activity and country	US$	Yes	A	Asian countries	APO1
Labour productivity ratio	Apparent productivity of labour of each branch to apparent productivity of the total	nos	No		EC	EC61 (10)
Productivity levels (current prices)	National, agriculture, manufacturing, electricity gas and water, construction, trade, transport and communication and finance	US$	Yes	A	Asian countries	APO1 (B.1-B.8)
Productivity levels (constant prices)	National, agriculture, manufacturing, electricity gas and water, construction, trade, transport and communication and finance	US$	Yes	A	Asian countries	APO1 (C.1-C.8)

34.9 PRODUCTION - INDUSTRIAL AND SECTORAL ACCOUNTS

34.9.1 Industrial Accounts

Subject	Categories	Units	Time series Yes/No	Frequency	Territorial coverage	Source (Table no.)
Agriculture, per person employed	Percentage change	%	Yes	A	OECD, EC	OECD32 (3.8)
Agriculture		%	No		MPS countries	UN16 (27B)
Agriculture		%	Yes	Selected	SNA countries	UN16 (27A)
Agriculture		% GDP	Yes	A	Central and South American countries	IADB1
Agriculture	Percentage change	%	Yes	A	OECD, EC	OECD32 (3.3)
Agriculture	Percentage of GDP	%	Yes	A	OECD, EC	OECD32 (5.1)
GDP	Constant prices by industry	nat curr	Yes	Q	OECD	OECD41 (3b)
GDP	Current prices by industry	nat curr	Yes	Q	OECD	OECD41 (3a)
GDP	At factor cost, by industry	ECU	No		EC	EC69 (III.3)
GDP	Market prices, by industry	ECU	No		EC	EC69 (III.2)
GDP	Market prices	ECU	Yes	A	EC	EC69 (III.1)
GDP by kind of activity prices	Current and constant	nat curr	Yes	A	World	UN38 (1.10, 1.11)
Gross value added (factor cost)	By industry	ECU	No	1985	EC	EC53 (3.2)
Gross value added per person employed (factor cost)	By industry	ECU	No	1985	EC	EC53 (3.7)
Gross value added (at market prices)	By branch	ECU, indices	Yes	A	EC	EC61 (-)
value added per head	by branch and yearly change of	nos, %	Yes	A	EC	EC61 (-)
Gross value added (at market prices)	By branch	nat curr, indices	Yes	A	EC	EC61 (-)
Gross value added: average annual growth rate	At market prices, at constant prices by branch	%	No		EC	EC61 (5)
Gross value-added (at market prices), share of branches in	By branch	%	No		EC	EC61 (1)
Gross value-added at market prices	By region	ECU, %	No	1984	EC	EC53 (7.2)
Industrial activity		%	No		MPS countries	UN16 (27B)
Industry, per person employed	Percentage change	%	Yes	A	OECD, EC	OECD32 (3.9)

Subject	Categories	Units	Time series Yes/No Frequency		Territorial coverage	Source (Table no.)
Industry		% GDP	Yes	A	Central and South American countries	IADB1
Industry	Percentage change	%	Yes	A	OECD, EC	OECD32 (3.4)
Industry	Percentage of GDP	%	Yes	A	OECD, EC	OECD32 (5.2)
Input, total intermediate	By branch and country		No		EC	EC63
Manufacturing, per person employed	Percentage change	%	Yes	A	OECD, EC	OECD32 (3.10)
Manufacturing		%	Yes	Selected	SNA countries MPS countries	UN16 (27A)
Manufacturing	Percentage change	%	Yes	A	OECD, EC	OECD32 (3.5)
Manufacturing	Percentage of GDP	%	Yes	A	OECD, EC	OECD32 (5.3)
Manufacturing activity	By country	%	Yes	A	World	WB6 (-)
Net material product	By kind of activity at current and constant prices	nat curr using MPS	Yes	A	World	UN38 (2a, 2b)
Net material product	By kind of economic activity	%	Yes	Selected years	DMECs, least developed countries	UNCTAD5 (2.2)
Production value	By industry	ECU	No	1985	EC	EC53 (3.3)
Services, per person employed	Percentage change	%	Yes	A	OECD, EC	OECD32 (3.11)
Services		% GDP	Yes	A	Central and South American countries	IADB1
Services	Percentage change	%	Yes	A	OECD, EC	OECD32 (3.6)
Services	Percentage of GDP	%	Yes	A	OECD, EC	OECD32 (5.4)
Share of GDP and growth rates	By country, by taxes, agriculture, industry, services, resource balance, expenditures	%	Yes	A	Developing countries	WB2 (-)
Share of individual industries in gross value added (factor cost)	By manufacturing industries	%	No	1985	EC	EC53 (3.6)
Share of industry in gross value-added	Current prices and exchange rates	%	No		EC, USA and Japan	EC53 (1.7)
Value added, gross agricultural	At current and 1985 prices and exchange rates, as % of final agricultural output, volume and price indices	ECU, %, indices	Yes	A	EC	EC26 (A.0.3)
Value added, net agricultural (factor cost)	At current prices and exchange rates and as % of EC net value added at factor cost	ECU, %	Yes	A	EC	EC26 (A.0.6)
Value added, gross agricultural (at market prices)	At current prices	nat curr	Yes	A	EC	EC26 (A.2.1-A.2.12)
Value added, gross agricultural (at factor cost)	At current prices	nat curr	Yes	A	EC	EC26 (A.2.1-A.2.12)
Value added, net agricultural (at factor cost)	At current prices	nat curr	Yes	A	EC	EC26 (A.2.1-A.2.12)
Value added, gross agricultural (at market prices)	At current prices and exchange rates	ECU	Yes	A	EC	EC26 (A.1-A.1.12)
Value added, gross agricultural (at factor cost)	At current prices and exchange rates	ECU	Yes	A	EC	EC26 (A.1-A.1.12)
Value added, net agricultural (at factor cost)	At current prices and exchange rates	ECU	Yes	A	EC	EC26 (A.1-A.1.12)
Value added, gross forestry (at market prices)	At current prices and exchange rates	ECU	Yes	A	EC	EC26 (B.1.1-B.1.12)
Value added, gross forestry (at factor cost)	At current prices and exchange rates	ECU	Yes	A	EC	EC26 (B.1.1-B.1.12)

Subject	Categories	Units	Time series Yes/No Frequency		Territorial coverage	Source (Table no.)
Value added, net forestry (at factor cost)	At current prices and exchange rates	ECU	Yes	A	EC	EC26 (B.1.1-B.1.12)
Value added, gross forestry (at market prices)	At current prices	nat curr	Yes	A	EC	EC26 (B.2.1-B.2.12)
Value added, gross forestry (at factor cost)	At current prices	nat curr	Yes	A	EC	EC26 (B.2.1-B.2.12)
Value added, net forestry (at factor cost)	At current prices	nat curr	Yes	A	EC	EC26 (B.2.1-B.2.12)
Value added, gross agricultural (at market prices)	By region	ECU	Yes	A	EC	EC26 (C.0.1)
Value added, gross agricultural (at factor cost)	By region	ECU	Yes	A	EC	EC26 (C.0.1)
Value added, net agricultural (at factor cost)	By region	ECU	Yes	A	EC	EC26 (C.0.1)
Value added	Agriculture, forestry, fishing, services and government	%	No		EC, USA, USSR, Canada, Japan	EC9 (2.5)
					EC regions and administrative units	EC9 (2.20-2.27)
Value added	Kind of activity at current and constant prices	nat curr	Yes	A	World	UN38 (4.1, 4.2)
	by cost components	nat curr	Yes	A	World	UN38 (4.3)
Value added (at market prices)	By branch and country		No		EC	EC63
34.9.2 Sectoral Accounts - see also under Capital Accounts (34.1) and Financial Accounts (34.4)						
Accounts for central government	By type of account by type of income or expenditure	nat curr	Yes	A	OECD	OECD29 (6.1)
Accounts for general government	By type of account by type of income or expenditure	nat curr	Yes	A	OECD	OECD29 (6)
Accounts for households and private unincorporated enterprises	By type of account by type of income or expenditure	nat curr	Yes	A	OECD	OECD29 (8)
Accounts for local government	By type of account by type of income or expenditure	nat curr	Yes	A	OECD	OECD29 (6.3)
Accounts for non-financial and financial corporate and quasi corporate enterprises	By type of account by type of income or expenditure	nat curr	Yes	A	OECD	OECD29 (7)
Accounts for private non-profit institutions serving households	By type of account by type of income or expenditure	nat curr	Yes	A	OECD	OECD29 (9)
Accounts for social security funds	By type of account by type of income or expenditure	nat curr	Yes	A	OECD	OECD29 (6.4)
Accounts for state or provincial government	By type of account by type of income or expenditure	nat curr	Yes	A	OECD	OECD29 (6.2)
Corporate and quasi-corporate enterprises – current income and outlay summary	By type	nat curr	Yes	A	World	UN38 (1.5)
Corporate and quasi-corporate enterprises – income and outlay account	By type and sector	nat curr	Yes	A	World	UN38 (3.22)
Corporate and quasi-corporate enterprises – capital accumulation account	By type and sector	nat curr	Yes	A	World	UN38 (3.23)
Corporate and quasi-corporate enterprises – capital finance account	By type and sector	nat curr	Yes	A	World	UN38 (3.24)
	By type and sector	nat curr	Yes	A	World	UN38 (3.24)
Cost components of value added by kind of activity		nat curr	Yes	A	OECD	OECD29 (13)
GDP, proportions of	Sector of origin	%	Yes	A	Africa and Asia	MAC1 (K2)

Subject	Categories	Units	Time series Yes/No Frequency	Territorial coverage	Source (Table no.)
GDP, proportions of	By sector of origin	nos	No	The Americas and Australasia	MAC2 (K1)
GDP	By country, by sector	US$	No	Arabian Gulf	CH1 (2.1)
GDP	By economic activity	ECU	No 1985	EC, USA and Japan	EC53 (1.5)
GDP	By economic activity	indices	No	EC, USA and Japan	EC53 (1.6)
GDP	By economic sector, by country	nat curr	Yes A	ASEAN	ASEANS1 (2.1.3)
GDP	By kind of economic activity at current factor cost	million CFA frs	Yes A	East and Southern Africa	UN4 (9)
GDP	By origin	indices, %	No	ACP states	EC1 (II-)
GDP	By origin	indices, %	No	Mediterranean countries	EC1 (IV-)
GDP	By sector	nat curr	Yes A	OECD	OECD29 (1)
GDP	By type of goods and owner, current and constant prices	nat curr	Yes A	OECD	OECD29 (4)
GDP	Factor cost by branch of economic activity, by country	ECU	Yes A	EC	EC78 (VIII.2.1)
GDP	By kind of economic activity at current factor cost	million CFA frs	Yes A	Central Africa	UN5 (9)
GDP	By kind of economic activity at 1970/1980 factor costs	million CFA frs	Yes A	Central Africa	UN5 (10)
GDP	By kind of economic activity at 1970/1980 factor costs	million CFA frs	Yes A	East and Southern Africa	UN4 (10)
GDP	By kind of economic activity at current factor cost	million CFA frs	Yes A	North Africa	UN2 (9)
GDP	By kind of economic activity at 1970/1980 factor costs	million CFA frs	Yes A	North Africa	UN2 (10)
GDP	By kind of economic activity at current factor cost	million CFA frs	Yes A	West Africa	UN3 (9)
GDP	By kind of economic activity at 1970/1980 factor costs	million CFA frs	Yes A	West Africa	UN3 (10)
GDP	Expenditure at 1970/1980 purchasers values	million CFA frs	Yes A	West Africa	UN3 (8)
GDP (constant prices)	By economic activity and country	nat curr, US$	Yes A	Asian countries	APO1
GDP (current prices)	By cconomic activity and country	nat curr	Yes A	Asian countries	APO1
GDP (current prices)	By economic activity and country by country, region	US$	Yes A	Asian countries	APO1
GDP by institutional sectors	By sector	nat curr	Yes A	World	UN38 (1.9)
GDP by kind of activity	Current and constant prices	nat curr	Yes A	OECD	OECD29 (12)
GDP by kind of economic activity at constant factor cost	Total, Agriculture, mining, manufacturing, other industries, services	millions US$	Yes A	African countries	UN1 (17)
GDP index (constant prices)	By economic activity and country	indices	Yes A	Asian countries	APO1
GDP real	By economic sector, by country	%	Yes A	ASEAN	ASEANS1 (2.1.4)
General government – income and outlay account	By type and sector	nat curr	Yes A	World	UN38 (3.12)
General government – capital accumulation account	By type and sector	nat curr	Yes A	World	UN38 (3.13)
General government – capital finance account	By type and sector	nat curr	Yes A	World	UN38 (3.14)
corporate and quasi-corporate enterprises – production account	By type and sector	nat curr	Yes A	World	UN38 (3.21)
General government – production account	Output, input by type and sector	nat curr	Yes A	World	UN38 (3.11)

Subject	Categories	Units	Time series Yes/No Frequency		Territorial coverage	Source (Table no.)
General government – receipts and disbursements, current	By type	nat curr	Yes	A	World	UN38 (1.4)
Generation of GDP	By country, by sector, SNA market prices	nat curr, %	No		EC	EC18 (16.6)
Household and private unincorporated enterprises production account	By type and sector	nat curr	Yes	A	World	UN38 (3.31)
Household and private unincorporated enterprises income and outlay account	By type and sector	nat curr	Yes	A	World	UN38 (3.32)
Household and private unincorporated enterprises capital accumulation account	By type and sector	nat curr	Yes	A	World	UN38 (3.33)
Household and private unincorporated enterprises capital finance account	By type and sector	nat curr	Yes	A	World	UN38 (3.34)
Households and non-profit institutions – current income and outlay	By type	nat curr	Yes	A	World	UN38 (1.6)
Origin of GDP	By country, by economic sector	nat curr	No		EC	EM1 (0311)
Origin of GDP	By country, by economic sector	%	No		EC	EM1 (0312)
Private final consumption expenditure	By type and purpose; current and constant prices	nat curr	Yes	A	OECD	OECD29 (2)
Private non-profit institutions serving households production account	By type and sector	nat curr	Yes	A	World	UN38 (3.41)
Private non-profit institutions serving households income and outlay account	By type and sector	nat curr	Yes	A	World	UN38 (3.42)
Private non-profit institutions serving households capital accumulation account	By type and sector	nat curr	Yes	A	World	UN38 (3.43)
Private non-profit institutions serving households capital finance account	By type and sector	nat curr	Yes	A	World	UN38 (3.44)
Production cost	By type and transition to collective consumption	nat curr	Yes	A	EC	EC49 (3)
Sector accounts, detailed	By transaction and sector	nat curr	No		EC	EC62 (2)
Total government outlays	By function and type	nat curr	Yes	A	OECD	OECD29 (5)

35 PARLIAMENT AND PUBLIC AFFAIRS

35 PARLIAMENT AND PUBLIC AFFAIRS

Subject	Categories	Units	Time series Yes/No Frequency	Territorial coverage	Source (Table no.)
35.1 ELECTIONS					
Dates of last elections		date	No	Selected countries	IPU2 (VIII)
Political parties	By ballots, elected	nos, %	No	Nordic countries	NCM1 (269)
35.2 PARLIAMENTS					
35.2.1 European					
Main interests	By country, by national politics, international politics	%	No	EC	EC72(12.6)
Opinions of Europeans on integration	By country	%	No	EC	EC72(12.7)
Turnout in European elections	By country	%	No	EC	EC35 (-)
Turnout in European elections	By country	%	No	EC	EC72(12.2)
35.2.2 National					
Distribution of seats	By sex	nos, %	Yes I	World	IPU1
35.3 PARTICIPATION OF MEN AND WOMEN IN PUBLIC AFFAIRS					
Parliamentary assemblies, number of seats	By sex, total	nos, %	No	World	UN16 (31)
Professional staff in the UN Secretariat	By sex, level of responsibility and nationality	nos, %	No	World	UN16 (32)
Professional staff in the UN System and related agencies	By sex, level of responsibility and nationality	nos, %	No	World	UN16 (33)
35.4 WOMEN AND POLITICAL POWER					
Appointed parliamentarians	By country and parliament	nos	No	Selected countries	IPU2 (VII)
Candidates, total		nos	No	Selected countries	IPU2 (VIII)
Female candidates		nos, %	No	Selected countries	IPU2 (VIII)
Membership of house	By country and parliament	nos	No	Selected countries	IPU2 (VII)
Participation in parliamentary assemblies	Lower, upper chamber	nos, % % difference	No	Africa	UN46 (28)
Participation in parliamentary assemblies	Lower, upper chamber	nos, % % difference	No	World	UN17 (29)
Seats reserved for women	By country and parliament	nos	No	Selected countries	IPU2 (VII)
Women in national parliaments	By chamber	%	No	World	IPU1
Women, right to vote and access to parliament		date	No	World	IPU1
Year granted right to vote		year	No	Africa	UN46 (28)
Year granted right to vote		year	No	World	UN17 (29)
Year of right to stand for election		year	No	Africa	UN46 (28)
Year of right to stand for election		year	No	World	UN17 (29)

36 POPULATION AND VITAL STATISTICS

Subject	Categories	Units	Time series Yes/No Frequency		Territorial coverage	Source (Table no.)

36.1 BIRTH CONTROL AND FAMILY PLANNING

Subject	Categories	Units	Time series Yes/No	Frequency	Territorial coverage	Source (Table no.)
Community-based distribution programmes	By villages, population covered, services, whether charged	nos, %	No		Developing countries	PC1 (12)
Contraceptive prevalence	By personal characteristics, age	nos	No		Developing countries	PC1 (9)
Contraceptive prevalence	By method, public, private sector	nos	No		Developing countries	PC1 (10)
Contraceptive prevalence rate	By country, region	%	No		UNICEF assisted countries	UNICEF2 (-)
Contraceptive use among currently married women of reproductive age	By method used, age group	%	No		World	UN17 (7)
Contraceptive use among currently married women of reproductive age	By method used, age group	%	No		Africa	UN46 (7)
Contraceptives, percentage of couples of reproductive ages using	By country, date, and method	%	No		World	PC1 (8)
Contraceptives import regulations, supplies available and price range	By contraceptive,	nos, US$	No		Developing countries	PC1 (25)
Facilities specifically allocated for family planning services	By total, by type of facility	nos	No		Developing countries	PC1 (29)
Family planning, health and total govt budgets	By health and family planning as % of total	nat curr, %	Yes	A	Developing countries	PC1 (21)
Family planning programme expenditures	By programme function	US$	No		Developing countries	PC1 (24)
Family planning programme expenditures	By type of expenditure	US$	No		Developing countries	PC1 (23)
Family planning programme effort scores (percentage of maximum)	By effort level, programme component, contraceptive prevalence	nos, %	No		Developing countries	PC1 (11)
Family planning services, percentage of population with access to	By contraceptive	%	No		Developing countries	PC1 (14)
Family planning services, no of acceptors of	By method, by year	nos	No		Developing countries	PC1 (15)
Family planning services, payments to personnel for	By country, type of service, personnel	US$ equivalent	No		Developing countries	PC1 (27)
Family planning services and supplies, charges to acceptors of	By country and supply of service	US$	No		Developing countries	PCI (26)
Funding for family planning programmes	By source	US$	Yes	A	Developing countries	PC1 (22)
Live births and low birth weight neonates and proportions of low birth weight neonates	By country	nos, %	No		SEAR	WHO1 (21)
Personnel specifically allocated for family planning services	By total, by type of personnel	nos	No		Developing countries	PC1 (28)
Population	By birth, death rates by family planning acceptors, by country	indices nos	Yes	A	Asia and Pacific	UN43 (-)
Population and vital statistics	By urban, growth rate, life expectancy, projections, density age structure crude birth, death fertility,infant mortality, child death rates, family planning	nos, %, years, sq km	No		Developing countries	WB1 (-)
Social marketing programmes	By % population covered, contraceptives sold	%, nos	No		Developing countries	PC1 (13)

Subject	Categories	Units	Time series Yes/No Frequency		Territorial coverage	Source (Table no.)
Vital statistics for adolescent women aged 15-19	By children born, surviving, age-specific fertility, contraception	nos, %	No		Developing countries	PC1 (7)

36.2 BIRTHS AND FERTILITY - see also under General Demographic Indicators (36.4)

Subject	Categories	Units	Time series Yes/No	Frequency	Territorial coverage	Source (Table no.)
Age of woman at first birth, average		years	Yes	A	EC	EC20 (E-3)
Birth rate, crude, projections		per thou	Yes	I	World, world regions and income groups	WB5 (B-4)
Birth rate, crude projections		per thou	Yes	I	World Bank regions and country departments	WB5 (B-8)
Birth rate, projections		per thou	Yes	5yr 25yr	World, world regions and income groups. World economies and territories	WB5 (-)
Birth rate, crude	By country, region	per thou	Yes	I	UNICEF assisted	UNICEF2 (-)
Birth rate, crude	By region and country or area, medium, high and low variants	per thou	Yes	5yr	World	UN54 (35-37)
Birth rate, crude	crude birth rate, total fertility rate, medium variant	per thou, nos	Yes	I	World, major regions	UN54 (16)
Birth rate, crude		per thou	Yes	A	ASEAN member countries	ASEANS1 (1.4)
Birth rate, crude		rate, per capita	Yes	A, M	World	UN35 (2)
Birth Rate		per thou	Yes	5yr	Central and South American countries	IADB1
Birth rate		rate	No		World macro regions and regions	UN19 (1)
Birth rate		rate	No		World macro regions	UN50 (2)
Birth rates	By country	%	No		EC	EM1 (0206)
Births		nos, %	No		EC	EC69 (I.2)
Births		nos, rate	No		World	UN39 (-)
Births		per thousand	No		EC, EC regions and basic administrative units	EC9 (3.2-3.9)
Births	by country, region	nos	Yes	5yr	UNICEF assisted countries	UNICEF2 (-)
Births	By age group, total urban and rural	nos, years	No		World	UN17 (6)
Births	By age group, total, urban and rural	nos, years	No		Africa	UN46 (6)
Births	By country	nos	No		EC	EC72 (1.17)
Births and deaths	By state	nos	No		EC	EC18 (3.6)
Children born out of wedlock	By country	%	No		EC	EC72 (2.13)
Completed fertility indicator	By country, by women of childbearing age	nos	No		EC	EC35 (-)
					countries	
Crude birth rate	By country, by year	nos	Yes	A	EC	CE1 (3.1)
Crude birth rate	By country, by year	nos	Yes	A	Non-member states of EC	CE1 (3.1*)

Subject	Categories	Units	Time series Yes/No Frequency		Territorial coverage	Source (Table no.)
Crude birth rate estimates	By country	nos	No		SEAR countries	WHO1 (12)
Excess of births	Mean population	nos	Yes	A	Nordic countries	NCM1 (23/24)
Expectation of life	Specified ages, sex	age, years	No		Nordic countries	NCM1 (33)
Extra-marital births	By country, by year	nos	Yes	A	EC	CE1 (3.2)
Extra-marital births	By country, by year	nos	Yes	A	Non-member states of EC	CE1 (3.2*)
Fertility, total	Evolution	nos	Yes	A	EC	EC20 (E-6)
Fertility		rate	No		World	UN19 (4)
Fertility		rate	No		World	UN50 (15)
Fertility	By country	nos	No		EC	EC72 (1.19)
Fertility	Comparison of estimates of total fertility and life expectancy, by region	nos	No		Africa, Asia, Latin America, more developed regions	UN54 (20, 22 ,24, 26)
Fertility	Live births, live births outside marriage, total fertility, gross reproduction rate, net reproduction rate	nos, per thou	Yes	A	EC	EC20 (E-1)
Fertility and life expectancy	Comparison of population, total fertility and life expectancy	nos, %	No		World, more and less developed regions, major areas of the world	UN54 (18)
Fertility and reproduction	Age-specific	rate	Yes	A	Nordic countries	NCM1 (28)
Fertility for female generations born 1940 to 1960	By country	nos	No		EC	CE1 (3.7)
Fertility projections		per woman	Yes	5yr 25yr	World, world regions and income groups World economies and territories	WB5 (-)
Fertility rate, per woman	Life expectancy, infant mortality	per thou, years, indices	Yes	I	World	WHO2 (1)
Fertility rate, total	Children, woman by country, region	nos	Yes	I	UNICEF assisted countries	UNICEF2 (-)
Fertility rate, total	By region and country or area, medium, high and low variants	nos	Yes	5yr	World	UN54 (41-43)
Fertility rate, total	Comparison of population, total fertility and life expectancy	nos, %	No		World, more and less developed regions, major areas of the world	UN54 (18)
Fertility rate		%	No		World	UN16 (2A)
Fertility rate		%	No		World	UN16 (2A)
Fertility rate		rate	No		World	UN16 (11)
Fertility rate	By country	%	No		EC	EM1 (0211)
Fertility rate	Crude birth rate, total fertility rate, medium variant	per thou, nos	Yes	I	World, major regions	UN54 (16)
Fertility rate	Total	rate	No		Africa	UN46 (6)
Fertility rate	Total	rate	No		World	UN17 (6)
Fertility rates, projections	Total	per woman	Yes	I	World, world regions and income groups	WB5 (B-4)
Fertility rates, projections	Total	per woman	Yes	I	World Bank regions and country departments	WB5 (B-8)
Fertility rates	By %, % change	%	No		Developing countries	PC1 (4)

Subject	Categories	Units	Time series Yes/No	Frequency	Territorial coverage	Source (Table no.)
Fertility rates	By age group	live births,	Yes	A	EC	EC20 (E-9)
Fertility rates	By country, by year, by age	nos	Yes	A	EC	CE1 (3)
Fertility rates	Number of children	nos	Yes	5yr	Latin American and Caribbean countries	UN45 (11)
Infant mortality	Life expectancy, fertility	per thou, years, indices	Yes	I	World	WHO2 (1)
Live births		nos, rate	No		World	UN19 (4)
Live births		nos, rate	No		World	UN50 (15)
Live births		nos	Yes	A	EC	EC20 (E-2)
Live births		per capita	No		World	NCM1 (1)
Live births	By country, by chronol-ogical order	nos	No		EC	EC72 (2.15)
Live births	By country	nos	No		EC	EM1 (0204)
Live births	Mean population	nos	Yes	A	Nordic countries	NCM1 (23/24)
Live births and crude live-birth rates	Urban, rural	nos, rate	Yes	A	World	UN19 (9)
Live births and late foetal deaths	By sex,extra marital	no, %	Yes	A	Nordic countries	NCM1 (25)
Live births by age of mother		age, years	No		Nordic countries	NCM1 (26)
Live births by age of mother	Sex,urban, rural	age, years	No		World	UN19 (10)
Live births by parity	First, second or third births, fourth or higher order births, total, by country	nos	Yes	A	EC	EC20 (E-4)
Live births of married mothers	By country, by year, by order of birth	nos, %	Yes	A	EC	CE1 (4)
Live births outside marriage	Absolute figures, births outside marriage	nos, per thou	Yes	A	EC	EC20 (E-5)
Live-birth rates specific for age of mother	Urban, rural	age, years	No		World	UN19 (11)
Maternal mortality, estimates of, and nos of live births	By mortality ratio, live births, maternal deaths	nos	No		World	PC1 (30)
Mean age of women at birth of any child	By country, by year	nos	Yes	A	EC	CE1 (3.5)
Mean age of women at birth of any child	By country, by year	nos	Yes	A	Non-member states of EC	CE1 (3.5*)
Mean age of women at birth of first child	By country, by year	nos	Yes	A	EC	CE1 (3.4)
Mean age of women at birth of first	By country, by year	nos	Yes	A	Non-member states of EC	CE1 (3.4*)
Natality	Average annual rates	per thou	Yes	5yr	Latin American and Caribbean countries	UN45 (8)
Natural increase		rate	No		World	UN19 (4)
Natural increase		rate	No		World	UN50 (15)
Net production rate	By country, by year	nos	Yes	A	EC	CE1 (3.6)
		nos, per thousand	No		EC, USA, USSR, Canada, Japan	EC9 (3.12)
Reproduction rate, gross	Evolution	nos	Yes	A	EC	EC20 (E-7)
Reproduction rate, net	Evolution	nos	Yes	A	EC	EC20 (E-8)
Reproduction rate, net	Year when net reproduction rate reaches 1	year	No		World, world regions and income groups	WB5 (B-3)
Reproduction rate, net	Year when net reproduction rate reaches 1	year	No		World Bank regions and country departments	WB5 (B-7)

Subject	Categories	Units	Time series Yes/No Frequency		Territorial coverage	Source (Table no.)
Reproduction rate, net	Year when net reproduction rate reaches 1	year	No		World and economies	WB5 (B-2)
Reproduction rate, net		?	Yes	5yr	World, world regions and income groups	WB5 (-)
		thou women				
Total fertility rate		rate	No		Africa	UN46 (3)
Total fertility rate		rate	No		World	UN17 (3)
Total fertility rate	By country, by year	nos	Yes	A	EC	CE1 (3.3)
Total fertility rate	By country, by year	nos	Yes	A	Non-member states of EC	CE1 (3.3*)
Total fertility rate	By country	nos	No		SEAR countries	WHO1 (13)
Total fertility rates	By %, % change	%	No		Developing countries	PC1 (4)
Vital statistics for adolescent women aged 15-19	By children born, surviving, age-specific fertility, contraception	nos, %	No		Developing countries	PC1 (7)
Women of reproductive age	By age group	nos	No		World	PC1 (5)

36.3 ECONOMIC ACTIVITY - see also Section 16

Subject	Categories	Units	Time series Yes/No Frequency		Territorial coverage	Source (Table no.)
Activity rates	Sex, age	%	No		EC	EC69 (II.3)
Activity rates	Sex, age group	%	No		Africa	ILO3 (2)
Activity rates	Sex, age group	%	No		African countries	ILO3 (2)
Activity rates	Sex, age group	%	No		Latin America	ILO4 (2)
Activity rates	Sex, age group	%	No		Latin American countries	ILO4 (2)
Activity rates	Sex, age group	%	No		Northern America EC, Oceania and USSR	ILO5 (2)
Activity rates	Sex, age group	%	No		World	ILO6 (2)
Activity rates	Sex. age group	%	No		Northern America EC, Oceania and USSR	ILO5 (2)
Activity rates by major age-groups in the OECD	Observations, projections	nos, indices	Yes	5 yr	OECD	OECD4 (II.8.)
Activity rates, total in the OECD countries	Observations, projections	nos, indices	Yes	5 yr	OECD	OECD4 (II.7.)
Activity, principal characteristics of	Sex, age	nos	No		EC	EC69 (II.1)
Age distribution of the active population	Observations, projections	%	Yes	5 yr	OECD	OECD4 (II.11.)
Age range 15-64	Percentage change	%	Yes	A	OECD EC, OECD, EC,	OECD32 (1.2)
Age range 15-64	Percentage of total population	%	Yes	A	OECD EC,	OECD32 (2.1)
Dependency rate of the economically inactive population	Observations, projections	nos, indices	Yes	5 yr	OECD	OECD4 (II.12.)
Economically active	By economic sectors, by country	%, nos	Yes	A	VICES countries	VICES1 (I/2)
Economically active	Over minimum school leaving age, total, attainment	nos	No		EC	EC11 (13)
Economically active foreign born population	Occupation, sex	nos	No		World	UN19 (35)
Economically active married women as percentage of total married women in each age group	%	No			EC	EC11 (7.1)
Economically active persons aged 15 years and over	By sex and age group	nos	No		EC	EC11 (6)

Subject	Categories	Units	Time series Yes/No Frequency	Territorial coverage	Source (Table no.)
Economically active persons as percentage of total persons in each age group	Sex	%	No	EC	EC11 (6.1)
Economically active persons aged 15 years or over	By sex, age group and occupational status	nos	No	EC	EC11 (9)
Economically active population		million US$, %	Yes	World	UN55
Economically active population	By country, by agricultural population, population economically active in agriculture	nos	No	GCC region	CH1 (7.3)
Economically active population	Industry and sex	nos 1000	No	Central Africa	UN5 (3)
Economically active population	Industry and sex	nos 1000	No	East & Southern Africa	UN4 (3)
Economically active population	Industry and sex	nos 1000	No	North Africa	UN2 (3)
Economically active population	Industry and sex	nos 1000	No	West Africa	UN3 (3)
Economically active population	Sex	nos	No	EC	EC11 (1)
Economically active population	Total population, agricultural population	nos, %	Yes A	World	FAO1 (3)
Economically active population by socio-economic group	Socio-economic status	nos, %	No	EC	EC11 (12)
Economically active population by sex and occupational status	Persons, males, females	nos	No	EC	EC11 (8)
Economically inactive not in full time education	Over minimum school leaving age, total, attainment	nos	No	EC	EC11 (13)
Labour force	Ages 15-64, labour force, sex	nos	No	OECD EC, OECD,	OECD32 (D)
Labour force	By occupation	nos	No	OECD EC, OECD, EC	OECD32 (D)
Labour force	Industry group	nos, %	No	Latin American countries	ILO4 (3)
Labour force	Percentage change	%	Yes A	OECD EC, OECD, EC,	OECD32 (1.1)
Labour force	Sex, age	nos	No	EC	EC69 (II.1,2)
Labour force	Sex, age group	nos	No	Latin American countries	ILO4 (1,2)
Labour force and participation rates	By gender, by age	nos, %	No	Arabian Gulf	CH1 (5.3)
Labour force by professional status and sex	Various categories	%	Yes 10 yr	OECD	OECD20 (0.4)
Labour force growth	15 to 64 years of age	%	Yes 5yr	Latin American and Caribbean countries	UN45 (3)
Labour force, distribution of	By high, middle, low income, by sector	%	No	World	CS1 (25)
Married women and economically active married women by age group	Married, nos, % economically active	nos, %	No	EC	EC11 (7)
Non-active population	Sex, age group	nos	No	EC	EC69 (II.1)
Numbers	Industry group	nos, %	No	African countries	ILO3 (3)
Numbers	Industry group	nos, %	No	Northern America EC, Oceania and USSR	ILO5 (3)
Numbers	Sex, age group	nos	No	Africa	ILO3 (1,2)
Numbers	Sex, age group	nos	No	African countries	ILO3 (1,2)
Numbers	Sex, age group	nos	No	Latin America	ILO4 (1,2)
Numbers	Sex, age group	nos	No	Northern America EC, Oceania and USSR	ILO5 (1,2)
Numbers	Sex, age group	nos	No	Northern America, EC, Oceania and USSR	ILO5 (1,2)
Persons in employment	By sex and occupational group	nos	No	EC	EC11 (11)

Subject	Categories	Units	Time series Yes/No Frequency	Territorial coverage	Source (Table no.)
Persons in employment	By economic	nos, %	No	EC	EC11 (1)
	activity in sector		No	EC	EC11 (1)
Persons in employment	By sex and	%	No	EC	EC11 (1)
	occupational status		No	EC	EC11 (1)
Persons in employment	By sex and branch of economic activity	nos	No	EC	EC11 (10)
Proportion of females in the active population	Observations, projections	nos, indices	Yes 5 yr	OECD	OECD4 (II.10.)
Rates of growth	Sex, age group	%	No	Africa	ILO3 (1,2)
Rates of growth	Sex, age group	%	No	African countries	ILO3 (1,2)
Rates of growth	Sex, age group	%	No	Latin America	ILO4 (1,2)
Rates of growth	Sex, age group	%	No	Latin American countries	ILO4 (1,2)
Rates of growth	Sex, age group	%	No	Northern America EC, Oceania and USSR	ILO5 (1,2)
Rates of growth	Sex, age group	%	No	Northern America EC, Oceania and USSR	ILO5 (1,2)
Unemployed	Sex, age	nos, %	Yes A	EC	EC69 (II.4)

36.4 GENERAL DEMOGRAPHIC INDICATORS

Subject	Categories	Units	Time series Yes/No Frequency	Territorial coverage	Source (Table no.)
Births, deaths, marriages, divorces, and legal abortions	By country, by year	nos	Yes A	EC	CE1 (2)
Demographic indicators, principal	Births, natural increase, <15, >65, life expectancy, fertility, infant mortality rate, population density	nos, %, years	No	World, major world regions	EC20 (D-2)
Demographic indicators	Total population (1988, 2000, 2020), births, deaths, natural increase, marriages, <15, >65, life expectancy, fertility rate, infant mortality rate, density,	nos, %, nos, sq km, per thou, years	No	EC and economic groups	EC20 (D-3)
Demographic situation	Total population (1988, 2000, 2020) births, deaths, natural increase, marriages, <15, >65, life expectancy, fertility rate, infant mortality rate, density	nos, %, years, nos, sq km per thou	No	Mediterranean countries	EC20 (D-4)
Demographic situation	Total population (1988, 2000, 2020) births, deaths, natural increase, marriages, <15, >65, life expectancy, fertility rate, infant mortality rate, density	nos, %, years, nos, sq km per thou	No	Mediterranean countries	EC20 (D-4)
Main indicators	By country, by population, population change, migration, marriage rate, fertility rate, infant mortality	nos, %	No	EC	CE1 (0.1-0.2)

36 POPULATION AND VITAL STATISTICS

Subject	Categories	Units	Time series Yes/No	Frequency	Territorial coverage	Source (Table no.)
Population, vital statistics	Area, density, population, births, deaths, natural increase, migration, total increase, population; <15 years, >65 years by country, region	sq km nos, sq km per thou, %, nos	No		EC and regions	EC20 (C-1)
Population, vital statistics	Growth, birth, death, migration by region	%, per thou	Yes	5yr	Regions of Europe, Less developed regions, Africa, Asia and Latin America	UN54 (5-7)
Population and vital statistics	By urban, growth rate, life expectancy, projections, density age structure crude birth, death fertility,infant mortality, child death rates, family planning	nos, %, years, sq km	No		Developing countries	WB1 (-)
Selected demographic characteristics	By population, urban population, nos of women, dependency ratio, density	nos, population sq km	No		World	PC1 (1)
Vital statistics	By age and sex, urban, rural, birth rate, death rate, natural increase, by country	nos, per thou	Yes	A	VICES countries and Yugoslavia	VICES1 (0/2)
Vital statistics	Population, natality, general mortality, natural increase	nos, per thou	No		World	WHO2 (8)
Vital statistics	Urban population as % of total, crude birth, death rate, infant mortality, life expectancy at birth	%, nos, per thou	No		World	UNCTAD1 (6.10A)
Vital statistics: rates per 1000 population	By countries	rate	Yes	A	Europe	MAC3 (A6)
Vital statistics: rates per 1000 population	By country, births, deaths	nos	Yes	A	Africa and Asia	MAC1 (B5)
Vital statistics: rates per 1000 population	Cities	Nos	No		The Americas and Australasia	MAC2 (B5)

36.5 HOUSEHOLDS - see also Section 23

Subject	Categories	Units	Time series Yes/No	Frequency	Territorial coverage	Source (Table no.)
Average number of persons per household	By country	nos	No		EC	EC35 (-)
					countries	
Distribution of private households	By country	%	No		EC	EC72 (2.5)
Family nuclei by type and by number of children in family nucleus		nos	No		EC	EC11 (18)
Family units composed of fathers living alone with one or more children	By country, by age of children	%	No		EC	EC72 (2.19)
Family units composed of mothers living alone with one or more children	By country, by age of children	%	No		EC	EC72 (2.20)
Household heads	By sex	nos	No		World	UN16 (11)

Subject	Categories	Units	Time series Yes/No	Frequency	Territorial coverage	Source (Table no.)
Household size	In urban and rural areas	nos	No		World	UN16 (11)
Household size	Total, urban and rural rounds	nos	No		World	UN17 (5)
Household size	Total, urban and rural rounds	nos	No		Africa	UN46 (5)
Households, private	Size of household	nos	No		EC, USA, USSR Canada, Japan	EC9 (3.13)
Households, private	By household type	%	Yes	10 yr	OECD	OECD20 (0.6)
Households	By country, by region	nos, %	No		EC	EM1 (-)
Households	By country, by socio-economic category of head of household	nos	No		EC	EC35 (-)
Households	By type, composition, and economic situation, according to the socio-economic category of the head of household, the type of household, the income category, the region and the urban, rural environment, by country	%	No		EC	EC42 (1/1-1/5)
Households receiving housing allowances		%	Yes	Selected	EC	MHPPE1 (-)
Members of households	By sex and age, according to the socio-economic category of the head of household, the type of household, the income category, the region and the urban, rural environment, by country	%	No		EC	EC42 (1/1-1/5)
Numbers		nos years	Yes	Selected	EC	MHPPE1 (-)
One-person households	By country, by age, gender	%	No		EC	EC72 (2.7)
Persons in private households	Total, private, not in private, % in private	nos, %	No		EC	EC11 (14)
Population in private households	By size of household	nos	No		Latin American and Caribbean	UN45 (108)
Private households, size	Average size, distribution of households according to size	nos, %	No		Latin American and Caribbean countries	UN45 (12)
Private households, members of private households and numbers of children	By type of household	nos	No		EC	EC11 (16)
Private households	By country, by children under 15	%	No		EC	EC72 (2.17)
Private households	By total number of persons and number of economically active persons in households	nos	No		EC	EC11 (17)
Private households	By the number of persons	nos	No		EC	EC11 (1)
Private households	By total number of persons and number of persons aged under 15 years	nos	No		EC	EC11 (17.1)
Private households	By total number of persons and number of aged 65 years and over	nos	No		EC	EC11 (17.2)
Private households and members of private households	By type and size of household	nos	No		EC	EC11 (15)

Subject	Categories	Units	Time series Yes/No Frequency		Territorial coverage	Source (Table no.)
Size, distribution		%	Yes	Selected years	EC	MHPPE1 (-)
Size, average		nos	Yes	Selected years	EC	MHPPE1 (-)
Women heads of households, census	By age group rounds	nos, %	No		World	UN17 (5)
Women heads of households	By age group rounds	nos, %	No		Africa	UN46 (5)
36.6 LIFE EXPECTANCY						
At birth		years	Yes	5yr	Latin American and Caribbean countries	UN45 (10)
At birth	Crude death rate, infant mortality rate, life expectancy at birth, medium variant	per thou, years	Yes	I	World, major regions	UN54 (17)
At birth	By region and country or area, by sex	years	Yes	5yr	World	UN54 (44)
Expectation of life	Specified ages, sex	age, years	No		World	UN19 (22)
	comparison of population, total fertility and life expectancy	nos, %	No		World, more and less developed regions, major areas of the world	UN54 (18)
Expectation of life at birth	Sex	nos	No		World	UN19 (4)
Expectation of life at birth	Sex	nos	No		World	UN50 (15)
Life expectancies	Comparison of population, total fertility and life expectancy	nos, % years	No		World, more and less developed regions, major areas of the world	UN54 (18)
Life expectancy, at birth	By sex, by country/region	years	Yes	I	UNICEF assisted countries	UNICEF2 (-)
Life expectancy, estimated	By country	years	No		SEAR countries	WHO1 (15)
Life expectancy, estimates	Comparison of estimates of total fertility and life expectancy, by region	nos	No		Africa, Asia, Latin America, more developed regions	UN54 (20, 22, 24, 26)
Life expectancy		years	No		Developing countries	WBI (-)
Life expectancy		years	Yes	A	ASEAN member countries	ASEANS1 (1.6)
Life expectancy		yrs at birth	Yes	5yr	Central and South American countries	IADB1
Life expectancy	Evolution, at certain ages, males, females	years	Yes	I	EC	EC20 (G-14)
Life expectancy	At specified ages, for each sex, by country	years	No		ESCAP countries	UN44
Life expectancy	By country, by gender	years	No		EC	EM1 (0212)
Life expectancy	By country, by gender	years	No		EC	EC35 (-)
Life expectancy	By gender	years	No		EC	EC72 (1.22)
Life expectancy	By sex	rate, nos	No		World	PC1 (2)
Life expectancy	By state, by gender	years	No		EC	EC18 (3.8)
Life expectancy	Infant mortality	per thou, years, indices	Yes	I	World	WHO2 (1)
Life expectancy	By country	years	No		SEAR countries	WHO1 (16)
Life expectancy	At age X (years): 0, 1, 15, 45, 65	years	No		World	WHO2 (9)
Life expectancy at birth, projections		years	Yes	I	World, world regions and income groups	WB5 (B-4)

Subject	Categories	Units	Time series Yes/No Frequency		Territorial coverage	Source (Table no.)
Life expectancy at birth, projections		years	Yes	I	World Bank regions and country departments	WB5 (B-8)
Life expectancy at birth		years	No		World	UNCTADI (6.10A)
Life expectancy at birth	infant mortality, fertility	per thou, years, indices	Yes	I	World	WHO2 (1)
Life expectancy at certain ages, around 1980	By country, by year	nos	No		EC	CE1 (4.3)
Life expectancy at certain ages, latest available year	By country, by year	nos	No		EC	CE1 (4.4)
Life expectancy at certain ages, around 1980	By country, by year	nos	No		Non-member states	CE1 (4.3*)
Life expectancy at certain ages, latest available year	By country, by year	nos	No		Non-member states	CE1 (4.4*)
Life expectancy by sex, vital rates	By birth, death rate population growth, life expectancy	rate, nos	No		World	PC1 (2)
Number of survivors out of 100,000 at birth	to age X (years): 0, 1, 15, 45, 65	nos	No		World	WHO2 (9)
Projections	At birth, at age ten, both sexes	years	Yes	5yr 25 yr	World, world regions and income groups world economies and territories	WB5 (-)
Survivors born alive	Sex, 100,000	nos	No		Nordic countries	NCM1 (34)
36.7 MARRIAGE AND DIVORCE						
Age at first marriage, average	Evolution, males, females	years	Yes	A	EC	EC20 (F-5)
Age at first marriage, average	By sex	years	No		World	UN16 (10)
Age at marriage, average	Evolution, males, females	years	Yes	A	EC	EC20 (F-3)
Divorce rate, crude	By country, by year	nos	Yes	A	EC	CE1 (2.4)
Divorce rate, total	By country, by year	nos	Yes	A	EC	CE1 (2.5)
Divorce rate, crude	By country, by year	nos	Yes	A	Non-member states of EC	CE1 (2.4*)
Divorce rate, total	By country, by year	nos	Yes	A	Non-member states of EC	CE1 (2.5*)
Divorce rate	By country	%	No		EC	EM1 (0210)
Divorces		nos, rate	No		Worlds	UN50 (15)
Divorces		nos, rate	No		World	UN19 (4)
Divorces		nos	Yes	A	EC	EC20 (F-1)
Divorces	By country	nos	No		EC	EC72 (2.11)
Divorces	Evolution, number per thou population	per thou	Yes	A	EC	EC20 (F-7)
Divorces	Evolution, number per thou existing marriages	per thou	Yes	A	EC	EC20 (F-8)
Divorces	Evolution	nos	Yes	A	EC	EC20 (F-6)
Divorces	Total	nos	Yes	A	Nordic countries	NCM1 (37)
Divorces and crude divorce rates		nos, rate	Yes	A	World	UN19 (25)
Marital status	By age group and sex, by average age at first marriage, by sex	years, %,	No		World	UN17 (4)
Marital status	By age group and sex, by average age at first marriage, by sex	years, %	No		Africa	UN46 (4)

36 POPULATION AND VITAL STATISTICS

Subject	Categories	Units	Time series Yes/No	Frequency	Territorial coverage	Source (Table no.)
Marital status	By sex and age group	%	No		World	UN16 (10)
Marriage rate, crude	By country, by year	nos	Yes	A	EC	CE1 (2.1)
Marriage rate, crude	By country, by year	nos	Yes	A	Non-member states of EC	CE1 (2.1*)
Marriage rate for females below the age of 50	By country, by year	nos	Yes	A	EC	CE1 (2.2)
Marriage rate for females below the age of 50	By country, by year	nos	Yes	A	Non-member states of EC	CE1 (2.2*)
Marriages, first	Per unmarried, sex, age	nos	Yes	A	Nordic countries	NCM1 (36)
Marriages, first	Evolution, males, females	nos	Yes	A	EC	EC20 (F-4)
Marriages		nos, rate	No		World	UN50 (15)
Marriages		nos, rate	No		World	UN19 (4)
Marriages		nos,	No		EC, USA, USSR	EC9 (3.12)
Marriages		rate	Yes	A, M	World	UN35 (4)
Marriages	Age, bride, groom	age, years	No		World	UN19 (24)
Marriages	By country	nos	No		EC	EC72 (2.8)
Marriages	Marriages, average age at marriage, persons marrying for the first time, average age at first marriage, divorces	nos, years, per thou	Yes	A	EC	EC20 (F-1)
Marriages	Total, mean population	nos	Yes	A	Nordic countries	NCM1 (35)
Marriages and crude marriage rates	Urban and rural	nos, rate	Yes	A	World	UN19 (23)
Marriages and gross marriage rate	Evolution, absolute figures, rate	nos, per thou	Yes	A	EC	EC20 (F-2)
Marrige rate	By country	%	No		EC	EM1 (0209)
Mean age of women at first marriage	By country, by year	nos	Yes	A	EC	CE1 (2.3)
Mean age of women at first marriage	By country, by year	nos	Yes	A	Non-member states of EC	CE1 (2.3*)
		per thousand			Canada, Japan	
Women married, cohabiting	By age group	%	No		Developing countries	PC1 (6)

36.8 MIGRATION - see also Sections 31 and 39

Subject	Categories	Units	Time series Yes/No	Frequency	Territorial coverage	Source (Table no.)
Emigration from Europe	By decades	nos	Yes	10 yr	EC	MAC3 (A8)
Foreign-born population	Sex	%	No		World	UN16 (2B)
Incidence of active population migration average annual rate of variation due to migration		nos	Yes	5 yr	OECD	OECD4 (II.9.2.)
Incidence of active population migration average annual incidence		nos	Yes	5 yr	OECD	OECD4 (II.9.1.)
Inter-regional migration	From, to, total	nos	No		EC	EC69 (I.4)
Internal migrations	Cities	nos	No		The Americas and Australasia	MAC2 (B7)
International migration	By country, by year	nos	No		EC	CE1 (5)
Migration	Cities	nos	Yes	A	EC	MAC3 (A9)
Migration rate, net international		per 1000	No		World	UN16 (2B)
Migration rate, net international		per 1000	No		World	UN16 (2B
Migration rate		per thous	No		EC, EC Regions and basic administrative units	EC9 (3.2-3.9)
Migration rates	By region	%, per thou	Yes	5yr	Regions of Europe, less developed regions, Africa, Asia and Latin America	UN54 (5-7)
National and ethnic groups, principal		%	No		World	UN16 (2B)

Subject	Categories	Units	Time series Yes/No	Frequency	Territorial coverage	Source (Table no.)
Natural and migratory rates of increase	Observations, projections	nos	Yes	5 yr	OECD	OECD4 (I.10.)
Net migration		Nos, %	No		EC	EC69 (I.2)
Net migration		per thou	Yes	A	EC	EC20(A-3)
Net migration	By country, by year	%	Yes	A	EC	CE1 (1.4)
Refugees		nos	No		World	UN16 (2B)

36.9 MORTALITY - see also under General Demographic Indicators (36.4)

Subject	Categories	Units	Time series Yes/No	Frequency	Territorial coverage	Source (Table no.)
Below 5 years of age, projections	Probability, both sexes	ratio	Yes	5yr	World, world regions and income groups World economies and territories	WB5 (-)
Causes	By sex and age, by country	per thou	No		World	WHO2 (10)
Causes of death	By cause, males, females	nos	Yes	I	EC	EC20 (G-15)
Causes, chances of dying from	By cause of death, at selected ages, by sex	per thou	No		World	WHO2 (9)
Child death rate		nos	No		Developing countries	WB1 (-)
Child, under 5's	Deaths, rate, by country, region	nos, per thou	Yes	5yr	UNICEF assisted countries	UNICEF2 (-)
Death	By countries per 1000 population	rate	Yes	A	EC	MAC3 (A6)
Deaths		nos	No		Developing countries	WB1 (-)
Deaths		nos	No		EC and economic groups	EC20 (D-3)
Deaths		nos	No		EC and regions	EC20 (C-1)
Deaths		nos	No		Mediterranean countries	EC20 (D-4)
Deaths		nos, %	No		EC	EC69 (I.2)
Deaths		nos, rate	No		World	UN19 (4)
Deaths		nos, rate	No		World	UN50 (15)
Deaths		per thou	No		EC, EC Regions and basic administrative units	EC9 (3.2-3.9)
Deaths	Age, sex, urban, rural	age, years	No		World	UN19 (19)
Deaths	By age group and sex	nos	No		EC	EC20 (G-3)
Deaths	By cause	nos	No		EC	EC69 (VII.2)
Deaths	By country	nos	No		EC	EM1 (0205)
Deaths	By major causes	nos	Yes	A	ASEAN member countries	ASEANS1 (9.4.4)
Deaths	By major causes, by country	nos	Yes	A	ESCAP countries	UN44
Deaths	Evolution, males, females	nos	Yes	A	EC	EC20(G-2)
Deaths	Mean population	nos	Yes	A	Nordic countries	NCM1 (23/24)
Deaths	Per thou population of each age group, males, females	per thou	No		EC	EC20 (G-4)
Deaths	Sex, age, mean population	nos	No		Nordic countries	NCM1 (29/30)
Deaths	Total, infant	nos, rate	No		World	UN39 (-)
Death rate		per thou	Yes	5 yr	Central and South American countries	IADB1

Subject	Categories	Units	Time series Yes/No Frequency		Territorial coverage	Source (Table no.)
Death rate		per thou	Yes	A	VICES countries and Yugoslavia	VICES1 (0/2)
Death rate		rate	No		World macro regions and regions	UN19 (1)
Death rate		rate	No		World macro regions and regions	UN50 (2)
Death rate	Crude death rate, infant mortality rate, life expectancy at birth, medium variant	per thou, years	Yes	I	World, major regions	UN54 (17)
Death rate, crude		per thou	Yes	A	ASEAN member countries	ASEANS1 (1.4)
Death rate, crude		rate, per capita	Yes	A/M	World	UN35 (3)
Death rate, crude	By country, by year	nos	Yes	A	EC	CE1 (4.1)
Death rate, crude	By country, by year	nos	Yes	A	Non-member states of EC	CE1 (4.1*)
Death rate, crude	By country, region	per thou	Yes	I	UNICEF assisted countries	UNICEF2 (-)
Death rate, crude	By region and country or area, medium, high and low variants	per thou	Yes	5yr	World	UN54 (38-40)
Death rate, crude, estimated	By country	nos	No		SEAR countries	WHO1 (14)
Death rate, infant mortality	By region and country or area, medium variant	per thou	Yes	5yr	World	UN54 (45)
Death rates		per 1000 population	Yes	A	Africa and Asia	MAC1 (B5)
Death rates	By country	%	No		EC	EM1 (0207)
Death rates	By region	per thou	Yes	5yr	Regions of Europe, less developed regions, Africa, Asia and Latin America	UN54 (5-7)
Death rates	Cities	per 1000 population	No		The Americas and Australasia	MAC2 (B5)
Death rates, specific	Age, sex, urban, rural	age, years	No		World	UN19 (20)
Deaths and crude death rates	Urban, rural	nos, rate	Yes	A	World	UN19 (18)
Deaths and death rates	Cause, 1965 revision	nos, rate	No		World	UN19 (21)
Deaths and death rates	Cause, 1975 revision	nos, rate	No		World	UN19 (21)
Deaths of infants under one year old per 1,000 live births	By country	nos	Yes	A	Africa and Asia	MAC1 (B6)
Fatalities	By country, by cause of death	nos	No		EC	EC18 (4.2)
Foetal deaths and ratios, late	Urban, rural	nos, ratio	Yes	A	World	UN19 (12)
Foetal deaths, late	By sex, extra marital	no, %	Yes	A	Nordic countries	NCM1 (25)
Infant and child mortality rates	By infant/under-5 mortality rates, number of deaths	nos	No		Developing countries	PC1 (34)
Infant deaths		nos	Yes	A	Nordic countries	NCM1 (31)
Infant deaths		nos, rate	No		World	UN19 (4)
Infant deaths	By country, by major cause group	%	No		Selected countries	WHO1 (27a,b)
Infant deaths and infant mortality rates	Age, sex, urban, rural	nos, rate	No		World	UN19 (16)
Infant deaths and infant mortality rates	Urban, rural	nos, rate	Yes	A	World	UN19 (15)
Infant deaths, causes	By sex and age, by country	nos, %	No		World	WHO2 (12)
Infant deaths, under 28 days		nos	Yes	A	EC	EC20 (G-7)
Infant deaths, under 28 days	Per thou live births	per thou	Yes	A	EC	EC20 (G-8)
Infant deaths, under 7 days		nos	Yes	A	EC	EC20 (G-9)
Infant deaths, under 7 days	Per thou live births	per thou	Yes	A	EC	EC20 (G-10)

Subject	Categories	Units	Time series Yes/No Frequency		Territorial coverage	Source (Table no.)
Infant deaths, under one year		nos	Yes	A	EC	EC20 (G-5)
Infant deaths, under one year	Deaths, rate, by country, region	nos, per thou	Yes	5yr	UNICEF assisted countries	UNICEF2 (-)
Infant deaths, under one year	Per thou live births	per thou	Yes	A	EC	EC20 (G-6)
Infant mortality		nos	No		Developing countries	WB1 (-)
Infant mortality		nos, per thous	No		EC, USA, USSR Canada, Japan	EC9 (3.12)
Infant mortality		per thou	No		World	UNCTAD1 (6.10A)
Infant mortality	Average annual rates	per thou	Yes	5yr	Latin American and Caribbean countries	UN45 (26)
Infant mortality	By country	nos	No		EC	EC72 (1.29)
Infant mortality	By country, by year	nos	Yes	A	EC	CE1 (4.2)
Infant mortality	By country, by year	nos	Yes	A	Non-member states of EC	CE1 (4.2*)
Infant mortality	By state	nos	No		EC	EC18 (3.7)
Infant mortality	Life expectancy, fertility	per thou, years, indices	Yes	I	World	WHO2 (1)
Infant mortality estimated	By country	nos	No		SEAR countries	WHO1 (24)
Infant mortality estimated by ESCAP, UNICEF and the WB	By country	nos	No		SEAR countries	WHO1 (26)
Infant mortality rate		per thou	Yes	5yr	Central and South American countries	IADB1
Infant mortality rate		per thous	No		EC and economic groups	EC20 (D-3)
Infant mortality rate		per thous	No		Mediterranean countries	EC20 (D-4)
Infant mortality rate		per thous	No		World, major world regions	EC20 (D-2)
Infant mortality rate	By country	%	No		EC	EM1 (0208)
Infant mortality rate, projections	Per thou live births	per thou	Yes	I	World Bank regions and country departments	WB5 (B-8)
Infant mortality rate, projections	Per thou live births	per thou	Yes	I	World, world regions and income groups	WB5 (B-4)
Infant mortality rate, projections	Per thou live births, both sexes	per thou	Yes	5yr, 25yr	World, world regions and income groups World economies and territories	WB5 (-)
Infant mortality rates	Cities	nos	No		The Americas and Australasia	MAC2 (B6)
Infant mortality rates	Cities	nos	Yes	A	EC	MAC3 (A7)
Infant mortality reported	By country	nos	No		SEAR countries	WHO1 (25)
Maternal deaths and maternal mortality rates		nos, rate	Yes	A	World	UN19 (17)
Maternal mortality rate	By country, region	per hun thou	No		UNICEF assisted countries	UNICEF2 (-)
Maternal mortality rates	By country	nos	No		SEAR countries	WHO1 (31)
Maternal mortality, estimates of and nos of live births	By mortality ratio, live births, maternal deaths	nos	No		World	PC1 (30)
Morbidity leading causes of	By country, by rank order	nos	No		SEAR countries	WHO1 (32)
Mortality		per thou	No		World countries	WHO2 (8)
Mortality	Average annual rates	per thou	Yes	5yr	Latin American and Caribbean countries	UN45 (9)

36 POPULATION AND VITAL STATISTICS

Subject	Categories	Units	Time series Yes/No	Frequency	Territorial coverage	Source (Table no.)
Mortality	Total mortality, infant mortality by age	nos, per thou	Yes	A	EC	EC20(G-1)
Mortality leading causes of	By country, by rank order	nos	No		SEAR countries	WHO1 (33)
Mortality rates	By country, by gender,	nos	No		EC	EC72 (1.27)
Mortality rates	By infant rate, perinatal rate	nos	No		Selected countries	WHO1 (23)
Perinatal deaths and death rates	By country, by year	nos	No		Selected countries	WHO1 (22)
Perinatal mortality	By country	nos	No		EC	EC72 (1.31)
Perinatal mortality rate	Per thou live births plus	per thou	Yes	A	EC	EC20 (G-13)
Population	By birth, death rates by family planning acceptors, by country	indices nos	Yes	A	Asia and Pacific	UN43 (-)
Rate, crude, projections		per thou	Yes	I	World Bank regions and country departments	WB5 (B-8)
Rate, crude, projections		per thou	Yes	I	World, world regions and income groups	WB5 (B-4)
Rate, per woman	Life expectancy, infant mortality	per thou, years, indices	Yes	I	World	WHO2 (1)
Rate, projections		per thou	Yes	5yr, 25yr	World, world regions and income groups. World economies and territories	WB5 (-)
Rates for selected causes	By sex, age standardized still births	per thou	No		World	WHO2 (11)
Still births		nos	Yes	A	EC	EC20 (G-11)
Still births	Per thou live births plus still births	per thou	Yes	A	EC	EC20 (G-12)
Stillbirths and infant mortality		nos	Yes	A	Nordic countries	NCM1 (32)
Under-five mortality rate	By birthweight, % of breast-feeding mothers, type of illness, food production, calorie supply, % household income	%, index	No		World	UNICEF1 (2)
Under-five mortality rate	Very high, high, middle low	US$, %	No		World	UNICEF1 (6)
Under-five mortality rates	By country, by gender	nos	No		SEAR countries	WHO1 (30)
Under-five mortality rates estimated	By country	nos	No		SEAR countries	WHO1 (28)
Under-five mortality rates reported	By country	nos	No		SEAR countries	WHO1 (29)
36.10 POPULATION						
36.10.1 Size and Structure						
Activity, principal characteristics of	Sex, age	nos	No		EC	EC69 (II.1)
Activity, by type	Various categories	%	Yes	10 yr	OECD	OECD20 (0.3)
Activity rate		%	Yes	A	EC	EC65 (-)
Activity rates	Observations, projections	nos, indices	Yes	5 yr	OECD	OECD4 (II.7.)
Activity rates	Sex, age group	%	No		World	ILO6 (2)
Activity rates	Sex, age group	%	No		Asian countries	ILO2 (2)
Activity rates by major age-groups	Observations, projections	nos, indices	Yes	5 yr	OECD	OECD4 (II.8.)

Subject	Categories	Units	Time series Yes/No	Frequency	Territorial coverage	Source (Table no.)
Administrative divisions, major, population of	By countries	nos	No		The Americas and Australasia	MAC2 (B3)
Adopted children	Sex, age, country of birth	nos	No		Nordic countries	NCM1 (27)
Age, sex, sex ratio for all ages		nos	No		World macro regions and regions	UN19 (2)
Age		%			Canada, Japan	(3.10-3.11)
Age	By age	nos	Yes	A	EC	EC29 (I/3)
Age	By country, by age	nos	No		EC	EC72 (1.9)
Age	Percentage of total for under 15 years, 15 to 64 years and 65 years plus	%	Yes	A	OECD	OECD19 (I)
Age	Total, under 15 years, from 15 to 64 years, 65 years plus, total male and female	nos	Yes	A	OECD	OECD19 (I)
Age 15-24 years	By sex	nos	Yes	A	EC	EC29 (I/2)
Age and sex		nos 1000	No		Central Africa	UN5 (2)
Age and sex		nos 1000	No		East & Southern Africa	UN4 (2)
Age and sex		nos 1000	No		North Africa	UN2 (2)
Age and sex		nos 1000	No		West Africa	UN3 (2)
Age and sex	By age and sex	nos, %	No		EC	EC20 (B-2-20)
Age breakdown	By country	nos, %	No			EM1 (0220)
Age distribution	By sex, age	%, index	No		EC	EC65 (-)
Age distribution of the active population percentages for age groups	Observations, projections	%	Yes	5 yr	OECD	OECD4 (II.11.)
Age of distribution		%	No		EC	MHPPE1 (-)
Age of population, median	By country	years	No		SEAR countries	WHO1 (6)
Age range 15-64	Percentage of total population	%	Yes	A	OECD, EC	OECD32 (2.1)
Age ranges		%	Yes		World	UN55
Age structure		nos	No		Developing countries	WB1 (-)
Age structure	Various categories	%	Yes	10 yr	OECD	OECD20 (0.2)
Ages, from 15 to 64 years old	Total and as a percentage of total population	nos, %	Yes	A	OECD, OECD countries and EC	OECD19 (2.0)
	Area	nos	No		EC, EC Regions and basic administrative units	EC9 (3.2-3.9)
By age and sex		nos, per thou	Yes	A	VICES countries and Yugoslavia	VICES1 (0/20)
By sex, age group and male, female ratio		nos, % years	Yes	Selected	World	UN16 (1)
Children	By country	nos	No		EC	EM1 (0217)
Cities, population of major	By city	nos	Yes	10 yr	Africa and Asia	MAC1 (B4)
Cities, population of major	Cities	nos	No		The Americas and Australasia	MAC2 (B4)
Cities, selected	By city	nos	No		EC	EC18 (3.11)
Cities, capital	City proper, urban	nos	No		World	UN19 (8)
Citizenship	Sex	nos	No		Nordic countries	NCM1(14)
City, largest	% AGR.	nos, %	Yes	10 yr	World	UN26
City, largest	Sex	nos	No		World	UN16 (3)
Community size	Various categories	%	Yes	10 yr	OECD countries	OECD20 (0.5) (1.2)
Density		inhabitants, sq km	Yes	A	EC	EC65 (-)
Density		inhabitants per sq km	Yes	A	OECD, World	OECD33 (14.3)
Density		no per sq km	No		World, EC, USA, USSR, Japan	EC9 (3.1)

Subject	Categories	Units	Time series Yes/No Frequency		Territorial coverage	Source (Table no.)
Density		nos, sq km	No		World, major world regions	EC20 (D-2)
Density		nos, per sq km	No		EC	MHPPE1 (-)
Density		per km	Yes	A	EC	EC34 (2.3)
Density		per sq km	No		Developing countries	WB1 (-)
Density		per sq km	No		World, macro regions	UN19 (1)
Density		per sq km	No		World	UN19 (3)
Density		per sq km	No		World	UN50 (14)
Density		per sq km	No		World macro regions and regions	UN50 (2)
Density		sq km	No		World	UNCTAD5 (-)
Density	Area, density nos, sq km	sq km	No		World and economic regions	UNCTAD1 (6.1)
Density	Area, GNP per capita	sq km, US$, nos, sq km	No		OPEC countries	OPEC1 (2)
Density	By country, by area	sq km, nos	No		EC	EC35 (-)
Density	By country	nos, sq km	No		EC	EM1 (0213)
Density	By country	nos	No		EC	EC72 (1.16)
Density	By region, by area	sq km, nos	No		SEAR countries	WHO1 (3)
Density	Mid-year estimates	per sq km, per capita	No		World	NCM1 (1)
Density	Mid-year estimates	per sq km	Yes	5 yr	World	UNESCO1 (1.1)
Dependency, demographic	Population <15 and >64 as % of population between 15 and 64 years of age	%	Yes	A	Latin American and Caribbean countries	UN45 (2)
Dependency rate of the economically inactive population	Observations, projections	nos, indices	Yes	5 yr	OECD	OECD4 (II.12.)
Dependency ratios	By country	nos	No		SEAR countries	WHO1 (18)
Dependency ratios and ageing indices	By country, by age group	%	No		EC	CE1 (1.6)
Distribution	By region	%	Yes	I	World	UN54 (9)
Economically active	Over minimum school leaving age, total, attainment	nos	No		EC	EC11 (13)
Economically active foreign born population	Occupation,sex	nos	No		World	UN19 (35)
Economically active married women as percentage of total married women in each age group		%	No		EC	EC11 (7.1)
Economically active persons	% of total persons in each age group by sex	%	No		EC	EC11 (6.1)
Economically active persons aged 15 years and over by sex and age group	Persons, males, females	nos	No		EC	EC11 (6)
Economically active persons aged 15 years or over by sex, age group and occupational status	Males, females	nos	No		EC	EC11 (9)
Economically active population by socio-economic group	Socio-economic status	nos, %	No		EC	EC11 (12)
Economically active population by sex and occupational status	Persons, males, females	nos	No		EC	EC11 (8)
Economically inactive not in full time education	Over minimum school leaving age,total, attainment	nos	No		EC	EC11 (13)
Females		%	No		EC	EC11 (1)
Females	By country	nos	No		EC	EM1 (0216)
Females in the active population	Observations, projections	nos, indices	Yes	5 yr	OECD	OECD4 (II.10.)
Females per 100 males	By age	%	No		EC	EC11 (1)
Foreign born	By sex	%	No		Africa	UN46 (3)
Foreign born	By sex	%	No		World	UN17 (3)

Subject	Categories	Units	Time series Yes/No Frequency		Territorial coverage	Source (Table no.)
Foreign born population by country or area of birth	Age, sex	age, years	No		World	UN19 (32)
Foreign born population in country or area for less than five years	Country of birth, age, sex	age, years	No		World	UN19 (33)
Foreign citizenship	By country, by year	nos	Yes	A	EC	CE1 (6)
Foreign nationals		nos, %	No		EC	EC65 (-)
Foreign resident	Total member countries, non-member countries	nos	Yes	A	EC	EC29 (I/4)
Foreign residents	Total, males females, by nationality	nos	No		EC	EC20 (H-1-3)
Foreign-born population	Sex	%	No		World	UN16 (2B)
Foreign-born population	Sex	%	No		World	UN16 (2B)
Inactive population, total population and dependency rate of with and without migration		Nos	No		OECD	OECD4 (II.13.)
Inactive population, variation due to migration and the dependency rate of	Relative variation in total population	%	No		OECD	OECD4 (II.14.)
Inactive population, variation in the dependency rate of		%	No		OECD	OECD4 (II.14.)
Income	By high, middle, low income, by area, by age	%	No		World	CS1 (24)
Industry group		nos, %	No		World	ILO6 (3)
Industry group		nos, %	No		Asian countries	ILO2 (3)
Labour Force	By occupation	nos	No		OECD, EC	OECD32 (D)
Localities, large	By population size	nos	No		World	UN16 (4)
Locality, size of		nos, %	No		World	UN16 (4)
Males	By country	nos	No		EC	EM1 (0215)
Married women and economically active married women by age group	Married, nos, % economically active	nos, %	No		EC	EC11 (7)
Migration rate, net international		per 1000	No		World	UN16 (2B)
Municipalities, biggest	Land area, sex, country	nos	No		Nordic countries	NCM1(19)
National and ethnic groups, principal		%	No		World	UN16 (2B)
Nationality	By gender	%, nos	No		Arabian Gulf	CH1 (5.8)
Nationality	Persons, males	nos	No		EC	EC11 (4)
Native and foreign-born population	Age, sex, urban, rural residence	age,years	No		World	UN19 (31)
Non-nationals as percentage of total population in each age group	Persons, males, females	%	No		EC	EC11 (5.2)
Non-nationals by sex and age group	Persons, males, females	nos	No		EC	EC11 (5)
Non-nationals: percentage distribution by age group	Persons, males, females	%	No		EC	EC11 (5.1)
Numbers	Age, sex	age, years	No		World	UN19 (7)
Numbers	Urban, rural residence residences	age, years	No		World	UN19 (7)
Percentage single in each age group	By age, sex	%	No		EC	EC11 (3.1)
Persons aged 65 and over	By country	nos	No		EC	EM1 (0219)
Persons in employment by sex and branch of economic activity	Branch, persons males, females	nos	No		EC	EC11 (10)
Persons in employment by sex and occupational group	By type of employment persons, males, females	nos	No		EC	EC11 (11)
Persons of working age	By country	nos	No		EC	EM1 (0218)
Population, estimates of	By nationality, by age	nos	No		Arabian Gulf	CH1 (5.2)
Population, estimated	By gender, by Kuwaiti, non-Kuwaiti	nos	No		Arabian Gulf	CH1 (5.7)
Population, total		nos	Yes	A	EC, USA and Japan	EC60 (O)
Population, occupied		nos	Yes	A	EC, USA and Japan	EC60 (O)
Population, esimated	By region	nos	No		SEAR countries	WHO1 (1)

36 POPULATION AND VITAL STATISTICS

Subject	Categories	Units	Time series Yes/No Frequency		Territorial coverage	Source (Table no.)
Population, most populous countries ranking	By country, by population, size, medium variant	nos	No		World	WHO1 (2)
Population, United Nations estimate	By state	nos	No		EC	EC18 (3.4)
Population, estimated mid-year		nos	Yes	A	World	UN19 (5)
Population, estimated mid-year		per sq km	No		World	NCM1 (1)
Population, estimated mid-year		nos	Yes	A	World	UN35 (1)
Population, mid-year	By country	Per capita	Yes	A	Asia and Pacific	UN43 (-)
Population, estimated	By sex and age group, mid-year	nos	No		Latin American and Caribbean countries	UN45 (106)
Population, mid-year	By region and country or area, medium variant	nos	Yes	A	World	UN54 (34)
Population, resident	By country, by EC foreigners, nationals	nos, %	No		EC	EC72 (1.32&33)
Population, EC	By age group	%		No	EC	EC35 (-)
Population, resident	By country, by community, non-community	nos, %	No		EC	EC35 (-)
Population, total		nos	Yes	A	EC	EC20 (B-1)
Population, 1970-1981	By country	nos	No		Arabian Gulf	CH1 (5.1)
Population, density	Population growth rates	nos, per sq km, %	Yes	A	World, ASEAN member countries	ASEANS1 (1.1)
Population, density	Population, <15 years, >65 years by country, region	nos, sq km	No		EC and regions	EC20 (C-1)
Population						
Population, share in world		% years	Yes	Selected	World, by development groups	UNCTAD5 (2.1)
Population		nos	No		EC	EM1 (-)
Population		nos	No		ECMT countries	ECMT1 (2
Population		nos	No		VICES countries and Yugoslavia	VICES1 (0/1)
Population		nos	Yes	A, M	World	IMF6 (-)
Population		nos	Yes	A, M	World	IMF7 (-)
Population		nos	Yes	A	EC	EC65 (-)
Population		nos	Yes	A	EC	EC73 (12)
Population		nos	Yes	A	EC by region	EC65 (-)
Population		nos	Yes	A	ESCAP region, developing ESCAP region	UN44 (p5,10)
Population		nos	Yes	A	OECD, World	OECD33 (14.1)
Population		nos	Yes	A	OPEC countries	OPEC1 (1)
Population		nos	Yes	A	World, ESCAP countries, developing ESCAP countries	UN44 (p1)
Population		nos	Yes	A/M	World	IMF6 (-)
Population		nos	Yes	A/M	World	IMF7 (-)
Population		nos	No		World	WHO2 (8)
Population		per thou	No		EC	WC1 (-)
Population		sq km, nos, %	Yes	A	World, ASEAN member countries	ASEANS1 (1.1)
Population	% urban	%	No		Developing countries	UNCTAD5 (1.4)
Population	Age and sex	nos %	No		EC, USA, USSR, Canada, Japan	EC9 (3.10-3.11)
Population	By age and sex	nos	No		ASEAN member	ASEANS1
Population	By country, by agricultural population, population economically active in agriculture	nos	No		GCC region	CH1 (7.3)
Population	By country, by region	nos	No		EC	EM1 (-)

Subject	Categories	Units	Time series Yes/No Frequency	Territorial coverage	Source (Table no.)
Population	By country, by age, gender	nos, %	No	EC	EC18 (3.9)
Population	By country, by age group	%	No	EC	EC35 (-)
Population	By country population change, area and density, by age and sex	nos, sq km, years	Yes A	ESCAP countries	UN44
Population	By country	nos	Yes A	Selected countries	ITC1 (-)
Population	By country	nos	Yes A	World	ISTA2(-)
Population	By sex	nos	Yes 10 A	Nordic countries	NCM1 (7)
Population	By sex and age	nos	Yes 10 A	Nordic countries	NCM1 (7/11)
Population	By sex and age	nos	Yes 10 A	Nordic countries	NCM1 (9/10)
Population	By type	nos	No	Nordic countries	NCM1 (20)
Population	Distribution, annual	nos, %	Yes I	Major regions worldwide	UN54 (14)
Population	Labour force and participation rates, by gender, by age	nos, %	No	Arabian Gulf	CH1 (5.3)
Population	Latest official estimate, latest population census, mid-year estimate	nos	No	World	UN39 (-)
Population	Mid-year total	nos,1000	Yes A	North Africa	UN2 (1-1)
Population	Mid-year total	nos,1000	Yes A	West Africa	UN3 (1-1)
Population	Mid-year total	nos,1000	Yes A	East & Southern Africa	UN4 (1-1)
Population	Mid-year total	nos,1000	Yes A	Central Africa	UN5 (1-1)
Population	Total, sex ratio, age ranges, urban and annual growth rate	millions,%	Yes	World	UN55
Population	Total, average annual growth in %	nos, %	No	World	UNCTAD5 (-)
Population	Total mid-year and urban	nos 1000,%	Yes A	North Africa	UN2 (1)
Population	Total mid-year and urban	nos 1000,%	Yes A	West Africa	UN3 (1)
Population	Total mid-year and urban	nos 1000,%	Yes A	East & Southern Africa	UN4 (1)
Population	Total mid-year and urban	nos 1000,%	Yes A	Central Africa	UN5 (1)
Population aged 15 years or over by sex, age group and marital status	Males, females	nos	No	EC	EC11 (3)
Population aged 15+ by sex and marital status	Males,females	%	No	EC	EC11 (1)
			No	EC	EC11 (1)
Population aged 60 years and more	By country	nos	No	SEAR countries	WHO1 (67)
Population and area	By state, by capital	sq km, nos	No	EC	EC18 (3.1)
Population at the last census	By state	nos	No	EC	EC18 (3.2)
Population by citizenship	Sex, urban, rural	nos	No	World	UN19 (34)
Population by income	By high, middle, low income	nos, years	No	World	CS1 (29)
Population by major age groups	By country, by surface area	nos, sq km	No	EC	CE1 (1.5)
Population by sex and age group	By countries	nos	No	The Americas and Australasia	MAC2(B2)
Population density		per sq km	No	VICES countries and Yugoslavia	VICES1 (0/1)
Population density		per sq km	Yes A	EC by region	EC65 (-)
Population density		per sqkm	No	ECMT countries	ECMT1 (3)
Population density	Growth rates	per sq km	Yes A	World, ASEAN member countries	ASEANS1 (1.1)
Population distribution	By country, by type of household	%	No	EC	EC72 (2.2)
Population estimates	By countries	nos	Yes A	EC	MAC3 (A5)
Population estimates	Comparison of population estimates by region	nos	No	Africa, Asia, Latin America, more developed regions	UN54 (19,21,23,25)

Subject	Categories	Units	Time series Yes/No Frequency	Territorial coverage	Source (Table no.)
Population in census years	By Kuwaiti, non-Kuwaiti, by gender	nos	No	Arabian Gulf	CH1 (5.6)
Population of countries	By country, gender	nos	Yes 10 yr	Africa and Asia	MAC1 (B1)
Population of countries at censuses	By countries	nos	No	The Americas and Australasia	MAC2 (B1)
Population of countries at censuses	By countries	nos	Yes A	EC	MAC3 (A1)
Population of major administrative divisions	By division	nos	Yes dec A	Africa and Asia	MAC1 (B3)
Population of major cities	Cities	nos	Yes 10 yr	EC	MAC3 (A4)
Population of major countries	By country, gender, age	nos	No	Africa and Asia	MAC1 (B2)
Population of major districts	By countries	nos	Yes A	EC	MAC3 (A3)
Population of working age		nos	No	VICES countries and Yugoslavia	VICES1 (0/1)
Population on 1st January	By country, by year	nos	Yes A	EC	CE1 (1.1)
Population on January 1st	By country,by sex, age group	nos, %	Yes A	EC	CE1 (1)
Population policies	By country, population growth		No	SEAR countries	WHO1 (4)
Refugees		nos	No	World	UN16 (2B)
Resident employees, characteristics of	By sex, age, employees full time, part-time, temporary	%	No	EC by region	EC65 (-)
Rural		%	Yes 5yr	Central and South American countries	IADB1
Rural	% AGR	nos, %	Yes 10 yr	World	UN26
Settlements, population	Proportion of population living in settlements >100 000 inhabitants, < 2 000 inhabitants	%	Yes 10yr	EC	EC34 (2.15-2.16)
Sex, urban, rural and density	Total population	nos	No	Nordic countries	NCM1(18)
Sex, age group		nos	No	World	ILO6 (1,2)
Sex, age group		nos	No	World	ILO6 (1,2)
Sex, age group		nos	No	Asian countries	ILO2 (1,2)
Sex		nos		Africa	UN46 (31A)
Sex		nos	No	EC, USA, USSR,	EC9
Sex		nos	Yes	World	UN19 (3)
Sex and age		age, years	No	EC	EC69 (I.3)
Sex and age group		%	No	World	UNESCO1 (1.3)
Sex and age group	Total, females by age group female, male ratio	nos, %	Yes 15 yr	World	UN17 (1)
Sex and age group	Total, females by age group female, male ratio	nos, %	Yes 15 yr	Africa	UN46 (1)
Sex and age group	By countries	nos	Yes A	EC	MAC3 (A2)
Sex and marital status		nos	No	Nordic countries	NCM1 (12)
Sex ratio		%	Yes	World	UN55
Sex ratio	By age group	ratio	No	EC	EC20 (B-4)
Size, most populous countries	Medium variant	nos, rank	Yes I	32 most populous countries worldwide	UN54 (15)
Size	Comparison of population, total fertility and life expectancy	nos, %	No	World, more and less developed regions, major areas of the world	UN54 (18)
Size and distribution of population	By sex, age group and male, female ratio	nos, % years	Yes Selected	World	UN16 (1
Size distribution	Distribution of countries according to population size, by region	nos, %	No	World	UN54 (10)
Structural changes, estimates of	By country, by age-group	%	No	SEAR countries	WHO1 (7)
Total, mid-year		nos	Yes A	World	UN10 (1)
Total		%, nos	No	World, OPEC, non-OPEC, ACP, EC	EC1 (I1)

Subject	Categories	Units	Time series Yes/No Frequency		Territorial coverage	Source (Table no.)
Total		nos, indices	Yes	A	OECD, EC	OECD19 (1.0)
Total		nos, years	Yes	Selected	EC	MHPPE1 (-)
Total		nos	No		ACP states	EC1 (II-)
Total		nos	No		Mediterranean countries	EC1 (IV-)
Total		nos	No		World	UN19 (1)
Total		nos	Yes	10 yr	OECD	OECD20 (0.1)
Total		nos	Yes	5yr	Central and South American countries	IADB1
Total		nos	Yes	A	EC	EC34 (2.1)
Total		nos	Yes	A	World	UN50 (1)
Total		nos	Yes	I	World	UN54 (1)
Total	total, annual average growth rate	nos, %	No		World and economic regions	UNCTAD1 (6.1)
Total	% AGR	nos, %	Yes	10 A	World	UN26
Total	Ages 15-64, labour force, male and female	nos	No		OECD, EC	OECD32 (D)
Total	Area	nos	Yes	A	World, EC, USA USSR, Japan	EC9 (3.1)
		no per sq km	No		EC, EC Regions and basic administrative units	EC9 (3.2-3.9)
Total	At mid year	nos	Yes	A	Latin American and Caribbean countries	UN45 (104)
Total	By sex	nos	Yes	A	EC	EC29 (I/1)
Total	By size of localities	nos	No		Latin American and Caribbean countries	UN45 (107)
Total	Sex, age		No		OECD	OECD4 (A-K,1,2)
Total	Sex	nos	No		World	UN50 (14)
Total population, international estimates	By country	nos, %	No		EC	EM1 (0201)
Total population, national estimates	By country	nos	No		EC	EM1 (0202)
Total population, latest official census year	By country, by gender, age	nos	No		EC	EM1 (0203)
Total population		indices, nos	Yes	A	EC	EC36
Total population		nos	No		EC	EC11 (1)
Total population	Agricultural population and economically active population	nos, %	Yes	A	World	FAO1 (3)
Total population by age		%	No		EC	EC11 (1)
Total population by sex	Males,females	nos	No		EC	EC11 (1)
Total population by sex and age group	Total, males, females	nos	No		EC	EC11 (2)
Urban, rural		nos	Yes	A	VICES countries and Yugoslavia	VICES1 (0/2)
Urban		%	Yes		World	UN55
Urban		nos	No		Developing countries	WB1 (-)
Urban	% AGR	nos, %	Yes	10 yr	World	UN26
Urban agglomerations with one million or more inhabitants	By country	nos	No		SEAR countries	WHO1 (11)
Urban and rural areas	Sex	nos	No		World	UN16 (3)
Urban and rural areas and in largest city	By sex, by % population urban, annual rate of growth	nos, %, rate	No		World	UN17 (2)
Urban and rural areas and in largest city, census rounds	By sex, by % population urban, annual rate of growth	nos, %, rate	No		Africa	UN46 (2)
Urban and rural population	By state	nos	No		EC	EC18 (3.10)
Urban and total population	Sex	nos, /%	No		World	UN19 (6)

36 POPULATION AND VITAL STATISTICS

Subject	Categories	Units	Time series Yes/No Frequency		Territorial coverage	Source (Table no.)
Urban concentration	% total population in main metropolitan area, main two metropolitan areas	%	Yes	10yr	Latin American and Caribbean countries	UN45 (6)
Urban crowding	indicators of urban crowding	%, nos, nos, sq km	No		Developing countries	UN25 (20)
Urban crowding	Indicators of urban crowding	%, minutes nos, sq km	No		Industrial countries	UN25 (41)
Urban population		%, nos, per thou	No		World	UNCTAD1 (6.10A)
Urban population		%	Yes	5yr	Latin American and Caribbean countries	UN45 (5)
Urban population		nos	No		VICES countries and Yugoslavia	VICES1 (0/1)
Urban population	By country	%	No		SEAR countries	WHO1 (9)
Urban population	Proportion of urban population, current and projected	%	Yes	I	ASEAN member countries	ASEANS1 (1.3)
Urbanization	By country, by urban population, city popul-ation, growth rates	nos, %	No		EC	EM1 (0214)
Urbanization	% total population in localities with 20 thousand inhabitants, 100 thousand inhabitants	%	Yes	10yr	Latin American and Carribean countries	UN45 (4)
Urbanization	By country, by conurb-ations, population	nos, %	No		EC	EC35 (-)
Women among elderly people	By country, by age	%	No		EC	EC72 (1.26)
Women by income	By high, middle, low income	%, years	No		World	CS1 (32)
Youth and population	By country, by gender	%	No		Member countries	OECD6 (C4)
36.10.2 Trends and Projections						
Active population, trend of in the OECD countries - results by zone and average annual rate of variation		nos	Yes	5 yr	OECD	OECD4 (II.2.)
Active population - trend of in the OECD countries - results by country	Observations, projections	nos, indices	Yes	5 yr	OECD	OECD4 (II.3.)
Age groups, projections	Males, females	%	Yes	10yr	EC	EC20 (I-9)
Age range 15-64	Percentage change	%	Yes	A	OECD, EC	OECD32 (1.2)
Annual increment, average	Medium, high, low variants	nos	Yes	5yr	World, more developed and less developed regions, least developed countries	UN54 (13)
Change	Factors affecting population size	nos, per thou	Yes	A	EC	EC20 (A-1)
Change	Factors affecting population size in 1988	nos, per thou	No		EC	EC20 (A-5)
Comparison of previous projections with actual trends	Births, deaths, natural excess,migratory	nos	No		OECD	OECD4 (I.1.)
Components of change	Increases and decreases by births and deaths	nos, %	Yes	A	OECD	OECD19 (I)
Dependency ratio, projections		ratio	Yes	5yr	World, world regions and income groups	WB5 (-)

Subject	Categories	Units	Time series Yes/No Frequency		Territorial coverage	Source (Table no.)
Discrepancy between the number of vital events projected and observed as compared with the average population	Balance, total excess					
Discrepancy between the numbers of vital events projected and observed as compared with the number of events recorded for each category	Births, deaths	%	No		OECD	OECD4 (I.2.)
Distribution, projections	Population and percentage distribution, by region	nos, %	Yes	I	World Bank regions and country departments	WB5 (B-5)
Distribution, projections	Population and percentage distribution, by region	nos, %	Yes	I	World, world regions and income groups	WB5 (B-1)
Distribution, projections	By broad age group,	%	Yes	5yr	World and economies	WB5 (B-11)
Growth, total		%	Yes	5yr	Latin American and Caribbean countries	UN45 (1)
Growth, phases	Crude birth rate, crude death rate, population growth rate	%, per thou	Yes	I	World	UN54 (3)
Growth		%	Yes	5yr	EC	EC34 (2.2)
Growth	Annual increment, annual growth rate	nos, %	Yes	I	World	UN54 (2)
Growth	By state	nos	No		EC	EC18 (3.3)
Growth rate, projections		%	Yes	5yr 25yr	World, world regions and income groups	WB5 (-)
Growth rate, net, projections		%	Yes	5yr, 25yr	World, world regions and income groups	WB5 (-)
Growth rate		%	No		Developing countries	WB1 (-)
Growth rate	Average annual rate,	%	No		World	UN54 (4)
Growth rate	Medium, high, low variants	nos, %	Yes	5yr	World	UN54 (11)
Growth rate of		%	Yes	Selected	World, by development groups	UNCTAD5 (2.1)
Growth rates		%	Yes	I	Less developed regions worldwide	UN54 (8)
Growth rates	By state	%	No		EC	EC18 (3.5)
Growth rates	Growth, birth, death, migration by region	%, per thou	Yes	5yr	Regions of EC, less developed regions, Africa, Asia and Latin America	UN54 (5-7)
Households - trends - results by country with and without migration	Observations, projections	nos	Yes	5 yr	OECD	OECD4 (I.11.)
Increase		per thou	Yes	A	EC	EC20 (A-4)
Increase and growth rate, annual	Projections	nos, %	Yes	I	World, world regions and income groups	WB5 (B-2)
Increase and growth rate, annual	Projections	nos, %	Yes	I	World Bank regions and country departments	WB5 (B-6)
Increase of population	Mean population	nos	Yes	A	Nordic countries	NCM1 (23/24)

36 POPULATION AND VITAL STATISTICS

Subject	Categories	Units	Time series Yes/No	Frequency	Territorial coverage	Source (Table no.)
Long-run and stationary population	1985, 2050, 2100, stationary. stationary ratio	nos, ratio	Yes	I	World Bank regions and country departments	WB5 (B-7)
Long-run and stationary population	1985, 2050, 2100, stationary. stationary ratio	nos, ratio	Yes	I	World, world regions and income groups	WB5 (B-3)
Momentum		ratio	No		World, world regions and income groups	WB5 (B-3)
Momentum		ratio	No		World and economies	WB5 (B-12)
Momentum		ratio	No		World Bank regions and country departments	WB5 (B-7)
Natural increase, rate of projections		%	Yes	5yr	World, world regions and income groups World economies and territories	WB5 (-)
Natural increase	By country, by year excess of births over deaths	%	Yes	A	EC	CE1 (1.3)
People age 75 and over, trends in OECD member countries - results by country	Observations, projections, sex	nos, indices	Yes	5 yr	OECD	OECD4 (I.8.)
Population, projections	1950, 1970, 1988, 2000, 2020	nos, %	Yes	I	Major world regions	EC20 (D-1)
Population, total	Total, by age, urban population, annual growth rate, by country, region	nos	Yes	I	UNICEF assisted countries	UNICEF2 (-)
Population	Size, percentage distribution, annual rate of increase, increment of population, medium variant	nos, %	Yes	I	Major regions worldwide	UN54 (14)
Population change, annual rate of	Age group	%	No		World	UN16 (2A)
Population change, annual rate of	Age group	%	No		World	UN16 (2A)
Population change	By births, deaths, natural increase, net migration, rates	nos	Yes	A	EC	EC72 (1.8)
Population change	By country, by year, natural increase, net migration	nos	Yes	A	EC	CE1 (7)
Population doubling	Year when population doubles	year	No		World, world regions and income groups	WB5 (B-3)
Population doubling	Year when population doubles	year	No		World Bank regions and country departments	WB5 (B-7)
Population dynamics	By country	nos	Yes	A	EC	EC72 (1.3)
Population growth rates	Age group, estimated population	%	Yes	10 yr	World	UNESCO1 (1.2)
Population growth rates	Age group, estimated population	%	Yes	10 yr	World	UNESCO1 (1.2)
Population growth rates	By country	%	Yes	A	Selected countries	WHO1 (5)
Population increase/decrease	By country, by year	%	Yes	A	EC	CE1 (1.2)

Subject	Categories	Units	Time series Yes/No	Frequency	Territorial coverage	Source (Table no.)
Population of working age (15-64) in the OECD countries, trend of	Observations, projections	nos, indices	Yes	5 yr	OECD	OECD4 (II.5.)
Population projection	By age group, by sex	nos	No		ASEAN member countries	ASEANS1 (1.9)
Population projections, the active population, trend of in the OECD countries - results by zone	Observations, projections, labour force	nos	Yes	5 yr	OECD	OECD4 (II.1.)
Population projections		nos	No		World, EC, USA, USSR, Japan	EC9 (3.1)
Population projections	1995, 2000, 2010, 2020, by sex	nos	No		EC	EC20 (I-5-8)
Population projections	1995, 2000, 2010, 2020	nos	No		EC	EC20 (I-1-4)
Population projections	By country, region or area, estimates, medium high, low and constant fertility rates	nos	Yes	5yr	Major regions, all countries	UN54 (46-47)
Population projections	By gender, by Kuwaiti, non-Kuwaitit, growth rates	%, nos	No		Arabian Gulf	CH1 (5.9)
Population projections	Total population (1988, 2000, 2020)	nos	No		EC and economic groups	EC20 (D-3)
Population projections official	By country	nos	No		EC	EM1 (0222)
Population stationary, projected and hypothetical	By high, middle, low income	nos	No		World	CS1 (26)
Population trends with migration	Sex, age		No		OECD	OECD4 (A-K,1,2)
Population trends without migration	Sex, age		No		OECD	OECD4 (A-K,1,2)
Projected demographic population	By country, by age, by gender	nos	No		EC	EM1 (0223)
Projected sex ratios	By country, by males per 100 females	nos	No		SEAR countries	WHO1 (8)
Projection indicators	Gross reproduction rate, life expectancy at birth	nos	Yes	5 yr	OECD	OECD4 (I.9.)
Projections		nos	No		Developing countries	WB1 (-)
Projections		nos	Yes	5yr, 25yr	World and economies	WB5 (B-9)
Projections	By age and sex	nos	Yes	5yr	World, world regions and income groups	WB5 (-)
Rate of change	By total, by age group, sex	rate, years	No		World	UN17 (3)
Rate of change	By total, by age group, sex	rate, years	No		Africa	UN46 (3)
Rate of change	Population, annual rate of change, medium low and high variants, by region and country or area	nos, %	Yes	5yr	World	UN54 (30-33)
Rate of increase		%	No		World macro regions and regions	UN19 (1)
Rate of increase		%	No		World	UN50 (14)
Rate of increase		%	No		World macro regions and regions	UN50 (2)
Rate of increase		%	Yes	A	World	UN19 (3)

Subject	Categories	Units	Time series Yes/No Frequency		Territorial coverage	Source (Table no.)
Rate of increase		per thou	Yes	A	EC, world,	EC20 (A-2)
Rate of increase	Medium variant	nos, %	Yes	5yr	World, more developed and less developed regions, least developed countries	UN54 (12)
Rates of growth	Sex, age group	%	No		World	ILO6 (1,2)
Rates of growth	Sex, age group	%	No		World	ILO6 (1,2)
Rates of growth	Urban, rural	%	No		World	UN16 (3)
Replacement level	Assumed period required to reach replacement level, medium variant	period by dates	No		African, Asian, Latin American countries	UN54 (27-29)
Sex and age	Projected	age, years	No		Nordic countries	NCM1 (17)
Size by sex and age group	Total, females by age group female, male ratio	nos, %	Yes	15 yr	World	UN17 (1)
Stationary population	Stationary population, stationary ratio	nos, ratio	No		World and economies	WB5 (B-12)
Total, projected	At mid-year	nos	Yes	5yr	Latin American and Caribbean countries	UN45 (105)
Total	Percentage change	%	Yes	A	OECD, EC	OECD32 (1.1)
Total population and the active population - trend of in the OECD countries - results by country		nos	Yes	5 yr	OECD	OECD4 (II.4.)
Total population trends	Age group, annual average increase	nos	Yes	5 yr	World	UNESCO1 (1.2)
Total population trends	Age group, annual average increase	nos	Yes	5 yr	World	UNESCO1 (1.2)
Total population trends in OECD countries with and without external migration - results by zone	Observations, projections, total	nos, indices	Yes	5 yr	OECD	OECD4 (I.3.)
Total population trends in OECD countries - results by country	Observations, projections, total	nos, indices	Yes	5 yr	OECD	OECD4 (I.4.)
Total population trends in OECD countries by sex and age group (with migrations) - results by zone	Observations, projections, sex and age	nos, proportions	Yes	5 yr	OECD	OECD4 (I.6.)
Total population trends in OECD countries by sex and age group - results by country	Observations, projections, sex and age	nos, proportions	Yes	5 yr	OECD	OECD4 (I.7.)
Total population trends in OECD countries - results by zone	Total	nos	Yes	5 yr	OECD	OECD4 (I.5)
Trend of the population of working age without migration		nos	Yes	5 yr	OECD	OECD4 (II.6.)
Urban and rural areas and in largest city	By sex, by % population urban, annual rate of growth	nos, %, rate	No		World	UN17 (2)
Urban population, growth rate of	By country	%	No		SEAR countries	WHO1 (10)
Urban population growth	Main metropolitan area, main two metropolitan areas	%	Yes	10yr	Latin American and Caribbean countries	UN45 (7)
Variations between 1970 and 1980 in total population and the number of young and older people per 100 persons of working age	Relative variation in total population, under 15 yrs, 65 and over	%, nos	No		OECD	OECD4 (II.15.)

37 PRICES

Subject	Categories	Units	Time series Yes/No Frequency		Territorial coverage	Source (Table no.)
37.1 AGRICULTURE - see also under Producer Prices (37.12), Trade (37.16) and Sections 2 and 5						
Agricultural prices	Producer prices, goods and services consumed, goods and services contributing to agricultural investment	deflated indices	Yes	A	EC	EC9 (5.20)
Agricultural prices	Producer prices, goods and services consumed, goods and services contributing to agricultural investment	nominal indices	Yes	A	EC	EC9 (5.20)
Agricultural prices received and paid by farmers	By country	indices	Yes	A	ESCAP countries	UN44
Agricultural prices, deflated price indices	By agricultural product, by country	indices	Yes	A	EC	EC4 (-)
Agricultural prices, nominal price indices	By agricultural product, by country	indices	Yes	A	EC	EC4 (-)
Agricultural prices, weighting scheme	By agricultural product by country	indices	No		EC	EC4 (-)
Agricultural production	By type of output and input	%	Yes	A	EC	EC2 (A5)
Agricultural production	Indices of final output	indices	Yes	A	EC	EC2 (A25)
Agricultural production	Indices of final output	indices	Yes	A	EC	EC2 (A26)
Agricultural production consumption in agriculture	Indices of intermediate	indices	Yes	A	EC	EC2 (A30)
Agricultural production	Indices of intermediate consumption in agriculture	indices	Yes	A	EC	EC2 (A31)
Agricultural products	Agricultural products, vegetable products, livestock products	indices	Yes	A, M	EC	EC36
Agricultural products	By products	indices	Yes	A	EC	EC6 (IF 4)
Agricultural products, main	Average prices received by farmers	indices	Yes	A	EC and North America	UN40 (1)
Agricultural products, miscellaneous	Unit price per kilo-calorie	PPS	No		Africa	EC1 (V3)
Agricultural products, miscellaneous	Unit price per 1000g of protein	PPS	No		Africa	EC1 (V4)
Animal products selling prices	By type	ECU/kg	Yes	A	EC	EC6 (IF 2)
Animal products, selling prices	By animal product, by country	nat curr, ECU	Yes	A	EC	EC4 (-)
Barley – all forms of utilization	Weighted average prices (unit values) received by farmers per 100 kg					
Barley – brewing	Average prices received by farmers per 100 kg	nat curr	Yes	A	EC and North America	UN40 (IIIB)
Barley – livestock	Average prices received by farmers per 100 kg	nat curr	Yes	A	EC and North America	UN40 (IIIA)
Beef	By cut	nat curr, kg	Yes	A, M	EC	MLC1 (-)
Beef	By forequarter, hind-quarter, side	nat curr, kg	Yes	A, M	EC	MLC1 (-)
Beef	Live adult bovine	ECU, kg	Yes	M, Q	EC	EC3 (-)
Beef and veal levies	Frozen	ECU, kg	Yes	M	EC	EC3 (-)
Beef or certain beef cuts, retail prices		nat curr, kg, indices	Yes	A, Q	Selected EC countries	UN34 (VI)
Beef prices	Received by producers	nat curr, kg, %	Yes	A	World	GATT1 (12)
Beef prices	Retail	nat curr, kg, %	Yes	A	World	GATT1 (13)
Beef prices, export	Average or representative	US$, tonnes	Yes	A	World	GATT1 (14)
Beef prices, import	Average or representative	US$, tonnes	Yes	A	World	GATT1 (14)
Bovine animal levies	Live	ECU, kg	Yes	M	EC	EC3 (-)

37 PRICES

Subject	Categories	Units	Time series Yes/No	Frequency	Territorial coverage	Source (Table no.)
Broilers or poultry, producer prices		nat curr, kg, lb	Yes	A, Q	Selected EC countries	UN34 (LI)
Butter and margarine	By retail prices	nat curr, kg	Yes	A	EC	MMB1(42)
Calf, finished	By type	nat curr, head, kg, lw	Yes	A, M	EC	MLC1 (-)
Calf, rearing	By type, liveweight	nat curr, head, kg	Yes	A, M	EC	MLC1 (-)
Calves	Live	ECU, kg	Yes	M, Q	EC	EC3 (-)
Cattle	Average prices received per 100 kg live weight for the most representative type of grade	nat curr	Yes	A	EC and North America	UN40 (VIIIA)
Cattle	Weighted average prices (unit values) received by farmers per 100 kg live weight for all types and grades of beef cattle (excluding calves)	nat curr	Yes	A	EC and North America	UN40 (VIIIB)
Cattle or beef, producer prices		nat curr, kg	Yes	A, Q	Selected EC countries	UN34 (VII)
Cattle, finished	By type of cattle	nat curr, kg dw	Yes	A, M	EC	MLC1 (-)
Cereals, prices and levies	All varieties	ECU, t	Yes	M, Q	EC	EC3 (-)
Cheeses, selected	By retail prices	nat curr, kg	Yes	A	EC	MMB1 (43)
Cocoa beans	Daily and indicator prices	SDR's, tonne, USc lb	Yes	A, M	World	ICC02 (15)
Cocoa beans	Daily prices	USc lb	Yes	A, M	World	ICC02 (16)
Cocoa beans, prices of international significance	London terminal market New York coffee, sugar and cocoa exchange	£, tonne, USc/lb	Yes	A, M	World	ICC02 (17)
Compound feed for dairy cows	At grass	ECU, kg	Yes	A, M	Ireland	EC58 (5.3)
Compound feed for dairy cows	Stall fed	ECU, kg	Yes	A, M	EC	EC58 (5.4)
Compound or mixed feed	Raw protein content, type of feed by kind of animal or fowl, prices paid by farmers per 100 kg of	%, nat curr, US$	Yes	A	EC and North America	UN40 (XV)
Crop products, selling prices	By crop product, by country	nat curr, ECU	Yes	A	EC	EC4 (-)
Crop products, selling prices	By type	ECU/kg	Yes	A	EC	EC6 (IF 1)
Crop products/animal and animal products, nominal indices		indices, %	Yes	Q	EUR 10	EC5 (1)
Crop products/animal and animal products, deflated indices		indices, %	Yes	Q	EUR 10	EC5 (1)
Crop products/animal products, rates of change of the price indices		indices, %	Yes	Q	Member states	EC5 (2)
Crops	Price series of international significance by crop	nat curr, US$, tonnes	Yes	A	World	FAO1 (119)
Crops and animal products	Nominal, deflated	indices, %	Yes	Q	EUR 11	EC81 (1)
Crops and animal products	Nominal, deflated	indices, %	Yes	Q	Member states	EC81 (2)
Egg prices	Ratios to prices paid by farmers for feed for laying hens	ratios	Yes	A	EC and North America	UN40 (7)
Eggs, prices and levies		ECU, kg	Yes	M, Q	EC	EC3 (-)
Fertilisers, mixed and complex		nat curr, US$	Yes	A	World	FAO5 (37)
Fertilizers	Nitrogenous, phosphatic, prices paid by farmers per metric ton of specified	%, nat curr, US$, tonnes	Yes	A	EC and North America	UN40 (XVIB, XVIIB, XVIIIB)
Fertilizers	Plant nutrient content prices paid by farmers per metric ton of specified	%, nat curr, US$	Yes	A	EC and North America	UN40 (XIX)

Subject	Categories	Units	Time series Yes/No Frequency		Territorial coverage	Source (Table no.)
Fertilizers	Weighted average prices	nat curr	Yes	A	EC and North America	UN40 (XX)
Fertilizers prices	Nitrogenous, phosphatic, potassic, weighted average paid by farmers per 100 kg of plant nutrient	nat curr	Yes	A	EC and North America	UN40 (XVIA, XVIIA, XVIIIA)
Foodstuffs, consumer price indices	By type	indices	Yes	A	EC	EC6 (IF 6)
Fowls for meat production	Average prices received for the most representative type of young chickens raised for meat production per 100 kg live weight	nat curr	Yes	A	EC and North America	UN40 (X)
Fowls for meat production	Ratios of prices to production to prices paid by farmers for feed for broilers	ratios	Yes	A	EC and North America	UN40 (6)
Goods and services	Nominal, deflated	indices, %	Yes	Q	EUR 11	EC81 (3)
Goods and services	Nominal, deflated	indices, %	Yes	Q	Member states	EC81 (4)
Grain feed	Weighted average prices paid by farmers per 100 kg, by type	nat curr	Yes	A	EC and North America	UN40 (XIIIA, B,C)
Grain, coarse, export prices	Based on official f.o.b quotations	US$, tonne	Yes	A, M	World	IWhC3 (A.8)
Hen eggs	Average prices received by farmers per 100 kg of eggs sold to wholesalers	nat curr	Yes	A	EC and North America	UN40 (XIA)
Hen eggs	Weighted average prices (unit values) received by farmers per 100 kg for all types of sales	nat curr	Yes	A	EC and North America	UN40 (XIB)
Lamb	By cut	nat curr, kg	Yes	A, M	EC	MLC1 (-)
Lamb, finished	By type, deadweight	nat curr, kg	Yes	A, M	EC	MLC1 (-)
Maize, cassava, fishmeal and soybean meal, prices on the international market	By product and quotation	US$, tonnes	Yes	A, Q	International market	UN34 (LVI)
Market prices, world	Commodity groups	indices	Yes	2 A	World	UN40 (3)
Meat	By cut	nat curr, kg	Yes	A	EC	MLC1 (-)
Milk – intervention price equivalent	Butter, skim powder	ECU, kg	No		EC	MMB1 (6)
Milk - producer price and target price	By ex-farm, levy, transport, deliveries	nat curr, kg	Yes	A	EC	MMB1 (40)
Milk - retail prices	By shop price	nat curr, kg	Yes	A	EC	MMB1 (41)
Milk - target and intervention prices	By product	ECU, kg, ppl £, tonne	Yes	A	EC	MMB1 (5II)
Milk - target and intervention prices	By product	nat curr per kg, litre	No		EC	MMB1 (5II)
Milk prices	By type of feed, ratios to prices paid by farmers for feed for dairy cows	ratio	Yes	A	EC and North America	UN40 (9)
Milk product levies		ECU, kg	Yes	M, Q	EC	EC3 (-)
Milk, producer prices	3.7% fat, ex-farm, exc VAT and co-responsibility levy	nat curr, ECU, kg	Yes	A	EC	MMB1 (39)
Milk, whole	Average fat content	%	Yes	A	Selected countries	UN40 (XIIA)
Milk, whole	Average prices received by farmers per 100 kg of milk delivered to dairies for all forms of utilization	nat curr	Yes	A	EC and North America	UN40 (XIIA)
Milk, whole	Weighted average prices (unit values) received by farmers per 100 kg for all types of sales	nat curr	Yes	A	EC and North America	UN40 (XIIB)
Nitrogenous fertiliser, producer prices		nat curr, US$	Yes	A	World	FAO5 (34)

37 PRICES

Subject	Categories	Units	Time series Yes/No	Frequency	Territorial coverage	Source (Table no.)
Nominal prices, change in	By type of output and input	%	Yes	A	EC	EC2 (A4)
Oats and maize - all forms of utilization	Weighted average prices (unit values) received by farmers per 100 kg	nat curr	Yes	A	EC and North America	UN40 (IVB, VB)
Oats and maize - feed oats	Average prices received by farmers per 100 kg	nat curr	Yes	A	EC and North America	UN40 (IVA, VA)
Oilcake and other feed prices, selected international	By type of feed	US$ per tonne	Yes	A	Selected countries	UN40 (8)
Oilcakes - prices paid by farmers	Raw material used	nat curr, US$	Yes	A	EC and North America	UN40 (XIV)
Oilseeds, food oils, fats, oilmeals,		indices	Yes	A	World	ISTA2(-)
Oilseeds, price premiums or discounts	Selected oils, fats, meals	US$, tonne	Yes	A	World	ISTA2(-)
Olive oil, prices and levies	All types	ECU, kg	Yes	M, Q	EC	EC3 (-)
Phosphate fertiliser, price, producer		nat curr, US$	Yes	A	World	FAO5 (35)
Pig meat	By price	nat curr, kg	Yes	A, M	EC	MLC1 (-)
Pig meat reference prices	By price	nat curr, kg dw	Yes	A, M	EC	MLC1 (-)
Pig prices	By type of feed, ratios to prices paid by farmers for feed for pigs	ratios	Yes	A	EC and North America	UN40 (5)
Pig, actual compound	Fattening pigs	ECU, nat curr	Yes	A, M	EC	MLC1 (-)
Pig, actual compound	Rearing pigs	ECU, nat curr	Yes	A, M	EC	MLC1 (-)
Pig, finished	By deadweight	nat curr, kg	Yes	A, M	EC	MLC1 (-)
Pigmeat levies		ECU, kg	Yes	Q	EC	EC3 (-)
Pigs	Average prices received per 100 kg live weight for the most representative grade	nat curr	Yes	A	EC and North America	UN40 (IXA)
Pigs	Weighted average prices (unit values) received by farmers per 100 kg live weight for all grades	nat curr	Yes	A	EC and North America	UN40 (IXB)
Pigs or pig meat, producer prices		nat curr, kg, indices	Yes	A, Q	Selected EC countries	UN34 (XXII)
Plant protection products	Active matter, physical state, packing, prices paid by farmers per 100 kg	%, nat curr, US$	Yes	A	EC and North America	UN40 (XXI)
Plant protection products, price indices of		indices	Yes	A	EC and North America	UN40 (12)
Pork	By cut	nat curr, kg	Yes	A, M	EC	MLC1 (-)
Pork	Pigs, cuts, piglets	ECU, kg PAB	Yes	M, Q	EC	EC3 (-)
Pork or certain pork cuts, retail prices		nat curr, kg, indices	Yes	A, Q	Selected EC countries	UN34 (XXI)
Potash fertiliser, producer prices		nat curr, US$	Yes	A	World	FAO5 (36)
Potatoes – all forms of utilization (main crop only)	Weighted average prices (unit values) received by farmers per 100 kg	nat curr	Yes	A	EC and North America	UN40 (VIB)
Potatoes – direct human consumption (main crop only)	Average prices received by farmers per 100 kg	nat curr	Yes	A	EC and North America	UN40 (VIA)
Poultry meat, retail prices		nat curr, indices	Yes	A, Q	Selected EC countries	UN34 (L)
Poultry, prices and levies		ECU, kg	Yes	Q, M	EC	EC3 (-)
Price series of international significance	By product and quotations	local units	Yes	A, M	World	FAO6 (68)
Prices paid by farmers, indices	By feed, fertilisers, plant protection products, agricultural wage rates	indices	Yes	A	EC and North America	UN40 (10)
Prices per unit of plant nutrient	By fertilizer, paid by farmers for fertilizers, indices of average	indices	Yes	A	EC and North America	UN40 (11)
Prices received by farmers and prices paid by farmers, index numbers of	All agricultural products, all requisites	indices	Yes	A	World	FAO1 (120)
Prices, producer	Cows milk	ECU, kg	Yes	A, M	EC	EC58 (5.2

Subject	Categories	Units	Time series Yes/No Frequency	Territorial coverage	Source (Table no.)
Purchase price of the means of agricultural production	By input	indices	Yes A	EC	EC6 (IF 5)
Purchase prices of the means of agricultural production	By feeding stuffs, fertilizers, motor fuels and fuels for heating	ECU/kg	Yes A	EC	EC6 (IF 3)
Purchase prices of the means of agricultural production, nominal indices	Goods and services	indices, %	Yes Q	EUR 10	EC5 (3)
Purchase prices of the means of agricultural production, deflated indices	Goods and services	indices, %	Yes Q	EUR 10	EC5 (3)
Purchase prices of the means of agricultural production, nominal	Goods and services	indices, %	Yes Q	Member states	EC5 (4)
Purchase prices of the means of agricultural production	By type, nominal price indices goods and services currently consumed by agriculture, goods and services contributing to agricultural investment, by country	nat curr, ECU indices	Yes A	EC	EC4 (-)
	Deflated price indices goods and services currently consumed by agriculture, goods and services contributing to agricultural investment, by country	indices	Yes A	EC	EC4 (-)
Purchase prices of the means, of agricultural production, deflated	Goods and services	indices, %	Yes Q	Member states	EC5 (4)
Rice, prices and levies	All varieties	ECU, t	Yes M, Q	EC	EC3 (-)
Rubber, natural		nat curr, tonne	Yes A	World	IRSG2 (14)
Rubber, natural	By grade	nat curr, tonne	Yes A, M	New York, London Tokyo, Kuala Lumpur Singapore	IRSG1 (44)
Rubber, natural		£ or $, tonne	Yes A	London, New York	IRSG2 (25)
Rubber, synthetic		nat curr, tonne	Yes A	World	IRSG2 (20)
Rubber, synthetic	By type	nat curr, tonne	Yes A, Q	UK, Germany, Italy	IRSG1 (45)
Rubber, SBR export values		nat curr, tonne	Yes A, M	USA, France, UK Germany, Japan, Republic of Korea Taiwan	IRSG1 (43)
Sheep and cattle, reference basic price		ECU, kg nat curr, kg	Yes A, M	EC	MLC1 (-)
Sheep meat or for certain cuts, retail price		nat curr, indices	Yes A, Q	Selected EC countries	UN34 (XXXVI)
Sheep or sheep meat, producer prices		nat curr	Yes A, Q	Selected EC countries	UN34 (XXXVII)
Sheep, prices and levies	Lambs	ECU, kg, PAB	Yes M, Q	EC	EC3 (-)
Sheep, representative market prices	By price	nat curr, kg dw	Yes A, M	EC	MLC1 (-)
Sheepmeat levies	Frozen	ECU, kg	Yes M, Q	EC	EC3 (-)
Sugar beet	Average prices realized per 100 kg for the whole of the harvest	nat curr	Yes A	EC and North America	UN40 (VIIB)
Sugar beet	Contract prices paid to producers per 100 kg	nat curr	Yes A	EC and North America	UN40 (VIIA)
Sugar levies	Dry, syrup	ECU, kg	Yes M	EC	EC3 (-)
Sugar prices	By London, New York and ISA daily price monthly averages	£ tonnes, US cents, US$	Yes A,D, M	World	ISO3 (-)

Subject	Categories	Units	Time series Yes/No	Frequency	Territorial coverage	Source (Table no.)
Sugar prices, daily spot	By sugar type, differentials	US cents per lb, %, SDR, US$, indices	Yes	A, M	World	ISO1 (-)
Sugar raw, daily spot prices	By highest, lowest	tonnes	Yes	D	London, New York, ISA	ISO2 (-)
Sugar, free market daily spot prices	By monthly averages, sugar type	US cents per lb f.o.b.	Yes	A, M	World	ISO1 (-)
Sugar, ISA daily price of	By monthly averages	US cents per lb	Yes	A, M	World	ISO1 (-)
Sugar, prices of white refined	By country and locality wholesale and retail	US cents	Yes	A	Selected countries	ISO3 (-)
Sugar, raw and white	Market prices	nat curr lb, nat curr, tonnes	Yes	D	Selected capitals	FOL2 (189)
Sugar, raw and white	Price premiums or discounts	nos	Yes	D	Selected capitals	FOL2 (190)
Tea - annual average prices (London)	By country	pence per kg	Yes	A	World	ITC1 (F3)
Tea - annual average prices (producing countries)	By type and country	nat curr per kg	Yes	A	Selected countries	ITC1 (F4-F5)
Tea - average prices (London)	By month	pence per kg	Yes	A, M	UK	ITC1 (F2)
Tea - monthly price quotations (London)	By type	pence per kg	Yes	A, M	UK	ITC1 (F1)
Tea - quantities sold and average prices	By country, cif, fob	tonnes, pence per kg	Yes	A	Selected countries	ITC1 (F7-F8)
Veal	By cut	nat curr, kg	Yes	A, M	EC	MLC1 (-)
Wage rates		indices	Yes	A	EC and North America	UN40 (13)
Wages paid by farmers for hired labour, increase in average	By type of job	%	Yes	A	EC and North America	UN40 (14)
Weaner	By liveweight	nat curr, head	Yes	A, M	EC	MLC1 (-)
Wheat and maize, selected international export prices		US$, kg	Yes	2 A	USA	UN40 (4)
Wheat and rye	Basic fixed prices paid to producers per 100kg	nat curr	Yes	A	EC and North America	UN40 (IA,IIA)
Wheat and rye	Weighted average prices (unit values) received by farmers per 100 kg	nat curr	Yes	A	EC and North America	UN40 (IB,IIB)
Wheat export prices	Based on official f.o.b. quotations	US$, tonne	Yes	A, M	World	IWhC3 (A.5)
Wine	All types	ECU	Yes	M, Q	EC	EC3 (-)

37.2 CHEMICALS – see also under Producer Prices (37.12) and Trade (37.16) and Sections 5 and 25

Prices	Home sales	indices	Yes	A	Western World	CIA1 (29)
Real prices	Annual % change	%	Yes	A	Western World	CIA1 (31)

37.3 COMMODITIES – see also under Agriculture (37.1) and Sections 2, 5, 21, 25, 32 and 33

Agricultural raw materials	Price index	indices	Yes	A	World	UN32 (K)
Commodities	By selected primary commodity	indices	Yes	A, Q	World	UNCTAD1 (2.7)
Commodities	Prices by commodity	lbs/US$/ tonne/kg	Yes	A, M	World	ISL2 (2.3.27)
Commodities	Prices for 18 individual commodities covered by the IPC	indices	Yes	A	Developing countries	UNCTAD1 (4.10)
Commodities	Prices, 55 commodities	US$/cents	Yes	A, M	World	IMF7 (-)
Commodities	Selected manufactured goods, by SITC group	indices	Yes	A	World	UNCTAD1 (2.8)
Commodity price index		indices	Yes	A	World	IMF7 (-)
Commodity prices	55 commodities	US$/cents	Yes	A, M	World	IMF6 (-)
Food and beverages	Price index	indices	Yes	A	World	UN32 (K)
Machinery and transport	Price index	indices	Yes	A	World	UN32 (J)

Subject	Categories	Units	Time series Yes/No	Frequency	Territorial coverage	Source (Table no.)
Market price and raw material price indices	By commodity	indices	Yes	A, M	World	ISL2 (2.3.26)
Metals (non-ferrous)	Price index	indices	Yes	A	World	UN32 (K)
Minerals	Price index	indices	Yes	A	World	UN32 (K)
Primary commodities market	Prices for selected , instability indices by commodity	indices	Yes	Selected years	Developing countries	UNCTAD5 (4.12)
Primary commodities market	Prices for selected primary , trends by commodity	US$	Yes	Selected years	Developing countries	UNCTAD5 (4.11)

37.4 CONSTRUCTION – see also under Producer Prices (37.12), Trade (37.16) and Section 7

Subject	Categories	Units	Time series Yes/No	Frequency	Territorial coverage	Source (Table no.)
Building materials		indices	Yes	Selected years	EC	MHPPE1 (-)
Building materials price indices	By type	indices	Yes	A	World	UN10 (15)
Construction costs, newly-built, subsidised, rental dwellings		ECU	No		EC	MHPPE1 (-)
House prices	Newly-completed dwellings	indices	Yes	Selected years	EC	MHPPE1 (-)
Input and output prices	Indices	indices	Yes	A	World	UN10 (13)
Land costs as percentage of total construction costs for social dwellings		%	Yes	Selected years	EC	MHPPE1 (-)
Non-residential construction	Implicit price index	%	Yes	A	OECD, EC	OECD32 (8.7)
Owner-occupied, previously used dwellings		indices	Yes	Selected years	EC	MHPPE1 (-)
Residential construction	Implicit price index	%	Yes	A	OECD, EC	OECD32 (8.6)

37.5 CONSUMER PRICES – see also Sections 5 and 34

Subject	Categories	Units	Time series Yes/No	Frequency	Territorial coverage	Source (Table no.)
Consumer goods	By country, by goods	nat curr	No		EC	EM1 (1504)
Consumer price	All groups, food groups	indices nos	Yes	Q	South Pacific countries	SPC1 (1,2)
Consumer price	By type of goods, by country	indices	Yes	A	ESCAP countries	UN44
Consumer price and rent indices		indices	Yes	A	World	UN10 (8)
Consumer price changes	At December and June for 12-months periods	nos	Yes	6 M	EC and North America	UN40 (2)
Consumer price indices	By country	indices	Yes	A	Selected countries	CIA1 (30)
Consumer price indices	By group	indices, nos	Yes	Q	South Pacific	SPC1 (4)
Consumer price indices	Food retail	indices	Yes	A	Western world	MLC1 (-)
Consumer prices			Yes	A	Central and South American countries	IADB1
Consumer prices		%	Yes	A, M	World	IMF6 (-)
Consumer prices		%	Yes	A, M	World	IMF7 (-)
Consumer prices		%, indices	Yes	A, M	World	IMF6 (-)
Consumer prices		%, indices	Yes	A, M	World	IMF7 (-)
Consumer prices	All items, food, energy	indices	Yes	A, M	OECD Total, EC Total Major Seven Total OECD EC	OECD22
Consumer prices	All items, food	indices	Yes	A, M	World	UN35 (51)
Consumer prices	All items, food	indices	Yes	A	Nordic countries	NCM1 (165)
Consumer prices	All items, all items less food, food, all goods less food, services less rent and rent	indices	Yes	M	OECD	OECD22 (-)
Consumer prices	All items, food	indices	Yes	A	World	UN50 (22)

37 PRICES

Subject	Categories	Units	Time series Yes/No	Frequency	Territorial coverage	Source (Table no.)
Consumer prices	All items, food and energy	indices	Yes	A, Q, M	OECD	OECD22 (-)
Consumer prices	By countries	nos	No		The Americas and Australasia	MAC2 (I2)
Consumer prices	By country	indices	No		EC	EM1 (1501)
Consumer prices	By country, by category	indices	No		Selected countries	EC35 (-)
Consumer prices	By country, index	indices	Yes	A	Africa and Asia	MAC1 (I2)
Consumer prices	By item	indices	Yes	A, M	OECD	OECD22
Consumer prices	By type of good and service	indices	Yes	M, Q, A	OECD	OECD23 (-)
	All, food, energy	indices	Yes	M, Q, A	OECD - total Major seven OECD EC, EC	OECD23 (-)
Consumer prices	General and food index	nos	Yes	A	African countries	UN1 (38)
Consumer prices	General level and food, average annual rates	indices	Yes	A	Latin American and Caribbean countries	UN45 (63)
Consumer prices	General, food, drinks, clothing and footwear, rent, fuel, power, household goods and services, transport, communications,	indices	Yes	A, M	EC, USA, Japan	EC36
Consumer prices		indices	Yes	A	EC	EC73 (12)
Consumer prices		indices	Yes	A	Western world	MLC1 (-)
Consumer prices		indices, %	Yes	A, Q, M	EC	EC59 (II.9)
Consumer prices	Food, excl drinks and meals out, drinks (home consumption), tobacco, clothing, footwear, inc repairs, rent, fuel, power, household goods and services, transport, communications, recreation, education, culture, fuel and power, goods and services, inc meals and drinks out	indices	Yes	A	EC, USA, Japan	EC9 (2.43)
Consumer prices	General level, food	indices	Yes	A	Latin American and Caribbean countries	UN45 (236)
Consumer prices	Monthly value, January, July	indices	Yes	A	EC	EC28
Consumer prices, percentage changes	All groups. food groups	%	Yes	Q	South Pacific countries	SPC1 (3)
Consumer prices, variation in	By high, middle, low income	%	Yes	A	World	CS1 (6)
Consumption		indices	Yes	Selected years	EC	MHPPE1 (-)
Cost of living/consumer prices	By countries	indices	Yes	A	EC	MAC3 (H2)
Cost-of-living price index	By country, by index group	indices	No		EC	EC18 (15.1)
Domestic prices, deflators	By country	indices	Yes	A	World	WB6 (-)
Durable goods	By type	nat curr, ECU, indices	No		EC	EC16
Food beverages and tobacco	By type	indices	No		EC	EC16
Food costs	By country, by selected food and drink	nat curr	No		EC	EM1 (1503)
Food prices	By country	indices	No		EC	EM1 (1502)
Food, beverages and tobacco	By type	nat curr, ECU, indices	No		EC	EC16
Inflation	By category	%	Yes	A	Developing countries, DMECs, Least developed countries	UNCTAD5 (3.7)
Price index	Consumer, general, food clothing, rent, fuel	nos	Yes	A	Central Africa	UN5 (40)

Subject	Categories	Units	Time series Yes/No Frequency		Territorial coverage	Source (Table no.)
Price index	Consumer, general, food clothing, rent, fuel	nos	Yes	A	East and Southern Africa	UN4 (40)
Price index	Consumer, general, food clothing, rent, fuel	nos	Yes	A	North Africa	UN2 (40)
Price index	Consumer, general, food clothing, rent, fuel	nos	Yes	A	West Africa	UN3 (40)
Price index	Total consumer index	nos	Yes	A	Central Africa	UN5 (8-1-1)
Price index	Total consumer index	nos	Yes	A	East and Southern Africa	UN4 (8-1-1)
Price index	Total consumer index	nos	Yes	A	North Africa	UN2
Price index	Total consumer index	nos	Yes	A	West Africa	UN3 (8-1-1)
Price indices	Index, % change	indices, %	Yes	A	ASEAN	ASEANS1 (8.1)
Price, general index	Price indices, rate of increase over one month, rate of increase over 12 months	indices, %	Yes	A, M	EC	EC17 (1)
Prices	Indices		Yes	A, M	World	IMF6 (-)
Prices	Indices		Yes	A, M	World	IMF7 (-)
Prices, general index	Price indices, rate of increase over one month, rate of increase over 12 months	indices, %	Yes	A, M	USA, Japan, Switzerland, Austria, norway, Sweden, Finland, Canada	EC17 (2)
Prices, housing costs in the consumer price index		indices	Yes	Selected years	EC	MHPPE1 (-)
Prices, indices	Annual rate of increase	nat curr, %, indices	Yes	A, M	EC	EC27 (V)
Primary products, trends		indices	No		World	GATT3 (A.2)
Rent	Social, private	indices	Yes	Selected years	EC	MHPPE1 (-)
Rent, fuel and power		indices	Yes	Selected years	EC	MHPPE1 (-)
Retail prices	Food products	US$	Yes	A	Nordic countries	NCM1 (163)
Retail prices, average	Selected commodities	$A	No		South Pacific	SPC1 (6)
Services	By country, by service	nat curr	No		EC	EM1 (1505)
Share of consumer product categories in the general price index	By country, by caregory	%	No		EC	EC35 (-)

37.6 ENERGY – see also under Producer Prices (37.12), Trade (37.16) and Section 17

Coal exports	By destination	US$	Yes	A	OECD	IEA2 (II.17)
Coal imports	By origin	US$	Yes	A	OECD	IEA2 (-)
Coal, coking	By country	nat curr per tonne	Yes	A, Q	OECD	IEA6 (IIB.1)
Coal, coking	By country	nat curr per tonne	Yes	A, Q	Non-OECD	IEA6 (IIIA.1)
Coal, coking	For industrial use	US$ per tonne/ toe	Yes	A	OECD	IEA6 (IID.15)
Coal, coking	For Industrial use by country	US$ per tonne/ toe	Yes	A	Non-OECD	IEA6 (IIIB.15)
Coal, coking: import	By country	indices	Yes	A, Q	OECD, EC	IEA6(I.12)
Coal, coking: import	By country	US$ per tonne	Yes	A, Q	OECD, EC	IEA6(I.11)
Coal, coking: import prices from non-EC to the EC	By country	US$ per tonne	Yes	A, Q	Selected non-EC countries	IEA6(I.13)
Coal, coking: import prices to Japan	By country	US$ per tonne	Yes	A, Q	World	IEA6(I.15)
Coal, export prices	Steam and coking coal	US$ per tonne indices	Yes	A, Q	Australia and USA	IEA6 (I.17-I.18)

37 PRICES

Subject	Categories	Units	Time series Yes/No	Frequency	Territorial coverage	Source (Table no.)
Coal, steam	By country incl. and excl. tax	nat curr per toe	Yes	A, Q	OECD	IEA6 (IIB.2)
Coal, steam	For industry and electricity generation	US$ per tonne/ toe	Yes	A	OECD	IEA6 (II(D.13-D.14))
Coal, steam	For industry and electricity generation by country	US$ per tonne/ toe	Yes	A	Non-OECD	IEA6 (III(B.13-B.14))
Coal, steam	For industry, electricity generation and households by country	nat curr per tonne	Yes	A, Q	OECD	IEA6 (IIB.1)
Coal, steam	For industry, electricity generation and household use by country	nat curr per tonne	Yes	A, Q	Non-OECD	IEA6 (IIIA.1)
Coal, steam	Incl. and excl. tax by country	nat curr per toe	Yes	A, Q	Non-OECD	IEA6 (IIIA.2)
Coal, steam: import prices from non-EC to the EC	By country	US$ per tonne	Yes	A, Q	Selected non-EC countries	IEA6 (I.7)
Coal, steam: imports	By country	indices	Yes	A, Q	OECD	IEA6 (I.6)
Coal, steam: imports	By country	US$ per tonne	Yes	A, Q	OECD	IEA6 (I.5)
Coal, steam import prices to Japan	By country	US$ per tonne	Yes	A, Q	World	IEA6 (I.9)
Crude oil	Dubai, Brent, WTI	US$/barrel	Yes	A, M	Rotterdam	IEA10 (I.13)
Crude Oil - prices	By product	US$ per bl	Yes	A, M	World	DSC2 (2.7)
Crude oil and products, freight costs		US$/barrel,	Yes	M	World worldscale points	OPEC2
Crude oil import	By country	indices	Yes	A, Q, M	OECD	IEA6 (I.3)
Crude oil import	By country	US$/bbl	Yes	A, Q, M	OECD	IEA6 (I.2)
Crude oil import	By type of crude	US$/bbl	Yes	A, Q, M	World	IEA6 (I.4)
Crude oil imports	By country	US$/barrel	Yes	A	IEA Countries	IEA10 (I.12)
Crude oil imports	By type of crude	US$/barrel	Yes	A, M	World, OECD, non-OECD	IEA10 (I.11)
Crude oil netback values	By API	$/bl per fob	Yes	A, M	UK, M East, Africa	BB1 (19.1)
Crude oil netback values	By country By product, API	$ per bl fob	Yes	A, M	World	BB2 (14.1)
Crude oil prices	By API,M average	$ per bl fob	Yes	A	OPEC	BB1 (17.1, 17.3)
Crude oil prices, OPEC	By country and product	$ per bl fob	Yes	A, M	OPEC	BB2 (14.3)
Crude oil prices, Saudi Arabian	By M average	$ per bl fob	Yes	A	Selected countries	BB1 (17.2)
Crude oil sales prices	By API	$ per bl fob	Yes	A, M	Non-OPEC	BB1 (17.4)
Crude oil sales prices, non-OPEC	By country and product	$/bl	Yes	A, M	Non-OPEC	BB2 (14.4)
Crude oil spot	By type of crude	US$/bbl	Yes	A, Q, M	World	IEA6 (I.1)
Crude Oil, f.o.b. loading ports	By type of crude and gravity API	US$/barrel	Yes	A	OPEC	OPEC1 (71)
Crude oil, freight rate index, general	% of worldscale	indices	Yes	A	World	OPEC1 (66)
Crude oil, freight rates, average spot	% of worldscale	dwt	Yes	A	World	
Crude Oil, spot		US$/barrel	Yes	M	OPEC	OECD2
Crude Oil, spot	By country, type of crude	US$/barrel	Yes	M	Selected non-OPEC countries	OPEC2
Crude Oil, spot	OPEC Basket and selected crudes	US$/barrel	No		World	OPEC2
Crude oil, spot prices	By API	$ per bl fob	Yes	A, M	World	BB1 (18)
Crude oil, spot prices	By change, product	$ per bl, %	Yes	A, M		BP2 (-)
Crude oil, spot prices	Price by country and product, API	$ per bl fob	Yes	A, M, W	World	BB2 (14.2)
Crude Oil, spot prices; NWE/ARA	By change, product	%, $ per tonnes	Yes	A, M		BP2 (-)

Subject	Categories	Units	Time series Yes/No Frequency		Territorial coverage	Source (Table no.)
Crude oil, spot prices; USG	By change, product	%, $ per bl, c/gal	Yes	A, M		BP2 (-)
Crude oil, spot tanker freight rates	By change, haul	%, $ per tonnes	Yes	A, M		BP2 (-)
Diesel oil, automotive		US$ per litre/ toe	Yes	A	OECD	IEA6 (IID.3)
Diesel oil, automotive	By country	US$ per litre/ toe	Yes	A	Non-OECD	IEA6 (IIIB.3)
Electricity	For industry and household use by country	nat curr per kWh	Yes	A, Q	Non-OECD	IEA6 (IIIA.1)
Electricity	For industry and household use by country	US$ per kWh/ toe	Yes	A	Non-OECD	IEA6 (III(B.8-B.9))
Electricity	For industry and households by country	nat curr per kWh	Yes	A, Q	OECD	IEA6 (IIB.1)
Electricity	For industry and household use	US$ per kWh/ toe	Yes	A	OECD	IEA6 (II(D.8-D.9))
Electricity for households	Using exchange rates and PPPs	US$ per kWh	Yes	A	OECD	IEA6 (IIE.4)
Electricity generation	By fuel type and by country incl. and excl. tax	nat curr per toe	Yes	A, Q	Non-OECD	IEA6 (IIIA.2)
Electricity generation	By fuel type and by country incl. and excl. tax	nat curr per toe	Yes	A, Q	OECD	IEA6 (IIB.2)
Electricity, domestic		nat curr/kWh ECUs/kWh PPS/kWh	Yes	A	EC	EC28
Electricity, domestic	Net of tax, VAT excluded, selling price, by country	nat curr/kWh PPS/kWh ECUs/kWh	Yes	A	EC, Selected Cities	EC28
Electricity, industry		nat curr/kWh ECUs/kWh PPS/kWh	Yes	A	EC	EC28
Electricity, industry	Net of tax, VAT excluded, selling price, by country	nat curr/kWh PPS/kWh ECUs/kWh	Yes	A	EC, Selected Cities	EC28
Energy	By fuel type wholesale and retail by country	indices	Yes	A, Q	Non-OECD	IEA6 (IIIA.3)
Energy pices for end-users	By country	indices	Yes	A, Q	OECD	IEA6 (IIA.5)
Energy prices	By fuel type wholesale and retail by country	indices	Yes	A, Q	OECD	IEA6 (IIB.3)
Energy prices - household consumers	By energy type, by country	nat curr, PPS, ECU	Yes	2 yr	EC	EC32 (-)
Energy prices - industrial consumers	By energy type, by country	nat curr, PPS, ECU	Yes	2 yr	EC	EC32 (-)
Energy prices, for end-users	By energy type for industry and households	indices	Yes	A, Q	OECD, EC USA and Japan	IEA6 (II(A.1-A.4))
Energy prices, supplied	Price comparison, household sector (all taxes included), industrial sector (VAT and deductible specific taxes excluded), by energy type	ECU/GJ	Yes	2 yr	EC	EC32 (-)

37 PRICES

Subject	Categories	Units	Time series Yes/No	Frequency	Territorial coverage	Source (Table no.)
Energy prices, useful	Price comparison, household sector (all taxes included), industrial sector (VAT and deductible specific taxes excluded), by energy type	indices	Yes	2 yr	EC	EC32 (-)
Fuel oil	By type and country incl. and excl. tax	nat curr per toe	Yes	A, Q	OECD	IEA6 (IIB.2)
Fuel oil	By type incl. and excl. tax by country	nat curr per toe	Yes	A, Q	Non-OECD	IEA6 (IIIA.2)
Fuel oil, heavy	For industry and electricity generation by country	nat curr per tonne	Yes	A, Q	Non-OECD	IEA6 (IIIA.1)
Fuel oil, heavy	For industry and electricity generation by country	US$ per tonne/ toe	Yes	A	Non-OECD	IEA6 (III(B.6-B.7))
Fuel oil, heavy	For industry and electricity generation	US$ per tonne/ toe	Yes	A	OECD	IEA6 (II(D.6-D.7))
Fuel oil, light	For industry and household use by country	nat curr per 'ooo Litres	Yes	A, Q	Non-OECD	IEA6 (IIIA.1)
Fuel oil, light	For industry and household use by country	US$ per 'ooo litres/toe	Yes	A	Non-OECD	IEA6 (III(B.4-B.5))
Fuel oil, light	For industry and household use	US$ per litre/ toe	Yes	A	OECD	IEA6 (II(D.4-D.5))
Fuel oil, light for households	Using exchange rates and PPPs	US$ per 'ooo litres	Yes	A	OECD	IEA6 (IIE.3)
Fuel oils	By type and country	nat curr per litre/tonne	Yes	A, Q	OECD	IEA6 (IIB.1)
Fuel to end users	Electricity generation and industrial use by fuel type	US$	Yes	A	OECD	IEA2 (-)
Fuel to end users	Electricity generation and industrial use by fuel type	US$ nat curr	Yes	A	OECD	IEA2 (-)
Fuels, automotive	By type and by country	nat curr per litre	Yes	A, Q	Non-OECD	IEA6 (IIIA.1)
Fuels, automotive	By type and country	nat curr per litre	Yes	A, Q	OECD	IEA6 (IIB.1)
Gas - gasworks gas prices for households	By region, by price net of tax, price excluding VAT, selling price	nat curr	Yes	A	EC	EC48 (-)
Gas - gasworks gas prices for industry	By region, by price net of tax, price excluding VAT, selling price	nat curr	Yes	A	EC	EC48 (-)
Gas - natural gas prices for households	By region, by price net of tax, price excluding VAT, selling price	nat curr	Yes	A	EC	EC48 (-)
Gas - natural gas prices for industry	By region, by price net of tax, price excluding VAT, selling price	nat curr	Yes	A	EC	EC48 (-)
Gas and oil prices	By country, product	US$ per Btu	Yes	A	Japan, OECD, USA	BP2 (-)
Gas natural prices	By source delivered	US$ per mm	Yes	A, M	World	DSC2 (3.4)
Gas, liquefied natural: imports		US$ per toe	Yes	A, Q	France and Japan	IEA6 (I.20)
Gas, natural	By country incl. and excl. tax	nat curr per toe	Yes	A, Q	OECD	IEA6 (IIB.2)

Subject	Categories	Units	Time series Yes/No	Frequency	Territorial coverage	Source (Table no.)
Gas, natural	For industry, electricity generation and household use by country	nat curr per 107 kCal	Yes	A, Q	Non-OECD	IEA6 (IIIA.1)
Gas, natural	For industry, electricity generation and households, by country	nat curr per Kcal	Yes	A, Q	OECD	IEA6 (IIB.1)
Gas, natural	For industry, electricity generation and household use	US$ per 107kcal/toe	Yes	A	OECD	IEA6 (II(D.10-D.12))
Gas, natural	For industry, electricity generation and household use by country	US$ per 107kCal/toe	Yes	A	Non-OECD	IEA6 (III(B.10-B.12))
Gas, natural	Incl. and excl. tax by country	nat curr per toe	Yes	A, Q	Non-OECD	IEA6 (IIIA.2)
Gas, natural		US$/btu	Yes	A	EC, Western EC, USA	BP1 (p25)
Gas, natural for households	Using exchange rates and PPPs	US$ per 107kcal		Yes	A	OECD IEA6 (IIE.5)
Gas, natural: exported by pipeline		US$ per toe	Yes	A, Q	Netherlands and Norway	IEA6 (I.21)
Gas, natural: imports by pipeline	By country	US$ per toe	Yes	A, Q	Selected OECD countries	IEA6 (I.19)
Gasoline		US$ per litre/ toe	Yes	A	OECD	IEA6 (IID.2)
Gasoline	By country	US$ per litre/ toe	Yes	A	Non-OECD	IEA6 (IIIB.2)
Gasoline	Using exchange rates and PPPs	US$ per litre	Yes	A	OECD	IEA6 (IIE.2)
Heavy fuel oil for industry	By country	nat curr/t	Yes	A, Q	France, Germany, Italy, Spain, UK, Japan, US	IEA10 (I.17)
Household fuel	By fuel type and by country incl. and excl. tax	nat curr per toe	Yes	A, Q	Non-OECD	IEA6 (IIIA.2)
Household fuel	By type and by country incl. and excl. tax	nat curr per toe	Yes	A, Q	OECD	IEA6 (IIB.2)
Light fuel oil for households	By country	nat curr/litre	Yes	A	France, Germany, Italy, Spain, UK, Japan, US	IEA10 (I.16)
LPG - prices in major markets	By product, market	US$ per tonne	Yes	A, Q	Major markets	BP2 (-)
Motor fuels	By fuel type	nat curr	No		EC	EC33 (-)
Oil products	By type of product and market, fob	US$/barrel	Yes	M	EC, US, Caribbean, Middle East, Singapore	OPEC2
Oil, crude spot	By type of crude	US$/barrel	Yes	A	USA	BP1 (p12)
Oil, spot	Dubai, Brent	US$/barrel	Yes	Q, M	World	OECD25 (XV)
Oil, spot refined product prices	By M average, product	$/tonnes, $/bl, c/gl	Yes	A, M	World	BB1 (19.2- 19.3)
Oil, spot refined product prices	By product, futures	$/tonne, $/bl, c/gal, %	Yes	A, M,	World	BB2 (15.1-15.2)
Petroleum products	Premium gasoline, LFO HFO 3% sulphur	US$/tonne US$/barrel	Yes	A, Q	Rotterdam	IEA10 (I.14)
Petroleum products, spot	November average	US$/barrel	No		World	OPEC2
Retail motor gasoline	By country	nat curr/litre	Yes	A, Q	France, Germany, Italy, Spain, UK, Japan, US	IEA10 (I.15)
Spot freight rates by tanker size	By ASFR, spot(dirty),	tonnes, % of WS, $ per tonne	Yes	A, M	World	BB2 (22)

37 PRICES

Subject	Categories	Units	Time series Yes/No	Frequency	Territorial coverage	Source (Table no.)
Useful energy prices	Price comparison, household sector (all taxes included), industrial sector (VAT and deductible specific taxes excluded), by energy type	ECU/GJ	Yes	2 yr	EC	EC32 (-)
37.7 FINANCIAL MARKETS - see also Section 19						
Share prices	Industrials, all shares	indices	Yes	A, M, Q	OECD	OECD22
37.8 IRON AND STEEL INDUSTRY – see also under Producer Prices (37.12), Trade (37.16), Minerals, Ores and Metals (37.9) and Sections 25, 32 and 33						
ECSC basic prices	By product	nat curr/tonne	Yes	A	EC	EC55 (8.2-8.13)
Iron and steel - spot prices, MB assessment, small merchants' and consumers' buying prices	By country, by product and basing point	nat curr	No		World	MB1 (-)
Iron and steel products continental producers	By type	US$ /tonne	Yes	I	OECD	OECD18 (28)
Iron and steel products, home	By type	US$, nat curr	No		OECD	OECD18 (27)
Iron ore prices	By country	nat curr	No		World	MB1 (-)
Iron ore prices in the major world markets	By company	US cents per 1%/dmt fob	Yes	A	World	DSC2 (5.3)
Iron ore prices, European	By country, by type	cents per tonne	No		Selected countries	MB2 (-)
Iron ore prices, Japan	By country, by type	cents per tonne	No		Selected countries	MB2 (-)
Iron-ore prices		nat curr indices	Yes	M	OECD	OECD18 (25)
Non-ferrous metal LME prices, comex daily prices, Chicago buying price, MB international quotation	By country, by metal	nat curr	No		World	MB1 (-)
Scap merchants' buying price, MB ferrous scrap index, MB assessment	By country, by type	nat curr	No		World	MB1 (-)
Scrap, prices		indices	Yes	A	OECD	OECD18 (26)
37.9 MINERALS, ORES AND METALS – see also under Producer Prices (37.12), Trade (37.16), Iron and Steel Industry (37.8) and Sections 25, 32 and 33						
Aluminium	By London Exchange cash settlement	$ per tonne,	Yes	A, M	World	WBMS2 (-)
Aluminium	By settlement, by 3 months	$ per tonne	Yes	D	World	WBMS2 (-)
Aluminium alloy	By settlement, by 3 months	$ per tonne	Yes	D	World	WBMS2 (-)
Aluminium, primary ingot	London Metal Exchange cash price	USc/lb	Yes	A	World	IBA1 (5)
Ammonium paratungstate	Low, high, average	US$/mtu	Yes	I	USA, EC	UNCTAD3 (1.4)
Copper	By London exchange cash settlement, US producer price	£ per tonne cents per lb	Yes	A, M	World	WBMS2 (-)

Subject	Categories	Units	Time series Yes/No Frequency		Territorial coverage	Source (Table no.)
Copper	By settlement, by 3 months, by producer price	£ per tonne cents per lb	Yes	D	World	WBMS2 (-)
Ferro-tungsten	Low, high, average	US$/kg	Yes	I	World	UNCTAD3 (1.3)
Gold	By London bullion dealers fixed price	$ per troy oz	Yes	A, M	World	WBMS2 (-)
Gold	By spot price	$ per troy oz	Yes	D	World	WBMS2 (-)
Lead	By London exchange cash settlement, US producer price	£ per tonne cents per lb	Yes	A, M	World	WBMS2 (-)
Lead	By settlement, by 3 months, by producer price	£ per tonne cents per lb	Yes	D	World	WBMS2 (-)
Lead, refined	London Metal Exchange, United States	£/tonne USc/lb	Yes	A, M	London, US	ILZSG1 (4)
Metal prices, average	By type	US$ tonnes, cents per lb, £ tonnes, pence per troy ounce, US$ troy ounce	Yes	A	World	WBMS3 (-)
Metal prices, averages	By metal type	£ and $	Yes	A, M	World	WBMS1 (-)
Metal prices, officially quoted	By metal	US$/tonne	No		World	MJ1 (2)
Metal prices, relative	By selected metal, by ratio relative to zinc	US cents	No		World	ILZSG2 (2)
Minerals	Price index	indices	Yes	A	World	UN32 (K)
Nickel	By London exchange cash settlement, producer price	$ per tonne, $ per lb	Yes	A, M	World	WBMS2 (-)
Nickel	By settlement, by 3 months	$ per tonne	Yes	D	World	WBMS2 (-)
Silver	By London bullion dealers fixed price By US producer price	pence per troy oz cents per troy oz	Yes	A, M	World	WBMS2 (-)
Silver	By spot price, 3, 6, 12 months, producer price	pence per troy oz, cents per troy oz	Yes	D	World	WBMS2 (-)
Silver price ratio to base-metals	By base metal	US cents	No		World	ILZSG2 (3)
Tin	By London Exchange cash settlement, US producer price	$ per tonne, cents per lb	Yes	A, M	World	WBMS2 (-)
Tin	By settlement, by 3 months, by Kuala Lumpur	$ per tonne, cents per lb	Yes	D	World	WBMS2 (-)
Tungsten carbide powder	Low, high, average	£/kg	Yes	I	World	UNCTAD3 (1.3)
Tungsten concentrates	Price and quantity	US$/mtu, tonnes, %, mtu	Yes	A, M	World	UNCTAD3 (1.2)
Tungsten concentrates	Wolframite, scheelite	US$/mtu, tonnes	Yes	A, M	World	UNCTAD3 (1.1)
Tungsten powder	Low, high, average	£/kg	Yes	I	World	UNCTAD3 (1.3)
Zinc	By London Exchange cash settlement, US producer price	$ per tonne, cents per lb	Yes	A, M	World	WBMS2 (-)
Zinc	By settlement, by 3 months, by producer price	$ per tonne, cents per lb	Yes	D	World	WBMS2 (-)
Zinc	London Metal Exchange, United States	US$/tonne USc/lb	Yes	A, M	London, US	ILZSG1 (29)

Subject	Categories	Units	Time series Yes/No Frequency		Territorial coverage	Source (Table no.)

37.10 NATIONAL ACCOUNTS PRICE DEFLATORS – see also under Consumer Prices (37.5) and Section 34

Subject	Categories	Units	Time series Yes/No	Frequency	Territorial coverage	Source (Table no.)
Consumer price indices		%	Yes	A	OECD, EC,	OECD32 (8.11)
Consumer price indices: all items less food		%	Yes	A	OECD, EC,	OECD32 (8.12)
Consumer price indices: energy		%	Yes	A	OECD, EC,	OECD32 (8.14)
Consumer price indices: food		%	Yes	A	OECD, EC,	OECD32 (8.13)
Exports of goods and services	Implicit price index	%	Yes	A	OECD, EC,	OECD32 (8.9)
Final domestic demand	Implicit price index	%	Yes	A	OECD, EC,	OECD32 (8.2)
Final uses, domestic origin: producers' prices	By country, NACE classification and final use	nat curr	No		EC	EC63
GDP price indices	Yearly value	indices	Yes	A	EC	EC28
Government final consumption expenditure	Implicit price index	%	Yes	A	OECD, EC,	OECD32 (8.4)
Gross fixed capital formation	Implicit price index	%	Yes	A	OECD, EC,	OECD32 (8.5)
Implicit price index, GDP	At market prices	indices	Yes	A	Latin American and Caribbean countries	UN45 (234)
Implicit price index, gross domestic product		%	Yes	A	OECD, EC	OECD32 (8.1)
Imports of goods and services	Implicit price index	%	Yes	A	OECD, EC,	OECD32 (8.10)
Imports, final uses: producers' prices	By country, NACE classification and final use	nat curr	No		EC	EC63
Inflation	Annual rate	%	Yes	A	Western World	MLC1 (-)
Inflation	GDP implicit price deflected	%	No		EC	WC1 (-)
Inflation rate	By country,region	%	No		UNICEF assisted countries	UNICEF2 (-)
Inflation rates	By country	%	No		EC	EM1 (0306)
Intermediate inputs of domestic origin: producers' prices	By country and NACE classification	nat curr	No		EC	EC63
Intermediate inputs, imports: producers' prices	By country and NACE classification	nat curr	No		EC	EC63
Intermediate inputs: producers' prices	By country and NACE classification	nat curr	No		EC	EC63
Machinery and equipment	Implicit price index	%	Yes	A	OECD, EC,	OECD32 (8.8)
Non-residential construction	Implicit price index	%	Yes	A	OECD, EC,	OECD32 (8.7)
Price indices	By country, by consumer prices, wholesale prices, GDP deflator, expenditures deflator	indices	Yes	A	Developing countries	WB2 (-)
Price shares, index numbers of	By type	indices	Yes	A, M	Nordic countries	NCM1 (185)
Prices, production, employment		indices	Yes	A, M	World	IMF7 (-)
Primary inputs: producers' prices	By country,type and NACE classification	nat curr	No		EC	EC63
Private consumption expenditure	Implicit price index	%	Yes	A	OECD, EC,	OECD32 (8.3)

Subject	Categories	Units	Time series Yes/No Frequency		Territorial coverage	Source (Table no.)
Producer price indices	By NACE sector total industry (NACE 1-4), intermediate goods, capital goods industries, consumer goods, total NACE 1, NACE 2-4	indices	Yes	A, M	EC	EC52 (-)
Producer price indices: manufacturing		%	Yes	A	OECD, EC,	OECD32 (8.15)
Producer price indices: basic metals		%	Yes	A	OECD, EC,	OECD32 (8.18)
Producer price indices: chemicals		%	Yes	A	OECD, EC,	OECD32 (8.17)
Producer price indices: metal products, machinery and equipment		%	Yes	A	OECD, EC,	OECD32 (8.19)
Producer price indices: textiles, clothing and leather		%	Yes	A	OECD, EC,	OECD32 (8.20)
Producer price indices: food, beverages and tobacco		%	Yes	A	OECD, EC,	OECD32 (8.16)
Residential construction	Implicit price index	%	Yes	A	OECD, EC,	OECD32 (8.6)
Share price index			Yes	A	EC	EC9 (2.34)

37.11 PAPER AND BOARD – see also under Producer Prices (37.12), Trade (37.16) and Section 25

Linerboard prices - Kraftliner	By country	nat currtonnes,	No		Selected countries	JP1 (-)
Newsprint prices	By market, grades,	nat curr/ tonnes, lb, grammes/sq m	No		Selected countries	JP1 (-)
Prices - fluting	By market, grades	tonnes/nat curr	No		USA, Germany	JP1 (-)
Prices of sack and other Kraft papers	By market, grades	nat curr/tonnes	No		Germany, USA	JP1 (-)
Printing and writings	By market, grades, country	nat curr/ tonnes	no		Selected countries	JP1 (-)
Pulp prices	By type, period	tonnes/nat curr, c.i.f,	No		Western EC, North America	JP1 (-)

37.12 PRODUCER PRICES – see also under Commodities (37.3) and Sections 2, 5, 7, 17, 21, 23, 25, 32, 33, 41 and 45

Machinery and transport	Price index	indices	Yes	A	World	UN32 (J)
Price indices	Index, % change	indices, %	Yes	A	ASEAN	ASEANS1 (8.2)
Price scissors of intermediate consumption	Nominal index of final output divided by the nominal index of prices of intermediate consumption, trends in	indices	Yes	A	EC	EC2 (A35)
Producer prices		indices	Yes	A	World	IMF7 (-)
Producer prices		indices	Yes	A, Q, M	OECD,	OECD22 (-)
Producer prices		nat curr, ECU	Yes	A	EC	EC55 (8.1)
Producer prices	By commodity group	indices	Yes	A, M	OECD	OECD22
Producer prices	By product and industry,	indices	Yes	M, Q, A	OECD	OECD23 (-)
	by manufacturing, all	indices	Yes	M, Q, A	OECD Total, EC Major Seven	OECD23 (-)
Producer prices	By sector	indices	Yes	Q, M	OECD	OECD15
Producer prices	Manufacturing	indices	Yes	A, M	OECD Total EC Total Major Seven Total	OECD22

Subject	Categories	Units	Time series Yes/No	Frequency	Territorial coverage	Source (Table no.)
Producer prices	Total, food and beverages, paper and allied industries, chemicals, basic metals, metal products, electrical machinery, petroleum and coal products	indices	Yes	A, Q, M	OECD	OECD22
Producers prices and wholesale prices	Product group	indices	Yes	A	World	UN50 (21)
Product prices	Individual products by NACE sector	ECU	No		EC	EC66 (2)
Product prices	Individual products by NACE sector	nat curr	No		EC	EC66 (1)
Wholesale price indices		indices	Yes	A	Latin American and Caribbean countries	UN45 (235)
Wholesale price indices	By countries	indices	Yes	A	EC	MAC3 (H1)
Wholesale price indices	By type of goods, by country	indices	Yes	A	ESCAP countries	UN44
Wholesale price indices	General, producers, consumers	indices	Yes	A	Nordic countries	NCM1 (164)
Wholesale price indices	By countries	nos	No		The Americas and Australasia	MAC2 (I1)
Wholesale price indices	By country, index	indices	Yes	A	Africa and Asia	MAC1 (I1)
Wholesale prices		%	Yes	A	World	IMF7 (-)
Wholesale prices		%, indices	Yes	A	World	IMF7 (-)
Wholesale Prices	By type of product	indices	Yes	A, M	Austria	OECD22
Wholesale prices and consumer price index numbers		indices	Yes	M	Asia and Pacific	UN43 (-)

37.13 RUBBER - see also under Producer Prices (37.12), Trade (37.16) and Section 5

Subject	Categories	Units	Time series Yes/No	Frequency	Territorial coverage	Source (Table no.)
Natural rubber prices		nat curr	Yes	M	Major cities	IRSG1 (44)
		nat curr	Yes	A	Major cities	IRSG2 (35)
Natural rubber prices - INRO daily market indicator	Daily high, low, monthly average	Singapore cents	Yes	M	Malaysia	IRSG2 (36)

37.14 SHIPPING – see also under Producer Prices (37.12), Trade (37.16) and Section 41

Subject	Categories	Units	Time series Yes/No	Frequency	Territorial coverage	Source (Table no.)
Average spot freight rates	By vessel size	% worldscale	Yes	M	World	BB3 (1)
Demolition prices		US$/LDT	Yes	A	Far East, Pakistan, India, Southern EC	UNCTAD2 (27)
Demolition prices	By area, type	$ per ldt	Yes	A, M	World	DSC1 (38)
Demolition prices by area	Second-hand prices of dry cargo vessels and tankers; average values; prices for new buildings; development of bunker market prices	US$	Yes	A	World	ISL2 (1.6.1-4)
Dirty spot, rates	Load, discharge, route no, cargo, fixtures	dwct, Ws, nos	Yes	A, M	World	DSC1 (4, 7)
Freight costs in world trade	Estimate and totals values	% import	Yes	A	World	ISL2 (2.2.7)
Freight costs in world trade, total	Estimate of total freight costs of imports, value of imports, freight costs as % of import value	US$	Yes	I	World, economic regions	UNCTAD2 (31)
Freight rate indices	By sources	indices, WS	Yes	A, M	World	ISL1 (-)

Subject	Categories	Units	Time series Yes/No	Frequency	Territorial coverage	Source (Table no.)
Freight rates	By haul	indices	Yes	A, M	World	COS1 (12.1 -12.3)
Freight rates, comparative	By selected commodity	US$/tonne	No		World	UNCTAD2 (29)
Freight rates, heavy grains	Port of origin to port of destination	US$/tonne	Yes	A, M	World Ports	IWhC3
Freight rates, tanker	Dirty, clean	%/dwt	Yes	A, M	World	ISL2 (5.7)
Futures prices, implied rates	By BFI route, commodity	$ per Dwct $ per day, %	Yes	M	World	DSC1 (41)
Indices and rates (Lloyds, Maritime Research)	By vessel and cargo type	indices, dwt, $ dwt per month	Yes	A, M	World	ISL1 (I 3.1-5)
Newbuilding prices	By type and size of vessel	US$	Yes	A	World	UNCTAD2 (20)
Newbuildings, contracting prices	By ship type	$, dwt/cu m	Yes	A	World	COS1(15.1)
Ocean freight rates by commodity	Major load,discharge areas	US$	No		World	WFP1 (15)
Oil, bunker market prices	By oil type, % change over period	US$ fob, % change, tonnes	Yes	A, M	Hamburg-Le Havre	ISL1 (-)
Oil, spot market dirty fixtures		US$	Yes	A, M	Arabian Gulf to north EC	ISL2 (5.8)
Prices, breaking		ldt, US$	Yes	A	EC, Far East	F1 (17)
Prices, contracting	By new ship type	US$, dwt	Yes	A	World South	F1 (16)
Representative prices	By area, vessel and oil type	US$ per tonne	Yes	A, Q, M	World	DSC1 (40)
Scrap prices	By region, % change over period	US$, % change	Yes	A, M	Selected countries	ISL1 (-)
Second hand prices	By ship type, when built, % change over period	US$, % change	Yes	A, M	World	ISL1 (-)
Secondhand average price	By ship type, age	nat curr	Yes	A	World	COS1(15.2)
Secondhand prices	By type, dwt, age	$	Yes	A, Q	World	DSC1 (36)
Shipping costs, prices	By bunker market prices, demolition prices by area	US$ fob, tonnes US$ per LDT, indices	Yes	A, M	World	ISL1 (I 1.6.1-2)
Spot fixtures dirty, clean	By period	nos, tonnes, $ per tonnes	No		World	BB3 (-)
World market prices		indices	Yes	A, M	World	ISL1 (-)

37.15 TEXTILES – see also under Producer Prices (37.12), Trade (37.16) and Sections 5 and 25

Cotton	Changes in consumer price	%	Yes	A	World	ICAC2 (p79)
Cotton (	Changes in domestic product	%	Yes	A	World	ICAC2 (p78)
Cotton (New York Futures)		USc/lb	Yes	A	New York	ICAC2 (pp61-63)
Cotton (north EC)		USc/lb	Yes	A, M	World	ICAC2 (pp56-59)
Polyester		nat curr/kg nat curr/lb	Yes	M	US, Taiwan, Italy Japan, Germany	ICAC2 (p60)

37.16 TRADE – IMPORTS AND EXPORTS – see also Section 27

Commodities, export	Price quotations, by country	US$	Yes	A	ESCAP countries	UN44
Export commodities, major	By commodity	value by weight	Yes	A	ASEAN	ASEANS1 (8.3)
Export price index numbers	Primary commodities, non-ferrous base metals	indices	Yes	A, M	World	UN35 (50)

37 PRICES

Subject	Categories	Units	Time series Yes/No Frequency		Territorial coverage	Source (Table no.)
Export price index numbers	Primary commodities and non-ferrous base metals	indices	Yes	A	Market economies	UN50 (13)
Food		indices	Yes	A	World	UN50 (1)
Import and export prices, terms of trade	By country, by index group	indices	No		EC	EC18 (15.2)
Minerals		indices	Yes	A	World	UN50 (1)
Non-food, of agricultural origin		indices	Yes	A	World	UN50 (1)
Prices	Import prices, export prices, terms of trade, by country	indices	Yes	A	VICES countries and Yugoslavia	VICES1 (III/1)
Primary commodities, export		indices	Yes	A, Q	World	GATT4 (A.18)
Trade, total		indices	Yes	A	World	UN50 (1)

38 PRODUCTION

38.1 AGRICULTURE, FOOD, DRINK AND TOBACCO
- 38.1.1 Outputs
- 38.1.2 Outputs and Inputs

38.2 CHEMICALS

38.3 CONSTRUCTION AND CONSTRUCTION MATERIALS

38.4 ENERGY

38.5 FISHING

38.6 FORESTRY

38.7 GENERAL
- 38.7.1 Production, Deliveries, Orders and Stocks – Total and by Industry
- 38.7.2 Production – By Type of Goods

38.8 MANUFACTURING

38.9 MINERALS, ORES AND METALS
- 38.9.1 Iron and Steel
- 38.9.2 Products other than Iron and Steel

38.10 MINING AND QUARRYING

38.11 PAPER AND BOARD

38.12 RUBBER

38.13 TEXTILES AND LEATHER

38.14 TRANSPORT EQUIPMENT
- 38.14.1 Motor Vehicles
- 38.14.2 Shipping

38 PRODUCTION

Subject	Categories	Units	Time series Yes/No Frequency		Territorial coverage	Source (Table no.)

38.1 AGRICULTURE, FOOD, DRINK AND TOBACCO - see also Sections 2 and 34

38.1.1 Outputs

Subject	Categories	Units	Time series Yes/No	Frequency	Territorial coverage	Source (Table no.)
Agricultural production, growth	By high, middle, low income, by GDP agriculture, industry	%	No		World	CS1 (4A)
Agricultural production, volume index numbers		indices	Yes	A	EC	EC6 (IG 3)
Agricultural production, value	Detailed figures at current prices and exchange rates	ECU	Yes	A	EC	EC6 (IG 4)
Agricultural production, value	Overall figures in percentage of final production of the EC at current prices and exchange rates	%	No		EC	EC6 (IG 5)
Agricultural production, value	Detailed figures in percentage of final production of each country at current prices and exchange rates	%	No		EC	EC6 (IG 6)
Agricultural production, growth	Total, per capita, anual average growth rates of agricultural production	%	Yes	A	World	UNCTAD1 ge (6.5)
Agricultural production	By production	tonnes	Yes	A	World	FAO1 (14)
Agricultural production	Broad groups	1000 ton	Yes	A	African countries	UN1 (22)
Agricultural production index	Agricultural production, food production, cereal production	indices	Yes	A	World, ASEAN	ASEANS1 (3.3)
Agriculture, production	By crop	%, tonnes	No		World, developing ACP	EC1 (I3-I12)
Agriculture, fishery, forestry	Selected commodities	1000 ton	Yes	A	African countries	UN1 (21)
Agriculture		indices	Yes	A, Q M	OECD	OECD22 (-)
Agriculture and production	By high, middle, low income	index, tones	No		World	CS1 (14)
Animal products	By type	tonnes	Yes	A	VICES region, VICES countries and Yugoslavia	VICES1 (I/5)
Animal products	Output	indices	Yes	A, M	Denmark	OECD22
Animals, slaughter weight	By type	kg/carcass	Yes	A	EC	EC7 (IV)
Animals and animal products	Gross indigenous production, usable production, by animal, product	tonnes	Yes	A	EC	EC7 (IV)
Animals slaughtered	By meat type and by country	nos	Yes	A	OECD	OECD26
Beef and veal, total		tonnes	Yes	A	OECD	OECD26
Beef and veal, slaughtered		tonnes	Yes	A	OECD	OECD26
Beef and veal		tonnes	Yes	A	ASEAN	ASEANS1 (4.1.5)
Beer		hectolitres	Yes	A	World	UN50 (97)
Beer	By country	hectolitres	Yes	A	Europe	MAC3 (D26)
Beer	By country	nos	No		The Americas and Australasia	MAC2 (E21)
Beer	By country	ha	Yes	A	Africa and Asia	MAC1 (E27)
Beverages	By product, total	h/tonnes	Yes	A	World	UN28 (-)
Butter		tonnes	No		EC, USA, USSR, Canada, Japan	EC9 (5.8)
Butter	By vegetable	tonnes	Yes	A	World	UN50 (92)

38 PRODUCTION

Subject	Categories	Units	Time series Yes/No	Frequency	Territorial coverage	Source (Table no.)
Cereal imports and production	By high, middle, low income	tonnes, kg	No		World	CS1 (15)
Cereals	By type	tonnes	No		World	EC9 (5.4)
Cheese		tonnes	No		EC, USA, USSR, Canada, Japan	EC9 (5.8)
Cheese		tonnes	Yes	A	World	UN50 (93)
Cigarettes		nos	Yes	A	World	UN50 (98)
Cocoa beans, grindings	By country	tonnes	Yes	A, Q	World	ICC02 (3)
Cocoa beans, summary data	Gross crop, grindings surplus, deficit, end of season stocks, buffer stocks, price	tonnes, %, US$/tonne, SDR's/tonne	Yes	A	World	ICC02 (1)
Cocoa beans	By country	tonnes	Yes	A	World	ICC02 (2)
Commodities, by type		indices	Yes	A	World	UN50 (1)
Crop yields	By type of crop	kg/ha	Yes	10 A	EC, USA, USSR,	EC9 (5.3)
Crops	Areas, yields and production, by product	tonnes, ha, kg/ha	Yes	A	EC	EC19 (II)
Crops	By type	tonnes	Yes	A	VICES region, VICES countries and Yugoslavia	VICES1 (I/5)
Crops	Usable production, by product	tonnes	Yes	A	EC	EC19 (V)
Dressed carcass weight	By meat type and by country	kg	Yes	A	OECD	OECD26
Eggs		tonnes	No		EC, USA, USSR, Canada, Japan	EC9 (5.8)
Eggs and poultry, chicks placed	By type of poultry, by type of stock	nos	Yes	M	EC	EC7 (II)
Eggs and poultry, hatcheries	Chicks hatched, eggs in incubation, by type of poultry, by type of stock	nos	Yes	M	EC	EC7 (II)
Fertilizers, nitrogenous		tonnes	Yes	A	World	UN50 (104)
Fertilizers, phosphate		tonnes	Yes	A	World	UN50 (105)
Fertilizers, potash		tonnes	Yes	A	World	UN50 (106)
Fertilizers		tonnes	Yes	A	Latin American and Caribbean countries	UN45 (344)
Fertilizers		tonnes	Yes	A	World	UN50 (1)
Fertilizers	Nitrogenous, phosphate, potash	tonnes	No		World	EC9 (4.7)
Food	By major foodstuffs, by country	tonnes	Yes	A	OECD	OECD12
Food	By product, total Food crops cereals livestock products wheat barley maize (corn) rice (paddy) potatoes cotton (lint) groundnuts (in shell) wool, greasy meat hens' eggs milk coffee, green tea cocoa (beans) tobacco	tonnes,	Yes	A	World	UN28 (-)

Subject	Categories	Units	Time series Yes/No Frequency		Territorial coverage	Source (Table no.)
Food and agricultural production		indices	Yes	A	World	UN50 (6)
Food and total agric production, index numbers per capita		indices	Yes	A	World	UN50 (7)
Food production, growth rates,	Total, per capita, annual average growth rates of food production	%	Yes	A	World	UNCTAD1 (6.5)
Food stocks, variation	By major foodstuffs, by country	tonnes	Yes	A	OECD	OECD12
Fruit	Pure stand areas, harvested production, by fruit	tonnes, ha,	Yes	A	EC	EC19 (III)
Fruit	Total fresh fruit, apple citrus, dried	tonnes	No		World	EC9 (5.5)
Grain production	By region	tonnes	Yes	A	World	DSC2 (7.3)
Grape vines, area planted		ha	Yes	4 yr	World	OIVV1 (A)
Grape vines, area planted	By type	ha	No		World	OIVV1 (B)
Grapes, table		q	Yes	4 yr	World	OIVV1 (O)
Grapes		q	Yes	4 yr	World	OIVV1 (C)
Grapes	Wine grapes, table grapes, grapes for drying	q	No		World	OIVV1 (D)
Horse meat, total		tonnes	Yes	A	OECD	OECD26
Horse meat, slaughtered		tonnes kilolitres, h	Yes	A	OECD	OECD26
Land use	Arable, crops, grassland wooded	ha	No		World	EC9 (5.1)
Land use	Arable - by crop, permanent grassland, permanent crops - by crop kitchen gardens	ha	No		EC	EC9 (5.2)
Livestock	By type	nos	Yes	A	VICES region, VICES countries and Yugoslavia	VICES1 (I/5)
Livestock	Cattle, pigs, sheep and goats	nos	No		World	EC9 (5.6)
Livestock numbers	By type	nos	Yes	A	OECD	OECD26
Meat, gross indigenous		tonnes	Yes	A	OECD	OECD26
Meat, slaughtered,		tonnes	Yes	A	OECD	OECD26
Meat, gross indigenous	By meat type and by country	tonnes	Yes	A	OECD	OECD26
Meat, net production	Slaughterings by type of animal	tonnes	Yes	M	EC	EC7 (I)
Meat, gross indigenous production	By type of animal	tonnes	Yes	M	EC	EC7 (I)
Meat		tonnes	Yes	M	Asia and Pacific	UN43 (-)
Meat	By type	tonnes	No		World	EC9 (5.7)
Meat	By type	tonnes	Yes	A	VICES region, VICES countries and Yugoslavia	VICES1 (I/5)
Meat	Kind	tonnes	Yes	A	World	UN50 (91)
Milk		tonnes	No		World	EC9 (5.8)
Milk and milk products	By type	tonnes	Yes	M	EC	EC7 (III)
Mutton, lamb and goat meat, total		tonnes	Yes	A	OECD	OECD26
Mutton, lamb and goat meat, slaughtered		tonnes	Yes	A	OECD	OECD26
Nuts		tonnes	No		World	EC9 (5.5)
Offal, edible		tonnes	Yes	A	OECD	OECD26
Offal, edible, slaughtered		tonnes	Yes	A	OECD	OECD26
Other meat, total		tonnes	Yes	A	OECD	OECD26
Other meat, slaughtered		tonnes	Yes	A	OECD	OECD26

38 PRODUCTION

Subject	Categories	Units	Time series Yes/No Frequency		Territorial coverage	Source (Table no.)
Output, agricultural gross	Total, crop, animal, index at constant prices, average annual growth rate at constant prices	indices, %	Yes	A	Vices region, VICES countries and Yugoslavia	VICES1 (I/5)
Pig meat, total		tonnes	Yes	A	OECD	OECD26
Pig meat, slaughtered		tonnes	Yes	A	OECD	OECD26
Poultry meat, total		tonnes	Yes	A	OECD	OECD26
Poultry meat, slaughtered		tonnes	Yes	A	OECD	OECD26
Raisins		q	Yes	4 yr	World	OIVV1 (R)
Slaughtered meat, total	By meat type and by country	tonnes	Yes	A	OECD	OECD26
Sugar, raw		tonnes	Yes	A	World	UN50 (1)
Sugar		tonnes	Yes	A	World	UN50 (95)
Sugar		tonnes	Yes	M	Asia and Pacific	UN43 (-)
Sugar	By country	tonnes	Yes	A, M	World	ISO2 (-)
Sugar	By imports, exports, consumption, stocks	tonnes	Yes	A	World	ISO3 (-)
Sugar	By sugar type, country	tonnes	Yes	A	World	ISO3 (-)
Tobacco	By product, total	tonnes, units	Yes	A	World	UN28 (-)
Tobacco	Cigars, cigarettes	nos, tonnes	No		EC, USA, USSR, Canada, Japan	EC9 (4.12)
Tomatoes		tonnes	No		World	EC9 (5.5)
Vegetables	Harvested crops area, harvested production, yield	tonnes, ha, kg/ha	Yes	A	EC	EC19 (III)
Viticulture	Vine area, production, by region	ha, hl	No		Principal wine producing countries	OIVV1(U)
Wheat flour		tonnes	Yes	A, M	World	UN35 (21)
Wheat flour		tonnes	Yes	A	World	UN50 (1)
Wheat flour		tonnes	Yes	M	Asia and Pacific	UN43 (-)
Wheat flour and flour of other cereals	Wheat, cereal	tonnes	Yes	A	World	UN50 (94)
Wine		hl	Yes	A	World	UN50 (96)
Wine		hl	No		World	OIVV1 (J)
Wine		hl	Yes	4 yr	World	OIVV1 (F)
Wine		tonnes	Yes	A	World	UN50 (1)
Yield, agriculture	By crop	q/h	Yes	A	VICES region, VICES1 countries and Yugoslavia	VICES1 (I/5)
38.1.2 Outputs and Inputs						
Final output, indices of		indices	Yes	A	EC	EC2 (A24)
Final output, change in		indices	Yes	A	EC	EC2 (A27)
Final output, indices of		indices	Yes	A	EC	EC2 (A28)
Intermediate consumption in agriculture, indices of		indices	Yes	A	EC	EC2 (A29)
Intermediate consumption in agriculture, indices of		indices	Yes	A	EC	EC2 (A32)
Intermediate consumption in agriculture, indices of		indices	Yes	A	EC	EC2 (A33)
Labour input, total, in annual work units (AWU)		indices	Yes	A	EC	EC2 (A36)
Labour input, family, in annual work units (AWU)		indices	Yes	A	EC	EC2 (A37)
Net value added at factor cost, share in net domestic product at factor cost		%	Yes	A	EC	EC2 (A1)
Values, nominal, indices of	By type of output and input	%	Yes	A	EC	EC2 (A6)

Subject	Categories	Units	Time series Yes/No Frequency		Territorial coverage	Source (Table no.)
Values, real, change in	By type of output and input	%	Yes	A	EC	EC2 (A7)
Volumes, change in	By type of output and input	%	Yes	A	EC	EC2 (A3)
38.2 CHEMICALS						
Ammonia		tonnes	No		World,	EC9 (4.7)
Asbestos (raw), phosphate rock, potash and sulphur	By type, country	tonnes	Yes	A	Africa and Asia	MAC1 (E15)
Caustic soda		tonnes	No		EC, USA, USSR, Canada, Japan	EC9 (4.6)
Caustic soda		tonnes	Yes	A	Latin American and Caribbean countries	UN45 (338)
Chemical industry	By NACE	tonnes, hl	Yes	A, Q	EC	EC51 (B)
Chemicals		tonnes	Yes	A	World	UN50 (1)
Chemicals and chemical products	By product, total	tonnes	Yes	A	World	UN28 (-)
Chlorine		tonnes	No		EC, USA, USSR, Canada, Japan	EC9 (4.6)
Fluorine		tonnes	Yes	A	EC	EC68 (-)
Fluorine	Fluorspar, hydrofluoric acid and aluminium fluoride	tonnes	No		EC	EC68 (-)
Output, per capita	World index	indices	Yes	A	Western World	CIA1(22)
Phosphates		tonnes	Yes	A	EC	EC68 (-)
Phosphates	Natural phosphates, phosphoric acid, slag and fertilizers	tonnes	No		EC	EC68 (-)
Production	World index	indices	Yes	A	Western World	CIA1(21)
Sulphuric acid, hydrochloric acid, nitric acid and caustic soda	By countries	nos	No		The Americas and Australasia	MAC2 (E18)
Sulphuric acid		tonnes	No		EC, USA, USSR, Canada, Japan	EC9 (4.6)
Sulphuric acid		tonnes	Yes	M	Asia and Pacific	UN43 (-)
Sulphuric acid	By countries	tonnes	Yes	A	Europe	MAC3 (D23)
Sulphuric acid	By country	tonnes	Yes	A	Africa and Asia	MAC1 (E24)
Urea, granular	Share of production	%	No		World	IFA1R (-)
Urea		tonnes, %	Yes	A	World	IFA1R (-)
38.3 CONSTRUCTION AND CONSTRUCTION MATERIALS - see also Sections 7, 23 and 34						
Building and civil engineering	Seasonally adjusted	indices	Yes	A, M	EC	EC53 (6.24)
Building construction, new authorized	By type	nos, cu m	Yes	A	World	UN18 (-)
Building materials	By type	nos, sq m tonnes, cu m	Yes	A	World	UN10 (14)
Buildings, new completed	By type of building	nos, cu m	Yes	A	World	UN18 (-)
Cement		tonnes, indices	Yes	A, M	EC, USA, Japan	EC36
Cement		tonnes	Yes	A, M	OECD	OECD22
Cement		tonnes	Yes	A	EC, USA and Japan	EC53 (1.14)
Cement		tonnes	Yes	A	Latin American and Caribbean countries	UN45 (340)
Cement		tonnes	Yes	A	World, ASEAN	ASEANS1 (4.1.3)
Cement		tonnes	Yes	A	World	EC9 (4.5)
Cement		tonnes	Yes	A	World	UN10 (16)
Cement		tonnes	Yes	A	World	UN50 (1)
Cement		tonnes	Yes	A	World	UN50 (107)

38 PRODUCTION

Subject	Categories	Units	Time series Yes/No Frequency		Territorial coverage	Source (Table no.)
Cement		tonnes	Yes	M	Asia and Pacific	UN43 (-)
Construction		indices	Yes	A, M	OECD	OECD22
Construction	Industrial production	indices	Yes	A, M	Japan	OECD22
Construction activity	By country or area	indices	Yes	A	World	UN18 (-)
Construction output	By country	index	No		EC	EM1 (0704)
Dwelling construction authorized	By location and investor	nos	Yes	A	World	UN18 (-)
Dwelling construction authorized	By type	nos, cu m	Yes	A	World	UN18 (-)
Dwellings		nos	No		EC, USA, USSR, Canada, Japan	EC9 (4.14)
Dwellings completed	By location and investor	nos	Yes	A	World	UN18 (-)
Dwellings completed	By type	nos, cu m	Yes	A	World	UN18 (-)
Output, total value of		nat curr	Yes	A	World	UN18 (-)
Output indices	Per working day, seasonally adjusted, building and civil engineering, construction of buildings, civil engineering	indices	Yes	A, M	EC	EC52 (-)
Rooms, authorized dwelling		nos	Yes	A	World	UN18 (-)
Rooms, dwellings completed		nos	Yes	A	World	UN18 (-)

38.4 ENERGY - see also Sections 17, 25 and 34

Subject	Categories	Units	Time series Yes/No	Frequency	Territorial coverage	Source (Table no.)
Coal, hard	By country	tonnes	Yes	A	ESCAP	UN44
Coal, lignite, coke-oven		tonnes	No		World	EC9 (4.24)
Coal		toe, % share % change	Yes	A	World	BP1 (p28)
Coal		tonnes	Yes	A	EC	EC9 (4.23)
Coal		tonnes	Yes	A	World, OECD and non-OECD	IEA7
Coal		tonnes	Yes	A	World	UN50 (1)
Coal		tonnes	Yes	M	Asia and Pacific	UN43 (-)
Coal	By country	nos	No		The Americas and Australasia	MAC2 (E2)
Coal	By country	tonnes	Yes	A	Europe	MAC3 (D2)
Coal	By country and type	tonnes	Yes	A	Africa and Asia	MAC1 (E2)
Coal	By type of coal	tonnes	Yes	A	World	BP1 (p28)
Coal and lignite		toe	No		World	EC9 (4.15)
Coal reserves	By type of coal	tonnes, % share R/P ratio	No		World	BP1 (p26)
Coal-brown coal mines, production structure	By country	tonnes	Yes	A	EC, USA	UN6 (3)
Coal-hard coal mines, production structure	By country	tonnes	Yes	A	EC, USA	UN6 (2)
Commercial energy	Total and by type	TJ	Yes	A	World	UN21 (3)
Crude oil,	Parent companies estimated gross share	barrels/day	Yes	A	OPEC	OPEC1 (44)
Crude oil		toe	No		World	EC9 (4.15)
Crude oil	By companies	barrels/day	Yes	A	OPEC	OPEC1 (42)
Crude oil	By country, since commencement	barrels	Yes	A	OPEC	OPEC1 (38)
Crude oil	By country	barrels/day	Yes	A	World	OPEC1 (39)
Crude oil	By region	barrels/day	Yes	A	World	OPEC1 (14)
Crude oil	Refinery input, refining capacity	tonnes	No		World	EC9 (4.25)
Crude oil and natural gas liquids		tonnes	Yes	A	World, OECD, non-OECD	IEA10 (I.18)

Subject	Categories	Units	Time series Yes/No Frequency		Territorial coverage	Source (Table no.)
Crude oil and NGL		tonnes, barrels/day	Yes	A	World, OECD and non-OECD	IEA7
Crude oil production excluding NGLs and condensates	By main countries, regions	tonnes	Yes	A, M	World	DSC2 (2.4)
Crude petrolelum and natural gas	Total	tonnes	Yes	A	World	UN28 (-)
Crude petroleum		cu m	Yes	M	Asia and Pacific	UN43 (-)
Crude petroleum		tonnes	Yes	A	World	UN50 (1)
Crude petroleum		tonnes,	Yes	A, M	OECD	OECD22
Crude petroleum	By countries	nos	No		The Americas and Australasia	MAC2 (E3)
Crude petroleum	By countries	tonnes	Yes	A	Europe	MAC3 (D3)
Crude petroleum	By country	tonnes	Yes	A	Africa and Asia	MAC1 (E3)
Crude petroleum	By country	tonnes	Yes	A	ESCAP	UN44
Electric energy, derivative energy	Gross production, thermo electric energy, hydro-electric energy resulting from pumping,	GWh	Yes	A	EC, USA, Canada	UN9 (1)
Electric energy, primary energy	Gross production, geothermal electric energy, hydro-electric energy, nuclear electric energy	GWh	Yes	A	EC, USA, Canada	UN9 (1)
Electric energy	By countries	GWh	Yes	A	Europe	MAC3 (D27
Electric energy	By countries	nos	No		The Americas and Australasia	MAC2 (E22)
Electric energy	By country	kWh	Yes	A	Africa and Asia	MAC1 (E28)
Electric energy	Produced by public power plants, self-producers	GWh	Yes	A	EC, USA, Canada	UN9 (1)
Electrical energy		GWh	Yes	A	EC, OECD	EC9 (4.31)
Electrical energy	Total, hydro, geothermal, nuclear, conventional thermal	GWh	No		World	EC9 (4.32)
Electricity, share of each fuel	By fuel type	%	Yes	I	OECD, selected	IEA3 (-)
Electricity, primary		toe	No		World, OECD	EC9 (4.15)
Electricity		GWh	Yes	A	World, OECD and non-OECD	IEA7
Electricity		kWh	Yes	A	Latin American and Caribbean countries	UN45 (350)
Electricity		kWh	Yes	A	World	UN50 (1)
Electricity		kWh	Yes	M	Asia and Pacific	UN43(-)
Electricity	By product, total	kWh	Yes	A	World	UN28 (-)
Electricity	By type	kW	Yes	A	World	UN21 (34)
Electricity	By type of plant	kWh	Yes	I	Latin American and Caribbean countries	UN45 (351)
Electricity	Hydro, thermal, by country	kWh	Yes	A	ESCAP	UN44
Electricity	Total	kWh	Yes	A	World	UN21 (35)
Electricity capacity, net maximum	Public utilities, autoproducers, by type of fuel; type of generation	MW	Yes	A	OECD	IEA8&9
Electricity generation, estimated	Total, nuclear	TWh, %	Yes	I	OECD	OECD31 (1)
Electricity production	Gross, net, by source	GWh	Yes	A	OECD	IEA8&9 (–)
Electricity input	By fuel type	toe	Yes	I	OECD	IEA3 (-)
Electricity output, share of each fuel	By fuel type	%	Yes	I	OECD OECD	IEA3 (-)
Electricity output	By fuel type	TWh	Yes	I	OECD	IEA3 (-)
Electricity production	By country, by thermal,	kWh	No		EC	EC18 (8.7)
Electricity production	Gross, net, by source	GWh	Yes	A	OECD	IEA8&9

38 PRODUCTION

Subject	Categories	Units	Time series Yes/No Frequency		Territorial coverage	Source (Table no.)
Energy, commercial (coal equivalent)	Total and by type	tonnes	Yes	A	World	UN21 (1)
Energy, commercial (oil equivalent)	Total and by type	tonnes	Yes	A	World	UN21 (2)
Energy converted, total	By form of energy and method of conversion	TJ	Yes	A	EC, USA, Canada	UN9 (2)
Energy production, consumption and trade	By high, middle, low income	tonnes, kg, %	No		World	CS1 (16)
Energy products from refineries	By type	tonnes	Yes	A	World	UN21 (26)
Feedstocks and other input supply	Imports, exports, refinery intake and losses and stock levels					
Gas, converted	By type of conversion and type of gas, by country	TJ	Yes	A	EC, USA	UN8 (1)
Gas, changes in stocks	By type of gas, by country	TJ	Yes	A	EC, USA	UN8 (1)
Gas, deliveries for final consumption	By industry, by type of gas, by country	TJ	Yes	A	EC, USA	UN8 (1)
Gas, length of mains for transport	Pipeline transmission system, distribution system	km	Yes	A	EC, USA	UN8 (5)
Gas, transfers	By type of gas, by country	TJ	Yes	A	EC, USA	UN8 (1)
Gas, natural		toe	No		World	EC9 (4.15)
Gas, natural		TJ	Yes	A	EC, W Germany, France, Ireland, Italy, Netherlands, UK	EC9 (4.29)
Gas, natural		cu m, TJ	No		World	EC9 (4.30)
Gas	Primary production, associated-dissolved and non-associated gases, derived production, by type of gas, by country	TJ	Yes	A	EC, USA	UN8 (1)
Gas produced by gas works	By product, total	TJ				
Gaseous fuels, primary energy	Total, natural gas, LPG`	TJ	Yes	A	EC, USA, Canada	UN9 (1)
Gaseous fuels, primary energy	Gasworks gas, coke-oven gas, blast furnace gas, substitute natural gas, LPG	TJ	Yes	A	EC, USA, Canada	UN9 (1)
Gases		TJ	Yes	A	World	UN21 (31)
Gases, other	By type	TJ	Yes	A	World	UN21 (30)
Gasoline		cu m	Yes	A	Latin American and Caribbean countries	UN45 (341)
GCC crude oil production	By country	barrels/day	No		Arabian Gulf	CH1 (3.2)
GCC gross production of natural gas	By country	cu m	No		Arabian Gulf	CH1 (3.5)
Heat		TJ	Yes	A	OECD	IEA8&9
Heat		TJ	Yes	A	OECD	IEA8&9
Hydro, other electricity		GWh	Yes	A	World, OECD and non-OECD	IEA7
Hydro-electric potential, estimates		MW	Yes	I	Latin American and Caribbean countries	UN45 (353)
Hydro-electric power	Share in generation of electricity	%	Yes	A	Latin American and Caribbean countries	UN45 (57)
Indices, industrial production	By selected industries	indices	Yes	A	World	UNCTAD1 (6.6)

Subject	Categories	Units	Time series Yes/No Frequency		Territorial coverage	Source (Table no.)
Lignite		tonnes	Yes	A	World, OECD and non-OECD	IEA7
Lignite and brown coal		tonnes	Yes	A	World	UN50 (1)
Liquid fuels, primary energy	Crude petroleum, total	tonnes	Yes	A	EC, USA, Canada	UN9 (1)
Liquid fuels, derivative energy	Light products, aviation and motor gasoline, jet fuel, kerosene, naphthas, heavy products: gas (diesel) oil, residual fuel oil	tonnes	Yes	A	EC, USA, Canada	UN9 (1)
Liquid fuels	By type	tonnes	Yes	A	World	UN21 (14,17-24)
LPG	By country	tonnes, % change, % share	Yes	A	World	BP2 (-)
Manufactured gas		TJ	Yes	A	ASEAN	ASEANS1 (4.1.1)
Natural gas, gross and marketed	Re-injected, flared, shrinkage	cu m	Yes	A	OPEC	OPEC1 (40)
Natural gas, marketed	By country	cu m	Yes	A	World	OPEC1 (41)
Natural gas, offshore production of	By country	cu m, % share	Yes	A	World	BP2 (-)
Natural gas		cu m	Yes	A, M	OECD	OECD22
Natural gas		cu m	Yes	M	Asia and Pacific	UN43 (-)
Natural gas		TJ	Yes	A	World, OECD and non-OECD	IEA10 (I.21)
Natural gas		TJ	Yes	A	World	UN21 (28)
Natural gas		toe, % share % change	Yes	A	World	BP1 (p20)
Natural gas		toe	Yes	A	World, OECD and non-OECD	IEA7
Natural gas		tonnes	Yes	A	World	UN50 (1)
Natural gas	By countries	cu m	Yes	A	Europe	MAC3 (D4)
Natural gas	By countries	nos	No		The Americas and Australasia	MAC2 (E4)
Natural gas	By country	cu m, % change, % share	Yes	A	World	BP2 (-)
Natural gas	By country	cu m	Yes	A, Q, M	Selected countries	DSC2 (3.6)
Natural gas	By country	cubic metres	Yes	A	Africa and Asia	MAC1 (E4)
Natural gas	Marketed, by region	cu m	Yes	A	World	OPEC1 (16)
Natural gas	Marketed	cu m	Yes	A	OPEC	OPEC1 (15)
Natural gas liquid plants	Production and capacity, by type	tonnes	Yes	A	World	UN21 (27)
Natural gas reserves, proven	By region	cu m	Yes	A	OPEC	OPEC1 (12)
Natural gas reserves, proven	By country	cu m	Yes	A	World	OPEC1 (34)
Natural gas reserves, proved		cu m, cu ft % share R/P ratio	No		World	BP1 (p18)
Non-energy product from refineries	By type	tonnes	Yes	A	World	UN21 (25)
Nuclear electricity		GWh	Yes	A	World, OECD and non-OECD	IEA7
Nuclear energy		toe	No		World	EC9 (4.15)

Subject	Categories	Units	Time series Yes/No	Frequency	Territorial coverage	Source (Table no.)
Nuclear power stations	Production and performance data for individual power stations	MW, GWh hours, %	Yes	A, M	IEA member countries	IAEA1 (-)
Oil, refinery capacities		barrels/day % share % change	Yes	A	World	BP1 (p14)
Oil, refinery throughputs		barrels/day % share % change	Yes	A	World	BP1 (p15)
Oil		barrels/day % share % change	Yes	A	World	BP1 (p5)
Oil		tonnes, % share % change	Yes	A	World	BP1 (p4)
Oil output		barrels/day	Yes	Q	World	OECD26 (XIII)
Oil reserves, proved		barrels, tonnes, % R/P ratio	No		World	BP1 (p2)
Other solid fuels		TJ	Yes	A	OECD	IEA8&9
Petroleum		cu m	Yes	A	Latin American and Caribbean countries	UN45 (333)
Petroleum and coal, products of	By product, total	tonnes, metres, TJ/ units	Yes	A	World	UN28 (-)
Petroleum production	By country, by barrels/ day	tonnes, nos	Yes	A	World	IP1 (-)
Petroleum products		cu m	Yes	M	Asia and Pacific	UN43 (-)
Petroleum products		tonnes	Yes	A	World, ASEAN	ASEANS1 (4.1.4)
Petroleum products	By type	tonnes	No		World	EC9 (4.26)
Petroleum products	Total production	tonnes	Yes	A	EC	EC9 (4.27)
Primary energy		tce	Yes	A	World, ESCAP, developing ESCAP countries	UN44 (p3)
Primary energy		TJ	Yes	A	EC, USA, Canada	UN9 (2)
Primary energy		toe	Yes	A	EC	EC9 (4.16)
Primary energy	By type	tce, %	Yes	I	World	UNCTAD1 (6.9)
Primary energy	By type by country	toe	Yes	I	VICES countries and Yugoslavia	VICES1 (V/2)
Primary energy	Coal and lignite, crude oil, gas, nuclear energy, primary electricity	toe	No		World	EC9 (4.15)
Primary energy supply, total	By fuel type	toe	Yes	I	OECD, selected	IEA3 (-)
Production, growth rates	Total, main sources, type	%	Yes	I	World	UNCTAD1 (6.9)
Production		1000MT oil	Yes		World	UN55
Production	Coal, oil, gas, total, per capita	toe	No		VICES countries and Yugoslavia	VICES1 (V/1)
Production and utilization of natural gas in the GCC region	By country, by production, flared, waste	cu m	No		Arabian Gulf	CH1 (3.4)
Refined products		barrels/day	Yes	A	OPEC	OPEC1 (19)
Refined products	By country	barrels/day	Yes	A	World	OPEC1 (48)
Refined products	By region	barrels/day	Yes	A	World	OPEC1 (20)
Refined products	By type	barrels/day	Yes	A	OPEC	OPEC1 (47)

Subject	Categories	Units	Time series Yes/No Frequency		Territorial coverage	Source (Table no.)
Refinery capacity, growth rates		%	Yes	I	World	UNCTAD1 (6.9)
Refinery distillation	Capacity, throughput and output	tonnes	Yes	A	World	UN21 (16)
Refinery output		tonnes	Yes	A	World, OECD, non-OECD	IEA10 (I.6)
Reserves	By energy resource	tonnes	No		World	UN21 (38)
Solid fuel	By type	tonnes	Yes	A	World	UN21 (5-6,8-13)
Solid fuels, recovered slurry	By fuel type, by country	tonnes	Yes	I	EC, USA	UN6 (1)
Solid fuels, bunkering	By fuel type, by country	tonnes	Yes	I	EC, USA	UN6 (1)
Solid fuels, energy converted	By fuel type, by type of plant, by country	tonnes	Yes	I	EC, USA	UN6 (1)
Solid fuels, derivative energy	Patent fuel coke total, coke-oven coke, gas coke, brown coal coke, brown coal briquettes	tonnes	Yes	A	EC, USA, Canada	UN9 (1)
Solid fuels, primary energy	Hard coal, brown coal and lignite, other	tonnes	Yes	A	EC, USA, Canada	UN9 (1)
Solid fuels	By fuel type, by country	tonnes	Yes	I	EC, USA	UN6 (1)
Steam and hot water	From geothermal sources, from public thermal power plants for combined generation of electric energy and heat	TJ	Yes	A	EC, USA, Canada	UN9 (1)
Steam and hot water	From geothermal and thermal sources	TJ	Yes	A	World	UN21 (36)
Supply, crude, NGL, refinery	Indigenous production,	tonnes	Yes	Q	OECD	IEA11
Supply, NGL	Indigenous production, imports, exports, refinery intake and losses and stock levels	tonnes	Yes	Q	OECD	IEA11
Supply, refinery feedstocks	Indigenous production, imports, exports, refinery intake and losses and stock levels	tonnes	Yes	Q	OECD	IEA11
Supply, other origins	Indigenous production, imports, exports, refinery intake and losses and stock levels	tonnes	Yes	Q	OECD	IEA11
Supply, total products	Indigenous production, imports, exports, gross and net consumption and stock levels	tonnes	Yes	Q	OECD	IEA11
Supply, naphtha	Indigenous production, imports, exports, gross and net consumption and stock levels	tonnes	Yes	Q	OECD	IEA11
Supply, LPG	Indigenous production, imports, exports, gross and net consumption and stock levels	tonnes	Yes	Q	OECD	IEA11
Supply, gasoline	Indigenous production, imports, exports, gross and net consumption and stock levels	tonnes	Yes	Q	OECD	IEA11

Subject	Categories	Units	Time series Yes/No	Frequency	Territorial coverage	Source (Table no.)
Supply, kerosene	Indigenous production, imports, exports, gross and net consumption and stock levels	tonnes	Yes	Q	OECD	IEA11
Supply, aviation kerosene	Indigenous production, imports, exports, gross and net consumption and stock levels	tonnes	Yes	Q	OECD	IEA11
Supply, gas, diesel oil	Indigenous production, imports, exports, gross and net consumption and stock levels	tonnes	Yes	Q	OECD	IEA11
Supply, heavy fuel oil	Indigenous production, imports, exports, gross and net consumption and stock levels	tonnes	Yes	Q	OECD	IEA11
Supply, other products	Indigenous production, imports, exports, gross and net consumption and stock levels	tonnes	Yes	Q	OECD	IEA11
Supply, natural gas	Indigenous production, imports, exports, consumption and stock levels	cu m	Yes	Q	OECD	IEA11
Supply balance	By fuel type	toe	Yes	Q	OECD	IEA11
Thermal electricity		GWh	Yes	A	World, OECD and non-OECD	IEA7
Transformation	Electricity; installed capacity, per thousand inhabitants. petroleum; refinery capacity as a percent of liquid fuel consumption	kW, %	Yes	I	World	UNCTAD1 (6.9)
Uranium		tonnes	Yes	A	World	UN21 (37)
Uranium production, natural	Actual, forecast	tonnes/year	Yes	5yr	OECD, World	OECD31 (5B)
Vegetable fuels		toe	Yes	A	Non-OECD	IEA7

38.5 FISHING - see also Sections 20 and 34

Subject	Categories	Units	Time series Yes/No	Frequency	Territorial coverage	Source (Table no.)
Catch, utilisation	By uses	tonnes, %	Yes	A	OECD	OECD43
Catch, landings and values	By method of production, product and port of landing, by country	tonnes	Yes	A	OECD	OECD43
Catch, total allowable	Allocations and catches, by country	nos	Yes	A	OECD	OECD43
Fish, total catch		tonnes	Yes	A, M	Iceland	OECD22
Fish, production		tonnes, indices	Yes	A	OECD	OECD43
Fish catches		tonnes	Yes	A	World	UN50 (1)

38.6 FORESTRY - see also Sections 21 and 34

Subject	Categories	Units	Time series Yes/No	Frequency	Territorial coverage	Source (Table no.)
Production		indices	Yes	A	EEC	EC6 (IIC 2)
Roundwood		tonnes	Yes	A	World	UN50 (1)
Sawn wood	By country	cu m	Yes	A	Africa and Asia	MAC1 (E25)
Sawnwood		cu m	Yes	A	World	UN50 (1)
Sawnwood		cu m	Yes	A	World	UN50 (99)
Timber	Roundwood, softwood, hardwood	cu m	No		World	EC9 (5.19)

Subject	Categories	Units	Time series Yes/No Frequency		Territorial coverage	Source (Table no.)
Timber industry indicators	By countries	nos	No		The Americas and Australasia	MAC2 (E19)
Timber industry indicators	By countries	tonnes, cu m,	Yes	A	EC	MAC3 (D24)
Wood fellings		cu m	Yes	A, M	OECD	OECD22
Wood in the rough, supplies of	By production	metres (length)	Yes	A	EC	EC6 (IIC 3)
Wood production	Total, by type	metres (length)	Yes	A	EC	EC6 (IIC 1)
Wooded area, breakdown of	By type, production	hectares	No		EC	EC6 (IIA 1)
38.7 GENERAL						
38.7.1 Production, Deliveries, Orders and Stocks - Total and by Industry						
Capacity utilisation	By industry sector	%	No		EC	EC70
	Capital goods s.a.	indices	Yes	A, M	EC	EC53 (6.3)
	Chemical industry, including man-made fibres industry s.a.	indices	Yes	A, M	EC	EC53 (6.8)
	Clothing industry s.a.	indices	Yes	A, M	EC	EC53 (6.18)
	Consumer goods s.a.	indices	Yes	A, M	EC	EC53 (6.4)
Deliveries	By sector	indices	Yes	Q, M	OECD	OECD15
	Electrical engineering s.a	indices	Yes	A, M	EC	EC53 (6.12)
Expectations	All industry intermediate goods, investment goods consumption goods	%	Yes	A, M	EC	EC36
	Food, drink and tobacco industry s.a.	indices	Yes	A, M	EC	EC53 (6.14)
	Food, edible oils and fats s.a.	indices	Yes	A, M	EC	EC53 (6.15)
	Footwear manufacture s.a.	indices	Yes	A, M	EC	EC53 (6.17)
Index numbers of industrial production	Total, by industry	indices	Yes	A	EC	EC6 (IA10)
Indices	Seasonally adjusted, per working day, indices of production, by NACE sector	indices	Yes	A, M	EC	EC52 (-)
Industrial	By branch, NACE branches in difficulty	indices	Yes	A	EC, USA, Japan	EC36
Industrial	NACE, turnover, seasonally adjusted	indices	Yes	A, M	EC, USA, Japan	EC36
Industrial	Total, manufacturing, by type of goods	indices	Yes	A, M	OECD	OECD22
Industrial output	By industrial production, country	indices	Yes	A, Q, M	World	DSC2 (1.5)
Industrial production		1000 tonnes	Yes	A	Central Africa	UN5 (5-1)
Industrial production		1000 tonnes	Yes	A	East & Southern Africa	UN4 (5-1)
Industrial production		indices	Yes	A	World	EC9 (4.1)
Industrial production		indices	Yes	A	World	UN27 (-)
Industrial production		nos	Yes	A	Central Africa	UN5 (20)
Industrial production		nos	Yes	A	East & Southern Africa	UN4 (20)
Industrial production	By country	indices	Yes	A	Africa and Asia	MAC1 (E1)
Industrial production	By country	indices	Yes	A	Europe	MAC3 (D1)
Industrial production, gross	By country	index	No		Europe	EC18 (8.5)
Industrial production	By country	indices	Yes	A, M	World	BB2 (26)
Industrial production	By country	nos	No		The Americas and Australasia	MAC2 (E1)
Industrial production	By country or area	indices	Yes	A	World	UN50 (81)
Industrial production	By industry	indices	Yes	A, M	World	EC53 (1.8)
Industrial production, volume index	By industry	indices	Yes	A	Nordic countries	NCM1(79)

38 PRODUCTION

Subject	Categories	Units	Time series Yes/No	Frequency	Territorial coverage	Source (Table no.)
Industrial, production		%/tonnes	No		World, developing countries, OPEC, non-OPEC, ACP	EC1 (I13-I17)
Industrial, total		indices	Yes	A, M	OECD total, Major Seven total, EC total, OECD Europe	OECD22
Industry		indices	Yes	A, Q, M	OECD	OECD22 (-)
Industry	Building and civil engineering s.a.	indices	Yes	A, M	EC	EC53 (6.24)
Industry	General, mining, manufacturing, electricity and gas	indices	Yes	M	Asia and Pacific	UN43 (-)
Industry	Intermediate products industry s.a.	indices	Yes	A, M	EC	EC53 (6.2)
Industry	Manufacture of metal articles s.a.	indices	Yes	A, M	EC	EC53 (6.9)
Industry	Manufacture of motor vehicles parts and accessories s.a.	indices	Yes	A, M	EC	EC53 (6.13)
Industry	Manufacture of office and data processing machinery s.a.	indices	Yes	A, M	EC	EC53 (6.11)
Industry	Manufacturing s.a.	indices	Yes	A, M	EC	EC53 (6.1)
Industry	Mechanical engineering s.a.	indices	Yes	A, M	EC	EC53 (6.10)
Industry	Mineral oil refining s.a.	indices	Yes	A, M	EC	EC53 (6.5)
Industry	Non-metallic mineral products s.a.	indices	Yes	A, M	EC	EC53 (6.7)
Industry	Total production, production index	%, GDP, indices 1000MT oil equivalent	Yes		World	UN55
	investment goods consumption goods					
Order books	All industry intermediate goods,	%	Yes	A, M	EC	EC36
Order books	By industry sector	indices	Yes	M	EC	EC70
Orders, new	By industry sector	indices	No		EC	EC70
Orders, new	By sector	indices	Yes	Q, M	OECD	OECD15
Orders, unfilled	By sector	indices	Yes	Q, M	OECD	OECD15
Output	In producers' prices	nat curr	Yes	A	World	UN27 (-)
Output	Printing industries s.a.	indices	Yes	A, M	EC	EC53 (6.21)
Output	Processing of plastics s.a.	indices	Yes	A, M	EC	EC53 (6.23)
Output, general industrial per working day	By country intermediate goods, capital goods industries, consumer goods	indices	No		EC	EM1 (0701)
Production		indices	No		EC, USA, Japan	EC53 (1.8)
Production		indices	Yes	A, M	World	IMF7 (-)
Production		indices	Yes	A, M	World	UN50 (8)
Production		indices	Yes	A, Q, M	OECD	OECD22 (-)
Production	Branch of activity	indices	Yes	A	World	UN27 (-)
Production	Branch of activity, by region	indices	Yes	A	World, excluding Eastern Europe and USSR	UN27 (-)
Production	Branch of activity, developed countries	indices	Yes	A	World, excluding Eastern Europe and USSR	UN27 (-)
Production	Branch of activity, developing countries	indices	Yes	A	World, excluding Eastern Europe and USSR	UN27 (-)

Subject	Categories	Units	Time series Yes/No Frequency		Territorial coverage	Source (Table no.)
Production	Branch of activity, total	indices	Yes	A	World, excluding Eastern Europe and USSR	UN27 (-)
Production	By country	tonnes	Yes	A	World	MJ1 (-)
Production	By country	tonnes	Yes	A	World	MJ1 (-)
Production	By NACE	ECU	Yes	A	EC	EC75 (1)
Production	By sector	indices	Yes	Q, M	OECD	OECD15
Production	Gross output, value added	million frs	Yes	A	Central Africa	UN5 (21)
Production	Gross output, value added	million frs	Yes	A	East & Southern Africa	UN4 (21)
Production	Gross output, value added	million frs	Yes	A	North Africa	UN2 (21)
Production	Industrial	1000 tonnes	Yes	A	North Africa	UN2 (5-1)
Production	Industrial	nos	Yes	A	North Africa	UN2 (20)
Production	Sectors and selected industries	indices	Yes	A	World	UN50 (8)
Production and labour indices		indices	Yes	A	Industrial countries	IMF7 (-)
	Production and preliminary processing of metals s.a.	indices	Yes	A, M	EC	EC53 (6.6)
Production expectations	By industry sector	indices	Yes	M	EC	EC70
Production indicators, basic	Total industry, intermediate goods, capital goods industries, consumer goods, turnover, no. of employees. per working day and seasonally adjusted	indices	No		EC, USA, Japan	EC52 (-)
Production indices,	Total industry,	indices	Yes	A, M	EC	EC52 (-)
Production value	By NACE	ECU	No		EC	EC75 (3.1)
Production, gross	By selected branches of industry, by country	nat curr	Yes	A	Vices region, VICES countries and Yugoslavia	VICES1 (I/4)
Production, growth of	By high, middle, low income, by manufacturing, construction, trade, communication	%	No		World	CS1 (4B)
Production, limits to	None, demand, labour, equipment, other, by industry sector	indices	No		EC	EC70
Production, structure of and indicators of openness	By high, middle, low income	US$, %,	No		World	CS1 (3)
	Pulp, paper and paperboard s.a.	indices	Yes	A, M	EC	EC53 (6.20)
Raw material stocks	By industry sector	indices	No		EC	EC70
	Rubber manufacture s.a	indices	Yes	A, M	EC	EC53 (6.22)
Services		indices	Yes	A, Q, M	OECD	OECD22 (-)
Stocks, finished products	All industry intermediate goods, investment goods consumption goods	%	Yes	A, M	EC	EC36
Stocks, finished products	By industry sector	indices	Yes	M	EC	EC70
	Textile industry s.a.	indices	Yes	A, M	EC	EC53 (6.16)
	Timber and wooden furniture s.a.	indices	Yes	A, M	EC	EC53 (6.19)
Total		indices	Yes	A	World	UN50 (1)
Total		indices	Yes	A, Q, M	OECD	OECD22 (-)
Total	By ISIC division	nat curr	Yes	A	OECD	OECD16
Trends	By industry sector	indices	Yes	M	EC	EC70

Subject	Categories	Units	Time series Yes/No	Frequency	Territorial coverage	Source (Table no.)
Turnover	Unadjusted, seasonally adjusted, by NACE sector	indices	Yes	A, M	EC	EC52 (-)
Value added	By NACE	ECU, %	Yes	A	EC	EC75 (1) (3.1)
Value added	In producers' prices	nat curr	Yes	A	World	UN27 (-)
38.7.2 Production - By Type of Goods						
Data processing equipment	By NACE	ECU, nos	Yes	A, Q	EC	EC51 (A)
Electric and electronic construction	By NACE	ECU, nos	Yes	A	EC	EC51 (A)
plastics		tonnes	No		World	EC9 (4.7)
Electrical appliances, domestic	By NACE	ECU, nos	Yes	A, Q	EC	EC51 (A)
Engines, turbines and machinery	By product, total	units, kilowatts, horsepower, spindles,kVA	Yes	A	World	UN28 (-)
Industry, production	Principal products	tonnes, TJ	No		ACP states	EC1 (II-)
Industry, production	Principal products	tonnes, TJ	No		Mediterranean countries	EC1 (IV-)
Mechanical		tonnes	Yes	A	World	UN50 (1)
Mechanical engineering products	By NACE	ECU, nos	Yes	A	EC	EC51 (A)
Miscellaneous manufactured articles	By product, total	units, metres	Yes	A	World	UN28 (-)
Output, growth in volume,	By major product group	%	Yes	A	World	GATT3 (2)
Output	By kind of economic activity	indices	Yes	A, M	World	IMF6 (-)
Output	Selected industrial products, by country	kWh, cu m, tonnes, nos, sq m, hl	Yes	A	VICES region, VICES countries and Yugoslavia	VICES1 (I/4)
Output by country income group	Total GDP, agriculture, industry, services	%	Yes	Selected years	Developing countries, DEMCs, least-developed countries	UNCTAD5 (1.1)
Output by major category	Total GDP, agriculture, industry, services	%	Yes	Selected years	Developing countries, DMECs, least-developed countries	UNCTAD5 (1.1)
Porcelain, china and glass, articles of	By product, total	tonnes, units, metres	Yes	A	World	UN28 (-)
Primary commodities, local processing of selected	By commodity	%	Yes	Selected years	Developing countries	UNCTAD5 (4.13)
Production	For 18 individual commodities covered by the IPC	tonnes	Yes	A	Developing countries	UNCTAD1 (4.10)
Production data	By country, product	US$	Yes	A	World	EAT2 (2.2)
Radio and television receivers, communication equipment and electrical appliances	By product, total	units/tonnes	Yes	A	World	UN28 (-)
Soaps and detergents, selected	By country, by product	tonnes	No		EC	EM1 (0707)
Wood and wood products	By product, total	metres/units	Yes	A	World	UN28 (-)
38.8 MANUFACTURING						
Elasticity of manufacturing	With respect to the GDP	indices	Yes	5yr	Latin American and Caribbean countries	UN45 (60)
Growth	Average annual rates	indices	Yes	A	Latin American and Caribbean countries	UN45 (58)
Industry	Total production, production index	%, GDP, indices	Yes		World	UN55
Manufactures, durable		indices	Yes	A, Q, M	OECD	OECD22 (-)

Subject	Categories	Units	Time series Yes/No	Frequency	Territorial coverage	Source (Table no.)
Manufactures, non-durable		indices	Yes	A, Q, M	OECD	OECD22 (-)
Manufactures, annual growth		%	Yes	A	World	UNIDO1 (1.15)
Manufacturing, deliveries, stocks and orders		nat curr	Yes	A, Q, M	OECD	OECD22 (-)
Manufacturing		indices	Yes	A, Q, M	OECD	OECD22 (-)
Manufacturing		indices	Yes	A	World	UN50 (1)
Manufacturing	Annual growth rates at 1980 factor cost	%	Yes	A	African countries	UN1 (25)
Manufacturing	By product, by country	tonnes	Yes	A	ESCAP	UN44
Manufacturing production	By country	indices	No		EC	EM1 (0703)
Manufacturing production index		indices	Yes	A	World, ASEAN	ASEANS1 (4.1)
MVA	By ISIC group	%	No		World	UNIDO1 (2.6)
MVA per employee	By ISIC group	US$	No		World	UNIDO1 (2.6)
MVA per employee	by ISIC group	US$	No		World	UNIDO1 (2.6)
MVA per employee	by ISIC group	US$	Yes	I	World	UNIDO1 (1.12, 2.5)
Output, value added	By ISIC group	%	No		World	UNIDO1 (2.6)
Production, annual growth	By ISIC group	%, indices	Yes	A	World	UNIDO1 (2.4)
Production	Manufacturing	1000 tons	Yes	A	Central Africa	UN5 (24)
Production	Manufacturing	1000 tons	Yes	A	East & Southern Africa	UN4 (24)
Production	Manufacturing	1000 tons	Yes	A	North Africa	UN2 (24)
Production	Manufacturing	1000 tons	Yes	A	West Africa	UN3 (24)
Share in the generation of the product	% of total GDP at constant prices	%	Yes	A	Latin American and Caribbean countries	UN45 (59)
Value added		nat curr	No		World	UN50 (90)
Value of output		nat curr	No		World	UN50 (90)

38.9 MINERALS, ORES AND METALS - see also under Mining and Quarrying (38.10) and Sections 25, 32, 33 and 34

38.9.1 Iron and Steel

Subject	Categories	Units	Time series Yes/No	Frequency	Territorial coverage	Source (Table no.)
Alloy steel, total		tonnes	No		OECD, EC	OECD18 (6)
Aluminium	By % of total production	tonnes	Yes	A	World	UN50 (1)
	By region, by country, total	tonnes	Yes	M	World	IISI4 (3, 3a)
Castings	Total, by type	tonnes	Yes	A	World	WBMS4 (-)
Coke production	By country, region	tonnes	Yes	A	World	IISI4 (26)
Coke-oven coke, national output		tonnes	No		OECD, EC	OECD18 (11)
Continuous cast semis	By production	tonnes	Yes	A	Developing countries	IISI3 (-)
Continuously cast steel	By country, by region % of total crude steel production	tonnes, %	Yes	A	World	IISI4 (5)
Continuously cast steel	By output	tonnes; %	Yes	A	World	IISI5 (-)
Crude steel		tonnes, indices	Yes	A, M	EC, USA, Japan	EC36
Crude steel		tonnes	Yes	A, M	OECD	OECD22
Crude steel		tonnes	Yes	A, Q, M	OECD	OECD22 (-)
Crude steel		tonnes	Yes	A	EC	EC9 (4.36)
Crude steel		tonnes	Yes	A	World, ASEAN	ASEANS1 (4.1.6)

38 PRODUCTION

Subject	Categories	Units	Time series Yes/No Frequency		Territorial coverage	Source (Table no.)
Crude steel		tonnes	Yes	A	World	UN50 (1)
Crude steel		tonnes	Yes	M	Asia and Pacific	UN43 (-)
Crude steel	By countries	nos	No		The Americas and Australasia	MAC2 (E9)
Crude steel	By countries	tonnes	Yes	A	EC	MAC3 (D9)
Crude steel	By process	tonnes; %	No		World	IISI5 (-)
Crude steel	By production	tonnes	Yes	A	Developing countries	IISI3 (-)
Crude steel	Growth rates	tonnes; %	Yes	A	World	IISI5 (-)
Crude steel	Total, percentage variation and percentage of world total	tonnes, %	No		World, OECD	OECD18 (2)
Crude steel	Total, percentage variation and amount of cast	tonnes, %	No		OECD	OECD18 (4)
Crude steel output	By process, total and percentage of steel output	tonnes, %	No		OECD	OECD18 (5)
Crude steel output per worker		indices	No		OECD	OECD18 (20)
Crude steel production, world summary	By production	tonnes	Yes	A	World	IISI4 (1)
Crude steel production, BOFs and EAFs	By country, region	tonnes, %	Yes	A	World	IISI4 (27,28)
Crude steel production	By country, by year	tonnes	Yes	A	World	ISSB1 (-)
Crude steel production	By country, total	tonnes	Yes	A	World	IISI4 (2)
Crude steel production	By country, region, % change	tonnes, % change	Yes	M, Q	EC	IISI2 (-)
Crude steel production	By process, by country	tonnes, %	Yes	A	World	IISI4 (4)
Crude steel production	Monthly average by country	tonnes	Yes	A, M	OECD	BB2 (28)
Crude steel production OHFs	By country, region	tonnes, %	Yes	A	World	IISI4 (29)
DR iron	By production, imports	tonnes	Yes	A	Developing countries	IISI3 (-)
Finished and semi-finished products for sale	By production	tonnes	Yes	A	Developing countries	IISI3 (-)
	Finished rolled products					
Flat products	By production, imports, exports	tonnes	Yes	A	Developing countries	IISI3 (-)
High speed steel	Total, in ingot and liquid forms for casting	tonnes	No		OECD	OECD18 (7)
Ingots	By production	tonnes	Yes	A	Developing countries	IISI3 (-)
Ingots	Total, by type	tonnes	Yes	A	World	WBMS4 (-)
Ingots and semis	By production, imports, exports	tonnes	Yes	A	Developing countries	IISI3 (-)
Iron		tonnes	Yes	A	Latin American and Caribbean countries	UN45 (332)
Iron	Availability: mining production, domestic recovery imports,	tonnes	No		EC, USA, Japan	EC9 (4.4)
Iron and major alloying metals	By metal type	tonnes	No		EC	EC68 (-)
Iron and steel	Pig iron, steel,	tonnes	No		World,	EC9 (4.34)
Iron and steel basic industries	By product, total	tonnes	Yes	A	World	UN28 (-)
Iron ore, merchantable	Total and by percentage iron content	tonnes	No		OECD, EC	OECD18 (8)
Iron ore		tonnes	Yes	A	World	UN50 (1)
Iron ore		tonnes	Yes	M	Asia and Pacific	UN43 (-)
Iron ore	By countries	tonnes	Yes	A	EC	MAC3 (D7)
Iron ore	By country	tonnes	Yes	A	Africa and Asia	MAC1 (E5)
Iron ore	By production, imports	tonnes	Yes	A	Developing countries	IISI3 (-)

Subject	Categories	Units	Time series Yes/No Frequency		Territorial coverage	Source (Table no.)
Iron ore	Total ore mined, % iron content	tonnes, %	No		World	EC9 (4.33)
Iron ore production	By country, region	tonnes	Yes	A	World	IISI4 (20)
Iron production, direct reduced	By country, region	tonnes	Yes	A	World	IISI4 (14)
Iron production	By country, region,by type	tonnes	Yes	A, M	World	IISI4 (17a)
Iron products of the steel industry	By type	tonnes	Yes	A, Q	EC, USA, Canada and Japan	UN11 (1)
Liquid steel for casting	By production	tonnes	Yes	A	Developing countries	IISI3 (-)
Long products	By product, imports, exports	tonnes	Yes	A	Developing countries	IISI3 (-)
Metal manufactures and machinery industries	Share of industrial output produced	%	Yes	A	Latin American and Caribbean countries	UN45 (62)
Output of iron ore	By countries	nos	No		The Americas and Australasia	MAC2 (E5)
Pellet production	By country, region	tonnes	Yes	A	World	IISI4 (15)
Pellets	By production, imports	tonnes	Yes	A	Developing countries	IISI3 (-)
Pig iron		tonnes	Yes	A	Latin American and Caribbean countries	UN45 (346)
Pig iron	By countries	nos	No		The Americas and Australasia	MAC2 (E8)
Pig iron	By countries	tonnes	Yes	A	EC	MAC3 (D8)
Pig iron	By country, region, % change	% change	Yes	M	EC	IISI2 (-)
Pig iron	By country	tonnes	Yes	A	Africa and Asia	MAC1 (E16)
Pig iron	By production, imports	tonnes	Yes	A	Developing countries	IISI3 (-)
Pig iron and crude steel	Pig iron and ferro-alloys, crude steel	tonnes	Yes	A	World	UN50 (108)
Pig iron and ferro-alloys		tonnes	Yes	A, M	World	UN35 (34)
Pig iron and ferro-alloys		tonnes	Yes	A	World	UN50 (1)
Pig iron production	By country, by year	tonnes	Yes	A	World	ISSB1 (-)
Pig iron production	By country, region	tonnes	Yes	A	World	IISI4 (17)
Pig-iron and ferro-alloys	Total, percentage variation and percentage of world total	tonnes, %	No		World, OECD	OECD18 (1)
Pig-iron and ferro-alloys	Total and percentage variation	tonnes, %	No		OECD	OECD18 (3)
Production, world	By country	tonnes	Yes	A	World	MJ1 (I)
Production, means of	By oxygen, electric, open hearth, other	tonnes	Yes	A	Developing countries	IISI3 (-)
Production	Total	tonnes	Yes	A	Western world	WBMS4 (-)
Raw steel production	By country	tonnes	Yes	A, M	World	DSC2 (4.3)
Rolled products	flat, non-flat	tonnes	Yes	A	Latin American and Caribbean countries	UN45 (348-349)
Seamless tube production	By country, region	tonnes	Yes	A	World	IISI4 (31)
Seamless tubes	By production, imports, exports	tonnes	Yes	A	Developing countries	IISI3 (-)
Sinter production	By country, region	tonnes	Yes	A	World	IISI4 (16)
Slabs, blooms and billets	Total, by type	tonnes	Yes	A	World	WBMS4 (-)
Stainless steel	Total, in ingot and liquid forms for casting	tonnes	No		OECD	OECD18 (7)
Stainless steel production	By country, region	tonnes	Yes	A	World	IISI4 (33)
Steel, crude		tonnes	Yes	A, M	World	UN35 (35)
Steel		tonnes	Yes	A	Latin American and Caribbean countries	UN45 (347)

Subject	Categories	Units	Time series Yes/No	Frequency	Territorial coverage	Source (Table no.)
Steel industry raw materials	By type	tonnes	Yes	A, Q	EC, USA, Canada and Japan	UN11 (1)
Steel ingots and castings	By country	tonnes	Yes	A	Africa and Asia	MAC1 (E17)
Steel production, world	By % change	tonnes, % change	Yes	A, M	Selected countries	ISL1 (-)
Steel products, finished and semi-finished	By type	tonnes	Yes	A, Q	EC, USA, Canada and Japan	UN11 (2)
Steel tube production	By country, region	tonnes	Yes	A	World	IISI4 (30)
Steel-producing companies, largest	Crude steel output	tonnes	Yes	A	World	IISI5 (-)
Steel-producing countries, major	Crude steel Utilization: consumption, exports	tonnes	Yes	A	World	IISI5 (-)
Welded tube production	By country, region	tonnes	Yes	A	World	IISI4 (32)
Welded tubes	By production, imports, exports	tonnes	Yes	A	Developing countries	IISI3 (-)
Wire rod		tonnes	Yes	A	Latin American and Caribbean countries	UN45 (345)
World steel trade as percentage of world steel production	By crude steel equivalent, finished steel	tonnes, %	Yes	A	World	IISI4 (9)
38.9.2 Production other than Iron and Steel						
Alumina		tonnes	Yes	A	World	IBA1 (2)
Aluminium, output of	By countries	nos	No		The Americas and Australasia	MAC2 (E10)
Aluminium, primary		tonnes	Yes	A	World	IBA1 (3)
Aluminium, secondary recovery		tonnes, %	Yes	A	Western world	IBA1 (6)
Aluminium, primary		tonnes	Yes	A	EC	EAA1 (-)
Aluminium, secondary		tonnes	Yes	A	EC	EAA1 (-)
Aluminium		tonnes	Yes	A	World	UN50 (109)
Aluminium	Availability: mining production, domestic recovery imports,	tonnes	No		EC, USA, Japan	EC9 (4.4)
Aluminium	By countries	tonnes	Yes	A	EC	MAC3 (D10)
Aluminium	By country	tonnes	Yes	A	Africa and Asia	MAC1 (E18)
Aluminium	By region	tonnes	Yes	A, M	World	DSC2 (8.3)
Aluminium	By type	tonnes	Yes	A	World	WBMS1 (-)
Aluminium	By type	tonnes	Yes	A	World	WBMS3 (-)
Aluminium	Primary, secondary	tonnes	Yes	A, M	World	UN35 (36)
Aluminium castings		tonnes	Yes	A	EC	EAA1 (-)
Aluminium extrusions		tonnes	Yes	A	EC	EAA1 (-)
Aluminium production and exports	By volume, by value	tonnes, nat curr	No		Bahrain	CH1 (8.2)
Aluminium products, semi-fabricated		tonnes	Yes	A	EC	EAA1 (-)
Aluminium rolled products		tonnes	Yes	A	EC	EAA1 (-)
Antimony	Availability: mining production, domestic recovery imports,	tonnes	No		EC, USA, Japan	EC9 (4.4)
Antimony	By type	tonnes	Yes	A	World	WBMS1 (-)
Antimony	Total	tonnes	Yes	A	World	WBMS3 (-)
Antimony ore	By country	tonnes	Yes	A	Africa and Asia	MAC1 (E12)
Bauxite		tonnes	Yes	A	Latin American and Caribbean countries	UN45 (328)
Bauxite		tonnes	Yes	A	World	IBA1 (1)
Bauxite	By country	tonnes	Yes	A	Africa and Asia	MAC1 (E11)

Subject	Categories	Units	Time series Yes/No Frequency		Territorial coverage	Source (Table no.)
Bismuth	Total	tonnes	Yes	A	World	WBMS3 (-)
Cadmium	By type	tonnes	Yes	A	World	WBMS1 (-)
Cadmium	Total	tonnes	Yes	A	World	WBMS3 (-)
Chromium, nickel and vanadium ores	By country	tonnes	Yes	A	Africa and Asia	MAC1 (E7)
Chromium	Availability: mining production, domestic recovery imports,	tonnes	No		EC, USA, Japan	EC9 (4.4)
Chromium	Total	tonnes	Yes	A	World	WBMS3 (-)
Coal		tonnes	Yes	A	Latin American and Caribbean countries	UN45 (329)
Cobalt	Availability: mining production, domestic recovery imports,	tonnes	No		EC, USA, Japan	EC9 (4.4)
Cobalt	Total	tonnes	Yes	A	World	WBMS3 (-)
Copper, smelter		tonnes	Yes	A, M	World	UN35 (37)
Copper, refined		tonnes	Yes	A, M	World	UN35 (38)
Copper		tonnes	Yes	A	Latin American and Caribbean countries	UN45 (330)
Copper		tonnes	Yes	A	World	UN50 (1)
Copper	Availability: mining production, domestic recovery imports,	tonnes	No		EC, USA, Japan	EC9 (4.4)
Copper	By type	tonnes	Yes	A	World	WBMS1 (-)
Copper	By type	tonnes	Yes	A	World	WBMS3 (-)
Copper	Smelter, refined	tonnes	Yes	A	World	UN50 (110)
Copper ore	By country	tonnes	Yes	A	Africa and Asia	MAC1 (E8)
Copper ore and concentrates		tonnes	Yes	M	Asia and Pacific	UN43 (-)
Fabricated metal products	By product, total	units/tonnes	Yes	A	World	UN28 (-)
Fluorine	Availability: mining production, domestic recovery imports,	tonnes	No		EC, USA, Japan	EC9 (4.4)
Gold	By content	tonnes	Yes	A	World	WBMS1 (-)
Gold	Total	tonnes	Yes	A	World	WBMS3 (-)
Gold and silver	By type, country	tonnes	Yes	A	Africa and Asia	MAC1 (E14)
Lead	Mine production	tonnes	Yes	A	EC, USA, Australia	ILZSG1 (2)
Lead	Mine production	tonnes	Yes	A, M	World	ILZSG1 (5)
Lead	Mine production metal production	tonnes	Yes	A	Eastern Europe. Socialist countries	ILZSG1 (9)
Lead, concentrates		tonnes	Yes	A, Q	Western World	ILZSG1 (1)
Lead, recovery of secondary lead	Refined lead and lead alloys, remelted lead and lead alloys	tonnes	Yes	A, Q	World	ILZSG1 (11)
Lead, refined		tonnes	Yes	A	EC, USA, Japan	ILZSG1 (2)
Lead, refined		tonnes	Yes	A, Q	Western World	ILZSG1 (1)
Lead, refined		tonnes	Yes	A, M	World	ILZSG1 (6)
Lead, totals	Mine production refined metal production	tonnes, %	Yes	A	World	ILZSG1 (25)
Lead, totals	Mine production refined metal production	tonnes, %	Yes	A	Western World	ILZSG1 (25)
Lead, reported metal stocks		tonnes	Yes	A, Q	Western Europe	ILZSG1 (1)
Lead, stocks	Producers, consumers London Metal Exchange	tonnes	Yes	A	EC, USA, Japan	ILZSG1 (3)
Lead, stocks	Consumers merchants primary secondary	tonnes	Yes	A, M	Selected countries	ILZSG1 (15,16,18, 20,23,24)

Subject	Categories	Units	Time series Yes/No Frequency		Territorial coverage	Source (Table no.)
Lead, refined metal stocks	Commercial stocks, (producers consumers merchants London Metal Exchange) non-commercial stocks	tonnes	Yes	A, M	World	ILZSG1 (8)
Lead		tonnes	Yes	A	World	UN50 (1)
Lead		tonnes	Yes	A	World	UN50 (111)
Lead	Ores and concentrates refined lead	tonnes	Yes	A, M	Selected countries	ILZSG1 (15-24)
Lead	Availability: mining production, domestic recovery imports,	tonnes	No		EC, USA, Japan	EC9 (4.4)
Lead	By type	tonnes	Yes	A	World	WBMS1 (-)
Lead	By type	tonnes	Yes	A	World	WBMS3 (-)
Lead	Primary, secondary	tonnes	Yes	A, M	World	UN35 (39)
Lead and zinc ores	By country	tonnes	Yes	A	Africa and Asia	MAC1 (E9)
Lead ores and concentrates		tonnes	Yes	M	Asia and Pacific	UN43 (-)
Magnesium		tonnes	Yes	A	World	UN50 (112)
Magnesium	Total	tonnes	Yes	A	World	WBMS3 (-)
Manganese	Availability: mining production, domestic recovery imports, exports	tonnes	No		EC, USA, Japan	EC9 (4.4)
Manganese	Total	tonnes	Yes	A	World	WBMS3 (-)
Manganese ore	By country	tonnes	Yes	A	Africa and Asia	MAC1 (E6)
Mercury, molybdenum, tungsten concentrates	By type, country	tonnes	Yes	A	Africa and Asia	MAC1 (E13)
Mercury	Availability: mining production, domestic recovery imports, exports	tonnes	No		EC, USA, Japan	EC9 (4.4)
Mercury	Total	tonnes	Yes	A	World	WBMS3 (-)
Metal ores, output of non-ferrous ores	By countries	nos	No		The Americas and Australasia	MAC2 (E6)
Metals, selected	By country, by metal	tonnes	No		EC	EM1 (0706)
Metals	Aluminium, copper, zinc, tin, lead	tonnes	No		World	EC9 (4.3)
Metals	By type	tonnes	Yes	A	EC	EC68 (-)
Metals	Mercury, antimony,	tonnes	No		EC	EC68 (-)
Mineral products,other non-metallic	By product, total	units, metres, tonnes	Yes	A	World	UN28 (-)
Mineral sector production	Selected commodities	tonnes, carats	Yes	A	African countries	UN1 (23)
Minerals, output of non-metallic	By countries	nos	No		The Americas and Australasia	MAC2 (E7)
Minerals, selected	By country, by mineral	tonnes	No		EC	EM1 (0705)
Molybdenum	Availability: mining production, domestic recovery imports, exports	tonnes	No		EC, USA, Japan	EC9 (4.4)
Molybdenum	By type	tonnes	Yes	A	World	WBMS1 (-)
Molybdenum	Total	tonnes	Yes	A	World	WBMS3 (-)
Nickel	Availability: mining production, domestic recovery imports, exports	tonnes	No		EC, USA, Japan	EC9 (4.4)
Nickel	By type	tonnes	Yes	A	World	WBMS1 (-)
Nickel	By type	tonnes	Yes	A	World	WBMS3 (-)
Niobium	Availability: mining production, domestic recovery imports, exports	tonnes	No		EC, USA, Japan	EC9 (4.4)

Subject	Categories	Units	Time series Yes/No Frequency		Territorial coverage	Source (Table no.)
Non-ferrous metals, main	By countries	tonnes	Yes	A	EC	MAC3 (D5)
Non-ferrous metals	By metal type	tonnes	No		EC	EC68 (-)
Non-ferrous metals	By product,,total	tonnes	Yes	A	World	UN28 (-)
Non-metallic minerals, main	By countries	tonnes	Yes	A	EC	MAC3 (D6)
Ores, metals and non-metallic minerals	By NACE	tonnes, cu m, sq m, nos	Yes	A, Q	EC	EC51 (B)
Output of refined copper, lead, tin and zinc	By countries, primary, secondary	nos	No		The Americas and Australasia	MAC2 (E11)
Phosphate	Availability: mining production, domestic recovery imports, exports	tonnes	No		EC, USA, Japan	EC9 (4.4)
Platinum	Total	tonnes	Yes	A	World	WBMS3 (-)
Refined production	By metal type	tonnes	Yes	A	World	WBMS1 (-)
Secondary production	By metal	tonnes	Yes	A	World	WBMS3 (-)
Semi-manufactures	By metal type	tonnes	Yes	A	World	WBMS1 (-)
Silicon carbide estimated production	By microgrits, powders, fibres, whiskers	tonnes, US$	Yes	A	World	EAT1 (4.3)
Silicon carbide grain production	By major producing countries	tonnes	Yes	A	Selected countries	EAT1 (4.1)
Silicon carbide production facilities	By location, capacity	tonnes	No		World	EAT1 (4.2)
Silver	By content	tonnes	Yes	A	World	WBMS1 (-)
Silver	Total	tonnes	Yes	A	World	WBMS3 (-)
Smelter production	By metal type	tonnes	Yes	A	World	WBMS1 (-)
Tantalum	Availability: mining production, domestic recovery imports, exports	tonnes	No		EC, USA, Japan	EC9 (4.4)
Tin		tonnes	Yes	A, M	World	UN35 (40)
Tin		tonnes	Yes	A	Latin American and Caribbean countries	UN45 (331)
Tin		tonnes	Yes	A	World	UN50 (1)
Tin		tonnes	Yes	A	World	UN50 (113)
Tin	Availability: mining production, domestic recovery imports, exports	tonnes	No		EC, USA, Japan	EC9 (4.4)
Tin	By content	tonnes	Yes	A	World	WBMS1 (-)
Tin	By type	tonnes	Yes	A	World	WBMS3 (-)
Tin concentrates	By country	tonnes	Yes	A	Africa and Asia	MAC1 (E10)
Tin metal		tonnes	Yes	A	World, ASEAN	ASEANS1 (4.1.2)
Tin metal		tonnes	Yes	M	Asia and Pacific	UN43 (-)
Titanium	Availability: mining production, domestic recovery imports, exports	tonnes	No		EC, USA, Japan	EC9 (4.4)
Titanium	By type titanium and zirconium	tonnes	Yes	A	World	WBMS3 (-)
Tungsten, co-production of other metals from mines	Tin, copper, bismuth, molybdenum sulphide	tonnes	Yes	A	World	UNCTAD3 (2.3)
Tungsten, ores and concentrates		tonnes	Yes	A	World	UNCTAD3 (2.1)
Tungsten	Availability: mining production, domestic recovery imports, exports	tonnes	No		EC, USA, Japan	EC9 (4.4)
Tungsten	By type of mine, number of mines operating	tonnes, nos	Yes	A	World	UNCTAD3 (2.2)

Subject	Categories	Units	Time series Yes/No Frequency	Territorial coverage	Source (Table no.)
Tungsten	Total	tonnes	Yes A	World	WBMS3 (-)
Tungsten products	By type	tonnes	Yes A	World	UNCTAD3 (2.6)
Uranium	Total	tonnes	Yes A	World	WBMS3 (-)
Vanadium	Availability: mining production, domestic recovery imports, exports	tonnes	No	EC, USA, Japan	EC9 (4.4)
Zinc, metal		tonnes	Yes A, M	World	ILZSG1 (31)
Zinc, mine production		tonnes	Yes A, M	World	ILZSG1 (30)
Zinc, recovery of secondary zinc	Refined zinc metal, remelted zinc and direct use of secondary materials	tonnes	Yes A, Q	World	ILZSG1 (36)
Zinc, totals	Mine production refined metal production	tonnes	Yes A	World	ILZSG1 (50)
Zinc, totals	Mine production refined metal production	tonnes	Yes A	Western world	ILZSG1 (50)
Zinc, metal stocks	Commercial stocks non-commercial stocks	tonnes	Yes A, M	World	ILZSG1 (33)
Zinc, stocks	Producers consumers merchants London Metal Exchange	tonnes	Yes A, M	Western World	ILZSG1 (26)
Zinc, stocks	Producers consumers merchants London Metal Exchange	tonnes	Yes A, M	EC, USA, Japan	ILZSG1 (28)
Zinc, stocks	Consumers merchants	tonnes	Yes A, M	Selected countries	ILZSG1 (40-49)
Zinc		tonnes	Yes A	Latin American and Caribbean countries	UN45 (334)
Zinc		tonnes	Yes A	World	UN50 (1)
Zinc		tonnes	Yes A	World	UN50 (114)
Zinc	Availability: mining production, domestic recovery imports, exports	tonnes	No	EC, USA, Japan	EC9 (4.4)
Zinc	By content	tonnes	Yes A	World	WBMS1 (-)
Zinc	By type	tonnes	Yes A	World	WBMS3 (-)
Zinc	Concentrates slab zinc	tonnes	Yes A, Q	Western World	ILZSG1 (26)
Zinc	Mine production refined zinc	tonnes	Yes A, M	EC, Canada Australia, Japan	ILZSG1 (27)
Zinc	Mine production metal production	tonnes	Yes A	Eastern European Socialist countries	
Zinc	Ores, concentrates refined zinc	tonnes	Yes A, M	Selected countries	ILZSG1 (40-49)
Zinc	Primary, secondary	tonnes	Yes A, M	World	UN35 (41)
Zinc ore and concentrates		tonnes	Yes M	Asia and Pacific	UN43 (-)
Zirconium	Availability: mining production, domestic recovery imports, exports	tonnes	No	EC, USA, Japan	EC9 (4.4)

38.10 MINING AND QUARRYING - see also under Energy (38.4), Minerals, Ores and Metals (38.9) and Sections 17 and 33

Coal	By type, total	tonnes	Yes A	World	UN28 (-)
Copper, joint production with lead and zinc	By production, by joint production	tonnes, %	No	World	ILZSG2 (10)
Copper, mine production	By ore type	%	No	World	ILZSG2 (11)

Subject	Categories	Units	Time series Yes/No Frequency	Territorial coverage	Source (Table no.)
Copper, mine production	By ore type	tonnes	No	World	ILZSG2 (12)
Degree of raw material dependence (technical)	By ores	import, export over consumption	No	EC, USA and Japan	EC53 (1.19)
				ESCAP and developing ESCAP countries	
Ferrous and non-ferrous metal ores	By type, total	tonnes, kilogrammes	Yes A	World	UN28 (-)
Lead, mine production	By ore type	%	No	World	ILZSG2 (7)
Lead, mine production	By survey coverage	tonnes, %	No	World	ILZSG2 (8)
Lead, mine production	By ore type	tonnes	No	World	ILZSG2 (9)
Mining		indices	Yes A	World	UN50 (1)
Mining	By product, by country	tonnes	Yes A	ESCAP	UN44
Mining	By type of industry	indices	Yes A	ESCAP and developing ESCAP region	UN44 (p5-13)
Mining	By type of industry	indices	Yes A	World,	UN44 (p2)
Mining production, growth in	Including, excluding petroleum, average annual rates	indices	Yes A	Latin American and Caribbean countries	UN45 (52)
Mining production, quantum indices	Including, excluding petroleum	indices	Yes A	Latin American and Caribbean countries	UN45 (327)
Mining production	By country	indices	No	EC	EM1 (0702)
Mining production index		indices	Yes A	World, ASEAN	ASEANS1 (4.2)
Non-metallic minerals and fertilizers	By type, total	tonnes. cu m, carats	Yes A	World	UN28 (-)
Ores	Copper, lead, zinc, tin, bauxite, potash	tonnes	No	World	EC9 (4.2)
Production	Mining	1000 tons	Yes A	Central Africa	UN5 (23)
Production	Mining	1000 tons	Yes A	East & Southern Africa	UN4 (23)
Production	Mining	1000 tons	Yes A	North Africa	UN2 (23)
Production	Mining	1000 tons	Yes A	West Africa	UN3 (23)
Raw material consumption	By ores	per capita	No	EC, USA and Japan	EC53 (1.20)
Silver, joint production with lead and zinc	By production, by joint production	tonnes, %	No	World	ILZSG2 (13)
Silver, mine production	By ore type	%	No	World	ILZSG2 (14)
Silver, mine production	By ore type	tonnes	No	World	ILZSG2 (15)
Silver, production	By ore type	g/tonne	No	World	ILZSG2 (16)
Zinc, mine production	By ore type	%	No	World	ILZSG2 (4)
Zinc, mine production	By survey coverage	tonnes, %	No	World	ILZSG2 (5)
Zinc, mine production	By ore type	tonnes	No	World	ILZSG2 (6)

38.11 PAPER AND BOARD

Subject	Categories	Units	Time series Yes/No Frequency	Territorial coverage	Source (Table no.)
Capacity					
Capacity					
Making, production capacity					
Making, production capacity					
Newsprint		tonnes	Yes A, M	World	UN35 (30)
Newsprint		tonnes	Yes A	Latin American and Caribbean countries	UN45 (337)
Newsprint		tonnes	Yes A	World	UN50 (1)
Newsprint		tonnes	Yes A	World	UN50 (101)

Subject	Categories	Units	Time series Yes/No Frequency		Territorial coverage	Source (Table no.)
Paper		tonnes	Yes	A, M	Finland	OECD22
Paper		tonnes	Yes	A	ASEAN	ASEANS1 (4.1.7)
Paper	Newsprint, wood pulp	tonnes	No		World	EC9 (4.13)
Paper and board	By country, total and annual variations	tonnes, %	Yes	A	OECD	OECD38 (V)
Paper and paper products	By product, total	tonnes, metres	Yes	A	World	UN28 (-)
Paper and paperboard, total	By type and by country	tonnes	No		OECD	OECD38 (II)
Paper and paperboard, production	By country	tonnes	No		OECD	OECD38 (VI)
Paper and paperboard, production	By country	tonnes	Yes	A	OECD	OECD38 (XI)
Paper and paperboard		tonnes	Yes	A	World	UN50 (100)
Paper pulp		tonnes	Yes	A	Latin American and Caribbean countries	UN45 (336)
Plywood		tonnes, cu m, sq m	Yes	A	ASEAN	ASEANS1 (4.1.8)
Production	By country	tonnes	Yes	A	World	BPB1 (-)
Pulp, paper and board	By NACE	tonnes	Yes	A, Q	EC	EC51 (A)
Pulp, total	By type and by country	tonnes	No		OECD	OECD38 (I)
Pulp and paperboard, comparison to industrial production	By country	%	Yes	A	OECD	OECD38 (III)
Wood pulp		tonnes	Yes	A, Q	OECD	OECD22
Wood pulp	By country	tonnes, dry weight	Yes	A	Africa and Asia	MAC1 (E26)
Wood pulp	Paper and board, newsprint	tonnes	No		World	EC9 (4.13)
Woodpulp	By country, total and annual variations	tonnes, %	Yes	A	OECD	OECD38 (IV)
Woodpulp for paper and paperboard	By country	tonnes	No		OECD	OECD38 (VI)
Woodpulp for paper and paperboard	By country	tonnes	Yes	A	OECD	OECD38 (VIII)

38.12 RUBBER - see also Section 5

Subject	Categories	Units	Time series Yes/No Frequency		Territorial coverage	Source (Table no.)
Cement		tonnes	Yes	A, M	World	UN35 (33)
Natural rubber, technically-specified		tonnes	Yes	M	World	IRSG1 (8)
Natural rubber		tonnes	Yes	A	World	UN50 (1)
Natural rubber		tonnes	Yes	M	World	IRSG1 (1, 7)
				A	World	IRSG2 (1, 7)
Rubber, natural	Production, stocks	tonnes	Yes	A, M	World	IRSG1 (1)
Rubber, natural, in producing countries		tonnes	Yes	A, M	World	IRSG1 (14)
Rubber, natural		tonnes	Yes	A, M	World	IRSG1 (13)
Rubber, natural		tonnes	Yes	A	World	IRSG2 (10)
Rubber, natural	Production, stocks	tonnes	Yes	A	World	IRSG2 (25)
Rubber, natural	Production, stocks	tonnes	Yes	A	World	IRSG2 (1)
Rubber, natural in producing countries		tonnes	Yes	A	World	IRSG2 (11)
Rubber, synthetic	Production, stocks	tonnes	Yes	A	World	IRSG2 (2)
Rubber, natural and synthetic		tonnes	Yes	A	World	IRSG2 (3)
Rubber, natural and synthetic		tonnes	Yes	A, M	World	IRSG1 (3)
Rubber, synthetic		%	Yes	A, M	World	IRSG1 (4)
Rubber, synthetic		%	Yes	A	World	IRSG2 (4)
Rubber, synthetic		tonnes	Yes	A	World	IRSG2 (18)
Rubber, synthetic	Production, stocks	tonnes	Yes	A, M	World	IRSG1 (2)
Rubber, synthetic		tonnes	Yes	A, M	World	IRSG1 (28)
Rubber, apparent consumption in non-reporting countries	By country	tonnes	Yes	A	World	IRSG2 (6)

Subject	Categories	Units	Time series Yes/No	Frequency	Territorial coverage	Source (Table no.)
Rubber	by country	tonnes	Yes	A	Malaysia, peninsular	IRSG1 (16)
					Singapore	IRSG1 (17)
					Indonesia	IRSG1 (18)
					Thailand	IRSG1 (19)
					Sri Lanka	IRSG1 (20)
Rubber	By major sector	tonnes	Yes	A	World	IRSG2 (5)
Rubber	By major sectors	tonnes	Yes	A, Q	World	IRSG1 (37)
Rubber	By type of rubber	tonnes	No		USA	IRSG1 (29)
					Brazil	IRSG1 (30)
					France	IRSG1 (31)
					Germany	IRSG1 (32)
					UK	IRSG1 (33)
					Australia	IRSG1 (34)
					India	IRSG1 (35)
					Japan	IRSG1 (36)
Rubber	Synthetic, reclaimed	tonnes	Yes	A	World	UN50 (102)
Rubber latex, natural		tonnes	Yes	A, M	World	IRSG1 (23)
Rubber products	By product/total	units, tonnes	Yes	A	World	UN28 (-)
Synthetic		tonnes	Yes	A, M	World	UN35 (31)
Synthetic rubber		tonnes	Yes	M	Asia and Pacific	UN43 (-)
Synthetic rubber		tonnes	Yes	M	World	IRSG1 (2, 24)
Tyres		nos	Yes	A	ASEAN	ASEANS1 (4.1.10)
Tyres		nos	Yes	A	Latin American and Caribbean countries	UN45 (335)
			Yes	A	World	IRSG2 (2, 19)

38.13 TEXTILES AND LEATHER - see also Section 5

Subject	Categories	Units	Time series Yes/No	Frequency	Territorial coverage	Source (Table no.)
Artificial and synthetic fibres	By countries	nos	No		The Americas and Australasia	MAC2 (E17)
Artificial synthetic fibres, output	By country	tonnes	Yes	A	EC	MAC3 (D21)
Cellulosic fibres		tonnes	Yes	A	World	UN50 (1)
Cellulosic: filament and staple	By country	tonnes	Yes	A	World	CIRFS1 (-)
Cotton, wool and man-made fibres by country	By fibre type, yarn,	tonnes, %	Yes	A	World	CIRFS1 (-)
Cotton		ha, tonnes	Yes	A	USA	ICAC1 (p9)
Cotton (all types)		bales	Yes	A	World	ICAC2 (p12-13)
Cotton (harvested area)		acres	Yes	A	World	ICAC2 (p14-15)
Cotton (total)		tonnes	Yes	A	China, US, CIS, India, Pakistan Brazil	ICAC1 (p2)
Cotton (yield)		lbs/acre	Yes	A	World	ICAC2 (p16-17)
Cotton fabric		tonnes	Yes	A	World	ICAC2 (p72-73)
Cotton spindles	By countries	nos	No		The Americas and Australasia	MAC2 (E13)
Cotton spindles	By country	nos	Yes	A	Africa and Asia	MAC1 (E19)
Cotton tissues	By country	nos	No		The Americas and Australasia	MAC2 (E15)
Cotton tissues, output	By country	tonnes, linear metres, sq m,	Yes	A	EC	MAC3 (D17)
Cotton yarn		tonnes	Yes	A, M	World	UN35 (22)
Cotton yarn		tonnes	Yes	A	World	ICAC2 (66-67)
Cotton yarn		tonnes	Yes	M	Asia and Pacific	UN43 (-)

38 PRODUCTION

Subject	Categories	Units	Time series Yes/No Frequency		Territorial coverage	Source (Table no.)
Cotton yarn	By country	nos	No		The Americas and Australasia	MAC2 (E14)
Cotton yarn	By country	tonnes	Yes	A	Africa and Asia	MAC1 (E20)
Cotton yarns and fabrics		tonnes	No		EC, USA, USSR, Canada, Japan	EC9 (4.11)
Detailed production of synthetics	By yarn, staple	tonnes	Yes	A	Selected countries	CIRFS1 (-)
Leather and footwear	By NACE	tonnes, sq m, nos	Yes	A, Q	EC	EC51 (A)
Leather and leather products	By product, total	tonnes, metres, pairs	Yes	A	World	UN28 (-)
Leather, non-leather	By country	pairs	Yes	A	World	SATRA1 (-)
Linen industry indicators	By country	tonnes	Yes	A	EC	MAC3 (D22)
Man-made fibres, textiles, clothing	By NACE	tonnes, sq m, nos	Yes	A, Q	EC	EC51 (A)
Man-made fibres	Cellulosic, yarn, staple, non-cellulosic, yarn, staple	tonnes	No		World	EC9 (4.10)
Non-cellulosic fibres	Continuous filaments, discontinuous filaments	tonnes	Yes	A, M	World	UN35 (29)
Non-cellulosic fibres		tonnes	Yes	A	World	UN50 (1)
Output of cotton yarn	By country	tonnes	Yes	A	EC	MAC3 (D16)
Raw cotton consumption	By country	nos	No		The Americas and Australasia	MAC2 (E12)
Raw wool consumption indicators	By country	tonnes	Yes	A	EC	MAC3 (D18)
Rayon and acetate filaments and fibres	Continuous filaments, discontinuous filaments	tonnes	Yes	A, M	World	UN35 (27)
Synthetic filament and staple yarn	By country	tonnes	Yes	A	World	CIRFS1 (-)
Synthetic filaments	By country	tonnes	Yes	A	Africa and Asia	MAC1 (E22)
Textiles, selected	By country, by textile	tonnes	No		EC	EM1 (0708)
Textiles	By product, total	tonnes, metres	Yes	A	World	UN28 (-)
Vegetable textile yarns, other than cotton	Flax, ramie, true hemp jute, other vegetable	tonnes	Yes	A, M	World	UN35 (24)
Wearing apparel	By product, total	pairs, units, metres, tonnes,	Yes	A	World	UN28 (-)
Wool industry indicators, yarn, tissues, wool	By countries, output, consumption	nos	No		The Americas and Australasia	MAC2 (E16)
Wool yarn		tonnes	Yes	A, M	World	UN35 (25)
Wool yarn	By country	tonnes	Yes	A	Africa and Asia	MAC1 (E21)
Wool yarn, output	By country	tonnes	Yes	A	EC	MAC3 (D19)
Wool tissues, output	By country	tonnes, linear metres, sq m	Yes	A	EC	MAC3 (D20)
Woollen fabrics and yarns		tonnes	No		World	EC9 (4.11)
Woollen woven cloth		sq m	Yes	M	Asia and Pacific	UN43 (-)
Woollen yarn		tonnes	Yes	M	Asia and Pacific	UN43 (-)
Woven cotton fabrics		units	Yes	A, M	World	UN35 (23)
Woven rayon and acetate fabrics	Metres	units	Yes	A, M	World	UN35 (28)
Woven woollen fabrics		units	Yes	A, M	World	UN35 (26)

38.14 TRANSPORT EQUIPMENT

38.14.1 Motor Vehicles - see also Section 45

Car production in selected countries	By country	nos	Yes	A, M	Selected countries	BB2 (27)
Cars, production of	By model	nos	Yes	A	Selected countries	SMMT2(-)
Cars, production of	By vehicle type, total	nos	Yes	A	Selected countries	SMMT2 (12)
Cars		nos	Yes	A	Selected countries	SMMT2 (10)

Subject	Categories	Units	Time series Yes/No Frequency		Territorial coverage	Source (Table no.)
Commercial		tonnes	Yes	A	World	UN50 (1)
Commercial motor vehicles	Commercial vehicle	nos, indices	Yes	A, M	EC, USA, Japan	EC36
Commercial vehicles		nos	Yes	A, M	OECD	OECD22
Commercial vehicles		nos	Yes	A	Latin American and Caribbean countries	UN45 (343)
Commercial vehicles		nos	Yes	A	Selected countries	SMMT2 (11)
Motor vehicles	By country, full production	nos	Yes	A	Africa and Asia	MAC1 (E23)
Motor vehicles, output and assembly of	By countries	nos	No		The Americas and Australasia	MAC2 (E20)
Motor vehicles	Passenger, commercial	nos	Yes	A, M	World	UN35 (42)
Motor vehicles	Production and assembly of, passenger cars, commercial vehicles	nos	No		World	EC9 (4.8)
Motor vehicles assembly	Passenger, commercial	nos	Yes	A, M	World	UN35 (43)
Motor vehicles assembly	Passenger cars, commercial vehicles	nos	Yes	A	ASEAN	ASEANS1 (4.1.9)
Motor vehicles, output	By countries	nos	Yes	A	EC	MAC3 (D25)
New cars, new registrations	By manufacturer	nos	No		Selected countries	SMMT1(-)
Passenger		tonnes	Yes	A	World	UN50 (1)
Passenger cars, production		nos	Yes	A, Q, M	OECD	OECD22 (-)
Passenger cars, production		nos	Yes	A, Q, M	OECD	OECD22 (-)
Passenger cars		nos, indices	Yes	A, M	EC, USA, Japan	EC36
Passenger cars		nos	Yes	A, M	OECD	OECD22
Passenger cars		nos	Yes	A	World	UN50 (117)
Passenger cars		nos	Yes	M	Asia and Pacific	UN43 (-)
Passenger motor vehicles		nos	Yes	A	Latin American and Caribbean countries	UN45 (342)
Production	Cars, commercial vehicles	nos	Yes	A	World	IRSG2 (39, 40)
Transport equipment, manufacture	By NACE	tonnes, nos,	Yes	A, Q	EC	EC51 (B)
Transport equipment	By product, total	units/grt/ horsepower	Yes	A	World	UN28 (-)
Tyres		nos	Yes	A, M	World	UN35 (32)
Tyres		nos	Yes	A	World	UN50 (103)
Vehicle production	Car	nos	Yes	A	World	IRSG2 (23)
Vehicles, commercial: production		nos	Yes	A, Q, M	OECD	OECD22 (-)
38.14.2 Shipping - see also Section 41						
Merchant vessels, tonnage launched		tonnes, gross	Yes	A	World	UN50 (116)
Ships completed, merchant vessels		tonnes, gross	Yes	A, Q	OECD	OECD22
Ships under construction, launched		tonnes, gross	No		World	EC9 (4.9)
Tonnage launched		tonnes, gross	Yes	A	World	UN50 (1)
Tonnage under construction		tonnes, gross	Yes	A	World	UN50 (1)

39 REFUGEES

Subject	Categories	Units	Time series Yes/No Frequency	Territorial coverage	Source (Table no.)
39.1 FINANCIAL ASSISTANCE					
Aid programmes	Source of funds, type of assistance	US$	No	World	UN51
Contributions to UNHCR assistance programmes	Governments, intergovernmental organizations, United Nations system, others	US$	No	World	UN41 (3)
Expenditure	By country or regional bureau, source of funds	US$	No	World	UN41 (1)
Expenditure	By country or regional bureau, main types of assistance activities	US$	No	World	UN41 (2)
39.2 NUMBERS OF REFUGEES					
Refugees		nos	No	World	UN16 (2B)

40 SCIENCE AND TECHNOLOGY

Subject	Categories	Units	Time series Yes/No Frequency		Territorial coverage	Source (Table no.)
40.1 INTERNATIONAL TRADE						
40.1.1 Export - Import Ratios						
Aerospace industry	By country	nos	Yes	A	OECD	OECD24 (84)
Drug industry	By country	nos	Yes	A	OECD	OECD24 (87)
Electrical, electronic industry	By country	nos	Yes	A	OECD	OECD24 (85)
Office machinery and computer industry	By country	nos	Yes	A	OECD	OECD24 (86)
Other manufacturing industries	By country	nos	Yes	A	OECD	OECD24 (88)
Total manufacturing	By country	nos	Yes	A	OECD	OECD24 (89)
40.1.2 Technology Balance of Payments						
Balance	By country	nat curr	Yes	A	OECD	OECD24 (81)
Coverage ratio	By country	nos	Yes	A	OECD	OECD24 (82)
Exports, developing country exports to DMECs by R&D intensity, market shares	By R&D intensity	%, years	Yes	Selected years	World, by development groups	UNCTAD5 (4.41)
Payments	By country	nat curr	Yes	A	OECD	OECD24 (80)
Receipts	By country	nat curr	Yes	A	OECD	OECD24 (79)
Technology related flows to developing countries	By type	US$, years	Yes	Selected years	World, by development groups	UNCTAD5 (4.40)
Total transactions	By country	nat curr	Yes	A	OECD	OECD24 (83)
Type of transfer	By country	nat curr	Yes	A	OECD	OECD3 (19)
40.2 PATENTS – see also Section 26						
Autosufficiency ratio, resident, national patent applications	By country	nos	Yes	A	OECD	OECD24 (76)
Dependancy ratio, non-resident, resident patent applications	By country	nos	Yes	A	OECD	OECD24 (75)
Inventiveness coefficient, resident patent applications/10000 population	By country	nos	Yes	A	OECD	OECD24 (77)
Patent applications	According to the relationship of patentee to patent office, by country	nos	Yes	A	OECD	OECD3 (20)
Patent applications	By country	nos	No		Selected countries	EC35 (-)
Patent applications	By country of origin and designated contracting states	nos	No		EC, USA, Japan	EPO1
Patent applications	By residence of applicants	nos, %	No		EC, USA, Japan	EPO1
Patent applications	Country of origin	nos	No		World	NCM1 (88)
Patent applications	Filed by non–residents	nos	No		Reporting countries	WIPO1 (IIA)
Patent applications	Filed by, granted to	nos	No		Reporting countries	WIPO1 (I)
Patent applications	Pending, according to year of filing	nos	No		Reporting countries	WIPO1 (V)
Patent applications	Priority claims according to country where first filing made	nos	No		Reporting countries	WIPO1 (IIIA)
Patent applications and patents granted		nos	No		World	WIPO3
Patent applications and patents granted	According to country of residence of applicant	nos	No		Reporting countries	WIPO1 (IVA)
Patent applications and patents granted	In certain countries according to technical units of IPC	technical units	No		Reporting countries	WIPO1 (IVB)
Patent applications, external	By country	nos	Yes	A	OECD	OECD24 (74)
Patent applications, external	By country of application,	nos	Yes	A	OECD	OECD3 (22)
Patent applications, foreign	By country of origin	nos	Yes	A	OECD	OECD3 (21)

40 SCIENCE AND TECHNOLOGY

Subject	Categories	Units	Time series Yes/No Frequency	Territorial coverage	Source (Table no.)
Patent applications, national	By country	nos	Yes A	OECD	OECD24 (71)
Patent applications, non-resident	By country	nos	Yes A	OECD	OECD24 (73)
Patent applications, resident	By country	nos	Yes A	OECD	OECD24 (72)
Patents	Applications, grants in force	nos	Yes A	World	UN50 (53)
Patents granted	According to year of filing of application	nos	No	Reporting countries	WIPO1 (VII)
Patents granted	Country of origin	nos	No	World	NCM1 (89)
Patents granted	Priority claims according to country where first filing made	nos	No	Reporting countries	WIPO1 (IIIB)
Patents granted to non–residents	According to country of residence of applicant	nos	No	Reporting countries	WIPO1 (IIB)
Patents in force	According to year of granting	nos	No	Reporting countries	WIPO1 (VI)
Patents valid		nos	Yes A	Nordic countries	NCM1 (87)
Rate of diffusion	By country	%	Yes A	OECD	OECD24 (78)

40.3 RESEARCH AND DEVELOPMENT – EMPLOYMENT

40.3.1 Branch of Economic Activity

Subject	Categories	Units	Time series Yes/No Frequency	Territorial coverage	Source (Table no.)
Agriculture, forestry, hunting and fishing		nos, %	No I	World	UNESCO1 (5.6)
Construction		nos, %	No I	World	UNESCO1 (5.6)
Extractive industries		nos, %	No I	World	UNESCO1 (5.6)
Manufacturing industries		nos, %	No I	World	UNESCO1 (5.6)
Other activities		nos, %	No I	World	UNESCO1
Personnel, business enterprise	R&D scientists engineers and researchers, by industry, by country	fte	Yes A	OECD	OECD3 (13)
Total		nos, %	No I	World	UNESCO1 (5.6)
Transport and communication		nos, %	No I	World	UNESCO1 (5.6)
Utilities		nos, %	No I	World	UNESCO1 (5.6)

40.3.2 Category of Personnel

Subject	Categories	Units	Time series Yes/No Frequency	Territorial coverage	Source (Table no.)
Auxiliary personnel		nos	No I	World	UNESCO1
Auxiliary personnel		per capita	No I	World	UNESCO1 (5.15)
Goverment RSE, compound annual growth rate	By country	%	Yes A	OECD	OECD24 (60)
Government RSE	By country	nos	Yes A	OECD	OECD24 (59)
Government RSE as a percentage of national total	By country	%	Yes A	OECD	OECD24 (61)
Higher education RSE	By country	nos	Yes A	OECD	OECD24 (50)
Higher education RSE as a percentage of national total	By country		Yes A	OECD	OECD24 (52) (5.5)
Higher education RSE, compound annual growth rate	By country	%	Yes A	OECD	OECD24 (51)
Scientists and engineers		nos	No	World	UN50 (49)
Scientists and engineers		nos	No I	World	UNESCO1 (5.5)
Scientists and engineers		per million population	No I	World	UNESCO1 (5.17)

Subject	Categories	Units	Time series Yes/No Frequency		Territorial coverage	Source (Table no.)
Scientists and engineers	Number, indices	per capita	No	I	World	UNESCO1 (5.15)
Scientists and engineers	Total, female	nos	No	I	World	UNESCO1 (5.3)
Scientists and engineers in R&D as of potential scientists and engineers		%	No	I	World	UNESCO1 (5.17)
Scientists and technicians engaged in research and development activities	Total manpower, scientists, potential technicians	nos	No		ASEAN	ASEAN (10.3.2)
Technicians		nos	No		World	UN50 (49)
Technicians		nos	No	I	World	UNESCO1 (5.5)
Technicians		per capita	No	I	World	UNESCO1 (5.15)
Technicians		per million population	No	I	World	UNESCO1 (5.17)
Technicians		per scientist or engineer	No	I	World	UNESCO1 (5.17)
Technicians	Total, female	nos	No	I	World	UNESCO1 (5.3)
Total in R&D and percentage by sector		nos, %	No	I	World	UNESCO1 (5.5)
40.3.3 Field of Study – see also Section 40.3.4						
Agricultural sciences		nos	No	I	World	UNESCO1 (5.4)
Agricultural sciences		nos, %	No	I	World	UNESCO1 (5.7)
Engineering and technology		nos	No	I	World	UNESCO1 (5.4)
Engineering and technology		nos, %	No	I	World	UNESCO1 (5.7)
Medical sciences		nos	No	I	World	UNESCO1 (5.4)
Medical sciences		nos, %	No	I	World	UNESCO1 (5.7)
Natural sciences		nos	No	I	World	UNESCO1 (5.4)
Natural sciences		nos, %	No	I	World	UNESCO1 (5.7)
Other sciences		nos, %	No	I	World	UNESCO1 (5.7)
Other fields		nos	No	I	World	UNESCO1 (5.4)
Social sciences and humanities		nos	No	I	World	UNESCO1 (5.4)
Social sciences and humanities		nos, %	No	I	World	UNESCO1 (5.7)
Total		nos	No	I	World	UNESCO1 (5.4)
Type of data	Full and part-time, sex		No	I	World	UNESCO1 (5.4)
40.3.4 General						
Government total R&D personnel	By country	nos	Yes	A	OECD	OECD24 (57)
Government total R&D personnel, compound annual growth rate	By country	%	Yes	A	OECD	OECD24 (58)
Higher education and the general service sectors		nos, %	No	I	World	UNESCO1 (5.7)
Personnel per thousand labour	By country	nos	Yes	A	OECD	OECD24 (9)

40 SCIENCE AND TECHNOLOGY

Subject	Categories	Units	Time series Yes/No	Frequency	Territorial coverage	Source (Table no.)
Personnel, business enterprise	R&D scientists engineers and researchers, by industry, by country	fte	Yes	A	OECD	OECD3 (13)
Personnel, business enterprise R&D personnel, compound annual growth rate	By country	%	Yes	A	OECD	OECD24 (27)
Personnel, business enterprise R&D as a percentage of national total	By country	%	Yes	A	OECD	OECD24 (28)
Personnel, business enterprise R&D	By country	nos	Yes	A	OECD	OECD24 (26)
Personnel, higher education	By field of science and occupation, by country	fte	Yes	A	OECD	OECD3 (17)
Personnel, higher education total R&D compound annual growth rate	By country	%	Yes	A	OECD	OECD24 (49)
Personnel, higher education total R&D personnel	By country	nos	Yes	A	OECD	OECD24 (48)
Personnel, total	By country	nos	Yes	A	OECD	OECD24 (7)
Personnel, total	By sector of employment and formal qualification, by country	fte	Yes	A	OECD	OECD3 (6)
Personnel, total	By sector of employment and occupation, by country	fte	Yes	A	OECD	OECD3 (5)
Personnel, total	By sector of employment and main scientific field, by country	fte	Yes	A	OECD	OECD3 (8)
Personnel, total business enterprise R&D	By industry, by country	fte	Yes	A	OECD	OECD3 (12)
Personnel, total, compound annual growth rate	By country	%	Yes	A	OECD	OECD24 (8)
R&D staff, total		nos	No	I	World	UNESCO1 (5.3)
R&D staff, total		per capita	No	I	World	UNESCO1 (5.15)
RSE per thousand labour force	By country	nos	Yes	A	OECD	OECD24 (12)
RSE, business enterprise	By country	nos	Yes	A	OECD	OECD24 (29)
RSE, business enterprise, as a percentage of national total	By country	%	Yes	A	OECD	OECD24 (31)
RSE, business enterprise, compound annual growth	By country	%	Yes	A	OECD	OECD24 (30)
RSE, compound annual growth rate	By country	%	Yes	A	OECD	OECD24 (11)
Scientific and technical manpower potential	Estimated number, per million population	nos	Yes		Continents, major areas and groups of countries	UNESCO1 (5.1)
Scientific and technical manpower	Total manpower, potential scientist and engineer, potential technicians	nos	No		ASEAN	ASEANS1 (10.3.1)
Scientists and engineers, RSE	By country	nos	Yes	A	OECD	OECD24 (10)
40.3.5 Potential						
Economically active, qualified manpower			No	I	World	UNESCO1 (5.2)
Scientists and engineers	Total, female	nos	No	I	Countries and territories	UNESCO1 (5.2)
Scientists and engineers, technicians		per capita	Yes	Selected years	World, by development groups	UNCTAD5 (4.39)

Subject	Categories	Units	Time series Yes/No	Frequency	Territorial coverage	Source (Table no.)
Scientists and engineers, technicians engaged in R&D		per capita	Yes	Selected years	World, by development groups	UNCTAD5 (4.39)
Scientists and technicians	Personnel, funding, by country	nat curr, nos	No		ESCAP countries	UN44
Technicians	Total, female	nos	No	I	Countries and territories	UNESCO1 (5.2)
40.3.6 Sector of Performance						
All sectors		nos	No	I	World	UNESCO1 (5.5)
General service		nos	No	I	World	UNESCO1 (5.5)
Higher education		nos	No	I	World	UNESCO1 (5.5)
Personnel engaged and number of man-years	By sector of performance	nos	Yes		Nordic countries	NCM1 (249)
Productive sector	Integrated, non-integrated	nos	No	I	World	UNESCO1 (5.5)
40.4 RESEARCH AND DEVELOPMENT – EXPENDITURE						
40.4.1 Business Enterprise Expenditure						
Agriculture forestry hunting and fishing		nat curr, %	No	I	World	UNESCO1 (5.12)
BERD	By country	nat curr	Yes	A	OECD	OECD24 (21)
BERD	By country	PPP	Yes	A	OECD	OECD24 (22)
BERD as a percentage of DPI	By country	%	Yes	A	OECD	OECD24 (24)
BERD as a percentage of GDP	By country	%	Yes	A	OECD	OECD24 (25)
BERD financed by industry	By country	%	Yes	A	OECD	OECD24 (32)
BERD financed by government	By country	%	Yes	A	OECD	OECD24 (35)
BERD financed by other national sources	By country	%	Yes	A	OECD	OECD24 (36)
BERD financed by abroad	By country	%	Yes	A	OECD	OECD24 (37)
BERD industry-financed, compound annual growth rate	By country	index	Yes	A	OECD	OECD24 (33)
BERD industry-financed as a percentage of DPI	By country	%	Yes	A	OECD	OECD24 (34)
BERD performed in the aerospace industry	By country	%	Yes	A	OECD	OECD24 (38)
BERD performed in the electrical, electronic industry	By country	%	Yes	A	OECD	OECD24 (39)
BERD performed in the office machinery and computer industry	By country	%	Yes	A	OECD	OECD24 (40)
BERD performed in the drug industry	By country	%	Yes	A	OECD	OECD24 (41)
BERD performed in all other manufacturing industries	By country	%	Yes	A	OECD	OECD24 (42)
BERD performed in non-manufacturing industry	By country	%	Yes	A	OECD	OECD24 (43)
BERD, compound annual growth rate	By country	index	Yes	A	OECD	OECD24 (23)
Branch of economic activity		nat curr, %	No	I	World	UNESCO1 (5.12)
Construction		nat curr, %	No	I	World	UNESCO1 (5.12)
Extractive industries		nat curr, %	No	I	World	UNESCO1 (5.12)

Subject	Categories	Units	Time series Yes/No	Frequency	Territorial coverage	Source (Table no.)
Intramural	By industry and source of funds, by country	nat curr	Yes	A	OECD	OECD3 (10)
Intramural	By industry and type of costs, by country	nat curr	Yes	A	OECD	OECD3 (11)
Intramural	By industry, by country	nat curr, constant US$	Yes	A	OECD	OECD3 (9)
Manufacturing industries		nat curr, %	No	I	World	UNESCO1 (5.12)
Other activities		nat curr, %	No	I	World	UNESCO1 (5.12)
Percentage of GERD financed by industry	By country	%	Yes	A	OECD	OECD24 (13)
Percentage of GERD performed by the business enterprise sector	By country	%	Yes	A	OECD	OECD24 (17)
Productive enterprise funds		nat curr, %	No	I	World	UNESCO1 (5.9)
Special funds		nat curr, %	No	I	World	UNESCO1 (5.9)
Total		nat curr, %	No	I	World	UNESCO1 (5.12)
Transport and communication		nat curr, %	No	I	World	UNESCO1 (5.12)
Utilities		nat curr, %	No	I	World	UNESCO1 (5.12)
Within the business enterprise sector, main data	Total	nat curr, %	Yes	2 yrly	Nordic countries	NCM1 (245)
40.4.2 General Expenditure						
Capital expenditure		nat curr	No	I	World	UNESCO1 (5.8)
Current	Total, labour, other	nat curr	No	I	World	UNESCO1 (5.8)
Current expenditure	% of GNP	nat curr, %	No	I	World	UNESCO1 (5.18)
Current expenditure	Amount, % of total	nat curr, %	No	I	World	UNESCO1 (5.16)
Current expenditure	Per capita	nat curr	No	I	World	UNESCO1 (5.18)
Current expenditure as percentage of total		%	No	I	World	UNESCO1 (5.8)
EC industry share of R&D spending	By country	%	No		Selected countries	EC35 (-)
EC internal spending on R&D	By country, by per capita, research workers	%, ECU, nos	No		Selected countries	EC35 (-)
EC national spending on R&D	By country, by per capita GDP, research workers, state, funding spent on defence, industry	ECU, %, nos	No		Europe	EC35 (-)
EC state share of R&D spending in	By country, by research funding	%	No		Selected countries	EC35 (-)
Expenditure	By source of finance, grants	%	Yes	2 yrly	Nordic countries	NCM1 (246)
Expenditure by field	Natural sciences engineering and technology medical sciences agricultural sciences social sciences and humanities other fields	nat curr, %	No	I	World	UNESCO1 (5.13)

Subject	Categories	Units	Time series Yes/No	Frequency	Territorial coverage	Source (Table no.)
Expenditure by major socio-economic aim	Earth, seas and the atmosphere civil space development of agriculture industrial development energy transport and communication education services health services socio economic services	nat curr, %	No	I	World	UNESCO1 (5.14)
	environment	nat curr, %	No	1	World	UNESCO1 (5.14)
	Advancement of knowledge	nat curr, %	No	1	World	UNESCO1 (5.14)
	Other aims	nat curr, %	No	1	World	UNESCO1 (5.14)
	Defence	nat curr, %	No	I	World	UNESCO1 (5.14)
Expenditure by sector	All sectors	nat curr, %	No	I	World	UNESCO1 (5.11)
Expenditure by source of funds	Foreign funds, other funds	nat curr, %	No	I	World	UNESCO1 (5.9)
Expenditure by type	Fundamental research applied research experimental development	nat curr, %	No	I	World	UNESCO1 (5.10)
Expenditure for research and experimental development	Capital, current	nat curr	No		World	UN50 (50)
Expenditure on R&D		ECU, % EDP per capita	Yes	A	EC	EC9 (2.11)
Expenditure on R&D, as percentage of GNP		%,	Yes	Selected years	World, by development groups	UNCTAD5 (4.39)
Expenditure per R&D scientist or engineer		nat curr	No	I	World	UNESCO1 (5.18)
Expenditure, current as percentage of total		%	No		World	UN50 (50)
	General service	nat curr, %	No	I	World	UNESCO1 (5.11)
Total		nat curr	No	I	World	UNESCO1 (5.16)
Total expenditure		nat curr	No	I	World	UNESCO1 (5.8)
Total expenditure	% of GDP	nat curr, %	Yes	2 yrly	Nordic countries	NCM1 (247)
Total expenditure	% of GNP	%	No		ASEAN	ASEANS1 (10.3.3)
Total expenditure	By sector of performance	nat curr, %	Yes	2 yrly	Nordic countries	NCM1 (244)
Total expenditure	Financed from public funds	nat curr, %	No	I	World	UNESCO1 (5.14)
40.4.3 Government Budget Appropriations or Outlays for R&D (GBAORD)						
Civil budget R&D as a percentage of total GBAORD	By country	%	Yes	A	OECD	OECD24 (65)
Defence budget R&D as a percentage of total GBAORD	By country	%	Yes	A	OECD	OECD24 (64)
Economic development programmes as a percentage of civil GBAORD	By country	%	Yes	A	OECD	OECD24 (66)
General university funds as a percentage of civil GBAORD	By country	%	Yes	A	OECD	OECD24 (70)
Health and environment programmes as a percentage of civil GBAORD	By country	%	Yes	A	OECD	OECD24 (67)
Non-oriented research programmes as a percentage of civil GBAORD	By country	%	Yes	A	OECD	OECD24 (69)
Research and development budgets	Final and provisional budgets by NABS chapter	nat curr, ECU	Yes	A	EC	EC50

40 SCIENCE AND TECHNOLOGY

Subject	Categories	Units	Time series Yes/No Frequency		Territorial coverage	Source (Table no.)
Space programmes as a percentage of civil GBAORD	By country	%	Yes	A	OECD	OECD24 (68)
Total GBAORD	By country					
Total GBAORD	By country	PPP	Yes	A	OECD	OECD24 (63)
Total GBAORD	By field of science and occupation,	fte	Yes	A	OECD	OECD3 (17)
Total government budget appropriat-ions or outlays for R&D, GBAORD	By country	nar curr	Yes	A	OECD	OECD24 (62)
40.4.4 Government Expenditure on R&D (GOVERD)						
GERD financed by government	By country	%	Yes	A	OECD	OECD24 (14)
GERD performed by the government sector	By country	%	Yes	A	OECD	OECD24 (19)
GOVERD	By country	PPP	Yes	A	OECD	OECD24 (54)
GOVERD as a percentage of GDP	By country	%	Yes	A	OECD	OECD24 (56)
GOVERD, compound annual growth rate	By country	index	Yes	A	OECD	OECD24 (55)
Government funds		nat curr, %	No	I	World	UNESCO1 (5.9)
Intramural expenditure	By country	nat curr	Yes	A	OECD	OECD24 (53)
40.4.5 Gross Domestic Expenditure on R&D (GERD)						
Civil GERD as a percentage of GDP	By country	%	Yes	A	OECD	OECD24 (6)
Current domestic expenditure	By sector of performance and type of activity, by country	nat curr	Yes	A	OECD	OECD3 (3)
GERD	By country	nat curr	Yes	A	OECD	OECD24 (1)
GERD	By country	PPP	Yes	A	OECD	OECD24 (2)
GERD	By sector of performance and type of costs, by country	nat curr	Yes	A	OECD	OECD3 (2)
GERD	By sector of performance and socio-economic objective, by country	nat curr	Yes	A	OECD	OECD3 (4)
GERD	By sector of performance and main scientific field, by country	nat curr	Yes	A	OECD	OECD3 (7)
GERD	By sector of performance and source of funds, by country	nat curr, constant US$	Yes	A	OECD	OECD3 (1)
GERD as a percentage of GDP	By country	%	Yes	A	OECD	OECD24 (5)
GERD financed by industry	By country	%	Yes	A	OECD	OECD24 (13)
GERD financed by government	By country	%	Yes	A	OECD	OECD24 (14)
GERD financed by other national sources	By country	%	Yes	A	OECD	OECD24 (15)
GERD financed by abroad	By country	%	Yes	A	OECD	OECD24 (16)
GERD per capita population	By country	PPP	Yes	A	OECD	OECD24 (4)
GERD performed by the business enterprise sector	By country	%	Yes	A	OECD	OECD24 (17)
GERD performed by the higher education sector	By country	%	Yes	A	OECD	OECD24 (18)

Subject	Categories	Units	Time series Yes/No	Frequency	Territorial coverage	Source (Table no.)
GERD performed by the private non-profit sector	By country	%	Yes	A	OECD	OECD24 (20)
GERD performed by the government sector	By country	%	Yes	A	OECD	OECD24 (19)
GERD, compound annual growth rate	By country, by constant prices	index	Yes	A	OECD	OECD24 (3)
40.4.6 Higher Education Expenditure on R&D (HERD)						
GERD performed by the higher education sector	By country	%	Yes	A	OECD	OECD24 (18)
HERD		nat curr, %	No	I	World	UNESCO1 (5.13)
HERD	By country	nat curr	Yes	A	OECD	OECD24 (44)
HERD	By country	PPP	Yes	A	OECD	OECD24 (45)
HERD as a percentage of GDP	By country	%	Yes	A	OECD	OECD24 (47)
HERD, compound annual growth rate	By country	index	Yes	A	OECD	OECD24 (46)
Higher education		nat curr, %	No	I	World	UNESCO1 (5.11)
Higher education expenditure	By field of science and source of funds, by country	nat curr	Yes	A	OECD	OECD3 (16)
Higher education intramural expenditure	By field of science, and type of costs, by country	nat curr	Yes	A	OECD	OECD3 (15)
Higher education intramural expenditure	By field of science, by country	nat curr, constant US$	Yes	A	OECD	OECD3 (14)
Productive sector	Integrated, non integrated	nat curr, %	No	I	World	UNESCO1 (5.11)
40.5 RESEARCH AND DEVELOPMENT – GENERAL						
Brain drain: skilled migration from developing countries and per capita income gap						
Income gap per capita		US$	Yes	Selected years	Developing countries	UNCTAD5 (4.42)
Number of skilled migrants		nos	Yes	Selected years	Developing countries	UNCTAD5 (4.42)
Framework programmes in the EC	By programme	%, nos	No		Europe	EC35 (-)
Main data	% of GDP, man-years, manpower	nat curr	Yes	2 yrly	Nordic countries	NCM1 (243)
Manufactures, selected indicators	By end-use and R&D intensity	indices	Yes	I	World	UNIDO1 (2.8)
Manufactures, selected indicators	By R&D intensity	indices	No		World	UNIDO1 (1.18)
Nobel prizes and scientific publications	By country	nos	No		Selected countries	
R&D for environmental protection, public		US$, %	Yes	A	Selected countries	OECD33 (13.3)
Research and development	Institutions, activities manpower, budget funding, by country	nos, %, nat curr	No		ASEAN	ASEANS1 (10.4-10.8)
Research in the EC	By programme	ECU, %	No		Europe	EC35 (-)
Total man-years and total man-years in relation to total manpower		nos, %	Yes	2 yrly	Nordic countries	NCM1 (248)

41 SHIPPING

Subject	Categories	Units	Time series Yes/No Frequency		Territorial coverage	Source (Table no.)
4.1 ACCIDENTS - see also Section 1						
Casualty returns	Total loss, total loss by casualty	grt/gt, dwt, nos,	Yes	A,Q,M	World	ISL1 (I 1.4.1-2)
Lives lost	By category, per capita	nos	Yes	A	World	LRS2 (-)
Losses	By flag	nos, tonnage	Yes	A	World	LRS2 (5)
Losses	By how lost	gross tonnage, % of tonnage, nos	No		World	LRS2 (-)
Losses	By how lost, flag, size, age	nos	No		World	LRS2 (1,2a,2b)
Losses	By how lost, geographical distribution	nos	No		World	LRS2 (-)
Losses	By ship type, how lost	nos, tonnage	No		World	LRS2 (3)
Losses reported world total	By age at time of loss	years/nos/ grt-gt	Yes	A	World	ISL2 (1.4.2)
Losses reported world total	By nature of casualty	nos/grt-gt/ grt-gt-%	Yes	A	World	ISL2 (1.4.3)
Losses reported world total	By flag	nos/grt-gt	Yes	A	World	ISL2 (1.4.1)
Merchant fleets	By how lost	nos, tonnage	Yes	A	World	LRS2 (8)
Ships lost, scrapped	Tankers, bulk carriers, general cargo, total	nos, grt	Yes	A	OECD, EC open registries, World	OECD25 (XXVIII)
Ships totally or partially lost at sea and loss of life	Ships, total/partial, life, accident/total partial	nos/gross tonnage	No		Nordic countries	NCM1 (140)
41.2 CHARTERING AND FREIGHT RATES AND COSTS						
Baltic freight rates		US$, indices			World	ISL2 (5.5.1-2)
Bulk freight market indices (dry cargo market)	By vessel type	index	Yes	A, M	World	DSC1 (19)
Bunker market prices	By oil type, % change over period	US$ fob, % change, tonnes	Yes	A, M	World	ISL1 (-)
Charter freight (development)	Dry cargo, tankers	indices	Yes	A, Q	World	OECD25 (XXIX)
Charterers	Route, charterer	dwct	No		World	DSC1 (2)
Charterers, time	By length	dwt, months	No		World	DSC1 (10)
Charterers, time	By size and length	dwt, months	No		World	DSC1 (8)
Chartering	By commodity, cargo size, ship type	dwct and nos of fixtures	No		World	DSC1 (23a, 23b)
Chartering activity, summary of (dry cargo market)	By size and type	dwct	Yes	A, M	World	DSC1 (20)
Chartering trends	Load, discharge, user	dwct	Yes	A, M	World	DSC1 (3, 6)
Chartering, grain	By loading zone, cargo, size, ship type	dwt, nos of charterers	No		World	DSC1 (24)
Charters	By commodity	dwct, nos	Yes	A, M	World	DSC1 (22)
Contracting of bulk tonnage	By ship type	no of ships, dwt	Yes	6 mnthly	World	F2 (5)
Contracting, world	By ship type	dwt	Yes	A	World	F1 (10)
Fixtures	Load, discharge,	nos	No		World	DSC1 (1, 5)
Freight - time charter	General, grain, miscellaneous	indices	Yes	A, M	World	ISL2 (5.4.1-6)
Freight costs in world trade	Estimate and totals values	% import	Yes	A	World	ISL2 (2.2.7)
Freight costs in world trade, total	Estimate of total freight costs of imports, value of imports, freight costs as % of import value	US$	Yes	I	World	UNCTAD2 (31)

41 SHIPPING

Subject	Categories	Units	Time series Yes/No Frequency		Territorial coverage	Source (Table no.)
Freight costs, estimates of, in world trade	Value, % of value	$US, %	Yes	Selected years	World, by development groups	UNCTAD5 (4.35)
Freight futures - implied rates from selected futures prices	By BFI route, commodity $ per day, %	$ per dwct	Yes	M	World	DSC1 (41)
Freight indices, tanker voyage	By type of tanker	worldscale points	Yes	A, M	World	OECD25 (XXXII)
Freight rate indices	By sources	indices, WS	Yes	A, M	World	ISL1 (-)
Freight rate indices	By type of vessel	indices	Yes	A, M	World	UNCTAD2 (30)
Freight rates	By haul	indices,	Yes	A, M	World	COS1 (12.1-12.3)
Freight rates	By route and charterer, dirty, clean, name of tanker, cargo	% worldscale, tonnes	No		World	BB3 (4.1-4.2)
Freight rates	By route and size, fixtures, cargo dirty, clean	nos, % worldscale, $ per tonne, tonnes	No		World	BB3 (3.1-3.2)
Freight rates	By charterer, fixtures, cargo dirty, clean	nos, % worldscale, $ per tonne, tonnes	No		World	BB3 (5.1-5.2)
Freight rates, bulk cargo	Voyages, timecharter	indices, dwt	Yes	A	World	F1 (14)
Freight rates, comparative	By selected commodity	US$, tonne	No		World	UNCTAD2 (29)
Freight rates, tanker	By ship type	indices, world scale points	Yes	A	World	F1 (13)
Freight rates, tankers Indices	By vessel size	% worldscale	Yes	M	World	BB3 (1) (XXX1)
Indices and rates	By vessel and cargo type	indices, dwt, $ dwt per month	Yes	A, M	World	ISL1 (I 3.1-5)
Prices, contracting	By new ship type	US$, dwt	Yes	A	World South	F1 (16)
Prices, world market		indices	Yes	A, M	World	ISL1 (-)
Rates, dirty spot	Load, discharge, route no, cargo, fixtures	dwct, Ws, nos	Yes	A, M	World	DSC1 (4, 7)
Representative prices (bunkers)	By area, vessel and oil type	US$ per tonne	Yes	A, Q, M	World	DSC1 (40)
Representative rates on key oil and dry routes(combined carriers)	By cargo and route	$ per dwct	Yes	A, M	World	DSC1 (15)
Shipping costs, prices	By bunker market prices, demolition prices by area	US$ fob, tonnes US$ per LDT, indices	Yes	A, M	World	ISL1 (I 1.6.1-2)
Short-term time, average reported	By vessel size, rate	$ per day, dwt	Yes	A, M	World	DSC1 (11)
Single voyage rates	By commodity and M average	$ per dwct	Yes	A, M	World	DSC1 (21)
Spot (dirty) freight rates, tankers	By haul, WS, $ per tonne	tonnes, % of	Yes	A, M	Selected countries	BB2 (23)
Spot (dirty) tanker fixtures and freight rates	By haul and company of WS, $ per tonne	nos, tonnes, %	No		World	BB2 (20)
Spot fixtures, tankers	By period dirty, clean	nos, tonnes, $ per tonnes	No		World	BB3 (-)
Spot freight rates by tanker size	By ASFR, spot (dirty) WS, US$ per tonne	tonnes, % of	Yes	A, M	World	BB2 (22)
Spot market dirty fixtures		US$	Yes	A, M	Arabian Gulf to North Europe	ISL2 (5.8)
Tanker freight rates	Dirty/clean	%, dwt	Yes	A, M	World	ISL2 (5.7)
Tanker freight rates, spot	By route	%, $/LT	Yes	A	World	OPEC1 (67)
Tanker time charters fixed	By charterer, vessel, period, rate, delivery	dwt, $	No			BB2 (21)
Time charter freight, dry cargo		indices	Yes	A, M	World	OECD25

Subject	Categories	Units	Time series Yes/No Frequency		Territorial coverage	Source (Table no.)
Time charters, tanker	By charterer, name of vessel, period,	$ per day, tonnes, dwt, rate	No			BB3 (2)
Time, charter, activity	By vessel size	dwt, nos	Yes	A, M	World	DSC1 (27)
Time, charter, duration	By month	dwt, nos	Yes	A, M	World	DSC1 (28)
Tonnage time chartered	By length	dwt, months	Yes	A, M	World	DSC1 (9)
Trip charter and liner freight indices, dry cargo voyage	Voyage charter, tramp trip charter, liner freight	indices	Yes	A, M	World	OECD25 (XXX)
Trip charter rates, representative	By vessel type	$ per day	Yes	A, M	World	DSC1 (26)
Trip charters, reported	By delivery zone	dwct, nos	Yes	A, M	World	DSC1 (25)
Worldwide-charter fixtures for coal and grain		nos, tonnes	Yes	A, M	World	ISL2 (5.6.1-2)
41.3 EMPLOYMENT						
Employment analysis (combined carriers)	By cargo	dwt, %	Yes	A, M	World	DSC1 (16)
Personnel (merchant marines)	By nationality	nos	No		OECD	OECD25 (XXXIV)
Personnel (merchant marines)	By occupation	nos	No		OECD	OECD25 (XXXIII)
41.4 FLEETS						
41.4.1 Broken-up						
Broken-up tonnage	By ship type, % change over period	dwt, grt, % change	Yes	A, M	World	ISL1 (-)
Bulk tonnage broken up and lost	By ship type	dwt	Yes	6 mnthly	World	F2 (7)
Merchant ships broken up etc	By country of disposal	nos, tonnage, %	Yes	A	World	LRS2 (7)
Merchant ships, broken up etc	By flag	nos, tonnage	Yes	A	World	LRS2 (6)
Ships broken up, analysis of	By ship type, age	nos, tonnage	No		World	LRS2 (4)
Ships broken up, summary of	By country	nos, tonnage	No		World	LRS2 (-)
Tonnage broken up	By year of build, ship type, flag	grt/gt, dwt, %, nos	Yes	A, M	World	ISL1 (I 1.3.1-3)
Tonnage broken up and lost	By ship type	dwt	Yes	A	World	F1 (5)
Tonnage reported sold for breaking	By type of vessel	dwt, %	Yes	A	World	UNCTAD2 (26)
Tonnage reported sold for breaking	By ship type, size	dwt	Yes	6 mnthly	World	F1 (6)
Tonnage reported sold for demolition	By type	dwt	Yes	A, M	World	DSC1 (37)
Tonnage, broken up	Tonnage sold for breaking, share of broken-up tonnage in the total world fleet	dwt, %	Yes	A	World	UNCTAD2 (25)
41.4.2 General						
Bulk fleet	By country of registry	no of ships, dwt	Yes	6 mnthly	World	F2 (10)
Bulk fleet	By ship type, argo/ miscellaneous	nos, %, grt, gt-%			World	ISL2 (1.1.3)
Bulk fleet	By size and ship type	no of ships, dwt	Yes	6 mnthly	World	F2 (8)
Bulk fleet	By size, age and ship type	no of ships, dwt	Yes	6 mnthly	World	F2 (9)
Bulk fleet	Flag distribution, by country of registry	no of ships, dwt	Yes	6 mnthly	World	F2 (4)
Bulk fleet	By ship type, size distribution	no of ships, dwt	Yes	6 mnthly	World	F2 (2)
Bulk fleet development	By ship type	no of ships, dwt	Yes	6 mnthly	World	F2 (1)
Bulk fleet storage	By ship type	no of ships/ dwt	Yes	6 mnthly	World	F2 (16)

41 SHIPPING

Subject	Categories	Units	Time series Yes/No Frequency		Territorial coverage	Source (Table no.)
Bulk fleet, estimated world	By ship type	dwt	Yes	A	World	F2 (17)
Cargo carrying ships	By age	nos, fwt	No		World	LRS4 (6)
Dry bulk carrier fleet	By age and size, year of build	dwt, nos	Yes	5 yrly	World	DSC1 (43)
Dry bulk carrier fleet	By dwt and flag	dwt, nos	No		World	DSC1 (45)
Dry fleet (bulk carriers)	By size, activity, changes	dwt	Yes	M	World	DSC1 (29)
Fleet	By principal types of vessel	dwt, %	Yes	A	World	UNCTAD2 (9)
Fleet	By ship type, trade, employment	grt/gt/nos, dwt/%/years	Yes	A	World	ISL2 (6.2.1.1-6.2.4.4.6)
Fleet	By size and age tonnage	nos, gross	No		Nordic countries	NCM1 (137)
Fleet	By type of vessel tonnage	nos, gross	No		Nordic countries	NCM1 (136)
Fleet	Total	nos/grt/gt	Yes	A	World	ISEL2 (1.1.1)
Fleet age distribution	World fleet, oil tankers ore and bulk carriers	nos, grt, %	No		World	OECD25 (XX)
Fleet development	By division of age, ship type	years/dwt-%/ nos/grt/gt			World	ISL2 (1.1.8)
Fleet development	By major flags, by ship type	nos, dwt, %			World	ISL2 (1.1.6)
Fleet development	By size class, by ship type	nos, dwt, %			World	ISL2 (1.1.7)
Fleet development	Oil tankers, ore and dry bulk carriers, total	nos, % change	Yes	A	World	OECD25 (XVIII)
Fleet development	Total fleet/by type	nos, %, grt, dwt	Yes	A	World	ISL2 (1.1.4)
		nos, grt, dwt, teu/dwt-%	Yes	A	World	ISL2 (1.1.5)
Fleet development		nos, grt, gt-%	Yes	A	World	ISL2 (1.1.1)
Fleet development	By major flags	nos, grt, gt-%	Yes	A	World	ISL2 (1.1.2)
Fleet size		nos	Yes	I	EC	EC80 (1.5)
Fleet size distribution	World fleet, oil tankers ore and bulk carrier	nos, grt, %	No		World	OECD25 (XIX)
Fleet, capacity in GRT		tonnes	Yes	I	EC	EC80 (1.5)
Fleet, container	Size, nos, %	ft, nos, %	No		IICL members	UNCTAD2 (35)
Fleet, percentage of EC fleet in GRT	By country	%	Yes	I	EC	EC80 (1.5)
Fleet, percentage of world fleet in GRT	By country	%	Yes	I	EC	EC80 (1.5)
Fleet, size of	By country	tonnes	No		EC	EM1 (2213)
Fleet, UK owned/world trading	By vessel type, owner	nos, dwt, %	No		World	COS1 (7)
Fleet, world	By ship type	dwt	Yes	A	World	F1 (8)
Fleet, world	By ship type	ships, dwt	Yes	A	World	F1 (3)
Fleet, World	By type and flag	nos	No		World	EC80 (5.2)
Fleets	All, oil tankers	nos, tonnes	No		EC	EC9 (7.7)
Fleets	Nos/gross	tonnage	Yes	A	Nordic countries	NCM1 (134)
Fleets - bulk (growth)	Oil tankers, dry bulk carriers, combination carriers	dwt	Yes	A	World	OECD25 (XXVI)
Fleets - world	By country of registration and type of vessel	grt, %	No		World	OECD25 (XXII)
Fleets - world	By country of registration	grt, dwt	No		World	OECD25 (XXI)
Fleets - world	By type of vessel and regional distribution	gt, %	No		World	OECD25 (XXV)
Fleets - world	By major national groups	grt, %	Yes	A	World	OECD25 (XXIV)
Fleets, open registry	Flags, type, age, size class	grt/gt/nos/ dwt/TEU/%/ years	Yes	A	World	ISL2 (6.1.3.1-4)

41 SHIPPING

Subject	Categories	Units	Time series Yes/No	Frequency	Territorial coverage	Source (Table no.)
Fleets, open-registry, major	By true nationality	dwt, %	No		World	UNCTAD2 (8)
Fleets, open-registry, major	Tonnage distribution by category of vessel	nos, dwt	No		Major open registry fleets, world	UNCTAD2 (7)
Fleets, ten largest trading	By rank and register	nos, dwt, grt	No		World	COS1 (5)
Inactivity (bulk carrier)	By vessel size	dwt, nos	Yes	A, M	World	DSC1 (32)
Maritime countries, most important	By number of vessels, by deadweight tonnage	nos, % tonnes	No		35 most important maritime countries	UNCTAD2 (5)
Merchant (fleet), age distribution	By type of vessel	years, %	No		World	UNCTAD2 (12)
Merchant fleet	By age and country	nos, tonne	No		World	EC80 (5.5)
Merchant fleet	By flag	nos, tonnes	Yes	A	World	EC80 (5.3)
Merchant fleet	By ship type, % change over period	dwt, % change	Yes	A, M	World	ISL1 (-)
Merchant fleet	By size group	nos	No		World	EC80 (5.4)
Merchant fleet	By summer draught and ship type	metres, nos, grt/gt	No		World	ISL1 (I 1.1)
Merchant fleet	By type and age	nos, tonnes	No		World	EC80 (5.6)
Merchant fleet	Flag state, ship type , age	nos, tonnes	No		World	LRS4 (1)
Merchant fleets	By flag of registration by types of ships, by groups of countries	grt, dwt	No		World, world economic regions	UNCTAD2 (III)
Merchant fleets	Gross register for vessels of 1000 tonnes and over, by type	nos	No		Latin American and Caribbean countries	UN45 (357)
Merchant fleets	Increase or decrease, by country	gt, %	No		World	OECD25 (XXIII)
Merchant shipping	By country, by principal type of vessel	tonnes	No		Europe	EM1 (2216)
Merchant shipping	Unloaded, loaded	tonnes	No		EC	EC9 (7.8)
Merchant shipping fleet		grt	Yes	A	ASEAN	ASEANS1 (5.3.1)
Merchant ships	By country	nos	No		Europe	EC18 (10.8)
Merchant ships registered	By countries	nos	No		The Americas and Australasia	MAC2 (G4)
Merchant ships registered	By countries	nos, tonnes	Yes	A	EC	MAC3 (F4)
Merchant ships registered	By country, ship type	gross tonnes nos	Yes	A	Africa and Asia	MAC1 (G4)
Motor and steam ships		nos, tonnes	Yes	A	World	EC80 (5.1)
Ship disposals and losses	By flag state, age	nos, tonnes	Yes	A	World	LRS4 (23)
Ship disposals and losses	By ship type category, age	nos, tonnes	Yes	A	World	LRS4 (24)
Ship type categories	By age, by type	nos, tonnes	No		World	LRS4 (5)
Ships (average size)	Ships in service, on order	dwt	Yes	A	World	OECD25 (XXVII)
Tanker fleet	By age and size, year of build	dwt, nos	Yes	5 yrly	World	DSC1 (42)
Tanker fleet	By flag and size	dwt, nos	No		World	DSC1 (44)
Tonnage	% share of world tonnage (dwt) by type of vessel and country groups	%	Yes	I	World, world continents and economic group	UNCTAD2 (10)
Tonnage oversupply	By vessel type	dwt	Yes	A	World	UNCTAD2 (19)
Tonnage oversupply, merchant fleet		dwt, %	Yes	A	World	UNCTAD2 (17)
Tonnage, distribution	Tonnage and % shares, increase in tonnage, by groups of countries of registration	dwt, grt	Yes	I	World, world continents and economic regions	UNCTAD2 (4)
Tonnage, flagged-out, distribution	By category of vessel	nos, dwt %		No	World	UNCTAD2 (6)
Total		grt	Yes	A	World	UN50 (134)

41 SHIPPING

Subject	Categories	Units	Time series Yes/No Frequency		Territorial coverage	Source (Table no.)
Vessels, international shipping	Entered, cleared	grt	Yes	A	ASEAN	ASEANS1 (5.3.2.1)
Vessels, productivity	By type of vessel	tonne-miles per dwt	Yes	A	World	UNCTAD2 (15)
Vessels, productivity	By type of vessel	tonnes per dwt	Yes	A	World	UNCTAD2 (16)
World fleet	By vessel type	nos, dwt, grt %	No		World	COS1 (1)
World fleet, UK owned/ UK registered	By average age, vessel	nos, dwt, grt type, owner	No		World	COS1 (3)
41.4.3 Laid-up						
Bulk fleet lay-up	By ship type	no of ships/ dwt	Yes	6 mnthly	World	F2 (15)
Flag	By ship type	nos/dwt/ dwt-%	Yes	A, M	World	ISL2 (1.2.7)
Laid-up tonnage	By ship type, % change over period	dwt, grt, % change	Yes	A, M	World	ISL1 (-)
Laid-up tonnage	By year of build, ship type, flag, tonnage reduction and addition, dwt rank	grt/gt, dwt-%, nos	Yes	A, M	World	ISL1 (I 1.2.1-4)
Lay-up area	By ship type	nos/dwt/ dwt-%			World	ISL2 (1.2.8)
Lay-up rate of world merchant fleet	Type of vessel	grt/gt	Yes	A	World	ISL2 (1.2.2)
Lay-up time	By ship type	%			World	ISL2 (1.2.9)
Ship type		grt/gt	Yes	A, M	World	ISL2 (1.2.3)
Size class	By ship type	nos/dwt/ dwt-%			World	ISL2 (1.2.6)
Tonnage laid up	By ship type	dwt	Yes	A	World	F1 (7)
Tonnage reduction and addition	By ship type	nos/dwt-%	Yes	M	World	ISL2 (1.2.4)
Tonnage, laid-up	Nos/gross	tonnage	Yes	A, Q	Nordic countries	NCM1 (135)
Tonnage, world laid-up tanker and combined carrier tonnage	By size	dwt	Yes	A	World	OPEC1 (64)
Type of vessel		nos/grt-gt/ dwt	Yes	A, M	World	ISL2 (1.2.1)
UK owned/world fleet,laid up	By vessel type, owner	nos, dwt, grt	No		World	COS1 (6)
Year of build	By ship type average age	nos/dwt/	Yes	4 yrly	World	ISL2 (1.2.5)
41.4.4 Type						
Bulk dry	By age	nos, dwt	No		World	LRS4 (10)
Bulk dry, oil	By age	nos, dwt	No		World	LRS4 (11)
Bulk fleet	By size and ship type	no of ships/ dwt	Yes	6 mnthly	World	F2 (8)
Bulk fleet development	By ship type	no of ships/ dwt	Yes	6 mnthly	World	F2 (1)
Bulk fleet development of size distribution	By ship type	no of ships/ dwt	Yes	6 mnthly	World	F2 (2)
Bulk fleet(age)	By size, age and ship type	no of ships/ dwt	Yes	6 mnthly	World	F2 (9)
Bulk fleet, world	By ship type	dwt	Yes	6 mnthly	World	F2 (17)
Cargo carriers, conventional, general, ro-ro ships, partly/ fully cellular containerships, barge carriers	By developed/developing economies	dwt/%/ indices	Yes	A	World	ISL2 (3.5-9)
Chemical	By age	nos, dwt	No		World	LRS4 (8)
Combined carrier shipments	By commodity	tonnes, %	Yes	A	World	F1 (15)
Container	By age	nos, dwt, TEU	No		World	LRS4 (14A-14B)
Dry cargo, bulk	Flag state, cargo type,	nos, tonnes age	No		World	LRS4 (2B)

Subject	Categories	Units	Time series Yes/No Frequency	Territorial coverage	Source (Table no.)
Dry cargo, other	Flag state, cargo type, age	nos, tonnes	No	World	LRS4 (2C)
Fish catching	By age	nos, tonnes	No	World	LRS4 (17)
Flagged-out tonnage, distribution	By category of vessel	nos, dwt %	No	World	UNCTAD2 (6)
Fleet	By principal types of vessel	dwt, %	Yes A	World	UNCTAD2 (9)
Fleet	By ship type, cargo/ miscellaneous	nos/%/grt/ gt-%		World	ISL2 (1.1.3)
Fleet	By ship type, trade, employment	grt/gt/nos/ dwt/%/years	Yes A	World	ISL2 (6.2.1.1-6.2.4.4.6)
Fleet		nos/grt-gt/ dwt/dwt-%	Yes A, M	World	ISL2 (1.3.7)
Fleet activities	Flag state, age	nos, tonnes,	No	World	LRS4 (2E)
	fleet development, by flag, major flags, year of build and by size class	nos/grt-gt/ berths/%	Yes A	World	ISL2 (1.5.9.1-5)
Fleet	By major flag, country and age, size and division of age, summer draught and dwt-size class	nos/grt-gt/ dwt/dwt-% years	Yes A	World	ISL2 (1.5.4.1-4)
Fleet average age	By ship type	age	Yes A	World	ISL2 (1.3.2)
Fleet by country groups	By ship type	nos/dwt/ groups		World	ISL2 (1.3.4)
Fleet by flag	By ship type	nos/dwt/ dwt-%		World	ISL2 (1.3.3-9)
Fleet by size class	By ship type	nos/dwt/		World	ISL2 (1.3.6)
Fleet by year of build	By ship type/ average age	nos/dwt/ dwt-%		World	ISL2 (1.3.5-8)
Fleet development		nos/dwt	Yes A	World	ISL2 (1.3.1)
Fleet development	By division of age, ship type	years/dwt-%/ nos/grt/gt		World	ISL2 (1.1.8)
Fleet development	By major flags, ship type	nos/dwt/%		World	ISL2 (1.1.6)
Fleet development	By size class, ship type	nos/dwt/%		World	ISL2 (1.1.7)
Fleet development	Total fleet/by type	nos/%/grt/ dwt	Yes A	World	ISL2 (1.1.4)
Fleet fishery development	Total/type of vessel	nos/grt-gt/%	Yes A	World	ISL2 (1.5.10.1)
Fleet fishery development	Total/type of vessel, by major flags	nos.grt-gt/%		World	ISL2 (1.5.10.2)
Fleet, OECD	Flag, type, age, size class, personnel employed	grt/gt/nos/ %/TEU/ years/dwt	Yes A	OECD	ISL2 (6.1.1.1-5)
Fleet of reefer ships	By major flag, size class and age, summer draught and dwt-size class	nos/grt-gt/ dwt/dwt-% years		World	ISL2 (1.5.6.6.1-3)
Fleet of special general cargo	By major flag, size class and age, summer draught and dwt-size class	nos/grt-gt/ dwt/dwt-% years		World	ISL2 (1.5.6.5.1-3)
Fleet, cargo passenger and total passenger	By ship type, total by major flags, total passenger and cargo passenger, size class and age, cargo/ passenger and ro-ro/ passenger ships by summer draught and grt/gt size, passenger ships by summer draught and grt/gt size	nos/grt-gt/ %/years	Yes A	World	ISL2 (1.5.8.1-5)

41 SHIPPING

Subject	Categories	Units	Time series Yes/No Frequency		Territorial coverage	Source (Table no.)
Fleet, chemical	By major flag, country and age, size and division of age, summer draught and dwt-size class	nos/grt-gt/ dwt/dwt-% years			World	ISL2 (1.5.2.1-4)
Fleet, fishery, fishing and offshore	Flag state, cargo type	nos, tonnes age	No		World	LRS4 (2D)
Fleet, fishery, fishing vessels and factory trawlers	By size and flag	nos, tonnes	No		World	EC80 (5.7)
Fleet, fishery, offshore service vessel	Type of vessel, year of build	nos/%	Yes	A	World	ISL2 (1.5.11)
Fleet, world	By ship type	dwt	Yes	A	World	F1 (8)
Fleet, world	By ship type	ships, dwt	Yes	A	World	F1 (3)
Fleet, world	By type and flag	nos	No		World	EC80 (5.2)
Fleet, world	By type of vessel, nos/gross	tonnage	No		Nordic countries	NCM1 (136) (137)
Fleets	All, oil tankers	nos, tonnes	No		EEC,	EC9 (7.7)
Fleets, open registry	Flags, type, age, size class	grt/gt/nos/ dwt/TEU/%/ years	Yes	A	World	ISL2 (6.1.3.1-4)
Fleets, world	By country of registration and type of vessel	grt, %	No		World	OECD25 (XXII)
Fleets, world	By type of vessel and regional distribution	gt, %	No		World	OECD25 (XXV)
Fleets, world	By vessel type	nos, dwt, grt %	No		World	COS1 (1)
Fully cellular containerships	Ships, TEU capacity and % shares, economic regions by groups of countries	nos, %	Yes	A	World	UNCTAD2 (11)
General cargo	By ship type	nos/grt-gt/ dwt/dwt-%/ TEU	Yes	A	World	ISL2 (1.5.6.1)
General cargo	By ship type/age/ capacity	nos/TEU/ years/teu-%	Yes	A	World	ISL2 (1.5.6.2)
General cargo multi-deck	By major flag, size class and age, summer draught and dwt-size class	nos/grt-gt/ dwt/dwt-% years	Yes	A	World	ISL2 (1.5.6.4.1-3)
General cargo single-deck	By major flag, size class and age, summer draught and dwt-size class	nos/grt-gt/ dwt/dwt-% years	Yes	A	World	ISL2 (1.5.6.3.1)
General cargo,including passenger	By age	nos, dwt	No		World	LRS4 (12)
Liquid cargo, bulk	Flag state, cargo type, age	nos, tonnes	No		World	LRS4 (2A)
Liquid cas carrier fleet	By size and type	cu m	No		World	OPEC1 (61)
Liquid gas carrier fleet	By major flag, country and age, size and division of age, summer draught and dwt-size class, pressurised	nos/grt-gt/ dwt/dwt-% years	Yes	A	World	ISL2 (1.5.3.1-4)
Liquid gas carrier fleet	By size and type	cu m	No		OPEC	OPEC1 (62)
Liquid gas carrier fleet	By vessel size, year of	nos, cu m build	Yes	A	World	G2 (1)
Liquid gas carrier fleet, semi-pressurised, refrigerated	By vessel size, year of build	nos, cu m	Yes	A	World	G2 (2)
Liquid gas carrier fleet, fully refrigerated	By vessel size, year of build	nos, cu m	Yes	A	World	G2 (3)
Liquid gas carrier fleet, existing LNG carriers	By vessel size, year of build	nos, cu m	Yes	A	World	G2 (4)
Liquid gas carrier fleet, existing liquified gas carriers	By vessel, flag, type	nos, cu m	No		World	G2 (5)
Liquified gas	By age	nos, fwt	No		World	LRS4 (7A)
Liquified gas	By gas capacity, age, insulated capacity	nos, cu m,	No		World	LRS4 (7B)

Subject	Categories	Units	Time series Yes/No Frequency	Territorial coverage	Source (Table no.)
Merchant fleet	By ship type, % change over period	dwt, % change	Yes A, M	World	ISL1 (-)
Merchant fleet	By summer draught and ship type	metres, nos, grt/gt	No	World	ISL1 (I 1.1)
Merchant fleet, age distribution	By type of vessel	years, %	No	World	UNCTAD2 (12)
Merchant fleets	By flag of registration, by types of ships, by groups of countries	grt, dwt	No	World	UNCTAD2 (III)
Merchant fleets	Gross register for vessels of 1000 tonnes and over, by type	nos	No	Latin American and Caribbean countries	UN45 (357)
Merchant fleets of the world	Flag state, ship type, age	nos, tonnes	No	World	LRS4 (1)
Merchant shipping	By country, by principal type of vessel	tonnes	No	EC	EM1 (2216)
Merchant ships registered	By country, ship type	tons gross nos	Yes A	Africa and Asia	MAC1 (G4)
Oil	By age	nos, dwt	No	World	LRS4 (9)
Oil chemical and combined carriers	By size, 10,000 dwt and over	dwt	Yes A	World	OPEC1 (63)
Oil chemical and combined carriers	By vessel size and age	nos dwt	No		G1 (-)
Oil chemical and combined carriers	By vessel size and type	nos, dwt	No		G1 (-)
Oil fleet	By total tonnage	dwt	Yes A, M	World	DSC1 (12)
Oil storage, tanker tonnage	Semi-permanent, short-term, total	nos, dwt	Yes 2 yr	World	UNCTAD2 (18)
Oil tankers		grt	Yes A	World	UN50 (134)
Oil tankers	By major flag, country and age, size and division of age, summer draught and dwt-size class	nos/grt-gt/ dwt/dwt-% years	Yes A	World	ISL2 (1.5.1.1-4)
Open-registry fleets, major	Tonnage distribution by category of vessel	nos, dwt	No	Major open registry fleets, world	UNCTAD2 (7)
Ore and bulk carrier fleets	By major flag, country and age, size and division of age, summer draught and dwt-size class	grt, nos/ grt-gt/dwt/ dwt-% years	Yes A	World World	UN50 (134) ISL2 (1.5.5.1-4)
Passenger	By age	nos, tonnes	No	World	LRS4 (16)
Refrigerated cargo	By age	nos, dwt	No	World	LRS4(15A)
Refrigerated cargo	Insulated capacity, age	nos, cu m,	No	World	LRS4 (15B)
Research fleet	By major flags, size class and division of age	nos/grt-gt/ %/years		World	ISL2 (1.5.12.1-2)
Ro-ro cargo	By major flag, size class and age, summer draught and dwt-size class	nos/grt-gt/ dwt/dwt-% years	Yes A	World	ISL2 (1.5.6.7.1)
Ro-ro cargo,including passenger	By age	nos, dwt	No	World	LRS4 (13)
Special fleets	By ship type, size, class age, flag	grt/gt, dwt %, nos, TEU	Yes A	World	ISL1 (I 1.5-1.5.6.2)
Tanker leet	By age, 10,000 dwt and over	dwt	Yes 5yr	World	OPEC1 (60)
Tanker fleet	By changes, vessel size, nos	dwt, %, nos	No	World	DSC1 (13)
Tanker fleet	By dwt	dwt, %	Yes A	World	IP1 (-)
Tanker fleet	Development	dwt	Yes A	OPEC	OPEC1 (59)
Tanker orderbook	By size, changes	dwt, %, nos	No	World	DSC1 (14)
Tanker tonnage	By country, by %	dwt, %	Yes A	World	IP1 (-)
Tankers	By type of tanker	nos, dwt	Yes A	World	IP1 (-)
Tankers, LPG, LNG and dry bulk carriers	Trade	dwt/%/ indices	Yes A	World	ISL2 (3.1-4)

41 SHIPPING

Subject	Categories	Units	Time series Yes/No Frequency		Territorial coverage	Source (Table no.)
Tonnage	% share of world tonnage (dwt) by type of vessel and country groups	%	Yes	I	World,	UNCTAD2 (10)
Tonnage oversupply	By vessel type	dwt	Yes	A	World	UNCTAD2 (19)
UK owned/world trading fleet	By vessel type, owner	nos, dwt, %	No		World	COS1 (7)
World fleet	By age	nos,tonnes	No		World	LRS4 (18)
41.5 SEABORNE TRADE - see also under Commodities (41.5.2) and Seaborne Traffic (41.6)						
41.5.1 Agriculture						
Coarse grains	Import and export, by destination	tonnes	Yes	A	World	ISL2 (2.3.17.4.1-2)
Coarse grains	Production and trade, by country/destination	tonnes	Yes	A	World	ISL2 (2.3.17.3-4)
Cocoa (beans)	Production and trade, by country	tonnes/%	Yes	A	World	ISL2 (2.3.23)
Coffee (green)	Production and trade by country	tonnes/%	Yes	A	World	ISL2 (2.3.21)
Fish	Catches, nominal and trade, by country	tonnes/%/ US$	Yes	A	World	ISL2 (2.3.25.1-2)
Grain	By export/import area, export/import matrix	tonnes/%	Yes	A	Region	ISL2 (2.1.8.1-3)
Grain	Canadian exports, by destination	tonnes	Yes	A, M	World	DSC2 (7.13)
Grain	Exports, by exporter	tonnes	Yes	A, M	Selected countries	DSC2 (7.9)
Grain	Imports, by country and region	tonnes	Yes	A	World	DSC2 (7.16)
Grain	Major exporters, by crop shipments and country	US$	Yes	A	Selected countries	DSC2 (7.5)
Grain	Origin and destination	tonnes	No		World	OECD25 (VIII)
Rice	Production and trade by country	tonnes	Yes	A	World	ISL2 (2.3.18)
Seaborne trade	From, to	tonnes	Yes	-	World	F3 (18)
Shipments by vessels	From, to	tonnes	Yes	-	World	F3 (20)
Soyabean	Production and trade by country	tonnes/%	Yes	A	World	ISL2 (2.3.19.1)
Soyabean oil	Import and export by country	tonnes/%	Yes	A	World	ISL2 (2.3.19.2)
Sugar (centrifugal and raw)	Production and trade by country	tonnes/%	Yes	A	World	ISL2 (2.3.20)
Tea	Production and trade by country	tonnes/%	Yes	A	World	ISL2 (2.3.22)
Tobacco (unmanufactured)	Production and trade by country	tonnes/%	Yes	A	World	ISL2 (2.3.24)
Trade, total	Export and import areas	tonnes-miles	Yes	A	World	F3 (19)
Wheat	Import and export, by destination	tonnes	Yes	A	World	ISL2 (2.3.17.2.1-2)
Wheat	Production and trade by region and country,	tonnes	Yes	A	World	ISL2 (2.3.17.2.1-2)
41.5.2 Commodities - see also Sections 5 and 27						
World Exports by Commodity						
All commodities	Quantity and alh	nautical miles, tonnes	Yes	A	World	UN31 (1)
Animal feeding stuff, by type	Quantity and alh	nautical miles, tonnes	Yes	A	World	UN31 (1)
Beverages	Quantity and alh	nautical miles, tonnes	Yes	A	World	UN31 (2)

Subject	Categories	Units	Time series Yes/No Frequency		Territorial coverage	Source (Table no.)
Beverages, by type	Quantity and alh	nautical miles, tonnes	Yes	A	World	UN31 (1)
Bulk liquid	Quantity and alh	nautical miles, tonnes	Yes	A	World	UN31 (1)
Bulk, dry	Quantity and alh	nautical miles, tonnes	Yes	A	World	UN31 (1)
Bulk, liquid	Quantity and alh	nautical miles, tonnes	Yes	A	World	UN31 (2)
Chemicals	Quantity and alh	nautical miles, tonnes	Yes	A	World	UN31 (2)
Coal and coke etc, by type	Quantity and alh	nautical miles, tonnes	Yes	A	World	UN31 (1)
Coffee	Quantity and alh	nautical miles, tonnes	Yes	A	World	UN31 (1)
Coffee	Quantity and alh	nautical miles, tonnes	Yes	A	World	UN31 (2)
Cotton	Production, trade and consumption	bales/%	Yes	A	World	ISL2 (2.3.13.1-2)
Cotton yarn	Production, by country	tonnes	Yes	A	World	ISL2 (2.3.16)
Crude minerals nes	Quantity and alh	nautical miles, tonnes	Yes	A	World	UN31 (2)
Crude petroleum etc	Quantity and alh	nautical miles, tonnes	Yes	A	World	UN31 (1)
Crude petroleum etc	Quantity and alh	nautical miles, tonnes	Yes	A	World	UN31 (2)
Crude rubber	Quantity and alh	nautical miles, tonnes	Yes	A	World	UN31 (1)
Crude rubber	Quantity and alh	nautical miles, tonnes	Yes	A	World	UN31 (2)
Energy petroleum products, by type	Quantity and alh	nautical miles, tonnes	Yes	A	World	UN31 (1)
Energy petroleum products, liquid	Quantity and alh	nautical miles, tonnes	Yes	A	World	UN31 (2)
Ferrous base metals, by type	Quantity and alh	nautical miles, tonnes	Yes	A	World	UN31 (1)
Fertilizers, by type	Quantity and alh	nautical miles, tonnes	Yes	A	World	UN31 (1)
Fuel gases	Quantity and alh	nautical miles, tonnes	Yes	A	World	UN31 (1)
Fuel gases, liquefied	Quantity and alh	nautical miles, tonnes	Yes	A	World	UN31 (2)
General cargo, dry	Quantity and alh	nautical miles, tonnes	Yes	A	World	UN31 (1)
General cargo, dry	Quantity and alh	nautical miles, tonnes	Yes	A	World	UN31 (2)
Grains, by type	Quantity and alh	nautical miles, tonnes	Yes	A	World	UN31 (1)
Machinery	Quantity and alh	nautical miles, tonnes	Yes	A	World	UN31 (2)
Machinery and equipment	Quantity and alh	nautical miles, tonnes	Yes	A	World	UN31 (2)
Manufactures of metal	Quantity and alh	nautical miles, tonnes	Yes	A	World	UN31 (2)
Metal scrap, by type	Quantity and alh	nautical miles, tonnes	Yes	A	World	UN31 (1)
Miscellaneous	Quantity and alh	nautical miles, tonnes	Yes	A	World	UN31 (2)
Non-energy petroleum products	Quantity and alh	nautical miles, tonnes	Yes	A	World	UN31 (2)
Non-ferrous base metals	Quantity and alh	nautical miles, tonnes	Yes	A	World	UN31 (2)
Oil seeds, nuts and kernels, by type	Quantity and alh	nautical miles, tonnes	Yes	A	World	UN31 (1)

41 SHIPPING

Subject	Categories	Units	Time series Yes/No Frequency		Territorial coverage	Source (Table no.)
Oils and fats	Quantity and alh	nautical miles, tonnes	Yes	A	World	UN31 (2)
Ores, by type	Quantity and alh	nautical miles, tonnes	Yes	A	World	UN31 (1)
Other bulk, by type	Quantity and alh	nautical miles, tonnes	Yes	A	World	UN31 (1)
Other bulk, dry, by type	Quantity and alh	nautical miles, tonnes	Yes	A	World	UN31 (1)
Other bulk, liquid	Quantity and alh	nautical miles, tonnes	Yes	A	World	UN31 (2)
Other crude materials	Quantity and alh	nautical miles, tonnes	Yes	A	World	UN31 (2)
Other dry cargo	Quantity and alh	nautical miles, tonnes	Yes	A	World	UN31 (2)
Other foods	Quantity and alh	nautical miles, tonnes	Yes	A	World	UN31 (2)
Other foods, by type	Quantity and alh	nautical miles, tonnes	Yes	A	World	UN31 (1)
Other manufactures	Quantity and alh	nautical miles, tonnes	Yes	A	World	UN31 (2)
Paper etc	Quantity and alh	nautical miles, tonnes	Yes	A	World	UN31 (2)
Refrigerated foods	Quantity and alh	nautical miles, tonnes	Yes	A	World	UN31 (2)
Refrigerated foods, by type	Quantity and alh	nautical miles, tonnes	Yes	A	World	UN31 (1)
Rubber, natural and synthetic	Production	tonnes	Yes	A	World	ISL2 (2.3.12.1-2)
Sugar, by type	Quantity and alh	nautical miles, tonnes	Yes	A	World	UN31 (1)
Tea and maté	Quantity and alh	nautical miles, tonnes	Yes	A	World	UN31 (1)
Tea and maté	Quantity and alh	nautical miles, tonnes	Yes	A	World	UN31 (2)
Textile fibres	Quantity and alh	nautical miles, tonnes	Yes	A	World	UN31 (2)
Textile fibres, by type	Quantity and alh	nautical miles, tonnes	Yes	A	World	UN31 (1)
Textiles	Quantity and alh	nautical miles, tonnes	Yes	A	World	UN31 (2)
Timber, by type	Quantity and alh	nautical miles, tonnes	Yes	A	World	UN31 (1)
Tobacco	Quantity and alh	nautical miles, tonnes	Yes	A	World	UN31 (2)
Tobacco, by type	Quantity and alh	nautical miles, tonnes	Yes	A	World	UN31 (1)
Woodpulp and paper waste	Quantity and alh	nautical miles, tonnes	Yes	A	World	UN31 (2)
Wool	Production, (dirty), by country	tonnes/%	Yes	A	World	ISL2 (2.3.14)
Wool yarn	Production, by country	tonnes	Yes	A	World	ISL2 (2.3.15)
41.5.3 Energy - see also under Commodities (41.5.2) and Sections 2 and 17						
Coal	Origin and destination	tonnes	No		World	OECD25 (VII)
Coal production and consumption	By country	toe/tonnes	Yes	A	World	ISL2 (2.3.3.1-2)
Coal trade	Size of vessels, export and import areas	%	Yes	A	World	F3 (17)
Coal, Australian exports	By product and destination	tonnes	Yes	A, M	Selected countries	DSC2 (6.6)
Coal, hard exports	By exporter	tonnes	Yes	A, M	Selected countries	DSC2 (6.1)
Coal, Japanese and EC-12 deliveries	By country, destination	tonnes	Yes	A, M	World	DSC2 (6.15)
Coal, Japanese and EC-12 imports	By exporter and product	tonnes	Yes	A, M	World	DSC2 (6.14)

Subject	Categories	Units	Time series Yes/No Frequency		Territorial coverage	Source (Table no.)
Coal, Japanese imports	By product and country of origin	tonnes	Yes	A, M	World	DSC2 (6.12-6.13)
Coal, Korean imports	By exporter	tonnes	Yes	A, M	Selected countries	DSC2 (6.10)
Coal, seaborne trade	From, to	tonnes	Yes	A	World	F3 (14)
Coal, seaborne trade by region	By export/import area, export/import matrix	tonnes/%	Yes	A	World	ISL2 (2.1.4.1-3)
Coal, shipments by vessels	From, to	tonnes	-		World	F3 (16)
Coal, trade, total	Export and import areas	tonnes-miles	Yes	A	World	F3 (15)
Coal, US exports	By product and destination	tonnes	Yes	A, M	Selected countries	DSC2 (6.7-6.8)
Crude oil shipments	Export and import areas, size of vessels	%, tonne-miles	Yes	A	World	F3 (8)
Crude oil	Oil (inter-regional movements), origin and destination	tonnes	No		World	OECD25 (XVI)
Crude oil	Oil output	b/d	Yes	Q	World	OECD25 (XIII)
Crude oil	Producing, reserves, refining, consuming, by country	tonnes/%	Yes	A	World	ISL2 (2.3.1.3.1-4)
Crude oil	Production excluding NGLs and condensates, by main countries/regions	tonnes	Yes	A, M	World	DSC2 (2.4)
Crude oil	Production, by country	tonnes/%	Yes	A	World	ISL2 (2.3.1.1)
Crude oil	Production, offshore daily average, by country	b/d,%	Yes	A	World	ISL2 (2.3.1.2)
Crude oil trade seaborne by region	By export/import area export/import matrix	tonnes/%	Yes	A	World	ISL2 (2.1.3.1-3)
Crude oil, exports estimated seaborne	By country	tonnes	Yes	A, Q, M	World	DSC2 (2.10)
Crude oil, imports OECD	By major source country	tonnes	Yes	A, Q, M	World	DSC2 (2.13 -2.14)
Crude oil, shipments by tankers and combined carriers	From, to	tonnes	Yes	A	World	F3 (6)
Crude oil, trade in tonne-miles	Total export and import areas	tonne-miles	Yes	A	World	F3 (5)
Crude oil, trade, seaborne	From, to	tonnes	Yes	A	World	F3 (4)
Natural gas	Production and reserves	cu m	Yes	A	World	ISL2 (2.3.2.1)
Natural gas reserves	Producing countries and	cu m	Yes	A	World	ISL2 (2.3.2.2.1-2)
Natural gas imports	By importers and exporters	cu m nge	Yes	A, M	World	DSC2 (3.7-3.8)
Natural gas production	By country	cu m	Yes	A, Q, M	Selected countries	DSC2 (3.6)
Natural gas, liquids and condensates	By OPEC and non-OPEC	tonnes	Yes	A, M	World	DSC2 (3.1)
Natural gas, offshore production	By country	cu ft/day, %	Yes	A	World	ISL2 (2.3.2.3)
Shipments by combined carriers	From, to	tonnes	Yes	A	World	F3 (7)
41.5.4 Fertilizers - see also under Commodities (41.5.2) and Sections 2 and 27						
Phosphate rock	Origin and destination	tonnes	No		World	OECD25 (X)
Phosphate rock trade by region	By export/import area, export/import matrix	tonnes/%	Yes	A	World	ISL2 (2.1.7.1-3)
Phosphate rock, Moroccan exports	By importer	tonnes	Yes	A, Q	World	DSC2 (9.3)
Potash, phosphate, nitrogenous	Production and trade	tonnes/%	Yes	A	World	ISL2 (2.3.11.1-3)
Seaborne trade, total	From, to	tonnes	Yes	A	World	F3 (24)
Shipments by vessels	From, to	tonnes	Yes	A	World	F3 (26)
Trade, total	Export and import areas	tonnes-miles	Yes	A	World	F3 (25)
41.5.5 General						
Bulk commodities	By major commodities	tonnes	Yes	A	World	OECD25 (XII)

41 SHIPPING

Subject	Categories	Units	Time series Yes/No Frequency		Territorial coverage	Source (Table no.)
Cargo tonnage carried	Cargo tonnage carried, tonne-miles performed per dwt of the total world fleet	tonnes, tonne-miles, (per dwt)	Yes	A	World	UNCTAD2 (14)
Cargo turnover and fleet ownership, comparison	Goods loaded/unloaded, total, merchant fleet, by groups of countries	tonnes, dwt, %	Yes	A	World	UNCTAD2 (13)
Chemicals, by type	Quantity and alh	nautical miles, tonnes	Yes	A	World	UN31 (1)
Combined carrier dry cargo shipments	From, to	tonnes	Yes	A	World	F3 (32)
Combined carrier shipments	By development	tonnes	Yes	A	World	F3 (31)
Container production	Number produced (TEU)	nos, %	No		World	UNCTAD2 (37)
Container services	Port calls, sailing frequency, units deployed, TEU capacity, by operator	nos, TEUs	No		Rhine region	UNCTAD2 (36)
Containers		nos, tonnes	Yes	A	EC	UN13 (27)
Crude materials, by type other	Quantity and alh	nautical miles, tonnes	Yes	A	World	UN31 (1)
Development in volume	Type of cargo	tonnes/% tonne-miles	Yes	A	World	ISL2 (2.1.1.1-2)
Development of bulk fleet, trade and distances	Type of cargo	dwt/tonnes/ miles	Yes	A	World	ISL2 (2.1.2)
Dry bulk shipments, commodities and areas	From, to	tonnes	Yes	A	World	F3 (30)
Dry bulk vessel shipments, total	From, to	tonnes	Yes	A	World	F3 (29)
Dry cargo, other	Quantity and alh	nautical miles, tonnes	Yes	A	World	UN31 (1)
Expenditure on transport and insurance of goods and services	% of f.o.b value of total imports	%	Yes	A	Latin American and Caribbean countries	UN45 (95)
Exporters of manufactures, world's leading		US$/%	Yes	A	World	ISL2 (2.2.3)
Goods loaded		tonnes	Yes	I	EC	EC80 (1.5)
Goods loaded in international seaborne trade	By country	tonnes	No		EC	EM1 (2214)
Goods transport, international by various modes	Imports/exports by various modes	tonnes/%	Yes	A	Nordic countries	NCM1 (133)
Goods unloaded		tonnes	Yes	I	EC	EC80 (1.5)
Goods unloaded in international seaborne trade	By country	tonnes	No		EC	EM1 (2215)
Goods unloaded/ loaded	By world, region, country or area	tonnes	Yes	A	World	UN32 (L)
Goods, international	Entering the country, leaving the country	tonnes	Yes	A	EC, USA	UN13 (4)
Goods, international shipping	Loaded, unloaded	tonnes	Yes	A	ASEAN	ASEANS1 (5.3.2.2)
Goods, international transport		tonnes	Yes	I	ECMT countries	ECMT2 (6-1-1)
Goods, international transport	Loading and unloading at origin and destination irrespective of registration country	tonnes	Yes	I	ECMT countries	ECMT2 (6-1-2)
International sea-borne shipping	Goods loaded and unloaded	tonnes	Yes	A	Nordic countries	NCM1 (139)
Machinery and equipment, by type	Quantity and alh	nautical miles, tonnes	Yes	A	World	UN31 (1)
Machinery, by type	Quantity and alh	nautical miles, tonnes	Yes	A	World	UN31 (1)
Major trading countries,	Unit value of export/import development and terms of trade	indices	Yes	A	World	ISL2 (2.2.4)

Subject	Categories	Units	Time series Yes/No Frequency		Territorial coverage	Source (Table no.)
Manufacturers, other	Quantity and alh	nautical miles, tonnes	Yes	A	World	UN31 (1)
Maritime trade	EEC-intra	grt/gt//nos/ dwt/TEU/%/ years/tonnes/ ecu	Yes	A	EC	ISL2 (6.1.2.1-7)
Maritime transport, international	Goods loaded/unloaded	tonnes	Yes	A, M	World	UN35 (49)
Merchandise exports by major areas	Destination	US$/%	Yes	A	World	ISL2 (2.2.2)
Merchandise trade	By leading exports/imports	US$/%	Yes	A	World	ISL2 (2.2.1)
Merchandise trade of selected countries with Central and Eastern Europe and the USSR		US$/%	Yes	A	World	ISL2 (2.2.6)
Miscellaneous, by type	Quantity and alh	nautical miles, tonnes	Yes	A	World	UN31 (1)
Oils and fats, by type	Quantity and alh	nautical miles, tonnes	Yes	A	World	UN31 (1)
Paper, by type	Quantity and alh	nautical miles, tonnes	Yes	A	World	UN31 (1)
Petroleum products, non-energy	Quantity and alh	nautical miles, tonnes	Yes	A	World	UN31 (1)
Ports, goods loaded/unloaded	International and national	indices	Yes	A	EC, USA, Canada	UN13 (25)
Sea and air transport	Goods/passengers	tonnes/nos	No		EC	EC69 (VI.5)
Sea-borne shipping - average annual growth rate	Loaded, unloaded	%	Yes	A	African countries	UN1 (41)
Seaborne trade	By type of cargo	tonne-miles	Yes	A	World	UNCTAD2 (2)
Seaborne trade	Goods loaded/unloaded by type, by geographical area	tonnes	Yes	I	World	UNCTAD2 (II)
Seaborne trade	Goods loaded/unloaded, by type of cargo, by country group	tonnes, %	Yes	A	World	UNCTAD2 (3)
Seaborne trade	By dry bulk carriers combined and bulk carriers	tonnes	No		World	OECD25 (V)
Seaborne trade (development)	Iron ore, grain, coal, bauxite and alumina, phosphate rock total	tonnes, tonne-miles	Yes	A	World	OECD25 (IV)
Seaborne trade (developments)	Dry cargo, oil, total	tonnes, % increase	Yes	A	World	OECD25 (I)
Seaborne trade (growth)	Tonnage shipments, tonne-mile performance	% variation per annum	Yes	A	World	OECD25 (II)
Seaborne trade (world)	Crude oil, coal, grain, iron ore, oil products, total	tonnes, tonne-miles	Yes	A	World	OECD25 (III)
Seaborne trade, development international	Tanker cargo, dry cargo, total goods, estimates of goods loaded	tonnes, %	Yes	A	World	UNCTAD2 (1)
Seaborne trade, UK	By tanker, cargo type, exports, imports	%, tonnes, tonne-km	Yes	A	World	COS1 (11.1-11.2)
Shipments by vessels	Combined carriers and large tankers	tonnes, tonne-miles	Yes	A	World	F3 (2)
Shipments by vessels	From, to	tonnes	Yes	A	World	F3 (28)
Shipping	Goods loaded/unloaded	tonnes	Yes	A	World, ESCAP countries, developing ESCAP countries	UN44 (p3)
Shipping - international	Goods loaded	1000 tonnes	Yes	A	Central Africa	UN5 (6-2-1)

41 SHIPPING

Subject	Categories	Units	Time series Yes/No Frequency		Territorial coverage	Source (Table no.)
Shipping - international	Goods loaded	1000 tonnes	Yes	A	East & Southern Africa	UN4 (6-2-1)
Shipping - international	Goods loaded	1000 tonnes	Yes	A	North Africa	UN2 (6-2-1)
Shipping - international	Goods loaded	1000 tonnes	Yes	A	West Africa	UN3 (6-2-1)
Shipping - international	Goods loaded, unloaded	tonnes	Yes	A	ESCAP region developing ESCAP region	UN44 (p6, 11)
Shipping - international	Goods unloaded	1000 tonnes	Yes	A	Central Africa	UN5 (6-2-2)
Shipping - international	Goods unloaded	1000 tonnes	Yes	A	East & Southern Africa	UN4 (6-2-2)
Shipping - international	Goods unloaded	1000 tonnes	Yes	A	North Africa	UN2 (6-2-2)
Shipping - international	Goods unloaded	1000 tonnes	Yes	A	West Africa	UN3 (6-2-2)
Shipping - sea-borne	Goods loaded, unloaded	1000 tonnes	Yes	A	Central Africa	UN5 (28)
Shipping - sea-borne	Goods loaded, unloaded	1000 tonnes	Yes	A	East & Southern Africa	UN4 (28)
Shipping - sea-borne	Goods loaded, unloaded	1000 tonnes	Yes	A	North Africa	UN2 (28)
Shipping - sea-borne	Goods loaded, unloaded	1000 tonnes	Yes	A	West Africa	UN3 (28)
Sugar	Origin and destination	tonnes	No		World	OECD25 (XI)
Textiles	Quantity and alh	nautical miles, tonnes	Yes	A	World	UN31 (1)
Trade and distance		dwt, tonnes, miles	Yes	A	World	F3 (3)
Tramp, trip charter		indices	Yes	A, M	World	ISL2 (5.3)
Travel expenses	% of f.o.b value of total imports of goods and services	%	Yes	A	Latin American and Caribbean countries	UN45 (97)
Woodpulp and paper waste	Quantity and alh	nautical miles, tonnes	Yes	A	World	UN31 (1)
World fleet and trade	By dry cargo tanker	dwt, tonnes, indices	Yes	A	World	COS1 (9)
World seaborne trade	By cargo	tonnes, %	No		World	COS1 (10)
World seaborne trade	Main bulk commodities	tonne-miles	Yes	A	World	F1 (2)
World seaborne trade	Main bulk commodities	tonnes	Yes	A	World	F1 (1)
World seaborne trade	Main bulk commodities	tonnes	Yes	A	World	F3 (1)
Goods Movement by Export Region and Destination						
All commodities	Quantity and alh	nautical miles, tonnes	Yes	A	World	UN31 (2)
Animal feeding stuff	Quantity and alh	nautical miles, tonnes	Yes	A	World	UN31 (2)
Bulk, dry	Quantity and alh	nautical miles, tonnes	Yes	A	World	UN31 (2)
Coal, and coke etc	Quantity and alh	nautical miles, tonnes	Yes	A	World	UN31 (2)
Ferrous base metals	Quantity and alh	nautical miles, tonnes	Yes	A	World	UN31 (2)
Fertilizers	Quantity and alh	nautical miles, tonnes	Yes	A	World	UN31 (2)
Grains	Quantity and alh	nautical miles, tonnes	Yes	A	World	UN31 (2)
Metal scrap	Quantity and alh	nautical miles, tonnes	Yes	A	World	UN31 (2)
Oilseeds, nuts and kernels	Quantity and alh	nautical miles, tonnes	Yes	A	World	UN31 (2)
Ores	Quantity and alh	nautical miles, tonnes	Yes	A	World	UN31 (2)
Other bulk, dry	Quantity and alh	nautical miles, tonnes	Yes	A	World	UN31 (2)
Sugar	Quantity and alh	nautical miles, tonnes	Yes	A	World	UN31 (2)
Timber	Quantity and alh	nautical miles, tonnes	Yes	A	World	UN31 (2)

Subject	Categories	Units	Time series Yes/No Frequency		Territorial coverage	Source (Table no.)
41.5.6 Minerals, Ores and Metals - see also under Commodities (41.5.2)						
Bauxite and alumina	Origin and destination	tonnes	No		World	OECD25 (IX)
Bauxite and alumina seaborne trade by region	By export/import area, export/import matrix	tonnes/%	Yes	A	World	ISL2 (2.1.6.1-3)
Bauxite and alumina seaborne trade, total	From, to	tonnes			World	F3 (21)
Bauxite and alumina shipments by vessels	From, to	tonnes	Yes	A	World	F3 (23)
Bauxite and alumina trade, total	Export and import areas	tonnes-miles	Yes	A	World	F3 (22)
Crude minerals, nes	Quantity and alh	nautical miles, tonnes	Yes	A	World	UN31 (1)
Crude steel production, trade in steel products, trade by area	By country, exports, destination	tonnes/%	Yes	A	World	ISL2 (2.3.5.1-3)
Iron ore	Origin and destination	tonnes	No		World	OECD25 (VI)
Iron ore trade seaborne, by region	By export/import area, export/import matrix	tonnes/%	Yes	A	World	ISL2 (2.1.5.1-3)
Iron ore, exports	By exporter and importer	tonnes	Yes	A, M	Selected countries	DSC2 (5.6, 5.7)
Iron ore, imports	By importer and exporter	tonnes	Yes	A, M	Selected countries	DSC2 (5.8, 5.10, 5.13)
Iron ore, seaborne trade	From, to	tonnes	Yes	A	World	F3 (9)
Iron ore, shipments by combined carriers	From, to	tonnes	Yes	A	World	F3 (12)
Iron ore, shipments by vessels	From, to	tonnes	Yes	A	World	F3 (11)
Iron ore, size of vessels	Export and import areas	%	Yes	A	World	F3 (13)
Iron ore, total seaborne trade	Export and import areas	tonnes-miles	Yes	A	World	F3 (10)
Lead	Production, consumption and trade	tonnes	Yes	A	World	ISL2 (2.3.10)
Manufactures of metal by type	Quantity and alh	nautical miles, tonnes	Yes	A	World	UN31 (1)
Non-ferrous base metals, by type	Quantity and alh	nautical miles, tonnes	Yes	A	World	UN31 (1)
Zinc	Production, consumption and trade	tonnes	Yes	A	World	ISL2 (2.3.9)
41.6 SEABORNE TRAFFIC – see also under Seaborne Trade (41.5)						
Coastal shipping-national traffic		tonne-kms	Yes	I	ECMT countries	ECMT2 (6-1-4)
Coastal shipping-national traffic	Goods unloaded	tonnes	Yes	I	ECMT countries	ECMT2 (6-1-3)
Container port traffic		TEUs, %	No		Developing countries and territories	UNCTAD2 (28)
Freight, traffic	Goods loaded/unloaded	tonnes	Yes	A	World	IRTU1
Goods traffic, international	By flag	tonnes	No		EC	EC80 (5.13)
Goods traffic, international	By NST/R chapter and relation	tonnes	No		EC	EC80 (5.14)
Goods traffic, national and foreign	By NST/R chapter and traffic relation	tonnes	No		EC	EC80 (5.15)
International maritime transport	Vessels entered/ cleared	nrt	Yes	A	World	UN50 (135)
International sea-borne shipping	Vessels entered and cleared	nos/gross tonnage	Yes	A	Nordic countries	NCM1 (138)
Sea traffic	By country, by type	nos	No		EC	EC18 (10.9)
Sea-air cargo traffic	From Japan	tonnes, %	No		World	UNCTAD2 (33)
Sea-air cargo traffic	From the Far East to Europe	tonnes	Yes	A	Far Eastern countries	UNCTAD2 (32)
Ship arrivals		nos, tonnes	Yes	A	EC	EC80 (5.8)
Traffic	By port	nos, tonnes	No		EC	EC80 (5.16)

41 SHIPPING

Subject	Categories	Units	Time series Yes/No Frequency		Territorial coverage	Source (Table no.)
Traffic	Goods unloaded and loaded	tonnes	Yes	I	Major seaports of ECMT countries	ECMT2 (6-1-5)
Traffic, goods	National and International	tonnes	Yes	A	EC	EC80 (5.11)
Traffic, goods (excl transit)		tonnes	Yes	I	EC	EC80 (1.5)
Traffic, international	By flag	%	No		World	EC80 (5.10)
Traffic, International	By flag arrivals and departures	nos, tonnes	No		World	EC80 (5.9)
Traffic, karge container	By port	nos, tonnes	No		EC	EC80 (5.17)
Traffic, petroleum products	Unloaded	tonnes, %	Yes	A	EC	EC80 (5.12)
41.7 SHIP PRICES						
41.7.1 New						
Contracting prices for new buildings	By ship type	$, dwt/cu m	Yes	A	World	COS1 (15.1)
Demolition prices by area, second-hand prices of dry cargo vessels and tankers, average values, prices for new buildings, development of bunker market prices		US$	Yes	A	World	ISL2 (1.6.1-4)
New building prices, development of	By vessel type	dwt, cu m, teu, US$	Yes	A, Q	World	DSC1 (34)
New building prices	By type and size of vessel	US$	Yes	A	World	UNCTAD2 (20)
41.7.2 Second-hand						
Cargo dry, second hand values	By ship type	US$	Yes	A	World	F1 (18)
Demolition prices by area, second-hand prices of dry cargo vessels and tankers, average values, prices for new buildings, development of bunker market prices		US$	Yes	A	World	ISL2 (1.6.1-4)
Second-hand average price	By ship type, age	nat curr	Yes	A	World	COS1 (15.2)
Second-hand prices	By ship type, when built,	US$, % change % change over period	Yes	A, M	World	ISL1 (-)
Second-hand prices, development of	By type, dwt, age	US$	Yes	A, Q	World	DSC1 (36)
Tankers, second-hand values	By ship type	US$	Yes	A	World	F1 (19)
41.7.3 Scrap						
Demolition prices		US$/LDT	Yes	A	Far East, Pakistan/India, Southern Europe	UNCTAD2 (27)
Demolition prices by area, second-hand prices of dry cargo vessels and tankers, average values, prices for new buildings, development of bunker market prices		US$	Yes	A	World	ISL2 (1.6.1-4)
Demolition values, development of	By vessel type	US$	Yes	A, Q	World, Japan	DSC1 (39)
Prices, breaking		ldt, US$	Yes	A	EC, Far East	F1 (17)
Prices, reported demolition	By area, type	US$ per ldt	Yes	A, M	World	DSC1 (38)
Scrap prices	By region, % change over period	US$, % change	Yes	A, M	Selected countries	ISL1 (-)

Subject	Categories	Units	Time series Yes/No Frequency		Territorial coverage	Source (Table no.)
41.8 SHIPBUILDING						
41.8.1 Completions and Deliveries						
All ships, showing principal types	Where built, ship type	nos, gt	No		World	LRS1 (2)
Bulk liquid cargo and bulk dry cargo, vessels completed	By cargo type, country of build	nos, tonnes	No		World	LRS4 (4A)
Cargo vessels completed	By ship type	nos, tonnes	No		World	LRS4 (3)
Completions	By country of build	nos, tonnes	Yes	A	World	LRS4 (21)
Completions	By ship type	nos, gt, dwt	Yes	A, M	World	ISL1 (-)
Completions	By shiptype category	nos, tonnes	Yes	A	World	LRS4 (22)
Completions	Ship type categories	nos, tonnes	No		World	LRS4 (5)
Completions, bulk dry		nos, dwt	No		World	LRS4 (10)
Completions, bulk dry, oil		nos, dwt	No		World	LRS4 (11)
Completions, cargo carrying ships		nos, dwt	No		World	LRS4 (6)
Completions, chemical		nos, dwt	No		World	LRS4 (8)
Completions, fish catching		nos, tonnes	No		World	LRS4 (17)
Completions, general cargo including passenger		nos, dwt	No		World	LRS4 (12)
Completions, liquified gas		nos, dwt	No		World	LRS4 (7A)
Completions, liquified gas	By gas capacity, insulated capacity	nos, cu m	No		World	LRS4 (7B)
Completions, oil		nos, dwt	No		World	LRS4 (9)
Completions, passenger		nos, tonnes	No		World	LRS4 (16)
Completions, principal merchant fleets	By flag state,age	nos, tonnes	Yes	A	World	LRS4 (19)
Completions, refrigerated cargo		nos, dwt	No		World	LRS4(15A)
Completions, refrigerated cargo	Insulated capacity, age	nos, cu m,	No		World	LRS4 (15B)
Completions, ro-ro cargo, including passenger		nos, dwt	No		World	LRS4 (13)
Completions, world fleet		nos,tonnes	No		World	LRS4 (18)
Container		nos, dwt, TEU	No		World	LRS4 (14A-14B)
Dry cargo vessels completed, other	By cargo type, country of build	nos, tonnes	No		World	LRS4 (4B)
Merchant ships	Where built, previous year total	nos, gt, % of world tonnage dwt	No		World	LRS1 (1)
Merchant vessels	Under construction, launched	tonnes gross	No		World, EC, USA, USSR, Canada	EC9 (4.9)
New ships delivered to the bulk fleet	By ship type	no of ships/ dwt	Yes	6 mnthly	World	F2 (6)
Newbuilding output	By country	dwt	Yes	A, Q	World	DSC1 (33)
Newbuildings, deliveries	By type of ship	nos, grt, dwt	Yes	A	World	UNCTAD2 (23)
Newbuildings, distribution of deliveries	By groups of countries of build	grt	Yes	A	World	UNCTAD2 (24)
Principal cargo carrying fleets	By flag state, age	nos, dwt	Yes	A	World	LRS4 (20)
Registration of all ships	Where built, country of registration	nos, gt	No		World	LRS1 (3)
Sale and purchase activity, reported	By type	dwt, nos	Yes	A, M	World	DSC1 (35)
Ships completed		grt	Yes	A, Q	OECD	OECD22
Ships launched	Size, where launched	gt	No		World	LRS1 (7)
Ships launched	Where launched, ship type	nos, gt	No		World	LRS1 (8)
Ships launched 1983-1992	Where built	nos, gt	Yes	A	World	LRS1 (5B)
Ships launched, merchant	Where launched, previous year total	nos, gt, % of world tonnage, dwt	No		World	LRS1 (6)
Ships of miscellaneous activities completed	By activity, country of build	nos, tonnes	No		World	LRS4 (4C)
Size	Where built,	gt	No		World	LRS1 (4)
Summary	Where built	nos, gt	Yes	A	World	LRS1 (5A)
World shipbuilding monthly contracts	By ship type and size	nos, dwt	Yes	A, M	World	ISL1 (II 1.1-1.1.2)

41 SHIPPING

Subject	Categories	Units	Time series Yes/No Frequency		Territorial coverage	Source (Table no.)
41.8.2 General						
Deliveries of new ships	By ship type	ships, dwt	Yes	A	World	F1 (4)
Development of dry fleet (bulk carrier)	By size	dwt, nos.	Yes	A, M	World	DSC1 (30)
Development(combined carriers)	By size, period, tonnage	dwt	Yes	A, Q, M	World	DSC1 (17)
Shipbuilding countries, ten largest	By completion	nos, dwt, grt	No		Selected countries	COS1 (8)
Shipbuilding figures	By country group, countries	nos, gt	Yes	A, M	World	ISL1 (-)
41.8.3 Order Books						
Bulk tonnage on order	By ship type, year of delivery	no of ships/ dwt	Yes	A	World	F2 (12)
Bulk tonnage on order	By ship type, country of build	no of ships/ dwt	Yes	A	World	F2 (13)
Bulk tonnage on order	By ship type, country of registry	no of ships/ dwt	Yes	A	World	F2 (14)
Bulk tonnage on order	By size and ship type	no of ships/ dwt	Yes	A	World	F2 (11)
Future deliveries (bulk carrier)	By size, current fleet	dwt, nos	Yes	A	World	DSC1 (31)
Order book	By ship type	nos, gt, dwt	Yes	A, M	World	ISL1 (-)
Order book, world	By ship size, dwt	dwt	Yes	A	World	F1 (11)
Order book, world	By ship type	ships, dwt	Yes	A	World	F1 (9)
Order book, world	Year of delivery	dwt	Yes	A	World	F1 (12)
Orderbook	By country	grt, %	Yes	A, Q	World	DSC1 (-)
Orderbook (combined carriers)	By size	dwt	No		World	DSC1 (18)
Tonnage on order	By type of vessel	dwt, %	Yes	Q	World	UNCTAD2 (21)
Tonnage on order	By type of vessel, by country/region of registry	dwt	No		World	UNCTAD2 (22)

42 SOCIAL INDICATORS

42.1 COMMUNICATIONS

42.2 CRIME AND CRIMINAL JUSTICE

42.3 EDUCATION AND LITERACY

42.4 EMPLOYMENT AND QUALITY OF WORKING LIFE
- 42.4.1 Distribution of Earnings
- 42.4.2 Fatal Occupational Injuries
- 42.4.3 Paid Annual Leave
- 42.4.4 Travel Time to Work
- 42.4.5 Unemployment
- 42.4.6 Work Environment Nuisances
- 42.4.7 Working Hours

42.5 ENVIRONMENT
- 42.5.1 Access to Outdoor Space
- 42.5.2 Basic Amenities
- 45.5.3 Indoor Dwelling Space
- 45.5.4 Pollution
- 45.5.5 Proximity of Selected Services

42.6 FOOD SUPPLY

42.7 HEALTH AND HEALTH SERVICES
- 42.7.1 Aids Cases
- 42.7.2 Disability
- 42.7.3 Life Expectancy and Mortality
- 42.7.4 Nutrition
- 42.7.5 Smoking and Drinking
- 42.7.6 Vital Statistics
- 42.7.7 Women's Health and Health Services

42.8 HOUSING AND HOUSEHOLDS

42.9 HUMAN DEVELOPMENT

42.10 HUMAN DISTRESS

42.11 INCOME AND WEALTH DISTRIBUTION

42.12 LEISURE

42.13 LIVING CONDITIONS

42.14 NATIONAL AND HOUSEHOLD INCOME AND EXPENDITURE

42.15 PERSONAL SAFETY

42.16 PUBLIC AFFAIRS AND POLITICAL PARTICIPATION

42.17 SANITATION

42.18 SOCIO-DEMOGRAPHIC STATISTICS

42.19 TRANSPORT

42.20 WATER

42.21 WEALTH AND POVERTY

Subject	Categories	Units	Time series Yes/No	Frequency	Territorial coverage	Source (Table no.)
42.1 COMMUNICATIONS - see also Section 10						
Book titles published		nos	No		World	UN16 (14A)
Films, long		nos	No		World	UN16 (14B)
Newspapers, numbers		nos	No		World	UN16 (14A)
Newspapers, circulation		per 100 population	No		World	UN16 (14A)
Paper consumption		kg per 1000 population	No		World	UN16 (14A)
Press	By country, by daily newspapers published, circulation	nos	No		EC	EC72 (11.16)
Radio licences	By country	nos	No		EC	EC18 (10.13)
Radio receivers in use		per thousand	No		World	UN17 (6.10B)
Radios		nos	No		World	UN16 (14B)
Radios		per 1000 population	No		World	UN16 (14B)
Radios and televisions	Receivers	nos per 1000	Yes	A	African countries inhabitants	UN1 (40)
Telephone lines		nos	No		World	UN16 (14B)
Telephone lines		per 1000 population	No		World	UN16 (14B)
Telephone lines, residential		%	No		World	UN16 (14B)
Telephones	By country	nos	No		EC	EC18 (10.12)
Television licences	By country	nos	No		EC	EC18 (10.14)
Television sets	By country	nos	No		EC	EC72 (11.14)
Television sets		nos	No		World	UN16 (14B)
Television sets		per 1000 population	No		World	UN16 (14B)
42.2 CRIME AND CRIMINAL JUSTICE - see also Section 9						
Crime record	Per 100,000 population % in largest city	nos rate %	Yes	Selected years	World	UN16 (34)
Criminal justice occupations	By police, prosecutors	nos, %	No		World	UN17 (33B)
Criminal justice occupations	By police, prosecutors occupations	nos, %	No		Africa	UN46 (30B)
Homicides, intentional	Number per 100,000 population	nos rate	Yes	Selected years	World	UN16 (34)
Persons apprehended	Number per 100,000 population	nos rate	Yes	Selected years	World	UN16 (34)
Persons apprehended	Per 100 crimes recorded					
Persons apprehended and prison population	By sex	nos	No		World	UN17 (33A)
Persons apprehended and prison population	By sex	nos	No		Africa	UN46 (30A)
Police personnel	Number per 1000 population	nos rate	Yes	Selected years	World	UN16 (34)
Prison population	By sex per 100,000 population	nos rate	Yes	Selected years	World	UN16 (34)
Seizures of cocaine and psychotropic substances reported to the United Nations	Cocaine, opiates	nos, kg	Yes	Selected years	World	UN 16 (35)
42.3 EDUCATION AND LITERACY - see also Section 15						
Adult literacy rates	By country, by gender	nos	No		SEAR	WHO1 (19)
Education attainment and illiteracy	By total, age group, sex urban and rural areas	%	No		Africa	UN46 (19)

Subject	Categories	Units	Time series Yes/No	Frequency	Territorial coverage	Source (Table no.)
Education attainment and illiteracy	By total, age group, sex, urban and rural areas	%	No		World	UN17 (20)
Education, regular, average years of ISCED levels	By characteristic		Yes	10 yrly	OECD	OECD20 (5.1-5.2)
Educational attainment and illiteracy	By age group, sex, urban and rural areas	%	No		World	UN16 (12)
Educational expenditure as percentage of GNP		%	No		World	UNCTADI (6.10B)
Enrolment in primary school	By country, by gender	%	No		SEAR	WHO1 (20)
Enrolment ratios		%	No		World	UNCTADI (6.10B)
Gross educational enrolment ratios	Higher education	%	Yes	A	African countries	UN1 (14)
Gross educational enrolment ratios	Secondary schools	%	Yes	A	African countries	UN1 (14)
Gross enrolment ratios for primary schools	Both sexes, by sex	%	Yes	A	African countries	UN1 (13)
Illiteracy	By sex	%	No		World	UN16 (21)
Illiteracy rate		%	No		World	UNCTAD1 (6.10B)
Illiterate population	Sex, age group	nos %	No		World	UN50 (42)
Literate population by sex	15 years of age and over	%	Yes	A	African countries	UN1 (12)
Population having participated in adult education	By selected characteristic	%	No		OECD	OECD20 (6.1)
Population with a level of education below "ISCED 2 completed"	By selected characteristic	%	No		OECD	OECD20 (5.4)
Population with a level of education at least "ISCED 3 completed"	By selected characteristic	%	No		OECD	OECD20 (5.5)
Population with at least some university or equivalent level (ISCED 6 and 7)	By selected characteristic	%	No		OECD	OECD20 (5.6)
Population, distribution by highest ISCED level		%	Yes	10 yrly	OECD	OECD20 (5.3)
Potential scientific and engineering workforce	By sex, annual rate of growth	nos, %	No		Africa	UN46 (21B)
Potential scientific and engineering workforce	By sex, annual rate of growth	nos, %	No		World	UN17 (22B)
Primary school enrolment		nos	No		Selected countries	WB1 (1)
Primary school enrolment		nos	No		Selected countries	WB1 (2)
Primary school enrolment ratios		%	Yes	Selected years	World, by development groups	UNCTAD5 (5.3)
School enrolment	By sex, annual growth, first, second and third levels, and primary , secondary enrolment ratio	nos, % rate	No		Africa	UN46 (20)
School enrolment	By sex, annual growth, first, second and third levels, and primary, secondary enrolment ratio	nos, %	No		World	UN17 (21)
School enrolment	First, second and third levels, and primary, secondary enrolment ratio, by sex	nos, %	Yes	Selected years	World	UN16 (13)
Teachers at first and second levels	By sex, annual rate of growth	nos, %	No		World	UN17 (22A)
Teachers at first and second levels	By sex, annual rate of growth	nos, %	No		Africa	UN46 (21A)

42.4 EMPLOYMENT AND QUALITY OF WORKING LIFE

42.4.1 Distribution of Earnings

Subject	Categories	Units	Time series Yes/No	Frequency	Territorial coverage	Source (Table no.)
Annual earnings of full-time adult employees	Deciles	%	No		OECD	OECD20(14.1)

Subject	Categories	Units	Time series Yes/No Frequency		Territorial coverage	Source (Table no.)
Frequency of low earnings among employees	By selected characteristics	%	No		OECD	OECD20 14.3)
Relative median earnings of full-time employees	By selected characteristics	%	No		OECD	OECD20(14.2)
42.4.2 Fatal Occupational Injuries - see also Section 1						
Number of fatal occupational injuries	By branch of activity	rate	Yes	10 yrly	OECD	OECD20(15.1)
42.4.3 Paid Annual Leave						
Employed working at night	By selected characteristics	%	No		OECD	OECD20(13.2)
Employed working on sundays and public holidays	By selected characteristics	%	No		OECD	OECD20(13.3)
Employees working in shifts	By selected characteristics	%	No		OECD	OECD20(13.1)
Public holidays and leave entitlement per year		nos	No		OECD	OECD20(12.1)
42.4.4 Travel Time to Work						
Daily commuters: distribution of	By travel time to work	%	No		OECD	OECD20(11.1)
Daily commuters: mode of transport		%	No		OECD	OECD20(11.2)
Daily commuters: with more than one hour of travel time to work	By selected characteristics	%	No		OECD	OECD20(11.4)
Daily commuters: with travel time to work up to 15 minutes	By selected characteristics	%	No		OECD	OECD20(11.3)
42.4.5 Unemployment - see also Section 16						
Discouraged workers rates	Selected characteristics	rate	No		OECD	OECD20(9.1)
Involuntary part-time work - persons in part-time employment who would prefer full-time status	Age, socio-economic status	%	No		OECD	OECD20(8.1)
Unemployed who are new entrants on the labour market	Sex	%	No		OECD	OECD20(7.2)
Unemployment rates	Sex and age, specific groups of population, household type and sex, by duration	%	Yes	5 yrly	OECD	OECD20(7.1)
42.4.6 Work Environment Nuisances						
Employed reporting exposure to specific nuisances in their work environment	By selected characteristics	%	No		OECD	OECD20(16.1)
42.4.7 Working Hours - see also Section 28						
Average number of hours actually worked in a week	By selected characteristics	hours	No		OECD	OECD20(10.3)
Distribution of employed by actual hours worked per week		%	No		OECD	OECD20(10.2)
Hours worked per week, trends		hours	Yes	10 yrly	OECD	OECD20(10.1)
Percentage of employed having worked long hours during the reference week	By selected characteristics	%	No		OECD	OECD20 (10.4bis)
Percentage of employed having worked 45 hours or more during the reference week	By selected characteristics	%	No		OECD	OECD20(10.4)
42.5 ENVIRONMENT - see also Section 18						
42.5.1 Access to Outdoor Space						
Households having access to an area of open space within a 20 minute walking time	By characteristics of head	%	No		OECD	OECD20(23.2)

42 SOCIAL INDICATORS

Subject	Categories	Units	Time series Yes/No	Frequency	Territorial coverage	Source (Table no.)
Households with access to an outdoor space adjacent to the dwelling	By characteristic of head	%	No		OECD	OECD20(23.1)
42.5.2 Basic Amenities - see also Section 23						
Households lacking some of the basic amenities in the dwelling	Amenities by characteristic by head	%	No		OECD	OECD20(24.2)
Population with basic amenities inside the dwelling		%	Yes	10 yrly	OECD	OECD20(24.1)
42.5.3 Indoor Dwelling Space - see also under Housing and Households (42.8) and Section 23						
Density of occupation of dwellings		%	Yes	Various	OECD	OECD20(22.2)
Households with more than one person per room	By characteristics of head	%	No		OECD	OECD20(22.3)
Number of persons per room, average		nos	Yes	10 yrly	OECD	OECD20(22.1)
42.5.4 Pollution						
Population exposure to transport noise	By source	%	No		OECD	OECD20(27.1)
Total emissions of traditional air pollutants	By type of pollutant	tonnes	No		OECD	OECD20(26.1)
42.5.5 Proximity of Selected Services						
Population having access to a primary school in the vicinity	By selected characteristics	%	No		OECD	OECD20 (25.2B)
Population having access to a post office in the vicinity	By selected characteristics	%	No		OECD	OECD20 (25.2C)
Population having access to a public transport stop in the vicinity	By selected characteristics	%	No		OECD	OECD20 (25.2D
Population having access to a store satisfying daily needs in the vicinity	By selected characteristics	%	No		OECD	OECD20 (25.2A)
Population within given walking distance to selected services	By service	%	No		OECD	OECD20 (25.1)
42.6 FOOD SUPPLY						
Calorie supply		nos	No		Selected countries	WB1 (1)
Calorie supply		nos	No		Selected countries	WB1 (2)
Food Security	Indicators of food security	indices, US$, tonnes, %	No		Developing countries	UN18 (13)
42.7 HEALTH AND HEALTH SERVICES - see also Section 22						
42.7.1 AIDS Cases						
Infected persons, estimated number	Female, male ratio, type of area	nos, ratio	No		World	UN16 (18A)
Reported AIDS cases	New, cumulative total	nos	No		World	UN16 (18C)
Symptomatic AIDS cases	Reported, estimated actual, projected	nos	No		World	UN16 (18B)
42.7.2 Disability						
Bed days	By selected characteristics	nos	No		OECD	OECD20 (3.2)
Disability days	By selected characteristics	nos	No		OECD	OECD20 (3.1)
Disability prevalence	By sex, male, female	rate	No		World	UN16 (21)
Disabled persons, distribution of	Urban, rural areas, age group, by sex	%	No		World	UN16 (21)
	per 100,000 population		ratio			

Subject	Categories	Units	Time series Yes/No	Frequency	Territorial coverage	Source (Table no.)
Population restricted in daily activities because of long-standing health conditions	By selected characteristics	%	No		OECD	OECD20 (4.1)
Population with certain types of functional disability	By age and sex	%	No		OECD	OECD20 (4.2)
42.7.3 Indicators of Life Expectancy and Mortality						
Death, causes of	By cause	%	No		World	UN16 (16A, B)
Distribution of causes of death, where registered	By sex	%	No		World	UN17 (24)
Expectancy of life	Specified ages, sex	age, years	No		World	UN19 (22)
Infant mortality		nos	No		Selected countries	WB1 (1)
Infant mortality		nos	No		Selected countries	WB1 (2)
Infant mortality rate		per 1000	Yes	A	African countries	UN1 (10)
Life expectancy	At birth and various ages		Yes	10 yrly	OECD	OECD20 (1.1-1.5)
Life expectancy at birth	By sex		Yes	Selected years	World	UN16 (15)
Life expectancy at birth	Life expectancy at birth		Yes	A	African countries	UN1 (10)
Mortality rates : child	By sex	rate	Yes	Selected years	World	UN16 (15)
Mortality rates, perinatal	By age of mother, by marital status of mother	rate	Yes	10 yrly	OECD	OECD20 (2.1-2.3)
Mortality rates: infants		rate	Yes	Selected years	World	UN16 (15)
Selected indicators of life expectancy and mortality	By sex and age	rate	No		World	UN17 (23)
Survival rates	Age group	rate	Yes	Selected years	World	UN16 (15)
42.7.4 Nutrition						
Calorie supply	% of requirements	%	Yes	Selected years	World	UN16 (19A)
Calories	Numbers Growth rate	nos %	No		World	UN16 (19A)
Food aid received in cereals		tonnes	Yes	Selected years	World	UN16 (19B)
Food aid, production ratio		ratio	Yes	Selected years	World	UN16 (19B)
Food and cereal production		tonnes	Yes	Selected years	World	UN16 (19B)
Protein per capita per day	Numbers, growth rate	nos %	No		World	UN16 (19A)
42.7.5 Smoking and Drinking						
Adults who smoke	By sex	%	No		World	UN16 (20)
Alcohol per capita		litres	Yes	Selected years	World	UN16 (20)
Beer per capita		litres	Yes	Selected years	World	UN16 (20)
Cigarette consumption and percentage of adults who smoke	By sex	%	Yes	15 yrly	World	UN17 (26)
Cigarette consumption and percentage of adults who smoke		%, nos	No		Africa	UN46 (26)
Cigarettes per adult		nos	Yes	Selected years	World	UN16 (20)
Wine per capita		litres	Yes	Selected years	World	UN16 (20)
42.7.6 Supply of Health Services and Personnel						
Population access to health services		%	Yes	A	African countries	UN1 (11)
Population access to safe water		%	Yes	A	African countries	UN1 (11)

Subject	Categories	Units	Time series Yes/No Frequency		Territorial coverage	Source (Table no.)
Population per hospital		nos	Yes	A	African countries	UN1 (9)
Population per nurse		nos	Yes	A	African countries	UN1 (9)
Population per physician		nos	Yes	A	African countries	UN1 (9)
Selected indicators	Proportion of infants immunized, access to water, expenditure on health as % of GNP, population per physician	%, nos, per thou	No		World	UNCTAD1 (6.10A)
42.7.7 Women's Health and Health Services						
Anaemia, women aged 15-49		%	No		World	UN16 (17)
Births attended by trained personnel		%	No		World	UN16 (17)
Contraceptives, currently married women using	Age group	%	No		World	UN16 (17)
Maternal mortality		rate	No		World	UN16 (17)
Selected indicators of female health and health services		%, nos	No		World	UN17 (25)
Selected indicators of female health and health services		%, rate	No		Africa	UN46 (24)
42.8 HOUSING AND HOUSEHOLDS						
Amenities	By electricity, transport, telephone	kWh per capita, nos	No		EC	EC69 (VII.5)
Amenities	By type, according to socio-economic category of head of household, income category, region and urban, rural environment, by country	%	No		EC	EC42 (1/1-1/5)
Capital formation in housing	Values at constant prices	nat curr	No		World	UN16 (6)
Consumer durables	By type, according to socio-economic category of head of household, type of household, income category, region and urban, rural environment, by country	%	No		EC	EC42 (1/1-1/5)
Consumption of electricity, motor gasoline and fuelwood	Total and per capita	HWU, %, KWh, WSR, Kg, CSR cu m	Yes	Selected years	World	UN16 (7)
Household size, average		nos	No		World	UN16 (5)
Households with electrical appliances	By country, by appliance	%	No		EC	EC35 (-)
Housing units, number		nos	No		World	UN16 (5)
Housing units: person per room, average		nos	No		World	UN16 (5)
Housing units: rooms, average number		nos	No		World	UN16 (5)
Housing units: without electricity		%	No		World	UN16 (5)
Housing units: without piped water		%	No		World	UN16 (5)
Housing units: without toilet		%	No		World	UN16 (5)
Population : without safe water		%	No		World	UN16 (5)
Population : without sanitation facilities		%	No		World	UN16 (5)
Rent, fuel and power (private final consumption) at constant prices		nat curr	No		World	UN16 (6)
Selected indicators of housing and human settlements conditions, census rounds	By population, housing characteristics, housing units	%, nos	No		World	UN17 (28)
Selected indicators of housing and human settlements conditions, census rounds	By population, housing characteristics, housing units	%, nos	No		Africa	UN46 (27)

Subject	Categories	Units	Time series Yes/No Frequency	Territorial coverage	Source (Table no.)
42.9 HUMAN DEVELOPMENT					
Female-male gaps	Indicators of human development	%	No	Developing countries	UN18 (10)
Female-male gaps	Indicators of human development	%	No	Industrial countries	UN18 (31)
Human deprivation	Indicators of deprivation	nos	No	Developing countries	UN18 (3)
Human development index	Indicators of human development	years, %, PPP$, ind	No	World	UN18 (1)
Human development, profile	Indicators of human development	years, %, US$, PPP$	No	Developing countries	UN18 (2)
Human development, profile	Indicators of human development	years, %, per 1000,nos, S$,PPP$	No	Industrial countries	UN18 (26)
Human development, trends	Indicators of human development	years, %, US$, PPP$	No	Industrial countries	UN18 (29)
Human development, trends	Indicators of human development	years, nos, %, PPP$	No	Developing countries	UN18 (4)
North-south human gaps, basic	Indicators of human development	indices	No	Developing countries	UN18 (7)
North-south human gaps, trends	Indicators of human development	indices	No	Developing countries	UN18 (6)
Rural-urban gaps	Population, access to services	%, indices	No	Developing countries	UN18 (9)
Social and economic characteristics	By GNP, % of government expenditure daily calories, legal age at marriage, % literate, % school enrolment	US$, %, nos, per capita	No	World	PC1 (3)
South-north, real expenditure	Food, health, education	indices	No	Developing countries	UN18 (8)
Weakening social fabric	Indicators of weakening social fabric	%, l, per 100 000, ratio	No	Industrial countries	UN18 (28)
42.10 HUMAN DISTRESS					
Indicators of human distress		per 100 000, %, ratio,	No	Industrial countries	UN18 (27)
42.11 INCOME AND WEALTH DISTRIBUTION - see also Section 24					
Distribution of disposable income of private households		%	No	OECD	OECD20 (19.1)
Distribution of total personal net worth of households		%	No	OECD	OECD20 (21.1)
Households classified by characteristics of head in the lowest quintile of the equivalent income distribution		%	No	OECD	OECD20 (20.1)
Households in each income decile with a number of income earners		%	No	OECD	OECD20 (19.2)
Income characteristics of households	By characteristics of head of household	index, nos	No	OECD	OECD20 (19.3)
Percentage distribution of income by percentile groups of households		%	Yes Selected years	World	UN16 (30)
Population in absolute poverty	Total, urban, rural	%	No	World	UN16 (30)
Population in each decile of the income distribution		%	No	OECD	OECD20 (19.2)

Subject	Categories	Units	Time series Yes/No Frequency	Territorial coverage	Source (Table no.)
Rate of household ownership of selected wealth items	By age of head of household	%	No	OECD	OECD20 (21.2)
	By socio-economic status of head of household	%	No	OECD	OECD20 (21.2)

42.12 LEISURE - see also Section 44

Subject	Categories	Units	Time series Yes/No Frequency	Territorial coverage	Source (Table no.)
Countries visited during main holidays	By country	%	No	EC	EC72 (11.2)
Distribution of total leisure time per week	Sex and status	%	No	OECD	OECD20 (17.1)
Free time per week	By sex and socio-economic status	hours	No	OECD	OECD20 (17.2)
Holiday destinations	By country, by seaside, countryside, mountains, towns or cities	%	No	EC	EC72 (11.4)
Household expenditure on leisure, entertainment and educational and cultural pursuits	By country	%	No	EC	EC72 (11.8)
Weekly hours of cultural time	By various factors	hours	No	OECD	OECD20(18.5)
Weekly hours of free time	By various factors	hours	No	OECD	OECD20(17.3)
Weekly hours of organised time	By various factors	hours	No	OECD	OECD20(18.6)
Weekly hours of reading time	By various factors	hours	No	OECD	OECD20(18.3)
Weekly hours of recreation time	By various factors	hours	No	OECD	OECD20(18.4)
Weekly hours of social time	By various factors	hours	No	OECD	OECD20(18.2)
Weekly hours of TV time	By various factors	hours	No	OECD	OECD20(18.1)

42.13 LIVING CONDITIONS - see also Section 30

Subject	Categories	Units	Time series Yes/No Frequency	Territorial coverage	Source (Table no.)
Urban crowding	Indicators of urban crowding	%, nos, sq km	No	Industrial countries	UN18 (41)
Urban crowding	Indicators of urban crowding	%, nos, nos, sq km	No	Developing countries	UN18 (20)

42.14 NATIONAL AND HOUSEHOLD INCOME AND EXPENDITURE - see also Section 34

Subject	Categories	Units	Time series Yes/No Frequency	Territorial coverage	Source (Table no.)
Agriculture, percentage of GDP		%	No	MPS countries	UN16 (27B)
Agriculture, percentage of GDP		%	Yes Selected years	SNA countries	UN16 (27A)
Consumption of the population		%	No	MPS countries	UN16 (27B)
Energy consumption per capita		kg of coal	Yes Selected years	World, by development groups	UNCTAD5 (5.3)
Exports		%	No	MPS countries	UN16 (27B)
Exports		%	Yes Selected years	SNA countries	UN16 (27A)
GDP	Value per capita	nat curr, $US, $int	Yes Selected years	World	UN16 (26A)
GDP	Value, per capita	%	Yes Selected years	SNA countries	UN16 (27A)
GDP or net material product, current and constant prices, and selected measures of consumption expenditure	By total and per capita per capita, % GDP,	nat curr,	No	World	UN17 (16)
GDP or net material product, current and constant prices,	GDP per capita,	nat curr,	No	Africa	UN46 (15)
GDP per capita		$US	Yes Selected years	World, by development groups	UNCTAD5 (5.3)
GDP per capita	Value per capita	%	Yes Selected years	SNA countries	UN16 (27A)
Government final consumption expenditure	% of GDP per capita	% $US, $int	Yes Selected years	World	UN16 (26A)

Subject	Categories	Units	Time series Yes/No	Frequency	Territorial coverage	Source (Table no.)
Government final consumption expenditure on selected categories of goods and services	By type, % of GDP, % of total, per capita	nat curr % $US, $int	No		World	UN16 (26B)
Government final consumption expenditure		%	Yes	Selected years	SNA countries	UN16 (27A)
Government social benefit expenditure		% GDP	No		World	UN17 (18)
Government social benefit expenditure		%			Africa	UN46 (17)
Government social security benefit expenditure, and private final consumption expenditure, current prices	GDP	nat curr, per capita, %	No		Africa	UN46 (18)
Government social security benefit expenditure, and private final consumption expenditure, current prices	GDP	nat curr, per capita, %	No		World	UN17 (19)
Government social security benefit expenditure	Valuee of GDP per capita	nat curr % nat curr, $US %	Yes	Selected years	World	UN16 (28)
Government, and private, and selected measures of consumption expenditure, total and per capita	per capita, final consumption expenditure	%, $US, $ int				
Imports		%	No		MPS countries	UN16 (27B)
Imports		%	Yes	Selected years	SNA countries	UN16 (27A)
Industrial activity, percentage of GDP		%	No		MPS countries	UN16 (27B)
Manufacturing share of in GDP		%	Yes	Selected years	World, by development groups	UNCTAD5 (5.3)
Manufacturing, percentage of GDP		%	Yes	Selected years	SNA countries	UN16 (27A)
Material consumption		%	No		MPS countries	UN16 (27B)
Net material product		%	No		MPS countries	UN16 (27B)
Private consumption expenditure on selected categories of goods and services	By category, % of GDP, % of total per capita	nat curr % $US	No		World	UN16 (26C)
Private final consumption expenditure	% of GDP per capita	% $US, $int	Yes	Selected years	World	UN16 (26A)
Private final consumption expenditure	By food and non-alcoholic beverages	%, per capita	No		Africa	UN46 (17)
Private final consumption expenditure	By food and non-alcoholic beverages	%, per capita $ int	No		World	UN17 (18)
Private final consumption expenditure		%	Yes	Selected years	SNA countries	UN16 (27A)
Rates of growth, average, selected economic accounts aggregates		rate	Yes	5 yrly	Africa	UN46 (16)
Rates of growth, average, selected economic accounts aggregates	By market economies, by centrally planned economies	rate	Yes	5 yrly	World	UN17 (17 A,B)

42.15 PERSONAL SAFETY - see also Section 1

Subject	Categories	Units	Time series Yes/No	Frequency	Territorial coverage	Source (Table no.)
Death from motor vehicle accidents	By sex and age, and distribution by mode of transport	rates, %	No		OECD	OECD20 (29.2)
Deaths from external causes	By cause	rate	Yes	10 yrly	OECD	OECD20 (29.1)
Persons afraid to walk alone in their neighbourhood at night	By selected characteristics	%	No		OECD	OECD20 (31.1)

Subject	Categories	Units	Time series Yes/No	Frequency	Territorial coverage	Source (Table no.)
Persons seriously injured in road accidents		rates	Yes	10 yrly	OECD	OECD20 (30.1A)
Persons seriously injured in road accidents	By sex and age groups	rates	No		OECD	OECD20 (30.1B)
Persons seriously injured in work accidents		rates	Yes	10 yrly	OECD	OECD20 (30.2A)
Persons seriously injured in work accidents	By selected characteristics	rates	No		OECD	OECD20 (30.2B)

42.16 PUBLIC AFFAIRS AND POLITICAL PARTICIPATION - see also Section 35

Subject	Categories	Units	Time series Yes/No	Frequency	Territorial coverage	Source (Table no.)
Professional staff in the United Nations Secretariat	By sex, level of responsibility and nationality	nos %	No		World	UN16 (32)
Professional staff in the United Nations System and related agencies	By sex, level of responsibility and nationality	nos %	No		World	UN16 (33)
Women's political participation	Lower, upper chamber % difference Participation in parliamentary assemblies Year granted right to vote Year of right to stand for election	nos, %	No		Africa	UN46 (28)
Women's political participation	Number of seats % female	nos %	No		World	UN16 (31)

42.17 SANITATION

Subject	Categories	Units	Time series Yes/No	Frequency	Territorial coverage	Source (Table no.)
Sanitation, access to	Total, urban, rural	%	Yes	I	World	WHO2 (3)
Sanitation, access to	By country, region	%	No		UNICEF assisted countries	UNICEF2(-)
Sanitation, access to	Total, urban and rural and % AGR	%	Yes	10 yearly	World	UN26

42.18 SOCIO-DEMOGRAPHIC STATISTICS - see also Section 36

Subject	Categories	Units	Time series Yes/No	Frequency	Territorial coverage	Source (Table no.)
Activity rates	Male, female	%	Yes	A	African countries	UN1 (8)
Age at first marriage, average	By sex	years	No		World	UN16 (10)
Age dependency ratio		%	Yes	A	African countries	UN1 (4)
Agricultural holders	By sex	nos, %	No		World	UN16 (25B)
Birth rate, crude		per 1000	Yes	A	African countries	UN1 (6)
Births	By age group, total urban and rural	nos, years	No		World	UN17 (6)
Births	By age group, total, urban and rural	nos, years	No		Africa	UN46 (6)
Contraceptive use among currently married women of reproductive age	By method used, age group	%	No		Africa	UN46 (7)
Contraceptive use among currently married women of reproductive age	By method used, age group	%	No		World	UN17 (7)
Death rate, crude		per 1000	Yes	A	African countries	UN1 (6)
Distribution of economically active population by sector	Agriculture, male/female industry, male/female services, male female	%	Yes	A	African countries	UN1 (7)
Economic dependency ratio	Male and female	%	Yes	A	African countries	UN1 (4)
Economically active and not economically active population	By sex and age	nos, %	No		World	UN16 (22, 23)
Economically active and not economically active populations, urban and rural, census rounds	By total, by age, by sex, % of total population	nos, years, %	No		World	UN17 (10)

Subject	Categories	Units	Time series Yes/No Frequency		Territorial coverage	Source (Table no.)
Economically active and not economically active populations, census rounds	By total, by age, by sex, % of total population urban and rural	nos, years, %	No		Africa	UN46 (10)
Economically active population in agriculture	By % of total, by sex; by % of population by sex	nos, %	No		Africa	UN46 (9)
Economically active population in agriculture	By % of total, by sex; by % of population by sex	nos, %	Yes	10 yrly	World	UN17 (9)
Economically active population	By sex and age group	nos, %	No		World	UN17 (8)
Economically active population	By sex and age group	nos, %	Yes	15 yrly	Africa	UN46 (8)
Economically active population	By sex and occupational group	nos, %	No		World	UN16 (24)
Economically active population in agriculture	By sex	nos, %	No		World	UN16 (25A)
Female economically active population, census rounds	By marital status and age group	by years, total, %, nos	No		World	UN17 (13)
Female economically active population, census rounds	By marital status and age group	years, total, %, nos	No		Africa	UN46 (13)
Fertility rate		rate	No		Africa	UN46 (3)
Fertility rate		rate	No		World	UN16 (11)
Fertility rate		rate	No		World	UN17 (3)
Fertility rate	% foreign born by sex	%	No		World	UN17 (3)
Fertility rate	Female	per woman	Yes	A	African countries	UN1 (5)
Fertility rate	Total	rate	No		Africa	UN46 (6)
Fertility rate	Total	rate	No		World	UN17 (6)
Household heads	By sex	nos	No		World	UN16 (11)
Household size	In urban and rural areas	nos	No		World	UN16 (11)
Household size, census rounds	Total, urban and rural	nos	No		Africa	UN46 (5)
Household size, census	Total, urban and rural rounds	nos	No		World	UN17 (5)
Labour force	By professional status and sex	%	Yes	10 yrly	OECD	OECD20 (0.4)
Localities, number of large	By population size	nos	No		World	UN16 (4)
Male, female wage ratios in non-agricultural economic activities		by ratio	No		World	UN17 (14)
Male, female wage ratios in non-agricultural economic activities		ratio	Yes	15 yrly	Africa	UN46 (14)
Marital status	By sex and age group	%	No		World	UN16 (10)
Marital status, census rounds	By age group and sex, by average age at first marriage, by sex	years, %,	No		World	UN17 (4)
Marital status, census rounds	By age group and sex, by average age at first marriage, by sex	years, %,	No		Africa	UN46 (4)
Mortality rate under-five	By adult literacy, radio and television sets, primary school enrolement, % reaching final grade, secondary school enrolement	nos, %	No		World	UNICEF1 (4)
Population	By age structure		Yes	A	African countries	UN1 (2)
Population	By annual rate of change By total, by age group, sex	rate, years	No		Africa	UN46 (3)
Population	By community size	%	Yes	10 yrly	OECD	OECD20 (0.5)
Population	By type of activity	%	Yes	10 yrly	OECD	OECD20 (0.3)
Population	In urban and rural areas, sex	nos	No		World	UN16 (3)
Population	Total	nos	Yes	10 yrly	OECD	OECD20 (0.1)

42 SOCIAL INDICATORS

Subject	Categories	Units	Time series Yes/No	Frequency	Territorial coverage	Source (Table no.)
Population	Urban and rural areas and in largest city, by sex, % population urban, annual rate of growth	nos, %, rate	No		World	UN17 (2)
Population	% foreign born by sex	%	No		Africa	UN46 (3)
Population by size of locality		nos, %	No		World	UN16 (4)
Population census rounds	Urban and rural areas and in, largest city annual rate of growth					
Population changes	By total, by age group, sex, by annual rate of change	rate, years	No		World	UN17 (3)
Population economically active, census rounds	By total, sex and occupational groups	nos, %	No		Africa	UN46 (12)
Population economically active, census rounds	By total, sex and occupational groups	nos, %	No		World	UN17 (12)
Population growth rates	Total and urban population	%	Yes	A	African countries	UN1 (3)
Population in largest city	Sex	nos	No		World	UN16 (3)
Population rate of change		%			Africa	UN46 (9)
Population rates of change		%	Yes	10 yrly	World	UN17 (9)
Population rates of change	By sex economically active and not economically active	%	Yes	15 yrly	World	UN17 (11)
Population size		nos, 1000	Yes	A	African countries	UN1 (1)
Population Size	Total, females by age group female, male ratio	nos, %	Yes	15 yrly	Africa	UN46 (1)
	By sex, by % population	nos, %, rate	No		Africa	UN46 (2)
Population size	Total, females by age group female, male ratio	nos, %	Yes	15 yrly	World	UN17 (1)
Population structure	By six	%	Yes	A	African countries	UN1 (1)
Population structure	Urban areas	%	Yes	A	African countries	UN1 (3)
Population, rates of growth	Urban, rural	%	No		World	UN16 (3)
Population: age structure	Various categories	%	Yes	10 yrly	OECD	OECD20 (0.2)
Populations rates of change economically active and not economically active	By sex	%	No		Africa	UN46 (11)
Private households	By household type	%	Yes	10 yrly	OECD	OECD20 (0.6)
Reproduction rate, gross	Female	per woman	Yes	A	African countries	UN1 (5)
Socio-economic indicators by country	By population, agriculture, health, education,	%, per capita, nos	No		Developing countries	UNCTAD5 (1.4)
Suicides	By sex-age group	rate	Yes	5 yrly	OECD	OECD20 (28.1)
Urban unemployment	By sex	nos, %	No		World	UN17 (15)
Women heads of households, census rounds	By age group	nos, %	No		Africa	UN46 (5)
Women heads of households, census rounds	By age group	nos, %	No		World	UN17 (5)

42.19 TRANSPORT - see also Section 45

Subject	Categories	Units	Time series Yes/No	Frequency	Territorial coverage	Source (Table no.)
Means of transport	By country, by means	%	No		EC	EC72 (11.7)
Motor vehicles and car ownership	By country, by type of vehicle	nos	No		EC	EC18 (10.4)
Passenger cars	Numbers in use per 1000 population	nos rate	Yes	Selected years	World	UN16 (29)

42.20 WATER

Subject	Categories	Units	Time series Yes/No	Frequency	Territorial coverage	Source (Table no.)
Access to drinking water	Total, urban and rural and % AGR.	%	Yes	10 yearly	World	UN26
Access to safe drinking water and sanitation	By urban, rural area	%	No		Developing countries	PC1 (39)

Subject	Categories	Units	Time series Yes/No Frequency	Territorial coverage	Source (Table no.)
Access to safe water	By country, region	%	No	UNICEF assisted countries	UNICEF2 (-)
Access to safe water	Total, urban, rural	%	Yes I	World	WHO2 (2)
Community water supply and sanitation problems and issues	By country, by institutional item, financial item, operational item		No	SEAR	WHO1 (60)
Water supply and sanitation coverage	By country	nos, %	No	SEAR	WHO1 (59)

42.21 WEALTH AND POVERTY - see also Section 24

Subject	Categories	Units	Time series Yes/No Frequency	Territorial coverage	Source (Table no.)
Wealth, poverty and social investment	Indicators of population wealth, poverty	PPP$, %, US$, ratio	No	Developing countries	UN18 (17)
Wealth, poverty and social investment	Indicators of population wealth, poverty	PPP$, %, US$, ratio	No	Industrial countries	UN18 (38)

43 TAXATION

Subject	Categories	Units	Time series Yes/No	Frequency	Territorial coverage	Source (Table no.)
43.1 CONSUMPTION TAXES						
Consumption taxes	As percentage of GDP	%	Yes	A	OECD	OECD42 (26)
Consumption taxes	As percentage of total taxation	%	Yes	A	OECD	OECD42 (27)
VAT rates	By Member State	%	No		EC	EC71 (EUR19)
43.2 CORPORATE TAXATION						
Taxes linked to production	Imports paid to EC	nat curr	Yes	A	EC	EC49 (7)
43.3 ENERGY TAXATION						
Coal, coking		nat curr per tonne	Yes	A, Q	Non-OECD	IEA6 (IIIA.1)
Coal, coking	By country	nat curr per tonne	Yes	A, Q	OECD	IEA6 (IIB.1)
Coal, steam	Industry	%	Yes	A	OECD	IEA6 (IIC.12)
Coal, steam	Industry, electricity generation and households, by country	nat curr per tonne	Yes	A, Q	OECD	IEA6 (IIB.1)
Coal, steam	Industry, electricity generation and household use, by country	nat curr per tonne	Yes	A, Q	Non-OECD	IEA6 (IIIA.1)
Diesel, automotive		%	Yes	A	OECD	IEA6 (IIC.2)
Electricity	Industry and household use, by country	nat curr per kWh	Yes	A, Q	Non-OECD	IEA6 (IIIA.1)
Electricity	Industry and households	%	Yes	A	OECD	IEA6 (II(C.7-C.8))
Electricity	Industry and households, by country	nat curr per kWh	Yes	A, Q	OECD	IEA6 (IIB.1)
Electricity sales	VAT	% of price before VAT	Yes	A	EC	EC28
Fuel oil, heavy	Industry and electricity generation, by country	nat curr per tonne	Yes	A, Q	Non-OECD	IEA6 (IIIA.1)
Fuel oil, heavy	Industry and households	%	Yes	A	OECD	IEA6 (II(C.5-C.6))
Fuel oil, light	Industry and household use, by country	nat curr per 'ooo litres	Yes	A, Q	Non-OECD	IEA6 (IIIA.1)
Fuel oil, light	Industry and households	%	Yes	A	OECD	IEA6 (II(C.3-C.4))
Fuel oils	By type and country	nat curr per litre/tonne	Yes	A, Q	OECD	IEA6 (IIB.1)
Fuels, automative	By type and country	nat curr per litre	Yes	A, Q	OECD	IEA6 (IIB.1)
Fuels, automotive	By type and by country	nat curr per litre	Yes	A, Q	Non-OECD	IEA6 (IIIA.1)
Gas, natural	Industry, electricity generation and households	%	Yes	A	OECD	IEA6 (II(C.9-C.11))
Gas, natural	Industry, electricity generation and household use, by country	nat curr per 107 kCal	Yes	A, Q	Non-OECD	IEA6 (IIIA.1)
Gas, natural	Industry, electricity generation and households, by country	nat curr per 107 Kcal	Yes	A, Q	OECD	IEA6 (IIB.1)
Gasoline		%	Yes	A	OECD	IEA6 (IIC.1)
43.4 PERSONAL TAXATION						
Income earners, incomes and taxes		nat curr	No		Nordic countries	NCM1 (170)

43 TAXATION

Subject	Categories	Units	Time series Yes/No	Frequency	Territorial coverage	Source (Table no.)
Tax payers	Total	nos	Yes	5 yrly	Nordic countries	NCM1 (171)
Taxation, incidence	Household sector (as % of price all taxes included), industry sector (as % of price VAT and deductible specific taxes excluded), by energy type	%	Yes	2/yr	EC	EC32 (-)
Taxes and contributions	By type	nat curr, % GDP	Yes	A	Nordic countries	NCM1 (207)
Taxes and contributions	Per capita	nat curr, US$	Yes	A	Nordic countries	NCM1 (206)
Taxes and social contributions	By category and receiving sub-sector	nat curr	Yes	A	EC	EC49 (6)

43.5 TAX RATES

Subject	Categories	Units	Time series Yes/No	Frequency	Territorial coverage	Source (Table no.)
ECSC levy share of	By country	%	Yes	A	EC	EC55 (9.2)
Iron and steel industry levy rate	By type of product	levy/tonne	Yes	A	EC	EC55 (9.1)
Taxation on corporate income, as percentage of GDP		%	Yes	A	OECD	OECD42 (12)
Taxation on corporate income, as percentage of total taxation		%	Yes	A	OECD	OECD42 (13)
Taxation on general consumption, as percentage of GDP		%	Yes	A	OECD	OECD42 (28)
Taxation on general consumption, as percentage of total taxation		%	Yes	A	OECD	OECD42 (29)
Taxation on goods and services, as percentage of GDP		%	Yes	A	OECD	OECD42 (24)
Taxation on goods and services, as percentage of total taxation		%	Yes	A	OECD	OECD42 (25)
Taxation on income and profits, as percentage of GDP		%	Yes	A	OECD	OECD42 (8)
Taxation on income and profits, as percentage of total taxation		%	Yes	A	OECD	OECD42 (9)
Taxation on payroll and workforce, as percentage of GDP		%	Yes	A	OECD	OECD42 (20)
Taxation on payroll and workforce, as percentage of total taxation		%	Yes	A	OECD	OECD42 (21)
Taxation on personal income, as percentage of GDP		%	Yes	A	OECD	OECD42 (10)
Taxation on personal income, as percentage of total taxation		%	Yes	A	OECD	OECD42 (11)
Taxation on property, as percentage of GDP		%	Yes	A	OECD	OECD42 (22)
Taxation on property, as percentage of total taxation		%	Yes	A	OECD	OECD42 (23)
Taxation on specific goods and services, as percentage of GDP		%	Yes	A	OECD	OECD42 (30)
Taxation on specific goods and services, as percentage of total taxation		%	Yes	A	OECD	OECD42 (31)

43.6 TAX REVENUES - see also Section 34

Subject	Categories	Units	Time series Yes/No	Frequency	Territorial coverage	Source (Table no.)
Central government	By major components	% total	No		World	IMF5 (pp36-37)
Central government	By type of revenue	% total	No		World	IMF5 (pp38-39)
Central government	Taxes on domestic goods and services, taxes on international trade and transactions	% total	Yes	A	World	IMF5 (pp54-55)

Subject	Categories	Units	Time series Yes/No Frequency		Territorial coverage	Source (Table no.)
Central government	Taxes on incomes and profits, social security contributions	% total	Yes	A	World	IMF5 (pp52-53)
Compulsory loans collected through the tax system	Gross amount	nat curr	Yes	A	OECD	OECD42 (110)
Local taxes as percentage of total tax revenues of local governments	Type	%	No	I	Unitary countries	OECD42 (128)
Local taxes, as percentage of GDP	Type	%	No	I	Unitary countries	OECD42 (127)
Main central government taxes, as percentage of total tax revenues of central government	Type	%	No	I	OECD	OECD42 (124)
Main central government taxes, as percentage of GDP	Type	%, market prices	No	I	OECD	OECD42 (123)
Main headings as a percentage of total taxation	Type	%	No		OECD	OECD42 (120)
Main headings as a percentage of total taxation	Type	%	No		OECD	OECD42 (117)
Main headings as percentage of GDP		%	No		OECD	OECD42 (6)
Main headings as percentage of total taxation		%	No		OECD	OECD42 (7)
Receipts from user taxation	By country, tax type, GNP	%, units of account	Yes	A	World	IRF1 (X)
Receipts, total from taxes and social contributions	By type	nat curr	Yes	A	EC	EC49 (8)
State and local taxes, as percentage of GDP	Type	%	No	I	Federal countries	OECD42 (125)
State and local taxes, as percentage of total tax revenues of these levels of government	Type	%	No	I	Federal countries	OECD42 (126)
Tax receipts	By type and receiving sub-sector	nat curr	Yes	A	EC	EC49 (-)
Tax revenues		nat curr	Yes	A	OECD	OECD42 (38-61)
Tax revenues		$ per capita	Yes	A	OECD	OECD42 (34)
Tax revenues	General government	% GDP	Yes	A	World	IMF5 (pp102-103)
Tax revenues	Total	$	Yes	A	OECD	OECD42 (32)
Tax revenues	Total	%, market prices	No		OECD	OECD42 (1)
Tax revenues	Total, annual percentage change	%, nat curr	Yes	A	OECD	OECD42 (35)
Tax revenues	Type	nat curr	No		OECD	OECD42 (115)
Tax revenues	Type	nat curr	No		OECD	OECD42 (118)
Tax revenues	Type	nat curr	No		OECD	OECD42 (111)
Tax revenues, as a percentage of GDP	Type	%	No		OECD	OECD42 (119)
Tax revenues, as percentage of GDP		%	No		OECD	OECD42 (113)
Tax revenues, as percentage of GDP	Total	%	Yes	A	OECD	OECD42 (3)
Tax revenues, as percentage of GDP excluding social security	Total	%	Yes	A	OECD	OECD42 (4)
Tax revenus, as percentage of GDP	Total	%, 3-yr average	Yes	A	OECD	OECD42 (5)
Tax revenues, as percentage of GDP excluding social security	Total	%, market prices	No		OECD	OECD42 (2)

43 TAXATION

Subject	Categories	Units	Time series Yes/No Frequency		Territorial coverage	Source (Table no.)
Tax revenues, as percentage of GDP	Type	%	No		OECD	OECD42 (116)
Tax revenues, as percentage of GDP	Type	%	No		OECD	OECD42 (112)
Tax revenues, as percentage of total OECD tax revenue		%	Yes	A	OECD	OECD42 (33)
Tax revenues, as percentage of total tax revenue	Sub-sectors	%	No	I	OECD	OECD42 (122)
Tax revenues, total		nat curr	Yes	A	OECD	OECD42 (129-152)
Taxable items, goods and services		nat curr	Yes	A	OECD	OECD42 (38-61, 129-152)
Taxable items, income, profits and capital gains		nat curr	Yes	A	OECD	OECD42 (38-61, 129-152)
Taxable items, other		nat curr	Yes	A	OECD	OECD42 (38-61, 129-152)
Taxable items, payroll and workforce		nat curr	Yes	A	OECD	OECD42 (38-61, 129-152)
Taxable items, property		nat curr	Yes	A	OECD	OECD42 (38-61, 129-152)
Taxation of five common categories of vehicles	By type	kms, tonnes	No		Selected countries	IRF1 (IX)
Taxes	Taxes, GDP, taxes as % of GDP	nat curr	Yes	A	ASEAN	ASEANS1 (7.1.2)
Taxes	Total production and imports, income and wealth, capital tax, social contributions	ECU, %	No		EC	EC9 (2.10)
Taxes, domestic goods and services	General government	% GDP	Yes	A	World	IMF5 (pp105)
Taxes, income, profits and capital gains	General government	% GDP	Yes	A	World	IMF5 (pp104)

44 TOURISM

44 TOURISM

Subject	Categories	Units	Time series Yes/No Frequency	Territorial coverage	Source (Table no.)

44.1 ACCOMMODATION

44.1.1 Capacity

Subject	Categories	Units	Time series Yes/No Frequency	Territorial coverage	Source (Table no.)
Accommodation capacity	Bed-places, rooms	nos	Yes A	World, major regions	WTO3 (pp 40-93)
Accommodation capacity	By accommodation type	nos	Yes A	OECD	OECD46 (13-14)
Accommodation capacity	Hotels and similar establishments, rooms, bed-places, by regions	nos	Yes A	World, regions of: Africa, Asia, Americas, EC, Oceania	WTO3 (6)
Accommodation, bed-places	Hotels and similar establishments, by country	nos	Yes A	World	WTO3 (pp 150-153)
Accommodation, residents	Travelling within their own country or abroad, staying at: hotel or similar, rented flat, apartment, secondary residence, friends or relatives, camping, caravanning site, youth hostel, others, by country	%	Yes A	OECD	OECD30 (-)
Accommodation, rooms	Hotels and similar establishments, by country	nos	Yes A	World	WTO3 (146-149)
Bed-places, hotels and similar		nos	Yes A	World	WTO1 (-)
Beds available	By country	nos	No	EC	EC18 (11.3)
Establishments offering accommodation	By country	nos	No	EC	EC18 (11.2)
Hotels and similar establishments capacity	By country, by establishment	nos	No	EC	EM1 (2308)
Private tourist accommodation	Dwellings, bedrooms, estimated bed-places,	nos	Yes A	EC and regions	EC78 (I.3.1)
Rooms, hotels and similar		nos	Yes A	World	WTO1 (-)
Supplementary accommodation	Supplementary accommodation establishments, bed-places, by type of accommodation	nos	Yes A	EC and regions	EC78 (I.2.1) EC78 (I.2.2)
Supplementary accommodation bed capacity	By country, by type	nos	No	EC	EM1 (2309)
Use of tourist accommodation	By country, by use	nos, %	No	Europe	EM1 (2306)

44.1.2 Guest Flows

Subject	Categories	Units	Time series Yes/No Frequency	Territorial coverage	Source (Table no.)
Accommodation establishments	Residents, non residents in the country, total, arrivals, nights, by country, region	nos	Yes A	EC and regions	EC78 (II.1.4)
Accommodation establishments	Residents, non-residents in the country, total, arrivals, nights, by type of accommodation, by country	nos	Yes A	EC	EC78 (II.1.1)
Hotels and similar establishments	Arrivals, nights, residents, non-residents in the country, by country	nos	Yes A, M	EC	EC78 (II.2.1)
Hotels and similar establishments	Residents, non residents in the country, total, arrivals, nights, by country, region	nos	Yes A	EC and regions	EC78 (II.1.2)

Subject	Categories	Units	Time series Yes/No Frequency		Territorial coverage	Source (Table no.)
Supplementary accommodation	Arrivals, nights, residents/non-residents in the country, by country	nos	Yes	A, M	EC	EC78 (II.2.2)
Supplementary accommodation	Residents, non residents in the country, total arrivals, nights, by country, region	nos	Yes	A	EC	EC78 (II.1.3)
44.1.3 Hotels						
Hotels and similar establishments	Bedrooms, bed-places	nos	Yes	A	EC	EC78 (I.1.1)
Hotels and similar establishments	Bedrooms, bed-places	nos	Yes	A	EC	EC78 (I.1.2)
Hotels and similar establishments	By country	nos	No		EC	EC35 (-)
Hotels and similar establishments	Utilization of bed-places, gross, net	indices	Yes	A	EC	EC78 (IV.1.2)
Hotels and similar establishments	Utilization of bed-places, gross, net	indices	Yes	A, M	EC	EC78 (IV.1.1)
Hotels, classification	By number of stars, establishments, bedrooms, bed-places	nos, %	Yes	A	EC	EC78 (I.4.1)
Hotels: ratios based on total revenues	$ per available room per year by av rooms, % of av daily rate per room av daily room per guest % double occupancy, revenues, dept costs, undistributed operating expenses, ratios to rooms revenue	%, US$	Yes	A	World	PKF2(2)
International hotels	By % of occupancy average daily rate per room, total revenues operating costs and expenses, income before fixed charges, energy costs	%	Yes	A	World	PKF2(1)
Market data, regions	By source of business, type of guests and reservation	%	No		World	HI1 (4)
Market data, trends	By source of business, type of guests and reservation	%	Yes	A	World	HI1 (3)
Performance measurements	By region, occupancy rate, av daily rate, total revenue, income before fixed charges	%, US$	No		World	HI1 (5)
44.1.4 Occupancy and Length of Stay						
Accommodation, all means	Arrivals, nights spent by tourists, by selected country of origin	indices, nos	Yes	A	OECD	OECD30 (-)
Accommodation, all means	Arrivals, nights spent by tourists from all foreign countries	indices, nos	Yes	A	OECD	OECD30 (-)

Subject	Categories	Units	Time series Yes/No Frequency		Territorial coverage	Source (Table no.)
Accommodation, all means	Nights spent by foreign tourists, from all foreign countries, from selected countries, by country	nos	Yes	A	OECD	OECD30 (-)
Accommodation, all means	Nights spent by foreign tourists, total, % share, % change, by country, region of origin, by country	nos, %	Yes	A	World	OECD30 (-)
Amount per available room	By occupancy, room rate, revenues, expenses, profit, region	%, US$	No		World	HI1 (I.12, II.12, III.12, IV.12, V.12)
Arrivals and nights in all means of accommodation	Of foreign tourists, by country of residence (Germany, Italy, Japan, Canada, France, US, Netherlands, UK)	indices	Yes	A	OECD	OECD46
Arrivals and nights in hotels	Of foreign tourists, by country of residence (Germany, Italy, Japan, Canada, France, US, Netherlands, UK)	indices	Yes	A	OECD	OECD46
Domestic tourist nights	In hotels and similar accommodation, in all types of accommodation, by country	nos	Yes	A	World	WTO1 (-)
Duration of trips, residents	Within their own country, abroad, by country	nos	Yes	A	OECD	OECD30 (-)
Hotels and similar establishments	Arrivals, nights spent by tourists, by selected country of origin	indices, nos	Yes	A	OECD	OECD30 (-)
Hotels and similar establishments	Arrivals, nights spent by tourists from all foreign countries	indices, nos	Yes	A	OECD	OECD30 (-)
Hotels and similar establishments	Bedrooms, bed-places	nos	Yes	A	EC	EC78 (I.1.1)
Hotels and similar establishments	Bedrooms, bed-places	nos	Yes	A	EC	EC78 (I.1.2)
Hotels and similar establishments	By country	nos	No		EC	EC35 (-)
Hotels and similar establishments	Nights spent by foreign tourists, from all foreign countries, from selected countries, by country	nos	Yes	A	OECD	OECD30 (-)
Hotels and similar establishments	Nights spent by foreign tourists. total, % share, % change, by country, region of origin, by country	nos, %	Yes	A	World	OECD30 (-)
Hotels and similar establishments	Utilization of bed-places, gross, net	indices	Yes	A	EC	EC78 (IV.1.2)
Hotels and similar establishments	Utilization of bed-places, gross, net	indices	Yes	A, M	EC	EC78 (IV.1.1)
Hotels, beds, guest nights	By nationality and camping sites	nos	No		Nordic countries	NCM1 (157)

44 TOURISM

Subject	Categories	Units	Time series Yes/No Frequency		Territorial coverage	Source (Table no.)
Hotels, classification	By number of stars, establishments, bedrooms, bed-places	nos, %	Yes	A	EC	EC78 (I.4.1)
International tourist nights	In hotels and similar accommodation, in all types of accommodation, by country	nos	Yes	A	World	WTO1 (-)
Length of stay	In the country, in accommodation, by country, nights stay	nos	Yes	A	World	WTO1 (-)
Length of stay, in tourist accommodation	Tourists from all foreign countries, from Europe (OECD), from North America (OECD), from Pacific (OECD)	nos	Yes	A	OECD	OECD46 (9)
Market data, regions	By source of business, type of guests and reservation	%	No		World	HI1 (4)
Market data, trends	By source of business, type of guests and reservation	%	Yes	A	World	HI1 (3)
Nights in accommodation	Total, resident, non-resident	%			EC	EC79 (-)
Nights spent	By foreign and domestic tourists, by type of accommodation	nos	Yes	A	OECD	OECD46 (10-12)
Nights spent	By foreign tourists, in registered tourist accommodation, by country of residence, by country of destination	nos, %	Yes	A	OECD	OECD46
Nights spent	By foreign tourists, in hotels, by country of residence, by country of destination	nos, %	Yes	A	OECD	OECD46
Nights spent	Total, by resident tourists, non resident tourists	nos, %	Yes	M, A	EC	EC79 (-)
Nights spent, residents	Travelling within their own country or abroad, by country	nos	Yes	A	OECD	OECD30 (-)
Nights, tourist	All accommodation establishments, by country	nos	Yes	A	World	WTO3 (pp 143-145)
Nights, tourists	From abroad, in all accommodation establishments, by country	nos, %	Yes	A	World	WTO4 (6)
Nights, tourists	From abroad, in hotels and similar establishments, by country	nos, %	Yes	A	World	WTO4 (5)
Non-resident guests	Arrivals, nights, by type of accommodation, by country of origin, by country	nos	Yes	A	EC	EC78 (III.1.1)
Occupancy rates		%	Yes	A	World	WTO1 (-)
Occupancy rates, hotels		%	No		EC	PKF1 (1)
Occupancy rates, hotels	Beds, rooms	nos	Yes	A, M	OECD	OECD46 (15)

Subject	Categories	Units	Time series Yes/No Frequency		Territorial coverage	Source (Table no.)
Occupancy: ratios based on total revenues,	$ per available room per year by av rooms, % of av daily rate per room, av daily room per guest % double occupancy, revenues, dept costs, undistributed operating expenses, ratios to rooms, revenues	%, $	Yes	A	World	PKF2 (2)
Overnight stays	By country	%	No		EC	EC35 (-)
Overnight stays	By country	nos	No		EC	EC18 (11.4)
Performance measurements	By region, occupancy rate, average daily rate, total revenue, income before fixed charges	%, US$	No		World	HI1 (5)
Tourism	Arrivals at frontiers, arrivals at all means of accommodation, nights spent in all means of accommodation by country, region of residence	nos, %	No		OECD	OECD46 (1-6)
44.1.5 Prices						
Amount per available room	By occupancy, room rate, revenues, expenses, profit, region	%, US$	No		World	HI1 (I.12, II.12, III.12, IV.12, V.12)
Room rates (hotels)		nat curr	No		EC	PKF1 (1)
Room rates: ratios based on total revenues	$ per available room per by av rooms, % of av daily rate per room av daily room per guest % double occupancy, revenues, dept costs, undistributed operating expenses, ratios to rooms revenue	%, US$	Yes	A	World	PKF2 (2)
44.2 ARRIVALS AND DEPARTURES						
Adults taking a holiday	By country, by holiday destination	%	No		EC	EM1 (2310)
Arrivals	By region, by mode of transport, by purpose of visit, by country	nos	Yes	A	World	WTO1 (-)
Arrivals	Visitors, tourists, excursionists, cruise passengers, by country	nos	Yes	A	World	WTO1 (-)
Arrivals and nights in all means of accommodation	Of foreign tourists, by country of residence (Germany, Italy, Japan, Canada, France, US, Netherlands, UK)	indices	Yes	A	OECD	OECD46
Arrivals and nights in hotels	Of foreign tourists, by country of residence (Germany, Italy, Japan, Canada, France, US, Netherlands, UK)	indices	Yes	A	OECD	OECD46
Arrivals at hotels	Of foreign tourists, by country of residence, by country of destination	nos, %	Yes	A	OECD	OECD46

44 TOURISM

Subject	Categories	Units	Time series Yes/No Frequency		Territorial coverage	Source (Table no.)
Arrivals, cruise passengers	By country	nos	Yes	A	World	WTO3 (pp 141-142)
Arrivals, excursionists	By country	nos	Yes	A	World	WTO3 (pp 139-140)
Arrivals, from abroad	Total, % of world arrivals, % change	nos, %, indices	Yes	A	World	WTO1 (-)
Arrivals, tourists	Annual change, by regions	%	Yes	A	World	WTO3 (pp 40-93)
Arrivals, tourists	At frontiers from abroad, by country	nos, %	Yes	A	World	WTO4 (1)
Arrivals, tourists	By country	nos	Yes	A	World	WTO3 (pp 135-138)
Arrivals, tourists	From abroad, in all accommodation establishments, by country	nos, %	Yes	A	World	WTO4 (4)
Arrivals, tourists	From abroad, in hotels and similar establishments, by country	nos, %	Yes	A	World	WTO4 (3)
Arrivals, tourists	Total, region of origin, by regions	nos, %	Yes	A	World	WTO3 (pp 40-93)
Arrivals, tourists	Trends, by selected economic groupings of countries	nos	Yes	A	World	WTO3 (pp 96-107)
Arrivals, tourists, business	From abroad, by country	nos, %	Yes	A	World	WTO4 (9.2)
Arrivals, tourists, by air	By region	%	Yes	A	World	WTO3 (pp 40-93)
Arrivals, tourists, by air	Country, region of origin, by country of destination	nos, %	Yes	A	World	WTO4 (7.1)
Arrivals, tourists, by rail	Country, region of origin, by country of destination	nos, %	Yes	A	World	WTO4 (7.4)
Arrivals, tourists, by road	Country, region of origin, by country of destination	nos, %	Yes	A	World	WTO4 (7.3)
Arrivals, tourists, by sea	Country, region of origin, by country of destination	nos, %	Yes	A	World	WTO4 (7.2)
Arrivals, tourists, holidays	From abroad, by country	nos, %	Yes	A	World	WTO4 (9.1)
Arrivals, tourists, visiting friends and relatives	From abroad, by country	nos, %	Yes	A	World	WTO4 (9.3)
Arrivals, visitors	At frontiers from abroad, by country	nos, %	Yes	A	World	WTO4 (2)
Arrivals, visitors, business	From abroad, by country	nos, %	Yes	A	World	WTO4 (10.2)
Arrivals, visitors, by air	Country, region of origin, by country of destination	nos, %	Yes	A	World	WTO4 (8.1)
Arrivals, visitors, by rail	Country, region of origin, by country of destination	nos, %	Yes	A	World	WTO4 (8.4)
Arrivals, visitors, by road	Country/region of origin, by country of destination	nos, %	Yes	A	World	WTO4 (8.3)
Arrivals, visitors, by sea	Country, region of origin, by country of destination	nos, %	Yes	A	World	WTO4 (8.2)
Arrivals, visitors, holidays	From abroad, by country	nos, %	Yes	A	World	WTO4 (10.1)
Arrivals, visitors, visit friends and relatives	From abroad, by country	nos, %	Yes	A	World	WTO4 (10.3)

Subject	Categories	Units	Time series Yes/No Frequency		Territorial coverage	Source (Table no.)
Characteristics, residents	Within country, abroad, total number, by age group, by socio-economic category, by country	nos, %	Yes	A	OECD	OECD30 (-)
Citizens travelling abroad	By country	nos	No		EC	EC18 (11.5)
Countries visited during main holidays	By country	%	No		EC	EC72 (11.2)
Departure rate, residents	Travelling within their own country and abroad, % travelling abroad	%	Yes	A	OECD	OECD30 (-)
Departures, travel abroad		nos	Yes	A	World	WTO1 (-)
Destinations, most popular	Arrivals, annual growth rate, share of world total, by country	nos, %	No		World	WTO3 (pp 130)
Destinations, principal	Residents travelling abroad. By destination, by country	%	Yes	A	OECD	OECD30 (-)
Distribution throughout the year, residents	Within their own country, abroad, by month, by country	%	Yes	A	OECD	OECD30 (-)
Foreign tourists	By country	nos	No		EC	EC18 (11.1)
Foreign tourists arrivals	By country, by arrivals at frontiers, arrivals at registered accommodation	nos	No		EC	EM1 (2303)
Foreign tourists arriving at frontiers	By selected country of origin	indices, nos	Yes	A	OECD	OECD30 (-)
Foreign tourists arriving at frontiers	Of foreign tourists and visitors, by country of residence (Germany, Italy, Japan, Canada, US, France, Netherlands, UK)	indices	Yes	A	OECD	OECD46
Foreign tourists arriving at frontiers	Total from all foreign countries	indices, nos	Yes	A	OECD	OECD30 (-)
Foreign tourists arriving at frontiers	Total, % share, % change, by country, region of origin	nos, %	Yes	A	World	OECD30 (-)
Foreign tourists arriving at frontiers	From all foreign countries, from selected foreign countries, by country	nos	Yes	A	OECD	OECD30 (-)
Foreign tourists arriving at frontiers	Of foreign tourists, by country of residence, by country of destination	nos, %	Yes	A	OECD	OECD46
Foreign tourists, countries of origin	By country	%	No		EC	EM1 (2307)
Main holiday destination	By country, by seaside, countryside, mountains, towns or cities	%	No		EC	EC72 (11.4)
Non-resident guests	Arrivals, nights, by type of accommodation, by country of origin, by country	nos	Yes	A	EC	EC78 (III.1.1)
Non-resident visitors	Arrivals at, principal seaports, principal airports, railways, motorways, by country of residence, by country	nos	Yes	A	EC	EC78 (VII.1.1)

44 TOURISM

Subject	Categories	Units	Time series Yes/No Frequency		Territorial coverage	Source (Table no.)
Purpose of trip	Holidays, visiting friends and relatives, others	%	Yes	A	OECD	OECD30 (-)
Residents' tourism	Holiday days at home, abroad	nos			EC	EC79 (-)
Tourism	Arrivals	nos 1000	Yes		World	UN55
Tourism	Arrivals at frontiers, arrivals at all means of accommodation, nights spent in all means of accommodation by country, region of residence	nos, %	No		OECD	OECD46 (1-6)
Tourism	International travel	nos 1000	Yes	A	Central Africa	UN5 (30)
Tourism	International travel	nos 1000	Yes	A	East and Southern Africa	UN4 (30)
Tourism	International travel	nos 1000	Yes	A	North Africa	UN2 (30)
Tourism	International travel	nos 1000	Yes	A	West Africa	UN3 (30)
Tourism from the USA	Number and expenditure of USA residents travelling abroad	US$, nos	Yes	A	World	OECD46 (7-8)
Tourism, development	Arrivals, receipts, exports, by region	%	Yes	A	World, developed market economies, developing countries and territories	WTO3 (8)
Tourism, development	Tourist arrivals, receipts from tourism, value of world exports	nos, indices US$	Yes	A	World	WTO3 (2)
Tourism, foreign	By mode of transport	nos, %	Yes	A	OECD	OECD46 (20)
Tourism, foreign	By purpose of visit	nos, %	Yes	A	OECD	OECD46 (19)
Tourists		nos	Yes	A	ASEAN	ASEANS1 (6.7)
Tourists	Arrivals from abroad, by regions	nos, % share	Yes	A	World, regions of: Africa, Asia, Americas, EC, Oceania	WTO3 (3)
Tourists	Arrivals from abroad, by regions	nos, indices % change	Yes	A	World, major regions	WTO3 (1)
Tourists arrivals and earnings	By high, middle, low income	nos, US$, %	No		World	CS1 (17)
Tourists, by country or area of definition		nos	Yes	A	World	UN50 (139)
Tourists, by region of origin		nos	Yes	A	World	UN50 (138)
Tourists, method of arrival	By country, by mode of transport	nos	No		EC	EM1 (2305)
Travel arrangements, residents	Travelling within their own country, abroad. Arrangements made by: traveller, travel agency, tour operator, club, company, school, others	%	Yes	A	OECD	OECD30 (-)
Trips made, residents	Within their own country, abroad, by country	nos	Yes	A	OECD	OECD30 (-)

Subject	Categories	Units	Time series Yes/No Frequency		Territorial coverage	Source (Table no.)
44.3 EMPLOYMENT						
Accommodation establishments and other tourist facilities	Self-employed, employees, total by type of establishment, by country, region	nos	Yes	A	EC	EC78 (VI.1.1) EC78 (VI.1.2)
Employment statistics	By region, employees	US$	No		World	HI1 (I.10, II.10, III.10, IV.10, V.10)
Staff employed in tourism	By sex, by sector of tourist industry	nos, %	Yes	A	OECD	OECD46 (21)
44.4 FINANCIAL DATA						
44.4.1 Balance of Payments						
Tourism in the balance of payments	By country, by income, expenditure, balance	%		No	EC	EC35 (-)
Tourism in the balance of payments	Receipts, expenditure, %	nat curr			EC	EC79 (-)
Transport, passenger	Credit, debit, net by country	ECU	Yes	A	EC	EC78 (X.3.1)
Transport, passenger	Credit, debit, net geographical breakdown of payments by country or region, by country	ECU	Yes	A	EC	EC78 (X.4.1)
Transport, passenger	Credit, debit, net by country	ECU	Yes	A, M	EC	EC78 (X.3.3)
Transport, passenger	Credit, debit, net by country	ECU	Yes	A, Q	EC	EC78 (X.3.2)
Travel	Credit, debits, net	ECU	Yes	A	EC	EC78 (X.1.1)
Travel	Credit, debits, net	ECU	Yes	A, M	EC	EC78 (X.1.3)
Travel	Credit, debits, net	ECU	Yes	A, Q	EC	EC78 (X.1.2)
Travel	Credit, debits, net, geographical breakdown of payments by country or region, by country	ECU	Yes	A	EC	EC78 (X.2.1)
44.4.2 Expenditure						
Costs, hotels	By type, % change, ratios to revenue	nat curr %	No		EC	PKF1 (-)
Expenditure, residents	Travelling within their own country, abroad, total, per trip, by country	nat curr	Yes	A	OECD	OECD30 (-)
Expenditure, tourism	Trends, by selected economic groupings of countries	nos	Yes	A	World	WTO3 (pp 119-127)
Expenditures	By regions	US$, % share	Yes	A	World, regions of: Africa, Asia, Americas, Europe, Oceania	WTO3 (5)
Expenditures, fare	By country	US$	Yes	A	World	WTO3 (pp 166-168)
Expenditures, top spenders	Expenditures, annual growth rate, share of world total, by country	US$, %	No		World	WTO3 (p 132)
Expenditures, tourism	By country	US$	Yes	A	World	WTO3 (pp 162-165)
Fare payments, international	Receipts, expenditure	US$	Yes	A	OECD	OECD46 (16)

44 TOURISM

Subject	Categories	Units	Time series Yes/No	Frequency	Territorial coverage	Source (Table no.)
International fare expenditures		US$	Yes	A	World	WTO1 (-)
International tourism expenditures		US$	Yes	A	World	WTO1 (-)
International tourist		current US$	Yes	A, M	World	OECD30 (-)
International tourist		indices, nat curr, current US$	Yes	A	OECD	OECD30 (-)
Payments	Receipts, fare receipts, expenditures, fare expenditures, by regions	US$	Yes	A	World	WTO3 (pp 40-93)
Receipts and expenditure	By region	US$, %	Yes	A	OECD	OECD46 (18)
Tourism expenditure		ECU, %			EC	EC79 (-)
Tourism expenditure	By country	US$	No		EC	EM1 (2302)
Tourism in the economies of EC member states	Receipts, expenditure, GNP, employment	%			EC	EC79 (-)
Tourist (consumer), total	Residents/non-residents in the country, residents abroad	ECU	Yes	A	EC	EC78 (VIII.1.1)
Tourist consumer prices, index	Consumer prices, hotel rates, restaurant prices, overall tourist prices	indices	Yes	A	EC	EC78 (IX.1.1)
44.4.3 General						
Tourism balance sheet	GNP/employment, by country	nos, %			EC	EC79 (-)
Tourism selected statistics	Value, share and growth rate	US$, %	Yes	A	World, by development groups	UNCTAD5 (4.33)
44.4.4 Prices						
International tourist, real prices		indices constant US$	Yes	A	OECD	OECD30 (-)
Prices, tourism	Trends, by sector of tourist industry	%	Yes	A	OECD	OECD46 (22)
Tourist (consumer), total	Residents, non-residents in the country, residents abroad	ECU	Yes	A	EC	EC78 (VIII.1.1)
44.4.5 Receipts						
Fare payments, international	Receipts, expenditure	US$	Yes	A	OECD	OECD46 (16)
Foreign currency receipts	By country	US$	No		EC	EC18 (11.6)
International fare receipts		US$	Yes	A	World	WTO1 (-)
International tourism receipts		US$	Yes	A	World	WTO1 (-)
International tourism receipts	Total, % of world receipts, % change	US$, % indices	Yes	A	World,	WTO1 (-)
International tourist		current US$	Yes	A, M	World	OECD30 (-)
International tourist		indices nat curr current US$	Yes	A	OECD	OECD30 (-)
International tourist	Total, % share, % change, by country, region of origin, by country	nat curr, current US$, %	Yes	A	OECD	OECD30 (-)
International tourist receipts		indices, US$	Yes	A	OECD	OECD33 (11.4)
Receipts	By regions	%	Yes	A	World	WTO3 (pp 40-93)
Receipts	Per arrival, as % of GNP, as % of exports, as % of services by regions	US$, %	Yes	A	World	WTO3 (pp 40-93)
Receipts and expenditure	By region	US$, %	Yes	A	OECD	OECD46 (18)

Subject	Categories	Units	Time series Yes/No Frequency		Territorial coverage	Source (Table no.)
Receipts and exports	Receipts, exports, share of receipts in exports, by regions	US$, % share	Yes	A	World, developed market economies, developing countries and territories	WTO3 (7)
Receipts, fare	By country	US$	Yes	A	World	WTO3 (159-161)
Receipts, from tourism	By regions	US$, % share	Yes	A	World, regions of: Africa, Asia, Americas, Europe, Oceania	WTO3 (4)
Receipts, from tourism	By regions	US$, indices % change	Yes	A	World, major regions	WTO3 (1)
Receipts, top earners	Receipts, annual growth rate, share of world total, by country	US$, %	No		World	WTO3 (pp 131)
Receipts, tourism	By country	US$	Yes	A	World	WTO3 (pp 155-158)
Receipts, tourism	Trends, by selected economic groupings of countries	nos	Yes	A	World	WTO3 (pp 108-118)
Tourism in the economies of EC member states	Receipts, expenditure, GNP, employment	%			EC	EC79 (-)
Tourism receipts	By country	US$	No		EC	EM1 (2301)
Tourism receipts		ECU, %			EC	EC79 (-)
Tourism, development	Arrivals, receipts, exports, by region	%	Yes	A	World, developed market economies, developing countries and territories	WTO3 (8)
Tourism, development	Tourist arrivals, receipts from tourism, value of world exports	nos, indices US$	Yes	A	World	WTO3 (2)
Tourism, payments	Receipts, fare receipts, expenditures, fare expenditures, by regions	US$	Yes	A	World	WTO3 (pp 40-93)
Tourist receipts		US$	Yes	A	World	UN50 (139)
44.5 HOTEL INDUSTRY						
Amount per available room	By occupancy, room rate, revenues, expenses, profit, region	%, US$	No		World	HI1 (I.12, II.12, III.12, IV.12, V.12)
Analysis of undistributed operating expenses	By region, administration, property operation and maintenance, marketing	%, US$	No		World	HI1 (I.8, II.8 III.8, IV.8, V.8)
Composition of sales	By region, sales type	%	No		World	HI1 (I.6, II.6, III.6, IV.6, V.6)
Employment statistics	By region, employees	US$	No		World	HI1 (I.10, II.10, III.10, IV.10, V.10)
Fixed charges	By region, charge type	US$	No		World	HI1 (I.11, II.11, III.11, IV.11, V.11)
Food and beverage statistics	By region, food, room service, beverage sales	%, US$	No		World	HI1 (I.9, II.9, III.9, IV.9, V.9)
Income, hotels	Per room	nat curr	No		Europe	PKF1 (2)
Market data	By region, source of business, type of reservation, guest and method of payment	%	No		World	HI1 (I.3, II.3, III.3, IV.3, V.3)

Subject	Categories	Units	Time series Yes/No Frequency		Territorial coverage	Source (Table no.)
Nationality of guests	By region	%	No		World	HI1 (I.4, II.4, III.4, IV.4, V.4)
Performance measurements	By region, room use, nos guests per room, daily rate, income	%, US$	No		World	HI1 (I.5, II.5, III.5, IV.5, V.5)
Ratio to total sales	By occupancy, room rate, revenues, expenses, profit, region	%, US$	No		World	HI1 (I.13, II.13, III.13, IV.13, V.13)
Revenue, hotels	Per room, by type, % change	nat curr	No		Europe	PKF1 (-)
Telephone and minor operated departments	By region, sales, rentals and expenses	%, US$	No		World	HI1 (I.7, II.7, III.7, IV.7, V.7)
44.6 TOURIST FACILITIES						
Tourist facilities	Restaurants, cafes, travel agencies, car rental, tourist boards, pleasure ports, libraries, museums etc. by country, region	nos	Yes	A	EC regions	EC78 (V.1.1, V.1.2)
44.7 TRAVEL METHOD						
Air transport	Tourist arrivals, passengers carried, passenger, kilometres, by regions	nos	Yes	A	World	WTO3 (pp 40-93)
Tourist travel, international	Summary, by country	nos, US$, days	Yes	A	ESCAP	UN44
Transportation, residents	Travelling within their own country, abroad by: train, car, coach, bus, plane, boat, others, by country	%	Yes	A	OECD	OECD30 (-)

45 TRANSPORT

45.1 AIR
- 45.1.1 Fleets
- 45.1.2 Freight Traffic
- 45.1.3 General
- 45.1.4 Passenger Traffic
- 45.1.5 Services,Traffic

45.2 EMPLOYMENT

45.3 ENERGY
- 45.3.1 Consumption
- 45.3.2 Transportation

45.4 FINANCE AND INVESTMENT

45.5 GENERAL

45.6 INLAND WATERWAYS
- 45.6.1 Energy
- 45.6.2 Freight Traffic
- 45.6.3 General
- 45.6.4 Networks
- 45.6.5 Vessels

45.7 PIPELINES

45.8 PRICES

45.9 RAIL
- 45.9.1 Accidents
- 45.9.2 Energy
- 45.9.3 Financial Accounts
- 45.9.4 Freight Traffic
- 45.9.5 General
- 45.9.6 Networks
- 45.9.7 Passenger Traffic
- 45.9.8 Rolling Stock

45.10 ROAD

- 45.10.1 Accidents
- 45.10.2 Energy Consumption and Prices
- 45.10.3 Finance and Taxation
- 45.10.4 Freight Traffic
- 45.10.5 General
- 45.10.6 Networks
- 45.10.7 Passenger Traffic
- 45.10.8 Speed Limits
- 45.10.9 Vehicles

45.11 SEA

- 45.11.1 Accidents
- 45.11.2 Energy
- 45.11.3 Fleets
- 45.11.4 Freight Traffic
- 45.11.5 Vessels

Subject	Categories	Units	Time series Yes/No Frequency	Territorial coverage	Source (Table no.)
45.1 AIR - see also Section 3					
45.1.1 Fleets					
Aircraft		nos	No	EC	EC9 (7.6)
Airlines		nos	No	EC	EC9 (7.6)
Engine driven aircraft	Registered aircraft by maximum take-off weight	kilogrammes, tonnes	Yes A	Nordic countries	NCM1 (150)
45.1.2 Freight Traffic					
Aircraft departures	International, domestic	nos, % change	Yes A	World, IATA, IATA members	IATA1 (-)
Available tonne kilometres	By airline, region,	% change	Yes A	World	AEA1 (-)
Available tonne kilometres	International, domestic	nos, % change	Yes A	World, IATA, IATA members	IATA1 (-)
Freight	By country	tonnes	No	EC	EM1 (2211)
Freight carried	International, domestic	nos, % change	Yes A	World, IATA, IATA members	IATA1 (-)
Freight carried	Scheduled Services by national flag carrier	tonnes	No	EC	EC80 (6.4)
Freight load-factor		%	No	EC	EC9 (7.6)
Freight rate index, general	% of worldscale	indices	Yes A	World	OPEC1(66)
Freight rates, average spot	% of worldscale	dwt	Yes A	World	
Freight-tonne kilometres	By airline, region, % change	% tonne km	Yes A	World	AEA1 (-)
Freight-tonnes carried	International, domestic	nos, % change	Yes A	World, IATA, IATA members	IATA1 (-)
Goods, international	Entering the country, leaving the country	tonnes	Yes A	EC, USA	UN13 (4)
Hours flown	International, domestic	nos, % change	Yes A	World, IATA, IATA members	IATA1 (-)
Kilometres flown	International, domestic	nos, % change	Yes A	World, IATA, IATA members	IATA1 (-)
Overall load factor	By airline, region, points	% change	Yes A	World	AEA1 (-)
Scheduled freighter services	By cargo traffic and revenue, aircraft operating data	tonnes, km, %	Yes A	World	AEA2 (-)
Tonne-kilometres	International, domestic passengers, freight and mail	nos, % change	Yes A	World, IATA, IATA members	IATA1 (-)
Tonne-kilometres performed	Freight, mail, international, domestic	nos, % change	Yes A	World, IATA, IATA members	IATA1 (-)
Total-tonne kilometres	By airline, region,	% change	Yes A	World	AEA1 (-)
Weight load factor	International, domestic	nos, % change	Yes A	World, IATA, IATA members	IATA1 (-)
45.1.3 General					
Aircraft movements		nos	Yes I	EC	EC80 (1.6)
Aircraft tonne-kilometres	All services by national flag carrier	tonne-km	No	EC	EC80 (6.4)
Aircraft tonne-kilometres	International and national	tonne-km	No	EC	EC80 (6.3)
Aircraft tonne-kilometres	Non-scheduled services by national flag carrier	tonne-km	No	EC	EC80 (6.4)
Aircraft tonne-kilometres	Scheduled services by national flag carrier, on offer, run	tonne-km	No	EC	EC80 (6.4)
Aircraft weight load factor	Scheduled services by national flag carrier	%	No	EC	EC80 (6.4)
Aircraft-kilometres	All services by national flag carrier	aircraft-km	No	EC	EC80 (6.4)
Aircraft-kilometres	International and national	aircraft-km	No	EC	EC80 (6.3)

45 TRANSPORT

Subject	Categories	Units	Time series Yes/No Frequency		Territorial coverage	Source (Table no.)
Aircraft-kilometres	Non-scheduled services by national flag carrier	aircraft-km	No		EC	EC80 (6.4)
Aircraft-kilometres	Scheduled Services by national flag carrier	aircraft-km	No		EC	EC80 (6.4)
Civil aircraft on register	By type	nos	No		EC	EC80 (6.1)
National airlines, kilometres flown	By country, by passengers, goods carried	nos, % tonnes,	No		EC	EM1 (2212)
Scheduled services: aircraft departures	International, domestic	nos, % change	Yes	A	IATA, IATA members	IATA1 (-)
Scheduled services: hours flown	International, domestic	nos, % change	Yes	A	IATA, IATA members	IATA1 (-)
Scheduled services: kilometres flown	International, domestic	nos, % change	Yes	A	IATA, IATA members	IATA1 (-)
Total distance flown	By country	km	No		EC	EM1 (2209)
45.1.4 Passenger Traffic						
Aircraft seat-kilometres	Scheduled services by national flag carrier	seat-km	No		EC	EC80 (6.4)
Civil aviation passenger-kilometres	By country	nos	No		EC	EM1 (2210)
Passenger aircraft, scheduled and charter operations	By haul type, number of aircraft, revenue hours per aircraft, airline	nos, hours, km	Yes	A	World	AEA2 (-)
Passenger-kilometres	By airline, region,	%, change km	Yes	A	World	AEA1 (-)
Passenger load factor	Scheduled services by national flag carrier	%	No		EC	EC80 (6.4)
Passenger load factor	By airline, region, points	% change	Yes	A	World	AEA1 (-)
Passenger numbers		nos	Yes	I	EC	EC80 (1.6)
Passenger traffic, developments	By country market change, passengers	nos, %	No		EC	AEA4 (-)
Passenger traffic, predictions and forecast	By traffic, real GDP and yield	%	Yes	A	EC	AEA4 (-)
Passenger traffic		no-km	No		EC	EC9 (7.6)
Passenger transport, relative importance of different modes	Urban railways and tramways, road, air	passenger, km %	Yes	I	Bulgaria, Italy, Netherlands, Norway, Portugal, Sweden, USA	UN13 (3A)
Passenger-kilometres	All services by national flag carrier	passenger-km	No		EC	EC80 (6.4)
Passenger-kilometres	International and national	passenger-km	No		EC	EC80 (6.3)
Passenger-kilometres	Non-scheduled services by national flag carrier	passenger-km	No		EC	EC80 (6.4)
Passenger-kilometres	Scheduled services by national flag carrier	passenger-km	No		EC	EC80 (6.4)
Passengers, embarking and disembarking	Total services	nos	Yes	A	Nordic countries	NCM1 (151)
Passengers	By airline, region,	%, change nos	Yes	A	World	AEA1 (-)
Passengers carried	international and national	nos	No			EC80 (6.3)
Passengers carried	Scheduled services by national flag carrier	nos	No		EC	EC80 (6.4)
Scheduled passenger services	By passenger cargo, total traffic and revenue aircraft operating data	km, %, nos, US$, US cents, hours, tonnes	Yes	A	World	AEA2 (-)
Seat availability		no-km	No		EC	EC9 (7.6)
Seat kilometres	By airline, region,	%, change km	Yes	A	World	AEA1 (-)
All Services of All Commercial Airlines						
Available Seat-Kilometres	International, domestic	nos, % change	Yes	A	World, IATA, IATA members	IATA1 (-)
Available Tonne-Kilometres	International, domestic	nos, % change	Yes	A	World, IATA, IATA members	IATA1 (-)

Subject	Categories	Units	Time series Yes/No Frequency		Territorial coverage	Source (Table no.)
Available tonne-kilometres	International, domestic	nos, % change	Yes	A	World, IATA, IATA members	IATA1 (-)
Passenger load Factor	International, domestic	nos, % change	Yes	A	World, IATA, IATA members	IATA1 (-)
Passenger-kilometres Flown	International, domestic	nos, % change	Yes	A	World, IATA, IATA members	IATA1 (-)
Passenger-kilometres flown	International, domestic	nos, % change	Yes	A	World, IATA, IATA members	IATA1 (-)
Passengers carried	International, domestic	nos, % change	Yes	A	World, IATA, IATA members	IATA1 (-)
Tonne-kilometres performed	International, domestic. passengers, freight and mail	nos, % change	Yes	A	World, IATA, IATA members	IATA1 (-)
Tonne-kilometres performed	International, domestic. passengers, freight and mail	nos, % change	Yes	A	World, IATA, IATA members	IATA1 (-)
Weight load factor	International, domestic	nos, % change	Yes	A	World, IATA, IATA members	IATA1 (-)
Charter Airlines, All Services						
Available tonne-kilometres	International, domestic	nos, % change	Yes	A	World, IATA, IATA members	IATA1 (-)
Passenger-kilometres flown	International, domestic	nos, % change	Yes	A	World, IATA, IATA members	IATA1 (-)
Tonne-kilometres performed	International, domestic. passengers, freight and mail	nos, % change	Yes	A	World, IATA, IATA members	IATA1 (-)
Charter Services, Total						
Available tonne-kilometres	International, domestic	nos, % change	Yes	A	World, IATA, IATA members	IATA1 (-)
Passenger-kilometres flown	International, domestic	nos, % change	Yes	A	World, IATA, IATA members	IATA1 (-)
Tonne-kilometres performed	International, domestic. passengers, freight and mail	nos, % change	Yes	A	World, IATA, IATA members	IATA1 (-)
Scheduled Airlines, All Services						
Available tonne-kilometres	International, domestic	nos, % change	Yes	A	World, IATA, IATA members	IATA1 (-)
Passenger-kilometres flown	International, domestic	nos, % change	Yes	A	World, IATA, IATA members	IATA1 (-)
Tonne-kilometres performed	International, domestic. passengers, freight and mail	nos, % change	Yes	A	World, IATA, IATA members	IATA1 (-)
Scheduled Airlines, Charter Services						
Available tonne-kilometres	International, domestic	nos, % change	Yes	A	World, IATA, IATA members	IATA1 (-)
Passenger-kilometres flown	International, domestic passengers, freight and mail	nos, % change	Yes	A	World, IATA, IATA members	IATA1 (-)
Tonne-kilometres performed	International, domestic.	nos, % change	Yes	A	World, IATA, IATA members	IATA1 (-)
Scheduled Services						
Available seat-kilometres	International, domestic	nos, % change	Yes	A	World, IATA, IATA members	IATA1 (-)

Subject	Categories	Units	Time series Yes/No Frequency		Territorial coverage	Source (Table no.)
Available tonne-kilometres	International, domestic	nos, % change	Yes	A	World, IATA, IATA members	IATA1 (-)
Freight tonnes carried	International, domestic	nos, % change	Yes	A	World, IATA, IATA members	IATA1 (-)
Passenger load factor	International, domestic	nos, % change	Yes	A	World, IATA, IATA members	IATA1 (-)
Passenger-kilometres flown	International, domestic	nos, % change	Yes	A	World, IATA, IATA members	IATA1 (-)
Passengers carried	International, domestic	nos, % change	Yes	A	World, IATA, IATA members	IATA1 (-)
Tonne-kilometres performed	International, domestic. passengers, freight and mail	nos, % change	Yes	A	World, IATA, IATA members	IATA1 (-)
Weight load factor	International, domestic	nos, % change	Yes	A	World, IATA, IATA members	IATA1 (-)
45.1.5 Services, Traffic						
Air traffic	Aircraft-km passengers carried, passenger-km, tonne-km of freight	nos	Yes	A	Latin American and Caribbean countries	UN45 (358)
Civil aviation traffic	By countries	nos	No		The Americas and Australasia	MAC2 (G7)
Civil aviation traffic	By country, traffic type	ton-kilometre, nos	Yes	A	Africa and Asia	MAC1 (G6)
Commercial traffic at the main international airports	By airport	nos, tonnes	No		EC	EC35 (-)
Tonne-kilometres performed	International, domestic, passengers, freight and mail	nos, % change	Yes	A	World, IATA, IATA members	IATA1 (-)
Total, all services	By cargo traffic and revenue on all service	tonnes, km, % US$, US cents	Yes	A	World	AEA2 (-)
Total traffic and capacity		%, tonnes, km	Yes	A	World	AEA2 (-)
Traffic, commercial	By EC airport and type	nos, tonnes	No		EC	EC80 (6.2)
Traffic, civil aviation	Km flown on: total scheduled services, international scheduled services	nos	Yes	A	ASEAN	ASEANS1 (5.4.1)
Traffic	Passenger-km and cargo tonne-km flown on: total scheduled services, international scheduled services	nos	Yes	A	ASEAN	ASEANS1 (5.4.2)
Traffic	Passengers, goods	nos, tonnes, passenger-km, tonne-km	Yes	A	World	IRTU1
Traffic	By country, by type	nos	No		EC	EC18 (10.10)
Traffic between countries of AEA airlines	By on-flight origin and destination, passengers flights, freight, mail	nos, tonnes	No		Selected countries	AEA3 (-)
Traffic between countries of AEA airlines and other countries in the AEA	By on-flight origin and destination, passengers flights, freight, mail	nos, tonnes	No		Selected countries	AEA3 (-)
Traffic of Finnair	Kilometres flown, revenue, freight, mail	kilometres nos, tonnes	No		World	NCM1 (152)
Traffic of Icelandair	Kilometres flown, revenue, freight, mail	kilometres, nos, tonnes	No		World	NCM1 (153)

Subject	Categories	Units	Time series Yes/No Frequency		Territorial coverage	Source (Table no.)
Traffic of Scandinavian airlines systems	Kilometres flown, revenue, freight, mail	kilometres, nos, tonnes	No		World	NCM1 (154)
45.2 EMPLOYMENT						
Employment	By sector of transport industry, by country	nos	Yes	A	World	IRTU1
Employment	By transport type	nos	Yes	A	ECMT countries	ECMT2 (1-0-5)
Staff		nos	Yes	A	EC, USA, Canada	UN13 (10)
Staff	By railway, by general management, railway operations, other oper- ations, total staff strength, permanent staff, supplied by con tractors	nos	No		World	IUR1 (31)
45.3 ENERGY - see also Section 17						
45.3.1 Consumption						
Energy consumption	Forms of energy	TJ	Yes	A	EC, USA, Canada	UN13 (5)
45.3.2. Transportation						
Carrier fleet, combined	By size, 10,000 dwt and over	dwt	Yes	A	World	OPEC1(63)
Crude oil and petroleum product	By traffic Type	tonne-km	Yes	A	EC	EC80 (7.3)
Crude oil and petroleum product	By traffic Type	tonnes	Yes	A	EC	EC80 (7.2)
Freight rate Index, general	% of worldscale	indices	Yes	A	World	OPEC1 (66)
Freight rates, average spot	% of worldscale	dwt	Yes	A	World	
Liquid gas carrier fleet	By size and type	cu m	No		OPEC	OPEC1 (62)
Liquid gas carrier fleet	By size and type	cu m	No		World	OPEC1 (61)
45.4 FINANCE AND INVESTMENT						
Expenditure on transport and insurance	% of f.o.b value of total imports of goods and services	%	Yes	A	Latin American and Caribbean countries	UN45 (95)
Income from transport and insurance	% of f.o.b value of total exports of goods and services	%	Yes	A	Latin American and Caribbean countries	UN45 (94)
Inland transport investment (equipment and infrastructure)	At current and 1985 exchange rates and prices	nat curr, ECU	Yes	A	ECMT countries	ECMT2 (1-0-1 to 1-4)
Travel expenses	% of f.o.b value of total imports of goods and services	%	Yes	A	Latin American and Caribbean countries	UN45 (97)
Travel income	% of f.o.b value of total imports of goods and services	%	Yes	A	Latin American and Caribbean countries	UN45 (96)
45.5 GENERAL						
Expenditure, transport	Total and by type	ECU	Yes	A	EC	EC80 (1.7)
Freight transport, domestic	By means of transportation	tonnes, kilometre	No		Nordic countries	NCM1 (156)
Goods and passenger transport	By country, by road, rail, inland waterways	tonnes, %	No		EC	EC35 (-)

45 TRANSPORT

Subject	Categories	Units	Time series Yes/No Frequency		Territorial coverage	Source (Table no.)
Means of transport	By country, by means	%	No		EC	EC72 (11.7)
Sea and air transport	Goods, passengers	tonnes, nos	No		EC	EC69 (VI.5)
Traffic, use of ECMT multilateral quota		tonne-km	Yes	5 yr	EC	ECMT3
Transport	International maritime, civil aviation traffic, registration of new vehicles, overseas migration		Yes	M	Asia and Pacific	UN43
Transport equipment	By country	nos	No		EC	EC35 (-)
45.6 INLAND WATERWAYS						
45.6.1 Energy						
Energy consumption	Forms of energy	TJ	Yes	A	EC, USA, Canada	UN13 (5)
45.6.2 Freight Traffic						
Danube traffic	Internal and international, country of destination	tonnes,	Yes	A		UN13 (23) UN13 (24)
Flow of goods by waterway		tonnes	Yes		EC and other countries	EC69 (VI.4)
Freight, market share of various modes	Rail, road, inland waterways	tonne-km	Yes	5 yr	EC	ECMT3
Freight	Rail, roads inland waterways pipelines	tonne-km	Yes	5 yr	EC	ECMT3
Freight transport	By ranges of distance	tonnes, tonne-km	Yes	A	Austria, Belgium, France, Germany, Italy, Netherlands, Yugoslavia	UN13 (21)
Freight transport	Entering the country, leaving the country	tonnes, km tonne-km	Yes	A	EC, USA	UN13 (20)
Goods, international	Entering the country, leaving the country entering and leaving, commodity group and mode of transport	tonnes	Yes	A	EC, USA	UN13 (4, 29)
Goods, international	Entering the country, leaving the country	tonnes	Yes	A	EC, USA	UN13 (4)
Goods carried		tonnes,	No		EC	EC9 (7.5)
Goods traffic	By type	tonne-km	Yes	A	EC	EC80 (4.11)
Goods traffic	By type	tonnes	Yes	A	EC	EC80 (4.10)
Goods transport, international	By traffic relations and NST, R chapter	tonnes	No		EC	EC80 (4.12)
Goods transported	National and International	tonnes, tonne-km	Yes	I	ECMT countries	ECMT2 (4-1-1)
Goods transported international	All vessels irrespective of registration country	tonnes	Yes	A	ECMT countries	ECMT2 (4-1-2)
Inland freight	By type of transport, length of rail, road, waterway	km, tonne-km,	No		Selected countries	UN22 (I-1.6.2)
Inland freight	By type of transport	km, tonne-km, length of rail, road, waterway	No		Selected countries	UN22 (I-1.6.2)
Inland freight transport, relative importance of different modes	Rail, road, pipelines inland waterways	% tonnes and % tonne-km	Yes	I	EC, USA	UN13 (3B)
Inland navigation traffic	By countries	tons, tonnes, km	Yes	A	EC	MAC3 (F5)
Inland waterway traffic	By country, by type	nos	No		EC	EC18 (10.7)
Traffic, total goods		tonnes	Yes	I	EC	EC80 (1.4)
Inland waterways	Goods loaded, unloaded	tonnes	Yes	A	World	IRTU1

Subject	Categories	Units	Time series Yes/No Frequency	Territorial coverage	Source (Table no.)
International traffic	By country and nationality of vessel	tonnes, km	No	EC	EC12 (2.3-2.4)
International traffic	By country and group of goods	tonnes, km	No	EC	EC12 (2.1-2.2)
International traffic	By link	km	No	EC	EC12 (2.6)
International traffic	By link and group of goods	tonnes	No	EC	EC12 (2.5.2)
International traffic	By link and NST, R chapter	tonnes	No	EC	EC12 (2.5.1)
Load capacity	Self-propelled, lighters and barges	tonnes	Yes I	EC	EC80 (1.4)
National, international and transit traffic	By group of goods	tonnes, km	No	EC	EC12 (1.1-1.2)
National, international and transit traffic	By nationality of vessel	tonnes, km	No	EC	EC12 (1.3-1.4)
National and international traffic	By link	tonnes	Yes M	EC	EC12 (1.6)
National traffic	By distance class and group of goods	tonnes, km	No	EC	EC12 (4.1-4.2)
National traffic	By region	tonnes	No	EC	EC12 (5.1)
National traffic	By region and group of goods	tonnes	No	EC	EC12 (5.2)
North America canal traffic	By countries	nos	No	The Americas and Australasia	MAC2 (G5)
Rhine traffic	At German-Dutch frontier by type	tonnes	Yes I	ECMT countries	ECMT2 (4-1-3)
Rhine traffic	National and international	tonnes, tonne-km tonne, km	Yes A		UN13 (22)
Total traffic	By type of vessel	tonnes, km	No	EC	EC12 (1.5)
Traffic, length and density		km, nos, tonnes, tonne-km	No	EC	EC80 (4.1)
Transit traffic	By country and nationality of vessel	tonnes, km	No	EC	EC12 (3.3-3.4)
Transit traffic	By country and group of goods	tonnes, km	No	EC	EC12 (3.1-3.2)
45.6.3 General					
Goods transport, enterprises		nos	No	EC	EC80 (4.9)
Inland passenger	By type of transport	nos	No	Selected countries	UN22 (I-1.6.1)
Inland passenger	By type of transport	nos	No	Selected countries	UN22 (I-1.6.1)
Tonne-kilometres hauled		tonne-km	Yes I	EC	EC80 (1.4)
45.6.4 Networks					
Length		km	No	EC	EC9 (7.5)
Length of transport networks	By country, by motorways, other roads, railways, inland waterways	km	No	EC	EC35 (-)
Navigable length	Kind of waterway and capacity of craft	km	Yes A	EC, USA	UN13 (16)
Navigable waterway length		km	Yes I	EC	EC80 (1.4)
Navigable waterway length	By group	km	No	EC	EC80 (4.2)
Transport networks	Railways, inland waterways, roads	km	No	EC	EC69 (VI.1)
Waterway length	By craft carrying capacity	km	Yes I	ECMT countries	ECMT2 (4-2-1)
45.6.5 Vessels - see also Section 41					
Craft in service	Number and capacity by type, by age and by cargo capacity	nos, tonnes	Yes I	ECMT countries	ECMT2 (4-3-1 to 4-3-3)
Craft in service	Type of craft	nos, tonnes, kW	Yes A	EC, USA	UN13 (17)

45 TRANSPORT

Subject	Categories	Units	Time series Yes/No Frequency		Territorial coverage	Source (Table no.)
Craft placed in service during year	Type of craft, new and used	nos, tonnes kW	Yes	A	EC, USA	UN13 (18)
Craft placed in service during year	Type of craft and year of construction	% by power, % by carrying capacity	Yes	A	EC, USA	UN13 (19)
Fleet change	By cause and vessel type	tonnes, kW	No		EC	EC80 (4.8)
Goods-carrying vessels, total	By type and year of construction	nos	Yes	I	EC	EC80 (4.7)
Goods-carrying vessels		nos, capacity	No		EC	EC9 (7.5)
Goods-carrying vessels		nos	Yes	I	EC	EC80 (1.4)
Goods-carrying vessels	By type, tugs and pushers, number	nos	Yes	I	EC	EC80 (4.3)
Goods-carrying vessels	By type, tugs and pushers, capacity	tonnes	Yes	I	EC	EC80 (4.4)
Goods-carrying vessels	By type and load-carrying capacity	nos, tonnes	No		EC	EC80 (4.5-4.6)
Load-carrying capacity, goods vessels		tonnes	Yes	I	EC	EC80 (1.4)
Load-carrying capacity, all vessels		tonnes	Yes	I	EC	EC80 (1.4)
45.7 PIPELINES						
Crude oil and refined products		tonne-km,	Yes	I	ECMT countries	ECMT2 (5-1-1)
Energy consumption	Forms of energy	TJ	Yes	A	EC, USA, Canada	UN13 (5)
Freight	Rail, roads inland waterways pipelines	tonne-km	Yes	5 yr	EC	ECMT3
Inland freight transport, relative importance of different modes	Rail, road, pipelines inland waterways	% tonnes and % tonne-km	Yes	I	EC, USA	UN13 (3B)
Length in service		km	Yes	I	ECMT countries	ECMT2 (5-2-1)
Oil pipeline length		km	Yes	A	EC	EC80 (7.1)
Pipelines, oil		km, tonnes, tonne-km	Yes	A	EC, USA	UN13 (28)
Pipelines, product	Length, diameter, operator	miles, inches	No		OPEC	OPEC1 (70)
Pipelines, gas	Length, diameter, operator	miles, inches	No		OPEC	OPEC1 (69)
Pipelines, crude oil	Length, diameter, operator	miles, inches	No		OPEC	OPEC1 (68)
Pipelines, long-distance	By country, by length, product, throughput	km, tonnes	No		EC	EC18 (10.11)
45.8 PRICES - see also Section 37						
Transport, communications		indices	Yes	A	EC, USA, Japan	EC9 (2.43)
45.9 RAIL						
45.9.1 Accidents - see also Section 1						
Accidents, killed or injured		nos	No		EC	EC80 (2.22)
45.9.2 Energy						
Energy consumption	Forms of energy	TJ	Yes	A	EC, USA, Canada	UN13 (5)
Tractive stock, energy consumption	By type total and unit consumption per 1000 tonne-km	tonnes, kWh	No		EC	EC80 (2.20)

Subject	Categories	Units	Time series Yes/No Frequency		Territorial coverage	Source (Table no.)
Energy consumption	Diesel, electricity and coal	tonnes, kWh	Yes	I	ECMT countries	ECMT2 (2-4-1)
45.9.3 Financial Accounts						
Balance sheet	By railway, by currency, assets, liabilities	nat curr	No		World	IUR1 (71)
Costs and revenues, specific	By railway, by currency, specific costs, specific receipts	nat curr	No		World	IUR1 (72)
Revenue-earning passenger traffic	By railway, by rail traffic, road traffic, shipping services, all traffic	nos, km, tonnes	No		World	IUR1 (51)
45.9.4 Freight Traffic						
Container traffic		nos, tonnes	Yes	I	EC, USA, Canada	UN13 (26)
Freight, market share of various modes	Rail, road, inland waterways	tonne-km	Yes	5 yr	EC	ECMT3
Freight		tonnes, km	Yes	A	EC,	EC9 (7.4)
Freight	Rail, roads inland waterways pipelines	tonne-km	Yes	5 yr	EC	ECMT3
Freight traffic	By railway, by rail traffic, road traffic, shipping services, all traffics	nos, km, tonnes, tonnes-km	No		World	IUR1 (61)
Freight traffic	National and international	tonnes, tonne-km	Yes	I	ECMT countries	ECMT2 (2-1-3)
Freight traffic and transport		nos, km, tonnes, days, %, indices	Yes	A	EC, USA, Canada	UN13 (8B)
Freight traffic on railways	By countries	nos	No		The Americas and Australasia	MAC2 (G2)
Freight traffic on railways	By countries	tonnes, km,	Yes	A	EC	MAC3 (F2)
Freight traffic on railways	By country	tonnes, ton-kilometres	Yes	A	Africa and Asia	MAC1 (G2)
Freight transport by ranges of distance		tonnes, %, tonne-km, %	Yes	A	EC	UN13 (9)
Goods, international	Entering the country, leaving the country	tonnes	Yes	A	EC, USA	UN13 (4)
Goods traffic, national	By distance	tonnes, tonne-km	Yes	A	EC	EC80 (2.18)
Goods traffic	By loading type	tonnes	Yes	A	EC	EC80 (2.17)
Goods traffic	Total, internal, received and dispatched to foreign countries and transit traffic	tonnes	Yes	A	EC	EC80 (2.15)
Goods traffic	Total, transit excluded	tonnes	Yes	I	EC	EC80 (1.2)
Goods transport, international	By traffic relations and NST, R chapters	tonnes	No		EC	EC80 (2.16)
Gross hauled tonne-kilometres of trains,	By railway, by rail gauge, type of traction	tonne-km	No		World	IUR1 (42)
Inland freight transport, relative importance of different modes	Rail, road, pipelines inland waterways	% tonnes and % tonne-km	Yes	I	EC, USA	UN13 (3B)
International freight traffic	For goods loaded to and from and in transit from foreign networks	tonnes,	Yes	I	ECMT countries	ECMT2 (2-1-4)
International traffic	By country and group of goods	tonnes, km	No		EC	EC13 (2.1-2.2)
International traffic	By link	km	No		EC	EC13 (2.4)
International traffic	By link and group of goods	tonnes	No		EC	EC13 (2.3.2)

45 TRANSPORT

Subject	Categories	Units	Time series Yes/No Frequency		Territorial coverage	Source (Table no.)
International traffic	By link and NST, R chapter 5	tonnes	No		EC	EC13 (2.3.1)
Motor vehicles traffic, accompanied	Units loaded, passengers Conveyed and net tonne-kilometres	nos, tonne-km	Yes	A	EC	EC80 (2.19)
National and international traffic	By group of goods	tonnes, km	No		EC	EC13 (1.1)
National and international traffic	By link	tonnes km	Yes	M	EC	EC13 (1.2)
National traffic	By distance class and group of goods	tonnes, km	No		EC	EC13 (4.1-4.2)
National traffic	By region	tonnes	No		EC	EC13 (5.1)
National traffic	By region and group of goods	tonnes	No		EC	EC13 (5.2)
Rail and road	Passengers, goods, rail, road journeys, by country	nos, tonnes	Yes	A	World	IRTU1
Railway freight carried	By country	tonnes	No		EC	EM1 (2207)
Railway traffic		net-tonne km	Yes	A	West Africa	UN3 (6-1)
Railway traffic		net-tonne Km	Yes	A	Central Africa	UN5 (6-1)
Railway traffic		net-tonne km	Yes	A	East and Southern Africa	UN4 (6-1)
Railway traffic		net-tonne km tonne-km	Yes	A	North Africa	UN2 (6-1)
Tonne-kilometres worked		tonne-km	Yes	I	EC	EC80 (1.2)
Traffic	Goods, length of haul, revenue	kilometres tonnes	Yes	A	Nordic countries	NCM1 (143)
Traffic	Passenger, freight	nos, tonnes-km	Yes	A	World	UN50 (132)
Traffic	Passenger, freight	nos, tonnes-km	Yes	A, M	World	UN35 (48)
Traffic	Passenger-km, net tonne-km	nos	Yes	A	ASEAN	ASEANS1 (5.1.3)
Traffic	Passengers, goods by country	tonnes, nos, passenger-km, tonne-km	Yes	A	World	IRTU1
Transit traffic	By country	tonnes, km	No		EC	EC13 (3.2-3.3)
Transit traffic	By group of goods	tonnes, km	No		EC	EC13 (3.1)
45.9.5 General						
Amount of traffic carried on the railways	By country, by type of traffic	nos	No		EC	EC18 (10.2)
Hauled vehicle-kilometres	Total and by type	vehicle-km	No		EC	EC80 (2.10)
National, international and transit traffic	By container and road, rail route	tonnes, nos	No		EC	EC13 (1.3)
Railway statistics of major national carriers	By country, by number of locomotives, passengers, journey length, goods carried	nos, km.	No		EC	EM1 (2208)
Railways	Length, rolling stock, traffic	km, nos, tonnes	Yes	A	North Africa	UN2 (26)
Railways	Length, rolling stock, traffic	km, nos, tonnes	Yes	A	West Africa	UN3 (26)
Railways	Length, rolling stock, traffic	km, nos, tonnes	Yes	A	East and Southern Africa	UN4 (26)
Railways	Length, rolling stock, traffic	km, nos, tonnes	Yes	A	Central Africa	UN5 (26)
Tonne-kilometres worked	By traffic type and mode of traction	tonne-km	No		EC	EC80 (2.12)
Tractive stock kilometres	Total and by type	vehicle-km	No		EC	EC80 (2.9)
Train kilometres	By railway, by rail gauge, type of traction	km	No		World	IUR1 (41)
Train-kilometres	By traffic type and mode of traction	train-km	No		EC	EC80 (2.11)

Subject	Categories	Units	Time series Yes/No Frequency		Territorial coverage	Source (Table no.)
Transport performance	Electric and diesel	train-km, tonne-km	Yes	I	ECMT countries	ECMT2 (2-1-6)
45.9.6 Networks						
Length		km	No		EC, USA, USSR, Canada Japan	EC9 (7.3)
Length and rolling stock	Total, state, private, carriages, goods	kilometres, nos	Yes	A	Nordic countries	NCM1 (141)
Length of public railway network operated	By country	km	No		EC	EM1 (2205)
Length of rail network	By country	km	No		EC	EC18 (10.1)
Length of railway line open	By countries	nos	No		The Americas and Australasia	MAC2 (G1)
Length of railway line open	By country	kilometres	Yes	A	Africa and Asia	MAC1 (G1)
Length of transport networks	By country, by motorways, other roads, railways, inland waterways	km	No		EC	EC35 (-)
Line length		km	Yes	I	EC	EC80 (1.2)
Line length	By current systems in use	km	No		EC	EC80 (2.3)
Line length worked	By number of tracks and traction type	km	Yes	A	EC	EC80 (2.1)
Line length worked	By traction type and nature of traffic	km	No		EC	EC80 (2.2)
Lines	By railway, by direction of train, rail gauge, length of lines worked at end of year, electrified operations, other operations	m, km	No		World	IUR1 (11)
Network length	Total and electrified	km	Yes	I	ECMT countries	ECMT2 (2-2-1)
Networks, other	Companies, line length, and locomotive numbers by type	nos	Yes	A	EC	EC80 (2.23)
Networks, other	Passenger carriages and goods wagons and passengers carried	nos	Yes	A	EC	EC80 (2.23)
Networks, other	Passenger kilometres, goods train haulage tonne-km	passenger-km	Yes	A	EC	EC80 (2.23)
Networks, other	Goods transport	tonnes	Yes	A	EC	EC80 (2.23)
Networks	Electrified, non-passenger,	passenger, km no. tracks	Yes	A	EC, USA Canada	UN13 (6)
Rail network, length	By country	km	No		EC	EC72 (9.17)
Rail network	Rolling stock, traffic, length of lines by country	km, nos, passenger-km, tonne-km	Yes	A	World	IRTU1
Railway network, total length		km	Yes	A	Latin American and Caribbean countries	UN45 (355)
Railways, length		km	Yes	A	ASEAN	ASEANS1 (5.1.1)
Railways	Length, rolling stock, traffic	km, nos, tonnes	Yes	A	North Africa	UN2 (26)
Railways	Length, rolling stock, traffic	km, nos, tonnes	Yes	A	West Africa	UN3 (26)
Railways	Length, rolling stock, traffic	km, nos, tonnes	Yes	A	East and Southern Africa	UN4 (26)
Transport networks	Railways, inland waterways, roads	km	No		EC	EC69 (VI.1)
45.9.7 Passenger Traffic						
International passenger traffic		nos passenger-km	Yes	I	ECMT countries	ECMT2 (2-1-2)

45 TRANSPORT

Subject	Categories	Units	Time series Yes/No Frequency		Territorial coverage	Source (Table no.)
Passenger kilometres		passenger-km	Yes	I	EC	EC80 (1.2)
Passenger numbers	Total and of which in second class	nos	Yes	A	EC	EC80 (2.13)
Passenger seat-kilometres		seat-km	Yes	A	EC	EC80 (2.13)
Passenger traffic, international	Total and by class	nos	No		EC	EC80 (2.14)
Passenger traffic		nos, km	Yes	A	EC, USA, Canada	UN13 (8A)
Passenger traffic	National and international traffic	nos, passenger-km	Yes	I	ECMT countries	ECMT2 (2-1-1)
Passenger traffic on railways	By countries	nos	No		The Americas and Australasia	MAC2 (G3)
Passenger traffic on railways	By country	nos, passenger-km	Yes	A	Africa and Asia	MAC1 (G3)
Passenger transport, relative importance of different modes	Urban railways and tramways, road, air	passenger-km %	Yes	I	Bulgaria, Italy, Netherlands, Norway, Portugal, Sweden, USA	UN13 (3A)
Passenger-kilometres	Total and of which in second class	passenger-km	Yes	A	EC	EC80 (2.13)
Passenger-km, inland		%	Yes	A	Bulgaria, Italy, Netherlands, Norway, Portugal, Sweden, USA	UN13 (3A)
Passenger-km		nos	No		EC, USA, USSR, Canada, Japan	EC9 (7.3)
Passengers, domestic conveyance	By means of transportation	per capita kilometre	No		Nordic countries	NCM1 (155)
Passengers carried		nos	Yes	I	EC	EC80 (1.2)
Rail and road	Passengers, goods, rail, road journeys, by country	nos, tonnes	Yes	A	World	IRTU1
Railway passenger-km	By country	nos	No		EC	EM1 (2206)
Railway traffic	Tonne-km, passenger-km,	nos	Yes	A	Latin American and Caribbean countries	UN45 (356)
Traffic	Passenger, freight	nos	Yes	A	World	UN50 (132)
Traffic	Passenger, freight	nos tonnes-km	Yes	A, M	World	UN35 (48)
Traffic	Passenger, length of journey, revenue	nos kilometres	Yes	A	Nordic countries	NCM1 (142)
Traffic	Passenger-km, net tonne-km	nos	Yes	A	ASEAN	ASEANS1 (5.1.3)
Traffic	Passengers, goods by country	tonnes, nos, passenger-km, tonne-km	Yes	A	World	IRTU1
45.9.8 Rolling Stock						
Double-stack trains, operation	By operator, route and frequency	nos	No		USA, Canada and Mexico	UNCTAD2 (34)
Freight transport stock	By railway, by rail gauge, stock at end of year, available annual mean fleet strength	nos, tonnes	No		World	IUR1 (23)
Length of lines and rolling stock	Total, state, private, carriages, goods	kilometres nos	Yes	A	Nordic countries	NCM1 (141)
Passenger transport stock	By railway, by rail gauge, stock at end of year, available annual mean fleet strength	nos	No		World	IUR1 (22)

Subject	Categories	Units	Time series Yes/No	Frequency	Territorial coverage	Source (Table no.)
Rolling stock, passenger	Number of seats by type	nos	No		EC	EC80 (2.7)
Rolling stock, goods	By type of wagon, number and capacity	nos, tonnes	No		EC	EC80 (2.8)
Rolling stock	By type, passenger and goods	nos	Yes	A	EC	EC80 (2.6)
Rolling stock	By type	nos	No		ECMT countries	ECMT2 (2-3-1)
Rolling stock	Locomotive, passenger cars, wagons	nos	Yes	A	ASEAN	ASEANS1 (5.1.2)
Rolling stock	nos, tonne-traffic	km, passenger-km	Yes	A	ESCAP region,	UN44 (p46, 11)
Rolling stock kilometres	By railway, by rail gauge, types of traction, wagons	km	No		World	IUR1 (43)
Tractive power	By traction type	kW, h.p.	No		EC	EC80 (2.5)
Tractive stock	By railway, by rail gauge, fleet strength at end of year, annual mean fleet strength	nos, kW	No		World	IUR1 (21)
Tractive stock	By traction type	nos	Yes	A	EC	EC80 (2.4)
Vehicles		nos, kW tonnes	Yes	A	EC, USA, Canada	UN13 (7)

45.10 ROAD

45.10.1 Accidents - see also Section 1

Subject	Categories	Units	Time series Yes/No	Frequency	Territorial coverage	Source (Table no.)
Accident severity indices killed per 1000 casualties	By road user category number	rate	No		ECMT countries	ECMT1 (6,7)
Accidents, killed or injured	By age	nos	Yes	A	Nordic countries	NCM1 (147)
Accidents, killed or injured	By category of road user	nos	Yes	A	Nordic countries	NCM1 (148)
Accidents, killed and injured, deaths		nos	Yes	5 yr	EC	ECMT3
Accidents, killed or injured		nos	Yes	I	EC	EC80 (1.3)
Accidents, killed or injured		nos	Yes	A	EC	EC80 (3.13)
Accidents, personal injury	Total and of which in built-up areas	nos	Yes	A	EC	EC80 (3.13)
Accidents, traffic casualties	By transport type	nos	No		EC	EC80 (3.14)
Accidents, traffic casualties	By sex and age group	nos	No		EC	EC80 (3.15)
Accidents, traffic casualties	By sex and age group	nos per 10 000 inhabitants	No		EC	EC80 (3.16)
Accidents, traffic casualties	By transport type and age	nos	No		EC	EC80 (3.17)
Accidents, elements involved	By pedestrian and vehicle type	nos	No		EC	EC80 (3.18)
Accidents	By country, by accidents, injuries, fatalities	nos	No		EC	EC18 (10.6)
Accidents	By country, injury to persons, number injured, number killed, rate per vehicle, km, % injury accidents	nos, vehicle, km, %	Yes	A	World	IRF1 (VII)
Accidents	Personal injury, death,	nos	Yes	A		EC9 (7.11)
Accidents causing casualties		%	No		ECMT countries	ECMT1 (1C)
Accidents causing casualties	By type of road	nos	No		ECMT countries	ECMT1 (10)

45 TRANSPORT

Subject	Categories	Units	Time series Yes/No	Frequency	Territorial coverage	Source (Table no.)
Accidents causing casualties	On motorways, overall road network, deaths within 30 days on motorways, overall road network casualties on motorways overall road network deaths within 30 days, 1000 accidents causing casualties on motorways deaths within 30 days, 1000 accidents causing casualties on other road deaths within 30 days, 100km of motorways	%, nos	No		ECMT countries	ECMT1 (11)
Accidents with personal injury	Traffic units involved	nos	Yes	A	Nordic countries	NCM1 (149)
Casualties, accidents causing casualties		ratio	No		ECMT countries	ECMT1 (3)
Deaths, number of road motor vehicles		ratio	No		ECMT countries	ECMT1 (3)
Killed		nos, % change	Yes	A	ECMT countries	ECMT1 (1A)
Killed	By road-user category	%	No		ECMT countries	ECMT1 (4)
Killed or injured		nos, % change	Yes	A	ECMT countries	ECMT1 (1B)
Killed or injured	By road-user category	%	No		ECMT countries	ECMT1 (5)
Road vehicle population	By vehicle category	nos	No		ECMT countries	ECMT1 (8)
45.10.2 Energy Consumption and Prices - see also Section 17						
Energy consumption	By mode	TOE	Yes	I	OECD	OECD33 (10.4)
Energy consumption	By mode	TOE	Yes	I	OECD	OECD33 (10.4)
Energy consumption	Diesel and petrol	toe	Yes	I	ECMT countries	ECMT2 (3-4-1)
Energy consumption	Forms of energy	TJ	Yes	A	EC, USA, Canada	UN13 (5)
Motor fuels	By country, fuel type, price, taxation, total consumption	%, tonnes, l	Yes	A	World	IRF1 (VI)
Road transport, energy consumption		toe, %, tonnes, TJ	Yes	A	EC	EC80 (3.11)
Road transport, retail fuel prices	By fuel type	nat curr, ECU	Yes	A	EC	EC80 (3.12)
45.10.3 Finance and Taxation						
Expenditure	Urban roads, non-urban roads	nat curr	Yes	A	EC, USA, Canada	UN13 (12)
Receipts from user taxation, annual	By country, tax type, GNP	%, units of account	Yes	A	World	IRF1 (X)
Road expenditure	By country, authority	SDR	Yes	A	World	IRF1 (XI)
Taxation of five common categories of vehicles, annual	By type	km, tonnes	No		Selected countries	IRF1 (IX)
45.10.4 Freight Traffic						
Flow of goods	From, to	tonnes	No		EC	EC69 (VI.2)
Freight, market share of various modes	Rail, road, inland waterways	tonne-km	Yes	5 yr	EC	ECMT3
Freight, total	All vehicles, hired vehicles	tonnes	Yes	A	EC, USA, Canada	UN13 (15)
Freight, international	Entered, left, transit	tonnes	Yes	A	EC, USA, Canada	UN13 (15)
Freight	Rail, roads, inland waterways pipelines	tonne-km	Yes	5 yr	EC	ECMT3
Freight traffic	National and international haulage	tonnes, tonne-km	Yes	I	ECMT countries	ECMT2 (3-1-2)

Subject	Categories	Units	Time series Yes/No Frequency		Territorial coverage	Source (Table no.)
Goods, international	Entering the country, leaving the country	tonnes	Yes	A	EC, USA	UN13 (4)
	entering and leaving, commodity group and mode of transport		Yes	A	EC, USA	UN13 (29)
Goods traffic, total		nos	Yes	I	EC	EC80 (1.3)
Goods traffic, national	By NST, R chapter	tonnes	Yes	A	EC	EC80 (3.7)
Goods traffic, national	By NST, R chapter	tonne-km	Yes	A	EC	EC80 (3.8)
Goods traffic, national	Total and of which for hire or reward	tonnes, tonne-km	Yes	A	EC	EC80 (3.9)
Goods transport, international	By traffic relations and and NST, R chapter	tonnes	No		EC	EC80 (3.10)
Goods transported by road	By country	tonnes	No		EC	EM1 (2204)
Inland freight transport, relative importance of different modes	Rail, road, pipelines, inland waterways	% tonnes, and % tonne-km	Yes	I	EC, USA	UN13 (3B)
International goods transport	By vehicles irrespective of registration country	tonnes	Yes	I	ECMT countries	ECMT2 (3-1-3)
International goods transport	By vehicles registered in the country	tonnes	Yes	A	ECMT countries	ECMT2 (3-1-4)
International goods transport	Loading and unloading at origin and destination for vehicles irrespective of registration country	tonnes	Yes	A	ECMT countries	ECMT2 (3-1-5)
International traffic, total	By country and group of goods	tonnes	No		EC	EC14 (1.3)
International traffic	By country and group of goods (own account)	tonnes	No		EC	EC14 (1.1)
International traffic	By country and group of goods (hire or reward)	tonnes	No		EC	EC14 (1.2)
International traffic	By country and type of carriage	km	No		EC	EC14 (1.4)
International traffic	By link	km	No		EC	EC14 (1.6)
International traffic	By link and NST, R chapter	tonnes	No		EC	EC14 (1.5.1)
International traffic	By link and group of goods	tonnes	No		EC	EC14 (1.5.2)
National traffic	By group of goods and type of carriage	tonnes, km	No		EC	EC14 (2.1)
National traffic	By length of journey and group of goods	tonnes,	No		EC	EC14 (2.2)
National traffic	By region	tonnes	No		EC	EC14 (3.1)
National traffic	By region and group of goods	tonnes	No		EC	EC14 (3.2)
Rail and road	Passengers, goods, rail, road journeys, by country	nos, tonnes	Yes	A	World	IRTU1
Traffic, goods	Inland, international by country	tonnes	Yes	A	World	IRTU1
Traffic, freight	Goods carried, by country	tonnes, km	Yes	A	World	IRTU1
Transport	Merchant fleet, commercial vehicles in use	dwt, nos	No		World	UNCTAD1 (6.10B)
45.10.5 General						
Motorway traffic, total traffic		%	No		ECMT countries	ECMT1 (10)
National, international and transit traffic	By container and road, rail route	tonnes, nos	No		EC	EC13 (1.3)
Road traffic	By country, traffic volume, distance, travelled by type, route type	nos, %, km tonnes	Yes	A	World	IRF1 (V)

Subject	Categories	Units	Time series Yes/No	Frequency	Territorial coverage	Source (Table no.)
Traffic carried on the road network	By country, by type of traffic	nos	No		EC	EC18 (10.5)
45.10.6 Networks						
International network length	"E" Routes	km	Yes	I	ECMT countries	ECMT2 (3-2-2)
Length of motorways		km, %	No		Selected countries	UN22 (I-1.6.3)
Length of transport networks	By country, by motorways, other roads, railways, inland waterways	km	No		EC	EC35 (-)
Motorway length		km	Yes	I	EC	EC80 (1.3)
Motorway network, length		km	No		ECMT countries	ECMT1 (10)
Motorway network, length		km, %	No		Selected countries	UN22 (I-1.6.3)
Motorway network length		km	No		ECMT countries	ECMT1 (11)
Road network, length	Type of road	km	Yes	A	EC, USA, Canada	UN13 (11)
Road network, length		km, %	No		Latin American and Caribbean countries	UN45 (354)
Road network, length	By type	kilometres	Yes	A	Nordic countries	NCM1 (146)
Road network, length		km	Yes	A	OECD countries	OECD33 (10.1A)
Road network, length	For roads open to the public by road type	km	Yes	I	ECMT countries	ECMT2 (3-2-1)
Road network, length	Total, of which: paved, gravel, earth	km	Yes	A	ASEAN	ASEANS1 (5.2.1)
Road network, length	Motorways, main, secondary, other	km	No		EC	EC9 (7.9)
Road network	By country, by type, density	nos, %, sq km	No		EC	EM1 (2201)
Road network	By country	km	No		EC	EC18 (10.3)
Road network	By country and area, road type, paved, density of network	km, %, sq km	Yes	A	World	IRF1 (I)
Road network	Main, secondary roads, by country	nos	Yes	A	World	IRTU1
Road network length	By category	km	Yes	A	EC	EC80 (3.1)
Road network length	By country	km	No		EC	EC72 (9.14)
Road transport	Length, type, vehicles	km, nos 1000	Yes	A	North Africa	UN2 (27)
Road transport	Length, type, vehicles	km, nos 1000	Yes	A	West Africa	UN3 (27)
Road transport	Length, type, vehicles	km, nos 1000	Yes	A	East and Southern Africa	UN4 (27)
Road transport	Length, type, vehicles	km, nos 1000	Yes	A	Central Africa	UN5 (27)
Roads (asphalted) and railways	Length	kilometres	Yes	A	African countries	UN1 (39)
Traffic volume on motorways overall road network		%	No		ECMT countries	ECMT1 (11)
Transport networks	Railways, inland waterways, roads	km	No		EC	EC69 (VI.1)
45.10.7 Passenger Traffic						
Distance travelled, car, average annual	By country	km	No		EC	EM1 (2203)
Passenger traffic	By vehicle type	passenger-km	Yes	1	ECMT countries	ECMT2 (3-1-1)
Passenger traffic	Rail buses and coaches private cars	passenger-km	Yes	5 yr	EC	ECMT3
Passenger transport, relative importance of different modes	Urban railways and tramways, road, air	passenger-km %	Yes	I	Bulgaria, Italy, Netherlands, Norway, Portugal, Sweden, USA	UN13 (3A)

Subject	Categories	Units	Time series Yes/No Frequency		Territorial coverage	Source (Table no.)
Passenger-kilometres	Vehicle type	nos	Yes	A	EC, USA, Canada	UN13 (15)
Rail and road traffic	Passengers, goods, rail, road journeys, by country	nos, tonnes	Yes	A	World	IRTU1
45.10.8 Speed Limits						
Maximum speed		km/h	No		ECMT countries	ECMT1 (11)
Speed limits		km/h	No		ECMT countries	ECMT1 (10)
45.10.9 Vehicles						
Car traffic volume	By country	km	No		EC	EM1 (2202)
Goods vehicles		nos	Yes	A	OECD, World	OECD33 (10.2C)
Goods vehicles		vehicle-km	Yes	A	OECD	OECD33 (10.3C)
Passenger cars, production		nos	Yes	A, Q, M	OECD	OECD22 (-)
Passenger cars		vehicle-km	Yes	A	OECD	OECD33 (10.3B)
Production and exports of motor vehicles	By country, vehicle type	nos	Yes	A	World	IRF1 (II)
Road traffic	By vehicle type	vehicle-km	Yes	I	ECMT countries	ECMT2 (3-1-6)
Total vehicles		vehicle-km	Yes	A	OECD	OECD33 (10.3A)
Vehicle production	Car commercial vehicle	nos	Yes	A	World	IRSG2 (23)
Vehicle traffic, entered country	Vehicle type	nos	Yes	I	EC, USA, Canada	UN13 (15)
Vehicle-kilometres	Vehicle type	nos	Yes	A	EC, USA, Canada	UN13 (15)
Vehicles, commercial : production		nos	Yes	A, Q, M	OECD	OECD22 (-)
Vehicle Registrations						
Assemblies	Cars, commercial vehicles	nos	Yes	A	World	IRSG2 (39a, 40a)
Buses, coaches	By seating capacity by country	nos	Yes	A	World	IRTU1
Cars, first registration		nos	Yes	I	EC	EC80 (1.3)
Commercial vehicles		1 000	Yes	A	World	UN50 (1)
Commercial vehicles	% AGR.	nos, %	Yes	10 yrs	World	UN26
First registration and imports of motor vehicles	By country, vehicle type	nos	Yes	A	World	IRF1 (III)
Lorries	By loading capacity by country	tonnes	Yes	A	World	IRTU1
Motor cars	Per thousand inhabitants	nos	Yes	A	VICES region, VICES countries and Yugoslavia	VICES1 (II/4)
Motor road vehicles	By type of vehicle by country	nos	Yes	A	World	IRTU1
Motor vehicle registrations, new		nos	Yes	A, M	OECD	OECD22
Motor vehicles, first registration	By category	nos	Yes	A	EC	EC80 (3.3)
Motor vehicles, total		nos	Yes	I	EC	EC80 (1.3)
Motor vehicles, cars		nos	Yes	I	EC	EC80 (1.3)
Motor vehicles, goods vehicles, road tractors and buses		nos	Yes	I	EC	EC80 (1.3)
Motor vehicles, cars per inhabitant		nos per 1000 inhabitant	Yes	I	EC	EC80 (1.3)
Motor vehicles	Passenger cars, commercial vehicles	nos per 1000 inhabitants	Yes	A	African countries	UN1 (40)
Motor vehicles and car ownership	By country, by type of vehicle	nos	No		EC	EC18 (10.4)

45 TRANSPORT

Subject	Categories	Units	Time series Yes/No Frequency	Territorial coverage	Source (Table no.)
Motor vehicles and car ownership	By country, by type of vehicle		nos	No	EC18(10.4)
Motor vehicles in use		per 1000 population	Yes	World	UN55
Motor vehicles in use	All roads, motorways	nos	Yes A	OECD, World	OECD33 (10.2A)
Motor vehicles in use	By countries	nos	No	The Americas and Australasia	MAC2 (G6)
Motor vehicles in use	By countries	nos	Yes A	EC	MAC3 (F6)
Motor vehicles in use	By country, vehicle type	nos	Yes A	Africa and Asia	MAC1 (G5)
Motor vehicles in use	Cars, commercial vehicles	nos	Yes A	World	IRSG2 (43, 44)
Motor vehicles in use	Passenger cars commercial vehicles	nos	Yes A	World	UN50 (133)
Passenger car registrations, new		nos	Yes A, M	OECD	OECD22
Passenger car registrations, new		nos	Yes A, M	OECD, EC, Major Seven Total	OECD22
Passenger cars, registration		nos	Yes A, Q, M	OECD	OECD22 (-)
Passenger cars		1 000	Yes A	World	UN50 (1)
Passenger cars	% AGR.	nos, %	Yes 10 yrs	World	UN26
Passenger cars in use		nos	Yes A	OECD	OECD33
Passenger cars in use		nos rate	Yes Selected years	World	UN16 (29)
Passenger vehicles registered	By type	nos	Yes I	ECMT countries	ECMT2 (3-3-1)
Production	Cars, commercial vehicles	nos	Yes A	World	IRSG2 (39, 40)
Registered vehicles and trailers	Road vehicles, motor coaches, trailer load capacity	nos, kgs, tonnes, per capita	No	Nordic countries	NCM1 (144)
Registrations	New cars, commercial vehicles	nos	Yes A	World	IRSG2 (41, 42)
Registrations (new) of motor vehicles and trailers	Road vehicles, motor coaches, trailer load capacity, private cars	nos, kgs, tonnes, per capita	No	Nordic countries	NCM1 (145)
Road freight vehicles registered	Amount and loading capacity by type	nos, tonnes	Yes I	ECMT countries	ECMT2 (3-3-2)
Road motor vehicles, population		ratio	No	ECMT countries	ECMT1 (3)
Road transport	Commercial motor vehicles in use	nos, 1000	Yes A	North Africa	UN2 (6-3-1)
Road transport	Commercial motor vehicles in use	nos, 1000	Yes A	West Africa	UN3 (6-3-1)
Road transport	Commercial motor vehicles in use	nos, 1000	Yes A	East and Southern Africa	UN4 (6-3-1)
Road transport	Commercial motor vehicles in use	nos, 1000	Yes A	Central Africa	UN5 (6-3-1)
Road transport	Length, type, vehicles	km, nos 1000	Yes A	North Africa	UN2 (27)
Road transport	Length, type, vehicles	km, nos 1000	Yes A	West Africa	UN3 (27)
Road transport	Length, type, vehicles	km, nos 1000	Yes A	East and Southern Africa	UN4 (27)
Road transport	Length, type, vehicles	km, nos 1000	Yes A	Central Africa	UN5 (27)
Road vehicle stocks	By country	nos	No	EC	EC72 (9.16)
Road vehicles		nos	Yes A	EC, USA, Canada	UN34 (6)
Roads and road vehicles	Summary, by country	km, nos	Yes A	ESCAP countries	UN44
Stock, goods vehicles and tractors	By category and transport type	nos, tonnes	No	EC	EC80 (3.4)
Stock, goods vehicles	By category, transport type	nos	No	EC	EC80 (3.5)
Vehicle stock	By category	nos	Yes A	EC	EC80 (3.2)
Vehicles, new registered	Vehicle type	number, seats,	Yes A	EC, USA	UN13 (14)

Subject	Categories	Units	Time series Yes/No	Frequency	Territorial coverage	Source (Table no.)
Vehicles, population	By vehicle category	%	No		ECMT countries	ECMT1 (9)
Vehicles	Passenger, goods, hire tonnes	number, seats	Yes	A	EC, USA, Canada	UN13 (13)
Vehicles	Passenger cars, commercial vehicles	nos	Yes	A	ESCAP region, developing ESCAP region	UN44 (pp6, 11)
Vehicles in use		nos,	No		EC	EC9 (7.10)
Vehicles in use	By country, vehicle type, population, number of cars per person, household, road	nos, per capita, km	Yes	A	World	IRF1 (IV)
Vehicles in use	Car commercial vehicle	nos	Yes	A	World	IRSG2 (24)
Vehicles in use	Total, of which: passenger cars, commercial vehicles	nos	Yes	A	ASEAN	ASEANS1 (5.2.2)
					World	(10.2B)
45.11 SEA - see also Section 41						
45.11.1 Accidents - see also Section 1						
Ships totally or partially lost at sea and loss of life	Ships, total, partial Life, accident, total partial	nos, gross tonnage	No		Nordic countries	NCM1 (140)
45.11.2 Energy- see also Section 17						
Energy consumption	Forms of energy	TJ	Yes	A	EC, USA Canada	UN13 (5)
45.11.3 Fleets - see also Section 41						
Fleet, capacity in grt		tonnes	Yes	I	EC	
Fleet, percentage of EC fleet in grt	By country	%	Yes	I	EC	EC80 (1.5)
Fleet, percentage of world fleet in grt	By country	%	Yes	I	EC	EC80 (1.5)
Fleet, world	By type and flag	nos	No		World	EC80 (5.2)
Fleet, merchant	By flag	nos, tonnes	Yes	A	World	EC80 (5.3)
Fleet, merchant	By size group	nos	No		World	EC80 (5.4)
Fleet, merchant	By age and country	nos, tonnes	No		World,	EC80 (5.5)
Fleet, merchant	By type and age	nos, tonnes	No		World	EC80 (5.6)
Fleet size		nos	Yes	I	EC	EC80 (1.5)
Fleet size	By country	tonnes	No		EC	EM1 (2213)
Fleets	All, oil tankers	nos, tonnes	No		EC	EC9 (7.7)
Fleets	nos, gross	tonnage	Yes	A	Nordic countries	NCM1 (134)
Merchant fleets	Gross register for vessels of 1000 tonnes and over, by type	nos	No		Latin American and Caribbean countries	UN45 (357)
Merchant shipping	By country, by principal type of vessel	tonnes	No		EC	EM1 (2216)
Merchant shipping fleet		grt	Yes	A	ASEAN	ASEANS1 (5.3.1)
Merchant ships registered	By countries	nos	No		The Americas and Australasia	MAC2 (G4)
Merchant ships registered	By country, ship type	tonnes gross, nos	Yes	A	Africa and Asia	MAC1 (G4)
Tanker fleet	By age, 10,000 dwt and over	dwt	Yes	5 yr	World	OPEC1 (60)
Tanker fleet	Development	dwt	Yes	A	OPEC	OPEC1 (59)
45.11.4 Freight Traffic						
Amount of sea traffic	By country, by type	nos	No		EC	EC18 (10.9)
Coastal shipping-national traffic		tonne-km	Yes	I	ECMT countries	ECMT2 (6-1-4)

Subject	Categories	Units	Time series Yes/No Frequency		Territorial coverage	Source (Table no.)
Coastal shipping-national traffic	Goods unloaded	tonnes	Yes	I	ECMT countries	ECMT2 (6-1-3)
Containers		nos, tonnes	Yes	A	EC	UN13 (27)
Freight, traffic	Goods loaded, unloaded	tonnes	Yes	A	World	IRTU1
Goods, international	Entering the country, leaving the country	tonnes	Yes	A	EC, USA	UN13 (4)
Goods, international shipping	Loaded, unloaded	tonnes	Yes	A	ASEAN	ASEANS1 (5.3.2.2)
Goods loaded		tonnes	Yes	I	EC	EC80 (1.5)
Goods loaded in international seaborne trade	By country	tonnes	No		EC	EM1 (2214)
Goods traffic, international	By flag	tonnes	No		EC	EC80 (5.13)
Goods traffic, international	By NST, R chapter and relation	tonnes	No		EC	EC80 (5.14)
Goods traffic, national and foreign	By NST, R chapter and traffic relation	tonnes	No		EC	EC80 (5.15)
Goods unloaded		tonnes	Yes	I	EC	EC80 (1.5)
Goods unloaded in international seaborne trade	By country	tonnes	No		EC	EM1 (2215)
International goods transport		tonnes	Yes	I	ECMT countries	ECMT2 (6-1-1)
International goods transport by various modes	Imports, exports	tonnes, %	Yes	A	Nordic countries	NCM1 (133)
International goods transport	Loading and unloading at origin and destination irrespective of registration country	tonnes	Yes	I	ECMT countries	ECMT2 (6-1-2)
International sea-borne shipping	Goods loaded and unloaded	tonnes	Yes	A	Nordic countries	NCM1 (139)
International sea-borne shipping	Vessels entered and cleared	nos, gross tonnage	Yes	A	Nordic countries	NCM1 (138)
Merchant shipping	Unloaded, loaded	tonnes	No		EC	EC9 (7.8)
Ports , goods loaded, unloaded	International and national	indices	Yes	A	EC, USA, Canada	UN13 (25)
Tanker freight rates, spot	By route	%, US$, LT	Yes	A	World	OPEC1 (67)
Traffic, goods (excl transit)		tonnes	Yes	I	EC	EC80 (1.5)
Traffic, international	By flag arrivals and departures	nos, tonnes	No		World	EC80 (5.9)
Traffic, international	By flag	%	No		World	EC80 (5.10)
Traffic, goods	National and international	tonnes %	Yes	A	EC	EC80 (5.11)
Traffic, petroleum products unloaded		tonnes, %	Yes	A	EC	EC80 (5.12)
Traffic, large container	By port	nos, tonnes	No		EC	EC80 (5.17)
Traffic	By port	nos, tonnes	No		EC	EC80 (5.16)
Traffic	Goods unloaded and loaded	tonnes	Yes	I	Major seaports of ECMT countries	ECMT2 (6-1-5)
Transport	Merchant fleet, commercial vehicles in use	dwt, nos	No		World	UNCTAD1 (6.10B)
45.11.5 Vessels						
Fishing vessels and factory	By size and flag	nos, tonnes	No		World	EC80 (5.7)
Merchant ships	By country	nos	No		EC	EC18 (10.8)
Motor and steam ships		nos, tonnes	Yes	A	World	EC80 (5.1)
Ship arrivals		nos, tonnes	Yes	A	EC	EC80 (5.8)
Shipping at individual ports	Goods unloaded, loaded	nos, gross tonnage	Yes	A	Oresund area	NCM1 (278)
Trawlers						
Vessels tonnage, world laid-up tanker and combined carrier tonnage	By size	dwt	Yes	A	World	OPEC1 (64)
Vessels, international shipping	Entered, cleared	grt	Yes	A	ASEAN	ASEANS1 (5.3.2.1)

Subject	Categories	Units	Time series Yes/No Frequency	Territorial coverage	Source (Table no.)
Vessels, tonnage	Nos, gross	tonnage	Yes A, Q	Nordic countries	NCM1 (135)
Vessels	Nos, gross, type	tonnage	No	Nordic countries	NCM1 (136)
Vessels	Nos, gross by size and age	tonnage	No	Nordic countries	NCM1 (137)

46 WELFARE

Subject	Categories	Units	Time series Yes/No Frequency		Territorial coverage	Source (Table no.)
46.1 POVERTY AND WEALTH – see also Section 24 and 30						
Household income share	Top 20%, bottom 40%, by country, region	ratio	No		UNICEF assisted countries	UNICEF2
Population in absolute poverty	Total, urban, rural	%	No		World	UN16 (30)
Population in absolute poverty	Urban, rural, by country, region	ratio	No		UNICEF assisted countries	UNICEF2
Poverty, rates of	By country, by households, persons	%, nos	No		Europe	EC72 (6.28)
Poverty, rates of	Households in a condition of poverty, national and urban	%	No		Latin American and Caribbean countries	UN45 (22)
Wealth, poverty and social investment	Indicators of population wealth, poverty	PPP$, %, US$, ratio	No		Developing countries	UN18 (17)
Wealth, poverty and social investment	Indicators of population wealth, poverty	PPP$, %, US$, ratio	No		Industrial countries	UN18 (38)
46.2 SOCIAL SECURITY BENEFITS						
46.2.1 Beneficiaries						
Basic, supplementary, means-tested welfare	By type of benefit	nos	Yes	A	EC	EC21 (II.1)
46.2.2 Expenditure						
Basic, supplementary, means-tested welfare	By type of benefit	nat curr	Yes	A	EC	EC21 (II.1)
Current expenditure on social protection		ratios	Yes	A	EC	EC73 (1)
Finance of social security expenditure as between central government, local authorities, employers and the insured	By main category	%	No		Nordic countries	NCM1 (216)
Social protection current expenditure	By type	ECU	Yes	A	EC	EC73 (2a)
Social protection current expenditure	By type	nat curr	Yes	A	EC	EC73 (6a)
Social protection current expenditure	By type	PPS	Yes	A	EC	EC73 (4a)
Social protection current expenditure	By type, constant prices	nat curr	Yes	A	EC	EC73 (8a)
Social protection current receipts	By sector of origin	ECU	Yes	A	EC	EC73 (3b)
Social protection current receipts	By sector of origin	nat curr	Yes	A	EC	EC73 (7b)
Social protection current receipts	By sector of origin	nat curr	Yes	A	EC	EC73 (9b)
Social protection current receipts	By sector of origin	PPS	Yes	A	EC	EC73 (5b)
Social protection current receipts	By type	ECU	Yes	A	EC	EC73 (3a)
Social protection current receipts	By type	nat curr receipts	Yes	A	EC	EC73 (7a)
Social protection current receipts	By type	nat curr	Yes	A	EC	EC73 (9a)
Social protection current receipts	By type	PPS	Yes	A	EC	EC73 (5a)

46 WELFARE

Subject	Categories	Units	Time series Yes/No Frequency		Territorial coverage	Source (Table no.)
Social protection expenditure	By function, costs, other expenditure, total current expenditure	%	Yes	A	EC	EC73 (10)
Social protection receipts:	By type, sector of origin, total	%	Yes	A	EC	EC73 (11)
Social security expenditure	By item	nat curr	No		Nordic countries	NCM1 (214)
Social security expenditure	Per capita	nat curr	No		Nordic countries	NCM1 (217)
46.2.3 General						
Benefits	% of GDP and per capita, by type of scheme	ECU	No		EC	EC21 (III.4,5)
Benefits	Basic and supplementary compulsory and means-tested schemes, all scheme	% of GDP, ECU, per capita	No		EC	EC22 (4,5)
Benefits	By type of scheme	ECU	No		EC	EC21 (III.1)
Benefits	By type, by country	ECU	No		EC	EC22 (1)
Benefits	ECU per capita PPS per capita		Yes	A	EC, EC, Scandinavian countries	EC9 (3.32-3.33)
Benefits	Sickness, invalidity, disability, employment injury, occupational diseases old age, survivors, maternity, family, voc. guidance, mobility, housing	ECU	Yes	A	EC	EC9 (3.36)
Benefits in cash and in kind	By groups of schemes, by country	ECU	No		EC	EC22 (8)
Benefits in cash and in kind	By type of scheme	ECU	No		EC	EC21 (III.8)
Benefits structure	By type of cash benefit	ECU	No		EC	EC21 (III.9)
Benefits structure	By type of scheme	ECU, %	No		EC	EC21 (III.6)
Benefits structure	By basic, supplementary, means-tested and by groups of schemes	ECU, %	No		EC	EC22 (6)
Benefits structured by type of cash benefit	By country, by type	ECU	No		EC	EC22 (9)
Benefits, index of amounts	By type of scheme	indices	No		EC	EC21 (III.2)
Benefits, index of amounts	By type, by country	nat curr, indices	No		EC	EC22 (2)
Benefits, trends	By country	nat curr, indices	Yes	A	EC	EC22 (3)
Benefits, trends	By type of scheme	indices	No		EC	EC21 (III.3)
Social benefits	By type and providing sector	nat curr	Yes	A	EC	EC62 (5.4)
Social protection benefits	By country, per capita	%	No		EC	EC72 (7.4)
Social protection benefits	By function	ECU	Yes	A	EC	EC73 (2b)
Social protection benefits	By function	nat curr	Yes	A	EC	EC73 (6b)
Social protection benefits	By function	nat curr	Yes	A	EC	EC73 (8b)
Social protection benefits	By function	PPS	Yes	A	EC	EC73 (4b)
Supplementary schemes	By total, compulsory schemes, voluntary schemes	ECU	No		EC	EC22 (7)
Supplementary schemes	By type of scheme	ECU	No		EC	EC21 (III.7)
46.2.4 Invalidity and Disability Benefits						
Beneficiaries	By country, basic schemes, supplementary schemes, means-tested welfare schemes	nos	Yes	A	EC	EC22 (2)
Benefits	By country, basic schemes, supplemen-	nat curr	Yes	A	EC	EC22 (1)

Subject	Categories	Units	Time series Yes/No Frequency		Territorial coverage	Source (Table no.)
	tary schemes, means-tested welfare schemes					
Old age and invalidity, workers and employees	Average monthly pension at current prices	nat curr	Yes	A	VICES countries and Yugoslavia	VICES1 (II/2)
Population covered	Insured population as % of total population, as % of total economically active population	%	No		Latin American and Caribbean countries	UN45 (34)
46.2.5 Old Age Benefits						
Expenditure, aggregate at constant prices	By type of scheme	ECU, %	No		EC	EC21 (III.B)
Expenditure, aggregate at current prices	By type of scheme	ECU, %	No		EC	EC21 (III.A)
Expenditure, aggregate rate of growth at constant prices	By total expenditure	nat curr	No		EC	EC21 (III.C)
Old age and invalidity, workers and employees	Average monthly pension at current prices	nat curr	Yes	A	VICES countries and Yugoslavia	VICES1 (II/2)
Old-age benefit expenditure	As % of GDP	%	No		EC	EC21 (III.D)
Old-age benefit expenditure	Per capita	ECU, nat curr, PPS	No		EC	EC21 (III.E)
Share of benefits in kind in the total of means-tested schemes	By type of scheme	%	No		EC	EC21 (III.F)
46.3 SOCIAL SECURITY CONTRIBUTIONS						
Contributions as percentage of GDP		%	Yes	A	OECD	OECD42 (14)
Contributions as percentage of total taxation		%	Yes	A	OECD	OECD42 (15)
Employees' contributions as percentage of GDP		%	Yes	A	OECD	OECD42 (16)
Employees' contributions as percentage of total taxation		%	Yes	A	OECD	OECD42 (17)
Employers' contributions as percentage of GDP		%	Yes	A	OECD	OECD42 (18)
Employers' contributions as percentage of total taxation		%	Yes	A	OECD	OECD42 (19)
Financing of social security benefits	Total	nat curr	Yes	A	OECD	OECD42 (62-85)
Social security contributions		nat curr	Yes	A	OECD	OECD42 (38-61)
Social security contributions (1975-1989)		nat curr	Yes	A	OECD	OECD42 (129-152)
Social security contributions	By type and receiving sector	nat curr	Yes	A	EC	EC62 (5.3)
Social security contributions and payroll taxes paid by government	Total	nat curr	Yes	A	OECD	OECD42 (86-109)
46.4 WELFARE INDICATORS – see also Sections 30 and 42						
Babies, low birth-weight	By country, region	%	No		UNICEF assisted countries	UNICEF2
Calories and proteins available	Per day, per capita, three year averages	calories, g	Yes	I	Latin American and Caribbean countries	UN45 (24)
Children enrolled in day care institutions for children and young persons		nos	Yes	A	Nordic countries	NCM1 (218)
Community water supply and sanitation problems and issues	By country, by institutional item, financial item, operational item		No		SEAR	WHO1 (60)

Subject	Categories	Units	Time series Yes/No Frequency		Territorial coverage	Source (Table no.)
Family day care	Approved homes	nos, %	No		Nordic countries	NCM1 (219)
Food supplies and nutrition	By high, middle, low income	index, %	No		World	CS1 (28)
Food, health and nutrition	Food production, calories and proteins population per physician, nurse and hospital bed access to safe water	indices, grammes, nos %	No		Developing countries	WB1 (-)
Health-related indicators	By high, middle, low income	nos, %	No		World	CS1 (30)
Housing allowances	Households receiving	%	Yes	Selected years	EC	MHPPE1 (-)
Mortality rate	By % life expectancy female/male, % literacy female/male, school enrolement female/male, contraception prevalence,pregnant women immunized against tetanus, % births attended by trained personnel, maternal mortality rate	%, nos	No		World	UNICEF1 (7)
Mortality rates	By % with access to safe water, % with access to health service, % immunized, ORT use rate	%, nos	No		World	UNICEF1 (3)
Mortality rates	By adult literacy, radio and television sets, primary school enrolement, % reaching final grade, secondary school enrolement	nos, %	No		World	UNICEF1 (4)
Mortality rates	By birthweight, % of breast-feeding mothers, type of illness, food production, calorie supply, % household income	%, index,	No		World	UNICEF1 (2)
Mortality rates	By GNP, GNP growth, inflation, population below poverty level, government expenditure, ODA inflows,debt as % of exports	US$, %	No		World	UNICEF1 (6)
Mortality rates	By population, growth rate, death rate, birth rate, life expectancy, fertility rate, population urbanized, growth of urban population	nos, %	No		World	UNICEF1 (5)
Mortality rates	By total population, births, deaths, GNP, life expectancy, adult literacy, % enrolled in primary school, % household income	nos, US$, %	No		World	UNICEF1 (1)
Pensioners	By type of pension	nos	Yes	A	Nordic countries	NCM1 (220)
Pensioners aged 65 and over	By type of dwelling	nos, %	No		Nordic countries	NCM1 (221)
Self-sufficiency	By product	%	No		EC	WC1 (-)
Social assistance	By family	nos, nat curr	No		Nordic countries	NCM1 (215)
Social housing	Newly-built social rental dwelling	%	No		EC	MHPPE1 (-)

Subject	Categories	Units	Time series Yes/No Frequency	Territorial coverage	Source (Table no.)
Underweight children	Weight for age, by country, region	%	No	UNICEF assisted countries	UNICEF2
Water supply and sanitation coverage	By country	nos, %	No	SEAR	WHO1 (59)

APPENDIX A

INDEX OF PUBLICATIONS

ARRANGED BY *instat* CODE

FULL BIBLIOGRAPHICAL DETAILS

INTRODUCTION TO APPENDIX A

Publications are referred to by code only throughout the main body of this book. The titles of the publications and other bibliographical details are presented in this Appendix arranged by ***instat*** code. Notes on the information provided are given below.

instat codes

The ***instat*** codes consist of two parts:

- an alphabetical prefix which denotes the organization responsible for compiling the publication
- a numerical suffix which distinguishes different publications of the same organization

Arrangement

All publications are listed here in alphanumeric order according to the ***instat*** codes referred to above.

Information provided

In addition to the ***instat*** code, the title of the publication and the full name of the organization responsible, the following information is provided:

- **Edition indexed**

  This indicates, as appropriate, the edition date and/or the volume number of the edition examined when compiling this book. Note that the edition date is *not* necessarily the same as the publication date (given separately)

- **Publisher**

  Name of the publisher. This is generally, but not necessarily, the same as the name of the sponsoring body for the publication

- **Frequency**

  This is the frequency of publication for serial publications

- **Date**

  This is the date of publication of the edition indexed when compiling this book

- **Place**

  Place of publication: town or city and country

- **ISBN and ISSN**

  International Standard Book Number and/or International Standard Serial Number, where applicable, of the edition indexed when compiling this book. A dash in this column indicates that the edition has neither an ISBN nor ISSN

instat code	Title	Edition indexed	Publisher Frequency Date Place	ISBN ISSN

AEA: ASSOCIATION OF EUROPEAN AIRLINES

AEA1	Association of European Airlines Yearbook	1992	AEA Annually 1992 Brussels, Belgium	—
AEA2	Statistical Appendices to AEA Yearbook	1992	AEA Annually 1992 Brussels, Belgium	—
AEA3	Intra-European Country to Country Traffic	1990 October	AEA Monthly 1991 Brussels, Belgium	—
AEA4	Medium-Term Forecast of European Scheduled Passenger Traffic	1992–96	AEA Irregular 1992 Brussels, Belgium	—

APO: ASIAN PRODUCTIVITY ORGANISATION

APO1	Comparative Information on Productivity Levels and Changes in APO Member Countries	1991	APO Irregular 1991 Tokyo, Japan	ISBN 9 2 833 1 613 4

ASEANS: ASSOCIATION OF SOUTH-EAST ASIAN NATIONS SECRETARIAT

ASEANS1	ASEAN Selected Statistics	1982–88	ASEANS Occasional 1990 Jakarta, Indonesia	—

BB: BASIL BLACKWELL LTD

BB1	Oil and Energy Trends, Annual Statistical Review	1992	Energy Economics Research/ Blackwell Annually 1992 Oxford, UK	ISSN 0953 1033
BB2	Oil and Energy Trends	1992 December	Blackwell Monthly 1992 Oxford, UK	ISSN 0950 1045
BB3	Tanker Charter Record	1993 January	Blackwell Monthly 1993 Oxford, UK	ISSN 0958 8787
BB4	World Oil Trade Review of International Oil Movements	1992 Vol 14	Blackwell Biannual 1992 Oxford, UK	ISSN 0950 1029

instat code	Title	Edition indexed	Publisher Frequency Date Place	ISBN ISSN

BGS: BRITISH GEOLOGICAL SURVEY

BGS1	World Mineral Statistics Vol 1 Metals and Energy	1986–90	BGS Annually 1992 Keyworth, UK	ISBN 0 85272 210 9
BGS2	World Mineral Statistics Vol 2 Industrial Minerals	1986–90	BGS Annually 1992 Keyworth, UK	ISBN 0 85272 211 7

BP: BRITISH PETROLEUM COMPANY PLC

BP1	BP Statistical Review of World Energy	1990	BP Annually 1990 London, UK	ISBN 0 86165 184 7
BP2	BP Review of World Gas	1992	BP Annually 1992 London, UK	—

BPB: BRITISH PAPER AND BOARD INDUSTRY FEDERATION

BPB1	Reference Tables	1991	BPB Annually 1991 Swindon, UK	—

CAA: CIVIL AVIATION AUTHORITY

CAA1	Fatal Accident Statistics for Passenger Air Transport Services CAA Paper 83014	1964–81	CAA Occasional 1983 London, UK	ISBN 0 86039 190 6

CBI: CONFEDERATION OF BRITISH INDUSTRY

CBI1	West European Living Costs	1991	CBI Annually 1991 London, UK	ISBN 0 85201 2829

CCS: CARIBBEAN COMMUNITY SECRETARIAT

CCS1	Caricom's Trade	1985–1990	CCS Irregular January 1993 Georgetown, Guyana	—
CCS2	A Digest of Trade Statistics	1970–80	CCS Irregular 1983 Georgetown, Guyana	—

instat code	Title	Edition indexed	Publisher Frequency Date Place	ISBN ISSN

CE: COUNCIL OF EUROPE

CE1	Recent Demographic Developments in Europe	1991	Council of Europe Press Annually 1991 Strasbourg, France	ISBN 92 871 1989 9

CH: CROOM HELM LIMITED

CH1	The Economies of the Arabian Gulf: A Statistical Source Book	1984	Croom Helm Irregular 1984 London, UK	ISBN 0 7099 1543 8

CIA: CHEMICAL INDUSTRIES ASSOCIATION

CIA1	Basic International Chemical Industry Statistics	1963–90	CIA Irregular 1991 London, UK	ISBN 0 900 623 640 ISSN 0961 7531

CIRFS: COMITE INTERNATIONAL DE LA RAYONNE ET DES FIBRES SYNTHETIQUES

CIRFS1	Information on Man-made Fibres	1986	CIRFS Annually 1986 Paris, France	—

COS: CHAMBER OF SHIPPING

COS1	Statistical Brief	1992 (4)	COS Quarterly 1992 London, UK	—

CS: COMMONWEALTH SECRETARIAT

CS1	Basic Statistical Data on Selected Countries	1992	Commonwealth Secretariat Annually 1992 London, UK	—

DSC: DREWRY SHIPPING CONSULTANTS LIMITED

DSC1	Shipping Statistics and Economics	1993 March	Drewry Monthly 1993 London, UK	ISSN 0306 1817
DSC2	Shipping Trade, Trends and Statistics	1992 December	Drewry Monthly 1992 London, UK	ISSN 0966 7032

instat code	Title	Edition indexed	Publisher Frequency Date Place	ISBN ISSN
EAA: EUROPEAN ALUMINIUM ASSOCIATION				
EAA1	European Aluminium Statistics	1991	EAA Annually 1991 Brussels, Belgium	—
EAT: ELSEVIER ADVANCED TECHNOLOGY				
EAT1	Silicon Carbide	1992 Vol 1	EAT Irregular 1992 Oxford, UK	ISBN 1 85617 151 5
EAT2	Telecommunications: Profile of the Worldwide Telecommunications Industry	1990	EAT Irregular 1990 Oxford, UK	ISBN 0946 395 594
EC: EUROPEAN COMMUNITY (EUROSTAT)[1]				
EC1	ACP Basic Statistics	1988	SOEC Annually 1989 Luxembourg	ISBN 92 825 8867 X
EC2	Agricultural Income	1991	SOEC Irregular 1992 Luxembourg	ISBN 92 826 4005 1
EC3	Agricultural Markets: Prices	1991 (4)	SOEC 5 per year 1991 Luxembourg	ISSN 1014 8159
EC4	Agricultural Prices: Price Indices and Absolute Prices	1980–89	SOEC Annually 1990 Luxembourg	ISBN 92 826 1721 1

1 In addition to the publications listed here, the EC (Eurostat) also publish a series entitled *Rapid Reports*, the purpose of which is to summarize the main results of surveys, studies or publications. These have not been indexed in this volume because their content varies from one report to another. Details of the series are as follows:

Rapid Reports – Agriculture, Forestry and Fisheries. ISSN 1017–5776.
Rapid Reports – Economy and Finance. ISSN 1016–0213.
Rapid Reports – Energy and Industry. ISSN 1016–0191.
Rapid Reports – Environment. ISSN 1017–5849.
Rapid Reports – External Trade and Balance of Payments. ISSN 1017–5792.
Rapid Reports – Population and Social Conditions. ISSN 1013–0535.
Rapid Reports – Regions. ISSN 1013– 0535.

***instat* code**	**Title**	**Edition indexed**	**Publisher Frequency Date Place**	**ISBN ISSN**
EC5	Agricultural Prices: Price Indices and Absolute Prices	1990 (2)	SOEC Quarterly 1990 Luxembourg	ISSN 1015 9924
EC6	Agriculture Statistical Yearbook	1990	SOEC Annually 1991 Luxembourg	ISBN 92 826 2596 6
EC7	Animal Production, Quarterly Statistics	1990	SOEC Quarterly 1990 Luxembourg	ISSN 0250 6580
EC8	Areas Under Vines, Results of the Annual Surveys	1979–89	SOEC Annually 1991 Luxembourg	ISBN 92 826 2965 1
EC9	Basic Statistics of the Community	1990	SOEC Annually 1990 Luxembourg	ISBN 92 826 1497 2
EC10	Balance of Payments: Geographical Breakdown	1980–84	SOEC Annually 1986 Luxembourg	ISBN 92 825 6382 0
EC11	Censuses of Population in the Community Countries 1981– 82	1981–82	SOEC Irregular 1988 Luxembourg	ISBN 92 825 7609 4
EC12	Carriage of Goods – Inland Waterways	1987	SOEC Annually 1989 Luxembourg	ISBN 92 825 9879 9
EC13	Carriage of Goods – Railways	1987	SOEC Annually 1989 Luxembourg	ISBN 92 825 9880 2
EC14	Carriage of Goods – Road	1987	SOEC Annually 1989 Luxembourg	ISBN 92 826 0690 2
EC15	Community Survey of Orchard Fruit Trees	1987	SOEC Irregular 1990 Luxembourg	ISBN 92 826 0782 8
EC16	Consumer Price Index	1992 (1)	SOEC Monthly 1992 Luxembourg	ISSN 1010 2779

instat code	Title	Edition indexed	Publisher Frequency Date Place	ISBN ISSN
EC17	Consumer Prices in the EEC	1988	SOEC Irregular 1990 Luxembourg	ISBN 92 826 1321 6
EC18	Country Reports, Central and Eastern Europe	1991	SOEC Irregular 1991 Luxembourg	ISBN 92 826 2371 8
EC19	Crop Production, Quarterly Statistics	1991 (4)	SOEC Quarterly 1992 Luxembourg	ISSN 0378 3588
EC20	Demographic Statistics	1990	SOEC Annually 1990 Luxembourg	ISBN 92 826 1481 6
EC21	Digest of Statistics on Social Protection in Europe Vol 1 Old Age	1980–88	SOEC Irregular 1992 Luxembourg	ISBN 92 826 3719 0
EC22	Digest of Statistics on Social Protection in Europe Vol 2 Invalidity/Disability	1980–88	SOEC Irregular 1992 Luxembourg	ISBN 92 826 3720 4
EC23	Earnings in Agriculture	1988	SOEC Annually 1990 Luxembourg	ISBN 92 826 1689 4
EC24	Earnings, Industry and Services	1991	SOEC Annually 1991 Luxembourg	ISBN 92 826 3355 1
EC25	EC External Trade Indices	1980–86	SOEC Irregular 1988 Luxembourg	ISBN 92 825 7787 2
EC26	Economic Accounts for Agriculture and Forestry	1984–89	SOEC Annually 1991 Luxembourg	ISBN 92 826 2401 3
EC27	ECU– EMS Information	1991 (11–12)	SOEC Monthly 1991 Luxembourg	ISSN 1011 0844
EC28	Electricity Prices	1985–91	SOEC Annually 1991 Luxembourg	ISBN 92 826 3068 4

***instat* code**	**Title**	**Edition indexed**	**Publisher Frequency Date Place**	**ISBN ISSN**
EC29	Employment and Unemployment	1989	SOEC Annually 1989 Luxembourg	ISBN 92 825 9734 2
EC30	Energy Balance Sheets	1988–89	SOEC Annually 1991 Luxembourg	ISBN 92 826 2244 4
EC31	Energy, Monthly Statistics	1991 (12)	SOEC Monthly 1991 Luxembourg	ISSN 0258 3569
EC32	Energy Prices	1978–90	SOEC 2 per year 1991 Luxembourg	ISBN 92 826 2354 8
EC33	Energy Yearly Statistics	1990	SOEC Annually 1992 Luxembourg	ISBN 92 826 3947 9
EC34	Environment Statistics	1989	SOEC Irregular 1990 Luxembourg	ISBN 92 826 1108 6
EC35	Europe in Figures	1992	SOEC Irregular 1992 Luxembourg	ISBN 92 826 3372 1
EC36	Eurostatistics – Data for Short-term Economic Analysis No 5	1992	SOEC Monthly 1992 Luxembourg	ISSN 0252 8266
EC37	External Trade: Analytical Tables A– L, Imports and Exports	1990	SOEC Annually 1991 Luxembourg	ISBN 92 826 2613 X
EC38	External Trade and Balance of Payments	1992	SOEC Monthly 1992 Luxembourg	ISSN 1017 6004
EC39	External Trade Statistical Yearbook	1958–89	SOEC Annually 1990 Luxembourg	ISBN 92 826 1666 5
EC40	External Trade, System of Generalized Tariff Preferences Imports 1988 Vol I	1988	SOEC Annually 1990 Luxembourg	ISBN 92 826 1110 8

***instat* code**	**Title**	**Edition indexed**	**Publisher Frequency Date Place**	**ISBN ISSN**
EC41	External Trade, System of Generalized Tariff Preferences Imports 1988 Vol II	1988	SOEC Annually 1990 Luxembourg	ISBN 92 826 1110 8
EC42	Family Budgets: Comparative Tables Vols I and II	1990	SOEC Irregular 1990 Luxembourg	ISBN 92 826 1568 5
EC43	Farm Structure: 1985 Survey Analysis of Results. Economic Size and Other Gainful Activities	1985	SOEC Irregular 1988 Luxembourg	ISBN 92 825 7706 6
EC44	Farm Structure: 1985 Survey Analysis of Results. Regional Structure of Agricultural Production	1985	SOEC Irregular 1991 Luxembourg	ISBN 92 826 1970 2
EC45	Farm Structure: 1985 Survey Main Results	1985	SOEC Irregular 1987 Luxembourg	ISBN 92 825 7626 4
EC46	Fisheries, Yearly Statistics	1990	SOEC Annually 1990 Luxembourg	ISBN 92 826 1914 1
EC47	Forestry Statistics	1980–84	SOEC Irregular 1987 Luxembourg	ISBN 92 825 6943 8
EC48	Gas Prices	1985–90	SOEC Annually 1990 Luxembourg	ISBN 92 826 1679 7
EC49	General Government Accounts and Statistics	1970–87	SOEC Annually 1990 Luxembourg	ISBN 92 826 1570 7
EC50	Government Financing of Research and Development	1980–90	SOEC Annually 1991 Luxembourg	ISBN 92 826 2885 X
EC51	Industrial Production Quarterly Statistics	1991 (2)	SOEC Quarterly 1991 Luxembourg	ISSN 0254 0649
EC52	Industrial Trends Monthly Statistics	1992 December	SOEC Monthly 1992 Luxembourg	ISSN 0258 1922

***instat* code**	**Title**	**Edition indexed**	**Publisher Frequency Date Place**	**ISBN ISSN**
EC53	Industry Statistical Yearbook	1988	SOEC Annually 1989 Luxembourg	ISBN 92 825 9038 0
EC54	International Comparisons of Energy Data	1988	SOEC Irregular 1991 Luxembourg	ISBN 92 826 2156 1
EC55	Iron and Steel, Yearly Statistics	1991	SOEC Annually 1991 Luxembourg	ISBN 92 826 3261 X
EC56	Labour Force Survey Results 1991	1991	SOEC Annually 1993 Luxembourg	ISBN 92 826 5414 1
EC57	Milk Quotas – their Effects on Agriculture in the European Community, Vol 1 Main Report	1990	SOEC Irregular 1990 Luxembourg	ISBN 92 826 1245 7
EC58	Milk Quotas – their Effects on Agriculture in the European Community, Vol 2 Annex	1990	SOEC Irregular 1990 Luxembourg	ISBN 92 826 1246 5
EC59	Money and Finance	1990 (4)	SOEC Quarterly 1991 Luxembourg	ISSN 0255 6510
EC60	National Accounts ESA Aggregates	1970–89	SOEC Annually 1991 Luxembourg	ISBN 92 826 2099 9
EC61	National Accounts ESA Detailed Tables by Branch	1989	SOEC Annually 1990 Luxembourg	ISBN 92 826 1001 2
EC62	National Accounts ESA Detailed Tables by Sector	1970–87	SOEC Annually 1990 Luxembourg	ISBN 92 826 1431 X
EC63	National Accounts ESA Input-Output Tables	1980	SOEC 5 yearly 1986 Luxembourg	ISBN 92 825 6539 4
EC64	Operation of Nuclear Power Stations	1989	SOEC Annually 1990 Luxembourg	ISBN 92 826 1531 6

instat code	Title	Edition indexed	Publisher Frequency Date Place	ISBN ISSN
EC65	Portrait of the Regions: Vol I Germany Benelux Denmark Vol II France United Kingdom Ireland Vol III Portugal Spain Italy Greece	1993	SOEC Irregular 1993 Luxembourg	ISBN 92 826 3222 9 ISBN 92 826 3223 7 ISBN 92 826 3224 5
EC66	Price Structure of the Community Countries in 1985	1985	SOEC Irregular 1988 Luxembourg	ISBN 92 825 7715 5
EC67	Quarterly National Accounts ESA	1990 (4)	SOEC Quarterly 1990 Luxembourg	ISSN 1010 1764
EC68	Raw Material EC Supply	1975–83	SOEC Irregular 1986 Luxembourg	ISBN 92 825 5837 1
EC69	Regions Statistical Yearbook	1989	SOEC Annually 1990 Luxembourg	ISBN 92 826 1198 1
EC70	Results of the Business Survey Carried Out Among Managements in the Community	1992 January	SOEC Monthly 1992 Luxembourg	ISSN 0378 4479
EC71	Retailing in the European Single Market 1993	1993	SOEC Irregular 1993 Luxembourg	ISBN 92 826 54583
EC72	A Social Portrait of Europe	1991	SOEC Irregular 1991 Luxembourg	ISBN 92 826 1747 5
EC73	Social Protection Expenditure and Receipts	1980–89	SOEC Irregular 1991 Luxembourg	ISBN 92 826 3251 2
EC74	Steel Consumption by User Branch	1970–84	SOEC Irregular 1986 Luxembourg	ISBN 92 825 6813 X
EC75	Structure and Activity of Industry: Annual Enquiry Main Results	1987–88	SOEC Annually 1991 Luxembourg	ISBN 92 826 3254 7
EC76	Structure and Activity of Industry: Data by Regions	1986–87	SOEC Annually 1991 Luxembourg	ISBN 92 826 2157 X

instat code	Title	Edition indexed	Publisher Frequency Date Place	ISBN ISSN
EC77	Structure and Activity of Industry: Data by Size of Enterprises	1986–88	SOEC Irregular 1991 Luxembourg	ISBN 92 826 2759 4
EC78	Tourism Annual Statistics	1988–89	SOEC Annually 1991 Luxembourg	ISBN 92 826 0530 2
EC79	Tourism in Europe, Trends	1989	SOEC Annually 1990 Luxembourg	ISBN 92 826 1581 2
EC80	Transport and Communications Annual Statistics	1970–87	SOEC Annually 1990 Luxembourg	ISBN 92 826 1564 2
EC81	Unemployment	1991 (1)	SOEC Monthly 1991 Luxembourg	ISSN 0252 9920

ECMT: EUROPEAN CONFERENCE OF MINISTERS OF TRANSPORT

ECMT1	Statistical Report on Road Accidents	1990	ECMT Annually 1992 Paris, France	ISBN 92 821 0174 6 ISSN 1012 9898
ECMT2	Statistical Trends in Transport	1965–88	ECMT Annually 1992 Paris, France	ISBN 92 821 0173 8
ECMT3	Trends in the Transport Sector	1970–90	ECMT Annually 1991 Paris, France	—

EDFM: E D & F MAN COCOA LIMITED

EDFM1	Cocoa Market Report	1993 No 347	EDFM 3 per year 1993 London, UK	—

EFTA: EUROPEAN FREE TRADE ASSOCIATION

EFTA1	EFTA Trade	1990	EFTA Economic Affairs Department Annually 1991 Geneva, Switzerland	ISSN 0531 4119

***instat* code**	**Title**	**Edition indexed**	**Publisher Frequency Date Place**	**ISBN ISSN**

EM: EUROMONITOR

EM1	European Marketing Data and Statistics	1993	Euromonitor Annually 1993 London, UK	ISBN 0 86338 457 9 ISSN 0071 2930

EPI: EUROPEAN PAPER INSTITUTE

EPI1	European Paper Institute Annual Statistics	1983–90	EPI Annually 1991 Paris, France	—

EPO: EUROPEAN PATENT OFFICE

EPO1	Facts and Figures	1991	EPO Annually 1992 Munich, Germany	—

F: FEARNLEYS

F1	Fearnley's Review	1987	Fearnleys Annually 1988 Oslo, Norway	ISSN 0801 5589
F2	World Bulk Fleet	1988	Fearnleys Half-yearly August 1988 Oslo, Norway	ISSN 0801 5007
F3	World Bulk Trades	1986	Fearnleys Annually 1987 Oslo, Norway	ISSN 0801 4086

FAO: FOOD AND AGRICULTURE ORGANISATION

FAO1	FAO Production Yearbook	1990 Vol 44	FAO Annually 1991 Rome, Italy	ISBN 92 5 003067 3 ISSN 0071 7118
FAO2	FAO Trade Yearbook	1986 Vol 40	FAO Annually 1987 Rome, Italy	ISBN 92 5 002596 3
FAO3	FAO Yearbook of Fishery Statistics: Catches and Landings	1986 Vol 62	FAO Annually 1988 Rome, Italy	ISBN 92 5 002627 7 ISSN 02515679

instat code	Title	Edition indexed	Publisher Frequency Date Place	ISBN ISSN
FAO4	FAO Yearbook of Fishery Statistics: Commodities	1986 Vol 68	FAO Annually 1988 Rome, Italy	ISBN 92 5 002628 5 ISSN 02515687
FAO5	Fertiliser Yearbook	1989 Vol 39	FAO Annually 1990 Rome, Italy	ISBN 92 5 002964 0
FAO6	Quarterly Bulletin of Statistics	1993 Vol 6 (3)	FAO Quarterly 1993 Rome, Italy	ISSN 1011 8780
FAO7	World Crop and Livestock Statistics	1948–85	FAO Irregular 1987 Rome, Italy	ISBN 92 5 002530 0
FAO8	Yearbook of Forest Products	1976–87	FAO Annually 1989 Rome, Italy	ISBN 92 5 002727 3

FNOCL: FEDERATION NATIONALE DES ORGANISMES DE CONTROLE LAITIER

FNOCL1	Situation de la Production Laitière et du Contrôle Laitier dans les Pays Members	1991	FNOCL Annually 1992 Paris, France	—

FOL: F O LICHT

FOL1	International Molasses and Alcohol Report	1992 Vol 29 No 17	F O Licht Bi-monthly 1992 Ratzeburg, Germany	—
FOL2	International Sugar and Sweetener Report	1993 14 April Vol 125	F O Licht Weekly 1993 Ratzeburg, Germany	—
FOL3	World Sugar and Sweetener Yearbook	1989	F O Licht Annually 1989 Ratzeburg, Germany	ISBN 3 9801139 0 6

G: E A GIBSON SHIPBROKERS LIMITED

G1	Oil, Chemical and Combined Carriers	1993 March	Gibsons Irregular 1993 London, UK	—

***instat* code**	**Title**	**Edition indexed**	**Publisher Frequency Date Place**	**ISBN ISSN**
G2	Register of Liquified Gas Carriers	1993	Gibsons Annually 1993 London, UK	—

GATT: GENERAL AGREEMENT ON TARIFFS AND TRADE

GATT1	The International Markets for Meat	1991–92	GATT Annually 1992 Geneva, Switzerland	ISBN 92 870 1053 6 ISSN 0259 8213
GATT2	The International Markets for Meat. Arrangement Regarding Bovine Meat 12th Annual Report	1991–92	GATT Annually 1992 Geneva, Switzerland	ISBN 92 870 1066 8 ISSN 0259 8213
GATT3	International Trade Statistics Vol I	1989–90	GATT Annually 1990 Geneva, Switzerland	ISBN 92 870 1057 9 ISSN 0072 064X
GATT4	International Trade Statistics Vol II	1989–90	GATT Annually 1990 Geneva, Switzerland	ISBN 92 870 1058 7 ISSN 0072 064X
GATT5	The World Market for Dairy Products	1991	GATT Annually 1991 Geneva, Switzerland	ISBN 92 870 1065 X ISSN 0259 8213

GP: GENERATION PUBLICATIONS

GP1	The Best 'N' Most in DFS	1992–93	General Publications Annually 1992 Örnsköldsvik, Sweden	ISBN 91 86166 15 8 ISSN 1100 3006

HI: HORWATH INTERNATIONAL

HI1	Worldwide Hotel Industry	1992	Horwath International Annually 1992 New York, USA	—

IADB: INTER-AMERICAN DEVELOPMENT BANK

IADB1	Pocket Profiles	1991	IADB Irregular 1991 Washington DC, USA	—

instat code	Title	Edition indexed	Publisher Frequency Date Place	ISBN ISSN

IAEA: INTERNATIONAL ATOMIC ENERGY AGENCY

IAEA1	Operating Experience with Nuclear Power Stations in Member States in 1990	1990	IAEA Annually 1991 Vienna, Austria	ISBN 92 0 159391 0 ISSN 1011 2634

IAHP: INTERNATIONAL ASSOCIATION OF HORTICULTURAL PRODUCERS

IAHP1	Yearbook of International Horticultural Statistics	1992 Vol 40	IAHP Annually 1992 The Hague, Netherlands	ISBN 90 74486 01 0

IARC: INTERNATIONAL AGENCY FOR RESEARCH ON CANCER

IARC1	Cancer Incidence in Five Continents	1987 Vol V	IARC 5 yearly 1987 Lyon, France	ISBN 92 832 1188X ISSN 0300 5085

IATA: INTERNATIONAL AIR TRANSPORT ASSOCIATION

IATA1	World Air Transport Statistics	1991 No 36	IATA Annually 1992 London, UK	ISBN 92 9035 454 2

IBA: INTERNATIONAL BAUXITE ASSOCIATION

IBA1	IBA Quarterly Review	1991 Vol 17	IBA Quarterly 1991 Jamaica	—

ICAC: INTERNATIONAL COTTON ADVISORY COMMITTEE

ICAC1	Cotton: Review of the World Situation	1992 Vol 45 No 3	ICAC 2 monthly 1992 Washington DC, USA	ISSN 0010 9754
ICAC2	Cotton: World Statistics, Bulletin of the International Cotton Advisory Committee	1991 Vol 45 No 1	ICAC Annually 1991 Washington DC, USA	—

ICAO: INTERNATIONAL CIVIL AVIATION ORGANIZATION

ICAO1	Accident/Incident Reporting (ADREP) Annual Statistics	1987	ICAO Annually 1991 Montreal, Canada	—

instat code	Title	Edition indexed	Publisher Frequency Date Place	ISBN ISSN
ICAO2	Civil Aviation Statistics of the World Doc 9180	1990	ICAO Annually 1991 Montreal, Canada	—
ICAO3	Digest of Statistics Series AF Airport and Route Facilities, Financial Data and Summary Traffic Data	Digest No 399 Series AF No 9 1991	ICAO Annually 1993 Montreal, Canada	—
ICAO4	Digest of Statistics Series AT Airport Traffic	Digest No 383 Series AT No 31 1990	ICAO Annually 1991 Montreal, Canada	—
ICAO5	Digest of Statistics Series F Financial Data, Commercial Air Carriers	Digest No 397 Series F No 45 1991	ICAO Annually 1993 Montreal, Canada	—
ICAO6	Digest of Statistics Series FP Fleet – Personnel, Commercial Air Carriers	Digest No 385 Series FP No 44 1990	ICAO Annually 1991 Montreal, Canada	—
ICAO7	Digest of Statistics Series OFOD On Flight Origin and Destination	Digest No 381 Series OFOD No 44 1990	ICAO Quarterly 1990 Montreal, Canada	—
ICAO8	Digest of Statistics Series R Civil Aircraft on Register	Digest No 382 Series R No 30 1990	ICAO Annually 1991 Montreal, Canada	—
ICAO9	Digest of Statistics Series T Traffic – Commercial Air Carriers	Digest No 379 Series T No 50 1986–90	ICAO Annually 1991 Montreal, Canada	—
ICAO10	Digest of Statistics Series TF Traffic By Flight Stage	Digest No 398 Series TF No 106 1991	ICAO Annually 1991 Montreal, Canada	—

ICCAT: INTERNATIONAL COMMISSION FOR THE CONSERVATION OF ATLANTIC TUNAS

instat code	Title	Edition indexed	Publisher Frequency Date Place	ISBN ISSN
ICCAT1	Statistical Bulletin	1989 Vol 20	ICCAT Annually 1989 Madrid, Spain	—

instat code	Title	Edition indexed	Publisher Frequency Date Place	ISBN ISSN
ICCO: INTERNATIONAL COCOA COUNCIL ORGANIZATION				
ICCO1	International Cocoa Organization Annual Report	1991–92	ICCO Annually 1992 London, UK	—
ICCO2	Quarterly Bulletin of Cocoa Statistics	1991 Vol XVIII No 1	ICCO Quarterly 1991 London, UK	ISSN 0308 4469
ICCO3	The World Cocoa Market: An Analysis of Recent Trends and of Prospects to the Year 2000	1993	ICCO Irregular 1993 London, UK	ISBN 1 85670 0054
IDF: INTERNATIONAL DAIRY FEDERATION				
IDF1	Bulletin–Consumption Statistics for Milk and Milk Products	1991 No 282	IDF Annually 1993 Brussels, Belgium	ISSN 0250 5118
IEA: INTERNATIONAL ENERGY AGENCY				
IEA1	Annual Oil Market Report	1990	OECD/IEA Annually 1991 Paris, France	ISBN 92 64 13550 2
IEA2	Coal Information	1991	OECD/IEA Annually 1991 Paris, France	ISBN 92 64 13536 7
IEA3	Electricity Supply in the OECD	1992	OECD/IEA Irregular 1992 Paris, France	ISBN 92 64 13599 5
IEA4	Energy Balances of OECD Countries 1980–89	1980–89	OECD/IEA Irregular 1991 Paris, France	ISBN 92 64 03500 1
IEA5	Energy Balances of OECD Countries 1990–91	1990–91	OECD/IEA Annually 1993 Paris, France	ISBN 92 64 03860 4
IEA6	Energy Prices and Taxes	1991 (4)	OECD/IEA Quarterly 1991 Paris, France	ISBN 92 64 13644 4

instat code	Title	Edition indexed	Publisher Frequency Date Place	ISBN ISSN
IEA7	Energy Statistics and Balances of Non-OECD Countries	1988–89	OECD/IEA Annually 1991 Paris, France	ISBN 92 64 03511 7
IEA8	Energy Statistics of OECD Countries 1980– 89	1980–89	OECD/IEA Irregular 1991 Paris, France	ISBN 92 64 03299 1
IEA9	Energy Statistics of OECD Countries 1989– 90	1989–90	OECD/IEA Annually 1992 Paris, France	ISBN 92 64 03534 6
IEA10	Oil and Gas Information	1988–90	OECD/IEA Annually 1991 Paris, France	ISBN 92 64 03507 9
IEA11	Quarterly Oil Statistics and Energy Balances	1991 (3)	OECD/IEA Quarterly 1991 Paris, France	ISSN 0378 6536
IEA12	World Energy Statistics and Balances	1985–88	OECD/IEA Irregular 1990 Paris, France	ISBN 92 64 03335 1

IFA: INTERNATIONAL FERTILIZER INDUSTRY ASSOCIATION

IFA1	Urea Statistics	1991	IFA Annually 1992 Paris, France	—

IISI: INTERNATIONAL IRON AND STEEL INSTITUTE

IISI1	Annual Report of the International Iron and Steel Institute	1992	IISI Annually 1992 Brussels, Belgium	—
IISI2	Monthly Crude Iron and Steel Production	1993 May	IISI Monthly 1993 Brussels, Belgium	—
IISI3	Steel Statistics of Developing Countries	1992	IISI Annually 1992 Brussels, Belgium	—
IISI4	Steel Statistical Yearbook	1992	IISI Annually 1992 Brussels, Belgium	—

instat code	Title	Edition indexed	Publisher Frequency Date Place	ISBN ISSN
IISI5	World Steel in Figures	1991	IISI Annually 1991 Brussels, Belgium	—

IISRP: INTERNATIONAL INSTITUTE OF SYNTHETIC RUBBER PRODUCERS

IISRP1	Worldwide Rubber Statistics	1993	IISRP Annually 1993 Houston, USA	—

ILO: INTERNATIONAL LABOUR ORGANIZATION

ILO1	Bulletin of Labour Statistics	1991 (4)	ILO Quarterly 1991 Geneva, Switzerland	ISSN 0007 4950
ILO2	Economically Active Population 1950– 2025 Vol I Asia	1986	ILO Irregular 1986 Geneva, Switzerland	ISBN 92 2 005345 4 ISSN 0258 0489
ILO3	Economically Active Population 1950– 2025 Vol II Africa	1986	ILO Irregular 1986 Geneva, Switzerland	ISBN 92 2 005346 2 ISSN 0258 0489
ILO4	Economically Active Population 1950– 2025 Vol III Latin America	1986	ILO Irregular 1986 Geneva, Switzerland	ISBN 92 2 005347 0 ISSN 0258 0489
ILO5	Economically Active Population 1950– 2025 Vol IV Northern America, Europe, Oceania and USSR	1986	ILO Irregular 1986 Geneva, Switzerland	ISBN 92 2 005348 9 ISSN 0258 0489
ILO6	Economically Active Population 1950– 2025 Vol V World	1986	ILO Irregular 1986 Geneva, Switzerland	ISBN 92 2 005349 7 ISSN 0258 0489
ILO7	Yearbook of Labour Statistics	1991	ILO Annually 1991 Geneva, Switzerland	ISBN 92 2 007339 0 ISSN 0084 3857

ILZSG: INTERNATIONAL LEAD AND ZINC STUDY GROUP

ILZSG1	Bulletin of the Lead and Zinc Study Group: Lead and Zinc Statistics	1992 Vol 32 No 2	ILZSG Monthly 1992 London, UK	—

instat code	Title	Edition indexed	Publisher Frequency Date Place	ISBN ISSN
ILZSG2	Joint Production of Lead and Zinc	1957–81	ILZSG Irregular 1983 London, UK	—

IMF: INTERNATIONAL MONETARY FUND

instat code	Title	Edition indexed	Publisher Frequency Date Place	ISBN ISSN
IMF1	Balance of Payments Statistical Yearbook Part I	1990 Vol 41	IMF Annually 1990 Washington DC, USA	ISBN 1 55775 157 9 ISSN 0252 3035
IMF2	Balance of Payments Statistical Yearbook Part II	1990 Vol 41	IMF Annually 1990 Washington DC, USA	ISBN 1 55775 157 9 ISSN 0252 3035
IMF3	Direction of Trade Statistics Yearbook	1991	IMF Annually 1991 Washington DC, USA	ISBN 1 55775 1773 ISSN 0252 306X
IMF4	Direction of Trade Statistics	1992 March	IMF Quarterly 1992 Washington DC, USA	ISSN 0252 306X
IMF5	Government Finance Statistics Yearbook	1991	IMF Annually 1991 Washington DC, USA	ISBN 1 5577 5178 1 ISSN 0250 7374
IMF6	International Financial Statistics	1992 Vol XLV No 2	IMF Monthly 1992 Washington DC, USA	ISSN 0020 6725
IMF7	International Financial Statistics Yearbook	1991 Vol XLIV	IMF Annually 1991 Washington DC, USA	ISBN 1 55775 223 0 ISSN 0250 7463

IMWF: INTERNATIONAL METALWORKERS' FEDERATION

instat code	Title	Edition indexed	Publisher Frequency Date Place	ISBN ISSN
IMWF1	The Purchasing Power of Working Time. An International Comparison	1989	IMWF Irregular 1990 Geneva, Switzerland	—

INPFC: INTERNATIONAL NORTH PACIFIC FISHERIES COMMISSION

instat code	Title	Edition indexed	Publisher Frequency Date Place	ISBN ISSN
INPFC1	International North Pacific Fisheries Commission Statistical Yearbook	1988	INPFC Annually 1991 Vancouver, Canada	ISSN 0535 1588

instat code	Title	Edition indexed	Publisher Frequency Date Place	ISBN ISSN
IP: INSTITUTE OF PETROLEUM				
IP1	Know More About Oil, World Statistics	1992	IP Annually 1992 London, UK	ISSN 0141 4305
IPHC: INTERNATIONAL PACIFIC HALIBUT COMMISSION				
IPHC1	International Pacific Halibut Commission, Annual Report	1990	IPHC Winterholm Press Annually Seattle, USA	ISSN 0074 7238
IPU: INTER-PARLIAMENTARY UNION				
IPU1	Distribution of Seats Between Men and Women in National Parliaments. Statistical Data from 1945 to 30 June 1991	1991	IPU Irregular 1991 Geneva, Switzerland	—
IPU2	Women and Political Power Survey carried out among the 150 National Parliaments existing as from 31.10.91	1991	IPU Irregular 1991 Geneva, Switzerland	—
IRF: INTERNATIONAL ROAD FEDERATION				
IRF1	World Road Statistics, 1986– 90	1991	IRF Annually 1991 Geneva, Switzerland	ISSN 0444 1419
IRRI: INTERNATIONAL RICE RESEARCH INSTITUTE				
IRRI1	World Rice Statistics, 1987	1987	IRRI Annually 1988 Manilla, Philippines	ISBN 971 104 204 5
IRSG: INTERNATIONAL RUBBER STUDY GROUP				
IRSG1	Rubber Statistical Bulletin	1993 Vol 47 No 11	IRSG Monthly 1993 London, UK	ISSN 0035 9548
IRSG2	World Rubber Statistics Handbook	1960–90 Vol 4	IRSG Irregular 1992 London, UK	—

instat code	Title	Edition indexed	Publisher Frequency Date Place	ISBN ISSN
IRTU: INTERNATIONAL ROAD TRANSPORT UNION				
IRTU1	World Transport Data	1990	IRTU Annually 1990 Geneva, Switzerland	—
ISL: INSTITUTE OF SHIPPING ECONOMICS AND LOGISTICS				
ISL1	Shipping Statistics	1993 April	ISL 10– 12 per year 1993 Bremen, Germany	ISSN 0721 3751
ISL2	Shipping Statistics Yearbook	1991	ISL Annually 1991 Bremen, Germany	ISSN 0721 3220
ISO: INTERNATIONAL SUGAR ORGANIZATION				
ISO1	Quarterly Market Review	1993	ISO Quarterly 1993 London, UK	—
ISO2	Statistical Bulletin	1993 Vol 51 No 4	ISO Monthly 1993 London, UK	—
ISO3	Sugar Yearbook	1991	ISO Annually 1992 London, UK	—
ISSB: IRON AND STEEL STATISTICS BUREAU				
ISSB1	International Steel Statistics Summary Tables	1988	ISSB Annually 1991 Croydon, UK	ISSN 0952 6803
ISSB2	World Trade Stainless, High Speed and Other Alloy Steel	1988	ISSB Bi-annually 1988 Croydon, UK	ISSN 0952 5742
ISSB3	World Trade Steel	1988	ISSB Quarterly 1988 Croydon, UK	—

***instat* code**	**Title**	**Edition indexed**	**Publisher Frequency Date Place**	**ISBN ISSN**
ISTA: ISTA MIELK GmbH				
ISTA1	Oil World	1992 31 January	ISTA Mielke Weekly 1992 Hamburg, Germany	—
ISTA2	Oil World Annual	1992	ISTA Mielke Annually 1992 Hamburg, Germany	—
ITC: INTERNATIONAL TEA COMMITTEE				
ITC1	Annual Bulletin of Statistics	1992	ITC Annually 1992 London, UK	ISSN 0305 2370
ITMF: INTERNATIONAL TEXTILE MANUFACTURERS FEDERATION				
ITMF1	Country Statements	1992	ITMF Annually 1992 Zurich, Switzerland	—
ITMF2	International Cotton Industry Statistics	1991 Vol 34	ITMF Annually 1992 Zurich, Switzerland	—
ITMF3	International Textile Machinery Shipment Statistics	1991 Vol 14	ITMF Annually 1992 Zurich, Switzerland	—
ITTO: INTERNATIONAL TROPICAL TIMBER ORGANIZATION				
ITTO1	Annual Review and Assessment of the World Tropical Timber Situation	1992	ITTO Annually 1993 Yokohama, Japan	—
ITU: INTERNATIONAL TELECOMMUNICATION UNION				
ITU1	Yearbook of Common Carrier Telecommunications Statistics	1981–90	ITU Annually 1992 Geneva, Switzerland	ISBN 92 71 1706 X
IUR: INTERNATIONAL UNION OF RAILWAYS				
IUR1	International Railway Statistics Statistics of Individual Railways	1991	IUR Annually 1993 Paris, France	—

instat code	Title	Edition indexed	Publisher Frequency Date Place	ISBN ISSN
IWC: INTERNATIONAL WHALING COMMISSION				
IWC1	International Whaling Statistics	1988	IWC Irregular 1988 Cambridge, UK	ISSN 0020 9090
IWhC: INTERNATIONAL WHEAT COUNCIL				
IWhC1	Food Aid Shipments	1987–88	IWhC Annually 1989 London, UK	—
IWhC2	Grain Market Report	1993	IWhC Monthly 1993 London, UK	—
IWhC3	Report for the Crop Year	1989–90	IWhC Annually 1991 London, UK	—
IWS: INTERNATIONAL WOOL SECRETARIAT				
IWS1	Wool Facts 1991–92	1992	IWS Annually 1992 London, UK	—
JM: JOHNSON MATTHEY				
JM1	Platinum	1993	Johnson Matthey Bi-annually 1993 London, UK	ISSN 0268 7305
JP: JAAKKO PÖYRY				
JP1	Short-term Review of International Pulp and Paper Markets	1992 No 58	Jaakko Pöyry 3–4 times yearly 1992 Vantaa, Finland	ISSN 0784 7289
LRS: LLOYDS REGISTER OF SHIPPING				
LRS1	Annual Summary of Merchant Ships Completed	1992	Lloyd's Register Annually 1993 London, UK	ISSN 0261 1848

instat code	Title	Edition indexed	Publisher Frequency Date Place	ISBN ISSN
LRS2	Casualty Return	1991	Lloyd's Register Annually 1992 London, UK	ISSN 0268 0815
LRS3	Merchant Shipbuilding Return	1993 March	Lloyd's Register Quarterly 1993 London, UK	ISSN 0261 0848
LRS4	World Fleet Statistics	1992 December	Lloyd's Register Annually 1993 London, UK	ISSN 0076 0234
MAC: MACMILLAN				
MAC1	International Historical Statistics, Africa and Asia	1982	Macmillan Irregular 1982 London, UK	ISBN 0 333 31630
MAC2	International Historical Statistics, The Americas and Australasia	1983	Macmillan Irregular 1983 London, UK	ISBN 0 333 31629 0
MAC3	International Historical Statistics, Europe 1750– 1988	1992 3rd edn	Macmillan[1] Irregular 1992 Basingstoke, UK	ISBN 0 333 56872 9
MB: METAL BULLETIN BOOKS LIMITED				
MB1	Iron and Manganese Ore Databook	1992	Metal Bulletin Irregular 1992 Worcester Park, UK	ISBN 0 947671 62 5 ISSN 0967 7925
MB2	Metal Bulletin's Prices and Data	1992	Metal Bulletin Annual 1992 Worcester Park, UK	ISBN 0 947671 58 7 ISSN 0269 1698
MHPPE: MINISTRY OF HOUSING, PHYSICAL PLANNING AND THE ENVIRONMENT (NETHERLANDS)				
MHPPE1	Statistics on Housing in the European Community	1992	MHPPE Annually 1992 The Hague, The Netherlands	—

[1] Published in the United States and Canada by Stockton Press, 1992. ISBN 1 56159 038 X

instat code	Title	Edition indexed	Publisher Frequency Date Place	ISBN ISSN
MJ: MINING JOURNAL				
MJ1	Metals and Minerals The Safer World of SGS	1992	Mining Journal Annually 1992 London, UK	ISBN 0 900117 58 3
MLC: MEAT AND LIVESTOCK COMMISSION				
MLC1	European Handbook, EEC and International Statistics	1992 Vol II	Meat and Livestock Commission Irregular 1992 Milton Keynes, UK	—
MMB: MILK MARKETING BOARD				
MMB1	EC Dairy Facts and Figures	1992	MMB Annually 1992 Thames Ditton, Surrey	—
NATO: NORTH ATLANTIC TREATY ORGANIZATION				
NATO1	The North Atlantic Treaty Organization 1949– 89, Facts and Figures	1949–89	NATO Irregular 1989 Brussels, Belgium	ISBN 92 845 0041 9
NCM: NORDIC COUNCIL OF MINISTERS AND THE NORDIC STATISTICAL SECRETARIAT				
NCM1	Yearbook of Nordic Statistics	1991	Nordic Council of Ministers and the Nordic Statistical Secretariat Annually 1991 Copenhagen, Denmark	ISBN (Denmark) 87 7303 529 7) ISBN (Sweden) 91 7996 303 X ISSN 0078 1088
NWAFO: NORTH WEST ATLANTIC FISHERIES ORGANIZATION				
NWAFO1	Statistical Bulletin, Fishery Statistics for 1988	1988 Vol 38	NWAFO Annually 1991 Dartmouth, Nova Scotia, Canada	ISSN 0250 6394

instat code	Title	Edition indexed	Publisher Frequency Date Place	ISBN ISSN

OECD: ORGANIZATION FOR ECONOMIC CO-OPERATION AND DEVELOPMENT [1]

instat code	Title	Edition indexed	Publisher Frequency Date Place	ISBN ISSN
OECD1	Balances of Payments of OECD Countries	1965–84	OECD Irregular 1986 Paris, France	ISBN 92 64 02836 6
OECD2	Bank Profitability: Statistical Supplement – Financial Statements of Banks	1981–89	OECD Irregular 1991 Paris, France	ISBN 92 64 03518 4
OECD3	Basic Science and Technology Statistics	1991	OECD Biennially 1991 Paris, France	ISBN 92 64 03501 X
OECD4	Demographic Trends in OECD Member Countries	1970–85	OECD Irregular 1974 Paris, France	ISBN 92 64 01262 1
OECD5	Economic Accounts for Agriculture	1976–89	OECD Irregular 1991 Paris, France	ISBN 92 64 03521 4
OECD6	Education at a Glance	1992	OECD Irregular 1992 Paris, France	ISBN 92 64 03692 X
OECD7	Education in OECD Countries	1987–88	OECD Annually 1990 Paris, France	ISBN 92 64 13425 5
OECD8	External Debt Statistics: The Debt and Other External Liabilities of Developing, CMEA and Certain Other Countries and Territories at end December 1987 and end December 1988	1989	OECD Annually 1989 Paris, France	ISBN 92 54 13305 4
OECD9	External Debt Statistics: The Debt and Other External Liabilities of Developing, Central and Eastern European and Certain Other Countries and Territories at end December 1988 and end December 1989	1989	OECD Annually 1990 Paris, France	ISBN 92 64 13427 1
OECD10	Financial Market Trends	1993 No 56	OECD 3 per year 1993 Paris, France	ISSN 0378 651X

[1] Publications of the International Energy Agency and the European Conference of Ministers of Transport are listed separately under IEA and ECMT respectively.

instat code	Title	Edition indexed	Publisher Frequency Date Place	ISBN ISSN
OECD11	Flows and Stocks of Fixed Capital: 1964– 89	1964–89	OECD Irregular 1991 Paris, France	ISBN 92 64 03514 1
OECD12	Food Consumption Statistics	1979–88	OECD Irregular 1991 Paris, France	ISBN 92 64 03513 3
OECD13	Foreign Trade by Commodities Vols I to V Series C	1990	OECD Annually 1992 Paris, France	ISSN 0474 540X
OECD14	Geographical Distribution of Financial Flows to Developing Countries, Disbursements, Commitments, Economic Indicators: 1986– 89	1991	OECD Irregular 1991 Paris, France	ISBN 92 64 03345 9 ISSN 1015 3934
OECD15	Indicators of Industrial Activity	1991 (4)	OECD Quarterly 1991 Paris, France	ISSN 0250 4278
OECD16	Industrial Structure Statistics	1989–90	OECD Irregular 1992 Paris, France	ISBN 92 64 03528 1
OECD17	International Direct Investment Statistics Yearbook	1993	OECD Annually 1993 Paris, France	ISBN 92 64 03887 6
OECD18	The Iron and Steel Industry	1990	OECD Annually 1992 Paris, France	ISBN 92 64 03530 3
OECD19	Labour Force Statistics	1969–89	OECD Annually 1991 Paris, France	ISBN 92 64 03510 9
OECD20	Living Conditions in OECD Countries: Compendium of Social Indicators	1986	OECD Irregular 1986 Paris, France	ISBN 92 64 12734 8
OECD21	Main Economic Indicators	1992 June	OECD Monthly 1992 Paris, France	ISSN 0474 5523
OECD22	Main Economic Indicators, Historical Statistics	1969–1988	OECD Irregular 1990 Paris, France	ISBN 92 64 03296 70

instat code	Title	Edition indexed	Publisher Frequency Date Place	ISBN ISSN
OECD23	Main Economic Indicators, Historical Statistics: Prices Labour and Wages 1962–91	1962–91	OECD Irregular 1993 Paris, France	ISBN 92 64 03873 6
OECD24	Main Science and Technology Indicators	1993 (1)	OECD Biannually 1993 Paris, France	ISSN 1011 792X
OECD25	Maritime Transport	1990	OECD Annually 1991 Paris, France	ISBN 92 64 13587 1 ISSN 0474 5884
OECD26	Meat Balances in OECD Countries	1982–88	OECD Irregular 1990 Paris, France	ISBN 92 64 03374 2
OECD27	Monthly Statistics of Foreign Trade, Series A	1992 May	OECD Monthly 1992 Paris, France	ISSN 0474 5388
OECD28	National Accounts Vol I Main Aggregates	1960–90	OECD Annually 1992 Paris, France	ISBN 92 64 03522 2 ISSN 0256 758X
OECD29	National Accounts Vol II Detailed Tables	1978–90	OECD Annually 1992 Paris, France	ISBN 92 64 03683 0 ISSN 0256 7571
OECD30	National and International Tourism Statistics	1974–85	OECD Irregular 1989 Paris, France	ISBN 92 64 03221 5
OECD31	Nuclear Energy Data	1991	OECD Nuclear Energy Agency Annually 1991 Paris, France	ISBN 92 64 03297 5 ISSN 1017 9402
OECD32	OECD Economic Outlook Historical Statistics	1960–89	OECD Annually 1991 Paris, France	ISBN 92 64 03348 3
OECD33	OECD Environmental Data Compendium	1991	OECD 2 yearly 1991 Paris, France	ISBN 92 64 03512 5
OECD34	OECD Financial Statistics Part 1, Section 1 International Markets	1992	OECD Monthly 1992 Paris, France	ISSN 0304 3371

***instat* code**	**Title**	**Edition indexed**	**Publisher Frequency Date Place**	**ISBN ISSN**
OECD35	OECD Financial Statistics Part 1, Section 2 Domestic Markets – Interest Rates	1992	OECD Monthly 1992 Paris, France	ISSN 0304 3371
OECD36	OECD Financial Statistics Part 2, Financial Accounts of OECD Countries (series of booklets – one for each country)	1976–91	OECD Annually 1993 Paris, France	ISSN 0304 3371
OECD37	OECD Financial Statistics Part 3 Non-Financial Enterprises Financial Statements	1991	OECD Annually 1992 Paris, France	ISSN 0304 3371
OECD38	The Pulp and Paper Industry	1988	OECD Annually 1991 Paris, France	ISBN 92 64 03509 5
OECD39	Purchasing Power Parities and Real Expenditures	1990	OECD Irregular 1992 Paris, France	ISBN 92 64 03686 5
OECD40	Quarterly Labour Force Statistics	1993 (2)	OECD Quarterly 1993 Paris, France	ISSN 0255 3627
OECD41	Quarterly National Accounts	1992 (4)	OECD Quarterly 1992 Paris, France	ISSN 0304 3738
OECD42	Revenue Statistics of OECD Member Countries	1965–90	OECD Annually 1991 Paris, France	ISBN 92 64 03504 4
OECD43	Review of Fisheries in OECD Member Countries	1989	OECD Annually 1991 Paris, France	ISBN 92 64 13541 3 ISSN 0078 6241
OECD44	Services: Statistics on International Transactions	1970–89	OECD Irregular 1992 Paris, France	ISBN 92 64 03681 4
OECD45	Steel Market in 1991 and the Outlook for 1992	1992	OECD Annually 1992 Paris, France	ISBN 92 64 13677 0
OECD46	Tourism Policy and International Tourism in OECD Member Countries	1989	OECD Annually 1990 Paris, France	ISBN 92 64 13424 7 ISSN 0256 7598

***instat* code**	**Title**	**Edition indexed**	**Publisher Frequency Date Place**	**ISBN ISSN**
OECD47	Uranium – Resources, Production and Demand	1989	OECD Irregular 1990 Paris, France	ISBN 92 64 13364 X

OIVV: OFFICE INTERNATIONAL DE LA VIGNE ET DU VIN

OIVV1	Bulletin de IOIV	1991 November– December	Office International de la Vigne et du Vin Bi-monthly 1991 Paris, France	ISSN 0029 7127

OPEC: ORGANIZATION OF PETROLEUM EXPORTING COUNTRIES

OPEC1	OPEC Annual Statistical Bulletin	1989	OPEC Annually 1990 Vienna, Austria	ISSN 0475 0608
OPEC2	OPEC Bulletin	1992 January	OPEC 10 issues per year 1992 Vienna, Austria	ISSN 0474 6279

PC: THE POPULATION COUNCIL

PC1	Family Planning and Child Survival Programs as Assessed in 1991	1991	The Population Council Irregular 1992 New York, USA	ISBN 0 87834 066 1

PKF: PANNELL KERR FORSTER

PKF1	Euro Trends Survey	1992	Panell Kerr Forster Annually 1992 London, UK	—
PKF2	Trends in the Hotel Industry	1989	Panell Kerr Forster Annually 1989 Houston, USA	—

PPI: PULP AND PAPER INTERNATIONAL

PPI1	Pulp and Paper International Annual Review	1992	PPI Annually 1992 Brussels, Belgium	—

instat code	Title	Edition indexed	Publisher Frequency Date Place	ISBN ISSN
SATRA: SATRA FOOTWEAR TECHNOLOGY CENTRE				
SATRA1	World Footwear Markets	1992	SATRA Annually 1992 Kettering, UK	ISSN 0266 0709
SFIA: SEA FISH INDUSTRY AUTHORITY				
SFIA1	European Supplies Bulletin	1989 December	SFIA Annually 1989 Edinburgh, UK	ISSN 0142 973X
SMMT: SOCIETY OF MOTOR MANUFACTURERS AND TRADERS LIMITED				
SMMT1	Monthly Statistical Review	1993 April	SMMT Monthly 1993 London, UK	—
SMMT2	Motor Industry of Great Britain: World Automotive Statistics	1992	SMMT Annually 1992 London, UK	—
SPC: SOUTH PACIFIC COMMISSION				
SPC1	Retail Price Indices, Statistical Bulletin of the South Pacific	1992 No 44	SPC Annually 1993 Noumea, New Caledonia	ISSN 1018 0958
SPC2	South Pacific Economies	1992	SPC Irregular 1992 Noumea, New Caledonia	ISBN 982 203 246 3
UN: UNITED NATIONS[1]				
UN1	African Socio-economic Indicators 1990– 91	1990–91	UN Irregular 1992 Addis Ababa, Ethiopia	ISBN 92 1 025034 6
UN2	African Statistical Yearbook 1988– 89 Vol I, Part 1 North Africa	1988–89	UN Annually 1992 New York, USA	—

[1] Publications of the International Civil Aviation Organization, International Telecommunication Union, the United Nations Conference on Trade and Development, the United Nations Educational, Scientific and Cultural Organization, the United Nations Children's Fund, the United Nations Industrial Development Organization, World Health Organization and the World Meteorological Organization are listed separately under ICAO, ITU, UNCTAD, UNESCO, UNICEF, UNIDO, WHO and WMO respectively.

instat code	Title	Edition indexed	Publisher Frequency Date Place	ISBN ISSN
UN3	African Statistical Yearbook 1988– 89 Vol I, Part 2 West Africa	1988–89	UN Annually 1992 New York, USA	—
UN4	African Statistical Yearbook 1988– 89 Vol II, Part 3 East and Southern Africa	1988–89	UN Annually 1992 Addis Ababa, Ethiopia	ISBN 92 1 025 030 3
UN5	African Statistical Yearbook 1988– 89 Vol II, Part 4 Central Africa, Others in Africa	1988–89	UN Annually 1992 Addis Ababa, Ethiopia	ISBN 92 1 025031 1
UN6	Annual Bulletin of Coal Statistics for Europe	1991	UN, ECE Annually 1991 Geneva, Switzerland	ISBN 92 1 016260 9 ISSN 0066 3808
UN7	Annual Bulletin of Electric Energy Statistics for Europe	1990	UN, ECE Annually 1991 Geneva, Switzerland	ISBN 92 1 016244 7 ISSN 0066 3816
UN8	Annual Bulletin of Gas Statistics for Europe	1991	UN, ECE Annually 1991 New York, USA	ISBN 92 1 016239 0 ISSN 0066 3824
UN9	Annual Bulletin of General Energy Statistics for Europe	1989 Vol 22	UN, ECE Annually 1991 New York, USA	ISBN 92 1 016259 5 ISSN 0377 9165
UN10	Annual Bulletin of Housing and Building Statistics for Europe	1980, 1986–89 Vol 33	UN, ECE Annually 1991 Geneva, Switzerland	ISBN 92 1 016243 9 ISSN 0066 3840
UN11	Annual Bulletin of Steel Statistics for Europe	1989 Vol 17	UN, ECE Annually 1990 New York, USA	ISBN 92 1 016241 2
UN12	Annual Bulletin of Trade in Chemical Products	1989 Vol 16	UN Annually 1991 New York, USA	ISBN 92 1 016262 5 ISSN 0250 9911
UN13	Annual Bulletin of Transport Statistics for Europe	1990 Vol 40	UN, ECE Annually 1990 Geneva, Switzerland	ISBN 92 1 016228 5 ISSN 0250 9911
UN14	Bulletin of Statistics on World Trade in Engineering Products	1988	UN Annually 1990 New York, USA	ISBN 92 1 016245 5 ISSN 0084 8174

instat code	Title	Edition indexed	Publisher Frequency Date Place	ISBN ISSN
UN15	Commodity Trade Statistics	1990 Vol XL	UN Approximately 28 issues per year 1990 New York, USA	—
UN16	Compendium of Social Statistics and Indicators	1988	UN Irregular 1988 New York, USA	ISBN 92 1 061145 4
UN17	Compendium of Statistics and Indicators on the Situation of Women	1986	UN Irregular 1989 New York	ISBN 92 1 061130 6
UN18	Construction Statistics Yearbook	1985	UN Annually 1988 New York, USA	ISBN 92 1 061126 8
UN19	Demographic Yearbook	1989	UN Annually 1991 New York, USA	ISBN 92 1 051074 7
UN20	Energy Balances and Electricity Profiles	1990	UN Irregular 1992 New York	ISBN 92 1 061147 0
UN21	Energy Statistics Yearbook	1989	UN Annually 1991 New York, USA	ISBN 92 1 061143 8
UN22	The Environment in Europe and North America: Annotated Statistics 1992	1992	UN Irregular 1992 New York, USA	ISBN 92 1 116537 7
UN23	Foreign Trade Statistics for Africa, Direction of Trade Series A	1990	UN Annually 1990 Addis Ababa, Ethiopia	ISBN 92 1 125058 7
UN24	Foreign Trade Statistics of Asia and the Pacific	1984–88	UN Irregular 1990 New York, USA	ISBN 92 1 119548 9 ISSN 1011 4858
UN25	Human Development Report	1991	Oxford University Press for the UN Development Programme Irregular 1991 Oxford, UK	ISBN 0 19 507147 6
UN26	Human Settlements Basic Statistics	1990	UN Irregular 1990 Nairobi, Kenya	ISBN 92 1 131098 9

***instat* code**	**Title**	**Edition indexed**	**Publisher Frequency Date Place**	**ISBN ISSN**
UN27	Industrial Statistics Yearbook, Vol I General Industrial Statistics	1989	UN Annually 1991 New York, USA	ISBN 92 1 161338 8
UN28	Industrial Statistics Yearbook, Vol II Commodity Production Statistics	1980–89	UN Annually 1991 New York, USA	ISBN 92 1 061146 2
UN29	International Narcotics Control Board – Narcotic Drugs, Estimated World Requirement Statistics for 1990	1990	UN Annually 1991 Geneva, Switzerland	ISBN 92 1 048050 3 ISSN 1013 3453
UN30	International Narcotics Control Board – Psychotropic Substances, Statistics for 1990	1990	UN Annually 1991 Geneva, Switzerland	ISBN 92 1 048051 1
UN31	International Sea-borne Trade Statistics: Yearbook 1984– 85	1984–85	UN Annually 1988 New York	ISBN 92 1 161285 3
UN32	International Trade Statistics Yearbook, Vol I Trade by Country	1989	UN Annually 1991 New York, USA	ISBN 92 1 061140 3
UN33	International Trade Statistics Yearbook, Vol II Trade by Commodity	1989	UN Annually 1991 New York, USA	ISBN 92 1 061140 3
UN34	The Livestock and Meat Market	1988 and 1989 Vol IV	UN Biennial 1990 New York, USA	ISBN 92 1 116483 4 ISSN 1011 3363
UN35	Monthly Bulletin of Statistics	1992 April	UN Monthly 1992 New York, USA	—
UN36	National Accounts Statistics: Analysis of Main Aggregates 1988– 89	1988–89	UN Annually 1991 New York	ISBN 92 1 161341 8
UN37	National Accounts Statistics: Compendium of Income Distribution Statistics	Series M No 79	UN Irregular 1985 New York, USA	ISBN 92 1 161253 5
UN38	National Accounts Statistics: Main Aggregates and Detailed Tables Parts I and II	1989	UN Annually 1991 New York, USA	ISBN 92 1 161339 6

***instat* code**	**Title**	**Edition indexed**	**Publisher Frequency Date Place**	**ISBN ISSN**
UN39	Population and Vital Statistics Report	XLV No 1	UN Quarterly 1993 New York, USA	—
UN40	Prices of Agricultural Products and Selected Inputs in Europe and North America	1990–91	UN Annual 1992 New York, USA	ISBN 92 1 116538 5 ISSN 0251 3986
UN41	Report of the UN High Commissioner for Refugees. General Assembly Official Records: 46th Session, Supplement No 12	1991	UN High Commission for Refugees Annually 1991 New York, USA	ISSN 0251 8023
UN42	Standardized Input-Output Tables of ECE Countries for Years Around 1975	1982	UN Irregular 1982 New York, USA	ISBN 011 907 7493
UN43	Statistical Indicators for Asia and the Pacific	1992 Vol XXII	UN Quarterly 1992 New York, USA	ISBN 92 1 119604 3 ISSN 0252 4457
UN44	Statistical Yearbook for Asia and the Pacific	1986–87	UN Economic and Social Commission for Asia and the Pacific Annually Bangkok, Thailand	ISBN 92 1 119447 4 ISSN 0252 3655
UN45	Statistical Yearbook for Latin America and the Caribbean	1990	UN Economic Commission for Latin America and the Caribbean Annually 1991 Santiago, Chile	ISSN 92 1 021029 8 ISBN 0251 9445
UN46	Statistics and Indicators on Women in Africa	1986	UN Irregular 1989 New York, USA	ISBN 92 1 061133 0
UN47	Statistics of Road Traffic Accidents in Europe	1991	UN, ECE Annually 1991 Geneva, Switzerland	ISBN 92 1 016261 7
UN48	Statistics of World Trade in Steel	1989	UN, ECE Annually 1990 New York, USA	ISBN 92 1 016242 0 ISSN 0501 3062
UN49	The Steel Market in 1991	1992	UN Annually 1992 Geneva, Switzerland	ISBN 92 1 116551 2 ISSN 0497 9478

instat code	Title	Edition indexed	Publisher Frequency Date Place	ISBN ISSN
UN50	UN Statistical Yearbook	1987	UN Annually 1990 New York, USA	ISBN 92 1 061131 4
UN51	UNHCR Activities Financed by Voluntary Funds. Report for 1990– 91 and Proposed Programmes and Budget for 1992. Part 1: Africa Part 2: Asia and Oceania Part 3: Europe and North America Part 4: Latin America Part 5: South West Asia, North Africa and the Middle East Part 6: Overall Allocations	1990–91	UNHCR Annually 1991 Geneva, Switzerland	—
UN52	World Investment Directory Vol I Asia and the Pacific	1992	UN Irregular 1992 New York, USA	ISBN 92 1 104389 1
UN53	World Investment Directory Vol II Central and Eastern Europe	1992	UN Annually 1992 New York, USA	ISBN 92 1 104402 2
UN54	World Population Prospects	1990	UN Bi-ennially 1991 New York, USA	ISBN 92 1 151223 9
UN55	World Statistics in Brief, United Nations Statistical Pocketbook	14th edn	UN Annually 1992 New York	ISBN 92 1 161344 2

UNCTAD: UNITED NATIONS CONFERENCE ON TRADE AND DEVELOPMENT

instat code	Title	Edition indexed	Publisher Frequency Date Place	ISBN ISSN
UNCTAD1	Handbook of International Trade and Development Statistics	1988	UNCTAD Irregular 1989 New York, USA	ISBN 92 1 012025 6 ISSN 0251 9461
UNCTAD2	Review of Maritime Transport	1989	UNCTAD Annually 1990 New York, USA	ISBN 92 1 112292 9 ISSN 0566 7682
UNCTAD3	Tungsten Statistics	1990	UNCTAD Annually 1991 New York, USA	ISBN 92 1 112298 8 ISSN 0049 4828
UNCTAD4	UNCTAD Commodity Yearbook	1992	UNCTAD Annually 1992 New York, USA	ISBN 92 1 012030 2 ISSN 1012 0793

instat code	Title	Edition indexed	Publisher Frequency Date Place	ISBN ISSN
UNCTAD5	UNCTAD Statistical Pocket Book	1989	UNCTAD Irregular 1989 New York, USA	ISBN 92 1 112281 3

UNESCO: UNITED NATIONS EDUCATIONAL, SCIENTIFIC, AND CULTURAL ORGANIZATION

UNESCO1	Statistical Yearbook	1990	UNESCO Annually 1990 Paris, France	ISBN 92 3 0027008 1

UNICEF: UNITED NATIONS CHILDREN'S FUND

UNICEF1	The State of the World's Children	1992	Oxford University Press Annually 1992 Oxford, UK	ISBN 0 19 262228 5 ISSN 0265 718X
UNICEF2	Statistics on Children in UNICEF Assisted Countries	1992	UNICEF Annually 1992 New York, USA	ISBN 92 806 1084 8

UNIDO: UNITED NATIONS INDUSTRIAL DEVELOPMENT ORGANIZATION

UNIDO1	Handbook of Industrial Statistics	1990	Edward Elgar Publishing Ltd for UNIDO Annually 1991 Aldershot, UK	ISBN 1 85278 440 7

VICES: VIENNA INSTITUTE FOR COMPARATIVE ECONOMIC STUDIES

VICES1	Comecon Data	1988	Macmillan Irregular 1989 Basingstoke, UK	ISBN 0 333 51798 9 ISSN 0263 3701

WB: THE WORLD BANK

WB1	Social Indicators of Development	1988	World Bank Irregular 1988 Washington DC, USA	ISBN 0 8018 3831 2 ISSN 1012 8026
WB2	Trends in Developing Economies	1992	World Bank Annually 1992 Washington DC, USA	ISBN 0 8213 2234 6
WB3	World Debt Tables, Vol 1 Analysis and Summary Tables	1992–93	World Bank Annually 1992 Washington DC, USA	ISBN 0 8213 2226 5

instat code	Title	Edition indexed	Publisher Frequency Date Place	ISBN ISSN
WB4	World Debt Tables Vol 2 External Finance for Developing Countries, Country Tables	1992–93	World Bank Annually 1992 Washington, USA	ISBN 0 8213 2227 3
WB5	World Population Projections	1989–90	John Hopkins University Press Irregular 1990 Maryland, USA	ISBN 0 8018 4094 5
WB6	World Tables	1991	John Hopkins University Press Annually 1991 Washington DC, USA	ISBN 0 8018 4252 2 ISSN 1043 5573

WBMS: WORLD BUREAU OF METAL STATISTICS

WBMS1	World Metal Statistics	1993	WBMS and Inco Europe Limited Monthly 1993 Ware, UK	ISSN 0043 8758
WBMS2	World Metal Statistics Quarterly Summary	1993 January	WBMS Quarterly 1993 Ware, UK	—
WBMS3	World Metal Statistics Yearbook	1991	WBMS Annually 1991 Ware, UK	—
WBMS4	World Stainless Steel Statistics	1990	WBMS and Inco Europe Limited Annually 1990 Ware, UK	ISSN 0141 0806

WC: WYE COLLEGE

WC1	Agrifacts: A Handbook of UK and EEC Agricultural and Food Statistics	1990	Harvester Wheatsheaf 1990 Hemel Hempstead, UK	ISBN 0 7450 0756 2

WFP: WORLD FOOD PROGRAMME

WFP1	The Food Aid Monitor: World Food Aid Flows, Transport and Logistics	1992	WFP Quarterly 1992 Rome, Italy	—

instat code	Title	Edition indexed	Publisher Frequency Date Place	ISBN ISSN
WHO: WORLD HEALTH ORGANISATION				
WHO1	Bulletin of Regional Health Information	1988–90	WHO 3 yearly 1992 New Delhi, India	—
WHO2	World Health Statistics Annual	1991	WHO Annually 1992 Geneva, Switzerland	ISBN 92 4 067910 3 ISSN 0250 3794
WIPO: WORLD INTELLECTUAL PROPERTY ORGANIZATION				
WIPO1	Industrial Property Statistics, Part I, Patents	1990 Part I	WIPO Annually 1992 Geneva, Switzerland	ISBN 92 805 0393 6
WIPO2	Industrial Property Statistics, Part II Trademarks and Service Marks, Utility Models, Industrial Designs, Varieties of Plants, Micro-organisms	1990	WIPO Annually 1992 Geneva, Switzerland	—
WIPO3	Industrial Property Statistics, Publication A (Supplement to Industrial Property) No 11	1990	WIPO Annually 1991 Geneva, Switzerland	—
WMO: WORLD METEOROLOGICAL ORGANIZATION				
WMO1	Climatological Normals (CLINO) for CLIMAT and CLIMAT Ship Stations	1931–60	WMO Irregular 1971 Geneva, Switzerland	—
WTO: WORLD TOURISM ORGANIZATION				
WTO1	Compendium of Tourism Statistics	1986–90	WTO Annually 1992 Madrid, Spain	ISBN 92 844 0016 3 ISSN 1014 1744
WTO2	Travel and Tourism Barometer	1992	WTO Monthly 1992 Madrid, Spain	ISSN 1014 7306
WTO3	Yearbook of Tourism Statistics Vol 1	1990	WTO Annually 1991 Madrid, Spain	ISBN 92 844 0014 7 ISSN 1011 8977
WTO4	Yearbook of Tourism Statistics Vol 2	1990	WTO Annually 1991 Madrid, Spain	ISBN 92 844 0014 7 ISSN 1011 8977

APPENDIX B

INDEX OF PUBLICATIONS

ARRANGED BY TITLE OF PUBLICATION

Title of publication	*instat* code	Name of organization
Accident/Incident Reporting (ADREP) Annual Statistics	ICAO1	International Civil Aviation Organization
ACP Basic Statistics	EC1	European Community
African Socio-economic Indicators 1990–91	UN1	United Nations
African Statistical Yearbook 1988–89 Vol I, Part 1 North Africa	UN2	United Nations
African Statistical Yearbook 1988–89 Vol I, Part 2 West Africa	UN3	United Nations
African Statistical Yearbook 1988–89 Vol II, Part 3 East and Southern Africa	UN4	United Nations
African Statistical Yearbook 1988–89 Vol II, Part 4 Central Africa, Others in Africa	UN5	United Nations
Agricultural Income	EC2	European Community
Agricultural Markets: Prices	EC3	European Community
Agricultural Prices: Price Indices and Absolute Prices	EC4	European Community
Agricultural Prices: Price Indices and Absolute Prices	EC5	European Community
Agriculture Statistical Yearbook	EC6	European Community
Agrifacts: A Handbook of UK and EEC Agricultural and Food Statistics	WC1	Wye College
Animal Production, Quarterly Statistics	EC7	European Community
Annual Bulletin of Coal Statistics for Europe	UN6	United Nations
Annual Bulletin of Electric Energy Statistics for Europe	UN7	United Nations
Annual Bulletin of Gas Statistics for Europe	UN8	United Nations
Annual Bulletin of General Energy Statistics for Europe	UN9	United Nations
Annual Bulletin of Housing and Building Statistics for Europe	UN10	United Nations
Annual Bulletin of Statistics	ITC1	International Tea Committee
Annual Bulletin of Steel Statistics for Europe	UN11	United Nations
Annual Bulletin of Trade in Chemical Products	UN12	United Nations
Annual Bulletin of Transport Statistics for Europe	UN13	United Nations
Annual Oil Market Report	IEA1	International Energy Agency
Annual Report of the International Iron and Steel Institute	IISI1	International Iron and Steel Institute

Title of publication	*instat* code	Name of organization
Annual Review and Assessment of the World Tropical Timber Situation	ITTO1	International Tropical Timber Organization
Annual Summary of Merchant Ships Completed	LRS1	Lloyds Register of Shipping
Areas Under Vines, Results of the Annual Surveys	EC8	European Community
ASEAN Selected Statistics	ASEANS1	Association of South-East Asian Nations Secretariat
Association of European Airlines Yearbook	AEA1	Association of European Airlines
Balance of Payments Statistical Yearbook, Part I	IMF1	International Monetary Fund
Balance of Payments Statistical Yearbook, Part II	IMF2	International Monetary Fund
Balance of Payments: Geographical Breakdown	EC10	European Community
Balances of Payments of OECD Countries	OECD1	Organization for Economic Co-operation and Development
Bank Profitability: Statistical Supplement - Financial Statements of Banks	OECD2	Organization for Economic Co-operation and Development
Basic International Chemical Industry Statistics	CIA1	Chemical Industries Association
Basic Science and Technology	OECD3	Organization for Economic Co-operation and Development
Basic Statistical Data on Selected Countries	CS1	Commonwealth Secretariat
Basic Statistics of the Community	EC9	European Community
The Best 'N' Most in DFS	GP1	Generation Publications
BP Review of World Gas	BP2	British Petroleum Company Plc
BP Statistical Review of World Energy	BP1	British Petroleum Company Plc
Bulletin–Consumption Statistics for Milk and Milk Products	IDF1	International Dairy Federation
Bulletin de IOIV	OIVY1	Bulletin de IOIV
Bulletin of Labour Statistics	ILO1	International Labour Organization
Bulletin of Regional Health Information	WHO1	World Health Organization
Bulletin of Statistics on World Trade in Engineering Products	UN14	United Nations
Bulletin of the Lead and Zinc Study Group: Lead and Zinc Statistics	ILZSG1	International Lead and Zinc Study Group
Cancer Incidence in Five Continents on	IARC1	International Agency for Research Cancer

Title of publication	*instat* code	Name of organization
Caricom's Trade	CCS1	Caribbean Community Secretariat
Carriage of Goods - Inland Waterways	EC12	European Community
Carriage of Goods - Railways	EC13	European Community
Carriage of Goods - Road	EC14	European Community
Casualty Return	LRS2	Lloyds Register of Shipping
Censuses of Population in the Community Countries 1981–82	EC11	European Community
Civil Aviation Statistics of the World, Doc 9180	ICAO2	International Civil Aviation Organization
Climatological Normals (CLINO) for CLIMAT and CLIMAT Ship Stations	WMO1	World Meteorological Organization
Coal Information	IEA2	International Energy Agency
Cocoa Market Report	EDFM1	E D & F Man Cocoa Limited
Comecon Data	VICES1	Vienna Institute for Comparative Economic Studies
Commodity Trade Statistics	UN15	United Nations
Community Survey of Orchard Fruit Trees	EC15	European Community
Comparative Information on Productivity Levels and Changes in APO Member Countries	APO1	Asian Productivity Organization
Compendium of Social Statistics and Indicators	UN16	United Nations
Compendium of Statistics and Indicators on the Situation of Women	UN17	United Nations
Compendium of Tourism Statistics	WTO1	World Tourism Organization
Construction Statistics Yearbook	UN18	United Nations
Consumer Price Index	EC16	European Community
Consumer Prices in the EEC	EC17	European Community
Cotton: Review of the World Situation	ICAC1	International Cotton Advisory Committee
Cotton: World Statistics, Bulletin of the International Cotton Advisory Committee	ICAC2	International Cotton Advisory Committee
Country Reports, Central and Eastern Europe	EC18	European Community
Country Statements	ITMF1	International Textile Manufacturers Federation

Title of publication	*instat* code	Name of organization
Crop Production, Quarterly Statistics	EC19	European Community
Demographic Statistics	EC20	European Community
Demographic Trends in OECD Member Countries	OECD4	Organization for Economic Co-operation and Development
Demographic Yearbook	UN19	United Nations
Digest of Statistics No 379, Series T – No 50, Traffic – Commercial Air Carriers	ICAO9	International Civil Aviation Organization
Digest of Statistics No 381, Series OFOD – No 44, On Flight Origin and Destination	ICAO7	International Civil Aviation Organization
Digest of Statistics No 382, Series R – No 30, Civil Aircraft on Register	ICAO8	International Civil Aviation Organization
Digest of Statistics No 383, Series AT – No 31, Airport Traffic	ICAO4	International Civil Aviation Organization
Digest of Statistics No 385, Series FP – No 44, Fleet – Personnel, Commercial Air Carriers	ICAO6	International Civil Aviation Organization
Digest of Statistics No 397, Series F – No 45, Financial Data, Commercial Air Carriers	ICAO5	International Civil Aviation Organization
Digest of Statistics No 398, Series TF – No 10, Traffic By Flight Stage	ICAO10	International Civil Aviation Organization
Digest of Statistics No 399, Series AF – No 9, Airport and Route Facilities, Financial Data and Summary Traffic Data	ICAO3	International Civil Aviation Organization
Digest of Statistics on Social Protection in Europe, Vol 1, Old Age	EC21	European Community
Digest of Statistics on Social Protection in Europe, Vol 2 Invalidity/Disability	EC22	European Community
A Digest of Trade Statistics	CCS2	Caribbean Community Secretariat
Direction of Trade Statistics	IMF4	International Monetary Fund
Direction of Trade Statistics Yearbook	IMF3	International Monetary Fund
Distribution of Seats Between Men and Women in National Parliaments. Statistical Data from 1945 to 30 June 1991	IPU1	Inter-Parliamentary Union
Earnings in Agriculture	EC23	European Community
Earnings, Industry and Services	EC24	European Community
EC Dairy Facts and Figures	MMB1	Milk Marketing Board
EC External Trade Indices	EC25	European Community

Title of publication	*instat* code	Name of organization
Economic Accounts for Agriculture	OECD5	Organization for Economic Co-operation and Development
Economic Accounts for Agriculture and Forestry	EC26	European Community
Economically Active Population 1950–2025, Vol I Asia	ILO2	International Labour Organization
Economically Active Population 1950–2025, Vol II Africa	ILO3	International Labour Organization
Economically Active Population 1950–2025, Vol III Latin America	ILO4	International Labour Organization
Economically Active Population 1950–2025, Vol IV Northern America, Europe, Oceania and USSR	ILO5	International Labour Organization
Economically Active Population 1950–2025, Vol V World	ILO6	International Labour Organization
The Economies of the Arabian Gulf: A Statistical Source Book	CH1	Croom Helm Limited
ECU-EMS Information	EC27	European Community
Education at a Glance	OECD6	Organization for Economic Co-operation and Development
Education in OECD Countries	OECD7	Organization for Economic Co-operation and Development
EFTA Trade	EFTA1	European Free Trade Association
Electricity Prices	EC28	European Community
Electricity Supply in the OECD	IEA3	International Energy Agency
Employment and Unemployment	EC29	European Community
Energy Balance Sheets	EC30	European Community
Energy Balances and Electricity Profiles	UN20	United Nations
Energy Balances of OECD Countries 1980–89	IEA4	International Energy Agency
Energy Balances of OECD Countries 1990–91	IEA5	International Energy Agency
Energy, Monthly Statistics	EC31	European Community
Energy Prices	EC32	European Community
Energy Prices and Taxes	IEA6	International Energy Agency
Energy Statistics and Balances of Non-OECD Countries	IEA7	International Energy Agency
Energy Statistics of OECD Countries 1980–89	IEA8	International Energy Agency
Energy Statistics of OECD Countries 1989–90	IEA9	International Energy Agency
Energy Statistics Yearbook	UN21	United Nations

Title of publication	*instat* code	Name of organization
FAO Yearbook of Fishery Statistics: Commodities	FAO4	Food and Agriculture Organization
Farm Structure 1985 Survey: Main Results	EC45	European Community
Farm Structure: 1985 Survey Analysis of Results. Economic Size and Other Gainful Activities	EC43	European Community
Farm Structure: 1985 Survey Analysis of Results. Regional Structure of Agricultural Production	EC44	European Community
Fatal Accident Statistics for Passenger Air Transport Services CAA Paper 83014	CAA1	Civil Aviation Authority
Fearnley's Review	F1	Fearnleys Review
Fertiliser Yearbook	FAO5	Food and Agriculture Organization
Financial Market Trends	OECD10	Organization for Economic Co-operation and Development
Fisheries, Yearly Statistics	EC46	European Community
Flows and Stocks of Fixed Capital: 1964–89	OECD11	Organization for Economic Co-operation and Development
The Food Aid Monitor: World Food Aid Flows, Transport and Logistics	WFP1	World Food Programme
Food Aid Shipments	IWhC1	International Wheat Council
Food Consumption Statistics	OECD12	Organization for Economic Co-operation and Development
Foreign Trade by Commodities, Vols I to V, Series C	OECD13	Organization for Economic Co-operation and Development
Foreign Trade Statistics for Africa, Direction of Trade Series A	UN23	United Nations
Foreign Trade Statistics of Asia and the Pacific	UN24	United Nations
Forestry Statistics	EC47	European Community
Gas Prices	EC48	European Community
General Government Accounts and Statistics	EC49	European Community
Geographical Distribution of Financial Flows to Developing Countries, Disbursements, Commitments, Economic Indicators: 1986–89	OECD14	Organization for Economic Co-operation and Development
Government Finance Statistics Yearbook	IMF5	International Monetary Fund
Government Financing of Research and Development	EC50	European Community

Title of publication	*instat* code	Name of organization
Grain Market Report	IWhC2	International Wheat Council
Handbook of Industrial Statistics	UNIDO1	United Nations Industrial Development Organization
Handbook of International Trade and Development Statistics	UNCTAD1	United Nations Conference on Trade and Development
Human Development Report	UN25	United Nations
Human Settlements Basic Statistics	UN26	United Nations
IBA Quarterly Review	IBA1	International Bauxite Association
Indicators of Industrial Activity	OECD15	Organization for Economic Co-operation and Development
Industrial Production Quarterly Statistics	EC51	European Community
Industrial Property Statistics, Part I, Patents	WIPO1	World Intellectual Property Organization
Industrial Property Statistics, Part II Trademarks and Service Marks, Utility Models, Industrial Designs, Varieties of Plants, Micro-organisms	WIPO2	World Intellectual Property Organization
Industrial Property Statistics, Publication A (Supplement to Industrial Property) No 11	WIPO3	World Intellectual Property Organization
Industrial Statistics Yearbook, Vol I General Industrial Statistics	UN27	United Nations
Industrial Statistics Yearbook, Vol II Commodity Production Statistics	UN28	United Nations
Industrial Structure Statistics	OECD16	Organization for Economic Co-operation and Development
Industrial Trends Monthly Statistics	EC52	European Community
Industry Statistical Yearbook	EC53	European Community
Information on Man-made Fibres	CIRFS1	Comité International de la Rayonne et des Fibres Synthétiques
International Cocoa Organization Annual Report	ICCO1	International Cocoa Council Organization
International Comparisons of Energy Data	EC54	European Community
International Cotton Industry Statistics	ITMF2	International Textile Manufacturers Federation
International Direct Investment Statistics Yearbook	OECD17	Organization for Economic Co-operation and Development

Title of publication	*instat* code	Name of organization
International Financial Statistics	IMF6	International Monetary Fund
International Financial Statistics Yearbook	IMF7	International Monetary Fund
International Historical Statistics, Africa and Asia	MAC1	Macmillan Press Limited
International Historical Statistics, The Americas and Australasia	MAC2	Macmillan Press Limited
International Historical Statistics, Europe 1750–1988	MAC3	Macmillan Press Limited
The International Markets for Meat	GATT1	General Agreement on Tariffs and Trade
The International Markets for Meat. Arrangement Regarding Bovine Meat 12th Annual Report	GATT2	General Agreement on Tariffs and Trade
International Molasses and Alcohol Report	FOL1	F O Licht
International Narcotics Control Board – Narcotic Drugs, Estimated World Requirement Statistics for 1990	UN29	United Nations
International North Pacific Fisheries Commission Statistical Yearbook	INPFC1	International North Pacific Fisheries Commission
International Narcotics Control Board – Psychotropic Substances, Statistics for 1990	UN30	United Nations
International Pacific Halibut Commission, Annual Report	IPHC1	International Pacific Halibut Commission
International Sea-borne Trade Statistics: Yearbook 1984–85	UN31	United Nations
International Railway Statistics, Statistics of Individual Railways	IUR1	International Union of Railways
International Steel Statistics Summary Tables	ISSB1	Iron and Steel Statistics Bureau
International Sugar and Sweetener Report	FOL2	F O Licht
International Textile Machinery Shipment Statistics	ITMF3	International Textile Manufacturers Federation
International Trade Statistics Vol I	GATT3	General Agreement on Tariffs and Trade
International Trade Statistics Vol II	GATT4	General Agreement on Tariffs and Trade
International Trade Statistics Yearbook, Vol I Trade by Country	UN32	United Nations
International Trade Statistics Yearbook, Vol II Trade by Commodity	UN33	United Nations
International Whaling Statistics	IWC1	International Whaling Commission
Intra-European Country to Country Traffic	AEA3	Association of European Airlines

Title of publication	*instat* code	Name of organization
Iron and Manganese Ore Databook	MB1	Metal Bulletin Books Limited
The Iron and Steel Industry	OECD18	Organization for Economic Co-operation and Development
Iron and Steel, Yearly Statistics	EC55	European Community
Joint Production of Lead and Zinc	ILZSG2	International Lead and Zinc Study Group
Know More About Oil, World Statistics	IP1	Institute of Petroleum
Labour Force Survey, Results 1991	EC56	European Community
Labour Force Statistics	OECD19	Organization for Economic Co-operation and Development
The Livestock and Meat Market	UN34	United Nations
Living Conditions in OECD Countries: Compendium of Social Indicators	OECD20	Organization for Economic Co-operation and Development
Main Economic Indicators	OECD21	Organization for Economic Co-operation and Development
Main Economic Indicators, Historical Statistics	OECD22	Organization for Economic Co-operation and Development
Main Economic Indicators, Historical Statistics: Prices Labour and Wages 1962–91	OECD23	Organization for Economic Co-operation and Development
Main Science and Technology Indicators	OECD24	Organization for Economic Co-operation and Development
Maritime Transport	OECD25	Organization for Economic Co-operation and Development
Meat Balances in OECD Countries	OECD26	Organization for Economic Co-operation and Development
Medium-Term Forecast of European Scheduled Passenger Traffic	AEA4	Association of European Airlines
Merchant Shipbuilding Return	LRS3	Lloyds Register of Shipping
Metal Bulletin's Prices and Data	MB2	Metal Bulletin Books Limited
Metals and Minerals, The Safer World of SGS	MJ1	Mining Journal
Milk Quotas – their Effects on Agriculture in the European Community, Vol 1 Main Report	EC57	European Community
Milk Quotas – their Effects on Agriculture in the European Community, Vol 2 Annex	EC58	European Community
Money and Finance	EC59	European Community

Title of publication	*instat* code	Name of organization
Monthly Bulletin of Statistics	UN35	United Nations
Monthly Crude Iron and Steel Production	IISI2	International Iron and Steel Institute
Monthly Statistical Review	SMMT1	Society of Motor Manufacturers and Traders Limited
Monthly Statistics of Foreign Trade, Series A	OECD27	Organization for Economic Co-operation and Development
Motor Industry of Great Britain: World Automotive Statistics	SMMT2	Society of Motor Manufacturers and Traders Limited
National Accounts ESA Aggregates	EC60	European Community
National Accounts ESA Detailed Tables by Branch	EC61	European Community
National Accounts ESA Detailed Tables by Sector	EC62	European Community
National Accounts ESA Input-Output Tables	EC63	European Community
National Accounts Statistics: Analysis of Main Aggregates 1988–89	UN36	United Nations
National Accounts Statistics: Compendium of Income Distribution Statistics	UN37	United Nations
National Accounts Statistics: Main Aggregates and Detailed Tables Parts I and II	UN38	United Nations
National Accounts, Vol I Main Aggregates	OECD28	Organization for Economic Co-operation and Development
National Accounts, Vol II Detailed Tables	OECD29	Organization for Economic Co-operation and Development
National and International Tourism Statistics	OECD30	Organization for Economic Co-operation and Development
The North Atlantic Treaty Organization 1949–89, Facts and Figures	NATO1	North Atlantic Treaty Organization
Nuclear Energy Data	OECD31	Organization for Economic Co-operation and Development
OECD Economic Outlook Historical Statistics	OECD32	Organization for Economic Co-operation and Development
OECD Environmental Data Compendium	OECD33	Organization for Economic Co-operation and Development
OECD Financial Statistics Part 1 Section 1 International Markets	OECD34	Organization for Economic Co-operation and Development
OECD Financial Statistics Part 1 Section 2 Domestic Markets – Interest Rates	OECD35	Organization for Economic Co-operation and Development

Title of publication	*instat* code	Name of organization
OECD Financial Statistics Part 2 Financial Accounts of OECD Countries	OECD36	Organization for Economic Co-operation and Development
OECD Financial Statistics Part 3 Non-Financial Enterprises Financial Statements	OECD37	Organization for Economic Co-operation and Development
Oil and Energy Trends	BB2	Basil Blackwell Limited
Oil and Energy Trends, Annual Statistical Review	BB1	Basil Blackwell Limited
Oil and Gas Information	IEA10	International Energy Agency
Oil World	ISTA1	Ista Mielk Gmbh
Oil World Annual	ISTA2	Ista Mielk Gmbh
Oil, Chemical and Combined Carriers	G1	E A Gibson Shipbrokers Limited
OPEC Annual Statistical Bulletin	OPEC1	Organization of Petroleum Exporting Countries
OPEC Bulletin	OPEC2	Organization of Petroleum Exporting Countries
Operating Experience with Nuclear Power Stations in Member States in 1990	IAEA1	International Atomic Energy Agency
Operation of Nuclear Power Stations	EC64	European Community
Platinum	JM1	Johnson Matthey
Pocket Profiles	IADB1	Inter-American Development Bank
Population and Vital Statistics Report	UN39	United Nations
Portrait of the Regions: Vol I Germany Benelux Denmark, Vol II France, United Kingdom, Ireland, Vol III Portugal, Spain, Italy	EC65	European Community
Price Structure of the Community Countries in 1985	EC66	European Community
Prices of Agricultural Products and Selected Inputs in Europe and North America	UN40	United Nations
The Pulp and Paper Industry	OECD38	Organization for Economic Co-operation and Development
Pulp and Paper International Annual Review	PPI1	Pulp and Paper International
The Purchasing Power of Working Time. An International Comparison	IMWF1	International Metalworkers' Federation
Purchasing Power Parities and Real Expenditures	OECD39	Organization for Economic Co-operation and Development

Title of publication	*instat* code	Name of organization
Quarterly Bulletin of Cocoa Statistics	ICCO2	International Cocoa Council Organization
Quarterly Bulletin of Statistics	FAO6	Food and Agriculture Organization
Quarterly Labour Force Statistics	OECD40	Organization for Economic Co-operation and Development
Quarterly Market Review	ISO1	International Sugar Organization
Quarterly National Accounts	OECD41	Organization for Economic Co-operation and Development
Quarterly National Accounts ESA	EC67	European Community
Quarterly Oil Statistics and Energy Balances	IEA11	International Energy Agency
Raw Material EC Supply	EC68	European Community
Recent Demographic Developments in Europe	CE1	Council of Europe
Reference Tables	BPB1	British Paper and Board Industry Federation
Regions Statistical Yearbook	EC69	European Community
Register of Liquified Gas Carriers	G2	E A Gibson Shipbrokers Limited
Report of the UN High Commissioner for Refugees. General Assembly Official Records: 46th Session, Supplement No 12	UN41	United Nations
Report for the Crop Year	IWhC3	International Wheat Council
Results of the Business Survey Carried Out Among Managements in the Community	EC70	European Community
Retail Price Indices, Statistical Bulletin of the South Pacific	SPC1	South Pacific Commission
Retailing in the European Single Market 1993	EC71	European Community
Revenue Statistics of OECD Member Countries	OECD42	Organization for Economic Co-operation and Development
Review of Fisheries in OECD Member Countries	OECD43	Organization for Economic Co-operation and Development
Review of Maritime Transport	UNCTAD2	United Nations Conference on Trade and Development
Rubber Statistical Bulletin	IRSG1	International Rubber Study Group
Services: Statistics on International Transactions	OECD44	Organization for Economic Co-operation and Development

Title of publication	*instat* code	Name of organization
Shipping Statistics	ISL1	Institute of Shipping Economics and Logistics
Shipping Statistics and Economics	DSC1	Drewry Shipping Consultants Limited
Shipping Statistics Yearbook	ISL2	Institute of Shipping Economics and Logistics
Shipping Trade, Trends and Statistics	DSC2	Drewry Shipping Consultants Limited
Short-term Review of International Pulp and Paper Markets	JP1	Jaakko Pöyry
Silicon Carbide	EAT1	Elsevier Advanced Technology
Situation de la Production Laitière et du Contrôle Laitier dans les Organismes Pays Members	FNOCL1	Federation Nationale des de Contrôle Laitier
Social Indicators of Development	WB1	The World Bank
A Social Portrait of Europe	EC72	European Community
Social Protection Expenditure and Receipts	EC73	European Community
South Pacific Economies	SPC2	South Pacific Commission
Standardized Input–Output Tables of ECE Countries for Years Around 1975	UN42	United Nations
The State of the World's Children	UNICEF1	United Nations Children's Fund
Statistical Appendices to AEA Yearbook	AEA2	Association of European Airlines
Statistical Brief	COS1	Chamber of Shipping
Statistical Bulletin	ICCAT1	International Commission for the Conservation of Atlantic Tunas
Statistical Bulletin	ISO2	International Sugar Organization
Statistical Bulletin, Fishery Statistics for 1988	NWAFO1	North West Atlantic Fisheries Organization
Statistical Indicators for Asia and the Pacific	UN43	United Nations
Statistical Report on Road Accidents	ECMT1	European Conference of Ministers of Transport
Statistical Trends in Transport	ECMT2	European Conference of Ministers of Transport

Title of publication	*instat* code	Name of organization
Trends in the Hotel Industry	PKF2	Pannell Kerr Forster
Trends in the Transport Sector	ECMT3	European Conference of Ministers of Transport
Tungsten Statistics	UNCTAD3	United Nations Conference on Trade and Development
UN Statistical Yearbook	UN50	United Nations
UNCTAD Commodity Yearbook	UNCTAD4	United Nations Conference on Trade and Development
UNCTAD Statistical Pocket Book	UNCTAD5	United Nations Conference on Trade and Development
Unemployment	EC81	European Community
UNHCR Activities Financed by Voluntary Funds. Report for 1990–91 and Proposed Programmes and Budget for 1992. Part 1: Africa Part 2: Asia and Oceania Part 3: Europe and North America Part 4: Latin America Part 5: South West Asia, North Africa and the Middle East Part 6: Overall Allocations	UN51	United Nations
Uranium – Resources, Production and Demand	OECD47	Organization for Economic Co-operation and Development
Urea Statistics	IFA1	International Fertilizer Industry Association
Western European Living Costs	CBI1	Confederation of British Industry
Women and Political Power Survey carried out among the National Parliaments existing as from 31.10.91	IPU2	Inter-Parliamentary Union
Wool Facts 1991–92	IWS1	International Wool Secretariat
World Air Transport Statistics	IATA1	International Air Transport Association
World Bulk Fleet	F2	Fearnleys
World Bulk Trades	F3	Fearnleys
The World Cocoa Market: An Analysis of Recent Trends and of Prospects to the Year 2000	ICCO3	International Cocoa Council Organization
World Crop and Livestock Statistics	FAO7	Food and Agriculture Organization
World Debt Tables, Vol 1, Analysis and Summary Tables	WB3	The World Bank
World Debt Tables, Vol 2, External Finance for Developing Countries, Country Tables	WB4	The World Bank

Title of publication	*instat* code	Name of organization
World Energy Statistics and Balances	IEA12	International Energy Agency
World Fleet Statistics	LRS4	Lloyds Register of Shipping
World Footwear Markets	SATRA1	Satra Footwear Technology Centre
World Health Statistics Annual	WHO2	World Health Organization
World Investment Directory Vol I Asia and the Pacific	UN52	United Nations
World Investment Directory Vol II Central and Eastern Europe	UN53	United Nations
The World Market for Dairy Products	GATT5	General Agreement on Tariffs and Trade
World Metal Statistics	WBMS1	World Bureau of Metal Statistics
World Metal Statistics Quarterly Summary	WBMS2	World Bureau of Metal Statistics
World Metal Statistics Yearbook	WBMS3	World Bureau of Metal Statistics
World Mineral Statistics Vol 1 Metals and Energy	BGS1	British Geological Survey
World Mineral Statistics Vol 2 Industrial Minerals	BGS2	British Geological Survey
World Oil Trade Review of International Oil Movements	BB4	Basil Blackwell Limited
World Population Projections	WB5	The World Bank
World Population Prospects	UN54	United Nations
World Rice Statistics, 1987	IRRI1	International Rice Research Institute
World Road Statistics, 1986–90	IRF1	World Road Federation
Worldwide Rubber Statistics	IISRP1	International Institute of Synthetic Rubber Producers
World Rubber Statistics Handbook	IRSG2	International Rubber Study Group
World Stainless Steel Statistics	WBMS4	World Bureau of Metal Statistics
World Statistics in Brief, United Nations Statistical Pocketbook	UN55	United Nations
World Steel in Figures	IISI5	International Iron and Steel Institute
World Sugar and Sweetener Yearbook	FOL3	F O Licht
World Tables	WB6	The World Bank
World Trade Stainless, High Speed and Other Alloy Steel	ISSB2	Iron and Steel Statistics Bureau
World Trade Steel	ISSB3	Iron and Steel Statistics Bureau

APPENDIX C

INDEX OF PUBLICATIONS

ARRANGED BY NAME OF ORGANIZATION

Name of organization	*instat* code	Title of publication
Asian Productivity Organization	APO1	Comparative Information on Productivity Levels and Changes in APO Member Countries
Association of European Airlines	AEA1	Association of European Airlines Yearbook
	AEA2	Statistical Appendices to AEA Yearbook
	AEA3	Intra-European Country to Country Traffic
	AEA4	Medium-Term Forecast of European Scheduled Passenger Traffic
Association of South-East Asian Nations Secretariat	ASEANS1	ASEAN Selected Statistics
Basil Blackwell Limited	BB1	Oil and Energy Trends, Annual Statistical Review
	BB2	Oil and Energy Trends
	BB3	Tanker Charter Record
	BB4	World Oil Trade Review of International Oil Movements
British Geological Survey	BGS1	World Mineral Statistics Vol 1 Metals and Energy
	BGS2	World Mineral Statistics Vol 2 Industrial Minerals
British Paper and Board Industry Federation	BPB1	Reference Tables
British Petroleum Company Plc	BP1	BP Statistical Review of World Energy
	BP2	BP Review of World Gas
Caribbean Community Secretariat	CCS1	Caricom's Trade
	CCS2	A Digest of Trade Statistics
Chamber of Shipping	COS1	Statistical Brief
Chemical Industries Association	CIA1	Basic International Chemical Industry Statistics
Civil Aviation Authority	CAA1	Fatal Accident Statistics for Passenger Air Transport Services CAA Paper 83014
Comité International de la Rayonne et des Fibres Synthétiques	CIRFS1	Information on Man-made Fibres
Commonwealth Secretariat	CS1	Basic Statistical Data on Selected Countries
Confederation of British Industry	CBI1	Western European Living Costs
Council of Europe	CE1	Recent Demographic Developments in Europe
Croom Helm Limited	CH1	The Economies of the Arabian Gulf: A Statistical Source Book

Name of organization	*instat* code	Title of publication
Drewry Shipping Consultants Limited	DSC1	Shipping Statistics and Economics
	DSC2	Shipping Trade, Trends and Statistics
E D & F Man Cocoa Limited	EDFM1	Cocoa Market Report
Elsevier Advanced Technology	EAT1	Silicon Carbide
	EAT2	Telecommunications: Profile of the Worldwide Telecommunications Industry
Euromonitor	EM1	European Marketing Data and Statistics
European Aluminium Association	EAA1	European Aluminium Statistics
European Community	EC1	ACP Basic Statistics
	EC2	Agricultural Income
	EC3	Agricultural Markets: Prices
	EC4	Agricultural Prices: Price Indices and Absolute Prices
	EC5	Agricultural Prices: Price Indices and Absolute Prices
	EC6	Agriculture Statistical Yearbook
	EC7	Animal Production, Quarterly Statistics
	EC8	Areas Under Vines, Results of the Annual Surveys
	EC9	Basic Statistics of the Community
	EC10	Balance of Payments: Geographical Breakdown
	EC11	Censuses of Population in the Community Countries 1981–82
	EC12	Carriage of Goods – Inland Waterways
	EC13	Carriage of Goods – Railways
	EC14	Carriage of Goods – Road
	EC15	Community Survey of Orchard Fruit Trees
	EC16	Consumer Price Index
	EC17	Consumer Prices in the EEC
	EC18	Country Reports, Central and Eastern Europe
	EC19	Crop Production, Quarterly Statistics
	EC20	Demographic Statistics

Name of organization	*instat* code	Title of publication
European Community	EC21	Digest of Statistics on Social Protection in Europe, Vol 1 Old Age
	EC22	Digest of Statistics on Social Protection in Europe, Vol 2 Invalidity/Disability
	EC23	Earnings in Agriculture
	EC24	Earnings, Industry and Services
	EC25	EC External Trade Indices
	EC26	Economic Accounts for Agriculture and Forestry
	EC27	ECU–EMS Information
	EC28	Electricity Prices
	EC29	Employment and Unemployment
	EC30	Energy Balance Sheets
	EC31	Energy, Monthly Statistics
	EC32	Energy Prices
	EC33	Energy Yearly Statistics
	EC34	Environment Statistics
	EC35	Europe in Figures
	EC36	Eurostatistics – Data for Short-term Economic Analysis, No 5
	EC37	External Trade: Analytical Tables A–L, Imports and Exports
	EC38	External Trade and Balance of Payments
	EC39	External Trade Statistical Yearbook
	EC40	External Trade, System of Generalized Tariff Preferences, Imports 1988, Vol I
	EC41	External Trade, System of Generalized Tariff Preferences, Imports 1988, Vol II
	EC42	Family Budgets: Comparative Tables, Vols I and II
	EC43	Farm Structure: 1985 Survey Analysis of Results. Economic Size and Other Gainful Activities
	EC44	Farm Structure: 1985 Survey Analysis of Results. Regional Structure of Agricultural Production
	EC45	Farm Structure 1985 Survey: Main Results

Name of organization	*instat* code	Title of publication
European Community	EC46	Fisheries, Yearly Statistics
	EC47	Forestry Statistics
	EC48	Gas Prices
	EC49	General Government Accounts and Statistics
	EC50	Government Financing of Research and Development
	EC51	Industrial Production Quarterly Statistics
	EC52	Industrial Trends Monthly Statistics
	EC53	Industry Statistical Yearbook
	EC54	International Comparisons of Energy Data
	EC55	Iron and Steel, Yearly Statistics
	EC56	Labour Force Survey, Results 1991
	EC57	Milk Quotas - Their Effects on Agriculture in the European Community, Vol 1 Main Report
	EC58	Milk Quotas - Their Effects on Agriculture in the European Community, Vol 2 Annex
	EC59	Money and Finance
	EC60	National Accounts ESA Aggregates
	EC61	National Accounts ESA Detailed Tables by Branch
	EC62	National Accounts ESA Detailed Tables by Sector
	EC63	National Accounts ESA Input-Output Tables
	EC64	Operation of Nuclear Power Stations
	EC65	Portrait of the Regions: Vol I Germany, Benelux, Denmark,, Vol II France ,United Kingdom, Ireland, Vol III Portugal, Spain, Italy
	EC66	Price Structure of the Community Countries in 1985
	EC67	Quarterly National Accounts ESA
	EC68	Raw Material EC Supply
	EC69	Regions Statistical Yearbook
	EC70	Results of the Business Survey Carried Out Among Managements in the Community

Name of organization	*instat* code	Title of publication
European Community	EC71	Retailing in the European Single Market 1993
	EC72	A Social Portrait of Europe
	EC73	Social Protection Expenditure and Receipts
	EC74	Steel Consumption by User Branch
	EC75	Structure and Activity of Industry: Annual Enquiry Main Results
	EC76	Structure and Activity of Industry: Data by Regions
	EC77	Structure and Activity of Industry: Data by Size of Enterprises
	EC78	Tourism Annual Statistics
	EC79	Tourism in Europe, Trends
	EC80	Transport and Communications Annual Statistics
	EC81	Unemployment
European Conference of Ministers of Transport	ECMT1	Statistical Report on Road Accidents
	ECMT2	Statistical Trends in Transport
	ECMT3	Trends in the Transport Sector
European Free Trade Association	EFTA1	EFTA Trade
European Paper Institute	EPI1	European Paper Institute Annual Statistics
European Patent Office	EPO1	Facts and Figures
Fearnleys	F1	Fearnley's Review
	F2	World Bulk Fleet
	F3	World Bulk Trades
Federation Nationale des Organismes de Contrôle Laitier	FNOCL1	Situation de la Production Laitière et du Contrôle Laitier dans les Pays Members
F O Licht	FOL1	International Molasses and Alcohol Report
	FOL2	International Sugar and Sweetener Report
	FOL3	World Sugar and Sweetener Yearbook
Food and Agriculture Organization	FAO1	FAO Production Yearbook
	FAO2	FAO Trade Yearbook
	FAO3	FAO Yearbook of Fishery Statistics: Catches and Landings

Name of organization	*instat* code	Title of publication
Food and Agriculture Organization	FAO4	FAO Yearbook of Fishery Statistics: Commodities
	FAO5	Fertiliser Yearbook
	FAO6	Quarterly Bulletin of Statistics
	FAO7	World Crop and Livestock Statistics
	FAO8	Yearbook of Forest Products
General Agreement on Tariffs and Trade	GATT1	The International Markets for Meat
	GATT2	The International Markets for Meat. Arrangement Regarding Bovine Meat 12th Annual Report
	GATT3	International Trade Statistics Vol I
	GATT4	International Trade Statistics Vol II
	GATT5	The World Market for Dairy Products
Generation Publications	GP1	The Best 'N' Most in DFS
E A Gibson Shipbrokers Limited	G1	Oil, Chemical and Combined Carriers
	G2	Register of Liquified Gas Carriers
Horwath International	HI1	Worldwide Hotel Industry
Institute of Petroleum	IP1	Know More About Oil, World Statistics
Institute of Shipping Economics and Logistics	ISL1	Shipping Statistics
	ISL2	Shipping Statistics Yearbook
Inter-American Development Bank	IADB1	Pocket Profiles
International Agency for Research on Cancer	IARC1	Cancer Incidence in Five Continents
International Air Transport Association	IATA1	World Air Transport Statistics
International Association of Horticultural Producers	IAHP1	Yearbook of International Horticultural Statistics
International Atomic Energy Agency	IAEA1	Operating Experience with Nuclear Power Stations in Member States in 1990
International Bauxite Association	IBA1	IBA Quarterly Review
International Civil Aviation Organization	ICAO1	Accident/Incident Reporting (ADREP) Annual Statistics
	ICAO2	Civil Aviation Statistics of the World, Doc 9180

Name of organization	*instat* code	Title of publication
International Civil Aviation Organization	ICAO3	Digest of Statistics No 399, Series AF – No 9, Airport and Route Facilities, Financial Data and Summary Traffic Data
	ICAO4	Digest of Statistics No 383, Series AT–No 31, Airport Traffic
	ICAO5	Digest of Statistics No 397, Series F – No 45, Financial Data, Commercial Air Carriers
	ICAO6	Digest of Statistics No 385, Series FP – No 44, Fleet – Personnel, Commercial Air Carriers
	ICAO7	Digest of Statistics No 381, Series OFOD – No 44, On Flight Origin and Destination
	ICAO8	Digest of Statistics No 382, Series R – No 30, Civil Aircraft on Register
	ICAO9	Digest of Statistics No 379, Series T – No 50, Traffic – Commercial Air Carriers
	ICAO10	Digest of Statistics No 398, Series TF – No 10, Traffic By Flight Stage
International Cocoa Council Organization	ICCO1	International Cocoa Organization Annual Report
	ICCO2	Quarterly Bulletin of Cocoa Statistics
	ICCO3	The World Cocoa Market: An Analysis of Recent Trends and of Prospects to the Year 2000
International Commission for the Conservation of Atlantic Tunas	ICCAT1	Statistical Bulletin
International Cotton Advisory Committee	ICAC1	Cotton: Review of the World Situation
	ICAC2	Cotton: World Statistics, Bulletin of the International Cotton Advisory Committee
International Dairy Federation	IDF1	Bulletin–Consumption Statistics for Milk and Milk Products
International Energy Agency	IEA1	Annual Oil Market Report
	IEA2	Coal Information
	IEA3	Electricity Supply in the OECD
	IEA4	Energy Balances of OECD Countries 1980–89
	IEA5	Energy Balances of OECD Countries1990–91
	IEA6	Energy Prices and Taxes
	IEA7	Energy Statistics and Balances of Non-OECD Countries

Name of organization	*instat* code	Title of publication
International Energy Agency	IEA8	Energy Statistics of OECD Countries 1980–89
	IEA9	Energy Statistics of OECD Countries 1989–90
	IEA10	Oil and Gas Information
	IEA11	Quarterly Oil Statistics and Energy Balances
	IEA12	World Energy Statistics and Balances
International Fertilizer Industry Association	IFA1	Urea Statistics
International Institute of Synthetic Rubber Producers	IISRP1	Worldwide Rubber Statistics
International Iron and Steel Institute	IISI1	Annual Report of the International Iron and Steel Institute
	IISI2	Monthly Crude Iron and Steel Production
	IISI3	Steel Statistics of Developing Countries
	IISI4	Steel Statistical Yearbook
	IISI5	World Steel in Figures
International Labour Organization	ILO1	Bulletin of Labour Statistics
	ILO2	Economically Active Population 1950–2025 Asia, Vol I
	ILO3	Economically Active Population 1950–2025 Africa, Vol II
	ILO4	Economically Active Population 1950–2025 Latin America, Vol III
	ILO5	Economically Active Population 1950–2025 Northern America Europe Oceania and USSR, Vol IV
	ILO6	Economically Active Population 1950–2025 World, Vol V
	ILO7	Yearbook of Labour Statistics
International Lead and Zinc Study Group	ILZSG1	Bulletin of the Lead and Zinc Study Group: Lead and Zinc Statistics
	ILZSG2	Joint Production of Lead and Zinc
International Metalworkers' Federation	IMWF1	The Purchasing Power of Working Time. An International Comparison
International Monetary Fund	IMF1	Balance of Payments Statistical Yearbook, Part I
	IMF2	Balance of Payments Statistical Yearbook, Part II
	IMF3	Direction of Trade Statistics Yearbook

Name of organization	*instat* code	Title of publication
International Monetary Fund	IMF4	Direction of Trade Statistics
	IMF5	Government Finance Statistics Yearbook
	IMF6	International Financial Statistics
	IMF7	International Financial Statistics Yearbook
International North Pacific Fisheries Commission	INPFC1	International North Pacific Fisheries Commission Statistical Yearbook
International Pacific Halibut Commission	IPHC1	International Pacific Halibut Commission, Annual Report
International Rice Research Institute	IRRI1	World Rice Statistics, 1987
International Road Federation	IRF1	World Road Statistics, 1986–90
International Road Transport Union	IRTU1	World Transport Data
International Rubber Study Group	IRSG1	Rubber Statistical Bulletin
	IRSG2	World Rubber Statistics Handbook
International Sugar Organization	ISO1	Quarterly Market Review
	ISO2	Statistical Bulletin
	ISO3	Sugar Yearbook
International Tea Committee	ITC1	International Tea Committee Annual Bulletin of Statistics
International Telecommunication Union	ITU1	Yearbook of Common Carrier Telecommunications Statistics
International Textile Manufacturers Federation	ITMF1	Country Statements
	ITMF2	International Cotton Industry Statistics
	ITMF3	International Textile Machinery Shipment Statistics
International Tropical Timber Organization	ITTO1	Annual Review and Assessment of the World Tropical Timber Situation
International Union of Railways	IUR1	International Railway Statistics, Statistics of Individual Railways
International Whaling Commission	IWC1	International Whaling Statistics
International Wheat Council	IWhC1	Food Aid Shipments
	IWhC2	Grain Market Report
	IWhC3	Report for the Crop Year
International Wool Secretariat	IWS1	Wool Facts 1991–92

Name of organization	*instat* code	Title of publication
Inter-Parliamentary Union	IPU1	Distribution of Seats Between Men and Women in National Parliaments. Statistical Data from 1945 to 30 June 1991
	IPU2	Women and Political Power Survey carried out among the National Parliaments existing as from 31.10.91
Iron and Steel Statistics Bureau	ISSB1	International Steel Statistics Summary Tables
	ISSB2	World Trade Stainless, High Speed and Other Alloy Steel
	ISSB3	World Trade Steel
Ista Mielk Gmbh	ISTA1	Oil World
	ISTA2	Oil World Annual
Jaakko Pöyry	JP1	Short-term Review of International Pulp and Paper Markets
Johnson Matthey	JM1	Platinum
Lloyds Register of Shipping	LRS1	Annual Summary of Merchant Ships Completed
	LRS2	Casualty Return
	LRS3	Merchant Shipbuilding Return
	LRS4	World Fleet Statistics
Macmillan Press Limited	MAC1	International Historical Statistics, Africa and Asia
	MAC2	International Historical Statistics, The Americas and Australasia
	MAC3	International Historical Statistics Europe, 1750–1988
Meat and Livestock Commission	MLC1	European Handbook, EEC and International Statistics
Metal Bulletin Books Limited	MB1	Iron and Manganese Ore Databook
	MB2	Metal Bulletin's Prices and Data
Milk Marketing Board	MMB1	EC Dairy Facts and Figures
Mining Journal	MJ1	Metals and Minerals, The Safer World of SGS
Ministry of Housing, Physical Planning and the Environment (Netherlands)	MHPPE1	Statistics on Housing in the European Community
Nordic Council of Ministers and the Nordic Statistical Secretariat	NCM1	Yearbook of Nordic Statistics
North Atlantic Treaty Organization	NATO1	The North Atlantic Treaty Organization 1949–89, Facts and Figures

Name of organization	*instat* code	Title of publication
North West Atlantic Fisheries Organization	NWAFO1	Statistical Bulletin, Fishery Statistics for 1988
Office International de la Vigne et du Vin	OIVV1	Bulletin de IOIV
Organization for Economic Co-operation and Development	OECD1	Balances of Payments of OECD Countries
	OECD2	Bank Profitability: Statistical Supplement – Financial Statements of Banks
	OECD3	Basic Science and Technology
	OECD4	Demographic Trends in OECD Member Countries
	OECD5	Economic Accounts for Agriculture
	OECD6	Education at a Glance
	OECD7	Education in OECD Countries
	OECD8	External Debt Statistics: The Debt and Other External Liabilities of Developing, CMEA and Certain Other Countries and Territories at end December 1987 and end December 1988
	OECD9	External Debt Statistics: The Debt and Other External Liabilities of Developing, Central and Eastern European and Certain Other Countries and Territories at end December 1988 and end December 1989
	OECD10	Financial Market Trends
	OECD11	Flows and Stocks of Fixed Capital: 1964–89
	OECD12	Food Consumption Statistics
	OECD13	Foreign Trade by Commodities, Vols I to V, Series C
	OECD14	Geographical Distribution of Financial Flows to Developing Countries, Disbursements, Commitments, Economic Indicators: 1986–89
	OECD15	Indicators of Industrial Activity
	OECD16	Industrial Structure Statistics
	OECD17	International Direct Investment Statistics Yearbook
	OECD18	The Iron and Steel Industry
	OECD19	Labour Force Statistics
	OECD20	Living Conditions in OECD Countries: Compendium of Social Indicators

Name of organization	*instat* code	Title of publication
Organization for Economic Co-operation and Development	OECD21	Main Economic Indicators
	OECD22	Main Economic Indicators, Historical Statistics
	OECD23	Main Economic Indicators, Historical Statistics: Prices Labour and Wages 1962–91
	OECD24	Main Science and Technology Indicators
	OECD25	Maritime Transport
	OECD26	Meat Balances in OECD Countries
	OECD27	Monthly Statistics of Foreign Trade, Series A
	OECD28	National Accounts, Vol I Main Aggregates
	OECD29	National Accounts, Vol II Detailed Tables
	OECD30	National and International Tourism Statistics
	OECD31	Nuclear Energy Data
	OECD32	OECD Economic Outlook Historical Statistics
	OECD33	OECD Environmental Data Compendium
	OECD34	OECD Financial Statistics Part 1 Section 1 International Markets
	OECD35	OECD Financial Statistics Part 1 Section 2 Domestic Markets – Interest Rates
	OECD36	OECD Financial Statistics Part 2 Financial Accounts of OECD Countries
	OECD37	OECD Financial Statistics Part 3 Non–Financial Enterprises Financial Statements
	OECD38	The Pulp and Paper Industry
	OECD39	Purchasing Power Parities and Real Expenditures
	OECD40	Quarterly Labour Force Statistics
	OECD41	Quarterly National Accounts
	OECD42	Revenue Statistics of OECD Member Countries
	OECD43	Review of Fisheries in OECD Member Countries
	OECD44	Services: Statistics on International Transactions
	OECD45	Steel Market in 1991 and the Outlook for 1992

Name of organization	*instat* code	Title of publication
Organization of Petroleum Exporting Countries	OECD46	Tourism Policy and International Tourism in OECD Member Countries
	OECD47	Uranium – Resources, Production and Demand
Organization of Petroleum Exporting Countries	OPEC1	OPEC Annual Statistical Bulletin
	OPEC2	OPEC Bulletin
Pannell Kerr Forster	PKF1	Euro Trends Survey
	PKF2	Trends in the Hotel Industry
The Population Council	PC1	Family Planning and Child Survival Programs as Assessed in 1991
Pulp and Paper International	PPI1	Pulp and Paper International Annual Review
Satra Footwear Technology Centre	SATRA1	World Footwear Markets
Sea Fish Industry Authority	SFIA1	European Supplies Bulletin
Society of Motor Manufacturers and Traders Limited	SMMT1	Monthly Statistical Review
	SMMT2	Motor Industry of Great Britain: World Automotive Statistics
South Pacific Commission	SPC1	Retail Price Indices, Statistical Bulletin of the South Pacific
	SPC2	South Pacific Economies
United Nations	UN1	African Socio-economic Indicators 1990–91
	UN2	African Statistical Yearbook 1988–89 Vol I, Part 1 North Africa
	UN3	African Statistical Yearbook 1988–89 Vol I, Part 2 West Africa
	UN4	African Statistical Yearbook 1988–89 Vol II, Part 3 East and Southern Africa
	UN5	African Statistical Yearbook 1988–89 Vol II, Part 4 Central Africa, Others in Africa
	UN6	Annual Bulletin of Coal Statistics for Europe
	UN7	Annual Bulletin of Electric Energy Statistics for Europe
	UN8	Annual Bulletin of Gas Statistics for Europe
	UN9	Annual Bulletin of General Energy Statistics for Europe
	UN10	Annual Bulletin of Housing and Building Statistics for Europe
	UN11	Annual Bulletin of Steel Statistics for Europe

Name of organization	*instat* code	Title of publication
United Nations	UN12	Annual Bulletin of Trade in Chemical Products
	UN13	Annual Bulletin of Transport Statistics for Europe
	UN14	Bulletin of Statistics on World Trade in Engineering Products
	UN15	Commodity Trade Statistics
	UN16	Compendium of Social Statistics and Indicators
	UN17	Compendium of Statistics and Indicators on the Situation of Women
	UN18	Construction Statistics Yearbook
	UN19	Demographic Yearbook
	UN20	Energy Balances and Electricity Profiles
	UN21	Energy Statistics Yearbook
	UN22	The Environment in Europe and North America: Annotated Statistics 1992
	UN23	Foreign Trade Statistics for Africa, Direction of Trade Series A
	UN24	Foreign Trade Statistics of Asia and the Pacific
	UN25	Human Development Report
	UN26	Human Settlements Basic Statistics
	UN27	Industrial Statistics Yearbook, Vol I General Industrial Statistics
	UN28	Industrial Statistics Yearbook, Vol II Commodity Production Statistics
	UN29	International Narcotics Control Board – Narcotic Drugs, Estimated World Requirement Statistics for 1990
	UN30	International Narcotics Control Board – Psychotropic Substances, Statistics for 1990
	UN31	International Sea-borne Trade Statistics: Yearbook 1984–85
	UN32	International Trade Statistics Yearbook, Vol I Trade by Country
	UN33	International Trade Statistics Yearbook, Vol II Trade by Commodity
	UN34	The Livestock and Meat Market
	UN35	Monthly Bulletin of Statistics

Name of organization	*instat* code	Title of publication
United Nations	UN36	National Accounts Statistics: Analysis of Main Aggregates 1988–89
	UN37	National Accounts Statistics: Compendium of Income Distribution Statistics
	UN38	National Accounts Statistics: Main Aggregates and Detailed Tables Parts I and II
	UN39	Population and Vital Statistics Report
	UN40	Prices of Agricultural Products and Selected Inputs in Europe and North America
	UN41	Report of the UN High Commissioner for Refugees. General Assembly Official Records: 46th Session, Supplement No 12
	UN42	Standardized Input-Output Tables of ECE Countries for Years Around 1975
	UN43	Statistical Indicators for Asia and the Pacific
	UN44	Statistical Yearbook for Asia and the Pacific
	UN45	Statistical Yearbook for Latin America and the Caribbean
	UN46	Statistics and Indicators on Women in Africa
	UN47	Statistics of Road Traffic Accidents in Europe
	UN48	Statistics of World Trade in Steel
	UN49	The Steel Market in 1991
	UN50	UN Statistical Yearbook
	UN51	UNHCR Activities Financed by Voluntary Funds. Report for 1990–91 and Proposed Programmes and Budget for 1992. Part 1: Africa Part 2: Asia and Oceania Part 3: Europe and North America Part 4: Latin America Part 5: South-West Asia, North Africa and the Middle East Part 6: Overall Allocations
	UN52	World Investment Directory Vol I Asia and the Pacific
	UN53	World Investment Directory Vol II Central and Eastern Europe
	UN54	World Population Prospects
	UN55	World Statistics in Brief, United Nations Statistical Pocketbook
United Nations Children's Fund	UNICEF1	The State of the World's Children

Name of organization	*instat* code	Title of publication
United Nations Children's Fund	UNICEF2	Statistics on Children in UNICEF Assisted Countries
United Nations Conference on Trade and Development	UNCTAD1	Handbook of International Trade and Development Statistics
	UNCTAD2	Review of Maritime Transport
United Nations Conference on Trade and Development	UNCTAD3	Tungsten Statistics
	UNCTAD4	UNCTAD Commodity Yearbook
	UNCTAD5	UNCTAD Statistical Pocket Book
United Nations Educational, Scientific, and Cultural Organization	UNESCO1	Statistical Yearbook
United Nations Industrial Development Organization	UNIDO1	Handbook of Industrial Statistics
Vienna Institute for Comparative Economic Studies	VICES1	Comecon Data
The World Bank	WB1	Social Indicators of Development
	WB2	Trends in Developing Economies
	WB3	World Debt Tables, Vol 1, Analysis and Summary Tables
	WB4	World Debt Tables, Vol 2, External Finance for Developing Countries, Country Tables
	WB5	World Population Projections
	WB6	World Tables
World Bureau of Metal Statistics	WBMS1	World Metal Statistics
	WBMS2	World Metal Statistics Quarterly Summary
	WBMS3	World Metal Statistics Yearbook
	WBMS4	World Stainless Steel Statistics
World Food Programme	WFP1	The Food Aid Monitor: World Food Aid Flows, Transport and Logistics
World Health Organization	WHO1	Bulletin of Regional Health Information
	WHO2	World Health Statistics Annual
World Intellectual Property Organization	WIPO1	Industrial Property Statistics, Patents, Part I

Name of organization	*instat* code	Title of publication
World Intellectual Property Organization	WIPO2	Industrial Property Statistics, Part II Trademarks and Service Marks, Utility Models, Industrial Designs, Varieties of Plants, Micro-organisms
	WIPO3	Industrial Property Statistics, Publication A (Supplement to Industrial Property) No 11
World Meteorological Organization	WMO1	Climatological Normals (CLINO) for CLIMAT and CLIMAT Ship Stations
World Tourism Organization	WTO1	Compendium of Tourism Statistics
	WTO2	Travel and Tourism Barometer
	WTO3	Yearbook of Tourism Statistics, Vol 1
	WTO4	Yearbook of Tourism Statistics, Vol 2
Wye College	WC1	Agrifacts: A Handbook of UK and EEC Agricultural and Food Statistics

APPENDIX D

NAMES AND ADDRESSES OF ORGANIZATIONS

ALPHABETICAL LISTING

ASIAN PRODUCTIVITY ORGANIZATION (APO)
4–14 Akasaka 8–Chome, Minato-ku, Tokyo 107, Japan

ASSOCIATION OF EUROPEAN AIRLINES (AEA)
Publications Department, Association of European Airlines, 350 Avenue Louise, Bte 4, 1050 Brussels, Belgium

ASSOCIATION OF SOUTH-EAST ASIAN NATIONS SECRETARIAT (ASEANS)
70A Kebayoran Baru, PO Box 2072, Jakarta 12110, Indonesia

BASIL BLACKWELL LTD (BB)
108 Cowley Road, Oxford, OX4 1JF, UK

BRITISH GEOLOGICAL SURVEY (BGS)
Keyworth, Nottingham, NG12 5GG, UK

BRITISH PAPER AND BOARD INDUSTRY FEDERATION (BPB)
Papermakers House, Rivenhall Road, Westlea, Swindon, SN5 7BE, UK

BRITISH PETROLEUM COMPANY PLC (BP)
Britannic House, 1 Finsbury Circus, London, EC2M 7BA, UK

CARIBBEAN COMMUNITY SECRETARIAT (CCS)
PO Box 10827, Bank of Guyana Building 3rd Floor, Avenue of the Republic, Georgetown, Guyana

CHAMBER OF SHIPPING (COS)
30–32 St Mary Axe, London, EC3A 8ET, UK

CHEMICAL INDUSTRIES ASSOCIATION (CIA)
King's Building, Smiths Square, London, SW1P 3JJ, UK

CIVIL AVIATION AUTHORITY (CAA)
Greville House, 37 Gratton Road, Cheltenham, Gloucestershire, GL50 2BN, UK

COMITE INTERNATIONAL DE LA RAYONNE ET DES FIBRES SYNTHETIQUES (CIRFS)
29 rue de Courcelles, 75008, Paris, France

COMMONWEALTH SECRETARIAT (CS)
Marlborough House, Pall Mall, London, SW1Y 5HX, UK

CONFEDERATION OF BRITISH INDUSTRY (CBI)
Centre Point, 103 New Oxford Street, London, WC1A 1DU, UK

COUNCIL OF EUROPE (CE)
Strasbourg, France

CROOM HELM LIMITED (CH)
c/o Routledge, 11 New Fetter Lane, London, EC4P 4EE

DREWRY SHIPPING CONSULTANTS LIMITED (DSC)
11 Heron Quay, London, E14 4JF, UK

E A GIBSON SHIPBROKERS LIMITED (G)
PO Box 278, Audrey House, 16–20 Ely Place, London, EC1P 1HP, UK

E D & F MAN COCOA LIMITED (EDFM)
Sugar Quay, Lower Thames Street, London, EC3R 6DU, UK

ELSEVIER ADVANCED TECHNOLOGY (EAT)
Mayfield House, 256 Banbury Road, Oxford, OX2 7DH, UK

EUROMONITOR (EM)
87–88 Turnmill Street, London, EC1M 5QU, UK

EUROPEAN ALUMINIUM ASSOCIATION (EAA)
Avenue de Broqueville, 12, B–1150 Brussels, Belgium

EUROPEAN COMMUNITY (EUROSTAT) (EC)
Bâtiment Jean Monnet, L–2920, Luxembourg

EUROPEAN CONFERENCE OF MINISTERS OF TRANSPORT (ECMT)
19 rue de Franqueville F–75775, Paris, Cedex 16, France

EUROPEAN FREE TRADE ASSOCIATION (EFTA)
9–11 rue de Varembé, CH–1211 Geneva 20, Switzerland

EUROPEAN PAPER INSTITUTE (EPI)
42 rue Galilé, 75116 Paris, France

EUROPEAN PATENT OFFICE (EPO)
Erhardtstrasse 27, D–800, Munich 2, Germany

FEARNLEYS (F)
PO Box 1158 Sentrum, 0107 Oslo 1, Norway

FEDERATION NATIONALE DES ORGANISMES DE CONTROLE LAITIER (FNOCL)
149 rue de Bercy, 75595 Paris, Cedex 12, France

F O LICHT (FOL)
PO Box 1220, D–2418 Ratzeburg, Germany

FOOD AND AGRICULTURE ORGANIZATION (FAO)
Via Delle Terme Di Caracella, 00100 Rome, Italy

GENERAL AGREEMENT ON TARIFFS AND TRADE (GATT)
Centre William Rappard, rue de Lausanne 154, CH–1211 Geneva 21, Switzerland

GENERATION PUBLICATIONS (GP)
PO Box 234, S–891 25 Örnsköldsvik, Sweden

HORWATH INTERNATIONAL (HI)
Headquarters, 415 Madison Avenue, New York, NY10017, USA

INSTITUTE OF PETROLEUM (IP)
61 New Cavendish Street, London, W1M 8AR, UK

INSTITUTE OF SHIPPING ECONOMICS AND LOGISTICS (ISL)
Universitätsallee GW1, Block A, D–2800, Bremen 33, Germany

INTER-AMERICAN DEVELOPMENT BANK (IADB)
Headquarters, 13000 New York Avenue, Washington DC, 20577, USA

INTERNATIONAL AGENCY FOR RESEARCH ON CANCER (IARC)
150 Cours Albert Thomas, F–69372 Lyon, Cedex 08, France

INTERNATIONAL AIR TRANSPORT ASSOCIATION (IATA)
3rd Floor, Sceptre House, 75–81 Staines Road, Hounslow, TW3 3HW, UK

INTERNATIONAL ASSOCIATION OF HORTICULTURAL PRODUCERS (IAHP)
Bezuidenhoutseweg 153, Postbus 93099, NL–2509 AB's–Gravenhage, Netherlands

INTERNATIONAL ATOMIC ENERGY AGENCY (IAEA)
Wagramerstrasse 5, PO Box 100, A–1400 Vienna, Austria

INTERNATIONAL BAUXITE ASSOCIATION (IBA)
36 Trafalgar Road, PO Box 551, Kingston 5, Jamaica

INTERNATIONAL CIVIL AVIATION ORGANIZATION (ICAO)
1000 Sherbrook Street W, Montreal PQ, H3A 2RZ, Canada

INTERNATIONAL COCOA COUNCIL ORGANIZATION (ICCO)
22 Berners Street, London, W1P 3DB, UK

INTERNATIONAL COMMISSION FOR THE CONSERVATION OF ATLANTIC TUNAS (ICCAT)
Calle Principe de Vergara 17–7, 28001 Madrid, Spain

INTERNATIONAL COTTON ADVISORY COMMITTEE (ICAC)
1901 Pennsylvania Av NW, Suite 201, Washington DC 20006, USA

INTERNATIONAL DAIRY FEDERATION (IDF)
41 Square Vergote, B–1040 Brussels, Belgium

INTERNATIONAL ENERGY AGENCY (IEA)
IEA 2 rue André Pascal, F–75775 Paris Cedex 16, France

INTERNATIONAL FERTILIZER INDUSTRY ASSOCIATION (IFA)
28 rue Marbeuf, 75008 Paris, France

INTERNATIONAL INSTITUTE OF SYNTHETIC RUBBER PRODUCERS (IISRP)
2077 South Gessner Road Suite 133, Houston, Texas 77063, USA

INTERNATIONAL IRON AND STEEL INSTITUTE (IISI)
rue Colonel Bourg, 120 B–11140 Brussels, Belgium

INTERNATIONAL LABOUR ORGANIZATION (ILO)
4 Route des Murillons, Ch–1211, Geneva 22, Switzerland

INTERNATIONAL LEAD AND ZINC STUDY GROUP (ILZSG)
Metro House, 58 St James Street, London, SW1A 1LD, UK

INTERNATIONAL METALWORKERS' FEDERATION (IMWF)
54 bis route des Acacias, Care Postale, 563, CH–1227 Geneva, Switzerland

INTERNATIONAL MONETARY FUND (IMF)
700 19th Street NW, Washington DC 20431, USA

INTERNATIONAL NORTH PACIFIC FISHERIES COMMISSION (INPFC)[1]
6640 Northwest Marine Drive, Vancouver, V6T 1X2, Canada

INTERNATIONAL PACIFIC HALIBUT COMMISSION (IPHC)
PO Box 5009, University Station, Seattle, WA 98145, USA

INTERNATIONAL RICE RESEARCH INSTITUTE (IRRI)
Headquarters, PO Box 933, 1099 Manila, Philippines

INTERNATIONAL ROAD FEDERATION (IRF)
CH–1202, 63 rue de Lausanne, Geneva, Switzerland

INTERNATIONAL ROAD TRANSPORT UNION (IRTU)
Centre International, BP 44, 3 rue de Varembé, CH–1211 Geneva 20, Switzerland

INTERNATIONAL RUBBER STUDY GROUP (IRSG)
York House, Empire Way, Wembley, HA9 0PA, UK

INTERNATIONAL SUGAR ORGANIZATION (ISO)
1 Canada Square, Canary Wharf, London, E14 5AA, UK

INTERNATIONAL TEA COMMITTEE (ITC)
Sir John Lyon House, 5 High Timber Street, London, EC4V 3NH, UK

INTERNATIONAL TELECOMMUNICATION UNION (ITU)
Head Office, Place des Nations, CH–1211 Geneva 20, Switzerland

INTERNATIONAL TEXTILE MANUFACTURERS FEDERATION (ITMF)
Am Schanzengraben 29, Postfach, 8039 Zurich, Switzerland

[1] To be replaced by the North Pacific Anadromous Fish Commission after 1993.

INTERNATIONAL TROPICAL TIMBER ORGANIZATION (ITTO)
International Organization Centre, SF/Pacifico–Yokohama, H–1 Minato-Mirai, Nishi-ku, Yokohama 220, Japan

INTERNATIONAL UNION OF RAILWAYS (IUR)
16 rue Jean-Rey, 75015 Paris, France

INTERNATIONAL WHALING COMMISSION (IWC)
The Red House, Station Road, Histon, Cambridge CB4 4NP, UK

INTERNATIONAL WHEAT COUNCIL (IWhC)
Haymarket House, 28 Haymarket, London, SW1Y 4SS, UK

INTERNATIONAL WOOL SECRETARIAT (IWS)
Development Centre, Valley Drive, Ilkley, West Yorkshire, LS29 8PB, UK

INTER-PARLIAMENTARY UNION (IPU)
Place du petit-saconnex, CP–438, CH–1211, Geneva 19, Switzerland

IRON AND STEEL STATISTICS BUREAU (ISSB)
Canterbury House, 2 Sydenham Road, Croydon, CR9 2LZ, UK

ISTA MIELK GmbH (ISTA)
2100 Hamburg 90, Langenberg 25, Germany

JAAKKO PÖYRY (JP)
Third Floor, Century House, Station Way, Cheam, Surrey, SM3 8SW, UK

JOHNSON MATTHEY (JM)
Blounts Court, Sonning Common, Reading, RG4 9NH, UK

LLOYDS REGISTER OF SHIPPING (LRS)
71 Fenchurch Street, London, EC3M 4BS, UK

MACMILLAN PRESS LIMITED (MAC)
Houndmills, Basingstoke, Hampshire, RG21 2XS, UK

MEAT AND LIVESTOCK COMMISSION (MLC)
PO Box 44, Winterhill House, Snowdon Drive, Milton Keynes, MK6 1AX, UK

METAL BULLETIN BOOKS LIMITED (MB)
Park House, Park Terrace, Worcester Park, Surrey, KT4 7HY, UK

MILK MARKETING BOARD (MMB)
Portsmouth Road, Thames Ditton, Surrey, KT7 OEL, UK

MINING JOURNAL (MJ)
60 Worship Street, London, EC2A 2HD, UK

MINISTRY OF HOUSING, PHYSICAL PLANNING AND THE ENVIRONMENT (MHPPE)
PO Box 20951, 2500 EZ The Hague, The Netherlands

NORDIC COUNCIL OF MINISTERS AND THE NORDIC STATISTICAL SECRETARIAT (NCM)
Store Strandstraede 18, DK–1255 Copenhagen K, Denmark, and
Nordic Statistical Secretariat, Sejøgade 11, DK–2100 Copenhagen Ø, Denmark

NORTH ATLANTIC TREATY ORGANIZATION (NATO)
Headquarters, B–1110, Brussels, Belgium

NORTH WEST ATLANTIC FISHERIES ORGANIZATION (NWAFO)
PO Box 638, Dartmouth BZY, 3Y9, Canada

OFFICE INTERNATIONAL DE LA VIGNE ET DU VIN (OIVV)
Paris 8e, 11 rue Roquepine, Paris, France

ORGANIZATION FOR ECONOMIC CO-OPERATION AND DEVELOPMENT (OECD)
2 rue André Pascal, F–75775, Paris, Cedex 16, France

ORGANIZATION OF PETROLEUM EXPORTING COUNTRIES (OPEC)
Obere Donaustrasse 93, A–1020 Vienna 11, Austria

PANNELL KERR FORSTER (PKF)
262 North Belt East, Suite 300, Houston, TX 77060, USA

THE POPULATION COUNCIL (PC)
1 Dag Hammarskjold Plaza, New York, NY 1007, USA

PULP AND PAPER INTERNATIONAL (PPI)
123a Chaussee de Charleroi, B–1060 Brussels, Belgium

SATRA FOOTWEAR TECHNOLOGY CENTRE (SATRA)
SATRA House, Rockingham Road, Kettering, Northamptonshire, NN16 9JH, UK

SEA FISH INDUSTRY AUTHORITY (SFIA)
Fishery Economics Research Unit, Sea Fisheries House, 10 Young Street, Edinburgh, EH2 4JQ, UK

SOCIETY OF MOTOR MANUFACTURERS AND TRADERS LIMITED (SMMT)
Forbes House, Halkin Street, London, SW1X 7DS, UK

SOUTH PACIFIC COMMISSION (SPC)
Anse Vata, BPD5, Noumea Cedex, New Caledonia

UNITED NATIONS (UN)
New York, NY 10017, USA
Economic and Social Commission for Asia and the Pacific, United Nations Building, Rajadamern Avenue, Bangkok 10200, Thailand
Economic Commission for Africa, PO Box 3001, Addis Ababa, Ethiopia
Economic Commission for Europe, Palais des Nations, Ch–1211, Geneva 10, Switzerland
Office of the UN Disaster Relief Coordinator, Palais des Nations, CH–1211, Geneva, Switzerland
United Nations Centre for Human Settlements, Habitat, PO Box 30030 Nairobi, Kenya
United Nations Centre for Regional Development, Nagono 1–41–1, Nakamura-Ku, Nagoya 450, Japan
United Nations Environment Programme, PO Box 30552, Nairobi, Kenya
United Nations Conference on Trade and Development, Palais des Nations, CH–1211 Geneva 10, Switzerland
United Nations Educational, Scientific, and Cultural Organization, 7 Place de Fontenoy, F–75700, Paris, France

UNITED NATIONS CHILDREN'S FUND (UNICEF)
Unicef House 3 United Nations Plaza, New York NY10017, USA

UNITED NATIONS CONFERENCE ON TRADE AND DEVELOPMENT (UNCTAD)
Palais des Nations, CH–1211, Geneva 10, Switzerland

UNITED NATIONS EDUCATIONAL, SCIENTIFIC, AND CULTURAL ORGANIZATION (UNESCO)
7 Place de Fontenoy, F–75700, Paris, France

UNITED NATIONS INDUSTRIAL DEVELOPMENT ORGANIZATION (UNIDO)
Vienna International Centre, PO Box 300, A–1400 Vienna, Austria

VIENNA INSTITUTE FOR COMPARATIVE ECONOMIC STUDIES (VICES)
Postfach 87, A–1103 Wein, Austria

THE WORLD BANK (WB)
Head Office, 1818 H Street, NW, Washington DC 2043, USA

WORLD BUREAU OF METAL STATISTICS (WBMS)
27 High Street, Ware, Hertfordshire, SG12 9BQ, UK

WORLD FOOD PROGRAMME (WFP)
426, Via Cristoford Colombo, I–00145 Rome, Italy

WORLD HEALTH ORGANIZATION (WHO)
CH–1211, Geneva 27, Switzerland

WORLD INTELLECTUAL PROPERTY ORGANIZATION (WIPO)
Case Postale 2300, 41 AV Giuseppe-Motta, CH–1211 Geneva 2, Switzerland

WORLD METEOROLOGICAL ORGANIZATION (WMO)
Case Postale 2300, 41 Av Giuseppe-Motta, CH–1211 Geneva 2, Switzerland

WORLD TOURISM ORGANIZATION (WTO)
Calle Capitan Haya 42, Madrid 28020, Spain

WYE COLLEGE (WC)
Wye College, University of London, Wye, Ashford, Kent, TN25 5AH, UK

Subject index

(*Note*: bold headings denote main subject sections)

Subject index